THE PADUMAWATI

BIBLIOTHECA INDICA
a
COLLECTION OF ORIENTAL WORKS
published by the
ASIATIC SOCIETY OF BENGAL

THE PADUMAWATI

OF

MALIK MUHAMMAD JAISI

EDITED, WITH A COMMENTARY, TRANSLATION, AND CRITICAL NOTES

By

G. A. GRIERSON

and

MAHAMAHOPADHYAYA SUDHAKARA DVIVEDI

IN VI FASCICULUS

COSMO PUBLICATIONS
2005 New Delhi

THE PADUMAWATI

First Published by Cosmo 2005

ISBN 81-307-0107-3

Published by
MRS. RANI KAPOOR
for COSMO PUBLICATIONS

Publishing Division of
GENESIS PUBLISHING PVT. LTD.
24-B, Ansari Road, Darya Ganj,
New Delhi-110 002,
INDIA

Printed at
Mehra Offset Press

INTRODUCTION.

(*Temporary*).

The following is an attempt to give a correct text and translation of the Padumāwati,[1] or Padmāvatī of Malik Muḥammad of Jāyas in Oudh. He flourished under S͟hēr S͟hāh in the year 1540 A.D., and numerous MSS. of his great poem are in existence.

The value of the Padumāwati consists chiefly in its age. Malik Muḥammad is, we believe, the oldest vernacular poet of Hindūstān of whom we have any uncontested remains. Cand Bar'dāī was much older, but the genuineness of his Prithīrāj Rāy'sā is denied by many competent scholars. Vidyāpati Ṭhākur, who lived in the year 1400 A.D., has only left us a few songs which have come down to us through five centuries of oral transmission, and which now cannot be in the form in which they were sung. The preservation of the Padumāwati is due mainly to the happy accident of Malik Muḥammad's religious reputation. Although profoundly affected by the teaching of Kabīr, and familiarly acquainted with Hindū lore, and with the Hindū Yōga philosophy, he was from the first revered as a saint by his Muḥammadan co-religionists.

He wrote his poem in what was evidently the actual vernacular of his time, tinged slightly with an admixture of a few Persian words and idioms due to his Musalmān predilections. It is also due to his religion that he originally wrote it in the Persian character, and hence discarded all the favourite devices of paṇḍits, who tried to make their language correct by spelling (while they did not pronounce) vernacular words in the Sanskrit fashion. He had no temptation to do this. The Persian character did not lend itself to any such false antiquarianism. He spelled each word rigorously as it was pronounced. His work is hence a valuable witness to the actual condition of the vernacular language of Northern India in the 16th century. It is, so far as it goes, and with the exception of a few hints in Alberuni's Indica, the only trustworthy witness which we have. It is trustworthy, however, only to a certain extent, for it often merely gives the consonantal frame work of the words, the vowels, as is usual in Persian MSS., being generally omitted. Fortunately, the vowels can generally be inserted correctly with the help of a few Dēvanāgarī MSS. of the poem which are in our possession.

Besides its interest as a key to a philological puzzle, the Padumāwati also deserves notice for its contents. In itself it is a fine poetical work, and one of the few original ones, not dealing with either Rāma or Krishṇa, with which we are acquainted in any Indian language. It is also remarkable for the vein of tolerance which runs through it,—a tolerance in every way worthy of Kabīr or of Tul'sī Dās. The story of the poem has been a favourite

[1] The author himself invariably spells the word thus.

one with eastern authors. Ḥusain Ghaznawī wrote a Persian poem on the subject, entitled *Qissae Padmāwat.* Rai Gōbind Munshī in 1652 A.D. wrote a version in Persian prose, called (after the chronogram of its date) *Tukfatu-l-Kulūb.* Again Mīr Ẓiyāu-d-dīn 'Ibrat, and Ghulām 'Alī 'Ishrat wrote a joint version in Urdū verse in 1796 A.D. Malik Muḥammad's poem was written in 1540 A.D.

Concerning the author little is known. He tells us himself that he was the disciple of Sayyad Muḥīud-d-īn. He studied Sanskrit Prosody and Rhetoric from Hindū Paṇḍits at Jāyas. He belonged to the *Cistiyā Niẓāmiyā,* that is to say, he was the eleventh disciple in descent from the well-known Niẓāmu-d-dīn, who died in 1325 A.D. Muḥīu-d-dīn's teacher was Shaikh Burhān, who resided at Kalpī in Bundēl'khaṇḍ, and who is said to have died at the age of a hundred years in A.D. 1562–63. The poet was patronized by Shēr Shāh.

The only other fact which we know for certain is that he was blind of one eye. I have collected the following traditions about him. One of Shēr Shāh's allies was Jagat Dēv, (enthroned 1527 A.D.: died 1573 A.D.), Mahārāj of Ghāzīpur and Bhōj'pur. He was present at the battle of Bagh'sar (Buxar) in which Shēr Shāh defeated Humāyūn. Malik Muḥammad is said to have attended his court. Two of Malik Muḥammad's four friends, whom he mentions in his poem (22) were also patronised by Jagat Dēv. These were Yūsuf Malik and Salōnē Siŋgh (whom Malik Muḥammad calls Miyā̃ as if he was a Muṣalmān). It is said that another attendant at Jagat Dēv's court was a *Katthak,* named Gandharv Rāj, who was skilled in the art of singing. Malik Muḥammad was greatly attached to him and gave him his blessing, prophesying that skill in song would always remain in his family, and, at the same time, begging him to take, as a sign of affection, his title of Malik. Ever since, Gandharv Rāj's descendants have called themselves Malik, and members of the family still live in Talūkā Rāipurā and at Haldī in Baliyā District, and are renowned singers.

It is said that the Rājā of Amēṭhī was childless, but was granted a son, in consequence of the prayers of Malik Muḥammad. When the poet died, he was buried at Amēṭhī, and his tomb is still shown, and worshipped by believers. Malik Muḥammad's two friends, Malik Yūsuf and Salōnē, died in what is now the district of Gōrakh'pur, from a surfeit of mangoes. Malik Muḥammad was with them at the time, and himself narrowly escaped. The mangoes are said to have been infested by poisonous insects.

The text of the Padumāwati, being in the ṭhēṭh Hindī language, and written in the Persian character, is very difficult both to read and to understand. It has been frequently transliterated into the Nāgarī character, but the transcriptions, whether MS. or printed, are full of mistakes, generally guesses to make the meaning clear. The best transliterated edition is that by Paṇḍit Rām Jasan of Banāras; but even in his case (putting instances of sanskritization out of sight) hardly a line is correct. There are several printed editions in the Persian character, but they too are all incorrect. We have been fortunate enough to become possessed of several old MSS. of the poem in the Persian character, and by diligent comparison we have endeavoured to reproduce, in the Nāgarī character, the actual words written by the poet. A glance at the critical notes will show the labour involved in the task.

For the purposes of these specimens, we have used the following MSS. :—

A. MSS. in Persian character (marked collectively as P).

(1) India Office Library, Pers. Cat. 1018. Dated 1107 Hij. =1695 A.D. (Ia).

(2) Ditto No. 1975. Vowel marks freely used. Correctly written. Dated 1109 Hij. =1697 A.D. (Ib).

(3) Ditto No. 1819. Vowel points inserted in red ink by a later hand. Dated 1114 Hij. =1702 A.D. (Ic).

(4) India Office Library, Urdu Catalogue, No. 3130. Few vowel points. In two different handwritings. No date, (Id).

All these Persian MSS. are very fairly correct. We have taken Ib. as the basis throughout.

B. MSS. in the Dēvanāgarī character (marked collectively as N).

(1) India Office Library, Sanskrit Catalogue, No. 2471. A magnificent copy, profusely illustrated. Written by Thānā Kāyath of Mirzāpur. No date. Spelling highly Sanskritized (Is).

We must here express our thanks to the authorities of the India Office Library, for the loan of the above MSS.

(2) A well written copy kindly lent me by the late Kavirāj Syāmal Dās, belonging to the library of the Mahārāj of Udaipur. Spelling not so Sanskritized. Dated Sambat 1895=1838 A.D. (U).

C. MSS. in the Kaithī character.

(1) A clearly written copy. With very irregular spelling: and many important variations in the readings. Written in Sambat 1812=1755 A.D. (K).

(2) A well written correct copy, but incomplete. The commencement, and several portions in the middle are missing. It also contains several interpolations. Written in *Sambat* 1758 (A.D. 1701), at Vaitāla-gaḍha, by Jaya-kṛṣṇa Dūbē, the son of Hari-rām. The last dōhā is numbered 739. (K^2).

(3) A fairly correct copy. Complete. Contains several interpolations. Commenced in *Sambat* 1879 (A.D. 1822). Writer's name not mentioned. (K^3).

These three books are full of various readings, and owing to the use of the Kaithī character, the spelling is very irregular. All the readings of K^2 and K^3, have not been inserted, but only those which illuminate doubtful points in the text.

As might be expected in a work sometimes written in the Persian, and sometimes in the Dēva-nāgarī character, the spelling of the MSS. is very capricious. In editing the text, we have adopted a system of spelling, and of representing grammatical forms, which, we believe, represents as nearly as possible the practice of the best copies. In a critical edition, a uniform system of spelling is absolutely essential, and as no single manuscript follows any rules on the subject we have allowed ourselves some latitude. The principal points are as follows :—

Spelling :—Prākrit words are spelt as in the Persian copies. When the Persian copies give vowels, those vowels are adopted. When no vowels are given, we have used our judgment in adopting the vowels given in the Dēvanāgarī and Kaithī copies.

On the other hand, for precisely similar reasons, we have generally adopted the spelling of Arabic and Persian words which is best vouched for by the Dēvanāgarī and Kaithī copies. Such words are phonetically spelt in that alphabet.

U and K uniformly write स as श. We have not followed them in this.

The termination نهہ *nh*, is capable of being read as equivalent to either the plural oblique termination न्ह, or to the singular oblique termination न्हिँ or न्हि. Unless the context showed that न्ह is required, we have transliterated it न्हि. Even in the best Persian MSS. the nasal is inserted so capriciously, that it is at least doubtful whether it should be used in the singular, and we have accordingly followed the best Dēvanāgarī MSS., in omitting it, in this case, throughout.

In Tadbhava words, a Sanskrit or Prakrit medial म becomes वँ (Cf. Hēma-candra's Prakrit Grammar, IV. 397). Thus the representative of the Sanskrit कमलम् is कवँल (not कँवल), and of स्मरणम्, सवँरन. This वँ, at the end of a word becomes उँ, thus नाउँ (not नाँउ), a name. When म or *anusvāra*, however, forms the first member of a compound, the *preceding* vowel is nasalized. Thus आँब (for Prakrit अम्ब), a mango, सँवारइ, (for संवारयति), he arranges.

In the preposition अव, the व becomes उ. Thus, अउगाहि, for अवगाहि, having bathed. In other cases after अ, ए, or ऐ, medial व remains unchanged. Thus पवन, wind, भवन, a house, सेवरा, a savage. After any other vowel, medial व is dropped. Thus भुअन (for भुवन), earth, जिअना (for जिवना), life. A final व always becomes उ. Thus जीउ (for जीव), life. Similarly for य, *e.g.* नयन.

Scheme of transliteration adopted in this work:—

अ *a*, आ *ā*, इ *i*, ई *ī*, उ *u*, ऊ *ū*, ऎ *e*, ए *ē*, ऒ *o*, ओ *ō*. ँ ˜, thus अँ *ã*, आँ *ā̃*, इँ *ĩ*, ईँ *ī̃*, and so on. ं *ṁ*.

The following vowels occur only in a few Sanskrit words, ऋ *ṛ*, ऐ *ai*, औ *au*. In Tadbhava words ऐ and औ do not occur. अइ is transliterated *ai* and अउ *au*. In Nāgarī MSS. when ऐ and औ occur, they are plainly stenographic signs for अइ and अउ. This is frequently shown by the metre. There is no danger of confusing अइ, अउ, and ऐ, औ, for they appear in distinct classes of words, अइ, अउ, are always in Tadbhava words, or in corrupted Tatsama words, ऐ and औ occur only in words lifted bodily from Sanskrit:—

क *k*, ख *kh*, ग *g*, घ *gh*, ङ *ṅ*.
च *c*, छ *ch*, ज *j*, झ *jh*, ञ *ñ*.
ट *ṭ*, ठ *ṭh*, ड *ḍ*, ढ *ḍh*, ण *ṇ*.
त *t*, थ *th*, द *d*, ध *dh*, न *n*.
प *p*, फ *ph*, ब *b*, भ *bh*, म *m*.
य *y*, र *r*, ल *l*. व *w*, (or in Sanskrit words *v*).
ष *ṣ*, स *s*, ह *h*.

श only occurs in Persian words, representing the Persian ش, or in pure Sanskrit words. In the former case it is transliterated sh, and in the latter by *ç*.

Arabic and Persian letters.

ث *s̤*, ح *ḥ*, خ kh, ذ *ẕ*, ز *z*, ژ zh, ص *ṣ*, ض *ẓ*, ط *ṭ*, ظ *ẓ̤*, ع ʻ, غ gh. ف *f*, ق *q*.

Grammar.

SUBSTANTIVES :—The oblique cases are all formed by adding हि or इ for the singular, and हिँ or इँ for the plural, before which, a final long vowel is shortened. Thus from राजा, a king, we have राजहि or राजइ, for the Instrumental (or Agent), Dative, Ablative, Genitive and Locative Singular. In the Plural, न्ह is sometimes substituted for हिँ, thus कानन्ह (38, 2), in (their) ears. The Nominative Plural is usually the same as the Nominative Singular. Postpositions are not often used. We find, however, कहँ for the Accusative and Dative, सउँ for Instrumental and Ablative, मँह, माँहा, पाँहा, and पइ for the Locative, and others. The following postpositions are found for the Genitive क or कै (fem. कइ), कर (fem. करि), केर (fem. केरि). At the end of a line we often have केरा (fem. केरी).

PRONOUNS :—1st Person; मइँ, or हउँ, obl. मोहि or मो, genitive मोर. Plural हम, &c.

2nd Person : तुँ or तुँह, obl. तोहि or तो, genitive तोर or तोहर. Plur. तुम्ह, &c.

Demonstrative : वह or उहइ, case of Agent, वेइ or उहइ, obl. ओहि or ओही : Plur., Nom. वह or वेइँ, Agent, वेइँ, Obl. उन्ह.

Relative : जो, Agent जेइ, Obl. जेहि or जा, Genitive जासु, &c. Plur. जे, जेइँ, Agent जेइँ, Obl. (including gen.) जिन्ह. जा is never used as an adjective.

So also the Correlative सो or तेइ.

Interrogative : को, who? का what?

Indefinite, कोइ or कोउ, anyone, obl. काहूँ. किछु, anything.

		Singular.	Plural.
VERBS :—*Present* :	1.	देखउँ, I see.	देखहिँ, देखइँ.
	2.	देखसि, देखहि, देखइ.	देखहु, देखउ.
	3.	देखसि, देखहि, देखइ, देखु.	देखहिँ, देखइँ.

The forms in हि and हिँ are rather rare.

		Singular.	Plural.
Past :	1.	देखेउँ ;	देखेहिँ.
	2.	देखेसि.	देखेहु.
	3.	देखेसि, देख (देखा)	देखेहिँ.

From देना, दीन्हेसि, he gave. So लेना.

		Singular.	Plural.
Future :	1.	देखिहउँ.	देखिहइँ.
	2.	देखिहइ.	देखिहउ.
	3.	देखिहइ.	देखिहइँ.

देखब, Fem. देखबि, may also be used for all persons of both numbers From देना, we have, 3rd. sg., दोहइ.

Pres. Part : देखत, Past, देख.

Conj. Part : देखि, देखि कइ. From देना and लेना we have देइ or देइ, and लेइ or लेइ.

The past tense of a neuter verb is thus conjugated.

	Singular.	*Plural.*
1.	गएउँ, fem. गइउँ, I went.	गए, fem. गईं.
2.	गएउ or गा, गइउ.	Do.
3.	गएउ or गा, गइउ.	Do.

The above does not, of course, pretend to be a complete grammar. It is only meant to show the spelling of the principal forms.

The **metre** of the poem consists of stanzas of seven *caupāīs* followed by a *dōhā*. In the latter, a *mātrā* is frequently omitted in the first half. In the *caupāīs*, accent is frequently used instead of quantity, a short accented syllable being treated as a long one, especially at the end of a line. Malik Muḥammad wrote long before Kēçava-dāsa laid down the canons of Hindī metre. Such accented short syllables we have marked, in transliteration with an acute accent, thus,—*niramárē* (2, 3).

TRANSLATION.

Canto I. The Preface.

(1). I bear in mind that one and only primal Maker, who gave life and made the world. First made He manifest the Light, then made He (for the Light) the mighty mountain Kailāsa.[1] He made the fire, the air, the water, and the dust, and, from them, made He forms[2] of varied hue. He made the Earth, and Heaven, and Hell; and He made incarnations in many persons.[3] He made the mundane egg[4] with its seven[5] continents. He made the universe with its fourteen[6] worlds. He made the sun for the day, and the moon for the night; He made the asterisms and the systems of the stars. He made coolness, sunshine and shade; He made the clouds and lightning (that abideth) in them.

1 By 'Light,' the poet refers to Mahādēva, who dwells in Kailāsa. Indian Musalmāns frequently consider Adam, the first man, as the same as Mahādēva. The fact that the poet expressly says that Kailāsa was made 'for' the Light, shows that he cannot be referring to light, the first of created things. In the system of the Nānak-panthīs, to which Kabīr, from whom Malik Maḥammad borrowed much, originally belonged, the Supreme Being is, in its essence, *jōti* or light, which, though diffused into all creatures, remains distinct from them. The Human Soul is also this light, a *scintilla animœ divinœ*, which has emanated from the absolute, and is itself immortal. See Trumpp, Ādi Granth, pp. ci and ff.

2 An Urdū gloss translates *urēha* by نقش, design, stamp, drawing. I have noted it also in *asa mūrata kē daī urēhī*, and in *bhaī urēha puhupa saba nāmā.* In the second the Urdū translation gives ظاهر کی and in the latter, the whole line is translated تو يهه معلوم هوتا تها كه رنگ برنگ پهول هر قسم کے هين. The word is still used in Oudh and Bihār by women, in the sense of *racanā*. It is derived from the Skr. *ullēkha.*

3 Apparently, incarnations in many castes. Alluding to the doctrine that incarnations have occurred in all religions in many parts of the world. Or it may, as the comm. suggests, only refer to the various *avatārs* of Viṣṇu.

4 *I. e.*, the universe, alluding to the well known tradition detailed in Manu.

5 The seven horizontal divisions of the world, *viz.*, Jambu, Plakṣa or Gōmēdaka, Çālmala, Kuça, Krauñca, Çāka, and Puṣkara.

6 There are seven worlds (lōka) above, *viz.*, Bhūr-lōka, Bhuvar-l., Svar-l., Mahar-l., Janar-l., Tapar-l., and Satya-l. or Brahma-l., and seven below, *viz.*, A-tala, Vi-tala, Su-tala, Rasā-tala, Talā-tala, Mahā-tala, and Pātāla. According to Musalmāns, there are seven regions (طبق) above (these are heavens), and seven below (earths).

All things are so made by Him, that naught is worthy to be compared with Him. First take I His name, and then in deep thought do I begin[1] my story.

2. He made the seven[2] shoreless oceans, and He made the mountains of Mēru and Kukhaṇḍa.[3] Rivers made He, and streams and springs; crocodiles and fish made He of many kinds. He made the oyster shell, and the pearl which filleth it; He made many flawless gems. Forests made He and roots;[4] tall trees made He, palmyras and date palms. He made the wild animals[5] which dwell in the forest; He made the fowl which fly whither they will. He made colours, white and black; He made sleep, and hunger, and rest. He made the betel-leaf and flowers, and the pleasures of taste; many medicines made He and many sicknesses.

He made them in less than the twinkling of an eye; all made He in a single instant. He fixed the Heavens in space without a pillar, and without a prop.

3. He made man, and gave him dominion; He made grain for his food. He made the king who taketh pleasure in his kingdom; He made elephants and horses for his array. He made for him many delights; some made He lords, and others slaves. Wealth made He from which cometh pride; He made longings which none can satisfy. He made life which all men ever desire; He made death, from which none can escape. Happiness made He and myriads of joys; sorrow made He, and care and doubt.[6] Some made He poor and others rich; He made prosperity and very deep adversity.

Some made He weak, and others strong. From ashes made He all, and again turned He all to ashes.

4. He made agallochum, musk, and the scented *khas* grass; He made the camphors,—*bhīmasēni*[7] and *cēna*.[8] He made the snake in whose mouth dwelleth poison; He made the snake-charm which carrieth off the bite. He made the Water of Life, which giveth eternal life to him who getteth it; He made the poison, which is death to him who eateth it. He made the sugarcane filled with sweet juice; He made the acrid creeper with its manifold fruit. He made the honey which the bee stores in its home; He made the humble bee, the birds and winged creatures. He made the fox, the rat and the ant; He made many creatures which dig the earth and dwell therein. He made demons, goblins and ghosts; He made ghouls and *Dēvas* and *Daityas*.

[1] Two Urdū glosses translate *augāhi* by شروع a meaning for which I can find no other authority. It means literally to plunge into water, hence to be immersed in anything, to have the mind fully occupied.

[2] These encircle the seven continents (*dvīpas*) mentioned in l. 5. Their names are, Lavaṇa (or Kṣāra), Ikṣu, Surā (or Madya), Ghṛta, Dadhi, Dugdha, Jala. The author, in the description of the seven seas, later on, gives a different enumeration, *viz.*, Khāra, Khīra, Dadhi, Jala, Sura, Udadhi, Kilakila.

[3] Mēru is the well-known mountain. It represents the northern hemisphere or pole, and is the abode of the Gods. Kukhaṇḍa is Kumēru, the southern hemisphere or pole, the region of the *daityas* or demons. The poet has mixed this up with Kiṣkindhā, also to the south of Oudh, and has confounded the two names.

[4] *Jari* is a root used for medicine, and *mūri* is a root used for food.

[5] *Sāuja* is any animal used for food.

[6] Two Urdū glosses translate *danda* by غم grief, but the dictionary meaning of the word is enmity (*dwandwa*). Here it means opposition of ideas, doubt.

[7] The *Bhīmasēna-karpūra* of Sanskrit.

[8] The *Cīna-karpūra* of Sanskrit.

He made eighteen thousand creations of varied kinds.[1] For all did He make meet provision, and thus gave food to all.

5. He indeed is a master of wealth, to whom belongeth the universe; to all He giveth continually, yet His storehouse minisheth not. To every creature in the world, aye, from the elephant even unto the ant, doth He day and night give its share of nourishment. His eye is upon all: none is forgotten, neither foe nor friend; nor bird nor grasshopper, nor aught whether manifest or hidden is forgotten. He deviseth dainty food of many kinds. All doth He feed thereof, yet eateth not Himself. His meat and His drink is this—that to all He giveth nourishment and life. All have hope in Him at every breath, nor hath He ever (turned) the hope of any to despair.

Æon after æon doth He give, yet never minisheth (His store). Yea, so doth He this with both hands, that whatever hath been given in this world, hath all been given by Him.

6. Let me tell of Him as that great primal king, whose rule is glorious from the beginning to the end of things. Ever all-bounteous doth He rule, and whom He willeth, rule to him He giveth. He maketh umbrellaless him who hath the umbrella of royalty; and He giveth its shade unto him who is without it; no other is there who is equal unto Him. The people all look as He upturneth the mountains, and maketh the ant (that crawleth from beneath them) equal unto the elephant. Adamant He maketh like unto straw and scattereth it, and again He maketh straw like adamant, and giveth it honour. For one created He food, and enjoyment and all happiness; another striketh He with beggary and a home of poverty. No one understandeth what He hath done, for He doeth that which is beyond the power of mind and thought.

All else is non-existent.[2] He alone is ever the same, whose wondrous creations are such as these. He createth one and destroyeth him, and, if He will, He formeth him again.

7, Invisible, formless and untellable is that Creator; He is one with[3] all, and all are one in Him. Whether manifest or hidden, He is all pervading; but only the righteous recognize Him, and not the sinful. He hath no son nor father nor mother, no family hath He, and no relations. He hath begotten none, nor is He begotten of any; but all created beings proceed from Him. All things, as many as exist, He made; nor was He made by any one. He was at the beginning, and He is now; He alone remaineth existent and no one else. All else that are, are mad and blind; for after but two or four days they do their work and die.

Whate'er He willed that He did, He doeth that He willeth to do. No one is there to prevent Him, and, by his mere will, He gave life to all.

8. In this manner know ye Him, and meditate upon Him, for so is

[1] There is no such enumeration of created beings in the works of Musalmān doctors, but, in poetry, both Persian and Hindūstānī, phrases like *hizhda hazār 'alm*, the eighteen thousand created beings, are of frequent occurrence;—more especially in the class of works called *maulūd*, which celebrate the Prophet's birth. The expression merely means an enormous quantity, like our 'thousand and one.'

[2] Urdū gloss فاني, transient.

[3] The Urdū gloss translates *baratā* by نزديک "near," but I know of no authority for this meaning. *Baratā* means *baṭā huā*, twisted as a rope is twisted, hence involved in, closely connected with. Compare *Bihārī Sat'saī*, 59, *dīṭhi barata bādhī aṭani*, twisting their (mutual) glances into a rope, they bind it from balcony to balcony.

the tale written in the holy book.[1] The Lord hath no life, and yet He liveth; He hath no hands, and yet He maketh all things. He hath no tongue, yet He telleth everything; He hath no bodily form, yet that which He shaketh, is shaken. Ears hath He not, yet heareth He all things; Heart hath He not, yet The Wise One discriminateth all things. He hath no eyes, yet all things doth He see; How can anyone discern as He doth? No one hath a form like unto His; nor, like Him, is any one so incomparable. He hath no abiding place, yet He is not without an abiding place (for He is omnipresent). He hath no form nor mark, yet His name is THE PURE.

He is not indiscrete, nor is He discrete, yet so doth He dwell (within the universe), and fill it (with Himself). To those who can see, He is near, but He is far from the foolish blind.

9. The simple-minded knoweth not the secret of the other priceless jewels which He hath given. He hath given us a tongue, and the pleasures of taste; He hath given us teeth, which brighten[2] a smile. Eyes hath He given us, to see the world; ears hath He given us with which to hear language. He hath given the throat in which dwelleth our speech; He hath given us fingers and noble arms. Graceful feet hath He given us with which we walk; that man knoweth the secret of all these blessings who hath none. Yea, it is the old who know the secret of youth; when they find not their young days though they (go bent forward) seeking them. The great man knoweth not the secret of poverty; but the poor man knoweth it, to whom poverty is come.

It is the sick man who knoweth the secret of the body, while the healthy man liveth careless; but the secrets of all are known to the Lord, who abideth ever in every body.

10. Very immeasurable are the makings of the Maker; no teller can tell them. If (all the writers of) the Universe took the seven heavens[3] for paper, and filled the seas[4] of the earth with ink; if they took as many branches as cover[5] all the forests in the world, and all the hairs and down (of animals), and all the feathers of birds; if they took the motes of dust and salt where'er they found them, and all the drops in the clouds and all the stars of heaven; and turned them all to pens and wrote, still then they could not write the shoreless ocean of his wondrous works. So hath He manifested all His skill, that even now not one drop of that ocean hath decreased. Think thou of this, and let not pride be in thy heart; for mad is he, who, in his heart, nourisheth pride.

Very full of holiness is the Lord. What He willeth, for Him that quickly is. So full of holiness can He make a man, that that man, himself, performeth countless holy actions.

1 Urdū gloss for *purāna*, قرآن, the Qur'ān. This is quite possible. It will be seen that Mallik Muḥammad frequently uses Hindū words as Musalmān technical terms. E. G., *cēlā*, xx, 4.

2 Lit., are fit for.

3 The seven Heavens, see note to i, 5.

4 The seven seas of Hindu tradition, see ii, 1. The general idea of this verse is taken from the *Kahf* or Cave Sūrah of the Qur'ān. Verse 109 runs 'Say, "were the sea ink for the words of my Lord, the sea would surely fail before the words of my Lord fail; aye, though we brought as much ink again."'

5 *Bana-dhā̃khā*, is equivalent to *bana kē ḍhākhanē-wālē*, (branches) which cover the forest. The subject of all these objects is *sansārū* in the fifth line.

11. Thus, made He one man without a blemish, named Muḥammad, glorious as the full moon. It was his radiancy that God first produced, and then for love of him He created the universe. He kindled that light and gave it to the world. The world became clear, and recognized its (true) way. If that bright man had not been, the dark path would not have been visible. The deity (Muḥammad) wrote the second place (in heaven) for those who learned his creed.[1] For those who have not taken (refuge in) his name throughout his life, God hath prepared a place in hell. God made him His messenger to the world, and whoever hath taken his name passes safely across both worlds.[2]

God will ask of each his virtues and his vices, (when) there will be the (great) casting up of accounts. But he (Muḥammad) will humbly bend before him, and will effect the salvation of the world.

12. Muḥammad had four friends, who (followed him) in his place, and the four had spotless names in both worlds. ABŪ BAKR ṢIDDĪQ, the Wise, who first truthfully (*ṣidq*) brought the faith (into the world).[3] Then 'UMAR, who adorned the title (of Caliph); justice came to the world when he adopted the faith. Then 'UṢMĀN, the learned and wise one, who wrote the Qur'ān, as he heard its verses. Fourth came 'ALĪ, the mighty lion; when he attacked, both heaven and hell quaked. All four had one mind, and one word, one path and one fellowship. Each preached the same true word, which became authoritative, and read in both worlds.

The very *Qur'ān*[4] which God[5] sent down (to this world), that holy book they read; and they who (have lost their way) in coming (into the world), when they hear it, find the path.[6]

1 *Lit.*, teaching. The Urdu gloss gives کلمہ, the Musalmān creed.

2 The *ihalōka* and *paralōka* of the Hindūs. This world and the world to come.

3 *Lit.*, brought.

4 Here again we have *purāna* used for the Musalmān sacred book.

5 Here *vidhi*, a Hindu technical term.

6 Abū Bakr ibn Abī Quḥāfa was Muḥammad's dearest friend and father-in-law, and one of his first converts. He enjoyed immense influence with his fellow citizens of Mecca, and earned by his probity the appellation of 'aṣ-ṣiddīq,' 'The True.' He accompanied Muḥammad in the Flight, and on his death (632 A.D.) he became the first Caliph. He died 634 A.D.

'Umar ibn Al-khaṭṭab was converted in the 6th year of the call (615 A.D.). His conversion carried with it so much weight that the Musalmān traditions relate it with miraculous attendant details. Abū Bakr by his eloquence and address, and 'Umar by his vigour and promptitude, supplied the want of the practical element in Muḥammad's character. 'Umar set the example of public (instead of private) prayer, which was followed by other Muslims. He was the leading spirit of the Emigrants (*muhājira*) who had left Mecca at the time of the Flight, and settled in Medina. He procured the nomination of Abū Bakr to be first Caliph, and, as a matter of course, succeeded him as second Caliph in 634. He was murdered at Medina in 644.

'Uṣmān ibn 'Affān was one of Muḥammad's first converts, and married his daughter. He was elected third Caliph on the death of 'Umar. The Qur'ān was compiled in its present form in his reign. He was killed at the age of eighty-two in 655, in the rebellion which arose in consequence of the movement, the ultimate aim of which was the deposition of 'Uṣman in favour of 'Alī.

'Alī ibn Abū Ṭālib was Muḥammad's cousin, and one of his first converts. He followed him to Medina three days after the Flight. He succeeded 'Uṣmān as fourth Caliph in 655, and was murdered in 660 A.D.

The first compilation of the Qur'ān was undertaken by Zāid ibn Ṣābit, who was ap-

13. Shēr Shāh is Sultan of Delhi, who warmeth the whole world[1] even as the sun. His kingdom and throne beseem him well; low on the earth have all kings laid their brows before him. By caste a Sūr[2] and with his sword a hero; wise is he and full of all skilfulness. In the nine regions the sun (or all heroes) hath set (or have bent low) before him,[3] and the seven continents[4] of the world have all bowed before him. All his kingdom he won with the might of his sword, as did Alexander, the Zū-l-qarnain.[5] On his

pointed to the work by the Caliph Abū Bakr at the instigation of 'Umar. Zāid had been an amanuensis of Muḥammad. This redaction had no canonical authority, and discrepancies in the text soon appeared. Accordingly, 'Usman confided to Zāid and three other Quraishites the preparation of an edition which was to be canonical for all Muslims. This text is the one which is now extant.

1 *Lit.*, the four quarters. The use of *khaṇḍa* is uncommon, but it is the only meaning which I can suggest here. An Urdū gloss gives چاروں طرف.

2 Here, and in the following stanzas there is a series of puns on the word *sūra*, which is not only the name of the Afghān tribe to which Shēr Shāh belonged, but also means a hero, and the sun.

3 *Lit.* 'In the nine regions there was a bending of *sūra*,' where, again, there is a pun on the word *sūra*, 'hero' or 'sun.' According to the most ancient Hindū Geographers, India was shaped like an eight-petalled lotus. These eight petals, together with the central division, formed the nine *khaṇḍas* or regions, *viz.*, Pañcāla (central), Kaliṅga (S. E.), Avanti (S.), Ānarta (S. W.), Sindhu-Sauvīra (W.), Hārahaura (N. W.), Madra (N.), Kauṇinda (N. E.). The Purāṇas give a different list of names, *viz.*, Indra (E.), Kasēru (N.), Tāmraparṇa, (? S.), Gabhastimat, Kumārikā (Central), Nāga, Saumya, Vāruṇa (W.), Gāndharva. See Cunningham's *Ancient Geography of India*, pp. 5 and 66. The Comm. gives Bhārata-varṣa, Kinnara-varṣa, Hari-vara, Kuru-varṣa, Hiraṇmaya-varṣa, Ramyaka-varṣa, Bhadrāçva-varṣa, Kētumālaka-varṣa, and Ilāvṛta; cf. Viṣṇu-Purāṇa, ii, 2.

4 See I, 5.

5 Zū-l-qarnain, means 'The Master of Two Horns.' Musalmān tradition varies about this name. According to some, the Zū-l-qarnain was not Alexander the Great, but another saint, who lived at the time of Khwāja Khiẓr, and who was so called from his having two curls hanging, one from each side of his forehead, or because he reached both sides of the world, or because he was noble by descent from both his parents, or because he went through both the light and dark parts of the world, or because he died when struck on one side of the forehead, and then was restored to life, and again died on being struck on the other side of the forehead, and again came to life.

Beale's *Oriental Biographical Dictionary* (Ed. Keene), says 'Master of Two Horns, a title of Alexander the Great, probably based on coins representing him in the character of Ammon.' Alexander's coins show his head adorned with two ram's horns. They were widely current in the East, and the Muḥammadans probably gave him that name after his coins.

The Musalmān idea of Alexander the Great is based upon legends contained in the Qur'āṇ and its commentaries. Thus, Burton, *Arabian Nights*, night ccccLxiv, says, 'Iskandar (*i. e.*, Alexander) was originally called Marzbān (Lord of the Marches), son of Marzabah, and, though descended from Yunān, son of Japhet, the eponymus of the Greeks, was born obscure, the son of an old woman. According to the Persians he was the son of the elder Dārāb (Darius Codomannus of the Kayaniaṇ or second dynasty), by a daughter of Philip of Macedon; and was brought up by his grandfather. When Abraham and Isaac rebuilt the Ka'abah they foregathered with him, and Allah sent him forth against the four quarters of the earth to convert men to the faith of the Friend or to cut their throats; thus he became one of the four world-conquerors with Nimrod, Solomon, and Bakht al-Nasr (Nabuchodonosor); and he lived down to generations of men. His Wazīr was Aristū (the Greek Aristotle), and he carried a couple of flags, white and black, which made day and night for him and facilitated his conquests.' The Comm. gives a well-known legend about the title given to him in the text. Alexander concealed the fact of his having horns from the public, and it was known only to his barber. One day, owing to sickness, this barber sent hand is Solomon's ring,[1] and, with it, he gave gifts to the world with full hand. Majestic is he, and a mighty lord of the earth; like a pillar he supporteth the earth and maintaineth the whole universe.

Muḥammad blessed him and said, Reign thou from age to age. Thou art the Emperor of the World. The world is a beggar at thy door.

14. I tell of the heroism of this king, Lord of the world, the weight of whose array is greater than the world can bear. When his army full of horsemen advanceth, covering the earth, mountains crash and fly away in powder, night cometh from the clouds of dust which eclipse the sun, so that man and bird alike goeth home to bed. The land taketh flight, and goeth up into the firmament; earth-dust covereth each continent,—yea the world, the

his son Babban Ḥajjām as his deputy. After the hair-dressing was finished Alexander warned Babban, that if he told any one about the horns he would lose his head. The secret burnt within the wretched man so that he was like to burst, till he relieved his feelings by whispering it to an old Jack-tree. The Jack-tree, unable to tell the secret, withered and died, and a carpenter bought it and made two fiddles and a drum out of the wood. These were bought for a concert at the palace, but when people tried to play them before Alexander, all that one fiddle could be got to say was, *sīg sīg, sīg* (horn, horn, horn), all that the other *kin, kin, kin* (who told? who told? who told?), and all that the drum, *Babban Ḥajjām, Babban Ḥajjām, Babban Ḥajjām.* The secret was thus divulged. Compare the story of Midas. Another well-known legend (referred to in the Padumāwati) is that he made friends with Kh̲wāja Kh̲iẓr, the Green Prophet, (see note to xx, 5) and was guided by him to Ẓalmāt, the Land of Darkness (called the *Kajjalī-ban* by Hindūs), where exists the Fountain of Life. He was, however, unable to drink of this Eternal Spring, and returned disappointed. His unsuccessful quest for the Water of Life has formed the basis of many stock poetical similes.

[1] This is the famous ring with which Solomon 'was wont to imprison Jinns, Marīds and Satans in cucurbites of copper, and to stop them with lead and seal them.' It was made of stamped stone and iron, copper and lead. According to others it consisted of four jewels, presented by as many angels, representing the Winds, the Birds, Earth (including sea), and Spirits, and the Gems were inscribed with as many sentences: (1) To Allāh belong Majesty and Might; (2) All created things praise the Lord: (3) Heaven and Earth are Allāh's slaves; and (4) There is no God but *the* God, and Muḥammad is his messenger. This ring gave Solomon power over all supernatural beings, and hence endowed him with unending wealth,—in fact the whole secret of his power lay in it. Solomon conquered the King of Sidon and married his daughter Jizādih. She so incessantly mourned for her father, that Solomon commanded the Jinns to make an image of him to console her, and to this she and her maids used to pay divine honours. To punish him for encouraging this idolatry, a Jinn named Sak̲h̲r one day obtained possession of the ring which Solomon had entrusted to his concubine Amīnah, while he had gone out for a necessary purpose. During his absence the Jinn transformed himself to Solomon's likeness, and came in and took it from her. Solomon also was changed in form and was not recognized by his subjects, and wandered forlorn about the world for forty days (the time during which the image had been worshipped in his house), while the Jinn reigned in his stead. At the end of that period the demon flew away, and flung the ring into the sea, where it was swallowed by a fish, which was afterwards caught and brought to Solomon who by this means recovered his kingdom and power. Solomon then imprisoned Sak̲h̲r in one of his cucurbites, and cast him into the lake of Tiberias where he still lies. This recovery of a ring by means of a fish is common to many legends. Compare those of Polycrates of Samos and of Çakuntalā.

This Sak̲h̲r was the Jinn who brought Solomon the throne of Bilkīs, the Queen of Sheba. She was a worshipper of the sun, and Solomon converted her to the worship of the true God, by this, and by his wisdom in answering her hard questions. He played one trick on her which is well-known all over the East. He heard that she had legs hairy like a goat, but could not ascertain the truth. So he made her walk over glass underneath which was water with fishes swimming in it. Believing that she had to wade through deep water, she tucked up her petticoats, and revealed to Solomon that the report whole creation and the universe.[1] The Heavens tremble, and Indra quaketh in fear; the snake-god Vāsuki fleeth and hideth himself in the lowest Hell.[2] Meru sinketh down, the oceans dry up, the forests break and are mingled with the dust. (When his army marcheth to a halting place) some of his advance-guard may receive a share of water and of grass for their horses, but for none of his rear-guard is there even sufficient mud.

Citadels which have never bowed to anyone, when he advanceth all become dust,—when the Lord of the World, S͟hēr S͟hāh, the Sun of the Universe attacketh them.

15. I tell of his justice,[3] how it is upon the earth. Not even to a crawling ant doth anyone (dare to) give pain. Naus͟hīrwān[4] was called 'The Just,' but even he was not equal to the justice of S͟hēr S͟hāh. He did justice like unto 'Umar,[5] for the shout of praise to him was (heard over) the whole world. No one dareth even to touch a nose-ring lying fallen on the ground, (much less to pick it up and appropriate it). On the very highways do men cast about gold (yet no one snatcheth it). The cow[6] and the tiger walk together on the same road, and both drink water together at the same landing-ford. He straineth milk and water (mixed together) in his court, and separateth the one from the other. He marcheth with piety, justice and sincerity, and the weak and the mighty he keepeth on even terms.

The whole earth blesseth him, folding its hands continually, and crying, May that head endure immortal as long as there is water in the Ganges and the Jamunā.

16. Again, how can I describe his comeliness, for all the world desireth the beauty of his countenance. His comeliness surpasseth in brightness even the full moon which God created. Sin abandoneth those who reverently gaze upon him, and the whole world maketh obeisance and blesseth him. As when the sun blazeth over the world, so, before him, all things hide their comeliness (in shame). Thus did the Sun[7] become a spotless man, with ten times more[8] beauty than the sun itself. No one can look upon him face to face, and if anyone see him, he remaineth with bent head. His comeliness

was true. Solomon begat a son upon her, who the Abyssinians say was Menelek, the founder of their royal race. She was not a very estimable character before her conversion. *Ṣa'labī*, in his History of the Prophets, gives an entertaining account of her wrong doings. She introduced the worship of the sun into her dominion, and when she was married to her first husband against her will, she treacherously slew him on her wedding night. It required a mighty man like Solomon to tame so independent a young person. Much of this note is taken from Burton's Arabian Nights, and from Palmer's translation of the Qur'ān.

1 The √ *maṇḍ* has two meanings, either 'to adorn' (*maṇḍana*) or 'to crush,' (*mardana*). The passage here is corrupt in all MSS., and the reading is very doubtful.

2 See note to line 5 of the first stanza.

3 This reference to S͟hēr S͟hāh's justice (*'adal*) may have a complimentary reference to his son 'Adal. See *J. A. S. B.*, Pt. I, 1890, p. 167.

4 The celebrated king of Persia, surnamed 'Ādil, or the Just. He ascended the throne 531 A.D. He was the Chosroes of the Greeks. Muḥammad (B. 571) used to boast of his good fortune in being born when so just a king reigned. He died 579 A.D.

5 The second Caliph in succession to Muḥammad. See note to 12, 9.

6 *Gōru* is properly any domesticated herbivorous animal.

7 Here again the word *sūra* is introduced with a threefold meaning, hero, sun and proper name.

8 *Āgari* means 'excellent.'

increaseth by a quarter, day by day, the Creator formed his beauty above the world.

Comely is he with a jewelled (tiara) on his brow, and the moon waneth as he waxeth; while the earth, craving to see him, standeth and humbly offereth its praises.

17. Again God hath made him so greatly generous, that none in the world hath ever given gifts like unto him. Bali[1] and Vikramāditya[2] were famed for their generosity, and Ḥātim Ṭāē[3] and Karṇa[4] were described as lavish; but none of them equalleth Shēr Shāh, for the very ocean and even Mount Mēru, are ever minishing (as they give up their jewels and gold). The kettle-drum of his generosity soundeth at his court, and the fame thereof hath gone even across the ocean. The world touched this Sun,[5] and became of gold compact, so that poverty fled and went beyond the borders of his kingdom. He who but once approacheth him and asketh, for all his life is free from hunger and from nakedness. Even that (King of old) who performed ten horse-sacrifices,[6]—even he gave not holy gifts like him.

So generous hath Sultan Shēr Shāh been born upon the world, that none hath e'er been like him, or will be, nor doth anyone give such gifts.

1 The well-known Daitya, who gave Viṣṇu his famous three and a half paces of ground.

2 'Clarum et venerabile nomen.' The well-known king of Avanti, many legends of whose generosity are given in the Siṁhāsana Battīsī.

3 Familiar to readers of the Bāgh-o-Bahār (story of the second Darwēsh). His liberality continued after his death. His tomb was surrounded by stone images of girls, which each night used to burst out into lamentations for so good a man. King Ẕū-l-karā'a camping near there one night, hearing the wailing, asked the reason, and was told it was the tomb of Ḥātim Ṭāē. He then cried out in jest, 'O Ḥātim Ṭāē, we are thy guests, and hungry.' Shortly afterwards one of his camels became violently ill and (as they say in Ireland) to prevent its dying, they killed it, and then, to make the best of a bad job, had a good feast on its flesh. Next day, while they were on the march, they were met by Ḥātim's son bringing a she-camel. He explained that his father had appeared to him on the preceding night, and said 'Ẕū-l-karā'a sought hospitality from me last night, and I had nothing to give him; so perforce I killed his camel, and do thou now give him one in exchange for the one I took.' History does not relate how the son appreciated his father's vicarious hospitality, but he certainly did accept the responsibility.

4 The famous Hero of the Mahābhārata. The son of Kuntī by Sūrya. He was famous for his generosity. Yudhiṣṭhira once asked Kṛṣṇa, who was the most generous member of his family. To his mortification Kṛṣṇa replied 'Karṇa.' The following is an example. A poor Brāhmaṇ woman had a child born to her, and her husband went to Yudhiṣṭhira and begged for some wood to make a fire to warm her. Yudhiṣṭhira ordered his steward to supply the fuel, but on the latter reporting that there was none just then available, he told the Brāhmaṇ to go away, and to come again in an hour or two, when he could be supplied. The Brāhmaṇ went on to Karṇa and made a similar request. It happened that, here too, the supply of fire-wood was temporarily deficient, and the steward asked Karṇa to tell the man to come again in an hour or two (as Yudhiṣṭhira had done). 'Fool,' replied Karṇa, 'shall I leave the poor woman to die of cold, while you are searching for fuel? Break up my beds till the Brāhmaṇ has enough wood for to-day, and tell him to come to-morrow for more.' 'This,' said Kṛṣṇa to Yudhiṣṭhira, 'is the difference between you and Karṇa. Had *you* no beds to break up?' The above legend is sung by the Vyāsas at the passage in Mahā-bhārata where Karṇa divested himself of the ear-rings and armour (with which he had been born), and gave them to Indra, (See Mahā-bhārata, Ādi-parvan, Adhyāya 67, Çlōkas 141–143).

5 Again the triple pun on the word *sūra*. Shēr Shāh is compared to a philosopher's stone which changed all that touched it into gold.

6 This is a reference to Brahmā, who completed ten Açva-mēdha sacrifices at Benares. The site of the Sacrifice is the well-known Daçāçva-mēdha ghāṭ in that city.

18. Saiyad Ashraf (Jahāngīr)[1] was an elect saint, and he it was who threw light upon my path. He lit the lamp of love within my heart; the light burned up, and my heart became pure. My way had been dark and invisible, and lo! it became bright and I understood. He cast my sins into the salt ocean, and making me as his disciple took me into the boat of virtue. He grasped my rudder firmly,[2] and I reached the landing place on the far bank. If a man hath such a steersman,[3] he graspeth him and bringeth to the other side. He is a protector, and one who succoureth in time of trouble, and, where (the water) is fathomless, there giveth he his hand.

His family title was Jahāngīr, pure like the moon. He was the Holy Master of the World, and I am the slave of his house.

19. In his house was a spotless jewel, Ḥājī Shaikh by name, fulfilled with good fortune. In his house were two bright lights, whom God created to show the way. Shaikh Mubārak glorious as a full moon, and Shaikh Kamāl spotless in the world. Both were stedfast, unmoveable like pole-stars, exalted even above Mēru and Kukhaṇḍa.[4] God gave them beauty and glory, and made them pillars of the world. On these two pillars supported He the earth, and under their weight the universe remained firm. Whoever saw them and reverently touched their feet, his sins were lost and his body became pure.

O Muḥammad, there is the road secure, where a saintly teacher beareth company. O my soul, when he hath a boat and a rower, a man quickly gaineth the other side.

20. Muḥīu-d-dīn was my preceptor, my steersman, and I served him. He crosseth speedily who hath him upon the ferry. Before him was Shaikh Burhān, who brought him on the path and gave him knowledge. His spiritual guide was the good Alhadād, who in the world was a light and beauteous in the faith. He was a disciple of Saiyad Muḥammad and even perfected men enjoyed[5] his fellowship. To him did Dāniyāl point out the path,—Dāniyāl, who consorted with Ḥazrat Khwāja Khiẓr.[6] The Ḥazrat Khwāja was pleas-

1 Saiyad Ashraf was one of the founders of the line of spiritual preceptors, whose representative in the first half of the 16th century (Muḥīu-d-dīn) taught the poet. For full particulars see note to stanza 20.

2 This is a difficult passage. *Kariā* is the same as *kaḍi*, an iron ring, or a beam, hence a rudder. Either meaning will do here. Other MSS., and printed editions have *unha mora kara būḍata kai gahā*, he grasped my hand as I was sinking. *Pōḍhi kai* means 'firmly.'

3 *Kanahāra* or *kanadhāra* is the Sanskrit *karṇadhāra*.

4 See line 1 of the second stanza.

5 *Lit.* sported in his company.

6 Khwāja Khiẓr, the Green Prophet, is a well-known figure in Muḥammadan legends. He has been identified by some with Elijah and by others with St. George. He is said to be still living, and sometimes aids travellers who have lost their way. As stated in the note to xiii, 5, he conducted Alexander the Great to the Land of Darkness, when the latter was searching for the Water of Life. He usually appears on horseback, dressed in green (hence his name). In India he is looked upon as a saint not only by Musalmāns but also by Hindūs. Lāl Bēgī Mihtars pay him divine reverence. Their first pīr is Jesus, the Lord of the Wand, their second Khwāja Khiẓr, the Master of the Water-cup, their third Muḥammad, the Great Interceder, and their fourth Lāl Bēg, the man of the Wild-flowing Tresses (see Greeven, *Knights of the Broom*, 45). Temple's *Legends of the Panjāb* are full of references to him. He is, in India more especially a water-god, or the god of the Flood. Under his special protection is the well at Safidam in the Jind state, which contains the Water of Life. Musalmān traditions make him out to have been a true believer in the Islām of his day and to have been Wazīr of Kai Qubād (6th century

ed with him, and brought him (as a disciple) to Saiyad Rājī Ḥāmid Shāh. From him (Muḥīu-d-din) did I win all my (good) deeds. My tongue was loosened,[12] and, a poet, (I learned to) tell my tale.[13]

He was my master and I his disciple, evermore do I bow before him as his slave. Through him did I obtain a sight of the Creator.

B. C.), the founder of the second or Kayanian dynasty of the kings of Persia, and ninth in ascent before the Darius, who was conquered by Alexander. In the text, all that is meant is that Khwāja Khiẓr appeared to Dāniyāl, and performed his customary office of guide.

[12] *Lit.* uncovered.

[13] The following account of Malik Muḥammad's spiritual ancestors is taken partly from what the poet himself tells us, and partly from the Urdū gloss and other sources

He belonged to the *Cishtiyā Niẓāmiyā*, that is to say he belonged to the spiritual descent which took its name from the celebrated Niẓāmu-d-dīn Auliyā, the teacher of Amīr Khusrō, who died about 1325 A. D. His disciple was Sīrāju-d-dīn, whose disciple was Shaikh 'Alāu-l-ḥaqq. 'Alāu-l-ḥaqq's son and disciple Shaikh Nūr Quṭb 'Ālam, the date of whose death is usually given as 1444 A. D. Chronologists, however, vary as to this; some say A. H. 808, *i.e.*, A. D. 1405, others A. H. 813, *i.e.*, A. D. 1410, others A. H. 818, *i.e.*, A. D. 1415, others A. H. 848, *i.e.*, A. D. 1444, and others again A. H. 851, *i.e.*, A. D. 1447. Mr. Beveridge in J. A. S. B. lxiv, Pt. I, 207, considers A. H. 818, A. D. 1415, as the true date. He lived at Paṇḍuā in Māldah, and another disciple was Saiyad Ashraf Jahāngīr (see 18, 1.) Ashraf's most famous disciple was Shaikh Ḥājī, whose disciples were Shaikh Mubārak, and Shaikh Kamāl. Shaikh Nūr Quṭb 'Ālam and Saiyad Ashraf Jahāngīr were fellow disciples (*pīr bhāī*) and from them eighth in descent came Malik Muḥammad (Fl. 1540 A. D.)

The full genealogical table is as follows:—

Niẓāmu-d-dīn (d. 1325 A. D.)

Sīrāju-d-dīn.

Shaikh 'Alāu-l-ḥaq.

Shaikh Nūr Quṭb 'Ālam of Paṇḍuā, and Saiyad Ashraf Jahāngīr (*vide* xviii, 1), (son of preceding.)

Shaikh Ḥashāmu-d-dīn of Mānikpur.

Saiyad Rājī Ḥāmid Shāh.

Shaikh Dāniyāl (d. 1486 A. D.).

Saiyad Muḥammad.

Shaikh Alhadād.

Shaikh Burhān.

Saiyad Muḥīu-d-dīn (*vide* xx, 1).

Malik Muḥammad, (1540 A. D.)

Shaikh Ḥājī.

Shaikh Mubārak and

Shaikh Kamāl.

From this it follows that the poet was not an actual disciple of Saiyad Ashraf Jahāngīr, as might be assumed from xviii, 1 and ff. Malik Muḥammad merely refers to him and praises him as his spiritual ancestor. A tradition makes him the poet's *mantra-guru*, while Muḥīu-d-dīn was his *vidyā-guru*, *i.e.*, the one initiated him, and the other taught him, which agrees with Malik Muḥammad's own language. Shaikh Dāniyāl, the fifth in the line before the poet, appears to have claimed to have had for a friend Khwāja Khiẓr, who introduced him to his preceptor, Saiyad Rājī Ḥāmid Shāh. Shaikh Burhān, Malik Muḥammad's spiritual grandfather resided at Kāl'pī in Bundēl'khaṇd, and is said to have died at 100 years of age in A. H. 970, or A. D. 1562-63. See Rep. Arch. Sur. Ind. xxi, 131.

21. Muḥammad was skilful, though he had but one eye,[1] and every poet who heard him was entranced. Even as God created the moon for the universe, so He put a dark spot upon her, while He made her bright. With that one eye the poet saw the whole world,[2] shining bright like Venus brilliant among the other stars.[3] Until there come black spots upon a mango-fruit, it hath no fragrant scent. God made the water of the ocean salt, but nevertheless He made it immeasurably boundless. Mount Mēru was destroyed by the trident, and then it became a mountain of gold,[4] and reached to heaven. Till black firestains defile the crucible (the ore) remaineth unsmelted, and becometh not pure gold.

The poet hath but one eye, but it is (bright) as a mirror, and that mirror's nature is pure. (Though he is uncomely), all that are beautiful clasp his feet, and with desire look upon his face.

As the prophet Muḥammad (see xii, 1) had four friends, so also had the poet Malik Muḥammad. He tells us their names were Malik Yūsuf, Salār Khādim, Miyā̃ Salōnē and Shaikh Baḍē. Concerning these, see the introduction to this edition, and xxii, 1 and ff.

The Urdū gloss concludes (we insert dates and other particulars in parentheses), Those who consider that Ḥazrat 'Abdu-l-Qādir Jilānī (b. 1078, d. 1166) (God's mercy be upon him) is descended from Saiyad Muḥīu-d-dīn, and that Saiyad Rājū Qattāl (d. 1403) is descended from Saiyad Rājī, are far from being in the right. It is clear that the line of Qadariyās is descended from Ḥazrat 'Abdu-l-Qādir Jilānī. His preceptor was Ḥazrat Abū Saiyad.

'Saiyad Rājū Qattāl was full brother of Ḥazrat Saiyad Jalālu-d-dīn of Bukhārā (who was known as Makhdūm Jahāniyān Jahān (Gasht Shaikh Jalāl), and was his disciple). He was a Suharwardiyā by sect.

'Another disciple of Ḥazrat Niẓāmu-d-dīn (the founder of Malik Muḥammad's line) was Shaikh Ruknu-d-dīn Abū-l-fatḥ Ma'āṣir (fl. 1310), who was also disciple of his own father Shaikh Ṣadru-d-dīn ('Ārif, d. 1309). This last was disciple of his father Shaikh Bahāu-d-dīn Zikariyā (d. 1266) of Mul'tān, who was disciple of Shaikh Shahābu-d-dīn (Suharwardiyā, d. 1234), who travelled from city to city as missionary (peace be upon him).'

Makhdūm Jahāniyān was a disciple of Ruknu-d-dīn abovementioned. The Suharwardiyās form a branch of the followers of the *çūfī* sect, and are named from Suharward, a town near Bagdad, the birth place of the founder Shahābu-d-dīn above mentioned.

1 According to tradition this was the result of an attack of small-pox, which not only destroyed the sight of one eye, but dreadfully disfigured his features. It is said that some Rājā once saw him, and loudly scoffed at his ugly face, not knowing who he was. Thereupon the poet said, 'scoffest thou at me, or at the Potter who fashioned me?' Struck by his reply, the Rājā repented, and became his disciple. The poet still, however thanks God for all His mercies, and points out that every great and good thing in Nature has some detraction.

2 That is to say other folk with two eyes can see but a short way, but the poet's single eye 'in a fine frenzy rolling, can glance from heav'n to earth and earth to heav'n.'

3 Çukra, the regent of the planet Venus, had but one eye. He lost it this way. He was guru of the demon Bali, who gave Viṣṇu, in his dwarf-incarnation, the famous three and a half steps of ground. Çukra, to prevent the success of Viṣṇu's stratagem, came and hid in a water-vessel. When, at the time of making the formal gift, water refused to flow from the vessel, Viṣṇu, under pretence of clearing out the spout with a stick, pierced Çukra's right eye.

4 According to tradition, mountains had once wings, and used to fly about. When they alighted after flight, they used to crush people under their weight, so Indra cut off their wings with his thunderbolts. The first to suffer amputation was Sumēru. It was a mountain of gold (Viṣṇu-purāṇa, ii, 2). The poet has substituted Çiva's trident (*triçūla*) for Indra's thunderbolt (*vajra*). This confusion between Çiva and Indra is constant throughout the poem.

22. The Poet Muḥammad[1] had four friends, and by gaining their friendship he raised himself to equality with them. One was Malik Yūsuf, the learned and wise, who first of all knew the secret meaning of words. The next was Salār Khādim, the discreet, whose arms were ever raised either in (wielding) the sword or in (distributing) gifts. The third was Miyā̃ Salōnē, a lion amidst unsurpassed heroes, a fighter with the sword in the battle-field. The fourth was Shaikh Baḍē, famed as a sage. Yea, even sages thought themselves honoured by performing his commands.[2] All four were learned in the fourteen[3] branches of knowledge, and God himself created their association (with the poet). Let a tree but dwell near a sandal-grove, and let but the odour of the sandal permeate it, and, lo, it becometh sandal-wood itself.

Muḥammad, when he had found these four friends, became of one soul with them. When he hath accomplished their companionship in this world, how can they be separated in the next?

23. The city Jāyas is a holy spot: there came the poet and told his lay. There humbly waited he upon Hindū scholars, and prayed them[4] to correct and mend the broken (metre) and arrangement (of his song). I am a follower of poets, and I go forward saying my say, and beating the drum with the drum-stick to proclaim it.[5] My heart is a treasure-house, and it holdeth a store of precious stones. I made my tongue the key of my palate and opened it. I spake words,—jewels, and rubies; sweet, filled with the wine of love, and priceless. He who is wounded by the words of love,[6]—What is hunger or sleep or shade to him? He changeth his appearance, and becometh a hermit, like a jewel covered and hidden in the dust.

O Muḥammad, the body which love hath, hath neither blood nor flesh. Whoever seeth the face of such a man laugheth, but when the lover heareth the laughter tears come (into his eyes).[7]

24. It was the year 947 (of the Hijra),[8] when the poet began to tell this tale in words. Of Ceylon and Queen Padmāvatī, whom Ratna-sēna brought to Citaur castle; of 'Alāu-d-dīn, the Sulṭān of Delhi, and how Rāghava-caitanya told him of her. How the Emperor heard, and besieged the castle, and how there arose the war between the Hindūs and the

1 So also had the Prophet Muḥammad, see 12, 1. Regarding these four men, see introductory remarks.

2 *Adēsa* also means the initiation of a *cēlā*, or disciple, by a *guru*, or spiritual preceptor.

3 The 4 Vēdas, the 6 Vēdāṅgas, the Purāṇas, the Mīmāṁsā, the Nyāya, and Dharma.

4 *Bhajā* or *Bhājā*, is equivalent to *bhrājā*, *i.e.*, *prakāçita kiā*, 'made manifest;' hence 'presented,' a petition.

5 *Ḍágā* is a drum-stick. The poet means that he is impelled to publish his lay by beat of drum, so to speak, *i.e.*, as loudly as possible, in order that other poets and learned men may hear it, and correct his mistakes. A simpler rendering is obtained by amending the text to *kichu kahi calata bōla dei ḍagā*, 'saying my say, I progress, setting down the feet of language;' in which language is metaphorically compared to a foot, or step (*ḍagā*).

6 Here we have the first instance of the poet's use of the word *biraha*. He uses it to mean love, especially unhappy love. In countless places it cannot possibly have the usual meaning of 'separation from a beloved one.' *Ghāyā* is translated in the Urdū Gloss by بھری 'full of.' We can find no authority for this.

7 The worldly imagine the distraught lover to be mad, and laugh at him. He, on the other hand, knowing that no jewel is so precious as the love which he has conceived, weeps at *their* madness.

8 1540 A.D.

Musalmāns. From beginning to end, just as the story runs, so wrote he it in the language of the people, and told it in verse. The poet, the bard,[1] and the lotus full of nectar, are near to what is far and far from what is near. That which is near is yet far, like the flower and the thorn (so near and yet so different), and that which is far is near, like sugar and the ants (who dwell so far from it, yet find it out).

So the bee[2] cometh from the (distant) forest, and findeth the odour of the lotus-nectar, while the frog ne'er findeth the odour, though he dwelleth (in the pond) close to (the flower).

CANTO II.

SIṀHALA.

25. Now sing I the tale of Siṁhala-dvīpa,[3] and tell of the Perfect Woman.[4] My description is like an excellent mirror, in which each form is seen as it really is. Happy is that land where the women are lights,[5] and where God created that (famous) Padminī (Padmāvatī). All people tell of seven lands, but none is fit to compare with Siṁhala. The Diyā-land[6] (or land of lamps) is not so bright as it. The land of Saran[7] cannot bear comparison with it. I say that Jambū-land[8] is nowhere like it, and that Laŋka-land cannot even fill (the excellence of) its reflection. The land of Kumbhasthala[9] fled to the forest (before it), but the land of

1 *Kabi* is one who makes poems, *biāsa* (*vyāsa*) is one who recites them.

2 *I.e.*, a prophet has no honour in his own country. The author means that he is aware that his own country-folk, and his own people (the Musalmāns) will not care for his poem, for it is in a Hindū dialect and not in Urdū; but, on the other hand men of distant lands and of other religions (the Hindūs) will be attracted by it, as the bee is attracted by the distant lotus. There is a tradition that Malik Muḥammad commenced the composition of the poem in his own village, where it was not thought much of. One of his disciples wandered to Jāyas and began to sing there the particular canto (Nāgmatī's song of the twelve months), which he had been taught. The Rājā of Jāyas was so pleased with what he heard, especially with the *dōhā* commencing *kawāla jo bigasata mānasara, binu jala gaeu sukhāi*, that he invited Malik Muḥammad to his city, and encouraged him to complete the work.

3 Ceylon. The word *dvīpa* means both island and continent.

4 A Padminī is one of the four classes of women and is supremely the best. The Singhalese women are all supposed to be Padminīs, *omne ignotum pro mirifico*.

5 Here there is a pun on the word (*dīpa* = *dvīpa*), a continent or island, and *dīpaka*, a light.

6 The poet now proceeds to compare Siṁhala, not with the seven continents of tradition, referred to in line 4, and catalogued in the note to stanza i, 5, but with half-a-dozen imaginary continents named after parts of the human body. *Diyā-dīpa*, the land of lights, means the land of fair women's eyes. *Sarana-dīpa* (*çravaṇa-dīpa*) means the land of their ears. *Jambū-dīpa*, Rose-apple-land, is the land of their raven hair, to which the black rose-apple is often compared. *Laŋka-dīpa*, is the land of waists. *Kumbha-sthala*, jar land, is the land of their rounded breasts; a. v. l. is *gabha-sthala* (*garbha-sthala*) the land of wombs; and finally *mahu-sthala* (*madhu-sthala*), is the land of secret parts. Under this highly figurative language the poet signifies that the women of Siṁhala surpassed all these imaginary lands, each in its own peculiar excellence.

7 The poet does not seem to be aware that *Sarana-dīpa* (*Saran-dīp*, Serendib) is actually Ceylon itself. Here, as pointed out above, the words also mean 'ear-land.'

8 Hindūstān, or bosom-land.

9 Or perhaps Gabhasthala, one of the nine divisions of Bhārata-varṣa (India); here used as equivalent to *garbha-sthala*, the land of wombs. The forest whither the bosoms fled is, of course, the necklaces, bodices, &c., under which they lay concealed.

Mahusthala[1] had destroyed mankind (and how therefore can I compare it with Siṁhala-dvīpa).

In the whole universe, in the world are seven lands, but none of them is excellent beside the land of Siṁhala.

26. Gandharva-sēna was a fragrant[2] prince, He was its king, and that was his dominion. I have heard of King Rāvaṇa in Laŋkā;[3] greater even than his was his majesty. Fifty-six times ten millions formed his battle-array, and over all were princes and commanders of forts. Sixteen thousand horses were in his stalls, black-eared and gallant steeds.[4] Seven thousand Singhalese elephants had he, each like the mighty Airāvata[5] of Kailāsa.[6] He is called the crown of lords of steeds, and with his goad he causeth to bow low the elephants of lords of elephants. Over lords of men I call him a second Indra, and in the world I also call him the Indra[7] of the lords of earth.

So universal[8] a monarch was he, that all the earth feared him. All men came and bowed their heads before him, no one dared to emulate him.

27. When a man approacheth this land, 'tis as though he approacheth Kailāsa the mount of heaven. Dense mango-groves lie on every side, rising from the earth to the very sky. Each tall tree exhaleth the odours of mount Malaya,[9] and the shade covereth the world as though it were the night. The shade is pleasant with its Malaya-breeze; e'en in the fiery month of Jyēṣṭha[10] 'tis cool amidst it. It is as though night cometh from that shade, and as though from it cometh the greenness of the sky.[11] When the wayfarer cometh thither, suffering from the heat, he forgetteth his trouble in his blissful rest, and whoso hath found this perfect shade, returneth ne'er again to bear the sun-rays.

So many and so dense are these groves, that I cannot tell their end. The whole six seasons of the year[12] do they flower and fruit, as though it were always spring.

28. The pleasant thick mango groves bear fruit, and the more fruit they bear, the more (humbly) do the trees bow their heads. On the

1 Or Mēwasthila.

2 There is here an alliteration between Gandharva, and *Gandha*, scent. Some of the MSS. have *Sēni* for *Sēna* throughout the poem. This would lead one to restore the word to the Sanskrit *Sainya*, or *Çyēna* (श्येन = A hawk, used like Siṁha) were there not a strong tradition in favour of *Sēna*.

3 The identification of Laŋkā with Ceylon is a very modern idea, *e. g.*, Varāha-mihira, *Bṛhat-saṁhitā*, xiv, 11, 15, mentions Laŋkā and Siṁhala as different countries.

4 *Çyāma-karṇa*, black-eared, is a technical name for a horse. It is the kind used in sacrifices. *Tukhāra* means 'horse.'

5 The name of Indra's elephant.

6 Çiva's heaven. Here taken for Indra's heaven, Indra-purī.

7 Here Indra is referred to in two aspects. First he is the mighty king of the lower gods, and hence supreme over lords of men; and secondly he is the storm-god giving refreshing showers to the earth, and hence an object of worship to everyone who lives by cultivation.

8 *Cakkawai* = *Cakravartī*.

9 The Western Ghauts (*ghāṭs*), famous for their growth of sandal trees.

10 The hottest month in the year, May-June, with its pitiless burning blue-grey sky.

11 This is an example of the rhetorical figure *utprēkṣā*, or Poetical Fancy, with the word expressing comparison omitted. The poet fancifully states that this shade is so dark, that from it is produced all night, while the green shade of the sky is its reflection.

12 Hindūs divide the year into six seasons of two months each.

main branches and trunks[1] of the jack trees, the jack fruit ripen, and fair appeareth the baṛhal[2] to him who looketh. The khirnī[3] ripeneth, sweet as molasses, and the black wild plum,[4] like black bees (among its leaves). Cocoanuts ripen and ripeneth the khurhur;[5] they ripen as though the orchards were in Indra's heaven. From the Mahuā[6] doth such sweetness exude, that honey is its flavour, and flowers its scent; and in these princes' gardens are other fruits, good to eat whose names I know not. They all appear with nectar-like branches, and he who once tasteth them remaineth ever longing for more.

Areca[7] and nutmeg, all fruits, are produced there luxuriantly. On every side are thick groves of tamarinds, of palmyras, and of date-palms.

29. There dwell the birds, singing in many tongues, and sporting joyfully as they look upon these nectar-branches. At dawn the honey-suckers are fragrant, and the turtle-dove cries out '’tis thou and only thou.'[8] The emerald-parroquets[9] sportively rejoice, and the rock-pigeons cry *kurkur*, and fly about. The hawk-cuckoo[10] crieth for its beloved, and the skulking warbler shouteth *tūhī̃ khī*. *Kuhū kuhū* ever crieth the cuckoo, while the king-crow[11] speaketh in many tongues. 'Tyre, tyre' crieth the milkmaid-bird,[12] while the green pigeon[13] plaintively telleth its tale of woe. The peacock's cry *kũ kũ* soundeth sweet to the ear, and loudly caw the crows.

Filling the orchards, sitteth every bird that hath a name, and each praiseth the Creator in his own tongue.

30. At every step one cometh upon a well or reservoir,[14] adorned with seats and steps. Many are the springs scattered about, one named after every holy place of pilgrimage. Around them are built convents and temples, where devotees sit in austerity and mutter prayer. Here are great saints,[15] Sannyāsins, devotees of Rāma, and Māsavāsins; Māhēçvaras,

1 The jack fruit grows only on the stems and main branches of the trees, not on the younger shoots.

2 *Artocarpus lakoocha*, Roxb., A sweet-acid fruit, yellowish red and nearly round.

3 *Mimusops hexandra*, Roxb.

4 *Eugenia jambolana*, L.

5 *Ficus cunia*, Ham.

6 *Bassia latifolia*, Roxb.

7 *Guā* and *supārī* are varieties of the areca or betel nut.

8 Its cry is *ēka-i tū-hī*, 'one alone, only thou.'

9 The *sārau* is a bright green parroquet.

10 The *Papīhā* or Hawk-cuckoo, (*Hierococcyx varius*, Vahl) is not a sparrow-hawk as the dictionaries say. Its cry is *piu piu*, 'beloved, beloved.' The ordinary native tradition is that it says *pī kahā̃* 'where is my beloved.' It is the 'Brain-fever bird' of Anglo-Indians.

11 The *Bhrṅgaka* or Racket-tailed Drongo (*Dissemurus paradiseus*, L.), is not a sparrow-hawk, as the dictionaries say. It is a sort of king-crow, it is an excellent talking-bird.

12 The *maharī* is said to be a bird like the *mahōkhā* (*cuculus costaneus*, Roxb.), but smaller. Its cry is *dahī, dahī*, 'tyre, tyre,' and hence it is also known as *gwālinī* or *ahirinī* *i.e.* milkmaid.

13 The cry of the *hāril* or green pigeon (*crocopus phœnicopterus*, Latham) is *hā hāri gaī* 'alas I have lost.' It lives in the various fig trees of India. It is said never to rest on the ground. When it descends to drink, it sucks up water, from a short distance aloft, through a straw. When it dies, it falls to the ground with its feet in the air, rather than allow them to touch earth.

14 A *bāwarī* is a large masonry well with steps leading down to the water.

15 Many of the sects mentioned in this list are described in Wilson's *Religious Sects of the Hindūs*. The Commentary also gives a full account of them. *Sannyāsins* (W. p 32) consider themselves dead to the world and go through a funeral ceremony in their life

Jaŋgamas, Yatins, worshippers of the left-hand and of the right-hand Dēvī. There are Brahmacārins, and there are Digambaras to whom it seemeth good to go naked. There are Sant s, Siddhas, Yōgins, and Pessimists seated on the path of hopelessness.

Sēvarās, and the like, Vāna-prasthas, Siddhi-sādhakas, are all seated there, mortifying their earthly frames.

31. What can be compared to the water of the Mānasarōdaka lake, full as the sea and as unfathomless? Its water clear as spotless pearls, like ambrosia scented with camphor. From the isle of Laŋkā have they brought the lapis lazuli,[1] and with it built the landing stages. On each side have been made

time. They lay aside the brahmanical cord and carry a staff *(daṇḍa)* which they never lay upon the ground, and which they consider as a witness of all their actions. They are hence also called *Daṇḍins* (W. 143, 191). *Rāma-yatins* are Vaiṣṇava mendicants, who worship Rāma, like the Vairāgins of Ayōdhyā. *Māsa-vāsins*, are those who abide for a month in one place, and then wander on. *Māhēçvaras* are mendicants who cover themselves with ashes, and adopt the traditional appearance of Çiva, whom they worship. *Jaŋgamas* (W. 219) are ever on the move. They usually worship Vīra-bhadra, who destroyed Dakṣa's famous sacrifice. This legend is a favourite subject of sculpture at Elephanta and Ellora. As regards *Yatins* see W. 317., They are Jains who have taken orders. Dēvī is the object of worship of the *vāma*, or left-hand *Çāktas*, and Satī of the *dakṣiṇa* or right hand ones. See W. 240, 254, 250. A *Brahmacārin* is a religious student, living under the supervision of his spiritual preceptor (W. 237). *Digambaras* are naked vagrants, such as *Paramahaṁsas, Nāgās* and the like. Some Vaiṣṇava sects call themselves *Digambaras*, but wear white clothes. Jainas are divided into *Digambaras* (naked) and *Çvētāmbaras* (white-dressed) (W. p. 276). *Santas* are merely religious people generally. *Siddhas* are Yōgins who have arrived at supreme perfection (adepts). They have eight supernatural powers *(siddhi)*, viz., *aṇimā*, the power of becoming infinitely small, *mahimā*, that of becoming infinitely great, *laghimā*, of becoming infinitely light, *garimā*, of becoming infinitely heavy, *prāpti* of reaching infinitely far, *prākāmya*, of obtaining at once whatever is desired, *īçatva*, of infinite sovereignty, *vaçitva*, of infinite power of subjection. *Yōgins* are Çaiva mendicants claiming spiritual descent from Gōrākṣa-nātha. They claim the power of acquiring, even in life, entire command over elementary matter by means of certain ascetic practices (W. 205). An adept *Yōgin* (or *Jōgī*) is a *Siddha* above described. Readers of the poem will have much to do with *Yōgins*, for king Ratna-sēna and his followers become such. A *Viyōgin* is a pessimist, soured by unhappy love. *Viyōga*, lit., dis-union, in this poem is specially used to mean the condition of a lover who is separated from his beloved. *Sēvaras* (the word is a corruption of the Sanskrit *Çabara*) go about in troops, with matted hair, and red-ochre-coloured garments. They call themselves *Çaivas*. To mark their triumph over sensual desires, they affix an iron ring and chain to the male organ, which they also mutilate. Wilson (236) calls them *Karā Liŋgins.* They extort money by pretended miracles, such as wringing Ganges-water out of their dry matted hair. *Khēwaras* are a sub-variety of the *Sēwara's* They carry skulls. One of their tricks is to turn spirituous liquor into milk, and then to drink it. Another is to rub the palms of their apparently empty hands together, till they bring forth Wheat, Gram, and the like. The name is a fanciful one, derived from *Sēwara*. A *Vāna-prastha* is a Brāhmaṇa of the third order who has retired from domestic life to the forest. A *Siddhi-sādhaka* is the same as a *Siddha*. An *Avadhūta* is a man who has shaken off restraint. Thus Rāmānanda called his Vaiṣṇava disciples *Avadhūta*, because they had shaken off the ties of caste and personal distinction. So Çaiva mendicants, such as *Paramahaṁsas* who go about naked are *Avadhūtas*. Each of these ascetics is represented as mortifying his *bhūtātman* or body considered as composed of grosser elements, into which it must ultimately be dissolved. The five grosser elements are earth, water, fire, air and ether. Hence *pañcatva*, or the condition of being five, is used to mean death. By mortifying these elements, the soul acquires ultimate release from the round of transmigration.

1 The lapis lazuli is the stone of Laŋka. It is popularly supposed to be the conglomerate ashes of that city after it was burnt by Rāma, the gold spots in it being the relics of the ornaments which were burnt at the same time.

winding steps on which the folk ascend and descend on all sides. The lotuses bloom there beautiously scarlet, with their clusters of thousands upon thousands of petals.[1] The swans overturn the shells, from which pearls fall out, which they pick up and sport as they do so. Beautiful swim these golden birds,[2] looking as it were statues cast in gold.

Above around lie the banks, with ambrosial fruit on every tree. He who hath but once seen the fairness of these lakes, loseth for aye both thirst and hunger.

32. The maidens come to draw the water, each in form and figure a Padminī.[3] Their limbs are odorous of the lotus (*padma*), and the black bees hover round them as they come. Waisted like lionesses, and with eyes like lotuses,[4] swan-like in their motions, sweet-voiced as the cuckoo. In numbers they come, row upon row, charming the eye with varied gaits. Over their moon-faces shine their golden jars,[5] as, in joy and sport, they come and go. Struck, as it were by a dagger, by her coquettish eyes, is he on whom the glance of one of them is fallen. The black cloud of her hair falleth from her head to her feet, from behind which flasheth the lightning of her teeth.

Like images of the God of Love[6] are these nymphs[7] of matchless charm. If these water-maidens are so beauteous, how lovely must be their queen!

33. To tell of the lakes and lakelets is more than I can do. So broad are they that vision cannot cross them. How many are the lilies that bloom there, like stars risen in the sky. The clouds come down to them, drink their water and ascend, while within the fish (carried up into the air) gleam like lightning. Happily with each other swim the feathered fowl upon the surface, white are they and yellow, and red of varied hue. There sport the ruddy goose and his mate, whose lot it is to wake the night apart, and meet by day.[8] There joyfully sporteth the Indian crane, (remembering that, not like the ruddy goose) he liveth and dieth in the company (of his spouse).[9] There are the lotus, the gold crane,[10] the stork, and the *lēdī*,[11] and countless fishes piercing the waves.

There, in those lakes, lie priceless jewels, shining, e'en by day, like lamps; and he who diveth therein, findeth the pearl-oyster.

34. On every side are ambrosial gardens, filled with perfect fruit, and carefully watched. There are the fresh coloured[12] lime and the pretty orange-citron, the almond, and figs of various kinds. Elephant lemons

[1] The excellence of a lotus depends on the number of its petals.

[2] The Golden Swan.

[3] The best of the four classes of women. The *Padminī*, *Citriṇī*, *Çaṅkhinī*, and *Hastinī*. In a later portion of the poem, Rāghava-caitanya, describes them to 'Alāu-d-dīn.

[4] *Sārãga* is like Mark Twain's *zug*. It may mean almost anything. Here it means a lotus or a deer.

[5] The sun is often compared to a golden jar.

[6] Maīna = Madana = Kāma-dēva.

[7] Acharī = apsaras.

[8] The fable about the *cak'wā* and *cakaī* is one of the commonplaces of Indian poetry.

[9] The legend is that a pair of these birds cannot bear to be separated. If one dies, the other dies also.

[10] A fish-eating bird which I have not identified. It is the *Ardea sibirica*, the same as the *sāras* above translated by Indian crane.

[11] Not identified. It is a fish-eating bird.

[12] Or perhaps *nau-rāga* may be for *naraṅgī* orange.

and citrons are ever ripe, and the glowing oranges are full of juice. Raisins[1] and apples with fresh leaves, pomegranates and vines delight the sight. Pleasant appeareth the Indian gooseberry, and the clusters of plantains are humbly bent (by their excessive weight). There fruit the mulberry, the averrhoa, and the red currant, the corinda, the jujube and the cirōnjī-nut.[2] There is the sorrel,[3] and the date, and other edible fruits both sweet and sour.

They lead the water from the wells through irrigation channels with many a dam,[4] and with the pulleys of the Persian wheel, water they the black currants.

35. Again, all around are flower-gardens, with trees imbued with sandal-odour. There bloometh the ghana-vallī,[5] with its many blossoms, the fragrant screw-pine, the fragrant yellow-flowered campaka,[6] and the Indian and Arabian jasmines.[7] Beauteous are the basils, the kudums,[8] and the kūjā-roses,[9] and scented are the Abelias, which only king Gandharva offered at the time of worship. The rose-chesnut, the marigold, the jasmine and the weeping-nyctanthes are in these gardens. The oleaster and the dog-rose bloom, the rūpa-mañjarī,[11] and the clove-scented aganosma.[12] There do men plant bunches[13] of the Spanish and of the Indian jasmine, and the flowers of the roseapple lend their charm. The maulasirī[14] creeper and the citron, all these bloom in varied hues.

Blessed and fortunate is the man whose head is crowned with these flowers. Fragrant do they ever remain, like spring and its (fragrant) festival.

36. When a man seeth Siṁhala's city, and how it is inhabited, he crieth 'Blessed is the king whose kingdom is so fair.' High are the gates, high are the palaces, high as Kailāsa[15] the abode of Indra. In every house each one, great or small, is happy, each one appeareth with a smiling face. They build their sitting platforms with sandal, and plaster them with aloes, *mēdā*[16] and saffron. Each pavilion hath its pillars of sandal, and therein sitteth, reclining, a lord with his councillors. Fair is the sight, as a council of the gods, as though a man gazed on the city of Indra. All the councillors are experient, wise, and learned, and all the words they utter are in the Sanskrit tongue.

Fairies build the roads, so that the city is bright as the heaven of Çiva, and in every house are fair Padminīs, whose beauty enchanteth the vision.

1 The poet does not seem to be aware that raisins are dried grapes.

2 *Buchanania latifolia*, Roxb. Its kernels are eaten like almonds.

3 The *Çaṅkha-drava*.

4 See *Bihār Peasant Life*, § 919.

5 The dictionaries give *Ghana-vallī* as a synonym of *Amṛta-sava*. The latter they say is 'a certain plant.' Dr. G. King suggests that it is probably the *Tinospora cordifolia*, Miers. Its blossoms are small in size, but numerous, as the poet says.

6 *Michelia champaca*, L.

7 *Jasminum pubescens*; Willd. (*kunda*), and the *jasminum sambac*, Ait. (*camēlī*).

8 *Anthocephalus cadamba*, Miq.

9 *Kūjā* is a kind of rose, *Rosa Brunoniana*, Lind.

10 *Abelia triflora*, Br.

11 Not identified.

12 *Aganosma caryophyllata*, Don.

13 *Bakucā* means a bundle or a bunch, and *bakucanha* is its obl. plur.

14 *Mimusops elengi*, L.

15 Again, Çiva's heaven is confused with Indra's.

16 A root like ginger.

37. Again I saw the markets of the city, all stocked with the prosperity of the nine treasures.[1] The golden markets are plastered with saffron, where sit the great merchants of the isle of Siṁhala. They cast the silver and hammer out the ornaments, and carve out images in countless shapes. Gold and silver lie abundantly scattered about, and the house-doors are hung with glistening curtains. Jewels and gems,[2] rubies and pearls, set in the doors, give forth a fine sheen, and the shops are filled with camphor, scented khas grass, musk, sandal and wood of aloes. What gain would any market be to him who bought not here?

Some there are who buy, and some who sell. Some come there and make a profit, some come there and lose their capital.

38. Again the mart of beauty[3] is a prosperous place, where sit the painted courtezans,—their lips red with the betel leaf, and their forms hidden 'neath safflower-coloured veils. From their ears hang jewel-studded earrings; with lute in hand they entrance the very deer. Who heareth their songs becometh enchanted, nor can he move his feet. Their brows are bows, their eyes are skilful archers, and, sharpening them on the whetstones of their glances, they discharge their arrows. On their cheeks swing pendent curls as they smile, and men's lives take they with each side look that they throw. The twin bosoms 'neath the bodice are two dice which they cast as it were upon the game-board,[4] as each, in her (wanton) nature, letteth her bosom-cloth slip aside. Many a gambler hath lost the game with them, and, wringing his hand,[5] hath gone away with broken heart.

Magic use they to captivate the heart, so long as the purse-knot in the swain's waistband is not untied. When once it is untied, beggared doth he wander forth and take the road, for no more do they recognize him or allow him to resort unto them.

39. There sit the flower-girls with flowers and their neatly arranged rows of betel unsurpassed. The perfume sellers sit with their goods, tying plenteous camphor and catechu.[6] Here, are learned men reading holy books, and telling the people of the path of virtue. There, are others reciting stories, and elsewhere men dance and leap. Here, buffoons bring their sights, and there, puppet-showmen make their dolls to dance. Here, is the sweet sound of singing, and there, actors and magicians show their skill. Here some practise the lore of ṭhags, and there (other villains) drug men, and drive them mad.

1 The nine mystic treasures of Kuvēra, the God of wealth. They are named *Padma*, *Mahāpadma*, *Çaṅkha*, *Makara*, *Kacchapa*, *Mukunda*, *Nanda*, *Nila* and *Kharba*. It is not at all clear what they are. They are possibly auriferous ores. See, however, Wilson's translation of the *Mēgha-dūta*, note to v. 534.

2 *Padāratha*, a gem, usually means, in this poem, a ruby (لعل), but here it is evidently used in its general sense.

3 The Courtezans' quarter.

4 *Caupār* or *sāra* is a game very like backgammon. As in that game, a man by itself is a blot, and can be taken up by the opponent. When two men of the same player come together on the same place, it is called *juga*, *i. e.*, the blot is covered, and the move is a decidedly winning one. The game is played with dice as in backgammon.

5 When a gambler is bankrupt, it is etiquette for him to wring his hands to show that they are empty.

6 *Khirauri* are pills of catechu wrapped up with other spices in betel leaf for chewing.

Agile thieves, knaves, robbers and pick-pockets all are there and dance their dance; and only the pockets of those escape, who are wide awake, and look ahead in this bazār.

40. And then a man approacheth Siṁhala's fort; how can I describe what seemeth to reach to the sky? Below, it reacheth down to Vāsuki's [1] back; above, it gazeth upon Indra's heaven. Surrounded is it by a deep and zigzag moat, so deep that no one dareth to peep (over its edge) or his limbs will tremble. Impassible, deeper than one can see, its very sight causeth fear. Who falleth therein, down down to the seven Hells will he go. Nine crooked gate-ways hath the fort, and nine stories. Who climbeth the nine will approach (the limit of) the mundane egg.[2] The golden bastions are studded with glass, and look like lightning filled with stars. That castle seemeth taller than that of Laṅkā, and wearieth the sight and soul that gazeth on it.

The heart cannot contain it. The sight cannot grasp it. It standeth upright like Mount Sumeru. How far can I describe its height? How far shall I tell of its circumference?

41. The sun and moon (cannot go over it but) make a circuit round it, or else the steeds and their chariots would be broken into dust.[3] The nine gateways are fortified with adamant, and a thousand thousand foot soldiers sit at each. Five captains of the guard[4] go round their watch, and the gateways tremble at the trampling of their feet. At each gateway of the fort is a molten image of a lion, filling the hearts of kings with fear. With great ingenuity were these lions cast, in attitude as if roaring and about to leap upon thy head. With lolling tongue they lash their tails. Elephants are filled with terror at them, lest they should fall upon them with a roar. A staircase fashioned of gold and lapis-lazuli, leadeth up into the castle, which shineth above, up to the very sky.

The nine stories, have nine portals, each with its adamantine gates. Four days' journey is it to the top, to him who climbeth honestly (without gainsay).

42. Above the nine portals is the tenth doorway, at which ring the hours of the royal water-clock[5]. There sit the watchers and count the hours, watch by watch, each in his own turn. As the clock filleth he striketh the gong and 'the hour, the hour,' it calleth forth. As the blow falleth, it warneth the whole world. 'Ye earthen vessels,' it crieth, 'why sleep ye void of care?

1 King of the serpents. He lives in hell.

2 The universe, shaped like an egg.

3 In the preceding stanza, the poet has compared the fort with Sumēru, the central mountain peak round which the heavenly bodies revolve. He now carries the simile further.

4 In the esoteric meaning of the poem, this city means the human body. The nine gates are the nine openings of the body, the mouth, the eyes, the ears, the nostrils, and the excretory organs. The five guardians are the five vital airs, the *prāṇa*, the air expired, up-wards, *apāna*, that expired downwards, *samāna*, that which circulates round the navel and is essential for digestion, *vyāna*, that which is diffused through the body, and *udāna*, that which rises up the throat and passes into the head. The adamantine gates are the bones, the warriors are the downy hairs of the body, and the King is the soul.

5 A kind of clepsydra. It is an empty bowl of a fixed weight and specific gravity, with a hole of a fixed size in its bottom. It is set floating in a larger vessel, gradually fills, and sinks after the lapse of a *ghaṛī* or twenty-four minutes. A gong is then struck. On the expiry of each *pahara* (of eight *ghaṛī*) a chime (*gajara*) is rung.

Ye are but soft clay, still mounted on the Potter's wheel. Still whirl ye round (in the circle of existence) nor can ye remain steadfast. As the clock is fulfilled, your life diminisheth. Tell me, why sleepest thou secure, O wayfarer? Yea, watch by watch, the chimes ring forth, yet your hearts are careless, and no soul awakeneth.'

Saith Muḥammad, Life is but the filling of water, as in a clock or in a Persian-wheel. The hour cometh, and life is filled. Then it is poured forth, and all man's days are gone.

43. In the fort are two rivers, the Nīra and the Khīra, each endless in its flow like unto (the store of) Draupadī.[1] Also there is a spring which is built of crushed pearls, whose water is nectar, and whose mud is camphor. Only the king drinketh its waters, which give him continual youth so long as he liveth. By it is a golden tree, like unto the wishing tree in Indra's palace.[2] Deep down to hell go its roots, and up to heaven go its branches. So life-giving a tree, who can reach it? Who can taste it? Its leaves are like the moon, and its flowers like the stars, so that by it is the whole city illumined. Some by austerities obtain its fruit, and eating it in old age obtain renewed youth.

Kings have made themselves beggars when they heard of its ambrosial delights. For he who hath obtained it becometh immortal, nor suffereth pain or disease.

44. Above the fort dwell only captains of castles, captains of horses, captains of elephants, captains of land, captains of men. All their palaces are decked out with gold, and each is as a king in his own house. Handsome wealthy, and fortunate, their very portals are overlaid with philosophers' stones. Ever enjoying happiness and magnificence[3] no one ever knoweth what is sorrow or care in his life. In every palace is there the game of *caupār*,[4] and there the princes sit and play upon the boards. They throw the dice, and fine is the game, each without an equal in his sword and in his generosity. Bards sing of glorious deeds, and receive as their gift elephants and horses of Siṁhala.

In every palace is a garden, odorous of perfumes and of sandal. There night and day is it spring, through all the six seasons and through all the twelve months.

45. Again went I forward and saw the royal gateway; (so great a crowd surroundeth it that) a man might wander round and round and not find the door. At the gate are tied elephants of Siṁhala, standing upright like unto living mountains. Some of them are white or yellow or bay; others sorrel or black as smoke. Of every hue are they, like clouds in the sky, and there they sit like pillars of that sky. My tale is of Siṁhalī elephants of Siṁhala, each one mightier than the other. Mountains and hills can they thrust aside; trees do they root up, and shake, and thrust into

[1] From their names we may assume that one flowed with water and the other with milk. According to the Mahābhārata (Vana-p.. 3. 72–74). Draupadī, the wife of the five Pāṇḍavas was a model housewife. No matter how little she cooked, it was always exactly enough to satisfy her five husbands, and it was impossible to empty her store room. As soon as she had eaten her meal, after her husbands, the store room was found empty for the time being.

[2] Again Indra's heaven, Amarāvatī, is confused with Çiva's.

[3] *Bhōga* means pleasures of the senses, *vilāsa* external magnificence.

[4] See verse xxxvi. The board on which the game is played is called *sāra*.

their mouths. *Must* ones, wild with fury, bellow in their bonds, and night and day their drivers sit upon their shoulders.

The earth cannot bear their weight; as they put down their feet it trembleth. The shell of the mundane tortoise cracketh, the hood of the serpent of eternity is split,[1] as these elephants proceed.

46. Again, there are fastened horses at the king's gate, but how can I tell the glory of their colours? The paces of the iron-grey, the dun, are famous in the world. The bay with black points,[2] the jet,[3] and the dark-brown,[4] do I tell of. I tell of the sorrel, the dark bay,[5] the liver chestnut of many kinds, the strawberry roan, the white, and the yellow-maned[6] in rows. Spirited horses were they, fiery, and graceful; eagerly curveting, they rear without urging. Swifter than thought, shake they their reins, and snort and raise their heads to heaven. As they hear their riders' voices they run upon the sea. Their feet sink not, and across they go. Stand still they cannot; in rage champ they their bits; they lash their tails, and throw up their heads.

Such appear the horses, like the charioteers of thought. In the twinkle of an eye do they arrive where their rider would have them go.[7]

47. I saw the royal-council seated there, and like Indra's council did it seem. Blessed is the king who hath such a council, which is glorious like unto a blooming garden.[8] There sit the princes with diadems on their heads,[9] each with an army whose drums loudly sound. Comely is each with jewels shining on his brow, as he sitteth on the throne with sunshade o'er his head. 'Tis as though the lotuses of a lake have flowered, so entrancing is that council. It is filled with fragrant odours of betel, of camphor, of *mēda*[10] and of musk. Throned on high, in the midst sitteth king Gandharva-sēna.

His sunshade reacheth to the sky; and as he giveth forth heat like the sun, the lotuses of his council all do bloom at the might of his countenance.

48. The king's palace is mighty as Kailāṣa,[11] of gold throughout from floor to roof. Seven stories high is it, only such a king could build it. The bricks are diamonds, and the mortar camphor; adorned with precious stones is it built up to heaven. Each painted design that is there designed, is marked out with jewels of each kind of colour. Varied are the carving and the sculptures arranged in rows. Rubies shine along the pillars which, e'en

1 It is on these that the universe is supported.

2 The *hāsul* is a bay (*kumēt*) with black feet.

3 The *bhawăr* or *mushkī* is black.

4 The *kiāh* is described as of the colour of the ripe fruit of the palmyra palm.

5 The *kurang* is the same as the *nīlā kumēt*.

6 The *bulāh* (Skr. *vollāha*) is a horse with light yellow mane and tail.

7 The names of these various kinds of horses has presented some difficulty. We have consulted many kind friends, more experienced in the veterinary lore of England and India than we are. For the curious in such matters, we may refer to the Sanskrit book on Veterinary Surgery, the *Açva-vaidyaka* of Jayāditya, quoted in the Commentary.

8 The poet alludes to the brilliant effect of the many-coloured garments of the courtiers.

9 That is to say they did not venture to remove their head-dresses in the presence of Gandharva-sēna. They were great, but he was greater.

10 *Mēda* comes from the Nēpāl Tarāī. It is a well known fragrant medicament—a root of cooling properties.

11 Çiva's heaven. Here probably, as usual, confused with Indra's.

by day, blaze like luminants. The very sun, moon and stars hide themselves before the glory of the palace.

As we have heard tales of the seven heavens,[1] so were arranged the seven stories each separately, one above the other.

49. I would tell of the women's quarter of the palace, like Kailāsa[2] filled with nymphs. Sixteen thousand queens, all Padminīs,[3] are there, each more beauteous than the other. Very lovely are they and very tender, living on betel and on flowers. Above them all is Queen Campāvatī, the chief queen of exquisite loveliness. She sitteth upon her throne in all her grace, reverenced by all the queens. Ever varying in her moods and brilliant is she,—in her first prime,[4] without a rival. Chosen from all lands was she, amongst them all a perfect sun.[5]

Maidens with all the thirty-two[6] points of excellence are there, and amongst them all is she matchless. Every one in Siṁhala telleth the tale of her beauty.

1 See v. i, 5.

2 Again, it is Indra's heaven, not Çiva's which is filled with houris.

3 See v. xxv, p. 1.

4 According to Hindu rhetoricians heroines are of three kinds, the *mugdhā* or the Artless, the *madhyā* or the Adolescent, and the *prauḍhā* or *pragalbhā*, the Mature, perfect in form, and experient in all the arts of love. Campāvatī was a *prauḍhā*.

5 The 12 kinds, refer to the twelve digits (*kalā*) of the sun. She was the sun in all its twelve digits, *i.e.*, complete.

6 The thirty-two points of a woman will be found described in the commentary. Some of them will not bear translation into English.

CRITICAL NOTES.

1\. 2. *Kīnhesi*, so apparently Ib, which seems to vocalize the final سِ. The word may, however, be also read *kīnhisa* for *kīnhesa*. The other copies in the Persian character simply have كينهس, which which may be read either *kīnhesi*, *kīnhasa*, or *kīnhasa*. Is and K have *kinheçi* for *kīnhesi*. U has *kīnhasa*. Throughout the poem a short *e* is inserted to form the past tense. Thus *dēkhasi*, he sees; *dēkhesi*, he saw. Ia *tinhahi prīti kabilāsū*, Ibc *parabata kabilāsū*, Id *parabata kailāsū*, Is *tēhi prīti ka bilasū*, U *tihi parabata ka bilāsū*. In the Persian character پريت and پربت and كيلاسو and كبلاسو are easily confused. In each case it is a question of a dot. There can be no doubt about the form *kabilāsū* for *kailāsū* being right. The word is of frequent occurrence in the poem and is invariably spelt thus in the best MSS. It is a curious corruption, and has puzzled all copyists with Sanskrit predilections. 3. Ib has *pawana agini*, K *agni pauna*, Is *bahutai*, UK *bahutē*, P give no clue. 4. Is *awatārū*.

5\. Ia *kīnhesi sapata dīpa brahamaṇḍā*
Ib „ „ *lōga*
Ic „ *sāta saraga* „
Id „ (illegible) ? *sēta pēta mahi bhaṇḍā*
Is *kīnhesi sata sata brahamaṇḍā* (*sic*)
U *kīnhasa sāta saraga*
K *kīnhesi* „ *dīpa* „

Two printed editions follow Ia, except having *mahī* instead of *dīpa*, Ia is adopted as making the best sense. 6. Ib *duniara*, U *dinakara*, K *duniā*. Printed editions *dinēsa*. 7. Is *kinhesi sīta ghāma*. 8. Id *kīnhasi saba asa*. Ias *dusarahi*, U *dusarahu*. 9. Ia *tā kara nāũ*, K *karatā kai nāũ lei*, Ia *kathā kahaũ*, Id اركاه, Is *arigāhũ*, printed editions and K *uragāhu*.

2\. 1. *Sāta-u*, so Ib, Ia U K have *hēma* (U reverses the order of the two hemistichs), Is *hĩwa*, Ic *sātō* with *hēma* as a v. 1. on margin. Id *sāta* (also Rām Jasan), Ic ? *bãwara*; كهكهند (Sanskrit किष्किन्ध for कुखण्ड) evidently puzzled the Nāgarī transcribers. Is has *khaṇḍa khaṇḍa*, U *kīnhasa parabata mēru apārā*. The P copies are undecided between *khikhinda* and *khikhiṇḍa*. The former is probably the correct reading. 2. K *mācha*, 3. U *wahu bhárē*, K *jehi bhálē*, *niramálē*. 5. U *ráhai*, *cáhai*, N *uḍai*. 7. U *phūla au*, Id K *aukhadha*. 8. Ia *gogana antaricha*, Ic *gagana antarikha*, Ib *khãbha*, U *lagai*, *rākhai*. K *nimikhi*, *karata tehi sabhai kīnha chana ēka*. Ias have *ohi*, Ibcd U *wahi*.

3\. The order of these sets of *caupāīs* is different in different copies. The above is the order of Iab U K, Icd begin 4, 3, and then go on as above. Is begins 15, 16, and then 3, 4, &c., like Ia. 1. Icd *dihesi baḍāī*; Iac *tehi pāī*, Id *tehi khāī*, Is *tinha jāī*. 2. Ib *bahu sājū*, Ic *tehi sājū*. 3. Iac U K *bilāsū*, U K *kou* for *koi*. 4. Iacs U *jehi hoi*. 5. Id transposes 11. 5 and 6. Is *jīu sadā sukha*, U *jiyuna sadā tinha* K *jīwa sadā saba*, U *kōū*. 6. Id U *kōṭi*, Is *bahu dandū*; Id *dhandū*, U K *anandā*, *dandā*. 7. U *kou*, Ia *ati ghánī*, Id K *puni ghánī*, Is *sāga ghánī*, U *jū ghánī*. 8. U *kou* for *koi*. 9. Iacd *chārahi*, Is *tinha chāra*, K *bahuri kīnha saba*.

4\. Icds *bhīwāsēni*, U *bhīmasainijā*. 2. P *mukha*, which spoils the metre. 3. Id makes this line the sixth, Is *amiya*, Ibd *jiuna jehi*, Ibd *tehi*, Iads U K *pāē*, *khāē*. 4. K *karui nīmi jō phārī*. 5. K *lāwai jo mākhī*, Icd K *bhawāra patāga*, Is *bhawāra nāga*. 6. Ia K *indura*, Icd doubtful, Ibs N clearly *undura*, Iacd *rahahī*. 7. So Iacd K, Ibs *kīnhasi rākasa dēwa daētā*, *kīnhasi bhōkasa bhūta parētā*, U similar except . . . *dēwa dayantā*, . . . *bhūta parantā*. 9. Icd K *dihisa*, Ib U *sabahī*.

5\. 1. Ias U *ohi*, K *dhanaita hai jehi kē san°*; Is U *kā*; P have *ka*; Iad *sabai*, J *nahi ghaṭai*. 3. K *sabhanha*, U *kou*. 4. Is puts verse 4 after verse 5, U *paragaṭi gupati*. 5.

Ib *khawāwai*, U *āpuni khāī*, K *āpuna khāī*, P might also be read thus. 6. K *uhai*, Iads *sō khā°*, Ic *sabahi bhuguti dēī au jianā*; Is K *sabahi dēī*, U *saba kahā̃ dēhi*. 7. Ia *sabahi so tā kari hērai āsā* | *ohi na kāhu*, &c. Is *hari sā̃sa, ohi*, U *sabai, tā kara, sā̃sā, ohi na kāhu kī āsa*, K *sabhai āsa tā kari hari phērī* | *ohi nahi āsa ahai kehu kērī*|| 8. Iac *ghaṭata*, U K *ghaṭai*, U *ubhai, tasi*. 9. Id *jo dēta*, U K *dēhi*, K *sabha tā kara*.

6. 1. Id *ādi ēka baranaū̃ sō rājā*; K *ādi anādi karata jehi chājā*. 2. Ibcd *karāī*, *dái* Iacs K *jehi, tehi*. Ibcd *achata*, Is *chatrahi achata nachatrahi*, U *nichatriya*, K *chatra nichatra nichatrihi*; K *dōsara kōi na sarabari*.' 4. Is *dēkha*, U K *dēkhu*, P give no clue a third person singular seems required by the sense, Is *lōgā, jōgā*, Is *ciṭhihi*, Ib *karahi*. U *sā̃jōgū*. 5. Iac K *trina, trinahi*, U *uḍhāī, tinhai bajara kī dēhi baḍhāī*, K *tōri u(?a)ḍāī*, 6. *kāhū bhī̃kha bhīkha dukha*, Ia *bhīkha* (?) *bahuta*, U *dukha bhārā*, K *bhauna bhīkha dukha bhārā*. 7. Ibs K *karai so jō mana cinta na hōī*, Ia *karai so jō mana cintā hōī*; K *karai sōi jo ohi mana hōī*. 8. U *asthirā* (which makes the metre right), Ias U *jehi*, K *tehi*. 9. U *aru bhā̃jai*, K *tehi bhā̃°*.

7. 1. Id reverses the order of ll. 1 and 2. U *baranaū̃ sō*, Ib *saba ohi saū̃ waha saba mahā̃ baraṭā*, K *oha saba sō saba mō̃ waha baratā*, Is has *saū̃*. 2. Is K *jo saraba*, U *paragaṭa guputi*, Ia *cīnha na cīnhata*, Id *cīnha na cīnhē*. 3. Ia *na ohi sā̃ga*, Id *na kōī sā̃ghātā*, U *na kou sā̃ghātā*. 4. Ic *na koi wahi jānā*, Is *na waha koi jānā*, U *na kou wē jānā*, K *ō kī sirajānā*. 5. Ias reverse order of ll. 5 and 6, K *waha saba*, Ib *wahu na kīnha*, Is *oha kīnha*, K *unha na kinha*. 6. Ia *hutā so pahilahi sō hai sōī*, Is *au hai aba sōī*, K *hutā pahilahi aba hai sōī* Ic *sō puni rahai rahai na na kōī*, U *sō puni*, K *rahai rahihi nahi kōī*. 7. Ia *auru jo hōhī*, U *aura kahai sō*, K *aura je rahai se bā°*, Ia *marahī kai*, K *marai kari*. 8. U *jō wai cāhas, kīnhasi*, K *jō oha cāha so kīnhasi*, Iak *karahī*, U *karahi ju cāhahi kīnha*. 9. U *na kāū̃*, Ic U *sabai cāhi*, K *sabhai oahahi*, U *jiya*.

8. 1. Id *cīnha jo*, K *cētahu*, Ib *purāna mē̃*, Is *giānā, bakhānā*. 2. Icds *jiu nāhī*, K *jīa nāhi* or *jia nāhī*, Ia *kara nāhī pai sabahi karāhī*, Is *karai sawāī*, U *karahī samāī*, K *karai saharāī* (?). 3. Ia reverses the order of ll. 3 and 4, Ib *jo ḍolāwe so ḍōlā*, Id *jo ḍolāwahi ḍōlā*. 4. Ic reverses the order of ll. 4 and 5, Is has *sūnā, gūnā*, Ia U *hiyā nāhi*, Id *hiyā nāhi pai guna saba gūnā*, U *guninā*. 5. Ic U K *bhā̃ti sō jāī*. 6. Ib *nā koi āhi na ohi kē rūpā*, Ic om. this line. Ias om. *hoi*, U *nā kou hai ohi*, K *na kōi hoi hai ohi*, Ia *nā kāhū asa rūpa anūpa*, Id *nā ohi kā̃ asa taisa anūpā*, Is *nā oha kāhu asa taisa sarūpā*, U *nā kōū asa taisa anūpā*, K *na oha kāhu asa rūpa anūpā*; possibly Ia fits in best with the rest of the passage. 7. K *na binu ohi ṭhā̃ū̃*, Ic *rūpa rēkha nahi*, K *niraguna nāū̃*. 8. Ic K *nā hai milā na bichurā*, U *nā hai milā na waiharā*. 9. U *andhi murakhi kahā̃ dūri*, Ibid *mūrakhahī*.

9. 1. Ic *puni jō dīnhesi ratana amūlā*, Is *sabahi jo dīnhesi*, U *dīnhasi*, K *jānahi* Throughout, Is K have *dīnhesi* and U *dīnhasa*, cf. I. 2, *n* 2. Is *bihū̃sī*, U *bihasē̃*, K *dasana bihasi mukha jōgū*, Iab *lōgū* for *jōgū*. 4. Iac U *jehi māhā*, U *tihi mā̃hā*, Ic reverses the order of ll. 4 and 5. 5. Iads *sōi jāna jehi dīnhesi nāhī̃*, K *sō pai marama janai jehi nāhī̃*. 6. Id *jāna hō*, Is *jāna hoi*, K *jōbana marama na jānai mū̃ḍhā*, Ia *milā nāhi tarunāpā ḍhū̃ḍha*, Ic *saba ḍhū̃ḍha*, K *cahai na tarunāpā cāhai ḍhūḍhā* (sic), Is has *mū̃ḍhē* and *ḍhū̃ḍhē*. 7. Id *sukha kara marama*, this makes better sense, and is also the reading of Rām Jasan, K *jehi kē dukhā bā°*. 8. K *bhōgi rahai anacinta*. 9. Ib *saba kara marama jānu karatā*, K, *ghaṭa raha ninta*.

10. 1. Ib *karatā kē karanā*, K *karatā kai karanī*, Iad *barani na kōī pāwai baranā*, Ic *barani na pāru kāhu kai baranā*, Is *barani na koı jō pārai karanā*, U *barani na jāī āhi bahu baranā*, K *barani na kāhu parai jo baranī*. 2. Ib *saraga sāta*, Ia *sāta saraga kāgada jaū̃ ka°*, Ic *kāgada hūī*, Is K *jaū̃ kāgada*, Ic *hūī* for *bharaī*, K *dharatī sāta saraga ma°*, U has *karahi, bharahi*. 3. Ic makes this line the sixth, Ib transposes ll. 3 and 4, Ib *rōma*, U *jāwāta kēsa rōma au pā̃khā*. 4. Ia *rēha khēha*, Icd U *khēha rēha duniyāī*, Ib *buna*, K *nakhata tarāī*. 5. U *likhai sansārā*, Ic *ati samū̃°*, Is *kabi amū̃°*, U *bidhi carita apārā*, K *kabi carita aparū* کب is evidently a misreading of گت. 6. Iacds *ēta guninha saba guna*, U *au saba guniyana guna paragáṭā*, K *aba guna para°*, Ib *tēhi samū̃da bū̃dahi nahī̃ ghāṭā*, Ia *bunda*, Id *aba-hu samū̃da mahā̃ bunda na gháṭā* Is *aba-hu samū̃da tehi bunda na gháṭā*, U *aba-hī bū̃da samū̃da nahī̃ ghāṭā*, K as in text, except *nīra* for *bū̃da*. 7. K *garaba na uṭhā*, K *garaba karai sō bāura jhūṭhā*. 8. Ib *bahu guna°*, U *asa guna°*, Iac *sō hoi tehi*, Ib *cahai sō tinha hō bēga*, U *sō hō tehi*, K *karai sō caha tehi bēga*, Rām Jasan *cahai sā̃warai bēga*. 9. Id *jō guna karahi anēga*, Is *jō guna cahai*, U *karai na nēga*.

11. 1. Ia *nāū*, U K *nāma*; U K *niramālā*, *kālā*; Id *pūnō* U *pūnou*, K *puniu* 2. Ia *unha kai*, Is *tinha kahā̃*, U *jōti tinha kī bidhi*, K *tā kara*, Is *tinha prīti*. 3. Iab U *dīpaka aisa*, U *bhā a(ā̃)jōra*. 4. Ibcd *jaū na hōta asa purukha ujyārā*. 5. Id *nāū*, U *ṭhāū daī* K *ṭhāwā̃ daā*, Is *likhē......sikhē*, K *likhā...sikhā*. Ia *paṛhatā*, K *bhau dharamī bhau paṇḍita sikhē*. 6. Is *jēi nahī*, Ia *ohi nāū*, K *janama bhara*. K *dīnha naraka māha*. Icd transpose ll. 6 and 7. 7. Ia *ohi kīnhā*. Ibds U *kinhē...līnhē*. K *utima basīṭha dīnha oi kīnhā*, Ibs U K *dui*, Icd *dō*. Is U K *juga*; Id U K *tarai nāma*. Icd *ohi* instead of *jai*, Is U K *unha*. 8. K *aiguna*, Ia *pūchihī*, U *hō kai*. 9. Iac *ohi*, Is U *unha*, Id *binawata*, K *unha āgē hama binaiba*, Id *karata*.

12. 1. Ia *cahū̃ dīnha*, Icd *cahū̃ kā duhū̃*. 2. Ia *taba ānē*, Ic *wei ānē*. Is *sidika daiya unha mānē*, K *uni ānē*, U *dīna oi jānē*. 3. Ibc U *puni jō*. Id *puni tehi*, Ia *jaba āē*, Ib *ohi āē*, Is *jāū āē*, K *jinha jaga adala dīna kahā̃ lāē*. 4. Ib *bahu gūnī*, Id *baḍa paṇḍita gūnī*, U *puni usi mahā baḍa paṇḍita*. Ia U K *likhā kurāna*. The correction is evidently a scribe's improvement. 5. Ia *bariārā*, K *bala tē kā̃pai*. Ias *saūhi na kōū rakā jujhārā* (Is° *rū*). 7. K *paramāna*. 8. K. *kurāna* for *purāna*,...*sōi likhā kari grantha*. 9. Is *tē saha*, K *tē suṭhi*.

13. 1. U *sēra sā̃ha*, K *sēra sāha*, U *sulatānā........bhānā*. Ia *cārihi*, Ic *cāri-u*. 2. Ib transposes ll. 1 and 2. Ib *ohi kahā̃ chāja chatara au pāṭā*, Is *chāja chālā au*. U *ōhī chātra sāju au*, K *ohi pai chāja chatra au*, Ia J K *pāṭā......lilāṭā*. Ib *rajai*, Ic *sabha rājā*, Id *sabha* (or *sabahi*) *rājanha* (or *rājahi*), Is K *saba rājanha*, U *saba rājānu* (?); 3. Ia K *gunawanta*, Icd *sabahi*, Ib *bidhi pūrā*, Is *nidhi pūrā*. 4. Is *nawāi nawa khā̃ḍuhu*, K *nāwa nau khā̃ḍahi*. The final word of the half line بهي may be transcribed either *bhaī* or *bhaē*. All N give the former, but printed editions give the latter. So also ني may be either *naī* or *naē*. We prefer *bhaī* and *naī* as giving the best sense. Iad *sātahi*. U *dīpa duniā*, Is *dīpa duniā sira*. 6. Ibds *tahā̃ lagi*. Ia *kharaga bala*, Icds *kh*° *para*; Ia *jala karana na kīnhā̃* (جل كرن نكينهان), Ib جولكرن Icd ذوالقران, U *julikandhara kīnhā̃*. 6. Ib *dēwai jabahi bhara mūṭhī*, U *juga kahā̃ jīwa dīnha*, K *joga kahā̃ jīti līnha gahi mūṭhī*. Ia *puhum*‖ *bhāra saba līnha samhārī* ‖ *ōhī sakai puhumipati bhārī* ‖ K *puhumi bhāra ohi ēka sā̃bhārā a tau thira rahai sakala sansārā* ‖ 9. Ia *pādashāha*, Ic *bādashāhā*, K *tuha jaga para jagē tohāra*.

14. 1. Id *sō sājā*. 2. Ia *hai kī rēnu*, Is *hai gai saina*. U *hai maimanti calai*. Ia *parabata phūṭi hōi sama dhūrī*. Ib *uṭhahī hoi*, Is *parabata phūṭi*, K *ṭūṭi jhikaṭi*. 3. Ia *sūra rainu hoi dinahi garāsā* Ib *parahi rainu*, Is K *raini rēnu*, Id omits this line. 3. K *pañchi*. 4. Iac U K *ūpara hoi chāwai brahamaṇḍā*. Ia *ḍōlai dharati au brahamaṇḍā*, U *naiwa khā̃ḍi dharati sakala brahamaṇḍā*, K *khanḍai dharatī bhau sata khaṇḍā*. 5. Ia transposes this and the next line. U *patālahi jhā̃pā*, Iac K *patārahi jhā̃pā*. 6. Is *bhai jāhī*. 7. U *ghara bā̃ṭā*. K *kharha kā̃ṭā*. Ia *pāchai parā sō kā̃daū*, Id *kahā̃ nahī*, K *kahā̃ kādau nahī āṭā*. 8. Ia *giri tariwara kahū̃ na rahā calata hōta saba cūra*. Id *hōhi sō cūra*. Is *saina calata giri tariwara hōhī sabai sata cūra*. U *jo gaḍha naai na nāai calata hōhi tē cūra*. K *jo giri tarai na kāhu tē calata hōi sabha cūra*. 9. Ias U K *jaba-hī*. Ia *calai*.

15. In Is this is No. 3. Ch. 1. Iabs *jasa prithimī hōī*. J *jasu*. K *kasa hōī*. Icd *cā̃ṭa*. Is *cīṭā*, K *bāṭa calata dukhawai nahī kōī*. 2. U *ādila áhā*, K *ādila kāhā*. Ib *sama sōu*. U *sō uni rāhā*. K *sari jūja na tāhā*. 3. Iab *adala jo kīnha umara*. Iab *bhaī āni*, U *sigarī*, K *kiriānā puhumī jahā̃ tā̃ī*. 4. U *kou*. Ib *sūna*. Icd *mānusa saū ujiārā*. 5. Is U *gāi siṅgha* K *gāe sēra*. Is *dua-u* (? *dūa-u*) *pāni*, U *dōnō*. K *dunau pāni pī*°. Ia *chīra*, Ib K *chānahī*, Is *chānī*. Ia *hōi ninārā*, Ibcd *karai nirārā*. K *pāni sō karahi ninārā*. 7 Ib *barihi*, Ic *wahū̃ sama*, Id *balī dū-hī sama*. Is *dubare baria dua-u*, U *baria ēka*, K *dūbara balī ēka*. 8. Icd *saba prithimī āsīsai*, Is *sabai prithimī asīsai*, U *saba prathimī mili asīsai*, K *sabhai prathimī asīsa dēi*. Ia *lāi lāi bhuī mātha*, Ic *dui hātha* Id *kara hātha* U *jōra jōra dou hātha*. 9. Ia *gā̃ga jamuna*, Ibd *gaṅgana jamuna*, Ics *gā̃ga jauna jau lahi jala*. U *gaṅga jamani jala jau lahi*, K *gaṅgā jauna jau lagi jala*. Ib *ammara nātha*, Is J *ammara mātha*, U *tau lagi*, Id *amara to mātha*.

16. In Is this is No. 4 1. Ib *kāhā*, *cāhā*. Id *sabahi*, K *muha*. 2. U *caudasi cā̃da dai sā̃wārā*. Iabc U *daī*, Is *daiya*. U K *tā hū*. Ic *cāhi adhika ūji*°. 3. K *jāi pāpa*. Is *pāpa ghaṭai jaū*, U K *jō*, P *jō* or *jau*. U *jagata juhārai dēi*. 4 Ic K *sabhai*. 5. Icd *purukha sūra niramārā* Is *bhā asa sūra pu*°. U *asi bhaye sūra purakhi naramālā* (sic). K *asa ohi sūra nāwa niramālā* Ibc *daha*. U *kālā*. K *ohi āgarı kālā*. 6. U *hēru*. Ia *jaī jaī dēkha rahai*, Ib *jō dēkhai so rahai*, U *jō dēkhā so rahā lubhāī*, K *jō dēkhai sō raha*

sharamāī. 7. Ic *saba ūpara.* Ib *surūpa.* Other Ps doubtful, N *sarūpa.* Is *darapawanta.* 9. Is K *mēdani darasa lobhānī.* U *mēdina darasi lu°.*

17. Here Is resumes the correct numbering. 1. Iabo U *daī,* Is *daiwa,* U *daā.* U *baḍi, asi dā̃ni.* 2. Icd K transpose *āhē* and *kāhē.* Icd U *Bali au Bīkrama dāni,* K *Bali au Kārna dātā baḍa.* Is *Hētama,* U *Hōtama,* K *Hētima.* 3. U *sara-pū̃ji,* Is K *ghaṭai,* U *sumēru bhā̃ḍārī dōū̃.* 4. Is *ḍāka dāna.* U *dā̃na ḍaṅka.* Ia *samū̃da kai,* Ib U *samundara pārā.* 5. U *kañcana barasi sūra kali.* K *kañcana barisa sūra kali.* 6. Ia *bāra eka mā̃gā.* Other P بر *bira* or *biri.* Iac *janama na hūi bhūkha au nā̃gā.* U *janama hōi nahi bhūkhā nā̃gā.* 7. Ibcs *jō kīnhā.* U K *dasi asimēda jagya jō.* Ia *tinha-hū surasari dāna na dīnhā.* Ib *dāna punna sari tāhu na dīnhā.* Id *sari saū̃hi.* Is *sē-u na* U *sō uni cīnhā.* K *unha sabha kē dīnhā.* 8. U K *jaga ūpara.* 9. U *kou dai asi.*

18. 1. Ia *jehi* (or *jinha*) *mohi,* Is *tinha mohi,* U *tē.* P (exc. Ia) *tinha* or *tehī.* 2. Ia *lēsē-hī eka pēma.* Ibd U K *prēma,* Is *pīrama* (sic). Ib *wahī jōti,* U *ōhi jōta,* Id *bhai sō jōti bhā,* Ic *bhai niramala,* K *bhau niramala.* 3. Ib *huta ā̃dhēra sō sūjhā,* Ic *huta jo ā̃dhēra asūjhā,* Id illegible, Is *māraga hato ā̃dhiāra so sūjhā,* so U but *ā̃dhēra,* K *māraga andha hōta sō sūjhā.* Ib *bhā ūjēra,* Ic U *jaga jānā̃,* Id *parā sūjha saba jānā.* 4. K *rākhu kai.* 5. N *unhi,* P *ohi* or *unha.* Ia کریتي, Ic *karī,* Id *ohi kara mōrā pō°.* Is *pōha kai,* U *pauḍhi kai,* K *unha mori kairihara* (?) *pauḍhi kai gāhī......ghāṭa jahā̃ rāhī.* Ia *jahā̃ āhā,* U *ghāṭi.* 6. Ib *jā kē,* Ic *jā kara aisa hōhi,* Id U K *jā kara hōhi aisa,* Ia *gahī bēga lei lāwai pārā,* Ib K *turita bēgi sō utarai,* Is *turita bēgi so pāwai.* U *turita ēi lai lāwai.* 8. Is *oi cistī,* K *rūpa jai se jaga cā̃da.* K *oi ati baḍē jagata mā̃ha.* Ic *hama unha.* Ic *unha kara.*

19. 1. Id *ohi* or *unha.* Is U *unha,* K *tinha,* U K *niramālā, bhālā.* Iad شيخ Ibc سيكه Ib *so bhāgai,* Ic *sabhā guna,* U *sabai guna.* K *sabhāgā.* Is U *tinha ghara.* K *tinha kē ghara dui dīpa,* Ic *ūjiārā, sā̃wārā.* Is *daiya sā̃°.* K *daū sā̃°.* 3. Iad شيخ Ibc سيكه, U *sēkha muhammada,* Ia U K *kālā, niramālā.* 4. Is *khanḍa khanḍa.* U *khakhanḍa tāhu,* K, *khikhida tāhī.* 5. Is *khā̃bha,* U *jaga kī nā̃ī.* 6. Ia *ṭēkā,* Is *tēkū taba.* U *duhū̃ ke bhāra srisṭi thira rāhī* | *dōna-hū̃ kara ṭēkī saba māhī.* K *tau tehi bhāra jagata thira.* 7. Is *jinha darasyau au parasyau,* K *jinha darasū parasā unha pāyā.* Is *bhau,* K *bhā.* 8. K *nicinta rahu.* 9. All copies insert *kariā* before *khēwaka,* except U *jehi rē nāwa hai kariyā,* and K *jehi rē nāwa kariyāā.* The omission of either *kariā* or *khēwaka* is required by the metre but, except U and K, all copies have both. K *bēgi sō lāwai tīra.*

20. 1. U *mohi dai khē°.* K *guru mahiudi kaha eka mai sēwā.* Iad *jā kara,* U *tinha kara,* K *jinha mohi khēwā.* 2. K *āgē,* Iad شيخ Ibc سيكه. U *baḍahānū̃;* Ic U *mohi dīnha* 3. U K *tinha kē gūrū,* Iad سر خرو Ibc سر كهرو Is K *surukhu rū,* U *surakhu rū.* 4. Ias *siddhanha purukhanha jehi sā̃ga khēlā* (Is has *jyaū̃*), Ic *jai rē siddha purukha sā̃ga khēlā.* K *jinha siddhyā purukhanha sā̃ga khēlā.* 5. U *lagāē,* K *dā̃nāra......dekhalāē,* Ibc U *jehi pāē,* K *mana lāē.* All P give خضر, N *khidira.* 6. Ia U K *tehi haj°.* Is *jē haj°.* U *āni milāē saiyada,* K *lau lagāe lei saidū rājē.* 7. Id *jō pāī karanī,* N *saba karanī,* P *jībha parama* (?) (پرم), N *kathā.* 8. *tehi ghara kā hañ cēlā,* Id *tehi guru kā haū̃,* K *waha rē guru,* U K *hwai cēra.* 9. Ia *ohi tai,* U *jehi tai,* K *dēkhana.*

21. 1. K *kali,* K *kali pūnī.* 3. Ids *asa,* K *uā sūra.* 4. U K *ā̃bā ḍā̃bha nahi.* Rām Jasan's edition gives *basāyana sōī* but all P give بساى نسوى 5. Ia *tau suṭhi,* Ib *tau asa,* Ic *taba ati,* Ids *tau ati kīnha,* K *tau waha, bhaeu.* 6. Ias *jaū̃.* 7. K *kā̃cu hōi kañcana kī kārā.* 8. U *tasa niramala tehi bhāu.* 9. K *rupavanta banā̃wahī,* Ia *rūpawanta gahi jōahī, sō karahī gahi pāu.* Ib *mukha cahahī kai,* J *mukha cāhai kai.* K *mukha dēkhana ke cāu.*

22. 1. P سر U *sira,* K *ora.* 2. Ia *yūsufa mallika panḍita gyānī,* Ib *bahu gyā̃°,* Id *baḍa gyā̃°,* K *jō panḍita gyā̃°.* All N have *isapha* for *yusupha.* Iac K *pahilahi,* K *pahilī* 3. Iac كادن, Ib گاجن, Id قارن Is *kandana.* Ib *khā̃ḍahi,* U *ubhai,* K *uṭhai jō bā̃°.* 4. U *apārā, jujhārā,* Ia *khēta au,* K *briga sitaraini* (?) *jō kharaga johārū.* 5. Iabc سيكه, Id شيخ Ib K *bakhānī, jānī* (K *mānī*), Iabd *baḍa jānā.* Is *sādhunha.* 6. Ia *catura guna dasa wei,* Ib K *dasau guna.* U *cārō catura au dasi guna* (sic), Icd *au sā̃ga jōga,* K *au saba jōga* Is repeats the last line by a mistake of the copyist. Printed editions have *simha jōga.* 7. Ib *jo rōpahi,* U *jo upajai.* K *purukha jo āpē* (آپى for آچهى). K *jau bēdhai bā̃sā.* 8. Icd *bhā.* 9. Ia *sātha nibāhā.* U *yaha jaga ōra nibāhā.* K *sātha jīwana bhā* (جيونبها for جيون بها for جونبها). Ia U *bichurahī.*

23. 1. Ibd *tahawã̄ bahu*, Ic *tahā̃ una kabitanha kī°*. Is *tahā̃ awara*, K *tahā̃ awani*. 2. Ibs U *au bi°*, Id *bīnatī kara*. U *kabitanha*. K *au paṇḍita sō binatī bhájā* Ib *bhākhē ... sākhē*, Is *bhājā ... sājā*. Iad *mērehu*. Is *meraehu*. U *ṭūṭi mirāi sãwārahu sájā*. K *ṭuṭala sãwāraba au merabai sájā*. 3. N *paṇḍitanha*, U *pachilāgā ... ḍāgā*. Is *gai ḍagā*. K *kichu kai cahau kathā kara āgā*. 4. Ia *jō kachu pũjī*, U *hiyã̄ bhā̃ḍāra āhi naga pũjī*. Is *khōlu*, U *lai kū̃°*. Is *tārā kī*. K *khōlau, tāla au kū̃°*. 5. Is U *bōlē bō.°* K *bōlau bō°*. Ia K *pēma rasa*,* Ids U *pēma mada*. 6. So Ia. Ib *kā̃hā̃ tehi bhū̃kha kahā̃ tehi kāyā*, Ic *kahā̃ tehi rūpa kahā̃ kai kāyā*, Id *kahā̃ tehi bhū̃kha kahā̃ tehi māyā*. Is *kā tehi bkū̃kha nīda kā māyā*. U K *kahā̃ tehi rūpa kahā̃ tehi māyā*. 7. Ia *lāaī bhēsa*. 8. *kayā*, so U K. It makes good sense. P *kabi jō prēma kā*. Is *kabi jo pīrama kā bhā tana rakata*. 9. Ic *sunā to*. Is *sunā tā̃*.

24. 1. Ia *áhā ... káhā*. K *áhī ... káhī*. All texts agree in giving the date (A. H.) as 947. Rām Jasan's edition gives 927 which is certainly wrong. Ia *tāhi dina káhā*. 2. *sēni*, so Is K. J has *saīna*. 3. Ia *suratānū*. Is *ḍhīlī sulitānū*, K *dīlī, cētani*, so all N. 4. N have *sāha* not *sāhi*, which is the usual spelling elsewhere. 5. Is *kathā áhī*. Ia *kathā jo ahī*, K *ādī anta kathā asi áhī ...... káhī*. U *bhākhā mai caupāī káhī*. 6. Ic K *biāsa jasa*. Ia *dūri jo niarahi niarē dūrī*, Ics *dūrihi niara niara bhā dūrī*, Id *dūrihi niara jo niarahi dūrī*. U *dūri su niarē niarē dūrī*. 7. Ids *sãga kā̃°*, U *sama kā̃°*. Ic K *duri niara jaisai gura*. Ids *dūri jo niarē sō gura*, U *dūri so niarē jasa*. 8. Ic U K *khaṇḍa tai*. Is *khaṇḍahū*. Id U *kī bāsa*, Is *kai bāsa*. Ib U *pāwahī*. 9. Ib *jō āchai ohi pāsa*. Id K *sadā jo āchai pāsa*. Is *āchahi*.

25. 1. Is K *gāwau, sunāwau*, U *gā̃wō̃, sunā̃wō̃*. Id *au bahu padumini*, J *barana*. 2. U *niramala dārapana*, K *badana kudana* (?) *jasa bhānu bisēkhā*, Ia *jō jehi bhā̃ti*. Ib *jehi jasa rūpa soī tasa dēkhā*, Id *jō jehi*, Is *jō jasa rūpa*, U *taisahi*, K *jehi jasa rūpa so taisahi dēkhā*. 3. Id *dhani waha dīpa*. Is *dhanya dēsa jehi dīpaka*. K *dhanya dīpa jehi*. Ia *daī ãwārī*, Ib *au bidhī padumini autārī*, Ia *au jō padumini daī sãwārī*, Is *daiya sãwārī*, U *asa paduminī daī autārī*, K *au paduminī daā autārī*. 4. Icds *saba baranai* (Is *baranahi*) *lōgū*. Ibc K *tehi sari*. Id *waha sari*. 5. Ib *wasa nahi ũji°*, U *nahi asa*, K *tasa nahi*. U transposes ll. 5 and 6. Is *sarada-dīpa*, U *sārāga-dīpa*, K *sarā-dīpa*. 6. U *sari nāhī*. Ia *laŋka-dīpa sari pūja na tahī*, Ib *laŋka-dīpa nahī pūjai chāhī*. Ic *laŋka-dīpa pūjai parichāhī*. Id *laŋka-dīpa pūja parichāhī*. U *laŋka-dīpa na pūjai chāhī*, K *laŋka-dīpa na puja parichāhī*. 7. *Kumbhasathala*, so Iab U, Ic *k-s-th-l*; Id, *k-s-sa-h-l*; Is *kūçasthila*, K *kōsathila*. Is U *pārā, hārā*, K *āra bakhānā*. Ia *mahasthala*, Ib *mai asthala*, Ic *mahūsthala*, Id U *mēwasthala*, Is *mahūsthila*, K *mēwasthila*. 8. Is K *prīthimī*, U *prathyumī*, Ia *au sāta-u saba dīpa*, Ib *au saba sāta-u dīpa*, U *aura ju sātō̃*, K *au yaha sata-u*. 9. Ia *na ūpamā*, Ib *na ūpara*, Ic *na pā̃ū̃*, U *uttama*, K *dīpa tehi sarī*.

26. 1. Is K *sēni*. U *Gandharpa saīna sukha hhaṇḍi*, Ia *dhana rājā*. Is *rājā au tā*. 2. U K *rājā...sājā*. U *tāhu cāhi baḍi*, K *tāhi*. 3. Ibc U K *dala*. K *cāraụ disā kaṭaka*, *Au gaḍha* is very doubtful. *Uragahī* is a possible reading of the Persian Character. The following are the readings of the various MSS. Iab اور کنه Ic ار کنه Id (درور کنه) Is *ōrāgē rājā*, U *ghara ghara rājā*, K *o raŋgana rājā*. All printed editions have *au gaḍha-rājā*. 4. U *sōrāhi sahāsa*, Id *sahāsa*, K *sōraha laccha*. Ib *sāwa karana bākā tu°*, Ic *jasa bāka*, Id *syāma karana bākā tumhārā*, Is *sāwa karana cālūko tōrākhāra* (sic), U *bara ganē tu°*, K *syāma karana turaākī jō* (sic) *tokhārā*. The text has no difficulty if the technical meaning of *çyāma-karṇa* is remembered, and if it is recognized that *tukhāra* means 'horse.' 5. Id *aru kailāsa*, Is *imi kapilā airāpati*, U *janu ka bilāsa airāpati*, K *sakā bandhi rāutapai* (sic) *ati bālī*. 6. Ia *sohāwai*, Is *asa-pati*, U *asu-pati kā, gaja-pati kā*, K *asu-patīnha*, K *gaja-pati sira aŋkusa gaja nāwai*. 7. Ia *nara-pati kahaū jo āhi narindū*, Ib *nara-patī ka au kahaū*, Is U *nara-pati ka kahāwa*, K *nara-pati mahā kahalāwai indū*, Ia *bhū-patī ka mahā*, Is *bhua-pati*, K *bhua-pati jaga para dōsara īndū*. 8. Ias U *bhai hōi*, K *mō̃ hōi*. 9. K *sabhai*.

27. 1. Ib *jōhu* (جوه), *niarāwē*, Icd *jō wahi dīpa*, K *jō wahi dīpa kē niarē jāī*. Ia *bhau āī*, Iabds U *kabilāsa*, K *kailāsa tinha niarē pāī*. 2. U K *ghani ãbarāī*, U *uṭhī bhūmī*, K *uṭhai bhūmi*, Is *lāga*. 3. U *tariwara ū̃cē sabai suhāō*, K *taruari sabhai milē ohi jāī*, Ib *bhai tasi chā̃ha*, Ic *sītala chā̃ha*, U *raini kai āē*, K *hō jaga chāha raini bhai āī*. 4. Ia *sohāwana*. 5. U *abu jamu chā̃ha*, K *au asi chāha raini bhā*. 6. Ia *jaū sahi āwai ghāmū*, U *panthika cali āwai sahi*. K *panthika pahū̃cai sahi kai ghāmā* Ibs K, *ghāmā̃, bisrāmā̃*, U *bisarai bhai sukha bisrāmā̃*, K *bisarai chana kai bisrāmā*. 7. Is K *jinha waha*, U *jō pāwai*

waha chā̃ha, Ia *sō dhūpā*, Ic *dukha dhūpā*, Id *tehi dhūpa*. 8. U *asi ā̃barāī suhāwani*, K *asi ā̃barāī saghani ghani*, Id *pārai*, Is *parahi*. 9. Ic *cahu disa*, K *phūlahī pharahī chaau*, U *mā̃nahu*.

28. Id *ambha* (? انبه), K *āma*. Id U *suhāē*. Ibc *suhāī*. Is K *sohāē*. Ia *aura jo*. 2. Id *pēḍa maū̃ pākē*. Id N Ia *ati anūpa phala tākai* Ib *baḍahari phara anūpa* Ic *baḍahara sē u*. U *au baḍihari anūpa suṭhi tākē*. 3 Is *pāka* Iad *jāmu jo pāki* Is *jā̃bu jo pāka*. 4. Iacds *pharai pharī* K *pharē au pharī khajurī*. Id *pharahī jānu*. Ib *sadā̃ jānu*. 5. Ia *mahuā cuai so adhika* Ic *puni mahu cuai so* Id *cuai jo mohuā so adhika* Is *puni madhu cuai so* U *puni mahuā sō bahuta* K *inha mō̃ cuai madhura mīṭhāsū*. Ia *asa mīṭhī—asa bāsū*. Ib *tasa bāsū*. Id *asa mīṭhi*. Is *mīṭha*. 6. Is *āwana*, U *atibala bhāū*. K *anawana nāū̃*. Ia *saba sōbhata*. Ic *sabha*. Id K *jasa rāuna*. U *dēkhē*. K[2] *aura khawahajā anawana nāū̃, dēkhi sabai rawanika ā̃barāū̃*. K[3] *awara rūkha jō āwa na nāū̃ dēkhā sabai sohāwana ṭhāū̃*. 7. Ia *rasa ambrita*. Is *lāgā*. K *lagā* Ia *jaī cākhā*. Is *kōi jaū̃ cākhā* U *jāi jō cākhā*, K *jō cāhai cākhā*. 8. Ic *lavā̃ga supārī*, Ia U K *jāiphala*. Ic *sabha*. U *au phara lāgu apūra*. K *phala pharē*. 9. K *abili*.

29. 1. Ia K *pañchi*. Ic *karata*. 2. Ib U K *hōta bōlahī*. Is K *pāṇḍuka*. Ics *tū̃hī* 3. Ia *sō raha*. Ic *sōra bahu karahī*, Is *rahasa karēhī*, U *sūgā sārō au kurarahī*, K *rahasya karāhī*. The latter half of the line runs as follows in the different MSS.

Ia کهون پریوا تنهه کرارهین

Ib کنّهنه پرپوا کرور کوهین

Ic کُرهین پربوا کُرکُر رهین

Id کرهین پربوا او کرو رهین

Is ठूरहि परेवा अउ कुररेहीं ॥

U बोलि पपीहा पिउ पिउ कहहीं ॥

K बोलहिँ परेवा अउ गुररहीं ॥

The verb √ *karawar* = *kalabalā* is frequently used in the poem. It must be some form of it which should stand at the end of the line. 4 Ib U make this the 6th line. Ia *karahī*, K *karai lāgē*. Ia *guḍurā*, Ib *kīhā*, Is *kaha gu°* Is *khēhā*. K *kai guru jō káhā*. 5. Iac *bahū bahū*. Is *bahō bahō*, K *bahau bahau*. Iacs *kōili kai*. 6. Ib *dahiu dahiu* 7. U K *kuhukai*, Is *kūkuhē*. U *kagawara karahī baiṭhi sō̃ kāgā*. K *kā̃gurī karahi pukārahi kā̃gā*. 8. Ia *pañchi ahai saba*, Ics *paṅkhi jagata kē*, U *paṅkhi āhi jaga*, K *pañchi kahi sravana, basahi sabhai ā̃barāu*. 9. Is *apanī apanī bhākhā*

30. 1. K *kūā̃ kulawārī*. Ia *sājī*. Ia *au caupāūrī*. Is *sājē panthi kahā̃ jō pāwarī*. K *au caupārī*. 2. Icds *kuṇḍa bahu*. Ic *sabha* Is *tinha kara* U *saba kē*. 3. Iads K *maṇḍapa* 4. Iac U K *kōi* (U *kōu*) *rikhēsura*. Is *kōi riṣēçvara*. Iacs U K *kōi rāma*. Icds U *janī* Iad *koi bisuāsī* Ibc *koi m s w āsī* Is K *masawāsī* U *koi dāsī*. 5. Iacs U K *kōi* (U *kōu*) *mahēsura*. Id *jōgī jatī*, Ib *kōī pu°* Id *koi sō*. 6. Ia *°caraja sō̃ lā°*. Is *brahmacarja* U *brahmacāra* K *brahmacārī*. Iacs U K *kōi* (U *kōu*) *di°*. 7 This line has many variants, Ib is however clear. Iad *koi sarasutī siddha*, Is *kōi sunata*, U *kou sati santa siddha*, K *kōī maunī suanī jōgī*. U K *pada*. K *gahē bi°*,

8. The various readings are

Ia *siurā khiurā bāna sabha*	*sidha sādhaka abadhūta*,
Ib *siura khēra nānaka panthi*	*s n k adhika audhūta*,
Ic *siura khiunā̃ bāna sikha*	*sādhaka au audhūta*,
Id *siurā khiunā sarasuti*	*sīkha sādhaka audhūta*,
Is *sewarā khewarā bāna para*	*sidha sādhaka abadhuta*,
U *jōgi jati sannyāsī*	*bahuta digambara dūta*,
K *sewarā khōnā banaspatī*	*sīkha sādhaka abadhata*,

9. Ia *jaṅgama jati sannyāsī siurā au audhūta*, Ib *baithi saba maṇḍapha pā̃ca at°*, Id K *pā̃ca āt°*

31. 1. Ia *dēkhaū̃* Is K *baranaū̃* U *mānasarōwara ati augāhā*. Ib *pala hara* (?) Ic K *jasa ati* Ids *asa ati* U *jahā̃ wāra pāra nahī thāhā* 2. Ia *jala mōtī*, Ia U *ambritawāna* Ib *ambritabāna* Id *ambrita nīra* K *ambrita pāni khīra su.°* 3. Ias *mā̃gāī* Ic ? *s dā u māī* K *sara silā*. U *kanaka silā gaḍhi sīḍhī lāī*. Is *so ghāṭa sohāī* U *bā̃dhāī*. 4. Ia *siḍhi upara*, Ib *bahutērī*, U *cahū̃ disi sīḍhi*. Icd U K *utarai caḍhai*, Is *utarai lāga* 5. Id U *phūlā rahā*. *rātī* so Ib, all

others *rātā*. U *kamala*. Ia *pātā*. 6. Ia *chitarāhī* K *ulathahī mōti mānika hīrā* Icds *cunahī*. U *cakāī cakawā kēli*. K *dakha dēkhī mana rahai na thīrā*. 7. Ic *lōnā*, Is K *paurahī*, Ia U *sãwārē sōnē*, Icd *kīnha saba*, Is *likhā saba*, K. *likhā gaḍhi*. 8. Ib *pāra*, K *beli cahũ*, Ib, *suphala s k h n bahu rūkha* Is K *phala* U *suphala pharai saba* 9. K *harai pyāsa*.

32. 1. Ibc *bharahī*, Ib *su-padumini*. 2 U *paduma bāsa*, Ia *saba saṅga*, K *saṅga uḍāhī* 3. Is *sārãga bainī*. 4. Ia *bahu pãtinha*, U *āwai sō saba pãtinha*. U. *barana barana au bhãtinha*. 5. Ids K interchange lines 5 and 7, Ia 5 and 6. 5. Ia *rahasi kūdi saba āwahī*. Ic *rahasi kūda saũ*, Is U *rahasa kōḍa saũ*, K *rahasa kēlī karata saba jāhī*. U *jā saũ cakhu hērahī panihārī*. U K *hanai*. 7. Ia K. *sira pā tāī*, Is *sira yō tāī*. U *meghāwara, pāi na tāī*. 8. Is *āchari*, U *acharī rūpa anūpa*. Is U *wē panihārī*, Iab *tē rānī*.

33. U omits the whole of this stanza. 1. Iad *talāwara barani*, Is K *talāu barani nahi*. Ia *jehī nāhī*, K *kachu nāhī* 2. Ia *phūlai kawãla kumuda*, K *gagana para*. 3. Is *maccha kaccha kī*. K *camakahī mēgha* 4. Ics K *bahu raṅgā*. 5. Is *karēhī* K *camakahi cakawā*. Ib *nisi bicharahī au dinahi*. Ic *bichōha so*, Id *bichōha jo*, K *nisi bichōha raha dibasa mi.*° 6. Ia *karahī hulāsā*. Is *kururahi*. Ic *jētahī muaī rāhahī eka*, K *mue-hu na bichurai hōhi sãga pāsā*. Ib gives v. l. *jiuna muaī āchaī eka pāsā*. 7. For the first word we have adopted, *kēwa*, a lotus, which however gives bad sense. Some fish eating bird is referred to. We can make nothing of P. Ia has ? *k n y bā*, Ib *n k ṭ hā*, Ic *b n sā* or *n b sā*. Id is entirely illegible. Is *baka* 8. Ib *unha*, K *uha sarawara*. K *barahi jōtī jasa* 9. K *hoi parai sō pāwai mōti sīpa*.

34. 1. U K *lāgī*. 2. Is *turuñja jābhīrā*, Icd U *jābhīrā*. Ia *au bādāma bēdāna*. Ibd *badāma bēḍa*, Is *bēda*. U *bēra*, K *badāma jo pēḍa*, 3. Is *gāgala surãga*, U *gala gala tūta*, K *nārãgi rakata rātē*. 4. Is *naubārā......mana tārā*. U *nau-bātā*. Ia U K *dārima*. 5. Ia *sohāwana harapā*, Ib *haraphā*, Is *sohāi su harapā*, K *alaga sohāī haraphā*. Is K *aunai rahī*, U *unhai*. Ia K *kēlanha*, Is *kērā*. 6. K *kamaraṅgā newajī*, Ia *diṭhā*. Ib *rāi sugandha cho*°. K *sīkha dāu* U has an altogether different couplet, *viz*.

पउनारी सो बहुत मिठासू ।
मधु जसु मीठि पुहुप जसु बासू ॥

35. 1. K *candana kē bāsā*. Is *phara au phūla*, K *pahupa phūla lagē gha*°. 2. Ics *keolā* 3. K *kuñjā*, Is *bikaurā*, K *bakāwarī*. 4. *satibaraga*, so N. It is the Persian صد برگ which is so spelt in P. 5. K *sōna basana*. Is *sewātī*. Is *rūpa-mãjari au mālati jātī*. All other MSS. have similarly a *mātra* missing at the beginning of the second half-line. Accent must be used for quantity. 6. Is K *bahuta suda*°. 7. *maulasarī (mimusops elengi)*,—whenever this word occurs in the poem the MSS. vary between *bōlasari* and *maulasarī*. Ia *maulasari jō bēli*. Ibc *bolasarī bēlā au*. Id *bōlasarī bēlī*. Is *mōlasarī*. U *maulisiri bēlī* K *maulasarī an bēili*. Icd K *sobhai* K *phula lāgai bahu*. 8. U *baḍi bhāga*. 9. U *sugandhi wē*, K *sabhai subāsa lai*. K *jasa basanta*.

36. 1. Ia *tasa bāsā*, Is *phiri bāsā*, U *jō bāsā*, K *siṅghala dēkhi āpuniu bãsā*. 3. Ids U K *raṅka*. K *sō saba hãsa-mukhī*. 4. U makes this line the last of the stanza and has *cūrī ...... kastūrī*. Id. *raci raci sājai candana khābhā*, *ṭhaṅghi sabhā-pati baithai sãbhā*. 5. K *sōnē khambhā—sabhā*, Ic *khãbhā—sābhā*, Id mixes up lines 4 and 5. U omits this and repeats 4 with slight variations. 8. *āhakā*, so Iads, Ib *ādhika* Ic *nāhaka* U K *au asi panthi*. Ia *sōbhata kalā anūpa*. Is *jasa si*°, U *janu kabilāsa anū*°, K *sēwahi lōga anūpa*, Ia *sabha darasana saba rūpa*, Icd U *saba acharinha kē rūpa*.

37. K has following order of verses 39, 40, 37, 38. 1. K *puni baranaũ*. 2. Ia *kumakuma* Ic *kūhikūhi*, Id *kumakūhi*, U *hāṭa kuṅkuma sō līpī*, K *kuṅkuma līpā——dīpā*, Is *baiṭha*, U *baiṭhi*, K *baisu*. 3. Ia *hāṭā racai saba rūpai*, K *racā hāṭa sabha rūpanha*. U *citara bicitara*. 4. Is *rūpa saba bha*°, U *bhala parā pa*°. Is *dhavala-srī*. U *pāṭā khirawārī*, K *paṭabahu kha*°. 5. *su anawana*, So Iabds K. The vowel points are carefully given in Ib. Ic *hīrā lāla p n sāna bahu jōtī*, U *hīra lāla suanimanu*. 6. K *agara dauna raha pūrī*. Ia *jaī isa hāṭa na līnha*. Id U *kīnha*, K *jō na hāṭa tehi*, Ia *nahi lāhā*, Is *kasa lāhā*, U K *kata*. S. U *kōu* throughout Ia K *lābha lai*. Iab U K *mūla*.

38. 1. Ia *hāṭa kai*, U K have *kai siṅgāra dhani baiṭhī* (K *baisī bahu*) *bēsā* । *mohai darasana raṅka* (K *rūpa*) *narēsā* || Ic *saba baiṭhi*. Icd *sira cira*, U *au cira*, 3. K *bēnu*, Ia *mōhita hōhī paiga nahi jāhī*. Icds U *nara mō*°, Is *guna paigu*. U *nara pai*°, K *nara paraga na*. 4. Ia *sāni wai*. 5. K *phãsi dēhī*. U K *kaṭacha jiu hari lēhī*. 6. K *mānahū*, Is *ṭārī*, U K *ḍārī*. 7. Ia *kētē kēli rahī tehī*. U *kitē kha*° K *kētē chaila rahahī*, Ia *jhāri kai*. 8. K *caḍhē turāi rahahi wahi tau lagi jau lagi gatha raha pheṭa*, Ia *gãtha hoi*, U *jaba*

lagi. 9. This line is very corrupt. Ia *uṭhi bhāgahī*, Ic om. *baṭāū*, Id *sā̃ṭhi nā̃ṭhi bhē̃ṭi na pāwaī*, U *sāṭhi nā̃ṭhi hwai calai baṭāu*, K *sā̃ta nighaṭā uṭhi bhaeu baṭau.* The reading given in the text is that of Ib. The metre is however wrong. U *puni pahicāni.*

39. 1. Ia K *baiṭhi siŋgāra hāṭa phulawārī.* Ib *phulahārī.* Id reverses the order of the two halves of the *caupāī.* Ic *pāna anūpa jo dha°* K *dharā.* 2. Is U *gandhī.* K *baisu.* Ia K *bahuta ka°*, Ib *mēli kapūra*, Ic U *phūla ka°.* Is U K *khiraurā.* 3. Ia U K *purānā—bakhānā.* Ib *dharama pāpa.* Is *dharama rāsi.* 4. K *kathā kabitta kaha kōī*, K *bahū hōī* 6. Ib *nāda bēda dhunī bhālā.* Is *cēṭaka cālā* 7. Ic *ṭhagaurī lāī*, Is *katahū̃ kānha ṭhaga*, U *katahū̃ ṭhaga ṭhaga bi°.* Ia *mānukha.* 8. U *rahahī tē nā̃ca.* 9. Is *jō tehi nā̃ca.* All MSS exc. U insert *agamanu* after *rahai.* The word is superfluous and spoils the metre. Ia *sō bā̃ca*, Id *tai bā̃ca*, Is *wai bā̃ca*, U *pai bā̃ca*, Is U K *gatha.* The reading of this *dōhā* is very doubtful.

40. 2. *Kuruma.* P give no vowel marks. Is *kurūbha.* U *jānahū̃ kūrama.* K *tarēhi rambha bā°.* Printed editions have *karēhī* which is a possible transliteration of P كرينة for كرنبة. U *parai ḍi.* 3. Ia *khāda phēra cahū̃°*, U *cārau disi bā̃kā.* 4. Id *parai jo*, Is *parai to.* 5. Ia U *jō unhi caḍhai*, Ic *tinha kī ca°*, Is K *nau-hū̃ jo caḍhai jāi.* 6. Ib *bharī naraka tahā̃ dīsa*, Is U *bharē, asi dīsā*, K *asa.* 8. All MSS insert *pahū̃cai*, after *nahī.* The word is superfluous and spoils the metre. U *lāgi sumēru.* 9. U *kahā̃ lagi karaū̃ baḍāī.*

41. K has following stanza order. 36, 39, 40, 37, 38, 43, 44, 45, 46, 47, 48, 41, 42, 49, 50. U om. 41. Ia *nāhi to hōī.* 3. Ia *tehī bhā̃°.* K *tē bhā̃°.* The latter half has an instant too many in all MSS. except Ic, Iad *pāi.* Ic *jāta* for *cā̃pata*, Is *kā̃pai jā̃gha.* K *kā̃pai jā̃gha dēkhata khana pā̃°.* 4. Ia *rāu.* Ic *ḍarapahī haṭi.* K *ḍarahi gainda dēkhī unha ṭhā°.* 6. K *rātē pū̃chi.* Is K *jīhā.* The second half varies greatly. Ia *līlē līhā.* Icd *guñjari kīnhā.* Is *kajala līhā.* K *dēkhi oi sīha.* All P have *jībhā* in the first half, which, however, does not rhyme. 8. K *nauu paurī bhau khaṇḍa tehi.* Id *au tehī nau kēwāra.*

42. 1. Ia *nau-unha*, Ic U K *nau paurī.* K *dasama.* K *tā para* 2. Ia *ghari jō.* Ic *gharī gharī so ganahī*, Ia *paharahi pahara so*, Ic *pahara pahara para*, Ids *pahara so apanī apanī bārī*, U *pahara so apanī apanī*, K om. the latter half of this *caupāī* and the former half of the next. 3. Ia *pūja taba mārā.* 4. U *parā su-ḍā̃ḍi.* Ic K *kara*, Id *khara.* Is *mā̃ṭī bhā̃ḍā* U *kati nicinta.* 5. Ic *tumha tō.* K *taba tehi.* Ia *bhaeu so phēri nāhī thira bā̃cē*, U *rahē na jama tē̃ thira.* 6. Ic *tumha jāū*, U *jo bajai ghaṭai*, K *ghari jo ghaṭai. ghaṭai.* Ia *ka nicinta aba sōu ba°*, Ib *sōai*, Is *nicinta hwai sōahu ba°*, U *kati nicinta*, K *nicinta bhai rahai baṭāū.* 7. Ia *hiā basana kā jī guna sōī*, Is *hia na sugāi*, U *hiya bajara pai jā°*, K *huā na suna nis͟hē jāgata kōī.* K adds *jau lagi dēva asta na hōī* । *tau lagi cēta karahu nara lōī* ‖ Ib also inserts this on the margin. 8. Ia *taja marana*, K *jīana dīna bharana*, Ia *jaisa rahaṭi kī rīti.* Ib *kaunai rahaṭi kī*, K *rahai gharī.* 9. Ia *āī marana kī*, Icds *gharī so āī.* U *jala bharī*, K *bharī so ḍhārī phiri bharī.* Ia U K *janama gaeu taha bīti.*

43. 1. Ia *gaḍha tara.* U *nīra chīra.* Ib *jānahū̃ du°.* U *pāni bharai āwai draupādī.* 3. U *jō sugandhi pānī waha pīā* 4. The latter half of the verse has an instant too much if we spell *indra* as *indara.* U has *kalapa brakṣa janu hai kabilāsā*, K *kalapa taru indra kabilāsā.* So Is has *indra kabilāsā.* 5. Ia *saraga kō sā.* Ib *saraga tehi sā°.* Id *mūra.* Ic *asa pāu*, Id *kou pāu na eā°.* Is U *pāwai kō cā°.* 6. Is *cā̃da pāta.* Id U *jagata jahā̃*, K *nētra jahā̃.* 9. U *sati guru milai to pāwai jō sādhai tapa jōga.*

44. 1. Is *cāri gaḍha°*, U *jāra gaḍhi-pātī.* 2. Ib U *saba kē.* Is K *dhaurāhara*, Ib *apanē apanē saba ra°.* Id K *saba apanē apanē.* 3. U *rūpawanta saba basahī sabha°.* 4. Icd N *bilāsa*, Is *sabai kau mā°*, K *sabai sudha*, Id *koi nāhī jā°*, Is *kou kahū̃ na jā°.* 5. U *tahā̃ khē°.* 6. U *pāsā sāra khēla tahā̃ kōī*, Ia K *khēli bahu*, U *kharaga gahē sara gūjani kōī.* 7. U *baranāwai kī°*, U *hasti-dāna siŋ°.* 8. U *achirī baiṭhī pāsa.* 9. Ib *khaṭa ritu*, U *chā̃ḍi basanta auru nahi khaṭi ritu, &c.*

45. 1. *Mahi ghū̃bia* the reading is very doubtful, Iab have مهه كهو بنهى so also Ic, omitting diacritical marks. Id مهِه كهو نهتي, Is *mahi khūbai*, U *mahi khū̃dē.* K *mahipati jhurī na pāwahi pārū.* 2. K *hāthī si°.* 3. Ic K *kōī-kōī.* U *dhūmarē kārē.* 4. U *barana sō jānahu mēghā.* Ia *bhāra baiṭhi gagana*, Ibc *gagana baiṭhi*, Ids U K *gagana pīṭhi.* 5. Is U *baranau*, U *janu airāpati kualī bālī.* Ia *pahāra parabata kahā̃ pē°*, Id *pahāra pannī kahā̃*, Is *pabai gahi pē°*, U *paina sō̃ pē°*, K *palau gahi pē°.* Is U *upāri.* K *ucāri ghāli.* 7. Icds K *mā̃ta nimata saba.* 8. Ic *mahi hāḷi.* U *kurama uṭhā hia sāla.* 9. Iac *bhūī phā°*, U *jabahi calai gayandawē̃ jagata parai bhūi cāla*, K *kurama pīṭhi puni phaṭai unha hastinha kē cāli.*

श्रीजानकीवल्लभो विजयते।

अथ सुधाकर-चन्द्रिका लिख्यते।

दोहा।

लखि जननी के गोद विच मोद करत रघु-राज।
होत मनोरथ सुफल सब धनि रघु-कुल सिरताज॥
जनक-राज-तनया सहित रतन-सिँहासन आज।
राजत कोशल-राज लखि सुफल करऊ सब काज॥
निहचै निज जन जानि जो ऊँच नीच तजि मान।
मिले हरखि निज बंधु ज्योँ ताहि भजऊ हित जान॥
का दुसाधु का साधु जन का विमान संमान।
लखऊ सुधाकर-चन्द्रिका करत प्रकाश समान॥
मलिक मुहम्मद मति-लता कविता कनक वितान।
जोरि जोरि सुवरन वरन धरत सुधाकर सान॥

अथ पदुमावति लिख्यते।

मूल ॥

अथ असतुति-खंड ।

चउपाई ।

सवँरउँ आदि एक करतारू । जेइ जिउ दीन्ह कीन्ह संसारू ॥
कीन्हेसि प्रथम जोति परगासू । कीन्हेसि तेहि परबत कबिलासू ॥
कीन्हेसि अगिनि पवन जल खेहा । कीन्हेसि बहुतइ रंग उरेहा ॥
कीन्हेसि धरती सरग पतारू । कीन्हेसि बरन बरन अउतारू ॥
कीन्हेसि सपत दीप ब्रहमंडा । कीन्हेसि भुअन चउदह-उ खंडा ॥
कीन्हेसि दिन दिनिअर ससि राती । कीन्हेसि नखत तराइन पाँती ॥
कीन्हेसि सीउ धूप अउ छाँहा । कीन्हेसि मेघ बीजु तेहि माँहा ॥

दोहा ।

कीन्ह सबइ अस जा कर दोसर छाज न काहि ।
पहिलइ तेहि कर नाउँ लेइ कथा करउँ अउगाहि ॥ १ ॥

टीका ॥

असतुति-खंड = स्तुति-खण्ड ।

यद्यपि खण्ड खण्ड में ग्रन्थ की रचना करना ग्रन्थ-कार के लेख से नहीं पाया जाता, तथापि बहुत पुस्तकों में खण्डों के नाम होने से अनुमान होता है कि पीछे से लोगों ने इस ग्रन्थ का पुराणवत् आदर करने के लिये पद्म-पुराण, स्कन्द-पुराणादि के ऐसा, इस में भी अनेक खण्ड कर डाले। इस खण्ड में ईश्वर और गुरु की ग्रन्थ-कार ने स्तुति की है। इसी लिये इस का स्तुति-खण्ड नाम पडा ॥

सवँरउँ = सुमिरउँ । जोति = ज्योतिः । परगासू = प्रकाश । कबिलासू = कैलास । खेहा = धूलि। उरेहा = उल्लेख, रचना। दिनिअर = दिनकर, सूर्य। तराइन = तारा-गण। सीउ = शीत । बीजु = विद्युत्, बिजुली । अउगाहि = अवगाहन कर, डूब कर ॥

मैं सब से आदि और एक (अद्वितीय) जो कर्त्तार (कर्त्ता = परब्रह्म) है उसे स्मरण करता हूँ। जिस ने जीव दिया और संसार को किया॥ जिस ने पहिले *ज्योतिः-स्वरूप (महादेव) को प्रकाश किया और तिस के लिये कैलास पर्वत को किया। (मुसल्मानों में कहावत है कि हिंदुओं का महादेव हमारे लोगों का आदम है)॥ जिस ने अग्नि, पवन (वायु), जल और खेह (मृत्तिका, धूलि) को किया। †(मुसल्मान लोग आकाश को तत्त्व नहीं मानते इसी लिये यहाँ पर चार-ही तत्त्वों का नाम कहा है)। इन्हीं चारो तत्त्वों से बहुतह (बहुत प्रकार के) रंगों का उरेह (रचना) किया अर्थात् इन्हीं चारो तत्त्वों से अनेक प्रकार के पदार्थों का रचना किया॥ जिस ने धरती (धरित्री = पृथ्वी), सरग (स्वर्ग), और पतार (पताल) को किया। जिस ने बरन बरन (तरह तरह) का अवतार धारण किया। मत्स्य, कूर्म, वराह, नृ-सिंह इत्यादि परब्रह्म ईश्वर के अवतार पुराणों में प्रसिद्ध हैं॥ जिस ने सपत (सप्त) दीप और ब्रह्माण्ड को किया। पुराणों में जम्बू द्वीप, शाक, शाल्मल, कुश, क्रौञ्च, गो-मेदक और पुष्कर ये सात द्वीप प्रसिद्ध हैं। जिस ने खण्ड खण्ड चौदह भुवन को किया। पुराणों में भूर्लोक, भुवर्लोक, स्वर्लोक, महर्लोक, जनलोक, तप- और सत्य- ये सात ऊपर के लोक, और अतल, वितल, सुतल, रसातल, तलातल, महातल और पाताल, ये सात नीचे के लोक, प्रसिद्ध हैं। दोनों सप्तकों के मिलाने से चौदह भुवन होते हैं। कभीं कभीं स्वर्ग-लोक, मर्त्य-लोक, और पाताल-लोक ले कर कवि लोग तीन-ही भुवन कहते हैं॥ जिस ने दिन में सूर्य और रात्रि में (प्रकाश के लिये) शशि (चन्द्र) को किया। जिस ने नक्षत्र और तारा-गण की पङ्क्ति को किया॥ जिस ने सीउ (शीत) धूप (घाम) और छाँह (छाया) को किया। जिस ने मेघ (बादल) और तिस के माँह (मध्य) विद्युत् को किया॥

ऐसा सब कुछ जिस का किया है दूसरे में काहि (कहीं भी) जिस का गुण शोभित नहीं, पहले उस का नाम ले कर (स्मरण कर) कथा को अउगाहि (ध्यान में डूब कर) करता हूँ। आगे की चौपाइयों में भी सर्वत्र "जिस ने" का योजना करना चाहिए॥ १॥

चउपाई।

कीन्हेसि सात-उ समुद अपारा। कीन्हेसि मेरु खिखिंद पहारा॥
कीन्हेसि नदी नार अउ झरना। कीन्हेसि मगर मच्छ बहु बरना॥

---

* नान्हकपन्थियों के मत में ज्योतिःस्वरूप से परब्रह्म लेते हैं।

† फारसी में कानूनचा नाम पुस्तक के २ पृष्ठ में लिखा है कि अग्नि, वायु, जल और पृथ्वी ये ही चार तत्त्व हैं।

कीन्हेसि सीप मोँति तेहि भरे। कीन्हेसि बहुतइ नग निरमरे ॥
कीन्हेसि बन-खँड अउ जरि मूरी। कीन्हेसि तरिवर तार खजूरी ॥
कीन्हेसि साउज आरन रहहीं। कीन्हेसि पंखि उडहिँ जहँ चहहीँ ॥
कीन्हेसि बरन सेत अउ सामा। कीन्हेसि नीद भूख बिसरामा ॥
कीन्हेसि पान फूल रस भोगू। कीन्हेसि बहु ओखद बहु रोगू ॥

दोहा।

निमिख न लाग करत ओहि सबहि कीन्ह पल एक।
गगन अंतरिख राखा बाजु खंभ बिनु टेक ॥ २ ॥

समुद = समुद्र। खिखिंद = किष्किन्धा, कुखण्ड, जिस के ऊपर दक्षिण ध्रुव है। इसे ज्यौतिष में कुमेरु भी कहते हैँ। निरमरे = निर्मल। बनखंड = पृथ्वी में वन-रूपी खण्ड (विभाग)। तरिवर = तरुवर, वृक्षोँ में बडा। साउज = श्वापद, मार कर खाने लायक जन्तु। आरन = अरण्य, वन। पंखि = पक्षी। सेत = श्वेत। सामा = श्याम। ओखद = औषधि। अंतरिख = अन्तरिक्ष। बाजु = वर्जयित्वा। टेक = आधार ॥

(जिस ईश्वर ने) अपार सातो समुद्र* को किया। मेरु और किष्किन्धा पहाड को किया॥ नदी, नारा और झरने को किया। (पहाड के तल से वा किसी बडे ताल से जो निकले उसे नदी, किसी ग्राम से नल-रूप हो कर बहते बहते किसी नदी में मिले उसे नारा (नल), और पहाड के छेदोँ से धीरे धीरे जो पानी बहता है उसे झरना कहते हैँ)। बहु (अनेक) बरन के मगर और मच्छ को किया॥ सीप को किया तिस में मोँती भरे हैँ। बहुत प्रकार के निर्मल नग को किया॥ पृथ्वी में बन-खंड (वन-रूपी विभाग), जडी, और मूरि को किया। प्रायः जडी औषधि के और मूरि खाने के काम में आती है। वृक्षोँ में बडा ताड और खजूर को किया॥ साउज (खाने लायक जन्तुओँ) को किया जो कि अरण्य (वन) में रहते हैँ। पक्षियोँ को किया जो कि जहाँ चाहते हैँ तहाँ उडते हैँ॥ श्वेत और श्याम वर्ण को किया। संसार में श्वेत और श्याम-ही वर्ण मुख्य हैँ, इस लिये इन्ही दोनोँ में मुख्यता समझ, इन्ही दोनोँ का ग्रहण किया। भूख, नीँद और विश्राम (आराम) को किया॥ पान, फूल, रस और भोग को किया। अनेक औषधि और अनेक रोग को किया॥

---

* क्षार, दुग्ध, दधि, घृत, इक्षु-रस, मद्य, स्वादु जल, इन के सात समुद्र पुराणोँ में प्रसिद्ध हैँ। परन्तु इन से भिन्न ग्रन्थ-कार ने कई एक नाम लिखे हैँ जो कि रत्नसेन की सिंहल-यात्रा में मिलेँगे।

पलक भजने में जो काल लगता है, उसे निमेष कहते हैं। सो ओहि (उस को) करने में एक निमेष न लगा। एक-ही पल में सब को किया। यहाँ पल से निमेष का पल लेना चाहिए। नहीँ तो जो पल प्रसिद्ध है, वह निमेष से बडा है तब पूर्वापर ग्रन्थ में असङ्गति होगी। निमेष का साठवाँ भाग निमेष का एक पल होता है।

अन्तरिच्छ में खंभा को बाजु (वर्जन कर अर्थात् छोड कर) विना आधार के गगन (आकाश) को रक्खा है। मुसल्मानों के मत से आकाश भी, और पदार्थों के ऐसा, एक पदार्थ है। परन्तु हमारे लोगों के मत से आकाश शून्य है॥ २॥

चउपाई।

कीन्हेसि मानुस दीन्ह बडाई। कीन्हेसि अन्न भुगुति तेइँ पाई॥
कीन्हेसि राजा भूँजइ राजू। कीन्हेसि हसति घोर तेहि साजू॥
कीन्हेसि तेहि कहँ बहुत बिरासू। कीन्हेसि कोइ ठाकुर कोइ दासू॥
कीन्हेसि दरब गरब जेहि होई। कीन्हेसि लोभ अघाइ न कोई॥
कीन्हेसि जिअन सदा सब चहा। कीन्हेसि मीँचु न कोई रहा॥
कीन्हेसि सुख अउ कोड अनंदू। कीन्हेसि दुख चिंता अउ दंदू॥
कीन्हेसि कोइ भिखारि कोइ धनी। कीन्हेसि सँपति बिपति बहु घनी॥

दोहा।

कीन्हेसि कोइ निभरोसी कीन्हेसि कोइ बरिआर।
छारहि तइँ सब कीन्हेसि पुनि कीन्हेसि सब छार॥ ३॥

मानुस = मनुष्य। भुगुति = भुक्ति = भोजन। भूँजइ = भोग करता है। राजू = राज्य। हसति = हस्ती। घोर = घोटक = घोडा। बिरासू = विलास। दरब = द्रव्य। गरब = गर्व। अघाइ = अघा जाना = पूर्ण हो जाना = तृप्त हो जाना। जिअन = जीवन। मीँचु = मृत्यु। कोड = करोड = कोटि। दंदू = दन्द। निभरोसी = जिस को किसी का भरोसा न हो = अत्यन्त दुर्बल। बरिआर = बलिष्ठ। छार = भस्म = राखी॥

मनुष्य को किया और उसे बडाई दिया। क्योंकि ईश्वर की सृष्टि में मनुष्य सब से बडा गिना जाता है। अन्न को किया जिसे तिस मनुष्य ने भोजन के लिये पाया॥ राजा को किया जो कि राज्य भोगता है। और तिस के साज के लिये हाथी और घोड़े को

किया ॥ तिस राजा के लिये बझत विलास को किया, (छच, सिंहासन, सुन्दर भोजन आदि अनेक सुखोपभोग विलास हैं)। किसी को ठाकुर (मालिक) और किसी को दास किया ॥ द्रव्य को किया जिस को हो कर (पा कर) गर्व (अभिमान) होता है। लोभ को किया जिस के कारण कोई अघाता नहीं (पूर्ण नहीं होता) ॥ जीवन को किया जिस को सदा (सर्वदा) सब कोई चाहता है। मृत्यु को किया जिस से कोई नहीं रहता है अर्थात् मृत्यु सब को मार लेती है ॥ सुख और करोड आनन्द को किया। दुःख, चिन्ता और दन्द अर्थात् ममत्व को किया ॥ किसी को भिक्षुक और किसी को धनी किया। सम्पत्ति (पुत्र, पौत्र, गो, धनादि वैभव) और अति घनी (कठिन) विपत्ति को किया ॥

किसी को अति दुर्बल किया और किसी को बली किया। सब वस्तु को छार-ही से किया और अन्त में फिर सब को छार कर दिया ॥ ३ ॥

चउपाई।

कीन्हेसि अगर कसतुरी बेना। कीन्हेसि भीमसेनि अउ चेना ॥
कीन्हेसि नाग मुखइ बिख बसा। कीन्हेसि मंच हरइ जो डसा ॥
कीन्हेसि अमीँ जिअइ जेहि पाई। कीन्हेसि बिख जो मीँचु तेहि खाई ॥
कीन्हेसि ऊख मीठ रस भरी। कीन्हेसि करुइ बेलि बहु फरी ॥
कीन्हेसि मधु लावइ लेइ माँखी। कीन्हेसि भवँर पंखि अउ पाँखी ॥
कीन्हेसि लोवा उंदुर चाँटी। कीन्हेसि बहुत रहहिँ खनि माँटी ॥
कीन्हेसि राकस भूत परेता। कीन्हेसि भोकस देव दएता ॥

दोहा।

कीन्हेसि सहस अठारह बरन बरन उपराजि।
भुगुति दीन्ह पुनि सब कहँ सकल साजना साजि ॥ ४ ॥

अगर = सुगन्धित एक वृक्ष। कसतुरी = कस्तूरी = मृगमद। बेना = वेण = खस। भीमसेनि = भीमसेनी कर्पूर। चेना = चीन देश का कर्पूर। मुखइ = मुखे = मुख में। अमीँ = अमृत। पाई = पान कर। करुइ = कटु। मधु = शहद। माँखी = मक्षिका = मक्खी। भवँर = भ्रमर। पंखि = पक्षी। पाँखी = जिन जन्तुओं को ऋतु-विशेष में पर उत्पन्न हो

जाता है। जैसे वर्षा ऋतु में दीँवक को। लोवा = लोमडी। उंदुर = मूसा। चाँटी = चीँटी। राकस = राचस। परेत = प्रेत। भोकस = बुभुचु = भुक्खड। दएता = दैत्य। उपराजि = उत्पन्न कर॥

अगर, कस्तूरी, और खस को किया। भीमसेनी और चीनी कपूर को किया॥ नाग (सर्प) को किया जिस के मुख में विष बसता है। मन्त्र को किया जो डसे ऊये विष को हर लेता है॥ अमृत को किया जिस को पान कर (प्राणी) जीता है। विष को किया, जो तिस को खाता है वह मृत्यु को प्राप्त होता है। यहाँ "मीँचु" के स्थान में "मरद" यह पाठ होने से सुन्दर अर्थ लग जाता है। जो तिस को खाता है वह मर जाता है॥ ऊख को किया जिस में मीठा रस भरा रहता है। कडुई बेलि को किया जो कि बऊत फरती है॥ मधु को किया जिस को ले कर मक्खी (छत्ते को) लगाती है। भ्रमर, पची, और पाँखी को किया॥ लोमडी, मूसा, और चीँटी को किया। बऊत ऐसा किया जो मट्टी को खन कर रहते हैं॥ राचस, भूत और प्रेत को किया। भुक्खड, देवता, और दैत्य को किया॥

तरह तरह उत्पन्न कर अठारह हजार को किया। (हमारे यहाँ चौरासी लाख योनि है परन्तु ग्रन्थ-कार ने अठार-ही हजार लिखा है। *मुसल्मानी मत में अठार-ही हज़ार योनि हैं)॥ सब तरह की साजना (तयारी) साज कर (बना कर) सब को भोजन दिया। अर्थात् जिस को जैसा चाहिए वैसी सब सामग्री समेत भोजन को दिया॥ ४॥

चउपाई।

धनपति उहइ जेहि क संसारू। सबहि देइ निति घंट न भँडारू॥
जावँत जगत हसति अउ चाँटा। सब कहँ भुगुति राति दिन बाँटा॥
ता करि दिसिटि सबहि उपराहीँ। मितर सतरु कोइ बिसरइ नाहीँ॥
पंखी पतंग न बिसरइ कोई। परगट गुपुत जहाँ लगि होई॥
भोग-भुगुति बहु भाँति उपाई। सबहि खिआवइ आपु न खाई॥
ता कर इहइ जो खाना पिअना। सब कहँ देइ भुगुति अउ जिअना॥
सबहि आस ता करि हर साँसा। ओहि न काहु कइ आस निरासा॥

---

* मुसल्मानीं के एक मौलूद में लिखा है कि "हिश्दह हज़ार आलम" अर्थात् अठारह हज़ार योनि हैं। बऊत से लोग कहते हैं कि यहाँ अठारह हज़ार से असंख्य समझना चाहिए।

चउपाई ।

अलख अरूप अबरन सो करता । वह सब सउँ सब ओहि सउँ बरता ॥
परगट गुपुत सो सरब बिआपी । धरमी चीन्ह चीन्ह नहिँ पापी ॥
ना ओहि पूत न पिता न माता । ना ओहि कुटुँब न कोइ सँग नाता ॥
जना न काहु न कोइ ओहि जना । जहँ लगि सब ता कर सिरजना ॥
वेइ सब कीन्ह जहाँ लगि कोई । वह न कीन्ह काहू कर होई ॥
हुत पहिलइ अउ अब हइ सोई । पुनि सो रहइ रहइ नहिँ कोई ॥
अउरु जो होइ सो बाउर अंधा । दिन दुइ चारि मरइ कइ धंधा ॥

दोहा ।

जो वेइ चहा सो कीन्हेसि करइ जो चाहइ कीन्ह ।
बरजन-हार न कोई सबहि चाहि जिउ दीन्ह ॥ ७ ॥

अलख = अलच्य । अबरन = अवर्ण = विना रङ्ग का, वा अवर्ण्य = वर्णन के योग्य नहीँ । बरता = बटा हुआ है । बिआपी = व्यापी । सिरजना = रचना किया हुआ । हुत = था) बाउर = बौरहा । कइ = कर के । धंधा = कार्य । चाहि = चाहना कर = इच्छा से ॥

वह जो कर्त्ता परब्रह्म ईश्वर है सो अलख, अरूप और अवरन (विना रङ्ग का, वा अवर्ण्य) है । वह सब से, और सब कोई उस से, बटे हुये हैँ (रस्सी की तरह) ॥ वह कहीँ प्रगट रूप से, कहीँ गुप्त रीति से, सर्वत्र व्याप्त है । परन्तु जो धर्मी हैँ वे लोग तो इस ईश्वर को पहचानते हैँ, और पापी नहीँ पहचानते ॥ न उस को पुत्र, न पिता, न माता है । न उस को कुटुम्ब है, और न किसी के संग उस का नाता (सम्बन्ध) है ॥ वह किसी को नहीँ जना (उत्पन्न किया), और न उस को कोई उत्पन्न किया । परन्तु जहाँ तक सब है, वह सब उसी का रचा हुआ है ॥ जहाँ तक जो कुछ है, सब उसी का किया हुआ है, परन्तु वह किसी का किया नहीँ है ॥ पहले भी वह था, और अब भी सोई ईश्वर है । फिर (आगे) भी वही रहता है, और उसे छोड कोई नहीँ रहता ॥ और जो होता है (संसार में) सो बौरहा और अंधा है । दो चार दिन धंधा (कार्य) कर मर जाता है ॥

जो उस ने चाहा सो किया, और जो करने चाहता है सो करता है । उस को कोई बर्जने-वाला नहीँ है, सब को अपनी इच्छा से जीव दिया है ॥ ७ ॥

चउपाई।

एहि बिधि चीन्हहु करहु गिआनू। जस पुरान मँह लिखा बखानू॥
जीउ नाहिँ पइ जिअइ गोसाईँ। कर नाहीँ पइ करइ सबाईँ॥
जीभ नाहिँ पइ सब किछु बोला। तन नाहीँ जो डोलाउ सो डोला॥
स्रवन नाहिँ पइ सब किछु सुना। हिअ नाहीँ गुननाँ सब गुना॥
नयन नाहिँ पइ सब किछु देखा। कवन भाँति अस जाइ बिसेखा॥
ना कोइ होइ हइ ओहि के रूपा। ना ओहि अस कोइ अइस अनूपा॥
ना ओहि ठाउँ न ओहि बिनु ठाऊँ। रूप रेख बिनु निरमर नाऊँ॥

दोहा।

ना वह मिला न बेहरा अइस रहा भरि पूरि।
दिसिटिवंत कहँ नीअरे अंध मुरुख कहँ दूरि॥८॥

गिआनू = ज्ञान। सबाईँ = सब को। डोलाउ = डोलाता है = चलाता है। स्रवन = श्रवण = कान। जाइ बिसेखा = विशेष रूप से वर्णन किया जाय। बेहरा = अलग। दिसिटिवंत = दृष्टिवन्त।

इस प्रकार से चीन्हो और ज्ञान करो, जैसा कि (उस ईश्वर का) पुराण में बखान (वर्णन) लिखा है॥ जीव नहीँ है, पर वह गोसाईँ (गो-स्वामी = सब इन्द्रियोँ का पति) जीता है। उस को कर (हाथ) नहीँ है, पर सब को करता है॥ "उस को" का सर्वत्र योजना करना चाहिए। जीभ नहीँ है, पर सब कुछ बोलता है। तन (तनु = शरीर) नहीँ है, पर जो डोलाता है वही डोलता है। श्रवण नहीँ है, पर सब कुछ सुनता है। हिअ (हृदय) नहीँ है, पर सब गुनना (विचार) को गुना (विचारा) करता है॥ नयन (नेत्र = आँख) नहीँ है, पर सब कुछ देखता है। किस प्रकार से ऐसे का विशेष रूप से वर्णन किया जाय॥ उस के रूप के ऐसा न कोई होता है और न कोई है। और न उस के ऐसा कोई है और न कोई ऐसा अनुपम है। यहाँ देहली दीप न्याय से यदि "कोई" का दोनोँ ओर अन्वय किया जाय तो ग्रन्थ लग जाता है! अथवा "अइस" के स्थान मेँ "होइ" पाठ किया जाय, तो उस के ऐसा कोई अनुपम नहीँ होता है, यह ठीक अर्थ बैठ जाता है। ऐसा न करने से "अस" और "अइस"

दोनों शब्द एक-ही अर्थ के बोधक एक के अपेक्षा एक व्यर्थ पड जाते हैं ॥ न उस को स्थान है, और उस के विना कोई स्थान-ही नहीं है, अर्थात् वह सर्वत्र व्याप्त है। रूप और रेखा (चिन्ह) के विना वह है, इसी से उस का निर्मल, मल कर के रहित, अर्थात् सच्चिदानन्द नाम पडा है ॥

न वह किसी से मिला है न किसी से अलग है, (संसार में) ऐसा भरा पूरा हो रहा है, कि देखने-वालों के तो नीअरे (नगीच) है, और अन्धे मूर्ख को दूर ॥ ८ ॥

चउपाई ।

अउरु जो दीन्हेसि रतन अमोला । ता कर मरम न जानइ भोला ॥
दीन्हेसि रसना अउ रस भोगू । दीन्हेसि दसन जो विहँसइ जोगू ॥
दीन्हेसि जग देखइ कहँ नयना । दीन्हेसि स्रवन सुनइ कहँ बयना ॥
दीन्हेसि कंठ बोलि जेहि माँहा । दीन्हेसि कर-पल्लउ बर बाँहा ॥
दीन्हेसि चरन अनूप चलाहीँ । सो पइ मरम जानु जेहि नाहीँ ॥
जोबन मरम जानु पइ बूढा । मिला न तरुनापा जग ढूँढा ॥
दुख कर मरम न जानइ राजा । दुखी जानु जा कहँ दुख बाजा ॥

दोहा ।

कया क मरम जानु पइ रोगी भोगी रहइ निचिंत ।
सब कर मरम गोसाईँ जानइ जो घट घट मँह निंत ॥ ९ ॥

रतन = रत्न । अमोला = अमूल्य । भोला = सीधा आदमी, भोलना । रसना = जिह्वा । दसन = दशन = दन्त । बयना = वचन । कर-पल्लउ = कर-पल्लव = अङ्गुली । बर = श्रेष्ठ । बाहाँ = बाहु । चलाहीँ = चलते हैं । तरुनापा = जवानी । बाजा = शब्द किया वा बजनी किया = लडाई किया । कया = काय = शरीर । निचिंत = निश्चिन्त = विना चिन्ता का । निंत = नित्य ।

और उस ईश्वर ने (इन्द्रिय-रूपी) अमूल्य रत्न को जो दिया है, सीधा आदमी उस के मर्म को नहीं जानता ॥ (देखो) जिह्वा को दिया, और उस के भोग के लिये अनेक रस को दिया । दाँतों को दिया जो हँसने के योग्य हैं ॥ संसार को देखने के लिये नेत्र को दिया । वचन को सुनने के लिये कान को दिया । कण्ठ को दिया जिस

के बीच मेँ बोली रहती है। अँगुली और श्रेष्ठ बाज्ज को दिया॥ अनुपम चरण को दिया जो कि चलते हैँ। इन सब का मर्म सोई जानता है, जिस को कि ये सब नहीँ हैँ॥ जवानी का मर्म निश्चय कर के (पद=अपि=निश्चय) बूढा जानता है। क्योँकि उस ने जग मेँ ढूँढा परन्तु जवानी न मिली। बूढे की कमर झुक जाती है, इस लिये वह पृथ्वी की ओर दृष्टि कर चलता है। कवि की उत्प्रेक्षा है, कि नीची दृष्टि कर के जो बूढा चलता है, वह जवानी को ढूँढ रहा है, जो कि फिर नहीँ मिलती॥ राजा दुःख का मर्म नहीँ जानता। दुःखी जो प्राणी है, जिस के ऊपर दुःख ने चढाई किया है, वह दुःख का मर्म जानता है॥ यहाँ "सुख" पाठ अच्छा है क्योँकि राजा सुख का मर्म नहीँ जानता, कि उस मेँ क्या आनन्द है। जिस पर दुःख ने चढाई किया है, वह दुःख निवृत्त होने पर सुख का पूरा अनुभव करता है। राजा का तो खस की टट्टी के नीचे जन्म-ही ज्जआ है, वह उस के सुख को कैसे जाने। जेठ की दुपहरी से झुलसा ज्जआ यदि खस के टट्टी की छाया मेँ आवे, तब उस को जान पडेगा, कि खस के टट्टी की छाया मेँ क्या आनन्द है॥

शरीर का मर्म रोगी जानता है, और भोगी तो निश्चिन्त रहता है, अर्थात् बे-फिकिर हो अपनी-ही शरीर के ऐसा सब का शरीर समझता है। गोसाईँ, जो ईश्वर, नित्य सब के घट घट मेँ रहता है, वह सब का मर्म जानता है॥ इस दोहे मेँ कई मात्रा बढी ज्जई हैँ। ईसी प्रकार इस ग्रन्थ मेँ दोहाओँ की मात्रा प्रायः घट बढ हैँ। दोहाओँ के मात्राओँ का ठीक न रहना, और सर्वत्र सात सात चौपाई के अनन्तर दोहे का रहना, इन सब का कारण २१ वेँ दोहे मेँ लिखा जायगा॥ ९॥

चउपाई।

अति अपार करता कर करना। बरनि न पारइ काह्न बरना॥
सात सरग जउँ कागद करई। धरती सात समुद मसि भरई॥
जावँत जगत साख बन-ढाँखा। जावँत केस रोवँ पँखि पाँखा॥
जावँत खेह रेह जहँ ताईँ। मेघ बूँद अउ गगन तराईँ॥
सब लिखनी कइ लिखु संसारू। लिखि न जाइ गति समुद अपारू॥
अइस कीन्ह सब गुन परगटा। अब-हूँ समुद बूँद नहिँ घटा॥
अइस जानि मन गरब न होई। गरब करइ मन बाउर सोई॥

दोहा ।

बड गुनवंत गोसाईं चहइ सो होइ तेहि बेग ।
अउ अस गुनी सँवारइ जो गुन करइ अनेग ॥ १० ॥

पारइ = पार हो सकता है । काह्न बरना = किसी भाँति = किसी प्रकार । साख = शाखा । बन-ढाँखा = वन के ढाँकने-वाले, अर्थात् वृक्ष । केस = केश = बार । रोवँ = रोम । पाँखा = पक्ष । लिखनी = लेखनी = कलम । अनेग = अनेक ॥

कर्त्ता (परब्रह्म) का करना (करण, अर्थात् कर्त्तव्य) अति अपार है। किसी प्रकार वर्णन कर पार नहीँ हो सकता ॥ सात स्वर्ग और धरती को यदि कागद करे, और सात समुद्र मेँ मसि (स्याही) को भरे ॥ जगत मेँ जितने वृक्षोँ की शाखा । जितने (मनुष्योँ के) बाल और रोम, जितने पक्षियोँ के पक्ष ॥ जितनी जहाँ तक मिट्टी और रेह। मेघ के बूँद, और आकाश के तारे हैँ ॥ सब कोँ कलम बना कर संसार (संसार भर के लिखने-वाले) लिखे। तो भी उस ईश्वर की समुद्र के ऐसी अपार जो गति है, वह लिखी न जाय ॥ ऐसा ईश्वर ने सब गुणोँ को प्रगट किया है (कि उन मेँ आज तक रत्ती भर भेद नहीँ ऊआ, ज्योँ के त्योँ बने हैँ, इस पर समुद्र का एक दृष्टान्त दिखाते हैँ)। आज तक समुद्र मेँ एक बूँद नहीँ घटा, अर्थात् जैसा का तैसा बना है ॥ ऐसा जान कर मन मेँ गर्व न होना चाहिए। जो मन मेँ गर्व करता है सो बौरहा है ॥

वह गोसाईं ऐसा गुनवन्त (गुण से भरा है) है, कि जिस के लिये जो चाहता है, तिस को सो बेग (शीघ्र) होता है। और ऐसा गुणी को बनाता है, जो स्वयं अनेक गुण करता है, अर्थात् जिस को स्वयं ऐसी शक्ति हो जाती है, कि अनेक गुण को बनावे । ऐसा ईश्वर ने किस को बनाया है। इस का सम्बन्ध अगली चौपाई मेँ लगा कर, ग्रन्थ-कार ने परब्रह्म का वर्णन समाप्त किया ॥ १० ॥

चउपाई ।

कीन्हेसि पुरुख एक निरमरा । नाउँ मुहम्मद पूनिउँ करा ॥
प्रथम जोति बिधि तेहि कइ साजी । अउ तेहि प्रीति सिसिटि उपराजी ॥
दीपक लेसि जगत कहँ दीन्हा । भा निरमर जग मारग चीन्हा ॥
जउँ नहिँ होत पुरुख उँजिआरा । सूझि न परत पंथ अँधिआरा ॥

दोसरे ठाउँ दई वेइ लिखे। भए धरमी जेइ पाढत सिखे॥
जेइ नहिँ लीन्ह जनम भरि नाऊँ। ता कहँ कीन्ह नरक मँह ठाऊँ॥
जगत बसीठ दई ओहि कीन्हा। दुहुँ जग तरा नाउँ जेइ लीन्हा॥

दोहा।

गुन अउगुन बिधि पूछब होइहि लेख अउ जोख।
वह बिनउब आगइ होइ करब जगत कर मोख॥ ११॥

पूनिउँ करा = पूर्णिमा की कला। लेसि = बार कर। पाढत = पाठ। बसीठ = दूत। अउगुन = अवगुण। पूछब = पूछेंगे। होइहि = होगा। बिनउब = बिनती करेँगे। करब = करेँगे। मोख = मोच॥

उस ईश्वर ने मुहम्मद नाम पूर्णिमा के चन्द्र के कला, ऐसा एक निर्मल पुरुष को किया॥ बिधि (ब्रह्मा) ने सब से पहले तिस की ज्योति को सजा और तिसी के प्रसन्नार्थ सृष्टि को उत्पन्न किया॥ (ब्रह्मा ने) जगत को दीपक बार कर दिया, अर्थात् जगत मेँ मुहम्मद को दीपक के ऐसा प्रज्वलित किया। इसी लिये संसार (संसार के लोग) निर्मल हो गया (= भा), और मार्ग को पहचान लिया॥ यदि ऐसा उँजियारा पुरुष न होता, तो अँधियारे मेँ पन्थ (राह) न सूझ पडती॥ वह दई (मुहम्मद देव) उन लोगोँ को दूसरे स्थान मेँ लिखे, जो लोग कि उन के पढाये ऊये पाठ को सिख लिये॥ और जिन लोगोँ ने जन्म भर (उन के पढाये ऊये पाठ का) नाम तक नहीँ लिया। उन के लिये नरक मेँ स्थान किया॥ पिछली चौपाई मेँ दूसरे स्थान से स्वर्ग लेना चाहिए। मुसल्मानोँ मेँ प्रसिद्ध है, कि धर्म्मी के लिये स्वर्ग और पापियोँ के लिये नरक लिखा जाता है। उसी लेख के अनुसार प्रलय मेँ विचार किया जाता है॥ देव (ईश्वर) ने जगत मेँ उस को (मुहम्मद को) अपना दूत किया (बनाया)। इस लिये जिस ने (मुहम्मद का) नाम लिया, वह दोनोँ जग (यह लोक और परलोक) को तैर गया। मुहम्मद का नाम लेने से, इस लोक मेँ मुहम्मद की कृपा से सुख, और परलोक मेँ, ईश्वर के दूत होने से, ईश्वर के यहाँ उस पुरुष की मुहम्मद ने जो प्रशँसा की, इस से सुख॥

(प्रलय के समय मेँ) ब्रह्मा गुण अवगुण पूछेँगे, और लेखा (हिसाब) जोखा (तौल) होगा। वही मुहम्मद आगे हो कर बिनती करेँगे, और जगत का मोच करेँगे॥ यहाँ ग्रन्थ-कार ने विधि (ब्रह्मा) और ईश्वर मेँ अभेद माना है॥ ११॥

चउपाई ।

चारि मीत जो मुहमद ठाऊँ। चहूँ क दुहुँ जग निरमर नाऊँ॥
अबा बकर सिद्दीक सयाने। पहिलइ सिदिक दीन वेइ आने॥
पुनि सो उमर खिताब सोहाए। भा जग अदल दीन जो आए॥
पुनि उसमान पँडित बड गुनी। लिखा पुरान जो आयत सुनी॥
चउथइ अली सिंघ बरिआरू। चढइ तो काँपइ सरग पतारू॥
चारिउ एक मतइ एक बाता। एक पंथ अउ एक सँघाता॥
बचन एक जो सुनावहिँ साँचा। भा परवाँन दुहूँ जग बाँचा॥

दोहा।

जो पुरान बिधि पठवा सोई पढत गरंथ।
अउरु जो भूले आवतहि तेहि सुनि लागहिँ पंथ॥१२॥

मीत = मित्र। मतइ = मते = मत मेँ। सँघात = संघात = साथ। परवाँन = प्रमाण॥

मुहम्मद के स्थान मेँ जो चारो मित्र थे, उन चारोँ का दोनोँ जगत मेँ निर्मल नाम है॥ पहले का नाम अबा बकर सिद्दीक (अबू बक्र सिद्दीक) था, वह बडे सयाने (चतुरे) थे, उन्होँ ने (संसार मेँ) सिद्दीक दीन (सत्य धर्म) को आने, ले आये, अर्थात् प्रगट किया॥ फिर दूसरे जो थे, सो उमर नाम के थे, जिन को कि (खलीफा की) पदवी शोभित थी। जो कि (जब मुहम्मद के) धर्म मेँ आए, तब जगत मेँ न्याय ऊआ, अर्थात जगत न्याय से छाय गया॥ फिर उन के अनन्तर, तीसरे उसमान नाम के थे, जो कि बडे पण्डित और गुणी थे, जिन्होँ ने कि उस पुरान (कोरान) को लिखा, जैसा कि आयतेँ (मन्त्रोँ) को (ईश्वर से) सुना॥ चौथे अली नाम के सिँह के ऐसे बलिष्ठ थे। जब वे लडाई करने को चढँ, तो स्वर्ग और पाताल कँपने लगे॥ चारो मित्र एक मत, एक बात, एक राह और एक साथ मेँ रहते थे॥ चारो जो एक सत्य वचन को सुनाते हैँ, वह (सर्वत्र) प्रमाण की गई, और दोनोँ जगत मेँ बाँची गई, अर्थात आदर से पढी गई। अथवा उस वचन का (जिस को) प्रमाण ऊआ, वह दोनोँ जग से बँच गया॥

ब्रह्मा ने जिस पुराण (कोरान) को भेज दिया था, उसी ग्रन्थ को वे लोग पढते हैँ। और लोग (ईश्वर के यहाँ से) आवने मेँ जो (ईश्वर की राह को) भूल गये हैँ, सो तिस ग्रन्थ को सुन कर पंथ (ईश्वर की राह) मेँ लग जाते हैँ॥१२॥

इस प्रकार से अपने मत के आचार्य का वर्णन कर अब अपने समय के राजा का वर्णन ग्रन्थ-कार करता है।

चउपाई।

सेर साहि देहिली सुलतानू। चारि-उ खंड तपइ जस भानू॥
ओही छाज राज अउ पाटू। सब राजइ भुइँ धरा लिलाटू॥
जाति सूर अउ खाँडइ सूरा। अउ बुधिवंत सबइ गुन पूरा॥
सूर-नवाँई नवो खँड भई। सात-उ दीप दुनी सब नई॥
तहँ लगि राज खरग बर लीन्हा। इसकंदर जुलकरन जो कीन्हा॥
हाथ सुलेमाँ केरि अँगूठी। जग कहँ जिअन दीन्ह तेहि मूठी॥
अउ अति गरू पुहुमि-पति भारी। टेकि पुहुमि सब सिसिटि सँभारी॥

दोहा।

दीन्ह असीस मुहम्मद करहु जुग हि जुग राज।
पातिसाहि तुम्ह जगत के जग तुम्हार मुहताज॥ १३॥

भानू = भानु = सूर्य। पाटू = पट्ट = सिंहासन। लिलाटू = ललाट = मस्तक। खाँडइ = खाँडे मेँ = तरवार मेँ। सूर = बहादुर। बुधिवंत = बुद्धिमान्। सूर-नवाँई = बहादुराँ की झुकावट अर्थात् नीचा होना। दुनी = दुनिया = प्राणी लोग। नई = झुक गई = नीचे पड गई। खरग = खड्ग। बर = बल। इसकंदर = सिकन्दर। जुलकरन = दो सीँगवाला। सुलेमान = यहूदी एक बादशाह। पुहुमि-पति = पृथ्वीपति। पातिसाहि = बादशाह। मुहताज = भिखमंगा = भिक्षुक।

दिल्ली का सुलतान (बादशाह) शेर शाह (पृथ्वी के) चारो (खण्ड) भाग मेँ अर्थात् पूर्व, पश्चिम, उत्तर, दक्खिन ऐसा तपता है जैसे सूर्य॥ उसी को (शेर शाह को) राज्य और सिंहासन सोहता है, (उस के आगे) सब राजाओँ ने पृथ्वी मेँ अपने मस्तक को धरा अर्थात् रख दिया (हार मान कर प्रणाम करने मेँ शिर को झुँका लिया)॥ वह बादशाह जाति मेँ सूर अर्थात् सूरवंश का है (सूर एक अफगानोँ के जाति का नाम है। उसी जाति मेँ शेर शाह उत्पन्न हुआ था) और तलवार मेँ भी सूर अर्थात् बहादुर है। और बुद्धिमान और सब गुणोँ मेँ पूरा है॥ जम्बूदीप के नवो खण्डोँ (भारतवर्ष,

किन्नरवर्ष, हरिवर्ष, कुरुवर्ष, हिरण्मयवर्ष, रम्यकवर्ष, भद्राश्ववर्ष, केतुमालकवर्ष और इलावृत) में (उस के आगे) बहादुरों की नवाँई हुई अर्थात् बहादुरों को नीचा खाना पडा। और (उस के आगे) सातो दीप (जम्बूदीप, शाक, शाल्मल, कुश, क्रौञ्च, गोमेदक और पुष्करदीप) की सब दुनिया (प्राणी) नय गई (झुक गई, अर्थात् सब कोई उस के शरण में आ गये)॥ उस ने अपने खड्ग के बल से तहाँ तक राज्य (अपने अधिकार में) ले लिया, जहाँ तक कि दो सींगवाला सिकन्दर बादशाह ने किया था॥

सिकन्दर के शिर में सींग का होना परम्परा से प्रसिद्ध है। कहावत है कि एक दिन बीमार पड जाने से सिकन्दर के हजाम ने बाल बनाने के लिये अपने पुत्र बब्बन हजाम को भेजा। बाल बनाने के अनन्तर सिकन्दर ने डाँट कर बब्बन से कहा कि खबर्दार मेरे शिर में सींग का होना किसी से न कहना, नहीं तो शिर कटवा लूँगा। उस का कहे विना पेट फूलने लगा, तब मनुष्यों से न कह कर, एक बगीचे में, जो बडा पुराना कटहर का पेंड था, उस से कह, अपने पेट को हलका किया (जड कटहर किस से जा कर कहे?)। निदान विना कहे उस का भी यहाँ तक पेट फूला कि कुछ दिनों में सूख गया। एक बढई ने उसे मोल ले कर, उस की दो सारंगी और एक सुन्दर तबला बनाया। कत्थकों ने उन सुन्दर सारंगियों को और तबले को मोल ले कर सिकन्दर के दर्बार में गाना सुनाने को गये। उन लोगों ने लाख उपाय किया परन्तु उन से कोई शब्द न निकले केवल एक सारंगी सींग सींग दूसरी किन किन कहे। इस पर तबले से आवाज निकले कि बब्बन हजाम। इस का भेद बादशाह को खुल गया। बब्बन को बुला कर एकान्त में पूछा कि तुम सच कहो मेरे शिर में सींग का होना तुम ने किसी से कहा?। अभय-दान पाने पर बब्बन ने कटहर से कहना कहा। अन्त में जान पडा कि उसी कटहर की ये सारंगियाँ और तबला हैं॥

(शेर शाह के) हाथ में सुलेमान की अँगूठी थी, तिसी मूठी से (जिस में अँगूठी थी) जग को (जगत भर के प्राणियों को) जीवन दान दिया॥

कहावत है कि जिस के हाथ में सुलेमान की अँगूठी हो, वह रात दिन लोगों को रुपया पैसा देता रहे, परन्तु उस की मूठी खाली न हो॥

और वह भारी पृथ्वी-पति (बादशाह) अत्यन्त गुरु था, अर्थात् भारी था, कि पृथ्वी को टेक कर (रोक कर) सब सृष्टि को सँभार लिया, अर्थात् सृष्टि में जितने प्राणी थे सब का बोझा (पालन, आच्छादनादि का) अपने शिर पर उठा लिया॥

मुहम्मद ने आशीर्वाद दिया कि तुम युग युग राज करो, (युग के लिये ५वेँ दोहे की टीका देखो) तुम जगत भर का बादशाह हो, और सारा जग (संसार). तुम्हारा मुहताज हो, अर्थात् सब कोई तुम से माँगने की आशा करे, और तुम सब के दाता कहावो। यहाँ मुहम्मद से मुसल्मानी मत के आचार्य और इस ग्रन्थ का कवि दोनोँ का ग्रहण करने से अर्थ मेँ भेद नहीँ पडता ॥१३॥

इस चौपाई मेँ ग्रन्थ-कार जो शेर शाह को गुरु बनाया। उस का समर्थन अगली चौपाई मेँ है ॥

चउपाई।

बरनउँ सूर पुहुमि-पति राजा। पुहुमि न भार सहइ जेहि साजा ॥
हय-मय सेन चलइ जग पूरी। परबत टूटि उडहिँ होइ धूरी ॥
रइनि रेनु होइ रबिहि गरासा। मानुस पंखि लेहिँ फिरि बासा ॥
भुइँ उडि अँतरिख गइ म्रित मंडा। खँड खँड धरति सिसिटि ब्रहमंडा ॥
डोलइ गगन इँदर डरि काँपा। बासुकि जाइ पतारहि चाँपा ॥
मेरु धसमसइ समुद सुखाहीँ। बन-खँड टूटि खेह मिलि जाहीँ ॥
अगिलहि काहु पानि खर बाँटा। पछिलहि काहु न काँदउ आँटा ॥

दोहा।

जो गढ नएउ नहिँ काहुही चलत होहिँ सब चूर।
जबहि चढइ पुहुमी-पति सेर साहि जग-सूर ॥१४॥

हय-मय = घोडे से भरी। रइनि = रात्रि = रजनी। रेनु = रेणु = धूरी। रबिहि = रवि को = सूर्य को। गरासा = ग्रास किया। बासा = वास-स्थान = बसेरा। म्रित = मृत् = मृत्तिका = मट्टी। मंडा = माँड दिया = मर्दन कर डाला। इँदर = इन्द्र। बासुकि = वासुकि = एक प्रकार का सर्प जो पृथ्वी के नीचे रहता है। चाँपा = चँपाया = दबाया। धसमसइ = धँस जाता है। बन-खँड = वन-खण्ड = वन-विभाग। अगिलइ = आगे को खर = तृण = घास। काँदउ = काँदो = कीचड। आँटा = पूरा पडा। नएउ = झुँका।

उस सूर जाति वा बहादुर और पृथ्वी के पति राजा (शेर शाह) का वर्णन करता हूँ, अर्थात् कैसा शुर राजा है उसका वर्णन करता हूँ। जिस राजा के साज (तयारी)

का भार पृथ्वी नहीँ सहती है ॥ (जिस समय) घोडे से भरी सेना जग को पूरा कर अर्थात् पृथ्वी भर में फैल कर चलती है, (उस समय) पर्वत टूट कर धूर हो कर उडने लगते हैँ ॥ धूर रात्रि हो कर सूर्य को ग्रास लेती है, अर्थात् छिपा लेती है, मनुष्य और पक्षी (रात समझ कर) फिर कर (लौट कर) बसेरा लेने लगते हैँ ॥ भूमि उड कर अन्तरिक्ष को चली गई, मृत्तिका ने धरती के खण्ड खण्ड (प्रत्येक विभाग) को, (विधि की) सृष्टि (माच) को और ब्रह्माण्ड को मर्दन कर डाला, अर्थात् सर्वत्र धूर व्याप्त हो गई, धूर छोड और कुछ नहीँ दिखाई देता है ॥ आकाश घूमने लगता है, इन्द्र (देवताओँ का राजा) डर कर काँपने लगता है, वासुकि जा कर पाताल को चाँपता है ॥ मेरु (देवताओँ का पर्वत) नीचे धँस जाता है, समुद्र सूख जाते हैँ वन-विभाग टूट कर, अर्थात् छिन्न भिन्न हो कर, मट्टी में मिल जाते हैँ ॥ आगे के (घोडोँ को) किसी किसी को पानी और घास बाँटा गया, (परन्तु) पिछले में किसी (घोडोँ) को काँदो तक न अँटा, अर्थात् न पूरा पडा ॥

जो गढ कभीँ भी नहीँ झुके थे, वह सब जब पृथ्वी का पति जग का बहादुर शेर शाह चढाई करता है (उस समय सेना के) चलते-ही चूर हो जाते हैँ, अर्थात् ऐसा गुरु (भारी) राजा है, कि उस के भार को कोई नहीँ सँभार सकता ॥ १४ ॥

चउपाई ।

अदल कहउँ पुहुमी जस होई । चाँटहि चलत न दुखवइ कोई ॥
नउसेरवाँ जो आदिल कहा । साहि अदल सरि सोउ न अहा ॥
अदल कीन्ह उम्मर कइ नाईँ । भइ आहा सगरी दुनिआईँ ॥
परी नाँथ कोइ छुअइ न पारा । मारग मानुस सोन उछारा ॥
गोरु सिंघ रेँगहिँ एक बाटा । दून-उ पानि पिअहिँ एक घाटा ॥
नीर खीर छानइ दरबारा । दूध पानि सब करइ निरारा ॥
धरम निआउ चलइ सत-भाखा । दूबर बरी एक सम राखा ॥

दोहा ।

पुहुमी सबइ असीसई जोरि जोरि कइ हाथ ।
गाँग जउँन जल जब लगि तब लगि अमर सो माथ ॥ १५ ॥

अद्ल = न्याय। नउसेरवाँ = नौशेरवाँ = एक बादशाह। आदिल = न्यायी। आहा = शाबशी = वाह वाह = प्रशंसा। दुनिआई = दुनिया में। नाँथ = नथ = स्त्रियों के नाक का एक आभूषण। पारा = सकता है। सोन = सोना = स्वर्ण। उछारा = उछालते हैं = लोकाते हैं। गोरू = गाय बैल इत्यादि जन्तु, जिन्हें पाल कर लोग चराते हैं। रँगहिं = रँगते हैं = चलते हैं। नीर = जल। खीर = क्षीर = दुग्ध। निरारा = अलग। निआउ = न्याय। बरी = बली। गाँग = गङ्गा। जउँन = यमुना॥

(शेर शाह के समय में) पृथ्वी में जैसा न्याय होता है उस को कहता हूँ, कि चलते में कोई चींटे को भी नहीं दुःख देता है॥ जो कि नौशेरवाँ न्यायी कहा गया है, शाह (शेर शाह) के न्याय की बराबरी में वह भी नहीं है, अर्थात् शेर शाह नौशेरवाँ से भी अधिक न्यायी है॥ उमर (जिस की चर्चा १२ वें दोहे में कर आये हैं) के ऐसा (शेर शाह ने) न्याय किया। सगरी (सब) दुनियाँ में आहा आहा हो गया, अर्थात् जहाँ देखो तहाँ शाह के न्याय के प्रशंसा की ध्वनि हो रही है॥ (राह में) पडी (गिरी) हुई नथ को कोई (उठाना तो दूर रहे) छू नहीं सकता। मार्ग में मनुष्य लोग सोने को उछालते हैं, अर्थात् सोने को लोकाते हुये चलते हैं, परन्तु किसी की सामर्थ्य नहीं कि छीने॥ गोरू और सिंह एक-ही बाट (राह) में चलते हैं, अर्थात् बादशाह के न्याय के भय से आपस का वैर भाव सब छोड दिये हैं। दोनों (गोरू और सिंह) एक-ही घाट पर पानी पीते हैं॥ (शेर शाह) दर्बार में पानी और दूध की छान करता है, (ऐसा छान करता है कि) दूध पानी सब अलग अलग कर देता है, अर्थात् जैसे दूध में पानी मिल जाने से दूध-ही ऐसा समझ पडता है, उसी प्रकार जिस मोकद्दमें में झूठ और सच दोनों मिल कर सब सच्च ही समझ पडता है, वहाँ भी खूब छान कर झूठ और सच्च अलग अलग कर डालता है॥ धर्म न्याय और सत्य-भाषा (सत्यवचन) से चलता है। दुर्बल और बली को एक सा रखता है॥

सब पृथ्वी (पृथ्वी पर के सब लोग) हाथ जोर जोर कर आशीर्वाद देती है, कि जब तक गङ्गा और यमुना में जल रहे तब तक वह जो माथ (सब के मस्तक के सदृश) है सो अमर रहे॥ १५॥

चउपाई।

पुनि रुपवंत बखानउँ काहा। जावँत जगत सबइ मुख चाहा॥
ससि चउदसि जो दई सवाँरा। ते-हु चाहि रूप उँजिआरा॥

पाप जाइ जउँ दरसन दीसा। जग जुहारि कइ देइ असीसा॥
जइस भानु जग ऊपर तपा। सबइ रूप ओहि आगइ छपा॥
अस भा सूर पुरुख निरमरा। सूर चाहि दस आगरि करा॥
सउँह दिसिटि कइ हेरि न जाई। जेइ देखा सो रहा सिर नाई॥
रूप सवाई दिन दिन चढा। बिधि सुरूप जग ऊपर गढा॥

दोहा।

रूपवंत मनि माँथइ चाँद घाटि ओहि बाढि।
मेदिनि दरस लोभानी असतुति बिनवइ ठाढि॥१६॥

रूपवंत = रूपवान्। काहा = क्या। चाहा = चाहता है। चउदसि = चतुर्दशी। चाहि = चय कर = बढ कर। दीसा = देखा। जुहारि = प्रणाम = सलाम। आगरि = अग्रा = श्रेष्ठ। सउँह = सौंह = सम्मुख। हेरि = देख। माँथइ = माँथे में। चाँद = चन्द्र। मेदिनि = मेदिनी = पृथ्वी॥

फिर (वह) ऐसा रूपवान है, कि क्या बखान करूँ। जगत में जितने लोग हैं, सब (उस के) मुख को चाहते हैं॥ ब्रह्मा ने चतुर्दशी के चन्द्रमा को जो बनाया है (पूर्णिमा के चन्द्रमा में विशेष कर के कलङ्क देख पडता है इस लिये यहाँ उसे छोड दिया है) तिस से भी बढ कर (उस का) उज्ज्वल रूप है॥ यदि दर्शन दीख पडा, अर्थात् उस के रूप का दर्शन हो गया तो पाप चला जाता है। जगत (जगत के सब लोग) सलाम कर कर के (उसे) आशीर्वाद देता है॥ जैसे जग के ऊपर सूर्य तपता है (उसी प्रकार यह भी तप रहा है, इसी लिये) उस के आगे सब रूप छिप गया॥ ऐसा (वह) सूर जाति वा बहादुर अथवा सूर्य निर्मल पुरुष हुआ, कि सूर से बढ कर दश गुनी (उस में) श्रेष्ठ कला है॥ (पहली चौपाई में जिस सूर को ग्रहण करना वही दूसरी में भी क्रम से लेना चाहिए)। सामने दृष्टि कर (वह) देखा नहीं जाता। जिस ने देखा वह शिर झुँका कर रह गया॥ (उस का) दिन दिन सवाई रूप चढता है। ब्रह्मा ने उस का सुन्दर रूप जग के ऊपर गढा है, अर्थात् सब से बढ कर बनाया है॥

ऐसा रूपवान है कि (उस के) माँथे में मणि (ज्योति) है। (जो बहुत रूपवान् होता है, उस का माँथा ऐसा चमकता है, मानों उस में मणि है)। उस के (रूप के) बाढ के आगे चाँद घट गया।

मेदिनी (पृथ्वी पर के लोग) (उस के) दर्शन के लिये लुभा गई, खडी हो कर (उस की) स्तुति की विनय करती है, अर्थात् बडे विनय से उस की स्तुति करती है ॥ १६ ॥

चउपाई ।

पुनि दातार दई बड कीन्हा । अस जग दान न काहु दीन्हा ॥
बलि बिक्रम दानी बड अहे । हातिम करन तिआगी कहे ॥
सेर साहि सरि पूज न कोऊ । समुद सुमेरु घटहिँ निति दोऊ ॥
दान डाँक बाजइ दरबारा । कीरति गई समुदही पारा ॥
कंचन परसि सूर जग भएऊ । दारिद भागि दिसंतर गएऊ ॥
जउँ कोइ जाइ एक बेरि माँगा । जनमहु भएउ न भूखा नाँगा ॥
दस असमेध जग्ग जेइ कीन्हा । दान पुन्न सरि सोउ न दीन्हा ॥

दोहा ।

अइस दानि जग उपजा सेर साहि सुलतान ।
ना अस भएउ न होइही ना कोइ देइ अस दान ॥ १७ ॥

बिकरम = विक्रम, अवन्ती का प्रसिद्ध दानी राजा, जिस का संवत् चलता है। हातिम = मुसल्मानों में प्रसिद्ध दानी । करन = कर्ण, भारत का प्रसिद्ध दानी । तिआगी = त्यागी । डाँक = डङ्का । दिसंतर = देशान्तर । असमेध = अश्वमेध । जग्ग = यज्ञ । पुन्न = पुण्य ॥

फिर ईश्वर ने (उस को) बडा भारी दाता किया। ऐसा दान जग में किसी ने नहीँ दिया ॥ बलि (पाताल का राजा जिस से भगवान् वामन-स्वरूप हो कर साढे तीन पैर भूमि माँगी थी) और विक्रम बडे दानी थे (= अहे)। हातिम और कर्ण को भी लोग त्यागी अर्थात् बडे दानी कहे हैँ ॥ परन्तु शेर शाह की बराबरी में कोई नहीँ पहुँचा। (जिस के दान के आगे) समुद्र और सुमेरु दोनों नित्य घटते हैँ, अर्थात् रत्नों के दान से समुद्र, और सुवर्ण के दान से सुमेरु, नित्य घट रहे हैँ ॥ दर्बार में दान का डङ्का बजता है, और समुद्र के पार कीर्त्ति (उस की) चली गई ॥ उस सूर को परसि (स्पर्श कर) संसार कञ्चन (सोना) हो गया, इस लिये दरिद्र भाग कर देशान्तर में चला गया, अर्थात् इस के राज्य से निकल कर दूसरे राज्य में चला गया ॥ यदि कोई जा कर (उस से) एक बेर भी माँगा, तो फिर वह जन्म भर भूखा और नंगा न हुआ ॥

हरा = हर गया = नष्ट हो गया। मुरसिद = गुरु । पीर = महानुभाव। नाउ = नाव। खेवक = खेने-वाला ।

तिन के (सैयद अशरफ के) घर में, एक निर्मल रत्न, सुभाग्य से भरे, शेख हाजी हुए॥ तिन के (शेख हाजी के) घर में, देव ने (ईश्वर ने) (जगत् को) पन्थ देने के लिये दो प्रज्वलित दीपक बनाया, अर्थात् उत्पन्न किया॥ एक का नाम शेख मुबारक, जिन की पूर्णिमा के चन्द्र के ऐसी कला (शोभा) थी। दूसरे शेख कमाल, जो जगत् में निर्मल अर्थात् जिन में एक भी अवगुण नहीं था॥ दोनों ध्रुव के ऐसे अचल (स्थिर) डोलते नहीं थे, अर्थात् चलायमान नहीं होते थे। मेरु जिस के ऊपर उत्तर ध्रुव, और खिखिंद, कुखण्ड, जिस के ऊपर दक्षिण ध्रुव हैं, तिन दोनों पहाडों के भी ऊपर हैं॥ गोसाईं (ईश्वर) ने (दोनों को) रूप और ज्योति दिया, और तिन दोनों को जग का खंभा किया॥ (ईश्वर ने) इन्ही दोनों खंभों से सब मही (पृथ्वी) को रोक रक्खा, इन्हीं दोनों के भार लेने से सृष्टि स्थिर रही है॥ जो दर्शन करे और (इन के) पैर को छूए, उन का (जानो) पाप नष्ट हो गया, और काया (शरीर) निर्मल हो गई॥

मुहम्मद कवि कहते हैं, कि जिस के संग में (ऐसे) महानुभाव गुरु हों, (वह जहाँ हो) तहाँ-ही निश्चिन्त पंथ है, अर्थात् उस की राह में किसी बात का डर नहीं। क्योंकि (रे मन) जिस को नाव और खेने-वाला है, सो (वह) शीघ्र तीर को पाता है, अर्थात् शीघ्र पार हो जाता है॥ यहाँ रे नीच-सम्बोधन है। और गुरु को खेवक और धर्म को नाव समझना चाहिए॥ इस दोहे और इस के पिछले दोहे से स्पष्ट है, कि सैयद अशरफ मलिक मुहम्मद के मन्त्र-गुरु थे॥ १९॥

चउपाई।

गुरु मोहिदी खेवक मइँ सेवा। चलइ उताइल जेहि कर खेवा॥
अगुआ भएउ सेख बुरहानू। पंथ लाइ जेहि दीन्ह गिआनू॥
अलहदाद भल तेहि कर गुरू। दीन दुनी रोसन सुरुखुरू॥
सैयद मुहमद के वेइ चेला। सिद्ध पुरुख संगम जेइ खेला॥
दानिआल गुरु पंथ लखाए। हजरत ख्वाज खिजिर तेइ पाए॥
भए परसन ओहि हजरत ख्वाजे। लेइ मेरए जहँ सइअद राजे॥
ओहि सउँ मइँ पाई जब करनी। उघरी जीभ कथा कबि बरनी॥

दोहा।

वेइ सो गुरु हउँ चेला निति बिनवउँ भा चेर।
ओहि हुत देखइ पाएउँ दिरिस गोसाईं केर॥२०॥

उतादल = शीघ्र। खेवा = बोझ से भरी नाव। अगुआ = आगे। पंथ = राह = मत। भल = अच्छे = श्रेष्ठ = भले। रोसन = प्रसिद्ध। सुरखुरू = सब के प्रिय। परसन = प्रसन्न। मेरए = मिलाए। करनी = करणी = योग्यता = लियाकत। उघरी = खुली। बरनी = वर्णन किया। चेर = चेला = दास। दिरिस = दृश्य = देखने-योग्य रूप॥

सेवक रूप जो मोहिदी (मुहिउद्दीन) जिन का खेवा बहुत शीघ्र चलता है, मैं ने उन की सेवा किया॥ मोहिदी के अगुआ, अर्थात् अग्र (गुरु), शेख बुर्हान हुए, जिन्हों ने जिस को (मोहिदी को) (अपने) पंथ (मत) में लगा कर ज्ञान दिया॥ तिन के (शेख बुर्हान के) अच्छे गुरु अलहदाद (अल्हदाद) थे, जो कि दीन (धर्म) में अर्थात् धर्म के विषय में दुनिया में रोशन (प्रसिद्ध) और सर्व-प्रिय थे॥ वे (अलहदाद) सैयद मुहम्मद के चेले थे, जिन्हों ने सिद्ध-पुरुषों के सङ्गम (समाज) में खेल किया था, अर्थात् बडे बडे सिद्धों को भी अपनी सिद्धाई से छका दिया था॥ उन को (सैयद मुहम्मद को) दानियाल गुरु ने पंथ (मत) को दिखाया, तिन्हों ने (दानियाल ने) हज़रत ख्वाज़ खिज़िर को पाया, अर्थात् उन से दानियाल की भेंट हो गई॥ हज़रत ख्वाज़ खिज़िर उन से (दानियाल से) प्रसन्न हुए, और जहाँ सैयद राजी (सैयद राजी हामिद शाह) थे, वहाँ ले जा कर (उन से) मिलाया, अर्थात् दानियाल को सैयद राजी का शिष्य बनाया॥ इस प्रकार की गुरु परम्परा में जो मेरे गुरु मोहिदी हैं, उन से जब मैं ने योग्यता को पाई, तब जीभ खुली, और कवि (मैं) ने कथा का वर्णन किया॥ अर्थात् उन के प्रसाद से कवि हुआ, और कथा (पदुमावती का वृत्तान्त) बनावने की शक्ति हुई॥

वे मोहिदी जो हैं, सो मेरे गुरु हैं, मैं (उन का) चेला हूँ, नित्य (उन का) दास हो कर विनय करता हूँ, अर्थात् प्रत्यह उन की स्तुति किया करता हूँ। उन्हीं से, अर्थात् उन की जो कृपा थी, उसी के प्रसाद से, ईश्वर का दृश्य रूप देखने पाया, अर्थात् उन्हीं के अनुग्रह से मैं भी सिद्ध हो गया॥

मुसल्मान लोग मलिक मुहम्मद को निज़ामुद्दीन औलिया के शिष्य परम्परा में कहते हैं। इसी लिये मलिक मुहम्मद को चिश्तिया निज़ामिया कहते हैं। निज़ामुद्दीन औलिया

मीर खुसरो का विद्या-गुरु था। यह सन् १३२५ ई॰ में मरा है। इस का चेला सिराजुद्दीन, और सिराजुद्दीन का चेला शेख अलाउलहक्क़ था। अलाउलहक्क़ का पुत्र और शिष्य, पण्डोई का नूर कुतुब आलम था, जो कि सन् १४१५ ई॰ में मरा है। अलाउलहक्क़ का दूसरा शिष्य सैयद अशरफ़ जहांगीर था जिस की चर्चा १८ वें दोहे में कवि ने किया है। सैयद अशरफ़ का बडा प्रसिद्ध शिष्य शेख हाजी था। शेख हाजी के दो शिष्य थे एक का नाम शेख मुबारक, दूसरे का शेख कमाल। शेख नूर कुतुब आलम और सैयद अशरफ़ जहांगीर दोनों गुरु-भाई थे, और इन दोनों की आठवीं पीढ़ी में मलिक मुहम्मद हुए हैं॥

मुसल्मान लोग इस प्रकार से इन के गुरु-परम्परा को लिखते हैं॥

निजामुद्दीन औलिया (जो सन् १३२५ ई॰ में मरे)।

सिराजुद्दीन।

शेख अलाउल हक्क़

पण्डोई का शेख कुतुब आलम। — सैयद अशरफ़ जहांगीर।

मानिक पुर का शेख हुसामुद्दीन; — शेख हाजी।

सैयद-राजी हामिद शाह। — शेख मुबारक। शेख कमाल।

शेख दानियाल (जो सन् १४८६ ई॰ में मरे)।

सैयद मुहम्मद।

शेख अल्हदाद।

शेख बुरहान।

शेख मोहिदी (मुहिउद्दीन)।

मलिक मुहम्मद (जायस के)।

इस गुरु परम्परा से और ग्रन्थ-कार के लेख से बहुत भेद है। लेख से तो स्पष्ट है कि मलिक मुहम्मद के मन्त्र-गुरु सैयद अशरफ़ और विद्या-गुरु मोहिदी थे॥

कालपी जो कि बुन्देल-खण्ड में है, वहाँ के रहने-वाले शेख बुरहान थे। ऐसा सुना जाता है, कि ये सौ वर्ष के हो कर ९७० हिजरी सन् (स.१५६२-६३ ई॰) में मरे हैं॥

गुरुश्रों के प्रसाद से जब मलिक मुहम्मद प्रसिद्ध कवि ऊए, तब अपनी प्रशंसा लिखने को तयार ऊए, नहीं तो अपनी प्रशंसा करना केवल अभिमान-सूचक है ॥२०॥

चउपाई।

एक नयन कबि मुहमद गुनी। सोइ बिमोहा जेइ कबि सुनी ॥
चाँद जइस जग बिधि अउतारा। दीन्ह कलंक कीन्ह उँजिआरा ॥
जग सूझा एकइ नयनाँहा। उआ सूक जस नखतन्ह माँहा ॥
जउ लहि आँबहि डाभ न होई। तउ लहि सुगँध बसाइ न सोई ॥
कीन्ह समुदर पानि जउ खारा। तउ अति भएउ असूझ अपारा ॥
जउ सुमेरु तिरसूल बिनासा। भा कंचन गिरि लागु अकासा ॥
जउ लहि घरी कलंक न परा। काँचु होइ नहिँ कंचन करा ॥

दोहा।

एक नयन जस दरपन अउ तेहि निरमर भाउ।
सब रुपवंतइ पाउँ गहि मुख जोहहिँ कइ चाउ ॥ २१ ॥

बिमोहा = मोहित हो गया। अउतारा = अवतार दिया। नयनाँहा = नयन से = आँख से। उआ = उदय ऊआ। सूक = शुक्र ग्रह। माँहा = मध्य = बीच। आँबहि = आम में। डाभ = दर्भ = कुश के ऐसा बौर वा मञ्जरी। बसाइ = बासा जाता है। तिरसूल = त्रिशूल। चाउ = चाह = इच्छा ॥

(यद्यपि) मुहम्मद कवि को एक-ही नयन है, (तौ भी) (मुहम्मद) ऐसे गुणी हैं, कि जिस कवि ने (इन की वाणी को) सुना सोई मोहित हो गया। कवि का अभिप्राय है कि यद्यपि मैं दोषी हूँ (काना होने से), तथापि उसी दोष के साथ मेरे में यह बडा भारी गुण है, कि मेरी कविता को जो सुनता है सोई आनन्द से मोहित हो जाता है ॥ ऐसा परम्परा से प्रसिद्ध है कि शीतला माता के निकलने से इन की एक आँख मारी गई, और चेहरा भी खराब हो गया। एक वार एक राजा ने इन को न पहचान कर, महा कुरूप मुख को देख कर, बडे स्वर से कुछ व्यङ्ग बचन सुना कर हँसा, इस पर इन्हों ने बडे धैर्य से उत्तर दिया कि "मोहिँ का हँससि कि कोहरहि," अर्थात् मुझे

हँसते हो, या कोहार को (जिस ने मेरी ऐसी-ही गढनि गढी है), इस पर उस राजा को ऐसा ज्ञान हो गया, कि उसी-चण इन का शिष्य ऊआ ॥

ब्रह्मा ने (मुहम्मद को) जग में जैसा चाँद है ऐसा-ही अवतार दिया है, कलङ्क दिया तो उज्ज्वल भी किया (जिस के प्रकाश से जगत् उज्ज्वलित होता है), कवि का अभिप्राय है, कि जैसे चन्द्रमा में कलङ्क-रूपी दोष, उसी प्रकार काना होना मेरे में दोष। जिस प्रकार जगत् को प्रकाश करना यह चन्द्रमा में गुण, उसी प्रकार मेरी कविता-द्वारा जगत् को जो आनन्द होना, यह मेरे में गुण है॥ (मुझे) एक-ही आँख से जग (भर) सूझ पडा, अर्थात् लोगों को दो आँख होती हैं, वे दो कोश तक भी पृथ्वी को नहीं देख सकते, और मैं एक-ही आँख से जग भर को देख लिया। जैसे नचत्रों के बीच में शुक्र उदित है (उसी प्रकार मैं संसार के लोगों के बीच में उदित हूँ)॥ वामन भगवान को जब बलि साढे तीन पैर भूमि दान देता रहा, उस समय उस के गुरु शुक्र विघ्न करने के लिये जल की झारी में आ बैठे। संकल्प करती समय झारी से जल न गिरे, तब कौतुकी भगवान् ने कुश से झारी के टोटी को साफ करने के व्याज से शुक्र की दहनी आँख फोड दिया, यह प्रसिद्ध कथा है॥

शुक्र की उपमा से जान पडता है, कि कवि की दहनी आँख फूटी थी। कवि का अभिप्राय है, कि जैसे सब नचत्रों के बीच काना शुक्र-ही अधिक प्रकाशवान् है, उसी प्रकार जगत् के लोगो में मैं सब से प्रसिद्ध हूँ॥ जब तक आम में बौर (मञ्जरी) नहीं होता, तब तक वह आम सुगन्ध से नहीं बासा जाता॥ आम के सब अंग को छेद छेद कर बौर उत्पन्न होते हैं। इस लिये छेद हो जाना यह दोष ऊआ, तो उसी के साथ सुगन्ध से बास जाना, यह गुण ऊआ॥ (ब्रह्मा ने) जो समुद्र का पानी खारा किया, (तो उसी के साथ) समुद्र अत्यन्त असूझ और अपार ऊआ (जिस के समान कोई नहीं है)॥ जो त्रिशूल से सुमेरु नष्ट किया गया, अर्थात् उस का पच्च काटा गया, तो उसी के साथ वह सोने का पहाड हो गया, और (इतना ऊँचा ऊआ कि) आकाश में लग गया॥ पुराणों में कथा है कि पहले पहाडों के चिडियों के ऐसा पच्च होते थे। उन से वे उड कर जहाँ चाहते थे तहाँ जा कर गाँव के लोगों को चापड कर देते थे। इस पर इन्द्र ने वज्र से सब के पच्चों को काट डाला। सब से पहले सुमेरु का पच्च काटा गया, और उस के अनन्तर उस ने बडी बडाई पाई। इस लिये सुमेरु-ही का ग्रहण कवि ने किया है। छन्द में वज्र का नाम समावेश न होने से त्रिशूल-ही को रख दिया॥

(इन सब दृष्टान्तों से यह स्पष्ट होता है, कि) जिस घडी तक कलङ्क (किसी प्रकार का एक दोष) नहीँ पडता, तब तक काँच (बे-गुण का मनुष्य) सोने के रूप (आदरणीय रूप) नहीँ होता ॥

(मेरी) एक आँख ऐसी है जैसा दर्पण (आईना), और तिस दर्पण का निर्मल भाव है, अर्थात् जैसे निर्मल दर्पण का स्वभाव है, कि पण्डित वा चाण्डाल जो उस में देखे, सब का प्रतिबिम्ब जैसा का तैसा देख पडता है, तिसी प्रकार मेरे नेत्र में सब लोगों का रूप जैसा का तैसा देख पडता है ॥ (यद्यपि मैं काना हूँ तथापि) सब रूपवान् लोग मेरे पैर को पकड कर इच्छा कर के (मेरे) मुख को जोहा (चुप चाप देखा) करते हैँ ॥ कवि का सिद्धान्त है, कि विना एक दोष ऊए गुण नहीँ उत्पन्न होता। इसी लिये इस ने अपने इस ग्रन्थ में भी चौपाइओँ की दो चौकडी के बदले, लँगडा कर, सात-ही पैर रक्खा, और दोहे के मात्रा को भी प्रायः घट बढ कर दिया। इस में ग्रन्थ-कार का यह आन्तरिक अभिप्राय है, कि मेरे भक्त लोग तो मेरे ग्रन्थ को आदर से पढे-हीँगे, परन्तु इस प्रकार का ग्रन्थ में दोष रहने से मेरे प्रतिस्पर्द्धी लोग भी हास्य-बुद्धि से इसे पढेँगे। इस प्रकार मेरे ग्रन्थ का सर्वत्र प्रचार हो जायगा ॥ २१ ॥

चउपाई।

चारि मीत कबि मुहमद पाए। जोरि मिताई सरि पहुँचाए ॥
युसुफ मलिक पंडित अउ ग्यानी। पहिलइ भेद बात वेइ जानी ॥
पुनि सलार कादिम मति-माँहा। खाँडइ दान उभइ निति बाँहा ॥
मिआँ सलोने सिंघ अपारू। बीर खेत रन खरग जुझारू ॥
सेख बडे बड सिद्ध बखाना। कइ अदेस सिद्धन्ह बड माना ॥
चारिउ चतुरदसा गुन पढे। अउ संजोग गोसाईँ गढे ॥
बिरिख जो आछहि चंदन पासा। चंदन होहिँ बेधि तेहि बासा ॥

दोहा।

मुहमद चारि-उ मीत मिलि भए जो एकइ चित्तु।
एहि जग साथ जो निबहा ओहि जग बिछुरहिँ कित्तु ॥ २२ ॥

मति-माँहा = मतिमान्। उभइ = उभडती है = उठती है। खेत = क्षेत्र। रन = रण=

सङ्ग्राम। जुझारू = योद्धा = युद्ध करने-वाले। अदेस = आदेश = आज्ञा। चतुरदसा = चतुर्दश = चौदह। संजोग = संयोग = सङ्ग। बिरिख = वृक्ष। आछहि = अच्छा। बेधि = विद्ध हो कर। बासा = सुगन्ध। किन्तु = कुतः = क्यों॥

मुहम्मद कवि ने चार मित्र को पाया, (जिन से) मिताई (मित्रता) को जोड कर (अपने को) उन की बराबरी मेँ पऊँचाया॥ प्रथम मित्र मलिक यूसुफ, पण्डित और ज्ञानी थे, (ऐसे वे ज्ञानी थे कि सब से) पहले बातेँ का भेद जान जाते थे॥ फिर दूसरे मतिमान् (बुद्धिमान्) सलार कादिम थे, जिन की बाँह नित्य खाँडे मेँ (तलवार चलाने मेँ) और दान मेँ (दान देने मेँ) उभडती है अर्थात् उठती है॥ तीसरे सलोने मियाँ थे, जो अपार वीरोँ मेँ सिंह थे, और रण-क्षेत्र मेँ खड्ग-योद्धा थे, अर्थात् तलवार से लडने-वाले थे। उन के ऐसा कोई तलवार नहीँ चला सकता था॥ चौथे मित्र शेख बडे थे, जिन को लोग बडा सिद्ध बखानते हैँ, जिन के आदेश (आज्ञा) को कर के सिद्ध लोगोँ ने भी (अपने को) बडा माना॥ चारो मित्र चौदहो गुण (विद्या) को पढे थे (चार वेद, छ वेदाङ्ग, पुराण, मीमांसा, न्याय, और धर्म-शास्त्र ये-ही चौदह विद्या हैँ), और ईश्वर ने चारो का एक संयोग (सङ्ग) गढा था, अर्थात् बनाया था॥ पहली चौपाई मेँ जो लिखा है कि मैँने उन से मित्रता को जोड कर, अपने को उन की बराबरी मेँ पऊँचाया, इस से उनके समान होने मेँ अपना सामर्थ्य प्रगट ऊआ, उस का निराकरण करने के लिये यह पिछली चौपाई लिखा है, कि मेरे मेँ कुछ सामर्थ्य नहीँ, कि उन के बराबर होऊँ, किन्तु जो वृक्ष अच्छा (बढियाँ) चन्दन के पास होते हैँ, वे चन्दन के बास से बिध कर आप चन्दन हो जाते हैँ। इस मेँ चन्दन का गुण है, न कि वृक्ष का। कवि का अभिप्राय है, कि उसी प्रकार उन चारो चन्दन-रूपी मित्रोँ के पास रहने से, मैँ भी उन्हीँ लोगोँ के ऐसा हो गया॥

चारो मित्रोँ से मिल कर मुहम्मद जो एक चित्त हो गये, अर्थात् उन चारो के चित्त मेँ अपने चित्त को मिला लिया, इस लिये (जिन का) इस जग (लोक) मेँ जो साथ निबह गया तो (वे) उस जग मेँ कहाँ बिछुडते हैँ, अर्थात् क्योँ बिछुडेँगे॥ २२॥

अब प्रसङ्ग से अपने ग्रन्थ के बनाने का स्थान कहते हैँ॥

चउपाई।

जाप्रस नगर धरम-असथानू। तहाँ आइ कबि कीन्ह बखानू॥
कइ बिनती पँडितन्ह सउँ भजा। टूट सँवारहु मेरवहु सजा॥
हउँ सब कबितन्ह कर पछ-लगा। किछु कहि चला तबल देइ डगा॥
हिअ भँडार नग अहइ जो पूँजी। खोली जीभ तारु कइ कूँजी॥
रतन पदारथ बोली बोला। सुरस पेम मधु भरी अमोला॥
जेहि कइ बोलि बिरह कइ घाया। कहँ तेहि भूख नीद कहँ छाया॥
फेरइ भेस रहइ भा तपा। धूरि लपेटा मानिक छपा॥

दोहा।

मुहमद कया जो पेम कइ ना तेहि रकत न माँसु।
जेइ मुख देखा तेइ हँसा सुनि तेहि आप्रउ आँसु॥ २३॥

असथानू = स्थान। भजा = सेवा किया। टूट = टूटा ऊआ = चुटि। मेरवऊ = मिला-दूये। सजा = साज = शोभा-योग्य पद। कबितन्ह = कवित्त बनाने-वाले = कवि। पछ-लगा = पीछे लगने-वाला = पीछे चलने-वाला = अनुगामी। तबल = तबला = डुग्गी। डगा = डागा = डुग्गी बजाने की लकडी। पूँजी = मूल-धन। तारु = तालू वा ताला। कूँजी = कुञ्जी = चाभी॥

जायस नगर जो धर्म का स्थान है, तहाँ पर आ कर कवि ने (इस कथा का) बखान किया॥ पण्डितों से विनती कर के (उन की) सेवा किया, (और कहा कि) टूटा अचर बनादूये, और इस में साज (शोभा-योग्य पद) को मिलादूयें॥ मैं सब कवियों का अनुगामी हूँ, डुग्गी के ऊपर लकडी को दे कर, अर्थात् डुग्गी को बजा कर कुछ कह चला हूँ, अर्थात् न मुझे आग्रह और न पाण्डित्य का अभिमान है, इस लिये सब पण्डित और कवि लोगों को मैं अपनी कविता सुनाता हूँ, और वे लोग जहाँ अनुचित कहें उसे मैं सुधारने पर प्रवृत्त हूँ। यहाँ 'किछु कहि चलत बोल देइ डगा' यह पाठ अच्छा है। यह पाठ उपलब्ध पुस्तकों में नहीं है, किन्तु मेरी कल्पना है तनिक पदों के हेर फेर से ऐसा हो सकता है॥ इस का तब 'मैं बोल (वाक्य) रूपी डग (पैर) दे कर कुछ कह चलता हूँ', यह अर्थ है॥ हृदय-रूपी भण्डार में जो नग पूँजी है, जीभ को तालु की

कूँजी बना कर उस पूँजी को (मैं ने) खोला। यहाँ पर कवि ने अपने हृदय को भण्डारा, उस में जो अनेक पद पदार्थ भरे हैं, उसे नग (रत्न) जो कि आगे की चौपाई से स्पष्ट है, तालु को उस भण्डारे का ताला और उस ताले की कुञ्जी (चाभी) जीभ को बनाया है। इस प्रकार से यहाँ रूपकालङ्कार है॥

अनेक जो बोली बोला (कहा) है, वेई रत्न-रूपी पदार्थ हैं। वे बोलियाँ कैसी हैं? कि प्रेम-रूपी जो सुरस (सुस्वादु रस) मधु (शहद) उस से भरी हैं, इसी लिये अमूल्य हैं॥

प्रेम में ऐसी क्या बात है, जो कि अमूल्य है? ऐसी कदाचित् शङ्का हो, तो उस के लिये आगे प्रेम का माहात्म्य कहते हैं॥ जिस को विरह के बोली का, अर्थात् प्रेम का, घाव लग गया, तिस को कहाँ भूख, कहाँ नींद, और कहाँ छाया (विश्राम) है॥ वह पुरुष अपने भेस (वेष) को फेर लेता है, अर्थात् अपने स्वरूप को छिपा लेता है, और तपस्वी (=तपा) हो कर रहता है। (उस की) ऐसी दशा हो जाती है, जैसे धूर से लपेटा माणिक्य छिपा हो॥ यहाँ कवि का यह अभिप्राय है, कि जो प्राणी प्रेम-मय हो गया, वह माणिक्य रत्न के ऐसा है। वह रत्न न खो जाय, इस लिये वह संसार से विरक्त हो, वेष बदल कर, तपस्वी बन कर रहता है॥

मुहम्मद कवि कहते हैं, कि जो प्रेम की कया (काय=शरीर) है, तिस में न रक्त है, न माँस है, अर्थात् अस्थि-मात्र है, क्योंकि ऊपर लिख आये हैं, कि प्रेमी को न भूख, न नींद, न विश्राम, कुछ भी नहीं होता। इसी लिये शरीर का रक्त माँस गल जाता है। केवल अस्थि रह जाती है। इसी लिये जिस ने उस प्रेमी का मुख देखा, तिस ने हँस दिया। हँसने का तात्पर्य यह, कि लोगों ने उस को बौरहा समझ लिया है। (उन के हास्य को) सुन कर, तिस प्रेमी को आँस (अश्रु) आ जाती है, अर्थात् उस प्रेमी की दृष्टि तो सर्वदा उस प्रेम-ही की ओर है; केवल कान से उन लोगों का सहास्य वचन को सुन कर, वह रोने लगता है, कि हाय जगद्विचित्र है, जिस में प्रेम नहीं वह भी कोई पुरुष है। सो उलटे ये बौरहे मुझी को बौरहा समझ हँसते हैं॥ यहाँ प्रेम से ईश्वर के चरण में अनुराग होना है। अथवा तिस प्रेमी का वृत्तान्त सुन कर, कि यह ईश्वर-चरणानुरागी पुरुष है, पीछे से उस हँसने-वालों को ग्लानि से अश्रु आ जाती है, कि हाय हाय विना समझे मैं ने हँसा, अर्थात् हँस कर अपने शरीर को कलुषित किया॥२३॥

चउपाई।

सन नउ सइ सइँतालिस अहे। कथा अरंभ बयन कबि कहे॥
सिंघल-दीप पदुमिनी रानी। रतन-सेन चितउर गढ आनी॥
अलउदीन देहिली सुलतानू। राघउ-चेतन कीन्ह बखानू॥
सुना साहि गढ छेंका आई। हिंदू तुरुकन्ह भई लराई॥
आदि अंत जस गाथा अही। लिखि भाखा चउपाई कही॥
कबि बिआस रस कवँला पूरी। दूरि सो निअर निअर सो दूरी॥
निअरहि दूरि फूल जस काँटा। दूरि जो निअरहि जस गुरं चाँटा॥

दोहा।

भवँर आइ बनखंड सउँ लेइ कवँल रस बास।
दादुर बास न पावई भलहि जो आछइ पास॥ २४॥

इति असतुति-खंड॥ १॥

नउ सइ = नव से। सइँतालिस = सैंतालीस। अहे = थे। गाथा = कथा = इतिहास। बिआस = व्यास = जो कि कथा पुराण बाँचते हैं। कवँला = कमल। गुर = गुड। भवँर = भ्रमर। दादुर = दर्दुर = मेघा। भलहि = भली-भाँति से = अच्छी तरह से। आछइ = शोभित है। पास = पार्श्व = निकट॥

जब कथा के आरम्भ का वचन कवि ने कहा, अर्थात् जब कवि ने कथा का आरम्भ किया, उस समय हिजरी सन् नव से सैंतालिस था (सन् १५४० ईशवी)॥ अब संक्षेप से वाल्मीकि-मूल-रामायण के ऐसा कथा की भूमिका लिखते हैं, कि सिंघल-द्वीप में जो पदुमिनी (पद्मिनी = पद्मावती) रानी थी, उसे रतन-सेन (राजा रत्न-सेन) चितउर (चित्रवर) गढ में ले आया॥ राघव-चेतन (एक व्यक्ति) ने उस पद्मावती के रूप का वर्णन दिल्ली के सुलतान (बादशाह) अलाउद्दीन से किया॥ शाह (अलाउद्दीन) ने प्रशंसा को सुना, और आ कर (पद्मावती के लेने के लिये) गढ (चित्तौर-गढ) को छेंक (घेर) लिया। हिन्दू तुरकों में लडाई ऊई॥ इत्यादि आदि से अन्त तक जैसी कथा थी, सब भाषा चौपाई लिख कर कहा है। कोई 'लिखि दोहा चौपाई कही' ऐसा

पाठ कहते हैँ ॥ भाषा से, कवि के देश की भाषा समझना, जिसे हम लोग आज पुरानी अवध की भाषा कह सकते हैँ ॥ जन्म-स्थान छोड कर, जायस नगर मेँ कवि का आना, और वहाँ पर कथा का प्रचार करना, इस पर दृष्टान्त दिखलाते हैँ, कि कवि, व्यास और रस से पूरी (भरा ऊआ) कमल, इन से जो दूर हैँ वे निकट, और जो निकट मेँ हैँ वे दूर हैँ, जैसे काँटा फूल के निकट-ही है, परन्तु दूर है, अर्थात् फूल के गुण को वह कभोँ नहीँ जानता, नहीँ तो फूल मेँ लपट कर रहता। इस लिये मानोँ वह फूल से दूर है। और जैसे चीँटा गुड के दूर रहता है, परन्तु निकट-ही है, अर्थात् चीँटा गुड से अन्यच कहीँ दूर अपनी बिल मेँ रहता है, परन्तु वायु-द्वारा गुड का सुगन्ध पाते-ही निकट हो जाता है ॥ निकट रहने पर दूर और दूर रहने पर भी जो निकट है, इस पर और एक दृष्टान्त दिखाते हैँ, कि देखो भ्रमर वन-विभाग से, अर्थात् बऊत दूर से, आ कर, कमल का बास लेता है, परन्तु दर्दुर जो भली भाँति से कमल के पास-ही शोभित है, उस कमल के बास को नहीँ पाता ॥ कवि का भाव है, कि अवध की भाषा मेँ काव्य होने से यद्यपि मुसल्मान लोग अनादर करँगे, तथापि हिन्दू जो मुझ से बऊत दूर हैँ मेरे काव्य का आदर करँगे। इसी प्रकार यह भी कवि का भाव है, कि मेरे जन्म-स्थान के लोग जो दिन रात मेरी कविता को सुना करते थे, कुछ भी आदर न किये; और जायस जो कि दूर है, वहाँ के लोगोँ ने बऊत-ही आदर किया ॥ इस विषय मेँ परम्परा से ऐसा प्रसिद्ध है, कि मलिक मुहम्मद पहले अपने जन्म-स्थान-ही मेँ रह कर, पदुमावति के दो चार खण्डोँ को बना कर, गाया करते थे। इन के साथ साथ चेले लोग भी गाते गाते उन खण्डोँ को अभ्यास कर लिये ॥ एक चेला रमते रमते जायस मेँ पऊँचा, और जो खण्ड उसे अभ्यास था, उस का गाना आरम्भ किया। वहाँ का राजा उस खण्ड की कविता पर ऐसा मोहित ऊआ, कि उस चेले के साथ अपने सरदार को भेज, बडे आदर से मलिक मुहम्मद को अपने यहाँ बुलाया, और पूरी कथा बनाने के लिये प्रार्थना किया ॥ बऊत लोगोँ से यह भी सुना जाता है, कि उस चेले को नागमती का बारह मासा याद था, और उसी को उस ने गाया था। उसी पर वहाँ का राजा मोहित हो गया, विशेष कर बारह मासे के इस दोहे पर 'कवँल जो विगसत मान-सर, विनु जल गयउ सुखाइ।' ॥ २४ ॥

इति स्तुति-खण्डं नाम प्रथम-खण्डं समाप्तम् ॥ १ ॥

अथ सिंघल-दीप-बरनन-खंड ॥ २ ॥

चउपाई।

सिंघल-दीप कथा अब गावउँ। अउ सो पदुमिनि बरनि सुनावउँ॥
बरनक दरपन भाँति बिसेखा। जो जेहि रूप सो तइसइ देखा॥
धनि सो दीप जहँ दीपक नारी। अउ सो पदुमिनि दइ अउतारी॥
सात दीप बरनइ सब लोगू। एक-उ दीप न ओहि सरि जोगू॥
दिया-दीप नहिँ तस उँजिआरा। सरन-दीप सरि होइ न पारा॥
जंबू-दीप कहउँ तस नाहीँ। लंक-दीप पूज न परिछाहीँ॥
दीप-कुँभसथल आरन परा। दीप-महुसथल मानुस-हरा॥

दोहा।

सब संसार पिरिथुमीँ आए सात-उ दीप।
एक-उ दीप न ऊतिम सिंघल-दीप समीप॥ २५॥

पदुमिनि = पद्मिनी = पद्मावती। बरनक = वर्णक = वर्णन। धनि = धन्य। कुँभसथल = कुम्भस्थल। मऊसथल = मधुस्थल। और जब गभसथल यह पाठ है, तब गभसथल = गर्भस्थल। पिरिथुमीँ = पृथिवी। ऊतिम = उत्तम॥

कवि कहता है, कि अब (स्तुति-खण्ड के अनन्तर) सिंघल-दीप के कथा को गावता हूँ, अर्थात् कहता हूँ, और उस पद्मिनी (के वृत्तान्त को) वर्णन कर के सुनाता हूँ॥ वर्णन करने में, यथार्थ बात नहीँ प्रगट होती, ऐसी यदि कोई शङ्का करे, तहाँ कहते हैं, कि

वर्णन एक विशेष दर्पण के भाँति है, इस लिये जो जिस रूप का है, सो तैसा-ही (उस दर्पण में) देख पडता है ॥ विशेष दर्पण कहने का यह भाव है कि बहुत से ऐसे भी दर्पण होते हैं, जिन में छोटे बडे रूप देख पडते हैं। उन सबों का निराकरण करने के लिये विशेष पद दिया ॥ धन्य सो (वह) दीप है जहाँ नारी (स्त्री-लोग) दीपक हैं, अर्थात् दीप के शिखा सी उज्ज्वल हैं, और जहाँ पर देव (ईश्वर) ने उस पद्मिनी का अवतार दिया ॥ सब लोग सात दीप का वर्णन करते हैं, (परन्तु) उस दीप के समता योग्य एक भी दीप नहीं है ॥ दिया-दीप अर्थात् सुन्दरी युवती का नेत्र, तैसा उज्ज्वल नहीं है। सरन-दीप (श्रवण-दीप), अर्थात् सुन्दरी का कर्ण, उस (सिंघल-दीप) के तुल्य होने को समर्थ नहीं है ॥ जम्बू-दीप, अर्थात् सुन्दरी के केश पाश, को भी कहता हूँ, कि तैसा (सिंघल-दीप सा सुन्दर) नहीं है। लंक-दीप, अर्थात् सुन्दरी की कटि, (सिंघल-दीप की) परिछाहीं (छाया) की समता को नहीं पूजती, अर्थात् नहीं पाती ॥ कवि कहता है कि कुम्भस्थल-दीप, अर्थात् सुन्दरी का पयोधर, अरण्य (जङ्गल) में पडा है, अर्थात् छिपा हुआ है, इस लिये वह क्या समता करेगा। अरण्य से मुक्ताहार, वस्त्राञ्चल इत्यादि समझना चाहिए। और मधुस्थल-दीप, अर्थात् सुन्दरी का गुह्याङ्ग, मनुष्य को नाश करने-वाला है (क्योंकि संसार उसी विषय-तृष्णा में पड कर, वार वार मरा करता है), इस लिये ऐसा दुष्ट पापी अङ्ग क्या समता करेगा ॥ जब गभसथल पाठ है, तब गर्भस्थल से सुन्दरी का उदर लेना, जिस में वार वार मनुष्य वास करता है, इसी लिये वह उदर मनुष्य को हरने-वाला, अर्थात् चोराने-वाला हुआ, तब वह चोर इस दीप की क्या समता करेगा ॥ कवि का अभिप्राय है, कि सुन्दरियों के सब उत्तम अङ्ग जब उस दीप की समता नहीं कर सकते, तब वहाँ की दीप-शिखा सी जो नारी हैं, उन की समता इतर सुन्दरियों से करना असम्भव है, अर्थात् उस दीप की नारी और उन के अङ्ग अनुपम हैं ॥ जैसे, कथा का प्रसङ्ग बैठाने के लिये, पञ्चतन्त्रादि में कर्पूर-दीप इत्यादि नाम कल्पना कर लिये हैं, उसी प्रकार जिस में श्लेष हो (अर्थात् दो अर्थ हो), ऐसा समझ कर, कवि ने दिया-दीप, सरन-दीप, कुम्भ-स्थल, और मधु-स्थल, ऐसा नाम कल्पना कर लिया है। जम्बू और लङ्का में आप-ही द्व्यर्थ है इस लिये इन को यथार्थ-ही ले लिया ॥

संसार में सब पृथिवी भर सातो दीप आये हैं, अर्थात् छाये हुये हैं, (परन्तु) सिंघल-दीप के समीप (निकट), अर्थात् उस के साथ तुलना करने में एक दीप भी नहीं उत्तम ठहरता है ॥ २५ ॥

चउपाई।

गँधरब-सेन सुगंध नरेसू। सो राजा वह ता कर देसू॥
लंका सुना जो रावन राजू। ते-हु चाहि बड ता कर साजू॥
छप्पन क्रोड(१) कटक दर साजा। सबइ छतर-पति अउ गढ राजा॥
सोरह सहस घेार घोर-सारा। सावँ-करन अउ बाँक तुखारा॥
सात सहस हसती सिंघली। जनु कबिलास इरावति बली॥
असु-पती क सिर-मउर कहावइ। गज-पती क आँकुस गज नावइ॥
नर-पती क अउ कहउँ नरिंदू। भू-पती क जग दोसर इंदू॥

दोहा।

अइस चक्कवइ राजा चहूँ खंड भय होइ।
सबइ आइ सिर नावँहीँ सरिबर करइ न कोइ॥ २६॥

गँधरब-सेन = गन्धर्व-सेन। नरेसू = नरेश। रावन राजू = रावन राजा। छतर-पति = छत्रपति। सहस = सहस्र = हजार। घोर-सारा = घोडे की शाला = घोटक-शाला। सावँ-करन = श्याम-कर्ण = जिन के सब अङ्ग श्वेत केवल कान काले होँ। बाँक = वक्र = तेज। तुखारा = घोडा। असु-पती = अश्वपति = घोडे पर चढने-वालेँ मेँ श्रेष्ठ। सिर-मउर = शिरो-मयूर = शिर पर मयूर के ऐसी टोपी। गज-पती = गजपति = हाथी पर चढने-वालेँ मेँ श्रेष्ठ। नर-पती = नर-पति = राजा। नरिंदू = नरेन्द्र। भू-पती = भू-पति = पृथ्वी के पति = जिमीदार लोग, जिन के अधिकार मेँ केवल जोतने बोने के लिये भूमि हो। इंदू = इन्द्र। चक्कवइ = चक्रवर्त्ती। सरिबर = बहस = सवाल जवाब॥

गन्धर्व-सेन जो सुगन्ध (सुन्दर गन्ध से भरा, अर्थात् जिस के शरीर से सुगन्ध महकती है) राजा, सो (वहाँ का) राजा है, और वह (सिंघल-दीप) तिसी (राजा) का देश है॥ लङ्का मेँ जो रावण राजा सुना है, तिस से भी बढ कर तिस का (गन्धर्व-सेन का) बडा साज (तयारी) है॥ छप्पन करोड कटक-दल (सेना का समूह) साजा हुआ है, सब (छप्पनो करोड) छत्रपति और (एक एक) गढ के राजा हैँ॥ (जिन के चलने मेँ) सेवक उन के शिर पर छत्र लगाते हुए चलेँ। (पहले बडे वीरोँ को यह प्रतिष्ठा प्राप्त

---

(१) तीसरे दोहे की ६वीँ चौपाई देखो।

होती थी।) (उस के) घोड-सार में सोरह हजार घोडे हैं, (जिन में बहुत से) श्याम-कर्ण और बाँके घोडे हैं ॥ सिंघल देश के सात हजार हाथी हैं, जानों कैलास (शिव-पुरी, परन्तु यहाँ इन्द्र-पुरी) के बली ऐरावत हाथी हैं। (ऐरावत श्वेत हाथी होता है, और उस पर देवताओं का राजा इन्द्र चढता है) ॥ (वह राजा) अश्व-पतियों का शिर-मौर कहाता है, गज-पतियों के गज (हाथी) को अङ्कुश से नवा देता है (झुका देता है), और (मैं उसे) राजाओं का नरेन्द्र (मनुष्यों में इन्द्र), और भू-पतियों का दूसरा इन्द्र कहता हूँ॥ इन्द्र वर्षा का पति है। भू-पतियों को अन्न होने में वर्षा-ही का भरोसा है। वह विना इन्द्र की कृपा से नहीं होती। इस लिये इन्द्र बनाया है॥ 'नर-पती' क कहउँ अउ नरिंदू', इस पाठ में, यति-भङ्ग दोष है। यदि 'कह-उँ-अउ' ऐसा शब्द को काट कर यति बनावें तो शब्दाबध दोष होता है॥

ऐसा चक्रवर्त्ती राजा है कि चारो भाग में (पूर्व, प. उ. द.), (उस का) भय होता है, सब कोई आ कर (उस के सामने) शिर को नवाते हैं (झुकाते हैं), और (उस के आगे) कोई सरबर नहीं करता है ॥ २६ ॥

चउपाई ।

जब-हि दीप निअरावा जाई। जनु कबिलास निअर भा आई॥
घन अँबराउँ लाग चहुँ पासा। उठे पुहुमि हुति लागु अकासा॥
तरिवर सबइ मलय गिरि लाई। भइ जग छाँह रइनि होइ छाई॥
मलय समीर सोहाई छाँहा। जेठ जाड लागइ तेहि माँहा॥
ओही छाँह रइनि होइ आवइ। हरिअर सबइ अकास देखावइ॥
पंथिक जउँ पहुँचइ सहि घामू। दुख बिसरइ सुख होइ बिसरामू॥
जेइ वह पाई छाँह अनूपा। बहुरि न आइ सहहिँ यह धूपा॥

दोहा ।

अस अँबराउँ सघन घन बरनि न पारउँ अंत।
फूलइ फरइ छव-उ रितु जानउँ सदा बसंत॥ २७॥

निअरावा = नगीच किया। घन = झुण्ड = ढेर का ढेर। अँबराउँ = आम-राज = अच्छे जाति का आम। जेठ = ज्येष्ठ महीना। पंथिक = पथिक = राही। सघन = गञ्जिन। छव-उ = छवो। जानउँ = जानों = मानों ॥

जिस घडी किसी ने जा कर (सिंघल) दीप को नगीच किया, अर्थात् जब कोई सिंघल के नगीच पङ्कँचा, (उस घडी ऐसा समझ पडता है) जानें (वह) आ कर कैलास के नगीच ङआ॥ चारो ओर (चङँ पासा) आम्र-राज के झुण्ड लगे हैं, जो पृथ्वी से उठे हैं, और आकाश में जा कर लगे ङए हैं॥ सब तरुवरों में (जानें) मलय-गिरि (मलय-चन्दन) लगाया ङआ है। (उन वृचों से) जग में छाँह हो गई, और (सर्वत्र वह छाया) रात्रि हो कर छा गई॥ वह छाया मलय-समीर (मलय-चन्दन-सहित वायु) से (ऐसी) शोभित ङई है, कि तिस के मध्य ज्येष्ठ महीने में भी जाडा लगती है॥ (कवि की उत्प्रेचा है कि निश्चय समझो) उसी छाया से (संसार में वार वार) रात हो आती है, और (वही छाया) सब आकाश को हरिअर (हरा) दिखलाती है, अर्थात् उसी छाया का प्रतिबिम्ब पडने से सब आकाश हरे वर्ण का हो गया है॥ यदि घाम को सह कर कोई पथिक (वहाँ) पङ्कँच जाय, तो (उस का) दुःख भूल जाता है, सुख होता है और खस्थता (विश्राम) होती है॥ जिन्हों ने उस अनुपम छाया को पाया, वे फिर (बङरि) (इस संसार में) आ कर इस धूप को नहीं सहते हैं॥

ऐसा आम्र-राज का गम्भिन झुण्ड है, जिस का वर्णन कर के अन्त तक नहीं पार हो सकता ङँ। कवि का अभिप्राय है कि जिन वृचों के छाया वर्णन में सात चौपाई हो गई उन के वर्णन में तो संभव है, कि एक ग्रन्थ तयार हो जाय॥ छवो ऋतु (वहाँ) फूलती फरती हैं, जानें (उस दीप में) सर्वदा वसन्त ऋतु है। ऋतुओं में वसन्त ऋतु राजा है, इस से वसन्त का ग्रहण किया है॥ २७॥

चउपाई।

फरे आँब अति सघन सोहाए। अउ जस फरे अधिक सिर नाए॥
कटहर डार पींड सउँ पाके। बडहर सो अनूप अति ताके॥
खिरनी पाकि खाँड असि मीठी। जाउँनि पाकि भवँर असि डीठी॥
नरिअर फरे फरी फरहरी। फरी जानु इँदरासन-पुरी॥
पुनि महुआ चुअ अधिक मिठास्ट। मधु जस मीठ पुहुप जस वास्ट॥
अउरु खजहजा आउ न नाऊँ। देखा सब राउन अवँराऊँ॥
लाग सबइ जस अंम्रित साखा। रहइ लोभाइ सोइ जो चाखा॥

दोहा ।

गुत्रा सुपारी जाइफर सब फर फरे अपूरि ।
आस पास घनि इविँली अउ घन तार खजूरि ॥ २८ ॥

आँब = आम्र । नाए = झुँकाये हैँ । पौँड = पँडी । ताके = देखने मेँ । जाउँनि = जामुन = जम्बू । डीठी = देख पडती है । फरुहरी = फरहरी = छोटे छोटे मेवे के वृच्च । इँदरासन = इन्द्रासन । चुत्र = चूता है । पुहुप = पुष्प । बासू = वास = सुगन्ध । खजहजा = खाद्य वृच्च, जिन के फल खाये जाते हैँ । अवँराऊँ = अमरावती = इन्द्र के बगीचा सा श्रेष्ठ बगीचा । अंत्रित = अम्मृत । गुत्रा = एक प्रकार की पूर्वी सोपारी । इबिँली = अमिली ॥

अत्यन्त सघन (गझिन) आम फरे हैँ और शोभित हैँ । और (जो आम) जैसा (अधिक) फरे हैँ, तैसा-ही अधिक शिर झुँकाये हैँ । तात्पर्य यह कि फल से भरे भी हैँ, तौ-भी अभिमान से रहित हो कर नम्र हो गये हैँ (शिष्ट पुरुष के ऐसा) ॥ कटहर डार और पँडी से लग कर पके हुए हैँ । (इस वृच्च का यही स्वभाव है कि डार और पँडी मेँ फरता है) । बडहर जो हैँ सो देखने (ताके) मेँ अति अनूप (अति सुन्दर) हैँ । (इस का फूल डारोँ मेँ ऐसा गुथा रहता है, कि देखने मैँ बडा मनोहर जान पडता है) ॥ पकी खिरनी खाँड ऐसी मीठी है । पकी जामुन भौँरा सी (काली) देख पडती है ॥ नरियर फरे हैँ, फरहरी (सब) फरी है । (इस प्रकार से) फरी (वाटिका) ऐसी शोभित है, जानोँ इन्द्रासन-पुरी अर्थात् अमरावती है ॥ फिर अत्यन्त मीठा महुआ चू रहा है । (वह), जैसा मधु (शहद) मीठा होता है, वैसा मीठा, और, जैसा पुष्प मेँ वास होता है, वैसा (उस मेँ) वास (सुगन्ध) है ॥ और जितने खजहजा (मेवे के वृच्च) हैँ, जिन का नाम नहीँ आता, उन सब को राव लोगोँ की अमरावती (वाटिका) मेँ देखा ॥ शाखाओँ मेँ सब (फल) ऐसे लगे हैँ जैसे अम्मृत, (उन को) जो चखता है सोई लोभाय रहता है ॥

गुत्रा, सुपारी, और जायफर सब (वृच्च) अपूर (भर पूर) फरे हैँ ॥ आस पास (अगल बगल) घनि (गझिन), अर्थात् बहुत, अमिली और बहुत तार, खजूर (लगे) हैँ ॥ वाटिका के भीतर इन की शोभा नहीँ होती, इस लिये किनारे पर लगना लिखा है ॥

चौथी चौपाई का 'नरिअर फरे भरी खुरुहरी । फरी जानु इँदरासन-पुरी ॥' ऐसा पाठ उत्तम जान पडता है, तब 'नरियर फरे हैँ (उन मेँ) खुरुहरी भरी है ।

(वाटिका ऐसी फरी है) जानों इन्द्रासन-पुरी (अमरावती) फरी ऊइ है', यह अर्थ करना चाहिए॥ गरी दो प्रकार की होती है, एक कडी और खाने में नीरस। दूसरी नर्म और खाने में मीठी, ऐसी मीठी और नर्म गरी को 'खुरुऊरी' कहते हैं॥ २८॥

चउपाई।

बसहिँ पंखि बोलहिँ बहु भाखा। करहिँ हुलास देखि कइ साखा॥
भोर होत बासहिँ चुहिचूही। बोलहिँ पांडुकि एकइ तूही॥
सारउ सुआ जो रहचह करहीँ। कुरहिँ परेवा अउ करबरहीँ॥
पिउ पिउ लागइ करइ पपीहा। तुहीँ तुहीँ करि गुडुरू खीहा॥
कुहू कुहू करि कोइलि राखा। अउ भँगराज बोल बहु भाखा॥
दही दही कइ महरि पुकारा। हारिल बिनवइ आपनि हारा॥
कुहुकहिँ मोर सोहावन लागा। होइ कोराहर बोलहिँ कागा॥

दोहा।

जावँत पंखि कही सब बइठे भरि अवँराउँ।
आपनि आपनि भाखा लेहिँ दई कर नाउँ॥ २९॥

हुलास = उल्लास = आनन्द। बासहिँ = फूलोँ के सुगन्ध से वास जाती हैँ। सारउ = सारा = दूर्वा = दूब। रहचह = चहचह = आनन्द के शब्द। कुरहिँ = कुरकुर करते हैँ। परेवा = कबूतर = पारावत। करबरहीँ = कलबलाते हैँ = इधर से ऊधर उडते हैँ। भंगराज = भृङ्गराज। कोराहर = कोलाहल। अवँराउँ = अमरावती॥

उस अमरावती मेँ पक्षी बसते हैँ, जो बहु भाषा (अनेक तरह की बोली) बोलते हैँ। और शाखा को देख कर (जिन मेँ पहले कह आये हैँ कि 'लाग सबइ जस अंम्रित साखा' अर्थात् अमृत फल लगे हैँ) हुलास (मन मेँ आनन्द) करते हैँ॥ भोर (प्रातःकाल) होते-ही चुहिचुही (फूल के रस को खाने-वाली चिडिया इस प्रान्त मेँ प्रसिद्ध है, जिसे बहुत लोग फुलचुही वा फुलसुंघी कहते हैँ) फूल के रस के सुगन्ध से बास जाती हैँ। और पाण्डुकी (पँडुकी जो कबूतर के तरह होती है। यह भी इस प्रान्त मेँ प्रसिद्ध है) 'एकइ तूही' 'एकइ तूही' बोलती हैँ। इस पक्षी की बोली मेँ ऐसी-ही धुनि जान पडती है॥ सारउ, दूब के ऐसे जो सुआ (शुक) हैँ, अर्थात् बडे

मनोहर मरकत के ऐसे जो शुक हैं, वे रहचह करते हैं (आपस में कल्लोल कर के बोलते हैं)। परेवा (कबूतर) कुरकुर करते हैं (इन की बोली में भी कुरकुर धुनि जान पडती है। कोई घुरघुर धुनि बतलाते हैं, उन के मत से घुरहिँ यह पाठ है), और कलबलाते हैं, अर्थात् इधर से उधर उडते हैं॥ पपीहा पीउ पीउ करने लगे हैं। (पपीहे की बोली से पीउ पीउ धुनि निकलती है)। गुडुरू तुहीँ तुहीँ कर के, खीहा, अर्थात् खी खी, करता है। अर्थात् इस की बोली में 'तुहीँ खी' 'तुहीँ खी' यह धुनि निकलती हैं॥ यह पत्ती हमारे प्रान्त में नहीँ प्रसिद्ध है॥ कोयल कुहू कुहू कर रक्खे हैं, अर्थात् कुहू कुहू बोल रहे हैं (कुहू कुहू कोयल के बोली की धुनि है)। और भृङ्गराज अनेक भाषा को बोलता है॥ (इस का ऐसा स्वभाव है, कि जिस की बोली सुने, वैसा-ही बोलने लगे। यह बहु-मूल्य और भुजङ्गे की तरह प्रसिद्ध पत्ती है। धनी लोग बोली सुनने के लिये पालते भी हैं)॥ महरि दही दही कर के पुकारती है। (दही दही इस के बोली की धुनि है। इस को बहुत लोग ग्वालिनि वा अहिरिनि कहते हैं। यह महोखे से कुछ छोटी, उसी जाति की इस देश में प्रसिद्ध है)। हारिल अपने हारे हुए की बिनती करती है, अर्थात् इस की बोली से यही धुनि निकलती है कि 'हा हारि गई' 'हा हारि गई'। (यह पत्ती सुग्गे की तरह हरे रंग का होता है, और बहुधा, बर, पीपर और पाकर पर रहता है। पृथ्वी पर नहीँ उतरता। यदि पानी पीने के लिये उतरना पडा, तो पञ्जे में तृण लिये हुए उतरता है, और उसी के आधार से पानी पी कर पेँड पर चला जाता है। पृथ्वी पर अपने पैर को नहीँ रखता। ऐसी कहावत है कि मारने से भी जब भूमि पर गिरता है, तब पैर को ऊपर किये हुए रहता है। इस देश में प्रसिद्ध है। खाने-वाले इसे खाते भी हैं)॥ मोर कुहकते हैं, जो (कुहकना) सोहावन (अच्छा) लगता है, (इस की बोली से कूँ कूँ धुनि होती है), और (जब) काग (कौए) बोलते हैं, (तब) कोलाहल हो जाता है, अथवा तब कोराहर होने लगता है, अर्थात् कर कर होने लगता है। (कौए की बोली की कर कर धुनि है)॥

जितने पत्ती कहे हैं, अर्थात् प्रसिद्ध हैं, सब अमरावती भर बैठे हैं। और अपनी अपनी भाषा में सब देव (ईश्वर) का नाम लेते हैं॥

तीसरी चौपाई में बहुत लोग 'सारी सुआ जो रहचह करहीँ', यह पाठ कहते हैं, परन्तु सब पुस्तकों में सारउ यही पाठ मिलता है। सारी (=सारिका=पहाडी मैना)

वाटिका का पच्ची नहीँ है। यह पहाडोँ में वा ऊँचे महुए के वृचोँ में बसती हैँ। इसी लिये जान पडता है कि कवि ने छोड दिया है ॥ २९ ॥

चउपाई ।

पइग पइग कूआँ बाउरी । साजे बइठक अउ पाउँरी ॥
अउरु कुंड सब ठाउँहिँ ठाऊँ । सब तीरथ अउ तिन्ह के नाऊँ ॥
मठ मंडफ चहुँ पास सँवारे । तपा जपा सब आसन मारे ॥
कोइ सु-रिखेसुर कोइ सनिआसी । कोइ सु-राम-जति कोइ मसबासी ॥
कोइ सु-महेसुर जंगम जती । कोइ एक परखइ देवी सती ॥
कोई ब्रहमचरज पँथ लागे । कोइ सु-दिगंबर आछहिँ नाँगे ॥
कोई संत सिद्ध कोइ जोगी । कोइ निरास पँथ बइठ बिओगी ॥

दोहा ।

सेवरा खेवरा बान सब　सिधि-साधक अउधूत ।
आसन मारे बइठ सब　जारहिँ　आतम-भूत ॥ ३० ॥

पइग = पग = प्रग = पद = पैर। कूआँ = कूप। बाउरी = बावली = वापी। पाउँरी = पौरी = द्वार वा सीढी। मठ = जहाँ विद्यार्थी वा साधु-लोग रहैं। मंडफ = मण्डप, जो चारो ओर खुला रहे, केवल ऊपर छाया रहे॥ तपा = तपस्वी, जो पञ्चाग्नि तापे, वा वृच में उलटे टंग कर धूम पीए, वा और प्रकार से शरीर को कष्ट दे॥ जपा = जप करने-वाले, जो किसी देवता को वश करने के लिये उस के मन्त्र को, आसन लगा कर, जपते हैँ॥ सु-रिखेसुर = सु-ऋषीश्वर = ऋषियोँ में श्रेष्ठ। जो मनुष्योँ की शक्ति को उल्लङ्घन कर जाते हैँ, इन में साधारण योग्यतानुसार, ऋषि, परमर्षि, महर्षि, राजर्षि, ब्रह्मर्षि और देवर्षि, ये भेद हैँ। वसिष्ठ और विश्वामित्र की लडाई में, बडी तपस्या से, तब चत्रिय विश्वामित्र ब्रह्मर्षि हुए हैँ। इस की कथा वाल्मीकि-रामायण बालकाण्ड में प्रसिद्ध है॥ सनिआसी = सन्न्यासी, जो जीते-ही अपना कर्म-न्यास कर डालता है, अर्थात् मरने पर जो गति के लिये क्रिया कर्म किया जाता है, सो वे लोग जीते-ही कर डालते हैँ, और शिखा सूत्र त्याग कर एक दण्ड धारण करते हैँ। उस दण्ड को जीवन

पर्यन्त पृथ्वी पर गिरने नहीं देते, और अपने सब कर्म का साक्षी उसी दण्ड को समझते हैं। इन्हें दण्डी भी कहते हैं। कोई कोई तीन दण्ड धारण करते हैं। मरने के समय, अशक्त होने पर, जो सन्यास है, उसे आतुर सन्यास कहते हैं। उस को जो ग्रहण करता है, उसे आतुर सन्यासी कहते हैं॥ राम-जति = राम-यति, जो राम की उपासना में विरक्त हो कर रहे, जैसे अयोध्या के वैरागी लोग॥ मस-बासी = मास-वासी, जो एक स्थान पर मास भर वास करें, फिर दूसरे स्थान पर जा कर वहाँ भी एक महीना रह कर उसे भी छोड तीसरे, चौथे इत्यादि पर बसते रहें॥ सु-महेसुर = सु-माहेश्वर, जो अपनी आकृति महादेव (महेश्वर) के ऐसी बनाते हैं, अर्थात् जटा, चन्द्र, रुद्राक्ष इत्यादि धारण करते हैं, और घर से विरक्त हो शिव का पूजन करते हैं॥ जङ्गम, जो एक जगह न रहें, सर्वदा घूमा करें। प्रायः ये लोग वीरभद्र (जो कि दक्ष के यज्ञ को विध्वंस किया था) की उपासना करते हैं॥ जती = यति, जो संयम अर्थात् आचार से रहे। जैनियों में बहुधा यति होते हैं, और ये घरबारू भी होते हैं॥ देवी = वाम-देवी॥ सती = दक्षिण देवी॥ ब्रहमचरज = ब्रह्मचर्य, जो यज्ञोपवीत होते-ही,—सन्ध्या गायत्री इत्यादि नित्य क्रिया है,—इस क्रिया को करते, गुरु के घर में रह कर, वेद को पढता है, उसे ब्रह्मचारी कहते हैं॥ दिगंबर = जिन का दशोदिशा-ही अम्बर (वस्त्र) है, जैसे परमहंस, नागा इत्यादि। वैष्णवों में भी दिगम्बरी और निर्वाणी, निर्मोही, इत्यादि अखाडा हैं। परन्तु इन अखाडाओं के साधु अब श्वेतवस्त्र धारण करते हैं॥ जैनियों में भी दिगम्बर होते हैं॥ सन्त = जो भगवत्कथावार्त्ता का प्रेमी हो॥ सिद्ध = जिसे अणिमा (छोटा हो जाना), महिमा (बडा हो जाना), लघिमा (हलका हो जाना), गरिमा (गुरु हो जाना), प्राप्ति (चाहे जिसे छू ले, जैसे अंगुली से चन्द्रबिम्ब को), प्राकाम्य (जो मनोरथ हो, सो शीघ्र हो जाय), ईशत्व (चाहे जिस का प्रभु हो जाय) और वशित्व (चाहे जिसे वश कर ले), ये आठो सिद्धि वश में हो॥ योगी = जो योग जानता हो, समाधि लगाता हो॥ बिओग = वियोग = किसी के वियोग से जो विरक्त हो गया हो॥ सेवरा = यह झुण्ड के झुण्ड चलते हैं। शिर पर जटा और वस्त्र गेरुआ रखते हैं। अपने को शैव कहते हैं। अपने मूत्रेन्द्रिय की नश को तोड डालते हैं। और उस में (मूत्रेन्द्रिय में) एक पीतल की सिकडी बाँधे रहते हैं। अपनी चमत्कारी से सूखी जटा में से पानी निकाल देते हैं, और कहते हैं कि गङ्गा-जल है॥ खेवरा, सेवरा-ही के एक भेद हैं, (जैसे गोसाइँओं मेँ रूखड, सूखड, भूखड, निरञ्जनी, इत्यादि भेद हैं)। हाथ में खप्पड

लिये रहते हैं, और, गोरख-नाथियों के ऐसा, मद्य को सब के सामने दूध बना कर पी जाते हैं। खाली हाथ से केवल हथेलियों को मल मल कर चना, गोहूँ इत्यादि निकाल कर लोगों को दिखलाते हैं ॥ वान = वान-प्रस्थ, जो स्त्री-पुरुष साथ वन में जा कर तपस्या करते हैं, अर्थात् जो ब्राह्मण विद्या पढने के अनन्तर, विवाह कर, फिर स्त्री के साथ वन में रहता है। इस का वर्णन मनु ने मनु-स्मृति में किया है ॥ सिधि-साधक = सिद्धि-साधक = अष्ट सिद्धि के साधने-वाले ॥ अउधूत = अवधूत, जो संसार के व्यवहार से अलग हो जाय। परमहंसों के ऐसा, प्रायः अवधूत भी मौन रहता है, और धूर लपेटे रहता है। गोरख-नाथ को लोग सच्चा अवधूत कहते हैं ॥ आतम-भूत = आत्म-भूत = अपना भूत, अर्थात् अपने पाञ्चभौतिक (शरीर) को ॥

उस अमरावती में पैर पैर पर कूएँ और बावली हैं, (जिन पर विश्राम के लिये) बैठक सजे हैं, और सीढियाँ लगी हैं ॥ और स्थान स्थान पर जो सब कुण्ड हैं वे सब तीर्थ (तीर्थ-स्वरूप) हैं, और तिन के नाम भी हैं, अर्थात् राम-कुण्ड, लक्ष्मण-कुण्ड, सीता-कुण्ड, द्रौपदी-कुण्ड, इत्यादि, उन के नाम रक्खे हुए हैं ॥ चारो तरफ (उन कुण्डों के) मठ और मण्डप बनाये गये हैं, जिन में तपस्वी और जपी सब आसन मारे (आसन को लगाये) हैं ॥ कोई सु-ऋषीश्वर, कोई सन्यासी, कोई राम-यति, कोई मास-वासी, कोई सु-माहेश्वर, कोई जङ्गम और कोई यति हैं। कोई एक देवी (वाम-देवी) को परखता है (परीक्षा करता है), अर्थात् वामोपासना में प्रवृत्त है, और कोई सती देवी (दक्षिण-देवी) को परखता है, अर्थात् शक्ति की उपासना करता है ॥ कोई ब्रह्मचर्य पथ में लगे हैं। कोई सुन्दर दिगम्बर हैं, जो नङ्गे होने पर भी अच्छे लगते हैं (आछहिं) ॥ कोई सन्त, कोई सिद्ध, कोई योगी हैं। और कोई वियोगी (प्रेमी) निरास पथ (नैराश्य मार्ग = प्रेम-मार्ग) में बैठा है ॥

सेवरा, खेवरा, वान (वान-प्रस्थ), सिद्धि-साधक, और अवधूत, सब आसन मार कर बैठे हैं, और सब अपने शरीर को जराते हैं ॥ ३० ॥

चउपाई।

मानसरोदक देखे काहा। भरा समुद जल अति अउगाहा ॥
पानि मोति असि निरमर ताहू। अंब्रित आनि कपूर सु-बाहू ॥
लंक-दीप कइ सिला अनाई। बाँधा सरवर घाट बनाई ॥

खँड खँड सीढी भई गरेरी । उतरहिँ चढहिँ लोग चहुँ फेरी ॥
फूले कवँल रहे होइ राते । सहस सहस पखुरिन्ह कइ छाते ॥
उलथहिँ सीप मोति उतराहीँ । चुगहिँ हंस अउ केलि कराहीँ ॥
कनक पंख पइरहिँ अति लोने । जानउँ चितर कीन्ह गढि सोने ॥

दोहा ।

ऊपर पाल चहूँ दिसा अंब्रित फर सब रूख ।
देखि रूप सरबर कर गइ पिआस अउ भूख ॥ ३१ ॥

मानसरोदक = मान-सर का पानी । अउगाह = अवगाह = अथाह । सिला = शिला । अनाई = मँगा कर । गरेरी = गले के ऐसी = घुमौआ । राते = रक्त = लाल । उलथहिँ = उलटते हैँ । उतराहीँ = उतराय आती हैँ । पइरहिँ = पौरते हैँ = तैरते हैँ । चितर = चित्र । पाल = पालि = पाली = तट = किनारा । पिआस = प्यास = पिपासा ॥

उस अमरावती के सरो-वर के जल को देखा क्या, जानोँ अति अथाह समुद्र के ऐसा जल भरा है ॥ जिस का पानी मोती के ऐसा निर्मल है, मानोँ अम्टत को ला कर (आनि), कर्पूर से सु-वासित किया है ॥ लङ्का-द्वीप की शिला अर्थात् सुवर्ण की शिला मँगा कर, उस सरो-वर का घाट बना कर (सुन्दर रचना कर के) बाँधा गया है ॥ खण्ड खण्ड (प्रत्येक भाग) में घुमौआ सीढी भई है, अर्थात् लगी है, जिन से चारो ओर (लोग) उतरते चढते हैँ ॥ उस सरो-वर में कमल फूले हैँ, और लाल हो रहे हैँ। ऐसे कमल हैँ जिन में हजार हजार पखुरिओँ के छाते (छत्र) हैँ। (जिन कमल के फूल में सहस्र पखुरियाँ होती हैँ वस्तुतः वे-ही कमल हैँ। अमरकोश में भी लिखा है कि 'सहस्र-पत्त्रं कमलं, शत-पत्त्रं कुशेशयम्', अर्थात् जिस में हजार पत्त्र हो वह कमल, और जिस में सौ पत्त्र हो वह कुशेशय कहलाता है ॥

हंस सीप को उलटते हैँ, (जिस से) मोती उतराय आती हैँ। और उन मोतियों को चुगते हैँ, और (आपस में) केलि को करते हैँ ॥ (वे हंस) अति सुन्दर (अति लोने) सोने के पत्त्र (पंख) से पैरते हैँ। जानोँ गढ कर सोने में चित्र, अर्थात् विचित्र रूप, किया है। (कवि लोग सुन्दरता के लिये प्रायः सुवर्ण-रूपी हंस को ग्रहण करते हैँ। नैषध के प्रथम सर्ग में भी लिखा है कि 'स तत्र चित्रं विचरन्तमन्तिके हिरण्मयं हंसमबोधि नैषधः') ॥

उस सरो-वर के पाली (तट) के ऊपर, चारो दिशा में, सब वृच (रूख) अमृत फल के लगे हैं। उस सरो-वर का रूप देख कर, प्यास और भूख गईं, अर्थात् चली जाती हैं ॥ २१ ॥

चउपाई।

पानि भरइ आवहिँ पनिहारी। रूप सरूप पदुमिनी नारी ॥
पदुम गंध तिन्ह अंग बसाहीँ। भवँर लागि तिन्ह संग फिराहीँ ॥
लंक-सिंघिनी सारँग-नयनी। हंस-गाविँनी कोकिल-बयनी ॥
आवहिँ झुंड सु पाँतिहिँ पाँती। गवँन सोहाइ सु भाँतिहिँ भाँती ॥
कनक-कलस मुख-चंद दिपाहीँ। रहसि केलि सउँ आवहिँ जाहीँ ॥
जा सउँ वेइ हेरहिँ चखु नारी। बाँक नयन जनु हनहिँ कटारी ॥
केस मेघावरि सिर ता पाईँ। चमकहिँ दसन बीजु कइ नाईँ ॥

दोहा।

मानउँ मयन मूरती अछरी बरन अनूप।
जेहि कइ असि पनिहारी सो रानी केहि रूप ॥ ३२ ॥

लंक = लङ्क = कटि = कमर। सिंघिनी = सिंहिनी। सारँग = सारङ्ग = कमल। गाविँनी = गामिनी। दिपाहीँ = दिपते हैं = चमकते हैं। रहसि = हँसी ठट्टा। चखु = चचु = नेच। हनहिँ = मारती हैं। मेघावरि = मेघावलि = मेघ के पङ्क्ति के ऐसा। ता पाईँ = पैर तक। बीजु = विद्युत = विजली ॥ मयन = मदन = काम-देव। अछरी = अप्सरा ॥

(जो) पनिहारी पानी भरने आती हैं, उन के रूप का स्वरूप (आकृति) पद्मिनी नारी के ऐसा है, क्योँकि २५वेँ दोहे में कह आये हैं कि 'धनि सो दीप जहँ दीपक नारी' ॥ तिन के अङ्ग पद्म-गन्ध (कमल के सुगन्ध) सा गमकते हैं (बसाते हैं), अर्थात् तिन के अङ्ग से पद्म के सुगन्ध का बास आता है। (जिन नारियोँ के अङ्ग मेँ पद्म का गन्ध हो, उन्हेँ पद्मिनी कहते हैं। नारियोँ का विस्तार से लचण, अलाउद्दीन से राघव-चेतन ने जहाँ नारियोँ का वर्णन किया है, तहाँ पर किया जायगा)। (जिस कारण से) भ्रमर लगे हुए तिन के संग फिरा करते हैं ॥ वे पनिहारियाँ लङ्क-सिंहिनी (सिंहिनी के

कटि सी जिन की कटि हो), सारङ्ग-नयनी (कमल सा जिन के नयन हेा), हंस-गामिनी (हंस की गति सी जिन की गति हो)। और कोकिला-वयनी (कोकिला सी जिन की बोली हो) हैं ॥ (ऐसी पनिहारियाँ) झुण्ड की झुण्ड सुन्दर पङ्क्ति पङ्क्ति में आती हैं, अर्थात् दश दश बीस बीस का झुण्ड, एक साथ पाँती लगा कर, पानी भरने के लिये आती हैं। उन का सुन्दर भाँति भाँति का (तरह तरह का) गवँन (गमन = चाल) सोहाता है ॥ (शिर पर) सोने के कलस से चन्द्र-रूपी मुख (और) दिपते हैं (चमकते हैं)। (आपस में) हँसी और केलि से, अर्थात् हँसी और विनोद करती ऊई, आती जाती हैं ॥ वे नारी (पनिहारियाँ) जिस से आँख लडाती हैं (हेरहिं), जानों (उसे अपनी) बाँक नयन (तिरछी आँख) से कटारी मार देती हैं (हनहिं), अर्थात् कटारी के चोट से जो मन को दुःख होता है, वैसा-ही उन के देखने से जो हृदय में मदनाग्नि उत्पन्न हो जाती है, उस से मनुष्य के मन को दुःख व्याप्त हो जाता है ॥ काली घटा की पाँति की तरह (मेघावली की तरह) शिर से पैर तक केश हैं। उस में (उस काली घटा में) दशन (दाँत) बिजली की तरह चमकते हैं ॥

(वे पनिहारियाँ) मानों काम की मूर्त्ति हैं, और उन का वर्ण अप्सरा से भी अनुपम (उत्तम) है। जिस रानी की ऐसी पनिहारियाँ हैं, (नहीं जानते कि) वह रानी (पद्मावती) किस रूप की होगी ॥ ३२ ॥

चउपाई ।

ताल तलाउ सो बरनि न जाहीँ । सूझइ वार पार तेहिँ नाहीँ ॥
फूले कुमुद केति उँजिआरे । जानउँ उए गगन मँह तारे ॥
उतरहिँ मेघ चढहिँ लेइ पानी । चमकहिँ मंछ बीजु कइ बानी ॥
पइरहिँ पंखि सो संगहिँ संगा । सेत पीत राते सब रंगा ॥
चकई चकवा केलि कराहीँ । निसि क बिछोहा दिनहिँ मिलाहीँ ॥
कुरलहिँ सारस भरे हुलासा । जिअन हमार मुअहिँ एक पासा ॥
केवा सोन ढेँक बग लेदी । रहे अपूरि मीन जल-भेदी ॥

दोहा ।

नग अमोल तिन्ह तालहिँ दिनहिँ बरहिँ जस दीप ।
जो मरजीआ होइ तेहिँ सो पावइ वह सीप ॥ ३३ ॥

ताल = जो कोसोँ तक लम्बे होते हैँ, और किसी के खोदे नहीँ होते, किन्तु पृथ्वी के नीची पड जाने से होते हैँ। तलाव = तडाग। वार = जिधर देखने-वाला खडा हो, उधर जो किनारा हो। पार = पाट का दूसरा किनारा। केति = कितने। मंछ = बडे मत्स्य। बानी = वर्ण = सदृश। कुरलहिँ = क्रीडहिँ = क्रीडा करते हैँ। केवा = कमल। सोन, ढेँक, और लेदी प्रसिद्ध ताल के पक्षी हैँ, इन को बहुधा लोग खाते हैँ। बग = बक = बकुला। मीन = मछली॥ मरजीआ = मर कर जो जीते हैँ, अर्थात् जो समुद्र में रत्न निकालने के लिये गोता लगाते हैँ (गोता-खोर)। ये जब गोता लगाते हैँ, तब मानोँ मर जाते हैँ। फिर जब उतराते हैँ, तब मानोँ जी जाते हैँ। इसी लिये मरजीआ कहाते हैँ॥

उस अमरावती में जो ताल के ऐसे तलाव हैँ, वे बरने नहीँ जाते। तिन का वार पार (कुछ भी) नहीँ सूझता है॥ उन में कितने उज्ज्वल कुमुद (कोईं) फूले हैँ। उन की शोभा ऐसी है, जानोँ गगन (आकाश) में तारे उए हैँ॥ (उन में पानी लेने के लिये) मेघ उतरते हैँ, और पानी ले कर (फिर आकाश को) चढ जाते हैँ। उस समय पानी के साथ जो मेघ-मण्डल में बडे बडे मत्स्य चले जाते हैँ, वे बिजली के सदृश चमकते हैँ॥ उन तालावो में सेत (श्वेत), पीत, और राते (लाल) सब रङ्ग के पक्षी सङ्ग सङ्ग में पैरते हैँ (तैरते हैँ)॥ चकई और चकवा (आपस में) क्रीडा करते हैँ। ये दोनोँ निशि (रात्रि) के विछोहा (वियोगी) हैँ, इस लिये दिन-हीँ में मिल लेते हैँ। (यह कहावत है, कि सन्ध्या होते-ही चकई (= चकवा की स्त्री) और चकवे (चक्र = चक्रवाक) में वियोग हो जाता है, ताल के इस पार एक दूसरे पार दूसरा एक एक के शोक में रात्रि भर चिल्लाया करते हैँ)॥ सारस उल्लास (आनन्द) में भरे आपस में क्रीडा करते हैँ। और (कहतें हैँ कि सच्चा) जीना हम लोगोँ का है, जो एक साथ (पास) मरते हैँ। (सारस के जोडे में ऐसी परस्पर प्रीति होती है, कि यदि एक पकड लिया जाय, तो दूसरा आप से आप उस के पास आ जाता है। इस लिये एक के मरने पर दूसरा उसी स्थान पर आ कर अपना भी प्राण गवाँ देता है)॥ केवा (कमल), सोन, ढेँक, बक, लेदी, और जल को भेदने-वाली, अर्थात् जल के भीतर रहने-वाली मछली, ये सब (उन तालावोँ में) भर पूर (अपूरि) रहे हैँ, अर्थात् भरे पडे हैँ॥ उन तालोँ में अमूल्य नग (रत्न) भरे हैँ, वे दिन-हीँ में ऐसे बरते हैँ, (चमकते हैँ) जैसे दीप। उन तालावोँ में जो मरजीआ (गोता-खोर) हो, सो उस सीप को पावे, जिस में वे नग रहते हैँ॥ २२॥

चउपाई ।

पुनि जो लागु बहु अंब्रित बारी । फरीँ अनूप होइ रखवारी ॥
नउ-रँग नीउँ सुरंग जँभीरी । अउ बदाम बहु भेद अँजीरी ॥
गलगल तुरुँज सदा-फर फरे । नारँग अति राते रस भरे ॥
किसिमिसि सेउ फरे नउ पाता । दारिउँ दाख देखि मन राता ॥
लागु सोहाई हरिफा-रेउरी । उनइ रही केला कइ घउरी ॥
फरे तूत कमरख अउ नउँजी । राइ-करउँदा बेरि चिरउँजी ॥
संख-दराउ छोहारा डीठे । अउरु खजहजा खाटे मीठे ॥

दोहा ।

पानि देहिँ खँडवानी कुअँहिँ खाँड बहु मेलि ।
लागी घरी रहंट कइ सीचहिँ अंब्रित बेलि ॥ ३४ ॥

नउ-रँग = नव-रङ्ग । नीउँ = निम्बू । जँभीरी = जम्बीर । गलगल = एक प्रकार का निम्बू । तुरुँज = तुरंज = निम्बू । सदा-फर = सर्वदा फरने-वाले । नारँग = नारङ्गी । सेउ = सेव । दारिउँ = दाडिम = अनार । दाख = द्राक्षा = अङ्गूर । हरिफा-रेउरी = हालफा-रेवडी । घउरी = घौर । नउँजी = लौंजी लीची । राइ-करउँदा = राय-करौंदा । संख-दराउ = शङ्ख-द्रावक = संख को गला देने-वाला निम्बू, यह उदर रोग के लिये बडे काम का है । खजहजा = मेवे के वृक्ष (२८वेँ दोहे की ६वीँ चौपाई को देखो) ॥ खँडवानी = गडुआ = झारी, यहाँ पर हजारा जिस से फूल, पैंड, सीँचते हैँ । घरी = छोटी छोटी गगरी । रहंट = चक्राकार जल निकालने का यन्त्र = एक प्रकार की पुरवट = आरघट्ट (संस्कृत मेँ) ॥

पुनः (फिर) और जो बहुत अमृत (के ऐसी) बारी (बगीचा) लगी हैँ, सो अनुपम (उत्तम) फरी हैँ, और उन की रखवारी होती है ॥ उन मेँ नव-रङ्ग, सुरङ्ग और जम्बीर निम्बू हैँ, और बदाम और बहुत भेद के, अर्थात् तरह तरह के, अञ्जीर हैँ ॥ गलगल, तुरँज (तुरंज = निम्बू, इसे बिजौडिया कहते हैँ, दवा मेँ बहुधा काम आता है), और सदा-फर फरे हैँ, नारंग फरे हैँ, जो रस भरे अति राते (खूब सुर्ख) हो गये हैँ ॥ किसमिस और सेव नये पत्ते से भरे फरे हैँ । (कोई नउ पाता से

नाशपाती लेते हैं, परन्तु यहाँ कवि का यही अभिप्राय जान पडता है, कि किसमिस (मडुआ के ऐसा) और सेव (अमरूत के ऐसा) नया पत्ता लेते-ही फरते हैं)। दाडिम (अनार) और दाख (अङ्गूर) को देख कर, (उन में) मन रक्त (राता) हो जाता है, अर्थात् लग जाता है। यही मन चाहता है, कि इन्हें देखा कीजिए॥ हालफा-रेवडी जो लगी है, वह अत्यन्त शोभित है। और केले का घौर (मारे बोझेँ के) झुंक (उनइ) रहा है॥ तूत, कमरख, नउँजो, राय-करौंदा, बेर, और चिरौंजो ये सब फरे हैं॥ संख-द्राव और छोहारा भी (उन बगीचेँ में) देखे जाते हैं, अर्थात् हैं, और खट्टे मीठे, जितने खजहजा (मेवे के वृक्ष) हैं, सब वहाँ पर देख पडते हैं, अर्थात् ऐसे मेवे के कोई वृक्ष नहीं जो वहाँ पर न लगे हों॥

(माली लोग) कूओँ में खाँड डाल कर (मेलि), हजारा से (इन मेवे के वृक्षेँ में) पानी देते हैं। और रहंट की घडी लगी ऊई हैं, जिन से अमृत-रूपी जो बेलि (वल्ली = लता) हैं, उन्हें सीँचते हैं॥ ३४॥

चउपाई।

पुनि फुल-वारि लागु चहुँ पासा। बिरिख बेधि चंदन भइ बासा॥
बहुत फूल फूली घन-बेइली। केवरा चंपा कुंद चवेँइली॥
सुरँग गुलाल कदम अउ कूजा। सुगँध-बकाउरि गँधरब पूजा॥
नागेसर सतिबरग नेवारी। अउ सिंगार-हार फुलवारी॥
सोनिजरद फूली सेवती। रूप-मंजरी अउरु मालती॥
जाही जूही बकुचन्द लावा। पुहुप सुदरसन लागु सोहावा॥
मउलसिरी बेइलि अउ करना। सबइ फूल फूले बहु बरना॥

दोहा।

तेहि सिर फूलचढहिँ वेइ जेहि माथहि मनि भागु।
आछहिँ सदा सुगंध भइ जनु बसंत अउ फागु॥ ३५॥

घन-बेइली, केवरा (= केवडा), चम्पा, कुन्द, चवँइली (= चमेली), सुरँग, गुलाल, कदम (= कदम्ब), कूजा, सुगँध-बकाउरि (= सुगन्ध-वकावली = गुल-बकावली), नागेसर, सतिबरग (= सदबरग), नेवारी, सिंगार-हार (= हरसिंगार = पारिजाता), सोनिजरद

सेवती (=सोने सी पीली सेवती, वा सोनि-जरद और सेवती), रूप-मञ्जरी, मालती, जाही, जूही, सुदर्शन, मउलसिरी (=मौलसिरी), बेइलि (=बेला), और करना, ये सब फूलोँ के नाम हैँ ॥

फिर उस बगीचे के चारो ओर फुलवारी लगी है, जो (अपने) बास (सुगन्ध) से वृक्षों को बेध कर चन्दन ऊई है, अर्थात् उस के सुगन्ध के लगने से सब वृक्ष सुगन्धित हो गये हैँ, इस लिये फुलवारी चन्दन हो गई है, (चन्दन का गुण धारण करती है। क्योँकि चन्दन मेँ यह गुण है, कि उस की सुगन्ध लगने से, और वृक्ष भी वैसा-ही सुगन्धित हो जाते हैँ)॥ घन-बेली बऊत फूल फूली ऊई है, और उस फुलवारी मेँ, केवडा, चम्पा, कुन्द, चमेली, सुरंग, गुलाल, कदम्ब, और कूजा लगे हैँ, सुगन्ध-बकावली भी है, जो कि राजा गन्धर्व-सेन के पूजा-योग्य है, अर्थात् केवल राजा गन्धर्व-सेन के यहाँ उस के फूल पऊँचते हैँ, दूसरे को दुर्लभ हैँ ॥ फुलवारी मेँ नागेसर, *सदवरग, नेवारी और हर-सिंगार (भी) हैँ ॥ सोनजर्द, सेवती, वा पीली सेवती, रूप-मञ्जरी, और मालती फूली ऊई हैँ ॥ जाही और जूही ढेर के ढेर (बकुचन्ह), अर्थात् बऊत, लगाई हैँ। (इस फूल का धर्म है, कि एक लगाने से कुछ दिनोँ मेँ हजारोँ हो जाते हैँ)। सुदर्शन फूल भी लगा ऊआ शोभित है ॥ मौलसिरी, बेला, और करना फूले हैँ, और अनेक वर्ण के फूल फूले हैँ ॥

वे फूल तिस के शिर चढते हैँ, जिस के माथे मेँ मणि (कान्ति) और भाग्य हो। (वहाँ) सर्वदा अच्छी सुगन्ध भई है, अर्थात् हो रही है, जानोँ (सर्वदा) वसन्त और फाग है ॥

बेला की साधारण चार जाति है, मुँगरा, मदन-बान, मोतिया, और बेइलि। मुँगरा के फूल मेँ बऊत पत्तियाँ होती हैँ। मदन-बान का फूल लम्बा और कुछ नोखीला होता है। मोतिया का फूल मोती के ऐसा होता है। और बेइलि के फूल मेँ पत्तियाँ अलग अलग होती हैँ। मुँगरे को घन-बेइलि भी कहते हैँ। रूप-मञ्जरी चार प्रकार की होती है, दो गुलाबी, एक लाल, और एक श्वेत। श्वेत बऊत मिलती है, और तीन बऊत कम। करना एक प्रकार का निम्बू है, इस के फूल मेँ सुगन्ध भी होता है। करने का अँतर कान मेँ छोडने से, कान की पीडा अच्छी हो जाती है। (६०वेँ दोहे को देखो) ॥ ३५ ॥

---

* फारसी सद (صد) = सौ। बर्ग (برگ) = पत्ती। जिस मेँ सौ पत्तियाँ होँ, अर्थात् हजारा ॥

चउपाई ।

सिंघल नगर देख पुनि बसा । धनि राजा असि जा करि दसा ॥
ऊँचो पवँरी ऊँच अवासा । जनु कबिलास इँदर कर बासा ॥
राउ राँक सब घर घर सुखी । जो दीखइ सो हँसता-मुखी ॥
रचि रचि साजे चंदन चउरा । पोते अगर मेद अउ गउरा ॥
सब चउपारिन्ह चंदन खँभा । ओठँघि सभा-पति बइठे सभा ॥
जनउँ सभा देओतन्हि कइ जूरी । परइ दिसिटि इँदरासन पूरी ॥
सबइ गुनी पंडित अउ ग्याता । संसकिरित सब के मुख बाता ॥

दोहा ।

आहक पंथ सँवारई जनु सिउ-लोक अनूप ।
घर घर नारी पदुमिनी मोहहिँ दरसन रूप ॥ ३६ ॥

पवँरी = पौरी = डेवढ़ी । अबास = आवास = निवास-स्थान । राँक = रङ्क = दरिद्र चउरा = चौतरा । मेद = कस्तूरी । गउरा = गोरोचन । चउपारि = चतुः-शाला = बैठक, जिस मेँ चारो ओर खुलता रहे । देओतन्हि = देवताओँ । ग्याता = ज्ञाता । संसकिरित = संस्कृत ॥ आहक = हाहा = गन्धर्व-विशेष ॥

फिर सिंघल-नगर बसा देखा गया है। (उस बसने को देख कर यही कहा जाता है, कि) धन्य वह (गन्धर्व-सेन) राजा है, जिस की ऐसी दशा है, अर्थात् भाग्योदय है ॥ (जिस स्थान पर राजा रहता है), उस की डेवढ़ी (दरवाजा) ऊँची है, और निवास-स्थान भी ऊँचा है। ऐसा ऊँचा निवास-स्थान, जानोँ इन्द्र का वास-स्थान कैलास है। (इन्द्र से यहाँ महेश से तात्पर्य है, क्योँकि महादेव का वास-स्थान कैलास है) ॥ क्या राजा, क्या रङ्क, सदा (अपने) घर घर सुखी हैँ, और जो देख पड़ता है, सब हँसता-मुखी (प्रसन्न-वदन) है ॥ सब कोई रच रच कर चन्दन का चऊतरा सजे हैँ, अगर, कस्तूरी और गोरोचन (उस चऊतरे मेँ) पोते हैँ ॥ जितने चउपार (चतुः-शाला) हैँ, सब मेँ चन्दन के खम्भे लगे हैँ, जिन मेँ (खम्भे मेँ) ओठँघ (लग) कर सभा मेँ (चतुः-शाला मेँ) सभा-पति लोग बैठे हैँ ॥ (उस घड़ी ऐसी शोभा है), जानोँ देवताओँ की

सभा जुटी (जूरी), अर्थात् लगी, है, (और उस चतुः-शाला पर दृष्टि पडने से यही जान पडता है), जानौँ इन्द्र के आसन (बैठक) की पुरी (अमरावती) पर दृष्टि पडती है ॥ सब गुणी, पण्डित, और ज्ञाता (विज्ञ) हैं। सब के मुख में संस्कृत की बात है, अर्थात् सब कोई संस्कृत बोलता है ॥

आहक (हाहा नाम का गन्धर्व) पन्थ (पथ = राह) को बनाता है, जानौँ अनुपम शिव-लोक है (वह सिंघल नगर)। और वहाँ घर घर पद्मिनी रानी हैं, जो अपने रूप के दर्शन से, अर्थात् रूप को दिखा कर, सब को मोह लेती हैं (मोहती हैं) ॥ ३६ ॥

चउपाई ।

पुनि देखी सिंघल कइ हाटा। नउ-उ निद्धि लछिमी सब पाटा ॥
कनक हाट सब कुंकुँहि लीपी। बइठ महाजन सिंघल-दीपी ॥
रचहिँ हतउडा रूपहि ढारी। चितर कटाउ अनेक सँवारी ॥
सोन रूप भल भएउ पसारा। धवर-सिरी पटवन घर-बारा ॥
रतन पदारथ मानिक मोती। हीरा पवँरि सो अनवन जोती ॥
अउ कपूर बेना कसतूरी। चंदन अगर रहा भरि पूरी ॥
जेइ न हाट एहि लीन्ह बेसाहा। तां कहँ आन हाट कित लाहा ॥

दोहा ।

कोई करइ बेसाहना काहू केर बिकाइ ।
कोई चलइ लाभ सउँ कोई मूर गवाँइ ॥ ३७ ॥

हाटा = हाट = हट्टा = बजार ॥ कुंकुँहि = कुंकुमा से = एक प्रकार की रोरी से। हतउडा = हथौडा; जिस से सोनार-लोग आभूषण बनाते हैं। रूपहि = रूप को, अर्थात् स्वरूप को। चितर = चित्र। कटाउ = कटाव = काट काट कर, अनेक फूल पत्ते की रचना। सोन = सोना = स्वर्ण। रूप = रूपा = रौप्य = चाँदी। पसार = प्रसार = फैलाव। धवर-सिरी = धवल-श्री = उज्ज्वल शोभा। पटवन = पट-बन्ध = पर्दा। पवँरि = डेवढी। अनवन = जो बनने के योग्य न हो, अर्थात् अनुपम, वा अन्य अन्य = अनेक। जोती = प्रकाश। बेना = खस-तृण। अगर = अगुरु, एक सुगन्धित काष्ठ। बेसाहा = खरीदा। कित = कुतः = कहाँ। लाहा = लाभ ॥ बेसाहना = खरीद की वस्तु। मूर = मूल-धन ॥

फिर सिंघल के हाट को देखा। जहाँ नवो निधि की सब लक्ष्मी पटी है॥ पद्म, महापद्म, शङ्ख, मकर, कच्छप, मुकुन्द, नन्द, नील, और खर्व, ये नवो निधि हैं। सोने की बाजार सब कुंकुमा से लीपी ऊई है। उस में सिंघल-दीप के महाजन बैठे हैं॥ (साँचे में) स्वरूप (मूर्त्ति) को ढार कर, तरह तरह के चित्र और कटाव को बना कर, हथौडे से (पीट पीट कर, जहाँ कुछ कसर रह गई है, उसे) बनाते हैं॥ (उस हाट में) सोने और चाँदी का अच्छा फैलाव ऊआ है, अर्थात् बेंचने के लिये, जहाँ देखो, तहाँ सोने रूपे के खेलौने इत्यादि फैलाये ऊए हैं। घर के बार, अर्थात् द्वार, में पर्दे लगे हैं, जिन की उज्ज्वल शोभा है, अर्थात् श्वेत वर्ण के सब पर्दे शोभित हैं॥ रत्न के पदार्थ, माणिक्य, मोती, और हीरे डेवढियों में जडे हैं, जिन की ज्योति अनुपम है। (कोई अनवन का अनेक अर्थ करते हैं, अर्थात् जिन की अनेक प्रकार की ज्योति है)॥ और कर्पूर, खस, कस्तूरी, चन्दन और अगर (हाट में) पूरे तौर से, अर्थात् चारो ओर, भर रहे हैं॥ जिधर देखो, तिधर सुगन्ध से हाट महमह महक रही है॥ जिन्हों ने इस हाट में नहीं खरीद किया, उन को दूसरी हाट में कहाँ लाभ, अर्थात् ऐसा कोई पदार्थ नहीं, जो इस हाट में न बिकता हो, और जो पदार्थ इस में नहीं है, सो फिर दूसरी हाट में कहाँ लाभ हो, क्योंकि सब हाटों से बढ कर, यह हाट है॥

कोई खरीद कर रहा है, किसी का (पदार्थ) बिक रहा है। कोई लाभ उठा कर, और कोई मूर को भी गवाँ कर, वहाँ से चलते हैं॥ ३७॥

चउपाई।

पुनि सिंगार हाट धनि देसा। कइ सिँगार तहँ बइठीँ बेसा॥
मुख तँबोल तन चीर कुसुंभी। कानन्ह कनक जराऊ खुंभी॥
हाथ बीन सुनि मिरिग भुलाहीँ। सुर मोहहिँ सुनि पइग न जाहीँ॥
भउँहँ धनुख तिन्ह नयन अहेरी। मारहिँ बान सानि सउँ फेरी॥
अलक कपोल डोलु हँसि देहीँ। लाइ कटाछ मारि जिउ लेहीँ॥
कुच कंचुकि जानउँ जुग सारी। अंचल देहिँ सुभाव-हि ढारी॥
केत खेलार हार तिन्ह पासा। हाथ झारि होइ चलहिँ निरासा॥

दोहा ।

चेटक लाइ हरहिँ मन जउ लहि गँठि होइ फेँटि ।
साँठि-नाँठि उठि भए बटाउ ना पहिचानि न भेँटि ॥ ३८ ॥

सिंगार = शृङ्गार। धनि = धन्य। बेसा = वेश्या। तँबोल = ताम्बूल। तन = तनु = शरीर, वा पतला। चीर = वस्त्र। कुसुंभी = कुसुमी = कुसुम-रङ्ग का। खुंभी = खुँभिया = काँप। बीन = वीणा। मिरिग = मृग। सुर = स्वर। पइग = पग = प्रग = पद। भउँह = भ्रू। अहेरी = अहेर करने-वाला। सानि = सान = शाण, जिस पर वाण, छूरी, इत्यादि फिरा कर चोखे किये जाते हैं। अलक = लट। कपोल = गाल। कटाछ = कटाच। कंचुकि = कञ्चुकी = चोलिया = चोली। जुग = युग = दो। सारी = पासा॥ चेटक = चटक मटक से टोना लगा देना, वा दूत। गँठि = ग्रन्थी = गठरी (रुपये पैसे की)। फेँटि = फेट = कमर में लपेटा हुआ वस्त्र। साँठि-नाँठि = बे पैसे कौडी के। साँठ ऊख को कहते हैं, और नाँठ नष्ट का अपभ्रंश है, अर्थात् वह ऊख, जो कि नष्ट, अर्थात् नीरस हो गई हो, यह शब्दार्थ है। अब निर्धनी के अर्थ में प्रचलित है। बटाऊ = बाट चलने-वाला = राही॥

फिर शृङ्गार की हाट, अर्थात् जहाँ रूप बिकते हैं, वह धन्य देश (स्थान) है। तहाँ शृङ्गार किये वेश्यायेँ बैठी हैं॥ मुख में ताम्बूल (पान) खाये हैं, शरीर में कुसुम-रङ्ग का वस्त्र पहिने हैं, वा कुसुम-रङ्ग का पतला वस्त्र पहिने हैं (जिस में ऊपर से अंग का झलक देख पडे)। कानों में जडाऊ (नग से जडी हुई) सोने की काँप, वा कर्ण-फूल, पहिने हैं॥ हाथ में वीणा को लिये हैं, जिन के शब्द को सुन कर मृग (हरिण) भूल जाते हैं। और उस के स्वर को सुन कर ऐसे मोह जाते हैं कि एक पैर नहीं चलते, अर्थात् चित्र से खडे रहते हैं॥ उन की आँखें शिकारी भौंह-रूपी धनुष से, सान पर फेर कर, वाण को मारती हैं। यहाँ दृष्टि-पात को वाण, और कटाच को सान समझना चाहिये, और इधर उधर पुतलियों का फेरना, मानों उस दृष्टिपात-रूपी वाण पर सान फेरना है॥ गालों पर जो लट लटकती हैं, वह उन के हँस देने पर डोलने लगती हैं, अर्थात् डोल कर पथिकों को अपने पास बुलाती हैं। वे वेश्यायें (पथिकों के सन्मुख होने पर) कटाच को लगा कर, अर्थात् अपनी बाँकी चितवन से, जीव मार लेती हैं, अर्थात् मूर्छित कर देती हैं॥ चोली के भीतर उन के

कुच (स्तन) जानों दो पासे हैं, जिन को स्वभाव-ही से अंचल ढार देते हैं, अर्थात् मैदान में फेंक देते हैं। कवि का यहाँ पर ऐसा आशय है, कि पथिकों को लुभाने के लिये वेश्यायें स्वभाव-ही से चण चण पर जो अञ्चल कुच पर से हटा लेती हैं, इस से पथिकों के दृष्टि-गोचर वे कुच हो जाते हैं, सो मानों अंचल ने पथिकों के सामने कुच-रूपी पासाओं को फेंक दिया, कि यदि खेलाडी हो, तो आओ, और इन पासों से खेलो ॥ तिन्ह पासों से कितने खेलाडी हार गये हैं। और हाथ झाड कर निरास हो कर चले जाते हैं, अर्थात् ऐसे जादू के वे पासे हैं, कि उन से, यदि कोई खेले, तो वेश्याओं से प्रत्यच में हार जाय। जुआरी जब हार जाता है, तब हाथ को साफ करने के लिये, झाड देता है, वस्तुतः वह झाडता नहीं किन्तु मन में पछता कर हाथ मलता है॥

जब तक कमर में गँठरी (रुपये पैसे की) रहती है, तब तक चटक मटक से टोना सा लगा कर, वा दूत को लगा कर, मन को हर लेती हैं। और जब निर्धनी हो जाता है, तब ऐसी चेष्टा करती हैं, जानों न कभीं की भेंट न पहिचान है। इस लिये वह बेचारा उठ कर, बटाऊ हो जाता है, अर्थात् अपने कर्तव्यता को सोचता, वहाँ से चलता होता है॥

यहाँ दीसा के स्थान में, तुक मिलाने के लिये, यदि कवि ने देसा किया हो, ऐसा मानो, तो पहली चौपाई का अर्थ 'फिर शृङ्गार हाट को धन्य, अर्थात् विचित्र, देखा,' यह करना चाहिए॥ सातवीं चौपाई में 'तिन्ह पासा' का तिन (वेश्याओं) के पास (निकट) कितने खेलाडी हार गये, यह भी अर्थ कर सकते हो॥ ३८॥

चउपाई।

लेइ लेइ फूल बइठि फुलवारी। पान अपूरब धरे सँवारी॥
सोँधा सवइ बइठु लेइ गाँधी। बहुल कपूर खिरउरी बाँधी॥
कतहूँ पंडित पढहिँ पुरानू। धरम पंथ कर करहिँ बखानू॥
कतहूँ कथा कहइ किछु कोई। कतहूँ नाँच कोड भल होई॥
कतहुँ छरहटा पेखन लावा। कतहुँ पखंडी काठ नचावा॥
कतहूँ नाद सबद होइ भला। कतहूँ नाटक-चेटक-कला॥
कतहुँ काहु ठग विदिआ लाई। कतहुँ लेहिँ मानुस बउराई॥

दोहा ।

चरपट चोर गँठि-छोरा मिलें रहहिँ तेहि नाँच ।
जो तेहि हाट सजग रहइ गँठि ता करि पइ बाँच ॥ ३९ ॥

फुलवारी = फूल-वाली = फूल बेँचने-वाली । अपूरव = अपूर्व । सेाँधा = सुगन्ध-द्रव्य = अँतर फुलेल । गाँधी = गन्धी = अँतर फुलेल बेँचने-वाला । बहुल = बहुत । खिरउरी = खिरौरी = मसालेदार खैर की गोली, जिस से पान में विशेष स्वादु उत्पन्न होता है। हमारे प्रदेशोँ में बहुत प्रसिद्ध है, जैसे व्यञ्जनोँ में मूँग, तिल, और कोहडे, इत्यादि से 'मुँगौरी', 'तिलौरी', 'कोँहडौरी', इत्यादि शब्द बने हैँ, उसी प्रकार खैर से 'खिरौरी' हुआ है। कोड = कूर्दन = कूदना । छरहटा = नकल करने-वाले = छार (भस्म) लपेटने-वाले । पेखन = प्रेक्षण = दृश्य = मेला । पखंडी = पाखण्डी = धूर्त्त = कठ-पुतली नचाने-वाला । नाटक-कला = नट लोगोँ की बाजी-गरी । चेटक-कला = चटक मटक से टोना लगा देने-वाली कला, जिस से मनुष्य विवश हो जाय । बिदिआ = विद्या । बउराई = बौरहा ॥ चरपट = चपाट = मूर्ख, जो जबरदस्ती अपने जोर से दूसरे की चीज को छीन ले । गँठि-छोरा = गठरी को छीन लेने-वाले, = चाई । सजग = सज्जित = सावधान । पद = अपि = निश्चय से ॥

(उस हाट में) फूल बेँचने-वाली मालिन फूलोँ को ले ले कर बैठी हैँ । और बना कर (सँवारि) अपूर्व (जो कि पहले न देखा गया हो) पान को धरे हुई हैँ ॥ गन्धी सब सुगन्ध द्रव्य को ले कर, और बहुत कपूर के साथ खिरौरी बाँध कर बैठा है । (यहाँ 'बहुल' के स्थान में 'मेलि' यह पाठ अच्छा है। तब 'गन्धी सब सुगन्ध द्रव्य को ले कर बैठा है' और कपूर डाल कर (मेलि) खिरौरी को बाँधा है, अर्थात् बनाया है) ॥ कहीँ पण्डित पुराण को पढते हैँ, और धर्म-पथ का वर्णन करते हैँ ॥ कहीँ पर कोई कुछ कथा कहता है। कहीँ पर अच्छी तरह नाँच और कूद हो रहा है ॥ कहीँ पर नकल करने-वाला मेला लगा रक्खा है । कहीँ पर कठ-पुतली नचाने-वाला काठ-ही को (काठ की पुतलियोँ को) नचा रहा है ॥ कहीँ पर (वाद्य का) नाद हो रहा है, जिस का शब्द भला (जान पडता) है ॥ कहीँ पर नटोँ का खेल, और चालाकोँ का हथ-फेर सम्बन्धी खेल हो रहा है ॥ कहीँ पर ठग ने किसी के ऊपर (ठगने के लिये) अपनी विद्या को लगाया है। कहीँ पर लोग (अपने यन्त्र मन्त्र से) मनुष्य को बौरहा कर लेते हैँ ॥

जबरदस्त, चोर, और चाईं उन नाचों में मिले रहते हैं, अर्थात् ऊपर जो कह आये हैं, कि कहीं कहीं अच्छी तरह से नाँच कूद हो रहा है, वहाँ पर उसी नाँच कूद में ये सब मिले रहते हैं। इस लिये जो कोई तिस हाट में सावधान रहता है, तिसी की निश्चय कर के गँठरी बचती है ॥ ३९ ॥

चउपाई।

पुनि आए सिंघल-गढ पासा। का बरनउँ जनु लागु अकासा ॥
तरहि कुरुम बासुकि कइ पीठी। ऊपर इँदर-लोक पर डीठी ॥
परा खोह चहुँ दिसि तस बाँका। काँपइ जाँघ जाइ नहिँ झाँका ॥
अगम असूझ देखि डर खाई। परइ सो सपत पतारहि जाई ॥
नउ पउरी बाँकी नउ खंडा। नउ-उ जो चढइ जाइ ब्रहमंडा ॥
कंचन कोट जरे कउ सीसा। नखतन्ह भरी बीजु जनु दीसा ॥
लंका चाहि ऊँच गढ ताका। निरखि न जाइ दिसिटि मन थाका ॥

दोहा।

हिअ न समाइ दिसिटि नहिँ जानउँ ठाढ सुमेरु।
कहँ लगि कहउँ उँचाई कहँ लगि बरनउँ फेरु ॥ ४० ॥

कुरुम = कूर्म = कच्छप। वासुकि = वासुकि-नाग। खोह = खन्धक। कउ = कइ-उ = कई ॥

फिर सिंघल-गढ के पास जो आए, (तो देखने से बुद्धि थकित हो जाती है)। उस का क्या वर्णन करूँ। (इतना ऊँचा है), जानों आकाश में लगा ऊआ है ॥ तले (तरहि) तो (वह) कूर्म और वासुकि के पीठ तक चला गया है, और उस के ऊपर देखने से इन्द्र-लोक पर दृष्टि पडती है, अर्थात् इस की नीँव कूर्म और वासुकि के पीठ पर है, और ऊँचा इतना है, कि उस पर से इन्द्र-लोक देख पडता है। (कूर्म और वासुकि-नाग पृथ्वी के आधारोँ में से हैं। पुराणोँ में कथा है, कि कूर्म, वाराह, शेष-नाग, वासुकि-नाग, और दिग्गज, ये सब पृथ्वी को धारण किये हैं, जिस से यह नीचे को नहीँ जाती। कभीँ कभीँ ये लोग जब बोझे से थक कर श्वास लेते हैं, तब भू-कम्प होता है) ॥ तैसा कठिन (बाँका) उस गढ के चारो ओर खन्धक पडा है, कि झाँका नहीँ जाता,

झाँकने से जाँघ कँपने लगती है ॥ अगम्य और असूझ उस खन्धक को देख कर, ऐसा डर (भय) उत्पन्न होता है, कि वह भय (शरीर) खाने लगता है। (यदि) कोई उस में पड जाय (गिर जाय), तो वह सातवें पाताल में चला जाय, अर्थात् खन्धक की गहराई सातवें पाताल तक चली गई है। अतल, वितल, सुतल, तलातल, महातल, रसातल, और पाताल ये सात नीचे के लोक हैं, जिन में सातवाँ पाताल है (भागवत, पञ्चम-स्कन्ध, २४वीं अध्याय के ७वें श्लोक को देखो)। उस गढ में नव खण्ड हैं, और बडी दुर्गम (बाँकी) नव डेवढी हैं। नवो डेवढियों पर जो चढ जाय, वह (जानों) ब्रह्माण्ड पर चढ गया, अर्थात् वह गढ नव-महला है, प्रत्येक महल पर चढने के लिये एक एक डेवढी है। नवो को लाँघ कर, तब ऊपर पहुँचना होता है, ऊपर पहुँचने पर जान पडता है, कि ब्रह्माण्ड के ऊपर पहुँच गये। सिद्धान्त शिरोमणि में भास्कराचार्य ने लिखा है कि—

कोटिघ्नैर्नखनन्दषट्कनगभूभृद्भुजङ्गेन्दुभि १८७१७६९२०००००००
र्ज्योतिःशास्त्रविदो वदन्ति नभसः कक्षामिमां योजनैः।
तद्ब्रह्माण्डकटाहसम्पुटतटे केचिज्जगुर्वेष्टनं — इत्यादि

अर्थात् जिस ब्रह्माण्ड के भीतर पृथ्वी, ग्रह, नक्षत्रादि, और सब लोक हैं, वह दो कराहे के सम्पुट ऐसा है, जिस का घेरा १८७१७६९२०००००००० योजन है॥ वह कोट (गढ) सोने का है, और उस में कई प्रकार के सीसे लगे हैं। उस से उस की ऐसी शोभा है, जानों नक्षत्रों से भरी बिजली देख पडती है॥ सुवर्ण बिजली, और सीसे नक्षत्र के सदृश समझो। उस गढ को लङ्का से भी ऊँचा देखा। निरख नहीं जाता, निरखने से (निरीक्षण करने से) दृष्टि और मन थक जाते हैं॥

(उस गढ की सब रचना) न हृदय में समाती, और न दृष्टि में समाती। जान पडता है कि गढ नहीं, सुमेरु पर्वत खडा है। कहाँ तक उस की उँचाई कहूँ, और कहाँ तक उस के फेर (परिधि) का वर्णन करूँ॥ कवि का आशय है, कि जब वह मन और दृष्टि से बाहर है, और उन में समाय नहीं सकता, तब कहाँ तक उस का वर्णन हो सकता है॥ सुमेरु सुवर्ण का पर्वत है, और उस के चारो ओर नक्षत्र घूमती हैं, इस लिये सुमेरु का उपमा देना योग्य है॥ ३९-४० दोहे में गावने-वाले अपने मन से कई पद मिला दिये हैं, जिन को मैं ने निकाल दिया है, क्योंकि छन्दो-भङ्ग दोष पडता था ॥४०॥

चउपाई।

निति गढ बाँचि चलइ ससि सूरा। नाहिँ त होइ बाजि रथ चूरा॥
पउरी नउ-उ बजर कइ साजी। सहस सहस तहँ बइठे पाजी॥
फिरहिँ पाँच कोटवार सो भवँरी। काँपइ पाउँ चँपत वेइ पउँरी॥
पउरिहि पउरि सिंह गढि काढे। डरपहिँ राइ देखि तिन्ह ठाढे॥
बहु बिधान वेइ नाहर गढे। जनु गाजहिँ चाहहिँ सिर चढे॥
टारहिँ पूँछि पसारहिँ जीहा। कुंजर डरहिँ कि गुंजरि लीहा॥
कनक-सिला गढि सीढी लाईँ। जगमगाहिँ गढ ऊपर ताईँ॥

दोहा।

नउ-उ खंड नउ पउरी अउ तेहि बजर केवार।
चारि बसेरे सउँ चढइ सत सउँ चढइ जो पार॥ ४१॥

बाँचि = बचा कर। ससि = शशि = चन्द्रमा। सूरा = सूर = सूर्य। बाजि = वाजी = घोडा। चूरा = चूर = चूर्ण। बजर = वज्र। पाजी = पत्ति = पैदल सिपाही = योद्धा। कोटवार = कोट-पाल = कोतवाल। भवँरी = भ्रमण = फेरा। राइ = राजा। नाहर = सिंह। टारहिँ = टारते हैँ = इधर उधर हिलाते हैँ। पसारहिँ = फैलाते हैँ। जीहा = जिह्वा = जीभ। कुंजर = हस्ती। गुंजरि = गुञ्जार कर = शब्द कर। लीहा = लेता है॥ बसेरा = निवास-स्थान। पार = समर्थ = कुशल॥

चन्द्रमा और सूर्य उस गढ (गाढ = दुर्ग = किला) को बचा कर नित्य चलते हैँ, नहीँ तो उन के घोडे और रथ चूर हो जाते (गढ के ठोकर से)। (इस से अत्यन्त गढ की उँचाई सिद्ध हुई, कि सूर्य चन्द्र की कक्षा भी उस के अधो भाग-ही में है, और पुराणों में कथा है, कि मेरु के चारो ओर चन्द्र, सूर्य घूमते हैँ। पिछले दोहे में गढ को सुमेरु कहा है, इस लिये पूर्णोपमा यहाँ पर हुई)॥ नवो डेवढी वज्र की सजी हुई है, जहाँ हजार हजार योद्धा लोग बैठे हैँ॥ और पाँच कोतवाल जो हैँ सो भवँरी फिरा करते हैँ, अर्थात् दिन रात कोट के चारो ओर फेरा किया करते हैँ। इस लिये उन पौरियों पर पैर चँपते-ही काँपता है॥ पौरी पौरी पर सिंह गढ कर काढे हैँ, अर्थात् बनाये गये हैँ। जिन्हेँ खडे देख कर राजा लोग (सच्चा सिंह समझ कर) डरते

हैं ॥ बहुत विधान (विधि) से वे सिंह गढे हुए हैं, अर्थात् सच्चे सिंह से उन से कुछ भेद नहीं समझ पडता है। वे ऐसे जान पडते हैं, जानों गरजते हैं, और शिर पर चढा चाहते हैं ॥ वे पूँछ को हिलाते हैं, और जीभ को फैलाते हैं। (इस चेष्टा को देख कर) हाथी डरते हैं, कि ये सिंह गुञ्जार कर अब लिया चाहते हैं ॥ सोने की शिला को गढ कर (गढ में) सीढी लगाई गई हैं, जो कि गढ के ऊपर तक जगमगाती हैं ॥

नवो खण्ड में नव डेवढियाँ हैं, और तिन में वज्र के केवाडे लगे हैं। जो कोई सत्य से, अर्थात् निष्कपट व्यवहार से, चढने में समर्थ है, वह चार दिन बसेरा कर (टिक कर), तब (उस गढ पर) चढता है, अर्थात् जिस को उस के सत्य व्यवहार से चढने की आज्ञा मिलती है, उसे गढ पर चढने में चार दिन लगते हैं ॥

यहाँ पर गढ को शरीर, और दो आँख, दो कान, दो नासिका के पूरे, और दो गुह्येन्द्रिय ये नव पौरी, और प्राण अपानादि पाँच वायु को कोतवाल, हड्डियों को वज्र कपाट, रोमादिकों को योद्धा, और अन्तःकरण-स्थ आत्मा को गढ का राजा मानने से, अर्थान्तर हो सकता है ॥ ४१ ॥

चउपाई ।

नवउँ पउरि पर दसउँ दुआरा। तेहि पर बाजु राज-घरिआरा ॥
घरी सो बइठि गनइ घरिआरी। पहर पहर सो आपनि बारी ॥
जबहिँ घरी पूजइ वह मारा। घरी घरी घरिआर पुकारा ॥
परा जो डाँड जगत सब डाँडा। का निचिंत माँटी के भाँडा ॥
तुम्ह तेहि चाक चढे होइ काँचे। आएउ फिरइ न थिर होइ बाँचे ॥
घरी जोँ भरइ घटइ तुम्ह आऊ। का निचिंत सोअहु रे बटाऊ ॥
पहरहि पहर गजर निति होई। हिआ निसोगा जागु न सोई ॥

दोहा ।

मुहमद जीअन जल भरन रहट घरी कइ रीति ।
घरी जो आइ जीअन भरी ढरी जनम गा बीति ॥ ४२ ॥

राज-घरिआरा = राजा का घण्टा। इस की पहले सूरत घरियार (जल-यन्त्र) के ऐसी होती थी। इसी लिये इस का घरियार नाम ऊआ। घरी = घटी = जल-घटी। पहले यह दश पल ताम्बे की छ अङ्गुल ऊँची, और बारह अङ्गुल विस्तृत गोलार्द्ध के आकार की ऐसी बनती थी, जिस में साठ पल पानी भरे। इस के नीचे तीन माशा और एक माशे की तिहाई सोने से जो गोल चार अङ्गुल लम्बा तार बने, उस से छेद किया जाता था, उसी छेद से कुण्ड में वा जल-पूर्ण पात्र में घटी को छोड देने से, साठ पल वा एक घडी (नाडी) में वह भर जाती थी। ऐसा-ही ज्योतिष सिद्धान्त में श्रीपति ने, जो कि ९६१ शाका (१०३९ ई०) में थे, लिखा है,—

'शुल्वस्य दिग्भिर्विहितं पलैर्यत् षडङ्गुलोच्चं द्विगुणायतास्यम्।
तदम्भसा षष्टिपलैः प्रपूर्यं पात्रं घटार्द्धप्रतिमं घटी स्यात्॥१॥
सत्र्यंशमाषत्रयनिर्मिता या हेम्नः शलाका चतुरङ्गुला स्यात्।
विद्धं तया प्राक्तनमत्र पात्रं प्रपूर्यते नाडिकया ऽम्बुना तत्॥२॥

घरिआरी = घण्टा बजाने-वाला। पहर = प्रहर। बारी = वार = क्रम = पारी। डाँड = डण्डा = घण्टा बजाने की लकडी। डाँडा = डाँटा = डपेटा। निचिंत = निश्चिन्त = बे-फिकिर। भाँडा = भाण्ड = वर्त्तन। चाक = चक्र, कोहार का। काँचे = कच्चे। थिर = स्थिर। आऊ = आयु। गजर = गर्जर = गजल। निसोगा = निशोक = निश्चय कर के जिसे शोक हो, अर्थात् अभागा। सोई = सो कर॥ रहट = पुरवट = आरघट्ट। जीअन = जीवन = जिन्दगी वा जल॥

नवीँ पौरी के ऊपर एक दशवाँ द्वार है, तिस पर राजा का घण्टा बजता है॥ घण्टा बजाने-वाला जो है, सो बैठ कर घडी को गिना करता है। ऐसा वे बजाने-वाले पहर पहर पर अपनी अपनी पारी में करते हैं, अर्थात् पहर पहर पर पहरा बदला जाता है। तब एक एक की पारी आती है॥ जब घडी (जल-घडी) भरती है (पूजती है) तब वह बजाने-वाला (घण्टे पर लकडी से) चोट मारता है, (इस प्रकार से) घडी घडी पर घण्टा पुकारा करता है॥ घण्टे पर जो डण्डा पडता है, सो (जानोँ) सब जगत (सब मनुष्य) को डाँटता है, कि हे मट्टी के वर्त्तन क्या निश्चिन्त हो॥ (तुम्हेँ नहीँ मालूम कि) तुम कच्चे हो कर तिस ईश्वर के चाक पर चढे हो, (इस लिये) तुम (इधर से उधर) फिरने के लिये आये हो। स्थिर हो कर बँच नहीँ सकते॥ और ज्योँ ज्योँ घडी भरती है, त्योँ त्योँ तुम्हारी आयु घटती है, (इस प्रकार जब तुम्हारी

ख़राबी हो रही है, तब) अरे मुसाफिर (बटाऊ) तुम क्या निश्चिन्त सोते हो ॥ कवि कहता है, कि आश्चर्य है, कि लोगों को सावधान करने के लिये पहर पहर पर नित्य गजल ऊआ करता है, (परन्तु) यह निसोगा (अभागा) हृदय सो कर जागता नहीं है॥

मुहम्मद कवि कहते हैं, कि पुरवट और घडी में जैसी जल भरने की रीति है, वैसा-ही यह (मनुष्य का) जीवन है। जो घडी आ कर जीवन को भरी, वही फिर ढर गई, अर्थात् खाली हो गई, (ऐसा-ही करते करते कई) जन्म बीत गये ॥ एक अर्थ में घडी से शरीर, और जीवन से जिन्दगी, दूसरे में घडी से जल-घडी, और जीवन से जल समझो ॥ ४२ ॥

चउपाई ।

गढ पर नीर खीर दुइ नदी। पानि भरहिँ जइसे दुरुपदी ॥
अउरु कुंड एक मोती चूरू। पानी अंब्रित कीचु कपूरू ॥
ओहि क पानि राजा पइ पीआ। बिरिध होइ नहिँ जउ लहि जीआ॥
कंचन बिरिख एक तेहि पासा। जस कलप-तरु इँदर कबिलासा॥
मूल पतार सरग ओहि साखा। अमर बेलि को पाउ को चाखा॥
चाँद पात अउ फूल तराईँ। होइ उँजिआर नगर जहँ ताईँ॥
वह फर पावइ तपि कइ कोई। बिरिध खाइ नउ जोबन होई ॥

दोहा ।

राजा भए भिखारी सुनि ओहि अंब्रित भोग।
जेइ पावा सो अमर भा न किछु बिआधि न रोग ॥ ४३ ॥

नीर = जल। खीर = क्षीर से पका चावल। दुरुपदी = द्रौपदी। पइ = परन्तु। बिरिध = वृद्ध। बिरिख = वृक्ष। कलपतरु = कल्प-तरु = कल्प-वृक्ष। पतार = पाताल। सरग = स्वर्ग। साखा = शाखा। बेलि = वल्ली = लता। जोबन = यौवन। बिआधि = व्याधि ॥

गढ पर नीर और खीर नाम की दो नदियाँ हैं। अर्थात् एक का पानी तो पानी-ही है, दूसरे का पानी खीर है। ये नदियाँ अपना अपना पानी भरती हैं, अर्थात् वहाँ के लोगों को देती हैं, जैसे द्रौपदी पाँचो पाण्डवों की स्त्री। (महाभारत में कथा है, कि द्रौपदी थोडा भी भोजन बना कर, सब किसी को खिला देती थी, और

भण्डारा नहीं खाली होता था। जब वह खा लेती थी, तब भण्डारा खाली हो जाता था (महाभारत, वनपर्व, ३ अध्याय का ७२—७४ श्लोक देखो)। कवि का अभिप्राय है, कि दोनों नदियों में भी द्रौपदी का सा धर्म है, कि सब लोग नीर और खीर को यथेच्छ रात दिन पीआ करते हैं, परन्तु घटती नहीं। (नदियाँ ज्यों की त्यों उन से भरी रहती हैं)॥ और एक मोती के चूर्ण का बना कुण्ड है, जिस का कीचड कपूर और पानी अमृत है॥ परन्तु (जैसे सब के लिये दोनों नदियाँ सुलभ हैं, वैसा यह कुण्ड नहीं)। इस का पानी केवल राजा-ही पीता है। इसी कारण जब तक जीता है, वृद्ध नहीं होता॥ तिस कुण्ड के पास एक कञ्चन (सोना) का वृक्ष है, (उस की ऐसी शोभा है), जैसे राजा इन्द्र के यहाँ कैलास में कल्प-वृक्ष शोभित हो॥ यहाँ भी कैलास से अमरावती समझना चाहिए। उस वृक्ष का मूल (जड) पाताल, और शाखा स्वर्ग तक (चली गई) है। ऐसी अमर-करने-वाली वेलि (वेलि के फल) को कौन पावे और कौन चक्खे, अर्थात् अत्यन्त काठिन्य से कोई भाग्यवान् पावे तो पावे॥ उस वृक्ष के पत्ते (पात=पत्र) चन्द्रमा, और फूल तारा-गण हैं, (इसी कारण रात को) जहाँ तक शहर है, तहाँ तक उसी से उजेला होता है॥ कोई तपस्या कर के (तपि) उस फल को पाता है। उस फल को वृद्ध खाय, तो उस का भी नया यौवन हो जाय॥

उस अमृत भोग (फल) को सुन कर (कितने) राजा भिखारी हो गये, अर्थात् राज-पाट छोड दिये। जो (उस फल को) पाया, वह अमर हो गया, (फिर) उस को न कुछ व्याधि हो और न रोग॥ यहाँ व्याधि से शरीर के बाहर का रोग, और रोग से आधि, अर्थात् शरीर के भीतर का रोग, समझो॥ ४३॥

चउपाई।

गढ पर बसहिँ झारि गढ-पती। असु-पति गज-पति भू-नर-पती॥
सब क धउरहर सोनइ साजा। अउ अपने अपने घर राजा॥
रूपवंत धनवंत सभागे। परस-पखान पउरि तिन्ह लागे॥
भोग बिरास सदा सब माना। दुख चिंता कोइ जनम न जाना॥
मँदिर मँदिर सब के चउपारी। बइठि कुअँर सब खेलहिँ सारी॥
पासा ढरइ खेलि भलि होई। खरग दान सरि पूज न कोई॥
भाँट बरनि कहि कीरति भली। पावहिँ घोर हसति सिंघली॥

दोहा।

मँदिर मँदिर फुलवारी चोआ चंदन बास ।
निसि दिन रहइ बसंत तहँ छवो रितु बरहो मास ॥ ४४ ॥

झारि = बराय कर = झाड कर = केवल = खाली । अस्सु-पती = अश्व-पति । धउर-हर = धरहरा = ध्रुवहर = ध्रुव के ऐसा ऊँचा स्थान । परस-पखान = स्पर्श-पाषाण = पारस । बिरास = विलास । चउपारी = चतुः-पाट = चतुः-शाला = बैठक । सारी = पासा । खरग = खड्ग । सिंघल = सिंघल का ॥ बरहो = बारहो ॥

गढ के ऊपर झार कर के, अर्थात् केवल, गढ-पति, अश्व-पति, गज-पति, भू-पति और नर-पति लोग बसते हैं । औरों को अधिकार नहीं कि गढ के ऊपर बसें ॥ जिन के अधिकार में एकाध गढो हो, वे गढ-पति कहलाते हैं । जिन के अधिकार में कुछ घोडे और हाथी हों, वे क्रम से अश्व-पति और गज-पति कहे जाते हैं । जिन के अधिकार में कुछ भूमि और कुछ मनुष्य अर्थात् सिपाही हों, उन्हें क्रम से भू-पति और नर-पति कहते हैं । सब लोगों के धरहरे (उच्च-स्थान) सोने से सजे हैं, और वे सब अपने अपने घर में राजा-ही के ऐसे हैं, अर्थात् राजा जिस प्रकार का सुख भोगता है, वैसा-ही ये लोग भी भोगते हैं ॥ सब लोग सर्वदा भोग और विलास-ही को मानते हैं, अर्थात् भोग विलास-ही में समय को व्यतीत करते हैं, कोई जन्म भर में भी दुःख और चिन्ता को नहीं जानते, कि क्या पदार्थ हैं ॥ इन्द्रियों की सुख-साधन सामग्री को भोग कहते हैं, और बाहर की शोभा को विलास कहते हैं ॥ सब के मन्दिर मन्दिर में बैठक (चउपारी) हैं, वहाँ (गढ-पति, अश्व-पति इत्यादि के) कुअँर (बालक) सब बैठ कर पासा (सारी) खेलते हैं ॥ पासा ढारा (फेँका) जाता है, और अच्छी तरह से खेल होती है। यह न कोई समझे, कि वे कुअँर केवल खेल-ही में दिन बिताते हैं, इस लिये अगली चौपाई में वर्णन करते हैं, कि खड्ग (चलाने) और दान (देने) में उन कुअँरों की बराबरी में कोई नहीं पऊँचता (पूजा), अर्थात् वे कुअँर खड्ग चलाने में और दान देने में बडे बहादुर हैं ॥ भाँट लोग उन कुअँरों की वर्णना कर, और अच्छी तरह से (कविता कर), उन की कीर्त्ति कह कर, घोडे और सिंघल के हाथी पाते हैं । अर्थात् कुअँर लोग ऐसे उदार हैं, कि एक एक प्रशंसा में घोडे और हाथिओं से भाँटों को अयाच्य कर देते हैं ॥

मन्दिर मन्दिर में फुलवारी से चोत्रा और चन्दन के वास आते हैं। तहाँ पर छवो ऋतु, और बारहो महीने में, रात दिन वसन्त ऋतु रहती है॥ केवल छवो ऋतु-ही के कहने से बारहो महीना का बोध हो जाता है। पृथक् महीनाँ का कहना दार्ढ्यार्थ है। अर्थात् अपने अर्थ को पुष्ट करने के लिये, महीनाँ को भी पृथक् कहा है॥४४॥

चउपाई।

पुनि चलि देखा राज-दुआरू। महि घूबिँअ पाइअ नहिँ बारू॥
हसति सिंघली बाँधे बारा। जनु सजीउ सब ठाढ पहारा॥
कवन-उ सेत पीत रतनारे। कवन-उ हरे धूम अउ कारे॥
बरनहिँ बरन गगन जनु मेघा। अउ तेहि गगन पीठि जस ठेंघा॥
सिंघल के बरनउँ सिंघली। एक एक चाहि एक एक बली॥
गिरि पहार हसती सब पेलहिँ। बिरिख उचारि फारि मुख मेलहिँ॥
माँते निमते गरजहिँ बाँधे। निसि दिन रहहिँ महाउत काँधे॥

दोहा।

धरनी भार न अँगवई पाउँ धरत उठ हालि।
कुरुम टूट फन फाटई तिन्ह हसतिन्ह के चालि॥४५॥

दुआर = द्वार = दरवाजा। महि = मही = पृथ्वी। घूबिँअ = घूमिये। पाइअ = पाइये। बारू = बारा = बार = द्वार। सजीउ = सजीव। कवन-उ = कश्चन = को ऽपि = कोई। सेत = श्वेत। पीत = पीला। रतनारे = रक्त = लाल। हरे = हरित। ठेंघा = आधार। पेलहिँ = ढकेलती हैं। माँते = मत्त = मस्त। निमते = विना मत के, बे-समझ, जो कहना न माने। महाउत = महामात्र = पीलवान्॥ धरनी = धरणी = पृथ्वी। अँगवई = अङ्गीकार करती है = सहती है। कुरुम = कूर्म = कच्छप॥

फिर चल कर राज-द्वार को देखा, जहाँ सब पृथ्वी घूमिये (परन्तु) द्वार न पाइये। अर्थात् इतनी भीर चारो ओर से डटी रहती है, जिस से समझ नहीं पडता, कि किस ओर द्वार है॥ द्वार पर सिंघल के हाथी बाँधे हैं। वे ऐसे जान पडते हैं, जानाँ सहित जीव के (जिन्दा हो कर) सब पहाड खडे हैं॥ कोई श्वेत, कोई पीले, कोई

लाल, कोई हरे, कोई धूम्र से, और कोई काले हैं ॥ (पीले, लाल, हरे रंग के हाथी नहीं देखने में आये हैं । रंग से रँग देने से रंग बदल जा सकता है)। जानों गगन (आकाश) में वर्ण वर्ण (रंग-रंग) के मेघे (बादल) हैं । और तिस आकाश में उन की पीठ ऐसी जान पडती है, जेसे ठँघा (आधार)। अर्थात् वे हस्ती इतने ऊँचे हैं, जानों अपनी पीठ से आकाश को रोके ऊए हैं ॥ सिंघल के हाथियों का वर्णन करता हूँ, कि एक से एक बढ कर, और एक से एक बली हैं ॥ सब हाथी गिरि और पहाड को ढकेल देते हैं, और वृच को उखाड कर (उचारि), और उन्हें फाड फाड कर, मुख में डालते हैं । (यहाँ गिरि से बडा पहाड, और पहाड से साधारण पर्वत लेना चाहिए। यदि गिरि के स्थान में 'गिर' पाठ हो, तो अच्छा । तब चौपाई का अर्थ 'मत्त हस्ती (जब) ढकेलते हैं, (तब) पहाड गिर पडता है', ऐसा करना चाहिये) ॥ मस्त हाथी बे-समझ हो कर, बँधे ऊए गरजते हैं, (इसी कारण उपद्रव के भय से) उन के कन्धे पर रात दिन महावत रहते हैं ॥

पावँ के धरते-ही, पृथ्वी उन के भार को नहीं सह सकती, हिल उठती है। उन हाथियों के चाल से कूर्म की पीठ टूट जाती है, और शेष का फण फट जाता है ॥ ४५॥

चउपाई ।

पुनि बाँधे रजबार तुरंगा । का बरनउँ जस उन्ह के रंगा ॥
लीले समुँद चाल जग जाने । हाँसुल भवँर किआह बखाने ॥
हरे कुरंग महुअ बहु भाँती । गरर कोकाह बुलाह सो पाँती ॥
तीख तुखार चाँडि अउ बाँके । तरपहिँ तबहिँ नाँचि बिनु हाँके ॥
मन तइँ अगुमन डोलहिँ बागा । देत उसाँस गगन सिर लागा ॥
पावहिँ साँस समुँद पर धावहिँ । बूड न पाउँ पार होइ आवहिँ ॥
थिर न रहहिँ रिस लोह चबाहीँ । भाँजहिँ पूँछि सीस उपराहीँ ॥

दोहा ।

अस तुखार सब देखे जनु मन के रथ-बाह ।
नयन पलक पहुँचावहीँ जहँ पहुँचइ कोइ चाह ॥ ४६ ॥

तुरंग = घोडा। लीले = नीले रंग का घोडा, आज कल भी इसी नाम से प्रसिद्ध है (नीलो नीलक एवाश्व इति जयादित्य-कृते ऽश्ववैद्यके)॥ समुंद = समुद्र के फेन सा जिस घोडे का रंग हो, इसे आज कल कोई समंद कोई बदामी कहता है॥ हाँसुल = कुमैत-हिनाई, अर्थात् मेहदी के रङ्ग सा सब बदन हो, और चारो पैर कुछ काला लिये॥ भवँर = भौंरे का सा रंग, जिसे आज कल मुश्की कहते हैं॥ किआह = (कियाह) जिस घोडे का रंग पके ताड के फल के ऐसा हो, (पक्वतालनिभो वाजी कियाहः परिकीर्त्तितः—इति जयादित्य-कृते ऽश्ववैद्यके)॥ हरे = हरे रंग का घोडा, इस रङ्ग का घोडा दुर्लभ है नहीं मिलता। पुराण में कथा है, कि सूर्य के रथ में हरे घोडे हैं। कवि ने प्रशंसार्थ लिख दिया है॥ कुरंग = कुलंग = लाखोरी, जिस का रंग लाह के ऐसा हो, इसे नीला कुमैत कहते हैं॥ मकुअ = मकुए के ऐसा जिस का रंग हो॥ गरर = इसे आज कल लोग गर्रा कहते हैं। जिस के एक रोएँ लाल, और एक सफेद, खिँचडी हो॥ कोकाह = कोका, सफेद घोडे को कहते हैं, (श्वेतः कोकाह इत्युक्तः—इति जयादित्य-कृते ऽश्ववैद्यके)। बुलाह = वोल्लाह, जिस के गर्दन और पूँछ के बाल पीले हों (वोल्लाहस्त्वयमेव स्यात् पाण्डुकेशरवालधिरिति हेम-चन्द्रः)। इन घोडों के लिये सन् १८८६ में छपा नं० ५७४ बङ्गाल एशियाटिक सोसाइटी के अश्व-वैद्यक के तीसरे अध्याय के १००—११० श्लोक और टीका देखो॥ तीख = तीक्ष्ण = तेज। तुखार = घोडा। चाँडि = चण्ड = प्रचण्ड = बडे बली। बाँके = वङ्क = टर्रे = कठिन। तरपहिँ = तडपहिँ = तडपते हैं। तवहिँ = तपहिँ = तपते हैं, जैसे आग के ऊपर पैर पड जाने से, पैर को छन छन पटकते हैं॥ अगुमन = अगाडी = पहले। डोलहिँ = डोलते हैं = चलते हैं। बाग = रास, जिसे पकड कर घोडे को हाँकते हैं, जो कि लगाम में लगाई जाती है, हिन्दुस्तानी सूत की, बिलायती चमडे की, होती है। (इसी बाग में जो घोडे को बाँधने के लिये डोरी लगा देते हैं, उसे बाग-डोर कहते हैं। उसाँस = उच्छ्वास = यहाँ, घोडे के चलाने के लिये "हूँ", ऐसा इशारा॥ साँस = श्वास, यहाँ इशारा॥ रिस = रोष से। लोह = लगाम। चबाहीं = चबाते हैं। भाँजहिँ = भाँजते हैं = फेरते हैं। सीस = शीर्ष = शिर॥ उपराहीं = ऊपर-ही = ऊपर॥ रथ-वाह = रथ हाँकने-वाला = सूत = कोच-वान = गाडी-वान॥ पलक = पलक भंजनें में जो काल॥

फिर राज-द्वार पर घोडे बँधे हैं, उन के जैसे रङ्ग हैं, उन का क्या वर्णन करूँ॥ कोई लीले और समुंद हैं, जिन की चाल को जग (जगत् के सब लोग) जानता है,

= पीढा = सिंहासन। मेद = मद = मृग-मद। अपूरी = भर-पूर। माँझ = मध्य। ऊँच = उच्च। इँदरासन = इन्द्रासन। बिगसद् = विकसती है॥

फिर बैठी ज़ुई राज-सभा को (जो) देखा, (तो समझ पडा, कि) जानें। (देव-राज) इन्द्र-सभा के ऊपर दृष्टि (डीठी) पड गई॥ धन्य वह राजा है, जिस ने ऐसी सभा की रचना की। जान पडता है, कि फुलवारी फूली है। लाल, पीले, हरे, इत्यादि विचित्र विचित्र वस्त्रों से सजे ज़ुए सभ्य राजा लोग, जो बैठे हैं, वे सभा-रूपी फुल-वारी के फूल ऐसे जान पडते हैं॥ सब राजा मुकुट बाँध कर बैठे हैं। (मुकुट बाँधने से गन्धर्व-सेन की प्रतिष्ठा सूचित होती है, अर्थात् उस सभा में किसी को अधिकार नहीं, कि मुकुट के विना प्रवेश करे)। जिन सब के (साथ) सेना है, और डंका बजता है॥ और बडे रूपवन्त हैं, ललाट कान्ति (मणि) से दिप रहा है, माथे पर (राज) छत्र है, ऐसे सब राजा (अपने अपने) पाट (सिंहासन) पर बैठे हैं॥ (उस घडी ऐसी शोभा जान पडती है) मानों सरो-वर में कमल खिले हैं। (सभा सरो-वर, और स्व-स्व-वेष-धारी सभ्य कमल समझो)। ऐसे सभा का स्वरूप देख कर मन भूल जाता है, अर्थात् और कामों को छोड कर उसी के दर्शन में अटक जाता है॥ (उस सभा में) पान, कर्पूर, और मृग-मद (मेद) जो कस्तूरी, इन की सुगन्ध (बास) सर्वत्र भर गई है॥ सभा के मध्य (सब से) ऊँचा इन्द्र के आसन सा आसन (सिंहासन) सजा है। तिस पर गन्धर्व-सेन राजा बैठा है॥

तिस का (गन्धर्व-सेन का) छत्र आकाश में लगा है, आप स्वयं जैसे सूर्य, तैसे तपता है, और (उस सूर्य के तेज से) सभा कमल सी खिली ज़ुई है। (राजा के) माँथे में बडा प्रताप (बडी कान्ति) है॥४७॥

चउपाई।

साजा राज-मँदिर कबिलासू। सोनइ कर सब पुहुमि अकासू॥
सात खंड धउराहर साजा। उहइ सँवारि सकइ अस राजा॥
हीरा ईंटि कपूर गिलावा। अउ नग लाइ सरग लेइ लावा॥
जावँत सबइ उरेह उरेही। भाँति भाँति नग लागेउ वे-ही॥
भा कटाउ सब अनवन भाँती। चितर होत गा पाँतिन्ह पाँती॥

लाग खंभ मनि मानिक जरे। जनु दीआ दिन आछहिँ बरे॥
देखि धउरहर कइ उँजिआरा। छपि गा चाँद सुरुज अउ तारा॥

दोहा।

सुने सात बइकुंठ जस तस साजे खँड सात।
बीहर बीहर भाउ तस खँड खँड ऊपर जात॥ ४८॥

गिलावा = गारा। उरेह = उल्लेख = चित्र = मूर्त्ति। कटाउ = कटाव। बीहर बीहर = अलग अलग। भाउ = भाव॥

राज-मन्दिर (राजा का मन्दिर) कैलास के ऐसा सजा है। उस की भूमि (नीचे का तल), और छत (ऊपर का भाग = आकाश), सब सोने की है॥ (उस मन्दिर में) सात खण्ड (सात-मजिला) का धरहरा (ध्रुव-हर) सजा है। वही ऐसा राजा है, कि ऐसा (धरहरा) बना सकता है॥ वह धरहरा हीरे की ईंट, और कपूर के गारे से बना है, और नगों को लगा कर उस धरहरे को ले कर स्वर्ग तक लगा दिया है, अर्थात् बडा ऊंचा बनाया है॥ जितनी हाथी, घोडे, पशु, पच्छी, देवता, इत्यादि की मूर्त्ति हैं, सब उस में उरेही हैं (खींची ऊई हैं), और उन में (वे-ही) तरह तरह के (जिस जिस अङ्ग में जिस जिस वर्णके उचित हैं) नग लगे हैं॥ (उस धरहरे में) और भी अनुपम वा अनेक (३७वें दोहे की ५वीं चौपाई को देखो) भाँति के कटाव भये हैं, जिन कटाव से पाँती पाँती में चित्र होते गये हैं॥ माणिक्य-मणि (लाल मणि) से जडे खंभे लगे हैं। (उन से ऐसा प्रकाश है), जानों दिन में अच्छी तरह से दीया (दीप) बरते हैं॥ धरहरे का प्रकाश (उँजेला = उँजिआरा) देख कर, चन्द्र, सूर्य, और तारा छिप गये, अर्थात् लज्जित हो कर कभीँ चन्द्र, कभीँ सूर्य, और कभीँ तारे अस्त के बहाने मुँह छिपा लेते हैं॥

जैसे सात वैकुण्ठ सुने जाते हैं, तैसे-ही उस धरहरे में सातो खण्ड सजे हैं, और तैसे-ही खण्ड खण्ड में ऊपर जाते अलग अलग भाव है, अर्थात् सातो खण्डों में भिन्न भिन्न सजाव, और भिन्न भिन्न (देखने से) आनन्दानुभव होता है, जैसा कि सातो वैकुण्ठ में है। (यहाँ वैकुण्ठ से भूर्लोक, भुवर्लोक, स्वर्लोक, महर्लोक, जनलोक, तपोलोक और सत्यलोक समझो, न कि केवल विष्णु का स्थान, जो कि एक-ही है)॥

चौथी चौपाई के उत्तरार्द्ध में, 'नग लागेउ वे-ही' के स्थान में, लेखक-प्रमाद से 'नग लाग उवेही' यह अशुद्ध पाठ समझना चाहिये॥ 'उवेही' कोई हिन्दी विशेषण शब्द नहीं है। यदि उबहना (=पानी को उलचना) क्रिया से भूत काल में उबाही के स्थान में तुक मिलाने के लिये उवेही मानें, तो अर्थसङ्गति होती है॥ ४८॥

चउपाई।

बरनउँ राज-मँदिर रनिवाँसू। अछरिन भरा जानु कबिलासू॥
सोरह सहस पदुमिनी रानी। एक एक तइँ रूप बखानी॥
अति सु-रूप अउ अति सु-कुवाँरी। पान फूल के रहहिँ अधारी॥
तिन्ह ऊपर चंपावति रानी। महा सुरूप पाट परधानी॥
पाट बइठि रह किए सिँगारू। सब रानी ओहि करहिँ जोहारू॥
निति नउ रंग सु-रंग मँ सोई। परथम बयस न सरबरि कोई॥
सकल दीप मँह चुनि चुनि आनी। तिन्ह मँह दीपक बारह बानी॥

दोहा।

कुवँरि बतीस-उ लक्खिनी अस सब माँह अनूप।
जावँत सिंघल-दीप मँह सबइ बखानहिँ रूप॥ ४९॥

इति सिंघल-दीप-बरनन-खंड॥ २॥

रनिवाँसू = रनिवास = रानियों का निवास-स्थान। अछरिन = अछरी का बहु-वचन, अछरी = अप्सरा। पदुमिनी = पद्मिनी। सु-कुवाँरी = सु-कुमारी। अधारी = आधार। चंपावति = चम्पावती। परधानी = प्रधान। जोहारू = जीव हार, जीव हार = हे हार जीव, अर्थात् हे गले के हार आप जीवें, यहाँ जीव और हार दो संस्कृत शब्द मिल कर हिन्दी का यह जोहार बना है, जिस का अब प्रणाम अर्थ है। मँ = मैं = मँह। परथम = प्रथम। बयस = वयः = अवस्था। बारह बानी = बारह वर्ण = बारहो सूर्य के वर्ण, अर्थात् द्वादशादित्य की कला। कुवँरि = कुमारी। लक्खिनी = लक्षणी॥

राज-मन्दिर में जो रनिवास है, उस का वर्णन करता हूं। जानों अप्सराओं से भरा कैलास है॥ उस रनिवास में, सोरह हजार पद्मिनी रानी हैं, जो कि एक से एक

(बढ कर) रूप में बखानी जाती हैं ॥ वे रानियाँ अत्यन्त सुन्दरी (सु-रूप) और अति कोमल (सु-कुवाँरी) हैं, (केवल) पान और फूल के आधार से रहती हैं, (अन्न नहीं खातीं) ॥ तिन सब के ऊपर रानी चम्पावती है, जो कि महा सु-रूपवती और पाट (सिंहासन) में प्रधान है, अर्थात् प्रथम-विवाहिता है, जिसे अधिकार है, कि राजा के संग सिंहासन पर बैठे ॥ वह शृङ्गार को किये अपने आसन पर बैठी रहती है, और सब रानियाँ उस को प्रणाम (जोहार) करती हैं ॥ वह (सोई) नित्य नये रङ्ग सुरङ्ग में रहती है, अर्थात् नित्य नित्य नये नाच रंग में आनन्द करती है। उस की प्रथम अवस्था है, अर्थात् वह प्रौढा है, और उस की बराबरी में (सदृश) कोई नहीं है ॥ राजा गन्धर्व-सेन सब दीपों में से जिन जिन रानियों को चुन चुन कर ले आये हैं, तिन में (चम्पावती) द्वादश वर्ण दीपक है, अर्थात् प्रज्वलित दीप-शिखा सी है ॥

वह कुवँरि (चम्पावती) बत्तीसों लक्षण से युत है, और इस प्रकार से सब रानियों में अनुपम है, और सिंहल-दीप में जितने लोग हैं, सब उस के रूप का बखान करते हैं ॥४९॥

बृहत्संहिता के स्त्री-लक्षण अध्याय में स्त्रियों के ये बत्तिस लक्षण लिखे हैं ।—

पैर का नख तामे के ऐसा १। पाद-पृष्ठ कूर्म के पृष्ठ सदृश २। गुल्फ (घुट्ठी) सुन्दर गोल देखने लायक ३। पैर की अङ्गुलियाँ आपस में सटी हुईं ४। पाद-तल (तरवा) कमल के ऐसा चमकीला, उस में अङ्कुश, मत्स्य, असि इत्यादि के चिन्ह हों ५। जङ्घा (पैर के ऊपर के भाग) दोनों बराबर, और गोल जिन में नस ऊपर न उभड आई हों ६। जानु (जङ्घे के ऊपर के भाग) दोनों बराबर और सुढार ७। ऊरु (जानु के ऊपर के भाग जो नितम्ब से मिले रहते हैं) आपस में सटे हाथी के सूँड ऐसे ८। भग बडी पीपल के पत्त ऐसी ९। पेंडू (भग के ऊपर का भाग) कूर्म-पृष्ठ के ऐसा ऊंचा १०। भग के बीच का भाग छिपा हुआ ११। नितम्ब (चूतर) फैले, मांस से भरे स्थूल १२। नाभी गम्भीर और दहिनी ओर घूमी हुई १३। नाभी के ऊपर का भाग विना रोम का और तीन वलि से संयुत १४। स्तन, समान, गोल, घन और कठोर १५। पेट, मृदु विना रोम का १६। ग्रीवा (गला) शङ्ख के ऐसी १७। ओठ जपा (उडहुल) फूल के ऐसे लाल और पुष्ट १८। दांत कुन्द के कली से १९। बोलना, स्पष्ट और मीठा २०। सुन्दर नासिका जिस के दोनों पूरे बराबर हों २१। आँख नीले कमल सी २२। भौंहें द्वितीया के चन्द्र सी टेढी जो आपस में मिली न हों २३। विना रोम का ललाट, अर्धचन्द्र के

सदृश न नीचा न ऊँचा २४। कान कोमल, पुष्ट और दोनों समान २५। बाल चिकने, नीले और घुघुराले २६। शिर चारो ओर से सुडौल २७। हथेली, शङ्ख, छत्र इत्यादि से युत २८। कलाई सुडौल और पतली २९। बाहु खिले कमल से चमकीले ३०। मणिबन्धन, जहाँ कङ्कण पहिना जाता है, कुछ नीचे की ओर दबा हुआ ३१। हाथ की अङ्गुलियाँ पतली जिन के पोर सुडौल हों ३२।

योग के ग्रन्थों में, विशेष कर के गोरखनाथियों के ग्रन्थों में, और-ही महा-पुरुषों के बत्तीस लक्षण लिखे हैं, वे लक्षण स्त्रियों में भी होने से महा-भाग्यवती स्त्री कहाती हैं॥

उन बत्तीसों के नाम नीचे लिखे हैं।

निरालम्ब १। निर्भ्रम २। निर्वास ३। निःशब्द ४। ज्ञान-परीक्षा में॥ निर्मोह ५। निर्बन्ध ६। निःशङ्क ७। निर्विषय ८। विवेक-परीक्षा में॥ सर्वाङ्गी ९। सावधान १०। सत्य ११। सार-ग्राही १२। विचार-परीक्षा में॥ निःप्रपञ्च १३। निस्तरङ्ग १४। निर्द्वन्द्व १५। निर्लेप १६। निरालम्ब-परीक्षा में॥ अयाचक १७। अवाञ्छक १८। अमान १९। स्थिर २०। सन्तोष-परीक्षा में॥ शुचि २१। संयमी २२। शान्त २३। श्रोता २४। शील-परीक्षा में॥ सुहृत् २५। शीतल २६। सुखद २७। स्वभाव २८। सहज-परीक्षा में॥ लय २९। लक्ष्य ३०। ध्यान ३१। समाधि ३२। शून्य-परीक्षा में॥ बनारस संस्कृत-कालेज के पुस्तकालय में गोरक्ष-कृत ग्रन्थ के उत्तरार्द्ध में ४४ पत्र में ये बत्तीसो लक्षण लिखे हैं॥

इति सिंहल-द्वीप-वर्णनं नाम द्वितीयं खण्डं समाप्तम्॥ २॥

अथ जनम-खंड ॥ ३ ॥

चउपाई ।

चंपावति जो रूप सँवारी । पदुमावति चाहइ अउतारी ।
भइ चाहइ असि कथा सलोनी । मेटि न जाइ लिखी जसि होनी ॥
सिंघल-दीप भण्उ तब नाऊँ । जो अस दिआ दीन्ह तेहि ठाऊँ ॥
प्रथम सो जोति गगन निरमई । पुनि सो पिता माँथइ मनि भई ॥
पुनि वह जोति मात घट आई । तेहि ओदर आदर बहु पाई ॥
जस अउधानु पूर भा तासू । दिन दिन हिअइ होइ परगासू ॥
जस अंचल झीनइ महँ दीआ । तस उँजिआर देखावइ हीआ ॥

दोहा ।

सोनइ मँदिर सँवारहीँ अउ चंदन सब लीप ।
दिआ जो मनि सिउ-लोक महँ उपना सिंघल-दीप ॥ ५० ॥

सलोनी = लावण्य = सुन्दर । दिआ = दीप । जोति = ज्योतिः-स्वरूप = देवी कला । निरमई = निर्माण किया । मात = माता । घट = शरीर । ओदर = उदर = पेट । अउधानु = अवधान = गर्भाधान = गर्भ-स्थिति । परगासू = प्रकाश । झीनइ = झीने में = पतले में = महीन में = झाँझर । उपना = उत्पन्न हुआ ॥

जो (जिस) ईश्वर ने चम्पावती के रूप को बनाया, वही पद्मावती को अवतारने (उत्पन्न करने) चाहता है॥ और (जिस पद्मावती के कारण) ऐसी सलोनी कथा भई चाहती है, कवि कहता है कि, कहाँ पद्मावती का स्थान और कहाँ उस के कथा का प्रचार, यह आश्चर्य है, सो जैसी होनी (कर्म में) लिखि है सो मिटाई नहीं जाती, अर्थात् वह अमिट है॥ ईश्वर ने जो तिस स्थान में ऐसा दिआ (दीपक) दिआ, तभी सिंहल-दीप का नाम भया (ऊआ), अर्थात् पद्मावती के जन्म से तब वह प्रसिद्ध ऊआ॥ प्रथम ईश्वर जो है, सो आकाश में उस ज्योति (प्रकाश-रूप दैवी कला) को निर्माण किया (बनाया)। फिर वह ज्योति (शरीर में वायुद्वारा प्रवेश कर) पिता (राजा गन्धर्व-सेन) के माथे में मणि (वीर्य) ऊई। भारतवर्षीय विद्वानों के मत से वीर्य का स्थान मस्तक है॥ फिर वही ज्योति (मैथुन द्वारा) माता (चम्पावती) के शरीर में आई, और तिस के (माता के) उदर में (वह ज्योति) बऊत आदर को पाई (अनेक सुखोपभोग से), अर्थात् सुन्दर अन्नपानादि के सेवन से वह ज्योति पुष्ट ऊई॥ जैसा जैसा तिस का (पद्मावती का) गर्भाधान पूरा होने लगा, तैसा तैसा दिन दिन (चम्पावती के) हृदय में प्रकाश होने लगा॥ जैसे झीने वस्त्राञ्चल में दीये का उँजेला झलकता है, तैसे-ही (माता के) हृदय में वह ज्योति उँजेले को देखाती है॥

सब (सिंहल के वासी) (अपने अपने) मन्दिर को सोने से सँवारते हैं, और चन्दन से लीपतें हैं। जो शिवलोक (कैलास) में मणि-रूपी दीया (दीप) था, सो (आकर) सिंहल-दीप में उत्पन्न ऊआ॥ ५०॥

चउपाई।

भए दस मास पूरि भइ घरी। पदुमावति कनिआ अउतरी॥
जानउँ सुरुज किरिनि हुति काढी। सुरुज करा घाटि वह बाढी॥
भा निसि महँ दिन कर परगास्। सब उँजिआर भएउ कबिलास्॥
इते रूप मूरति परगटी। पूनिउँ ससि सो खीन होइ घटी॥
घटतहि घटत अमावस भई। दुइ दिन लाज गाडि भुइँ गई॥
पुनि जो उठी दूइज होइ नई। निहकलंक बिधि ससि निरमई॥
पदुम-गंध बेधा जग बासा। भवँर पतंग भए चहुँ पासा॥

(जन्म के अनन्तर) छट्ठी की रात ऊई। (लोगों ने) छट्ठी का सुख मनाया। (ज्यौतिषियों के मत से ब्रह्मा प्राणी का शुभाशुभ कर्म छट्ठी के दिन लिखता है, इस लिये उस के प्रातःकाल से तब ज्यौतिषी लोग बालक के शुभाशुभ का विचार करते हैं।

ललाटपट्टे लिखिता विधात्रा षष्ठीदिने या ऽक्षरमालिका च।
तां जन्मपत्री प्रकटीकरोति दीपो यथा वस्तु घनान्धकारे॥

यह श्लोक जन्मपत्री की प्रशंसा में प्रसिद्ध है)। खेल कूद से वह रात बीती। (छट्ठी के दिन स्त्रियाँ रात भर गाना बजाना करती हैं, और बच्चे की माँ बडी सावधानी से रहती है, जिस में भूत प्रेत इत्यादि की बाधा बच्चे को न हो। यह कहावत प्रसिद्ध है, कि कृष्ण की माता यशोदा ने छट्ठी के रात कुछ तिरछा रख कर कृष्ण को दूध पिलाया, इसी से कृष्ण की एक आँख तिरछी हो गई)। प्रातःकाल ऊआ, पण्डित लोग आये, पुरान (फल कहने की पुस्तक) को काढ कर (निकाल कर) जन्म का अर्थ किये, अर्थात् कैसी घडी में जन्म ऊआ इस का विचार करने लगे॥ (विचार से जान पडा, कि) तिस का (पद्मावती का) उत्तम घडी में जन्म ऊआ। (पण्डितों ने कहा, कि) कन्या नहीं ऊई, भूमि में चन्द्र का उदय ऊआ, जिस से आकाश दीप्त हो गया (उज्ज्वलित हो गया)। जग में (ब्रह्मा ने) कन्या राशि का उदय किया है, अर्थात् इस के जन्म समय में चन्द्रमा कन्या राशि में था, इस लिये इस का दिया ऊआ नाम, अर्थात् शास्त्रोक्त राशि-नाम "पद्मावती" ऐसा ऊआ॥ (कन्या राशि में उत्तरफाल्गुनी का तीन चरण, हस्त और चित्रा का आधा होता है, जिन के क्रम से टो, प, पी, पू, ष, ण, ट, पे, पो ये अक्षर हैं। पकारादि नाम होने से उत्तरफाल्गुनी नक्षत्र के तीसरे चरण में कन्या राशि का तीन अंश बीस कला बीत जानेँ पर पद्मावती का जन्म ऊआ)। मानों सूर्य और पारस-पाषाण से संयोग ऊआ, इस लिये किरण जम कर (किरण समेत) हीरा नग उत्पन्न ऊआ। (सूर्य राजा गन्धर्व-सेन, पारस चम्पावती दोनों के संयोग से किरण समेत, अर्थात् कान्तियुत हीरा नग पद्मावती ऊई)। तिन से (पद्मावती से) भी अधिक (ज्योति में) पदार्थ की कला, अर्थात् उत्तम पदार्थों का तत्त्व रूप अंश, योग्य (जोग), और निर्मल रतन उत्पन्न ऊआ है। (रतन से ज्यौतिषियों ने सङ्केत से रत्न सेन को बताया।) सिंहल-दीप में इस का अवतार ऊआ, और जम्बू-दीप में जा कर यमालय में जायगी, अर्थात् मरेगी॥

पण्डित लोग कहते हैं कि, यह कन्या सिंहल-द्वीप में वैसी-ही उत्पन्न ऊई है जैसे बत्तीसो लक्षण के साथ अयोध्या में राम। जैसे रूप (राम के रूप) को देख कर रावण लुभा गया उसी प्रकार इस पद्मावति के रूप को देख कर सब भूल गये, जैसे दीपक को देख कर पतङ्ग॥ ५२॥ ३२ सो लक्षणों के लिये ४९ वें दोहे की टीका देखो।

चउपाई।

अही जनम-पतरी सो लिखी। देइ असीस बहुरे जोतिखी॥
पाँच बरिस महँ भई सो बारी। दीन्ह पुरान पढइ बइसारी॥
भइ पदुमावति पंडित गुनी। चहू खंड के राजन्ह सुनी॥
सिंघल-दीप राज घर बारी। महा सुरूप दई अउतारी॥
एक पदुमिनि अउ पंडित पढी। दहुँ केइ जोग दई असि गढी॥
जा कहँ लिखी लच्छि घर होनी। सो असि पाउ पढी अउ लोनी॥
सपत दीप के बरइ ओनाहीँ। उतर न पावहिँ फिरि फिरि जाहीँ॥

दोहा।

राजा कहइ गरब सउँ हउँ रे इँदर सिउ-लोक।
को सरि मो सउँ पावई का सउँ करउँ बरोक॥ ५३॥

अही = आसीत् = थी। जनम-पतरी = जन्मपत्री। बहुरे = फिरे = लौटे। जोतिखी = ज्यौतिषी = गणक। बरिस = वर्ष। बारी = बालिका = कन्या। बइसारी = बैठाया। दहुँ = क्या जानें = देखें। लच्छि = लक्ष्मी। लोनी = लावण्यता से भरी = सुन्दरी। बरइ = वर लोग = विवाह करने-वाले। उतर = उत्तर। बरोक = बरेखी = बरच्छा = वरपरीक्षा = जिस से विवाह करना होता है, उसे कुछ दे कर, और विवाह का नियम कर, उसे वचन-बन्ध करते हैं; फिर विवाह चाहे जब हो, परन्तु वह दूसरी जगह विवाह नहीं कर सकता। यह रीति विवाह में सब से पहले भारतवर्ष में क्या नीच क्या उच्च कुल सर्वत्र होती है। देश विशेष से इस रीति के बरेखी, बरच्छा, सगाई, टेंका इत्यादि ये अनेक नाम हैं॥

जैसी जन्म-पची थी सो ज्यौतिषियों ने लिखा, और असीस (आशीर्वाद) दे कर (अपने घर) लौट गये॥ जब वह (सो) कन्या पाँचवें वर्ष में ऊई, अर्थात् जब पद्मावती को पाँचवाँ वर्ष लगा, तब पुराण पढने के लिये (गुरु के यहाँ) बैठाय दिया (उन के पिता ने)। ज्यौतिष-फलित की आज्ञा है कि बालक को जब पाँचवाँ वर्ष लगे तब अक्षरारम्भ कराना चाहिए, इसी लिये कवि ने पाँचवें वर्ष का नाम लिया है॥ (पृथ्वी के) चारो खण्ड के राजाओं ने सुना कि, पद्मावती (पढ लिख कर) पण्डित और गुणी ऊई॥ सिंहल-दीप के राजा के घर में देव (ईश्वर) ने महा सुन्दरी कन्या (बारी) का अवतार दिया॥ एक तो (स्वयं वह) पद्मिनी, दूसरे पढी पण्डित, क्या जानें ईश्वर ने ऐसी सुन्दरी को किस के योग्य गढा (रचा) है॥ जिस के घर मे लक्ष्मी का होना (कर्म में) लिखा है, सो ऐसी पढी और सुन्दरी (लोनी) को पता है॥ सातो दीप के वर लोग (विवाह करने के लिये) झुंकते हैं (ओनाहीं), परन्तु उत्तर नहीं पाते हैं, (लाचार हो कर घर) फिर फिर जाते हैं॥

राजा (गन्धर्व-सेन) गर्व से कहता है कि, अरे मैं शिव-लोक का इन्द्र (शिव) ऊं, मुझ से कौन समता (सरि) को पाता है, अर्थात् मेरी बराबरी कौन करता है; किस से मैं बरेखी करूं॥ रीति है कि विवाह, वैर, और प्रीति समान में सोहती है। सो राजा अपने समान किसी को नहीं पाता है, जिस से कि सम्बन्ध करे; इसी लिये किसी को कुछ उत्तर नहीं देता। अन्त में लाचार हो कर वर-लोग फिर फिर जाते हैं॥ ५३॥

चउपाई।

बारह बरिस माँह भइ रानी। राजइ सुना सँजोग सयानी॥
सात खंड धउराहर तासू। सेा पदुमिनि कहँ दीन्ह निवासू॥
अउ दीन्ही सँग सखी सहेली। जो सँग करहिँ रहसि रस केली॥
सबइ नउलि पिअ संग न सेाईं। कवँल पास जनु बिगसी कोईं॥
सुआ एक पदुमावति ठाऊँ। महा-पँडित हीरामनि नाऊँ॥
दई दीन्ह पंखिहि असि जोती। नयन रतन मुख मानिक मोती॥
कंचन बरन सुआ अति लोना। मानउँ मिला सोहागहि सोना॥

दोहा।

रहहिँ एक सँग दुअउ पढहिँ सासतर बेद।
बरम्हा सीस डोलावई सुनत लाग तस भेद ॥ ५४ ॥

सँजोग = संयोग = पति-संयोग। सयानी = बडी। सहेली = साथ रहने-वाली। नउलि = नवल = नई। बिगसी = विकसित हुई। कोईं = कुमुदिनी। सुआ = शुक = सुग्गा। ठाऊँ = ठावँ = स्थान। हीरामनि = हीरा-मणि। सासतर = शास्त्र। बरम्हा = ब्रह्मा। भेद = अन्तर = फर्क।

बारहवेँ वर्ष मेँ जब रानी (पद्मावती) भई, अर्थात् पद्मावती को जब बारहवाँ वर्ष लगा, तब राजा (गन्धर्व-सेन) ने सुना कि पद्मावती (पति के) संयोग लायक सयानी हुई॥ इस लिये तिस का (गन्धर्व-सेन का) जो सात खण्ड का धरहरा था, सो पद्मिनी (पद्मावती) को निवास-स्थान दिया, अर्थात् आज्ञा दिया कि, आज से पद्मिनी धरहरे पर रहे (एकान्त समझ कर धरहरे पर रहने के लिये राजा ने आज्ञा दिया, जिस मेँ पर-पुरुष की दृष्टि न पडे), और संग मेँ साथ रहने-वाली सखियोँ को दिया (जिस मेँ पद्मावती का मन बहला रहे उदास न हो), जो कि संग मेँ आनन्द (रहसि) और रस लिये क्रीडा (रस-केलि) करती हैँ॥ ये सहेलियाँ सब नई हैँ, और पति के सङ्ग सोई नहीँ हैँ, अर्थात् सब पद्मावती के समान अनूढा हैँ। उन सहेलियोँ की ऐसी शोभा है, जानोँ कमल के संग कोईँ खिली हुईँ। (कमल पद्मावती और कोईँ सहेली सब हैँ)॥ पद्मावती के स्थान (पास) मेँ एक सुग्गा है, जो कि महा-पण्डित है और जिस का नाम हीरा-मणि है॥ देव ने पची को ऐसी ज्योति दिया है, कि आँख तो रत्न, और मुख माणिक्य और मोती है, अर्थात् मुख का वर्ण माणिक्य (लाल मणि), और मुक्ता के ऐसा है॥ वह कञ्चन (सुवर्ण) वर्ण (बरन) का शुक अति सुन्दर (लोना) है, मानोँ सोहागा मेँ सोना मिला है (सोहागे के मिलने से सोने का रङ्ग और बढ चढ जाता है)॥

दोनोँ (पद्मावती और हीरा-मणि) एक संग रहते हैँ, और शास्त्र, वेद को पढते हैँ। उन के पढने को सुनते-ही तैसा भेद (हृदय मेँ) लग जाता है, अर्थात् हृदय मेँ उन का पढना ऐसा चुभ जाता है, कि (प्रेम से विकल हो कर) ब्रह्मा शिर को डुलाने लगता है, अर्थात् धन्य-वाद-मुद्रा प्रगट करता है॥ ५४ ॥

चउपाई ।

भइ उनंत पदुमावति बारी। धुज धवरी सब करी सँवारी॥
जग बेधा तेहि अंग सो बासा। भवँर आइ लुबुधे चहुँ पासा॥
बेनी नाग मलय-गिरि पइठी। ससि माँथहि होइ दूइज बइठी॥
भउँहइँ धनुख साधि सर फेरी। नयन कुरंगि भूलि जनु हेरी॥
नासिक कीर कवँल मुख सोहा। पदुमिनि रूप देखि जग मोहा॥
मानिक अधर दसन जनु हीरा। हिअ हुलसइ कुच कनक जँभीरा॥
केहरि लंक गवँन गज हारे। सुर नर देखि माँथ भुइँ धारे॥

दोहा ।

जग कोइ दिसिटि न आवई अछरी नयन अकास।
जोगि जती सनिआसी तप साधहिँ तेहि आस॥५५॥

उनंत = उन्नत = ऊँची = जवान। धुज = ध्वजा। धवरी = धवल = उज्ज्वल। करी = कली। कुरंगि = हरिनी = कुरङ्गी। कीर = शुक। अधर = ओठ। दसन = दशन = दाँत। हुलसइ = हुलास करता है = उल्लसित होता है। केहरि = केहरी = सिंह। लंक = लङ्क = कटि = कमर। गवँन = गमन = गति। जोगि = योगी। जती = यती। सनिआसी = सन्यासी। आस = आशा = उम्मेद॥

पद्मावती कन्या (बारी) जवान (उनंत) हुई, (ईश्वर ने) उज्ज्वल (धवरी) ध्वजा-रूप सब कलियोँ को, अर्थात् पद्मावती के सब अङ्ग को, सँवारा (सुडौल किया)। यहाँ बारी, कन्या और बगीचा, दोनोँ अर्थ बैठने के लिये (करी) कली का प्रयोग किया है॥ तिस के (पद्मावती के) अङ्ग का जो वास (सुगन्ध) है, सो जग को बेध दिया, अर्थात् अङ्ग की सुगन्धि सारे जगत् में फैल गई। इसी कारण चारो ओर (चहुँ पास) से भौँरे आ कर लुभाय गये॥ नाग-रूप बेनी (शिर का गुथा हुआ सर्पाकार केश) मलयगिरि में पैठ गई (मलयगिरि से पद्मावती का सुगन्धित शिर समझो)। चन्द्रमा दुइज का हो कर माथे पर बैठा, अर्थात् माथा ऐसा चमकने लगा जैसे द्वितीया का चन्द्र॥ भौँहेँ धनुष साध कर शर (वाण) फेरने लगीँ, अर्थात् भौँहेँ धनुष सदृश और कटाच शर से हो गये। नयनोँ की शोभा ऐसी हो गई जानोँ भूल कर, अर्थात् अपने

साथियों से बिछुड कर, हरिनी ने हेरी है, साथियों को ढूँढ रही है॥ हरिनी जब साथियों से बिछुड जाती है, तब चारो ओर आँखें फेर फेर कर देखती है, उस समय उस की स्वाभाविक चञ्चल और बडी आँखें और भी चञ्चल और बडी हो जाती हैं, इस लिये कवि की उक्ति है, कि पद्मावती की आँखें अत्यन्त बडी और चञ्चल हो गईं॥ कीर ऐसी नासिका और कमल सा मुख सोहने लगा। पद्मिनी का रूप देख कर जग मोह गया॥ जानों ओठ माणिक्य और दाँत हीरे हैं। हृदय (छाती) में कुच (स्तन) कनक (सुवर्ण) के जम्बीर नीबू से झलसते हैं, अर्थात् सोहते हैं॥ कटि (लङ्क) से केहरी (सिंह) और गमन (गति) से गज (हाथी) हार गये, (ऐसे रूप को देख कर)। देवता (सुर) और मनुष्य (नर) भूमि में माथा धरते हैं, अर्थात् माथा टेकते हैं॥ अर्थात् पद्मावती को देवी कला समझ आदर से शिर को भूमि में टेक कर प्रणाम करते हैं॥

(पद्मावती के रूप के आगे) जग में कोई दृष्टि नहीं आता है, तिस पद्मावती की आशा से अप्सराओं के नयन आकाश में हैं, अर्थात् सदा उन की आँखें खुली रहती हैं। और योगी, यती, और सन्यासी तप साधते हैं॥ अप्सराओं की पलक नहीं भँजती। आँखें सदा खुली रहती हैं। यह उन की स्वाभाविक बनावट है। तहाँ कवि की उत्प्रेक्षा है, कि पद्मावती के रूप-दर्शन से तृप्ति नहीं होती, इसी लिये अप्सरायें अपनी आँख को आकाश में लगाये रहती हैं, अर्थात् सदा खोले रहती हैं॥ और योगी यती इत्यादि जो ईश्वर-दर्शन के लिये तप साधते हैं, तहाँ भी कवि की उत्प्रेक्षा है, कि तिस पद्मावती के दर्शन की आशा से वे लोग तप साधते हैं॥ ५५॥

चउपाई।

एक दिवस पदुमावति रानी। हीरामनि तइँ कहा सयानी॥
सुनु हीरामनि कहउँ बुझाई। दिन दिन मदन सतावइ आई॥
पिता हमार न चालइ बाता। चासहि बोलि सकइ नहिँ माता॥
देस देस के बर मोहि आवहिँ। पिता हमार न आँखि लगावहिँ॥
जोबन मोर भएउ जस गंगा। देह देह हम लागु अनंगा॥
हीरामनि तब कहा बुझाई। बिधि कर लिखा मेटि नहिँ जाई॥
अगिआ देउ देखउँ फिरि देसा। तोहि लायक बर मिलइ नरेसा॥

दोहा ।

जउँ लगि मइँ फिरि आऊँ मन चित धरहु निबारि ।
सुनत रहा कोइ दुरजन राजहि कहा बिचारि ॥ ५६ ॥

मदन = काम । सतावइ = सन्ताप देता है । चालइ = चलाता है । मोहि = मोह कर । अनङ्ग = काम । अगिआ = आज्ञा । निबारि = निवार्य = निवारण कर के । दुरजन = दुर्जन ।

एक दिन चतुर (सयानी) पद्मावती रानी ने हीरा-मणि से कहा कि, मैं बुझा कर (समझा कर) कहती हूँ, हे हीरामणि, तुम सुनो, (मुझे) मदन (काम-देव) आ कर दिन दिन सताता है ॥ हमारे पिता (विवाह के विषय में कुछ) बात ही नहीं चलाते हैं, चास (डर) से मेरी माता (पिता से) कुछ कह नहीं सकती ॥ (मेरी सुन्दरता पर) मोह कर देश देश के वर आते हैं, परन्तु हमारे पिता (उन को) आँख नहीं लगाते, अर्थात् उन्हें तुच्छ समझ आँख उठा कर देखते नहीं विवाह की क्या चर्चा है ॥ मेरा योवन ऐसा ऊआ है, जैसे गङ्गा, अर्थात् ऐसा बढ रहा है जैसे गङ्गा, और हमारे अङ्ग अङ्ग (देह देह) में काम (अनङ्ग) लग गया है ॥ इस पर तब समझा कर हीरा-मणि ने कहा, कि ब्रह्मा का लिखा मिटाया नहीं जाता वा मिट नहीं जाता ॥ तुम आज्ञा दो तो मैं देश देश फिर कर देखूँ कि, तेरे लायक नरेश (राजा) वर (कहाँ) मिलता है ॥

जब तक मै फिर कर आता हूँ, तब तक मन और चित्त को निवारण कर के धरो, अर्थात् मन और चित्त को रोक रक्खो । पद्मावती और हीरा-मणि का यह संवाद कोई दुर्जन सुनता रहा, सो उस ने विचार कर (सब वृत्तान्त) राजा से (गन्धर्व-सेन से) कहा ॥

मन, ग्यारहवीं इन्द्रिय है जो कि उभयात्मक है, अर्थात् ज्ञान, कर्म, दोनों में है । सङ्कल्प विकल्प करना इस का धर्म है । चित्त, आत्मा की चेतन शक्ति में साहाय्य करता है । आत्मा के सहायक मन, बुद्धि, चित्त और अहङ्कार हैं । बऊत से इन में से अहङ्कार को छोड देते हैं । कितने लोग मन-ही को प्रधान मानते हैं ॥

इस चौपाई में मदन, सतावई, हमार, आँखि लगावहिं, लायक यह ऐसे पद पडे हैं, जिन का प्रयोग अन्यच प्रायः कवि ने नहीं किया है । और यहाँ सातवीं चौपाई में पद्मावती से आज्ञा माँगना लिखा है, और १८० वें दोहे में पद्मावती का सुग्गे से पूछना यह सब प्रायः असङ्गति सा जान पडता है । और जहाँ हीरा-मणि पची नर को छोड

कोई दूसरा मनुष्य रहता ही न था तहाँ दुर्जन का पहुँचना और इन के बात चीत का सुनना यह भी असम्भव प्राय है, इन सब बातों से जान पडता है कि यह चौपाई चेपक है। बहुत पुस्तकों में यह पाई भी नहीं जाती ॥ ५६ ॥

चउपाई ।

राजइ सुना दिसिटि भइ आना । बुधि जो देइ सँग सुआ सयाना ॥
भएउ रजाएसु मारहु सूआ । सूर सुनाउ चाँद जहँ ऊआ ॥
सतुर सुआ के नाऊ बारी । सुनि धाए जस धाउ मँजारी ॥
तब लगि रानी सुआ छपावा । जब लगि आउ मँजारि न पावा ॥
पिता कि आएसु माँथइ मोरे । कहहु जाइ बिनवँइ कर जोरे ॥
पंखि न कोई होइ सुजानू । जानइ भुगुति कि जानु उडानू ॥
सुआ जो पढइ पढाए बयना । तेहि कित बुधि जेहि हिअइ न नयना ॥

दोहा ।

मानिक मोती देखि वह हिए न गिआन करेइ ।
दारिउँ दाख जानि कइ तब-हिँ ठोर भरि लेइ ॥ ५७ ॥

आना = अन्य । बुधि = बुद्धि । रजाएसु = राजाज्ञा । सूर = सूर्य । सुनाउ = सुनावता है । ऊआ = उदय हुआ । सतुर = शत्रु । नाऊ = नापित = नाई । बारी = जो उच्छिष्ट पत्तल उठाता है। मशाल ले कर उँजेला करने-वाला। धाए = दौडे। मँजारी = मार्जारी = बिलैया। आएसु = आज्ञा। बिनवँइ = विनती करती है। कर = हाथ। जोरे = मिलाये। पंखी = पची। सुजान = सुज्ञ = जान-कार। भुगुति = भुक्ति = भोजन। उडानू = उड्डयन = उडना। बयन = वचन। गिआन = ज्ञान। दारिउँ = दाडिम = अनार। दाख = द्राचा = अङ्गूर वा मुनक्का। ठोर = चोँच ॥

राजा (गन्धर्व-सेन) ने सुना कि (पद्मावती के) सङ्ग में जो चतुर तोता (सुआ) है, वह (पद्मावती को) बुद्धि देता है, अर्थात् सिखाता है, इस लिये (पद्मावती की) दृष्टि दूसरी हो गई, अर्थात् अब उसे पुरुष की इच्छा हुई है॥ (इस लिये) राजाज्ञा हुई (भई) कि तोते को मारो, (क्योँकि) जहाँ चन्द्र का उदय हुआ है, वहाँ सूर्य को

तोहि सेवा बिछुरन नहिँ आखउँ । पीँजर हिअइ घालि कइ राखउँ ॥
हउँ मानुस तूँ पंखि पिआरा । धरम पिरीति तहाँ को मारा ॥
का पिरीति तन माँह बिलाई । सेा पिरीति जिउ साथ जेा जाई ॥
पिरिति भार लेइ हिअइ न सेाचू । ओहि पंथ भल होइ कि पोचू ॥
पिरिति पहार भार जो काँधा । तेाहि कित छूट लाइ जिउ बाँधा ॥

दोहा ।

सुआ न रहइ खुरुकि जिउइ अब-हिँ काल सेा आउ ।
सतुर अहइ जो करिया कब-हुँ सेा बेारइ नाउ ॥ ५९ ॥

इति जनम खंड ॥ ३ ॥

उतर = उत्तर । मया = मौया = करुणा । किमि = कैसे । कया = काय = शरीर । परान = प्राण । परेवा = पारावत, यहाँ साधारण पक्षी । बिछुरन = विछुरण = विच्छेद = जुदाई । आखउँ = आखा करती हूँ = चालती हूँ, आखा एक जालीदार महीन वस्त्र वा चर्म से लगा ऊआ एक मेडरे-दार पात्र होता है, जिस मेँ मेाँटे आँटे को रख कर चालने से मैदा निकलता है। यह एक प्रकार की चलनी है। पीँजर = पञ्जर = पिँजडा । घालि = डाल कर । मानुस = मनुष्य । पंखी = पक्षी । पिआरा = प्रिय । धरम = धर्म । पिरीति = प्रीति । तन = तनु = शरीर । बिलाई = विलय होय = नाश हो जाय । सेाचू = शोच । पोचू = पोच = नीच = खराब, बुरा । पहार = प्रहार = पहाड । कित = कुतः = कहाँ । खुरुकि = खेाटका = खटका = संशय = डर । जिउइ = जीव मेँ। करिया = कर्णी = कर्णधार = पतवार पकडने-वाला मल्लाह । बेारइ = बेारता है = डुबा देता है । नाउ = नाव ॥

(तोते के कहने पर) रानी ने करुणा कर के उत्तर दिया, कि (हे हीरा-मणि) यदि जीव चला जाय तो (फिर) शरीर कैसे रहे, अर्थात् तूँ मेरे जीव के समान है, तेरे चले जाने से मेरी शरीर नहीँ रह सकती॥ इस बात को अगली चौपाई से स्पष्ट करती है, कि, हे हीरा-मणि, तूँ (मेरा) प्राण-पक्षी है, तेरी सेवा मेँ धोखा नहीँ लगा, अर्थात् मैँ ने तेरी सेवा मेँ धोखा नहीँ लगाया॥ (सो) तेरी सेवा मेँ बिछुडने को

नहीँ चालती हूँ, अर्थात् तेरी सेवा-रूपी शुद्ध पदार्थ मेँ बिछुडन-रूपी दुष्ट पदार्थ का कण चाल कर नहीँ मिलाया चाहती हूँ, किन्तु हृदय-रूपी पिँजडे मेँ (तुझे) डाल कर रखना चाहती हूँ॥ मैँ मनुष्य हूँ, तूँ मेरा प्रिय पची है, और (तेरे मेरे मेँ) धर्म की प्रीति है, तहाँ कौन (तुझे) मार सकता है, अर्थात् पाप कर्म करने के लिये, यदि किसी से दुष्ट प्रीति हो, तो वह अवश्य ईश्वर की अकृपा से मारा जाता है, और धर्म प्रीति मेँ तो यदि कोई मारने के लिये दुष्टता भी करे, तो ईश्वर आप सहायक हो बचा लेता है॥ वह प्रीति-ही क्या, जो (शरीर से उठी और फिर) शरीर मेँ लय हो गई। प्रीति वही है जो जीव के साथ जाय, अर्थात् जीवन्न पर्यन्त कभीँ न टूटे, दिन दिन बढती और पुष्ट होती जाय॥ प्रीति का भार ले कर (उठा कर), अर्थात् उठाने पर हृदय मेँ सोच नहीँ रहता, (चाहे) उसे (प्रीति) पथ मेँ भला हो वा बुरा॥ प्रीति-रूपी पहाड का भार जो काँधे पर है, वह कहाँ छूटे। (क्योँकि वह तो) जीव से लगा कर बाँधा है, अर्थात् जब जीव शरीर से छूट कर अलग हो जाय, तब प्रीति भी छूट सकती है, क्योँकि दोनोँ साथ बँधे हैँ॥

कवि कहता है, कि यद्यपि पद्मावती ने बहुत कुछ कहा परन्तु वह शुक नहीँ रहता, अर्थात् नहीँ रहने चाहता, क्योँकि वह (नाऊ-बारी-रूप) काल अभीँ आता है, यह खटका उस के जी मेँ समाय गया। (और मन मेँ वह शुक सोचता है, कि) जो कर्णधार शत्रु है, वह कभीँ (अवश्य) नाव को डुबा देता है॥ (यहाँ कर्णधार राजा गन्धर्व-सेन, और शुक और पद्मावती प्राणी हैँ जो प्रीति-रूपी नाव पर चढे हैँ)॥ ५९॥

कोई संस्कृत-आख्यान-पद से आखा को बना मानते हैँ, तब "आखउँ" का अर्थ "कहती हूँ" ऐसा कहते हैँ। तुझे सेवा (इस लिये) बिछुडने को नहीँ कहती हूँ। अर्थात् जो तूँ वनवास के लिये कहता है, उस को मैँ नहीँ कहतीँ, ऐसा तीसरी चौपाई का अर्थ करते हैँ॥

इति जन्म-खण्डं नाम तृतीय-खण्डं समाप्तम्॥ ३॥

अथ मानसरोदक-खंड । ४ ।

चउपाई ।

एक दिवस पूनिउँ तिथि आई । मानसरोदक चली अन्हाई ॥
पदुमावति सब सखी बोलाई । जनु फुलवारि सबइ चलि आई ॥
कोइ चंपा कोइ कुंद सहेली । कोइ सो केत करना रस-बेली ॥
कोइ सो गुलाल सुदरसन राते । कोइ बकउरि बकुचन बिहँसाते ॥
कोइ सो मउलसिरि पुहुपावती । कोइ जाही जूही सेवती ॥
कोई सोनिजरद कोइ केसर । कोइ सिंगार-हार नागेसर ॥
कोइ कूजा सतिबरग चँबेइली । कोई कदम सुरस रस-बेइली ॥

दोहा ।

चली सबइ मालति सँग फूली कवँल कुमोद ।
बेधि रहे गन गंधरब बास परिमलामोद ॥ ६० ॥

पूनिउँ = पूर्णिमा । मानसरोदक = मानसर-उदक, उदक = पानी । जिस का पानी मानसरोवर, जो कि मेरु पर है, उस के ऐसा हो । चंपा । कुंद । केत = केतकी । करना = एक प्रकार के नीँबू का पुष्प । रस-बेली = रस की लता, गुलाल = गुलाली रंग का गुलाब । सुदरसन = सुदर्शन । राते = लाल । बकउरि = बकावली । बकुचन = ढेर =

बकुत । मउलसिरि = मौलसिरी । पुहुपावती = पुष्पवती = फूल से भरी । जाही । जूही । सेवती । सोनिजरद = सोनजर्द, जिस का सोने-सा पीला फूल हो । केसर, सिंगार-हार = हर-शृङ्गार = पारिजात । नागेसर = नागेश्वर । कूजा = एक प्रकार का गुलाब । सतिबरग = सद्वर्ग = सौ पत्तियाँ जिस के फूल में हों अर्थात् हजारा । चँबेली = चँबेली । कदम = कदम्ब । सुरस = जिस में सुन्दर रस हों, रसबेइली = घनबेली । (३५ वें दोहे की टीका देखो) ॥

एक दिन पूर्णिमा तिथि आई, (पूर्णिमा पर्व समझ कर) (पद्मावती), जिस मानस-रोदक की प्रशंसा २१ वें दोहे में कर आये हैं, उस में स्नान करने को चली ॥ (स्नान करने के लिये) पद्मावती ने सब सखियों को बुलाया। (सुनते-ही) सब की सब चली आईं । (उस समय ऐसी शोभा ऊई), जानों (पद्मावती के निकट) फुलवारी चली आई । (यहाँ सखियों का झुण्ड फुलवारी है, उस में रङ्ग रङ्ग के वस्त्र आभूषण से सुशोभित सखियाँ फूल-सी जान पडती हैं)॥ उस झुण्ड-रूपी फुलवारी में कोई सखी चंपा, कोई सखी (सहेली) कुन्द, कोई जो केतकी है सो, कोई करना, कोई रस की लता (रस बेली), कोई जो गुलाल है सो, कोई लाल (राते) सुदर्शन, कोई खिले ऊए (बिहँसते) बकावली के ढेर (बकुचन), कोई फूल से लदी (पुहुपावती) मौल-सिरी, कोई जाही, कोई जूही, कोई सेवती, कोई सोनजर्द, कोई केसर, कोई हरसिंगार, कोई नागेश्वर, कोई कूजा, कोई सदवर्ग, कोई चँबेली, कोई सुरस कदम्ब, और कोई रस-बेली (घन-बेइली = मुँगरा बेला) हैं ॥

सब सखी मालती के संग चलीं, अर्थात् मालती-रूप पद्मावती के संग चलीं। सब सखी ऐसी फूली ऊई हैं, अर्थात् प्रसन्न हैं ॥ जैसे कमल और कुमुद (कोई) उन फूल-रूपी सखियों के आमोद परिमल (आनन्द देने-वाला पुष्प-रस, अर्थात् सुगन्ध-द्रव्य) के बास (सुगन्ध) राजा गन्धर्व-सेन के गण (नौकर चाकर जो कि रक्षा के लिये दूर दूर हैं) को बेध रहे हैं, अर्थात् उन के अन्तःकरण में प्रविष्ट हो रहे हैं ॥९०॥

चउपाई ।

खेलत मानसरोदक गईं । जाइ पालि पर ठाढी भईं ॥
देखि सरोवर रहसहिँ केली । पदुमावति सउँ कहहिँ सहेली ॥
अइ रानी मनु देखु बिचारी । एहि नइहर रहना दिन चारी ॥

जउ लहि आहि पिता कर राजू। खेलि लेहु जो खेलहु आजू ॥
पुनि सासुर हम गवँनब काली। कित हम कित यह सरवर पाली ॥
कित आउन पुनि. अपने हाथा। कित मिलि कइ खेलब एक-साथा ॥
सासु ननद बोलिन जिउ लेहीँ। दारुन ससुर न निसरइ देहीँ ॥

दोहा।

पिउ पिआर सब ऊपर पुनि सो करइ दहुँ काह।
दहुँ सुख राखइ की दुख दहुँ कस जनम निबाह ॥ ६१ ॥

पालि = प्रान्त = तट। रहसहिँ = क्रीडती हैँ = खेलती हैँ। नइहर = मातृगृह। आहि = है। सासुर = श्वशुरगृह। गवँनब = जायँगी। काली = कल। सरवर = सरोवर। आउन = आवना। सासु = श्वश्रू। ननद = ननन्दा = पति की बहिन। लेहीँ = लेँगी। दारुन = दारुण = कठिन। ससुर = श्वशुर। निसरइ = निकलने = निसरने। देहीँ = देगा। निबाह = निर्वाह ॥

सब सखियाँ खेलती हुई मानसरोदक गईँ, और जा कर पाली पर (किनारे पर) खडी हुईँ ॥ सरोवर को देख कर केलि (क्रीडा) से रहसती हैँ (खेल कूद करती हैँ), और सब सहेलियाँ पद्मावती से कहती हैँ ॥ कि अये (अइ) रानी, विचार कर मन मेँ देख। इस नैहर (बाप के घर) मेँ चार दिन का रहना है॥ (इस लिये) जब तक पिता का राज्य है, अर्थात् जब तक हम लोग पिता के अधिकार मेँ हैँ, तब तक जो आज खेलना हो खेल लो॥ फिर (जब) हम कल सासुर (श्वशुरगृह, अर्थात् पति के घर) जायँगी, तब कहाँ हम, कहाँ यह सरोवर-तट॥ कहाँ फिर अपने हाथ (यहाँ का) आना, और कहाँ मिल कर एक साथ खेलना है॥ (जब हम सासुर जायँगी, वहाँ) सासु और ननद बोलियोँ से, अर्थात् व्यङ्ग वचनोँ से, जीव लेँगी, और दारुण श्वशुर (घर से) निकलने नहीँ देगा ॥

सब से ऊपर प्रिय पति है, सो क्या जानेँ, वह क्या करे। क्या जानेँ सुख से रक्खे अथवा दुःख से, देखेँ (क्या जानेँ) कैसे जन्म (भर) निर्वाह होता है ॥ ६१ ॥

चउपाई ।

मिलहिँ रहसि सब चढहिँ हिँडोरी । झूलि लेहिँ सुख बारी भोरी ॥
झूलि लेहु नइहर जब ताईँ । फिरि नहिँ झूलन दीही साईँ ॥
पुनि सासुर लेइ राखिहि तहाँ । नइहर चाह न पाउबि जहाँ ॥
कित यह धूप कहाँ यह छाँहा । रहबि सखी बिनु मंदिर माँहा ॥
गुनि पूँछिहि अउ लाइहि दोखू । कउनु उतर पाउबि कित मोखू ॥
सासु ननद कित भउँह सकोरे । रहबि सँकोचि दुअउ कर जोरे ॥
कित यह रहसि जो आउबि करना । ससुरइ अंत जनम दुख भरना ॥

दोहा ।

कित नइहर पुनि आउबि कित सासुर यह खेलि ।
आपु आपु कहँ होइही परबि पंखि जस डेलि ॥ ६२ ॥

बारी = बालिका = थोडी उमरवाली । भोरी = भुलनी । नइहर = मातृ-गृह । दीही = देगा । पाउबि = पावैँगी । साईँ = स्वामी । चाह = इच्छा । गुनि = गुनना कर के = समझ विचार के । पूँछिहि = पूँछेगा । लाइहि = लगावेगा । दोखू = दोष । कउनु = कौन = क नु । कित = कुतः = कस्मात् = कैसे । मोखू = मोच । कित = कियत् । भउँह = भ्रू । सकोरे = सिकोडैँगी = चढावैँगी । रहबि = रहैँगी । सँकोचि = सङ्कोच कर के = दब करके । दुअउ = दोनोँ । आउबि = आवैँगी । ससुरइ = सासुर मेँ = श्वशुर के गृह मेँ । आउबि = आवैँगी । परबि = पडैँगी । डेलि = डेली = बाँस वा रहट्टे की झाँपी जिस मेँ बहेलिये पची को फँसा कर रखते हैँ ॥

खेल कूद से (रहसि) सब (सखियाँ आपस मेँ) मिलती हैँ और हिंडोले पर चढती हैँ, और सब बारी भोरी (थोडे उमर की भुलनी) झूल झूल कर सुख लेती हैँ ॥ (और आपस मेँ कहती हैँ कि) जब तक नइहर मेँ हो, तब तक झूल लो। फिर स्वामी पति (ससुरे मेँ) नहीँ झूलने देगा ॥ फिर (स्वामी) ले कर ससुरे मेँ तहाँ पर रक्खेगा, जहाँ पर हम लोग नइहर (जाने) की इच्छा (तक) न करने पावैँगी ॥ फिर कहाँ यह (सरोवर के तट की) धूप, कहाँ छाँह । सखी के विना, अर्थात् अकेली, मन्दिर मेँ रहैँगी ॥ (कभीँ कभीँ) कुछ समझ बूझ कर (स्वामी कुछ हम

लोगों से) पूछेगा, और (व्यर्थ) दोष लगावेगा (कि तुमने यह अनुचित कर्म किया)। (उस घडी) कौन उत्तर से कैसे मोच पावैंगी, अर्थात् उस दोष से निर्मुक्त होंगी ॥ कितनी वार सासु और ननद (ननन्दा = पति की बहिन) (क्रोध से) भौंह सिकोडैंगी, (उस समय सङ्कोच से (दब कर) (उन के आगे) दोनों हाथ जोडे रहैंगी ॥ (फिर) कहाँ यह खेल कूद करने आवैंगी, ससुरे में जन्म से अन्त तक, अर्थात् मरण पर्यन्त दुःख भरना पडेगा ॥

फिर कहाँ नैहर में आवैंगी, और ससुरे में फिर कहाँ यह खेल (सब किसी को)। आप आप की होगी, अर्थात् आप आप की पडेगी, हम लोग (मन्दिर के भीतर ऐसी) पडैंगी, जैसे डेली में पची (जहाँ से निकलना कठिन होगा) ॥ ६२ ॥

चउपाई ।

सरवर तीर पदुमिनी आई । खोपा छोरि केस मुख लाई ॥
ससि मुख अंग मलय-गिरि रानी । नागिनि झाँपि लीन्ह अरघानी ॥
ओनए मेघ परी जग छाँहा । ससि कइ सरन लीन्ह जनु राँहा ॥
छपि गइ दिन-हिँ भानु कइ दसा । लेइ निसि नखत चाँद परगसा ॥
भूलि चकोर दिसिटि तहँ लावा । मेघ घटा मँह चंद देखावा ॥
दसन दाविँनी कोकिल भाखी । भउँहइँ धनुख गगन लेइ राखी ॥
नयन खँजन दुइ केलि करेहीँ । कुच नारँग मधुकर रस लेहीँ ॥

दोहा ।

सरवर रूप विमोहा हिअइ हिलोर करेइ ।
पाउँ छुअइ मकु पावऊँ एहि मिस लहरइ देइ ॥ ६३ ॥

सरवर = सरोवर । खोपा = जूरा । केस = केश । अरघानी = आघ्राण = सुगन्ध । ओनए = झुके । राँहा = राहु । दसा = दशा = तेज । नखत = नक्षत्र । परगसा = प्रकाश किया । दसन = दशन = दाँत । दाविँनी = दामिनी = बिजली । भाखी = भाषा । भउँहइँ = भ्रू = भौहैं । खँजन = खञ्जन । नारँग = नारङ्गी । मधुकर = भ्रमर । हिलोर = हलोरा = तरङ्ग । पाउँ = पैर । मकु = मैं ने कहा = मैं कहता हूँ = जानों । मिस = मिष = व्याज = बहाना ॥

पद्मिनी सरोवर के तीर पर आई, जूरे को छोड कर (मलने के लिये), बालोँ को मुँह में लगाया, अर्थात् मुँह की ओर किया। (यह रीति है कि जूड़े को छोड कर स्त्री लोग मलने के लिये केशोँ को मुँह की ओर झटका देती हैँ)॥ केशोँ से ढपे मुख की शोभा कैसी है जानोँ मलयगिरि-रूपी पद्मावती रानी के शशि-रूप मुख अङ्ग को नागिनियोँ (सर्पिणीगण) ने ढाँप कर (तोप कर) (उस का) आघ्राण (सुगन्ध) लिया है॥ (वा केश नहीँ हैँ) मेघ झुँक पडे हैँ, जिन से जग (संसार) में छाया (अन्धकार) पड गई है, वा जानोँ राहु ने चन्द्र (शशि) का शरण लिया है (राहु काले केश, और मुख चन्द्र हैँ)॥ (उन केशोँ की अँधियारी से) दिन-ही में भानु की दशा (तेज) छिप गई, (जानोँ) चन्द्रमा नक्षत्रोँ को ले कर रात्रि में प्रकाश किया (काले केश निशि, पद्मावती का मुख चन्द्र और सहेलियोँ के मुख नक्षत्र हैँ)॥ चकोर ने समझा, कि मेघ की घटा में चन्द्र देख पडता है, इस लिये भूल कर तिसी स्थान में अपनी दृष्टि को लगाया (काले केश मेघ और पद्मावती का मुख चन्द्र है)॥ उस काले केश-रूपी मेघ-घटा में (पद्मावती के) दाँत बिजली, और भाषा (बोली) कोकिल हैँ, और भौँह-रूपी धनुष (इन्द्र-धनुष) को ले कर गगन (आकाश) में रक्खा है॥ नयन-रूपी दो खञ्जन क्रीडा करते हैँ, और कुच-रूपी नारङ्ग का रस मधुकर (भ्रमर) लेते हैँ॥

(पद्मावती के) रूप से सरोवर विमोहि (मोहि) गया। इस लिये हृदय में हिलोरा करता है, अर्थात् चञ्चल हो कर इधर उधर दौडता है। तहाँ कवि की उत्प्रेक्षा है, कि मैं कहता हूँ, कि सरोवर की ऐसी इच्छा है, कि मैं (पद्मावती के) पाँव को छूने पाऊँ। इसी मिस (व्याज) से लहर को देता है, अर्थात् लहरा मारता है॥ ६३॥

चउपाई।

धरीँ तीर सब कंचुकि सारी। सरवर महँ पइठीँ सब बारी॥
पाइ नीर जानउँ सब बेली। हुलसहिँ करहिँ काम कइ केली॥
करिल केस बिसहर बिस भरे। लहरइ लेहिँ कवँल मुख धरे॥
उठी कोँपि जस दारिउँ दाखा। भई उनंत पेम कइ साखा॥
नवल बसंत सँवारइ करी। होइ परगट जानउँ रस भरी॥

सरवर नहिँ समाइ संसारा। चाँद नहाइ पइठि लेइ तारा॥
धनि सो नीर ससि तरई ऊई। अब कित दिसिटि कवँल अउ कूई॥

दोहा।

चकई बिछुरि पुकारई कहा मिलउँ हो नाँह।
एक चाँद निसि सरग पर दिन दोसर जल माँह॥ ६४॥

कंचुकि = कञ्चुकी = चोलिया। सारी = साडी। बारी = बालिका = थोडी उमर की। बेली = वल्ली = लता। करिल = करइत = काले। कोई कुटिल पाठ शुद्ध कहते हैं, तहाँ कुटिल = टेढे। बिसहर = विषधर = सर्प। बिस = विष। कोंपि = नवीन पल्लव। दारिउँ = दाडिम। दाखा = द्राचा। उनंत = उन्नत = ऊँची। पेम = प्रेम। साखा = शाखा। नवल = नूतन = नया। बसंत = वसन्त ऋतु। करी = कली। समाइ = समाता है। ऊई = उदय हुई। कूई = कोई। चकई = चक्रवाक की स्त्री। नाँह = नाथ। सरग = स्वर्ग॥

सब थोडी उमर की (बारी) सखियाँ कञ्चुकी और सारी को तीर पर धरीं, और सरोवर में (स्नान करने के लिये) पैठीं॥ (उस घडी ऐसी शोभा है) जानों वे सब बेली-(लता)-रूप नीर (जल) को पा कर हुलास करती हैं (उल्लासित होती हैं), और काम की क्रीडा करती हैं। अर्थात् जिन क्रीडाओं से काम-देव जगत् को मोह लेता है, उन्हीं क्रीडाओं को सखियाँ करती हैं॥ सखियों के केश काले, वा कुटिल, विष से भरे विषधर (सर्प) हैं। वे मुख में कमल को पकडे (धरे) लहरें लेते हैं। यहाँ कवि का ऐसा भाव है, कि शिर में जो लगे केश हैं, वे जानों काले सर्प हैं, जो कि अपने मुख में सखियों के मुख कमल को पकडे हुए हैं॥ बाँस के अङ्कुर को करिला कहते हैं। इस लिये यहाँ बहुत लोग ऐसा अर्थ करते हैं, कि केश का जो करिला है, अर्थात् लट, सो विष से भरे विषधर हैं॥ विष से भरे के कहने का यह तात्पर्य है, कि साधारण सर्प जब काटता है, तब प्राणी को विष चढता है। ये ऐसे विष से भरे विषधर (सर्प) हैं, कि जो इन्हें देखता है, उस के ऊपर देखने-ही से विष चढ बैठता है॥ फिर कवि की उत्प्रेचा है कि सखियों की शोभा ऐसी है, जैसे दाडिम और दाख में कोंप उठी हों, अर्थात् नव पल्लव निकल आये हों, (सखियाँ दाडिम, दाख उन के भूषण नव पल्लव हैं)। अथवा सखियाँ नहीं हैं, जानों प्रेम की

शाखायेँ उन्नत (ऊँची) ऊई हैँ ॥ अथवा सखियाँ नहीँ हैँ, जानौँ वसन्त ऋतु नई नई कलियोँ को सँवारा है (लगाया है), और रस से भरी वे कलियाँ प्रगट होती हैँ, अर्थात् प्रगट ऊई हैँ ॥ सरोवर (आज आनन्द से भरा) संसार मेँ नहीँ समाता है, (क्योँकि धन्य वह सरोवर है जहाँ) चन्द्र ताराओँ को ले कर पैठ कर नहाता है। पद्मावती चन्द्रमा सखियाँ तारा के समान हैँ ॥ धन्य वह (सो) नीर (पानी) है, जहाँ चन्द्र और तरैयाँ उदय ऊई हैँ। (भला जहाँ चन्द्र और तारे उदित हैँ, तहाँ) अब कमल और कोईँ पर कहाँ दृष्टि पडे ॥

चन्द्रमा और तारे रात को उदित होते हैँ, इस लिये रात समझ कर चकई और चकवे बिछुड गये। तब बिछुड कर चकई पुकारती है, कि हे नाथ (नाँह) अब कैसे मिलूँ, क्योँकि एक चन्द्र तो रात्रि (निशि) मेँ स्वर्ग पर रहता है, और दूसरा (अब) दिन को जल के बीच उदय ऊआ ॥ ६४ ॥ चकई चकवे के विषय मेँ ३३ वेँ दोहे की टीका देखो ॥

चउपाई।

लागीँ केलि करइ मँझ नीरा। हंस लजाइ बइठु तेहि तीरा ॥
पदुमावति कउतुक कहँ राखी। तुम्ह ससि होहु तरायन साखी ॥
बाद मेलि कइ खेलि पसारा। हार देइ जउँ खेलत हारा ॥
सवँरिहि सावँरि गोरिहि गोरी। आपनि आपनि लीन्ह सो जोरी ॥
बूझि खेलि खेलहु एक साथा। हार न होइ पराए हाथा ॥
आजु-हि खेलि बहुरि कित होई। खेलि गए कित खेलइ कोई ॥
धनि सो खेलि खेलहिँ रस पेमा। रउताई अउ कूसर खेमा ॥

दोहा।

मुहमद बारि परेम कइ　जउ भावइ तउ खेल।
तेलहि फूलहि संग जउँ　होइ फुलाएल तेल ॥ ६५ ॥

मँझ = माँझ = मध्य। कउतुक = कौतुक। तरायन = तारा-गण वा डूबने-वाली। साखी = साक्षी। बाद = झगडा = बाजी। मेलि = लगा कर। पसारा = प्रसरण किया = फैलाया। हार = मुक्ताहार = गले का हार। सावँरि = श्याम वर्ण की = श्यामली।

वह अचेत हो गई कि मेरा (अब) मणि-हार गया॥ कमल के डार को पकड कर (गहि) विकल हो गई, (और अपने मन में कहने लगी, कि) अपने हार के लिये किस से पुकार करूँ॥ (अपने मन में पछताने लगी, कि हा) क्यों इस साथ में खेलने आई, (कि) हार गवाँ कर (खाली) हाथ से (अब) चली॥ घर पैठते-ही (गुरु-जन) इस हार को पूछेंगे, (कि हार क्या हुआ उस घडी) कौन उत्तर से (घर के भीतर) पैठने पाऊँगी॥ (इसी दुःख से उस के) सीप-रूपी नयन में आँसू तिस तरह से भर गये (भरे), जानों उस सीप में मोती भर गई हों। (फिर वे मोती से आँसू) ढर ढर कर गिरती हैं, अर्थात् गिरने लगीं॥ सखियों ने कहा कि हे बौर-ही कोकिला (कोकिला-सी बोलने-वाली), कौन ऐसा पानी है, जिस में पवन (हवा) न मिला हो, अर्थात् पानी में भी अवश्य पवन मिला रहता है, सो डूबने पर भी पवन के आधार से बहुत देर तक प्राण रहता है। सो हार गवाँ कर प्राणी ऐसा-ही रोता है? अर्थात् नहीं रोता है। यदि (हार) खो गया हो, तो (रोने से क्या फल)। हेरि हेराय लो (डूबेने से हम लोग न मरजायँगी)॥

(इतना कह कर) एक-ही साथ डूब डूब कर सब मिल कर हेरने लगीं। कोई हाथ में मोती ले कर उठीं (उतराईं), और कोई घोंघी॥ ६६॥

चउपाई।

कहा मानसर चहा सो पाई। पारस-रूप इहाँ लगि आई॥
भा निरमर तिन्ह पायन्ह परसे। पावा रूप रूप के दरसे॥
मलय-समीर बास तन आई। भा सीतल गइ तपनि बुझाई॥
न जनउँ कउनु पवन लेइ आवा। पून दसा भइ पाप गवाँवा॥
ततखन हार बेगि उतराना। पावा सखिन्ह चंद बिहँसाना॥
बिगसी कुमुद देखि ससि-रेखा। भइ तहँ ओप जहाँ जो देखा॥
पावा रूप रूप जस चहा। ससि-मुख सब दरपन होइ रहा॥

दोहा।

नयन जो देखी कवँल भइ निरमर नीर सरीर।
हँसति जो देखी हंस भइ दसन जोति नग हीर॥ ६७॥

इति मानसरोदक-खंड॥४॥

चहा = चाहा = इच्छा किया। पारस = पारसपाषाण। निरमर = निर्मल। परसे = स्पर्श करने से। दरसे = दर्शन करने से। समीर = वायु। सीतल = शीतल = ठण्ढा। तपनि = तपन = ताप = दाह। बुझाई = बुझ गई। पून = पुण्य। दसा = दशा = समय। ततखन = तत्क्षण। कुमुद = कोईं। ससि-रेखा = शशि-रेखा = चन्द्र-किरण। ओप = कान्ति। दरपन = दर्पण = ऐना। दसन = दशन = दाँत। जोति = ज्योति = कान्ति॥

मानसर (सरोवर) ने कहा, कि जो इच्छा किया था (चाहा) सो पाया, पारस-पाषाण-रूपी (सखियाँ) यहाँ तक (इहाँ लगि), अर्थात् पानी के नीचे तक, (पहुँचीं) आईं। (सच्चे पारस का धर्म है, कि जिसे छूवे उसे अपना सा कर दें, तैसे-ही सखियाँ जिसे छूवें वही मनोहर सुन्दर हो जाय)॥ (वह सरोवर) तिन सखियों के पैरों को स्पर्श करने से निर्मल हो गया, और उन के रूप का दर्शन करने से रूप को (भी) पाया, अर्थात् स्वयं आप भी मनोहर रूपवान् हो गया॥ मलय-चन्दन से मिश्रित वायु की बास (सुगन्धि) जो (सखियों के) तन (तनु = शरीर) से आई, (इस से) (वह सरोवर) ठण्ढा हो गया, और तपन बुझ गई, अर्थात् बहुत दिनों से पद्मावती और सखियों के मिलने की चिन्ता से जो सरोवर के हृदय में तपन थी सो बुझ गई॥ (सरोवर कहता है, कि) नहीं जानता (जनउँ) कि (आज) कौन वायु (पवन) (इस सुगन्धि को) ले कर आया, (जिस से मेरी) पुण्य-दशा (पुण्य का काल) प्राप्त हुई, और (मैं ने) पाप को (गवाँवा) नष्ट किया॥ तिसी क्षण में (सरोवर की प्रेरणा से) हार उतराय (ऊपर उठ) आया, और सखियों ने (उसे) पाया, (जिस पाने को देख कर) चाँद (पद्मावती, क्योंकि पहले सखियों ने कहा है कि 'तुम शशि होड तराइन साखी') ने हँस दिया॥ हँसने से जो शशि-रेखा, अर्थात् मुख-चन्द्र से किरणें छूटीं, उन से कोईं सब खिल उठीं (विगसी), और उस शशि-रेखा को जहाँ जहाँ जिस ने देखा, तहाँ तहाँ तिस को कान्ति (उत्पन्न) हो गई॥ जिस को जिस प्रकार के रूप की इच्छा थी, उस ने उस शशि-रेखा से वैसा-ही रूप को पाया, अर्थात् उस को वैसा-ही रूप मिल गया। (उस समय) सब कोई उस शशि-मुख (पद्मावती के मुख-चन्द्र) का दर्पण हो रहा है, अर्थात् जैसे दर्पण में प्रतिबिम्ब पडता है, उसी प्रकार पद्मावती के मुख-चन्द्र का सब के अङ्ग में प्रतिबिम्ब पड गया। इस कारण सब कोई उस शशि का दर्पण हो गया॥

कमल ने पद्मावती के आँख को जो देखा, तो उस की (कमल की) शरीर निर्मल हो गई, अर्थात् उज्ज्वल-नेत्र-दर्शन से वह भी उज्ज्वल हो गया। हंस ने जो पद्मावती को हँसते देखा तो उस की शरीर निर्मल हो गई, अर्थात् उज्ज्वल-सुधा-रूप पद्मावती के हाँसी के दर्शन से हंस की शरीर उज्ज्वल हो गई। पद्मावती के दाँत की ज्योति से हीरे नग में ज्योति आ गई है, अर्थात् पद्मावती के दन्त-ज्योति का प्रतिबिम्ब पडने से हीरा नग चमकता है ॥ ६७ ॥

इति मानसरोदक-खण्डं नाम चतुर्थ-खण्डं समाप्तम् ॥ ४ ॥

अथ सुआ-खंड ॥ ५ ॥

चउपाई।

पदुमावति तहँ खेल दुलारी। सुआ मँदिर मँह देख मँजारी ॥
कहेसि चलउँ जउ लहि तन पाँखा। जिउ लेइ उडा ताकि बन-ढाँखा ॥
जाइ परा बन-खँड जिउ लीन्हे। मिले पंखि बहु आदर कीन्हे ॥
आनि धरे आगइ सब साखा। भुगुति न मेटइ जउ लहि राखा ॥
पाई भुगुति सुक्ख मन भएऊ। अहा जो दुक्ख बिसरि सब गएऊ ॥
अइ गोसाइँ तूँ अइस विधाता। जावँत जिउ सब कर भख-दाता ॥
पाहन मँह न पतंग बिसारा। जहँ तोहि सवँर देहि तूँ चारा ॥

दोहा।

तउ लहि सोग बिछोह कर भोजन परा न पेट।
पुनि बिसरा भा सवँरना जनु सपने भइ भेँट ॥ ६८ ॥

दुलारी = दुलरुई = अपने माँ बाप की बडी प्यारी। पाँखा = पक्ष। ताकि = देख कर। बन-ढाँखा = बन के ढाँकने-वाले = वन-वृक्ष। बन-खँड = वन-खण्ड = वन-विभाग। सुक्ख = सुख। दुक्ख = दुःख। बिसरि = विस्मृति = भूल। गोसाइँ = गोसाईं = गोस्वामी = ईश्वर। अइस = ऐसा। बिधाता = विधान करने-वाला = पोषण करने-वाला = पालन

करने-वाला। जावँत = यावन्तः = जितने। भख = भक्ष्य। दाता = देने-वाला। पाहन = पत्थल। सवँर = स्मरण करे। चारा = चर्वण = भोजन। सोग = शोक। बिछोह = वियोग॥

तिस सरोवर में (तहाँ) कुआरी पद्मावती (तो) खेलती है, और (यहाँ) मन्दिर में शुक ने बिलैया को देखा॥ (जी में) कहने लगा, कि जब तक शरीर (तन = तनु) में पक्ष (डैने) हैं, तब तक (यहाँ से) चलूँ (चल दूँ, तो अच्छा)। (ऐसा शोच कर) वन-वृक्षों को देख कर, अर्थात् वन-वृक्षों की ओर दृष्टि कर, जीव ले कर उडा॥ जीव को लिये वन-विभाग में जा कर पडा। (वहाँ पर) पक्षी सब (उस से) मिले, और (उस का) बहुत आदर किये॥ (पलुआ पक्षी को बनैले पक्षी देख कर मारने लगते हैं, परन्तु यहाँ पक्षियों का मिलना, और आदर करना, यह हीरा-मणि के गुण का प्रभाव है, इस लिये इस वाक्य से कवि ने हीरा-मणि की आन्तरिक प्रशंसा किया है)॥ सब पक्षियों ने (जिस शाखा पर हीरा-मणि बैठा था, उस) शाखा के आगे (अग्र-भाग में) (भोजन को) आन कर धरे, कवि कहता है, कि (ईश्वर की ओर से) जब तक (भोजन) रक्खा है, तब तक भुक्ति (भोजन) नहीं मिटती, अर्थात् प्राणी चाहे जहाँ जाय, परन्तु ईश्वर की ओर से उस के लिये जो पहले-ही से भोजन रक्खा है, वह अवश्य उसे मिलता है, ऐसा नहीं कि वह भूखों मरे॥ (शुक ने) भोजन को पाया, और उस के मन में सुख हुआ। जो कुछ (मार्ग का) दुःख था, सो सब भूल (बिसरि) गया॥ कवि कहता है कि, हे (अइ = अयि) गोसाईं, तूं ऐसा विधाता (पोषण करने-वाला) है। जितने जीव हैं सब को (तूं) भक्ष्य (भक्षण) देने-वाला है॥ पत्थल में भी तैं ने कीट (पतङ्ग) को नहीं भुलाया है, अर्थात् पहाडों में पत्थल के नीचे जो पडे हुये कीट हैं, उन की भी खबर तूं लेता है, ऐसा नहीं कि भूल जा। जहाँ तुझे स्मरण करे, तहाँ-ही तूं चारा (भोजन) देता है॥

वियोग (बिछुडने) का तब तक शोक रहता है, जब तक कि पेट में भोजन नहीं पडा। (भोजन पडने पर) फिर वह वियोग भूल जाता है, स्मरण-मात्र हो जाता है, और (वह जो दिन रात की भेंट) सो ऐसी जान पडती है, जानों सपने में भेंट हुई थी॥ कवि का तात्पर्य है, कि पद्मावती से बिछुडने का जो शोक, उसे भोजन करने पर हीरा-मणि ने भुला दिया, और जो दिन रात की भेंट, सो सपने की भेंट सी हो गई॥ ६८॥

चउपाई।

पदुमावति पहँ आइ भँडारी। कहेसि मँदिर मँह परी मँजारी॥
सुआ जो उतर देत अहा पूँछा। उडि गा पिँजर न बोलइ छूँछा॥
रानी सुना सूखि जिउ गएऊ। जनु निसि परी असत दिन भएऊ॥
गहनहिँ गही चाँद कइ करा। आँसु गगन जनु नखतन्ह भरा॥
टूट पालि सरवर बहि लागे। कवँल बूड मधुकर उडि भागे॥
एहि बिधि आँसु नखत होइ चुए। गगन छाँडि सरवर भरि उए॥
छिहुरि चुईं मोतिन्ह कइ माला। अब सँकेत बाँधा चहुँ पाला॥

दोहा।

उडि यह सुअटा कहँ बसा खोजहु सखि सेा बासु।
दहुँ हइ धरती की सरग पवन न पावइ तासु॥ ६९॥

भँडारी = भण्डारी = भण्डार में रहने-वाली। मँदिर = मन्दिर। अहा = था। छूँछा = खाली। सूखि = सूख = शुष्क। असत = अस्त। गहनहिँ = ग्रहण में। गही = पकड गई। करा = कला = तेज। आँसु = अश्रु। पालि = प्रान्त = तट = किनारा। छिहुरि = छटक छटक कर = छहर छहर कर। सँकेत = सङ्केत = सङ्कोच। चहु = चारो। पाला = किनारा। सुअटा = सुअना = सुगना = शुकना = नर शुक = सुग्गा। बासु = वास = बसने का स्थान। दहुँ = क्या जानैं। धरती = धरित्री = भूमि। की = वा, अथवा। सरग = स्वर्ग॥

पद्मावती के यहाँ भण्डारी ने आ कर कही, कि (आप के) मन्दिर में बिलैया (मार्जारी) (आ) पडी॥ (इस लिये) पूछने से जो शुक उत्तर (जवाब) देता था, सो उड गया खाली (छूँछा) पिँजडा (पिंजर = पञ्जर) नहीँ बोलता, अर्थात् पिँजडा खाली है, उस में से आवाज नहीँ आती है॥ रानी ने (इस बात को) सुना (सुनते-ही) जीव सूख गया, (ऐसी कान्ति मलिन हो गई), जानैं दिन अस्त हो गया, और रात्रि (निशि) (आ) पडी॥ (रानी का मुख-चन्द्र ऐसा मलिन हो गया, जानैं) ग्रहण में चन्द्रमा की कला (राहु से) पकड गई हो, (अँधेरा हो जाने से रात्रि में नक्षत्रोँ की चमक और संख्या बढ जाती है, इस लिये) अन्तरिक्ष में

आँसुओँ की ऐसी शोभा है, जानोँ नचत्रोँ से भरा आकाश (गगन) है ॥ (आँसुओँ की धारा से) किनारा (पालि) टूट गया, और सरोवर (जल के बढने से) बहने लगा। (अश्रु-जल के बाढ से) (सरोवर के) कमल बूड गये, भ्रमर (मधुकर) उड कर भाग गये ॥ इस प्रकार से आँसू नचत्र हो कर (सरोवर मेँ) चू पडे, (जानोँ) आकाश को छोड कर (सब नचत्र) सरोवर भर मेँ उदय हुए हैँ ॥ (पहले कह आये हैँ कि अश्रु-जल के बाढ से सरोवर बह चला, तो सरोवर के बाढ से शहर क्योँ नहीँ बह गया। इस पर समाधान करते हैँ, कि (पद्मावती के) मोतियोँ की माला छटक छटक कर गिरी (चुई)। इस से अब सङ्केत (सङ्कोच) हो गया, और (मोतियोँ ने सरोवर के) चारो किनारेँ को (बाँध दिया)। इस से पानी ठहर गया, शहर बूडने से बँच गया ॥

(सखियोँ से पद्मावती कहती है, कि) हे सखि, यह शुक उड कर कहाँ बस गया। तुम लोग उस वास को खोजो। क्या जानँ (वह शुक) पृथ्वी मेँ है, वा स्वर्ग मेँ। (क्या) तिस (शुक) को पवन (हवा) भी नहीँ पाता है? अर्थात् बडा उडने-वाला है? पवन से भी उस की गति अधिक है? ॥ ६९ ॥

चउपाई ।

चहूँ पास समुझावहिँ सखी। कहाँ सो अब पाइअ गा पँखी ॥
जउ लहि पिंजर अहा परेवा। रहा बाँद कीन्हेसि निति सेवा ॥
तेहु बंद हुति छूटइ पावा। पुनि फिरि बंद होइ कित आवा ॥
वह उडान-फर तहिअइ खाए। जब भा पंखि पाँख तन पाए ॥
पिंजर जेहि क सउँपि तेहि गएऊ। जो जा कर सो ता कर भएऊ ॥
दस बाटइँ जेहि पिंजर माँहा। कइसइ बाँच मँजारी पाँहा ॥
एहि धरती अस केतन लीले। तस पेट गाढ बहुरि नहिँ ढीले ॥

दोहा ।

जहाँ न राति न दिवस हइ जहाँ न पवन न पानि।
तेहि बन होइ सुअटा बसा को रे मिलावइ आनि ॥ ७० ॥

पाइअ = पावैँगो। गा = अगात् = चला गया। बाँद = बन्द = कैद। सउँपि = समर्थ = समर्पण कर के। बाटइँ = बाट = राह। केतन = कितने को। लीले = खा गई। गाढ = कठिन वा गडहा। ढीले = बाहर निकासी ॥

(पद्मावती को) चारो ओर (चहूँ पास) से सखी (सब) समुझावती हैं, कि वह (सो) पक्षी चला गया (गा), अब (हम लोग) कहाँ पावेंगी ॥ जब तक (वह) पक्षी (परेवा = पारावत) पिँजडे मेँ था, तब तक कैद था, (इसी लिये) नित्य (निति) सेवा किया ॥ तिस कैद से (जो) छूटने पाया, (तो) फिर (पुनि) लौट कर (फिरि) क्योँ (कित) कैद होने आवे ॥ उस ने तिसी दिन (तदहनि = तहिअइ) उडान-फर को खाया (जिस फर के खाने से उडने की शक्ति हो, उसे उडान-फर (= फल) कहते हैँ)। जिस दिन (जब) पक्षी हुआ, और तन मे (तन = तनु) पक्षोँ (पाँख) को पाया ॥ (सो) जिस का पिँजडा था तिसे (उस पिँजडे को) सौँप कर (वह) चला गया (गयऊ), (इस लिये) जो जिस का था, सो तिस का हुआ ॥ (सखियोँ को निश्चय हो गया, कि उसे बिलैया ने तोड खाई, इस लिये कहती हैँ, कि जो जिस का था, सो तिस का हुआ, अर्थात् तेरा पिँजडा तेरे पास रह गया, और वह शुक जहाँ से (वन वा स्वर्ग से) आया था, वहाँ चला गया) ॥ (सखियाँ शुक के मरने का और पक्का अनुमान करती हैँ, कि) जिस पिँजडे (शरीर) मेँ दश राह हैँ (दो कान, दो नाक के पूरे, दो आँख, एक गुदा, एक मूत्रेन्द्रिय, और गल-नाल के आगे घण्टी के कारण से दो छिद्र, इस प्रकार से दश छिद्र दश राह हुये), उस मेँ मार्जारी (काल) से (पक्षी प्राण) कैसे बँचे ॥ मरने के अनन्तर फिर वह प्राणी मिल सकता है कि नहीँ, इस पर सखियाँ कहती हैँ, कि यह पृथ्वी ऐसे (शुक ऐसे) कितने को लील गई है (खा गई है), और इस का तैसा कठिन पेट है वा पेट-रूपी गडहा है, कि उस मेँ से फिर (बहुरि) नहीँ (उस प्राणी को) ढीलती, अर्थात् निकाल देती ॥

सखियाँ और भी मरने को पक्का करती हैँ, कि जिस स्थान मेँ न रात न दिन है, अर्थात् जहाँ रात दिन नहीँ होते, और जहाँ न पवन न पानी है, तिस (घोर) वन मेँ (यम-पुरी मेँ) जा कर (होइ), वह सुगना बसा, सो रे पद्मावति उस को आन कर (अब) कौन मिलावे, अर्थात् किसी को सामर्थ्य नहीँ कि अब उस को आन कर मिलावे ॥ ७० ॥

चउपाई ।

सुअइ तहाँ दिन दस कलि काटी । आइ बिआध ढुका लेइ टाटी ॥
पइग पइग भुइँ चाँपत आवा । पंखिन्ह देखि हिअइ डर खावा ॥

देखहु किछु अचरज अनभला। तरिवर एक आवत हइ चला॥
एहि बन रहत गई हम आऊ। तरिवर चलत न देखा काऊ॥
आजु जो तरिवर चल भल नाहीँ। आवहु एहि बन छाँडि पराहीँ॥
वेइ तउ उडे अउरु बन ताका। पंडित सुआ भूलि मन थाका॥
साखा देखि राजु जनु पावा। बइठ निचिंत चला वह आवा॥

दोहा।

पाँच बान कर खोँचा लासा भरे सो पाँच।
पाँख भरे तन अरुझा कित मारइ बिनु बाँच॥ ७१॥

कलि = कल = विश्राम, इस का विरोधी कल में वि उपसर्ग लगाने से विकल। काटी = विताया। बिआध = व्याध। ढुका = छिपा। टाटी = टट्टी। पइग = पद = पैर = पग = प्रग। भुइँ = भूमि। अचरज = आश्चर्य। अनभला = बुरा फल देने-वाला। तरिवर = तरुवर = बडा वृक्ष। आऊ = आयु। काऊ = क्वापि वा को ऽपि। पराहीँ = परायँ = पलायन करँ = भागँ। ताका = देखा = तर्क किया। साखा = शाखा। राजु = राज्य। निचिंत = निश्चिन्त। बान = वाण। खोँचा = खोँचने के लिये वंश-दण्ड। लासा = लसी-दार द्रव पदार्थ जो परोँ में चफन जाय। बहेलिये प्रायः वर के दूध को तेल में मार कर लासा बनाते हैं॥

तहाँ (जिस वन की चर्चा ६८ वें दोहे में कर आये हैं) शुक ने दश दिन विश्राम से काटा, अर्थात् बिताया, (तब तक) व्याध (बहेलिया) आ कर टट्टी ले कर (फँसाने के लिये) ढुका॥ (बहेलिये वन में पक्षियेँ को फँसाने के लिये हरे हरे वृक्षोँ के शाखा पल्लवोँ से एक ऐसी टट्टी बनाते हैं जो देखने-वालोँ को वृक्ष-ही समझ पडती है। इस प्रकार शेर के शिकार मेँ भी लोग मचान मेँ वृक्षोँ के डार पात लगा कर उस को वृक्ष ऐसा बना लेते हैं॥ (वह व्याधा) पैर पैर पृथ्वी को चाँपते ऊए आया (जिस मेँ पैर का शब्द पक्षियेँ के कान मेँ न पडे)। पक्षी (इस लीला को) देख कर हृदय में डर खाये, अर्थात् डर गये॥ आपस मेँ कहने लगे (कि, भाई,) देखो यह बुरा फल देने-वाला आश्चर्य है, कि एक वडा वृक्ष चला आता है॥ इस वन मेँ रहते हम लोगोँ की (इतनी) आयु गई, (परन्तु) कभीँ बडे वृक्ष को चलते नहीँ देखा, वा किसी ने बडे वृक्ष को चलते नहीँ देखा (तरिवर कहने से आश्चर्य ऊआ.

क्योंकि घास-पात-वाले छोटे वृक्ष प्रायः हवा में चलते हैं, इस लिये उन में विशेषता नहीं है)॥ सो आज जो वृक्ष चलता है (इस से जान पडता है कि) भला नहीं है, (सो) आओ इस वन को छोड कर भाग चलें॥ (ऐसा आपस में सलाह कर) वे (सब पक्षी) तो उडे (और) दूसरे (अउरु = अपर) वन को देखा, (परन्तु वृक्षों की हरियारी और फलों में) भूल कर पण्डित-शुक (हीरा-मणि) का मन थक गया, अर्थात् उन्हीं फूल-फलों में लुभा कर इस का मन रह गया। इस लिये अन्यत्र न जा सका॥ क्योंकि (इस को बहुत काल पर वृक्षों के) शाखाओं को देख कर (इतना आनन्द हुआ), जानों राज्य पा गया, इस लिये बेफिक्र (निश्चिन्त) बैठा रहा, (और) वह (व्याधा) (इस के पास) चला आया॥

(उस बहेलिये का) पाँच बाण का खोंचा था, अर्थात् उस खोंचे के शिर पर पाँच बाण लगे थे, और वे पाँचो जो थे सो लासा से भरे थे। (उस खोंचे से बहेलिये ने जो मारा, तो वह खोंचा हीरा-मणि की) पक्ष से भरी शरीर (तनु) में अरुझ गया, फिर (वह हीरा-मणि अब) मारे विना कैसे बँचे॥ ७१॥

चउपाई।

बँद भा सुआ करत सुख केली। चूरि पाँख धरि मेलेसि डेली॥
तहवाँ पंखि बहुत खरभरहीँ। आपु आपु मँह रोदन करहीँ॥
बिख-दाना कित होइ अँगूरा। जेहि भा मरन डहन धर चूरा॥
जउँ न होत चारा कइ आसा। कित चिरि-हार ढुकत लेइ लासा॥
एइ बिख-चारइ सब बुधि ठगी। अउ भा काल हाथ लेइ लगी॥
एहि झूठी माया मन भूला। चूरइ पाँख जइस तन फूला॥
यह मन कठिन मरइ नहिँ मारा। जार न देखु देखु पइ चारा॥

दोहा।

हम तउ बुद्धि गवाँई बिख-चारा अस खाइ।
तूँ सुअटा पंडित हता तूँ कित फाँदा आइ॥ ७२॥

बँद = बाँद = कैद। चूरि = चूर्ण कर। मेलेसि = डाल दिया। डेली = झाँपी, जिस में बहेलिये पची को फँसा कर रख लेते हैं। खरभरहीं = खरभराते हैं। बिख = विष। उडन = उड्डयन = डैना। धर = धड = गले के नीचे का शरीर-भाग। चूरा = चूर्ण किया। आसा = आशा = उम्मेद। चिरि-हार = चटक-हर = चिडियों का मारने-वाला = बहेलिया। बुधि = बुद्धि। लगी = लग्गी = लगुड = वंश-दण्ड। चूरइ = चूर्ण करता है। जार = जाल। चारा = भच्य। गवाँई = खो दिया। हता = आसीत् = था। फाँदा = फंदे में पडा ॥

सुख से क्रीडा (केलि) करते (-ही) शुक कैद हो गया। (बहेलिये ने जो पंखे लासा से भर गये थे उन्हें) चूर कर (शुक को) पकड कर (धरि), डेली में डाल दिया ॥ तहाँ पर बहुत पची खरभराते हैं, अर्थात् हीरा-मणि की यह गति देख बहुत पची खरभराने लगे, और आप आप में (आपस में) रोदन करतें है (रोने लगे) ॥ (हीरा-मणि की यह दुर्गति देख पचियों को वैराग्य सूझा, इस लिये वेदान्त की कथा कहने लगे, कि) (यह) अङ्कूर अर्थात् अङ्कूर से सुन्दर वृच विष का दाना क्यों देता है (क्योंकि इसी के फल के लोभ से उडना नहीं होता), जिस (विष के दाने से फल के कारण) से (इस हीरा-मणि का) मरना हुआ, और डैना और धड चूर किया गया ॥ यदि चारे की आशा (उम्मेद वा लोभ) न होती, तो चिडि-हारा क्यों लासा ले कर ढुकता, अर्थात् चारे-ही की आशा से एक स्थान पर पचियों का रहना होता है, जिस से फँसाने के लिये बहेलियों को अवसर मिलता है ॥ इसी विष चारे ने (हीरा-मणि के) सब बुद्धि को ठग लिया, और हाथ में लग्गी ले कर (इस का) काल हुआ ॥ (सो हम लोगों का) मन झूठी माया में भूला हुआ है, (यह नहीं जानता कि अभिमान से) जैसे-ही शरीर (तनु) फूलती है, तैसे-ही (ईश्वर के कोप से) पंखे चूर होते हैं ॥ (सो) यह मन कठिन है मारने से नहीं मरता, अर्थात् इसे कितना-हू रोको, नहीं रुकता, (क्योंकि चारे पर अन्धा हो कर ऐसा टूटता है, कि) जाल, जिस में निश्चय है, कि फँस जायँगे, उसे नहीं देखता पर चारे को देखता है ॥

पची सब कहते हैं, कि हम लोगों नें तो ऐसे विष चारे को खा कर बुद्धि को खो (गवाँ) दिया है। (परन्तु) तूँ तो, रे शुक, पण्डित था; तूँ क्यों आ कर फँस गया, अर्थात् फंदे में पडा ॥ ७२ ॥

चउपाई।

सुअइ कहा हम-हूँ अस भूले। टूट हिँडोल गरब जेहि झूले॥
केला के बन लीन्ह बसेरा। परा साथ तहँ बइरिन्ह केरा॥
सुख कुरआर फरहरी खाना। बिख भा जबहिँ बिआध तुलाना॥
काहे क भोग-बिरिख अस फरा। आड लाइ पंखिन्ह कहँ धरा॥
होइ निचिंत बइठे तेहि आडा। तब जाना खोँचा हिअ गाडा॥
सुख निचिंत जोरत धन करना। यह न चिंत आगइ हइ मरना॥
भूले हम-हुँ गरब तेहि माँहा। सो बिसरा पावा जेहि पाँहा॥

दोहा।

चरत न खुरुक कीन्ह जब तब रे चरा सुख सोइ।
अब जो फाँद परा गिउ तब रोए का होइ॥ ७३॥

गरब = गर्व। बसेरा = वास-स्थान। बइरिन्ह = वैरी लोग वा वैर वृक्ष (वदरी)। कुरआर = कुलालय = कुल का गृह। फरऊरी = फरहरी = अनेक प्रकार के फल। बिआध = व्याध। तुलाना = तुलना किया = पहुँचा। बिरिख = वृक्ष। आड = ओट = आवरण। जोरत = जोडते हैँ = एकट्ठा करते हैँ। करना = करण = सुख-साधन-सामग्री। बिसरा = भूल गया = विस्मरण हो गया। खुरुक = खोटका = खटका = संशय। गिउ = ग्रीव = गरा॥

सुग्गे ने कहा, कि (जैसे तुम लोग भूले हो माया मेँ) ऐसे-ही हम भी भूले। जिस गर्व-रूपी हिण्डोल पर झूले थे, वह टूट गया, अर्थात् जिस डैने का बडा गर्व था, वह टूट गया॥ (सुख की इच्छा से मैँ ने) केला के वन मेँ वसेरा लिया, तहाँ भी वैरियोँ का साथ पडा॥ (वैरि से शत्रु और वैर-वृक्ष ये दोनोँ अर्थ की सङ्गति के लिये केला का उपादान किया। वैर पास होने से उस के काँटोँ से केले के अङ्ग भङ्ग हो जाते हैँ)॥ (सो) सुख से कुल-गृह मेँ फरहरियोँ का खाना विष हो गया जब, कि व्याधा आ पहुँचा॥ शुक रोता है, कि हा, (यह) भोग-वृक्ष (सुख-साधन-वृक्ष) काहे को ऐसा (सुस्वादु फल को) फरा, (जिस का) आड लगा कर (व्याधे लोग) पक्षियोँ को

धरते हैं (पकडते हैं)॥ (हा,) तिसी (फर) के आड में निश्चिन्त हो कर हम भी बैठे, (जब बहेलिये ने) हृदय में खोँचे को गाड दिया, तब जाना, अर्थात् तब जान पडा, कि फँसे॥ (हा, प्राणी) सुख से निश्चिन्त हो कर धन और सुख-साधन-सामग्री को जोडता है, (परन्तु) यह चिन्ता (चिंत) नहीँ करता, कि आगे मरना है॥ (हाय,) तिन्ही (सुख-साधन-सामग्री) में गर्व से हम भी भूले, (इस लिये) जो सुख जिस (ईश्वर) के यहाँ से पाया था वही ईश्वर भूल गया, अर्थात् गर्व से उसी को भुला दिया; उसी का यह फल है, कि फंदे में फँसे॥

जब तक चरते संशय नहीँ किया, अरे, तब तक तो सुख से उन फलोँ को (सोद्) चरा (खाया)। अब जो गला फंदे में फँसा तब रोने से क्या हो, अर्थात् अब उसी ईश्वर का ध्यान करना उचित है, जिसे गर्व से भुला दिया था, और अब रोने से कुछ फल नहीँ॥ ७३॥

चउपाई।

सुनि कइ उतर आँसु सब पोँछे। कउनु पंख बाँधे बुधि ओछे॥
पंखिन्ह जउँ बुधि होइ उँजिआरी। पढा सुआ कित धरइ मँजारी॥
कित तीतर बन जीभ उघेला। सो कित हँकारि फाँद गिउ मेला॥
ता दिन ब्याध भएउ जिउ-लेवा। उठे पाँख भा नाउँ परेवा॥
भइ बिआधि तिसिना सँग खाधू। सूझइ भुगुति न सूझ बिआधू॥
हमहिँ लोभ वह मेला चारा। हमहिँ गरब वह चाहइ मारा॥
हम निचिंत वह आउ छपाना। कउनु बिआधहि दोस अपाना॥

दोहा।

सो अउगुन कित कीजिए जिउ दीजिअ जेहि काज।
अब कहना किछु नाहीँ मसटि भली पँखि-राज॥ ७४॥

इति सुआ-खंड॥ ५॥

कउनु = कौन = को नु। पंख = पच। बुधि = बुद्धि। ओछे = तुच्छ = हलका। तीतर = तित्तिर। जीभ = जिह्वा। उघेला = उद्घाटन किया = उघारा = खोला। हँकारि =

अहङ्कार कर के = चिल्ला के। गिउँ = ग्रीवा = गला। मेला = डाला। जिउ-लेवा = जीव लेने-वाला। नाउँ = नाम। बिग्राधि = व्याधि = रोग। तिस्विना = तृष्णा = लालच। खाधू = खाद्य = भच्य। दोस = दोष। अपाना = अपना। अउगुन = अवगुण। मसटि = मष्ट = मुष्ट = मूसा हुआ = चुराया हुआ। मसटि भली = चुराये हुये धन के ऐसा भला है, अर्थात् हृत-धन का जैसा सन्तोष होता है, वैसा-ही सन्तोष अच्छा है। पँखि-राज = पचि-राज = हीरा-मणि शुक॥

(हीरा-मणि के) उत्तर को सुन कर सब पचियोँ ने (अपनी अपनी) आँसुओँ को पोँछा (प्रोचण किया), (और कहने लगे, कि) ऐसे ओछे बुद्धि-वाले (पचियोँ) के (अङ्ग में) किस ने पच बाँध दिया है, अर्थात् बुद्धिमान के अङ्ग में पच रहना चाहिये, जिस से वह विशेष कार्य्य ले, न कि पचियोँ के जो कि उन पचोँ से विशेष कार्य्य लेना तो दूर है अपना प्राण भी नहीँ बचा सकते॥ (क्योँकि) यदि पचियोँ को उज्ज्वल (उँजिआरी) बुद्धि हो, तो पढे हुए शुक को मार्जारी कैसे धरे (पकडे)॥ और वन में तीतर क्योँ अपनी जीभ को उघेले, और वह (सो) क्योँ हंकार कर के (बोल कर = चिल्ला कर) अपने गले में फंदे को डाले॥ (तीतर का धर्म है, कि प्रातः-काल और सन्ध्या को बडे उच्चस्वर से बोलता है। बहेलिये उस की बोली से पता लगा कर फँसा लेते हैं)॥ (पची सब कहते हैं, कि) जिस दिन पची (परेवा) नाम पडा, और (शरीर में) पच उठे, तिसी दिन (हमारे लोगोँ का) जीव लेने-वाला व्याधा हुआ॥ (हमारे लोगोँ के) अङ्ग में भोजन की तृष्णा जो है वही व्याधि हुई, (उस रोग के वेग में) भोजन (भुगुति)-ही सूझता है, व्याधा नहीँ सूझता, (जो, कि प्राण लेने-वाला है)॥ हम लोगोँ को लोभ (लालच) है, (इस लिये) उस ने चारा को डाला (मेला)। हम लोगोँ को गर्व है, (इस लिये) वह मारने चाहता है॥ हम लोग बेखबर (निश्चिन्त) हैं, वह छिप कर आता है, (इस लिये) व्याधे का कौन दोष है (सब) अपना दोष है॥

ऐसा वह (सो) अपराध (अवगुण)-ही क्योँ किया जाय, जिस के कर्त्तव्य (कार्य = काज) से अपना प्राण दीजिए (सो), हे पचि-राज (हीरा-मणि), अब कुछ कहना नहीँ है, अब मष्ट करना-ही भला है॥ ७४॥

इति शुक-खण्डं नाम पञ्चम-खण्डं समाप्तम्॥ ५॥

अथ बनिजारा-खंड ॥ ७ ॥

चउपाई ।

चितउर गढ कर एक बनिजारा । सिंघल-दीप चला बइपारा ॥
बाम्हन हत एक नसट भिखारी । सो पुनि चला चलत बइपारी ॥
रिनि काहु कर लीन्हेसि काढी । मकु तहँ गए होइ किछु बाढी ॥
मारग कठिन बहुत दुख भएऊ । नाँघि समुदर दीप ओहि गएऊ ॥
देखि हाट किछु सुझ न ओरा । सबइ बहुत किछु देखु न थोरा ॥
पइ सुठि ऊँच बनिज तहँ केरा । धनी पाउ निधनी मुख हेरा ॥
लाख करोरिन्ह बसतु बिकाहीँ । सहसन्ह केरि न कोइ ओनाहीँ ॥

दोहा ।

सब-ही लीन्ह बिसाहना अउ घर कीन्ह बहोर ।
बाम्हन तहवाँ लेइ का गाँठि साँठि सुठि थोर ॥ ७६ ॥

बनिजारा = वणिक् = वणिज = बनिया । बइपारा = व्यापार । बाम्हन = ब्राह्मण । हत = हता = आसीत् = था । नसट = नष्ट = अधम = नीच । भिखारी = भिक्षुक । बइपारी = व्यापारी । रिनि = ऋण = कर्जा । बाढी = वृद्धि । नाँघि = लङ्घयिला = लाँघ कर । समुदर = समुद्र । ओरा = ओर = वार = किनारा । सुठि = सुष्ठु = अति-उत्तम । बनिज = वाणिज्य । निधनी = निर्धनी । हेरा = हेरता है = देखता है । लाख = लक्ष । करोरिन्ह

= कोटिन = करोडोँ। बसतु = वस्तु = चीज। सहसन्ह = सहस्रन्ह = हजारोँ। ओनाहीँ = झुकते हैँ। बिसाहना = सामग्री = विसाधन = अपने अपने काम की चीज। बहोर = फेरा॥

चित्तौर गढ का एक बनिया व्यापार के लिये सिंहल-दीप को चला॥ (वहाँ) एक अधम भिखारी ब्राह्मण था, वह भी (पुनि = पुनः) व्यापारी को चलते (देख कर) (सिंहल-दीप को) चला॥ किसी के यहाँ से ऋण काढ लिया, और (मन मेँ कहने लगा, कि) क्या जानेँ, तहाँ पर (सिंहल-दीप मेँ) जाने से (गये) कुछ बढती (वृद्धि) हो॥ कठिन मार्ग मेँ (जाते), (उसे) बहुत दुःख हुआ, (अन्त मेँ वह) समुद्रोँ को लाँघ कर, उस (सिंहल)-दीप मेँ गया॥ हाट को देख कर उसे कुछ ओर (किनारा) नहीँ सूझता, अर्थात् यह नहीँ समझ पडता, कि इस हाट का कहाँ तक हद्द है। सभी (चीज) बहुत (ढेर के ढेर) हैँ, कुछ (भी चीज वह) थोडी नहीँ देखता है॥ निश्चय कर के (पइ = अपि) तहाँ का वाणिज्य (व्यापार) अति ऊँचा है, धनी (तो चीजोँ को) पाता हैँ, और निर्धनी (खडा लोगोँ का) मुख देखता है॥ लाखोँ और करोडोँ की वस्तु विकती हैँ, हजार की (वस्तु पर) कोई झुँकता-ही नहीँ॥

सब किसी ने अपने अपने काम की वस्तुओँ को लिया, और (अपने अपने) घर का फेरा किया, अर्थात् अपने अपने घर की ओर लौटे। तहाँ पर (भिखारी) ब्राह्मण क्या ले, (क्योँकि) गाँठ मेँ साँठि (द्रव्य) अति थोडी थी, अर्थात् गठरी मेँ धन बहुत थोडा था॥ (गाँठि = ग्रन्थि), साँठि के लिये ३८ वाँ दोहा देखो॥ ७६॥

चउपाई।

झुर-इ ठाढ काहे क हउँ आवा। बनिज न मिला रहा पछितावा॥
लाभ जानि आएउँ एहि हाटा। मूर गवाँइ चलेउँ तेहि बाटा॥
का मइँ मरन सिखाओन सिखी। आएउँ मरइ मीचु हति लिखी॥
अपने चलत सो कीन्ह कु-बानी। लाभ न देख मूर भइ हानी॥
का मइँ बोआ जनम ओहि भूँजी। खाइ चलेउँ घर-हु कइ पूँजी॥
जेहि बेवहरिआ कर बेवहारू। का लेइ देब जउँ छेकिहि बारू॥
घर कइसइ पइठब मइँ छूँछे। कउनु उतर देबउँ तिन्ह पूँछे॥

दोहा ।

साथि चला सत बिचला भष्र बिच समुद पहार ।
आस निरासा हउँ फिरउँ तूँ बिधि देहि अधार ॥ ७७ ॥

झुर-इ = झूर-ही = सूखा छुआ = विना फल का । पछितावा = पश्चात्ताप । सिखाओन = सिखावन = शिक्षा । हति = थी । कु-बानी = कुत्सित वाणिज्य = खोटी बनिअई । मूर = मूल-धन । बोआ = बोया । भूँजी = भूँज कर । पूँजी = पुञ्ज (मूल-धन की) = मूल-धन । बेवहरिआ = व्यवहारी = व्यवहार करने-वाला = महाजन । बेवहारु = व्यवहार । छेकिहि = छेकेगा = रोकेगा । बारू = वार = द्वार । छूँछे = खाली । साथि = साथी । सत = सत्य । बिचला = विचल गया = टल गया । समुद = समुद्र । पहार = प्रहार = पहाड । आस = आशा । निरासा = निराशा । बिधि = ब्रह्मा । अधार = आधार = अवलम्ब ॥

(५ वीँ चौपाई मेँ जनम के स्थान मेँ जरम पाठ भी है। उस का भी अर्थ जनम है। पश्चिमोत्तर-प्रदेश मेँ छोटी जातियोँ मेँ अब तक "जरम" प्रचलित है। कवि प्रायः सर्वत्र जनम प्रयोग करता है, इस लिये हम ने जनम पाठ रक्खा है)॥ (ब्राह्मण पछताता है, कि हाय,) मैँ झूरे-ही खडा हूँ काहे को यहाँ आया। (हाय,) वाणिज्य (वस्तु) न मिला (केवल) पछतावा रह गया॥ इस हाट मेँ लाभ जान कर आया, (सो) मूर गवाँ कर तिसी राह मेँ (जिधर से आया था उसी राह मेँ) चला॥ क्या मैँ मरने-ही की शिक्षा सिखी थी, (क्या) मौत (मीचु) लिखी थी (जो) मरने को (यहाँ) आया॥ अपने चलते अर्थात् सामर्थ्य रहते (मैँने) सो खोटी बनिअई कर्म को किया, (जहाँ) लाभ को (तो) नहीँ देखता हूँ (परन्तु) मूर की हानि (नुक्सान) छुई (यह अवश्य) देखता हूँ, (देख क्रिया का दोनोँ ओर अन्वय है)॥ क्या मैँ उस जन्म मेँ भूँज कर (कर्म-बीज को) बोया था, (जिस का फल न देखने मेँ आया), (भूँज कर बीज बोने से वृक्ष नहीँ उत्पन्न होते इस लिये फल होना असम्भव है), (जो) घर की भी पूँजी खा कर चला॥ जिस व्यवहरिया का व्यवहार है, अर्थात् जिस महाजन से लेन देन है, वह यदि द्वार छेँकेगा (रोकेगा), तो क्या ले कर (उसे) देँगे॥ खाली हाथ (छूँछे) घर कैसे पैठूँगा, तिन (महाजन) लोगोँ से पूछने पर कौन उत्तर देऊँगा॥

(हाय, मेरा) साथी चला, और सत्य भी टला, अर्थात् जो नियम कर के व्रण लिया था, लाभ न होने से, वह भी बिगडा। और (मेरे और घर के) बीच समुद्र और पहाड हो गये। (हाय, मैं अब) आशा से नैराश्य हो कर फिरता हूँ, (सो) हे ब्रह्मा, तूँ (कुछ) आधार (अवलम्ब) दे॥ ७७॥

चउपाई।

तब-हिँ बिआध सुआ लेइ आवा। कंचन बरन अनूप सोहावा॥
बेँचइ लाग हाटि लेइ ओही। मोल रतन मानिक जेहि होही॥
सुअ को पूँछइ पतँग मदारे। चलन देख आछइ मन मारे॥
बाम्हन आइ सुआ सउँ पूँछा। दहुँ गुनवंत कि निरगुन छूँछा॥
कहु परबते जो गुन तोहि पाँहा। गुन न छपाइअ हिरदइ माँहा॥
हम तुम्ह जाति बराम्हन दोऊ। जाति-हि जाति पूँछ सब कोऊ॥
पंडित हहु तो सुनावहु बेदू। बिनु पूँछे पाइअ नहिँ भेदू॥

दोहा।

हउँ बाम्हन अउ पंडित कहु आपन गुन सोइ।
पढे के आगे जो पढइ दून लाभ तेहि होइ॥ ७८॥

बिआध = व्याध। सुआ = शुक। कंचन = कञ्चन = सुवर्ण। बरन = वर्ण = रङ्ग। अनूप = अनुपम। हाटि = हाट में। पतँग = पतङ्ग = फतिङ्गा = कीट। मदारे = मदार का (मदार एक वृक्ष होता है, जिस का फूल महादेव को चढता है। इसे संस्कृत में अर्क, भाषा में आक भी, कहते हैं। यह औषधि में भी बडे काम का है)। आछइ = अच्छी तरह से। दहुँ = दो में से एक = देखें = क्या जानें। परबते = पार्वतीय = पर्वत का = पहाडी। बराम्हन = ब्राह्मण। भेदू = भेद = पता। दून = दूना = द्विगुण॥

(ब्राह्मण ताप करता-ही था) तिसी समय (तब-हीँ) व्याध शुक को ले कर आया, (जिस का) सुवर्ण सा वर्ण अनुपम शोभित था॥ (व्याध उस हाट में) उस (शुक) को (ओही) ले कर बेँचने लगा, जिस (हाट) में रत्न और माणिक्योँ (मानिक) का मोल होता है, अर्थात् जहाँ अनेक रत्न बिक रहे हैँ॥ (जिस हाट में "लाख करो-

रिन्ह बसतु बिकाही" यह ७६ वँ दोहे में कह आये हैं, तहाँ) मदार के कीट (सदृश) शुक को कौन (को) पूँछता है। (मदार का कीट हरित शुक-ही के सदृश होता है। मदार का कीट कहने का यह तात्पर्य है, कि जहाँ मदार-ही को बौरहे महादेव को छोड, और कोई नहीं पूँछता, तहाँ उस के कीट को कौन पूँछे)। (वह शुक) अच्छी तरह मन को मारे, अर्थात् चुप चाप (अपने) चलने को देखता है, (कि देखेँ कहाँ पर चलना होता है)॥ (वह भिखारी) ब्राह्मण आ कर शुक से पूछा (अपने मन में शोच कर, कि) देखेँ यह गुणवान (गुनवंत) है, अथवा (कि) खाली (छूँछा) निर्गुण (निरगुन = गुण से रहित) है॥ (पूँछा, कि) हे पहाडी (शुक), जो तेरे पास गुण हो, (उसे) कहो, हृदय में गुण को न छिपाइये॥ (क्योंकि) हम तुम दोनोँ जाति में ब्राह्मण हैं। (प्रसिद्ध है, कि पच्चियों में शुक ब्राह्मण है, इसी लिये उस के जूठे फल को लोग खा लेते हैं)। सब किसी में (सब कोऊ) (यह रीति है, कि) जाति-ही को जाति पूँछती है, (शास्त्र में भी लिखा है कि "स्ववर्गे परमा प्रीतिः")॥ (सो यदि) पण्डित हो, तो बेद को सुनावो, (क्योंकि) बिना पूँछे पता (भेद) नहीँ पाया जाता, (कि कौन क्या जानता है)॥

(भिखारी ब्राह्मण कहता है, कि मैं भी) ब्राह्मण और पण्डित हूँ, सो (मेरे सामने) अपना गुण कहो। (क्योंकि) पढे हुए (पण्डित) के आगे जो पढता है, तिसे (तेहि) दूना लाभ होता है, (एक अपना पढा हुआ पाठ शुद्ध हो जाता है, दूसरे वह पण्डित वैसा-ही उपयोगी दूसरा नया पाठ अपनी पाण्डित्य दिखलाने के लिये बता देता है। यों दूना लाभ होता है)॥ ७८॥

चउपाई।

तब गुन मोहिँ अहा हो देवा। जब पिंजर हुति छूट परेवा॥
अब गुन कउनु जो बँद जजमाना। घालि मँजूसा बेँचइ आना॥
पंडित होइ सो हाट न चढा। चहउँ बिकान भूलि गा पढा॥
दुइ मारग देखउँ एहि हाटा। दइउ चलावइ दहुँ केहि बाटा॥
रोअत रकत भएउ मुख राता। तन भा पिअर कहउँ का बाता॥
राते सावँ कंठ दुइ गीवा। तहँ दुइ फाँद डरउँ सुठि जीवा॥
अब हउँ कंठ फाँद गिउ चीन्हा। दहुँ गिउ फाँद चाह का कीन्हा॥

दोहा।

पढि गुनि देखा बहुत मइँ　हइ आगे डरु सोइ।
धुंध जगत सब जानि कइ　भूलि रहा बुधि खोइ॥ ७९॥

गुन = गुण। अहा = आसीत् = था। हो देवा = हे देव। पिंजर = पञ्जर। ऊति = से। छूट = छूटा ऊआ। कउनु = कौन = क नु। बँद = बाँद = कैद। जजमाना = यजमान। घालि = डाल कर। मँजूसा = मञ्जूषा = सन्दूक = डेली। आना = अन्य। बिकान = बिकाना। गा = अगात् = गया। पढा = पाठ पढा ऊआ। मारग = मार्ग = राह। दइउ = देव = ईश्वर। दऊँ = क्या जानेँ = देखेँ = दोनोँ मेँ से। बाटा = वाट = राह। रकत = रक्त = रुधिर। राता = रक्त = लाल। तन = तनु = शरीर। पिअर = पीत = पीली। राते = रक्त = लाल। सावँ = श्याम = काला। कंठ = कण्ठ = कण्ठा = गले की धारी। गीवा = ग्रीवा = गला। सुठि = सुष्ठु = अच्छी तरह = अति। गिउ = ग्रीवा = गला। चीन्हा = पहचाना। धुंध = धुन्ध = अन्धकार। बुधि = बुद्धि। खोइ = खो कर = गवाँ कर॥

(शुक कहता है, कि) हे (ब्राह्मण) देव, तब मेरे मेँ गुण था, जब पिँजडे से छूटा ऊआ (पर-दार) पची (परेवा = पारावत = परिंद) था॥ अब जो (यह) यजमान बन्द (कैद) है, (उस मेँ) कौन गुण है (जो) दूसरा (आना = अन्य) मञ्जूषे (डेली) मेँ डाल कर बँच रहा है॥ (ब्राह्मण को बड़ा समझ कर देव बनाया, और अपने को उस का यजमान बनाया। इसी बात से अपनी बुद्धि और विद्या का परिचय दे दिया)॥ (सो) जो पण्डित होता है वह (सो) हाट मेँ (बिकने के लिये) नहीँ चढता, (मैँ तो अब) बिकने चाहता हूँ, (इस लिये) पढा ऊआ भूल गया॥ (मैँ) इस हाट मेँ दो बाट (मारग = मार्ग) देखता हूँ, (एक पूर्व की ओर दूसरी पश्चिम की ओर), (देखेँ) ईश्वर दोनोँ मेँ से किस बाट मेँ चलाता है॥ रोते (रोते) (अश्रु) रक्त से मुख रक्त हो गया, शरीर (तनु) पीली हो गई, (सो अब) क्या बात कहूँ॥ मेरे गले (ग्रीवा) मेँ लाल और काले दो कण्ठे हैँ, तहाँ पर जो दो फन्दे हैँ तिन से अत्यन्त (सुठि) प्राण (जीव) के लिये डरता हूँ॥ (नर सुग्गोँ के गले मेँ जवानी पर लाल काले दो कण्ठे फूटते हैँ, जिन से गले मेँ दो फन्दे बन जाते हैँ। उस पर शुक की उत्प्रेक्षा है, कि इन्ही दोनोँ फन्दे से डरता हूँ, कि ये जीव न ले लेँ, अर्थात् इन्हीँ की सुन्दरता से लोग मोहित हैँ, इस लिये व्याध हमेँ फँसाते हैँ)॥ (शुक कहता है, कि)

अब (फँसने पर) गले के कण्ठे-रूपी फन्दे को मैं ने पहचाना, देखें (आगे) गले के फन्दे (कण्ठे) क्या किया चाहते हैं ॥

मैं ने बज्जत (कुछ) पढ गुन कर देखा, कि आगे वही (सो) (प्राण जाने की) डर है। (इस लिये) सब जगत् अन्धकार जान कर, बुद्धि खो कर, (पंढा) भूल रहा हूँ ॥ ७९ ॥

चउपाई ।

सुनि बाम्हन बिनवा चिरि-हारू। करु पंखिन्ह कहँ मया न मारू ॥
कित रे निठुर जिउ बधसि परावा। हतिआ केर न तोहि डरु आवा ॥
कहसि पंखि-खाधुक मानावा। निठुर तेइ जो पर-मँस खावा ॥
आवहि रोइ जाहि कइ रोना। तब-हुँ न तजहि भोग सुख सोना ॥
अउ जानहि तन होइहि नासू। पोखहि माँस पराए माँसू ॥
जउँ न होत अस पर-मँस खाधू। कित पंखिन्ह कहँ धरत बिआधू ॥
जो रे बिआध पँखिन्ह निति धरई। सो बेंचत मन लोभ न करई ॥

दोहा ।

बाम्हन सुआ बेसाहा सुनि मति बेद गरंथ ।
मिला आइ साथिन्ह कहँ भा चितउर के पंथ ॥ ८० ॥

चिरि-हारू = चटक-हर = व्याध। मया = माया = मोह = दया। निठुर = निष्ठुर = कठोर। हतिआ = हत्या = पाप। खाधुक = खाद्यक = भक्षण = भोजन। मानावा = मानव = मनुष्य (खावा का तुक मिलाने के लिये मानावा किया है)। पर-मँस = पर-मांस = दूसरे की मांस। आवहि = आता है। रोइ = रो कर। जाहि = जाता है। तजहि = त्याग करता है। सोना = सयन। जानहि = जानता है। नासू = नाश। पोखहि = पुष्णाति = पोषता है = पालता है। बेसाहा = खरीदा। गरंथ = ग्रन्थ ॥

(शुक की बातें) सुन कर ब्राह्मण ने व्याधे से विनय किया, (कि) पक्षियों के ऊपर दया कर मार मत (न)॥ रे निष्ठुर (व्याध), क्यों दूसरे (परावा) को बध करता है (कोई परेवा का अपभ्रंश परावा को कहते हैं तब "अरे निष्ठुर व्याध, क्यों

पची को बध करता है" यह अर्थ करना)। तुझे हंत्या (पाप) का डर नहीँ आता॥ कहता है, कि पची मनुष्य (मानव) का भोजन है, (सो मैँ तो तिसे मनुष्य नहीँ, किन्तु) निठुर (कठोर = क्रूर) (समझता हूँ), जो कि पराये (दूसरे) की मांस खाता है॥ (रे व्याध, निश्चय समझ, कि तूँ) रो कर आता है (जन्म लेता है), और रो-ही कर के जाता है (मरता है), तब भी भोग और सुख से सोना यह नहीँ तजता॥ और जानता है, कि शरीर (तन = तनु) नाश होगी, तब भी पराये की मांस से (अपनी) मांस को पोसता है (पालता है)॥ (ब्राह्मण कहता है, कि सत्य है,) यदि ऐसा (अस) पर-मांस-भोजन न होता, तो व्याधा क्योँ पचियोँ को धरता (पकडता)॥ रे (मन), जो व्याधा नित्य (निति) पचियोँ को धरता है (पकडता है), वह (सो) बँचते मन मैँ छोभ नहीँ करता, अर्थात् उस के मन मैँ दया नहीँ आती, कि ऐसे मनोहर पची को क्योँ बँचता हूँ, सम्भव है, कि खरीदने-वाला इसे मार कर खा जाय॥

(अन्त मैँ) ब्राह्मण ने (शुक की) मति (बुद्धि) से वेद के ग्रन्थोँ को अर्थात् वेद-पाठ को सुन कर शुक को खरीदा। और आ कर साथियोँ को मिला, और चित्तौर गढ के पन्थ (राह) मैँ हुआ, अर्थात् चित्तौर गढ की राह पकडी॥ ८०॥

चउपाई।

तब लगि चितर-सेन सिउ साजा। रतन-सेन चितउर भा राजा॥
आइ बात तेँहि आगे चली। राजा बनिज आए सिंघली॥
हहिँ गज-मोँति भरी सब सीपी। अउरु बसतु बहु सिंघल-दीपी॥
बाम्हन एक सुआ लेइ आवा। कंचन बरन अनूप सोहावा॥
राते सावँ कंठ दुइ काँठा। राते डहन लिखा सब पाठा॥
अउ दुइ नयन सोहावन राता। राते ठोर अमीँ-रस बाता॥
मसतक टीका काँध जनेऊ। कबि बिआस पंडित सहदेऊ॥

दोहा।

बोलि अरथ सोँ बोलई सुनत सीस पइ डोल।
राज-मँदिर मँह चाहिअ अस वह सुआ अमोल॥ ८१॥

चितर-सेन = चित्र-सेन। सिउ = शिव। बनिज = वणिज = वनिया। हहिँ = हैँ। गज-मोँति = गज-मुक्ता। राते = रक्त = लाल। सावँ = श्याम। कंठ = कण्ठ = गला। काँठा = कण्ठा = गले की धारी। डहना = डैना। पाठा = पट्ठा = डैने और पीठ का जोड। अमीँ-रस = अमृत-रस। मसतक = मस्तक। टीका = तिलक। काँध = स्कन्ध = कन्धा। जनेऊ = यज्ञोपवीत। बिआस = व्यास = पुराणोँ के कर्त्ता। सहदेउ = सहदेव = युधिष्ठिर के सब से छोटे भाई। बोलि = बोली। अरथ = अर्थ। सीस = शीर्ष। पइ = अपि = निश्चय कर के। डोल = डोलता है = हिलता है। अमोल = अमूल्य॥

(जब तक ब्राह्मण बनिजारे के साथ सिंहल-द्वीप को जाय और वहाँ से शुक को खरीद कर ले आवे), तब तक (तब लगि) राजा चित्र-सेन शिव (लोक) की तयारी किया (साज़ा), अर्थात् शरीर छोड स्वर्ग को गया, और रत्न-सेन चित्तौर (गढ) का राजा हुआ॥ तिस के (तेहि) आगे आ कर यह बात चली, अर्थात् लोगोँ ने यह बात कही, कि हे राजन् (राजा), सिंहल के बनिये आये हैँ॥ (उन के पास) गज-मुक्ता सी मोतियोँ से भरी सब सीपी (शुक्ति) हैँ, और बहुत सिंहल-द्वीप की वस्तु हैँ॥ एक ब्राह्मण एक शुक को ले आया है जिस का सुवर्ण (कञ्चन) सा वर्ण (वरण) अनुपम (अनूप) शोभित है॥ कण्ठ (गले) मेँ लाल और काले दो कण्ठे हैँ। डैने और पट्ठे सब लाल वर्ण से लिखे हैँ अर्थात् चित्रित हैँ॥ और दोनोँ रक्त नयन, रक्त अधर (ठोर) शोभित हैँ, और बात (जानोँ) अमृत-रस है, अर्थात् बातोँ से अमृत-रस टपकता है॥ मस्तक मेँ टीका (तिलक), और कन्धे मेँ (तीन धारी जानोँ) जनेऊ है, (उस के स्वरूप से और बातोँ से जान पडता है, कि) व्यास के ऐसा कवि और सहदेव के ऐसा पण्डित है॥ (भारत मेँ प्रसिद्ध है, कि सहदेव बडे पण्डित थे, और भारत और १८ पुराणोँ के कर्त्ता व्यास जगत्प्रसिद्ध कवि हैँ॥)

(वह शुक) अर्थ से बोली बोलता है, अर्थात् उस की बोली अनर्थ नहीँ होती। (उस की बोली) सुनते-ही (प्रेम से गद्गद होने से) निश्चय कर के शीश हिलने लगता है। ऐसा वह अमूल्य शुक है, इस लिये उसे राज-मन्दिर मेँ (रखना) चाहिये॥ ८१॥

चउपाई।

भई रजाएसु जन दउराए। बाम्हन सुआ बेगि लेइ आए॥
बिपर असीसि बिनति अउधारा। सुआ जीउ नहिँ करउँ निरारा॥

पइ यह पेट भएउ बिसुआसी। जेइ सब नाए तपा सनिआसी ॥
डासन सेज जहाँ जेहि नाहीँ। भुइँ परि रहइ लाइ गिउ बाहीँ ॥
आँध रहइ जो देख न नयना। गूँग रहइ मुख आउ न बयना ॥
बहिर रहइ जो स्रवन न सुना। पइ यह पेट न रह निरगुना ॥
कइ कइ फेरा निति बहु दोखी। बारहि बार फिरइ न सँतोखी ॥

दोहा।

सो मोहिँ लेइ मँगावई लावइ भूख पिआस।
जउँ न होत अस बइरी केहु काहू कइ आस ॥ ८२ ॥

रजाएसु = राजाज्ञा। जन = मनुष्य = नोकर-चाकर। दउराए = दौडाये गये। बिपर = विप्र = ब्राह्मण। असीसि = आशिषा कर = आशीर्वाद कर। बिनति = विनय। अउधारा = अवधारण किया = आरम्भ किया। निरारा = निरालय = घर से बाहर = अलग = दूर। बिसुआसी = विश्वाशी = विश्व (संसार) को खाने-वाला। नाए = नाये = नवाय दिया = झुका दिया। तपा = तपस्वी। सनिआसी = सन्यासी (३० वां दोहा देखो)। डासन = दर्भासन = बिछौना। सेज = शय्या। भुइँ = भूमि। परि = पड कर। लाइ = लगा कर। गिउ = ग्रीवा = गला। बाहीँ = बाहँ = बाऊ। आँध = अन्ध = अन्धी। गूँग = गूँगा = मूक। बयना = वचन। बहिर = बधिर = बहिरा। स्रवन = श्रवण = कर्ण = कान। निरगुना = निर्गुण = बे गुण का। दोखी = दोषी = दोष से भरा। बारहि बार = वारंवार = फिर फिर, वा द्वार द्वार = दरवाजे दरवाजे। सँतोखी = सन्तोषी = सन्तोष से भरा। लेइ = ले कर। मँगावई = मँगवाता है। लावइ = लगाता है। भूख = बुभुक्षा = क्षुधा। पिआस = पिपासा = प्यास। बइरी = वैरी = शत्रु। आस = आशा = उम्मेद ॥

राजा की आज्ञा ऊई, नोकर-चाकर (जन) दौडाये गये, (वे लोग) शीघ्र (बेगि) ब्राह्मण और शुक को ले आये॥ ब्राह्मण ने आशीर्वाद कर विनय को आरम्भ किया, कि (हे राजन्), शुक-प्राण (जीव) को अलग न करता॥ परन्तु यह पेट संसार को खाने-वाला ऊआ है। जिस ने सब तपस्वी और सन्यासियों को (अपनी ओर) झुंकाया है॥ जहाँ पर जिस को बिछौना और शय्या नहीँ होती। (तहाँ पर वह) गले में बाहँ लगा कर, अर्थात् बाहँ की गल-तकिया लगा कर, भूमि में पड रहता है, अर्थात्

उसी से निर्वाह कर लेता है, परन्तु भूखे निर्वाह नहीँ होता ॥ जो आँख नहीँ देखती वह अन्ध रहती है, अर्थात् नयन का गुण देखना है, उस गुण के न रहने पर भी आँख अन्धी रहती है। जिस मुख मेँ वचन नहीँ आता, अर्थात् जो मुख नहीँ बोलता, वह गूँगा रहता है। तात्पर्य यह, कि मुख का गुण बोलना जो है, उस के न रहने पर भी गूँगा मुख रहता है ॥ (इसी प्रकार) जो कान नहीँ सुनता, वह बधिर रहता है, अर्थात् सुनना गुण न रहते भी बहिरा कान रहता है। परन्तु (ऐसा नहीँ होता, कि) निर्गुण पेट रहे, अर्थात् जैसे देखना, बोलना, सुनना जो गुण हैँ उन के विना भी आँख, मुख, कर्ण रहते हैँ, और प्राणी का जीवन भी बना रहता है, उसी प्रकार ऐसा नहीँ होता, कि भोजन करना जो पेट का गुण है, उस के विना पेट रहे, और प्राणी का जीवन बना रहे ॥ नित्य फेरा कर कर (इधर उधर घूम कर) यह अत्यन्त (बड़) दोषी (दोष से भरा) वारंवार वा द्वार द्वार फिरता है, (परन्तु) सन्तोषी नहीँ होता ॥

(राजन्), सो (वही) पेट मुझे (अपने संग मेँ) ले कर (भिक्षा) मँगाता है, और भूख प्यास लगाता है। यदि ऐसा वैरी (पेट) न होता, तो किसी को किसी की आशा रहती? अर्थात् यदि पेट न होता तो किसी को किसी की आशा (उम्मेद) न रहती, स्वतन्त्र हो कर सब कोई विहार करता, इसी के भरने के लिये लोग दूसरे की आशा करते हैँ ॥ ८२ ॥

चउपाई।

सुअइ असीस दीन्ह बड साजू। बड परतापु अखंडित राजू ॥
भागवंत बिधि बड अउतारा। जहाँ भाग तहँ रूप जोहारा ॥
कोइ केहु पास आस कइ गवँना। जो निरास डिढ आसन मवना ॥
कोइ बिनु पूँछे बोलि जो बोला। होइ बोलि माँटी के मोला ॥
पढि गुनि जानि बेद मति भेऊ। पूँछे बात कहइ सहदेऊ ॥
गुनी न कोई आपु सराहा। जो सो बिकाइ कहा पइ चाहा ॥
जउ लहि गुन परगट नहिँ होई। तउ लहि मरम न जानइ कोई ॥

दोहा ।

चतुर-बेद हउँ पंडित हीरा-मनि मोहिँ नाउँ ।
पदुमावति सउँ मइँ रवँउँ सेव करउँ तेहि ठाउँ ॥ ८३ ॥

परतापु = प्रताप । अखंडित = अखण्डित = पूर्ण = अखण्ड । राजू = राज्य । भागवंत = भाग्यवान् = भाग्यवन्तः । बड = वर = बडा । अउतारा = अवतार दिया । भाग = भाग्य । जोहारा = जीव-हार देता है = दण्डवत करता है (४९ वाँ दोहा देखो) = गुलाम होता है = दास होता है । पास = पार्श्व = निकट । गवँना = गमन करता है = याचा करता है । निरास = नैराश्य = बे-परवाह । डिढ = दृढ = मज़बूत = पक्का । मवन = मौन = चुप । बोलि = बोली = बचन । माँटी = मृत् = मट्टी । मोला = मूल्य । मति = सम्मति । भेउ = भेद । सहदेउ = सहदेव (८१ वाँ दोहा देखो) । सराहा = सराहता है (श्लाघा करना = सराहना) । पइ = अपि = निश्चय कर के । परगट = प्रगट = प्रकट । मरम = मर्म = गुप्त-भेद । चतुर-बेद = चारो वेद । रवँउँ = रमउँ = रमण करता हूँ । सेव = सेवा = टहल । ठाउँ = स्थान ॥

(शुक ने अवसर को देख कर विचारा, कि अब अपनी विद्या प्रगट करूँ जिस से राजा मोहित हो कर मुझे ले, यह शोच कर) शुक ने आशीर्वाद दिया, कि आप का बडा साज (तयारी हाथी घोडे इत्यादि की), बडा प्रताप और अखण्ड-राज्य (पृथ्वी भर पूर्ण राज्य) हो ॥ (आप को) ब्रह्मा (विधि) ने बडा भाग्यवान् उत्पन्न किया, (अउतारा), (इस लिये) जहाँ भाग्य रहती है तहाँ रूप भी (आ कर) दण्डवत करता है, अर्थात् दास होता है, तात्पर्य यह, कि जैसी आप की भाग्य है, वैसा-ही ब्रह्मा ने रूप भी दिया है ॥ (सो, हे राजन्), कोई किसी के पास आशा कर के जाता है, और जो बे-परवाह (निरास) है, वह (अपने) आसन-ही पर मौन हो कर दृढ (पक्का = अचल) रहता है ॥ (हे राजन्), विना पूँछे कोई जो बोली बोलता है, वह बोली मट्टी के मोल की होती है, अर्थात् उस का अनादर हो जाता है ॥ पढ, गुन और वेद के सम्मति का भेद जान कर सहदेव पूँछने से बात कहता है, अर्थात् सकल-विद्या-निधान सहदेव भी विना पूँछे अनादर के भय से नहीँ बात करते थे ॥ (आप यह मन मेँ न शोचेँ, कि यह तुच्छ है; आप-ही से अपने विषय मेँ कह रहा है, मैँ भी जानता हूँ, कि) कोई गुणी अपने को आप नहीँ सराहता, (परन्तु) जो बिकाता है,

वह अवश्य (पइ = अपि) अपना गुण कहने चाहता है ॥ (क्योंकि) जब तक गुण नहीं प्रगट होता, तब तक कोई (किसी का) मर्म नहीं जानता ॥

(सो) मैं चारो वेद का पण्डित हूँ, हीरा-मणि मेरा नाम है। मैं पद्मावती से रमण (क्रीडा) करता हूँ, और तिसी स्थान में (पद्मावती की) सेवा करता हूँ ॥ ८३ ॥

चउपाई ।

रतन-सेन हीरा-मनि चीन्हा । लाख टका बाम्हन कहँ दीन्हा ॥
बिपर असिस देइ कीन्ह पयाना । सुआ सो राज-मँदिर मँह आना ॥
बरनउँ कहा सुआ कइ भाखा । धनि सो नाउँ हीरा-मनि राखा ॥
जो बोलइ राजा मुख जोआ । जनउँ मोति हिअ हार परोआ ॥
जउँ बोलइ सब मानिक मूँगा । नाहिँ त मवन बाँधि रह गूँगा ॥
मनहुँ मारि मुख अंब्रित मेला । गुरु होइ आपु कीन्ह जग चेला ॥
सुरुज चाँद कइ कथा जो कहा । पेम क कहनि लाइ चित गहा ॥

दोहा ।

जो जो सुनइ धुनइ सिर राजा पिरिति अगाहि ।
अस गुनवंत नहीं भल (सुअटा) बाउर करिहइ काहि ॥ ८४ ॥

इति बनिजारा-खंड ॥ ७ ॥

टका = टङ्क = पाँच तोले का छठवाँ भाग = पुराना रुपया । पयान = प्रयाण = यात्रा । आना = आनीत हुआ = लिआया गया । कहा = कथम् = क्या = कैसे । भाखा = भाषा = बोली । धनि = धन्य । नाउँ = नाम । जोआ = जोहा = जोह कर = रुख देख कर । परोआ = प्रोत किया है = पहिराया है । मउन = मौन = चुप । बाँधि = बाँध कर । मारि = मार कर । अंब्रित = अमृत । सुरुज = सूर्य । चाँद = चन्द्र । पेम = प्रेम । कहनि = कथन = कहानी । गहा = पकड लिया । पिरिति = प्रीति = प्रेम । अगाहि = अगाध = अपार । गुनवंत = गुणवान् = गुणवन्तः । बाउर = वातुल = बौरहा = पगला । करिहइ = करेगा । काहि = किसी को ॥

राजा रत्न-सेन ने हीरा-मणि को पहचाना, (चीन्हा) (कि यह कोई विचित्र जीव है)। (इस लिये) ब्राह्मण को लाख रुपया दिया (शुक का दाम)॥ ब्राह्मण ने आशीर्वाद दे कर याचा किया, और शुक जो था सो राज-मन्दिर में लिआया गया॥ कवि कहता है, कि शुक के भाषा का कैसे वर्णन करूँ, धन्य वह (पुरुष) है, जिस ने हीरा-मणि यह नाम रक्खा है॥ राजा के मुख का रुख देख कर, जो बोलता है, सो जानों हृदय-रूपी हार में मोतियों को पिरोता है (पिरोआ = प्रोत करता है = पिरोता है)॥ यदि बोलता है, तो सब माणिक्य और मूँगा, अर्थात् माणिक्य और मूँगा के सदृश, नहीं तो मौन बाँध कर चुप (गूँगा) रहता है॥ मानों मार कर मुख में अमृत डाल देता है, (मेला) अर्थात् किसी किसी विरह-वाक्य से तो सुनने-वालों को मार डालता है, फिर मार कर दूसरी अमृत-मय वाक्य से मानों मुख में अमृत डाल देता है। (इस प्रकार से) आप गुरु हो कर, जगत को चेला कर लिया (कीन्ह)॥ सूर्य और चन्द्र की जो कथा है, उस को (लोगों से) कहा, (अर्थात् सूर्य कौन है, कैसे तेजो-मय हुआ, और चन्द्र कौन है, कैसे अमृत-मय हुआ, दोनों का समागम कैसे होता है, इत्यादि कथा को सुनाया) और प्रेम की कहानियों को लगा कर, अर्थात् सुना कर, (सब के चित्त को) पकड लिया॥

जो जो (उस की मनो-हर भाषा) सुनता है, (प्रेम से विह्वल हो) शिर धुनता है, (इस पर) राजा की प्रीति अपार होती जाती है। (आपस में लोग कहते हैं, कि) ऐसा (शुक) भला (अच्छा) नहीं, (यह अपनी प्रेम-कहानी से) किसी को पागल करेगा, अर्थात् इस की कहानी सुन प्रेम से कोई घर बार छोड बौरहा बनेगा॥ ८४॥

इति वणिज-खण्डं नाम सप्तम-खण्डं समाप्तम्॥ ७॥

अथ नागमती-सुआ-संवाद-खंड ॥ ८ ॥

चउपाई ।

दिन दस पाँच तहाँ जो भए। राजा कतहुँ अहेरइ गए ॥
नाग-मती रुपवंती रानी। सब रनिवास पाट परधानी ॥
कइ सिँगार कर दरपन लीन्हा। दरसन देखि गरब जिउ कीन्हा ॥
हँसत सुआ पहँ आइ सो नारी। दीन्ह कसउटी अउपन-वारी ॥
भलहि सुआ अउ प्यारे नाहा। मोरहि रूप कोई जग माँहा ॥
सुआ बानि कसि कहु कस सोना। सिंघल-दीप तोर कस लोना ॥
कउनु दिसिटि तोरी रुप-मनी। दहुँ हउँ लोनि कि वेइ पदुमनी ॥

दोहा ।

जउँ न कहसि सत सुअटा तोहि राजा कइ आन ।
हइ कोई एहि जगत मँह मोरहि रूप समान ॥ ८५ ॥

कतहुँ = कुत-हि = कहीँ। अहेरइ = अहेर मेँ = आखेट मेँ। नाग-मती = नाग (सर्प) की ऐसी जिस की मति (बुद्धि) हो। रुपवंती = रूपवती = सुन्दरी। रनिवास = राज्ञी-वास = रानियाँ के रहने का स्थान। पाट = पट्ट = पीढी = सिंहासन। परधानी = प्रधाना। सिँगार = शृङ्गार। कर = हाथ। दरपन = दर्पण = आईना। दरसन = दर्शन = प्रतिबिम्ब। गरब = गर्व। हँसत = हँसती हुई। सो =

वह । नारी = स्त्री = नाग-मती । जब एक पद है, तब सोनारी = स्वर्णकारिणी = सोनारिन । कसउटी = कषवटी = सोना कसने की काले पत्थल की बटिया । श्रउपन-वारी = श्रोपने-वारी = सोने के वर्ण को दिखाने-वारी = सोने के श्राब को दिखाने-वाली । भलहि = भला = श्रच्छा = सुन्दर । नाहा = नाथ = स्वामी । बानि = वर्ण । कसि = कस कर । कस = कैसा । सोना = स्वर्ण । लोना = लवण = सुन्दर । कउनु = कौन = क नु । दिसिटि = दृष्टि । रूप-मनी = रूप-मणि । सत = सत्य । श्रान = श्राज्ञा = शपथ = कसम ॥

तहाँ पर दश पाँच दिन जो (रहते) ऊये, (इसी में) राजा कहीँ श्राखेट मेँ गये ॥ (इतने में) रूप-वती नाग-मती (राजा की) रानी जो कि सब रनिवास श्रौर पाट में प्रधान थी, शृङ्गार कर हाथ में दर्पण लिया, (उस में) (श्रपने) दर्शन (प्रतिबिम्ब) को देख कर जीव में गर्व किया, (कि मेरे समान कोई नहीँ) ॥ वह (सो) नारी वा वह सोनारिन हँसती ऊई, शुक के पास श्रा कर, (शुक को) श्रोपने-वारी कसौटी को दिया, श्रर्थात् रूप-स्वर्ण की परीक्षा करने को कहा ॥ कि हे भले शुक श्रौर स्वामी (नाह) के प्यारे, जग में मेरे रूप का कोई है ॥ हे शुक, (रूप-रूपी सोने के) वर्ण को कस कर कह, कि कैसा सोना है, श्रौर तेरा सिंहल-द्वीप कैसा सुन्दर (लोना) है ॥ तेरी (तोरी) रूप-मणि (पद्मावती) कौन दृष्टि की है, श्रर्थात् उस का दर्शन कैसा है, दोनों में से (कह), कि मैं सुन्दरी हूँ, श्रथवा वह (तेरी) पद्मिनी (पद्मावती) ॥

हे शुक (सुश्रटा), तुझे राजा की शपथ है, जो सत्य न कह। (बताव) इस जगत में मेरे रूप के समान कोई है ॥ ८५ ॥

चउपाई ।

सवँरि रूप पदुमावति केरा । हँसा सुश्रा रानी मुख हेरा ॥
जेहि सरवर मँह हंस न श्रावा । बकुली तेहि जल हंस कहावा ॥
दई कीन्ह श्रस जगत श्रनूपा । एक एक तइँ श्रागरि रूपा ॥
कइ मन गरब न छाजा काहू । चाँद घटा श्रउ लागेउ राहू ॥
लोन बिलोन तहाँ को कहा । लोनी सोइ कंत जेहि चहा ॥
का पूँछहु सिंघल कइ नारी । दिनहि न पूजइ निसि श्रँधिश्रारी ॥
पुहुप सुगंध सो तिन्ह कइ काया । जहाँ माँथ का बरनउँ पाया ॥

दोहा ।

गढीँ सो सोनइ सोँधई भरीँ सो रूपइ भाग ।
सुनत रूखि भइ रानी हिअइ लोन अस लाग ॥ ८६ ॥

सवँरि = स्मरण कर के । हेरा = देखा । सरवर = सरो-वर । बकुली = बक की स्त्री । दई = देव = ईश्वर । अनूपा = अनुपम । आगरि = अग्य्र = श्रेष्ठ । छाजा = सोहा = शोभित ह्रुआ । चाँद = चन्द्र । लोन = सुन्दर । बिलोन = विना नमक के = विना सुन्दरता के । पूजइ = पूजती = बराबरी करती । अँधिआरी = अन्धकारिणी = अँधेरी । पुहुप = पुष्प । माँथ = मस्तक । पाया = पद । सोँधई = सुगन्ध-द्रव्य । रुखि = रूखी = रूच । लोन = नोन ॥

शुक ने पद्मावती के रूप को स्मरण कर हँस दिया, और रानी (नाग-मती) के मुख की ओर देखने लगा (हेरा) ॥ (और कहने लगा, कि) (जिस सरो-वर में हंस नहीँ आता, तिस के जल में बकुली हंस कहाती है, (कहावत है, कि जहाँ कोई रूख नहीँ तहाँ रेँड-ही रूख) ॥ ईश्वर ने ऐसा अनुपम जगत बनाया है (कीन्ह), (जिस में) एक से एक श्रेष्ठ रूप हैँ ॥ मन में गर्व कर के किसी का अच्छा नहीँ होता (छाजा)। देखो, रूप का गर्व करने से) चन्द्रमा घट गया, अर्थात् चीण होने लगा, और (उस के पीछे) राहु (दैत्य) लगा ॥ अपने रूप पर चन्द्रमा का गर्व करना यह कथा प्रसिद्ध पुराणों में नहीँ पाई जाती । कदाचित् किसी पारसीग्रन्थ में हो, अथवा कवि की केवल उत्प्रेचा हो ॥ (हे रानी, ऐसी दशा में) तहाँ पर कौन (किस को) सुन्दर (लोन) वा असुन्दर कहे । (सो, मैं तो यही समझता हूँ, कि) जिसे (कान्त = कन्त) पति चाहे, वही सुन्दरी (लोनी) है ॥ सिंहल की स्त्रियों (नारियोँ) को क्या पूँछती हो, (इतनी-ही बात समझ लो, कि) अँधेरी रात दिन की बराबरी नहीँ करती, अर्थात् सिंहल की स्त्रियाँ दिन के समान उज्ज्वल हैँ, और यहाँ की काली रात्रि के समान काली हैँ ॥ सो (हे रानी), तिन्ह (सिंहल की नारियोँ) की काया (काय = शरीर) में पुष्प का सुगन्ध है, (इस लिये लोग देवी समझ कर उन के पैर में माँथा टेकते हैँ सो जिस पैर में सब का) माँथा है, अर्थात् माँथा लगा है, उस पैर का क्या वर्णन करूँ ॥

वे स्त्रियाँ (सो) सुगन्ध-द्रव्य-मिलित सुवर्ण से गढी हैँ । और वे (सो) रूप और भाग्य (भाग) से भरी हैँ । (इतना) सुनते-ही रानी (नाग-मती) रूखी हो गई,

(जल गई), इस से शुक की बात हृदय में नोन सी लग गई, अर्थात् शुक की बात सुन कर कलेजा छरछराने लगा, जैसे जले पर नोन छिडक दिया जाय ॥ ८६ ॥

चउपाई।

जउँ यह सुआ मँदिर मँह अहई। कब-हुँ होइ राजा सउँ कहई ॥
सुनि राजा पुनि होइ बिओगी। छाँडइ राज चलइ होइ जोगी ॥
बिख राखे नहिँ होत अँगूरू। सबद न देइ बिरह तमचूरू ॥
धाइ धामिनी बेगि हँकारी। ओहि सउँपा हिअ रिस न सँभारी ॥
देखु सुआ यह हइ मँद-चाला। भण्उ न ता कर जा कर पाला ॥
मुख कह आन पेट बस आना। तेहि अउगुन दस हाटि बिकाना ॥
पंखि न राखिअ होइ कु-भाखी। लेइ तहँ मारु जहाँ नहिँ साखी ॥

दोहा।

जेहि दिन कहँ हउँ निति डरउँ रइनि छपावउँ सूर।
लेइ चह दीन्ह कवँल कहँ मो कहँ होइ मजूर ॥ ८७ ॥

अहई = है। होइ = हीति = हि + इति = निश्चय कर के = हो न हो। बिओगी = वियोगी। जोगी = योगी। बिख = विष = जहर। अँगूरू = अङ्कुर। सबद = शब्द = आवाज। बिरह = विरह = वियोग। तमचूरू = ताम्रचूड = मुर्गा। धाइ = धाई = धात्री = बचपन में दूध पिलाने-वाली। धामिनी = धाविनी = दौडने-वाली (जो नागिन तेज दौडती है, उसे भी लोग आज कल भाषा में धाविनी का अपभ्रंश धामिनी वा धामिनि कहते हैं)। बेगि = शीघ्र। हँकारी = पुकारी। सउँपा = समर्पण किया। रिस = रोष = क्रोध। सँभारी = सम्भार लिया। मँद-चाल = मन्द-चाल = बुरा चाल। पाला = पालित = पोषित। आन = अन्य। अउगुन = अवगुण। कु-भाखी = कु-भाषी = खोटी भाषा कहने-वाला। साखी = साक्षी = गवाह। निति = नित्य। रइनि = रजनी = रात्रि। सूर = सूर्य। मजूर = मयूर पक्षी, सर्प का शत्रु = मोरेला = मोर ॥

(रानी अपने मन में सोचने लगी, कि) यदि यह शुक मन्दिर में रहे, और कभीँ निश्चय कर के (इस सिंहल के स्त्रियोँ की सुन्दरता को) राजा से कहे ॥ फिर

राजा सुन कर वियोगी (विरक्त) हो कर, राज्य (राज) को छोड कर योगी हो (सिंहल-द्वीप को) चले ॥ (क्योंकि) विष के रखने से (विष-ही होता है) अङ्कुर नहीं होता। (सो) विरह-रूपी मुर्गा शब्द न दे, अर्थात् अपनी आवाज से राजा को जगा न दे, कि क्या अँधेरी रात-रूपी नागमती के रूप में मोहा है; उठ, भोर ऊआ, दिन (पद्मावती) की शोभा देख॥ (ऐसा सोच कर) शीघ्र दौडने-वाली (धामिनी = धाविनी) जो धाई थी, उसे पुकारा, (शीघ्र दौडने-वाली धाई के पुकारने का यह तात्पर्य है, कि झट पट काम पूरा हो जाय, कोई देखने न पावे)। और हृदय में रोष को सँभार न सकी, उस (शुक) को (इस के हाथ) सौंपा॥ (और कहा, कि) देख यह शुक बुरी चाल का है, जिस का (पद्मावती का) यह पाला है, तिस का भी नहीं ऊआ (वहाँ से उड कर चल दिया)॥ मुख से दूसरी (अन्य) बात कहता है, पेट में दूसरी बात बसती है, तिसी अवगुण से दश हाट में विका है॥ (सो) ऐसे कु-भाषी पची को नहीं रखना चाहिए, इसे ले कर तहाँ मार (डाल) जहाँ (कोई) गवाह (साची) न मिले॥

जिस दिन को (पति वियोग को) मैं नित्य डरती हूँ, सूर्य (रत्न-सेन) को रात्रि (अपने काले रूप) में छिपाती हूँ, अर्थात् छिपाये हूँ। (उस सूर्य को) ले कर (यह शुक) लेरे लिये मयूर हो कर कमल (पद्मावती) को दिया चाहता है॥ (नागमती अपने को नागिनी बनाया, इस लिये शुक को, शत्रु समझ, मयूर कहती है)॥ ८७॥

चउपाई।

धाइ सुआ लेइ मारइ गई। समुझि गिआन हिअइ मति भई॥
सुआ सो राजा कर बिसरामी। मारि न जाइ चहइ जेहि सामी॥
यह पंडित खंडित पइ रागू। दोस ताहि जेहि सूझ न आगू॥
जो तिआइ के काज न जाना। परइ धोख पाछे पछिताना॥
नागमती नागिनि-बुधि ताऊ। सुआ मजूर होइ नहिँ काऊ॥
जो न कंत कइ आएसु माँहा। कउनु भरोस नारि कइ बाँहा॥
मकु यह खोज होइ निसि आई। तुरइ रोग हरि माँथइ जाई॥

दोहा।

दुइ सो छपाए ना छपहिँ एक हतिआ एक पापु।
अंत-हु करहिँ बिनास पुनि सइ साखी देइ आपु ॥ ८८ ॥

धाइ = धाई = धात्री। गिआन = ज्ञान। बिसरामी = विश्रामी = विश्राम देने-वाला। सामी = स्वामी = मालिक। खंडित = खण्डित = रहित = दूर = विभक्त = अलग। रागू = राग = आपस की डाह। दोस = दोष। आगू = आगे। तिआइँ = स्त्रियाँ। काज = कार्य। ताज = ताहृ = तिस को। मजूर = मयूर। काऊ = क्वापि = कभी। कंत = कान्त = पति। आएसु = आज्ञा। भरोस = भराशा = पूर्णाशा = विश्वास। बाँहा = बाहु। मकु = मैं ने कहा = क्या जानें। तुरइ = त्वरी = घोडा। हरि = वानर = बन्दर। हतिआ = हत्या = ब्रह्महत्यादि महापाप। पापु = पाप साधारण। अंत-हु = अन्त में। बिनास = विनाश। सइ = से। साखी = साक्षी ॥

धाई शुक को ले कर मारने गई, (राह में) समुझ कर ज्ञान हुआ और बुद्धि (मति) हुई ॥ (कि), शुक जो है, सो राजा को विश्राम (आराम) देने-वाला है, (इस लिये) जिसे स्वामी चाहता है, वह मारा नहीँ जाता ॥ यह शुक पण्डित है, और राग (द्वेष) से दूर है, अर्थात् निष्पक्षपात सत्य कहने-वाला है, (सो) जिस को आगे न सूझे तिसी का दोष जानना चाहिए ॥ जो स्त्रियोँ के कार्य को नहीँ जानता (कि क्षण क्षण में बदला करता है), उसे धोखा (खाना) पडता है, और पीछे से पछताना पडता है ॥ (सो) नागमती जो है, तिस की बुद्धि नागिनि सी है, (जिसे भले बुरे का कुछ पहचान नहीँ रहता। काट कर सब का प्राण लेती है), (उसे जो यह डर है, कि यह शुक मेरे लिये मयूर है, सो) कभीँ शुक मयूर नहीँ होता ॥ जो अपने पति-ही (जो दोनोँ लोक के लिये स्त्री को प्रधान पूज्य है) की आज्ञा में नहीँ रहती, ऐसी नारी के बाहु का कौन भरोसा है, अर्थात् कुछ भरोसा नहीँ ॥ (सो) क्या जानँ रात्रि में (राजा के आने पर) इस का (शुक का) खोज हो, और (ऐसा न हो, कि) घोडे का रोग बन्दर के माथे जाय। (कहावत प्रसिद्ध है, कि अश्व-शाला में बन्दर के रहने से घोडोँ को बीमारी नहीँ होती; यदि बीमारी आई भी, तो वह बन्दर के शिर जाती है, अर्थात् घोडे की बला बन्दर ले लेता है, और उस रोग (बला) से बन्दर-ही मर जाता है, घोडे अच्छे रहते हैं। इसी प्रकार

आदमियों की बला लाल चिडिया के शिर जाती है)। अर्थात् रानी का अपराध रानी के नट जाने से मेरे ऊपर आवे॥

सो एक हत्या और एक पाप ये दोनों छिपाये से नहीं छिपते। (चाहे कुछ काल तक छिपे रहें), परन्तु फिर अन्त में आप-ही से साची दे कर विनाश करते हैं, अर्थात् पाप अकेले में भी किया जाय, तौ भी आप-ही गवाह हो कर प्रगट हो जाता है॥ ८८॥

चउपाई।

राखा सुआ धाइ मति साजा। भएउ खोज निसि आएउ राजा॥
रानी उतर मान सउँ दीन्हा। पंडित सुआ मँजारी लीन्हा॥
मइँ पूँछी सिंघल पदुमिनी। उतर दीन्ह तुम्ह को नागिनी॥
वह जस दिन तुम्ह निसि अँधिआरी। जहाँ बसंत करील को बारी॥
का तोर पुरुख रइनि कर राऊ। उलू न जान दिवस कर भाऊ॥
का वह पंखि कोटि मँह गोटी। अस बडि बोलि जीभ कह छोटी॥
रुहिर चुअइ जो जो कह बाता। भोजन बिनु भोजन मुख राता॥

दोहा।

माँथइ नहिँ बइसारिअ सुठि सुआ जउँ लोन।
कान टूट जेहि आभरन का लेइ करब सो सोन॥ ८९॥

साजा = सजा = बनाया = किया। मान = अभिमान। करील = एक काला वृक्ष व्रज में बहुत होता है, वसन्त ऋतु में भी पत्ते इस में नहीं होते, भर्तृहरि ने भी लिखा है कि "पत्त्रं नैव यदा करील-विटपे दोषो वसन्तस्य किम्"। पुरुख = पुरुष। रइनि = रजनी = रात्रि। राऊ = राजा। उलू = उलूक = खूसट = कुचकुचवा। भाऊ = भाव। पंखि = पची। कोटि मँह = कोट में = किले में। जो कोई कोटि से करोर कहते हैं सो ग्रन्थ-कार का अर्थ नहीं जान पडता, क्योंकि ग्रन्थ-कार करोर के अर्थ में क्रोड का प्रयोग करते हैं। ३ रे दोहे की ६ वीं चौपाई देखो। गोटी = खेलने के लिये काठ वा पत्थल के रंग-दार छोटे छोटे टुकडे। जीभ = जिह्वा। रुहिर = रुधिर,

जैसे वधिर से बहिर। राता = रक्त = लाल। बइसारिअ = बैठाइये। सुठि = सुष्ठु। कान = कर्ण। आभरन = आभरण = गहना। सोन = स्वर्ण = सोना।

धाई ने ऐसी मति साज (कर) शुक को रक्खा, अर्थात् रख छोडा। रात्रि में (जब) राजा आया (शुक का) खोज हुआ॥ रानी ने मान (अभिमान) से उत्तर दिया, कि पण्डित शुक को बिलैया ने ले लिया॥ (शुक के मरने का ताप राजा को न हो, इस लिये शुक की निन्दा करने लगी, कि) मैं ने सिंहल के पद्मिनी को पूछा, (कि वह कैसी है)। (इस पर उस ने) उत्तर दिया, कि तुम नागिनी (उस के आगे) कौन हो, अर्थात् कुछ नहीं हो॥ वह ऐसी है जैसे दिन और तुम अँधेरी रात हो। जहाँ वसन्त ऋतु है, वहाँ करील की बारी (बगीचा) की कौन गणना है॥ रात्रि (काली नागमती) का राजा तेरा पुरुष (स्वामी, राजा रत्न-सेन) क्या है, अर्थात् कुछ नहीं। उलू (उलूक) दिन का भाव (प्रभाव) नहीं जानता (क्योंकि वह रात्रि-चर है)॥ (सो) कोट में गोटी-सा जो पक्षी, वह क्या है, अर्थात् कुछ भी आदर योग्य नहीं है। (जो दुष्ट) छोटी जीभ से ऐसी बडी बोली कहता है॥ जो जो (वह) बात कहता है सो (जानों उस के मुख से) रुधिर चूता है। और (उस का) मुख भोजन करने, वा भोजन न करने, पर लाल-ही रहता है, अर्थात् प्रेम से खिलाइये वा न खिलाइये, सर्वदा क्रोध से लाल मुख किये रहता है॥

(सो) यदि शुक (चाहे) भली भाँति सुन्दर (भी) हो, तो (भी) उसे माथे पर नहीं बैठाना चाहिए। (क्योंकि) उस सोना-ही को ले कर क्या करँगे, जिस के गहने से कान टूट जाय, अर्थात् यद्यपि देखने में शुक मनो-हर है, तथापि उस की बोली से हृदय विदीर्ण हो जाता है। इस लिये ऐसे शुक का न रहना-ही उत्तम है॥ ८९॥

चउपाई।

राजइ सुनि बिओग तस माना। जइस हिअइ बिकरम पछिताना॥
वह हीरा-मनि पंडित सूआ। जो बोलइ मुख अंब्रित चूआ॥
पंडित दुख-खंडित निरदोखा। पंडित हुते परइ नहिँ धोखा॥
पंडित केरि जीभ मुख सूधी। पंडित बात कहइ न निबूधी॥
पंडित सु-मति देइ पँथ लावा। जो कु-पंथ तेहि पँडित न भावा॥

चउपाई ।

चाँद जइस धनि उँजिअरि अही । भा पिउ रोस गहन अस गही ॥
परम सोहाग निबाहि न पारी । भा दोहाग सेवा जब .हारी ॥
एतनिक दोस बिरचि पिउ रूठा । जो पिउ आपन कहइ सो झूठा ॥
अइसइ गरब न भूलइ कोई । जेहि डर बहुत पिआरी सोई ॥
रानी आइ धाइ के पासा । सुआ भुआ सेवँरि कइ आसा ॥
परा पिरिति कंचन मँह सीसा । बिथरि न मिलइ सावँ पइ दीसा ॥
कहाँ सोनार पास जेहि जाउँ । देइ सोहाग करइ एक ठाउँ ॥

दोहा ।

मइँ पिउ पिरिति भरोसइ गरब कीन्ह जिअ माँह ।
तेहि रिस हउँ परहेली रूसेउ नागरि नाह ॥ ९१ ॥

चाँद = चन्द्र। जइस = जैसी । धनि = धन्या = नागमती । उँजिअरि = उज्ज्वलित । अही = थी । पिउ = प्रिय = पति = रत्न-सेन । रोस = रोष = क्रोध । गहन = ग्रहण । गही = पकडी गई। परम = अत्यन्त। सोहाग = सौभाग्य = पति-सुख। निबाहि = निर्वाह। पारी = सकी। दोहाग = दौर्भाग्य = दुःख। एतनिक = इतना = एतावान्। दोस = दोष। बिरचि = रच कर के = कर के। रूठा = रुष्ट ऊआ। गरब = गर्व। पिआरी = प्यारी = प्रिया। भुआ = भूआ = सेमर के फल की रूई। सेवँरि = सेमर = शाल्मलि। पिरिति = प्रीति। कंचन = काञ्चन = सुवर्ण। सीसा = सीसक। बिथरि = विश्लथ हो कर = भ्रष्ट हो कर = बिथुर कर = फट कर = अलग हो कर = चारो ओर से विदीर्ण हो कर। सावँ = श्याम = काला। दीसा = दीखा = देखा जाता है। सोनार = स्वर्णकार। सोहाग = सौभाग्य वा सोहागा जो सोने को शीघ्र गला देता और विशेष कान्तिमान कर देता है। ठाउँ = स्थान। रिस = रोस = क्रोध। परहेली = परहेलित ऊई = अवहेलित ऊई = अनादृत ऊई = आदर से रहित ऊई। नागरि = हे नागरी = चतुरी धाई। नाह = नाथ = स्वामी = पति। यहाँ परहेला = अवहेला = अनादर ॥

भामिनी-विलास के प्रास्ताविक-विलास में लिखा है कि “समुपागतवति दैवादवहेलां कुटज मधुकरे मागाः। मकरन्दतुन्दिलानामरविन्दानामयं महामान्यः॥” गीतिः ॥

नागमती जैसा चाँद तैसी जो उज्ज्वलित थी, (उस उज्ज्वल चन्द्र में) (जब) पति का रोष हुआ, (तब) ग्रहण के ऐसी पकड गई, अर्थात् पति के रुष्ट होने से, जो मुख-चन्द्र उज्ज्वलित था, वह ऐसा मलिन हो गया, जैसा ग्रहण में चन्द्र राहु के पकडने से मलिन हो जाता है॥ (नागमती) परम सौभाग्य को न निवाह सकी, अर्थात् पति को प्रसन्न न कर सकी। जब सेवा से चूक गई (हारी) तब दौर्भाग्य (उत्पन्न) हुआ॥ (अपने मन में कहने लगी कि), इतना-ही दोष के करने से पति रूठ गया, (सो) जो पति को अपना कहता है, सो झूठा है॥ (कवि कहता है, कि जैसे गर्व में नागमती भूली) ऐसे-ही गर्व में कोई न भूले। जिस को (पति का) डर है, वही (सो-ई) (पति की) बहुत प्यारी होती है॥ (ऐसा सोच कर) रानी धाई के पास, सेमर के भूआ (सदृश) शुक की आशा से आई॥ (और कहने लगी, कि) प्रीति-रूपी कञ्चन (सुवर्ण) में (पति-रोस-रूपी) सीसा पड गया। (सो सुवर्ण) फट कर (बिथरि) नहीँ मिलता है, (सीसे की) श्यामता, अर्थात् काली दाग, अवश्य (पइ = अपि = निश्चय) देखी जाती है, अर्थात् देख पडती है॥ (सो, हे सखि,) सोनार कहाँ हैँ, जिस के पास (मैँ) जाऊँ, (और वह) सौभाग्य वा सोहागा दे कर (फटे प्रीति-रूपी सोने को) एक स्थान में करे॥

मैँ पति की प्रीति के भरोसे जी में गर्व किया। (तिसी से जो शुक पर रिस किया), तिसी रिस से बे-आदर की हुई हूँ, (क्योँकि), हे नागरि (चतुरी) धाई, पति (नाह) रूस गया है॥ ९१॥

चउपाई।

उतर धाइ तब दीन्ह रिसाई। रिस आपु-हि बुधि अउरहि खाई॥
मइँ जो कहा रिस करहु न बाला। को न गएउ एहि रिस कर घाला॥
तूँ रिस भरी न देखेसि आगू। रिस मँह का कहँ भएउ सोहागू॥
बिरस बिरोध रिस-हि पइ होई। रिस मारइ तेहि मार न कोई॥
जेहि रिस तेहि रस जोगि न जाई। बिनु रस हरदि होइ पिअराई॥
जेहि कइ रिस मरिअइ रस जीजइ। सो रस तजि रिस कोह न कीजइ॥
कंत सोहाग न पाइअ साधा। पावइ सोइ जो ओहि चित बाँधा॥

दोहा ।

रहइ जो पिउ के आएसु अउ बरतइ होइ खीन ।
सोइ चाँद अस निरमर जरम न होइ मलीन ॥ ९२॥

उतर = उत्तर । धाइ = धाई = धात्री । रिसाई = क्रोध कर = रोष कर । आपु-हि = अपनी-ही । बुधि = बुद्धि । अउरहि = अपरहि = दूसरे को । खाई = खाता है । बाला = बालिका = कन्या = बेटी । कर = हाथ । घाला = नाश । सोहागू = सौभाग्य । बिरस = विरस = फीका-पन । बिरोध = वैर-भाव । पइ = अपि = निश्चय । जोगि = योग कर के = नियम कर के । बिनु = विना । हरदि = हरिद्रा । पिअराई = पीला-पन । मरिअइ = मर जाइये । जीजइ = जी जाइये । कोह = क्रोध । साधा = श्रद्धा । बरतइ = व्रत करें । खीन = क्षीण = दुर्बल । निरमर = निर्मल । जरम = जन्म । मलीन = मलिन = मैला ॥

तब धाई ने रिस कर के उत्तर दिया, (कि) रिस से अपनी-ही बुद्धि औरोँ को खाती है, अर्थात् रिस से अपनी बुद्धि, चाण्डाल-स्वरूपा हो कर, और निरपराधियोँ को खाने लगती है ॥ मैँ ने जो कहा, कि बेटी (बाला) रिस न करो, (क्योँकि) इस रिस के हाथ (कर) से कौन (को) नाश (घाला) को नहीँ प्राप्त हुआ (गएउ) ॥ (परन्तु तैँ न मानी, और) रिस से भरी आगे नहीँ देखी, (कि क्या होने-वाला है)। (सो सुन तो सही) रिस में किस को सौभाग्य हुआ है, अर्थात् भला हुआ है ॥ निश्चय (समझो) रिस-ही से विरस और विरोध होता है। (जो) रिस को मारता है, अर्थात् रोकता है, तिसे कोई नहीँ मारता ॥ जिसे रिस है, तिस के यहाँ नियम से, रस नहीँ जाता। और जहाँ रस-ही नहीँ है, अर्थात् नीरस है, तहाँ रस के विना हरदी के ऐसी पिअराई होती है, अर्थात् नीरस होने से उस का चेहरा सर्वदा हरदी के ऐसा पीला रहता है ॥ जिस रिस को कर (पीला होते होते) मर जाइये, और जिस रस से जी जाइये। उस (सो) रस को त्याग कर (तजि), रिस और क्रोध (कोह) न कीजिये। (जो क्रोध शरीर के भीतर-ही रहता है, प्रगट नहीँ होता, उसे रोष वा रिस कहते हैँ, वही प्रगट होने से क्रोध कहाता है)॥ कान्त (कंत) का सौभाग्य, अर्थात् पति-सौख्य, (केवल) श्रद्धा, अर्थात् इच्छा से नहीँ पाया जाता। (उस सुख को) वही (सोई) पाता है, जो (अपने) चित्त (=चित) को उस में (ओहि), अर्थात् उस पति में, बाँध देता है ॥

जो पति की आज्ञा में रहे, और (उस के प्रसन्न के लिये) चीण हो कर व्रत करे। सो (स्त्री) चन्द्र के ऐसा निर्मल हो, और जन्म भर मलिन न हो ॥ ९२ ॥

चउपाई।

जुआ-हारि समुझी मन रानी। सुआ दीन्ह राजा कहँ आनी ॥
मानु मती हउँ गरब न कीन्हा। कंत तुम्हार मरम मइँ लीन्हा ॥
सेवा करइ जो बरह-उ मासा। एतनिक अउगुन करहु बिनासा ॥
जउँ तुम्ह देइ नाइ कइ गीवा। छाँडहु नहिँ बिनु मारे जीवा ॥
मिलत-हि मँह जनु अहउ निरारे। तुम्ह सउँ अहहि अँदेस पिआरे ॥
मइँ जाना तुम्ह मो-हीँ माँहा। देखउँ ताकि त सब हिअ माँहा ॥
का रानी का चेरी कोई। जा कहँ मया करहु भल सोई ॥

दोहा।

तुम्ह सउँ कोइ न जीता हारे बररुचि भोज।
पहिलहि आपु जो खोअई करइ तुम्हारा खोज ॥ ९३ ॥

इति नागमती-सुआ-संवाद-खंड ॥ ८ ॥

जुआ = जूआ = द्यूत। मानु = मानो। मती = मति = बुद्धि। गरब = गर्व = अभिमान। कंत = कान्त = पति। मरम = मर्म = भेद। बरह-उ = बारहो। एतनिक = इतना = एतावान्। अउगुन = अवगुण। बिनासा = विनाश। नाइ = नवाँ कर = झुँका कर। गीवा = ग्रीवा = गला। निरारे = निरालय = अलग = दूर। अँदेस = अँदेसा = संशय = डर। पिआरे = हे प्रिय। ताकि = तर्क कर, वा आँख उठा कर। त = तो = तदा। चेरी = चेटिका = लौंडी। मया = माया = दया = कृपा। बररुचि = वररुचि = विक्रम के नवरत्नों में से एक रत्न-रूपी पण्डित, जिस ने प्राकृत का व्याकरण बनाया है। बहुत से लोग प्राकृत व्याकरण के कर्त्ता को दूसरा वररुचि कहते हैं, और इस का दूसरा नाम कात्यायन कहते हैं ॥ भोज = धारा के राजा प्रसिद्ध संस्कृतानुरागी ॥

(अन्त में धाई ने शुक को दिया। शुक के पाने पर) रानी ने मन में जुआ-हार समझी, अर्थात् जैसे जुआ की हारी चीज फिर हेर फेर से मिल जाती है, उसी

जुआ-हार के समान शुक का मिलना रानी ने समझा। जुआरी लोग हाथों में जब चाहते हैं तब कौडी को छिपा लेते हैं फिर प्रगट कर देते हैं। सो आन कर (आनी) राजा को शुक दे दिया। (और कहने लगी, कि) मति को, अर्थात् इस मेरे कहने को, मानो। मैं ने गर्व नहीं किया था। (किन्तु), हे कान्त, मैं ने तुम्हारा मर्म लिया, अर्थात् तुमारा भेद लिया, (कि तुम मुझे कैसा चाहते हो)॥ (सो समझ लिया, कि) बारहो मास जो (तुम्हारी) सेवा करे, (उस का भी) इतने-ही अवगुण पर (तुम) विनाश कर डालते हो, (इस में संशय नहीं)॥ यदि तुम्हें झुका कर (नाइ) (अपनी) गला भी दे दे, (तो भी) विना जी मारे न छोडो॥ (सो तुम) मिलते-ही में जानों अलग हो, अर्थात् यद्यपि प्रतिदिन आप से समागम होता है, तथापि आप ऐसे निर्मोही हो, जानों कभी की भेंट मुलाकात नहीं। सो, हे प्यारे, तुम से (मुझे) डर है, (कि कभी किसी के प्रेम में फँस कर मुझ से दूर न हो जाव)॥ मैं ने जाना था कि तुम मेरे-ही में हो, अर्थात् मुझे छोड अन्य से कुछ भी संबन्ध नहीं रखते हो, परन्तु तर्क कर के, वा आँख उठा कर, देखती हूँ, तो (तुम) सब के हृदय में हो॥ (सो) क्या रानी, क्या कोई चेरी, जिस के ऊपर (तुम) मया (दया) करो, वही (सोई) भली है, अर्थात् रूप का गर्ब करना व्यर्थ है, जिस को तुम चाहो वही भली रूपवती और सौभाग्यवती है॥

(सो) तुम से कोई नहीं जीता, वररुचि ऐसे विद्वान, और भोज ऐसे योगि-राज (जिस की बनाई सांख्य-सूत्र पर वृत्ति है) भी तुम से हार गये। जो कोई पहले (समाधि लगा कर वा आप के नाम को रट रट कर) अपने को खोवे, अर्थात् इस संसार से विरक्त हो जाय तब, वह तुम्हारा खोज करे (तो पावे तो पावे)॥ यहाँ पति को पर-ब्रह्म मानने से पर-ब्रह्म के पक्ष में भी दोहा समेत सब चौपाइयाँ बैठ जाती हैं॥ ९३॥

इति नागमती-शुक-संवाद-खण्ड-नामाष्टम-खण्डं समाप्तम्॥ ८॥

अथ राजा-सुआ-संवाद-खंड ॥ ९ ॥

चउपाई।

राजइ कहा सत्त कहु सूआ। बिनु सत कस जस सेवँरि भूआ ॥
होइ मुख रात सत्त कइ बाता। जहाँ सत्त तहँ धरम सँघाता ॥
बाँधी सिसिटि अहइ सत केरी। लछिमी आहि सत्त कइ चेरी ॥
सत्त जहाँ साहस सिधि पावा। अउ सत-बादी पुरुख कहावा ॥
सत कहँ सती सँवारइ सरा। आगि लाइ चहुँ दिसि सत जरा ॥
दुइ जग तरा सत्त जेइ राखा। अउरु पिआर दइहि सत-भाखा ॥
सेा सत छाँड जो धरम बिनासा। का मति हिअइ कीन्ह सत-नासा ॥

दोहा।

तुम्ह सयान अउ पंडित अ-सत न भाखहु काउ।
सत्त कहहु तुम्ह मो सउँ दहुँ का कर अनिआउ ॥ ९४ ॥

सत्त = सत्य। सत = सत्य। सेवँरि = सेमर = शाल्मली। भूआ = सेमर के फल की रूई। रात = रक्त = ललित। धरम = धर्म। सँघाता = संघात = समूह। सिसिटि = सृष्टि। लछिमी = लक्ष्मी। आहि = है। चेरी = चेटिका = लौंडी। सिधि = सिद्धि। सत-बादी = सत्य-वादी = सत्य बोलने-वाला। पुरुख = पुरुष। सती = जो स्त्री मृत-पति के साथ भस्म होने चलती है। सरा = शर = चिता। पिआर = प्यार = प्रिय। दइहि = ईश्वर को = देव को। भाखा = भाषा। बिनासा = विनाश किया। सत-नासा = सत्य-नाश

करने-वाली। सयान = सज्ञान = चतुर = माननीय। अ-सत = अ-सत्य। काउ = कभी = क्वापि। दऊ = दोनों में से। अनआउ = अन्याय॥

राजा ने कहा, कि, हे शुक, सत्य कह। (क्योंकि) विना सत्य के ढुँ कैसा है? जैसे सेमर का भूआ (जो कि फूंक देने से उड जाता है)॥ (क्योंकि) सत्य की वार्त्ता (कहने) से मुख लक्षित होता है, अर्थात् रहता है। और जहाँ पर सत्य है तहाँ धर्म का समूह रहता है (क्योंकि शास्त्रों में भी लिखा है, कि सत्यान्नास्ति परो धर्मः)॥ सत्य-(-ही) की बाँधी सृष्टि है, सत्य-(-ही) की चेरी लक्ष्मी है॥ जहाँ पर सत्य है, तहाँ साहस से (सहसा से) (भी) सिद्धि पाई जाती है, अर्थात् प्रसिद्ध है, कि साहस से कार्य की सिद्धि नहीं होती, परन्तु जहाँ सत्य है, तहाँ साहस करने से भी कार्य की सिद्धि होती है। और जहाँ सत्य है, वह पुरुष सत्य-वादी कहाता है॥ सत्य-(सत्य-लोक-)-ही के लिये सती चिता (सरा) को रचती है (सँवारइ), और सत्य-ही से, अर्थात् विवाह के समय जो पति से सप्त-पदी के समय कहा है, कि आप के दुःख सुख दोनों में साथ रहूँगी, इस वचन को सत्य करने-ही के लिये चारो दिशा में आग (अग्नि) को लगा कर जलती है॥ जिस ने सत्य को रक्खा, वह दोनों जग को, अर्थात् इस लोक और परलोक को, तर गया (पार हो गया), और ईश्वर को (दइहि) भी सत्य-भाषा प्यारी है॥ ऐसे सत्य को जो धर्म का विनाश करता है, वही (सो) छोडता है। (सो, हे शुक,) क्या तुम ने हृदय में सत्य-नाश करने-वाली मति को किया, अर्थात् खेद की बात है, कि व्यर्थ तुम ने "उलू न जान दिवस कर भाऊ" (८९ वाँ दोहा) इत्यादि वाक्य से मेरी निन्दा की॥

(सो) तुम सयाने और पण्डित हो। तुम कभी अ-सत्य नहीं कहते हो (भाखऊ)। तुम मुझ से सत्य कहो, कि (नाग-मती और तुम इन) दोनों में से किस का अन्याय है, अर्थात् सच मुच तुम ने मेरी निन्दा की, वा नाग-मती ने अपने मन से बात बना कर मुझ से कह दिया है॥ ९४॥

चउपाई।

सत्त कहत राजा जिउ जाऊ। पइ मुख अ-सत न भाखउँ काऊ॥
हउँ सत लेइ निसरा एहि पतेँ। सिंघल-दीप राज घर हतेँ॥
पदुमावति राजा कइ बारी। पदुम-गंध ससि बिधि अउतारी॥

ससि-मुख अंग मलय-गिरि रानी। कनक सुगंध दुआदस बानी॥
इहिँ पदुमिनि जो सिंघल माँहा। सुगँध सुरूप सो तेहि कइ छाँहा॥
हीरा-मनि हउँ तेहि क परेवा। काँठा फूट करत तेहि सेवा॥
अउ पाएउँ मानुस कइ भाखा। नाहिँ त पंखि मूठि भर पाँखा॥

दोहा।

जउ लहि जिअउँ राति दिन सवँरि मरउँ ओहि नाउँ।
मुख राता तन हरिअर दुहूँ जगत पइ जाउँ॥ ९५॥

सत्त = सत्य। जिउ = जीव। अ-सत = अ-सत्य। निसरा = निःसरण किया, निकला। पतैँ = पत्तन मेँ = देश मेँ। हतेँ = थे। पदुमावति = पद्मावती। बारी = बालिका = कन्या। पदुम = पद्म = कमल। गंध = गन्ध = सुगन्ध = खुशबू = महक। ससि = शशि = चन्द्रमा। बिधि = विधि = ब्रह्मा। अउतारी = अवतार दिया। मलय-गिरि = मलयाचल = मलय-पहाड जहाँ पर मलय चन्दन होता है। दुआदस = द्वादश। बानी = वर्ण। पदुमिनि = पद्मिनी। छाँहा = छाया = प्रतिविम्ब। परेवा = पारावत = पक्षी। काँठा = कण्ठा। मानुस = मनुष्य। पंखि = पक्षी। पाँखा = पक्ष। जउ लहि = जब तक। राति = रात्रि। सवँरि = स्मरण कर के। राता = रक्त = ललित। हरिअर = हरित वर्ण = हरा। दुहूँ = दोनोँ। पइ = अपि = निश्चय = अवश्य॥

(शुक ने कहा, कि), हे राजा, सत्य कहते (चाहेँ) जी (चला) जाय, परन्तु (पइ) (मैँ) कभीँ अ-सत्य नहीँ कहता॥ सत्य-ही को ले कर (मैँ) इस देश मेँ (पतैँ) निकला हूँ, अर्थात् निकल कर आया हूँ, (नहीँ तो) सिंहल-द्वीप मेँ राजा के घर मेँ (हम) थे॥ (मेरा वृत्तान्त सुनिये), (सिंहल-द्वीप) के राजा की पद्मावती कन्या है। (उस की ऐसी शोभा है, जानोँ) ब्रह्मा ने कमल के सुगन्ध सहित शशि (चन्द्र) का अवतार दिया है॥ उस रानी का मुख तो चन्द्रमा (शशि) और अङ्ग मलयाचल है, (उस का वर्ण ऐसा है, जानोँ) सुगन्ध सहित द्वादश वर्ण अर्थात् द्वादशादित्य के ऐसा प्रज्वलित वर्ण (उत्तम सुवर्ण) सुवर्ण (कनक) हो॥ सिंहल मेँ और जो पद्मिनी (स्त्रियाँ) हैँ, सो (सब) सुगन्ध और सुरूप मेँ तिस (पद्मावती) की छाया (प्रतिविम्ब) हैँ॥ तिस पद्मावती का (मैँ) हीरा-मणि पक्षी हूँ। तिसी की सेवा करते (मेरा) कण्ठा फूटा अर्थात् जवान हुआ॥ (सुग्ग जब जवान होते हैँ

तब उन के गले में लाल-काली एक धारी जिसे कण्ठा कहते हैं निकलती है। उसी को लोग कहते हैं कि कण्ठा फूटा) और मनुष्य की भाषा पाया, नहीं तो मुट्ठी (मुष्टि) भर पंख रखने-वाला पक्षी हूँ (मेरे में क्या विशेषता)॥

(सो) जब तक जीता हूँ, उसी (पद्मावती) का नाम स्मरण कर के मरता हूँ, अर्थात् उस के उपकार को भुला कर कृतघ्न नहीं बना चाहता, किन्तु अपनी सत्यता से उस के उपकार को स्मरण कर मरता हूँ, कि हा मैं ने उस का कुछ उपकार न किया, (और इसी सत्यता के कारण, कि मैं उस के उपकार को मानता हूँ)। दोनों जगत् में, अर्थात् इस लोक और परलोक में, जहाँ जाऊँ अवश्य मेरा सुख ललित और शरीर (तन=तनु) हरित रहेगी (क्योंकि मै सत्य-वादी हूँ, झूठे का मुँह काला और शरीर पीली हो जाती है)॥ ९५॥

चउपाई।

हीरा-मनि जो कवँल बखाना। सुनि राजा होइ भवँर भुलाना॥
आगे आउ पंखि उँजिआरे। कहे सो दीप पनिग के मारे॥
रहा जो कनक सुबासिक ठाऊँ। कस न होए हीरा-मनिं नाऊँ॥
को राजा कस दीप उतंगू। जेहि रे सुनत मन भएउ पतंगू॥
सुनि सो समुद चखु भए किलकिला। कवँलहि चहउँ भवँर होइ मिला॥
कहु सुगंध धनि कस निरमरी। दहुँ अलि संग कि अब-हीँ करी॥
अउ कहु तहँ जो पदुमिनि लोनी। घर घर सब के होहिँ जस होनी॥

दोहा।

सबद बखान तहाँ कर कहत सो मो सउँ आउ।
चहउँ दीप वह देखा सुनत उठा तस चाउ॥ ९६॥

हीरा-मनि=हीरा-मणि। कवँल=कमल। भवँर=भ्रमर। पंखि=पक्षी। उँजिआरे=उज्ज्वल। दीप=दीया वा द्वीप। पनिग=पन्नग=सर्प=नाग। मारे=मार दिया। कनक=सुवर्ण। सुबासिक=सुगन्धवान्=गमकदार। ठाऊँ=स्थान। पतंग=पतङ्ग=फतिङ्गा=कीट, जो दीप को देख कर उस के यहाँ दौड कर जाता है, और उस की ज्वाला से भस्म हो कर प्राण देता है। समुद=समुद्र। चखु=चक्षुः=नेत्र। किलकिला=सातवाँ

समुद्र, जिस का वर्णन रत्न-सेन की याचा में कवि ने खयं किया है कि "पुनि किलकिला समुद मँह आए"। धनि = धन्या = पद्मावती। कस = कैसी। निरमरी = निर्मला। दङ्ँ = क्या जानेँ = दोनोँ मेँ से। अलि = भ्रमर। करी = कली = कलिका। पदुमिनि = पद्मिनी। लोनी = सुन्दरी = लवण से युक्त। बखान = वर्णन। आउ = आवो। चाउ = चाह = इच्छा॥

हीरा-मणि ने जो कमल (पद्मावती) का बखान किया, (तो उस बखान को) सुन कर, राजा भ्रमर हो कर (उस कमल में) भूल गया॥ (लगा कहने, कि) हे उज्ज्वल पची, आगे आ, जिस दीप को (तै ने) कहा, उस ने (सो) (तो) सर्प को (पन्नग को) मार दिया। (यहाँ दीप-पद में श्लेष है, अर्थात् दीप से दीये को ले कर राजा कहता है, कि दीप अपनी प्रज्वलित शिखा से छोटे छोटे कीटों को मारता है, परन्तु इस दीप (दीये) ने तो पन्नग, जो मैं, तिसी को मार दिया। वा पन्नग, जो नाग-मती, तिस को मार दिया, क्योँकि मैं उसे अब त्याग कर कमल (पद्मावती) में भूल गया॥ (सो) जो तूँ कनक (सुवर्ण) गमक-दार (सुवासिक) स्थान में, अर्थात् सिंहल-दीप में, रहा, (तब) कैसे न तेरा नाम हीरा-मणि हो, अर्थात् ऐसे सुन्दर स्थान में रहने-ही से, तूँ ने हीरा-मणि ऐसा सुन्दर नाम पाया॥ (सो कह, कि वहाँ का) कौन राजा है, और वह दीप कैसा उतङ्ग (उत्तुङ्ग = ऊँचा) है, जिस (दीप = दीये) को सुनते-ही, रे (शुक), मेरा मन फतिंगा हो गया॥ (और जिस को) सुन कर मेरे नेच किलकिला समुद्र हो गये, अर्थात् जैसे लहरोँ से किलकिला समुद्र व्याकुल रहता है, तैसे-ही उस के दर्शन के उमङ्ग में नेच व्याकुल हो रहे हैं॥ (सो) कह, कि वह सुगन्ध से भरी धन्या (पद्मावती) कैसी निर्मल है, भ्रमर (अलि) के सङ्ग है, वा अभीँ कलिका (कली) है, अर्थात् विवाह हो गया है, वा कुआँरी है॥ और तहाँ जो सुन्दर पद्मिनी हैं, और सब के घर घर जैसे कृत्य (होनी) होते हैं (उन का भी वृत्तान्त) कह॥

तहाँ का मुझ से सब बखान कहता आव। मैं उस दीप को देखा चाहता हूँ। (तिस दीप का नाम) सुनते तैसी-ही (देखने की) चाह (इच्छा) उठी है॥ ९६॥

चउपाई।

का राजा हउँ बरनउँ ताह्र। सिंघल-दीप आहि कबिलाह्र॥
जो गा तहाँ भुलानेउ सोई। गइ जुग बीति न बहुरा कोई॥

घर घर पदुमिनि छतिस-उ जाती। सदा बसंत दिवस अउ राती ॥
जेहि जेहि बरन फूल फुलवारी। तेहि तेहि बरन सु-गंध सो नारी ॥
गँधरब-सेन तहाँ बड राजा। अछरिन्ह माँह इँदर बिधि साजा ॥
सो पदुमावति ता करि बारी। अउ सब दीप माँह उँजिआरी ॥
चहूँ खंड के बर जो ओनाहीँ। गरबहि राजा बोलइ नाहीँ ॥

दोहा।

उअत सूर जस देखी चाँद छपइ तेहि धूप।
अइसइ सबइ जाहिँ छपि पदुमावति के रूप ॥ ९७ ॥

आहि = है। कबिलासू = कैलास। जुग = युग। बहुरा = फिरा। छतिस-उ = छत्तीसो। राती = रात्रि। बरन = वर्ण = रङ्ग। फूल = फुल्ल = पुष्प। फुलवारी = पुष्प-वाटिका। गँधरब = गन्धर्व। अछरिन्ह = अप्सरा-गण। इँदर = इन्द्र। बारी = बालिका = कन्या। दीप = द्वीप वा दीया। उँजिआरी = उज्ज्वल। चहूँ = चारो। ओनाहीँ = झुँकते हैँ। गरब = गर्व। उअत = उदय होते। सूर = सूर्य। चाँद = चन्द्र। धूप = धाम = तेज। पदुमावति = पद्मावती ॥

(शुक कहता है, कि) हे राजा, तिस (सिंहल-द्वीप) का क्या बर्णन करूँ। (यही समझो, कि) सिंहल-द्वीप कैलास है ॥ जो (कोई) वहाँ गया, कि वह (सोई) भुलाया। युग बीत गया (परन्तु वहाँ से फिर) कोई न लौटा बहुरा ॥ (कवि के मत से युग स्त्री-लिङ्ग है, इस लिये गइ का प्रयोग किया है। संहिता-कारोँ के मत से ४३२०००० सौर वर्ष का एक युग होता है, और ज्यौतिष-वेदाङ्ग के मतानुसार एक युग पाँच सौर वर्ष का होता है। यही बात ५ वँ दोहे की टीका मेँ भी है ॥ (वहाँ) घर घर छत्तीसो जाति पद्मिनी हैँ। (चार प्रकार की स्त्री होती हैँ, हस्तिनी, शङ्खिनी, चित्रिणी और पद्मिनी। इन मेँ पद्मिनी सब से उत्तम और मनोहर होती हैँ। इसी ग्रन्थ मेँ जहाँ राघव चेतन ने बादशाह से पद्मावती का वर्णन किया है, तहाँ सब का लक्षण लिखा है। पद्मिनी सिंहल-द्वीप छोड और अन्यत्र कहीँ नहीँ उत्पन्न होती ॥ ब्राह्मण दश-विध, पञ्च-गौड, और पञ्च-द्राविड। पञ्च-गौड मेँ सारस्वत १। कान्यकुब्ज २। गौड ३। मैथिल ४। उत्कल ५ ॥ पञ्च-द्राविड मेँ, कार्णाटक १। द्राविड २। गुर्जर ३। महाराष्ट्र ४।

तैलङ्ग ५ ॥ १ ॥ चत्रिय। सूर्य-वंशी, चन्द्र-वंशी, इत्यादि प्राचीन समय के। वैस, बघेला, चन्देला, चौहान, पमार, उज्जैन, गहरवार, बिसेन, इत्यादि आजकल के॥ २ ॥ वैश्य। अगर-वाला इत्यादि ॥ ३ ॥ सोनार ॥ ४ ॥ कलवार ॥ ५ ॥ बनिया ॥ ६ ॥ कायस्थ ॥ ७ ॥ पटवा (पट-हारा) ॥ ८ ॥ बारी ॥ ९ ॥ ठठेर ॥ १० ॥ अहीर ॥ ११ ॥ गूजर ॥ १२ ॥ तमोली, बरई ॥ १३ ॥ रङ्गरेज ॥ १४ ॥ नाऊ ॥ १५ ॥ लोहार ॥ १६ ॥ भाट ॥ १७ ॥ तेली ॥ १८ ॥ माली ॥ १९ ॥ गन्धी ॥ २० ॥ छीपी ॥ २१ ॥ नट ॥ २२ ॥ डोम ॥ २३ ॥ ढोल=कोल, भिल्ल ॥ २४ ॥ हेला=हलालखोर=सहनाई बजानेवाला ॥ २५ ॥ धोबी ॥ २६ ॥ चमार ॥ २७ ॥ कोहार ॥ २८ ॥ कुनुबी ॥ २९ ॥ कोइरी ॥ ३० ॥ कहार, भूँजा, गोँड, काँदू ॥ ३१ ॥ मल्लाह, केवट, धीवर, धानुक, बहेलिया ॥ ३२ ॥ नोनिया ॥ ३३ ॥ भर, पासी, दुसाध ॥ ३४ ॥ खटिक ॥ ३५ ॥ गडेरिया ॥ ३६ ॥ इस प्रान्त में ये ३६ जाति प्रधान हैं। देश विशेष में कुछ इन्ही में हेर फेर है)॥ और सदा (सर्वदा) दिन और रात वसन्त ऋतु (ऋतु-राज) रहता है॥ फुलवारी में जिस जिस वर्ण के फूल होते हैं, तिसी तिसी वर्ण की सु-गन्ध से भरीं वहाँ नारियाँ हैं। तहाँ का प्रधान (बड=वर) राजा गन्धर्व-सेन है, ब्रह्मा (विधि) ने (उसे) अप्सराओं (अप्सरा सदृश युवतियों) के बीच इन्द्र (ऐसा) सजा (शोभित किया) है॥ तिसी (राजा) की कन्या वह (सो) पद्मावती है, और वह (कन्या) सब दीपों (सब दीये-सी और युवतियों) में उज्ज्वलित है॥ (विवाह के लिये) चारो (चहूँ) ओर (खण्ड) के जो वर (वहाँ) झुकते हैं (ओनाहीं)। राजा (गन्धर्व-सेन) गर्व से (उन से) बोलता नहीं, अर्थात् अपने समान न देख उन्हें तुच्छ समझता है॥

जैसे सूर्य उदय होता हो (वैसी-ही पद्मावती की कान्ति) देखी है, अर्थात् देख पडती है। (जैसे) तिस सूर्य के तेज (धूप) से चान्द छिप जाता है, ऐसे-ही पद्मावती के रूप के आगे सब छिप जाते हैं, अर्थात् उस की कान्ति के आगे सब की कान्ति फीकी पड जाती है॥ ९७॥

चउपाई।

सुनि रबि नाउ रतन भा राता। पंडित फेरि इहइ कहु बाता॥
तुइँ सु-रंग मूरति वह कही। चित मँह लागि चितर होइ रही॥
जनु होइ सुरुज आइ मन बसी। सब घट पूरि हिअइ परगसी॥
अब हउँ सुरुज चाँद वह छाया। जल बिनु मीन रकत बिनु काया॥

किरिनि करा भा पेम अँकूरू। जउँ ससि सरग मिलउँ होइ सूरू ॥
सहस-उ करा रूप मन भूला। जहँ जहँ दिसिटि कवँल जनु फूला ॥
तहाँ भवँर जिउ कवँला गंधी। भइ ससि राहु केरि रिनि-बंधी ॥

दोहा।

तीनि लोक चउदह खँड सबइ परइ मोहिँ सूझि।
पेम छाँडि किछु अउरु न (लोना) जो देखउँ मन बूझि ॥ ९८ ॥

नाउँ = नाम। रतन = रत्न (रत्न-सेन)। राता = रक्त। बाता = वार्त्ता। तुइँ = त्वया = तै ने। सु-रंग = सु-रङ्ग = सुन्दर-वर्ण। मूरति = मूर्त्ति। चित = चित्त। चितर = चित्र। सुरुज = सूर्य। पूरि = पूर्ण हो कर। परगसी = प्रकाशित ऊई। रकत = रक्त। काया = काय = शरीर। किरिनि = किरण। करा = कला। पेम = प्रेम। अँकूरू = अङ्कुर = अँखुआ। ससि = शशी। सरग = स्वर्ग। सूरू = सूर्य। सहस-उ = सहस्र-उ। करा = कर = किरण। दिसिटि = दृष्टि। कवँल = कमल। भवँर = भ्रमर। गंधी = गन्ध से भरा। रिनि = ऋण। बंधी = बँधा गया। चउदह = चौदह = चतुर्दश। खँड = खण्ड (भुवन)।

(पिछले दोहे में हीरा-मणि ने जो पद्मावती के वर्णन में कहा, कि "उअत सूर जस देखी," इस) रवि के (पद्मावती के) नाम को सुन कर रत्न-सेन रक्त हो गया, अर्थात् जैसे सूर्य के प्रकाश से सूर्य-कान्त मणि अग्नि-मय हो रक्त हो जाती है, उसी प्रकार यहाँ पद्मावती रवि के नाम-ही सुनने से यह रत्न (रत्न-सेन) लाल हो गया। (जानों उस रवि का तेज इस के शरीर में पैठ गया, और लगा कहने, कि) रे पण्डित, (हीरा-मणि), फिर वही बात कह, अर्थात् पद्मावती का वर्णन कर ॥ (क्योंकि) तै ने जो उस सु-रङ्ग मूर्त्ति को कहा, अर्थात् जो उस सु-रङ्ग मूर्त्ति का वर्णन किया, वह चित्त में लग कर, अर्थात् सट कर, चित्र (तसबीर) हो रही है ॥ जानों (वह मूर्त्ति) सूर्य हो कर (मेरे) मन में बस गई, और सब घट (शरीर) में पूर्ण हो कर, अर्थात् भर कर, हृदय में प्रकाशित (विकसित) ऊई ॥ "अब मैं सूर्य उस चन्द्र (पद्मावती) की छाया (प्रतिबिम्ब) हूँ, अर्थात् ज्यौतिष-शास्त्र से तो यह सिद्ध है, कि रवि के प्रतिबिम्ब से चन्द्रमा में कान्ति आती है, परन्तु यहाँ उलटा हो गया, चन्द्र-रूपी पद्मावती-ही के प्रतिबिम्ब से अब रत्न-सेन सूर्य कान्तिमान् हो सकता है, (नहीं तो, अब मेरी ऐसी

दशा है, जैसे) जल के विना मीन (मत्स्य), वा रक्त के विना शरीर (काय)॥ (सूर्य-रूपी पद्मावती की मूर्त्ति जो हृदय में विकसित ऊई, उस के) किरण के कला (प्रभाव) से (हृदय में) प्रेम का अङ्कुर उत्पन्न ऊआ, (सो) यदि स्वर्ग में भी वह शशी (पद्मावती) हो, तो भी सूर्य हो कर (उस से) मिलूँ॥ प्रेम से राजा विकल हो गया, इसी से अपने और पद्मावती में अभेद समझ, कभीँ पद्मावती को सूर्य, कभीँ चन्द्र कहता है। सहस्रों किरण-वाला, अर्थात् सूर्य-सा जो (पद्मावती का) रूप, उस में (मेरा) मन भूल गया, (इस लिये) जहाँ जहाँ दृष्टि करता हूँ, तहाँ जानों कमल-ही फूला है, अर्थात् जहाँ दृष्टि करता हूँ, तहाँ पद्मावती कमल-ही देख पडती है, अर्थात् कीट भृङ्ग की दशा हो गई है॥ भृङ्ग पर-दार एक प्रसिद्ध कीट है, जिसे भाषा में बिलनी कहते हैं। उस का स्वभाव है, कि किसी विजातीय कृमि को ले आ कर अपने घर में रख देता है। रखने के समय उस को एक डङ्क मार देता है। उस की वेदना से उस कीट को बडा भय हो जाता है, और दिन रात भृङ्ग-ही के ध्यान में मग्न हो जाता है, कि फिर आ कर डङ्क न मारे। सो भृङ्ग के ध्यान में मग्न रहते रहते कुछ दिनों में वह कीट भृङ्ग-स्वरूप हो जाता है। वेदान्ती लोगों का सिद्धान्त है, कि जिस प्रकार भृङ्ग के एकाग्र ध्यान से कीट भृङ्ग-स्वरूप हो जाता है, उसी प्रकार यह जीव ब्रह्म के एकाग्र ध्यान से ब्रह्म-मय हो जाता है। (सो) जहाँ पर सु-गन्ध से भरा कमल (पद्मावती) है, तहाँ जीव भ्रमर हो गया, (और) चन्द्रमा (शशी) राज्ञ के रूप से बँध गया, अर्थात् चन्द्र-रूपी पद्मावती मेरे प्रेम-रूपी राज्ञ से बँध गई, अब यह प्रेम अवसर पाने पर अवश्य पद्मावती शशी को पकडेगा॥ कवि के मत से शशी स्त्री-लिङ्ग है, इस लिये भद्द का प्रयोग किया है (५१ वाँ दोहा देखो।) पुराणों में कथा है, कि देवासुर संग्राम में जब भगवान् ने मोहिनी स्वरूप को धारण किया, तब देव असुर दोनों ने रूप से मोहित हो, यह कह कर संग्राम समाप्त किया, कि अमृत-का घट इस सुन्दरी को सौंपो, यह हम लोगों में अमृत को बाँट देगी। इस बात को जब सब ने स्वीकार किया, तब मोहिनी ने एक पङ्क्ति में देव दूसरी में राक्षसों को बैठा कर देवों में अमृत और राक्षसों में सुरा को बाँट दिया। उस समय छल से राज्ञ देव-पङ्क्ति में सूर्य और चन्द्र के बीच जा बैठा। ज्यो-हीँ अमृत-पान किया त्यो-हीँ सूर्य और चन्द्र ने विष्णु से कहा, कि यह दैत्य है, छल से यहाँ बैठ गया है। इस पर मोहिनी-रूप विष्णु ने क्रुद्ध हो सुदर्शन चक्र से इस के शिर को काट डाला,

परन्तु अमृत के प्रभाव से रुण्ड, और मुण्ड, दोनों जीते-ही रह गये। ऐसी दुर्दशा में राहु को देख कर ब्रह्मा ने इसे वर-दान दिया, कि तुम पर्व में सूर्य और चन्द्र को ग्रास कर लिया करोगे, और उस समय जो लोग दान पुण्य हवन इत्यादि करेंगे सब के भोक्ता तुम होगे। इस प्रकार ब्रह्मा के वर-दान से सूर्य और चन्द्र दोनों राहु के ऋण से बँधे हैं, अर्थात् जैसे ऋण देने-वाला ऋणी को पकड लेता है, और वह बेचारा कुछ नहीं बोलता, उसी प्रकार, वर-दान के प्रभाव से, यह राहु सूर्य और चन्द्रमा को पकड लेता है, और ये बेचारे ऋणी ऐसे कुछ नहीं बोलते॥

(रत्न-सेन कहता है, कि पद्मावती की मूर्त्ति सूर्य जो कि मेरे हृदय में पैठ गई है, इस से) तीन लोक और चौदहो भुवन (खण्ड) सब मुझे (इस घडी) सूझ पडते हैं। (सो) जो मैं मन में बूझ (समझ) कर देखता हूँ, तो प्रेम छोड (जगत में) और कुछ (भी) सुन्दर नहीं है॥ ९८॥

चौपाई।

पेम सुनत मन भूलु न राजा। कठिन पेम सिर देइ तो छाजा॥
पेम फाँद जउँ परइ न छूटा। जीउ दीन्ह बहु फाँद न टूटा॥
गिरिगिट छंद धरइ दुख तेता। खन खन रात पीत खन सेता॥
जानि पुछारि जो भा बन-बासी। रोवँ रोवँ परे फाँद नग-वासी॥
पाँखन्ह फिरि फिरि परा सो फाँदू। उडि न सकइ अरुझइ भइ बाँदू॥
मुएउँ मुएउँ अह-निसि चिललाई। ओहि रोस नागन्ह धरि खाई॥
पाँडक सुआ कंठ वह चीन्हा। जेहि गिउ परा चाहि जिउ दीन्हा॥

दोहा।

तीतर गिउ जो फाँद हइ निति-हि पुकारइ दोख।
सो कित हँकारि फाँद गिउ (मेलइ) कित मारे होइ मोख॥ ९९॥

पेम = प्रेम। छाजा = छाजता है = सोहता है। फाँद = फन्दा। गिरिगिट = गिर्गिटान। छंद = छन्द = रचना = रङ्ग रङ्ग का रूप। तेता = तितना = तावान्। खन = चण। रात = रक्त = लाल। पीत = पीला। सेता = श्वेत = सफेद। जानि = जान कर। पुछारि = पिच्छालि = मयूर = मोरैला = मोर। रोवँ = रोम। नग-वासी = नाग-पाशी = नाग-पाश का। पाँखन्ह = पचों। भइ = हो कर। बाँद = कैद। मुएउँ = मोरैले के बोली का

अनुकरण। अह-निसि = अहर्निश = दिन-रात। चिललाई = चिल्लाता है। रोष = रोष = क्रोध। नागन्ह = सर्पों को। पाँडुक = पाण्डुक = पँडुकी। गिउ = ग्रीवा = गला। चाहि = इच्छा कर के = चाह से। तीतर = तित्तिरपक्षी। निति-हि = नित्य-हि = नित्य-ही। दोख = दोष = पाप। कित = क्यों। मोख = मोक्ष॥

(शुक ने कहा, कि) राजा प्रेम को सुनते-ही मन में न भूलो। प्रेम कठिन होता है। इस के लिये शिर दे दे तब (तो) (यह प्रेम) छाजता है (सोहता है), अर्थात् विना शिर दिये प्रेम की शोभा नहीं॥ प्रेम के फन्दे में यदि पडा, तो (फिर वह) नहीं छूटता। बज्जतों ने जी दे दिया (परन्तु प्रेम का) फन्दा नहीं टूटा, अर्थात् जी के सङ्ग-हीं गया॥ जितना गिरिगिट छन्द को धरता है, अर्थात् रूप को बदलता है, तितना (इस प्रेम मार्ग में) दुःख है। (इस में पड कर प्राणी) क्षण क्षण में लाल, पीला, और क्षण में श्वेत होता रहता है॥ प्रेम-ही को जान कर, मयूर जो है, सो वन-वासी ज्जआ, अर्थात् गृह से विरक्त ज्जआ, (और इस के) रोम रोम में नग-वासी (नाग-पाश) के फन्दे पडे॥ वही (सो) नग-वासी फन्दा घूम घूम कर (फिरि फिरि) (इस के) पक्षों में पडा, (इसी कारण यह) उड नहीं सकता, और कैद हो कर, अरुझा रहता है, अर्थात् फँसा रहता है (मयूर के रोओं और पक्षों के ऊपर जो चित्र-कारी है, सो नाग-पाश फन्दे के ऐसी जान पडती है)॥ (फँसने-ही से दुःखी हो कर) मुऐँ मुऐँ (मरा, मरा) ऐसा चिल्लाता है, और उसी रोष से, (कि नाग-पाश के फन्दे में मैं फँसा हूँ), नागों को धर कर (पकड कर) खाता है॥ पँडुकी और शुक के कण्ठ में भी वही (फन्दे का) चिह्न है, (सो) जिस के गले में (फन्दा) पडा, वह चाह से (अपना) जी देता है॥

तीतर के गले में जो फन्दा है, (उसी लिये) (वह) नित्य-ही (अपने) दोष को पुकारता है। (ऐसा न होता, तो) वह (सो) क्यों पुकार कर (हँकारि) गले में फन्दे को डालता (मेलइ), और क्या मारने से मोक्ष होता है, अर्थात् नहीं होता॥ यहाँ कवि की उत्प्रेक्षा है, कि तीतर के गले में जो कण्ठ-रूपी फन्दा है, उसी से दुःखी हो कर, तीतर बोलता है, जिस की बोली सुन, व्याधे उसे फन्दे में फँसा लेते हैं, और मार डालते हैं, तब, जी के जाने पर भी, उस के गले का फन्दा नहीं टूटता, इस लिये ऊपर जो कह आये हैं, कि "जीउ दीन्ह बज्ज फाँद न टूटा" यह बज्जत ठीक है॥९९॥

BIBLIOTHECA INDICA:

A

COLLECTION OF ORIENTAL WORKS

PUBLISHED BY

THE ASIATIC SOCIETY OF BENGAL.

NEW SERIES No. 951.

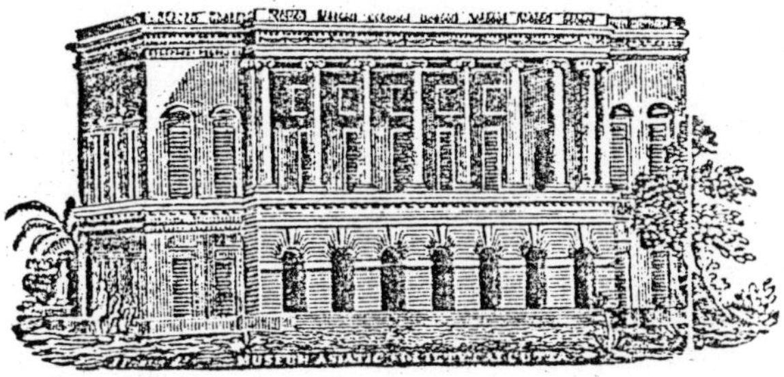

THE PADUMĀWATI

OF

MALIK MUHAMMAD JAISĪ

EDITED, WITH A COMMENTARY, TRANSLATION, AND CRITICAL NOTES,

BY

G. A. GRIERSON, C.I.E., PH.D., I.C.S.,

AND

MAHĀMAHŌPĀDHYĀYA SUDHĀKARA DVIVĒDI, F. A. U.

FASCICULUS III.

CALCUTTA:

PRINTED AT THE BAPTIST MISSION PRESS,

AND PUBLISHED BY THE ASIATIC SOCIETY, 57, PARK STREET.

1899.

54. 1. K *barakha kai bhai*, UK *rājaĩ kahā*, 2. U *padumāwati kahā̃*. 2. U *sakhi sayāni —rasa jānī*. 3. Ia *nisi dina karahi*, U *sō saba karahĩ kēli rasa jānī*. K *jehi sā̃ga karai sahaja rasa-kēlī*. | 4. K *kawala sātha jasa upajai kōi*. 5. UK *rājā kē ṭhāū̃*, K *paṇḍitā paḍhā hī*.° 6. Is *daiyā dī*,° UK *hirdai buddha hīrāmani jōtī*. 7. U *sō puni dīnhā suā salōnā*. K *sō dīnhā saba gunī salōnā*. 8. K *paḍhahī so sāstara*. 9. K *sunata bāta rasa-bhēda*.

55. 1. *unanta*, so Ic K. The word has puzzled all copiests. Ia has *ananda*, Ib اوستا with marginal v. l *utapati*, Ids *utapati*, U *sayāna*, | U *dhujā dhaurahar karī*. U *dhuja añcala bica kalī*. 3. N *pīṭhī.........īṭhī*, (U *baīṭhī*.) 4. K *kuraŋga citauna hērī*. 6. Ia K *dasana naga hī*.° U *dārima dasana damaka jasu hīrā*. 7. U *bhūi dārē*. 8. K *na lāwai*, U *kou drishti.........achari chapī akāsa*. 9. K *tapā tapahī tehī*.

56. This set of *caupāis* is wanting in all MSS. except K, from which it is taken. It is inserted, as necessary to understanding the story. Stanza 57 is unintelligible without it. Most probably it is not genuine, but is a clumsy insertion by a later bard.

57. 1. U *kubudhi dēi*, | K *kumati dēi*. 2. Ia *sūra sunī*, Ic *sūra sunā̃*, U *sūra na āu*, K *sūra na uā*. 3. I *nāuni bārī*. Is *tau lahi........ jau lahi*. K *tau lagi......jau lagi*, P *jaba lagi...taba lagi*, Is *jau lahi byādhi suā pahā̃ āwā*. 6. Ia *paŋkhi na hō kahe hōi*. Ic *paŋkhi na katahū̃ hōi*, U *jō tuha paŋkhi dīnha parawā̃nā* | *cāhai bhugati ki cāhi uḍānā*. K *jehi pañchihi dīnhā tuha dānū* | *jānai bhuguti*, &c. 7. Ia om. *jahā̃*, Is *tehi kata jībha hiē hō nainā̃*. U *hiē kati nainā̃*. K *tehi kata budhi andha jasa nainā̃*. 9. Ia *amahū̃ phōri gahi lēi*. Ib *ā̃ba ṭhōra*, Is *ā̃bahi ṭhōra, gahi lēi*.

58. 1. Icd K *suā*. 2. Icd *sukha pāū̃*, K *sira āū̃*, Ic *hoū̃ paŋkhī bana-bāsa kahā̃ jāū̃*, Ic *bāsa gahi jā̃*,° K *hau aba calau bāsa gahi pāū̃*. 3. U *mōti malīna hōi jo kalā.........niramalā*, K *kalā* | *bahuri na paniyā hoi niramalā*. 4. Iad U *sēwaka kara*, Ic *waha sēwaka* K *kauna ubārā*. 5. K *pañchī nāma na jīu so bā̃cā*. 6. K *tua rāja*, Uk *jau mā̃gahu dai jāi*. 7. Ib *bhau pachi*,° Is *bhā*. 8. Is *mārī sōi na suaṭā*, K *marai sāi jo suaṭahī*.

59. 2. K *dōkha na tōra kichu nahi dēwā*. 3. Ia *tohi sēwaka bichurata nahi ākhaū̃* | Ib *tohi kō̃ bichurana haū̃ nahi ākhaū̃* | Ic *tumha sēwā̃ bichurana kā̃* (or *gā̃*) *ākhaū̃* | Ids *tohi sēwā bichurana nahi ākhaū̃* | U *tohi saū̃ haū̃ bichurana nahi ākhaū̃* | K *tohi sēwaka bichurana kimi bhākhaū̃* | Ids U *ghāli tohi rākhaū̃*, K *hiē mēli kai*. 4. K *dharama bīca tahā̃ tohi kō*. 5. Ia U *baḍāī*. U *kauna prīti*, Ia *prīti soi jie sāthahī jāī*, Icd *jehī sāthahī iāī*, U *jīu saŋgahi jāī*, K *prīti sōi*. 7. Ias *sō kita*, U *tehi kata chā̃ḍa āna jiu bā̃dhā*, K *teh. kata chōra lāi*. 9. Icd *jehī karatā*.

60. 1. Iacs *kauni-u tithi*. U *kauna-u ti*,° K *kawanō ti*,° Ia UK *mānasarōara*. 3. IsK *koi kētuki karanā̃*. 4. Ic om. *bakauri*, Iad have *b. kāu*, Is *bikāu*, U *bakāu*, K *bakāwari kaca bi*,° U *bihisātī*, cf. *xxvl*, 3. 5. Id *bōlasari*, Is *mōlasari*. 6. Ia *jama kēsari*, Ibds °*jarada jyaū̃ kēsari*, Ic *janu kē*,° Is *kēsari...nāgēsari*. 7. Iacd *sadabaraga*, Is UK *kunda sati*°, K °*baraga sahēlī*, Is *su-rasa rasa-kēlī*. 8. U *calī sabai mila gōhanē*. K *calī sabhai jō mālatī*. 8. *kumōda*, so we vocalize the word, taking it as equivalent to *kumud*. All have *kamōda* which, however, gives bad sense, the word being the name of a drug not of a flower.

61. 1. Iads UK *mānasarōwara*. 2. Ia U *sarōwara hā̃sanhi kēlī*. Ib *dēkhi sarōwara hā̃sahī kulēlī*, Id *sarōwara karahī jo kēlī*, Is *dēkhi saraura hā̃sanha kai kēlī*, K *dēkhā sarawara hasanha kēlī*. 4. U *jaba lagi ahai*, K *jau lagi*. Icds U *ahai pitā*. Is *khēlahu khēli khēli lehu ājū*. 5. U *kālhī..... pālhī*, Ic *saraura-tālī*. 6. Ia *āuba*, Ib *hāṭā......sāṭā kata khēlana puni .....* | *katā khēlai āuba ē sāthā*, K *kai tuha hama khēlaba eka sāthā* | Ics *na āwai dēhī*, Id *na ūtara dēhī*, UK *na āwana dēhī*. 8. Ia *sē dahū̃ karai kāha*, U *sō dhaū̃ karahai kāhu*, K *sō dahu kara puni kāha*. 9. Iab *kai sukha*.

62. Iacd U om. this stanza. 1. IsK *hiḍōlē—lhōlē*, Ia *lēhu sakhi bālē*, K *lēhu saba bālī* 2. Ia *puni kata jhūlana*, K *phiri kata jhū*.° 3. Ib *naihara pauna na*, K *nisari jāē na*. 4. K *kahā̃ yaha dhūpa*. Ib *rahaba so kaisē̃ mandira*, K *rahaba sabhai puni mandira*. 5. K *kauna pūcha bōlā eha dōkhū* | *kauna utara kata pāuba mōkhū* || Ib is unintelligible here. 7. Ib *kita mili rahasa cān asa karanā*. K *kata naihara jō āeba*.

Ia substitutes for 62 following—

Cau.|| *suni sāsura padumāwati ḍārī* | *jala binu sūkhi kawā̃la kai kārī* ||
aba lagi sakhī sravana nahi sūnā̃ | *ḍarapā jīu hiẽ mā̃ha gūnā̃* ||
kāhā karaũ sakhī tora cērī | *kahu phiri bāta sakhī piu kērī* ||
ekasara jāba ki dōsari saŋgā̃ | *subhara pantha kī āhi karaŋgā* ||
ihai dīpa sakhı āhi ki dūā | *ihai sūra kī dōsara ūā* ||
kaisa nagara kaisana basagīṭī | *kahu aba tahā̃ kaisi hai rītī* ||
cakhu ghabarāi dharaka sõ hīyā | *daī māna tarahēlī tīyā* ||

Dō|| *kasa re milana kasa ādara kaisa nagara kara lōga* |
kaisa pantha dahū kanta kasa kaisa milai sukha bhō̃ga ||62||

Cau.|| *kahā sakhī khēlata sā̃ga āhaī* | *aba so bāta padumāwati kāhaī* ||
jasa naihara sāsura hai kāhā̃ | *jarana jharana ahaī nija tāhā̃* ||
sēwā sõ sāsura pada bhāgū | *jauna so kanta to sadā sohāgū* ||
sēwā sāsu nanā̃da basa kariye sēwā māna sauti kara hariyē ||
sañjama sawā̃ra basahī bhala hōī | *dewara jēṭha ḍara bōli na kōī* ||
sajana parāwā hōihi apanā | *naihara hōihi rainī sapanā* ||
kahā̃ tumha rānī kahā̃ hama sakhiā | *jhuri jhuri maraba na dēkhaba ā̃khiā* ||

Dō|| *kahā̃ khēli kahā̃ sarawara kahā̃ sakhī kahā̃ rāni* |
sakhī bujhāwahī āpu kahā̃ samajhi so sabai to āni ||62a ||

63. 2. U *malai-giri bāsā......cahū pāsā* Ia has for second half *kanaka su-gandha duādasi bānī*. K *lēhi so ghrānī*. 3. Ia *cā̃da ki sarana*. U *canda ko pāchu līnha*. K *cā̃da ke pāchu lāgu janu*. 4. Ia *chapi gā*. K *chapi gau*. K *bhau nisi nakhata dīpa para*.° 5. Ia *dishṭi mana*. Is U *ghaṭā tara*. Is *cā̃da*. K *ghaṭā jasa cā̃da capāwā*. 7. K *naina kā̃ula*. This makes better metre. 9. Iabd *laharai lēi*. K *tehi niti laharaī*.

64. 1. Ibcds *saba cuni kai sā*.° 2. Ia *pānī nīra jānu*. Ibc *pāī tīra jānu*. Icd *pā nīra jānu*, U *pāi nīra jānahū rasa bēlī*. K *pāwā nīra jaba sabai sahēlī* | *hulasī kēlī karama ki bēlī* || 3 Ia UK *kuṭila kēsa* K *bikhidhara bisi bharē*. 4. Ib *bhaī aṭapaṭi parēma*, Is *pīrama kai*. 5. Ia K *basanta saba bārī kārī*, U *basanta kamala mukha kārī*. Ia N *paragaṭa cāhai rasa*.

65. 1. Is *kēri karai*, Ids U *baiṭha hoi tīrā̃*. 2. Iad *kantaka kara*, Is K *kautuka kaha*. U *kautuka kai*. U *tarāini*. 3. Is K *khēḍa pasārā*. 4. U K *sā̃wari sā̃wari gōrī gōrī*. The second half varies much in different MSS. Iad *jo jehī jōga so tehi kai*, (Id *tā kara*) *jōrī*. U *līnhasi jōrī*, K *cuni cuni lēhi so apanī jōrī*. 6 Ib *kita* both times, U *kati*. 7. Id N *kūsala*. Iabc quite clear. 8. Is *bāri pīrama kā*. U *bāra ju prēma kē*, K *muhamad khēli prēma kī*. 9. U *saŋga milā*. K *tēla phūl jaū saŋga hōi*.

66. 1. Id *cita acēta bhai hāra gā̃wānā*. 2. Ib *ḍāra sō bhai*. Is *ḍāra kahā̃ bhau bi*,° UK *gahi bhau bi*.° Iac UK *kā saū pu*° but this spoils the metre, Ib *kāsu*, Id *kāhu* (??hi ??ha,) Is *kāgu*. 3. *tehi sāthā*, U *yaha sā*,° K *inha sā*,° Iacds *gā̃wāi caleū saī hāthā*. 4. Ia U *jaba hārū*, Ib *kahā̃ hārū*, Id *bahu hārū*, K *paisata*. 5. Ic (second half) *sīpa bahuta jami mōtī jhārē*. U *mōtī girē tasa ḍhārē*. K *mānahu mōti girai hia ḍhārē*. 6. K (second half) *niramala nīra pauna jau milā*. Ib *pauḍi pauḍi eka*, U *ḍūba ḍūba eka*.

67. 1. Ia K *cāhi*, Id *kahā̃ mānasara jahā̃ so pānī* | *pārasa rūpa ahā eka rānī*, U *kahā mānasara rūpa sohāī*, Ia *pāwā———āwā*. Ia *ihā̃ sō āī*, U *ihā̃ lahi āī*, K *ihā̃ cali āī*. 3. Ias U *sītala tana tapani*, K *tapani batāī* (for *butāī*). 5. *tata khina*. 6. Ia *bhā tahā̃ rūpa harā jaī dēkhā*, Ibd *bhai tahā̃ rūpa jahā̃*. 7. Ia *tehī tasa rūpa jaisana jaī cāhā*. U *pāwā rūpa rūpa kē darasē* | *sasi-mukha darapana bhūi kē parasē*. K *pāwa rūpa jōti jasa cānī........ rāhī* 8. Ia U *dēkhā kawā̃la bhā*, Is *dēkhe hansa bhae*. 9. Ia U *dēkhā, bhā*. K *hērata nīra samīra*.

Ia inserts the following two stanzas—

Cau|| *jehi kara sīpa caḍhā sō hāsā* | *ghōgha sewāra pāu sō nāsā* ||
padumini sabai sakhinha saū pū̃chā | *kehi sai lābha phirā kō chū̃chā* ||
hēri hāra saba karahī tawānā | *jō jehi āhi so tahā̃ bhulānā* ||
kāhu na sūjhā sarawara tālā | *janu bikha bujhā āi ura sālā* ||

murachi parī padumāwati rānī | sakhī jagāu mēli mukha pānī ||
pū̃chahī sakhī nāri kara ṭōī | aukhada sō jo biādhi na hōī ||
naga amōla harawā mahā̃ áhā | campāwati pū̃chai kā káhā ||
Dō|| *roai rāni padumāwati hār harā ehi ṭhāū̃ |*
sabai sakhī rahi māna saū̃ haū̃ kubujī ehi gāū̃ ||66(*a*)
Cau|| *bolahī̃ sakhī sabai eka bānī | jō dukha tumhahī̃ hamahī̃ sō rānī ||*
tumha rōahu gandhrapa kī bārī | hama kuā̃rihī̃ kehi māna bicārī ||
cā̃dara phāra rāni taba jhā̃khī | mānata nā̃hi bujhāwata sákhī ||
khēlata mahā̃ maī̃ samū̃da roāwā | koi rōwai koi karahi bujhāwā ||
tumha jānahu jani hamarī hārā | tumha saī̃ hamahī̃ hōi dukha bhārā ||
saba mili kai kara jōri pukārā | dēhi hāru aba samū̃da hamārā ||
sabai khēli aba bhā kura khēlā | sukha sanēha hama dukha kai mēlā ||
Dō|| *kahā̃ jāū̃ kā pahū̃ kahaū̃ hāru samū̃da mora līnha |*
hēri kawā̃la jala mīna pahū̃ nā jānaū̃ kā kīnha ||66(*b*)||

68. (1) Id U *khēla dhamārī,* Is *khēla duārī,* K *khēlu piārī.* Ic *parī mā̃°* U *dēkhi mā̃°* (2) Is K *kahesi.* U *kahisa.* K *bana sākhā.* (3) Ibs *ḍaru līnhē̃.* (4) Ia *bhala sākhā.* Id *bhara sākhā.* Is *bahu sākhā.* U K *phala sākhā.* Ia *jaba lagi rākhā.* Ids *mēṭa jau lahi bidhi rākhā.* K inserts *tana* between *lahi* and *rākhā.* (5) *sukkha.* This doubling of the final consonant is required by metre. Is K have *saukhya.* U has *sukhya.* Neither of these is supported by P. *Dukkha* is also required by the metre. Icd have *pāchila dukha bisari.* Is *dukha* which will not scan. (6) Ia *jīu sabhani.* Ib *saba kā.* Is *jāwata jaga saba kara.* K *jaha lagi jīu saba kē bhakha.* 7. *jahā̃ tahā̃.* 8. Ias *taba lagi.* Id *jau lahi.* U K *tau lagi.* Ia K *jaba* (K *jau*) *lagi bharai na pēṭa.* (8) Ia *puni sawā̃rana bhā bichurana.* U *puni pāchē bhā sumaranā.* K *puni bichurana bhā sumirana.*

The Ūrdū printed edition inserts the following:—

Cau || *Padumāwati tahā̃ khēli dhamārī | suā mā̃dira mahā̃ parī mā̃jārī ||*
cērī katahū̃ jāi urajhānī | tahā̃ so bhōga jāi rasa mānī ||
līnhesi rāni ke phūla tā̃bōlā | bōlā suā tahā̃ eka bōlā ||
tā kara puhupa chuasi rē cērī | jūlanihāra hai jehi kērī ||
pāna phūla tehī̃ saū̃pa na kōī | jō tū̃ lōbhī hai kō hōī ||
pāna phūla lījiyē to pāē̃ | au na dījiyē hātha parāē̃ ||
kā jānē dahū̃ hiyā ki mōkā | kō tehi pāna phūla kā dhōkā ||
Do || *suā kahē rē cērī | baurī bhaī akāja |*
lihisa phūla rānī kē | tohi mana āwa na lāja, || 68 (1) ||
Cau || *cērī au dō māna birāgā | suā ka bōli janahū̃ bikha lāgā ||*
bāuri andhi piriti kara lāgū | sō na dhasī nahi sūjhī āgū ||
sunatē hiē̃ māna anabhāū | yaha kī ghāli kiā ghara rāū ||
bhā nisi bhōra kōha mukha khōlā | tā tamacūra rahē anabōlā ||
suā jo ahā piñjara sukha bhārī | dharisa āi janu dharisa mā̃jārī ||
cūrisa paṅkha mirōrisa gīwā | ehi bidhi bidhi nē rākhā jīwā ||
sūā paṅknī pai budhi ōchī | līnhesi bhā̃ḍa khāla kī kōchī ||
Dō || *sīsa dhunē tasa sōṭā | bhā bhōjana sukha ṭhā̃ū |*
rahaū̃ eka tariwari caḍhi | caḍhaū̃ saba ā̃barā̃ū || 68 (2) ||
Cau || *kachu na basāi bhūli gā páḍhā | barahī̃ pāū̃ jo jōdhā cáḍhā ||*
sataruhi kōi pāu jō bā̃dhā | chā̃ḍi niripa kahā̃ karai biyādhā ||
bairī dāwa pāu jō kōī | lāgā ghāta rahai puni sōī ||
jau ri sayāna hoē tō bā̃cē | hōe ayāna to bihā̃si ke nā̃cē ||
āgū̃ dēkhi karai tehi kājā | ḍarē brithā āpai mana lājā ||
budhi cī̃ṭī parabata lē kā̃dhā | budhi kē hīna hasti gā bā̃dhā ||
aba budhi karō to bā̃cō súā | jiata jo marē na mārē̃ múā ||
Dō || *hārē sōi nisōtā | ḍarai jo kāja akāja |*
harakha na bisamau jānai | duhū̃ niwārai lāja || 68 (3) ||
Cau || *bhā̃ḍā āē khaṇḍa jahā̃ kūā̃ | kahesi māri mēlaū̃ aba sūā ||*

	dēkhata pāe so agumana tānī |	*kuā̃ mēli kai bahuta risānī* ||
	paŋkhi na ḍōlē ēkau nainā̃ |	*parā kūpa mahā̃ kahi taba bainā̃* ||
	kahesi tōhi suīraū̃ haū̃ ēkā |	*jina mahā̃ gā̃gana ā̃tara kā ṭēkā* ||
	agina mā̃ha rākhā jina saurā |	*kuā̃ parā tē rōwaī baurā* ||
	dharī jalandhara jōgī khā̃cā |	*bikarama saraga hutī kara bā̃cā* ||
	karihaū̃ nahī ḍahana nā pā̃khā |	*rahaū̃ kūpa mahā̃ rākas rākhā* ||
Dō ||	*jō prabhu rākhā cāha sē* |	*ṭūṭa na ēkau rōa* |
	nāhī tō kā mō̃ jugati |	*jō bhāwē sō hōa* || 68 (4) ||
Cau ||	*jau niçcai suīraū̃ bidhi nāū̃* |	*tahā̃ kahā̃ ṭēka duhū̃ jaga ṭhāū̃* ||
	kā dēkhē tariwara kō mā̃hā |	*pipara tīra au sītala chā̃hā* ||
	paratē̃ kahesi ḍāra sō̃ sūā |	*bhā kailāsa bisara gā kūā* ||
	phara sē tariwara dēkhē sākhā |	*bhuguti na mēṭai jau lahi rākhā* ||
	bisarā dukha paŋkhana kara cūrā |	*gā sō sōga bhūla bhā pūrā* ||
	kachu na basāe bhūla gā pāḍhā |	*naina mā̃ha bhari dīnha so cāḍhā* ||
	pāhana mahā̃ na pataŋga bisārā |	*kasa na kūda mūha parabasa cārā* ||
Dō ||	*gharī ēka kē sukkha mē̃* |	*bīsara gai saba jhaŋkha* |
	phara gai dishṭi suā kara |	*jaba laū̃ apanē paŋkha* || 68 (5) ||
Cau ||	*pā̃kha kuriāra ke dēkhē suriā* |	*paŋkhī kīnha paŋkha kara kuriā* ||
	kahasi calaū̃ jau lahi tana pā̃khā | &c., as in 69 (2)	

The above is an evident interpolation by a later hand. The language is quite different from that of the rest of the poem.

69. (1) Ic *padumāwati tahā̃.* U *pahi* K *paha dhāi bhā̃°.* U *kahisa* K *sua maṇḍila mahā̃ dēkhu mājārī.* (2) Ic *dēta huta.* Is *dēta tahā̃* U *dai tahā̃* K *dēta tuha pū̃°.* Ia *uḍi gā hansa piñjarā chū̃chā.* (3) Icd U *sukha saba gacū* U *sunatahī* Is *sūkhi taba.* K *rānī jabahī cāha asa pāī* \| *janu dina mā̃jha raini bhā āī* \|\| (4) Iu *ā̃su tehi nakhata gagana saba bhārā* \|\| (metre incorrect). K *ā̃su nakhata asa nainanha jhārā* \|\| (5) Iac *ṭuṭi ṭuṭi parī pāli para lāgī* U *ā̃su ṭūṭi pāla para lāgē.* K *bahi bahi nakhata pāli bahi lāgē.* U *kamala ḍūba.* (6) U *ā̃su naina tē cūē* \| Uk *saraura mahā̃ ūē.* K *saraga chāḍi.* (7) Ib *janahū̃ ṭūṭa mōtinha* Ic *jharahi cuahī mō°* Is *cīra cuai* U *cihura cuai jyaū̃ mōtī mālā* K *mōtī jasa mālā.* Ia *sakēta kai bā̃dhahu bālā* \|\| Id *puni hama phēri bā̃dha cahū̃ bālā* Is *sā̃kēta bā̃dhā caha bālā* U *aba hama phēri bā̃dha cahai bālā* K *hama aba phēri bā̃dhai cahai bālā.*

70. (1) K *cārau pāsa bujhāwahī.* Ia *kahā̃ so pāī uḍi gā pā̃khī* \| Id *gā so kahā̃ pāī aba pā̃khī.* Is K *pāiaga* U *so pāī gā aba pā̃khī* \| (2) Ia *jaba lahi pījarā* K *jau lagi pījara rahā parēwā.* Ia *bā̃nda* Ic *ahā bā̃da* Id K *ahā bā̃dhi* Is *ahā bandi* U *rahā banda.* (3) Ia *tāhi banda tē̃ chū.°* Ibcd U insert *jo* before *chuṭai* which spoils the metre. Is *tēhu bandi hutī* K *tēhi bandi sau chuṭai jo pāwā.* Ibc *phiri bā̃da* Id *bhā̃da* (sic.) Is *phiri bandi* K *puni sō bandi hoē kahā̃ dhāwā.* \| (4) Ib *uḍāna bahu pharahari khāī* Ic *phara tehi dina (?) khāē* K *sō uḍāna phara tei waha khāwā.* Ic *tana āē.* Id U *tana lāē.* K *jehi bhā......tana pāwā.* \| (7) The second half line is very corrupt in all copies. The various readings are as follows:—

Ia *aisa gāḍhi abahū̃ nahi ḍhīlē* \|\|
Ib *asa baḍa-pēṭa lagā hō ḍhīlā* \|\|
Icds *tasa peṭa-gāḍha bahuri nahi ḍhīlē* \|\|
U *aisa pēṭa gahi bahuri na ḍhīlē* \|\|
K *asa paṭa-gāḍha na nisarē ḍhīlē* \|\|
K2 *asa kai pakarē bahurī na ḍhīlē*
K3 *yehi dharatī asa kētika līlā* \| *tasa baḍa gāḍha bahuri nahi mīlā* \|\|

8. Here again there is much corruption in the second half:—

Ia *tahū̃ na pauna na khāna* \|
Ib *tahā̃ piuna nahi khāna* \|
Icd *jahā̃ na pauna na pāni* \| Id gives a marginal correction to the same as Ib.
Is *jahā̃ pauna na lei araghāni* \|
U *jahā̃ pauna nahi pāni* \|
K *jahi na pauna na ghrāni* \|

9. Ia *tehi bana sua-ṭā cali basā* U *bana waha sua-ṭā* K *bana bhai sua-ṭā.*

71. 1. Ic *jāe biādha.* 2. Icd U *dēkhi sabanhi ḍa°.* Is *sabahũ,* K *sabhai.* U *ḍari khāwā.* 3. Is *acarija* U *acaraju ika bhálā.* Id *ēka jō āwata cálā* U *ek āwē tahā̃ cálā* K *āwata janu cálā.* 4. Ib *dēkhī.* All others *dēkhā.* All N have *calata.* The vowel point is not given in P. 5. Ia *taruari āju calā bhala nāhī̃* | U *āju so.* K *taruari āyu* (sic.) *calata bhala nāhī.* Ib *aba'hama yaha bana.* 6. Ia K *āna bana* K *bhūli raha thākā.* 7. Ia *rāhā nicinta,* U *rahā acēta calā* K *bhaē nicinta.* 9. Ias K *bharā.*

72. 1. Is *mēlesi.* U *mēlisa.* K *phādā suā karata rasa-kēlī* | *pā̃khi cūri mēlā dukha ḍēlī* || 2. Ia *pañchi.* Uk *rōdana,* P *rōdana* or *rōana,* The MSS. are not clearly legible. In رووں, the third letter may be read either as *wau* or as *dāl.* 3. Ia *bikha cārā.* Is *ā̃kūrē,* U *ā̃kūrā.* Ibc *ā̃gūrā,* other P doubtful. K *kata daiā sūrē* | Iad *ḍaina.* Is *ḍaina bidhi cū°.* U *ḍaina dhai cū°* K *ḍaina dukha cū°.* 4. Ia K *cirimāra* Ics *carihāra* U *cirahāra.* 5. U *ūbhā kāla.* 7. Ias U K *jāla na dē°.* Is U *dēkhi dēkhi.* Ia *dēkhai dēkha cārā.* 8. Ias U *hama to kubuddhi.* Is *kubuddhi gāwāwa* U *kubuddhi kamāī.* 9. Is *tūha suaṭā asa panḍita ihā̃ katā bā̃jhehu āi* || Ia *sō katā bā̃jhehu āi* Id *katā rai phā̃dā āi* U *kasi tū̃ phā̃dē āi.* K *tū̃ kata bhūlei āi* ||

73. 1. Ia K *tasa bhūlē.* K *ṭūṭai ḍaina garaba.* 2. Ias *kērā.* Ics U *bairī kērā.* 3. Ia U *sukha kuriāri* K *sukha niruāra kuruharī* Ias K *bhā tabahī̃* U *bhā jabahi.* 4. Ia كاهي كون Ib *kāhe ka bhūla bi°* Icd *kāhe kahā̃.* Is K *kāhē bhōga* U *kāhē phūla bi°* Ib *uḍā lāi.* 5. Ia *kō̃cā jiba gā̃°.* Uk *jānā̃ jaba khō̃cā gāḍā.*

6. The various readings are :—

Ia *sukhī nicinta jōrē bidhi karanā̃* |
Ib *sukha kai cinta dinahī̃ dina karanā̃* |
Ic *saba kē jī jōrana dhana karanā̃* |
Id *sukhī nicinta jōrē dhana karanā̃* |
Is *sukha nicinta jōrata dhana karanā* |
U *sukha cintā jōrō dhani karanā* |
K *sukha cinta jō bandhana karanā* | *aba nicinta pāchē dukha bharanā* ||

7. U *sō bichurā.* 8. Ia *kīnha taba jaba cārā sukha.*

74. 1. *ā̃su tasa pō̃°* Ibd K *ā̃su taba pō̃°.* Id Uk *bā̃dhā* Is *bā̃cē būdhi.* U K *kauna.* 2. Ia *paṅkhinha budhi jau hota ūji°* Id *jau budhi hota* Is *hou.* Is K *kata.* In Ib the vowel points are clearly marked as *kita.* 3. *ughēlā,* so in all copies except Is which has *ughēlē. kita,* so again plainly Ib. N have *kata.* 4. K, second half *uḍi na sakā sō pañchi parēwā.* 5. Ia *bhā byādhā trishnā mana khūdhū.* Ic *phira biā°* U *bhai agādhi trisnā.* 6. Id *hama lōbhī......hama garabī.* 7. K *dōsa na byādhahi dōsa apānā.* 9. U *pachirāja.*

75. 1. Is K *sēni.* U *sēna.* P give no indication. Ia *kōṭi laṅka sama sājā.* Icd *citra sama sājā* K *citra sabha.* 2. Is K *sēni.* U *sēna,* as in line one. Icd *dhani sō jehī̃ janamā̃.* 3. Is *rūpa au lakhana* K *lakhana cinha saba rūpa bisēkhahī̃.* 4. The MSS. differ greatly, as follows :—

Ia *Ratana sēni jō kula niramārā* |
Ib *Ratana sēni bahu naga autārā* |
Icd .... *yaha kula* ....
Is Uk .... *naga autarā* |

Is U *bārā* K *jarā* (sic). 5. Ia *jasa jagata ā̃jōrī.* 7. Ia *citaura gaḍha āwā.* 9. U *lagana.*

76. 1. Ids *gaḍhi ka ēka.* 2. Iabc *nashṭha.* Is *nisaṭha,* K *nishṭa.* 3. *rini,* so Is K. U *rina.* 5. Uk *dēkhu......sūjhi.* Ia *kachu āhi na.* Is *kachu hai nahi thōrā.* 9. Ia K *gā̃ṭhi dūma suṭhi.*

77. 1. Ia *jhurawai ṭ*   *i kahā̃ maī̃ āwā* |
Ib *jhurai ṭhō*   *he ka haū̃ āwā* |
Ic *jhurawai ṭ*   *kāhe ka maī̃ āwā* |
Id .... *kahā̃ huū̃ āwā* |

Is *jhūrai ṭhāḍha kāhe kāhā āwa* |
U *jhurawai ṭhāḍhi haū kahē āwā* |
K *jhurawai ṭhāḍha kahā maĩ āwā* |

Ib *banija na lāga*. 2. U *ehī sāthā* | *mūla gawāĩ calē use hāthā* || 4. Ib *kīnha giānī*. Is *calata je kīnha*. U *ju kīnha*. Ia *bhā hānī*. Ibcd *bhai hānī*. 5. Ia *bōū janame ehi* Is *jarama jē bhūjī*. U K *kā maĩ bayā janama waha bhūjī*. 7. Is *utara pauba tinha*. 9. Is K *dēhi* K *dēhi ahāra*.

78. 1. Ias Uk *tabahī biādha*. 3. The various readings of the first half are
Ia *sua kauna pūcha patāga madārī* |
Ib ..... *kō* .... *paḍhaka mana ḍārī* | Marg. note, *paḍhaka* or *paḍhika* = *cirīmār*, a fowler.
Icd .... *pūchahi patāga madārē* | Ic has marg. v. l. (?) *anēka mārē*.
Is .... *pūcha*........... *madōrē* |
U *sua kō dēkhī patāga milārē* |
K *suahī pūchai matāga ninārē* |

5. K *guna na chapāwahu*. 7. Ia *ahahu sunāwahu*. Ibd *paṇḍita hō tō*. Uk *pūchē nahi pāia bhēdū*. (9) K *dūnā lābhā hōi* ||

79. 1. Ia U *jaba pījarā tē* Ib *piñjara mahā ahā parēwā* Is *piñjara sau chū°* K *pījarē mō rahā parēwā*. 2. Ia *banda mahā ānā*. Is *aba guna bandi kawana jaja°* U *guna kauna banda* K *kauna bandi*. U *bēcahi*. 3. Is *paṇḍita sō jō hāṭa*. Ia *cahaū bikāi*. 4. Iad U *daī ca°* Ia *ḍaiya ca°*. K *daā ca°*. 5. Ib *tana bhā pīta*. 6. K *syāma cinhā dui*. Ia *tehi ḍara adhika darī sō jiwā* Id *tahā dui cinha ḍaraū*. U *tē dui ādi ḍaraū* K *tē suṭhi ḍarai dēkhi kai jīwā*. 7. Ia *abahī* Ids *phāda giū* U *phāda kai* K *phāda kara*. Is *dahū kai bandi cāha* U K *dahū karatāra cahai kā*. 9. N have *dhandha*. Ia *jagata jiu jāni* U *baiṭhi raheu budhi*.

80. 1. Is *carihārū* U *cirahārū* K *caraihārū*. Iac *c r māru* K *puni bābhana*. U *kara*. K *pañchinha* Ia *dayā na mārū*. 2. Ia *jiu hatasi parāwā* Is *kata re* U *kati re* K *kasa re*...... *badhahi*. 3. Ia *khādhuka mana lāwā*. Ib *manāwā* Is *kahesi*......*manāwā* U *kahisa jo paŋkhī byādhi manāwā* K *kahesi paŋkhi khājī mānāwā*. Ia U *niṭhura sōi* Icd *niṭhura te kahahī je* (Id *jo*) *para°* Is *niṭhura sō jō* K *niṭhura jīu tai kabahi na khāwā* || 4. Ia *roanā* Is U *rōwana* K *āwahi rōwana jā kē rōwana*. Ia *tajahu bhōga sukha soanā*. Is U *sōwana* K *bahutanha tajā bhōga sukha sōwana*. 5. Ia *au tehi jana kara hōihi*. Ib *au jānō*. U *jānahi hoihai tana nāsū* Ias *pōkhahi āpu parāē* U *pōkhē*. 6. Iacs U K *jau na hōta* Ibd *jau na hōhi*. Ib *dharē*. U *kata* K *kata pañchinha*. 7. Ias *jō byādhā* U *jata paŋkhī byādhā saba dharaī* | *sō bēcati mana lōbha na karaī* || K *jata pacchī byādhā niti dharaī* | *sō bēcata mana* etc., as in U. 8. Ia *suni paṇḍita beda grantha*. 9. Is *milāi kai sāthinha bhā* UK *milā āi kai bhā sāthinha bhā*.

81. 1. U *citra-sēna* K *tau lagi* U *ratana-sēna*. 2. K *jāi bāta unha āgē*. Ias K *āē siŋ°* Ib *āuru bahuta banija siŋ°*. 3. Ib U K *haī gaja°* U *bharē tē sīpī* K *bharē naga sīpī* Ia U *bastu saba siŋ°*. 4. Id *brāmbhana*. U *bāmhana* K *brāmhana*. K *ceṭaka barana*. 5. Ia *rātē ṭhōra kanṭha dui kanthā* U K *kanṭha dui rēkhā* K *rātā*. Ia *rātē ḍaina likhē saba panthā* U *rātē ḍaina likhā saba pēkhā* K *rātā* &c., as U. 6. Ids K *rātā ṭhōra* Is K *amia*. 7. Ia *māthaī ṭikā*. 8. Is *sō bōlō* Ia *sīsa saba ḍōla* K *sunata sabhanha sira ḍōla*. 9. Ia *mandilu* U *cāhiyē* Ia *aisana sūa amōla*.

82. 1. Ib *jana dui dui dhāē* U *bhaī rajāisi* K *bhaiu rajāesa* Id *brāhmana*. 2. K *asīsa au binai johārā* | Ias U K *ninārā* Ib *suā janama nahī* U *suā na jiu tē karaū*. 3. Ibd *pēṭa mahā bi°* Ia U *jina nāē saba tapā*. Ic *jaī saba nāwā* Id *jaī saba nawāē* Is *jehi saba nawā* K *jau saba nāe*. 4. Iad U K *dārā sēja* Is *jehi hai nida sēja jaū nāhī* K *dārā sēja jehi kē nāhī* Is *giu bāhī* U *gala bāhī* K *gale bāhī*. 5. Ia *andhā rahai so jehi nahi nainā* U *jō sūjha na* K *andha* Ib *mukha kahai na* U *mukha bōle na*. 6. Ia *bahira rahai sarawana nahi sunā*. Is has for ll. 6 and 7. The following—

dēkhā rāja bahuta sukha pāwā | *cārau bēda paḍhata subha āwā* ||
harē barana kāṭha rātē rēkhā | *jyaū syāma mahā bi jasa dēkhā* (sic) ||

7. U *phēri anta bahu pōkhī* K *kai kai bāra anta jau pōkhī* | U *nisa tōkhī.* K *bāra bāra bhariē na sā°.* 8. Ia U *mohi liē phirāwai.* Ic *jō mohi.* 9. Is *hōta asa patita* Ia *kita kāhū* Is *tō kou kāhū ka na āsa* (sic) U *tau kāhu ki āsa* K *kōi na kāhu ka āsa.*

83. 1. Iads *suā asīsa* K *sājā*———*rājā.* 2. Ib *bidhi budhi autārā* Is *bidha jehi autārā* K *bidha nai aūtarā.* 3. Iad *kō kehu.* Is U *kou kehu* U *jō nirāsa tehi āsā dēṇā* K *jō nirāsa tehi āswau* (sic) *dainā.* 4. Ia *anapūchaī bōlī jō bōlā* Id *binu pūchā* Is *kou binu pūchā* U *kou binu pūchē* Is U *hōhī bōla māṭī kō mōlā* K *hōē bōla.* 5. Is *bēda huti bhēū.* 6. Ia om. this line. Is *kaunu kōi jō āpu,* U *kōu* Is *jaū so.* 7. K *jau lagi......tau lagi* Ia makes this line No. 6, and has for No. 7.

suaī so apanā guna darasāwā | *hīrāmani taba nāu kahāwā* ||

8. Ia *cāri bēda.* 9. Is *padumāwati kara suaṭā.* K *padumāwati yaha hōtiū* Ia *saba ṭhāū* Id *jehi ṭhāū* Is *ohi ṭhāū* K *sēwā karaū gahi pāu.*

84. 1. Ia *hīrāmani līnhā* Icds *ēka lākha bābhana* U *ēka lākha bāmhanu* K *laccha ṭakā brāhmana.* 2. Ia *asīsana minati audhārā.* K *bhā data dārida kīnha payānā* Is K *mādila.* 3. Ic *baranaū kāhu suā* Ic K *dhani sō nāma* see note to l. 7. The readings of the second half line are as follows—

Ia K *cuai mōti hie hāra parōā*
Ibcd *janahū*......................
Is *mānika mōti māṅa parōa*
U *cuni cuni mōtī hāra parōa.*

5. Ias U K *bōlai tau mānika* Id *bōlai sō mā°.* Ib K *bādhi hō gūga* Id *bādhi hue* Is *nāhite pauna bādhi hō.* 6. Ib *cahai ṭhāri mukha* Is *jībha cāri mukha* Ia *guru bhā āpu* Is *guru bhai* U *guru hwai kīnha āpu jaga* K *bhā guru āpu.* 7. Ia *cāda sūra kai kathā jo kahē* K *cāda suruja* &c., as Ia. Is *pēma ka gahana* K *prēma ka lubudha lāgi cita rahā* U om. this line, and inserts after l. 3.

hiradai budhi hīrāmāni jōtī | *naina ratana mukha mānika mōtī.*

8. Ia *sunai sisa dhunai.* Ia *p r t k h hui augāha* Id *p r t k hūi āgāha* Is *sunata pēma hoi tāhi* U *prīti ka hōi agāha* K *prīti kahai augāha.* 9. Ia *gunawanta suā bhala nāhi* U *gunawanti su suaṭā* Is *asa gunawantā nahi bhalā bāura* &c. K *asa gunawanta bhala suaṭā.* The reading given is that of Ibcd, which however is bad metre. Ia U *bāura kīnha jo chāha* K *bāura kiā jō.*

85. 1. Ia K *bhaeu......gaeu.* 2. Ias *raniwāsa.* 3. Iacds *jiya kīnhā.* 4. Ib *āi nārī* Is *āi so bārī.* The readings of the line are as follows—

Ia *bhalaī suā haū sō pii(?)nāhā* | *mōrē rūpa ko asa jaga māhā* ||
Ib *bhalahī ... au pyārī*............ | *mōrahī rūpa koī jaga* .... ||
Ic .... *waru* .... | *mōrē*................................ ||
Id .... *aru* .... | *moraī* .... ||
Is *bhaleha sohāi piārī*........... | *mōrē rūpa ki koi jaga* .... ||
U *bhalē su aura* .... | *morē*................................ ||
K *bhaleha so* .... | *mōrē rupa sama kō jaga* ... .. ||

6. Ia *suā bāni dahū kasa sōnā* |
Ibc *suā bāni kasi k(?g)ahu kasa sōnā* |
Id .... *dahū k(?g)ahu kasa sōnā* |
Is *suā bāna dēkhī kasa sōnā* |
U *suā bāna dahū gahu kasa sōnā* |
K *suā bāṭa dahu kasu kasa sōnā* |
K2 *suā barana kahu dahu kasa sōnā* |
K3 *suā barana dēkhī kasa sōnā* |
} &c.

7. Ias *kaunu siṣṭi mōrē rupa manī* K *kaunu rūpa tōrī.*

86. 1. U *sāwara(i) rūpa.* K *sauri rūpa.* 2. Ia *bakulā tehi sara* Is *bakulī tehi sara* U *bagulī* K *tehi sara bakulē hansa.* 3. Is *daiyā kīnha.* 4. K *pai mana garaba.* Ia *cāda ghaṭē jama lagē rāhū.* U K *lāgā.* 5. Ia *koi kāhā.* K *lōni bilōni.* 6. Ib *pūchasi* Ids *bārī* for *nārī* Is *dinahi ki pūjai* K *dewasa na pūjai.* 7. Icd *kā kāgā* Is *puhupa su-bāsā so* K

unha kai K koi *baranai pāyā*. 8. K *rūpanha bhāga*. 9. Iac *sunata sūkhi gai rānī* Is *bhau rānī* K *sunata rōsa bhai* K *lōna janu lāga*.

87. 1. Ias K *mãdila* Is *kabahū ke hoi*. 2. U K *rājā taba hōi* U *calai kai jōgī* K *calai bhai jōgī*. 3. Is *rākhau* U *ãkūrū* K substitutes for this line *mārai abahi dēi bikhi mūrī* | *jaū lagi nāhi bāja tamacūrī* || The 2nd half line reads as follows in the other MSS.

Ias U *sabada na dēi biraha tamacūrū*
Ib *sẽdura dei rahai tamacūrū*
Ic *sabada hai biraha tana cūrū*
Id *sabada dēi na hōi tamacūrū*. We have followed the majority

4. Ia *dhāi jo dāmini* Ic *saũpā jō risa* Is *ohi saũpā jia rīsanha bhārī* U *suā dīnha lai risa* 5. *dēkhu dhāi suaṭẽ mãda*° Ic *dēkhahu yaha sōṭā mãda*° Id *dēkhahu sōṭā hai mãda*° Is *dēkhu yaha suā hai mãda* K *dēkhai suā kēra mãda*° Iacd *bhaeu na tā kahā̃* Ia K *pēṭa kaha ānā*. 7. K *ahai ku-bhākhī* U *lē kara māra* K *lē ehi mārahu deu mai sākhī*. 8. Ia *tā dina kahā̃* Ia *chapāwai*. 9. K *lēi calai so kawala puhā̃* Ia U *hōi mayūra*. K *hōta mayūra*.

88. 1. K *mārana gāī* Iad *upajā gyāna* Ics *hiaĩ ḍaru bhāī*. 2. Ia *jehi sāmī*. 3. U *jehi sōca na*. 4. Ia *jaĩ tīwāi kai marama na* Ib *jo tiriyā kara kāja* Id *jō tīwā̃* Is *jaū tiwāni kai* U *jō tīwai kai* K *jō tiwāna kai* Ia *parai dōsa*. Is K *pachatanā̃*. 5. K *nāgini sama tāhū* | ......*kāhū* || Ia U *suā mayūra* K *suā mãjāri hōi*. 6. Is *nāri kō nāhā̃* K *nāri kai tā̃hā̃*. 7. Ia *kai maku khōja hōe risa āī*. U *maku sō khōja hō ini suhāī* Ia *turai dōkha* U *turī dōkha* K *turai ka rōga kapi mātha bisāī*. 8. P and Is *eka hutiā au pāpu*. 9. Iacs U *binūsa lai* Id *bināsa dai* K *bināsa waha* U *sau sākhī*.

89. 1. Ia *khōja jaba āeu*. 3. Ia N *maĩ pūchā* Ia *dīnha tō kyā pa*° K *tai kā pa*.° 4. Iac U *wai jasa* K *tu raini ā̃dhiārī* Ia *karīla kē* Is K *karīla kā* U *karīla kubārī*. 5. K *uruanha pūjai dewasa ka bhāū*. 6. U *kōṭi mahā̃ khōṭā* | *ati baḍa bōla jībha kara chōṭā*|| K *ati baḍa, jībha kara*. 7. K *rudhira cuai* K *asa hatiāra laai mukha rātā*. 8. Ia *jaū suaṭā suṭhi lōna* Ic *sūā sō lōna* Is *suā baḍa lōna* U *jō suṭhi suaṭā lōna* K *suṭhihi suā jaū lōna*. 9. N *kāna ṭuṭa jehi pahiraĩ* Ia *kahā karaba sō* K *kā karabai sō sōna*.

90. 1. Ia *jasa hiradāi bikarama* Is K *pachatānā*. 2. Is *āu hirāmani* Is *jaū bōlai taū ambrita*. 4. Ic K *jīha mukha*. Is *kahai nirabūdhī* Ia U K *bāta na kahai birūdhī*. 5. Ia *tehi pā̃ḍita caḍhāwā* K *tehi pā̃ḍita dekhāwā*. 6. Ia *hatiāra rudhira jaĩ dēkhā* Ids U *ruhira pai dēkhā* K *rudhira asa dēkhā*. 7. Ia *ghaṭa rākhahu matī* Is *gae parāna* K *kai pranāma ānahu nagamātī* Id *suaĩ sā̃ga* U *nā̃hi to hōhu bēgi sā̃ga sātī* K *kai hoihau tehi kārana jātī*. 8. Ia *mā̃dila karahu sukha* Ia K *mandila hō* U *kai mandila sukha*.

91. 1. Is *dhani ujari āhī* U *dhani niramala rāhī* K *jaisa ujiārī rāhī* Ia *gahana gā gāhī* N *gāhī*. 2. U *prēma suhāga* K *parama sohāgi* Is K *sēwā jitihārī* U *sēwa citahārī*, *jaba hārī* is quite plain in all P. The readings of the first half are as follows—

Ia *etanika dōkha lāgi piu rūṭhā* |
Ib *etanika dūsa biraji piu rūṭhā* |
Icd *etanika dōsa b r j* .... |
Ids *etanika dōsa birāci*............ |
U *etana ki dōsa biruci* .... |
K *etanika dōkha biraci* .... |.

4. Ic *na bhūlō kōī*. Id *aisa garaba jani bhūlai kōī*. 5. In Ib the second half is *tasa mukha sūkhi na tana mahā̃ swāsā*. 6. U *bichura na milai* K *bichuri na milai syāma asa dīsā*. 9. Is *tehi dukha hau* U *yaha auguna parahēlī* K *nahi janaū paratē jaba*. The last half runs as follows :—

Ia *n g n rūsa bahu nā̃ha* ||
Ib as in text
Ic *nagar rūsa kī nā̃ha* ||
Id *nīka (? nēga) rūsa kī nā̃ha* ||
Is *nerā̃ga rōsa kia nā̃ha* ||
U *niṭhura rōsa kai nā̃ha* ||
K *niṭhura rōsa kia nā̃ha* ||

92. 1. U *āpuhi rasa aurahi* K *hatha āpuhi*. 3. U *dēkhisa* K *dēkhahi* Iads K *kā kara bhaeu*. 5. Ia *jā kahā̃ risa rasa jōgi* Ib *rasa kōi na jāī* Is *rasa jōgai na jāī* U *rasa cākhi na jāī* K *jahā̃ risa rasa jōgai na jāī*. 6. In the different MSS. the 1st half runs as follows—

Ia K *jahawā̃ risa mārai rasa pījai*
Ibcd as in text
Is *risahi jo mariai au rasa jījai*
U *sēwā chā̃ḍi birasa jiu dījai*

Ia U K *risa kabahū̃ na kījai* Is *sō rasa tajia na rīsa na kījai*. 7. Icds *sohāga ki pāia* U *sohāgani* K *sōi jo piu mana bā̃dhā*. 8. K *baratai tana khīna* Ic has *chīna* for *khīna*. 9 Iac K *soi dēkhu cā̃da asa niramala* U *canda dēkhisa nisi niramala*.

93. 1. K *samujhī jiu rānī* Is K *suā līnha* Ics K *rājā pahā̃ ānī*. U *rājā pahi ānī*. 2. Ia K *nāgamatī maĩ garaba jo kīnhā* Icd *mānamatī maĩ garaba na kīnhā* Is *nāgamatī hia garaba jo kīnhā* U *mānamatī maĩ garabha* (sic) *jo kīnhā*. Is K *kanta tohāra*. 3. K *etanika aiguna kiehu nirāsā*. 4. K *jau tohi daii* Ia *chā̃ḍahu tāhi na mārahu jīwā̃* K *chā̃ḍahu nahi tuha tā kara jīwā̃*. 5. U *milatahī mahā̃ tuma ahau ninārē* K *janu ajahu ninārē* Iads *tumha saũ ahau* K *tuha tē hōi adēsa*. 6. Ia *tumha hahu mohi mā̃hā̃* Is *tumha mana mohi pā̃hā̃* U *tumhā hō mohi pā̃hā̃* K *tuha mōhī cāhā̃*. The second half is as follows in the various MSS.

Ia *dēkhaū̃ tāki tu saba jaga pā̃hā̃* ||
Ib as in text
Ic *dēkhaū̃ tāki tūha saba pā̃hā̃* ||
Ids *dēkhaū̃ tāki tu hahu saba pā̃hā̃* ||
U *dēkhā bū̃jhi to hahu saba mā̃hā̃* ||
K *dēkheū̃ bū̃jhi basahu saba māhā̃* ||
K2 *dēkheū̃ tāki ta hahu saba pā̃hā̃* ||
K3 *dēkhaū̃ tākī ta hau saba mā̃hā̃* ||

8. U *kāu na jītā*. 9. Ia U K *āpuhi khōi kai*. K *karai tohāra*.

94. 1. Id has for second half, *sati na kahasi mā̃thahi muri chūā*. U *binā satta jyaū̃ sēmara bhūā*. K *binā satta jas sēmara bhūā*. 2. U *hahu mukha rāti kahahu sati bātā* K *hō mukha rāta sata kahahu bātā*. 3. Ias *sisṭi jo sattahi kērī* U *bā̃dhī drisṭi sattahī kērī* K *bā̃dhī srisṭi sabai sata kērī*. 5. U K *āgi lāi kai cahū̃ disi jārā* 6. Is K *au piāra daiyahi sata°* U *piāra daī sata°*. 7. Is *sē sata chā̃ḍi* U *sō sata chā̃ḍi jo* Is *bhā mati hīna satta jeĩ nāsā* U *kā mati-hīna kīnha sati nāsā* K *kā mati-hīna kīnha tapa-nāsā*. The word هين may be read either *hiaī* or *hīna*. We have adopted the former on the authority of the usually correct Id which has هئي *hiai*. 9. U *kahahu hama āgē* K *dahū̃ kā kiehu durāu*.

95. 2. Is *haū̃ ehi sata nisarā lai pāthē*, U *mai sati lai nikasā tehi mātē* K *mai lai sata nisareu ohi mātē*. All P have distinctly *pātē* پتين to which Ib gives a gloss *i'tibār*, trust. 3. Ia *paduma-gandha sō daī sā̃wārī* Id *sasi daī sā̃wārī* Is *paduma-gandha sō bidhi autārī* U *padama sugandha daī autārī* K *paduma-gandha tehi daā sā̃wārī*. 4. Is om. this verse and inserts before 3.

padumāwati kara kieu bakhānū | *nāgamatī risa mana mahū̃ ānū* ||

U also omits this line, and inserts a new line after 7, see below. K has *malai-gira ghrānī*
5. Id *ahahĩ jo padumini siŋghala* Is U *kaṇṭha phūṭa* K *kaṇṭha khuleu karata tinha sēwā*
Ia *nāhĩ to kahā mūṭhi* K *nāhī tau kā muṭhi* Here U inserts

kā̃ṭō jībha karō dasa ṭhāū̃ | *tajau na aba padumāwati nāū̃* ||

8. Is *sumiraū̃ maraū̃ to ohi lai nāū̃* (sic). K *maraū̃ to uhai lai nāū̃*. 9. Is ins. *kīnhī* after *hariara* Ia *duhū̃ jaga jasa lai jāū̃* Id *duhū̃ jagata kai jāū̃* Is U *jagata lai jāū̃* K *dunuhā juga lē jāū̃*.

96. 1. Ia K *hīrāmani jaba kā̃wā̃la*. 2. K *pañchi*. The second half line is very corrupt. The following are the readings—

Ia *kahē jo dīpa patā̃ga kē mārē* ||
Ib *kahu so dīpa jahā̃ pana naga bārē* ||
Ic *kahē so dīpa paŋkhi kē bārē* ||
Id *kahu sō dīpa p n k(g) bārē* ||

Is *kahē so dīpa paniga kē mārē* ||
U *kahē so dīpa phaniga kē mārē* ||
K *kahē jo dīpa phaniga kē mārē* ||

3. Ias UK *subāsita* Is *ahā jo kanaka.* 4. Ia *kasa rājā kasa dēsa utaŋgū* Ic *kō rājā asa dīpa* 5. Ia *suni samunda* Id *cakhu bhae kōkilā* U *suni samundra cakha bhā kila*° K *suni samuda cakhu bhā kilakílē* K *kaūla jo milai bhaūra bhai sílī.* 6. Ic N *niramálē* Ia *bhai ali sāga kí ajahū̃ kárī* Is U K *bhā ali sāga* Ic N *kálī.* 7. U K *au kahu tahā̃ paduminī lōnī* Iad U K *ghara ghara sabahi hō*°. 8. Is *sahai bakhāna bhāu jasa.* 9. Ia *dīpa waha dēkhaū̃* Is *jau rē dīpa waha dēkhaū̃* K *jānahū̃ dīpa waha dēkheu* U *uṭha muhi cāu* K *suni upajā mana cāu.*

97. 1. Ia K *rājā maĩ baranaū̃.* 2. Ia U *bhulānā* Ia *bīti na palaṭā kōī* Ic *bahureu* Is *bahurō* K *juga tīni na.* 3. U *ghara ghara nārī padumini jātī* U *basanta hōi dina rātī.* 5. Ib *tahā̃ kara rājā.* U *gandhrapa-sēna* U *māha īdara jasu sājā* K *māha dēi jasa sājā.* 7. Ia *barē onāhī.* Is *cahū̃ khā̃ḍa kēra barēkhi onāhī̃* K *barē ohi āwahi.* U substitutes for this line

sōraha sahasa paduminī rānī | *sō saba siŋghala-dīpa bakhānī* ||

Ia K have second half *utara na pāwahi phiri phiri jāhī̃* K *phēri siḍhāwahi* || Ic *rājā garaba ke bōlai.* 9. Ia *aisaĩ chapi saba rānī.*

98. 1. U *suni yaha bāta ratana.* 3. U *janu hwai āi sūra mana bāsī* K *janu hoi suraja hiaĩ paragāsā* | *saba ghaṭa pūri āi mana bāsā* || 4. U see below. K *aba maĩ cā̃da suraja waha chāyā.* 5. Ia *prīti ka ābhā* (?) *pēma* Ib *girata kirini bhā* K *kirini kalā bhau pēma* K *saraga caḍhaū̃ bhai sūrū.* 6. Ia *kalā* for *karā* Is K *kaū̃la tahā̃ phūlā.* 7. K *aba kaū̃la jiu bhaū̃rā gandhī* K *jasa sasi.* U has for the last four lines

tū̃ paṇḍita tasa baranī bālā |	*janu kai lāgi campa kī mālā* ||
sunata-hī sō padumāwati nāma |	*hirdai āi pēma rāga jāma* ||
rātē naina wahī rāga bhūlē |	*dēkhahū̃ jāi phūla jasu phūlē* ||
naina bhaē darasana kē bhūkhē |	*dharatē saraga samāhī na dūkhē* ||

8. Ia K *caudaha bhuana.* 9. Id U om. *lōnā*, thus saving the metre. Iad Uk *dēkhā.*

99. 1. Ib *mana bhūlā na* (sic) Ic *mana bhūlā rāja.* Id U K *prēma* Iac U *dēi na chājā* Id *dei tohi chājā.* 2. Iacd U *jo parā na* U *phā̃da mahā̃ pa*° K *chūṭai......ṭūṭai* U *giragaṭa chāha* (?) *parā dukh jētā* K *girigiṭa chaā parai* Ia *khina hoi rātā* U *khana rātā khana piarā sētā* K *khinu khinu rātā pīta au sētā.* 4. Is *puni puchāri jaū̃ bhā bana* K *jo bhau bana*° Ia *rōmahī rōma phā̃da* Ic *rō̃ō rō̃ phā̃da parai naga*° Id *rō̃ rō̃ phā̃da parai naga*° Is *rō̃a rō̃a pare phā̃da naga*° U *rō̃ana phā̃da parā naga*° K *rōma rōma pare phā̃da naga*°. 5. Ia *pañchinha phiri phiri parā jo phā̃dū* Is *pā̃khanha* U *pañchinha phira phira parā* K *saba pañchinha gia para jō phā̃du.* 6. Ib *mueū̃ mueū̃ kara āhi cilaī* U *muyau muyau nisu dinu cilalāhī* | *tehi rōsana nāgini dhai khāhī* K *tehi rōsanha nāganha dhai khāī.* 9. Ia K om. *mēlai*, which improves the metre. Iacs *kita mārai* U *hōi māra kabi mōkha* K *hōi mōra kaba mōkha.*

100. 1. Icd *ūbhi mana sā̃*° Is *ūbhi bhari sā̃*° K *ubhai bhari sā̃*° Id K *bōla nahi bōlu* Is *jani bōlu* K *bōla nī bōlu.* 2. Ic *pahilahī pēma* N *bhaleha pēma* Is *pēma jeī khēlā* U *duhū̃ jaga tarā pēma jē̃.* 3. Ia *dukha kē maddhu pēma mada rākhā.* Ic *dukha bhītara so pēma-madhu* Ids *dukha bhītara so pēma-mada rākha* U *bhitara dukkha pēma-mada* K *dukha bhītara pēma-mada.* The readings of the second half verse are as follows—

Ia *gañjana marana cahai jō cākhā* ||
Ib *kañcana barana sahai sō cākhā* ||
Ic *kañcana barana bhaē jō cākhā* ||
Id *ganjana marana sahai jō cākhā* ||
Is .... *sō* ....
U .... *cahai jō* ....
K *rāja taji mirana* (sic ? *marana*) *rahai so cakhā.*

4. Ia *kāhe kō āwā* Ic *kāhe kē* Id *kahe kahā̃* Is *prithimī mahā̃ kāhe ko* U *sōu autara bhuī kāhē̃ āwā* K *sō prithimī mahā̃ kāhē āwā.* 5. Id *pēma pantha sira* Is K *pēma pāya sira* U *aba haū̃ pēma pantha sira.* Iacd U *pāi na.* 6. Is *jeĩ na dēkh* U K *jō na dēkhi kā jāni sarēkhā.* 7. Is K *tau lagi* Ia *milatahī kōna janama dukha* Ic *milatahī gaeu* Id *jō bhē̃ṭā jara mahā̃ dukha.* Is *milā to gā jarama* U K *bhē̃ṭā dukkha janama kā mēṭā.* 8. U K *anūpa tc baranī* (K *baranā*). U *nakha sikha jaisa sīgāra.* 9. Ia *milana kai* K *hiai hiai rasa pūrai.*

101. 2. U *prathamahi kahaũ kasturī.* K *aura jō sēsā.* 3. U *lēhi uraghānī,* K *bisahara murī lēhi sō ghrānī.* 4. Ib *chōra chāra jō mārā.* 5. Ia *kuṭila kēsa bisahara naga kārē.* 7. U K *ghughurārī.* U *sãkara pēma,* K *sakati pēma.* 8. All copies except Ia and U insert *rājā,* which spoils the metre. K *parē sēsa giu kāsa.* 9. *Asṭā-u,* &c. This passage is very corrupt. P have اسٹوکلي. Is *asṭa-u kūrī,* U K *asṭa-u kurī.*

The following are the full readings of this line :—

Ia	*asṭa-u kulī nāga wē* |	*bhae kēsahī kī bãda* ||
Ibc	*asṭa-u kulī nāga urkānyō (?)* |	*bhaē kēsa kī bãda* ||
Id	„ „ *urk(g)hānī* |	„ „ ||
Is	*asṭa-u kūrī nāga saba auraṅgē* |	*bhai kēsanha kē bãda* ||
U	*aṣṭa-u kurī uragānē* |	*bhae kēsanha kē bãdi* ||
K	*asṭa-u kurī nāga oragāena* |	*bhae kēsanha kē pāsa* ||

It will be observed that in this line again, except in Ia and U there are a number of extra syllables.

102. 1. *sēdura aja-hu,* 2. Ib *pantha gagana mahã.* 4. Ia *sūra kirana.* Is K *mãjha surasarī dēkhi,* Ia *jamunā mãjha janu surasari.* 5. Iad *khãḍai rēkha ruhira,* 6. U *dharē gaja mōtī.* 8. Ia U K *caḍhā suhāga.* 9. *sēwā karahĩ nakhata au taraī.* The metre here is corrupt again. The above is the readings of all P, and Is K. U has *sēwā karaī su taraī* The latter half of the verse is also corrupt. The following are the readings :—

Iad	*gagana caḍhī jasa gãga* ||
Ibcs	*uē gagana* „ „ ||
U	*gagana caḍhī sō mãga (? gãga)* ||
K	*gagana caḍhē nisi gãga* ||

103. 2. U *jō kirana dipāē.* 4. Ib *puni gahana girāsā.* 5. Ibs *duija pāsa.* U has for last half of line, *bēḍhō sō jo tilaka waha ḍīṭhā.* 6. *atara,* U K *antara,* P اتر. Is has *asira.* 8. *cakrabāna,* so all copies. Ic *duhu jaga māraka (? ga) nāũ,* U *māra rakatana nāũ* K *duī jaga jītanē tehi jāu* (sic). 9. All copies insert *rājā.* K *sua-hi bhaeu pachatāu* K[2] *mai eka pareũ kuṭhāũ.* K[3] *mō kō bhā eka ṭhāũ.*

104. 1. Is *hēru lāgu bikha,* K *jā saũ phēru māru cakhu bānā.* 2. Is U K *hanai dhanuka.* 6. Ia K *āpu bēdha jaga.*

105. 3. Ia *jānahu ulathahĩ hī mūha lāgā,* Icd *cāhahī ulatha gagana.* 4. U *jhakōrahi bahai.* 6. Iabd *bhaũha cakara kē.* 7. Ibc. *samũda hĩḍōlā.*

106. 1. Ia U *dvai ánī.* K *bāna dhanukha dui ánī.* 3, Ia U *wārahũ pāra.* The second half is as follows :—

Ia	*jā kahã chūṭi māra bikha bãdhē* ||
Ibds	as in text
Ic	*jā saũ hēra māra bikha bãdhē* ||
U	*jā kahã chūṭi lāi* „ ||
K	„ „ *lāgu* „ ||

4. *kō ko na mārā,* so all copies, except K which has *bānanha kō kō nahi mārā.* U has. *bānani sō kō ko* &c. U *sigarō* for *sagara-u.* 5. U *nakhata jo dīsahi ghánē* K *nakhata dīsahi ati ghánē.* Ia has *saba jāhī* for *jasa jāhī.* Iads *tē saba.* 6, Ic *bahu rākhī,* Id *phiri rā°* K *kai rākhī.* Is *dharatī bēdhi jānu saba rākhī.* Is *sākhā ṭhākha (? ṭhāḍha) dēhi saba sākhī.* U *sākhā sākha dēi saba.* K *sākhā sākhī dēi ohu sākhī.* 7. Iab U *rōma rōma.* 8. Ib U *bāna jasa.* Is *bāna saba.* For *upanī,* Is has *ōpahã,* U *ōpahai,* K *ōpaha.* All P give اوپنهٔ which may be read as *ōpahã,* or as in the text. Ibc *bēdhi rahē tana ḍhaṅkha.* K has *dhãkha.* 9. The following are the various readings. That of Ibds U has been adopted.

Ia	*sāuja tana saba rōma hai* |	*pañchihĩ tana saba paṅkha* ||
Ic	*saujahi tana jita rōwã* |	*paṅkhihĩ tana jita paṅkha* ||
K	*sravahi pasēwa rōwa rōwa* |	*paṅkhinha tana bhā pãkha* ||

107. 2. Ia has second half *bēsara saraka sukara hoi ūā,* U *hvai ūā,* K *bhai ūā.* 3. Ia *suā so hīrāmani bhā lājā.* Ib *suā so hīrāmani mana lājā.* U *suā ju pīta rahā mana lājā.* K *piura bhaē mana.* 4. *pãwārī,* so most MSS. Ib has *tēwārī* with *pãwārī* as a v. l. on the.

margin. It also gives a gloss, translating *tēwārī*, by *tēz*. U has *pannārī*. A printed edition has *banawārī*. 5. Ib has *pāsā* for *āsā*. 7. U *naina khãjana dui kēli*. U *dahũ waha rasa pāwai kou nāhī*. K *dahũ waha rahasa kawāla kē nāhī*. K has for the last *dōhā*

dēkhi adhara-rasa (ā)sraminha | *bhaiu nāsikā kīra*||
paunā bāsa pahũcāwai | *āsana* (or *āsa na*) *chāḍala tīra*||

108. 2. Ics *phūla parai jō*. Ia *jita jita kaha bātā*. 3. Ic *hīrā kīnha*. Is U *liyē*. K *hīrā lai bidaruma para dhārā*. Ic *bihãsata hasata jagata ũji°*. K *bihasata taisē hoi*. 4. Ia *au majīṭha*. 5. Id K *asa wai*. V *aisē amī adhara bhari*. Is *abahī achūta*. K *ahai achūta*. 6. The following are the readings of the first half :—

Ia	*mukha*	*tãbōra*	*rãga*	*ḍhārahī*	*rásā* |
Ib	*mukha*	*tãbōla*	*rãga*	*adharahī*	*rásā* |
Icd	*mukha*	*tãbōla*	*rãga*	*ḍhārahī*	*rásā* |
Is	*mukha*	*tãbōla*	*rasa*	*ḍhārahī*	*rásā* |
U	*mukha*	*tãbōla*	*adhara*	*rãga*	*rásā* |
K	*mukha*	*tamōla*	*rasa*	*dhārinha*	*rásā* |

8. K *adhara amia bhari rākhā sabha jaga*, &c. 9. Iacd *kā kahũ*. K *kā kara*.

109. Ib. *dasana jōga*. K. *naga syāma gãbhīrā*. 2. This differs in all MSS. Thus :—

Ia	*janu bhādō nisi dāmini dīsī* |	*camaka uṭhai janu b h y n batīsī*
Ibd	„ „ *kahã* „ „ |	„ „ *tasa banī* „
Ic	„ *dāmini bhādō nisu dīsī* |	„ „ „ *b h w n* „
Is	„ *bhādaũ nisi dāmini dīsī* |	*camaki uṭhita sibhini* (sic) „
U K	„ „ „ „ „ |	„ *uṭhai tasa badana* „

3. Is *hīrā jōti so*. U K *hīrā dipai so*. 4. U *bahutani jōti dēkhi kai bhāī*. Some MSS. place this line seventh. 6. *sobhāona*. So Ib. Iac U *sobhāiana*. Id سبهایه. Is *sobhāwē* K *sobhāwatē*. 7. Ias *auru kō dūjā*. 8. With regard to this line the MSS. are practically unanimous. We have

Ia	*bihãsata hãsata dasana jo camakeu*	*pāhana uṭheu jharakki* |	
Ibs	„ „ „ *tasa camakai*	„ *uṭhai* „	(Is *jharaŋki*).
Ic	„ „ „ „ „	„ *uṭheu* „	
Id	„ „ „ *wai* „	„ *uṭhai jarakki* |	
U	„ *dasana jo camakai*	*pāhana uṭhai jharāki* |	
K	„ *hãsata badana tasa camakai*	*pāhana uṭhai jharaki* |	

Of these U is the only one which will scan. 9. *tarakki*. So all, exc. Is *daraŋki*, U *tarāki*, and K *karaki*.

110. 1, Ib *rasanā khōla jo kahi*. U *rasanā mukha jo kahai*. K *rasanā śunai*. 2. Ia *harai sarasa* (or *sarisa*). Id *hōai nisa cātaka au kō°*. Is *so sīra* U K *hārē sura*. Is *binu basanta waha bainu na*. U *bīna bãsurī bainani milā*. K *binā basanta waha baina na*. 3. Is *cātaka kōkila sari na karāhī*. U *kōkila cātaki kahai so nāhī*. K *cātrika kōkila rarata jo āhī*. Is *bōli* for *bayana*. 4. Is *pēma-madhu* U *māthi jhamī kai ḍōlā*. K *ghurumi kai*. Iads *riga juga*. 7. Is *aratha būjhi*. U *amara su bhāratha piŋgala gītā* | U K *aratha cōja*. 8. The following are the various readings :—

Ia	*bhāwasatī byākarana sata piŋgala pāṭha purāna* |
Ib	„ „ *saba* „ „ „ |
Ic	„ „ *sama* „ „ „ |
Id	„ „ *sarasī* „ „ „ |
Is	„ „ *sata sata saũ paḍhai*„ |
U	*bhāwasatta byākarna saba sāstara bāca* „ |
K	*bhāwasatī au byākarana piŋgala kōka purāna* |

9. The verse ends as follows :—Ia *janu lāgata sara jāna*. Ibc *tasa janu lāgahī bāna*. Id *jasa rakhahī bisa bāna*. Is *sajananha lāgai bāna*. U *janu lāgai bikha bāni*. K *janu lāwai rasa bāna*.

111. 2. *paŋga-rasa*. So clearly Iab. Ic and Id omit the diacritical dots and have ٮٮک رس. Is *paŋka-asa*. U *pāka jasa*. K *paŋka-rasa*. Is *kyaũ yaha su°*. U *kē asa su*..

K *kai asa surāga khiraudā*. 3. *jeĩ*, so all P. Is K *jō*. U *jō dēkhā sō tila*. 4. K *agni-bāna*. 5. N *lākha dui*. So Id. 6. Is *sō tila kāla...... aba waha kāla kāla*. Ic *aba waha kāla jagata kahā̃ bhaeu*. K *sītala lāgeu bhēṭi na gaeu | au waha gāla kāla sama bhaeu*.|| 7. Is *tehi tana rāta*. U K *saba-tana*. 8. Iacd *gagana kieu*. 9. Ia has last half *tehi tila jāi jo chāḍi*. K *tilahi uṭhai tila būḍai nahi choḍaiṭhā* (?) *chāḍi*.

112. 2. Is *jhamakahĩ .. janu kaudhāra kīnha duhū̃*. U *jhalakaĩ*. K *jhamakaĩ*. 4. U *tehi khuṭilā dīpaka dwai bārē*. K *tā para khuṭilā dipa dui bārē*. Is *dui dhua duau khū̃ṭa waisī pīārī* (sic). U *dwai dhruwa tahā̃ āna baiṭhārē*. K *duau khū̃ṭa dui disā sā̃wārē*. 5. K *pahirē khuṭilā*. *Kacapacī* has puzzled the copiests. Ib has *gaja-mōtī*. Ic has کچس without a single dot. Id has کچپوتھڈ. Ia and N are clear. 6. Ia *khana khana cīra jabahĩ kara gáhā*. Is K *khana khana jabahĩ cīra sēra gáhā*. 8. Ia *srawana-sīpa asa*. Is *srawana dīpa hiya dōu* (sic). Uk *srawana dipahi asa*. 9. Is *gōhanē*. U *gahinai*.

113. 1. *kū̃ja kai rīsī*. So Iabcs U. Ib has *dīsī*. K *rāsī ...... sāsī*. Ib *kañca tāra maku lāgeu sīsī*. Ic as Ib exc. *janu* for *maku*. Is *kanaka tāra janu lāgeu*. 2. Is *kūdērai phēri*. The printed editions all give कूँड़े but the cerebralised ड़ is not borne out by any MSS. So in कुँदेरइ in the next set of *caupāīs*. 2. Ia UK *hāri*. 4. Id *jahāna* for *jānu*. Is *kaṅka* for *bāga*. K *bā̃ka turaṅga*. 6. Ias *ghū̃ṭata pīka*. 7. Ia *dhani giū̃ dīnha b dhā taĩ bhāū*. Ic *dhani gīū̃ dīnheu bidhi*. Id *dai ohi*. Is *dhanẓa gīu dīnhē bikha bhāū*. K *dhana bidha nā dīnhā giu bhāū*. Iad *kā kahā̃*. 8. Iacds *mukutāhala*. U *mālā sōhai gīu*. The word *mālā* is in all copies but spoils the *dōhā*. U corrects the metre by omitting *abharana*.

114. 1. Ia *danḍa bhuja banī ka°*. K *kundī banōī*. 2. Ic *khā̃bha*. Ids K *gā̃bha*. 4. Iad K *rakata* for *ruhira*. U *au ā̃gurī naga*. K *au ā̃gurinha naga kanaka ā̃gūṭhī*. Ia *ati lōnī*. K *sōha gati*. 7. The first half runs as follows.

Ia	*khana jiu dēi khanahi lei jāī*			
Ib	*jānahu gati saturana dekharāī*			
Ic	„ „ *pērana*	„		
Id	„ „ *pahiraī*	„		The word *pahiraī* is corrected to *bēḍana* or *bēḍina*.
Is	*bā̃hū gati pairi*	*dai lāī*		
U	*jānahu gati pāturi*	*dikharāī*		
K	„ „ *acharī*	*dekharāī*		

All printed copies have *bēḍina* or *bērena*, which they translate by *ṭawāif*. 9. Is *bējha bhā̂*. U *ṭhāū̃ ṭhāū̃ saba bidhi bhaē*. K *ṭhāwā̃hi ṭhāū̃ bēdha bhai ubhai sā̃sa lēhi jō nitta*.

115. 1. Is *kañcana lāhī ...... janu cāhī*. Ic *uṭhai hoi cāḍū*. K *uṭhai kuca cāḍū*. 2. Ia *kundana kanaka bhalē janu*. UK *kundana kanaka bēla janu*. Is *ambrita ratāna mauna dai mū̃dē*. UK *ratana dei mū̃°*.

4. Ia	*jōbana*	*bāsa*	*lēhĩ*	*rasa*	*bāgā*	*cāhahĩ sō nahi* (?)	*hiaĩ*	*mahā̃*	*lāgā*	||
Ib	„	*pāni*	*lēhĩ*	*nahi*	„	*cāhahĩ hulasi*	*hulasi*	*hia*	*lāgā*	||
Icd	„	*bāna*	„	„	„	„	„	*hiai lei*	*lāgā*	||
Is	„	*bāga*	„	„	„	„	„	„ *haṭha*	*lāgā*	||
U	„	*turai*	„	„	„	„	„	„	„	||
Is	„	*bāga*	„	„	„	„	*ulathī akāsahĩ*		*lāgā*	||

6. Id *chui kō pāu*. 7. Ia *nahi cākhā*. K *binu cākhē*. 9. Ia K *pāwā*. Ids *pāreu*.

116. U *pēṭa patra jānahū̃ sō lāwā | kuṅkuma candana barana*. K *pēṭa patra asa jānahū̃ lāwā*, &c., as U. 2. N *sukumārī ...... adhārī*. 5. Is *nāginha kai*. Ia *candana kū̃hakū̃ha*. Id *candana khāni bāsa lai*. Is *bāsa gau*. U *bāsa-rasa*. 6. *Kālindari* so all MSS. Ib *gai kā°*. Id *parāga*. Ic *nābhī kunḍa so*. Is *nābhī kunḍara bīca banārasī*. 8. All MSS. have plainly *sira karawata tana karasī lai lai*, except that U and K omit *lai lai*. 9. Ia has for second half, *bahutaka muē nirāsa*.

117. 1. *bairini*. The MSS. all differ as follows. Ia بیرن, Ib پاتر, Icd پیرن, Is पैरिनि, U बैरन, K पैरनी. Printed editions have चोटी. U *jānahu calī apa°*. 3.

Is *lahari lēta jānahu piṭhi caḍhā ...... kãcukī māḍhā.* U *lahirẽ dēi piṭhi para caḍhī* | *cīra ohāra kãcukī māḍhī.* 4. Ib *piṭhī kīnhī.* Ib and K have *bhuaŋgama.* Icds and U have *dīnhī* instead of *kīnhī.* 5. The following are the readings :—

Ia *kārī kisuna caḍhē ohi māthē* | *taba so chūṭa aba chūṭa na nāthē* ||

Ib *kisuna karā caḍhē ohi māthē* | " " " " " " " ||

Ic *kusatana(?) caḍhā nātha waha* " | " " " " " " " ||

Id *kirisuna ke karā caḍhā* " " | " " " " " " " ||

Is *kīsna karā caḍhā ohi* " | " " " " " " " ||

U *krasna caḍhā kālī kē māthē* | *taba sō chūṭa achūṭi na nāthē* ||

K *kisnā so caḍhē* " " " | *taba so chūṭa aba chūṭa* " " ||

7. K *sō dēkhai jehi mathē bhāgū.* 9. Ia *auru sĩghāsana yaha sakai.* Is *sō pāwaī jinha ḍīṭhi.*

118. The first line differs greatly in the various MSS. as follows.

Iacs *laŋka puhumi asa āhi na kāhū* | *kēhari kahaũ na ohi sari tāhu,* ||

Ib *chīna laŋka* " " " " | " " " " " " ||

Id *laŋka upama* " " " " | " " " " " " ||

U *kahaũ laŋka sari pūja na kēhara* | *laŋka bhriŋga kai jānahu lēhara* ||

K " " " " " *keharī* | " *siŋgha jānahu leharī* ||

We have followed the majority. 2. *basā.* So all P. Is K have *bisā.* Ib has marginal gloss '*bhawãra.*' U makes this line fourth, and has *wārõ cāha laŋka so khīnī* | *tēhũ cāha barana jaga jhīnī* ||. 3. Here again the MSS. greatly differ. We have

Ia *parihãsi piara tehi rīsā* | *lēhĩ ḍaŋka lōgahī kahã ḍīsā* ||

Ib " *dēhĩ piara* " *bāsa* | *liē ḍãka lōganha kahã ḍāsā* ||

Ic " *piara bhaē* " *bāsā* | *lēhĩ ḍhaŋka* " " " ||

Id " " " " *bīsā* | " *ḍaŋka lōgahī kahã ḍīsā* ||

Is " *ari bhai bana-bāsā* | *lihē laŋka nāganha kahã ḍāsā* ||

U " *piara bhaī tē nāsā* | *liē ḍaŋka mānusa kō ḍāsā* ||

K *paripari piarī bhaī tehi bāsā* | *līnhē ḍaŋka mānukha kahã ḍāsā* ||

We have followed, Ic and Id which give the best sense. 4. Id *kanaka tār.* U *duhũ bīca taisẽ rahi.* K *muri gaē.* 5. Ibd *bāgā* for *tāgā.* Ibs U K have *gati* for *kita.* 7. U *bājaī sabai.* K *rāgahī sabai.*

119. 1. Is *nābhī kōḍara ma°.* U K *kunḍala ma°.* 5. *tīwai,* so Ibs. Ia *nawala.* Ic بنوي or نبوي, Id *tana waha.* U *nābhī.* K *nībī.* 6. Iad *asa* for *dahũ.* Is has an altogether different line, *viz* :—

madana bhãḍāra romāvali gāī | *janu darapana kai mūṭhi sobhāī.* ||

120. 1. Ia U K *kahaũ* for *baranaũ.* U *jaŋgha* for *laŋka.* 2. Ia *jãgha.* Iad *khambha.* N have *gābh* for *khãbha.* 3. U K *bhūmi* for *puhumi.* Ia has *rahahĩ pahumi para pāṭa nahi.* So K *rahai bhūmi.* 4. Ic *pagu parai.* Is *paga para jahã.* 6. Is *jarā cãda.* U K *bīju* for *bīcu.* Is U K *camakārā* for *jhanakārā.* 8. Ia K *jaisa sĩgāra.* U *tasa kachu barana na janau, nakhasikha jaisa sĩgāra.* 9. Ia *jō nāra.* Ic *kehi jōga.* Id *jō jōga.* U K *tehi nāra.*

121. U *murajhāī.* K *murujhāī.* P are all quite plain. 3. Is *lēi bisã.°* 4. U K *khana khana.* 5. U *khanahi acēta ḍūba.* Iacs have *nisarai.* K om. this ine. 7. Is *pēma-awasthā.* K *kaṭhina biraha.* The second half runs as follows.

Ia *nā nija jiu na marana kara sthā(?)* ||

Ib *nã jehi jīu na dusaũ awasthā* ||

Ic *bãjahi* " " *dasaī* " ||

Id *nã jiu jaī na sahai* " ||

Is *jānahu jīu na sakai bewasthā* ||

U *nā nija jīwaī dasõ awasthā* ||

K *nā nija jīwa na marana awasthā* ||

K² *bhā jiya jiai na hōi bewasṭhā* ||

K³ *nā nija marana na jiana newāsā* ||

8. Ic *jinha nihāra nahī līnha.* K² *janu naiharanha līnha jiu.* K³ *janu lōhāra līnha kari.*

122. 1. K *rājā rāu*. 4. Ia *lachimana*. Ibc *lakhimana*. Ics U K *lakhana*. Is *mōhai apachārā*. U *mōhā hai pára*. K *mōhī kai párā*. Ias U K *nā sō rāma*. Id *nahi sō*.

6. Ia *binai karahī̃ cētahu gaḍha-pátī* |
Ib As in text. |
Ic *binai karahī̃ jita ga°*. |
Id *binau karahī̃ cētai ga°*. |
Is „ „ *cētahu* „ |
U K *binai* „ „ „ |
K² K³ *binai karahī̃ cētahu ga°* |

8. Ib *dasa rōga*. K³ *dasa ṭhōka*. 9. Ib *ānahu saba tehi rōga*.

123. Ias K *sōi kai jā°*. 2. Ia *jagata āwa jasa bālaka*. U *āi jagata jasa bā°* | *uṭhā so rōi gyāna saba khōā*|| K *uṭhā rōi tasa gyāna jo khōā*|| 3. N have *jáhā̃* and *káhā̃*.

3. The following are the readings.

Ia K *kaī̃ apakāra marana kara kīnhā̃* | *sakati jagāi jīu hari līnhā̃*||
Ib U „ *upakāra* „ „ „ | „ *hā̃kāri* „ „ „ ||
Ic „ „ „ *kau* „ | „ *jagāi* „ „ „ ||
Id „ „ „ *kara* „ | „ „ „ „ „ ||
Is „ *upacāra* „ *kai* „ | „ *jīu jeī̃ kari kai* „ ||
K² *kei upakāra marana kā kīnhā* | *kehi re jagāi jīu hari līnhā*||
K³ *sakati hā̃kāri jīu hari līnhā* | *kē upakāra marana kahi dīnhā*||

6. Is U have to *prāna*, instead of *paāna*. 7. The latter half is as follows :—

Ia *ghaṭana nīka lē jīu na sāthā* ||
Ib *kaṭhina nīka pai* „ „ „ ||
Ic *ghaṭata bēga lē jīwana sāthā* ||
Id „ *nīka pai jīu na* „ ||
Is *ghaṭana nīka pai jīu niswāthā*||
U *ghaṭana nīka jīwana pai sāthā*||
K omits the whole line.
K² *ghaṭai na nikarai pai jiu sāthā*||
K³ *ghaṭata nīka pai jīwana sāthā*||

8. *ahuṭha* so all N. Ia has اهتّه, Ib اهت, Ic اهته, Id اُدهت.

124. 1. The second half runs as follows :—

Ia *jūjhi kāla sō kaī̃ na chājā* ||
Ib *kālahu taī̃ kachu jūjhi na chājā* ||
Ic *kāla s nā̃ kē* „ „ „ ||
Id „ *satē̃ kai* „ „ „ ||
Is „ *sēti kai* „ „ „ ||
U „ *sēti* „ „ „ „ ||
K „ „ *koi* „ „ *sājā* ||
K² „ „ „ *jūjha* „ „ ||
K³ „ *so jūjha kīnha nahī̃ chājā*||

2. Ia has *taja na kishuna jāta gō°*. Is *jāṭa na kisuna na jāta gō°*. Iū has an altogether different line which has been partly defaced. So far as we can make it out it runs,—

تاسون دوکه کهي اى سيرا | جهه سن کر لاکی پر پيرا || .

4. Ib *punī jō*. Id U *puni suṭhi*. 5. *ahuṭha*, so all copies, exc. Id which has اونه, and Ib which has اونه. 7. Ib *pāu dharē*.

125. 1. Iad *suai kahā mō saū̃ sunu rājā* |
Ib „ „ *sunu cētahu* „ |
Ics K² „ „ *mana samajhahu* „ |
K³ „ „ *mana būjhahu rājā* |
UK as in text.

अर्थात् दोनों जग से निस्तार पाता है, पर-ब्रह्म में लीन हो जाता है॥ दुःख के भीतर (भीतर=अभ्यन्तर) जो प्रेम-मधु रक्खा है, उस को वही चखता है जो गञ्जन और मरने को सहता है, अर्थात् अपमान और मरण से जो न डरे, वह प्रेम-मधु को चक्खे॥ प्रेम-पथ में जिस ने (अपने) शीस को नहीं लगाया, वह काहे को पृथिवी में आया, अर्थात् प्रेम के विना पृथ्वी में आना व्यर्थ है॥ (सो, हे शुक,) मैं ने तो अब (अपने) शिर में प्रेम-फंदें को डाला। (सो तूं मेरे) पैर को (उस प्रेम-मार्ग से) न टाल (हटाव)। (मुझे) चेला कर के रख, अर्थात् तूं गुरु हो, और मुझे चेला बना कर प्रेम-मार्ग में चलने का उपदेश दे, उस से निराश मत कर॥ (तुझे इस लिये गुरु बनाता हूं, कि) प्रेम-द्वार को वही (सो) कह सकता है, अर्थात् बता सकता है, जिस ने कि उसे देखा हो। और जिस ने (उस द्वार को) नहीं देखा, वह क्या जाने कि उस में क्या विशेष (गुण) है। (प्रेम-द्वार में) तभीं तक दुःख है, जब तक कि प्रियतम से भेंट न हो, (और जब प्रियतम मिल गया,) तो (फिर) जन्म भर का दुःख मिट जाता है॥

(तो, हे शुक, पद्मावती को) जैसा अनुपम तैं ने देखा है, (तैसा-ही) नख से शिखा तक (उस के) शृङ्गार का वर्णन कर। मुझे (पद्मावती के) मिलने की इच्छा है, यदि कर्त्ता (ब्रह्मा) मिलावे (तो)॥ १००॥

इति राज-शुक-संवाद-खण्ड-नाम नवम-खण्डं समाप्तम्॥ ९॥

अथ नखसिख-खंड ॥ १० ॥

चउपाई ।

का सिँगार ओहि बरनउँ राजा । ओहि क सिँगार ओही पइ छाजा ॥
प्रथम-हि सीस कसतुरी केसा । बलि बासुकि को अउरु नरेसा ॥
भवँर केस वह मालति रानी । बिसहर लरहिँ लेहिँ अरघानी ॥
बेनी छोरि झारु जो बारा । सरग पतार होइ अँधिआरा ॥
कोवँल कुटिल केस नग कारे । लहरइँ भरे भुअंग बिसारे ॥
बेधे जानु मलय-गिरि बासा । सीस चढे लोटहिँ चहुँ पासा ॥
घुँघुर-वार अलकइँ बिख-भरी । सँकरइँ पेम चहहिँ गिउ परी ॥

दोहा ।

अस फँद-वारि केस वेइ (राजा) परा सीस गिउ फाँद ।
असट-उ कूरी नाग सब उरझ केस के बाँद ॥ १०१ ॥

सिँगार = शृङ्गार । केसा = केश = बार । बासुकि = वासुकि = नागोँ का राजा । बिसहर = विषभर = विष से भरे । वा बिसहर = बेसँभार = बेखबर = मस्त । वा बिसहर = विषधर । अरघानी = आघ्राण । लेहिँ अरघानी = आघ्राण लेते हैँ = सूँघते हैँ = सुगन्ध लेते हैँ । बेनी = वेणी = चोटी । सरग = स्वर्ग । पतार = पाताल । अँधिआरा = अन्धकार । कोवँल = कोमल । नग = नाग = सर्प । वा नग = पर्वत । भुअंग = भुजङ्ग = सर्प ।

बिसारे = विस्मरण कर दिये = भुला दिये। वा बिसारे = बइसारे = बैठाये हैं। मलय-गिरि = मलयाचल। बासा = वास = सुगन्ध। घुँघुर-वार = घुघुरू के ऐसे गोल गोल। अँलकईं = अलक का बक्कवचन = लटैं। बिख = विष। सँकरईं = शृङ्खला = सीकड। पेम = प्रेम॥ फँद-वारि = फंदे से भरे। असट-उ = आठो। कूरी = कुली = कुल के। बाँद = बंदी = कैद॥

(हीरा-मणि शुक कहता है, कि) हे राजा (रत्न-सेन), उस के (पद्मावती के) शृङ्गार का (मैं) क्या वर्णन करूँ। उस का शृङ्गार उसी पर छाजता है, अर्थात् उस के अङ्ग का शृङ्गार अङ्ग के ऊपर ऐसा सोहता है, कि वह देखे-ही बन आता है, कोई उस का वर्णन कर पार नहीं पा सकता॥ प्रधान कवि लोग देवता के वर्णन में नख-वर्णन से आरम्भ कर केश-वर्णन कर समाप्त करते हैं और मनुष्य-वर्णन में केश से आरम्भ कर नख-वर्णन तक वर्णन कर समाप्त करते हैं। पद्मावती मानुषी व्यक्ति है इस लिये कवि ने केश से वर्णन करना आरम्भ किया, जैसा कि श्री-हर्ष ने नैषध के सातवें सर्ग में दमयन्ती के केश-ही से वर्णन आरम्भ किया और अन्त में स्पष्ट लिखा कि

इति स चिकुरादारभ्यैतां नखावधि वर्णयन्
हरिणरमणीनेत्रां चित्राम्बुधौ तरदन्तरः।
हृदयभरणोद्वेलानन्दः सखीकृतभीमजा-
नयनविषयीभावे भावं दधार धराधिपः॥

लोक-रीति भी है, कि अनुरागी अनुराग से भरा अपने प्रेमी के देखने के लिये प्रथम ऊपर-ही की ओर दृष्टि करता है, जिस से पहले केश-ही का दर्शन होता है, और उपासक भक्त श्रद्धा से भरा अपने उपास्य देवता के प्रणाम के लिये पहले उस के चरण-ही की ओर दृष्टि करता है, जिस से पहले-ही नख-दर्शन होता है।

पहले-ही कस्तूरी से काले और सुगन्धित जो केश हैं, उन पर वासुकि सर्प बलि हो जाता है। (फिर), हे राजा (नरेसा = नरेश), और (दूसरा) कौन है (जिस की उपमा दी जाय)। अर्थात् वासुकि अपने को तुच्छ समझ (कि हाय मैं तो केवल काला-ही हूँ ये केश सुगन्ध से भरे अतिशय काले मुझ से भी बढ कर हैं) मूर्छित हो, इन केशों को अपना पूज्य समझ इन पर अपने को बलि करता है। कस्य (ब्रह्मणः) ईशः (क + ईशः =) केशः, ऐसा विग्रह करने से ये ब्रह्मा के ईश स्वामी ऊए, अर्थात् साचात् भगवान् विष्णु ऊए, फिर इन पर वासुकि का बलि होना कुछ अनुचित नहीं। यदि नरेसा को

सम्बोधन न मानो तो, 'जिन केशोँ पर वासुकि बलि हो जाता है तो और (अन्य = अपर) नरेश क्या हैँ, अर्थात् जो सर्प प्राणी मात्र का वैरी है वह जिन केशोँ की शोभा से मोहित हो बलि हो जाता है, तो उस शोभा को देख कर और नरेशोँ की क्या गिनती है। वे लोग तो पहले-ही बलि हो जायँगे,' यह अर्थान्तर कर सकते हो॥ रानी (पद्मावती) (सुगन्ध से भरी जानोँ) मालती है और (घूघर-वारे) केश (जानोँ गुथे ऊए) भ्रमर हैँ। वे विष-धर भ्रमर (एक के ऊपर एक सुगन्ध लेने के लिये जानोँ) लड रहे हैँ, और (उस मालती के) सुगन्ध को ले रहे हैँ॥ (पद्मावती) यदि (=जो) बेनी (=चोटी) को छोड कर बालोँ को झारने लगती है, (तो वे ऐसे काले और लंबे बाल हैँ, कि उन की कालिमा से) स्वर्ग से पाताल तक अँधेरा हो जाता है॥ यदि पद्मावती को प्रकृति मानो तो 'वह यदि परस्पर कर्म से बँधी ऊई वस्तु-बेनी को छोड कर, अर्थात् अलग अलग कर, जिस समय बारोँ को, अर्थात् रव्यादि सप्त वारोँ को, झाड देती है, अर्थात् वार-द्योतक सूर्यादि को जब हरण कर लेती है, तो स्वर्ग से पाताल तक अन्धकार हो जाता है,' यह अर्थान्तर कर सकते हो। साङ्ख्य-शास्त्र मेँ लिखा है, कि जब प्रकृति मेँ सूर्यादि सब पदार्थ लीन हो जाते हैँ तब वही प्राकृतिक लय कहाता है जिस मेँ अन्धकार-मात्र सर्वत्र व्याप्त रहता है॥ वे कोमल और कुटिल (टेढे टेढे) केश (जानोँ) नग (पर्वत) पर सर्प (=कारे) हैँ, वा (नग कारे) काले नाग हैँ, (जिन की शोभा से) लहर से भरे सर्प को भुला देते हैँ, अर्थात् जिन की शोभा के आगे साधारण सर्पोँ की शोभा भूल जाती है॥ यदि 'बैसारे' का अपभ्रंश 'बिसारे' मानो तो 'वे कोमल और कुटिल केश (ऐसे जान पड़ते हैँ जानोँ) काले पहाड पर लहर से भरे साँप बैठाये गये है'॥ (यहाँ शिरः-पृष्ठभाग काला पर्वत और उस पर काली लंबी लटैँ सर्प समझो)॥ जानोँ वे केश-सर्प मलयाचल के बास से बिद्ध हो गये हैँ, (इस लिये) शिर पर चढे चारो ओर लोट रहे हैँ (बास से अर्थात् सुगन्ध से बिद्ध हो कर अन्यत्र जाने मेँ असमर्थ हैँ।) (सुगन्ध से भरी पद्मावती को मलयाचल समझो)॥ वे घूघर-वारी लटैँ विष से भरी, अर्थात् विष से बुझाई, प्रेम की शृङ्खला हैँ, (जो कि दर्शकोँ के) गले मेँ पडना चाहती हैँ॥

ऐसे फंदे-वारे केश (उस के) शिर पर पडे हैँ (जो कि दर्शकोँ के) गले के फंदे हैँ। आठो कुल के जो नाग हैँ वे सब (आपस मेँ) उरझ कर (उस केश के) कैदी हो गये। अर्थात् कई एक सर्प जो आपस मेँ अरुझ कर बैठे रहते हैँ। वहाँ पर कवि की

उत्प्रेक्षा है, कि वे अयोग्य, पद्मावती के केश की समता करने की जो इच्छा किये इसी अपराध से वे आपस में अरुझ-रूपी बन्धन से बँधवा कर कैद किये गये ॥

मनु इत्यादिकों के मत से यद्यपि नाग और सर्प में भेद है तथापि भाषा में इन का अभेद है (मनु-स्मृति के १ अध्याय का ३७ वाँ श्लोक 'यक्षरक्षःपिशाचांश्च गन्धर्वाप्सरसोऽसुरान्। नागान् सर्पान् सुपर्णांश्च पितॄणां च पृथग् गणान्') ॥

अष्टकुल नाग के ये हैं — वासुकि १। तक्षक २। कुलक ३। कर्कोटक ४। पद्म ५। शङ्खचूड ६। महापद्म ७। धनञ्जय ८॥

वासुकिं तक्षकं चैव कुलं कर्कोटकं तथा।
पद्मं च शङ्खचूडं च महापद्मं धनञ्जयम् ॥
पूजयेद्गन्धमाल्याद्यैर्नागानष्टौ प्रयत्नतः।
(वास्तुरत्नावली पृ. ८७) ॥१०१॥

चउपाई ।

बरनउँ माँग सीस उपराहीँ। सेँदुर अब-हिँ चढा जेहि नाहीँ॥
बिनु सेँदुर अस जानउँ दिआ। उँजिअर पंथ रइनि मँह किआ॥
कंचन-रेख कसउटी कसी। जनु घन मँह दाविँनि परगसी॥
सुरुज किरन जनु गगन बिसेखी। जवँुना माँझ सरसुती देखी॥
खाँडइ धार रुहिर जनु भरा। करवत लेइ बेनी पर धरा॥
तेहि पर पूरि धरी जो मोती। जवँुना माँझ गाँग कइ सोती॥
करवत तपा लीन्ह होइ चूरू। मकु सो रुहिर लेइ देइ सेँदूरू॥

दोहा ।

कनक दुआदस बानि होइ चह सोहाग वह माँग।
सेवा करहिँ नखत अउ (तरई) उए गगन जस गाँग॥१०२॥

उपराहीँ = उपरि। सेँदुर = सिन्दूर। दिआ = दीप = दीया। रइनि = रजनी = रात। कसउटी = कष-वटी = सोना कसने के लिये काले पत्थर की बटिया। दाविँनि = दामिनी = सौदामिनी = बिजली। परगसी = प्रकाश हुई। सुरुज = सूर्य। जवँुना = यमुना नदी। सरसुती = सरस्वती। खाँडइ = खाँडा = खण्डक = तलवार। रुहिर = रुधिर।

करवत = करपत्र = आरा । बेनी = वेणी = चोटी, वा यमुना सरस्वती का सङ्गम = प्रयाग । गाँग = गङ्गा । सोती = स्रोत = धारा । तपा = तपस्वी । चूरू = चूर्ण । मकु = क्या जानैं ॥ दुआदस = द्वादश = द्वादशादित्य । बानि = वर्ण । सोहाग = सौभाग्य वा सोहागा, जिस से सोने में और अधिक चमक आ जाती है ॥

इस प्रान्त में स्त्रियाँ पहले मुखाभिमुख शिरो-भाग के केशों को अलग कर नासिकाग्र और भ्रू-मध्यगत रेखा से उन का समान दो भाग कर एक भाग को दहिनी ओर दूसरे को बाईं ओर झार सँवार कर ले जाती हैं, और उन को तीसी के लबाब से चिक्कन कर शिर में चिपका देती हैं उन्हीं को पटिया कहते हैं। दोनों पटियों के बीचो बीच जो एक शिर के ऊपर चमकीली धारी सी शिरःपृष्ठावयव चमकता देख पडता है उसे माँग कहते हैं। विवाह के समय पति अपने हाथ से अपनी पत्नी के माँग में सेंदुर भरता है, उसी दिन से सधवा सर्वदा अपनी माँग को सेंदुर से भरी रखती है। जब तक कन्या का विवाह नहीं होता तब तक माँग खाली रहती है। कभीं कभीं शोभा के लिये कुछ केश और लाल डोरे की एक चोटी बना कर उस पर रख देती हैं। राजा बाबुओं के घर लाल डोरे के स्थान में मोतियों की लड रहती है। पटियों के केशावयव जो शिर के नीचे लटकते रहते हैं उन को गुह कर एक एक बेनी बना ली जाती है और शिर के पिछले भागों के केशों को भी एकट्ठाँ कर एक बेनी तयार की जाती है। फिर स्त्री लोग इन तीनों बेनियों को पीछे की ओर एकट्ठाँ कर रंग विरंग के तार मिला कर उन से जूरा बनाती हैं। जूरा खसक न जाय इस लिये उसे काले-ही ऊन वा सूत के डोरे से कस कर बाँध देती हैं। इस प्रकार इस प्रान्त में पति-संयुक्ता स्त्री त्रिवेणी अर्थात् तीन वेणी से अपने शिर को सँवारती है, और पति-वियुक्ता पति-वियोग-दुःख से सब केशों को एकट्ठाँ कर एक ही वेणी बना शिर में लपेट लेती है। इस प्रान्त में यह रीति चिर काल से प्रचलित है। पति-वियुक्ता सीता के वर्णन में महर्षि-वाल्मीकि ने भी लिखा है, कि 'एक-वेणी-धरा दीना त्वयि चिन्ता-परायणा' (सु. का. ६५ सर्ग का १४ वाँ स्लोक देखो)। जिस दिन स्त्री विधवा होती हैं उसी दिन अपने माँग का सेंदुर धो कर निकाल डालती हैं और फिर माँग में सेंदुर नहीं डालतीं। सेंदुर और चूरी के न रहने से विधवा का सङ्केत यह लौकिक रीति है। सधवा होने में सेंदुर का प्राधान्य किसी हमारे वैदिक कर्म में नहीं मिलता।

सीस के ऊपर जो माँग है उस का वर्णन करता हूँ, (पद्मावती के कुआँरी होने से) जिस पर अभी सेंदुर नहीं चढा है॥ विना सेंदुर की (वह माँग) ऐसी (चमकती) है जानों दीया, (वा वह माँग ऐसी जान पडती है मानों किसी ने) रजनी में अर्थात् अँधेरी रात में उँजेली राह (पन्था) की है अर्थात् बनाई है। (दोनों काली पटिया अँधेरी रात है उस में चमकती माँग की धारी उँजेली राह है)॥ (अथवा उस माँग की ऐसी शोभा है जानों) कसौटी पर कसी सुवर्ण-रेखा हो। (दोनों पटिया मिल कर जानों कसौटी है उस पर सोने सी चमकती माँग की धारी कसे हुए सोने की रेखा सी झलकती है)। (वा उस माँग की ऐसी शोभा है) जानों मेघ (घन) में बिजली प्रकाश हुई हो। (काली पटिया मेघ और माँग की धारी विद्युल्लता है)॥ (वा माँग नहीं है नीले) आकाश में एक विशिष्ट सूर्य-किरण है। (पटिया नीला आकाश और माँग की चमकती धारी एक विशेष सूर्य-किरण है)। (अथवा माँग नहीं है जानों) यमुना के मध्य में सरस्वती नदी देखी है, अर्थात् देख पडती है। (पटिया यमुना और कुछ लालिमा लिये चमकती माँग की धारी सरस्वती नदी है)॥ (अथवा शिर के चर्म के ललाई की आभा से कुछ लाली लिये चमकती माँग की धारी ऐसी शोभित है) जानों रुधिर से भरी तलवार की धार है। (अथवा माँग की धारी जानों) आरा है जिसे ले कर (किसी ने) बेनी के ऊपर धर दिया हो। [काले केश-कूपों से स्थान स्थान पर छिन्न हो जाने से वह माँग की धारी आरा (करपत्र=करवत) सी जान पडती है]॥ तिस माँग पर जो मोती पूर कर धरी है अर्थात् मोती की लड रक्खी है, (उस की ऐसी शोभा है जानों) यमुना के मध्य में गङ्गा की सोती आ गई हो। (पटिया यमुना और माँग पर मोती-लड गङ्गा की सोत है)॥ इस प्रकार यमुना और गङ्गा का सङ्गम बेनी (शिर की चोटी) पर होने से पद्मावती की बेनी साक्षात् बेनी (=प्रयाग) हुई, जहाँ शरीर चिरवाने के लिये माँग-रूपी आरा (करवत) भी मौजूद है। प्रसिद्ध कथा है कि दूसरे जन्म में मनो-वाञ्छित-फल पाने के लिये बहुत से लोग अपनी शरीर को आरा से चिरवा डालते थे इस के लिये वहाँ गङ्गा-यमुना के सङ्गम पर एक आरा भी रक्खा रहा था। शाहजहाँ बादशाह ने इस कु-रीति के दूर करने के लिये उस आरा को तोडवा डाला॥ इस पर कवि की उत्प्रेक्षा है, कि बहुत से तपस्वी (तपा) जो चूर्ण हो कर, अर्थात् अपनी शरीर को छिन्न भिन्न कर, आरे को लिये, अर्थात् पकडे,

राहु गरास लेता है, अर्थात् खा जाता है, (इस से वह मलिन हो जाता है) और वह ललाट-रूपी चन्द्र तो विना राहु के सदा प्रकाशित रहता है। द्वितीया के चन्द्र की जैसी टेढी आकृति होती है उसी के सदृश ललाटाकृति समझ कर कवि ने पहले द्वितीया के चन्द्र की उपमा दिया। फिर उस में ललाट सी चमक न पा कर उस को हटाया और ललाट-कान्ति की उपमा मन-ही में पूर्ण-चन्द्र से दे कर फिर अनुचित समझ प्रकाश में 'का सरि बरनक दिअउँ मयंकू' इत्यादि वाक्यों से पूर्ण-चन्द्र को भी तुच्छ ठहराया॥ तिस ललाट के ऊपर जो तिलक बैठा है, अर्थात् टीका दिया हुआ है, (उस की ऐसी शोभा है) जानों द्वितीया के चन्द्र-रूपी पाट (सिंहासन) पर ध्रुव (बैठा) देख पडता है। पुराणों में कथा है, कि एक दिन ध्रुव के पिता उत्तानपाद ध्रुव को गोद में लिये बैठे थे। उसी समय वहाँ पर ध्रुव की सौतेली माँ अपने लडके को लिये आई और ध्रुव को गोद में से ढकेल बाहर कर अपने लडके को उत्तानपाद के गोद में बैठा दिया, और अनेक कटु वचनों से ध्रुव का अनादर किया। इस पर ध्रुव ग्लानि से घर छोड वन में जा कर कठिन तपस्या करने लगे, जिस पर भगवान् ने प्रसन्न हो कर उन को सब से ऊँचा और अचल स्थान दिया। वही ध्रुव आकाश में अपने अचल स्थान पर सदा देख पडता है, और उसी के चारो ओर सदा सब ग्रह और तारा-गण घूमते दिखाई पडते हैं। बेध करने से ज्यौतिषियों ने सिद्ध कर दिया है, कि आज कल जिसे लोग आकाश में ध्रुव कहते हैं वह अचल स्थान पर स्थिर नहीं है, किन्तु नाडी-मण्डल के पृष्ठीय केन्द्र के चारो ओर १° २८' द्युज्याचापांश-वृत्त में घूमा करता है। इसी पर कमलाकर ने कहा है कि 'ध्रुवतारां स्थिरां ग्रन्थे मन्यन्ते ते कुबुद्धयः। सार्कं तैस्तु विवादोऽपि सतां मूढत्वमेव हि'॥ (तत्त्वविवेक के मध्यमाधिकार का ७८ वाँ श्लोक देखो)॥ यहाँ चमकता हुआ दुइज के चन्द्र सा टेढा ललाट पाट और उस पर का उज्ज्वल तिलक ध्रुव है॥ (अथवा ललाट और तिलक की ऐसी शोभा है) जानों सोने के सिंहासन पर (कोई) राजा बैठा है, (ललाट सोने का सिंहासन और तिलक राजा है), (और वह राजा, पद्मावती के) सब शृङ्गार-रूपी अस्त्रों को ले कर सज्जित है, अर्थात् लडने को तैयार है। मन्त्र-प्रयोग से जो चलाये जाते हैं और जिन की शक्ति कभीं नष्ट नहीं होती उन्हें अस्त्र कहते हैं॥ उस ध्रुव के आगे कोई स्थिर नहीं रहता, अर्थात् जैसे ध्रुव अपनी शक्ति से आप अचल हो सब तारा-गणों को अपने चारो ओर घुमाया करता है, उसी प्रकार यह तिलक-रूपी

राजा ध्रुव ने सब दर्शकों के मन को चञ्चल कर भ्रान्त कर दिया है। (सो) देखें किस के लिये ऐसा संयोग एकट्ठाँ हुआ है, अर्थात् देखें कौन ऐसा भाग्यवान् है, जो ऐसे ध्रुव-राज से संयोग, अर्थात् मैत्री रूप से समागम कर एकत्र स्थित शृङ्गार-रूपी अस्त्रों की लीला देखे॥

खड्ग (नासिका का अग्र), धनुष (भौंहें), चक्र (आखें की पुतलियाँ), और बाण (कटाक्ष), तिस तिलक-रूपी राजा के पास हैं। (इस लिये उस राजा का) नाम जग-मारन है, अर्थात् वह राजा जगत् के प्राणी मात्र को मारने-वाला है। इतना सुनते-ही (राजा रत्न-सेन) मूर्छित हो कर गिर पडा (और कहने लगा, कि हाय ये सब अस्त्र) मुझ को कु-ठावँ में भये, अर्थात् मुझ को मर्म स्थान हृदय में लग गये (सो अब जीना कठिन है)॥ १०३ ॥

चउपाई।

भउँहइ सावँ धनुख जनु ताना। जा सउँ हेर मारु बिख बाना॥
ओही धनुख ओहि भउँहहिँ चढा। कोइ हतिआर काल अस गढा॥
ओही धनुख किसुन पहँ अहा। ओही धनुख राघउ कर गहा॥
ओही धनुख राओन संघारा। ओही धनुख कंसासुर मारा॥
ओही धनुख बेधा हुत राहू। मारा ओही सहस्सर-बाहू॥
ओही धनुख मइँ ता पहँ चीन्हा। धानुक आपु बोझ जग कीन्हा॥
ओहि भउँहहिँ सरि कोइ न जीता। अछरइँ छपीँ छपीँ गोपीता॥

दोहा।

भउँह धनुख धन धानुक　दोसर सरि न कराइ।
गगन धनुख जो उग्गवइ　लाजइ सो छपि जाइ॥ १०४॥

भउँहइ = भौंह = भ्रू। सावँ = श्याम। बिख = विष। हतिआर = हत्यारा। किसुन = कृष्ण। अहा = आसीत् = था। राघउ = राघव = राम-चन्द्र। गहा = ग्रहण किया। राओन = रावण। संघारा = संहार किया। राहू = रोहू = रोहितक = एक प्रकार का मत्स्य। सहस्सर-बाहू = सहस्र-बाहु। धानुक = धानुष्क = धन्वी = धनुष चलाने-वाला।

चउपाई ।

नयन बाँक सरि पूज न कोऊ। मान समुँद अस उलथहिँ दोऊ॥
राते कवँल करहिँ अलि भवाँ। घूमहिँ माति चहहिँ अपसवाँ॥
उठहिँ तुरंग लेहिँ नहिँ बागा। जानउँ उलथि गगन कहँ लागा॥
पवन झकोरहिँ देइ हिलोरा। सरग लाइ भुइँ लाइ बहोरा॥
जग डोलइ डोलत नयनाँहा। उलटि अडार चाह पल माँहा॥
जबहिँ फिराहिँ गगन गहि बोरा। अस वेइ भउँह भवँर के जोरा॥
समुँद हिलोर करहिँ जनु झूले। खंजन लरहिँ मिरिग बन भूले॥

दोहा ।

सु-भर समुँद अस नयन दुइ मानिक भरे तरंग।
आवहिँ तीर फिरावहीँ काल भवँर तेहि संग॥ १०५॥

बाँक = वक्र = कठिन = कुटिल वा टेढे। मान = अभिमान। समुँद = समुद्र। वा मान-समुँद = मान-समुद्र = संमानयोग्य-समुद्र = चीर-सागर। उलथहिँ = उलटते हैँ। राते = रक्त = लाल। अलि = भ्रमर = भौँरा। भवाँ = भौँरी = भ्रमण। माति = मत्त हो कर। अपसवाँ = अपसरण = भागना। तुरंग = तुरङ्ग = तुरग = घोडा। बागा = वागुर वा वल्गा = लगाम में लगी डोर, जिस से चाहे जिधर घोडा फिर सकता है। सरग = स्वर्ग। भुइँ = भूमि। बहोरा = अवहरति = अवहरण करते हैँ = फिर ले आते हैँ। अडार = अडलक = जो डाली में न समाय = ढेर का ढेर। गहि = गृहीला = ग्रहण कर के = पकड के। बोरा = बोरते हैँ = डुबाते हैँ। भवँर = भ्रमर = आवर्त्त। जोरा = जोडा = युग्म, वा जोरा = जोडे ऊए = मिलाये ऊए। हिलोर = हिल-लोल = हिलने से चञ्चल। खंजन = खञ्जन पची, शरदृतु में जिस के प्रथम दर्शन से संहिताकारों ने शुभाशुभ फल कहा है। मिरिग = मृग = हरिण॥ सु-भर = शुभ्र = उज्ज्वल। मानिक = माणिक्य। काल = काला, वा सब का प्राण लेने-वाला। भवँर = भ्रमर, वा भौँर = आवर्त्त, जो नद, नदी वा समुद्रोँ में पानी चक्कर खाता है॥

नयन ऐसे बाँके हैं जिन की बराबरी में कोई नहीं पूरा पडता (पूजता), (क्योंकि आगे कवि ने इन्हें समुद्र बनाया है, और समुद्र तो अनन्वय है, इसी पर कवि ने जो यह कहा है, कि इन की बराबरी में कोई नहीं है यह ठीक है। अनन्वयालङ्कार का उदाहरण कुवलयानन्द में भी लिखा है, कि 'सागरः सागरोपमः'), ऐसे (नीचे से ऊपर और ऊपर से नीचे ये दोनों उलटते हैं (जैसे) मान से अर्थात् अभिमान से समुद्र वा चीर-सागर (उलटता पलटता हो)॥ (उस नयन-समुद्र में) लाल (रक्त=राते) कमल पर भ्रमर भ्रमण करते हैं, अर्थात् सु-गन्ध से मोहित हो भावँरी फिरते हैं। (कुछ लाली लिये कोए लाल-कमल, और उस पर घूमती काली पुतलियाँ भावँरी भरते भ्रमर ऐसी हैं)। (वे भ्रमर सु-गन्ध से) मत्त हो कर घूम रहे हैं अर्थात् घुमरी खाते हैं (और) भागना चाहते हैं (परन्तु सु-गन्ध के नशे से विवश हैं)॥ (काली पुतली समेत कोए जिस घडी ऊपर की ओर उठते हैं, उस घडी ऐसा जान पडता है) जानों घोडे उठते हैं जो कि बाग को नहीं लेते हैं, अर्थात् मोरने से नहीं मुरते हैं, और उलट कर आकाश में लगते हैं। (यहाँ काली पुतली समेत श्वेत-रक्त-कोआ उच्चैःश्रवा घोडा है, जो कि चीर-सागर से निकाला गया है, और चतुर्दश-रत्न में एक रत्न है)॥ (वे नयन-समुद्र ऐसे चञ्चल हैं जानों) पवन झकोरते हैं (जिस से समुद्र) हिलोरा देता है, अर्थात् जल नीचे से ऊपर और ऊपर से नीचे की ओर जाता आता है। (इस लिये वह समुद्र एक बेर जल को) स्वर्ग में लगा कर (लाइ) फिर पृथ्वी में लगा कर फेरता है, अर्थात् जल को नीचे ऊपर नचा रहा है॥ कवि की उत्प्रेचा है, कि जब पद्मावती के नयन-समुद्र ऊपर की ओर उठते हैं तो दर्शकों के जीवन (जल) स्वर्ग को चले जाते हैं, और जब नीचे को फिरते हैं तो साथ-ही साथ जीवन भी नीचे पृथ्वी पर, अर्थात् दर्शकों के शरीर में, आ जाते हैं॥ नयन के डोलते-ही जग डोलने लगता है, अर्थात् जगत के प्राणी-मात्र चञ्चल हो जाते हैं, कि हाय अब इस नयन-समुद्र की बाढ से कैसे प्राण बचँ। क्योंकि समुद्र की बाढ से तो जगत का लय-ही हो जाता है, कहीं आधार-ही नहीं रहता जहाँ कि प्राणी विश्राम ले। (सो वे नयन-समुद्र) एक पल में अडार अर्थात् प्राणियों के ढेर का ढेर उलटा चाहते हैं, अर्थात् प्रलय किया चाहते हैं॥ (उस नयन-समुद्र में) ऐसे भौंह-रूपी भवँर के जोडे हैं, अर्थात् आवर्त्त के एक जोडे हैं, कि जब वे फिरने लगते हैं, अर्थात् घूमने लगते हैं, तब आकाश को भी गह कर बोर देते हैं (डुबा देते हैं)॥ (चिच्छक्ति

पद्मावती के भ्रू-कुटी-विलास से ब्रह्माण्ड का लय वा प्रादुर्भाव ऊआ-ही करता है, इस में कोई चित्र नहीँ है)॥ बक्रतेाँ के मत से 'केइ जोरा' यह पाठ है। तब 'उस समुद्र में ऐसे भौँह-रूपी भवँर को किस ने जोडा है, अर्थात् लगाया है, कि जब घूमते हैँ, तब आकाश को पकड कर बोर देते हैँ,' यह अर्थ करना चाहिए॥ (जिस समय वे नयन इधर उधर) झूलने लगते हैँ, अर्थात् चञ्चल हो जाते हैँ, (दोनोँ नासिका की ओर चल चल कर कान की ओर फिर जाते हैँ, उस समय ऐसी शोभा है) जानोँ समुद्र हिलोर करते हैँ, वा खञ्जन (आपस में) लडते हैँ, वा वन में भूले मृग (इधर उधर फिरते) हैँ॥ [दोनोँ नयन-समुद्रोँ का नासिका की ओर वार वार आना हिलोर करना है वा नयन-खञ्जनोँ का वार वार नासिका की ओर आना आपस में लडना है, अथवा नयन-मृगोँ का वार वार नासिका की ओर आ आ कर कानन की ओर फिर जाना, जानोँ उन मृगोँ का भटकना है। खञ्जन के गले की कालिमा नेत्र की कालिमा से मिलती है, इस लिये नेत्र की उपमा खञ्जन से दी जाती है। किसी का मत है, कि खञ्जन बडा चञ्चल होता है, इस लिये चाञ्चल्य-धर्म ले कर कवि लोग इस की उपमा नेत्र से देते हैँ, और मृग के नेत्र बडे और चञ्चल होते हैँ, इस लिये वैपुल्य और चाञ्चल्य-धर्म ले कर मृग की उपमा नेत्र से दी जाती है। जब खञ्जन लडने लगते हैँ तब क्रोधावेश से गले की कालिमा वा चञ्चलता और बढ जाती है, और जब मृग भूल जातें हैँ, अर्थात् अपने साथियोँ से बिछुड जाते हैँ, तब साथियोँ से मिलने की चाह से उन के स्वाभाविक विपुल और चञ्चल नेत्र और भी विपुल (बडे) और चञ्चल हो जाते हैँ। इस लिये कवि का 'खञ्जन लरहिँ मिरिग बन भूले' यह कहना बक्रत-ही रोचक है]॥

इस प्रकार से दोनोँ नयन शुभ्र-समुद्र, अर्थात् क्षीर-सागर हैँ, जिन में माणिक्य और तरङ्ग भरे हैँ (नेत्र में लाल-डोरे माणिक्य और चाञ्चल्य तरङ्ग हैँ)। तिस (समुद्र) के सङ्ग काल से वा काले ऐसे (भौँह-रूपी) भवँर (आवर्त्त) हैँ, [जो कि जो लोग उस समुद्र के तीर (तट)] आते हैँ उन को फिराने लगते हैँ, अर्थात् जो कोई काल का मारा उस नयन-समुद्रोँ की लहर लेने के लिये तीर (पास) आया, कि भौँह-रूपी भवँरोँ की कुटिलता से चक्कर खाने लगा, फिर उस की सामर्थ्य नहीँ कि उस चक्कर के फेर से फिर कर अपने को सँभाले और अपने घर वार की सुधि ले। उसी में पडा प्राणान्त-पर्यन्त सडा करता है। भ्रान्त और श्रान्त हो कर ठोकर खाता फिरा करता

है। प्रकृति-रूपा पद्मावती की प्रेरणा से भी जो जगत्समुद्र के तीर पर पहुँचा वह काल-भ्रमर (काल-चक्र) के चक्कर में पड कर नाना प्रकार की योनि में फिरा करता है, विना भगवदनुग्रह से उस चक्कर से उस का उद्धार पाना दुर्घट है॥ १०५॥

चउपाई।

बरुनी का बरनउँ इमि बनी। साधी बान जानु दुहुँ अनी॥
जुरी राम रावन कइ सइना। बीच समुंद भए दुइ नइना॥
वारहिँ पार बनाउरि साधे। जा सउँ हेर लाग बिख-बाँधे॥
उन्ह बानहिँ अस को को न मारा। बेधि रहा सगर-उ संसारा॥
गगन नखत जस जाहिँ न गने। वेइ सब बान ओही के हने॥
धरती बान बेधि सब राखे। साखा ठाढ ओही सब साखे॥
रोवँ रोवँ मानुस तन ठाढे। सूतहिँ सूत बेध अस गाढे॥

दोहा।

बरुनि बान अस उपनी बेधी रन बन-ढंख।
सउजहिँ तन सब रोवाँ पंखिहिँ तन सब पंख॥ १०६॥

बरुणी = वारणी = आँख में धूल इत्यादि को वारण करने-वाली = नीचे ऊपर के पलकों की रोमावली। अनी = अनीक = सेना। जुरी = जुटी = युक्त ऊई = एकट्ठीँ ऊई। रावन = रावण। सइना = सेना। समुंद = समुद्र। नइना = नयन। वार = जिधर खडे हो उस ओर का तट। बनाउरि = वाणावलि = वाणोँ की पङ्क्ति। सगर-उ = सकल-अपि = सब। जस = ओजस् = चमकीले। हने = हनन किये गये। धरती = धरित्री = पृथ्वी। साखा = शाखा = वृचोँ की डार। साखे = शाखी = वृच। रोवँ रोवँ = रोम रोम। मानुस = मानुष = मनुष्य। सूत = सूच, यहाँ नापने के लिये एक मान। चार सूत की एक पइन और चार पइन का एक तसू और चौबीस तसू का एक इमारती गज होता है। तसू एक इञ्च से कुछ बडा होता है। बारह तसू में प्रायः तेरह इञ्च होते हैं॥ उपनी = उत्पन्न ऊई। रन = रण = संग्राम। बन-ढंख = बन के ढाँकने-वाले अर्थात् वृच। सउज = शवज = शिकार, यहां साधारण चौपाये पशु। पंखि = पची। तन = तनु। पंख = पच॥

(हीरा-मणि कहता है, कि) बरुनी का क्या बर्णन करूँ, अर्थात् वर्णन नहीँ कर सकता। वह ऐसी (इमि=इव) बनी है, जानोँ दोनोँ सेनाओँ ने बाणोँ को साध रक्खा है, (ऊपर की पलक-ओर एक सेना और नीचे पलक की ओर दूसरी सेना है, और एक एक पङ्क्ति में खडे दोनोँ ओर बरौनी के बार सधे ऊए बाणोँ के समान हैँ)॥ (एक ओर) राम (और दूसरी ओर) रावण की सेना (जानोँ) जुटी है। और दोनोँ नयन (उन सेनाओँ के) बीच में समुद्र ऊए हैँ॥ [ऊपर की पलक पर राम-सेना है जो कि समुद्र उतर लङ्क (कटि) की ओर आने चाहती है, और निचली पलक पर रावण-सेना है। इस में आश्चर्य यही है, कि रावण की ओर सुग्रीव (पद्मावती की सुन्दर ग्रीवा), हनु, और अङ्गद (बाऊ का भूषण) मिल गये हैँ। ऐसी कल्पना से यहाँ कविता में बऊत-ही रोचकता प्राप्त होती है।] (उस समुद्र के) वार पार (सैन्य के योद्धा-गण) बाण-पङ्क्तियोँ को साधे ऊए हैँ, विष से बँधी (विष-बाँधे), अर्थात् विष-मय, वे बाण-पङ्क्ति जिस की ओर हेरती हैँ (देखती हैँ), उसे-ही लग जाती हैँ, अर्थात् यह ऐसी विलक्षण बाण-पङ्क्ति है, कि इस के सन्मुख जो गया, देखते-ही उस के अङ्ग में लग जाती है, और दर्शक बेचारा इस की विष-वेदना से व्याकुल हो, कुल-मर्यादा को तोर, तोर मोर करता उसी की ओर कर मरोर मरोर मरा जाता है, और वह बाण-पङ्क्ति ज्योँ कि त्योँ अपने स्थान पर अचल खडी दर्शक-लीला देख देख लहराया करती है॥ ऐसे कौन कौन हैँ, जो जो कि उन बाणोँ से न मारे गये होँ, अर्थात् संसार में ऐसा कोई हई नहीँ है जिसे वह बाण न लगा हो, (इस लिये) वह बाण समग्र संसार को बेध रहा है॥ आकाश में चमकीले तारे जो गिने नही जाते, अर्थात् असङ्ख्य हैँ, वे सब उसी बाण (बरौनी-बाण) से हने गये हैँ (जिस से आज तक वे आकाश में जहाँ के तहाँ मुर्दा से अचल पडे हैँ, बरौनी-बाण के भय से धरती पर नहीँ आते, यह कवि की उत्प्रेक्षा है)॥ वे बाण धरती में सबँ को बेध रक्खे हैँ। (पृथ्वी में) वृक्षोँ में जितनी शाखायेँ खडी हैँ, उन्हेँ शाखा न समझो, वे सब बरौनी-बाण के रूपान्तर हैँ॥ मनुष्य के तन (=तनु) में रोएँ रोएँ (निश्चय समझो, कि वे-ही बरौनी-बाण) खडे हैँ, ये बरौनी-बाण ऐसे कठिन (गाढ) हैँ, कि (मनुष्य-तनु को रोम-व्याज से) सूत सूत पर बेध डाले हैँ, अर्थात् छिद्र कर डाले हैँ॥

इस प्रकार से यह बरौनी बाण ऐसी उत्पन्न ऊई है, जो कि रण (अर्थात् रण में योद्धाओँ को) और बन के वृक्षोँ को बेध डाला। पशुओँ के तन में जितने रोम हैँ,

और पक्षियों के शरीर में जितने पक्ष हैं, वे सब निश्चय समझो, कि बरौनी-बाण-ही हैं। इस प्रकार कवि ने 'बेधि रहा सगर-उ संसारा' इस वाक्य का समर्थन किया। वरुणस्य-इदं, वारुणी (अर्थात् जल-देवता) का अपभ्रंश यदि बरुनी को मानो, तो उस जल-देवता-ही के प्रसाद से आकाश के नक्षत्र, जिन्हें भारत के ज्योतिषी जल-मय कहते हैं, वृक्ष की डारें, पशु और मनुष्य के रोएँ और पक्षि के पक्ष सब जीवन-स्वरूप जल-देवता-ही के अनुग्रह से सु-रचित हैं, और सब में उसी जल-देवता का अंश वर्त्तमान है, इस प्रकार यह अर्थान्तर भी यहाँ कर सकते हो॥ १०६॥

चउपाई।

नासिक खरग देउँ केहि जोगू। खरग खीन वह बदन सँजोगू॥
नासिक देखि लजानेउ सूआ। सूक आइ बेसर होइ ऊआ॥
सुआ जो पिअर हिरा-मनि लाजा। अउरु भाउ का बरनउँ राजा॥
सुआ सो नाक कठोर पँवारी। वह कोवँल तिल पुहुप सँवारी॥
पुहुप सु-गंध करहिँ सब आसा। मकु हिरिकाइ लेइ हम बासा॥
अधर दसन पइ नासिक सोभा। दारिउँ देखि सुआ मन लोभा॥
खंजन दुहुँ दिसि केलि कराहीँ। दहुँ वह रस को पाउ को नाहीँ॥

दोहा।

देखि अमीँ-रस अधरन्ह भएउ नासिका कीर।
पवन बास पहुँचावई असरम छाँड न तीर॥ १०७॥

नासिक = नासिका = नाक। खरग = खड्ग = तलवार। जोगू = योग्य। खीन = क्षीण = पतली। बदन = वदन = मुख। सँजोगू = संयोग। सूआ = शुक = सुग्गा। सूक = शुक्र ग्रह जो असुरों का गुरु है (२१वें दोहे की टीका देखो)। बेसर = विसर = विशिष्ट सर (मोतियों की लड़) = मोतियों से बना नाक का एक आभूषण। ऊआ = उदय हुआ। पिअर = पीत = पीला। लाजा = लज्जा से। पँवारी = प्रवरी = प्रवर-गोत्र कह कह कर स्तुति करने-वाला पौंरिया। कोवँल = कोमल = मृदु। पुहुप = पुष्प। सँवारी = सम्मार्जित हुई = बनाई गई। आसा = आशा = उम्मेद। हिरिकाइ = नगीच कर = लगा

कर = हिरुक्। बासा = वास = सु-गन्ध, वा बास = बसावे = बास दे। अधर = ओठ। दसन = दशन = दाँत। पट = उपरि = ऊपर। सोभा = शोभित है। दारिउँ = दाडिम = अनार। कराहीँ = करते हैँ वा कराहते हैँ, अर्थात् कहरते हैँ ॥ अमीँ-रस = अमृत-रस। कीर = शुक। असरम = आश्रम = स्थान। तीर = तट ॥

खड्ग की धार जैसी पतली होती है, उसी तरह पतली नाक होने से नाक की उपमा खड्ग से दी जाती है। इसी प्रकार शुक के ठोर ऐसी नोखीली होने से नासिका की उपमा शुक से भी दी जाती है ॥ (हीरा-मणि कहता है, कि) नासिका-खड्ग किस के योग्य है जिसे देऊँ, अर्थात् जिस के सदृश कहूँ, (क्योँकि) वह खड्ग से भी पतली मुख से संयोग किये है, अर्थात् मुख से मिली है (सो खड्ग तो हाथ से मिला रहता है, और यह खड्ग से भी पतली मुख से मिली ऊई है, इस लिये खड्ग इस की समता को नहीँ प्राप्त कर सकता, यह कवि का अभिप्राय है)॥ नासिका को देख कर शुक लज्जित हो गया, (इसी से वन-वृक्षोँ के कोटर मेँ छिप कर रहने लगा)। (नासिका की शोभा देखने के लिये) शुक भी आ कर बेसर-स्वरूप हो कर उदय ऊआ। कवि की उत्प्रेक्षा है, कि पद्मावती के नाक मेँ जो बेसर की बडी मुक्ता पडी है, वह मुक्ता नहीँ है, जानोँ नासिका की शोभा देखने के लिये शुक मुक्ता का रूप हो कर उदय ऊआ है)॥ (मैँ) हीरा-मणि शुक जो हूँ, सो भी (नासिका की समता-योग्य न होने से) लज्जा से पीला हो गया हूँ, (सो) हे राजा (रत्न-सेन), (अब) दूसरे (अउर) भाव का क्या वर्णन करूँ, अर्थात् जिस की समता मैँ न कर सका, और इस लज्जा से पीला पड गया तो मैँ उस की प्रशंसा करने मेँ असमर्थ हूँ॥ सो (मैँ) शुक तो (उस नासिका की स्तुति करने-वाला) पौँरिया (उस) नाक से कठोर हूँ, (सो कठोर की समता अयोग्य है, क्योँकि) वह (नासिका) कोमल और तिल-रूपी पुष्प से (और भी) सँवारी है, अर्थात् नासिकाग्र पर जो काला तिल तिल-पुष्प सदृश है, उस से वह कोमल नासिका और भी शोभित है, इस लिये उस की बराबरी कठोर शुक कैसे कर सकता है॥ सब पुष्प और सु-गन्ध (द्रव्य अँतर फुलेल इत्यादि) यही आशा करते हैँ, कि क्या जानेँ (हम लोगोँ की ऐसी भाग्य है, कि पद्मावती अपनी नासिका मेँ हम लोगोँ को) लगा कर हम लोगोँ की बास ले वा हम को ले कर और हिरिका कर हम को भी (उस नाक-स्थान मेँ) बास (निवास) दे॥ ओठ और दाँतोँ के ऊपर नासिका (ऐसी) सोहती है, (जानोँ) अनार को देख कर शुक का मन लुभा गया है, (लाल ओठ

और श्वेत दन्त दोनों मिल कर अनार दाने से झलकते हैं, उस पर नासिका लुब्ध-शुक सी जान पडती है)॥ खञ्जन अर्थात् आँखें (नासिका के दोनों ओर उस दाडिम के लिये अनेक) केलि करती हैं, (परन्तु उस के रस को नहीं पा सकतीं), (सो कवि कहता है, कि) देखें उस दाडिम रस को कौन पाता है कौन नहीं। यदि रलयोः सावर्ण्यात् केलि को केरि समझो तो 'खंजन दुऔ दिसि केरि कराहीं' इस का 'दोनों दिशा की खंजनें (उस अनार के रस पाने के लिये) कराहती हैं,' यह अर्थान्तर हो सकता है॥

ओठों के अमृत-रस को देख कर, कीर नासिका हो गया, अर्थात् नासिका न समझो किन्तु उस अधरामृत के पान के लिये जानों शुक आ कर ठहरा है। (वार वार) वायु जो (उस अधरामृत की) वास (उस नासिका-शुक के पास) पऊँचाता है, (इसी लोभ से वह नासिका-रूपी शुक) आश्रम के तट को नहीं छोडता। अर्थात् उस वास से मोहित हो उस अमृत-पान की लालसा से एक-ही स्थान में अचल बैठा ऊआ है। पद्मावती के श्वासोच्छ्वास-द्वारा उस अधरामृत की वास वार वार नासिका में पऊँचती-ही रहती है, इस पर कवि की उत्प्रेक्षा है, कि उसी वास से लुब्ध हो वह नासिका-रूपी शुक उस अमृत की ताक में घात लगाये अचल एक स्थान पर बैठा ऊआ है॥ अधर में अमृत-रस है इस के कहने से संक्षेप-रूप में ओठों का भी वर्णन हो गया। विशेष वर्णन के लिये कवि ने आगे की चौपाई आरम्भ की॥ १०७॥

चउपाई।

अधर सुरंग अमीँ-रस भरे। बिंब सुरंग लाजि बन फरे॥
फूल दुपहरी जानउँ राता। फूल झरहिँ जो जो कह बाता॥
हीरा लेहिँ सु-बिद्रुम धारा। बिहँसत जगत होइ उँजिआरा॥
भइ मजीठ पानन्ह रँग लागे। कुसुम रंग थिर रहइ न आगे॥
अस कइ अधर अमीँ भरि राखे। अज-हुँ अछूत न काह्रु चाखे॥
मुख तँबोल रँग ढारहिँ रसा। केहि मुख जोग सो अंब्रित बसा॥
राता जगत देखि रँग-राती। रुहिर भरे आछहिँ बिहँसाती॥

दोहा।

अमीँ अधर अस राजा सब जग आस करेइ।
केहि कहँ कवँल बिगासा को मधुकर रस लेइ॥ १०८॥

सु-रंग = सु-रङ्ग = सुन्दर-रङ्ग = सुन्दर-वर्ण। वा सुरंग = सुराङ्ग = सुरा-अङ्ग = मदिरा का अङ्ग, अर्थात् मदिरा का अंश। वा सुरङ्ग = सुराङ्ग = सुर-अङ्ग = देवता का अंश। बिंब = विम्ब-फल = कुँदरू = डुलडुल, जिसे बुलबुल बहुत खाते हैं, और जो पकने पर गहिरा लाल लोहू सा हो जाता है। दुपहरी = दोपहर के समय फूलने-वाला पुष्प-विशेष। राता = रक्त = अनु-रक्त। बाता = वार्ता = बात। हीरा = हीर = वज्र। सु-विद्रुम = सु-विद्रुम = सुन्दर मूँगा। मजीठ = मजीठ के फल का रंग, जो कि बहुत लाल होता है। पान = पर्ण = ताम्बूल। कुसुम = बरैं का फूल जो रक्त-पीत होता है, और जिस के रङ्ग को बसन्ती रङ्ग कहते हैं। थिर = स्थिर। अकूत = विना कूआ = पवित्र। काहु = कहि = कोई। तँबोल = ताम्बूल = पान। रसा = रस। अंब्रित = अमृत। रँग-राती = रङ्ग-रक्ता = रंग से रँगी। रुहिर = रुधिर। आछहिँ = स्वच्छ = अच्छी तरह से॥ बिगासा = विकसित हुआ। मधुकर = भ्रमर = कमल का रस लेने-वाला॥

सुन्दर वर्ण वा कुछ मदिरा का अंश लिये अथवा देवांश के सदृश अधर अमृत-रस से भरे हैं। (उन के लाली की शोभा देख कर निश्चय समझो, कि) लज्जा से (लाजि) सु-रङ्ग विम्ब वन में जा कर फरे हैं, अर्थात् वैसी अमृत-रस-भरी अधर की लाली अपने फल में न देख कर-ही वह बन में छिप कर फरता है, यह कवि की उत्प्रेक्षा है॥ अधर की उपमा परम्परा से लोग विम्ब-फल से देते चले आये हैं, इसी लिये संस्कृत में सुन्दर लालित्य-अधर-वाली बाला को विम्बोष्ठी कहते हैं। कभीँ कभीँ कवि लोग अधर की उपमा बन्धुजीव-पुष्प (उडहुल-पुष्प) से भी देते हैं, जैसा कि श्री-हर्ष ने नैषध के १८वें सर्ग में दिया है कि —

'वीक्ष्य पत्युरधरं कृशोदरी बन्धुजीवमिव भृङ्गसङ्गतम्।
मञ्जुलैर्नयनकज्जलैर्निजैः संवरीतुमशकत् स्मितं न सा॥'

(उन अधरोँ की ऐसी शोभा है), जानोँ लाल लाल दुपहरी के फूल हैँ। (दुपहरी वृक्ष के फूल गहिरे लाल रङ्ग के होते हैँ, और अच्छी तरह खिल जाने पर आप से आप झड पडते हैँ; इस पर कवि की उक्ति है, कि पद्मावती) जो जो बात कहती है (वह जानोँ उस दुपहरी वृक्ष से) फूल झरते हैँ। (अथवा बात कहने मेँ जो अधरोँ के बीच में दाँत झलक पडते हैँ, उन की ऐसी शोभा है जानोँ) हीरा सुन्दर-विद्रुम की धारा (धार = नदी) को लेते हैँ, अर्थात् जानोँ सुन्दर-विद्रुम की नदी में हीरोँ की पङ्क्ति पडी चमकती हो। हाँसी की उपमा कवि लोग श्वेत वर्ण से देते हैँ, इस हेतु

कवि की उक्ति है, कि पद्मावती के बिहँसते (दन्त-ज्योति के प्रकाश से) जगत् में उँजेला हो जाता है॥ पानों के रङ्ग लगने से (उन अधरों की लाली में और गहिरा-पन आने से वह लाली) मजीठ (की लाली) हो गई। (इस लिये उस लाली के) आगे कुसुम-रङ्ग स्थिर नहीं रहता है, अर्थात् उडा ऊआ फीका समझ पडता है॥ इस प्रकार से, अर्थात् ऐसे यत्न से उन अधरों में अमृत भर रक्खे हैं, (कि) आज तक वह अछूत है, और किसी ने (उस के स्वादु को) नहीं चक्खा है, अर्थात् अधरों के भीतर वह अमृत-रस बंद है, इस लिये जब तक अधर में चत न हो, तब तक उस का मिलना कठिन है। ईश्वर की बडी-ही कृपा जिस भाग्यवान् पर हो, वह अधर-चत कर के उस का पान कर सकता है॥ (चिर काल तक अमृत-रस के रहने से बिगड जाने की आशङ्का न हो, इस पर कवि की विशेषोक्ति है, कि) मुख के पान उस रस में रंग ढारते रहते हैं, (जिस से उस अमृत-रस में विशेष सुगन्ध और रंगत चढी रहती है, फिर बिगडने की क्या बात है) सो (देखें) वह बसा (स्थित वा वासा ऊआ) अमृत किस के मुख-योग्य है, अर्थात् कौन ऐसा है जो अपने मुख से उस अधर-मध्यस्थित अमृत को पीवे॥ (उस) रँग-राती (पद्मावती) को देख कर, (उस में) सब जगत् रक्त हो गया, अर्थात् पद्मावती के रूप से मोहित हो, जगत् के सब प्राणियों की दशा चन्द-चकोर सी हो गई। (जिस समय) अच्छी तरह से (पद्मावती) विहँसती है (उस समय विहँसने के श्रम से कुछ और विशेष लाल हो जाने से अधर ऐसे जान पडते हैं, जानों) रुधिर से भरे हैं॥

शुक कहता है, कि, हे राजा (रत्न-सेन), ऐसा (अस) वह अधरामृत है, कि जगत् के सब (प्राणी) (उस के मिलने की) आशा करते हैं, अर्थात् सब को यही लालसा है, कि वह अधरामृत मुझे मिले। (सो नहीं कह सकता, कि) किस के लिये वह (ललित-अधर-रूपी) कमल विकशित ऊआ है, अर्थात् खिला है, और कौन (ऐसा) है जो भ्रमर हो कर (उस अधर-कमल का) रस लेता है॥ योग-ग्रन्थों में लिखा है, कि जब योगी सिद्ध हो जाता है, तब वह ब्रह्मामृत को पाता है (सोऽमृतमश्नुते), इस लिये कवि का अभिप्राय है, कि विना सिद्ध ऊए उस अमृत-रस के स्वादु को कोई नहीं पा सकता। यों तो जड चेतन सभी को इच्छा बनी रहती है, कि ब्रह्मामृत-पान से अमर हो जाऊँ, परन्तु वह आशा मृग-तृष्णा-सी व्यर्थ है, केवल अनर्थ-ही कारक है॥१०८॥

चउपाई ।

दसन चउक्क बइठे जनु हीरा। अउ बिच बिच रँग सावँ गँभीरा ॥
जनु भादउ निसि दाविँनि दीसी। चमकि उठइ तस बनी बतीसी ॥
वह सो जोति हीरा उपराहीँ। हीरा देहि सो तेहि परिछाहीँ ॥
जेहि दिन दसन-जोति निरमई। बहुतइ जोति जोति वह भई ॥
रबि ससि नखत दिपहिँ तेहि जोती। रतन पदारथ मानिक मोती ॥
जहँ जहँ बिहँसि सोभाओन हँसी। तहँ तहँ छिटकि जोति परगसी ॥
दाविँनि चमकि न सरिवरि पूजा। पुनि ओहि जोति होइ को दूजा ॥

दोहा ।

(बिहँसत) हँसत दसन तस चमकइ पाहन उठइ झरक्कि ।
दारिउँ सरि जो न कइ सका फाटेउ हिआ तरक्कि ॥ १०९ ॥

दसन = दशन = दाँत । चउक = चतुःकोण = चौकोन पीढा वा पिसान से पूरा ऊत्रा चौकोन चेच, जिस के ऊपर लोग मङ्गल-कार्य में बैठते हैं । रँग = रङ्ग । सावँ = श्याम = काला । गँभीरा = गम्भीर = गहिरा । भादउ = भाद्रपद = भादो मास । निसि = निशि = राची । दाविँनि = दामिनी = विद्युल्लता । दीसी = दृष्टि पडी । देहि = देह = शरीर । परिछाहीँ = परिच्छाया । जोति = ज्योति । निरमई = निर्मित ऊई = बनाई गई । रबि = रवि = सूर्य । ससि = शशी = चन्द्र । नखत = नचत्र । दिपहिँ = दीप्त होते हैं = प्रज्वलित हैं = चमकते हैं । रतन = रत्न । पदारथ = पदार्थ । मानिक = माणिक्य । मोती = मुक्ता । जहँ जहँ = यत्र यत्र = जहाँ जहाँ । सोभाओन = स्व-भावेन = सहज-ही । तहँ तहँ = तत्र तत्र = तहाँ तहाँ । छिटकि = छटक कर = उच्छलित हो कर । परगसी = परकाशित ऊई = प्रकाशित ऊई । सरिवरि = बराबरी में = सादृश्य-पर । पूजा = पूरा पडा । दूजा = द्वितीय = दूसरा ॥ चमकइ = चमकता है । पाहन = पाषाण = पत्थल । उठइ = उठता है = उत्तिष्ठते । झरक्कि = झलक । दारिउँ = दाडिम । सरि = सादृश्य = साम्य । हिआ = हृदय = हिया । तरक्कि = तडक कर ॥

दाँत (ऐसे जान पडते हैं) जानौं चौक के ऊपर हीरा बैठ हैं (मस-गुर चौक और उज्ज्वल चमकीले दाँत हीरा से हैं)। और (उन दाँतों के) बीच बीच (शोभा के लिये मिस्सी के लगाने से) गहिरा श्याम रङ्ग हो गया है॥ जैसे काली भादौं की रात में बिजली देख पडती है, तैसा-ही (पद्मावती के हँस देने से) बनी ऊई बतीसी (बत्तीसो दाँतों की लड) चमक उठती है॥ यहाँ जनु=यथा=जैसे, ऐसा समझना चाहिए। बऊतों का मत है, कि यथा और तथा का नित्य संबन्ध रहने से 'जस भादउ निसि दाविँनि दीसी' ऐसा पाठ चाहिए। 'बनी' से यह तात्पर्य है, कि मिस्सी के लगाने से ऐसी बतीसी बनी ऊई है, जैसे भादौं की रात में बिजली। (दाँतों की सन्धि सन्धि में बैठी ऊई मिस्सी काली भादौं की रात है, और उस में चमकते ऊए श्वेत दाँत बिजली से हैं)॥ वह (दाँतो की) ज्योति जो है सो हीरा के ऊपर है, अर्थात् हीरा की चमक से बढ कर है। हीरा की शरीर में तिस (ज्योति) की परछाहीं है, अर्थात् दन्तों के प्रतिविम्ब पड जाने-ही से हीरा में कान्ति आ गई है, जिस से वह चमकता है,— ऐसा कवि का आशय है॥ जिस दिन (पद्मावती की) दन्त-कान्ति बनाई गई, (उसी दिन से) वह ज्योति बऊतों में ज्योति भई है, अर्थात् उसी दन्त-ज्योति के प्रतिविम्ब से उसी दिन से बऊत पदार्थों में ज्योति आ गई है॥ (प्रकृति-रूपा पद्मावती-ही की ज्योति से जगत् में सब ज्योतिर्मय हैं, इस लिये पद्मावती को प्रकृति मानने से आगे की चौपाइयाँ प्रकृति-पक्ष में भी लग जाती हैं)। तिसी (दन्त-)ज्योति से रवि, चन्द्र, और नक्षत्र दिप रहे हैं। जितने रत्न पदार्थ माणिक्य, मुक्ता (इत्यादि) हैं, उन में भी वही ज्योति है, अर्थात् उसी दन्त-कान्ति के प्रतिविम्ब-ही से सब रत्नों में चमक है, जिस से वे दिपते रहते हैं॥ जहाँ जहाँ (पद्मावती ने) विहँस कर के (विहास्य=विशेष रूप से हँस कर), अर्थात् मुख खोल कर सहज स्वभाव-ही से हँस दिया, तहाँ तहाँ वह (दन्त-)ज्योति छटक छटक कर प्रगट हो गई॥ यहाँ 'विहँसि' के स्थान में 'विगसि' यदि हो तो बऊत-ही उत्तम। तब 'पद्मावती ने विकशित हो कर, अर्थात् मुख खोल कर जहाँ जहाँ स्वभाव-ही से हँस दिया' ऐसा स्पष्ट अर्थ उत्पन्न हो जाता है॥ (जिस दन्त-कान्ति की) बराबरी में बिजली की, चमक न पूरी पडी, (भला) फिर (पुनि=पुनः) उस ज्योति के ऐसा दूसरा कौन हो, अर्थात् उस ज्योति के सदृश वही ज्योति है, दूसरा ऐसा कोई नहीं जो ज्योति में इस ज्योति की बराबरी कर सके॥

हँसते मेँ तिस तरह से दाँत चमक उठता है, जैसे पाहन (हीरा-पाषाण), अर्थात् वज्र, झलक उठे। (उन लाल मस-गुर मिले उज्ज्वल दाँतोँ की) बराबरी दाडिम जो (अनार) न कर सका (इसी ग्लानि और सन्ताप से) तडक कर (उस दाडिम का) हृदय फट गया। अनार जब पकते हैँ, तब स्वभाव-ही से फट जाते हैँ। तहाँ कवि की उत्प्रेचा है, कि जान पडता है, कि दाडिम पद्मावती के दाँतोँ के समान अपने को न देख कर, रात दिन चिन्ता करते करते, आकुल हो गया, और उसी चिन्ताग्नि-ज्वाला से उस का हृदय विदीर्ण हो गया है। किसी कवि ने आम्र की प्रशंसा मेँ भी कहा है, कि

ह्रिया श्यामा जम्बू स्फुटितहृदयं दाडिमफलं
सदा धत्ते शूलं हृदय अभिमानेन पनसः।
कठोरे श्रीलक्ष्मीफल इह रुजा वारि जठरे
समुद्भूते चूते जगति फलराजे प्रभवति ॥

इस प्रकार कवि की उक्ति अतिशय चमत्कृत है ॥ १०९ ॥

चउपाई ।

रसना कहउँ जो कह रस-बाता। अंम्रित बयन सुनत मन राता ॥
हरइ सो सुर चातक कोकिला। बीन बंसि वेइ बयन न मिला ॥
चातक कोकिल रहहिँ जो नाहीँ। सुनि वेइ बयन लाजि छपि जाहीँ ॥
भरे पेम-मधु बोलइ बोला। सुनइ सो माति घूमिँ कइ डोला ॥
चतुर बेद मति सब ओहि पाँहा। रिग जजु सावँ अथरबन माँहा ॥
एक एक बोल अरथ चउ-गुना। इँदर मोहि बरम्हा सिर धुना ॥
अमर पिँगल भारथ अउ गीता। अरथ जो जेहि पंडित नहिँ जीता ॥

दोहा ।

भावसती ब्याकरन सब पिंगल पाठ पुरान।
बेद भेद सउँ बात कह तस जनु लागहिँ बान ॥ ११० ॥

रसना = जिह्वा = जीभ। रस-बाता = रस-वार्त्ता = रस की बात। अंम्रित = अमृत। बयन = वचन = बोली। राता = रक्त हो जाता है = लग जाता है। हरइ = हरति = हरती है। सुर = स्वर = वाणी। चातक = एक पक्षि-विशेष, जो इस प्रान्त मेँ वसन्त से

ले कर स्वात्यर्क तक 'पी कहाँ, पी कहाँ' ऐसा बोला करता है। फिर मौन हो कर कहीँ अन्यत्र चला जाता है, वा रूपान्तर से यहीँ रहता हो। क्योँकि स्वात्यर्क के अनन्तर फिर वह यदि पकड कर पिँजडे मेँ बन्द न किया जाय, तो वाटिकाओँ मेँ कहीँ भी देख नहीँ पडता। कोकिला = कोयल = एक पक्षि-विशेष, यह भी इस प्रान्त मेँ बहुत प्रसिद्ध पक्षी है। इस की बोली मेँ 'कुहू कुहू' ऐसा अनुकरण जान पडता है। यह भी वसन्त से ले कर वर्षा-ऋतु तक इस प्रान्त मेँ बोलता हुआ, इधर उधर दिखाई देता है। फिर यदि पकड कर न रक्खा जाय तो नहीँ देख पडता। बीन = वीणा = सरस्वती का प्रसिद्ध बाजा। बंसि = वंशी, एक प्रसिद्ध वाद्य-विशेष। पेम-मधु = प्रेम-मधु = प्रेम का मद्य-विशेष। माति = मत्त हो कर। घूविँ = घूर्मित हो कर = घुमरी खा कर। डोला = डोला करता है = फिरा करता है। चतुर = चत्वारः = चारो। रिग = ऋग्। जजु = यजुष् = यजुर्वेद। सावँ = साम। अथरबन = अथर्वण वेद। चउ-गुना = चतुर्गुण = चार-गुणा। इँदर = इन्द्र = देव-राज। बरम्हा = ब्रह्मा। सिर = शिर। धुना = धुनते हैँ = पीटते हैँ। अमर = अमरकोश, अमर सिंह का बनाया प्रसिद्ध संस्कृत का कोश-ग्रन्थ जो अग्नि-पुराण मेँ भी पाया जाता है। पिँगल = पिङ्गल, पिङ्गल नाग का बनाया प्राकृत भाषा मेँ प्रसिद्ध छन्दो-ग्रन्थ। भारथ = भारत, व्यास का बनाया प्रसिद्ध संस्कृत का इतिहास-ग्रन्थ। गीता = भगवद्गीता = भारत के भीष्म-पर्व का एक खण्ड, जिस मेँ कृष्णार्जुन संवाद है, और जो अनेक टीका टिप्पणादि से सर्वत्र बहुत-ही प्रसिद्ध है॥ भावसती = भास्वती, शतानन्द का बनाया प्रसिद्ध ज्यौतिष का एक करण-ग्रन्थ (मेरी बनाई गणक-तरङ्गिणी देखो)। ब्याकरन = व्याकरण, जिस के इन्द्र। चन्द्र। काश्यप। पिशलि। शाकटायन। पाणिनि। अमरसिंह। जिनेन्द्र। ये आठ आचार्य हैँ। उन मेँ अब केवल पाणिनि का व्याकरण अष्टाध्यायी सर्वत्र प्रसिद्ध है। सब = इतर वेदाङ्ग = ज्यौतिष, निरुक्त, कल्प, शिक्षा। पिँगल = पिङ्गल = इतर छन्दो-ग्रन्थ वृत्तरत्नाकरादि। पाठ = पाठ्य-ग्रन्थ = धर्म-शास्त्र, मीमांसा और न्याय। पुरान = पुराण॥

शुक कहता है, कि (अब) रसना को कहता हूँ, अर्थात् पद्मावती के रसना का वर्णन करता हूँ, जो कि (सदा) रस-ही की बात कहती है। (इस लिये रस से भरी उस) अमृत-वचन को सुनते-ही (सब का) मन रक्त हो जाता है, अर्थात् उस वचन-ही मेँ सब का मन लग जाता है, और यही चाहता है, कि सदा इस वचन को सुना करेँ॥ वह (सो) रसना चातक और कोकिला के स्वर को हरण करती है, अर्थात् उस

रसना की ऐसी वाणी है, जिस के सुनने के लिये चातक और कोयल भी मौन हो जाते हैँ। उस पर कवि की उत्प्रेक्षा है, कि वे मौन जो हो गये, सो जानौं उस रसना ने उन की वाणी को चुरा लिया, इसी कारण वाणी-रहित हो गये। (उस के) वचन से, वीणा और वंशी के मधुर शब्द नहीँ मिलते, अर्थात् उस की वाणी में वीणा और वंशी के माधुर्य से भी बढ कर माधुरी है॥ चातक और कोयल जो (सर्व-काल) नहीँ रहते हैँ, अर्थात् वसन्त से वर्षा तक दिखाई दे कर, फिर जो अदृश्य हो जाते हैँ, (उस का यही कारण है, कि) उस (पद्मावती के) वचन को सुन कर (वैसी माधुरी अपनी वाणी में न पा कर) लज्जा से छिप जाते हैँ॥ (वह रसना) प्रेम-मधु से भरे बोल (वचन) को बोलती है, (इस लिये) जो सुनता है वह (सो) मत्त हो कर और घुमरी खा कर डोलने लगता है, अर्थात् कर्ण-विवर की राह से जहाँ वह प्रेम-मदिरा से भरी वाणी अन्तः-करण में पहुँची, कि प्राणी उस की नशा से मात और घुमर कर डोलने लगता है॥ उस के पास, अर्थात् उस रसना में, चारो वेद की सब मति (बुद्धि) है, वा चतुर जनौं की और वेदौं की सब मति है, जो कि सब मति, अर्थात् सब विद्या, ऋग्, यजु, साम और अथर्वण में (भरी हुई) हैँ॥ एक एक बोली में चउ-गुने अर्थ हैँ, अर्थात् उस के एक एक शब्द में अनेक अर्थ भरे हैँ। जिस की मति चतुरौं के मति की ऐसी और वेद-मति सी है, उस के एक एक शब्द में अनेक-अर्थ का रहना समुचित-ही है, क्योँकि चतुरौं के शब्द ऐसैं-ही होते हैँ। कहावत है, कि कृष्ण से एक गोपी ने भोजन के लिये पत्तल माँगा, दूसरी ने कहा, कि आज मेरे घर पधारिये, तीसरी ने कहा, कि मुझे कर्ण-फूल पहनाइये, चौथी ने कहा, कि मुझे आग चाहिए, पाँचवीँ ने कहा, कि मुझे फूल ला दीजिये, और छठवीँ ने कहा, कि मुझे जल लाइये। इस पर चतुरे कृष्ण ने एक-ही वाक्य 'बारी नहीँ' कह कर, सब को उत्तर दे दिया। पहली के उत्तर में बारी, जो कि पत्तल बनाता है, वह नहीँ है। दूसरी के उत्तर में बारी=पारी, तेरे घर आने की, नहीँ। तीसरी के उत्तर में बारी=बाली कान की, जिस में कर्ण-फूल डाल देने से अटक रहता है नहीँ है। चौथी के उत्तर में बारी, अर्थात् आग जलाई, नहीँ है। पाँचवीँ के उत्तर में बारी अर्थात् फुल-वारी यहाँ नहीँ है, और छठवीँ के उत्तर में बारी=वारि=जल नहीँ है। यह वाक्यार्थ करना चाहिए। इस पर किसी कवि का नीचे लिखा हुआ सोरठा है।

पतरी दै घर आव करन-फूल पहिराव मोँहि।
आगि फूल जल लाव कृष्ण कही बारी नहीँ॥

इस पर गोपियोँ ने कृष्ण की प्रशंसा नीचे लिखे हुए दोहे से की है।

जस कदली के पात मेँ पात पात मेँ पात।
तस चतुरन के बात मेँ बात बात मेँ बात॥

इसी प्रकार वेद की श्रुतियाँ भी ऐसी होती हैँ, जिन के अनेक अर्थ होते हैँ। इसी लिये श्रुति को काम-दुघा कहते हैँ, जिस से जो चाहिए सो निकल सकता है। जैसे

चत्वारि शृङ्गा त्रयो अस्य पादा द्वे शीर्षे सप्त हस्तासो अस्य।
त्रिधा बद्धो वृषभो रोरवीति महो देवो मर्त्याँ आविवेश॥

इस श्रुति को वैयाकरण व्याकरण-पक्ष मेँ, ज्यौतिषी ज्यौतिष-पक्ष मेँ, वल्लभ-संप्रादय के लोग कृष्ण की मुरली-प्रशंसा मेँ, इसी प्रकार प्रायः सभी मत-वाले अपने अपने पक्ष मेँ लगाते हैँ। इस प्रकार वेद और चतुरोँ की सी मति होने से उस की एक एक बोली मेँ अनेकार्थ का भरा रहना कोई चित्र नहीँ है। (इस प्रकार की अनेकार्थ गुम्फित वाणी को सुन कर) इन्द्र और ब्रह्मा (दोनोँ) मोहित हो कर (अपनी वाणी मेँ वैसे अनेकार्थ को न पा कर) शिर पीटते हैँ। इन्द्र के ऐसा चतुर-पण्डित कोई नहीँ। भगवान् वामन के पढाने की वेला मेँ सब किसी ने यही कहा, कि इन्द्र से बढ कर चतुर-पण्डित दूसरा नहीँ। और जिस के मुख से चारो वेद निकले उस ब्रह्मा के समान दूसरा वेद जानने-वाला कौन हो सकता है। सो जब ये दोनोँ पद्मावती की वाणी से मोहित हो शिर पीटने लगे, तब दूसरे इतर जनोँ की क्या सामर्थ्य है, कि पद्मावती सी अनेकार्थ और रस-भरी वाणी को बोल सके॥ अमरकोश, पिङ्गल, भारत और भगवद्गीता के अर्थ करने मेँ भी वह जो (पद्मावती) है, (सो एक-ही है) जिसे पण्डित लोग भी नहीँ जीतते हैँ, अर्थात् जीत सकते हैँ॥

भारती, व्याकरण, सब षडङ्ग, पिङ्गल-ग्रन्थ, पाठ्य धर्मशास्त्रादि, पुराण और वेद जो हैँ, सब के (मत) भेद से तैसी (वह) बात कहती है, अर्थात् चतुर्दश-विद्या की संमति से वह तैसी बात कहती है, (चतुर्दश विद्या शास्त्र-कारोँ ने 'अङ्गानि वेदाश्चत्वारो मीमांसा न्यायविस्तरः। पुराणं धर्म-शास्त्रं च विद्या ह्येताश्चतुर्दश॥' यही कहा है। इसी का भावार्थ २२ वेँ दोहे की टीका मेँ लिख आये हैँ।) (कि सुन कर हृदय मेँ) जानोँ बाण लग जाता है, अर्थात् बाण के ऐसा उस का असर कलेजे पर पहुँच जाता है॥

इस प्रकार कवि का भावार्थ है, कि जिस की वाणी से वाणी का पति ब्रह्मा-ही मोहित हो कर, शिर पीटने लगता है, उस वाणी की समता ब्रह्मा की पत्नी वाणी (सरस्वती) कैसे कर सकती है। इस लिये जिस वाणी से सरस्वती और ब्रह्मा दोनों स्त्री-पुरुष हार कर शिर पीटते हैं, वह वाणी अनुपम और वर्णनातीत है। अर्थात् चिच्छक्ति-रूपा पद्मावती के अंग-रूप विष्णु के नाभी से निकले ब्रह्मा और उस की पत्नी सरस्वती की क्या सामर्थ्य जो प्रकृति के वाणी का भेद पावे। इसी लिये वेचारे चारो वेद 'यतो वाचो निर्वतन्ते' इत्यादि कह कह कर लाचार हो हार मान कर चुप हो रहे हैं ॥ ११० ॥

चउपाई।

पुनि बरनउँ का सुरँग कपोला। एक नारँग के दुअ-उ अमोला ॥
पुहुप पंग रस अंब्रित साधे। केइ यह सुरँग खिरउरा बाँधे ॥
तेहि कपोल बाएँ तिल परा। जेइ तिल देख सो तिल तिल जरा ॥
जनु घुँघुँची ओहि तिल कर-मुहाँ। बिरह-बान साधेउ सामुहाँ ॥
अगिन-बान तिल जानउँ सूझा। एक कटाछ लाख दस जूझा ॥
सो तिल गाल मेटि नहिँ गएऊ। अब वह गाल काल जग भएऊ ॥
देखत नयन परी परिछाहीँ। तेहि तइँ रात साँव उपराहीँ ॥

दोहा।

सो तिल देखि कपोल पर गगन रहा धुव गाडि।
खनहिँ उठइ खन बूडइ डोलइ नहिँ तिल छाडि ॥ १११ ॥

कपोला = कपोल = गाल। नारँग = नारङ्ग = नारंगी। दुअ-उ = दोनोँ। अमोला = अमूल्य। वा अमोला = अमोरा = विना मोरे, अर्थात् उठे ऊए। पुऊप = पुष्प। पंग = अपाङ्ग = नेत्र के नीचे का कपोल-भाग। साधे = साधे ऊए हैँ = साने ऊए हैँ। खिरउरा = खैर के बडे बडे गोले। (खिरउरी का पुंलिङ्ग, ३९ वेँ दोहे की टीका देखो। पुंलिङ्ग होने से उसी वस्तु की आकृति कुछ बडी समझनी चाहिए, जैसे हथउडी से हथौडा, गिलउरी से गिलउरा, दउरी से दउरा, कराही से कराहा इत्यादि)। तिल =

तिल अन्नविशेष के ऐसा चिह्न। परा = पडा है। तिल = तिलान्न के लंबाई चौडाई परिमाण का प्रदेश। वा, तिलतिल = तिल-तिर = तिल-तीर। जरा = जल जाता है = भस्म हो जाता है। वा, जरा = जडा = जड जाता है। कर-मुहाँ = काले मुहँ का = काल-मुख। सामुहाँ = सम्मुख = सामने। अगिन-बान = अग्नि-वाण, जिस के चलाने से अग्नि वर्षा होती है। कटाछ = कटाच = नयन-कोर की चितवन। जूझा = जूझे = जूझइ (युध्यते) का भूतकाल = जीव से रहित ऊए = जूझ गये। काल = सब को मारने-वाला। रात = रक्त = लाल। सावँ = श्याम = काला। धुव = ध्रुव नचत्र। गाडि = गड कर। खन = चण। बूडइ = बूड जाता है = डूब जाता है॥

फिर सु-रङ्ग (सुन्दर वर्ण) कपोलोँ का क्या वर्णन करूँ। (जान पडते हैँ, कि वे) दोनोँ अमूल्य, वा उठे ऊए, एक-ही नारंगी के हैँ, अर्थात् एक-ही काल के एक-ही नारंगी से उठे और लाल लाल ऐसे गोल गोल बने हैँ, कि दोनोँ के रूप रंग मेँ तनिक भी भेद नहीँ समझ पडता। अपाङ्ग-रूपी पुष्प के रसामृत से साने ऊए (नहीँ जानते, कि) किस ने इन सु-रंग खिरौरोँ को बाँधा है, अर्थात् कपोलोँ की शोभा ऐसी है, जानोँ अमृत से सने ऊए दो सुन्दर खिरौरे हैँ। अथवा जान पडता है, कि 'ब्रह्मा (के-इ = क-एव = ब्रह्मा-एव) ने इन सु-रंग खिरौरोँ को बाँधा है', यह अर्थान्तर हो सकता है॥ तिस बायेँ कपोल के ऊपर एक तिल चिह्न है। उस तिल को जो देखता है, सो (उस की दीप्ति से) तिल तिल भस्म हो जाता है, वा देखने से वह दर्शकोँ के नेत्र मेँ ऐसा समाय जाता है, कि उस के तिल तिल (अङ्गावयव) मेँ ज्रटित हो जाता है, अर्थात् आँख मेँ तिल समा जाने से वह उस आँख से जिस अङ्गावयव को देखता है, वहाँ वह तिल-ही देख पडता है। वा जो उस तिल को देखता है सो तिल-तीर (तिल-रूपी तीर) से भस्म हो जाता है॥ सामुद्रिक-शास्त्र मेँ प्रसिद्ध है, कि पुरुष को दक्षिण और स्त्री को वाम भाग मेँ तिल, मशा, इत्यादि चिह्न शुभ-फल-दायक हैँ। इसी लिये कवि ने बायेँ का ग्रहण किया है। और स्वाभाविक धर्म है, कि नायिकाओँ के बायेँ गाल का तिल विशेष छवि-मय हो नायकोँ के मन को विशेष से मोहित करता है। इस हेतु और अवयवोँ को छोड गाल-ही का ग्रहण किया गया। कवियोँ की तिल-लसित वाम कपोल के ऊपर अनेक उत्प्रेक्षा है, जैसा किसी ने कहा है कि

'प्यारी तेरे गाल पर सोहत है तिल श्याम।
मानोँ चंद बिछाय के बैठे सालिगराम॥'

जिन सुन्दरी गौर-वर्ण युवतियोँ के बायेँ गाल पर स्वभावतः तिल नहीँ रहता, वे लोग अपनी शोभा बढाने और रसिकोँ के मन को विशेष कर अपनी ओर दौडाने और रिझाने के लिये उस पर तिल-सदृश एक गोदना गोदा लेती हैँ । यह इस प्रान्त मेँ इतना प्रसिद्ध है, कि ग्राम्य लोग भी अपनी कविता मेँ 'गोरे गाल पर काला गोदनवाँ रिझिहैँ तोर सजना' इत्यादि गाया करते हैँ ॥ जानोँ उसी कर-मुहँ तिल से घुँघुंची (उत्पन्न ऊई) है, (नीचे गाल की लाली मिल कर तिल की शोभा ऐसी है, जानोँ इसी शोभा से घुँघुँची बनी है)। (अथवा तिल की ऐसी शोभा है, जानोँ) सामने विरह-बाण साधा है। कवि की उत्प्रेक्षा है, कि तिल देखने पर ऐसा चित्त बे-चैन हो जाता हैँ, जानोँ पद्मावती ने तिल-रूपी विरह-बाण को सामने जो साधा है, उसे देख कर घबडा गया है, कि कदाचित् चला कर प्राण न ले ले ॥ कवि कहता है, कि मुझे यह सूझ पडता है, कि जानोँ तिल अग्नि-बाण है, क्योँकि एक कटाक्ष से, अर्थात् एक नयनकोर-चितवन-सहित तिल-बाण के चलाने से, दश लाख जूझ गये हैँ, अर्थात् दश लाख दर्शक एक-ही तिल-बाण से मूर्छित हो गये हैँ, सो यह धर्म तो केवल अग्नि-बाण-ही मेँ है ॥ अथवा यदि 'लाख' 'लक्ष्य' का अपभ्रंश मानो तो 'एक-ही कटाक्ष से (दर्शकोँ के) दशो (इन्द्रिय-रूपी) लक्ष्य मर गये हैँ, अर्थात् दशो इन्द्रियाँ मूर्छित हो शक्ति-रहित हो गई हैँ', ऐसा अर्थ कर सकते हो ॥ 'एक कटा छ लाख दस जूझा' ऐसा लिखने से, दश लाख = १०,००,००० इस मेँ से एक को काट लेने से ०००००० ये छ शून्य (व्यर्थ होने) से दशो लाख की संख्या नष्ट हो गई। इसी प्रकार तिलाग्नि-बाण से एक (दर्शकोँ का मन) कट जाता है, जिस से छ (छ अङ्ग, नासिका, कान, नेत्र, मुख, हाथ, और पैर सब) व्यर्थ होने से दश लाख (दर्शक) जूझ जाते हैँ, ऐसा बऊत लोग वागाडम्बर से दूसरा अर्थ करते हैँ ॥ पद्मावती को प्रकृति और तिल को उस की माया मानने से उस माया-बाण से दश लाख, अर्थात् अनन्त प्राणी लोग, जूझ जाते हैँ, यह कवि का कहना ठीक-ही है॥ (शुक कहता है, कि राजन्,) वह गाल का तिल मिट नहीँ गया हैँ, (किन्तु जवानी मेँ जैसे सब अङ्ग बढ कर सु-रङ्ग और मनोहर हो जाते हैँ, तैसे-ही बढ कर प्रबल हो), अब वह गाल (का तिल) जग का काल हो गया है, अर्थात् जगत् के प्राणियोँ का प्राण लेने-वाला हो गया है ॥ (हीरा-मणि शुक कहता है, कि उन तिलोँ को) देखते (मेरे) नयनोँ मेँ (उस तिल की) परछाँही पड गई है। तिसी से

(आँखों के) ऊपर (उपराहीं) लाल और काला, अर्थात् घुंघुची के ऐसा चिह्न हो गया है॥ हीरा-मणि सुग्गे की आँख घुंघुची सी होती हैं; तहाँ हीरा-मणि की उक्ति है, कि उसी घुंघुची-सदृश तिल को देखते देखते उसी की परछाहीं मेरी आँखों में पड गई है, अर्थात् मेरे आँखों की शोभा उस तिल के प्रतिबिम्ब से है॥

उस कपोल पर के तिल को देख कर ध्रुव (मोहित हो) आकाश में गड कर, अर्थात् एक स्थान में अचल हो कर, ठहरा हुआ है। चण में उठता है (उगता है), चण में डूब (अस्त हो) जाता है, (इसी प्रकार रात दिन उठता बैठता रहता है, परन्तु उस) तिल को छोड कर (दूसरे स्थान पर) नहीं डोलता है, अर्थात् नहीं जाता है। कवि की उत्प्रेचा है, कि ध्रुव एक स्थान में अचल हो, जो सदा रात को उठा और दिन को बैठा करता है, सो उस की यह मतवाले सी गति गाल के तिल-दर्शन-ही से हुई है॥ १११॥

चउपाई।

स्रवन सीप दुइ दीप सँवारे। कुंडल कनक रचे उँजिआरे॥
मनि-कुंडल चमकहिँ अति लोने। जनु कउँधा लउकहिँ दुहुँ कोने॥
दुहुँ दिसि चाँद सुरुज चमकाहीँ। नखतन्ह भरे निरखि नहिँ जाहीँ॥
तेहि पर खूँट दीप दुइ बारे। दुइ ध्रुव दुहूँ खूँट बइसारे॥
पहिरे खुंभी सिंघल-दीपी। जानउँ भरी कचपची सीपी॥
खन खन जोहि चीर सिर गहा। काँपत बीजु दुहूँ दिसि रहा॥
डरपहिँ देओ-लोक सिंघला। परइ न टूटि बीजु एहि कला॥

दोहा।

करहिँ नखत सब सेवा स्रवन दीन्ह अस दो-उ।
चाँद सुरुज अस गहने अउरु जगत का कोउ॥ ११२॥

स्रवन = श्रवण = कर्ण = कान। सीप = शुक्ति = सीपी, जिस में मोती रहती है। कुंडल = कुण्डल = कान का गहना = कर्णपूर। मनि-कुंडल = मणि-कुण्डल = मणि का कुण्डल। लोन = लावण्य = ललित = सुन्दर। कउँधा = कन्ध = जल को धारण करने-वाला = मेघ वा विद्युत्। लउकहिँ = लोकहिँ = प्रकाशहिँ = प्रकाशित होती हैं = चमकती

हैं । (लोक-दीप्तौ इस संस्कृत-धातु से बना है)। कोने = कोणे = कोण में । दिसि = दिशि = दिशा में । चाँद = चन्द्र । सुरुज = सूर्य । निरखि = निरीक्षण = देख। खूँट = कान का एक खूँटी-दार गहना, जिसे इस प्रान्त में विरिया कहते हैं। दीप = दीपक = दीया। बारे = बारे हैं = जलाये हैं। धुव = ध्रुव-नक्षत्र। बइसारे = बैठाये हैं। खुंभी = खुँभिया = काँप, जो कान की ललरी में छेद कर, पहनी जाती है। इस में छोटे छोटे अनेक नग जडे रहते हैं। सिंघल-दीपी = सिंहल-द्वीपी = सिंहल-दीप की। कचपची = कृत्तिका-नक्षत्र, जिस में छ छोटे छोटे चमक-दार तारे हैं। जोहि = जोह कर = देख कर। चीर = वस्त्र = कपडा। बीजु = विद्युत् = बिजली। देश्रो-लोक = देव-लोक = देव-लोग। कला = अंश = टुकडा ॥ गहने = गहना = आभूषण। वा, गहने = ग्रहणे = रेहन ॥

सीप के ऐसे श्रवण (जानों) दो दीपक रचे गये हैं। (उन दीपकों में) सुवर्ण के कुण्डल उँजेले को रचे हैं, अर्थात् सुवर्ण-कुण्डल की कान्ति जो है, वही उस दीपक की प्रज्वलित शिखा है॥ अत्यन्त सुन्दर (अति-लोने) मणि-कुण्डल (ऐसे) चमकते हैं, जानों दोनों कोण में, अर्थात् कपोलों के दोनो ओर, बिजली प्रकाशित होती है॥ (अथवा वे दोनों मणि-कुण्डल ऐसे जान पडते हैं, जानों) दोनों दिशाओं में (क्रम से) चन्द्र और सूर्य चमकते हैं, अर्थात् पद्मावती का मुख पूर्णिमा तिथि है, इस लिये यदि उत्तर की ओर मुख मान लिया जाय, तो पश्चिम का मणि-कुण्डल अस्त-क्षितिज के पास का सूर्य, और पूर्व का कुण्डल पूर्व-क्षितिज में उदय-गत चन्द्र के सदृश है, क्योंकि केवल पूर्णिमा में यह संभव है, कि युगपत् एक ओर सूर्य और दूसरी ओर चन्द्र देखा जा सकता है। (वे दोनों सूर्य और चन्द्र) नक्षत्रों से भरे हैं, (इस लिये बहुत चमक बढ जाने से वे दोनों) निरख (देखे) नहीं जाते हैं। (मणि-कुण्डलों में जो अनेक नग जडे हुए हैं उन की शोभा ऐसी जान पडती है, जानों कुण्डल-रूपी सूर्य-चन्द्र में नक्षत्र भरे हुए हैं, इसी लिये उन दोनों की ऐसी चमक बढ गई है, कि आँखों में चकाचौंधी लग जाने से, देखे नहीं जाते हैं। इस प्रकार उदय और अस्त के चन्द्र, सूर्य स्वभावतः कान्ति-हीन होने पर भी, नग-नक्षत्रों के साथ अति-कान्तिमान् हो जाने से 'नखतन्ह भरे निरखि नहिँ जाहीँ' यह कवि की सूक्ति है)॥ तिस (मणि-कुण्डल) पर विरिया (खूँट) जो है, (सो जानों उन कुण्डल-रूपी सूर्य-चन्द्र के ऊपर) दो दीपक बारे हैं। (उन खूटों के ऊपर के जो गोल भाग हैं, उन की ऐसी शोभा है,

जानेँ) दोनेँ खूटोँ के ऊपर दोनेँ (उत्तर और दक्षिण के) ध्रुव बैठाये गये हैँ ॥ ज्योतिष-शास्त्र मेँ नाडीमण्डल के पृष्ठ-केन्द्र स्वरूप मेरु और कुमेरु के ऊपर उत्तर और दक्षिण ध्रुव प्रसिद्ध हैँ । भास्कराचार्य ने भी अपने गोलाध्याय मेँ लिखा है, कि

'सौम्यं ध्रुवं मेरुगताः खमध्ये याम्यं च दैत्या निजमस्तकोर्ध्वे ।
सव्यापसव्यं भ्रमदृक्षचक्रं विलोकयन्ति क्षितिज-प्रसक्तम् ॥'

(भास्कर के लिये गणकतरङ्गिणी देखो)

(पद्मावती उन कानेँ मेँ) सिंहल-द्वीप की बनी हुई खुंभी (काँप) पहरे है। (उन की ऐसी शोभा है) जानेँ कचपची से भरी सीपी हो [चाँदी की षट् कोण काँप सीपी, उस मेँ जडे हुए छ नग कचपची (कृत्तिका) से जान पडते हैँ]॥ (मनुष्योँ को) जोह (देख) कर (लज्जा से) क्षण क्षण पर शिर का वस्त्र (चीर) पकडा जाता है, अर्थात् वार वार लज्जा से पद्मावती शिर ढाँकने के लिये शिर के वस्त्र को सरकाया करती है; (उस व्यापार से शिर हिलने से जो काँप, काँप उठती है, उस की ऐसी शोभा है, जानेँ) दोनेँ दिशा मेँ बिजली कँप रही है ॥ देवता लोग डरते हैँ, कि सिंहल मेँ इस (काँप-रूपी) बिजली की एक कला, अर्थात् टुकडा, न टूट पडे, (नहीँ तो सिंहल के सब लोग चमक और आघात से मर जायँगे)॥

ऐसे दोनेँ श्रवण (ब्रह्मा ने) दिया है, अर्थात् बनाया है, कि सब नक्षत्र (नक्षत्र ऐसे नग-गण) (उन कानेँ की) सेवा करती हैँ । कवि की उत्प्रेक्षा है, कि मणि-कुण्डल, और काँपोँ के नग नहीँ है, जानेँ श्रवण को पवित्र श्रुति (वेद) समझ, नक्षत्र उनकी सेवा के लिये तत्पर हैँ ॥ (और जिन श्रुतियोँ के) चन्द्र और सूर्य के ऐसे गहने हैँ (आभूषण हैँ), वा जिन श्रुतियोँ के यहाँ चन्द्र और सूर्य गहने (रेहन) पडे हैँ, उन श्रुतियोँ के आगे जगत् मेँ और कौन है ?, अर्थात् श्रुतियोँ के सदृश जगत् मेँ कोई नहीँ है॥ (यहाँ कर्ण के जो दो मणि-कुण्डल हैँ, और जिन के लिये पहले कह आये हैँ, कि दुहुँ दिसि चाँद सुरुज चमकाहीँ, वे-ही दोनेँ क्रम से चन्द्र और सूर्य हैँ) ॥ ११२ ॥

चउपाई ।

बरनउँ गीउ कूँज कइ रीसी । कंचन तार लागु जनु सीसी ॥
कूँदइ फेरि जानु गिउ काढी । हरइ पुछारि ठगी जनु ठाढी ॥
जनु हिअ काढि परेवा ठाढा । तेहि तइँ अधिक भाउ गिउ बाढा ॥

चाक चढाइ साँच जनु कीन्हा। बाग तुरंग जानु गहि लीन्हा ॥
गिउ मजूर तम-चूर जो हारे। उंह-इ पुकारहिँ साँझ सकारे ॥
पुनि तेहि ठाउँ परी तिरि रेखा। घूँट जो पीक लीक सब देखा ॥
धनि ओहि गीउ दीन्ह बिधि भाऊ। दहुँ का सउँ लेइ करइ मेराऊ ॥

दोहा।

कंठ सिरी-मुकुताओली (माला) सोहइ अभरन गीउ।
को होइ हार कँठ (ओहि) लागइ को तपु साधा जीउ ॥ ११३ ॥

गीउ = ग्रीवा = गला। कूँज = कुञ्ज = वन। रीसी = ऋश्या = ऋश्य, मृग-विशेष का मादा (गोकर्णपृषतैणर्श्यरोहिताश्चमरो मृगाः। अमरकोश, सिंहादिवर्ग, श्लो० ५२९)। कूँदइ = कुंदा को (काठ के सुन्दर सुडौल गोले गोले टुकडे को कुंदा कहते हैं)। फेरि = फिरा कर = खराद पर चढा कर, और सुडौल गोल कर। काढी = काढी गई है = बनाई गई है। हरइ = हरण करती है = चोराती है। पुच्छारि = पिच्छालि = मयूर का मादा = पिचार। काढि = काढ कर = निकाल कर। परेवा = पारावत = कबूतर। भाउ = भाव। चाक = चक्र (कोहार का)। साँच = साँचा, जिस से ढार ढार कर चाहे जितने गले बना डालो। बाग = घोडे के लगाम की डोर। तुरंग = तुरङ्ग = घोडा। मजूर = मयूर = मोर पक्षी। तम चूर = ताम्र-चूड = मुर्गा। तिरि = त्रि = तीन। घूँट = घोंटती है = लीलती है = पीती है। पीक = पान का लाल रस। लीक = लिकारी = रेखा। धनि = धन्य। बिधि = विधि = ब्रह्मा, वा विधान। मेराऊ = मिलाव = मिलाप ॥ सिरी-मुकुताओली = श्री-मुक्तावली = लक्ष्मी की मुक्ता-माला। अभरन = आभरण = गहना ॥

ग्रीवा का वर्णन करता हूँ, जो कि वन (कुञ्ज) के ऋश्या (के सदृश) है। ऋश्य हरिण-विशेष की ग्रीवा सुन्दर सु-ढार गोल होती है, इसी लिये कवि ने इस की उपमा दिया है। इस ग्रीवा-वर्णन में जो जो कवि ने उपमा दिया है, वे प्रायः प्राचीन ग्रन्थों में नहीं पाये जाते, इस से जान पडता है, कि वे सब कवि की स्वयं कल्पना है। (अथवा जान पडता है, कि गला नहीं है, किन्तु) सोने के तार में सीसी लगी है। (गले की नसें सोने की तार सी, और उस में लगा ऊआ गला काँच के सीसी

सदृश जान पडता है, जिस मैं से उन नख-रूपी तारेाँ की झलक देख पडती है)॥ जानेाँ कुंदे को फेर कर, अर्थात् खराद से सुडौल गोल कर, (उस मेँ ब्रह्मा ने उस गले को) काढा है, अर्थात् खोदा है। (अथवा गले की ऐसी शोभा है), जानेाँ खडी ऊई ठगिन पिचार को हरण करती है, अर्थात् गले की शोभा पिचार के गले की शोभा को चोरा लेती है॥ (अथवा गले की ऐसी शोभा है), जानेाँ (देखने-वाले का) हृदय काढ (निकाल) कर, कबूतर खडा हो। (अथवा) तिस से भी अधिक भाव ग्रीवा मेँ बढा ऊआ है, अर्थात् कबूतर के गले से भी बढ कर वह ग्रीवा है॥ (अथवा ब्रह्मा कुलाल ने) चाक पर चढा कर, जानेाँ (पद्मावती के गले को) साँचा बनाया (कीन्ह) है, अर्थात् जगत् मेँ इतर प्राणियेाँ के ग्रीवाओँ का साँचा पद्मावती की ग्रीवा है; इसी से और लोगेाँ की ग्रीवा उत्पन्न ऊई है। (अथवा) जानेाँ (किसी ने) घोडे की बाग पकड ली हो, (जिस से वह घोडा लाचार हो, गर्दन उठाये अचल ज्योँ का त्योँ खडा है), अर्थात् गर्दन उठाये ऊए घोडे की ग्रीवा के ऐसी पद्मावती की ग्रीवा है॥ मयूर और मुर्गा जो (पद्मावती की) ग्रीवा से हार गये हैँ, (इसी लिये) सन्ध्या और प्रातःकाल मेँ उसी (हार) को पुकारा करते हैँ, अर्थात् पद्मावती की ग्रीवा-शोभा से अपनी ग्रीवा-शोभा के घट जाने से जो इन दोनेाँ की हार हो गई, इसी से व्याकुल हो सन्ध्या और प्रातःकाल मेँ, मयूर 'मुरुउँ मुरुउँ' और मुर्गा 'क्या कहूँ क्या', चिल्लाया करते हैँ। यह कवि की उत्प्रेक्षा है॥ फिर तिसी स्थान मेँ, अर्थात् तिस गले मेँ तीन रेखा पडी ऊई हैँ (उस स्वच्छ काँच की सीसी-सदृश गले के भीतर पद्मावती) जो (पान की) पीक घेाँटती है, उस की सब लीक (उन तीनेाँ रेखा-दार से) देख पडती है, (जिस से और भी ग्रीवा की शोभा चढ बढ गई है)॥ ब्रह्मा ने उस की ग्रीवा मेँ धन्य भाव, अर्थात् विलक्षण शोभा दिया है, (सो) देखेँ (पद्मावती के गले को ले कर) किस से मिलाव करता है, अर्थात् देखेँ कौन ऐसा सर्वोत्तम भाग्यशाली है, जिस के गले मेँ ब्रह्मा पद्मावती के गले को मिलाता है॥

कण्ठ मेँ श्री-मुक्तावली माला और और ग्रीवा के आभरण, कंठी, कंठा, टीक इत्यादि सोहते हैँ। (सो देखेँ) कौन हार हो कर, (उस के) कण्ठ मेँ लगता है, कौन जीव से तप को साधा है, अर्थात् किस की ऐसी उग्र तपस्या है, जो कि पद्मावती के गले का हार हो कर, उस के गले मेँ लगे॥ ११२॥

चउपाई ।

कनक-डंड दुइ भुजा कलाई । जानउँ फेरि कुँदेरइ भाई ॥
कदलि-खंभ कइ जानउँ जोरी । अउ राती ओहि कवँल-हथोरी ॥
जानउँ रकत हथोरी बूडी । रबि परभात तात वेइ जूडी ॥
हिआ काढि जनु लीन्हेसि हाथा । रुहिर भरी अँगुरी तेहि साथा ॥
अउ पहिरे नग-जरी अँगूठी । जग बिनु जीउ जीउ ओहि मूठी ॥
बाँह्ह कंगन टाड सलोनी । डोलत बाँह भाउ गति लोनी ॥
जानउँ—गति बेडिन देखराई । बाँह डोलाइ जीउ लेइ जाई ॥

दोहा ।

भुज उपमा पउ-नारि न (पूजइ) खीन भई तेहि चित्त ।
ठाउँहि ठाउँ बेध भइ (हिरदइ) ऊभि साँस लेइ नित्त ॥ ११४ ॥

कनक-डंड = कनक-दण्ड = सुवर्ण का दण्ड (यष्टि)। भुजा = भुज = हाथ। कलाई = केहुनी से मिला नीचे का भुज-भाग। कुँदेरइ = कुँदेरे से (लकडी के सुडौल रंग विरंग के कुंदे से जो तरह तरह के लट्टू, चकई, फिरहरी, भौंरे, सिंधोरे इत्यादि खेलौने खराद खराद कर, बनाते हैँ, उन्हेँ इस प्रान्त मेँ कुँदेरा कहते हैँ, यह प्रसिद्ध शब्द है)। कदलि-खंभ = कदली-स्तम्भ = केले का खंभा। जोरी = जोडी = युग्म = युगल। राती = रक्त वर्ण की = लाल। कवँल-हथोरी = कमल-हस्ततल = कमल के ऐसी हथेली। रकत = रक्त = लोहू। बूडी = बूड गई है = डूब गई है। रबि = रवि = सूर्य। परभात = प्रभात = प्रातःकाल। तात = तप्त = गर्म। जूडी = जड हैँ = ठंढी हैँ। रुहिर = रुधिर = लोहू। अँगुरी = अङ्गुल्यः = अँगुलियाँ। साथा = सार्थ = सहित। पहिरे = पहने हैँ = परिधान किये हैँ। नग-जरी = नग-जटित = नग से जडी हुई। अँगूठी = अङ्गुलीयक = मुदरी। मूठी = मुष्टि। कंगन = कङ्कण = कडा। टाड = टडिया = बाँह का एक आभूषण, जो बाजू के ऊपर स्त्रियाँ पहनती हैँ। यह पश्चिम अयोध्या, परतापगढ, सुलतापुर इत्यादि जिले मेँ बहुत प्रसिद्ध है, पहले ताडङ्क के ऐसा ताल-पत्र का बनता था, इसी से (ताल = ताड) यह नाम पडा। इस की आकृति अनन्त के ऐसी होती है। स-लोनी = स-लवण = नमकीन = रुचि-दार। गति = गमन = चाल = इधर उधर बाहु का

फेरना = गत। बेडिन = पहाड में रहने-वाले बेडे जाति की स्त्री, जो नाचने में बज्जत-ही प्रसिद्ध हैं। विन्ध्याचल में चैच के नवराच में ये सब पहाड से उतर बज्जत-ही तमाशा दिखाती हैं। आँखों से डोरे को पकड कर सुई के छेद में डाल देती हैं। अपने गुह्याङ्ग से जमीन में पडे पैसे रुपये को विना हाथ लगाये उठा कर लोगों को देखा देती हैं। इस प्रकार लोगों को अनेक हाव भाव से लोभा कर बज्जत कुछ कमा लेती हैं। मिर्जापुर के प्रान्त में ये बज्जत-ही प्रसिद्ध हैं। अङ्गरेजी राज्य के प्रभाव से अब इन में भी बज्जत कुछ सभ्यता आ गई है, इस लिये दिनों दिन अब अपने दुराचारों को कम करती जाती हैं। पउ-नारि = पयो-नाली = जल में कमल की नाली = मृणाली = कमल की डंडी। ऊभि = उद्विग्न हो कर = घबडा कर। साँस = श्वास। नित्त = नित्य = प्रत्यह = नित॥

दोनों भुजा और कलाई सुवर्ण-दण्ड हैं, अर्थात् सोने के डंडे ऐसी दोनों जान पडती हैं। यहाँ भुजा से केहुनी और कंधे के बीच का भाग, जिसे बाँह कहते हैं लेना चाहिए। (वे बाँह और कलाई मिल कर ऐसी) भाती (भाई) हैं, अर्थात् सोहती हैं, जानों कुँदेरे से (सुडौल करने के लिये खराद पर) फेरी हैं॥ (उन दोनों बाँह कलाइयों की ऐसी शोभा है) जानों केले के खंभे की जोडी हैं। (कंधे से केहुनी तक गोल सुढार एक खंभा और केहुनी से मणि-बन्ध तक दूसरा खंभा समझो), और उस कलाई में लाल कमल के ऐसी हथेली हैं, अर्थात् आश्चर्य शोभा है, कि केले के खंभे में लाल कमल फूला है॥ (वह लाल हथेली ऐसी जान पडती हैं), जानों लोह में डूबी हों, अर्थात् रक्त से भरी हैं, और उस में ऐसी गहरी लाली है, जानों जान पडता है, कि उस में से अभीं लोह के बूंद टपके चाहते हैं। (उस लाल हथेली की उपमा यदि प्रातःकाल के सूर्य से दें, तो अनुचित है, क्योंकि) प्रातःकाल का सूर्य तो (अग्नि-पुञ्ज होने से) तप्त रहता है, और यह तो जूडी (ठण्ढी) है, (तो शीतल की उपमा तप्त से कैसे हो सकती है)। [कवि का अभिप्राय है, कि रवि के कर तो मनुष्य के अङ्ग में लग कर ताप को बढाते हैं, और इस हथेली के कर मनुष्य के विरहाग्नि-ताप को बुझा कर, शीतल कर देते हैं, इस लिये यद्यपि प्रभात के रवि में हथेली सी लालिमा है, तथापि रवि में विपरीत धर्म होने से हथेली की उपमा रवि से नहीं दी जा सकती। उदय काल का रवि क्षितिज में रहने के कारण मनुष्य की दृष्टि से दूर रहता है, और उस के सब किरणों का तेज दृष्टि में न

लगने से और भू पर न आने से, वह बडा और विना किरण का लाल, कुलाल के चक्र ऐसा देख पडता है, इसी लिये श्री-पति ने अपने सिद्धान्त-शेखर में लिखा है, कि

वसुन्धरागोलनिरुद्धधामा दूरस्थितोऽयं सुखदृश्यबिम्बः ।
महीजवृत्तोपगतो विवस्वानतो महान् भात्यरुणो विरश्मिः ॥
(श्री-पति के लिये गणकतरङ्गिणी देखो)]

(जान पडता है, कि पद्मावती ने नयन-कटाक्ष से दर्शकों को मार कर उन के) हृदय को जानों हाथ से निकाल लिया है, (इसी से) तिस हथेली के साथ अँगुलियाँ रुधिर से भरी हैं, अर्थात् हृदय काढने की बेला कलेजे में घुस जाने के कारण अँगुलियों में रुधिर भर गये हैं। इस से कवि ने यह देखलाया, कि अँगुलियों की लाली सब से बढ कर है॥ और (उन अँगुलियों में पद्मावती अमूल्य) नग से जडी अँगुठी को पहने है। जगत् विना जीव का हो गया है, और जीव उसी मूठी में है, अर्थात् पद्मावती की अनूठी अँगूठी-सहित बँधी मूठी को देख कर, जगत् के प्राणी-मात्र का जीव उस मूठी-ही में खिँच कर चला जाता है, इस लिये मूठी में जीव के आ जाने से लोग विना जीव के हो जाते हैं। (यदि प्रकृति-रूपा पद्मावती की माया, मोहने-वाली अँगूठी हो, तो उस माया को ले कर मूठी बाँध लेने से, अर्थात् समग्र माया को बटोर लेने से, साङ्ख्य-मत से प्राकृतिक-लय हो जाता है, इस लिये जगत् विना जीव के और जीव के प्रकृति के अन्तः-प्रविष्ट हो जाने से, कवि का कथन प्रकृति-पक्ष में भी यथार्थ हो गया)॥ बाहु (भुज) में सुन्दर कङ्कण और टडिया हैं, जिन की लोनी गति, अर्थात् सुन्दर इधर से उधर घूमना, बाहु के (स्वाभाविक) डोलने में भाती है (भाउ), अर्थात् सोहती है॥ (पद्मावती के स्वाभाविक बाहु डोलाने में ऐसी शोभा जान पडती है, कि) जानों (नृत्य-चातुरी से भरी) बेडिन ने गति देखाई है। (अनेक प्रकार से रङ्ग-शाला में पद-विन्यास-पूर्वक ताल लिये घूघुरू का बजाना, ऊर्ध्वाधर-तिर्यक् भुजों का प्रक्षेपण करना, और विचित्र-रूप से चारो ओर घूम कर, केवल अङ्ग-भङ्गी से अनेक भावों का प्रगट करना गति है। इसी प्रकार बजनिये हस्त-चातुरी से बाजे में भी ताल लिये मनोहर सुरों के सहित अनेक गति बजाते हैं)। (इस प्रकार बेडिनों के ऐसा वह पद्मावती अपने) बाहु को डोला कर (सब का) जीव ले जाती है, अर्थात् उस गति-लीला को देख कर देखने-वाले विना जीव के ऐसे मूर्छित हो जाते हैं॥

भुज की उपमा में मृणाली नहीं पूरी पडती है, (इसी लिये अपने को अयोग्य समझ) तिसी (अयोग्यता के) चित्त से क्षीण हो गई। और स्थान स्थान पर विद्ध हो गई (कण्टकों से), और नित्य ऊब कर (अपने को अयोग्य समझ अयोग्य जल में निमग्न होने से व्याकुल हो, ठंढी) साँस लिया करती है। कमल का मृणाल बडा क्षीण, अर्थात् पतरा होता है, और उस में स्थान स्थान पर काँटे चुभे रहते हैं, और उस का यह धर्म है, कि चाहे जल कितना-ही बढे, परन्तु उस का अग्र, जल से बाहर-ही रहता है। इस पर कवि की उत्प्रेक्षा है, कि भुज के उपमा-योग्य न होने-ही से उस की यह दशा हुई है। भुज की उपमा मृणाल से देना यह प्राचीन रीति है। श्री-हर्ष ने भी नैषध में लिखा है, कि—

'बाहू प्रियाया जयतां मृणालं द्वन्द्वे जयो नाम न विस्मयोऽस्मिन्।
उच्चैस्तु तच्चित्रममुष्य भग्नस्यालोक्यते निर्व्ययनं यदन्तः॥
अजीयताऽऽवर्त्तशुभंयुनाभ्या दोर्भ्यां मृणालं किमु कोमलाभ्याम्।
निःसूत्रमास्ते घनपङ्कमृत्सु मूर्त्तासु नाकीर्त्तिषु तन्निमग्नम्॥'

(७ स०। श्लो० ६८-६९)

'किं नर्मदाया मम सेयमस्या दृश्याऽभितो बाहुलता मृणाली।
कुचौ किमुत्तस्थतुरन्तरीपे स्मरोष्मशुष्यत्तरवाल्यवारः॥'

(७ स०। श्लो० ७३)॥ ११४॥

चउपाई।

हिआ थार कुच कंचन लाडू। कनिक कचउरि उठइ कइ चाडू॥
कुंदन बेल साजि जनु कूँदे। अंब्रित भरे रतन दुइ मूँदे॥
बेधे भवँर कंट केतकी। चाहहिँ बेध कीन्ह कंचकी॥
जोबन बान लेहिँ नहिँ बागा। चाहहिँ हुलसि हिअइ महँ लागा॥
अगिन-बान दुइ जानउँ साधे। जग बेधहिँ जउँ होहिँ न बाँधे॥
उतँग जँभीर होइ रखवारी। छुइ को सकइ राजा कइ बारी॥
दारिउँ दाख फरे अन-चाखे। अस नारँग दहुँ का कहँ राखे॥

दोहा ।

राजा बहुत मुए तपि , लाइ लाइ भुइँ माँथ ।
काहु छुअइ न पाएउ गए मरोरत हाथ ॥ ११५ ॥

हिआ = हृदय = छाती । थार = थाली । लाडू = लड्डू = मोदक । कनिक = कनी = कणी, जिस में कण हो, रवे रवे, स्वच्छ गेहूँ का आँटा जिस से पूरी कचौरी इत्यादि पक्वान्न बनते हैं । कचउरि = कचौरी, एक प्रकार का घृत-पक्व । उठइ = उठती है = फूलती है = खिलती है । चाडू = चण्ड = वेग = बल । कुंदन = सब से बढियाँ सुवर्ण । बेल = बिल्व-फल । साजि = सज कर = भूषित कर । कूँदे = कुंदन किये गये हैं । रतन = रत्न । मूँदें = मुद्रित किये गये हैं = बंद किये गये हैं । कंट = कण्टक = काँटा । केतकी = पुष्पविशेष, जो सर्वत्र प्रसिद्ध है । कंचकी = कञ्चुकी = चोलिआ । जोबन = यौवन, यहाँ कुच । ऊलसि = उल्लसित हो कर = ऊँचे हो कर । उतँग = उत्तुङ्ग = अति-ऊँचे । जँभीर = जम्बीर = एक प्रकार का निम्बू । बारी = कन्या (बालिका), वा बगीचा (वाटिका) । दारिउँ = दाडिम । दाख = द्राक्षा = अङ्गूर । अन-चाखे = विना रक्खे = साफ = पवित्र । नारँग = नारङ्ग = नारङ्गी ॥ तपि = तप कर = तपस्या कर । मुए = मरे = मर गये ॥

हृदय थार में कुच कञ्चन का लड्डू है । (अथवा कुचों की शोभा ऐसी है, जानों) बल कर के कनिक की कचौरी उठती है, अर्थात् फूल रही है । (चक्राकार उठते ऊए स्तन, कराही में फूलती ऊई बदामी रंग की कनिक-कचौरी से जान पडते हैं)॥ (अथवा स्तनों की ऐसी शोभा है), जानों (दो) बिल्व-फल, बढियाँ सुवर्ण से भूषित कर, कूँदे गये हैं, अर्थात् सुवर्ण-भूषित-बिल्वों के ऊपर कुंदन करने से जैसी चमकीली कान्ति होती है, उसी प्रकार के गोल गोल बिल्व-फल-सदृश चमकीले कुच हैं । (अथवा कुच नहीं हैं, जानों) दो रत्न (के कलस) अमृत से भरे मूँदे ऊए हैं, (जिस में दह अमृत-रस बाहर गिर कर नष्ट न हो जाय) । (यहाँ स्तन के नीचे का गोल भाग उठा ऊआ कलस है, और कुचाग्र उस कलस के मुख का ढकना है)॥ (वे काले कुचाग्र ऐसे जान पडते हैं, जानों) केतकी के कण्टक से भ्रमर विद्ध हो गये हैं, (इस लिये केतकी के पुष्प के ऊपर अटके ऊए हैं)। (नीचे के स्तन-भाग केतकी के पुष्प-सदृश, और उन पर काले कुचाग्र जिन्हें संस्कृत में चूचुक कहते हैं, कण्टक-विद्ध भ्रमर हैं)। केतकी का अग्र सूच्याकार होता है, इसी लिये श्री-हर्ष ने भी लिखा है, कि —

'त्वदग्रसूची-सचिवः स कामिनोर्मनोभवः सीव्यति दुर्यशःपटौ।
स्फुटं च पत्रैः करपत्त्रमूर्त्तिभिर्वियोगिहृद्दारुणि दारुणायते॥'

(१ स०। श्लो० ८०)

और युवावस्था के समय कुचाग्रों पर श्यामता आ जाती है, जो कि गर्भाधान होने पर विशेष कृष्णता प्राप्त करती है। यह प्रसिद्ध है; इसी पर कालिदास ने रघुवंश में कहा है, कि—

'दिनेषु गच्छत्सु नितान्तपीवरं तदीयमानीलमुखं स्तनद्वयम्।
तिरश्चकार भ्रमराभिलीनयोः सुजातयोः पङ्कजकोशयोः श्रियम्॥'

(३ स०। श्लो० ८)

(वे ऐसे नोखीले कुचाग्र हैं, कि) चोलिया में बेध, अर्थात् छेद किया चाहते हैं॥ वे कुच (योवन) बाण हैं, (जो) बाग नहीं लेते हैं, अर्थात् मोरने से भी नहीं मुरते हैं। (किन्तु) हुलस कर (देखने-वालों के) हृदय में लगा चाहते हैं, (लाचार हैं, कि छाती में बँधे हुए हैं)॥ (वे कुच) जानों दो अग्नि-बाण, अर्थात् तोप के गोले साधे हुए हैं। (इस लिये) यदि (छाती में) बाँधे न होते, तो जगत् को बेधते, अर्थात् बेध डालते॥ (वे कुच जानों) ऊँचे (सरस) जम्बीर (निम्बू) हैं, (जिन की चोलिया इत्यादि वस्तु से और सखियों से) रखवारी होती है, (इस लिये) कौन (उन) राजा के वारी (कन्या वा वाटिका) के निम्बुओं को छू सकता है, अर्थात् किसी की सामर्थ्य नहीं, कि उन निम्बुओं को छूवे, क्योंकि जिस राजा का गढ सहस्र सहस्र पदातियों से और पाँच कोतवालों से सुरक्षित है, (४१ वाँ दोहा देखो) उस गढ तक पहुँचना-ही अत्यन्त कठिन है, फिर विना तपो-बल के उस के भीतर बारी में, और बारी के भीतर सुरक्षित निम्बू तक पहुँचने की चर्चा-ही करना व्यर्थ है। गढ को शरीर, उस के भीतर के स्थल को जहाँ षट् कमल [योग-ग्रन्थ में गुद-मूल से शिरो-भाग तक शरीर के मध्य आधार (=गुदस्थान), अधिष्ठान (=मूत्रेन्द्रिय का निकट भाग), नाभि, हृदय, कण्ठ, भ्रूमध्य और ब्रह्म-रन्ध्र (ब्रह्माण्ड) में एक एक चक्राकार कमल मानते हैं।

'चतुर्दलं स्यादाधारे स्वाधिष्ठाने च षट्दलम्।
नाभौ दशदल पद्मं सूर्यसंख्यादलं हृदि॥

कण्ठे स्यात् षोडशदलं भ्रूमध्ये द्विदलं तथा ।
सहस्रदलमाख्यातं ब्रह्मरन्ध्रे महापथे ॥'

(गोरक्ष-शतक । श्लो० १५-१६)]

हैं वाटिका, मन को राजा और आत्मा को निम्बू मानने से योग-पक्ष में भी लगा सकते हो ॥ (वे कुच नहीं हैं, जानों उस बारी में) विना चक्खे, अर्थात् पवित्र, ज्यों के त्यों दाडिम और द्राक्षा हैं। (अथवा कुच नहीं हैं, जानों उस बारी में सुन्दर नारंगी हैं, सो) देखें किस के लिये ऐसी नारंगियाँ रक्खी झई हैं। (नारङ्ग पुलिङ्ग है, इस लिये कवि ने 'राखे' का प्रयोग किया है)॥

हे राजा, बझत लोग, (वा राजा को सम्बोधन न मानो, तो) बझत राजा लोग तपस्या कर भूमि में माथे को लगा लगा कर, अर्थात् रगड रगड कर, मर गये, (और बझत से) हाथ मरोरते (निराश हो कर) चले गये, (परन्तु) कोई (उन जम्बीर के ऐसे ऊँचे, दाडिम-द्राक्षा के ऐसे रस-भरे, और नारंगी के ऐसे रँग-दार कुचों को) छूने न पाया ॥ ११५ ॥

चउपाई ।

पेट पतर जनु चंदन लावा । कुंकुँह केसर बरन सोहावा ॥
खीर अहार न कर सु-कुवाँरा । पान फूल लेइ रहइ अधारा ॥
सावँ-भुअंगिनि रोवाँवली । नाभी निकसि कवँल कहँ चली ॥
आइ दुहूँ नारँग बिच भई । देखि मजूर ठमकि रहि गई ॥
जनउँ चढी भवँरन्ह कइ पाँती । चंदन-खाँभ बास गइ माती ॥
कइ कालिंदरि बिरह सताई । चलि पयाग अरइल बिच आई ॥
नाभी कुंडर बानारसी । सउँह को होइ मीचु तेहि बसी ॥

दोहा ।

सिर करवत तन करसी (लेइ लेइ) बहुत सीझ तेइ आस ।
बहुत धूवँ घुँटि मुए देखे उतर न देइ निरास ॥ ११६ ॥

पतर = पत्र वा पतला = कृश । लावा = लगाया है । कुंकुँह = कुङ्कुम = रोरी बरन = वर्ण । खीर = क्षीर = दुग्ध । अहार = आहार = भोजन । सु-कुवाँरा = सु-कुमार

कोमल = मृदु। पान = पर्ण, ताम्बूल का। अधारा = आधार = अवलम्बन। सावँ-भुअंगिनि = श्याम-भुजङ्गिनी = काली नागिनि। रोवाँवली = रोमावली = रोम-पङ्क्ति। निकसि = निःकसित हो कर = निकल कर। मजूर = मयूर = मोर पची। पाँती = पङ्क्ति। चंदन-खाँभ = चन्दन-स्तम्भ = चन्दन का खंभा। बास = वास = सु-गन्ध। माती = मत्ता = मात। कालिंदरि = कालिन्दी = कलिन्द की कन्या = यमुना नदी। सताई = सन्तप्त ऊई = दुःखित ऊई। पयाग = प्रयाग = तीर्थ-राज, जो अलाहाबाद में प्रसिद्ध है। अरदल = एक स्थान का नाम, जहाँ पर यमुना गङ्गा से मिली है। उस प्रान्त को प्रयाग में अभीँ तक अरदल वा अरिल कहते हैँ। अरदल = अडदल = अड जाने-वाला, वा अड जाने-वाली। जैसे यह 'घोडा अडदल है'। वहाँ पर यमुना अड गई है, इसी से जान पडता है, कि उस स्थान का नाम, अरदल पड गया है। कुंडर = कुण्ड। बानारसी = बनारस का = काशी का। बानारसी कुण्ड = काशी करवट का कूआँ। [यह कुआँ ज्ञान-वापी के पूर्व-उत्तर की ओर पास-ही मेँ है। आगे लोग इसी स्थान मेँ 'काशी-मरणान्मुक्तिः', इस विश्वास से आत्म-हत्या करते थे। यह ऐसे गुप्त-स्थान मेँ है, कि अब भी बक्रत से पण्डे यात्रियोँ को वहाँ ले जा कर सब कुछ हरण कर लेते थे। (यात्रियोँ को पूजा के बहाने दण्डवत कराते थे, जब यात्री दण्डवत् करता था, तब कई मन के पत्थर के नादिया को, जो वहाँ अब तक मौजूद है, उस के ऊपर रख देते थे। यात्री बेचारा प्राण के भय से सब कुछ दे देता था)। मैँ जब दर्भङ्गा राजा की पाठशाला मेँ अध्यापक था, तब प्रायः उसी राह से आने जाने मेँ, यात्रियोँ के मुख से यह कु-रीति की कथा सुन, उस के निवारणार्थ बडा आन्दोलन मचाया। तब से सर्कार की ओर से अब वहाँ पर सिपाहियोँ का पहरा रहता है, और उस स्थान की चाभी थाने मेँ रहती है। और वह स्थान भी प्रति सोमवार को सन्ध्या समय पूजा के लिये खोला जाता है, फिर बंद कर दिया जाता है।] सउँह = संमुख। मीचु = मृत्यु। सिर = सिरा = अग्र-भाग। करवत = कर-पत्र = आरा। तन = तनु = शरीर। करसी = कर्षित की = खिँचवाई। सीझ = सीझ गये = पक गये। आस = आशा = उम्मेद। धूवँ = धूम = धूआँ। घूँटि = घोँट कर = पी कर। उतर = उत्तर = जवाब। निरास = निराशा = ना-उम्मेद ॥

(पद्मावती का) पेट जानोँ पत्र पर चन्दन लगा ऊआ है, अर्थात् सु-गन्धित पेट ऐसा पतला है, जानोँ पतले कागज (पतर = पत्र) पर चन्दन लगाया ऊआ है, जिस से

सुगन्ध का अनुभव तो अवश्य होता है, परन्तु यह नहीँ समझ पडता, कि पेट है, कि नहीँ है। स्त्रियोँ का कृश-उदर होना प्रशंसा में है, इसी लिये सुन्दरी युवती को कृशोदरी कहते हैँ। श्री-हर्ष ने भी नैषध में लिखा है, कि—

सरसीः परिशीलितुं मया गमिकर्मीकृतनैकनीवृता।
अतिथित्वमनायि सा दृशोः सदसत्संशयगोचरोदरी ॥
(२ स०। श्लो० ४०)

कुंकुम और केसर वर्ण का (वह पेट) शोभित है। यदि 'वर न' ऐसा दो पद मानो तो (उस पेट के आगे) वर (श्रेष्ठ) कुंकुम और केसर भी नहीँ शोभित हैँ, अर्थात् सु-गन्धित और सु-वर्ण उदर की शोभा से कुंकुम और केसर भी मन्द पड गये हैँ, यह अर्थान्तर हो सकता है॥ (वह पेट ऐसा) सु-कुँआर है, कि खीर का भी आहार नहीँ करता है, अर्थात् दूध भी नहीँ उस के भीतर पच सकता है। (केवल) पान-फूल ले कर (पा कर), अर्थात् मुख-द्वारा पान का रस, नासिका-द्वारा पुष्प का रस पा कर, (उसी रस के) आधार से रहता है, (दूसरी वस्तु के पचानें की सामर्थ्य-ही नहीँ है)॥ (उस पेट के बीचो बीच नाभी से ले कर कुचोँ के बीच तक जो लंबी) रोमावली है, वह (जानोँ) काली नागिन है, जो कि नाभी-(रूपी बिल) से निकल कर, कमल (कमल-रूपी पद्मावती के मुख) के यहाँ चली है॥ आ कर (वह नागिन) दोनोँ नारंगियोँ के, अर्थात् नारंगी के ऐसे दोनोँ कुचोँ के, बीच मैँ ऊई, अर्थात् कुचोँ के बीच तक पऊँची। (परन्तु आगे) मयूर को, अर्थात् मयूर-रूपी गले को देख कर, (आगे भय से न जा सकी, वहीँ पर) ठमक कर, अर्थात् रुक कर, रह गई। संस्कृत मेँ भी किसी कवि ने इस प्रकार का रूपक बाँधा है—

'वदनकञ्जमगादिलनाभितस्तनुरुहावलिरूपसुसर्पिणी ।
अथ रुमीच्य मयूरशिरोधरां स्थितवती भयतस्तनयोस्तटे'॥

किसी कवि ने ऐसा भी रूपक बाँधा है—

'नाभीविलान्तरविनिर्गतपन्नगीयं संप्रस्थिता नयनखञ्जनभक्षणाय ।
नासामुदीक्ष्य गरुडभ्रमसुद्दहन्ती शृङ्गेव पीनकुचपर्वतयोरधस्तात् ॥'

नैषध-कार ने काम-देव-हस्ती के बन्धन-रज्जु से इस रोमावली की उपमा दी है। नाभी को उस खूँटे का स्थान, जिस मेँ कि वह मत्त-हस्ती उस रज्जु-द्वारा बँधा था, और कुचोँ को उस हस्ती के सूतने का स्थान बनाया है, उस की कविता यह है—

'उन्मूलितालानविलाभनाभिच्छिन्नस्खलच्छृङ्खलरोमदामा।
मत्तस्य सेयं मदनद्विपस्य प्रस्वापवप्रोच्चकुचाऽस्तु वास्तु॥'
(७ स०। श्लो० ८४)

(उस रोमावली की ऐसी शोभा है), जानेाँ (बास लेने के लिये उस पेट के ऊपर) भैारेाँ की पङ्क्ति चढी है, जो कि चन्दन-स्तम्भ के, अर्थात् चन्दन-स्तम्भ-सदृश उस उदर के बास से मात गई है, अर्थात् मत्त हो गई है, (जिस से बे-सुधि हो कर, जहाँ की तहाँ पडी ऊई है)॥ अथवा (=कइ) (जान पडता है, कि वह रोमावली) यमुना नदी (की काली धारा) है, जो (यमुना, कृष्ण के) विरह से सन्तप्त ऊई है, (इस लिये दूसरे जन्म में कृष्ण का विरह न हो, इस मनोरथ से) चल कर प्रयाग के, अर्थात् पद्मावती के शिरोभागस्थ वेणी के (पास), अरदूल-नामक स्थान के (पद्मावती के कुच-स्थान के) बीच में आई है॥ (उस पेट पर) नाभी, बनारस का कुण्ड है, अर्थात् काशी-करवट का कूप है, (जहाँ मुक्ति पाने की इच्छा से 'काशी-मरणान्मुक्तिः' इस महा-वाक्य के विश्वास से, लोग, आगे अपना प्राण दे देते थे)। सो उस के सामने कौन हो, (क्योंकि संमुख होने से) तिस के पास मृत्यु बस जाती है, अर्थात् तिस के यहाँ मृत्यु का डेरा पड जाता है, जिस से बचना कठिन है॥

बऊत से लोग (प्रयाग में उस कुण्ड-दर्शन के मनोरथ से) आरे के शिरे पर तनु को खिँचवा डाले। बऊत से लोग तिसी कुण्ड-दर्शन की आशा से (अनेक तपस्या से) सीझ गये, और ऐसे भी बऊत से देखे गये, जो (उसी आशा से) धूम्र-पान कर मर गये, (परन्तु किसी को कुछ) उत्तर न दिया, अर्थात् जवाब न मिला, (सब) निराश हो गये।

'वटमूलं समासाद्य यस्तु प्राणान् परित्यजेत्।
सर्वान् लोकानतिक्रम्य रुद्रलोकं स गच्छति॥'
(मत्स्यपुराणान्तर्गत प्रयागमाहात्म्य, अध्या० ४। श्लो० १२)

(प्रसिद्ध कथा है, कि एक मुकुन्द-ब्रह्मचारी, बादशाह होने की इच्छा से, अपनी शरीर को आरे पर चिरवा डाला। वही दूसरे जन्म अकबर बादशाह ऊआ।)

कवि का अभिप्राय है, कि उस कुण्ड-दर्शन-मनोरथ से अनेक लोग अनेक प्रकार की तपस्या में प्रवृत्त ऊए, परन्तु आज तक ऐसी उग्र तपस्या किसी की न ऊई, जिसे ईश्वर की ओर से उत्तर दिया जाय, कि अब तुम उस नाभी के दर्शन योग्य ऊए। इस लिये आज तक किसी की आशा पूरी न ऊई। सब निराश ही हैँ। कवि भी

उस नाभी-कुण्ड के वर्णन में अभीँ अपने को अयोग्य समझ, वहाँ से हट कर, बुद्धि को तीक्ष्ण करने के लिये, पीठ और कटि की ओर चला गया, कि इन दोनोँ के वर्णन से बुद्धि को और वर्णन की परिपाटी अभ्यास हो जायगी, तब अधिक वर्णन-सामर्थ्य होने पर, फिर इस कुण्ड के वर्णन में बुद्धि को लगावेँगे ॥ ११६ ॥

चउपाई ।

बइरिनि पीठि लीन्ह वेइ पाछे। जनु फिरि चली अपछरा काछे ॥
मलयागिरि कइ पीठि सँवारे। बेनी नाग चढा जनु कारे ॥
लहरइ देत पीठि जनु चढा। चीर ओढावा केँचुलि मढा ॥
दहुँ का कहँ अस बेनी कीन्ही। चंदन बास भुअंगइ लीन्ही ॥
किरिसुन करा चढा ओहि माँथे। तब सो छूट अब छूट न नाथे ॥
कारे कवँल गहे मुख देखा। ससि पाछे जनु राहु बिसेखा ॥
को देखइ पावइ वह नागू। सो देखइ माँथहि मनि भागू ॥

दोहा ।

पंनग पंकज मुख गहे खंजन तहाँ बईठ ।
छात सिँघासन राज धन ता कहँ होइ जो डीठ ॥ ११७ ॥

बइरिनि = वैरिणी = वैरिन। पीठि = पृष्ठ = पीठ। पाछे = पश्चिमे = पश्चिमावयव में = पीछे। अपछरा = अप्सरा = इन्द्र के यहाँ की नर्त्तकी। काछे = काछ काछे हुई = अलङ्करादि से भूषित। मलयागिरि = मलयगिरि = मलयाचल। बेनी = वेणी = चोटी। कार = काला। लहरइ = लहर को। केँचुलि = कञ्चुक = केँचुर = केँचुरी। मढा = मण्डित किया = छादित किया। भुअंगइ = भुजङ्ग ने = सर्प ने। किरिसुन = कृष्ण = वसुदेव-देवकी के पुत्र। करा = कला = लीला, वा अवतार। नाथे = नाथने से। कारे = काला नाग। ससि = शशी। मनि = मणि। भागू = भाग्य ॥ पंनग = पन्नग = सर्प। पंकज = पङ्कज = कमल। खंजन = खञ्जन = पक्षि-विशेष। बईठ = बैठा है। छात = छत्र। सिँघासन = सिंहासन। राज = राज्य। डीठ = देखे ॥

वह (पद्मावती अपने) पीछे की ओर बैरिन पीठ को लिये है। जिस के दर्शन-मात्र से शरीर विना प्राण की हो जाय, वह जगत्-मात्र की वैरिणी-ही है, इसी हेतु

इस पीठ को जगत् की बैरिन समझ, कवि ने 'बैरिनि' का विशेषण दिया है। (उस पीठ की ऐसी शोभा है) जानों अलङ्कारादि से भूषित अप्सरा फिर कर चली हो (जिस से उस की पीठ-मात्र देख पडती है), अर्थात् अप्सरा की पीठ-सदृश पद्मावती की पीठ है। अथवा (उस पीठ की ऐसी शोभा है), जानों (उस पीठ की शोभा से लज्जित हो कर, भूमि से) फिर कर, अलङ्कारादि से भूषित अप्सरा (स्वर्ग को) चली गई है॥ (वह) पीठ मलय-गिरि से सँवारी ऊई है, अर्थात् पीठ नहीं है, जानों मलयाचल है। (और उस के ऊपर पडी ऊई) बेनी, जानों (उस मलयाचल पर) काला नाग चढा ऊआ है॥ (जानों वह नाग देखने-वालों को अपने विष से) लहर देता ऊआ, (उस) पीठ पर चढ गया है। (और उस के ऊपर पद्मावती का) ओढाया ऊआ चीर (वस्त्र) (ऐसा जान पडता है, कि वह नाग) केंचुर से मढा है॥ देखें किस के लिये ऐसी बेनी की गई है, अर्थात् बनाई गई है। (उस बेनी की ऐसी शोभा है, जानों) भुजङ्ग ने चन्दन के बास को लिया है॥ उस बेनी-रूपी नाग का मुख पद्मावती के शिर से अलग क्यों नहीं हो जाता है, इस पर कवि की उत्प्रेक्षा है, कि उस (नाग) के माथे पर कृष्ण (अपनी) कला से चढे हैं। सो तब कृष्णावतार के समय, तो (वह कालिय नाग अपनी पत्नी के कृष्ण-स्तुति-करने के कारण) छूट गया था, (परन्तु) अब नाथे विना नहीं छूटता, अर्थात् भगवान् कृष्ण इस को नाथने के लिये पकड रक्खे हैं, इसी कारण से यह पद्मावती के शिर में लगा ऊआ है। इस प्रकार वेणी-नाग का सदा पीठ और शिर के ऊपर अचलत्व स्थापन करना यह अतिशयोक्ति है। 'किरिसुन' को एक वचन होने से एक-वचन क्रिया का 'चढा' प्रयोग है। हम ने आदरार्थ टीके में बऊवचन का प्रयोग किया है॥ (उस वेणी-नाग की ऐसी शोभा है, जानों) काला नाग मुख में कमल को पकडे ऊए देखा जाता है, अर्थात् देख पडता है, (पद्मावती के शिर के ऊपर के केश मूलों का पुञ्ज वेणी-नाग का बाया ऊआ मुख, और उस में सटा ऊआ पद्मावती का मुख कमल है)। (अथवा पद्मावती के मुख-सहित वेणी-नाग की ऐसी शोभा है), जानों (किसी कारण) विशेष से शशि (चन्द्र) के पीछे राऊ है। (पद्मावती का मुख चन्द्र और बेनी नाग राऊ है)। बऊतों के मत से राऊ सर्पाकार है। वराह-मिहिर ने भी अपनी संहिता में लिखा है, कि—

'मुखपुच्छविभक्ताङ्गं भुजङ्गमाकारमुपदिशन्त्यन्ये।
कथयन्त्यमूर्त्तमपरे तमोमयं सैंहिकेयाख्यम्॥'

इस लिये कवि की उपमा पूर्णोपमा है ॥ (कवि कहता है, कि) कौन उस नाग (वेणी-नाग) को देखने पाता है, अर्थात् किसी की सामर्थ्य नहीँ, कि उस वेणी-नाग के दर्शन को पावे। (उस नाग को) वही (सो) देखता है, (जिस के) माथे में भाग्य की मणि हो, अर्थात् जिस के माथे मेँ भाग्य-मणि चमकती हो, सो उस नाग के दर्शन को पा सकता है, दूसरा नहीँ। अर्थात् नाग के दर्शन से संहिता-कारोँ ने अशुभ फल लिखा है, परन्तु इस नाग-दर्शन से ब्रह्मानन्द-प्राप्ति हैं, इस लिये जो बडा-ही भाग्यवान् हो, सो इस के दर्शन को पावे। वराह-मिहिर ने अपनी संहिता मेँ लिखा है, कि—

'जाहकाहिशशक्रोडगोधानां कीर्त्तनं शुभम्।
रुतं संदर्शनं नेष्टं प्रतीपं वानरर्क्षयोः ॥'
(अ० ८५। श्लो० ४२)

नाग (अपने) मुख में कमल को पकडे है, और तहाँ, अर्थात् उस कमल के ऊपर, खञ्जन (खिडरिच पक्षी) बैठा है। ऐसे खञ्जन को जो देखे तिसे छत्र, सिंहासन, राज्य और धन होता है, अर्थात् देखने-वाला छत्र, सिंहासन, राज्य और धन से समन्वित राजा हो जाता है। [वेणी नाग, पद्मावती का मुख कमल, और उस पर बैठा हुआ खञ्जन का एक जोड पद्मावती का नेत्र-युगल है। सर्प के शिर और कमल पर बैठे हुए खञ्जन के दर्शन से राज्य-प्राप्ति होती है, ऐसा ज्यौतिष के संहिता-कारोँ ने लिखा है। वराह-मिहिर ने भी अपनी संहिता में लिखा है, कि—

'अब्जेषु मूर्धसु च वाजिगजोरगाणां राज्यप्रदः कुशलकृच्छुचिशाद्वलेषु।
भस्मास्थिकाष्ठतुषकेशतृणेषु दुःखं दृष्टः करोति खलु खञ्जनकोऽब्दमेकम् ॥'
(अ० ८७। श्लो० २०)] ॥ ११७॥

चउपाई।

लंक पुहुमि अस आहि न काहू। केहरि कहउँ न ओहि सरि ता-हू ॥
बसा लंक बरनइ जग झीनी। तेहि तइँ अधिक लंक वह खीनी ॥
परिहँसि पिअर भए तेहि बसा। लिए डंक लोगन्हि कहँ डसा ॥
मानउँ नलिनि खंड दुइ भए। दुहुँ बिच लंक तार रहि गए ॥
हिअ सेा मोड चलइ वह तागा। पइग देत कित सहि सक लागा ॥

छुदर-घंट मोहहिँ नर राजा। इँदर-अखाड आइ जनु बाजा॥
मानउँ बीन गहे काविँनी। गाअहिँ सबद राग रागिनी॥

दोहा।

सिंघ न जीतइ लंक सरि हारि लीन्ह बन बास।
तेहि रिस रकत पिअइ मनुस खाइ मारि कइ माँस॥ ११८॥

लंक = लङ्क = कटि = कमर। पुहुमि = भूमि = पृथ्वी। आहि = आस्ते = है। काहु = किसी को। केहरि = केसरी = सिंह। ता-हु = तथा-हि = तौ-भी। बसा = बर्रै = वटर। झीनी = चीण = पतली। खीनी = चीण। परिहँसि = परिहास से। डंक = आर। डसा = दंशित करते हैँ = डस लेते हैँ। नलिनि = नलिनी = कमलिनी, यहाँ कमल का नाल। तार = तन्तु। तागा = सूत = तन्तु। पदग = प्रग = पेर। कित = कुतः = कस्मात् = क्योँ = कैसे। लागा = लगा हुआ = जुडा हुआ = बँधा हुआ। छुदर-घंट = चुद्र-घण्टिका = घुघुरू-दार करधनी। नर = मनुष्य, वा नर = नल राजा। इँदर = इन्द्र। अखाडा = अचालय = अचावाट = क्रीडागृह = खेल कूद का घर। बाजा = बजा है। बीन = वीणा। काविँनी = कामिनी = वेश्या। गाअहिँ = गावहिँ = गाती हैँ। राग = छ राग, जो कि सङ्गीत-शास्त्र मेँ प्रसिद्ध हैँ। रागिनी = रागिणी, छत्तीस हैँ। ये भी सङ्गीत-शास्त्र मेँ प्रसिद्ध हैँ॥ सिंघ = सिंह। सरि = सादृश्य = साम्य मेँ। हारि = हार कर। रिस = रोष = क्रोध। रकत = रक्त = लोहू। मनुस = मनुष्य = आदमी। खाइ = खाता है। माँस = मांस।

पृथ्वी मेँ (पद्मावती के कटि) ऐसी किसी की कटि नहीँ है, अर्थात् वह कटि अनुपम है। (यदि उस कटि के सदृश) सिंह (केहरि) को कहूँ, तथापि (वास्तव मेँ विचार करने से सिंह की कटि) उस कटि के सदृश नहीँ है, (क्योँकि सिंह की कटि तो बडे बडे रोआँ से भरी भयङ्कर देख पडती है, और यह निर्लोम सूक्ष्म चुद्र-घण्टिका-सहित कटि बडे भाग्य से देख पडती है)। जगत् मेँ (लोग) बर्रै की कटि को (बहुत) पतली (झीनी) वर्णन करते हैँ, (परन्तु) तिस से भी अधिक पतली (चीण) (पद्मावती की) कटि (लंक) है॥ (जगत् मेँ लोगोँ ने यह कह कर, कि 'तुमारी वेसी पतली और मनोहर कटि नहीँ है जेसी, कि पद्मावती की है', बर्रै का परिहास किया, अर्थात् हँसी किया। सो तिसी परिहास (के ताप) से बर्रै पीली हो गई, (और खिसिआ कर) डंक लिये लोगोँ को डसने लगी। (यह कवि की उत्प्रेचा है)॥ (जान पडता है, कि) मानोँ कमल-नाल (नलिनी) के दो खण्ड हुए हैँ, और उन

दोनोँ (खण्डोँ) के बीच (वह) लङ्क (तन्तु) तार रह गया है, अर्थात् जो विना टूटा तन्तु उन दोनोँ खण्डोँ के बीच रह गया है, उसी के सदृश वह लङ्क है ॥ सो (वह पद्मावती) (जिस समय) हृदय को मोरती है, (मोड, अर्थात् स्वभावतः इधर उधर छाती को हिलाती है), (उस समय केवल छाती-ही के भार से) वह तागा (=तन्तु-रूपी लङ्क) चलने लगता है, अर्थात् हिलने लगता है। (सो चलने के समय पृथ्वी मेँ) पैर देते (वह दोनोँ खण्डोँ मेँ) लगा हुआ तागा (लङ्क-तार) कैसे (सर्वाङ्ग का भार) सह सकता है, (यह परम आश्चर्य है)॥ हे राजा (राजन्) (उस लङ्क की) क्षुद्र-घण्टिका (करधनी) (अपनी मधुर धुनि से) नरोँ को मोह लेती हैँ, वा नल को मोह लेती हैँ। उन की धुनि ऐसी सोहावनी लगती है) जानोँ इन्द्र के अखाडे (स्वर्ग) से (कोई वाद्य विशेष आ कर, दैवी शक्ति से) बजता है॥ (अथवा उस की धुनि ऐसी मनोहर जान पडती है), मानोँ कामिनी (काम को उत्पन्न करने-वाली मनो-हारिणी युवतियाँ) वीणा को लिये (गहे) सब राग और रागिनियोँ को गाय रही हैँ। सङ्गीत-शास्त्र मेँ राग छ हैँ और एक एक राग की छ छ रागिनी भार्या हैँ इस प्रकार सब रागिनी छत्तीस हैँ।

छ राग, मालव १। मल्लार २। श्रीराग ३। वसन्त ४। हिन्दोल (=हिँडोल) ५। कर्णाट ६। हैँ।

मालव की भार्या छ रागिनी — धानसी (=धनास्री) १। माजसी २। रामकीली ३। सिन्धुडा ४। आशावरी ५। भैरवी ६।

मल्लार की भार्या — बेलावली (=बिलावल) १। पूरवी (=पुर्बी) २। कानडा (=कान्हरा) ३। माधवी ४। कोडा ५। केदारिका (=केदारा) ६।

श्रीराग की भार्या — गान्धारी १। सुभगा २। गौरी ३। कौमारिका ४। बेलोयारी ५। वैरागी ६।

वसन्त की भार्या — तुडी (=टोडी) १। पञ्चमी २। ललिता ३। पटमञ्जरी ४। गुर्जरी (=गुजरी) ५। विभाषा (=विभास) ६।

हिन्दोल की भार्या — मायूरी १। दीपिका २। देशकारी ३। पाहिडी ४। बराडी ५। मोरहाटी ६।

कर्णाट की भार्या — नाटिका १। भूपाली २। रामकेली (=रामकली) ३। गडा ४। कामोदा ५। कल्याणी ६।

सङ्गीत-शास्त्र के वचन हैं—

'आदौ मालवरागेन्द्रस्ततो मल्लारसंज्ञितः।
श्रीरागश्च ततः पश्चात् वसन्तस्तदनन्तरम्॥
हिन्दोलश्चाथ कर्णाट एते रागाः षडेव तु
षट्त्रिंशद्रागिणीभेदाः क्रमशः कथिता मया॥
धानसी मालसी चैव रामकीली च सिन्धुडा।
आशावरी भैरवी च मालवस्य प्रिया इमाः॥
बेलावली पूरवी च कानडा माधवी तथा।
कोडा केदारिका चापि मल्लारदयिता इमाः॥
गान्धारी सुभगा चैव गौरी कौमारिका तथा।
बेलोयारी च वैरागी श्रीरागस्य प्रिया इमाः॥
तुडी च पञ्चमी चैव ललिता पटमञ्जरी।
गुर्जरी च विभाषा च वसन्तस्य प्रिया इमाः॥
मायूरी दीपिका चैव देशकारी च पाहिडी।
वराडी मोरहाटी च हिन्दोलस्य प्रिया इमाः॥
नाटिका चाथ भूपाली रामकेली गडा तथा।
कामोदा चाथ कल्याणी कर्णाटस्य प्रिया इमाः॥'

(सङ्गीत-दामोदर। वाचस्पत्य-कोश देखो)।

भरत के मत से छ रागों के नाम—

भैरव १। कौशिक २। हिन्दोल ३। दीपक ४। श्रीराग ५। मेघराग ६।

भरत का वचन—

'भैरवः कौशिकश्चैव हिन्दोलो दीपकस्तथा।
श्रीरागो मेघरागश्च रागाः षडिति कीर्त्तिताः॥'

(सङ्गीत-दामोदर। वाचस्पत्य-कोश देखो)।

प्रायः आज कल भरतमतानुसार-ही रागों के नाम प्रसिद्ध हैं। भरत मुनि को लोग सङ्गीत का प्रधान आचार्य मानते हैं। इन राग-रागिनियों के पुत्र पौत्रादि अनेक सन्तान, खेमटा, घाँटो, दादरा, चैती, होली, कजरी इत्यादि देश विदेश में सर्वत्र प्रसिद्ध हैं।

(पद्मावती के) लङ्क की समता में सिंह नहीं जीतता है। (इसी से लज्जित हो) हार कर (सिंह ने) वन-वास लिया, अर्थात् वन में जा कर बसा और तिसी रिस से, (कि मैं लङ्क की बराबरी में हार गया हूँ), (पद्मावती के जाति) मनुष्य(-मात्र) का रक्त पीता है, और (मनुष्यों को) मार कर (उन की) मांस को खाता है। यह कवि की उत्प्रेक्षा है। बर्रै का बसा नाम इस प्रान्त में प्रसिद्ध नहीं है। 'बसा' यह किसी बर्रै-वाची संस्कृत शब्द का अपभ्रंश भी नहीं है। यदि विष जिस में रहे उसे विषी कहैं, तो इस का अपभ्रंश संभव है, कि विसी वा विसा अथवा बसा हो सकता है ॥ ११८ ॥

चउपाई ।

नाभी कुँडर सो मलय-समीरू । समुद भवँर जस भवँइ गँभीरू ॥
बहुतइ भवँर बवंडर भए । पहुँचि न सके सरग कहँ गए ॥
चंदन माँझ कुरंगिनि खोजू । दहुँ को पाउ को राजा भोजू ॥
को ओहि लागि हेवंचल सीझा । का कहँ लिखी अइस को रीझा ॥
तीवइ कवँल-सु-गंध सरीरू । समुद लहरि सोहइ तन-चीरू ॥
झूलहिँ रतन पाट के झोँपा । साजि मयन दहुँ का पहँ कोपा ॥
अबहिँ सो अहइ कवँल कइ करी । न जनउँ कवनु भवँर कहँ धरी ॥

दोहा ।

बेधि रहा जग बासना परमल मेद सु-गंध ।
तेहि अरघानि भवँर सब लुबुधे तजहिँ न बंध ॥ ११९ ॥

कुँडर = कुण्ड । समीरू = समीर = वायु । भवँर = भ्रमर = आवर्त्त = भौंर । भवँइ = भ्रमति = घूमता है = फिरता है । गँभीरू = गम्भीर = गहिरा । बवंडर = वात्या = बबूला = वायु-चक्र = हवा का चक्कर । सरग = स्वर्ग = आसमान । माँझ = मध्य = बीच । कुरंगिनि = कुरङ्गी = हरिणी । खोजू = खोज = चिह्न । ('खोज मारि रथु हाँकहु ताता । आन उपाय बनिहि नहिँ बाता ॥' तुलसीदास-रामायण अयोध्या-काण्ड ८५ वाँ दोहा)। भोजू = भोज, धारा का प्रसिद्ध राजा । ओहि लागि = उस के लिये । हेवंचल = हिमाचल = हिमालय पहाड । सीझा = सिद्ध हुआ, वा पक गया (तपस्या से)। रीझा = रक्त

ऊआ = अनुरागी ऊआ। तीवह = तीव्र = तीक्ष्ण। सरीरू = शरीर। तन-चीरू = तनु-चीर = पतला वस्त्र। रतन = रत्न। पाट = पट्ट = रेशम की डोर। झोंपा = झम्पा = झब्बा = लटकन। मयन = मदन = काम-देव। कोपा = कोप किया। करी = कली = कलिका। कवनु = क-नु = कौन॥ बासना = वासना = सु-गन्ध। परमल = परिमल = पराग = सु-गन्ध-धूलि। मेद = कस्तूरी। अरघानि = आघ्राण के लिये = सूँघने के लिये। बंध = बन्धन = बँधना॥

जब शक्ति मन्द हो जाती है, तब उस को बढाने के लिये लोग शोधित विष का सेवन करते हैं। इस लिये कवि भी नाभी-कुण्ड के वर्णन में बुद्धि-शक्ति को मन्द देख कर, वेणी-नाग और कटि-बर्रे के वर्णन-व्याज से दोनों विषेले जन्तुओं के शोधित विषों का सेवन कर, फिर नाभी-कुण्ड के वर्णन में तत्पर ऊआ।

सो (जो) नाभी-कुण्ड है (जिस का कुछ वर्णन पहले कर आये हैं, वहाँ) जैसे समुद्र का भौंर घूमा करता है, तैसा-ही मलय का समीर, अर्थात् मलयचन्दन के सु-गन्ध से भरा वायु, भ्रमा करता है। अर्थात् नाभी-कुण्ड में आवर्त्त के कारण जो सीढी के ऐसा ऊपर से नीचे तक फेरा पड गया है, उसी में जगत्प्राण-स्वरूप मलयानिल नीचे ऊपर फिरा करता है॥ बझत से (समुद्र के) भौंर [इस नाभि-कुण्ड के मनोहर आवर्त्त (भौंर) के देखने के लिये] बवंडर (वात्या) ऊए। (परन्तु वहाँ तक) पऊँच न सके, (अन्त में) स्वर्ग को (चले) गये, अर्थात् बिलाय गये। यह कवि की उत्प्रेक्षा है॥ (उस नाभी की ऐसी शोभा है, जानों) चन्दन के बीच में हरिणी (कुरंगिन) के जाने का चिन्ह है, अर्थात् चन्दन के बीच में हो कर, जो हरिणी गई है, उस के खुर का चिन्ह है। (चन्दन-मय पद्मावती का उदर उस में खुर-चिन्ह-रूप नाभी है) वा नाभी में कस्तूरी का विशेष सु-गन्ध होने से विश्वास होता है, कि इस में से हो कर हरिणी गई है, जिस के मृग-मद का सु-गन्ध इस द्वार से निकल रहा है। (सो) देखें कौन (उस पद्मावती के उदर के ऊपर विहार करने-हारी मनो-हारिणी हरिणी को, जो कि पद्मावती के नेत्रों में वा नाभी द्वारा हृदय में आ बसी है) पाता है, (और) कौन राजा भोज (के ऐसा भाग्यवान्) है, (जिसे संसार के सभी पदार्थ सु-लभ थे)॥ (देखें) कौन उस (कुरंगिन) के लिये हिमालय में (तपस्या कर के) सीझा है, किस के (भाग्य में यह कुरंगिन) लिखी है, और कौन ऐसा रीझा (प्रेमी) है, (जिस के प्रेम से मोहित हो कर, स्वयं यह हरिणी मिलने की चाह प्रगट करे)॥

(एक) शरीर में, अर्थात् मदन-मन्दिर में, तीव्र कमल-सुगन्ध है, अर्थात् उस में तीव्र कमल के ऐसा सु-गन्ध है, (और उस के ऊपर) पतला वस्त्र (पवन के झकोर से) समुद्र के लहर के ऐसा (लहराता) सोहता है॥ (उस के ऊपर) रेशम-डोर में गुहे रत्न के अनेक झब्बा झूलते हैं, (सो) नहीं जानते, कि मदन ने (इस प्रकार से) तयारी कर, किस के ऊपर कोप किया है॥ सो (वह शरीर, अर्थात् मदन-मन्दिर) अभीं कमल की कलिका है। नहीं जानते कि कौन भ्रमर के लिये धरी है॥ मदन-मन्दिर(=गुह्याङ्ग=योनि) का स्पष्ट-रूप से नाम ले कर वर्णन करना रसाभास दोष में गिना जाता है, इस लिये सत्कवि-जन इस गुह्याङ्ग का गुप्त-ही रीति से वर्णन करते हैं, इसी लिये श्री-हर्ष ने भी दमयन्ती के नख-शिख वर्णन में इस अङ्ग का गुप्त-रीति से नाम ले कर, वर्णन किया है, जैसा कि नैषध में लिखा है, कि—

'अङ्गेन केनापि विजेतुमस्या गवेष्यते किं चलपत्त्रपत्त्रम् ।
न चेद्विशेषादितरच्छदेभ्यस्तस्यास्तु कम्पस्तु कुतो भयेन ॥'

(सर्ग ७। श्लो० ८९)

इस गुप्त-रीति के वर्णन से स्पष्ट होता है, कि मलिक-महम्मद संस्कृत-साहित्य में सब बातों के तत्त्व-वेत्ता थे॥

(पद्मावती के उदर पर, वा उदर में हरिणी विहार करती है, यह उत्प्रेक्षा पहले लिख आये हैं। उसी को और दृढ करते हैं, कि) कस्तूरी के परिमल सु-गन्ध की वासना (गमक) से जगत् विद्ध हो रहा है, अर्थात् उस हरिणी की नाभी में जो कस्तूरी (मृग-मद) भरी है, उस की गमक जगत् भर में छा गई है। तिस की सु-गन्ध लेने के लिये सब भौँरे वा भौँर-रूपी अनेक राजा महाराज लोभाये ऊए हैं। (उसी के लोभ से) उस बन्धन (झब्बे की रेशम-डोर) को नहीं छोडते हैं, अर्थात् उसी पर एक टक दृष्टि लगाये अचल गडे ऊए हैं॥ ११९॥

चउपाई ।

बरनउँ नितँब लंक कइ सोभा। अउ गज-गवँन देखि सब लोभा॥
जुरे जंघ सोभा अति पाए। केला खाँभ फेरि जनु लाए॥
कवँल-चरन अति-रात बिसेखी। रहइ पाट पर पुहुमि न देखी॥
देओता हाथ हाथ पगु लेहीँ। जहँ पगु धरइ सीस तहँ देहीँ॥

माँथइ भाग को दहुँ अस पावा। कवँल-चरन लेइ सीस चढावा॥
चूरा चाँद सुरुज उँजिआरा। पाइल बीच करहिँ झनकारा॥
अनवट बिछिआ नखत तराईँ। पहुँचि सकइ को पाइन ताईँ॥

दोहा।

बरनि सिँगार न जानेउँ नखसिख जइस अभोग।
तस जग किछू न पाएउँ उपम देउँ ओहि जोग॥ १२०॥

इति नखसिख-खंड॥ १०॥

नितँब = नितम्ब = चूतर। लंक = लङ्क = कटि = कमर। सोभा = शोभा। गज-गवँन = गज-गमन = हाथी के ऐसी चाल। जुरे = जुटे ऊए = सटे ऊए। जंघ = जङ्घ। केला = कदली = केरा। फेरि = घुमा कर = उलटा कर = फिरा कर। लाए = लगाये हैं। कवँल-चरन = कमल-चरण = कमल के ऐसे पैर। अति-रात = अति-रक्त = अति लाल। पाट = पट्ट = पीढा। देओता = देवता। पगु = प्रग = पैर। चूरा = चूडी के ऐसा पावँ का आभूषण = छडा। पाइल = पायल = पायजेब, जो कि चूरा के नीचे पैर में पहना जाता है। झनकारा = झणत्कार = झन झन ऐसा झन-कार। अनवट = पैर के अँगूठे का आभूषण। बिछिआ = वृश्चिक (बिच्छी) के आकार का पैर के अँगुलियोँ का आभूषण। नखत = नक्षत्र। तराईँ = तारा-गण। पाइन = पायँ (पैर) का बक्र-वचन। ताईँ = तक = तदन्त॥ सिँगार = शृङ्गार। जइस = जैसा = यादृश। अभोग = आभोग = भोग-योग्य, वा अभोग = विना भोग किया, अर्थात् अछूत (पवित्र)। तस = तादृश = तैसा। जग = जगत्। वा, जग = जग कर = सावधान हो कर = जाग्रित हो कर। उपम = उपमा। जोग = योग्य = लायक॥

(कवि कहता है, कि अब) नितम्ब का वर्णन करता हूँ, जो कि लङ्क की शोभा है, अर्थात् जिस नितम्ब-ही के कारण कटि सोहती है। (यदि स्थूल नितम्ब न हो तो छश-कटि की कुछ सुन्दरता-ही न प्रगट हो)। और (उस स्थूल नितम्ब-ही के कारण पद्मावती में) गज के ऐसी चाल है, जिसे देख कर, सब कोई लोभाय गये हैं। (अर्थात् स्थूल नितम्ब-ही के भार से पद्मावती की मन्द मन्द चाल गज-गमन-सी जान पडती है)॥ जुटे ऊए, अर्थात् सटे ऊए (दोनोँ) जंघे अत्यन्त शोभा को पाये ऊए हैँ।

(उन दोनों की ऐसी शोभा है), जानों केले के खंभे फिरा कर, अर्थात् उलटा कर जिस में मूल ऊपर की ओर और अग्र नीचे की ओर हो (नितम्बों में) लगाये हुए हैं ॥ कमल के ऐसा चरण, विशेष कर के अत्यन्त रक्त है, अथवा कमल (चिन्ह) के सहित चरण, विशेष कर के अत्यन्त रक्त है, जो कि (सदा) पाट-ही पर रहता है, पृथ्वी को (कभी) देखा-ही नहीं ॥ (चलने के समय भूमि के आघात से चोट न लग जाय, इस लिये) देवता लोग (उस) पैर को हाथो हाथ लिये रहते हैं। और जहाँ (कहीं पद्मावती) पैर धरती है, (उस स्थान को पारस-रूपी पाद-स्पर्श से विशिष्ट देव-पीठ समझ, वे देवता लोग) तहाँ, अर्थात् उस स्थान में, (अपने को कृतार्थ होने के लिये अपने) शिर को देते हैं, अर्थात् शिर को रगडते हैं ॥ कवि कहता है, कि जिस पैर के पड जाने से स्थान की ऐसी महिमा हो गई, कि देवता लोग वहाँ शिर रगडने लगे, तो देखें, कि कौन माथे में ऐसी भाग्य को पाया है, कि (उस साक्षात्) कमल-चरण को ले कर (अपने) शिर पर चढावे, अर्थात् धन्य उस पुरुष को भाग्य है, जो कि उस कमल-चरण को ले कर अपने शिर पर रक्खे॥ (जिस पैर के) चूरा के बीच चन्द्र और पायजेद (पाइल) के बीच उज्ज्वल सूर्य (रात दिन) झणत्कार शब्द करते हैं, अर्थात् चूडा के मिष चन्द्र और पायजेब के मिष सूर्य, उस पैर के यहाँ आ कर, उस की रक्षा के लिये दिन रात झणत्कार-शब्द-व्याज से चौकीदारों के ऐसे पुकारा करते हैं ॥ और अनवट, (जो कि पैर के अँगूठे के नख के ऊपर बैठी है) और बिछिया, (जो कि पैर के और अँगुलियों के नख के ऊपर हैं) वे सब जानों (उस पैर की रक्षा के लिये) नक्षत्र और तारा-गण हैं। (सो जिस पैर की रक्षा के लिये जहाँ चन्द्र, सूर्य, नक्षत्र और तारा-गण चौकीदार हो कर, रात दिन लोगों को सावधान करने के लिये झणत्कार-शब्द-व्याज से पुकारा करते हैं, तहाँ भला उन) पैरों तक कौन पहुँच सकता है। कवि का आशय है, कि जिन पैरों की ऐसी कडी रखवाली हो रही है, उन के निकट पहुँच कर, अवयवों का देखना तो दूर है, किन्तु दूर से खडे हो कर, नेत्रों से एक बेर उन अवयवों की झाँकी ले लेना भी चन्द्र, सूर्य, नक्षत्र और तारा-गणों के युगपत् तेजः-पुञ्ज से चका-चौंधी के कारण सामर्थ्य से बाहर है, तो भला जहाँ दृष्टि तक नहीं पहुँच सकती, मन, वचन से भी जो पैर पर-ब्रह्म के ऐसा परे है, (किन्तु पर-ब्रह्म से भी बढ कर है, क्योंकि उपनिषदों में पर-ब्रह्म के विराटाकृति के नेत्र, चन्द्र और सूर्य, कहे हैं, वे यहाँ चौकीदारी में नियुक्त हैं), उस के अवयवों का वर्णन मेरी प्राकृत-बुद्धि

से कैसे हो सकता है। बस इतना-ही कह सकते हैं, कि पेर में चन्द्र के ऐसा चूडा और प्रज्वलित सूर्य के ऐसा पायजेब है, और पैर के नखों के ऊपर नक्षत्र और तारा-गण के सदृश अनवट और बिछिया हैं, अर्थात् समझ लो, कि जिन नखों के आभूषण नक्षत्र और तारा-गण हैं, वे नख अनुपम हैं, उन के उपमा-योग्य जगत् में कोई वस्तु-ही नहीं है। कवि इस प्रकार से नख-शिख का वर्णन कर उन अवयवों की और भी अधिक प्रशंसा के लिये, अर्थात् उन को अनुपम और अपने वर्णन को अधम ठहराने के लिये दोहा कह कर, इस खण्ड का उपसंहार करता है॥

(कवि शुकोक्ति को कहता है, कि) जैसे (पद्मावती के) अभोग (विना भोग किये ऊए, अर्थात् पवित्र) नख से शिखा तक (शृङ्गार से भूषित) अवयव हैं, (उन के) शृङ्गार का वर्णन करना मैं जाना-ही नहीं, अर्थात् मेरे में उस वर्णन करने की विद्या-ही नहीं, जिस से यथावत् उस शृङ्गार का वर्णन हो। मैं ने उस शृङ्गार-भूषित-अवयव के योग्य जगत् में, वा सावधानी से ढूँढने पर भी, तैसा कुछ पाया-ही नहीं, जिस की उपमा (योग्य समझ कर) देऊँ॥ (अर्थात् जिस के पैर की सेवकाई चन्द्र और सूर्य करते हैं उस प्रकृति-पुरुष के चोभ करने-वाले पर-ब्रह्म के वर्णन में वेद भी 'यतो वाचो निवर्त्तन्ते' इत्यादि कह कह कर, लाचार, हार कर, चुप रह जाता है, तहाँ मेरी क्या सामर्थ्य, कि यथावत् वर्णन कर, पार हो जाऊँ। सो, हे राजन् रत्न-सेन, आप की आज्ञा से जो कुछ बात बुद्धि में आई सो कह सुनाई, नहीं तो मैं ने आदि-ही में कह दिया है, कि 'का सिँगार ओहि बरनउँ राजा। ओहि क सिँगार ओही पंइ छाजा॥' इन सब बातों से शुक ने राजा को सूचित कर दिया, कि केवल वाग्-वर्णन से पद्मावती की शोभा किसी के मन में नहीं आ सकती। पर-ब्रह्म का ज्ञान वाग्-विलासों से नहीं साक्षात्कार हो सकता। जो योगी हो कर, उस के खोजने के लिये अपने को खोवे, और योग-बल के प्रभाव से उस का दर्शन करे, उस की शोभा को नेत्र-द्वारा हृदय में चुरा कर, देखे, तब वह उस के शोभा का आनन्द पा सकता है॥ १२०॥

इति नखशिख-खण्ड-नाम दशम-खण्डं समाप्तम्॥ १०॥

अथ पेम-खंड ॥ ११ ॥

चउपाई ।

सुनत-हि राजा गा मुरुछाई । जानउँ लहरि सुरुज कइ आई ॥
पेम-घाओ दुख जान न कोई । जेहि लागइ जानइ पइ सोई ॥
परा सो पेम-समुंद अपारा । लहरहिँ लहर होइ बिसँभारा ॥
बिरह भवँर होइ भाउँरि देई । खन खन जीउ हिलोरा लेई ॥
खनहिँ निसाँस बूडि जिउ जाई । खनहिँ उठइ निसँसइ बउराई ॥
खनहिँ पीत खन होइ मुख सेता । खनहिँ चेत खन होइ अचेता ॥
कठिन मरन तइँ पेम-बेवसथा । ना जिउ जाइ न दसउँ-अवसथा ॥

दोहा ।

जनउँ लोहारइ लीन्ह जिउ हरइ तरासइ ताहि ।
एतना बोल न आओ मुख करइ तराहि तराहि ॥ १२१ ॥

गा = गया = अगात् । मुरुछाई = मूर्छित । लहरि = लहरी = लहर । पेम-घाओ = प्रेम-घात । घाओ = घाव । पइ = अपि = निश्चय । समुंद = समुद्र । बिसँभारा = विसंभरण = जो अपने को सँभार न सके = बे-खबर । भवँर = भ्रमर = आवर्त्त । भाउँरि = भ्रामरी = घुमरी । खन = क्षण । हिलोरा = हिल-लोल = इधर से उधर डवाँ-डोल ।

निसाँस = निःश्वास = बे-दम। निसँसइ = निश्वास लेता है = हाँफता है। बउराई = बातुल हो कर। पीत = पीला। सेता = श्वेत = सफेद। चेत = चैतन्य = सावधान। पेम-बेवसथा = प्रेम-व्यवस्था = प्रेम की स्थिति। जिउ = जीव। दसउँ = दशम = दसईं। अवसथा = अवस्था = समय॥ लोहारइ = लोह-कार ने = लोहार ने। हरइ = हरण करता है। तरासइ = चासता है = डेरवाता है। वा, तरासइ = तरासता है = कतरता है। द्रतना = दूयत्। आओ = आता है। करइ = करोति = करता है। तराहि = चाहि = रच॥

राजा (रत्न-सेन, शुक के मुख से पद्मावती के नख-शिख का वर्णन सुनते-ही) मूर्छित हो गया। (उस की ऐसी दशा हो गई) जानौं सूर्य की लहर आ गई, अर्थात् सूर्य के तेज के लहर से जैसे जेठ में मनुष्य व्याकुल हो कर मूर्छित हो जाता है, उसी प्रकार ज्योतिः-स्वरूपा पद्मावती के वर्णन सुनने से कर्ण-द्वारा सूर्य से भी अधिक तेजो-मय वह ज्योति राजा के हृदय में धँस गई; इस से राजा अचेत हो गया॥ (कवि कहता है, कि) प्रेम-घात का दुःख कोई नहीं जानता, वही निश्चय कर के जानता है जिसे, कि यह आघात लगता है, अर्थात् जो इस दुःख को भोग चुका है, वही इस के मर्म को जान सकता है, दूसरा क्या जाने; कबीर-दास ने भी कहा है कि, 'जेहि तन परइ सोई तन जानइ दोसरा का जानइ रे भाई'। और लोक में भी कहावत है, कि 'जा के पैर न फटी बेवाई। सो का जानइ पीर पराई॥' वह (सो) (राजा रत्न-सेन) अपार, जिस का पारावार नहीं, ऐसे प्रेम के समुद्र में पड गया, (इस लिये उस समुद्र के) लहर लहर पर बे-खबर होता जाता है। एक एक अङ्ग के सुन्दरता का स्मरण होना-ही उस प्रेम-समुद्र का लहर है, जिस के कारण वार वार बे-खबर हो रहा है॥ (उस समुद्र में पद्मावती का) विरह जो है, सोई भवँर (आवर्त्त) हो कर, (राजा को) भावँरी देता है, अर्थात् घुमा कर, नीचे ऊपर ले जा रहा है, (जिस के कारण) क्षण क्षण जीव हिलोरा को लेता है, अर्थात् क्षण क्षण जीव नीचे ऊपर डवाँ-डोल हो रहा है॥ एक क्षण में विना श्वास का हो जाता है, अर्थात् बे-दम हो जाता है, (और उस समुद्र में) जीव डूब जाता है, (नाडी का चलना बंद हो जाता है, शरीर विना जीव के हो जाती है)। (और फिर एक) क्षण में (घबडा कर) उठता है, (और) पागल हो कर, साँस छोडता है, अर्थात् विरह से ठण्ढी साँस लेता है॥ क्षण में चेहरा (मुख) पीला होता है, क्षण में सफेद हो जाता है; (राजा) क्षण में चैतन्य हो जाता है, क्षण में अचेत हो जाता है, अर्थात् उस प्रेम-समुद्र में

पडा राजा डूब उतरा रहा है, इसी कारण राजा को कभी चेत हो जाती है और कभी बे-होशी में गाफिल पडा रहता है ॥ (कवि कहता है, कि) प्रेम-व्यवस्था मरण से, अर्थात् मरणा-ऽवस्था से, भी कठिन है, (क्योंकि मरणा-ऽवस्था में तो प्राणी दुःख से छुटकारा पा जाता है, परन्तु इस प्रेमा-ऽवस्था में तो) न जीव जाता है, और न दूसरी अवस्था अर्थात् मरणा-ऽवस्था आती है। अर्थात् प्राण तो निकलता नहीं, जिस से मरणा-ऽवस्था हो कर, प्राणी इस दुःख से छुटकारा पावे; किन्तु यह जीव विरहा-ऽग्नि से तप्त हो कर इधर से उधर तडपा करता है, जिस से रात दिन दुःख बढता-ही रहता है ॥ स्मृति में नीचे लिखी आठ अवस्थायें हैं।

कौमारं पञ्चमाब्दान्तं पौगण्डं दशमावधि।
कैशोरमापञ्चदशात् यौवनं च ततः परम् ॥
आषोडशाद्बालस्तरुणस्तत उच्यते।
वृद्धस्तु सप्ततेरूर्ध्वं वर्षीयान् नवतेः परम् ॥
(दशमस्कन्ध भागवत, १२ वें अध्याय की बालप्रबोधिनी टीका)

कौमार १। पौगण्ड २। कैशोर ३। यौवन ४। बाल ५। तरुण ६। वृद्ध ७। वर्षीयान् (अति-वृद्ध) ८॥ भारत के मोक्ष धर्म की टीका में नीलकण्ठ ने एक गर्भा-ऽवस्था और दूसरी अन्त में मरणा-ऽवस्था मान कर दश अवस्था कहा है, इसी लिये दशमा-ऽवस्था से मरणा-ऽवस्था लिया है ॥

(राजा की ऐसी दशा हो गई है) जानों (किसी) लोहार ने (उस के) जीव को लिया है, और (वह लोहार) तिसे (जीव को) हरता तरासता है, अर्थात् कतर छाँट करता है। (राजा के) मुख से इतना, अर्थात् कुछ भी बोल नहीं आती है, अवाक् हो गया है (केवल ध्याना-ऽवस्था में पद्मावती से यही प्रार्थना) करता है, कि राखि राखि, अर्थात् रक्ष रक्ष, (रक्षा करो रक्षा करो, प्राण बचावो प्राण बचावो) ॥ १२१ ॥

चउपाई ।

जहँ लगि कुटुँब लोग अउ नेगी। राजा राइ आए सब बेगी ॥
जावँत गुनी गारुरी आए। ओझा बइद सयान बोलाए ॥

चरचहिँ चेसटा परखहिँ नारी। निअर नाहिँ ओखद तेहि बारी॥
इइ राजहि लखिमन कइ करा। सकति-बान मोहइ हिअ परा॥
तहँ सो राम हनिवँत बडि दूरी। को लेइ आउ सजीअनि मूरी॥
बिनउ करहिँ जेते गढ-पती। का जिउ कीन्ह कउनि मति मती॥
कहउ सो पीर काहि बिनु खाँगा। समुद सुमेरु आउ तुम्ह माँगा॥

दोहा।

धावन तहाँ पठावहु देहु लाख दस रोक।
इइ सो बेल जेहि बारी आनहु सबहिँ बरोक॥ १२२॥

जहँ लगि = जहाँ तक। कुटुँब = कुटुम्ब = घर के प्राणी। लोग = लोक = प्राणी। नेगी = नेग लेने-वाले = मान्य-लोग = बडे लोग = पूज्य। राइ = राय = राजा से कुछ न्यून जिन की प्रतिष्ठा है। बेगी = बेग = शीघ्र। जावँत = यावन्तः = जितने। गुनी = गुणी। गारुरी = गारुडिक = सर्प-विष उतारने-वाला। ओझा = उपाध्याय = भूत-प्रेत उतारने-वाले। बइद = वैद्य। सयान = सज्ञान = चतुर। चरचहिँ = चरचते हैँ = उपचार करते हैँ। चेसटा = चेष्टा = चेहरा। परखहिँ = परखते हैँ = परीक्षा करते हैँ। नारी = नाडी। निअर = निकट = पास = नगीच। ओखद = औषधि। बारी = वाटिका। लखिमन = लक्ष्मण, राम के भाई। करा = कला = दशा। सकति-बान = शक्ति-बाण, जिस से मेघनाद ने लक्ष्मण को मारा था। हनिवँत = हनुमन्त = हनुमान्। आउ = आवे। सजीअनि = सञ्जीविनी = जिलाने-वाली। मूरी = मूली = मूलिका = जडी। बिनउ = विनय। कउनि = क नु = कौन। मति = बुद्धि। मती = मत ऊई = संमत ऊई = स्वीकृत ऊई। पीर = पीडा = पीरा। खाँगा = खाङ्ग = शून्य = घटा॥ धावन = दूत। रोक = रोकड = रुपया। बेल = वल्ली = लता। बरोक = बलौकः = बल का घर, अर्थात् सेना॥

(राजा की यह दशा सुन कर) जहाँ तक कुटुम्ब, प्राणी, और नेगी, राजा (जो कि रत्न-सेन के आश्रित थे), और राय, सब कोई शीघ्र (राजा को देखने के लिये) आये॥ (राजा को मूर्छित देख, लोगोँ को बीमारी की आहट न लगने से) जितने गुणी (जो कि यन्त्र, मन्त्र, टोटका इत्यादि से अच्छा करते हैँ), और गारुडिक

(सर्प-विष उतारने-वाले) ये सब आये, और ओझा, वैद्य और चतुर लोग भी बोलाये गये, (कि परीक्षा से यह तो मालूम हो, कि राजा को कौन बीमारी है)॥ (सब कोई राजा की) चेष्टा को परचते हैँ, अर्थात् चेहरे की रंगत से पता लगाते हैँ, कि राजा को क्या ऊआ है; और नाडी को (भी) परखते हैँ। (परीक्षा से लोगोँ ने निश्चय किया, कि राजा को जो रोग है, उस की) औषधि निकट तिस (राजा) की वाटिका में नहीँ है॥ (क्योँकि) राजा को लक्ष्मण की दशा ऊई है, हृदय में पडा शक्ति-बाण मोह रहा है, अर्थात् मूर्छित कर रहा है। [लक्ष्मण के पक्ष में शक्तिरेव बाणः शक्ति-बाणः ऐसा कर्मधारय से विग्रह करना चाहिए, और राजा रत्न-सेन के पक्ष में शक्तेः (शक्तिरूपायाः पद्मावत्याः) बाणः शक्ति-बाणः ऐसा षष्ठी तत्पुरुष से विग्रह करना चाहिए]॥ तहाँ, अर्थात् शक्ति-बाण के प्रभाव के हरण करने में राम और हनुमान-ही प्रधान हैँ, सो (वे राम-हनुमान्) तो बडी दूर हैँ, अर्थात् देव-स्वरूप हो विष्णु-लोक में विहार करते हैँ, (फिर) कौन सञ्जीविनी मूरि को ले आवे (जिस से राजा अपने चेत में हो, अर्थात् सब ने निश्चय किया, कि रोग असाध्य है, विना भगवद-ऽनुग्रह से नहीँ अच्छा हो सकता)॥ जितने गढ-पति हैँ (सब राजा से) विनय करते हैँ (गढ-पति के लिये ४४ वेँ दोहे की टीका देखो), (कि आप ने) क्या जीव किया है, अर्थात् कैसा छोटा जीव किया है? और कौन (बात आप की) मति मेँ मत गई है?॥ किस के विना (आप का घर) सूना (शून्य) है? उस (सो) पीडा को कहिये, (क्योँकि आप के लिये जगत् में कोई पदार्थ दुर्लभ नहीँ है, आप का ऐसा प्रताप है, कि यदि) आप (तुम्ह) माँगेँ (तो) समुद्र और सुमेरु (जो रत्नमय और सुवर्णमय हैँ) (भी आप के प्रताप के भय से चले) आवैँ, (औरोँ की क्या गिनती है)॥

जिस वाटिका में वह बल्ली है (जिस के लिये आप मरे जाते हैँ) तहाँ दूत को पठाइये, लाख दश रुपये दीजिये, अर्थात् खर्च कीजिये, और सब सेना से (उस बेल को) आनिये, अर्थात् ले आइये, (कादरोँ के ऐसा रोने गाने से क्या फल)। गढ-पतियोँ ने तीनोँ राज-नीति को देखा दिया, कि यदि किसी के मेल से मिले तो मेल के लिये दूत भेजिये, द्रव्य से मिले तो द्रव्य खर्चिये, और यदि युद्ध से मिले तो सेना को भेजिये; आप के पास सब सामग्री मौजूद है, कादर होने से जगत् में केवल उपहास छोड और कुछ भी प्राप्ति नहीँ है॥ १२२॥

चउपाई।

जो भा चेत उठा बइरागा। बाउर जनउँ सोइ अस जागा ॥
आवत जग बालक जस रोआ। उठा रोइ हा ग्यान सो खोआ ॥
हउँ तो अहा अमर-पुर जहवाँ। इहाँ मरन-पुर आएउँ कहवाँ ॥
केइ उपकार मरन कर कीन्हा। सकति हँकारि जीउ हरि लीन्हा ॥
सोअत अहा जहाँ सुख साखा। कस न तहाँ सोअत बिधि राखा ॥
अब जिउ तहाँ इहाँ तन सूना। कब लगि रहइ परान बिहूना ॥
जो जिउ घटिहि काल के हाथा। घटन नीक पइ जीअन साथा ॥

दोहा।

अहुठ हाथ तन सरवर हिआ कवँल तेहि माँह।
नयनहिँ जानउँ नीअरे कर पहुँचत अउगाह ॥ १२३ ॥

बइरागा = वैराग्य। बाउर = वातुल = बौराहा। रोआ = रौति = रोता है। ग्यान = ज्ञान। खोआ = खो दिया = नष्ट कर दिया। अहा = आसीत् = था। अमर-पुर = मुक्ति-स्थान। जहवाँ = यत्र। मरन-पुर = मरण-पुर = मरण-स्थान = मृत्यु-लोक। कहवाँ = कुत्र = कहाँ। संकति = शक्ति = एक प्रकार का अस्त्र जिस से मेघनाद ने लक्ष्मण को मारा था। हँकारि = हे क्त्वा = आह्वानं क्त्वा = हँकार कर = पुकार कर। हरि लीन्हा = हरण कर लिया = चुरा लिया। साखा = शाखा। बिधि = ब्रह्मा। सूना = शून्य = खाली = छूँछा। परान = प्राण। बिहूना = विहीन = विना। घटिहि = घटेगा = क्षीण होगा। काल = प्राण लेने-वाला। हाथा = हस्त = हाथ। घटन = घटना = कम होना। नीक = अच्छा। पइ = किन्तु = परन्तु। जीअन = जीवन। साथा = सार्थ = सङ्ग॥ अहुठ = अनुठ = अनुत्थ = न उठने योग्य। तन = तनु = शरीर। सरवर = सरोवर = तड़ाग। हिआ = हृदय। माँह = मध्य। नीअरे = निकट = नगीच। कर = हस्त = हाथ। पहुँचत = पहुँचने में। अउगाह = अवगाढ = अति कठिन = दुर्गम॥

(राजा को) जो चेत हुआ (भा = अभूत्), (तो) वैराग्य से उठा, अर्थात् चेत होने पर जो उठा तो संसार से विरक्त हो गया, (और उस अचेतनावस्था से) ऐसा

जागा जानौं बौरहा सो कर जागा हो ॥ जैसे जगत् में आने के समय, अर्थात् जन्म के समय बालक रोता है, (उसी प्रकार राजा भी) रो उठा, अर्थात् 'कहाँ कहाँ' करने लगा। जन्म के समय जब बालक माता के उदर से बाहर धरती पर आता है, तब उस के रोने में 'कहाँ कहाँ' ऐसी ध्वनि होती है। इस पर पुराणों में कथा है, कि माता के उदर में मलाशय के पास नाल से वेष्टित बालक अधोमुख पडा रहता है, और उसे गर्भ के भीतर अहर्निश भगवान् का दर्शन होता रहता है, जिस से वह सर्वदा प्रार्थना किया करता है, कि हे भगवन्, इस गर्भ-कारागार और नाल-बन्धन से मुझे निर्मुक्त करो, मैं बाहर निर्मुक्त होने पर सर्वदा आप का भजन करता रहूँगा। बाहर आने पर उस भगवान् को न देख कर, वह बालक रो रो कर, लोगों से पूछता है, कि वह दिव्य-पुरुष 'कहाँ है, कहाँ है?' इसी से उस के रोने में 'कहाँ कहाँ' ध्वनि होती है। संसार में आने पर विषय-वासना में अवलिप्त हो कर, वह बालक भगवान् से भजन करने, और संसार के विषयों से दूर रहने की प्रतिज्ञा को भुला देता है; इसी पर विहारी ने सतसई में लिखा है, कि—

'भजन कह्यौ ता तैं भज्यौ भज्यौ न एक-ऊ वार।
दूर भजन जा तैं कह्यौ सो तूँ भज्यौ गवाँर॥
(लाल-चंद्रिका। दो० ६७१)

कवि कहता है, कि हा, वह (सो) (राजा रत्न-सेन ने अपने) ज्ञान को खो दिया, अर्थात् बौरहा हो गया॥ (और लगा कहने, कि) मैं तो जहाँ अमर-पुर है, तहाँ था, अर्थात् प्रेम-मय हो ध्यानावस्था से मुक्ति-स्थान में पहुँच गया था, यहाँ कहाँ मरण-पुर, अर्थात् मृत्यु-लोक, में आया॥ किस ने (मेरे) मरने का उपकार किया है, अर्थात् मुझे मारने के लिये यत्न किया है, कि इस मरण-पुर में मुझे ले आया है। किस ने शक्ति (=पद्मावती, राजा के पक्ष में) को पुकार कर (मेरा) जीव हरण कर लिया॥ जहाँ सुख की शाखा (चारो ओर से फैली थी तहाँ सुख से) सोता था, ब्रह्मा ने क्यों नहीं (कस न) तिसी स्थान में (मुझे) सोता हुआ रक्खा॥ (सो हा), अब तो जीव तहाँ (मुक्ति-स्थान में बसा), और यहाँ (विना जीव के) तनु शून्य, प्राण विना कब तक रहेगी॥ यदि (जो) काल के हाथ से जीव क्षीण होगा, (तो वह) क्षीण होना अच्छा है, किन्तु (शरीर) जीवन के साथ, अर्थात् शरीर में रहते, यदि जीव क्षीण होता जाय तो अच्छा, क्योंकि क्षीण होते होते जीव और शरीर दोनों एक साथ-ही नष्ट होंगे, इस

लिये एक के विरह से दूसरे को ताप न होगा। और यह अच्छा नहीं, कि जीव अलग हो कर शरीर के लिये तडपे और विना जीव की शरीर जीव के लिये पछाडा खाय॥

राजा कहता है, कि (मेरा) हाथ तो अछुठ है, अर्थात् शक्ति के लग जाने से सामर्थ्य-हीन हो कर, बे-काम हो गया, और (मेरी) तनु सरोवर है, तिस (सरोवर) के हृदय मध्य, अर्थात् बीच में, कमल, अर्थात् पद्मावती बसी ऊई है। (सो) नयनों के लिये (तो) जानों (वह कमल) निकट-ही है, क्योंकि मैं अपने भीतर के नेत्रों से स्पष्ट उस कमल को देख रहा हूँ, (परन्तु उस कमल तक) हाथ के पऊँचने में अति कठिनता है, क्योंकि हाथ का व्यापार तो शरीर के बाहर होता है, और यह कमल तो शरीर-सरोवर के भीतर बसा है, इस लिये वहाँ पर शक्ति-हीन हाथ का पऊँचना तो अत्यन्त दुर्घट है॥ १२३॥

चउपाई।

सबन्ह कहा मन समुझहु राजा। काल सेति कइ जूझ न छाजा॥
ता सउँ जूझ जात जो जीता। जात न किसुन तजी गोपीता॥
अउ न नेहु काहू सउँ कीजिअ। नाउँ मीठ खाए जिउ दीजिअ॥
पहिलइ सुख नेहहि जब जोरा। पुनि होइ कठिन निबाहत ओरा॥
अहुठ हाथ तन जइस सुमेरू। पहुँचि न जाइ परा तस फेरू॥
गगन दिसिटि सेा जाइ पहूँचा। पेम अदिसिटि गगन तइँ ऊँचा॥
धुव तइँ ऊँच पेम-धुव ऊआ। सिर देइ पाउँ देइ सेा छूआ॥

दोहा।

तुम्ह राजा अउ सुखिआ करहु राज सुख भोग।
एहि रे पंथ सेा पहुँचइ सहइ जो दुख बीओग॥ १२४॥

समुझहु = समुझइ (संबुध्यते) का लोट् में मध्यमपुरुष का बहु-वचन। सेति = से। कइ = कृत्वा = कर के। जूझ = युद्ध। छाजा = सोहता। ता सउँ = तिस से = तस्मात्। जात = जायते = जाता है। किसुन = कृष्ण, नन्द-यशोदा के पुत्र। तजी = तत्याज = त्याग दिया = छोड दिया। गोपीता = गोप-पत्नी = गोपी = ग्वालिन। अउ = अपि = अपर = और। नेहु = स्नेह = प्रीति = मैत्री। काहू सउँ = किसी से = कैरपि सह। कीजिअ = करिये = कीजिये। नाउँ = नाम। मीठ = मिष्ट। खाए = खादनात् = खाने से।

जिउ = जीव । दीजिअ = दीजिये । पहिलइ = पहले = प्रथम । नेहहि = स्नेह को । जब = यदा । जोरा = योजना किया = मिलाया । निबाहत = निर्वाहतः = निबाहने में । ओरा = अपर प्रान्त = अन्त में । अऊठ = अनुठ = अनुत्थ = न उठने योग्य । तन = तनु = शरीर । जइस = यथा = यादृश = जैसे । सुमेरू = सुमेरु = सुवर्ण का पर्वत, जिस के शिर के ऊपर उत्तर ध्रुव है । परा = प्राप्त हुआ = पड गया । तस = तथा = तादृश = तैसा । फेरू = फेर । गगन = आकाश । दिसिट = दृष्ट । पेम = प्रेम । अदिसिट = अदृष्ट । गगन तइँ = गगनतोऽपि = आकाश से भी । ऊँचा = उच्च । ऊआ = उदय हुआ = उद्गमन हुआ । सिर = शिर ॥ सुखिआ = सुखी = सुख की इच्छा करने-वाला । राज = राज्य । पंथ = पन्थाः = राह । सहइ = सहति = सहता है । दुख = दुःख । बीओग = वियोग ॥

(राजा को व्याकुल देख कर) सभोँ ने कहा, कि हे राजा मन में समझो, काल से युद्ध कर के नहीं सोहता है, अर्थात् अच्छा नहीं होता, (क्योँकि प्राण देने के अतिरिक्त और कोई फल नहीं) ॥ जो कि जीता जाता हो, अर्थात् जिसे जीत सकते हो, युद्ध तिस से करना चाहिए । कृष्ण, जीते नहीं जाते थे, अर्थात् जीतने के योग्य न थे, इस लिये गोपियोँ ने (उन्हेँ) त्याग दिया, अर्थात् जब कंस की आज्ञा से अक्रूर, कृष्ण को लेने के लिये नन्द के यहाँ आये, और कृष्ण को ले कर चलने लगे, उस समय गोपियोँ ने समझ लिया, कि कृष्ण का लौटाना सामर्थ्य से बाहर है, इस लिये प्राण-प्रिय कृष्ण को अजीत समझ, लाचारी से छोड दिया, (सो हे राजन्, जो अजीत है, उस से युद्ध करना उचित नहीं) ॥ और (यह तो सिद्धान्त-ही समझिये, कि) किसी से स्नेह न कीजिये, (क्योँकि स्नेह का) नाम (तो सुनने में बडा चिकना और) मीठा है, (परन्तु) खाने से जीव दे दिया जाता है, अर्थात् स्नेह, उदर के भीतर जहाँ पहुँचा, कि प्राणी का प्राण गया ॥ जब (किसी व्यक्ति से) पहले स्नेह जोडा जाता है (तब जोडने के समय बडा) सुख होता है; फिर अन्त तक निबाहने में कठिन होता है, अर्थात् स्नेह जोडना तो सहज है, परन्तु अन्त तक उस का निबाहना बहुत-ही कठिन है ॥ जैसे शरीर का हाथ उठने योग्य न हो (तो वह) सुमेरु तक नहीं पहुँच जाता है, अर्थात् नहीं पहुँच सकता है, तैसा-ही (इस प्रेम की चोटी तक पहुँचने में) फेर पडा है । कवि का अभिप्राय है, कि जैसा सुवर्ण और रत्न-मय सुमेरु है, उसी प्रकार स्नेह भी सुवर्ण और रत्न-मय है; परन्तु जैसे सुमेरु की चोटी, जो ब्रह्मा, विष्णु और महादेव का निवास-स्थान है, अत्यन्त ऊंची है, जहाँ बडे बडे प्रलम्ब-बाहुओँ का

शक्ति-पूर्ण हस्त भी नहीं पहुँच सकता, वहाँ शरीर का शक्ति-रहित अनुठ हाथ तो कथमपि नहीं पहुँच सकता, वैसे-ही प्रेम-की चोटी तक पहुँचना मनुष्य-शक्ति से बाहर है। ब्रह्मा, विष्णु और महादेव के सदृश, यदि तपो-बल से मनुष्य हो जाय, तो सुमेरु-शिखा-समान प्रेम-चोटी तक पहुँच सकता है॥ गगन दृष्ट है, अर्थात् देख पडता है, (इस लिये) वह (सो) पहुँचा जाता है, अर्थात् आकाश तक लोग पहुँच सकते हैं। (परन्तु) प्रेम (तो) अदृष्ट है (इस लिये पर-ब्रह्म के ऐसा यह) आकाश से भी ऊँचा है॥ प्रेम-रूपी ध्रुव, ध्रुव से भी ऊँचा है (क्योंकि वह तो आकाश-ही में रहता है और अदृष्ट-प्रेम तो आकाश से भी ऊँचा है)। (इस लिये जो पहले अपने) शिर को दे कर, (उस शिर के ऊपर) पावँ दे कर, (यदि इस प्रेम-परब्रह्म के छूने की इच्छा करे तो) वह (सो) छूवे, अर्थात् ऐसा हठ-योग का साधन करे जिस में अपना शिर तक काट कर हवन कर डाले, तब यदि सिद्ध हो जाय तो उस प्रेम के स्पर्श-योग्य हो सकता है, अन्यथा प्रेम तक पहुँचना बडा कठिन है। इसी पर किसी कवि ने यह दोहा लिखा है, कि—

‘सीस काटि आगे धरो ता पर राखो पाँव।
प्रेम बाग के बीच में ऐसा हो तो आव॥’

(सब लोग कहते हैं, कि राजन्,) तुम राजा और सुखिया हो, (सो तुम) राज्य का सुख भोग करो। रे (राजन्), इस (प्रेम) पन्थ में (चल कर, प्रेम तक) वह (सो) पहुँचता है, जो कि दुःख और (राज्य, सुख, सम्पत्ति इत्यादि का) वियोग सहता है॥ १२४॥

चउपाई।

सुअइ कहा सुनु मो सउँ राजा। करब पिरीति कठिन इइ काजा॥
तुम्ह अब-हीँ जेइअ घर पोई। कवँल न बइठ बइठ तहँ कोई॥
जानहिँ भवँर जो तेहि पँथ लूटे। जीउ दीन्ह अउ दिग्र-उ न छूटे॥
कठिन आहि सिंघल कर राजू। पाइअ नाहिँ राज के साजू॥
ओहि पँथ जाइ जो होइ उदासी। जोगी जती तपा सनिआसी॥
जोग जोरि वह पाइत भोगू। तजि सो भोग कोइ करत न जोगू॥
तुम्ह राजा चाहहु सुख पावा। जोगी भोगिहि कित बनि आवा॥

दोहा ।

साधहि सिद्धि न पाइअ जउ लहि साध न तप्प ।
सेा पइ जानइ बापुरा सीस जो करइ कलप्प ॥ १२५ ॥

सुअइ = शुक ने । कहा = अकथयत् । सुनु = शृणु = सुनो । मो सउँ = मुझ से । करब = करण = करना = कर्त्तव्य । पिरीति = प्रीति । हइ = अहइ = अस्ति । काजा = कार्य । अब-हीँ = अभीँ । जेइअ = जेमति वा, जमति = जँवते हैँ = खाते हैँ । घर = गृह । पोई = पकी हुई = पकी पकाई । बइठ = बइठा = बैठा = उपविष्ट हुआ । बइठ = बइठे = बैठे । तहँ = तत्र । कोई = कोऽपि । वा, कोई = कोँई = कुमुदिनी । पँथ = पन्थाः = पथ = राह । लूटे = लुण्ठित हुए = लूटे गये । छूटे = छुटे = छुटकारा पाये = मुक्त हुए । आहि = अहइ = अस्ति । सिंघल = सिंहल-द्वीप । राजू = राज्य । पाइअ = पाई जाती है । राज = राजा । साजू = साज = तयारी । उदासी = उदासीन = संसार से विरक्त । जोगी = योगी । जती = यती । तपा = तपस्वी । सनिआसी = सन्न्यासी । (योगी, यती, तपस्वी और सन्न्यासी के लिये ३० वेँ दोहे की टीका देखो) । जोग = योग । जोरि = जोडयित्वा = जोड कर । पाइत = पाया जाता है । भोगू = भोग । तजि = त्यक्त्वा = त्याग कर । कित = कुतः = कहाँ ॥ साधहि = श्रद्धा से = इच्छा से । साध = साधे = साधयेत् । तप्प = तप = तपस्या । बापुरा = वापुरः = बपुरा = गरीब । सीस = शीर्ष = शिर । कलप्प = कल्पन = छेदन (कृपू छेदने, आक्षिप्त अर्थ) ॥

शुक ने कहा, (कि) राजा, मुझ से सुनो, प्रीति करना कठिन कार्य है ॥ तुम अभीँ घर (बैठे) पकी पकाई जँवो, (सो जिस के मन मेँ) कमल नहीँ बैठा है, अर्थात् कमल नहीँ बसा है, तहाँ, अर्थात् तिस के मन मेँ, (चाहे) कोई बैठे, अर्थात् बसे, वा तहाँ कोँई बैठे ॥ (परन्तु जिस के मन मेँ कमल बस गया फिर वह दूसरे की चाह नहीँ करता, उसी कमल के लिये तडपा करता है; इस बात को) भ्रमर जानते हैँ, जो कि तिस (कमल की) राह मेँ लुट गये हैँ, और जीव को (भी) दे दिये हैँ; (परन्तु जीव) देने पर (भी) छुटकारा नहीँ पाये, अर्थात् कमल-वासना की लालसा से जो मरे, तो दूसरे जन्म मेँ भी भ्रमर-ही हो कर फिर इसी दशा मेँ प्रवृत्त हुए, क्योँकि भगवद्गीता मेँ भगवान् कृष्ण का वाक्य है, कि

'अन्तकाले च मामेव स्मरन्मुक्त्वा कलेवरम् ।
यः प्रयाति स मद्भावं याति नास्त्यत्र संशयः ॥
यं यं वापि स्मरन् भावं त्यजत्यन्ते कलेवरम् ।
तं तमेवैति कौन्तेय सदा तद्भावभावितः ॥'

(८ अध्या० । श्लो० ५-६)

(सो) सिंहल का राज्य (बडा) कठिन है। राजा की तयारी से, अर्थात् सेना, धन, इत्यादि बल से, (वह राज्य) नहीँ पाई जाती है, अर्थात् कोई चाहे, कि बङ्गत सा धन अँकोर दे कर, वा बडी भारी सेना की चढाई से जीत कर, उसे लें, तो असंभव है; क्योँकि सिंहल के राजा के यहाँ असंख्य धन है, इस लिये वहाँ के मन्त्री लोग धन के लोभ में नहीँ आ सकते। और उस के यहाँ अनन्त सेना भी है, जिस का जीतना असंभव है॥ उस (राज्य की) राह में वही जाता है, अर्थात् वही जा सकता है, जो (संसार से) उदासीन हो कर, योगी, यती, तपस्वी वा सन्यासी हो जाय॥ योग जोड कर, अर्थात् योग कमा कर, उसी योग-बल की कमाई से वह (राज्य का) भोग पाया जाता है, (और दूसरी कोई उपाय-ही नहीँ जिस से वह मिले)। सो कोई भोग को त्याग कर, योग (क्लेश के भय से) करता नहीँ, (इसी से आज तक वह राज्य-भोग किसी को प्राप्त नहीँ ऊआ है)॥ तुम राजा हो, चाहते हो, (कि) सुख प्राप्त हो, (सो) भोगी से योगी बन आना कहाँ, अर्थात् जो रात दिन भोग-ही में अपनी आधी अवस्था बिताया, उस भोगी से यह कहाँ बन आवे (बन पडे), कि योगी हो। (सो राजा, निश्चय समझो, कि विना योगी बने उस भोग का भोग लगाना असंभव है, यह शुक का अभिप्राय है)॥.

(शुक कहता है, कि राजन्,) साध-ही से सिद्धि नहीँ पाई जाती, अर्थात् केवल मन की इच्छा-ही से मनोरथ की सिद्धि नहीँ होती, कहावत है, कि 'मन-मोदक नहिँ भूख बुताई', अर्थात् मन के लड्डू से भूख नहीँ बुझती, (सो) जब तक (योगी हो कर) तप न साधे (तब तक मनोरथ-सिद्धि नहीँ होती)। (मनोरथ-सिद्धि में जो क्लेश होता है, उसे) निश्चय से (पइ = अपि) सो (वह) गरीब जानता है, जो (उस सिद्धि के लिये अपने) शिर का छेदन करता है, अर्थात् कर डालता है॥ १२५॥

चउपाई ।

का भा जोग कहानी कथे । निकसु न घीउ बाजु दधि मथे ॥
जउ लहि आप हेराइ न कोई । तउ लहि हेरत पाउ न सोई ॥
पेम पहार कठिन बिधि गढा । सो पइ चढइ सीस सउँ चढा ॥
पंथ सूरि कर उठा अँकूरू । चोर चढइ कइ चढ मनसूरू ॥
तुइँ राजा का पहिरसि कंथा । तोर-इ घरहि माँझ दस पंथा ॥
काम करोध तिसिना मद माया । पाँच-उ चोर न छाडहिँ काया ॥
नउ सेँधइ जेहि घर मँझिआरा । घर मूसहिँ निसि कइ उँजिआरा ॥

दोहा ।

अजहूँ जाग अजाना होत आउ निसि भोर ।
पुनि किछु हाथ न लागिहइ मूसि जाहिँ जब चोर ॥ १२६ ॥

भा = अभूत् = भया = हुआ । कहानी = कथना = कथनी = कथा । कथे = कथन से = कहने से । निकसु = निःकसति = निकसता है । घीउ = घृत = घी । बाजु = वर्जयित्वा = विना । मथे = मन्थन से = मथने से = महने से । आप = आत्मा = स्वयम् । हेराइ = हेराता है = हारयति । पाउ = पाता है । पेम = प्रेम । पहार = प्रहार = पहाड = पर्वत । सूरि = शूली = फाँसी । उठा = उत्थित हुआ । अँकूरू = अङ्कुर = अँखुआ । मनसूरू = मनसूर = सूफी मत-वाले मुसल्मानों का आचार्य । पहिरसि = परिदधासि = प्रदधासि = पहिरता है । कंथा = कन्था = कथरी । तोर-इ = तेरे-ही = तवैव । माँझ = मध्य । दस = दश । पंथा = पन्थाः = मार्ग । काम = अभीष्ट । करोध = क्रोध = कोह = गुस्सा । तिसिना = तृष्णा = लालच = लोभ । मद = अभिमान । माया = ममतादि । छाडहिँ = छाडइ का बहु-वचन, छाडइ = छुडति = छोडता है = छाडता है । काया = काय = शरीर । नउ = नव । सेँधइ = सन्धि = सेँध । मँझिआरा = मध्यालय = मध्य-स्थान । मूसहिँ = मूसइ का बहु-वचन, मूसइ = मूषति = मूसता है = चोराता है । निसि = निशि = रात्रौ = रात्रि में । उँजिआरा = उज्ज्वलन = प्रकाश । जाग = जागृहि = जागो = सो कर उठो । अजाना = अज्ञानी = अयानी = बे-समझ । भोर = (भूरिः = इन्द्रः, उस से उत्पन्न भोर) = प्रभात = सबेरा । पुनि = पुनः । किछु = किञ्चित् । लागिहइ = लगेगा = प्राप्त होगा । मूसि = मूस कर । जाहिँ = जाइ का बहुवचन, जाइ = याति = जाता है ॥

(शुक कहता है, कि राजन्,) योग की कहानी कहने से क्या भया, अर्थात् क्या होता है, उस से कुछ भी फल-सिद्धि नहीं, व्यर्थ बक-वाद से समय नष्ट करना है, (क्योंकि) विना दही के महने से घी नहीं निकसता है॥ जब तक कोई आप नहीं हेराय जाता है, अर्थात् अपने को नहीं खो देता है, तब तक हेरता (ढूँढता) हुआ उस प्रेम को (सोई) नहीं पाता॥ ब्रह्मा ने (इस) प्रेम-रूपी पहाड को (ऐसा) कठिन बनाया (गढा) है, (कि इस पर पैर से कोई नहीं चढ सकता, परन्तु) वह (सो) निश्चय से (पइ) चढता है, जो कि शिर से चढता है, अर्थात् संसार के प्राणी मात्र से जो उलटा चले वह इस प्रेम-पहाड पर चढे। इस लिये सब प्राणी के चलने का व्यापार जो पैर से होता है, उस से विपरीत-व्यापार से, अर्थात् शिर के बल से, जो चलना स्वीकार करे सो इस प्रेम-पहाड पर चढे॥ (जिस के हृदय में प्रेम का अङ्कुर उठा, उसे समझो, कि) शूली के राह (जाने) का अङ्कुर उठा। (सो उस शूली पर दूसरे की सामर्थ्य नहीं, कि चढे; क्योंकि उस पर) चोर चढता है, अथवा मनसूर (ऐसा था जो) चढा। बैज़ा का रहने-वाला शेख हुसेन हल्लाज धुनिये का पुत्र मनसूर हल्लाज* था। बहुत मुसल्मानों का मत है, कि यह बडा ब्रह्म-ज्ञानी वेदान्ती था, और बहुतों का मत है, कि यह बडा-ही फरेबी था; फरेब-ही से बहुतों को ठग कर, अपने में विश्वास दिला कर, ब्रह्म-ज्ञानी बना था। यह अपने को भारतवर्षीय वेदान्ती साधुओं के ऐसा 'अनुल हक (सोऽहं),' अर्थात् 'मैं ही ईश्वर हूँ' कहता था, इस पर रुष्ट हो कर बगदाद के खलीफा मक्तदिर ने इसे सन् ९१९ ईसवी (३०६ हिजरी) में शूली पर चढा दिया। इब्न-खलीकान् के मत से यह घटना सन् ९२२ ई०, मार्च की २६ वीं (३०९ हि०, ज़ीकअद की २४ वीं) तारीख को हुई। मुसल्मानों में कहावत है, कि शूली के समय मनसूर के अङ्ग से जो रक्त-विन्दु गिरते थे, उन प्रत्येक में से 'अनुल हक, अनुल हक' ऐसा शब्द होता था। खलीफा ने मनसूर की मृत-देह को भस्म करवा डाला। एक रूमी मौलाना ने उस में की थोडी राख शीशी में रख, घर ले आया, और अपनी सयानी कन्या से कहा, कि यह अलभ्य वस्तु है इसे बडे यत्न से रक्खो। उस ने इसे अपूर्व पदार्थ समझा इस लिये थोडी-सी राख निकाल कर, खा गई। उस के खाने से गर्भ रहा। लडका होने पर उस कन्या के पिता रूमी मौलाना ने उस लडके को जारज समझ, वन में फँकवा दिया। पीछे से वही

* See Beale's Oriental Biographical Dictionary, s. v. Manṣūr Ḥallāj.

बालक शम्सतबजेर नाम से बडा सिद्ध ऊश्रा, अपने नाना को भी अपना शिष्य बनाया, और जगत् में बडा-ही प्रसिद्ध ऊश्रा। सूफी संप्रदाय के मुसल्मान लोग मन्सूर को अपने मत का आचार्य मानते हैं। सो महम्मद कवि का अभिप्राय है, कि जैसे मन्सूर की शरीर में ब्रह्म-मय होने से शूली चढने पर भी प्रति रक्त-विन्दु में ब्रह्म-ही ब्रह्म समाय गया था, उसी प्रकार जिस की शरीर में प्रेम समाय जाय, जिस में शूली चढने पर और मर जाने पर भी प्रति रक्त-विन्दु से प्रेम, प्रेम, वा जिस के लिये प्रेम लग गया हो, उस के नाम की ध्वनि निकले, वह इस प्रेम-पहाड पर चढ सकता है॥ (सो हे राजा) तूँ क्या कंथा (साधुओं की गेरुश्रा रंग की गुदडी जो गले में डाले रहते हैं) पहनता है, अर्थात् पहन सकता है। (क्योंकि) तेरे तो घर-हीं (शरीर-ही) के मध्य दश राह हैं, अर्थात् दशो (हाथ, पैर, नेत्र, कान, नाक, त्वचा, गुदा, जिह्वा, वाणी और लिङ्ग) इन्द्रियाँ अपनी अपनी राह में ले जाने के लिये तुझे प्रतिक्षण खींच रही हैं, तो तूँ क्योंकर प्रेम-मार्ग में जा सकता है; इस लिये गुदडी पहन कर, तेरा योगी का बनना व्यर्थ है॥ काम, क्रोध, तृष्णा, मद और माया ये पाँचो चोर तेरी काया को नहीं छोडते हैं, अर्थात् रात दिन तेरी शरीर के बीच में बैठे हैं॥ (सो) जिस घर (शरीर) के बीच में (दो आँख, दो कान, दो नासिका के पूरे, एक मुख, एक लिङ्ग और एक गुदा ये) नव सँध हैं (चाहे जिस राह से पाँचो चोर पैठ सकते हैं), (सो उन सँधों की राह से वे पाँचो घुस कर) रात में, अर्थात् अज्ञानान्धकार से पूरित तेरे हृदय में, उँजेला कर, अर्थात् हम चोर हैं ऐसा प्रत्यक्ष डङ्का बजा कर, तेरे घर (शरीर) को मूस रहे हैं (और तुझे खबर नहीं)। फिर तूँ क्या योगी बन कर, प्रेम-मार्ग में चलने को तयार होता है। पहले घर में घुसे पाँचो चोरों को मार कर, अपना घर शुद्ध कर ले, तब उस में प्रेम-रत्न रखने की इच्छा से प्रेम के ढूँढने के लिये योगी बने तो उचित है; अन्यथा केवल विडम्बना मात्र है॥

(सो अज्ञान) निशा में भोर ऊश्रा आता है, अर्थात् रात बीतती जाती है, अब भी, हे अज्ञानी (राजा), जाग। जब (पाँचो) चोर (घर को) मूस ले जाते हैं अर्थात् तेरी शरीर को नष्ट कर जायँगे, (तब) फिर (सेवाय पछताने के और) कुछ हाथ न लगेगा; अर्थात् शुक, राजा का गुरु बन कर, उपदेश देता है, कि माया-रूपी निशा में पडा पडा मत सो। अब जाग, और अपने शरीर की ओर चेत कर, जिस में पाँचो चोर बे-डर से तेरे मनो-मणि को लूट रहे हैं, और तुझे लट्टू सा चारो ओर

फिरा रहे हैं, सो जब तक उस मनो-मणि को वे चोर बाहर निकाल कर, नहीं ले जाते हैं, इस के बीच-ही में जाग कर यत्न कर, जिस में वे चोर-ही भागें, और तेरी भाग जागे ॥ १२६ ॥

चउपाई।

सुनि सो बात राजा मन जागा। पलक न मार टकटका लागा ॥
नयनहिँ ढरहिँ मोति अउ मूँगा। जस गुड खाइ रहा होइ गूँगा ॥
हिअ कइ जोति दीप वह सूझा। यह जो दीप अँधेरा बूझा ॥
उलटि दिसिटि माया सउँ रूठी। पलटि न फिरइ जानि कइ झूठी ॥
जउ पइ नाहीँ असथिर दसा। जग उजार का कीजिअ बसा ॥
गुरू बिरह-चिनगी पइ मेला। जो सुलगाइ लेइ सो चेला ॥
अब कइ पनिग भिरिँग कइ करा। भवँर होउँ जेहि कारन जरा ॥

दोहा।

फूल फूल फिरि पूँछउँ जो पहुँचउँ वह केत।
तन नेउछाउरि कइ मिलउँ जउँ मधुकर जिउ देत ॥ १२७ ॥

इति पेम-खंड ॥ ११ ॥

जागा = जाग्रित हुआ = जगा। टकटका = टकटकी = तकतक = ताकते ही रह जाने का व्यापार, जिस में न पलक भँजे और न पुतली घूमे। ढरहिँ = ढरते हैं = गिरते हैं। मोति = मौक्तिक। मूँगा = मुद्ग के सदृश विद्रुम के खण्ड। गूँगा = गुँ गुँ करने-वाला = मूक। हिअ = हृदय। जोति = ज्योतिः। सूझा = सूझइ का भूत काल में प्रयोग, सूझइ = शुध्यति। अँधेरा = अन्धकार। बूझा = बूझइ का भूतकाल में प्रयोग। बूझइ = बुध्यते। उलटि = उल्लुय = उलट कर। दिसिटि = दृष्टि। माया = धन, दारा इत्यादि। रूठी = रुष्ट हो गई। पलटि = प्रलुय = पलट कर। फिरइ = स्फुरति = फिरती है। झूठी = झुण्टः = काँटे ऐसी, अर्थात् असत्य। वा झूठ = उच्छिष्ट, अर्थात् अपवित्र। वा झूठ = झटः (झट उपघाते) वा जूष्टः (जूष हिंसायाम्) वा झूठ = झट् (झष आदानसंवरणयोः। भावे क्विप्)। असथिर = स्थिर = अचल। दसा = दशा = स्थिति। जग = जगत्। उजार = उज्जारण। कीजिअ = कीजिये। गुरू = गुरु = उपदेशक। चिनगी = अग्नि-कण = चिन-

गारी। मेला = मेलयति = मिलाता है। सुलगाद = सु-लग्गद से णिजन्त, जैसे जगद से जगाय, भगद से भगाय, पढद से पढाय इत्यादि। सु-लग्गद = सु-लगति (शकादीनां द्दित्वम् ५.२। प्राकृत-प्रकाश, अष्टमपरिच्छेद, शक्नोति = सक्कद। लगति = लग्गद) सुन्दर-रीति से लगाना। चेला = शिष्य। पनिग = पतङ्ग = फनगे। भिरिँग = भृङ्ग = कीट विशेष। करा = कला = विद्या। कारन = कारण। जरा = जर गया हूँ = जरा हूँ॥ फूल = फुल्ल = पुष्प। फिरि = फिर फिर कर = घूम घूम कर। पूँछउँ = पृच्छानि = पूँछूँ। केत = निकेत = स्थान = घर, वा केत = केतक = केतकी का फूल। नेउछाउरि = नेवछावर कर। जउँ = ज्यों = यथा = जैसे। मधुकर = भ्रमर = भौंरा। देत = देता है॥

(हीरा-मणि शुक से १२५-१२६ दोहे की) बातें को सुन कर, राजा (रत्न-सेन) का मन जाग उठा, (और जैसे कोई किसी वस्तु के ध्यान में काठ के ऐसा हो जाता है, उसी प्रकार राजा को) टकटकी लग गई; पलक नहीं मारता है, अर्थात् विना पलक भाँजे टकटकी लगा कर, एक ओर अचल दृष्टि लगा कर, ताकने लगा॥ (और) नयनों से मोती और मूँगा ढरते हैं (ढरने लगे), अर्थात् कभीं जल-विन्दु मुक्ता-सदृश और कभीं रक्त-विन्दु मूँगा-सदृश राजा की आँखों से टपकने लगे; (और राजा) गूँगा हो कर, रह गया; जैसे (कोई) (जादू का) गुड खा कर, गूँगा हो कर, रह जाता है, खट्टा वा मीठा कुछ भी नहीं कह सकता॥ (शुक के ज्ञानोपदेश से राजा को) हृदय की वह ज्योतिः-स्वरूप (परमात्म-रूप) दीया सूझी, (इस लिये) यह जगत् के जो (जम्बू, शाक, शाल्मल, कुश, क्रौञ्च, गोमेदक, और पुष्कर) दीप हैं वे अन्धकार-मय हैं, यह समझ पडा॥ (रात दिन जो धन, दारा इत्यादि माया-ही की ओर दृष्टि रहती थी, वह) दृष्टि उलट कर, माया से रूठ गई, अर्थात् माया से विरक्त हो गई; (सो माया को) झूठी जान कर, (अब माया की ओर) पलट कर, नहीं फिरती है॥ (कवि कहता है, वा राजा अपने मन में विचार करता है, कि) जब (यह जगत् की) स्थिति (दशा) निश्चय से स्थिर नहीं है, (तब इस) उजार जग में बस कर, क्या कीजिये, अर्थात् जब निश्चय है, कि यह संसार क्षण-भङ्गुर है, तब इस के बीच वास करने से क्या फल॥ (राजा कहता है, कि) गुरु (तो) निश्चय कर, विरह (परमात्मा के मिलने के लिये प्रेम) की (एक) चिनगारी (केवल) मिला देता है, अर्थात् शिष्य के हृदय में डाल देता है; (परन्तु असल) वही (सो) चेला है, जो कि (उस चिनगारी से आग को) सुलगा लेता है, अर्थात् पक्का चेला वही जो

विरहाग्नि-कण को गुरु से पा कर बडे यत्न से अपने रक्त, मांस इत्यादि को लगा कर उस विरह-(प्रेम)-अनल की राशि तयार कर ले, जिस के प्रकाश से सकल भूत-मय परमात्मा देख पडने लगे। और यदि अलभ्य चिनगारी पा कर, अपनी असावधानता से उसे बुझा दिया, तो बडे श्रम से जो गुरु ने उस चिनगारी को उत्पन्न किया वह श्रम व्यर्थ ऊई, और चेले का भी समय नष्ट होने से वह चेला न इस लोक न परलोक के योग्य ऊआ, चौगान के गेँद के ऐसा इधर उधर मारा फिरेगा॥ (सो राजा कहता है, कि) अब पतङ्ग (कीट) भृङ्ग की कला कर, अर्थात् जैसे भृङ्ग की चिन्ता से कीट (पतङ्ग) भृङ्ग हो जाता है (९८ वँ दोहे की टीका देखो), उसी प्रकार पद्मावती-कमल की चिन्ता से पद्मावती-मय हो जाऊँ, (और) जिस (कमल के) कारण जल गया हूँ, (उस के लिये) भ्रमर होऊँ॥

परमात्म-स्वरूप पद्मावती पुष्प का स्वरूप तो दृष्टि-गोचर न होने से अपरिचित है, इस लिये राजा कहता है, कि उस पुष्प के लिये घूम घूम कर, फूल फूल से पूछूँ, (और) यदि (जो) उस स्थान मेँ पऊँचूँ (जहाँ पद्मावती है), वा यदि उस केतकी (पद्मावती) के यहाँ पऊँचूँ, (तो) शरीर नेवछावर कर, अर्थात् शरीर का बलि-दान कर, (उस केतकी-रूपा पद्मावती से) मिलूँ, जैसे (केतकी के मिलने के लिये) भ्रमर जी दे देता है। केतकी के पत्र कर-पत्र (आरा) सदृश होते हैँ, और उस का गुच्छादार श्वेत-पुष्प भी कण्टक से भरा रहता है, इस लिये विना अङ्ग भङ्ग ऊए भ्रमर उस का रस नहीँ पा सकता। पद्मावती का मिलना भी विना अङ्ग भङ्ग ऊए कठिन है, इस लिये पूर्णोपमा के लिये कवि ने पद्मावती को उपमा केतक से दी। और राजा ने भी मन मेँ निश्चय समझ लिया, कि विना शरीर नेवछावर किये, अर्थात् विना शरीर दिये पद्मावती का मिलना असम्भव है॥ १२७॥

इति प्रेम-खण्ड-नाम-एकादश-खण्डं समाप्तम्॥ ११॥

अथ जोगी-खंड ॥ १२ ॥

चउपाई ।

तजा राज राजा भा जोगी । अउ किँगरी कर गहेउ बिओगी ॥
तन बिसँभर मन बाउर लटा । उरुझा पेम परी सिर जटा ॥
चंद-बदन अउ चंदन देहा । भसम चढाइ कीन्ह तन खेहा ॥
मेखल सीँगी चकर धँधारी । जोगोटा रुदराछ अधारी ॥
कंथा पहिरि डंड कर गहा । सिद्ध होइ कहँ गोरख कहा ॥
मुँदरा स्रवन कंठ जप-माला । कर उदपान काँध बघ-छाला ॥
पावँरि पाँय लीन्ह सिर छाता । खप्पर लीन्ह भेस कइ राता ॥

दोहा ।

चला भुगुति माँगइ कहँ साजि कया तप जोग ।
सिद्ध होउँ पदुमावति (पाए) हिरदइ जेहि क बिओग ॥ १२८ ॥

तजा = अत्यजत् = त्यागा । राज = राज्य । भा = भया = बभूव । जोगी = योगी । किँगरी = किन्करी = किन् किन् करने-वाली = एक तरह की चिकारी जो पैँरिये वा भर्त्तृहरि के गीत गाने-वाले योगी लिये रहते हैँ । गहेउ = गहइ का भूत-काल, गहइ = गृह्णाति । बिओगी = वियोगी = जिसे किसी का (जैसे यहाँ पद्मावती का) वियोग (विरह) हो । बिसँभर = विसम्भर = बेसँभार = जो सँभर न सके । बाउर =

वातुल = बौरहा। लटा = लट, वा लटा = रटा = रटइ (रटति) का भूत-काल। अरुझा = अरुझइ (आरुह्यते) का भूत-काल। पेम = प्रेम। परी = परइ (पतति) का भूत-काल। सिर = शिर। जटा = केशों के मिल जाने से शिर पर जो रस्सी-सौलट पड जाती हैं। चंद-बदन = चन्द्र-वदन = चन्द्र-मुख = चाँद के ऐसा मुख। चंदन = चन्दन = सुगन्ध-द्रव्य। देहा = देह = शरीर। भसम = भस्म = राख। चढाइ = चढा कर। खेहा = खेह = धूली = मट्टी। मेखल = मेखला = मूँज के रस्सी का कटि-बन्धन (कमर-बंद) जैसा कि यज्ञोपवीत होने के समय वटु पहनता है। सींगी = शृङ्गी = हरिण के सींग का बाजा जो मुह से बजाई जाती है, जैसे शङ्ख। चकर = चक्र = गोल। धंधारी = धन्धन के योग्य, (धन्धन = चिन्तन) = धंधा। धंधारी-चक्र = गोरख-धंधा। गोरख-पन्थी साधु लोहे वा लकडी के शलाकाओं के हेर फेर से चक्र बना कर उस के बीच में छेद कर कौडी को वा मालाकार डोरे को डाल देते हैं, और उसी कौडी वा डोरे को वार वार कुछ मन्त्र पढ पढ कर, निकाला करते हैं, और उस चक्र को गोरख-धंधा वा गोरख-धंधारी कहते हैं। विना क्रिया जाने उस चक्र में से सहसा किसी से वह कौडी वा डोरा नहीं निकलता। चक्र की सलाकाओं में ऐसा अरुझ जाता है, कि निकालना कठिन पड जाता है। जो निकालने की क्रिया को जानता है वह सहज में निकाल लेता है। गोरख-पन्थियों का विश्वास है, कि मन्त्र पढ पढ कर, गोरख-धन्धे के बीच से डोरा निकालने से गोरख की कृपा से ईश्वर प्रसन्न हो संसार-चक्र के बीच में पडे ऊए डोरे के सदृश उस प्राणी को निकाल बाहर कर, मुक्त कर देता है। लोक में कौतुक के लिये जो बटुआ, सन्दूक, वा कोई यन्त्र ऐसे बनाये जाते हैं, जिन के बीच में रक्खे ऊए पैसे इत्यादि खोलने की क्रिया न जानने-वालों से नहीं निकलते, उन को भी अब लोग गोरख-धंधारी कहते हैं। यह शब्द इस देश में ऐसा प्रसिद्ध है, कि यदि किसी से किसी वस्तु का भेद न खुले तो वह झट कह देता है, कि यह वस्तु गोरख-धंधा वा गोरख-धंधारी है। जोगोटा = योगोटा = योग को ओटने-वाला = योग को शुद्ध करने-वाला = योग को साफ करने-वाला, जैसे ओटने से रूई साफ होती है। जिस यन्त्र से रूई साफ की जाती है उस को पश्चिमोत्तर और अवध के प्रान्त में ओटनी वा ओटा कहते हैं। वा जोगोटा = योगोटा = योग का ओटा = योग का आधार। जिस पर बैठ के स्त्रियाँ जाँता पीसती हैं, उसे इस प्रान्त में ओटा कहते हैं। रुदराछ = रुद्राच = एक वृच का फल, जिस में रुद्र के नेच (अच)

सदृश चिन्ह रहते हैं; तन्त्र-शास्त्र के मत से शिव-मन्त्र जपने के लिये इस की माला बहुत पवित्र समझी जाती है। इस रुद्राच के दाने में खरबूजे की फाँक ऐसी कई रेखा होती हैं; उन्हें मुख कहते हैं; जप में प्रायः पञ्च-मुखी रुद्राच का विशेष माहात्म्य है। कहावत है, कि जैसे जिस के घर में वामावर्त्त शङ्ख रहे उस के घर में सदा लक्ष्मी का निवास रहता है, उसी प्रकार जिस के गले में एक-मुखी रुद्राच बँधा हो उस के ऊपर शस्त्र की शक्ति नहीं काम करती। एक-मुखी रुद्राच की परीचा के लिये लोग भँडे के गले में इसे बाँध कर भँडे के गले के ऊपर बल-पूर्वक तलवार मारते हैं; यदि तलवार से भँडे के गले में कुछ भी चोट न लगे तो समझना चाहिए, कि सच्चा एक-मुखी रुद्राच है। रुद्राच नेपाल और दचिण-प्रान्त में बहुत होता है। अधारी = आधार = काठ के डंडे में लगा काठ का पीढा, (आसा) जिसे योगी लोग प्रायः लिये रहते हैं; जहाँ कहीं इच्छा हुई तहाँ भूमि पर डंडे को खडा कर उस पीढे पर बैठ जाते हैं। जैसे विना अभ्यास किये बाइसिकिल (bicycle) पर लोग नहीं बैठ सकते, तैसे-ही अभ्यास के विना इस पीढे पर भी नहीं बैठा जाता। कंथा = कन्था = गेरुए रंग के सुजनी का चोलना जो गले में डाल देने से अङ्ग को ढाँक लेती है; इसे योगी लोग गुदरी कहते हैं; फटे, पुराने चिथडों को जोड जोड कर इसे बनाते हैं। डंड = दण्ड = डंडा = सोंटा, जो झाड फूँक करने के लिये योगी लोग रखते हैं; यह हाथ डेढ हाथ का काले रूलर (सीधी रेखा खींचने के लिये सीधी और लम्बी गोल काष्ठ की शलाका) के ऐसा होता है। बहुत से योगी इसे भैरव-नाथ का बहुत से गोरख-नाथ का सोंटा कहते हैं। गोरख = गोरच-नाथ = गोरख-नाथ = एक प्रसिद्ध सिद्ध अवधूत जो कि मछंदर-नाथ (मत्स्येन्द्र-नाथ) के प्रधान शिष्य थे। कहावत है, कि शिष्य हो कर गोरख-नाथ तप के लिये वन में चले गये और बहुत वर्षों पर लौटे। इस बीच में मछंदर-नाथ विषय-वासना में लिप्त हो कर, अपना योग भ्रष्ट कर दिया था। जिस समय गोरख अपने गुरु के द्वार पर पहुँचे, उस समय गुरु मछंदर जी एक वेश्या की नाच देख रहे थे। इस लीला को देख गोरख ने अपनी सिद्धता से ऐसी लीला की, कि, तबलची कैसा-ह, यत्न करे, परन्तु तबले से 'जाग मछंदर गोरख आये', इस आवाज को छोड दूसरी आवाज-ही न निकले। अन्त में मछंदर को ज्ञान हुआ, और गोरख को बुला कर कहा, कि अब तैं मेरा गुरु हुआ। गोरख-पन्थियों के मत से नव-नाथ हैं। उन के नाम नीचे लिखे हैं —

एक-नाथ १। आदि-नाथ २। मत्स्येन्द्र-नाथ ३। उदय-नाथ ४। दण्ड-नाथ ५। सत्य-नाथ ६। सन्तोष-नाथ ७। कूर्म-नाथ ८। जलन्धर-नाथ ९। इन नवों की उत्पत्ति गोरख-नाथ (जिन्हें श्री-नाथ भी कहते हैं) से कहते हैं, गोरख-ही के नव-विध ये अवतार हैं। गोरख-पन्थियों का सिद्धान्त है, कि गोरख-ही भिन्न भिन्न समय में अवतार ले कर भिन्न भिन्न नाथान्त नाम से नव नाथ हुए हैं, और गोरख-ही अनादि अनन्त पुरुष हैं, उन्हीं की इच्छा से ब्रह्मा, विष्णु, महादेव इत्यादि हुए हैं। कहा = कहइ का भूत-काल, कहइ = कथयति। मुँदरा = मुद्रा, जो कि स्फटिक वा हाथी-दाँत की मुद्रिकाकार होती है, और कान को चिरवा कर उस में जिसे गोरख-पन्थी पहनते हैं। गोरख-पन्थी लोग एक शुभ-दिन (प्रायः वसन्त पञ्चमी) में कान को चिरवा कर मन्त्र के संस्कार से इस मुद्रा को पहनते हैं, और कान पक न जाय इस भय से जब तक घाव अच्छा नहीं होता केवल फलाहार करते हैं। उन लोगों को निश्चय है, कि स्त्रियों के दर्शन से भी घाव पक जाता है, इस लिये घाव अच्छे होने तक एकान्त एक कोठरी के भीतर रहते हैं, जिस में स्त्रियों का दर्शन न हो। स्रवन = श्रवण = कान। जप-माला = जप करने के लिये माला = रुद्राक्ष-माला। उदपान = उदक (जल) पान (पीने) का पात्र = कमण्डलु। काँध = स्कन्ध = कंधा। बघ-छाल = व्याघ्र-छाल = व्याघ्राम्बर = बघंबर = व्याघ्र का चर्म। पावँरि = पामरी = पादुका = खराऊँ वा लतरी। पाँय = पद। छाता = छत्र। खप्पर = खर्पर = मट्टी के घडे का फोरा हुआ एक खण्ड, जिस में भिक्षा को योगी लोग लेते हैं; अब यह दर्य्यायी नरियर का बनता है। बहुत से योगी लोग काँसे का भी भिक्षा-पात्र रखते हैं, इस लिये खप्पर को काँसा भी कहते हैं। होली में योगीडे में गुरु लोग चौडे मुह के मट्टी के घडे में आग को रख कर जादू से उसे हाथ पर लिये फिरते हैं, उस घडे को भी खप्पर कहते हैं। भेस = वेष = सूरत। राता = रक्त = लाल = गेरुआ रँग॥ चला = चलइ (चलति) का भूत-काल। भुगुति = भुक्ति = भोग। माँगइ = माँगने। साजि = सज्जयित्वा = साज कर। कया = काय = काया = शरीर। जोग = योग्य। हिरदइ = हृदय। बिओग = वियोग = विरह॥

(हीरा-मणि शुक से सब बात को सुन कर) राजा (रत्न-सेन) ने राज्य को त्याग दिया, (और पद्मावती के पाने के लिये) योगी हुआ (बना)। (वह) वियोगी (विरही) हाथ (कर) में किंगरी को पकडा॥ (जैसे योगी लोग अपनी शरीर की खबर नहीं लेते, तैसे-ही राजा को) तनु (भी) बे-खबर हो गई, (और) मन बौरहा हो गया,

अर्थात् पागल के ऐसा राजा हो गया। मन में प्रेम के लट उरझ गये, वा (राजा का) मन बौरहा हो गया (और पद्मावती, पद्मावती,) रटने लगा। (उस मन में) प्रेम उरझ गया, (और शरीर की खबर न लेने से) शिर पर जटा पड गई॥ (जो) चन्द्र के ऐसा मुख और चन्दन से भूषित देह थी; (उस पर) भस्म को चढा कर (लपेट कर) शरीर को मट्टी कर डाला॥ मेखला, शृङ्गी, योग को शुद्ध करने-वाला धंधारी चक्र, रुद्राच (गले की कंठी) और आधार (आसन के लिये पीढा) इन सब को धारण किया॥ कंथा को पहर कर, कर में सेांटे को लिया। सिद्ध होने के लिये 'गोरख गोरख' कहने लगा, अर्थात् गुरु-वर गोरख-नाथ का नाम जपने लगा॥ कान में मुद्रा, कण्ठ में जप करने की (रुद्राच-)माला, हाथ में कमण्डलु और कंधे पर (आसन के लिये) व्याघ्र-चर्म को, और पैरों में पावँरी, शिर के ऊपर छाता, और (बगल में) खप्पर को लिया, अर्थात् धारण किया। वेष लाल कर सब को धारण किया, अर्थात् जिन वस्तुओं के ऊपर नाम गिना गये हैं, उन सब को गेरुये रँग से रँग कर तब धारण किया। (इस प्रकार से राजा पूरा गोरख-पन्थी योगी हुआ, और गोरख-नाथ के नाम जपने से गोरख-नाथ को अपना गुरु बनाया)॥

(इस प्रकार) तपस्या के योग्य अपनी शरीर को बना कर (साजि), भुक्ति (पद्मावती-प्राप्ति) माँगने के लिये चला। (और मन में यही सोचता है, कि) जिस का हृदय में वियोग (विरह) है, (तिसी) पद्मावती से सिद्ध होऊँ, अर्थात् तिसी पद्मावती की प्राप्ति होने-ही से मैं अपने को सिद्ध समझूँगा॥ १२८॥

चउपाई।

गनक कहहिँ गनि गवँन न आजू। दिन लेइ चलहु होइ सिध काजू॥
पेम-पंथ दिन घडी न देखा। तब देखइ जब होइ सरेखा॥
जेहि तन पेम कहाँ तेहि माँसू। कया न रकत न नयनन्ह आँसू॥
पंडित भूल न जानइ चालू। जीउ लेत दिन पूँछ न कालू॥
सती कि बउरी पूँछइ पाँडे। अउ घर पइठि न सइँतइ भाँडे॥
मरइ जो चलइ गंग-गति लेई। तेहि दिन कहाँ घडी को देई॥
मइँ घर-बार कहाँ कर पावा। घर काया पुनि अंत परावा॥

दोहा ।

हउँ रे पखेरू पंखी जेहि बन मोर निबाहु ।
खेलि चला तेहि बन कहँ तुम्ह आपन घर जाहु ॥ १२९ ॥

गनक = गणक = ज्योतिषी, जो किसी काम के लिये शुभ-दिन बताते हैं। गनि = गणयित्वा = गन कर = विचार कर। गवँन = गमन = यात्रा, अर्थात् यात्रा का शुभ-दिन = मुहूर्त्त = साइत। आजू = अद्य = आज। दिन = शुभ-दिन = मुहूर्त्त = साइत। सिध = सिद्ध = पूर्ण = पूरा। काजू = कार्य = मनोरथ। पेम-पंथ = प्रेम-पथ = प्रेम का मार्ग। घडी = घटी = समय। सरेखा = सु-लेख = समझ-दार = समझने के योग्य। कहाँ = क्व, वा कथम्। माँसू = मांस। कया = काय = शरीर। रकत = रक्त = रुधिर = लोहू। आँसू = अश्रु = आँस। भूल = भ्रम = गलती। चालू = चाल = चालन = चलाने की रीति, अर्थात् मुहूर्त्त। पूँछ = पूँछता है = पृच्छति। कालू = काल = प्राणियों का मारने-वाला। सती = महादेव की स्त्री और दक्ष-प्रजापति की कन्या यहाँ सती से ऐसी स्त्री, जो पति-वियोग से मृत-पति के शरीर के साथ चिता में बैठ कर भस्म हो जाय। बउरी = वातुला = बौरही = पति-वियोग से पगली। पूँछइ = पृच्छति = पूँछती है। पाँडे = पाण्डेय, यहाँ पण्डित। पइठि = प्रविश्य = पैठ कर। सइँतइ = संयतते = सहेजती है = यत्न से रखती है। भाँडे = भाण्ड = वर्त्तन = पात्र। मरइ = मरने को = मरने के लिये। गंग-गति = गङ्गा-गति (गङ्गायां गतिः = मोक्षः) = गङ्गा में मोक्ष। घर-बार = गृह-द्वार = घर-दुआर = घर इत्यादि। अंत = अन्त। परावा = परीय = पर का = दूसरे का॥ पखेरू = पक्षी। पंखी = पक्षी। निबाहु = निर्वाह। खेलि = खेलयित्वा = खेल कर। आपन = अपने। जाहु = याहि = जाव॥

ज्योतिषी लोग गणना कर के कहते हैं, कि आज गमन नहीं है, अर्थात् आज यात्रा के लिये शुभ-दिन नहीं है, (सो राजन्) शुभ-दिन ले कर चलो, अर्थात् साइत से यात्रा करो, (जिस में) कार्य सिद्ध हो॥ (कवि कहता है, कि) प्रेम-पथ में (जो चलने लगता है, वह) दिन घडी नहीं देखता है, अर्थात् आज शुभ वा अशुभ दिन है, इस का कुछ भी विचार नहीं करता। (क्योंकि) जब समझने के योग्य हो, तब तो (दिन घडी को) देखे (प्रेम-रस पान से तो बे-खबर हो गया है)॥ (सो) जिस की तनु में प्रेम है, अर्थात् प्रेम समाय गया है, (फिर उस की) शरीर में कहाँ

मांस, (क्योँकि) काया मेँ रक्त नहीँ रहता है। (इस लिये रक्त-मूलक मांस का अभाव हो जाता है), और (उस प्रेमी के) नयनोँ मेँ आँसू (भी) नहीँ रहती। (प्रेम-रस की नशा से टकटकी बँध जाती है, और पुतली पथरा जाती है, फिर पत्थर-सी पुतली मेँ कहाँ आँसू की आशा पाई जाय)॥ पण्डित की, अर्थात् गणक की, भूल है; (वह) चाल, अर्थात् यात्रादि के मुहूर्त्त को जानता-ही नहीँ, अर्थात् उसे इतना ज्ञान-ही नहीँ, कि किस कार्य के लिये मुहूर्त्त देखना आवश्यक है, और किस कार्य के लिये अनावश्यक है। (क्योँकि) काल (प्राणियोँ के) जीव लेती बेला दिन (मुहूर्त्त) नहीँ पूँछता। (जिस समय उस की इच्छा होती है, उसी समय जीव को ले लेता है)॥ (और) क्या (पति-वियोगा-ऽऽतुरा) बौरही सती पण्डित (पाँडे) से पूँछती है, (कि आज पति-शरीर के संग भस्म होने के लिये शुभ-दिन है?)। और (यदि दैवात् शुभ-दिन न हुआ तो क्या वह) घर मेँ पैठ कर, अर्थात् घर के भीतर जा कर, (अपने) भाण्डादिकोँ की रचा करती है,? अर्थात् क्या पति-वियोग-दुःख को भूल कर घर के वस्तुओँ की रचा मेँ लग जाती है?॥ (जिस दिन) जो मरने के लिये चलता है, और गङ्गा मेँ (शरीर-पात कर) गति (मोच) को लेता है, उस दिन (उस को) कोई कहाँ दिन (मुहूर्त्त) देता है। [इन सब बातोँ से कवि ने सूचित किया, कि ऐसे ऐसे अवसर मेँ मुहूर्त्त अनावश्यक है। घर मेँ आग लगने पर, उस के बुझाने के लिये, यदि ज्यौतिषी से मुहूर्त्त पूँछो, और यदि उस के विचार से ९ घडी भर भद्रा हो (भद्रा मेँ लोग कोई शुभ कार्य नहीँ करने, इस का विशेष वर्णन सिंहल से चित्तौर गढ को जहाँ रत्न-सेन ने यात्रा किया है वहाँ पर किया जायगा) तो ९ घडी भर ठहर जाने मेँ सब घर-ही भस्म हो जायगा; फिर बुझावोगे क्या?। इसी पर यह कहावत चली है, कि 'घडी मेँ घर जलै नव घडी भद्रा' सो ऐसे ऐसे अवसर मेँ ज्यौतिषी की मूर्खता है, कि मुहूर्त्त लेने के लिये हठ करे]॥ (ज्यौतिषियोँ के कहने पर राजा ने कहा, कि) मैँ ने कहाँ का घर-बार पाया। घर-(बार) (और) शरीर अन्त मेँ दूसरे की है, अर्थात् दुर्मुहूर्त्त से घर-बार सम्पत्ति और शरीर-ही का न नाश होता है; सो ये तो अन्त मेँ नाशवान् हैँ-हीँ; इन के रचा के लिये क्या मुहूर्त्त का पूँछना। ये तो सब पराये की थाती हैँ। सो यदि अपनी वस्तु हो, तो भला रचा के लिये मुहूर्त्तादि से यत्न उचित है। पराये की थाती मेँ क्या वश, जब चाहे तब ले ले॥

(सो) रे पखेरू, अर्थात् रे पक्षि-रूप ज्योतिषी, मैं (तो) पक्षी हूं। जिस वन में मेरा निर्वाह है, उस वन में (यहाँ) खेल कर चला। तुम अपने घर जाव (मुझे मुहूर्त्त से 'कुछ प्रयोजन नहीं, क्योंकि ऐसे अवसर में मुहूर्त्त का पूछना अपने मनोरथ का भङ्ग करना है)॥ १२९॥

चउपाई।

चहुँ दिस आनि साँटिया फेरी। भइ कटकाई राजा केरी॥
जावँत अहहिँ सकल उरगाना। साँबर लेहु दूर हइ जाना॥
सिंघल-दीप जाइ सब चाहा। मोल न पाउब जहाँ बेसाहा॥
सब निबहइ तहँ आपुन साँटी। साँटी बिनु सेा रह मुख माटी॥
राजा चला साजि कइ जोगू। साजउ बेगि चलउ सब लेागू॥
गरब जो चढेहु तुरइ कइ पीठी। अब भुइँ चलहु सरग सउँ डीठी॥
मंतर लेहु होहु सँग-लागू। गुदर जाइ सब होहिहिँ आगू॥

दोहा।

का निचिंत रे मानुसइ अपनी चिंता आछ।
लेहु सजुग होइ अगुमन पुनि पछिताउ न पाछ॥ १३०॥

चहुँ = चतुर्षु = चारो। दिस = दिशा। आनि = आज्ञा = शपथ-पूर्वक आज्ञा = दोहाई। साँटिया = सोँटिया = सेाँटे-बर्दार = यष्टिक। कटकाई = कटक = सेना = फौज। केरी = की। जावँत = यावन्तः = जितने। अहहिँ = हैं, अहइ (अस्ति) का बहु-वचन। सकल = सब। उरगाना = उडुकान = जिस के कारण रुक जाना पडे। साँबर = संबल = राह की सामग्री। जाना = यानम् = गमनम्। चाहा = चाहते हैं। मोल = मोल से = मूल्येन = खरीदने से। पाउब = पावँगे। जहाँ = यत्र। बेसाहा = विसाधनम् = सामग्री = खाने पीने की वस्तु। निबहइ = निर्वहति = निर्वाह होता है। साँटी = यष्टिः = छडी = दण्ड, यहाँ लक्षणा से सामर्थ्य। माटी = मृत् = मट्टी। गरब = गर्व = अभिमान। तुरइ = लरी = शीघ्र-चलने-वाला = घोडा। पीठी = पृष्ठ = पीठ। सरग = स्वर्ग = आकाश। डीठी = दृष्टि। मंतर = मन्त्र। सँग-लागू = संग-लगू = संग लगने-वाले। गुदर = गूदड = चिथडा = जिस से गुदडी बनती है। होहिहिँ = होंगे। आगू = अग्रे = आगे॥ का = किम् = क्योँ। निचिंत

= निश्चिन्त = बे-खबर । मानुसह = मानुष = मनुष्य । आछ = अच्छ = स्वच्छ = अच्छी । सजुग = सयुग् = सहित योग के, अर्थात् सावधान । अगुमन = अग्रत:, वा आगमनत: = आगे-ही से । पछिताउ = पछिताइ (पश्चात् तपति) का विध्यर्थ में लोट लकार के मध्यम-पुरुष का एक-वचन । पाछ = पश्चात् = पीछे ॥

सेाँटे-बर्दार (सिपाही-लोग) (नगर में) चारो ओर आज्ञा को फिराया, अर्थात् घूम घूम कर राजा के हुक्म को सुनाया, कि राजा की कटक भई है, अर्थात् राजा की सेना चलने को तयार हुई है ॥ (सो) जितनी सब सामग्री हैं, जिन के विना (राह में) रुकावट होती है, अर्थात् रुक जाना पडता है, उन सब को ले लेव (क्योँकि) दूर जाना है, अर्थात् एक दो दिन की बात हो, तो सामग्री के विना कष्ट को सह सकते हो। यहाँ तो कई महीनेाँ की यात्रा है, इस लिये सब सामग्री को ले लेना चाहिए ॥ (क्योँकि) सब कोई सिंहल-दीप को जाया चाहते हैं, जहाँ (राह में) मोल से (कोई) सामग्री न पावैंगे, अर्थात् राह में कोई सामग्री-ही न मिलेगी, खरीदैंगे कहाँ से ॥ तहाँ, अर्थात् तिस राह में, सब (कुछ) अपनी साँटी से (दण्ड से), अर्थात् सामर्थ्य से निबहता है। सामर्थ्य के विना (जो उस मार्ग में जाता है) सो (राह-ही में) रह जाता है, (और उस का) मुख मट्टी हो जाता है, अर्थात् सामर्थ्य के विना (सामग्री विना) राह में मर कर गल-पच जाता है, शरीर मट्टी में मिल जाती है ॥ (सो) राजा (उस राह में) योग को सज कर, अर्थात् योगी बन कर चला है, (इस लिये) सब लोग तयारी करो, और शीघ्र चलो ॥ (सब लोग) गर्व से जो घोडे की पीठ पर चढते थे, (सो अब उस चढने के व्यापार को छोडो) अब भूमि में चलो (और) स्वर्ग की ओर दृष्टि करो, अर्थात् उस राह से लौटना कठिन है, सो स्वर्ग की ओर दृष्टि लगावो जो कि स्वामि-कार्य में शरीर पात करने से अवश्य मिलता है ॥ (सो सब लोग चलो गुरु राजा से), मन्त्र लेव, (और राजा के) सँग-लगू हो; (क्योँकि) आगे जा कर सब कोई गूदड होँगे, अर्थात् गुदडी पहन कर अपनी अपनी शरीर को गूदड सदृश करैंगे, अर्थात् योगी बनैंगे ॥

(कवि कहता है, कि) अरे मनुष्य क्या बे-खबर (बैठा) है। (यह बे-खबरी अच्छी नहीँ किन्तु) अपनी चिन्ता करना (कि कौन हम हैं कहाँ से आये, कौन मेरा प्रभु है, किस प्रकार से उस प्रभु से भेँट हो इत्यादि) अच्छा है ॥ (और) आगे-ही से सावधान हो कर (सब कुछ) ले लो, और उत्तम कमाई कर लो, (जिस में) पीछे

फिर पछताना न पड़े, अर्थात् जब तक पौरुष है, तब तक पर-लोक के लिये उपाय कर लो। असमर्थ होने पर केवल पछताना छोड़, और कुछ हाथ न लगेगा। भर्तृहरि ने भी लिखा है, कि—

यावत् स्वस्थमिदं शरीरमरुजं यावज्जरा दूरतो
यावच्चेन्द्रियशक्तिरप्रतिहता यावत् क्षयो नायुषः।
आत्मश्रेयसि तावदेव विदुषा कार्यः प्रयत्नो महान्
सन्दीप्ते भवने तु कूपखननं प्रत्युद्यमः कीदृशः॥
(भर्तृहरि, वैराग्यशतक)॥ १३०॥

चउपाई।

बिनवँइ रतन-सेन कइ माया। माथइ छात पाट निति पाया॥
बेलसहु नउ लख लच्छि पिआरी। राज छाडि जनि होहु भिखारी॥
निति चंदन लागइ जेहि देहा। सो तन देखि भरत अब खेहा॥
सब दिन रहेहु करत तुम्ह भोगू। सो कइसइ साधब तप जोगू॥
कइसइ धूप सहब बिनु छाँहा। कइसइ नीँद परिहि भुइँ माँहा॥
कइसइ ओढब काँथरि कंथा। कइसइ पाउँ चलब तुम्ह पंथा॥
कइसइ सहब खनहि खन भूखा। कइसइ खाब कुरुकुटा रूखा॥

दोहा।

राज पाट दर परिगह तुम-हीँ सउँ उँजिआर।
बइठि भोग रस मानहु कइ न चलहु अँधिआर॥ १३१॥

बिनवँइ = विनमति = विनय करती है। रतन-सेन = रत्न-सेन। माया = माता = मा। माथइ = मस्तके = माथ के ऊपर। छात = छत्त्र = छाता। पाट = पट्ट = पीढा, यहाँ सिंहासन। निति = नित्य। पाया = पाद = पाँय = पैर। बेलसहु = बिलसहु = विलसइ (विलसति) का लोट-लकार में मध्यम-पुरुष का आदरार्थ, यहाँ बहु-वचन। नउ = नव। लख = लक्ष = लाख। लच्छि = लक्ष्मी। पिआरी = प्रिया। राज = राज्य। छाडि = संछुद्य = छोड कर। जनि = मत = न। भिखारी = भिक्षाकः = भिक्षुकः = भिख-मंगा। लागइ = लगति = लगता है। देखि = दृष्ट्वा = देख कर। भरत = भरति =

भरते हो। खेहा = धूर (खस्य आकाशस्य ईहा इच्छा यस्य)। भोगू = भोग। कइसइ = कथम् = कैसे। नीँद = निद्रा। परिहि = पडेगी। भुइँ = भुवि, यहाँ भू। माँहा = मध्ये = में। ओढब = ओढियेगा = अवधारण करियेगा। काँथरि = कथरी = गुदरी। कंथा = चोलना। पाउँ = पावँ = पैर। चलब = चलियेगा। पंथा = पन्थाः = राह। सहब = सहियेगा। खनहि खन = चण चण। भूखा = बुभुचा = भूख। खाब = खाइयेगा। कुरुकुटा = कर्करः = कडा = कंकड पत्थर से भरा = खर कतवार मिला। रूखा = रूच॥ दर = स्थान, वा दर = दल = सेना = फौज। परिगह = परिग्रहः = आश्रित-जन = प्रजा-लोग 'प्रमदानां सहस्राणि तव राजन् परिग्रहे' (वाल्मीकि-रा०, अरण्यका०, २८ स०, श्लो ३०)। उँजिआर = उज्ज्वल। बइठि = उपविश्य = बैठ कर। मानहु = मानिये। कइ = कला = कर के। चलहु = चलिये। अँधिआर = अन्धकार = अँधेरा॥

(राजा) रत्न-सेन की माता विनय करती है, (कि बेटा, तुमारे) माथे के ऊपर नित्य छाता (लगा रहता है, और) पैर के नीचे पाट (सिंहासन)॥ (सो) नव लाख लच्मी (के सदृश) प्रियाओं (भार्याओं) के साथ विलास करो, अर्थात् रनिवास में एक से एक लाखों सुन्दरी रानियाँ हैं, जिस से जी रमे, उस से सुख विलास करो। एक पद्मावती के लिये यह क्या सवाँग बनाते हो। (सो बेटा, मेरा कहा मानो,) राज्य छोड कर भिखारी मत बनो॥ (हा,) जिस देह में नित्य चन्दन लगता (रहा) है, सो (उस) देह (तनु = तन) को देख (देख) कर (जिस में कोई अवयव विना भस्म के बाकी न रहे) अब (उस में) भस्म (खेह) भरते हो, अर्थात् उस चन्दन-योग्य देह के ऊपर भस्म चढाते हो॥ तुम (तो) सब दिन (सुख) भोग करते रहे हो, सो (अब) कैसे तप (और) योग को साधियेगा॥ कैसे (योग साधने के लिये) छाया के विना धूप (सूर्य की दीप्ति = घाम) सहियेगा। कैसे (आप को) भूमि में नीँद पडेगी॥ कैसे (इस कोमल अङ्ग के ऊपर) कथरी और कंथा को ओढियेगा। कैसे आप (तुम्ह) पैरों से, अर्थात् पैदल, राह में चलियेगा॥ (जो आप यहाँ चण चण पर मेवा मिठाई इत्यादि कुछ न कुछ खाते-ही रहते थे, सो) कैसे चण चण पर (अब उस) भूख को सहियेगा। (समय कु-समय पर जहाँ कहीं जो कुछ) सूखा रूखा खर कतवार से भरा (अन्न दैव-संयोग से मिल जायगा, उसे मेवा पकान्न के जेवँने-वाले आप) कैसे खाइयेगा। माता का कहना है, कि बेटा, योग साधने में ऊपर कहे हुए कष्ट-ही कष्ट हैं, सो आप से योग नहीं सधेगा, आप राज्य छोड कर योगी न बनिये; यही मेरी विनती है॥

BIBLIOTHECA INDICA:

COLLECTION OF ORIENTAL WORKS

PUBLISHED BY

THE ASIATIC SOCIETY OF BENGAL.

NEW SERIES NO. 1024.

THE PADUMĀWATI

OF

MALIK MUḤAMMAD JAISĪ

EDITED, WITH A COMMENTARY, TRANSLATION, AND CRITICAL NOTES,

BY

G. A. GRIERSON, C.I.E., PH.D., I.C.S.,

AND

MAHĀMAHŌPĀDHYĀYA SUDHĀKARA DVIVĒDI, F.A.U.

FASCICULUS IV.

CALCUTTA:

PRINTED AT THE BAPTIST MISSION PRESS,

AND PUBLISHED BY THE ASIATIC SOCIETY, 57, PARK STREET.

1902.

2. Ia U K *baiṭhahu baiṭhahu kōī*. K[2] *baiṭha baiṭha jō kōī*. K[3] *baiṭheu baiṭheu kōī*. 3. Id *kaṭhina ahai*. 6. Ia has, || ایسي روپ نپای بهوگو | تپ سو روپ کوی کرت نجوگو K[2] *bhōga tajē waha pāwahi bhōgū* | K[3] *aisē rūpa na pāia bhōgū* | U *bhōgahi sē̃ pāiye tapa bhōgū*. 7. Is *jōgihi bhōgihi nyāwa na āwā*. 8, 9. U K *tāpa, kalāpā*.

126. 1. K *kala bhā*. Ia *nikasai ghīu na binu dadhi*. 3. Ia *sō pai pāu sīsa dei caḍhā* 5. Iabs *tōrai ghaṭahi* K *jāna sīsa dei*. 6. *Mada*, so Ia U K. Ibd have *mana*; the others, *au*. *Mada*, is necessary for the sense. 7. Ia *naau sē̃dhi tinha kai ḍiṭhiārī* .... *ũjhiārī* Is *ādhiārā* U K. *naau sē̃dhi unhi kai ḍiṭhiārī*.........*ãdhiārī*.

127. Icds U *palaka na māri pēma cita lāgā* K *palaka na lāgu*. 4. Ia *palaṭi na bhiraï*. 7. K *aba maĩ*........ *bhawãra hoi joti kārana*. 9. *jaũ madhukara, &c.*, so all copies exc. U which has *jiu na ganaũ jiu dēta*. Ib had originally *jiu karaũ ohi bhẽṭa*, corrected on margin to the text.

127*a*. Printed editions give the following set of caupāēs, which is wanting in all our MSS. except Id, in the margin of which it has been added:—

Cau.	*Hindū mīta bahuta samujhāwā*	*māna na rājā gawãna bhulāwā*	||
	upajai pēma-pēra jehi āē	*parabōdhata hoi adhika so āē*	||
	ambrita bāta kahata bikha jānā	*pēma ko bacana mīṭha kai mānā*	||
	jō wah bikhai māri kai khāī	*pũchahu tāhī pēma-miṭhāī*	||
	pũchahu bāta bharatharahi jāī	*ambrita rāja tajeu bikha khāī*	||
	au mahēsa baḍa siddha kahāwā	*una-hũ bikhahi kanṭha pai lāwā*	||
	hōta uai rabi kirana nikāsā	*hanumãta hoi kō dēi suāsā*	||
Do.	*tumha saba siddhi manāwahu*	*hoi ganēsa sidha lēhu*	|
	cēlā kō na calāwā	*milai gurū jehi bhēhu*	|| 127*a* ||

128. 2. Icd *raṭā* for *laṭā*. 3. K has second half, *bhaē malīna bharē saba khēhā*. 3. This runs as follows in the different MSS.

Ia UK	*mēkhaia*	*siṅgī*	*cakara adhārī*	*jō gōṭā rudarācha dhãdhārī*		||
Ib	„	*sīgī*	„ *dhãdhārī*	*jōgā tāra*	„ *adhārī*	||
Icds	„	*siṅgi*	„ „	*jō* (Is *au*) *gōṭā rudarācha adhārī*		||
K[2]	„		„	*jōgawaṭi*	„ „	||
K[5]	„		„	*jōga chāṛa*	„ „	||

Id. has on margin the following *v.l.* *līnha hātha tirasūla sãbhārī* ||

The printed editions have *ḍhiḍhārī* (ढिढारी), but the MSS. have *dhãdhārī* (धँधारी) quite clearly. We have followed Icd. 6. Ia لت اديان. Ib كراوپان. Icd كرلت اديان Is कर उद्यान U कर उदयान K करौ उद्यान K[2] कर उदवान K[3] गुरु क ध्यान कांधे धिग छाला। We have followed Icds and U. Two printed editions give the same, and one translates the word by सुमिरिनी. 8. Ias U K *sādhi kayā*. Id U *siddha hōi*. K. *hōe*.

129. 1. Id *kahahĩ karu gawãna*. Iacd *calahu phirai sidha*. K. *dina lei lēhu purai saba kājā* (*rājā* at end of previous hemistych.) 2. *jaba dēkhai taba hōi*. K. *taba jānai*. Is K *nayana nahi*. 4. Icd K *bhulāna jāra na cālū*. 6. Ia *mari jō*. 7. Ia *kāyā jiu anta*. 9. U K *apanē*.

130. *Sãṭiyā*. So Ia. The MSS. all differ. Ia has سانٹیا, Ib سنٹویا, Ic (?) سونٹهی, Id (?) سوئیر, Is साटिचन्ह, U सउँटियं K दसोटिन्ह. K[2] सठाइन्ह. K[5] साटउन्ह. One printed edition gives سوتیٹو, and two others सोडउडे। Ia has second half *calai kaṭaka jōrā°*. 3. Ia U K *pāuba tahā*. 4. Second half. Ibd *sãṭhī puni*. Is *sãwar binā*. 6. Ia *caḍhahu*. Ics *aba sō tajahu*. 7. U *mātrā lēhu*. K *mātrā tajahu lēhu sãga*. I *jō hwai. saba āgū*. 8. Ia U K *rē baurehu*. 9. Ics *phiri pachi°*.

131. Ia U *niti chāyā*. 2. Ia K *naula jo lachimi*. Id *parasahu*. 3. Is *sō tumha dēha bharaba*. Ia UK *bharaba*. 4. Ia *nisi dina karahu kāma asa bhōgū*. U *nisi dina*. K *sukha bhōgū*. 7. K. *karakuṭa sukhā*. 8. K. *dhana pari°*.

132. 1. K *kā kara dhana kāyā*. Iac *jō nidāna*. Ia U *nidāna pai*. Is *jō niāna puni*.

4

142. 1. Ib *siŋghala kē ghaṭa.* 2. Is K *sēni.* 3. Is *cāhia.* U *kawana dēsa.* 5. Ia *kahā hamārā.* 6. The following are the readings—

Ia	*so tumha kahahu jo hamahu na bhāū*	*jō nirāsa tehi lāu nasāū* ‖
Ib	*newatahu tehi jehi mahā̃ yaha bhāū*	*jō nirabhau bhā* „ ‖
Ic	*sō tehi kahā̃* „ „ „ „	*jo nirabhāū lāu na syāū* ‖(?)
Id	„ „ „ „ „ *bahu* „	*jō nirabhau waha lāu nasāu* ‖
Is	*sō tina kahu jinha mahā̃ nahi* „	*jau nirabhau tā* „ „ ‖
U	*sō tina kājana kā nahi* „	*jō nirabhai tehi* „ „ ‖
K	*sōi prīti jinha mahā̃ satbhāu*	*jō nisatā* „ „ „ ‖
K²	*sō pā̃tha kahahu bēgi haū̃ jāū*	*jō nirabhau tehi lēu nasāū* ‖
K³	*sō tehi kahahu jāi nā bhāū*	*jo nisacai tehi lāu nasāū* ‖

7. U has second half, *jehi caḍhi sīhala-dīpa pahi jāū̃*‖. 9. Is om. *re* and has *baharaū̃* for *phiraū̃*. UK *thāra* for *bāra*.

143. 1. Ia *bohilā nāu na hōihi.* 2. Ic *bōhila āni dēū̃.* 4. U *sāta samūda sata kīnha sā̃bhārā.* UK *maccha gōha ghari°.* 6. Ib *eta dukha sahahu kahau kehi.* Is U *atē jo khīsa sahia kehi.* K² *eta dukha sahau so kaunē kājā.* K³ *ati jōkhiwā̃ sahahī kehi kājā.* 8. Is *kalakalā akūlā.* K² *au kilakilā akūtā.*

144. 1. Icd *suni kai sīū.* N *pagu dēī...muē kēri kā mueu karēī.* 3. U *dukha saŋgahi.* K *dukha bāsā ... taba payāna.* 4. U *jehi jiu bithā.* 5. Ias *bū̃da bara.* UK *bū̃da kari.* 6. K *kīnha pasārū.* 8. K *tā kara nātha tehi hātha.* 9. Id *jabahi nātha.*

145. 1. K *atihi augāhā.* 2. The following are the readings—

Ia	*jau waha samūda kahā ehi parē* ‖	
Ibc	„ „ „ *gāha* „ „ ‖	
Id	*jehi samūda augāhi ehi parē* ‖	
Is	*jau waha samūda kāha ehi parē* ‖	
U	„ *yaha* „ *kāha kai parai* ‖	
K	„ „ „ „ *hoi parē* ‖	
K²	*jau ohi samudara kaha eha pārē*	*sō augāhā hā̃sa hō tārē* ‖
K³	*jehi eha samuda khāra māha pārē*	*jīu gawāi hā̃sa ke bihatārē* ‖

Iac *ati augāha.* U *hansa kai tāraī.* K *jō augāha samuda mahā̃ tārē.* 3. K *disiṭi na dēkhu.* 4. UK *jiu kāth°.* 5. U *aba yaha samūdā hōū̃ maī mārā* ‖ *pēma so mōra phaniga kai kārā.* K *hōu mai jārā.* K² *aba ehi samuda pāreū̃ hoi mārā* ‖ 6. The following are the readings—

Ia	*bahaū̃ kahū̃ kōī lai jāū* ‖
Ib	*mara hoi bahā katahū̃ lai jāū* ‖
Ic	„ „ *bahaū̃* „ „ „ ‖
Id	*muehi bahāū̃* „ „ „ ‖
Is	*mara bhāu haū̃* „ „ „ ‖
U	*kara nibāha* „ „ „ ‖
K	*mastā bahā* „ „ „ ‖
K²	*mara bahāi katahū̃ lei jāī* ‖
K³	*mara bhai bahau kehū lai jāū* ‖

Ias K *kōi lai khāū.* U *dhai khāū.* 9. K *uḍahī* for *uṭhahī.* K³ *mayana kauṛiā hoi rahē.*

146. 1. Ibcs have *jarama* for *jarata.* 2. Ia *dēkhahi āgi kachū nahī̃ pānī.* Ics UK. *dēkhai kachu na āgi au pānī.* 3. Iac UK *āgihī bhāwā.* Is *saū̃hai cāwā.* U *saū̃ha sadhāwā.* 4. Ia has second half *jehi pī̃tha jāi sōi pā̃tha sūjhā.* Ib *jō yaha bhā°.* Is *jau nita.* U *kaunō.* K *taunō.* 5. The second half runs as follows :—

Ia	*jahā̃ parai tahā̃ āpuhi dēkhā* ‖
Ibd	as text.
Ic	*jahā̃ parā tahā̃ āpuhi dēkhā* ‖
Is	*āpuhi jāna pāra bhā dēkhā* ‖
U	*jāna pāra bhā āpuhi dēkhā* ‖
K	*janu so pāra* „ „ ‖

K2 *āpuhi jānahu parabhā dēkhā* |
K3 *jānahu paratakha āpuhi dēkhā* |

6. Ia K have *sīha* for *siŋgha*. 9. Iacds *kehi kē sata*. U *kehi satta saũ*. K *satta taĩ*.

147. 1. Iacds *jīā* for *hīā*. U has second half *ũca hātha jē jaga mãha dīā*. K *ũca hātha kai jei jaga dīā*. 3. Ia *dēkhi dharamī mukha*. 4. Iad *ihā̃ jo diā uhũ saba pāwā*. Ics U *uhā̃ sō pāwā*. K *uhā̃ tei pāwā*. 5. U *niti* for *nisi*. K *mō̃* for *nisi*. 6. The following are the readings—

Ia *hātima diā awani mãha sīkhā* |
Ib as text
Ic *hātima dāna diē jaũ sīkhā* |
Id *hātima āi diā* ,, ,, |
Is *hētima awani* ,, ,, ,, |
U ,, *āi* ,, ,, ,, |
K *hōtima karana deī* ,, ,, |
K2 *hātima āi diā jō sīkhā* |
K3 *hātima dāna diā* ,, |

Is *uhā* for *rahā*.

148. 1. K has for second half, *rājā sata ṭārahu tumha māti*|| 2. Ia *āpu nāhi kāyā hai kanthā* | U *āpu nāhi kāyā mãha kanthā* | K2 *āpuna nā̃hī kayā au kānthā* | K3 *apanah kayā āpunehi kanthā* | 4. Is *dīnha nai sājū*. K *dīnha nau sājū*. 5. Is *pēma jei khēlī*. 6. Is has second half *bahuri na āi sahai waha jhāra*|| UK *pahũcā bārā*. 9. Is U *gana sādhu*.

149. 1. Iacs UK *ratha raini*. Ias UK *gā*. 5. Ic *cālha birājī*. K *calhā ura bājī* ...... *gājī*. 7. Ib *sãjōga* for *sãjūta*.

150. 1. *gawẽjā* so all P U and K. Ib has marg. gloss '*nā-mardī*.' Is has *kawẽjā*. K has for second half *kuãra na jāna samudara ka tējā*. 4. Ia *paŋkhi eka tahã* U *paŋki aisē*. K *paŋkhi puni asa*. 5. U *ṭhōra bhari lēhī*. K *thōra kari*. 6. UK have *jō lei uḍau samũda saba ḍōlā* | *garajai gagana khāi sō jhōlā*. 7. U *jahā̃ na canda*. K *suraja ũjiārā* ...... | *cadhai so āe apana jiu hārā* ||. 9. Ia *tau re kusala*. Ic *tau-hi kusala*. Id *taba kūsala*. Is *tau kūsala*. U *taba re kusala*. K *taba he kusala*. K2 *taba kūsala au khēma*. K3 *tau pai kūsala chēma*.

151. 1. Ia *kīnha jeĩ*. U *kīnha jō*. Ia *tā kahã kahā kusala au khēmā* || Ic *jahā̃ pēma kita kũ°*. Id *tehi re*. U *taba re kahā aba kũ°*. K *jō sō kahā kusala au khēmā* || 2. Is *tumha khēwaka khēwai jau pā̃°*. U *tumha khēwaka jō khēwai*. 4. Is *pira dōū*. Ia *bīca na rākhai kōu*. Ids *jiu rākha*. U om. this line. K *bīca so bā̃ca*. 5. U *pēma pantha sira dēta na khā̃°*. 6. U *sō sata dēkhi to nayanani dīyā*. 7. Ia *pāũ ratana*. U *taba laga, jaba laga milai padāratha*. 8. U *saraga patāra*. K *khōji jaga*. 9. K *sāta somũda*.

Some printed editions insert the following, which do not, however occur in any of our MSS.

Cau||	*Bāta kahata bhala dēsa gohārī*	| *kewaṭahi cālha samũda mãha mārī*	||
	hastī lāi sista sāba ḍhīlā	| *dawaḍi āi eka cālhai līlā*	||
	kēwaṭa lāga lāga saba bāli	| *phirai na cālha jāi bāhi cāli*	||
	bōhita sahasa jāhī̃ cahũ ōrā	| *hōi kalōla jāhī̃ tari bōrā*	||
	suni kai āi caḍhā sō rājā	| *au saba lōga dēsa mili bājā*	||
	bhāla bā̃sa khā̃ḍai bahu parahī̃	| *jānu pakhāla bāji kai caḍhahī̃*	||
	cārā lila jo mā̃chara bājhī	| *kahā̃ jāi jō jā kara khājhī*	||
Dō.||	*Mā̃chara kara bikha hiradai*	*tehi sādhē bikha bāna*	|
	sabahī̃ pahũci kai mārā	*cālhai tajā parāna*	||151*a*||
Cau||	*Jasa dhawalagiri parabata hōī*	| *tēhi bhā̃ti utarāneu sōī*	||
	sabai dēsa mili tairahī̃ ānā	| *liē kulhā̃ḍī lōga jahānā*	||
	janu parabata kahã lāgahī̃ cā̃ṭī	| *lei gae mā̃sa rahī̃ saba kā̃ṭī*	||
	pā̃jari parī kōsa dasa bēḍī	| *pā̃jari kasa jasa khēta barēḍī*	||
	nayana so jānu kōṭi kai pawārē	| *keta asa gahē phirahī̃ tehi bhawārē*	||

ratana-sēna sō suni kai kahahī	| *asa asa maccha samũda mãha ahahī* ||
rājā tumha cāhahu tahã gawãna	| *hōhu sajōga bahuri nahi awanā* ||
Dō.|| *Tumha rājā auru guru*	*hama sēwaka au cēra* |
kīnha cahahī saba āesu	*aba gawãnahu ohi phēra* || 151*b* ||

152. 1. Is *sãyara tīrai.* UK *tīra.* K^2 *tīra.* K^3 *tarō.* Ia *jau sata saŋga to kāyara sūrā.* Is *jehi jiu.* UK *jō sata kiai to kāyara sūrā.* 2. Ia has second half *sahasā pawana paŋkha tasa bāē.* Is *paŋkha para lāē.* U *paŋkha lai dhāē.* K *paŋkha bhai dhāē.* 3. *sahiwārū,* so Icds. 'Ia has *mahabārū.* Ib *sata bhārā.* UK *kãḍahārā.* K *sata karu hathiyārā.* K^3 *sata karai sansārā.* Ib *satai kiē lei lāwai pārā*\|\| Ic *satī gahī lai lāwai pārū.* 4. Ia K *jehi jehi māraga maccha.* 5. Ia *janu paraĩ pahārā.* Icd U *janu uṭhahĩ.* Is *lahari nahī jāi sãbhārā.* K *carai lahari janu carai pahārā* \| *uṭhai saraga,* &c., \| 6. Ia *khinahi tarai khina ūpari jāhī.* Id *khina tara hōhĩ khina.* 7. Is *tarai giri.* U *karia kara kãdhā.* K *bariau kãdhā.* 9. Id *behara behara saba nīra.* Ia K *bēgara bēgara.*'

153. Ia *chīra, chīrū.* 2. Ias K *mana rahai.* 3. Ia *mānukha cã°.* Id *panthahi cã°.* 4. Ia UK *chai jāni mana mār°.* 7. Ia K *bahuta ghara mūsē.* Is K *panthik.* 8. Ia *chīra.* Io K *puni nã°.* Id *sō lãghā.* 9. Id *jō haĩ bāura pēma kē.*

154. 1. Iad N *pai sáhā.* 2. Is *pēma so dādhā* . ... *dahī mãha mãthi.* UK *dādhā.* 3. Ia *chīrū ...... kãjī dūdha.* Ibc *bũda binasa hoi nīrū.* Id *būda taisa hoi.* U *jamai.* K *jasa khīrū.* 4. Iacd *sãsa ḍiḍha* (? ديڙه). Ib *suãsa dadhi.* Is *swãsa waiṭha.* U *suãsu baiḍhi mathānī.* K^2 *sō asa waiḍhi mathai kai gāṛhī* \| K^3 *abasa waḍhai mana mathanī gāḍhī* \| *hiē jōta binu phūla na sãḍhi*\|\| K *suai jo āi mathānī.* Ibd *jōta binu.* 5. K *sītala tehi āgī.* The second half has the following readings—

Ia	*pēma bihūna phiri na bairāgī* ||	
Ib	„ „ *bibhrama ḍari bhāgī* ||	
Ic	„ „ *phiri nahi abhāgī* ||	
Id	„ *na hōi bharahĩ ḍari bhāgī* ||	
Is	„ *bhuana ḍara rahi tē bhāgī* ||	
U	„ *bihūna ḍarai piri* (sic.) „ ||	[reading.
K	„ „ *phirai ḍari* „ ||	K seems to have the original
K^2	*pēma bihūna phirai ḍara bhāgī* ||	
K^3	*pēma ki āgi jarai jō kōī* „ *bhāgahi*||	

6. Ia *dukha na mirathā.* UK *dukha na birathā.* K^3 *dukha tā kara sō aghrita hōī* \|\| 7. U *binu sata hiē karai kā pārā.* 9. Ias U *parau* for *parai* and *parahĩ.*

155. 2.	Ia	*upanā waha huta kāḍhī*	| *khina na bujhāē āgi tasa bāḍhī* ||
So	Id	*upani hiē* „ „	| „ „ „ „ „ „ ||
	U	„ *so tahã kāḍhī*	| „ „ „ *gāta saba bāḍhī* ||
	K	„ *tehī kara āgī*	| *khana bujhāi khana karai jo lāgī* ||
3.	Ia	*upanā uha-i samundā*	| *laŋkā jarī so ēkahi bundā* ||
So	Id	„ „ „	| „ „ *wahī eka* „ ||
	U	„ *wahī* „	| „ „ „ *kē* „ ||
	K	„ „ „	| „ „ *so ohi kē* „ ||
	K^2	*biraha jo upanā wēhi te kāḍhā*	| *khina na bujhāi jaisa tana bāḍhā*||
	K^3	*āgi jo upanī kahu tē gāḍhī*	| *khinu na bujhāi jagata mō bāḍhī* ||

In other words the second and third lines have got mixed up in these MSS. Is *khina na bujhāi jā sata na bāḍhā*\|\|. 4. U *jahā biraha tahã āgi.* K *jehi bhau biraha āgi so ḍiṭhī.* 6. K *sādha na kā pāwai.* 9. Id *bũdā na parata samīra.*

Ic *bunda samunda.* K *bunda na sahata sarīra.*
K^2 *bēdha* „ K^3 *buḍā samunda samīru.*

156. Ics *puni rājā.* K *jau rāiā* 2. K *piai curu ēka lēi.* Icd *jō tehi parai.* Ia K *pãtha paraga.* U *patha paiga na ō* 3. Ia *jahi kē mana.* Is UK *hia mãhā.* 5. Is *jaga* *kāṭhī.* 6. Ia *pōtai hiā—jasa diā.* Ic *janu diā.* Id *hoi diā.* Is *barai jē hiā.* U *barā jo diā.* K *tehi diā.* 7. K² *biraha sīka hoi.* 8. U *mada jō prēma kā.* Is *kiē dīpa.* 9. Iacds *taba lagi.* K *pataṅga jau.*

157. Id second half *kila kila uṭhā dēkhi ḍaru.* Is has *kala kalā* and *kala kala* throughout. U and K *kilakilā*, &c. P are not vocalised. 2. Ia *puni uṭhai.* Id second half *gā ḍhīraja wei dēkhi hilōrā* (mixing up this and the preceding line. U *kilakilāi kai uṭhai.* 3. Ia UK *hoi bahurai.* U *jōjana dasa.* K *jōjana sai.* 4. Ia *saraga kahā̃.* Ib and U have *saraga lahu.* 5. Ia *mahā̃ta arāmbha.* Ia UK *samū̃da mā̃ha.* Ia *mahana arambha.* U *mahānarambha.* K *mahānāra samū̃da.* 6. Ib *jaisai bhawā̃i.* K *jōjana sai ... jānahu phirai.* Ia K *paralai* in both instances,—*jabahī̃, tabahī̃.*

158. 1. Ias *ā̃i sata.* K *samudra sata hīe na ḍōlā.* 2. Ia *siṅghala-pantha jo.* 3. Is K *kalakalā.* K *so lāgai tīrū.* 4. Ia UK *asa rēkha.* Iac N *ninārā.* 5. Ib *tē̃tisa sahasa kōsa kai.* Id U *kai bāṭā.* K *ati sā̃kara cali sakai ko bāṭā.* 6. Ids K *paini jahā̃ tā̃i.* K *jā kai paturā̃ī.* 7. Ibs make this the second line of the set. Ia *aisē ṭhā̃ū̃.* K² *ehī ṭhā̃ū̃ kō guru sā̃ga kijay | guru sā̃ga hōi pāra tau lījai ||* K³ *aisē ṭhā̃ū̃ gurū sā̃ga kījai | guru sā̃ga hōi pāra tau dījai ||* Icd U and K have a different line, *viz* :—

Ic	*ihai pantha saba kāhū jānā*	*hōi dusara bisuāsa nidānā*	||
Id	*wahī* „ „ „ „	„ „ *punu swāsa* „	||
U	„ „ *jānā saba kāhū*	*wahī pāntha mā̃ha hōi nibāhū*	||
K	„ „ „ „ „	„ „ *jau* „ „	||

8. U *ōhī.* K *hāihai nirāsahi āsa.*

159. In Ia This set of *caupais* comes immediately after No, 148. It is omitted by U. 1. Is *sura saba hōhu.* 2. Ia *ṭhākura jehi ka sūra jia hōī | sēwaka tehi ka niḍara jia sōī ||.* Ic *mana hōī.* 3. Ia second half, *sira saū̃ dēi ughāri na kā̃dhā.* K *sira lē dēi bhāra nahi kā̃dhā* 5. Ia *au baikū̃tha saū̃ nāhina kājū.* Ia *naraka hutē̃.* 6. Id *nēha pā̃tha.* Ia *āni pantha ehī lāwā.* K *jō mohi ihai pantha lagāwē* (*pāwē* at end of preceding hemistych). 7. *kāṭha lāgi gāḍhahu ohi ḍhīlā | būḍaū̃ samū̃da,* &c. Is *kō tehi kōha gārha kā ḍhīlā |* K has *jō kichu likhā sōi pai hōī | au saba mithā̃ karai jō kōī ||* 8. K *kahi samū̃°.* 9. Ic *kōi kachū* Id K *kou.*

160. Ic *bīju para.* Id *parachāhī̃.* Is *bīju asa.* K *koi camakai bijulī parachāhī̃.* U has *kou* or *kōu* throughout. 2. Ia *kōi calā baila.* K *baila asa wārū.* 3. Ia *bhāra saū̃.* Ic *bhāra tehi.* Id *bhāra bhai.* Is *bhāra lā̃ī.* U *garua jāni kai thākā.* K *jāni mana.* 4. Ia *pōhī kara.* Ia *sira mā̃°.* U *kōū būḍi.* K *kōī būḍi gaē gali māṭī.* 5. Ia K *jasa ḍōlā.* Ic *para ḍō°.* Ids *jyau ḍō°.* U *sama ḍō°.* 6. K *kōī phirai.* UK *phirā karai.* K² *kōī karari pāta janu ḍōlā |* K³ *kōī karahī pāta para ḍōlā |* 8. K *kōi milā adharāti.* 9. The following are the readings—

Ia	*jā kara*	*jasa huta saū̃ nija*
Ib	„	*jō huta sāju jasa*
Ic	„	*sāju jaisa huta*
Id	„	*huta jasa sāju*
Is	„	*jaisa sāju hōta*
U	„	*huta jasa khēwā*
K	„	*hōta sāju jasa*
K²	„	*hatā sāju jasa*
K³	„	*jaisā sāja huta*

Id *tehi ghāṭa.* K *sō āwā tehi.*

161. 2. U *bhayau hulāsa hiē tana chāwa.* K *purī tana chāwā.* 4. U *asta astaī* Is and K have *astu.* No vowels in P. K *andha jo rahai.* 5. Ia *kawā̃la bigāsata bigas. dēhī.* Ic *bhawā̃ra bāsa hoi.* U *kamala bigāsa taisa bhā hiā | bhawā̃ra kamala mili kai rasa piā ||* K *bhawā̃ra darasa.* 6. *kirīrā* P do not vocalise, exc. B. which has کریرا *karērā.* All N have किरीरा. K² K³ *karīrā.* Ia K *cugahī ratana.* 8. Ia *bāsa lēhi ohi āi.* U *līnha kamala rasa bāsa.* 9. Ia K *sūkhā kāṭha cabhāi.* U *dādara bāsa na kai sakā bhalē jo āchai pāsa.*

162. 1. Ib has this line No. 3. Its first line is given below. Icd *dina ūā*. 2. Ia *cā̃dana tana*. 3. Icd *sirāna sarīrū*. 5. Id *gagana kahā̃*. 6. Iab *au sō kacapaci bhaeu girāsā*. K *tehi para pūniu sasi*. 7. K last hemistych, *sabahi ṭhāū ūā janu tāra* ‖. 9. Ic *aisa bāsa jaga*. U *tasa saba lakhai subhāu*. K *jasa īchā jehi kē mana sō tahawā̃ gaa pāu* ‖. Ib substitutes for this set of caupāis the following—

Cau.‖	*Rājai disiṭi pantha naga dēkhī*	*bhai pāthara saba mōrī tēkhī* ‖
	kā lei karaū pāra nirabhāra	*taba jo līnha kā karia bhā̃ḍārā* ‖
	kachu mohi hātha lāga jō chā̃ḍā	*ṭhāwahī ṭhāu rahā saba gā̃ḍā* ‖
	siddha purukha saba jā saū bhāgē	*jeī sētē̃ tahā̃ hātha na lāge* ‖
	asthira hōī bhāra so khā̃cā	*panthī lei pātha jīa na bā̃cā* ‖
	sātau parabata kie gā hāthā	*sāta-u gurū duhū̃ jaga sātha* ‖
	kawā̃la lāga bhawā̃rā jasa garahī	*maku jiu jāi bēgi nahi tarahī* ‖
Do.‖	*Dhana au daraba mōra padumawati*	*haū bēdhā jehi pēma* |
	sāta-u samūda dēaū nechāwara	*milaū tau jaba taba pēma*‖162*a*‖
Cau.‖	*Sāta samūda jasa pantha bakhānī*	*sāta-u nā̃ghi dīpa niarānī* ‖

pawana bāsa, &c., as in text; besides this first line given here, all the seven *caupāis* (making eight in all) of the text are given.

163. 1. Iac *tuī*. 3. Is K *machīdura*. 4. Is *pēma tū̃*. K *bhūmi akāsū*. 5. Ia UK *bijurī kanaka*. Ic *bijurī loai*. Id *bijurī ghaṭai*. Ib has *kanai*, with v. l. on margin *loai*. 6. Ia *tehi sasi ēka ka°* ...... *mandila*. Id *mōtī naga*. 7. Ia *nakhata ahai*. Id *ū̃cha āsā*. U *nakhata āchi*. 8. U *aura tarāini pāsa*. K *gagana tarāī pāsa*. 9. Ia UK *tū̃ rabi āū*.

164. 1. Iac *kara gā na pahū̃°*. Id *kara khāni pahū̃°*. Is *kāna*. U *nayana dēkha pai kara na pahū̃°*. K *dēkha magu jā na pa°*. 3. U *dhāi bāju saū mānusa sūdhā*. 4. Ia U *cā̃da sūra*. Ia *ātaricha*. 5. Ia U *mārā cakara āi bhuī rāhā*. 6. Iad UK *nidānā*. 7. Is U *pāni uṭhā uṭhi*. K *mēgha uṭhā uṭhi*. 8. *rāwana saūha bilōkatahi*.

165. 2. UK *budhi ēka*. U *pahilaī darasana hō taba bhōgū*. 3. U *manḍapha*. 4. Iac K *waha khikhinda* (see ii, 1) *parabata jasa* (K *tasa*) *merū*. Is *yaha khā̃ḍa hai jasa*. U *waha khanḍahi sō parabata*. Icd *taba phērū*. U *tasa phē°*. K *asa phē°*. 6. Ias K *pūjai āi* U *āu*. K *sabai sansārū*. 7. Ia *darasa merā°*. K *hoihai ehi bidhi*. 9. Ids UK *pūjihi mana kai āsa*.

166. 1. Iad U *gagana caḍhi dhāwaū*. K *parbata kahā saraga para dhā°*. 2. Iad *pāū̃*. 3. UK *mō mana oha ū̃cē kara cāū̃* | K second half *dina dina ū̃cē rākhaū pāū̃*‖. 4. K *nāū̃* for *pāū̃*. 5. Ia UK *ū̃ca sēia darabārū*. 6. Iad K *caḍhata*. Iad *ū̃ca budhi bū°*. UK *ū̃cai rā̃dhi ū̃ca mati* (K *budhi*). 7. Iad U *ū̃ca kāja jīu*. 8. U *ū̃cai kara*. K *ū̃cai mana*. Iab K insert the following here. It is evidently not genuine—

Cau.‖	*nīcai sā̃ga niti hōi nicāī*	*jaisai hansa kāga kai nāī* ‖
	nīcai kaba-hū̃ na hōi bhalāī	*nīcai saū saba jāi muḍāī* ‖
	nīca na kaba-hū̃ jia mauna rākhai	*nīca na kaba-hū̃ mū̃ha saū bhākhai* ‖
	nīca na kaba-hū̃ āwai kājā	*nīcai rahai na ēka-ū̃ tājā* ‖
	nīcai saū sā̃ga kaba-hū̃ kījai	*nīca pantha pāu nahī dījai* ‖
	nīcai nahi līji̇a bewahārū	*nīcai nāhi dījia bhā̃ḍārū* ‖
	nīca ṭhāū̃ na bā̃dhia ghārā	*nīcai ṭhāū būḍa jala mārā* ‖
Do.‖	*hōī nīca na kaba-hū̃*	*jehi ū̃cai mana bhāu* |
	nīca jo ū̃ca bināsahī	*nīca ka ihai subhāu* ‖

There are minor differences of reading which it is not necessary to quote.

167. 2. K *kai parabōdha caleu parabātā*. 3. Ic U *mā̃ḍapha*. 4. Ia *amī sadā phara pharai apū°*. Is *ā̃brita karī phara*. Is UK *au bahu lāga*. 5. Ic U *manḍapha*, and so always. This spelling will not be recorded again.

168. 1. N K^2 and K^3 *sahasa bīsa*. 4. Iads *kā mohi*. Ic *kā tumha*. Ic *kā lahi*. UK *kā maī*. 6. K *hōhu dayāla niraguna ke dātā*. 7. K *tū̃ dēnihāra nirāsinha āsā* | *purawanihāra dēna sukha bāsā* ‖. 8. Iacd UK *vidhi kahai na*.

these to sport, that I have lost a necklace from my hand?[1] When I return home, all will ask me what hath happened, and with what answer shall I manage to gain entrance to my house?' Her shell-like eyes filled with tears, which fell as though they were a shower of pearls. Her friends cried, 'O simple Kōkilā,[2] where was there ever water without air commingled with it?[3] Why dost thou weep so at losing thy necklace? Search for what is lost until thou find it.'

They all began to search, diving and diving together. Some came up with pearls in their hands, and some with only cockle-shells.

67.[4] Said the lake, 'What I have desired, that have I found. A philosopher's stone hath touched me down to here.[5] My waters have become clear with the touch of their feet, and, seeing their beauty, have I too, become beautiful. My body hath become fragrant with the odour of a sandal breeze. It hath become cool and its fever is extinguished. I know not what breeze hath brought this fragrance, my condition hath become pure and my sins have disappeared.' Immediately he gave up the necklace; and, as the damsels took it, the moon-face smiled.[6] The lilies bloomed at beholding the digit of the moon, and a glory shone where'er it was seen. Each received the image (in its heart) which it had longed for, and the moon-faces all appeared reflected in them as in a mirror.

As the lotuses saw her eyes, their bodies in the water became pure like them. When the swans[7] saw her smile (their forms became pure white), and when the jewels and diamonds saw her teeth, they became all bright and glorious.[8]

[1] Here we have a rare occurrence of a post-position preceding, instead of following its noun, *sai hātha*, for *hātha sai*. Compare note 9, p. 43.

[2] *i.e.*, one who hath a voice sweet as that of a Cuckoo (*kōkila*).

[3] *i.e.*, one can always remain longer under water than one would imagine.

[4] The MS. Ia inserts two stanzas here, which serve as an introduction to this one. According to them Padmāvatī laments the loss of the necklace, and her friends to comfort her call upon the lake (called only here *samũda*, ocean) to give it up. The stanzas are evident interpolations.

[5] Down to its inmost depths. A philosopher's stone converts everything it touches to its own substance: hence, the pure bodies of the girls had converted the lake to purity.

[6] In stanza lxv Padmāvatī is named the moon, and the companions the stars.

[7] A pun on the word *haṁça*, swan, and *hãs'nā*, to smile.

[8] The poet makes each peculiar virtue of the lotuses, the swans, and the diamonds in the lake, due only to some virtue of Padmāvatī, and borrowed from it.

72. Captured thus was the parrot in the midst of his delight, and the fowler broke his feathers and thrust him in his basket. Thereupon many birds became distressed, lamenting among themselves. 'How can grapes produce such poison seeds, by which hath come his death, and his crushed frame and wings? Had he not had a desire for food, why should the bird-catcher have entered (the forest) with his lime, and hidden himself. By this poison-food hath Hīrā-maṇi's wisdom been deceived, and death hath come with his (limed) stick in hand. This false illusion of the world hath led us astray, and hath broken our wings, even as our body began to swell (with egoism). This heart is hard that dieth not at once when struck; and, intent on seeing food, seeth not the net.[1]

'Eating thus this poison-food, we have lost our wisdom; but thou, O Parrot, wast a paṇḍit, how didst thou become entangled?'

73. The parrot said, 'I also thus went astray. The cradle of my pride, in which I swung, broke down. I took up my dwelling in a plantain forest, and there fell into companionship with jujubes (or enemies).[2] My food, eaten happily in the home of my tribe, became poison when the fowler approached.[3] Why did the tree of pleasure bear such fruit, so that from behind it as a screen he hath caught birds? Secure I sat behind the screen, and knew it not till the gin struck my heart. Happy and secure men count their wealth and deeds, and have no care that in front of them is death. So also I was led away by that pride, and forgot Him from whom I had received these things.

'When there is no anxiety in eating, then only is eating pleasant. Now that the noose is on my neck, what good is there in weeping.'

74. On hearing his reply they wiped away their tears, and said 'Who fixed wings on things with feeble wisdom such as birds? Brilliant is not the wisdom of birds, or how could a cat seize a learned parrot? Why doth the partridge thrust forth its tongue in the forest, and why doth it utter the call which placeth the noose upon its neck.[4] On the day on which our feathers first grew and our name of "bird"[5] was invented, on that day also was born the hunter to take our lives. Greed with covetousness hath become our disease.[6] We see the food but see not the hunter. Because of our lust he spread the bait: because of our pride he desired to slay us. Because we were secure he came stealthily. What fault was the hunter's? Ours was the sin.

'Why shouldst thou do that sin, in the doing of which thou givest thy life? Now there is naught to be said, and, O king of birds, silence is the best.'

1 All this is Vēdāntik philosophy.

2 Here there is a series of elaborate puns. *Bairī* means an enemy, and also the jujube tree, which is covered with thorns.

3 *Kuraāra* is for *kulālaya*. *Pharahurī* is the same as *pharuhurī* in xxviii, 4, and means trees which bear small fruit. The translation '*khurhur*' on p. 16 is a slip of the pen, based on a reading since discovered to be incorrect.

4 Fowlers track the partridge by its loud evening and morning cry. Cf. xcix, 9.

5 Literally, feathered one.

6 Here there is the play upon the word *biādha*, a hunter, and *biādhi*, disease.

Canto VI.

The Birth of Ratna-sēna.

75. Citra-sēna[1] was King of Citra-pura (Citaur), who built a fortress and a castle, decorated as a picture.[2] In his line was born the illustrious Râtna-sēna. Blessed was the mother that gave birth to such a boy. Paṇḍits calculated according to the lore of body-marks and looked upon him. They gazed on his beauty and found his special stellar conjunction. Said they, 'In Ratna-sēna,[3] have many gems taken bodily form. Brilliant is his form as a jewel. On his head gleameth the precious stone (of good fortune). A thing glorious as a gem is written as his mate.[4] Glorious will they be, as the sun and moon together. As the bee is distraught apart from the jasmine, so will he be for her, and become an ascetic. To Siṁhala will he go, and there obtain her, and having become successful in his quest,[5] to Citaur will he bring her.

'E'en as Bhōja[6] enjoyed delights; e'en as Vikrama,[7] founded an era, so will he.' Thus having tested Ratna, the jewel, like jewel-testers, did they write down all his marks.

1 Some Mss. have *sēni*. See p. 15, note 2.

2 Citaura is a corruption of Citra-pura, the picture-fort. We shall henceforth use the more familiar name of *Citaur*.

3 Ratna means 'jewel.'

4 Throughout the poem, the comparisons of Ratna to a diamond, and of Padmāvatī to a ruby are of frequent occurrence.

5 Or perfected in spiritual knowledge. There is a double meaning here.

6 Bhōja was the celebrated king of Dhāra in Mâlwâ, in whose reign (about the 10th or 11th Century A.D.) the civilization of India is traditionally said to have reached its culminating point.

7 Vikrama or Vikramāditya,—see page 9, note 2. The well-known *sambat*-era is referred to him. It is considered the height of glory to be the founder of an era, and such eras are temporarily founded at the present day. For instance an era is used by some people dating from the Poet Hariçcandra of Benares, who died the other day. It is called the *Hariçcandra-sambat*.

Canto VII.

The Merchant.

76. A certain merchant of Citaur went to Siṁhala to trade, and there was a very poor Brāhmaṇa who went thither with him when he set forth. From some one did he borrow money in the hope that perchance by going thither he might increase it. The way was hard, and much toil did he pass through, and finally he crossed the ocean and arrived at the Isle. He gazed at the markets, so vast that he could not see the other side, and of every thing was there much and of nothing little. But very high is the trading there. The wealthy man getteth what he wanteth, but the wealthless can only gaze in wonder. Things were sold there by myriads and by millions; to things worth thousands did not any one bend himself.

All (his companions) bought and returned to their home. What would the Brāhmaṇa get there, for very small was the money in his poke.[1]

77. (He lamented, saying), 'Dried up do I stand. Why did I come? I have got no merchandize and naught has remained to me but regret. I came here to market, expecting a profit, and by walking on that road, I have lost even my capital. Why have I learned the lesson of dying? I am come to die, for death was written in my fate. While I had still power to move, I made a foolish bargain. I see no profit, but only the loss of my capital. Did I sow parched grain[2] in a former life, that I am come and have eaten even the savings of my house? The merchant with whom I did my business,—if

[1] *Gāṭhi* is the knot in a man's waist band in which he carries his money. For *sāṭhi*, see xxxviii, 9, comm. The word literally means sugarcane. *Sāṭhi-nāṭhi*, means crushed sugarcane, whence all the juice has been expressed. It is hence used to mean 'squeezed out,' hence 'without wealth.' From this idiom *sāṭhi* has come to mean 'wealth.'

[2] He refers to his *karma*, or (good) actions in a former birth. These he compares to seed which he then sowed, and of which he should now be enjoying the fruit. He now says, he must have sown parched seed (*i.e.*, have done something to nullify his *karma*), which has produced no fruit.

he wait at my door for payment of my debt, what am I to give him? How am I to enter my house empty? What answer am I to give him if he ask me?

'My companions are gone. My fair fame (will be) destroyed. Between us are oceans and mountains. Hopeless of hope do I return. O God, give thou unto me subsistence.

78. Just then the fowler came up with the parrot, all golden in its colour and matchless in its beauty. He offered it for sale in the market, where the price of jewels and rubies was settled.[1] But who would buy the parrot, the fly of a Madāra tree,[2] which was looking intently to see where it was to go? The Brāhmaṇa came up and asked himself, 'Is this parrot possessed of wisdom, or wisdomless and empty?' Said he, 'Tell me, thou mountain-born, if wisdom be with thee, and conceal it not within thy heart. Thou[3] and I are both Brāhmaṇas, and everyone asketh another his caste. If thou art a *paṇḍit*, then recite thou the Vēda; for without asking is no essential attribute discovered.

'I am a Brāhmaṇa and a learned man. Tell me thine own wisdom. For if a man recite before him who is well taught, the gain is two-fold.'

79. The parrot replied, 'Sir, I once had wisdom, when I was a bird escaped from the cage. Now what wisdom doth thy disciple possess, for he is a prisoner, thrust into a basket and brought for sale. Learned men are not brought to market. But I wish to be sold, and therefore is all my learning forgotten. Two paths[4] see I in this market: along which of them will God drive me? Weeping blood my countenance hath become red, and my body pallid. What tale can I tell? Red and black upon my throat are two collar-like marks. They are as it were nooses, and I fear for my life exceedingly.[5] Now have I recognized these nooses on my throat and neck. Let us see what these nooses are about to do.

'Much have I read and studied, and that fear is still before me. I see the whole world dark. All my knowledge have I lost, and I sit bewildered.'

80. When the Brāhmaṇa heard these words he entreated the fowler, 'Be merciful and slay not birds. O cruel one, why dost thou take another's life? Hast thou not fear of the guilt of murder? Thou sayest that birds are food for men, but he is cruel who eateth other's flesh. Weeping dost thou come into this world, and with weeping dost thou depart; yet, natheless, dost thou sleep in enjoyment and happiness. Thou knowest that thine own body will suffer destruction, still nourishest thou thy flesh with the flesh of others. If

1 According to verse lxxvi, prices ruled high.

2 The *Madāra* or *Arka* (*Asclepias gigantea*) is a plant used as medicine. It is of little account, except that its flowers are offered to the mad God Mahādēva. This in fact is one reason for its light estimation. A bright green fly settles on it, which, of course, is of still less value, and to it the bright green parrot is compared. The parrot is anxiously looking to see what its fate is to be.

3 The Parrot is the Brāhmaṇa of the bird tribe.

4 One to the east, the other to the west.

5 Male parrots, when full-grown, have two ring-like marks, one red and the other black round their neck. These are often compared to nooses. Compare xcv, 6, and xcix, 7.

there were not men so greedy of others' flesh, why then would fowlers capture birds? So the fowler who continually captureth birds, selleth them, nor desireth them in his own heart.'

The Brāhmaṇa bought the parrot, when he heard its knowledge of the Vēdas and Holy books. Then joined he his fellow travellers and started for Citaur.

81. In the meantime King Citra-sēna had gone to Çiva's (paradise) and Ratna-sēna had become monarch of Citaur: and behold there came a report to him: 'O King, merchants are come from Siṁhala. There are pearl oysters filled with elephant-pearls, and many goods of Siṁhala's isle. A Brāhmaṇa hath brought a parrot, all golden in its colour, and of matchless beauty. Red and black upon its neck are two (lines like) necklets, and its wings and shoulders[1] are all inscribed with scarlet. Its two eyes glow like rubies, ruby-coloured is its beak, and its speech is nectar-like. On its forehead is the caste-mark, and on its shoulder a Brāhmaṇa's thread. 'Tis a poet like unto Vyāsa, and 'tis learned like unto Saha-dēva.[2]

'What words it speaketh have meaning: and those who hear it wag their heads in admiration. So priceless a parrot should be in the King's palace.'

82. Forth went the King's command, and they sent men running, who quickly brought the Brāhmaṇa and the parrot. The Brāhmaṇa gave his blessing and began his supplication: 'Never would I separate myself from this parrot, which is like my soul; but this belly is a devourer of the universe, before which bow, yea, all ascetics and devotees. If a man hath no coverlet or bed, he can lay himself upon the ground with his arm beneath his neck. A man's eyes may refuse to see, and then he is but blind. His mouth may refuse to utter words, and then he is but dumb. His ears may cease to hear, and then he is but deaf: but this belly never loseth its peculiar function. Many and many a time[3] is it continually at fault, and must go begging from door to door, or else it is not satisfied.

[1] *Pāṭhā* or *paṭṭhā* is the joint of the wings with the body.

[2] Vyāsa was the celebrated composer or arranger of the Mahā-bhārata. Saha-dēva was one of the five Pāṇḍava brothers, heroes of the Mahā-bhārata, and was celebrated for his learning.

[3] The word *bāra* has many meanings, owing to many Sanskrit words having phonetically developed into it. The following story illustrates this.

Sūra-dāsa, the celebrated blind poet and singer once sung the following verse in Akbar's court.

Jasudā bāra bāra yaha bhākhai |
Hai kou hitū hamārō Braja mē calata Gopālahi rākhai ||

The Emperor asked the meaning of the words *bāra bāra*. Some said it meant 'repeatedly' (Skr. *vāraṁ-vāraṁ*); others that it meant 'at every door' (*dvāraṁ-dvāraṁ*); others 'to all the children' (*bālaṁ-bālaṁ*); others 'to all the girls' (*bālāṁ-bālāṁ*); others 'stopping continually' (*varja varja kara*); others 'may I be sacrificed' (*balaiyā lē lē kara*); others 'lighting lamp after lamp' (*dīpaka bāra bāra kara*); others 'with water water' (Skr. *vāri vāri*), *i.e.*, weeping; others 'day by day'; others 'raving' (*varvara*). At length the Emperor asked the poet, and he explained that the verse meant 'every hair (Skr. *bāla bāla*) of Yaśōdā cries out, "is there any friend in Vraja, who will take care of Gōpāla (the infant Kṛṣṇa) as he crawls about."'

'This is that which calleth me here, and which bringeth me hunger and thirst. If there were no enemy such as this, what unsatisfied desire of aught would any have?'

83. The parrot gave a blessing, promising mighty pomp, mighty prowess, and an unbroken rule. 'Full of fortune hath God created thee. Where there is good fortune, there beauty standeth reverently in attendance.[1] Some men come to a man in the hope (of obtaining a favour), while he who is without hope sitteth silent on his seat. Others without being asked say their say; and when they speak, their say, as clay, is worthless. When a man is learned and educated, and knoweth the mind-secrets of the Vēdas, then, when he is spoken to, he replieth like unto Saha-dēva.[2] No learned man praiseth himself, but if he is brought for sale, he desireth to speak; for so long as his virtues are not made manifest, so long no one knoweth the secret concerning them.

'(Therefore say I) "I am a paṇḍit learned in the four Vēdas. Hīrā-maṇi is my name. With Padmāvatī did I sport, and there used I to serve her."'

84. Ratna-sēna recognized Hīrā-maṇi as a learned bird, and bought him from the Brāhmaṇa for a hundred thousand rupees. So the Brāhmaṇa gave his blessing and departed, and the parrot was brought into the royal palace. How can I describe this parrot's speech? Blessed be he that first dubbed him Hīrā-maṇi (or the diamond-jewel). Whene'er he spake, he looked towards the King, and his words were like the pearls of the necklace which has the hearer's heart for its thread. All that he spake was rubies and coral, otherwise he remained silent like one that is dumb. (He would tell tales of love, and), as it were, strike (his hearers) dead, and then would he revive them with words of nectar. He became a spiritual guide, and the whole world became his disciples. He used to tell the tale of the sun and moon,[3] and with the story of passion did he ravish all hearts.

All who heard him wagged their heads (in admiration), and the King's love for him became unfathomable. (They would cry): 'So wise a parrot is there not aught other. Whom will he drive distracted?'

1 *i.e.*, Thou art not only fortunate but beautiful.

2 See note 2 on p. 40, above.

3 A side reference to Ratna and Padmāvatī. The tale of the sun and moon seems to mean that he gave lectures in astronomical physics. He used to combine instruction with amusement.

i.e., some day, he will drive some one to distraction with his tales of love.

Canto VIII.

Nāgamatī and the Parrot.

85. When five or ten days had passed, the king departed somewhither to hunt. Nāgamatī, his beauteous queen, was the chief of his harem. She adorned herself, and took a mirror in her hand; and, as she looked at the reflection, she became filled with vanity. Smiling went the Lady to the Parrot, and offered to him a touchstone of polish.[1] 'Parrot,' she said, 'Thou art worthy and the beloved of my Lord. In the whole world is there any so fair as I? Test thou the colour (of my beauty). How fair is this gold, and how fair is thine Isle of Siṁhala? How fair to look upon are the beauties there? Am I the more fair to see, or is the Padumanī (Padmāvatī)?

'Parrot, if thou tell me not the truth,—I adjure[2] thee by the King. Is there any on this earth so fair as I?'

86. When he thought of the beauty of Padmāvatī, the parrot laughed and looked the queen in the face. Replied he, 'In the lake to which the swan cometh not, there the paddy bird in the water is called a swan. God so perfectly did make this world, that every creature excelleth[3] another (in some beauty). Vanity becometh no one's soul. The very moon waneth and is devoured by Rāhu.[4] Who can call a woman fair or unfair? Fair alone is she, who is beloved of her lord. Why asketh thou me concerning the

[1] So literally. It means that she called upon the parrot to apply the touchstone of beauty to her. *Ōpanā* is polish, and *aupana-wārī* means that which gives polish, or which shows the true polish of the gold which is being tested. There is a pun in the words *so nārī*, 'the Lady.' They may also be translated as *sonārin* 'the goldsmith's wife,' who owns the gold to be tested.

[2] *Ānā* equals the Skr. *ājñā*.

[3] *Āgara* = *Agrya*, excelling.

[4] We are unable to trace any legend of the vanity of the moon being the cause of its waning or of its eclipse. Rāhu is the demon of eclipse who swallows the moon on that occasion, see note to v. xcviii.

women of Siṁhala, for the dark night cannot be compared with the day. Their bodies are fragrant as flowers. Why should I describe their feet,[1] to which every head (is bowed).

Compounded are they of gold and fragrant essence. Filled are they with beauty and good fortune?' When the queen heard this she was enraged, as if salt had been thrown upon her heart.[2]

87. (Cried she) 'If this parrot remain in the palace, he may sometime tell this unto the King. If the King hear he will became enamoured. He will desert his kingdom and become an ascetic. By storing poison it becometh not grapes. See that this chanticleer of love give not forth his note.'[3] She called her quick-running maid-servant, and no longer able to restrain her anger in her heart, gave unto her the parrot. 'See this parrot. He is an evil-worker. He doth not even belong to her who cherished him.[4] With his mouth he sayeth one thing, and in his belly dwelleth another; and for this fault hath he been sold in half a score of markets. Keep not a bird that speaketh such evil things. Take him and kill him where no one can see thee.

'This is the day-time, that I ever dreaded. In the night, have I hid my sun.[5] He desireth to give (the sun) to the lotus, and to be to me a peacock.'[6]

88. The maiden went off with the parrot to kill him, but, while she considered, wisdom came into her heart. 'The parrot,' quoth she, 'giveth ease unto my lord. He whom the master loveth should not be killed. He is a paṇḍit with his passions all subdued, and blame lieth at the door (not of such, but at the door) of him who looketh not before him. She who understandeth not a woman's actions, falleth into error and afterwards lamenteth. Nāgamatī hath but the wisdom of a serpent,[7] and no parrot ever hath become a peacock. What hope can there be in the arm of a woman that obeyeth not her Lord? Perhaps when the King returneth at nightfall, the bird will be sought for, and then will the horse's disease fall upon the monkey's head.[8]

'Two things, murder and sin, cannot be kept hidden, even though a man try to hide them. In the end they cause destruction, themselves bearing the witness.'[9]

1 The humblest part of their body. 'Ex pede Herculem.'

2 Her heart was like a blazing fire, which crackled ominously when salt was thrown upon it.

3 The cock-crow of love will awaken the king, and warn him to search for the day of Padmāvatī, now that the night of Nāgamatī is past.

4 *i.e.*, He deserted his late mistress.

5 Nāgamatī was black but comely, Padmāvatī fair as the day. Nāgamatī has kept her beloved (her sun) devoted to the night (herself). Now he will leave the night, and seek the day.

6 The peacock eats snakes. Nāgamatī refers to her name, in which *nāga* means 'snake.' The lotus is Padmāvatī.

7 Again a pun on the name, see note to last stanza. A serpent cannot distinguish between good and evil, and bites every one (good and bad) indifferently.

8 *i.e.*, The punishment due to the queen will fall on me. According to tradition, if you wish to keep your horses well, keep a monkey in the stable. It is believed that all diseases, to which horses are liable, leave them and fly to the monkey.

9 Here again the postposition (*sai*) precedes the noun (*āpu*) to which it belongs. Cf. v. lxvi, 3.

89. So the maiden made up her mind and put the parrot (in a place of safety); and at even, when the King returned, he sought for him. The Queen replied in angry tones, 'A cat hath carried off thy parrot. I asked him about the Padminī of Siṁhala, and he replied "What art thou, O Nāginī? She is like the day and thou art as the dark night. Where spring is ever blooming, who (careth for) a garden of the thorny *karīla*?[1] What is thy husband but the king of the night? Doth an owl know the nature of the day time?" So, what is that bird but a pawn in a fort,[2] whose little tongue speaketh such mighty words? Whene'er he speaketh, he distilleth blood. Whether he eat or be without food, his face is red.[3]

'Set not a parrot on thine head, even though it be exceeding fair. Why shouldst thou wear a golden earring, if it tear thine ear?'[4]

90. The king heard these words and became desolate, as Vikrama[5] lamented in his heart. 'That Hīrā-maṇi, was my scholar-parrot, from whose mouth distilled nectar when he spake. A scholar whose sorrows have been subdued, of blameless life. A scholar from whom fell no guile. A scholar

1 *Capparis aphylla*, Roxb., a thorny leafless plant which grows in the desert.

2 *Gōṭī*, which I have translated 'pawn,' is a wooden or stone back-gammon piece, or such like. In a great castle, such a petty thing is of no account.

3 Alluding to the red colour of the parrot's face. His face is ever red, whether you feed him or not. A red face implies anger. Hence he is angry even when you treat him kindly and feed him.

4 This is a well-known proverb, *phaṭa parē waha sōnā, jehi sē ṭūṭē kāna*.

5 Regarding Vikrama, See vv. xvii, and lxxv. The story of Vikrama and the Parrot is as follows.—He had a parrot named, like the parrot of the text, Hīrā-maṇi, who one day obtained leave to take a holiday in the forest, promising to bring back an '*amara-phala*,' or fruit of the Tree of Life, the eating of which prevented old-age and death. The leave was granted, and after a time, the parrot returned from his travels with an *amara-phala* in his beak, which he presented to his master and mistress. The king gave it to his gardener, with instructions to plant it and grow a fruit-bearing tree from it. This the gardener did, and in time it sprouted, and began to bear fruit. The king gave orders that as soon as a fruit ripened and fell from the tree, it was to be given to his queen. It happened that, at length, one night, a ripened fruit did fall, and, that attracted by its scent, a poisonous snake approached it and licked it all over. The fruit thus became poisoned, and lost its own property. In the morning the gardener picked it up and presented it to Her Majesty. As it was a new kind of fruit, she first fed a dog experimentally with it. Thereupon, the dog, there and then, fell down dead. The queen enraged with the parrot for bringing so poisonous a fruit into the house, had the bird killed at once, and told the king what had occurred. Some time after, the old wife of the gardener had a quarrel with him, and determined to commit suicide. As the easiest way of doing this, she decided to eat a fruit of the terrible poison tree, the seed of which had been brought by the parrot. She went and ate one, and immediately became young and beautiful. Her old husband went out searching for her, and at length found her under the tree, and, to his amazement, entirely changed in appearance. She told him what she had done, and what the consequences had been, so he took another fruit himself, and equally immediately, became young and handsome. Afterwards, when he brought the customary morning basket of fruit to the king, the latter noticed his good looks, and asked and was told the reason. Then the king knew that his parrot Hīrā-maṇi had, after all, been faithful, and that he had been unjustly put to death by the queen. Thereupon, he lamented so much that the phrase 'Lamentations like those of Vikrama' has become a proverb.

whose tongue and mouth were pure. A scholar who ne'er said a foolish word, A scholar, who gave me wisdom and who led me on The Way. 'Tis the way of evil that such a scholar loveth not. A scholar wise hath a lovely[1] countenance. It is a murderer whose contenance seemeth red as blood. Either, Nāgamatī, bring thou me back the life of my body, or else go thou, and with the parrot immolate thyself.'

(Saith Muḥammad), 'Think not that, by committing sin, there will be a reign of bliss within thy palace. When once a husband's command hath been broken, then who hath aught result but misery?'

91. Be a Lady as glorious as the moon, natheless is she eclipsed by her beloved's wrath. She could not carry out perfect happiness (by consoling her Lord), for when she failed in her devotion misery alone was born. So great a fault had she committed that her Beloved was wroth, so that though she call him her own, 'twas false. With such vanity let no one err: she, alone is the greatly beloved one who feareth her husband. The queen approached her maid, her hope in the silk of the cotton tree of the parrot.[2] In the midst of the (molten) gold of my love hath fallen lead. The gold is scattered, and will no more combine. Yea, naught but the dark mark of the lead is visible. Where is there a goldsmith that I may go to him, to apply a flux and unite the gold together.[3]

'Trusting in my beloved's affection, I showed vanity in my heart. Through his anger have I obtained but despite; for I, O clever maid, have made my beloved wroth.'

92. Then answered wrathfully the maiden, 'From anger doth one's own wisdom (become an ogress) and eat other unoffending ones.[4] Lady, I said unto thee, "Be not enraged, who hath not been ruined by this anger?" Thou wast full of anger, nor didst thou look before thee. In anger, for whom hath ever wedded bliss been born? Upon anger is born dis-love and discord, but no one beateth him who beateth down his own wrath. She who hath anger, to her, meetly, love cometh not; and without love she becometh yellow as turmeric.[5] Therefore let her not create anger and wrath,[6] from which she dieth; and let her not abandon love, from which she liveth. The love of a husband cannot be gained by a mere wish. She only obtaineth it, who hath fixed her heart upon him.

'She who obeyeth the behests of her mate, and humbly offereth her service, appeareth like unto a spotless moon, and her life hath no stain.'

93. [7]The queen felt in her heart like unto a gambler who hath gained

1 *Rātā* means both red and beautiful hence the allusion.

2 *I.e.*, she was hopeless. The *sīmal* or silk cotton tree is the proverbial example of disappointed hope. It is beautiful to look upon, but its fruit is only fluff.

3 A pun on the word *sohāg*, which means both the flux borax, and wedded happiness.

4 This stanza is a series of puns in the words *risa* 'anger,' and *rasa*, 'love,' both of which are written similarly in the Persian character, thus رس.

5 The jaundiced gaze of jealousy.

6 *Risa* means inward anger, of which *krōdha*, wrath, is its outward expression

7 The maid must be presumed to have given the parrot to the Queen.

once more what he hath lost, and she brought the parrot and gave it to the king. 'Heed thou my words; I was not vain. I but wished to test thine affection, O my love. Wouldst thou destroy for so small a fault one who hath faithfully been thy slave from year's end unto year's end. (So pitiless art thou, that) even though one humbly bend his neck before thee, thou dost not dismiss him without an order for his death. Even when I meet thee, thou art as it were far away: and hence, O dear one, is my heart full of fear (that thou lovest me no longer). I thought that thou dost pervade me alone, yet now I look and see that thou art enshrined in every heart. Whether Queen, or whether slave-girl, she alone is good, on whom thou showest mercy.

'No one can conquer thee. The Bhōja[1] and Vara-ruci are defeated before thee. But one doth not learn to seek for thee, till after one hath lost himself.'[2]

[1] Regarding *Bhōja*. see v. lxxv. Vara-ruci, the celebrated grammarian, was one of the 'Nine jewels,' who attended his court.

[2] *i.e.*, Had seen that I was not an individual, but only an emanation from the Supreme. The well-known Vēdāntik theory. The whole verse may be interpreted throughout in a Vēdāntik sense.

Canto IX.

The King and the Parrot.

94. The King said, 'O Parrot tell me truly. Without truth unto what art thou like? Thou art (useless) like unto the fluff of the silk-cotton tree.[1] From speaking truth the face acquireth beauty. Where there is truth, there virtue is its companion. Creation itself hath been composed in truth. Lakṣmī[2] herself is the handmaiden of truth. Where there is truth, daring gaineth success, and the speaker of truth is known as "the truthful man." For the sake of truth doth she who becometh suttee[3] prepare her funeral pyre, and for truth (at the marriage ceremony) do women put four fires (round the couple). They who cling to truth pass through this world and the next, and beloved of the Almighty are they who speak the truth. He who abandoneth truth, destroyeth virtue. (So tell me Parrot), didst thou form in thine heart a truth destroying thought, (when thou didst tell the tale of the Padminī)?

'Thou art a learned scholar, speak not that which is false. Tell thou me now the truth, to whom hath injustice been done?'[4]

95. 'O King,' quoth the parrot, 'I will tell the truth; and may my life depart, but still I will not speak untruth from my mouth. My truth was all that I brought with me to this country, or else should I have been in the king's palace in the isle of Siṁhala. Padmāvatī is the king's daughter. The Creator in her hath made incarnate a moon of lotus-odour. Her face is like the moon, and her limbs are odorous of sandal. Scented gold is she, and perfect in all her parts.[5] Many are the Padminīs in the isle of Siṁhala, but in fragrance

1 See note to stanza xci.

2 The Goddess of Prosperity.

3 Suttee is literally *satī*, the base of which word is the same as the base of the word *satya* truth.

4 *i.e.*, Has Nāgamatī told true or false stories about you when she said that you had spoken evil of me.

5 Compare the modern Hindī *bārah bāni*, accomplished, perfect, possessing the twelve

and in beauty, they are but her shadow. I, Hīrā-maṇi, was her bird, and in her service did I become full grown.[1] Thus did I gain the speech of men; otherwise what would I have been but a bird,—a fistful of feathers.

'As long as I live, night and day, do I e'er bear her name in memory, and, (as I do so), I die (of shame, that I serve her no more). My face is red, and my body green, and them will I carry with me in both worlds, (for I speak the truth.)'

96. As Hirāmaṇi described the lotus, the king, like the fabled bee,[2] became enamoured. 'Come hither, my bright bird. This island hath killed the serpent.[3] Thou, who hast dwelt in the home of golden fragrance, how art thou not well named Hīrā-maṇi?[4] Who is the king? How lofty is that island, at the mere hearing of which my soul hath become a moth enchanted by a candle.[5] When I hear it mine eyes become agitated like the Kilakilā Ocean.[6] Tell me of the spotless fragrance of the lady. Hath she found a bee for a companion, or is she still but a bud, and not an opened flower? And tell me also of the beauteous Padminīs there, and how the fate of each is in her own abode.

'Come, tell me all the tale of them. I long to see that isle. My desire hath arisen at hearing thy recital.'

97. 'O King, how can I tell all that? The isle of Siṁhala is like unto Kailāsa.[7] Whoe'er hath gone there hath been fascinated, and ages may pass, but none hath e'er returned. In every house are Padminīs of the thirty-six castes,[8] and it is ever spring both day and night. With whatever here a flower-garden bloometh, there, of that colour, flowereth a fragrant damsel. Gandharva-sēna is there the mighty king—created by God like Indra amidst his heavenly nymphs. This Padmāvatī is his daughter, glorious amongst all lights. Suitors from all lands have bowed themselves for her, but to all, in his pride, the king refuseth an answer.

'Even as when the sun riseth, the moon concealeth herself in his glory, so there all hide themselves before Padmāvatī's beauty.'

98. When Ratna, the Jewel, heard the name of the Sun, his face became flushed.[9] 'Tell me, Learned One, again this tale. Thou hast told me of her

colours, or the twelve different kinds of brilliancy. There are twelve *Ādityas* or forms of the sun, each of which lends a different kind of brilliancy.

1 Literally, the two lines (black and red) round my throat, which indicate full growth, appeared. Cf. lxxix, 6 and xcix, 7.

2 The love of the bee for the lotus is one of the common-places of Indian poetry.

3 This is impossible to translate literally. It has two meanings. It may mean either 'this light (*dīpa*) which has hitherto killed merely small moths, has killed me, the great serpent.' Or it may mean 'this (description of the) island has killed the snake (*i.e.*, Nāgamatī), and I cease to care for her.'

4 Diamond-jewel.

5 Here again, there is a pun on the two meanings of the word *dīpa*, an island, and a light.

6 One of the seven Oceans, with a particularly stormy sea. *Vide* p. 2, note 2.

7 Çiva's heaven. The poet, as usual, confuses it with that of Indra.

8 The castes are usually enumerated in a catalogue of thirty-six. See Hindī Comm.

9 Or, if we take Ratna as meaning 'a jewel,' especially the gem called *sūrya-kānta*, or

fair complexion and of her form, and they are now imprinted like a picture on my heart. Her form hath, as it were, become the Sun, which hath taken up its dwelling in my soul, and which, filling my whole being, hath become manifest in my heart. Now, though thus I have become the Sun, and she the Moon, yet 'tis I who borrow my radiance from her (and not she from me). Were this not so, I should be but a fish without water,—a body without blood. In the radiance of her beams, shoots of young love have sprung up (within my heart). Even if this Moon be in the heavens, I, as the Sun, will meet her there.[1] Her rays are thousandfold, and bewilder my soul. Where'er I gaze, the whole universe seemeth to be but one lotus;[2] and where that lotus is, there my soul hath become the bee, and the moon hath found itself in debt to Rāhu.[3]

Sun-stone, which gives out a blazing light in the Sun, the line means, 'The jewel became ruby-coloured in the blaze of the Sun' mentioned at the end of the last verse.

[1] In his agitation, the king compares, sometimes himself, and sometimes Padmāvatī to the Sun.

[2] This absorption of one's whole self, and all one's sentient powers, in one idea, is expressed in Hindī by the phrase 'The worm has become the ichneumon.' The *bhṛṅga*, or ichneumon, is a wasp-like insect, of the order Hymenoptera, the female of which, by means of its ovipositor, first stings and stupefies some other insect or caterpillar, and then deposits its eggs in its body. In process of time, the larvæ are hatched, and find their food by devouring, bit by bit, the interior of their living, but still stupefied, host. When nothing but the empty shell remains, they come forth into public life. The *bhṛṅga* is wrongly described in the dictionaries as a kind of wasp. The Indian tradition differs from the actual facts of natural history. It is said that when the ichneumon stings the insect, the pain to the latter is so severe that it is filled with terror, which renders it motionless and compels it to remain night and day doing nothing but meditating in rapt absorption on the ichneumon. So intent is this absorption, that the insect gradually abandons its own nature, and ultimately, itself, becomes an ichneumon. This is a favourite simile of teachers of the Vedantic school. Like the insect stung by the ichneumon, the soul, by absorption in contemplation on the Deity, gradually becomes, itself, a portion of the Deity. Here, Ratna-sēna represents himself as gradually becoming, in the same way, one with Padmāvatī. The more usual Hindī name for an ichneumon is *bilanī*.

[3] *i.e.*, as Rāhu, the demon of the Eclipse, covets and claims the moon, so I covet and claim her. When the Gods and Demons fought for possession of the nectar produced at the Churning of the Ocean, Viṣṇu took the form of a beautiful woman, named Mōhinī, and she persuaded the combatants to make over the jar of the precious liquor to her, to divide amongst them. She arranged the Demons in one line, and the Gods in another. To the former, she only gave the wine which also appeared from the Ocean when it was churned, and to the latter she distributed the immortality-giving nectar. The Demon Rāhu, who was the ascending Node of the Moon, disguised himself, and stood in the row of the Gods between the Sun and the Moon. Mōhinī handed him the jar of nectar in his turn, and as he commenced to drink, the Sun and the Moon told her that this was a Demon, not a God, and that he had no right to be there. In her rage, Mōhinī there and then cut off Rāhu's head with Viṣṇu's discus. Owing to the nectar which he had drunk, Rāhu's head and body both remained alive, though severed from each other. To console him, Brahmā gave him the boon that whenever the Sun and the Moon came into conjunction, he might swallow one of them, and that all dedications, sacrifices, and good works done during the time of swallowing should be his by right. In this way, it is said that the Sun and the Moon are in

'The three worlds, the fourteen regions,[1] have all come before my vision. But, except Love, naught else that my heart can understand, is fair.'

99. 'At hearing the tale of love be not distraught, O King. Love is hard, and unless one offer his head for it, it adorneth not. If a man fall into the noose of love, he escapeth not. Many have given up their lives, but that noose breaketh not. It hath so many pangs as the chameleon hath changes of colour; sometimes turning red and sometimes yellow and sometimes white. The peacock knoweth this, and hath become a hermit in the forest, and beareth on every hair the marks of the serpent-lasso.[2] Again and again doth this noose fall upon his wings. He cannot fly for it, and remains bound in its entanglement. Crying night and day "*mueũ mueũ*," "I am dead, I am dead," in his rage doth he devour snakes.[3] The turtle dove and the parrot have the same marks of the noose upon their necks; and on whose neck it falleth, he must give up his life.

'The partridge hath the noose upon his neck, and ever proclaimeth his guilt. Else, why calleth he out till the hunter's noose falleth on his neck? Vain is the hope that death will give him release.'[4]

100. The king heaved a deep sigh, and cried, 'Say not so hopeless a speech. Whether love be full of happiness or sorrow, it is hard; but, still, he who hath played the sport of love, hath safely passed this world and the world to come. Within (the casket of) sorrow is placed the honey of love, and he who tasteth it must bear contempt and death. Why doth he e'er come upon this earth, who layeth not his head upon the path of love? Now have I placed my head in love's noose. Thrust not aside my feet (from the path), but take me as thy disciple. He alone can tell of the door of love who hath seen it; and how can he who hath not seen it, know its secrets? Till the beloved is met, so long must pain be felt; and when she *is* met, the pain of all one's life is wiped away for ever.

'As thou hast seen the matchless one, so now describe to me her beauty from head to foot.[5] Hope have I of meeting her, if the Creator but bring us together.'

debt to Rāhu, and he has the right to seize them in payment of his debt. The swallowing of the Sun or the Moon causes an eclipse of that heavenly body, but as Rāhu's head has been cut off, he only swallows it, to let it out at the back of his head where it was separate from his trunk.

[1] See Notes 5 and 6 on p. 1.

[2] The *Nāga-pāça* or serpent-noose, is the name of a special kind of noose used in battle; a kind of lasso.

[3] The round spots on the peacock's tail are the marks of the noose. The peacock is said to be a great devourer of snakes. The poet's fancy is that his hatred for the reptile is caused by the *Nāga-pāça*, the 'serpent-lasso' of love in which he is entangled.

[4] Cf. lxxiv, 3. The Partridge's lamentations attract the hunter, and it is killed; but even then the lasso mark remains upon its neck.

[5] Lit. 'From toe-nail to top-knot.' A *nakha-sikha* is a technical term for a class of poetry describing a woman, limb by limb.

Canto X.

Love's Inventory.

101. (Quoth the Parrot), 'My Liege, how can I tell the tale of her charms. Charms verily hath she, but such as become her alone. *Imprimis*—A head[1] crowned with musk-scented locks, before which Vāsuki, not to speak of earthly kings, doth immolate himself.[2] 'The Princess is as it were a jasmine, and her tresses are black bees, attracted by her fragrance and impetuously struggling to imbibe her nectar. When she looseneth the braid and shaketh out her hair, darkness o'erspreadeth the universe from Heaven unto Hell. Soft and waved are her tresses like black snakes seated in wavy undulations on a mountain. For pervaded is she with the sandal odour of Mount Malaya, and therefore have they climbed her head and drag their slow lengths around it.[3] Full of deadly poison are her curls, chains of love ready to fall upon the neck of the beholder.

The locks upon that head are nooses which inevitably snare each neck, and hence all the eight tribes[4] of serpents are tangled in the fillets of her hair.

102. '*Item*—the parting of her hair yet untouched by vermilion.[5] Pure

[1] In describing a divine being it is usual to begin at the feet and work up to the head. In describing a human being the order is reversed.

[2] Vāsuki is the king of serpents, the most potent of which are black. So are Padmāvatī's locks, but they are also odorous, thereby surpassing the Lord of Snakes who immolates himself in consequence at their shrine. There is, however, a pun in the original. *Kēsa* the word for hair also means Viṣṇu (see the commentary) whom Vāsuki would naturally adore.

[3] Mount Malaya is celebrated for two things, its sandal trees and its snakes. Padmāvatī's head has the sandal-fragrance so that the snakes imagine it to be their natural abode. This comparison of wavy hair with serpents is unpleasing to European taste but is one of the most popular commonplaces of Indian poetry.

[4] The eight tribes of the *nāgas* or serpents are (1) Vāsuki, (2) Takṣaka, (3) Kulaka, (4) Karkōṭaka, (5) Padma, (6) Çaŋkha-cūḍa, (7) Mahāpadma, (8) Dhanañjaya.

[5] The *Māg* (Skr. *mārga*, or path) is the parting of the hair. Vermilion is first put upon it when a girl is married and she uses it during her married life. The flat folds of hair

white shineth it as though it were a shaft of light beaming bright upon a path through the night.[1] 'Tis like unto the bright line left by gold upon the (black) touchstone; 'Tis like the lightning flashing through the clouds. 'Tis a bright sunbeam shining across the sky; 'Tis the shining stream of the Sarasvatī in the midst of the (black torrent of the) Yamunā. Pink is it like an ensanguined sword-edge; (slightly uneven is it) as though it were a saw laid upon the braids. On it lieth a string of pearls, white as the stream of the Ganges amid the Yamunā.[2] At this holy confluence there thus lieth ready the saw for cutting the devotee in two (who sacrificeth himself that, perchance), she may take his blood and use it for vermilion.[3]

It is gold perfect in all its qualities, and longeth for its flux.[4] The stars and planets are its slaves. It is the Galaxy shining in the skies[5].

103. '*Item*—A forehead, bright as the young moon of its second day,—but where in the world is the young moon so bright; for the thousand-rayed sun himself who shineth in the sky setteth in shame when he beholdeth that brow. How can I compare it with even the full orb of night? for the moon is blemished, and it is without spot. Moreover the moon suffereth eclipse while it remaineth ever in its glory. And on that forehead

on each side are termed *paṭiyā*. When a topknot is worn it is called *cōṭī*. The ends of the *paṭiyās* and of the hair hanging down behind are tied into three braids (*bēnī*). When these three are twisted together at the back of the head, the coil is named *jūrā*. These three *bēnīs* are known as *tribēṇī*. When a woman is separated from her husband she ties her hair in one *bēnī* instead of three (Compare Vālmīki-Rām., v, 65, 14). When a woman becomes a widow she washes the vermilion out of the parting of her hair, and never applies it again.

1 The night, of course, is the two black *paṭiyās* on each side of the parting.

2 The Ganges and Jumna meet at Allahabad. There also is said to flow the Sarasvatī by an underground channel. The three streams unite and form the *tribēṇī* (Compare note 5 page 51 above). Each has waters of a different colour. The Ganges-water is plain to every eye for some way below the confluence. The Jumna (Yamunā) waters are much darker.

3 This is an elaborate comparison between the parting of the hair and the *Prayāga* or confluence of the three rivers (with a pun on the two meanings of *tribēṇī*). At this confluence a saw is supposed to be laid down. Its object is for the devoted lover to sacrifice himself with it, so that his blood may supply the vermilion of her parting, and thus make her a married woman. This is a reference to the true confluence (*tribēṇī*) at Prayāga (*i.e.*, Allahabad). According to tradition a saw was kept at this holy place, wherewith devotees cut themselves in two in order to obtain final emancipation. The action was considered so meritorious a one, and the self-sacrificers were considered so holy, that large crowds used to attend these dreadful functions, the women anointing the partings of their hair with the blood of the victim in the hope of obtaining long and happy wedded lives. It is said that Shāh Jahān put a stop to the practice by destroying the saw. The parting of the hair is compared to a saw because its edges are slightly jagged.

4 Here again there is a pun. *Sohāga* means both the flux which is added to gold to enhance its brilliancy, and also happy married life, (*saubhāgya*). Regarding the gold 'of twelve colours' see stanza xcv, note 5.

5 The Galaxy is the Ganges flowing in Heaven; which, of course, the stars and planets worship.

lieth a beauty-spot, like Dhruva seated on his new-moon throne.[1] Like a monarch seated on a golden throne, he hath been endowed with every charm-weapon from the armoury (of love). Before him none can remain firm ;[2] for (the destruction of) what (poor mortal) was such a union made?

For she hath endowed this monarch with a scymitar, with bows and discus' twain, and with (a quiver-full of) arrows.[3] "World-Slayer" is his name. At these words Ratna-sēna fell fainting and cried: 'Alas, those weapons have all smitten me in a mortal spot!'

104. '*Item*—Two eye-brows, black bows ready strung, from which she speedeth mortal shafts at whomsoe'er she casteth but a glance. Upon each eye-brow is fixed this bow, and (who knoweth) who it was that fashioned this weapon of Death. This was the bow which Kṛṣṇa bore; this was the bow which was grasped by Rāma's hand. With this bow was Rāvaṇa slain; with this bow did Kaṁsa meet his fate.[4] With this bow (Arjuna) smote the fish ;[5] with this bow was Sahasra-bāhu sent to his last account.[6] It is this bow which I recognized to be in her possession, and with it she, like a fair huntress, hath turned the world into a heap of slain. None hath e'er obtained the mastery over it. The Angels of Heaven, nay the well-guarded Goddesses[7] themselves, have hidden themselves before it.

No other bow beareth comparison with the brow-bows of this lady huntress. India's rainbow itself when it riseth in the sky, seeth them and disappeareth in its shame.

105. '*Item.*—Two eyes, arch beyond compare, which rise and fall like the ocean in its pride. Therein two black bees flutter upon a coral-pink lotus. Intoxicated with its fragrance they dart around and seek to flee.

1 The *tilaka, i.e.*, forehead-ornament, which I translate by 'beauty-spot' is compared to Dhruva, or the pole-star, seated on the new-moon as on a throne. Dhruva was the son of Uttānapāda. One day his step-mother thrust him from his father's arms, and placed therein her own son instead. Smarting under the slight he wandered forth and took to severe austerities. At length Viṣṇu, pleased at his devotion, made him the pole-star so that he might occupy the highest and most immoveable position possible. He has remained there ever since, with all the stars circling round him in his honour.

2 Just as no star except Dhruva is immoveable; all must go circling round him.

3 The scymitar is her nose; the bow, her eyebrows; the discuses, the pupils of her eyes; the arrows, her glances.

4 Viṣṇu's bow was named Çārṅga. Kṛṣṇa slew Kaṁsa, and Rāma slew Rāvaṇa. Both were incarnations of Viṣṇu.

5 *Rāhū* is said to be for *rōhū*, the name of a kind of fish. There is a well-known story Mahā-bhārata of how Arjuna won Draupadī for his bride by shooting a fish, after merely aiming at its reflection. His bow was named Gāṇḍīva.

6 Sahasra-bāhu's daughter Rēṇukā was married to Jamadagni, a famous saint. Jamadagni was subsequently murdered by his father-in-law in order to obtain the famous cow of plenty. In revenge for his father's death Jamadagni's son Paraçu-rāma slew Sahasra-bāhu and exterminated all the Kṣattriyas (to which caste Sahasra-bāhu belonged) from the face of the earth. Paraçu-rāma was one of Viṣṇu's incarnations. His usual weapon was a halbert (*paraçu*).

7 So *gōpitā* is explained in the commentary. The word might also be interpreted as meaning the *Gōpīs* or herd-maidens, beloved of Kṛṣṇa.

Like are they to horses that obey not the bridle, but rise and rear until they touch the skies.[1] The tempest bloweth, the waves arise and dash up to heaven and again fall to earth.[2] When this eye-ocean moveth, the whole world is moved, and it threateneth to overwhelm all creation in an instant.[3] Beneath those eye-brows are a pair of whirlpools, which, when they are set in motion, seize the very skies and drown them. When they turn from side to side, the sea moveth its waves, *khañjana*-birds quarrel among themselves, and deer wander lost through the forest.[4]

Each eye is an ocean of milk,[5] filled with gems and waves. In each is a deep-black whirlpool which carrieth away all who approach its bank.

106. '*Item.*—Eyelashes passing description. (Over each orb) they are as it were two opposed armies with their arrows drawn.[6] The troops of Rāma on the one side and of Rāvaṇa on the other are in array, and between them lie the two eyes,—the Ocean.[7] On each shore is the line of arrows ready drawn; and at whomsoe'er they are aimed, to him they give the tortures of a poisoned wound.[8] Who is there who hath not been smitten by these shafts, for the whole universe hath been pierced by them? The bright stars in the sky, which are beyond all count, have all been wounded by those arrows (and lie there cold and still). Everything upon the earth have they pierced; the very branches standing out upon the trees (are not branches) but are the arrows of her eyelashes. So is every hair of the down on men's bodies, which they have pierced and in which on every space[9] they are firmly buried.

1 It must be remembered that the simile of the ocean is preserved throughout. The lotus (*i.e.*, the eyeballs) over which the bees (the pupils) hover are growing in this ocean, and, if we take *mānasamūda*, in the sense of the sea of milk which was churned by the gods, then the greatest of all horses, *Uccaiḥ-çravas*, issued from it on that occasion.

2 A simile to the rapid rise and fall of the eyes. When they rise the hopes of the beholder are raised to heaven, when they fall his hopes are dashed to earth.

3 That is to say, the whole world will be drowned in the flood of the ocean.

4 A *mālōpamā* or 'garland' of similes. The glancing eyes are first compared to the waves of the sea. Next they are compared to *khañjana*-birds (*motacilla alba*). (This bird is a favourite subject of comparison when describing a lady's eyes. It has a jet black neck, and a very swift and darting manner of flying. When a number of them quarrel amongst themselves these peculiarities are of course heightened). Next they are compared to deer wandering lost in the forest. The large and liquid eyes of a deer are never at rest. This peculiarity is heightened when it is lost and anxious.

5 The celebrated ocean of milk which was churned by the gods.

6 The upper and lower lashes are each an army. Each hair represents an arrow.

7 In stanza cv. the eyes have been compared to the ocean. Rāma had to cross the ocean in order to attack Rāvaṇa. The upper eyelash represents Rāma's army, and the lower one Rāvaṇa's. The commentary points out that on the lower (*i.e.*, Rāvaṇa's) side are Padmāvatī's lovely neck (*su-grīva*), jaw (*hanu*), and armlets (*aŋgada*), although, according to legend Hanumān, and Aŋgada were allies of Rāma.

8 The mere aiming is sufficient to wound the unhappy wight upon whom Padmāvatī's glances fall.

9 Literally on every *sūt* or thread. The *sūt* is a unit of measurement, about the 16th of an inch. Four *sūt*=1 *pain* : 4 *pain* =1 *tasū* : 24 *tasū* =1 '*imāratī gaz* or mason's yard. A *tasū* is about an inch.

So were these eyelash-arrows created, that they have smitten alike the warrior on the field and the tree in the forest. Under the form of hair have they pierced every animal, and, under the form of feathers, every bird.

107. '*Item.*—A nose, thin as the edge of a glaive. With what can I compare it, for it is thinner than a sword and is joined unto her face?[1] When it saw her nose the parrot[2] tribe was filled with shame. The planet Venus herself came down to be the pearl-stud that adorneth it. On account of it even I, Hīrā-maṇi thy parrot, have become yellow in my jealousy; and, in that case, why need I, my Liege, tell the fate of others. I, thy parrot, who sing her praises,[3] have a slender beak it is true, but it is hard, and *her* nose is tender and is adorned with a sweet flower-like mole. Every flower and every scent liveth in but one hope, to wit that some day it may be brought near that nose and have its odour thereby inhaled. Over her lips and teeth its loveliness calleth to mind a parrot gazing at a pomegranate with soul entranced.[4] On each side of that parrot sport two *khañjanas.*[5] Who is it that is fated to have the bliss of tasting the nectar (of that pomegranate), and who is fated not?

When it beheld the nectar of those lips the parrot transformed itself to that nose. It abideth ever by that shrine, for thither the zephyr of her breath doth waft the nectar's fragrance.

108. '*Item.*—A lip, scarlet, full of nectar. The blood-red wild-gourd[6] because of it hath humbly betaken itself to the depths of the forest that it may bear its fruit. Poets have called the midday-flower[7] crimson, but it is when she speaketh that it really raineth its blossoms. Then is it as though diamonds[8] were swimming in a stream of coral, and when she smileth, the whole world becometh full of light. Her lips have become a still deeper scarlet[9] with the betel dye; and before them the red saffron-flower appeareth as though it had faded away. Brimful are they of nectar, for up till now they are untouched and none hath sipped it. The betel within her mouth ever poureth new colour into it; (happy will he be) for

1 An ordinary sword is held by the hand, not by the face.

2 A nose is frequently compared to a parrot's beak.

3 A *pañriyā* is properly a rhapsodist who sings the praises of the *Pravara* or *Pramara* clan. Hence any panegyrist in general.

4 Parrots are very fond of pomegranate seeds. The colour of these is partly a delicate pink and partly a pure white. Hence the comparison with the lips and teeth.

5 The eyes. See stanza cv.

6 The *bimba* (*momordica monadelpha*) is a forest gourd with a bright red fruit to which lips are frequently compared. In Sanskrit *bimbōṣṭhī*, is a synonym for a pretty girl with coral lips.

7 The *Dupaharī* or *bandhujīva* (*pentapeteṣ phœnicea*) is a plant with deep ruby bunches of flowers. They bloom at midday, and immediately wither and fall off. The poet says that when Padmāvatī speaks, her lips appear like the shower of the red flowers of the *dupaharī.*

8 Her teeth.

9 *Majīṭh* is the dark red madder dye. When she chews betel, her lips become redder still.

whom that fragrant nectar is destined. At the sight of that blooming beauteous one the whole world is inflamed with passion; but when she fully smileth those lips yet become more encarmined, and appear filled with the vital fluid.

Such, my Liege, is the nectar of her lips, that every world hath hopes but for them. For whom hath that lotus blossomed forth? What bee will sip its honey?

109. '*Item.*—Her teeth, like diamonds on a pedestal: between each, deep deep black.[1] Like a gleam of lightning in a dark Autumn[2] night, so are these thirty-two caused to flash. Their sheen exceedeth that of diamonds,—nay, the sheen of diamonds is but their reflection. From the day that that sheen was created, the sheen of many things is but their sheen. The sun, the moon, the stars, jewels, diamonds, rubies, pearls all owe their glory but to it. Whene'er she openeth her lips, the smile that cometh thereby scattereth drops of light around. The brightness of summer lightning cannot equal it; verily, no other brilliance approacheth it.

When she smileth or laugheth adamant blazeth forth in glory, the pomegranate could not equal her teeth in beauty, and hence its heart did burst.[3]

110. '*Item.*—A tongue, whose words are full of savour, inflaming the heart of him who heareth its nectar speech. It hath stolen the song of the *cātaka*[4] and of the cuckoo; nor can the melody of flute and lute compare with it. The *cātaka* and the cuckoo abide not[5] with us, for they hear her voice and hide themselves in shame. It speaketh words full of the wine of love, and he who heareth it becometh drunken, and staggereth in giddiness. On it is all the wisdom of the tetrad of the *vēdas*,—all that is within the *Ṛc*, the *Yajus*, the *Sāman*, and the *Atharvan*.[6] Not a sentence speaketh it that hath not four different meanings.[7] Indra and Brahmā, astonished at her

1 The pedestal is the gums. The interstices between the teeth are blackened with *misī*, which is a powder made up of yellow myrobalan, gall-nut, iron-filings, vitriol, and other ingredients.

2 *Bhādō* is an Autumn month of the rainy season. Its nights are black with clouds. The *misī* represents the dark clouds.

3 It has already been stated (stanza cvii) that teeth are often compared to pomegranate seeds. When this fruit ripens it bursts and scatters its seeds. The poet said this is a case of a burst or broken heart.

4 The pied cuckoo (*cuculus melanoleucus*).

5 These two birds only sing during spring and the rainy season.

6 The names of the four *vēdas*.

7 Students of Indian classics need not be told of the immense admiration exhibited for language capable of being interpreted with a double meaning. It is one of the great tests of learning. One time Kṛṣṇa was in company with six herd-maidens.

The first asked him for a leaf-platter for her food.
The second said 'come to my house to-day.'
The third said 'fasten my ear-pendant.
The fourth said 'give me a light.'
The fifth said 'pluck me a flower.'
The sixth said 'bring me water.'

(बेटा,) राज्य, पाट (सिंहासन), स्थान वा फौज, और (सब पुर के) प्रजा-लोग (ये सब) तुम्हीँ से उज्ज्वलित हैँ, अर्थात् तुम्हारे-ही से इन सब की शोभा है, विना दुलहा के बरात की शोभा नहीँ होती। (सो मेरे बुढापे की ओर निहार कर, मेरी विनती को स्वीकार करो। यहीँ) बैठ कर (इसी स्थान के सुख) भोग को रस मानो, अर्थात् यहाँ के जो सुखोपभोग हैँ, उन्ही को सुरस समझो। (पद्मावती के रस-भोग की लालसा मेँ फँस कर, घर बार को विध्वंस कर, ऊपर कहे ऊए सब पदार्थों को) अँधेरे मेँ कर, न चलो, अर्थात् तुम घर के चिराग हो, तुमारे बाहर होते-ही सब अँधेरे मेँ पड, तडप तडप और कलप कलप, विकल हो, मर जायँगे, सो इन को अनाथ कर आप न जाइये ॥ १२१ ॥

चउपाई।

मोहिँ यह लोभ सुनाउ न माया। का कर सुख का कर यह काया ॥
जो निआन तन होइहि छारा। माटी पोखि मरइ को भारा ॥
का भूलउँ एहि चंदन चोवा। बइरी जहाँ अंग के रोवाँ ॥
हाथ पाउँ सरवन अउ आँखी। ए सब भरहिँ आपु पुनि साखी ॥
सूत सूत तन बोलहिँ दोखू। कहु कइसइ होइहि गति मोखू ॥
जउ भल होत राज अउ भोगू। गोपिचंद नहिँ साधत जोगू ॥
उह-उ सिरिसिटि जउ देख परेवा। तजा राज कजरी-बन सेवा ॥

दोहा।

देखि अंत अस होइहइ गुरू दीन्ह उपदेस।
सिंघल-दीप जाब मइँ माता मोर अदेस ॥ १३२ ॥

माया = माता, वा राज्यादि सुखोपभोग सामग्री। काया = काय = शरीर। निआन = निदान = अन्त मेँ। तन = तनु = शरीर। छार = क्षार = भस्म। माटी = मृत् = मट्टी। पोखि = आपोष्य = पोषण कर = पाल कर। भारा = भार = बोझा। का = क्व = क्या। भूलउँ = भूलूँ। चोवा = च्युत द्रव्य = चुवा कर जो सुगन्ध द्रव्य बने। बइरी = वैरी = शत्रु। अंग = अङ्ग। रोवाँ = रोम = रोआँ। हाथ = हस्त। पाउँ = पावँ = पाद = पैर।

सरवन = श्रवण = कान । आँखी = अचि = आँख । भरहिँ = भरती हैँ = पूरी करती हैँ। आपु = आप = स्वयम् । पुनि = पुनः = फिर । साखी = साची = गवाही । सूत सूत = सूच सूच, सूत = एक परिमाण (१०६ दोहे की टीका देखो)। दोखू = दोष । कहु = कहो । होइहि = होगी । गति = प्राप्ति । मोखू = मोच । जउ = यदि । गोपिचंद = गोपी-चन्द = एक बंगाले का राजा । साधत = साधते । जोगू = योग । उह-उ = सोऽपि = वह भी । सिसिटि = सृष्टि = संसार । जउ = जो = यदा = जब । देख = देखा । परेवा = पराये की । वा, परेवा = पारावत, यहाँ साधारण पची । कजरी-बन = कज्जलि-वन, वा कदली-वन । सेवा = सेवन किया = रहने लगा ॥ अंत = अन्त । अस = एतादृश = ऐसा । होइहइ = होगा । गुरू = गुरु । उपदेस = उपदेश = शिचा = ज्ञान । जाव = जाऊँगा । अदेस = आदेश = कथन = कहना ॥

(राजा ने कहा, कि) माता मुझे यह लोभ न सुना, वा मुझे इस माया का लोभ न सुना (जो, कि पिछले दोहे में विस्तार-पूर्वक वर्णित है)। (क्योंकि यह संसार का सुख और शरीर चण-भङ्गुर हैं, सो) किस का सुख और किस की शरीर है, अर्थात् न किसी का सुख और न किसी की शरीर है, सब नाशवान् हैं ; उस की भूल है जो अपना समझता है ॥ जब (निश्चय है, कि) तनु अन्त में (एक दिन) छार हो जायगी, (तो) कौन (ऐसा मूर्ख है, जो इस) मट्टी का पालन कर, बोझे से मरे, अर्थात् शरीर को लालन पालन से मोटी कर, केवल बोझा बढाना है, और कुछ फल-सिद्धि नहीँ ॥ (और जो तैँ ने चन्दन-चोवे का पिछले दोहे में वर्णन किया, सो मैं) इस चन्दन-चोवे में क्या भूलूँ, अर्थात् नहीँ भूल सकता, (क्योंकि) जहाँ, अर्थात् जिस चन्दन-चोवे के लेपन में, अङ्ग के रोएँ वैरी हैं, अर्थात् लेपन में भी सुख नहीँ है, जहाँ असावधानी झई, कि मर्दन से रोएँ टूटे, फिर बरतोर की पीडा से लेपन का सुख सूखा, और हाय हाय पडी । यहाँ रोवाँ में अर्द्ध-चन्द्र होने से अनुप्रास का भङ्ग 'नानुस्वारविसर्गौ चित्रभङ्गाय' (वाग्भटविरचितकाव्यानुशासन १ अध्याय) इस वचन से नहीँ होता। अनुप्रास इत्यादि सब चित्र काव्य-ही में परिगणित हैं जैसा, कि साहित्यदर्पण के चतुर्थपरिच्छेद में लिखा है—

'प्रधानगुणभावाभ्यां व्यङ्ग्यस्यैवं व्यवस्थिते ।
उभे काव्ये ततोऽन्यद्यत्तच्चित्रमभिधीयते ॥'

(हे माता), हाथ, पैर, कान और आँख, ये सब इन्द्रियाँ फिर आप साची भरती

हैं, अर्थात् मनुष्य के पाप-पुण्य को सदा साक्षी देने के लिये देखा करती हैं॥ और सूत सूत पर (सब अङ्ग) इस तनु में दोष-ही बोलते हैं, अर्थात् शरीर के प्रति अवयव दुष्ट-ही कर्म करने की चाह रखते हैं, (तो भला) कहो (कि) कैसे मोक्ष-प्राप्ति होगी॥ (सो, हे माता, सुन तो सही) यदि राज्य और (सुख) भोग भले होते, अर्थात् इन्हीं से यदि जीव निस्तार पा जाता, (तो) (राजा) गोपी-चन्द (इन को त्याग कर) योग न साधते, (क्योंकि जब सुखोपभोग-ही से मोक्ष-प्राप्ति हो तो कौन ऐसा मूर्ख है जो, कि अतिकष्ट-साध्य योग-साधन में शरीर को तपावे)। गोपी-चन्द बङ्गाले के एक राजा थे, भर्तृहरि की बहिन मैनावती इन की माता थी; इस प्रकार भर्तृहरि के भैने गोपी-चन्द हुए। गोरख-नाथ ने जिस समय भर्तृहरि को ज्ञानोपदेश दिया था, उसी समय मैनावती भी गोरख-नाथ से दीक्षा ली थी, और गोरख-नाथ के अनुग्रह से समझ लिया था, कि संसार की विषय-वासना में फँसने से इस जीव का निस्तार नहीं हो सकता। मैनावती बङ्गाले के राजा से व्याही गई थी, और इस को एक पुत्र गोपी-चन्द और एक कन्या चन्द्रावली ये दो सन्तान हुए थे। चन्द्रावली का विवाह सिंहल-द्वीप के राजा उग्र-सेन से हुआ था। पिता के मर जाने पर गोपी-चन्द बङ्गाले का राजा हुआ, और सुख विलास करने लगा। एक दिन पुत्र के शरीर की शोभा निरख, मैनावती ने सोचा, कि संसार की विषय-वासना में फँस जाने से मेरे पुत्र की यह कान्तिमान् शरीर इस के पिता के शरीर की नाईं नष्ट भ्रष्ट हो जायगी। सो पुत्र को बुला कर, ज्ञानोपदेश दिया, कि बेटा, यदि अमर हो कर, जीवन-मुक्त हुआ चाहे तो जलन्धर-नाथ से, जो इस समय रमते रमते भाग्यवश तेरी वाटिका में आ उतरे हैं, शिष्य हो, योग साधन करो। इस पर गोपी-चन्द को ज्ञान हुआ और राज-पाट छोड कर, जलन्धर-नाथ से दीक्षा ले योग साधन के लिये कज्जलिवन (कदली-वन) चला गया, और सिद्ध हो गया, और पीछे से अपनी बहिन चन्द्रावली को अति विनती से उसे भी दीक्षा दे कर, योगिन बनाया। गोरख-पंथियों के सम्प्रदाय में जब कोई चेला हो कर, नया योगी बनता है, तब पहले गुरु की यह आज्ञा होती है, कि अपने घर जा कर, अपनी पत्नी को माता कह कर, अन्न-भिक्षा माँगो, और जब वह देने लगे, तब उस से 'पुत्र भिक्षा लो' यह कहवा कर, भिक्षा ग्रहण करो। इस प्रकार वह नया योगी भिक्षा ले कर, उस भिक्षा को जब गुरु को देता है, तब गुरु को विश्वास होता है, कि इस से योग सधेगा। सो जिस समय नया योगी हो, योग के सब चिन्ह

मेखला, शृङ्गी, सेली, गुदरी, खप्पर, कर्ण-मुद्रा, कौपीन, कमण्डलु, भस्म (राख), व्याघ्राम्बर, झोला इत्यादि को धारण किये, गोपी-चन्द प्रधान पट्ट-रानी पाटम-देवी से भिक्षा माँगने के लिये आया है; उस समय पाटम-देवी और उस से जो जो बातेँ हुई हैँ, उन को संप्रति योगी लोग नाना प्रकार की गीतेँ मेँ गाया फिरते हैँ। बहुतेरे ऐसे मनोहर स्वर से गाते हैँ, कि उस करुणामय-वृत्तान्त को सुनने से सहृदय पुरुषोँ के नयनोँ से आँस की धारा बहने लगती है। योगियोँ से गीतोँ का संग्रह कर, आज कल बहुत लोगोँ ने कुछ अपनी कल्पना से हेर फेर कर, इस कथा को पुस्तकाकार मेँ छपवा भी डाला है। गोपी-चन्द को एक कन्या थी; भिक्षा माँगने की वेला मेँ इस ने भी बहुत माया कर, चाही थी, कि पिता मेरा योग तज दे। यद्यपि योगी लोग अपनी गीतोँ मेँ गोपी-चन्द को बङ्गाले का राजा कह कह कर, गाया करते हैँ, तथापि बङ्गाले मेँ इस कथा का अल्प, और और-ही प्रकार से प्रचार होने से (मानिक-चन्द्र-राजार गान* और पूरण-प्रसाद का छपवाया गोपी-चन्द, की कथा देखो), और राजपुताने और मालवा प्रान्त मेँ इस आख्यायिका का विशेष कर प्रचार होने से मुझे ऐसा अनुमान होता है, कि यह गोपी-चन्द राजपुताने वा मालवे का कोई राजा रहा हो तो आश्चर्य नहीँ। इतिहास-वेत्ताओँ को इस का पूरा पता लगाना चाहिए॥ वह (गोपी-चन्द ने) भी जब देखा, कि (यह संसार की) सृष्टि परछाईं है, वा पक्षी के सदृश (जो एक स्थान पर स्थित नहीँ रहते, इधर उधर उड़ फिरा करते हैँ) है, (तब) राज को तजा (और योग साधने के लिये) कदली-वन का रुख किया॥ देहरा दून से ले कर हृषीकेश, वदरिकाश्रम, और उस के उत्तर के हिमालय के प्रान्त सब कजरी-वन कहे जाते हैँ। संस्कृत मेँ इस वन को कदली-वन कहते हैँ। लोक मेँ इसी कदली का अपभ्रंश कजरी हो गया है। इस वन मेँ केले (कदली) के वृक्ष विशेष रहते हैँ, इसी से इस का नाम कदली-वन पड़ा। इस वन मेँ हाथी बहुत रहते हैँ, और यह सिद्धोँ के रहने का स्थान है। विना सिद्ध हुए मनुष्य इस वन मेँ नहीँ प्रवेश कर सकता। इस वन मेँ आज तक अमर-स्वरूप हनुमान् जी सुख से विश्राम करते हैँ। द्रौपदी के सहित पाण्डव लोग जब वदरिकाश्रम मेँ पहुँचे हैँ, तब नर-नारायण के दर्शन करने पर छ रात्रि तक वहाँ ठहरे थे। उसी समय वायु मेँ उड़ता हुआ एक सहस्र-पत्र का कमल सुगन्ध से भरा द्रौपदी के

---

* J. A. S. B., Vol. xlvii, 1878, Part I, pp. 135 and ff.

दृष्टि-गोचर हुआ। द्रौपदी इस कमल को पा कर, बहुत प्रसन्न हुई और भीम-सेन से प्रार्थना की, कि नाथ इस कमल के अनेक और पुष्प ले आइये। इस पर भीम-सेन ढूंढने चले। मार्ग में हनुमान् जी मिले।

(स भीम-सेनस्तच्छ्रुत्वा सम्प्रहृष्टतनूरुहः।
शब्दप्रभवमन्विच्छंश्चचार कदली-वनम्॥
कदली-वन-मध्यस्थमथ पीने शिलातले।
ददर्श स महाबाहुर्वानराधिपतिं तदा॥
भारत वन-पर्व, १४६ अध्याय, श्लो० ७५-७८)

हनुमान् जी ने भीम-सेन से कहा, कि इस वन में आगे सिद्धों के विना गति नहीं।

(अतः परमगम्योऽयं पर्वतः सुदुरारुहः।
विना सिद्ध-गतिं वीर गतिरत्र न विद्यते॥
देवलोकस्य मार्गोऽयमगम्यो मानुषैः सदा।
कारुण्यात् त्वामहं वीर वारयामि निबोध मे॥
भा० वन-प०, १४६ अ०, ९१-९२ श्लो०)

अन्त में हनुमान् और भीम-सेन से परस्पर परिचय होने से हनुमान् की कृपा से भीम-सेन ने कुवेर की वाटिका में उस पद्म के अनेक पुष्पों को पाया। भारत, वन-पर्व, अध्याय १४५-१५६ में इस की सविस्तर-कथा लिखी हुई है। प्रसिद्ध है, कि अश्वत्थामा, बलि, व्यास, हनुमान्, विभीषण, कृपाचार्य और परशुराम ये सात चिर-जीवी इसी कदली-वन में रहते हैं। इस वन में अमृत-फल होते हैं॥ इस वन में कज्जल के ऐसे हाथी बहुत रहते हैं इसी कारण कदाचित् किसी ने इस का नाम कज्जलि-वन रक्खा हो। परन्तु इस नाम का कहीं पता नहीं लगता। इसी कदली-वन के अन्तर्गत-ही शिमला है, जो कि आज कल यहां पर ग्रीष्म में यूरोप के वासियों का प्रधान-स्थान है॥

अन्त में (सब की दशा) ऐसी-ही होगी, अर्थात् सब नष्ट हो जायँगे, (इस बात को) देख कर, गुरु (शुक, वा ध्यान में 'सिद्ध होइ कहँ गोरख कहा' इस से गोरख-नाथ) ने (मुझे) उपदेश दिया है। (सो) मैं सिंहल-द्वीप (अवश्य) जाऊँगा (और), हे माता, (यही) मेरा कहना है, अर्थात् यही मेरी आप से विनती है; आप मेरी माता हैं, सो विघ्न न पडिये, हर्ष से वहाँ जाने के लिये आज्ञा दीजिये॥ १३२॥

चउपाई ।

रोअहिँ नाग-मती रनिवासू । केइ तुम्ह कंत दीन्ह बन-बासू ॥
अब को हमहिँ करिहि भोगिनी । हम-हूँ साथ होब जोगिनी ॥
कइ हम लावहु अपनइ साथा । कइ अब मारि चलहु सइँ हाथा ॥
तुम्ह अस बिछुरइ पीउ पिरीता । जहवाँ राम तहाँ सँग सीता ॥
जव लहि जिउ सँग छाड न काया । करिहउँ सेव पखरिहउँ पाया ॥
भले-हि पदुमिनी रूप अनूपा । हम तइँ कोइ न आगरि रूपा ॥
भवँइ भलहिँ पुरुखन्ह कइ डीठी । जिन्ह जाना तिन्ह दीन्ह न पीठी ॥

दोहा ।

देहिँ असीस सबइ मिलि तुम्ह माथइ निति छात ।
राज करहु गढ चितउर राखहु पिअ अहिवात ॥ १३३ ॥

रोअहिँ = रोअइ (रोदिति) का बहु-वचन। नाग-मती = रत्न-सेन की प्रधान पट्ट-रानी। रनिवासू = राज्ञी-वास = रनिवास = अन्तःपुर, यहाँ अन्तःपुर में रहने-वालीँ और रानियाँ। कंत = कान्त = मनोरम पति। बन-बासू = वन-वास। को = कः = कौन। करिहि = करेगा। भोगिनी = भोग जिस को हो, अर्थात् भोग करने-वाली। साथ = सार्थ = सङ्ग। होब = होंगी। जोगिनी = योगिनी = योगिन। कइ = की = या तो। लावहु = लगावो। अपनइ = अपने। मारि = मारयित्वा = मार कर। सइँ = से। बिछुरइ = विच्छुडति = बिछुडता है। राम = अयोध्या के राजा, जगत्प्रसिद्ध रावण-संहार-कर्त्ता। सीता = जो सीत, अर्थात् हल के अग्र से भूमि जोतने की वेला उत्पन्न हुई, मिथिलेश जनक की मानी हुई पुत्री, जो रामायण की कथा से जगत्प्रसिद्ध है। करिहउँ = करूँगी। सेव = सेवा = टहल। पखरिहउँ = पखारूँगी = पखारइ (प्रक्षालयति) का भविष्यत्-काल। पाया = पाद = पैर। पदुमिनी = पद्मिनी = पद्मावती। अनूपा = अनुपमा। तइँ = तेँ = से। कोइ = कोऽपि पुंलिङ्ग में, यहाँ कापि = कोई। आगरि = अग्रा = श्रेष्ठा = आगरी = बढ कर। रूपा = रूप में। भवँइ = भ्रमति = घूमती है। पुरुखन्ह = पुरुख (पुरुष) का बहु-वचन। डीठी = दृष्टि। जिन्ह = जिन्हँ = यान् = जिन को। जाना = जानइ (जानाति) का भूत-काल। तिन्ह = तिन्हँ = तान् = तिन के प्रति। दीन्ह = देइ (ददाति)

का भूत-काल = दिये। पीठी = पृष्ठ = पीठ॥ देहिँ = देह का बहु-वचन। असीस = आशिष् = आशीर्वाद। मिलि = मिलित्वा = मिल कर। राखहु = राखह (रक्षति) के लोट लकार में मध्यम-पुरुष का बहु-वचन। पिउ = प्रिय = पति। अहिवात = आधिपत्य = सौभाग्य = सोहाग॥

नाग-मती (और) रनिवास की और रानियाँ रोती हैं, (और कहती हैं, कि) हे कान्त, आप (तुम्ह) को किस ने वन-वास दिया, अर्थात् किस ने ऐसा बहकाया, कि (राम-चन्द्र के ऐसा) राज छोड कर, योगी हो चले॥ (सो) अब हम-लोगों को कौन भोगिनी करेगा, अर्थात् अब हम-लोग किस के संग भोग-विलास करेंगी। (सो हे नाथ,) हम-लोग भी (आप के) साथ योगिन होंगी॥ (हम-लोगों की प्रार्थना है, कि) या तो हम-लोगों को अपने साथ लगावो, अर्थात् अपने साथ ले चलो, या अब, अर्थात् अभी, (अपने) हाथों से (हम-लोगों को) मार कर, (तब) चलो, अर्थात् जावो॥ (क्योंकि) आप ऐसे प्रीति के करने-वाले (पिरीता = प्रीति-कर्त्ता, वा पिरीता = प्रीतः = प्रसादितः) हमारे-लोगों की सेवा से प्रसन्न प्रिय (पीउ) (जब) बिछुडते हैं, (तब यहाँ आप के विना हम-लोगों का क्या काम, (क्योंकि) जहाँ राम तहाँ संग में सीता (का रहना भी उचित है), अर्थात् जहाँ आप तहाँ हम-लोगों का भी रहना नीति-संमत है॥ (हे प्राण-प्रिय, हम-लोग मार्ग में आप को तनिक भी कष्ट न देंगी, किन्तु) जब तक शरीर के संग को जीव न छोडेगा, अर्थात् जब तक जीती रहेंगी, (आप की) सेवा करेंगी (और थकने पर धूल से भरे आप के) पैरों को धोयेंगी॥ (मान लिया, कि) भले से, अर्थात् अच्छी तरह से पद्मावती का रूप अनूप हो, (परन्तु, नाथ, निश्चय जानिये, कि) रूप में हम-लोगों से बढ कर कोई नहीं है॥ (रानियाँ विनय करती करती हार गईं, तब आपस में कहती हैं, कि आश्चर्य है कि) पुरुषों की दृष्टि (तुरन्त-ही) भलहिं, अर्थात् अच्छी तरह से, घूम जाती है, अर्थात् फिर जाती है, (और पुरुषों का विलक्षण स्वभाव है, कि) जिन (पदार्थों) को जान लिया, अर्थात् समझ लिया, कि ये मेरे योग्य हैं, तिन (पदार्थों) के लिये पीठ नहीं दिये, अर्थात् उन की लालसा में पुरुष-लोग प्राण तक दे देते हैं परन्तु पीछे नहीं हटते॥

सब मिल कर आशीर्वाद देती हैं, (कि नाथ,) आप के माथे के ऊपर नित्य छत्र लगा करे, अर्थात् आप सर्वदा राजा बने रहें। (सो) (प्राण-)प्रिय, (हम-लोगों

की यही अभ्यर्थना है, कि) चित्तौर गढ का राज्य कीजिये, (बाहर योगी बन, वन वन न फिरिये) (और हम-लोगोँ का) अहिवात रखिये ॥ १३३ ॥

चउपाई ।

तुम्ह तिरिआ मति हीन तुम्हारी । मूरुख सो जो मतइ घर नारी ॥
राघउ जो सीता सँग लाई । राश्रोन हरी कउन सिधि पाई ॥
यह संसार सुपन जस मेरा । अंत न आपन को केहि केरा ॥
राजा भरथरि सुनि न अजानी । जेहि के घर सोरह सइ रानी ॥
कुचन्ह लिए तरवा सोहराई । भा जोगी कोउ संग न लाई ॥
जोगिहि कहा भोग सउँ काजू । चहइ न मेहरी चहइ न राजू ॥
जूड कुरुकुटा पइ भखु चहा । जोगिहि तात भात सउँ कहा ॥

दोहा ।

कहा न मानइ राजा तजी सबाई भीर ।
चला छाडि सब रोअत फिरि कइ देइ न धीर ॥ १३४ ॥

तिरिया = स्त्री । मति = बुद्धि । हीन = अल्प = कम । मूरुख = मूर्ख = बेवकूफ । मतइ = मत करता है = सलाह करता है । घर = गृह । नारी = स्त्री से । राघउ = राघव = दश-रथ के पुत्र, राम । सीता = राम-पत्नी । लाई = लगाई = लिया । राश्रोन = रावण = लङ्का का प्रसिद्ध राजा । हरी = हरइ (हरति) का भूत-काल । कउन = क नु = कौन । सिधि = सिद्धि । पाई = पावइ (प्राप्नोति) का भूत-काल । सुपन = स्वप्न = सपना । जस = यथा = जैसा । मेरा = मेला = जहाँ बहुत से लोग एकट्ठे होते हैँ । को = क नु = कौन । केहि केरा = किस का । भरथरि = भर्तृहरि = संवत्-कर्त्ता-प्रसिद्ध उज्जयिनी के राजा, विक्रम के छोटे भाई । सुनि = सुनी = सुनइ (शृणोति) का स्त्री-लिङ्ग मेँ भूत-काल । अजानी = अयानी = अज्ञानिनी । सोरह = षोडश । सइ = शत = से । रानी = राज्ञी । कुचन्ह = कुच (स्तन = छाती) का बहु-वचन । तरवा = पाद-तल = तल-पाद । सोहराई = सोहरावइ (सु-हारयति) का भूत-काल । भा = अभूत् = भया = हुआ । जोगी = योगी । जोगिहि = योगी को । कहा = क हि = क्या = किम् । काजू = कार्य = काम । चहइ = (चदति वा चतति) = चाहता है । चह परिकल्कने । (कल्कनं शाठ्यम् ।

इति सिद्धान्तकौमुद्याम्) धातु दुष्ट होने के अर्थ में है, इस लिये चहति से चहइ का बनना अर्थासङ्गति होता है। परन्तु प्राकृत में जाने से धातुओं का अर्थ बदल भी जाता है, इस लिये दहइ (दहति), सहइ (सहते), वहइ (वहति), उजहइ (उज्जहाति) के ऐसा चहति से चहइ का होना विशेषत: संभव है। बहुतों के मत से इस का मूल इच्छति और बहुतों के मत से पाली चघति, जिस का गमन अर्थ है, है। मेहरी = मेहर (कृपा) करने-वाली = स्त्री। राजू = राज्य। जूड = जड = जूडा = ठंढा। कुरुकुटा = कर्कर: = खर कतवार मिला। पइ = अपि = निश्चय। भखु = भक्ष्य = भक्षण = भोजन। चहा = चहइ का भूत-काल। तात = तप्त = गर्म। भात = भक्त॥ मानइ = मन्यते = मानता है। तजी = तजइ (त्यजति) का स्त्रीलिङ्ग में भूत-काल। सबाई = सर्वापि = सभी। भीर = भीरु: = भय से, अर्थात् राजा के विना हम-लोगों की क्या गति होगी, इस भय से डरी हुईं रानियाँ। छाडि = आकुड्य = छोड कर। रोअत = रोती हुईं। धीर = धैर्य॥

(रानियों के विनय करने पर राजा ने कहा, कि) तुम लोग स्त्री हो, तुमारे लोगों को कम बुद्धि होती है, (और) वह (सो) मूर्ख है जो घर में (बैठ) नारी से सलाह करता है॥ (तुम लोग सीता-राम का जो दृष्टान्त दिया उस का वृत्तान्त सुनो) जो राम ने सीता को संग लिया, (तो उस सीता को) रावण ने हर लिया (सो बे-चारे राम उसी के ढूँढने में समय को बिता दिया; योगी बनने पर भी) कौन सिद्धि को पाया, अर्थात् विना सिद्ध हुए जैसे गये थे, वैसे-ही घर लौट आये; यदि सीता को न ले गये होते, तो अवश्य निश्चिन्त हो पर-ब्रह्म के ध्यान से सिद्धि को प्राप्त करते॥ (सो) यह संसार वैसा-ही है जैसे स्वप्न का मेला, अर्थात् जैसे कोई सपने में देखे, कि किसी मेले में हैं, जहाँ लाखों मनुष्य एकट्ठे हैं, फिर आँख खुलने पर वह मेला झूठा ठहर जाता है, और वह मनुष्य अकेला-ही खाट पर पडा, अनेक बाट पर मन दौडाया करता है। उसी प्रकार इस संसार में जो अनेक भाई, बन्धु, धन, दारा देख पडते हैं, वे सब अन्त में कोई भी अपने नहीं हैं, अर्थात् यदि वे सब अपने होते तो अन्त में प्राण छूटने पर अवश्य अपने साथ चलते। (सो रानी-लोग, निश्चय समझो, कि अन्त में) कोई किसी का नहीं, (सब कोई जैसे अकेला आता है, उसी प्रकार अकेला-ही हाथ पसारे उठ जाता है, एक तिनका भी कोई अपने साथ नहीं ले जा सकता)॥ (तुम-लोग) अयानी हो, वा हे अयानी, (तुम लोगों ने) राजा भर्तृहरि को नहीं सुना है, जिस के घर में सोरह से रानियाँ थीं॥ (और वे सब

अपने) स्तनों को लिये (उन्हीँ स्तनों से रात दिन राजा भर्तृहरि के) तरवे को सुहराया करती थीँ, (परन्तु राजा भर्तृहरि ने एक सेवा को भी न स्वीकार किया और) योगी हो गया, (और) किसी (रानी) को संग न लिया॥ धारा नगरी के राजा गन्धर्व-सेन की चत्रिया स्त्री से शङ्ख, विक्रम, और भर्तृहरि, तीन पुत्र थे। राजा के मरने पर बडा पुत्र शङ्ख राजा हुआ। कुछ दिन बीते अवसर पा कर विक्रम, अपने विक्रम से शङ्ख को मार, आप राजा हुआ। विक्रम, बहुत वर्षों तक राज-सुखोपभोग कर, अपने छोटे भाई भर्तृहरि को राज्य का भार सौंप, आप संसार के चरित्रोँ को देखने के लिये देशाटन करने को चला गया। भर्तृहरि राज्य को पा कर खूब विषय-वासना में भूले; सोरह सै रानियोँ से विवाह किया, जिन में अनूपा-देवी, चम्पा-देवी, पिङ्गला, और श्याम-देवी, ये प्रधान हैँ। राजा के नगर में एक ब्राह्मण तपस्या करता था; तपः-सिद्धि होने पर उस के देवता ने एक अमर-फल दिया और कहा, कि जो इसे खायगा वह सदा अमर हो कर, युवा बना रहेगा। ब्राह्मण फल को ले कर घर आया और इस वृत्तान्त को अपनी ब्राह्मणी से कह सुनाया। ब्राह्मणी वृत्तान्त को सुन कर, बहुत रोई और कहने लगी, कि इस दरिद्रावस्था में फल खा कर, और अमर हो कर, अनन्त-काल तक मानापमान धो कर, भिचा माँगते माँगते, इधर उधर ठोकर खाना पडेगा, जिस से भला मैं मर जाना समझती हूँ। सो आप इस फल को किसी धनी के हाथ बेंचिये, जिस से अधिक धन मिले, और हम लोगोँ का सुख से जीवन निवहे। ब्राह्मण इस बात को सुन कर, राजा भर्तृहरि के पास गया, और उस फल का माहात्म्य सुनाया। राजा ने लाख रुपये पर उस फल को खरीदा। सन्ध्या समय उस फल को लिये राजा श्याम-देवी के घर आया, और फल की महिमा सुना कर, कहा, कि तुम मेरी सब रानियोँ से प्यारी हो, इस लिये मैं तुम्हेँ यह फल देता हूँ, और तुम इसे खा जाना; खा जाने से तुमारा यह मनोहर यौवन ऐसा-ही मनोहर बना रहेगा। श्याम-देवी राजा के कोतवाल से मिली थी। राजा के चले जाने पर उस ने अपना प्राण-प्रिय समझ, उस फल को कोतवाल के हवाले किया, और कहा, कि इस के खाने से तुम सदा अमर हो कर ऐसे-ही जवान बने रहोगे। कोतवाल उस फल को लिये अपने घर आया, और एक वेश्या को, जिसे वह प्राण से भी अधिक चाहता था, दिया, और कहा, कि इस के खाने से तेरा यह मनोहर रूप ऐसा-ही अचल मनोहर बना रहेगा। वेश्या उस फल को लिये अपने घर आई,

और सोचने लगी, कि इस फल को खा कर, अमर और अजर हो कर, अनन्त काल तक व्यभिचार दुराचार से कहाँ तक पाप की गठरी भारी करती रहूँगी, सो उत्तम यह, कि यह फल राजा को दूँ। इस बात को मन में ठान, वह राजा भर्तृहरि के पास गई, और फल-स्तुति के साथ उस फल को राजा के कर कमल में समर्पण किया। राजा ने फल को पहचाना, और वेश्या को बहुत सा धन दे, विदा कर, महल में जा, श्याम-देवी से पूछा, कि तुम ने उस फल को क्या किया; उस ने सहज स्वभाव से हँस कर, मनोहर वाणी से कही, कि आप का प्रसाद समझ कर, आदर-पूर्वक खा गई। इस पर राजा ने रानी को फल देखा कर, लज्जित किया, और संसार की यह गहन लीला देख, अपने को, तथा रानी इत्यादि को—

'यां चिन्तयामि सततं मयि सा विरक्ता सा चान्यमिच्छति जनं स जनोऽन्यसक्तः।
अस्मत्कृते च परितुष्यति काचिदन्या धिक् तां च तं च मदनं च इमां च मां च॥'

इस श्लोक से धिक्कार देता हुआ, राजा पाट छोड, संसार से विरक्त हो, गोरख-नाथ से दीक्षा ले, योगी बन, देश विदेश फिरने लगा। एक दिन चाँदनी रात में भर्तृहरि-योगी ने राह में पडे हुए तथा चमकते हुए उज्ज्वल थूँक को रुपया समझ, उठाने के लिये झुक कर, हाथ फैलाया, और जब नीचे की ओर निकट दृष्टि पहुँची तब थूँक पहचान कर, हाथ को हटा लिया, और अपनी तृष्णा को धिक्कार देता—

'भ्रान्तं देशमनेकदुर्गविषमं प्राप्तं न किञ्चित् फलं
त्यक्त्वा जातिकुलाभिमानमनिशं सेवा कृता निष्फला।
भुक्तं मानविवर्जितं परगृहे स्वाऽऽशङ्कया काकवत्
तृष्णे जृम्भिणि पापकर्मनिरते नाऽद्यापि सन्तुष्यसि॥'

इस श्लोक को बनाया। राजा भर्तृहरि संस्कृत के बडे पण्डित थे। इन्हों ने व्याकरण के ऊपर बहुत कारिका बनाई है, और संस्कृत में इन के बनाये नीति-शतक, वैराग्य-शतक, और शृङ्गार-शतक सर्वत्र बहुत-ही प्रसिद्ध हैं। ऊपर का प्रथम श्लोक नीति-शतक और दूसरा वैराग्य-शतक का है। योगी लोग, जो सारंगी बजा कर, इन की गीत गाया करते हैं, उन के मत से इन के योगी होने की ऐसी कहानी है, कि रानी श्याम-देवी ने इन से एक दिन कहा, कि आप राजा हैं, परन्तु आप को शिकार खेलते कभीँ नहीँ देखा। इस पर एक दिन राजा शिकार खेलने के लिये वन में गया। वहाँ एक काले मृग पर जैसे-ही बाण को साधा तैसे-ही उस की

मृगी ने कहा, कि राजा इसे मत मारो, इस के मारने से हम लोग राँड हो जायँगी। राजा ने मृगी की बात अनसुनी कर, उस कारे मृग को मार डाला। इस पर मृगी ने शाप दिया, कि इस को मार कर, आप ने जैसा मुझे अनाथ किया, इसी प्रकार तीन दिन के बीच में आप के योगी होने से आप की सब रानियाँ अनाथ हो जायँगी। निदान राजा उस कारे मृग को मार कर, घर ले चला। राह में गुरु-गोरख-नाथ को देख कर, बडे आदर से दण्डवत् किया। इस पर बडे क्रोध से गोरख ने ललकारा, कि तैं ने इस काले मृग को मार कर, सत्तर मृगियों को राँड बनाया। सो तूँ महा पापी है, तेरा दण्डवत् मैं नहीँ स्वीकार करता। इस पर भर्तृहरि ने व्यङ्ग से कहा, कि आप तो बडे सिद्ध हो, इस मरे मृग को जिलाय क्यों नहीँ देते, जिस से मेरा पाप कट जाय। गोरख ने भर्तृहरि को राज-मद में भूला समझ, अपना परिचय देने के लिये, झोली से एक चुटुकी भभूत निकाल, मरे मृग के ऊपर फेँका। फेँकते-ही वह मृग सजीव हो, चौकडी भरने लगा। इस आश्चर्य को देख, राजा गोरख के पैरों पर पडा, और उन से दीक्षा ले, घर बार छोड, योगी हो गया। राजा योगी हो कर, जिस समय अपनी रानी श्याम-देवी को माता कह कर, अन्न-भिक्षा माँगने लगा है, और रानी से विनय करने लगा है, कि हे रानी, तुम मुझे पुत्र कह कर, अन्न-भिक्षा दे दो, बाजी योगियों के मुख से उस समय की मनोहर गीत बहुत-ही प्यारी मालूम होती हैं। सुनने से रोएँ खडे हो जाते हैं, रुलाई आने लगती है॥ (राजा रानियों से कहता है, कि) योगी को भोग से क्या काम। (योगी) न स्त्री चाहता है, न राज्य को चाहता है॥ (किन्तु) निश्चय कर के ठंढा (और रूखा सूखा) खर कतवार मिला भोजन चाहता है। योगी को गर्म भात से क्या काम॥

राजा (किसी का) कहना नहीँ मानता है, सभी (रोती और डरती) रानियों को तज दिया। सब रोती हुई (रानियों) को छोड कर चला, (ऐसा निष्ठुर हो गया, कि) फिर कर, (रानियों को) धीरज भी नहीँ देता है, (कि घबडावो मत, कुछ दिन बीते सिंहल की सैर कर, मैं फिर आप लोगों से आ कर, मिलूँगा और सुख-भोग करूँगा)॥ १३४॥

चउपाई।

रोअइ मता न बहुरइ बारा। रतन चला जग भा अँधिआरा॥
बार मोर रज बाउर-रत्ता। सो लेइ चला सुआ परवत्ता॥

रोअहिँ रानी तजहिँ पराना। फोरहिँ बलइँ करहिँ खरिहाना॥
चूरहिँ गिउ-अभरन अउ हारू। अब हम का कहँ करब सिँगारू॥
जा कहँ कहीँ रहसि कइ पीऊ। सोई चला का कर यह जीऊ॥
मरइ चहहिँ पइ मरइ न पावहिँ। उठइ आगि सब लोग बुझावहिँ॥
घरी एक सुठि भएउ अँदोरा। पुनि पाछइ बीता होइ रोरा॥

दोहा।

टूट मनइ नउ मोती फूट मनइ दस काँच।
लीन्ह समेटि सब अभरन होइ गा दुख कर नाँच॥ १३५॥

रोअइ = रोदिति = रोती है। मता = माता = मा = महतारी। बहुरइ = अवहो-लति = वहोलति = बहुरता है = फिरता है। बारा = बाल = बालक। रतन = रत्न = रत्न-सेन। चला = चलइ (चलति) का भूत-काल। भा = अभूत् वा अभवत् = भया = हुआ। अँधिआरा = अन्धकार। बार = बाल = बालक = बेटा। मोर = मेरा। रज = रजस् = रजो-गुण। बाउर = वातुल = बौरहा। रत्ता = रक्त = संयक्त। बाउर-रत्ता = वातुल-रक्त = बौरहे के ऐसा रक्त (वातुलवत्-रक्तः)। सुआ = शुक = सुग्गा। परबत्ता = पर्वतीय = पर्वत का। पराना = प्राण। फोरहिँ = फोरइ (स्फोटयति) का बहु-वचन। बलइँ = वलय = कङ्कण, यहाँ कङ्कणाकार काँच की चूरी। खरिहाना = खड-स्थान = धान्य-राशि रखने का स्थान = खरिहान = जहाँ धान्य को काट कर एकट्ठा करते हैँ। चूरहिँ = चूरइ (चूर्णयति) का बहु-वचन। गिउ-अभरन = ग्रीवा-आभरण = गले का गहना, झमेल, हँसुली, टीक, दुलरी, तिलरी, इत्यादि। हारू = हार = मोतियोँ की माला। करब = करँगी (प्राकृत करअव्वम् = कर्त्तव्यम्)। सिँगारू = शृङ्गार। रहसि = रहस = क्रीडा। कइ = कर। पीऊ = प्रिय। जीऊ = जीव। मरइ = मरना। चहहिँ = चहइ = (चहति) का बहु-वचन। कोई इच्छति कोई पाली चयति से चहइ बना है ऐसा मानते हैँ (२५७ पृष्ठ देखो)। पइ = अपि = यहाँ परन्तु। उठइ = उत्तिष्ठते = उठती है। आगि = अग्नि। बुझावहिँ = बुझावइ (बोधयति) का बहु-वचन। घरी = घटी = घडी। सुठि = सुष्ठु = अच्छी तरह से। अँदोरा = आन्दोलन = कोलाहल। पाछइ = पश्चात् = पीछे। बीता = बीतइ (व्यत्येति) का भूत-काल। रोरा = रोरुदा = अति-रोदन॥ टूट =

टूटइ (त्रुट्यति) का भूत-काल। मनइ = मण = मन = चालीस सेर का एक परिमाण। नउ = नव = नौ। मोती = मौक्तिक = मुक्ता। फूट = फूटइ (स्फुट्यति) का भूत-काल। समेटि = समेत्य = बटोर। अभरन = आभरण। दुख = दुःख। नाँच = नाट = नृत्य॥

(रत्न-सेन की) माता रोती है (परन्तु) पुत्र (बालक) (रत्न-सेन) नहीँ फिरता है, (सो) रत्न-सेन (सिंहल की ओर) चला, (जिस से) जग, अर्थात् चित्तौर गढ, मेँ अँधेरा हो गया॥ (माता रो रो कर कहती है, कि जो) मेरा बेटा रजो-गुण मेँ, अर्थात् हाथी घोडे इत्यादि के सुखोपभोग मेँ, बौरहे के ऐसा रक्त था; सो (उस को यह) पर्वत का शुक (हीरा-मणि) (बहका कर) ले चला॥ रानी लोग रोती हैँ, (अपने) प्राण को तजती हैँ, अर्थात् तजा चाहती हैँ। (और) चूरियोँ को फोरती हैँ, (और उन चूरियोँ के चूर का) खरिहान करती हैँ॥ (छाती पीट पीट कर) ग्रीवा के आभरण और हार को चूर करती हैँ। (और रो रो कर, उच्च-स्वर से विलपती हैँ, कि) अब हम लोग किस के लिये (का कँह) शृङ्गार करेँगी॥ जिस को खेल कूद कर, प्रिय प्रिय कहा, वही (रत्न-सेन) चला। (सो अब) यह जीव किस का है, अर्थात् किसी का नहीँ है। अब इस जीव के रहने से कुछ फल नहीँ, इस को शरीर से बाहर-ही कर देना उचित है, क्योँकि सच्चा जीव-रूप पति-ही जब चला तो इस अधम जीव के रखने से क्या फल॥ (इस प्रकार मन मेँ सोच विचार, हाथ मार मार, सब रानियाँ) मरना चाहती हैँ, अर्थात् मरने के लिये छूरी माऊर लेती हैँ, परन्तु (क्या करेँ) मरने नहीँ पातीँ। (जब पति-विरह की दुःसह) आग (हृदय मेँ) उठती है (जिस के ज्वाला को न सह कर सब मरना चाहती हैँ, उस समय) सब लोग (नाना प्रकार की सीता, दमयन्ती) संबन्धिनी कथा को कह कह कर, उस विरहाग्नि को) बुझा देते हैँ॥ (निदान राजा के चले जाने पर) एक घडी तक बडा कोलाहल हुआ (जहाँ देखो, तहाँ रोदन-ही के शब्द)। फिर पीछे महा-रोदन हो कर, बीत गया, अर्थात् सब कोई रो विलप कर, शान्त हो गये। ईश्वर की प्रबल इच्छा समझ, 'हरेरिच्छा गरीयसी' इस सिद्धान्त को सत्य विचार, लोगोँ ने हृदय मेँ धीरज को बाँध लिया॥

(रानियोँ के विकल हो कर, हार और चूरियोँ के तोडने फोडने से) नव मन मोती टूटी, (और) दश मन काँच, अर्थात् चूरी, फूटी। (सब रानियोँ ने और) सब आभरणोँ को समेट लिया, अर्थात् अङ्ग से उतार, अलग कर दिया। (उस समय

चित्तौर गढ में) दुःख का नाँच हो गया, अर्थात् सर्वत्र ऐसा राजा के वियोग से शोक छा गया, जानों दुःख नट का वेष कर, चारो ओर नाँच रहा है। जहाँ देखो तहाँ हाय हाय मच रही है ॥ १२५ ॥

चउपाई।

निकसा राजा सिंगी पूरी। छाडि नगर मेला होइ दूरी ॥
राए रंक सब भए बिओगी। सोरह सहस कुअँर भए जोगी ॥
माया मोह हरी सइँ हाथा। देखेन्हि बूझि निआन न साथा ॥
छाडेन्हि लोग कुटुँब सब कोऊ। भए निनार दुख सुख तजि दोऊ ॥
सवँरइ राजा सोई अकेला। जेहि रे पंथ खेलइ होइ चेला ॥
नगर नगर अउ गाउँहि गावाँ। चला छाडि सब ठाउँहि ठावाँ ॥
का कर घर का कर मढ-माया। ता कर सब जा कर जिउ काया ॥

दोहा।

चला कटक जोगिन्ह कर। कइ गेरुआ सब भेसु।
कोस बीस चारि-हुँ दिसि। जानउँ फूला टेंसु ॥ १३६ ॥

निकसा = निकसइ (निष्कषति, कष गतौ भ्वादि) का भूत-काल। सिंगी = शृङ्गी = हरिण के सींग का बाजा। पूरी = पूरइ (पूरयति) का स्त्री-लिङ्ग में भूत-काल। मेला = मिला = मिलइ (मिलति) का भूत-काल। होइ = भूला = हो कर। दूरी = दूर। राए = राय = राजा, अर्थात् छोटे राजा। रंक = रङ्क = दरिद्र। बिओगी = वियोगी। सोरह = षोडश। सहस = सहस्र = हजार। कुअँर = कुमार = राज-कुमार। जोगी = योगी। हरी = हरइ (हरति) का स्त्री-लिङ्ग में भूत-काल। देखेन्हि = देखइ (बौद्धों के संस्कृत में द्रक्ष्यति = पश्यति) का भूत-काल में बहु-वचन। बूझि = बुद्ध्वा = बूझ कर = समझ कर। निआन = निदान = अन्त में। साथा = सार्थ = संग। छाडेन्हि = छाडइ = छोडति (कुडति) का भूत-काल में बहु-वचन। लोग = लोक = प्राणी। कुटुँब = कुटुम्ब = घर के लोग। निनार = निरालय = निराल = अलग। सवँरइ (स्मरयति) = स्मरण करता है। अकेला = एकाकी = एकलः (प्राकृत एक + इल्ल स्वार्थे)। खेलइ = खेलति।

चेला = शिष्य। गाउँ = गावँ = ग्राम। ठाउँ = ठावँ = स्थान। मढ-माया = मठ-माया = मठ का विभव = घर का ऐश्वर्य॥ गेरुआ = गैरिक। भेसु = वेष = सूरत। कोस = क्रोश। बीस = विंशति। फूला = फूलइ (फुल्लति) का भूत-काल। टेंसु = पलास॥

राजा (घर से बाहर) निकसा (और) सिंगी को पूरा, अर्थात् बजाया, (और) नगर को छोड कर, दूर हो कर, अर्थात् नगर छोड, दूर जा कर, (साथियों से) मिला॥ (राजा की नगरी में जितने) राय और रङ्क थे, सब वियोगी भये, अर्थात् सब राजा के वियोग से व्याकुल हो कर, घर-बार से मन मोर, वैराग्य धारण किये। (और) सोरह हजार राज-कुमार (राजा के संग) योगी ऊए॥ (सब राज-कुअँरों ने) माया और मोह को हाथ से हर लिया, अर्थात् योग की लालसा से माया और मोह को अपनी मुट्ठी में कर लिया, (और) अन्त में समझ बूझ कर (ज्ञान-दृष्टि से राज-कुअँरों ने) देख लिया, [कि इस असार संसार में (अन्त में किसी का) साथ नहीं है। सब कोई साथ छोड देंगे, अकेले-ही उस ईश्वर के यहाँ जाना पडेगा। इस से उत्तम है, कि जो लोग अन्त में मेरे संग को छोडेंगे, मैं पहले-ही से उन लोगों का संग तजूँ]॥ (यह सोच विचार कर के) सब किसी ने कुटुम्ब लोगों को छोड दिया। (और इस प्रकार से ज्ञान-चचुषा सब सुख-दुःख को असार समझ, सब राज-कुअँर विरक्त हो, ईश्वर में मन को लगा कर) दुःख और सुख दोनों को तज कर, (संसार से) अलग हो गये॥ राजा (रत्न-सेन) अकेला उसी को (सोई) स्मरण करता है, जिस के मार्ग में चेला हो कर, खेलता है, अर्थात् कवि कहता है, कि रे (मन, वा प्रेमी जन,) राजा जिस पद्मावती के लिये शुक का चेला बन कर, मार्ग में खेलता है, अर्थात् बौरहे के ऐसा नाचते कूदते चल रहा है; हृदय में अकेला, अर्थात् केवल उसी पद्मावती को स्मरण करता है, अर्थात् सब से परे प्रकृति-रूप परब्रह्म पद्मावती-ही को मान कर, उसी के ध्यान में निमग्न हो रहा है॥ (राजा) सब को छोड कर, नगर नगर, और गावँ गावँ, और स्थान स्थान, चला, अर्थात् पद्मावती के ढूँढने के लिये नगर से नगर, गावँ से गावँ, और स्थान से स्थान को, चला॥ (मुहम्मद कवि कहते हैं, कि जब हृदय की आँख खुल गई तो निश्चय हो गया, कि) किस का घर और किस की मठ-माया, अर्थात् घर की सम्पत्ति। सब कुछ तिस का है, जिस का, कि जीव और शरीर है, अर्थात् जिस सच्चिदानन्द का दिया यह जीव और शरीर है, उसी का सब कुछ है। जो अपना कहे, सो झूठा और संसार की माया में भूला ऊआ है॥

सब गेरुए रंग का वेष कर, अर्थात् गुदरी इत्यादि सब पहिरावा गेरुआ से रँगा कर, योगियों की (सोरह हजार कुअँरों की) सेना चली। (उस घडी ऐसी शोभा है) जानों बीस कोस तक चारो ओर पलाश फूला हुआ है। फूल लगने की बेरा में पलाश के पत्ते सब झड जाते हैं, बहुत दिनों तक पलाश-वन में चारो ओर फूल की ललाई-ही अनल-ज्वाला के ऐसी दिखाई देती है; इसी पर बिहारी ने अपनी सत-सई में उत्प्रेक्षा किया है, कि

'फिरि घर कौं नूतन पथिक चले चकित चित भागि।
फूल्यौ देखि पलास-बन समुहैं समुझि दवागि॥'
(लाल-चन्द्रिका, दोहा ५६७)

पत्तों के झड जाने पर टेसू जो फूलता है, उस पर किसी कवि ने अन्योक्ति से पलाश से पत्ते का उलाहना देना कहा है, कि

'सीत सहे बरषा सहे आतप सहे पचास।
हम बिछुडे तुम फूलिहो ऐसे मीत पलास'॥

इस पर पलाशान्योक्ति यह है, कि

'फूले फूले कहत हैं भूले हैं सब लोग।
मीत तुमारे सोग से हम लीन्हे हैं जोग॥' ॥ १३६ ॥

चउपाई।

आगइ सगुन सगुनिअइ ताका। दहिउ माँछ रूपइ कर टाका॥
भरे कलस तरुनी चलि आई। दहिउ लेहु ग्वालिनि गोहराई॥
मालिनि आइ मउर लेइ गाँथइ। खंजन बइठु नाग के माथइ॥
दहिनइ मिरिग आइ गा धाई। प्रतीहार बोला खर बाईं॥
बिरिख सवँरिआ दाहिन बोला। बाईं दिसि गीदर तहँ डोला॥
बाएँ अकासी धोबइनि आई। लोवा दरस आइ देखराई॥
बाएँ कुररी दहिनइ कूचा। पहुँचइ भुगुति जइस मन रूचा॥

दोहा ।

जा कहँ सगुन होहिँ अस अउ गवँनइ जेहि आस ।
असट-उ महासिद्धि तेहि जस कबि कहा बिआस ॥ १३७ ॥

आगइ = अग्रे = आगे । सगुन = शकुन = कार्यारम्भ के समय और पदार्थों के दर्शन वा चेष्टा से कार्य की सिद्धि वा असिद्धि जान लेना । सगुनिअइ = शाकुनी = शकुन-विद्या (शाकुन) के जानने-वाला = सगुनिया । ताका = ताकइ (तर्क्यते) का भूत-काल = तर्क किया, वा देखा । दहिउ = दधि, वा स्वार्थे क प्रत्यय से दधिकम्, प्राकृत में दहिओ = दही । माँछ = मत्स्य = मछली = मच्छ । रूपइ = रौप्य = रूप्य = चाँदी । टाका = टाङ्क-पात्र, जो टाँकी से गढ कर बनाया गया हो । भरे = भरे हुए = भरित । कलस = घट । तरुनी = तरुणी = सौभाग्यवती युवती । लेहु = लेइ (लाति) का लोट लकार में मध्यम-पुरुष का बहु-वचन । ग्वालिनि = गो-पालिनी = अहिरिन । गोहराई = (घर्घरायते) = पुकारती है = गोहराती है । मालिनि = माली की स्त्री = मालिनी । मउर = मयूर = मयूर के आकृति की फूल पत्ते की टोपी, जो विवाह के समय दुलहे के शिर पर मङ्गल समझ कर, बाँधी जाती है । गाँथइ = ग्रथ्नाति = गाँथती है । खंजन = खञ्जन = खिडरिच = एक प्रसिद्ध पक्षी, जो शरदृतु में देख पडता है, और स्थान विशेष में जिस के दर्शन से बहुत शुभाशुभ फल कहा जाता है । नाग = सर्प, वा नाग = हस्ती । माथइ = मस्तक = माथ । दहिनइ = दक्षिणे = दहिने भाग में । मिरिग = मृग = हरिण = एक हरिण । प्रतीहार = द्वारपाल = डेवढी-दार । बोला = बोलइ (वल्गति) का भूत-काल । बाईं = वामे = वाम भाग में = बाईं ओर । बिरिख = वृष = बैल । सवँरिआ = श्यामलक = काला । गीदर = गीदड = शृगाल = सिआर । अकासी = आकाशीय = आकाश की । धोबइनि = धोबिन = धावनी, यहाँ आकाश में उडने-वाली लाल चील्ह, जिसे क्षेम-करी भी कहते हैं । लोवा = लोमाशिका = लोमडी । दरस = दर्शन । कुररी = कुरला = टिटिहरी = टिट्टिभ । कूचा = क्रौञ्च = कराकुल = ताल का पक्षी जो पङ्क्ति बाँध कर अकाश में उडते हैं । भुगुति = भुक्ति = भोग । जइस = जैसा = यथा । रूचा = रुचा = रोचते ॥ गवँनइ = (गम्यते) । आस = आशा = उम्मेद = इच्छा । असट-उ = अष्टापि = आठ-हु । कबि = कवि । बिआस = व्यास = प्रसिद्ध भारत के रचयिता तथा अष्टादश पुराण के कर्त्ता ॥

(राजा के यात्रा-समय) आगे, अर्थात् राजा के संमुख, शकुन के जानने-वालोँ ने शकुन को देखा, कि (कोई) चाँदी के पात्र में दही और मत्स्य ले कर आया। शाकुन-शास्त्र में नीचे लिखे ५० मङ्गल द्रव्य हैँ जो यात्रा वा शुभाशुभ-कार्य मेँ देख पडने से शुभ फलद हैँ—

'दध्याज्यदूर्वाक्षतपूर्णकुम्भाः सिद्धान्नसिद्धार्थकचन्दनानि।
आदर्शशङ्खामिषमीनमृत्स्नागोरोचनागोमयगोमधूनि॥
गीर्वाणवीणाफलभद्रपीठपुष्पाञ्जनालङ्करणायुधानि।
ताम्बूलयानासनवर्द्धमानध्वजातपत्रव्यजनाम्बराणि॥
अम्भोजभृङ्गारसमृद्धवह्निगजाजवाद्याङ्कुशचामराणि।
रत्नानि चामीकरताम्ररूप्यं बद्धैकपश्वोषधयः सुरा च॥
वनस्पतिर्नूतनशाकमेव माङ्गल्यपञ्चाशदियं प्रसिद्धा।
शुभेषु कार्येष्वशुभेषु चैव कार्योद्यतानां शुभदः सदैव॥'

(वसन्तराज-शाकुन, पञ्चमवर्ग, २—६ श्लोक)

दही १। घृत २। दूर्वा (दूब) ३। चावल ४। जल-पूर्ण कलश ५। पका हुआ अन्न ६। सरसो (शर्षप) ७। चन्दन ८। दर्पण ९। शङ्ख १०। मांस ११। मत्स्य १२। मृत्तिका (मट्टी) १३। गोरोचन १४। गोबर १५। गौ १६। शहद १७। देवता की प्रतिमा १८। वीणा १९। फल २०। भद्रपीठ (सिंहासन) २१। पुष्प २२। अञ्जन (काजर वा सुरमा) २३। अलङ्करण (आभूषण) २४। शस्त्र २५। ताम्बूल (पान) २६। सवारी (यान) २७। आसन २८। वर्द्धमान (जैनियोँ का एक विशिष्ट चिह्नमय पात्र) २९। ध्वजा ३०। छाता ३१। पङ्खा ३२। वस्त्र ३३। कमल ३४। भृङ्गार (सुराही) ३५। बरती आग ३६। हाथी ३७। बकरा ३८। बाजा ३९। अङ्कुश ४०। चामर (चवँर) ४१। रत्न (हीरा इत्यादि) ४२। सुवर्ण (सोना) ४३। तामा ४४। चाँदी ४५। बँधा हुआ पशु ४६। ओषधि ४७। सुरा (मदिरा) ४८। वनस्पति (वन-वृक्ष) ४९। नया साग ५०॥ ४५ वाँ मङ्गल-द्रव्य चाँदी है, इस लिये चाँदी के पात्र में दधि और मत्स्य के कहने से तीन मङ्गल-द्रव्य (१,१२,४५ वाँ०) हो गये॥ कलस को (जल से) भरे सौभाग्यवती युवती चली आई। (सामने से) ग्वालिन 'दही लो (दही लो') पुकारने लगी॥ मालिन (राजा के सामने) आ कर, मौर ले कर, गाँथती है, अर्थात् मालिन मौर को गाँथने लगी, अर्थात् २२ वाँ

मङ्गल-द्रव्य पुष्य का दर्शन भी राजा को हुआ। खञ्जन, नाग (=सर्प वा हस्ती) के माथे पर बैठ गया (जिस का दर्शन भी राजा को हो गया) ऐसे खञ्जन के दर्शन से शाकुनज्ञों का वाक्य है, कि राज्य-प्राप्ति होती है—

'तुरङ्गमातङ्गमहोरगेषु सरोजगोछत्रवृषेषु येन।
पूर्वं च दृष्टोऽहनि खञ्जरीटो निःसंशयं तस्य भवेन्नृपलम्'॥

(वसन्तराज०, १० वर्ग, १४ श्लो०)

'राजा की दाहिनी ओर दौड कर, एक हरिण आ गया। दक्षिण भाग में ओज (विषम, अर्थात् १, ३, ५ इत्यादि) हरिण शुभफलद हैं।

ओजाः प्रदक्षिणं शस्ता मृगाः सनकुलाण्डजाः।

(बृहत्सं० ८५ अ०, ४३ श्लो०)

प्रतीहार और खर बाईं ओर बोला, अर्थात् जैसे द्वार-पाल राजा को देख कर अदब से बाईं ओर खडा हो कर, जय बोलने लगा, उसी प्रकार बाईं ओर खडा हो कर गदहा भी अपनी भाषा में राजा के लिये मङ्गल-ध्वनि करने लगा।

'ओजा मृगा व्रजन्तोऽति धन्या वामे खरस्वनः।'

(मुहूर्त्त-चिन्तामणि, यात्रा-प्रकरण, १०४ श्लो०)॥

काला वृष दाहिनी ओर बोलने लगा। शाकुन में साधारण किसी बैल का दक्षिण ओर शब्द शुभ लिखा है। कवि ने कृष्णा गौ के सदृश कृष्ण बैल को पवित्र समझ कर, कृष्ण विशेषण दिया है।

'वामोऽनुलोमस्य रवः खुरेण शृङ्गेण चाग्रे खननं पृथिव्याः।
प्रशस्यते दक्षिणतश्च चेष्टा तथा निशीथे निनदो वृषस्य॥'

(वसन्तरा० १० व०, १० श्लो०)

तहाँ पर, अर्थात् जहाँ राजा था वहाँ बाईं ओर गीदड (आ कर) डोलने लगा। शकुन के सब ग्रन्थों में बाईं ओर शृगाल का आ कर, न चलना अशुभ फल को देने-वाला है, इस लिये लेखक-प्रमाद से जो 'नहिँ' लिख गया था उस स्थान में 'तहँ' किया है। और गादुर, जिसे चमगादुर भी कहते हैँ, रात्रि-चर है, दिन को उस के दर्शन से अशुभ फल होता है, क्योँकि सामान्यतः रात्रि-चर जन्तु, प्रायः दिन को निर्भय हो कर दिखाई देँ तो शाकुन में अशुभ-फल कहा है, इस हेतु 'गादुर' के स्थान में 'गीदर' किया है।

'अनर्थहेतुर्गतिशब्दहीनः सदा शृगालः खलु दृष्टमात्रः।
शस्ताङ्कि वामा गतिरस्य शस्तो वामो निनादो निशि यो बहूनाम् ॥'
(वसन्त०, १४ व०, ४० श्लो०)॥

आकाश की धोबिन, अर्थात् क्षेम-करी, बायेँ भाग में आई। कहावत है, कि जब वसुदेव कृष्ण को नन्द के घर पहुँचा कर, वहाँ से यशोदा की कन्या को उठा लाये, और कंस ने उसी कन्या को देवकी के अष्टम-गर्भ की बालिका समझ, पत्थर पर पटकने के लिये, उस बालिका के पैर को हाथ से पकड कर, ऊपर की ओर घुमाने लगा; उस समय वह बालिका इसी क्षेम-करी का रूप धारण कर, कंस के हाथ से निकल, कंस को शाप देती हुई, आकाश में उड चली। फिर मिर्जापुर के पास विन्ध्याचल पहाड के ऊपर देवी-स्वरूप हो कर ठहरी, जो अब तक सब लोगों से पूजित है। देवीपुराण के ४० वें अध्याय में लिखा है, कि

'क्षेमान् देवेषु सा देवी कृत्वा दैत्यपतेः क्षयम्।
क्षेमङ्करी शिवेनोक्ता पूज्या लोके भविष्यसि ॥'

इस के दर्शन के समय उसी स्थान में

'कुङ्कुमारुणसर्वाङ्गि कुन्देन्दुधवलानने।
मत्स्यमांसप्रिये देवि क्षेमङ्करि नमोऽस्तु ते ॥',

यह प्रणामार्थ मन्त्र भी लिखा है॥ संप्रति प्रसिद्ध संस्कृत शाकुन-ग्रन्थों में इस पक्षी का कोई विशेष फल नहीं लिखा है, परन्तु लोक में प्रसिद्ध है, कि यात्रा में इस का दर्शन शुभ है। तुलसी-दास ने भी अयोध्या से जनक-पुर में बरात चलती समय लिखा है, कि 'छेमकरी कह छेम बिसेखी'। कवि ने स्त्री-लिङ्ग होने के कारण, अथवा कुररी के सदृश समझ, शुभ-फल के लिये बायेँ का ग्रहण किया है। लोमडी आ कर (राजा को अपना) दर्शन दिखाया, अर्थात् दर्शन दिया। शाकुन-शास्त्र में लिखा है, कि

'सिद्धौ सदा सर्वसमीहितानां स्याल्लोमशी दर्शनमात्रसेव।'
(वसन्त०, १४ व०, ४४ श्लो०)॥

बायेँ भाग में कुररी (टिटिहरी) और दहिने भाग में क्रौञ्च बोलते देख पडे। (प्राणी को) जैसा मन में रुचे वही भोग (उस के पास) पहुँचता है, (जिन के दर्शन से प्राणी मनो-वाञ्छित भोग को पाता है)।

'वामं प्रवासे रटितं हिताय तथोपरिष्टादपि टिट्टिभस्य।
टिटीति शान्तं टिटिटीति दीप्तं शब्दद्वयं चास्य बुधा वदन्ति ॥'

(वसन्त०, ८ व०, १३ श्लो०)

शकुन-शास्त्र में एक जोडे क्रौञ्च के दर्शन से फल कहा है, और यह जोडा चाहे जिस दिशा में देख पडे सर्वत्र शुभ-ही फल है। इस पक्षी का धर्म भी है, कि सारस के ऐसा सदा नर-मादे दोनों संग-ही रहते हैं। इस लिये यहाँ 'कूचा' से एक जोडा कूचा समझना चाहिए। और सब भाग की अपेक्षा दहना भाग विशेष कर के उत्तम है। इस लिये ग्रन्थ-कार ने 'दहिनद्द' यह लिखा है। सारस के जोडे के ऐसा क्रौञ्च के जोडे का भी फल लिखा है।

'इष्टार्थसिद्धिः सकलासु दिक्षु स सारसद्वन्द्वविलोकनेन'।

(वसन्त०, ८ व०, ९ श्लो०)

'स वेदितव्यः कथितोऽर्थकारी क्रौञ्चद्वयस्याप्ययमेव मार्गः।'

(वसन्त०, ८ व०, ११ श्लो०)॥

जिस को ऐसे शकुन होते हैं, और (वह इन शकुनों से) जिस की आशा से गमन करता है। तिस की (वह आशा पूरी होती है, और) आठो महा-सिद्धि प्राप्त होती है, जैसा कि (महा) कवि व्यास ने कहा है। (आठो सिद्धि के लिये ४६ पृष्ठ में १८-२२ पङ्क्ति देखो)। भारतवर्षीय विद्वानों को विश्वास है, कि अन्धकासुर मारने के लिये पहले महादेव जी ने इन शकुनों को प्रगट किया; उस के पीछे तारकासुर के मारने के लिये, जब महादेव के पुत्र स्वामी कार्त्तिकेय जी उद्यत हुए तब शिव ने इन को उन शकुनों को बताया। फिर जम्भदैत्य के मारने की वेला में स्वामी कार्त्तिकेय ने इन्द्र को इस शाकुन को बताया। इन्द्र से कश्यप, कश्यप से गरुड ने इस ज्ञान को पाया। शिव जी के अनुग्रह से ऋषि, गर्ग, भृगु, व्यासादिकों ने पाया। इस परम्परा से यह शाकुन-शास्त्र पृथ्वी पर आया। भारत और वाल्मीकि रामायण में भी अनेक स्थानों पर निमित्तों का, अर्थात् शुभाशुभ शकुनों का वर्णन है। ऋषियों में भगवान के चौबीस अवतार के मध्य १७ वें अवतार में व्यास की गणना होने से, कवि ने व्यास को महान् समझ कर, व्यास-ही का ग्रहण किया॥ १३७॥

चउपाई।

भएउ पयान चला पुनि राजा। सिंगि-नाद जोगिन्ह कर बाजा॥
कहहिँ आजु किछु थोर पयाना। काल्हि पयान दूरि हइ जाना॥
ओहि मेलान जउ पहुँचइ कोई। तब हम कहब पुरुख भल सोई॥
हहिँ आगइ परबत कइ पाटी। बिखम पहार अगम सुठि घाटी॥
बिच बिच नदी खोह अउ नारा। ठाउँहि ठाउँ उठहिँ बटपारा॥
हनुवँत केर सुनब पुनि हाँका। दहुँ को पार होइ को थाका॥
अस मन जानि सँभारहु आगू। अगुआ केर होहु पछ-लागू॥

दोहा।

करहिँ पयान भोर उठि पंथ कोस दस जाहिँ।
पंथी पंथा जे चलहिँ ते का रहहिँ ओनाहिँ॥ १३८॥

पयान = प्रयाण = यात्रा। सिंगि-नाद = शृङ्गी-नाद = शृङ्गी बाजे का शब्द। बाजा = बजइ (वाद्यते) का भूत-काल। किछु = किञ्चित्। थोर = थोड = थोडा = कम। पयाना = पयान। काल्हि = कल्यम् = बीता ऊआ दिन, परन्तु अब भाषा में बीता और आगामि दोनों दिनों के लिये व्यवहार किया जाता है = कल। दूरि = दूर। जाना = यानम् = गमनम्। मेलान = मेलन = मिलान = मेल में बराबर। जउ = यदि = जौं। कहब = कहँगे। पुरुख = पुरुष = आदमी। भल = भर = भला = भव्य। सोई = स एव = वही। हहिँ = हइ का बऊ-वचन = अहहिँ। आगइ = अग्रे = आगे। परबत = पर्वत। पाटी = पट्टिका = पटिया = शिला। वा पाटी = परम्परा = एक के बाद दूसरा। बिखम = विषम = कठिन = नीँचे ऊँचे। पहार = प्रहार = पर्वत। अगम = अगम्य = जाने योग्य नहीँ। सुठि = सुष्ठु = अच्छी तरह से = अत्यन्त। घाटी = घट्टी = सङ्कुचित राह। बिच बिच = बीच बीच। खोह = खन्धक = कन्दरा। नारा = नल = नार। ठाउँ = ठावँ = स्थान। उठहिँ = उठइ (उत्तिष्ठते) का बऊ-वचन। बटपारा = वाट-पाल = राह के मालिक = डाँकू। हनुवँत = हनुमन्तः = हनुमान्। सुनब = सुनियेगा। हाँक = ऊङ्कार = गर्जना। दऊँ = देखेँ = क्या जानेँ। थाका = स्थगित होता है = थकइ (स्थगति) का भूत-काल। अगुआ = अग्रग वा अग्रुक (प्राकृत में उकः स्वार्थे) = आगे जाने-वाला। पछ-लागू = पश्चाल्लग्न =

पीछे लगने-वाला ॥ भोर = भूरि = प्रातःकाल = दिन = सबेरा । कोस = क्रोश । दस = दश । जाहिँ = जाइ (याति) का बज-वचन । पन्थी = पथिकी पंथा = पन्थाः = मार्ग । जे = ये । चलहिँ = चलइ (चलति) का बज-वचन । का = किम् = क्या । रहहिँ = रहइ (रहति) का बज-वचन । ओनाहिँ = ओनाइ (अवनमति) का बज-वचन = झुक जाते हैँ ॥

यात्रा ऊई और (पुनः) राजा चला । (चलने के समय) योगियोँ का शृङ्गी-नाद बजा, अर्थात् यात्रा में मङ्गल के लिये चलती बेला योगियोँ (सोरह हजार कुअँरोँ) ने अपनी अपनी सिंगी को बडे उच्च-स्वर से बजाया ॥ (मार्ग में सब योगी आपस में) कहते हैँ, कि आज (तो) कुछ थोडी-ही यात्रा है, अर्थात् 'स्वल्पारम्भः क्षेमाय भवति' (किसी कार्य के करने में आरम्भ में उस का थोडा करना भला होता है), इस सिद्धान्त से आज तो थोडा-ही चलना है, (परन्तु) कल से पयान में दूर जाना है, अर्थात् कल से मंजिल कडी होगी ॥ (सो) यदि कोई उस (ओहि) (मंजिल में) मेल से पऊँचे, अर्थात् पीछा न दे बराबर साथ देता रहे, तब हम (लोग) कहँगे, कि वह भला, अर्थात् उत्तम मनुष्य है ॥ (क्योँकि) आगे पर्वतोँ की शिला हैँ, अथवा पर्वतोँ की परम्परा हैँ, (और वे) पहाड (बडे-ही) विकट (विषम) हैँ, (उन की) घाटी अत्यन्त अगम्य हैँ ॥ बीच बीच में (उन पहाडोँ के) नदी, कन्दरा और नारे हैँ । स्थान स्थान पर राह के मालिक, अर्थात् ठग वा डाँकू लोग, जो पर्वतोँ में अपनी अपनी सीमा बाँध कर, उन सीमाओँ तक के राजा बन बैठे हैँ, वे लोग (अपनी सीमा के भीतर पथिकोँ के आने पर 'कर-झुलौनी' कर के लिये, वा विशेष धनी समझ लूटने के लिये) उठते हैँ ॥ (योगी लोग कहते हैँ, कि फिर आगे दक्षिण लङ्का के निकट हम लोग) हनुमान् की हाँक सुनँगे, (उस हाँक को सुन कर) देखँ कौन (साहस कर, विना घबडाये) पार होता है, (और) कौन (घबडा कर) थक जाता है, अर्थात् थक कर, वहीँ रह जाता है । कहावत है, कि जब राम-चन्द्र लङ्का को जीत कर, इस पार सेतु-बन्ध के पास आये, तब वहाँ के साधु-जन बडे विनय से कहे, कि कुछ काल बीते राक्षसोँ के सन्तान जब बऊत बढ जायँगे, तब फिर वे लोग इस पार आ कर, हम लोगोँ को नाना प्रकार की पीडा देँगे । सो हे भगवन्, भक्तवत्सल, अनुग्रह कर, हम लोगोँ के कल्याण के लिये कुछ उपाय कर जाइये । इस पर राम-चन्द्र ने हनुमान् को आज्ञा दिया, कि तुम अपने अंश का एक दिव्य पुरुष नियत कर, उसे यहाँ चौकी-दार कर दो, जिस में राक्षस लोग भय से इस पार न आवैँ । इस आज्ञा से

हनुमान अपना एक द्वितीय रूप बना कर समुद्र के तट पर स्थापित कर दिया, जो समय समय पर हाँक मारा करता है, और उस हाँक के भये से राचस लोग आज तक इधर नहीं बढते॥ (योगी लोग आपस में कह कर औरों को सावधान करते हैं, कि) ऐसा मन में (दुर्गम मार्ग को) जान कर (सब कोई) आगे (अपने को) सँभारो; (और खबर्दार, संग न छोडो) आगे-वाले के पछ-लगू हो, अर्थात् जो आगे चले उस के पीछे पीछे क्रम से लगे हुए सब कोई चलो जिस में संग न छूटे॥

(इस प्रकार योगी लोग सावधान हो कर प्रत्यह) भोर को उठ कर यात्रा करते हैं (और प्रति दिन) दश कोश जाते हैं (कहीं रुकते नहीं हैं)। (कवि कहता है, कि) जो पथिक, मार्ग में चलते हैं, वे (ते) क्या रह जाते हैं? (और किसी अन्य पदार्थ के लिये वे लोग राह में) क्या झुक जाते हैं?; अर्थात् वे लोग सदा अपनी मंजिल पूरी किया करते हैं, और राह में रुकते नहीं, और दूसरी वस्तु की लालसा से उस ओर झुकते नहीं। जो वस्तु मन में बस गई है, उसी के ध्यान में उसी के आश्रम में पहुँचने का यत्न करते हैं॥ १३८॥

चउपाई।

करहु दिसिटि थिर होहु बटाऊ। आगू देखु धरहु भुइँ पाऊ॥
जो रे उबट होइ परहिँ भुलाने। गए मारे पँथ चलहिँ न जाने॥
पायन्ह पहिरि लेहु सब पवँरी। काँट चुभइ न गडइ अँकरवरी॥
परेउ आइ अब बन-खँड माहाँ। डंडाकरन बीझ-बन जाहाँ॥
सघन ढाँख-बन चहुँ दिसि फूला। बहु दुख मिलिहि उहाँ कर भूला॥
झाँखर जहाँ सो छाडहु पंथा। हिलगि मकोइ न फारहु कंथा॥
दहिनइ बिदर चँदेरी बाएँ। दहुँ केहि होब बाट दुहुँ ठाएँ॥

दोहा।

एक बाट गइ सिंघल दोसर लंक समीप।
हहिँ आगइ पँथ दूअउ दहुँ गवँनब केहि दीप॥ १३९॥

दिसिटि = दृष्टि = आँख = नज़र। थिर = स्थिर। बटाऊ = वाटेहः (वाटस्य-ईहा-इच्छा यस्य) = बटोही = राही। आगू = आगे = अग्रे। देखु = देखइ (दृश्यते) का

चउपाई ।

तत-खन बोला सुआ सरेखा । अगुआ सोई पंथ जेइ देखा ॥
सो का उडइ न जेहि तन पाँखू । लेइ सो पलासहि बोडइ साखू ॥
जस अंधा अंधइ कर संगी । पंथ न पाउ होइ सह-लंगी ॥
सुनु मति काज चहसि जउ साजा । बीजा-नगर बिजइ-गिरि राजा ॥
पूँछहु जहाँ गोंड अउ कोला । तजु बाएँ अँधिआर खटोला ॥
दक्खिन दहिनइ रहहिँ तिलंगा । उत्तर माँझहि करहकटंगा ॥
माँझ रतनपुर सीह-दुआरा । झारखंड देइ बाउँ पहारा ॥

दोहा ।

आगइ बाउँ उडइसा बाएँ देहु सो बाट ।
दहिनावरत देइ कइ उतरु समुद के घाट ॥ १४० ॥

इति जोगी-खंड ॥ १२ ॥

तत-खन = तत्क्षणे = उसी बेला में । बोला = बोलइ (भलते, भल परिभाषणहिंसा-दानेषु भ्वा. वा वदति, वद व्यक्तायां वाचि भ्वा.) का भूत-काल । सुआ = शुक । सरेखा = सु-लेख = श्रेष्ठ । अगुआ = अग्रुक वा अग्रग = आगे चलने-वाला । सोई = सोऽपि = स एव = वही । पंथ = पन्थाः = मार्ग । जेइ = येन = जिस ने । देखा = देखइ (दृश्यते) का भूत-काल । का = क = किम् = क्या । उडइ = उडे = उडइ (उड्डीयते) का लिङ् लकार में प्रथम-पुरुष का एक-वचन । तन = तनु = शरीर । पाँखू = पक्ष = पंखा । पलासहि = पलास को (पलाशम् = पत्र = पत्ता) = पत्ते को । बोडइ = बोरइ (बोडयति) = बोरता है = बुडाता है = डुबाता है । साखू = शाखा = डार । अंधा = अन्ध । अंधइ = अन्धे । संगी = सङ्गी = साथी । पाउ = पावे = पावइ (प्राप्नोति) का लिङ् लकार में प्रथम-पुरुष का एक-वचन । होइ = भवति = होता है । सह-लंगी = सह-लग्न = साथ-लगा, वा सह-लंगी = सह-लङ्घी = साथ साथ लाँघने-वाला । सुनु = शृणु = सुनो । काज = कार्य । चहसि = (चतसि वा चदसि वा चहसि) चहइ का मध्यम-पुरुष में एक-वचन । साजा = सज्जित करना = पूरा करना । बीजा-नगर = विजय-नगर । बिजइ-गिरि = विजय-गिरि = विजय-नगर का पहाड । गोँड = एक जङ्गली मनुष्य-जाति = कहारोँ का एक भेद = गोण्ड

(संस्कृत)। कोल = एक जङ्गली मनुष्यजाति = भीलोँ का एक भेद, जो मध्य-प्रदेश नाग-पुर-इत्यादि मेँ विशेष कर पाये जाते हैँ। तजु = तजइ (त्यजति) का लोट् लकार म मध्यम-पुरुष का एक-वचन। बाएँ = वामे = बाईँ ओर। अँधिआर खटोला = अन्धक-टोला = अन्धकोँ का स्थान। यदुवंशियोँ के प्रभेद मेँ एक जाति। पाणिनि ने अपने व्याकरण मेँ लिखा है, 'ऋष्यन्धकवृष्णिकुरुभ्यश्च' अष्टाध्यायी (अ॰ ४ पा॰ १ सू॰ ११४) काव्यप्रकाश मेँ लिखा है, कि

'येन ध्वस्तमनोभवेन बलिजित् कायः पुरा स्त्रीकृतो
यश्चोद्वृत्तभुजङ्गहारवलयो गङ्गां च योऽधारयत्।
यस्याहुः शशिमच्छिरो हर इति स्तुत्यं च नामामराः
पायात् स स्वयमन्धकक्षयकरस्त्वां सर्वदो माधवः॥'

(सप्तम उल्लास)

यह श्लोक शिवपक्ष और विष्णुपक्ष दोनोँ मेँ है। शिवपक्ष मेँ अन्धक = राक्षस, और विष्णुपक्ष मेँ अन्धक = यदुवंशियोँ का प्रभेद। यह अन्धक-नगरी समुद्र के तट पर बसी है, जब कि भगवान् कृष्ण मथुरा को छोड कर, द्वारिका को चले गये। दक्खिन = दक्षिण। दहनइ = दक्षिणे = दहनी ओर। तिलंगा = तैलङ्ग देश के रहने-वाले = पञ्चद्राविड मेँ एक जाति। करहकटंगा = कर्णाटक। रतन-पुर = रत्नपुर = रत्नगिरि। सीह-दुआरा = सिंह-द्वार = जगन्नाथ जी के यहाँ जाने के लिये प्रधान द्वार, जहाँ से हो कर, लोग जगन्नाथ पुरी मेँ प्रवेश करते हैँ। झारखंड = झारखण्ड = एक पहाड, जो वैद्यनाथ महादेव के पास से होता हुआ जगन्नाथ-पुरी के प्रान्त तक चला गया है॥ उडइसा = उड्र-देश = उत्कल-देश = जहाँ उत्कल-जातीय ब्राह्मण होते हैँ। ...रत = दक्षिणावर्त्त = दहिना फेरा = प्रदक्षिणा। उतरु = उत्तरइ (उत्तरति) का लोट् लकार मेँ मध्यम-पुरुष का एक-वचन। समुद = समुद्र। घाट = घट्टः = जहाँ, कि उतार का सुभीता हो = उतरने योग्य समुद्र का तट॥

(लोगोँ को, विशेष कर, राजा को राह न जानने से घबडाहट मेँ देख कर) उसी बेला मेँ श्रेष्ठ शुक (हीरा-मणि) बोला, (कि घबडावो मत) आगे वही है, जो कि राह को देखे हुए है, अर्थात् मैँ राह का देखने-वाला आगे हूँ घबडाने की कोई बात नहीँ॥ जिस के तनु मेँ पक्ष नहीँ है वह (सो) क्या उडे, अर्थात् वह नहीँ उड़ सकता। वह (सो) (तो) पत्ते को ले कर, शाखा को डुबा देता है, अर्थात् वह पत्ते-

ही को अपनी मूर्खता से बडी नाव समझ उस के ऊपर बडी डार को धर कर, ले चलता है, जिस कर्म से डार-ही बूड जाती है। शुक का तात्पर्य है, कि आप लोग पच से विहीन हैं, सो आप लोगोँ की सामर्थ्य नहीँ, कि इस मार्ग को पूरा कर पद्मावती के देश मेँ पऊँचँ, और आप लोगोँ का साहस करना वैसा-ही है, जैसे पत्ते के ऊपर डार (शाखा) को धर उस को समुद्र-पार ले जाना॥ (और) जैसे अन्धा अन्धे का साथी हो, (और ठीक) राह को न पावे (और लाचार हो कर उस अन्धे के) साथ लगा होता है, अर्थात् हैरान होने पर भी उस अन्धे के साथ साथ लगा रहता है (तैसे-ही यहाँ आप लोगोँ की दशा है), अर्थात् आप लोग इस समय अन्धे के सदृश मेरे हाथ मेँ हैँ, मैँ जिधर चाहूँ उधर आप लोगोँ को फिरा सकता हूँ॥ (सो मैँ पची हूँ, आकाश-मार्ग से चाहे जिधर उड कर जा सकता हूँ; मेरे पीछे लगने से काम न चलेगा। राजन्) मति को सुनो, अर्थात् मुझ से मति लो। यदि (अपना) कार्य पूरा करना चाहते हो (तो), (आगे) विजय-नगर मेँ विजय-गिरि का राजा है॥ जहाँ, अर्थात् तिस की राजधानी मेँ (अनेक जङ्गली) गोँड और कोल हैँ, (उन से ठीक ठीक राह को) पूछो। और (आगे) बाईँ ओर अन्धक-टोला (पडेगा) उस को छोड दो, अर्थात् बहक कर, उस की ओर न जावो॥ (जिस) दचिण (दिशा मेँ चलना है उस राह की) दहनी ओर तैलङ्गी लोग रहते हैँ, और उत्तर की ओर बीच मेँ कर्णाटक लोग रहते हैँ॥ (आगे) बीच मेँ (माँझ), अर्थात् राह-ही मेँ रत्नपुर, और सिंह-द्वार है (जहाँ से लोग जगन्नाथ-पुरी जाते हैँ)। झार-खण्ड पहाड को बायेँ दे कर अर्थात् बाईँ ओर छोड कर॥

(और उस के) आगे बाईँ ओर उडीसा है, सो (उस) बाट को भी बायेँ दो, अर्थात् उसे भी बाईँ ओर छोडो, (इस प्रकार) दहिनावर्त्त दे कर, अर्थात् दाहिनी-ही ओर झुँकते झुँकते समुद्र के घाट पर उतरो॥ १४०॥

ऊपर जो अर्थ लिख आये हैँ वह परम्परा से देशोँ के नाम और स्थान विना जाने पुराने लोगोँ का है। आचार्य के समय जिन जिन देशोँ के जो नाम प्रसिद्ध थे उन के परिचय के लिये प्राचीन ग्रन्थोँ से ले कर, कुछ वृत्तान्त लिखते हैँ। इस विषय मेँ मुझे पूर्णतया सहाय, पण्डित भैरवदत्त, गवर्नमेण्ट क्वीन्स कालेज के पुस्तकालयाध्यच ने दी है। इस लिये उन को जहाँ तक धन्यवाद देँ सब थोडा है।

मृगारण्य जो कि १४१ वेँ दोहे मेँ है और जहाँ पहले डेरा पडा

'मिरगारन मँह भयउ बसेरा' इस पाठ के अनुसार, यह वह स्थान है, जहाँ पहले दिन नर्मदा के तट पर   रहरे। जो कि पहले विजय-नगर में था और आज कल नीमार में है। यहाँ तीन पर्वतों के कुछ ऊँचे शिखरों के निवेश से नर्मदा के छोटे छोटे तीन खण्ड हो गये हैं। और वे शिखर एक पुल के तीनि ताखे से जान पडते हैं जिन्हें हरिण सहज में कूद जाते हैं। इसी लिये इस का नाम हरिण-पाल पडा है। यह आज तक एक विशिष्ट तीर्थ समझा जाता है। (See Malcolm's Central India. Vol. I., p. 13).

बिदर — बाँसवाडा, डोंगरपुर, परतापगढ, बरोदा, खानदेश इत्यादि सब बिदर में है, जैसा कि Cunningham साहब के प्राचीन भारतवर्षीय भूगोल के नक्शे से स्पष्ट है। और Col. Tod साहब के राज-स्थान, (Tod's Rājasthān, Vol. I., p. 166, ed. 2nd, 1877), नामक पुस्तक से भी विदित है।

चँदेरी — ग्रन्थ-कार के समय बुँदेलों के अधिकार में थी। और इस की सीमा मालवा तक थी। परन्तु अब छोटा सा एक नगर ग्वालियर के राज्य में चँदेरी नाम का रह गया है, जिस का उत्तर अक्षांश २४°। ४२′। और ग्रीनविच से पूर्वदेशान्तर ७८°। ११′॥ यहाँ की पगडी (मण्डील) और डुपट्टे इत्यादि बहुत प्रसिद्ध हैं। और यह नगर अकबर के समय में मालवे के सूबे के बारह सर्कारों में से एक सर्कार था। उस समय इस की दक्षिण-सीमा उज्जयन के सर्कार से मिली हुई थी। सरोंज, जो कि उज्जयन के निकट है, वह भी इसी के अन्तर्गत था। (See Thornton's Gazetteer. p. 194, and Āīn-i-Akbarī, Vol. II., pp. 201–203, Jarrett's translation).

बिजय-गढ — ग्रन्थकार के समय में नर्मदा के दोनों ओर फैला हुआ प्रसिद्ध राज्य था। परन्तु समय के फेर फार से अब एक छोटा सा नगर इन्दोर के राज्य में रह गया है, जो कि नर्मदा के दाहिने तट पर है। यह अकबर के समय, सूबे मालवा के बारह सर्कारों में से एक सर्कार था। इस का उत्तर अक्षांश और देशान्तर नीमार के आसन्न अक्षांश २२°। ३०′। पू॰ दे॰ ७७°। १′। ग्रन्थकार के कथनानुसार यहाँ के गावने-वाले बहुत प्रसिद्ध थे। 'बीजानगर केर बड गुनी' ऐसा रत्न-सेन के सभा-वर्णन में कहा है, जब कि अलाउद्दीन चढ आया था। यहाँ पर गोंड, भील, और कोल बहुत रहते थे और यह देश नीमार से ले कर दक्षिण-पूर्व की ओर गोंडवाने के नाम से प्रसिद्ध था। आज कल खानदेश और उडीशा के मध्यगत देश

गोंडवाने के नाम से प्रसिद्ध हैं। और किसी समय में यह सब देश गढ-मण्डला के राज्याधिकार में थे, जहाँ गोंड-लोग राज्य करते थे, और अब भी गोंड-लोग वहाँ बहुतायत से बसते हैं।

अँधियार (Anjārī) = अकबर के समय विजय-गढ के २९ महालों में से एक महाल था, जिस का क्षेत्रफल १२७१२ बीघा था, आमदनी १७०७०९२ दाम थी। यह नर्मदा के तट पर एक छोटा सा राज्य था। कदाचित् अन्जार नदी के तट पर अब भी इस के खँडहर मिलें जो, कि हुशङ्गाबाद और हँडिया के जिले से होती हुई नर्मदा में दक्खिन की ओर से मिलती है। अन्जार का अपभ्रंश अँधियार जान पडता है। आज कल अब इस का पता नहीं मिलता (See Āīn-i-Akbarī, Vol. II., pp. 204–206; and, for Anijala river, Hunter's Gazetteer, Vols. V., X., pp. 442 and 327 respectively, under Hoshangābād and Nimār).

खटोला — का राज्य अँधियार के राज्य से लगा हुआ उत्तर की तरफ था, जिस से आज कल, सागर, दमोह, शाहगढ इत्यादि जिले बने हैं। यह राज्य गढ-मण्डला के राज्य का पश्चिम-भाग था। जिस की राजधानी बुन्देल-खण्ड में कहीं शाहगढ के निकट खटोला के नाम से प्रसिद्ध थी। ईशा के ११ वें शतक में यह राज्य गढ-मण्डला के राज्य से अलग हुआ जिस को कि १५ वें शतक के अन्त में राजा वीर-सिंह देव ओरछावाले ने नष्ट किया। (See Hunter's Gazetteer, Vol. IV., p. 108, History of Damoh; Āīn-i-Akbarī, Vol. II., p. 200). और यह नगर अकबर के समय सूबा मालवा के सर्कार कन्नौज (गढ-मण्डला) के ५७ महालों में से एक महाल था, जिस की आमदनी १२१००० दाम थी। और अकबर की तरफ से ५०० सवार और ५०००० सिपाही रहते थे। उस समय भी यह गोंडों की बस्ती खटोले-ही के नाम से प्रसिद्ध थी। इस खटोले से स्पष्ट विदित होता है, कि अन्जार ही ग्रन्थ-कार का अँधियार है।

तिलङ्गा — तैलंगाना (See Hamilton's Description of Hindustan, Vol. II., p. 121). उस समय वर्हाड (बरार) देश को तैलंगाना कहते थे और अब भी वर्हाड तैलंगाना के नाम से इतिहासों में प्रसिद्ध है।

करह-कटंगा = गढ-कटंग (See History of the Garha-maṇḍala Rājās, by Sleeman, in J. A. S. B., Vol. VI., pp. 621 and also Āīn-i-Akbarī, Vol. II., pp. 199–200. See also Blochmann's translation, Vol. I., Index). गढ यह

एक प्राचीन नगर नर्मदा के तट पर संप्रति जबलपुर के दक्षिण की ओर तीन मील पर था। इस का उत्तर अक्षांश २३°। ९'। पूर्व देशान्तर ८०°। १६'। जबलपुर का अक्षांश २३°। ११'। पू० दे० ८०°। १६'। जो कि बहुत काल तक समग्र गोंडवाने का प्रधान राजस्थान था। कटंगी — एक टूटा-फूटा नगर भाँउर पहाडी के निकट हिरण्य-नदी के उत्तर तट पर जबलपुर से २२ मील वायुकोण पर सागर की सडक पर है। अक्षांश० २३°। २६'। ३०"। दे० ७९°। ५०' पूर्व इस का है। यहाँ पहले बन्दूक अच्छी बनती थी। गढ-कटंग वा गढ अकबर के समय सूबे मालवा के बारह सर्कारों में से एक सर्कार था। यह आज कल जबलपुर रेल के स्टेशन के निकट पड जाने से सब भ्रष्ट हो गया। केवल एक मदन-महल नामक स्थान बच गया है॥

रतन-पुर = रत्न-पुर — (See Hamilton's Description of Hindustan, Vol. II., p. 22; and also Cunningham's Archæological Survey of India, Vol. VII., pp. 214–216). जो कि आज कल बिलास-पुर के जिले में है। उस समय भी इसी नाम से प्रसिद्ध था। इस का उ० अ० २२°। २१' और पू० दे० ८२°। २५'॥

सीह-दुआरा (Chhindwara). (See Thornton's Gazetteer, p. 903 and p. 203, ed. of 1857; and also the Atlas of the Society for the Diffusion of Useful Knowledge, Vol. I., Map of India No. 6).

'छिन्दारा', जो कि मध्य-प्रदेश में आज कल एक जिला है, पहले यही सिंदवारा के नाम से प्रसिद्ध था। इस का उ० अ० २२°। २'। ३०" दे० ७८°। ५९' पू०।

झारखंड — छत्तीसगढ और गोंडवाने के उत्तर-भाग को मुसल्मानों ने अपने इतिहास-ग्रन्थों में झारखंड नाम से लिखा है। इस में उत्तरीय गोंडवाने का बहुत भाग पहाडी-भाग है जो कि सर्कार चुनार और सूबे बिहार तक चला गया है। (See Hamilton's Description of Hindustan, Vol. II., p. 6; and Āīn-i-Akbarī, Vol. I., Index).

उडीसा — यह आज तक इसी नाम से प्रसिद्ध है।

गज-पति — कलिङ्गदेशाधिपति, महेन्द्राधिपति (राजमहेन्द्री) उत्तरीय-सर्कार के प्राचीन राजाओं की पदवी है, जो कि समुद्र के अधिपति कहलाते थे। (रघुवंश, ७ स०। श्लो० ५४)। और जिस का बडा बन्दर कोरिङ्गा नदी के किनारे पर (जो कि महानदी की एक शाखा है) है। यह बन्दर प्राचीन समय से प्रसिद्ध है। कोरिङ्गा का उ० अ० १६°। ४०'॥ दे० ८२°। ४४' पू०। राजमहेन्द्री का उ० अ० १६°। ५९'॥

दे० ८१°। ५२' पू०। अलाउद्दीन ने (१२९५ ई०) जब दक्षिण पर चढाई की थी। फिरिश्तः (فرشتہ) ने राजमहेन्द्री के राजाओं को स्वतन्त्र राजा कहा है। (See Hamilton's Description of Hindustan, Vol. II., p. 80).

इन सब से सिद्ध होता है, कि 'माँझ रतन-पुर सीह-दुआरा' का रतन-पुर और सिंदवारा दोनों के बीच से होते। और झारखण्ड के पहाडी-भाग को बाईं ओर छोडते (झार-खंड देइ बाउँ पहारा) चलना चाहिए ऐसा अर्थ करना चाहिए। इन सब देशों के अनुसार जिस मार्ग से राजा रत्न-सेन चित्तौर से समुद्र-घाट तक पहुँचा उस का नक्शा अलग पत्र पर लिखा है। विशेष संभव है, कि उस समय यही राह रही हो।

राह में आज कल जो नगर पडते हैं उन के नाम—

चित्तौर, निंबारा (Nimbārā), नीमच, मण्डलेश्वर, जौडा, रतलाम, इन्दोर, नीमार (मृगारण्य = हरिण-पाल), बीजानगर, हँडिया, हुशंगाबाद (अँधियार, खटोला), मण्डला, लाँजी, नवागढ, जयपुर, राजमहेन्द्री, करिङ्गा।

हरिण-पाल तक सब देश राजा के परिचित थे। इस लिये वहाँ तक सुगमता से यात्रा हुई। इसी लिये इस का वर्णन अनावश्यक समझ कवि ने नहीं किया। फिर वहाँ से प्रति दिन दश दश कोस चलने पर एक महीने के आसन्न में लोग गज-पति के यहाँ पहुँचे 'मासेक लाग चलत तेहि बाटा'। नक्शे में हरिण-पाल से राजमहेन्द्री तक नापने से राह ७५० अँगरेजी* मील होती है, जिन के हिन्दुस्तानी कोस ३३० होते हैं जो कि प्रतिदिन दश कोस चलने से ३३ दिन में पूरे पडते हैं। इस नियम से जो राह नक्शे में है वह प्रायः ठीक मालूम होती है। कवि ने मध्य-प्रदेश से विशेष परिचित होने के कारण, वहाँ के अनेक स्व-समय के प्रसिद्ध देशों के नामों को लिखा है। फिर आगे झारखण्ड, उडीसा कह, झट गज-पति तक पहुँचा दिया। उस समय उधर डाँकुओं के रहने के कारण बहुत प्रसिद्ध नगर भी नहीं थे॥

---

* हिन्दुस्तानी कोस = ८००० हाथ। अँगरेजी मील = ५२८० फु० = ३५२० हाथ, इस लिये यदि य, हिन्दुस्तानी कोस में र, मील समझो तो ८००० य = ३५२० र। ३२० का अपवर्त्तन देने से २५ य = ११ र इस लिये यदि य = ११, तो र = २५। अर्थात् अँगरेजी २५ मील में हिन्दुस्तानी ११ कोस होते हैं॥

अथ राजा-गजपति-संबाद-खंड ॥ १३ ॥

चउपाई।

होत पयान जाइ दिन केरा। मिरगारन महँ होत बसेरा ॥
कुस-साँथरि भइ सेज सुपेती। करवट आइ बनी भुइँ सेती ॥
कया मइल तस पुहुमि मलीजइ। चलि दस कोस ओस तन भीजइ ॥
ठावँ ठावँ सब सोअहिँ चेला। राजा जागइ आपु अकेला ॥
जेहि के हिअइ पेम-रँग जामा। का तेहि भूख नीँद बिसरामा ॥
बन अँधिआर रइनि अँधिआरी। भादउ बिरह भएउ अति भारी ॥
किँगरी हाथ गहे बइरागी। पाँच तंत धुनि यह एक लागी ॥

दोहा।

नयन लागु तेहि मारग पदुमावति जेहि दीप।
जइस सेवातिहि सेवई बन चातक जल सीप ॥ १४१ ॥

पयान = प्रयाण = यात्रा = गमन। मिरगारन = मृगारण्य = जिस वन मेँ केवल मृग-ही रहते हैँ। बसेरा = वास = शिविर = डेरा। कुस-साँथरि = कुश-संस्तर = कुश का बिछौना = कुश का आसन। सेज = शय्या। सुपेती = सौप्तिकी = सूतने के योग्य। करवट = प्राकृते कडिवट्टी = संस्कृते कटि-वृत्तिः = करवट करना वा लेना वा बदलना = सूतने मेँ इधर से उधर फिर जाना। बनी = वर्ण्या = वर्णन के योग्य शोभित है।

भुइँ = भूमि । सेती = से । कया = काय = शरीर । मद्दल = मल = मैल । पुहुमि = पृथिवी = पुहुमी । मलीजइ = मलिन होती है (मलिनायते)। दस = दश। कोस = कोश । ओस = अवश्याय, यहाँ पसीने का जल-बिन्दु । तन = तनु = शरीर । भीजइ = भ्रेजते = चमकती है = भीँगती है । वा, भीजइ = भिनत्ति = भिद्यमान होती है । ठावँ = स्थान । सोअहिँ = सोअइ (शेते) का बहु-वचन । जागइ = जागर्त्ति = जागता है । आपु = आप = आत्मा = स्वयम् । अकेला = एकलः । हिअइ = हृदये = हृदय मेँ । पेम = प्रेम । रँग = रङ्ग । जामा = जन्म लिया, वा जम गया । भूख = बुभुक्षा । नीँद = निद्रा । बिसरामा = विश्राम = आराम । अँधिआर = अन्धकार । रइनि = रजनी = रात । अँधिआरी = अँधिआर का स्त्रीलिङ्ग । भादउ = भाद्रपद = भादव महीना, जो वर्षा-ऋतु के मध्य मेँ होता है । बिरह = विरह = वियोग । किँगरी = वैरागियोँ की सारंगी, वाद्य-विशेष । गहे = ग्रहण किये । बइरागी = वैराग्यी = वैरागी = योगी । पाँच = पञ्च । तंत = तन्तु = किँगरी के तार । धुनि = शब्द = आवाज । लागी = लगी । मारग = मार्ग = राह । पदुमावति = पद्मावती । दीप = द्वीप = सिंहल-द्वीप । जइस = यथा = जैसा । सेवातिहि = स्वाती को । सेवई = सेवइ = सेवते । चातक = पपीहा (दोहे की टीका देखो)। सीप = सीपी = शुक्ति, जिस मेँ मोती उत्पन्न होती है ॥

दिन को यात्रा होती जाती है, अर्थात् लोग दिन भर चलते हैँ, (जब संध्या का समय आता है, तब) मृगारण्य मेँ डेरा पडता है, अर्थात् जिस वन मेँ व्याघ्रादि प्राणि-हिंसक जन्तु नहीँ रहते, केवल मृग-ही रहते हैँ, ऐसे वन मेँ, प्राण जाने का भय न रहने से, लोग ठहर जाते हैँ । वा अपने परिचित स्थानोँ के बाहर जाने के लिये लोगोँ ने नर्मदा के तट पर मृगारण्य (हरिण-पाल) मेँ पहला वास किया ॥ कुश की चटाई (साँथरि) (वही) सोने योग्य शय्या हुई है, अर्थात् जो लोग मखमल की शय्या पर सोते थे, वे लोग अब कुश की चटाई पर सोते हैँ । करवट भूमि से आ कर बनी है, अर्थात् भूमि-ही पर करवट लेने की शोभा है, क्योँकि चारपाई पर तो सावधानी से करवट लेना पडता है; सावधानी न रखने से भूमि पर गिर जाना पडता है, और भूमि मेँ तो बे-खटके चाहो करवट लेते कई बल खाते जाओ, परन्तु गिरने का डर नहीँ; सो लोग जमीन-ही पर करवट लेते हैँ ॥ (राह मेँ चलते चलते पदाघात-धूलियोँ से शरीर भर जाती है, इस लिये) जैसी भूमि (खर कतवार, धूर इत्यादि से) मलिन होती है; उसी प्रकार (लोगोँ की) शरीर मलिन हो जाती है।

दश कोस चल कर, अर्थात् दश कोस की कडी मंजिल करने से, शरीर खेद-कण (ओस) से भीँग जाती है। दश के ग्रहण से कवि ने स्पष्ट किया, कि प्रतिदिन लोग दश कोस चलते थे, जो राजकुअँरो के लिये बहुत है॥ (डेरा पडने पर) सब चेला, अर्थात् कुअँर लोग, (यथा योग्य) स्थान स्थान में सोते हैँ, (परन्तु) राजा आप अकेला (पडा) जागा करता है॥ (राजा को क्योँ नहीँ निद्रा आती इस पर कवि कहता है, कि) जिस के हृदय में प्रेम-रङ्ग का जन्म हुआ, वा जिस के हृदय में (गाढा हो कर) प्रेम-रङ्ग जम गया, (फिर) तिस को क्या भूख, निद्रा और विश्राम, अर्थात् इस प्रेम-रस की ऐसी नशा है, कि इस में भूख, प्यास, निद्रा, विश्राम, सब शरीर से बाहर हो जाते हैँ; हृदय, आँख, नाक, कान, बुद्धि, सब में वही प्रेम-रस बस कर तरङ्ग मारा करता है॥ (सघन वन-वृक्षोँ के कारण) अन्धकार वन में, (और) अँधेरी रात में (राजा के लिये पद्मावती का) अत्यन्त भारी विरह (जो है सोई जानेँ) भादव (वर्षा के बीच का मास) हो गया (भएउ)॥ (ऐसी भादोँ की अँधेरी घन-घेरी रैन में) वैरागी, अर्थात् संसार से विरक्त हुआ राजा रत्न-सेन, हाथ में किँगरी को लिये (गहे), (बजा रहा है, जिस के) पाँचो तारोँ की धुनि में यही एक (पद्मावती) लगी है, अर्थात् 'पद्मावती, पद्मावती' यही पाँचो तारोँ में से धुनि निकलती है (जैसे वैरागी सिद्ध होने के लिये अपनी शरीर-रूपी सारंगी के पञ्चतत्त्वरूप वा पञ्चप्राण-रूप तारोँ से 'राम राम' यही धुनि लगाये रहता है)॥

(राजा के) नयन तिसी मार्ग में लग गये, जिस द्वीप में कि पद्मावती है, (जैसे योगी के नयन हृदय-द्वीपान्तर्गत परब्रह्म-रूपा प्रकृति पद्मावती-ही की ओर लग जाते हैँ)। जैसे वन में चातक, जल में सीपी, (ये दोनोँ) स्वाती को सेवते हैँ, अर्थात् स्वाती-ही का भजन किया करते हैँ, (तैसे-ही राजा ने सब संसार के जाल से बाहर हो, केवल 'पद्मावती पद्मावती' रट लगाया है)। आर्द्रा, पुनर्वसु, पुष्य, आश्लेषा, मघा, पूर्वफाल्गुनी, उत्तरफाल्गुनी, हस्त, चित्रा और स्वाती। इन दशोँ नक्षत्रोँ में जब तक सूर्य रहता है, तब तक वर्षा ऋतु रहती है, परन्तु यह प्रसिद्ध कहावत है, कि चातक (पपीहा) स्वाती-ही का जल पीता है। तुलसी-दास ने भी इसी कहावत पर लिखा है, कि

तुलसी के मत चातकहि केवल प्रेम पियास।
पियत स्वाति जल जान जग जाँचत बारह मास॥ (दोहावली) ३०८ दो०।

पपीहे को लोग पालते हैं, और वह सब नक्षत्रों का जल पीता है। मैं नही कह सकता, कि कैसे यह कहावत भारतवर्ष में प्रसिद्ध ऊई। कदाचित् पालने से पपीहे की प्रकृति बदल जाती हो। यह भी प्रसिद्ध कहावत है, कि समुद्र में जो सीपी, एक जन्तु-विशेष, रहता है, वह समुद्र में रह कर भी केवल स्वाती-ही का पानी पीता है, और उस पानी-ही से उस के पेट में मोती का जन्म होता है। किसी मुसल्मानी कवि ने इसी कहावत पर समुद्रान्योक्ति कहा है,

ऐ समंदर देख ली हम ने तेरी दरया दिली।
तिश्ने लब रक्खा सदफ् को बूँद पानी की न दी॥

اى سمندر ديكهه لي همنے تيري دريا دلي
تشنه لب ركها صدف كو بوند پاني كي ندي ॥ १४१ ॥

चउपाई।

मासेक लाग चलत तेहि बाटा। उतरे जाइ समुद के घाटा॥
रतन-सेन भा जोगी जती। सुनि भेँटइ आवा गज-पती॥
जोगी आपु कटक सब चेला। कवन दीप कहँ चाहहिँ खेला॥
भलेहिँ आए अब माया कीजिअ। पहुनाई कहँ आएसु दीजिअ॥
सुनहु गज-पती उतरु हमारा। हम तुम्ह एक-इ भाउ निनारा॥
नेवतहु तेहि जेहि महँ यह भाऊ। जो निरभउ तेहि लाउ नसाऊ॥
इह-इ बहुत जउ बोहित पावउँ। तुम्ह तइँ सिंघल-दीप सिधावउँ॥

दोहा।

जहाँ मोहिँ निजु जाना कटक होउँ लेइ पार।
जउ रे जिअउँ तब लेइ फिरउँ मरउँ त ओहि के बार॥ १४२॥

मासेक = मासेक = एक महीना। लाग = लगा। उतरे = उतरइ (उत्तरति) के भूत-काल का बऊ-वचन। घाटा = घट्ट = घाट। जोगी = योगी। जती = यती। भेँटइ = भेँटने। आवा = आयात् = आया। गज-पती = गज-पति = कलिङ्ग देश का राजा, जो आज कल विजयनगर का राजा मद्रास हाते में है, इस राजा के यहाँ दश हजार हाथी रहते थे; इसी हाथियों की अधिकता से इसे लोग गज-पति कहते थे। आज कल जो ईजानगर के राजा हैं उन के नाम के संग भी 'गज-पति' यह उपाधि लगी ऊई है।

जिस राजा की आज्ञा से प्रोफेसर म्याक्समूलर ने दूसरी वार ऋग्वेद को छपवाया है उस का नाम पशुपति-आनन्द-गजपति-राज था। कालिदास भी कलिङ्ग राजा को प्रशंसा में लिखते हैं, कि

प्रतिजग्राह कालिङ्गस्तमस्त्रैर्गजसाधनः।
पक्षच्छेदोद्यतं शक्रं शिलावर्षीव पर्वतः॥
(रघुवंश, ४सर्ग, ४० श्लो०)

असौ महेन्द्राद्रिसमानसारः पतिर्महेन्द्रस्य महोदधेश्च।
यस्य क्षरत्सैन्यगजच्छलेन यात्रासु यातीव पुरो महेन्द्रः॥
(रघुवंशः ६स० ५४ श्लो०)

जिस प्रकार कलिङ्ग-राजा बहुत हाथी के रहने से गज-पति कहाता है, उसी प्रकार बहुत घोडों के रहने से केकय-राजा को (जिस की पुत्री कैकेयी, अयोध्या के राजा दशरथ से व्याही थी) अश्व-पति कहते हैं। वाल्मीकि ने लिखा है, कि

स तत्र न्यवसद्भ्रात्रा सह सत्कारसत्कृतः।
मातुलेनाश्वपतिना पुत्रस्नेहेन लालितः॥
(वाल्मी० रामा०, अयो० का०, १स० २ श्लो०)

चाहहिँ = चाहइ (चदति, चहति वा इच्छति) का बहु-वचन। खेला = क्रीडा = सैर। माया = करुणा = कृपा = दया। कीजिअ = कीजिये। पहुनाई = प्राघुणीयः = पाहुन के योग्य सत्कार = पहुनई। मुरारिनाटक में लिखा है, कि पाहुणहत्येण सप्पमारणं खु एदं (प्राघुणहस्तेन सर्पमारणं खल्वेतत्)। आएसु = आज्ञा। दीजिअ = दीजिये। उतरु = उत्तर। भाउ = भाव = अभिप्राय। निनारा = निराला = निरालय। नेवतहु = नेवतइ (निमन्त्रयति) का लोट् लकार में मध्यम-पुरुष का एक-वचन। भाऊ = भाव। निरभउ = निर्भाव = विना भाव का। लाउ = लगावो (लगयत)। नसाऊ = नसावो = (नाशय)। इह-इ = यही। जउ = यदि = जो। वोहित = बडी नाव = जहाज। तुम्ह तइँ = तुम्ह तेँ = तुम से। सिधावउँ = सिधाइ (सेधति) का लोट् लकार में उत्तम-पुरुष का एक-वचन = जाऊँ॥ निजु = निज = स्वयम् = आप। बार = द्वार = डेवढी॥

तिस बाट में चलते एक मास लगा। (लोग) समुद्र के घाट (पर) जा कर उतरे॥ (उस घाट का अधिपति कलिङ्गाधिराज) गज-पति, यह सुन कर, कि

(चित्तौर गढ का राजा) रत्न-सेन योगी यती ऊआ है, अर्थात् योगी यती हो कर आया है, भैंट करने आया ॥ (और विनीत हो कर कहा, कि) आप योगी, (और) सब सेना (आप के) शिष्य, कौन द्वीप की सैर किया चाहते हैँ ॥ (बऊत दिनौँ से लालसा थी, कि आप का दर्शन हो, सो) अच्छा ऊआ (भलेहिँ) (कि आप) आये, अब (मेरे ऊपर) अनुग्रह (माया) कीजिये; और पऊनाई के लिये (मुझे) आज्ञा दीजिये, अर्थात् मेरे ऊपर अनुग्रह कर मेरे आतिथ्य को स्वीकार कीजिये ॥ (इस बात को सुन कर राजा रत्न-सेन ने कहा, कि) हे गज-पति, हमारे उत्तर को सुनिये; (इस में संशय नहीँ, कि राज्य, धन, यश, प्रताप, कुल, गोत्र, गौरव इत्यादि मेँ) हम तुम्ह एक-ही हैँ, अर्थात् कुल, गोत्र और राज्य-श्री के नाते से हम आप एक-ही* हैँ, (समान मेँ पऊनई करना शास्त्र-संमत-ही है, परन्तु इस समय मेरा) भाव निराला है, अर्थात् मैं राज्य-श्री से विरक्त हो कर योगी हो गया हूँ, और आप राज्य-श्री मेँ अनुरक्त हैँ, सो योगी और भोगी की कैसी पऊनाई, यह लोक-विरुद्ध है॥ (सो) जिस में यह भाव हो, अर्थात् जो तुमारे ऐसा राज्य-श्री में अनुरक्त हो, तिसे नेवतो। (और) जो निर्भाव है, अर्थात् जो राज्य-श्री से विरक्त हो गया है, तिसे (जो आतिथ्य को) लगावो, अर्थात् उस का जो आतिथ्य करो (तो उसे) नसावो, अर्थात् उस के तप को नाश करो, अर्थात् योगी को भोग-विलास की ओर ले जाना मानो उस के योग को नष्ट करना है॥ (सो मेरे लिये) यही बऊत (सत्कार है, जो आप से) जहाज को पाऊँ, और (आप के अनुग्रह से) सिंहल-द्वीप को जाऊँ। अर्थात् आप यहाँ के प्रधान अधि-पति हैँ, सो विना रोक-टोँक के जहाज इत्यादि के साहाय्य से मुझ सिंहल-द्वीप को पऊँचा देँ, यही मेरे लिये सब से बढ कर सत्कार है॥

जहाँ, अर्थात् जिस सिंहल-द्वीप में, मुझे स्वयं जाना है, (सो भी अकेले नहीँ, किन्तु) कटक ले कर पार होऊँ, अर्थात् कटक ले कर पार होना चाहता हूँ। (सो) अरे गज-पति, जो जीऊँ, अर्थात् यदि जीव है, मर न गया, (तो यही इच्छा है, कि पद्मावती को) ले कर तब फिरूँ; और मरूँ तो उसी (पद्मावती) के द्वार पर मरूँ, अर्थात् या तो पद्मावती को संग-ही ले कर फिरूँगा, या उस की डेवढी पर प्राण तजूँगा ॥ १४२॥

---

* इतिहासोँ से स्पष्ट है कि चित्तौर-राज-वंश ही का गज-पति था। आज कल के जो विजयनगर के राजा हैँ वह भी अपने को उदयपुर (चित्तौर) महाराज के वंश मेँ बतलाते हैँ ॥

चउपाई।

गज-पति कहा सीस पर माँगा। एतनी बोलि न होइहि खाँगा ॥
ए सब देउँ आनि नउ-गढे। फूल सोई जो महेसहि चढे ॥
पइ गोसाइँ सउँ एक बिनाती। मारग कठिन जाब केहि भाँती ॥
सात समुदर असूझ अपारा। मारहिँ मगर मच्छ घरिआरा ॥
उठइ लहरि नहिँ जाइ सँभारी। भागहिँ कोइ निबहइ बइपारी ॥
तुम्ह सुखिआ अपनइ घर राजा। एत जोखीउँ सहहु केहि काजा ॥
सिंघल-दीप जाइ सो कोई। हाथ लिए आपन जिउ होई ॥

दोहा।

खार खीर दधि जल-उदधि सुर किलकिला अकूत।
को चढि नाँघइ समुद ए (सात-उ) हइ का कर अस बूत ॥ १४३ ॥

गज-पति = समुद्र-तट का अधिपति = कलिङ्ग का राजा। सीस = शीर्ष = शिर। माँगा = माँगा हुआ = याचना। एतनी = इयत्। बोलि = बोली = वचन। होइहि = होगी। खाँगा = खञ्ज = खाली। आनि = आनीय = ले आ कर = आन कर। नउ-गढे = नव-गढे नये गढे हुए। महेसहि = महेश को। पइ = अपि = परन्तु। गोसाइँ = गो-स्वामी = गो (इन्द्रियाँ) के स्वामी = इन्द्रियों को अपने आधीन रखने-वाला। सउँ = सोँ = से। बिनाती = विनति = विज्ञप्तिका = विनय। मारग = मार्ग = राह। जाब = जाइयेगा = जाइ (याति) का भविष्यत्काल। भाँती = भङ्गी = रीति, जो काठिन्य को भग्न करे = प्रकार। सात = सप्त। समुदर = समुद्र। असूझ = असूह्य = जो ऊहा योग्य नहीँ = जो न देख पडे वा असूझ = अशुद्ध। अपारा = अपार = जिस का पार न हो। मगर = मकर = एक विशिष्ट जल-जन्तु। मच्छ = मत्स्य = रोहू, पहिने, तिमिङ्गिलादि। घरिआरा = ग्राह = घरियार। भागहिँ = भाग्येभ्यः = भाग्योँ से। निबहइ = निर्वहति = निबहता है। बइपारी = व्यापारी व्यापार करने-वाला = वणिक्। सुखिआ = सुखी = सुख-चाहने-वाले। अपनइ = अपने। एत = इयत् = इतना। जोखीउँ = जोखिम = नुकसान = हानि। सहहु = सहइ (सहते)

का लोट् लकार में मध्यम-पुरुष का बहु-वचन ॥ खार = चार = खारा । खीर = चीर = दुग्ध = दूध । जल-उदधि = जल का समुद्र । सुर = सुरा = मद्य । किलकिला = 'किल-किला' ऐसा जल के लहरोँ से घोर शब्द करने-वाला समुद्र । अकूत = अकूतः = जिस को कूत न सकैं कि, इतना है, अर्थात् जो असंख्य रत्नोँ से परिपूरित हो, इस का नाम कवि ने १६१ वेँ दोहे में 'मान-सर' कहा है । नाँघइ = लाँघइ = लङ्घयेत् = नाँघे = लाँघे । बूत = भूति = पराक्रम ॥

गज-पति ने कहा, कि (आप की यह) याचना, (कि मुझे बोहित मिलैँ, जिन से सेना समेत, समुद्र पार हो कर, सिंहल-दीप को जाऊँ) मेरे शिर पर है, अर्थात् आप की आज्ञा शिरो-धार्य है। इतने वचन में चुटि (कसर) न होगी, अर्थात् आप के इस वचन को मैं अवश्य-ही पूरा करूँगा ॥ ये सब (जहाजों) को (मैं) नये गढे हुए देऊँ, अर्थात् जो जहाज नये-गढे हुए हैं, जिन से आज तक अभी काम नहीं लिये गये हैं, उन सब को ला कर आप के लिये मैं दे सकता हूँ; (क्योंकि) जो फूल महेश (महादेव) को चढे, वही फूल फूल है, अर्थात् महादेव के शिर पर चढने-ही से फूल का नाम फूल पडा है, नहीं तो वे किस काम के। इसी प्रकार आप ऐसे महानुभावोँ की उचित सेवा करने-ही से मैं गज-पति कहलाता हूँ, नहीं तो मैं दक्षिण का रहने-वाला किस गिनती में। इस लिये जैसे चुन चुन के उत्तम प्रसून ईशान के पूजन के लिये लोग रखते हैं इसी प्रकार मैं भी चुन चुन कर, अति नूतन-ही बोहितोँ को आप की सेवा में समर्पण करूँगा ॥ परन्तु गो-स्वामी से, अर्थात् आप योगि-राज से, एक विनती है, कि (सिंहल की) राह कठिन है, (आप) किस प्रकार से जाइयेगा, अर्थात् आप के जाने योग्य सिंहल की राह नहीं है ॥ (क्योंकि उस राह में) असूझ और अपार सात समुद्र हैं, (जिन में) मगर, मच्छ और घरियार (प्राणियोँ को) मार डालते हैं ॥ (उन सातो में ऐसी) लहर उठती हैं जो सँभारी नहीं जाती हैं, अर्थात् उन के धक्कोँ से बडे बडे जहाज नहीं सँभर सकते, मनुष्योँ की क्या गिनती है। भाग्योँ से (हजारोँ में) कोई (एकाध) बैपारी निबह जाता है, अर्थात् उन सातोँ के पार हो जाता है ॥ (सो) आप, हे राजा, अपने घर के (सदा के) सुखिया हो, किस काम के लिये इतना जोखिम सहते हो, अर्थात् काहे जी के ऊपर खेलते हो ॥ (राजन्, निश्चय जानिये) वह कोई (विरला) सिंहल-दीप को जाता है, जो कि अपने जीव को हाथ में लिये हो, अर्थात् जो अपने जीव को,

काल के दानार्थ, संकल्प करने के लिये हाथ मैं लिये हो, वह सिंहल-दीप को जा सकता है; आप ऐसे सदा के सुखियों का काम नहीं, कि सिंहल-दीप जाने का साहस करे॥

चार, चीर, दधि, जलोदधि, सुरा, किलकिला और अकूत, ये सात समुद्र हैं। कौन (ऐसा है जो जहाज पर) चढ कर, इन सातो समुद्रों को नाँघे; (और) किस का ऐसा पराक्रम है (जो इन सातो के लाँघने के लिये साहस करे)। पुराणों मैं सर्वत्र चार, चीर, दधि, घृत, इचु-रस, सुरा, और खादु-जल के समुद्र लिखे हैं; इन में चार, चीर, दधि, सुरा, खादु-जल = जल, ये मलिक महम्मद के कहे ऊए समुद्रों से मिलते हैं; केवल इचु-रस और घृत इन दोनों के स्थान में यहाँ किलकिला और अकूत हैं। ऊख के रस को जब कराहे में खौलाते हैं, तब वह भी भयङ्कर तरङ्ग और किलकिला अव्यक्त शब्द करने लगता है, (भारत शल्य पर्व, अध्याय ३०, श्लो, ४६ में भी लिखा है कि 'ततः किलकिला शब्दः प्रादुरासीद्विशाम्पते'।) और दूध से दधि, दधि-मन्थन से तब सब दूधों का रत्न-रूप घृत उत्पन्न होता है। इस लिये जान पडता है, कि कवि ने भयङ्कर किलकिला शब्द को ले कर इचु-रस के स्थान में 'किलकिला', और रत्नों से भरा रत्न-रूप, मानसर वा अकूत, रत्न-रूप घृत के स्थान में रक्खा। ऐसे तात्पर्य से एक-वाक्यता हो जाती है॥१४३॥

चउपाई।

गज-पति यह मन-सकती सीऊ। पइ जेहि पेम कहाँ तेहि जीऊ॥
जो पहिलइ सिर देइ पगु धरई। मूए केरि मीचु का करई॥
सुख सँकलपि दुख साँबरि लीन्हा। तउ पयान सिंघल कहँ कीन्हा॥
भवँर जान पइ कवँल पिरीती। जेहि महँ बिथा पेम कइ बीती॥
अउ जेइ समुद पेम कर देखा। तेइ एहि समुद बूँद परि-लेखा॥
सात समुद सत कीन्ह सँभारू। जउ धरती का गरुअ पहारू॥
जेइ पइ जिउ बाँधा सत बेरा। बरु जिउ जाइ फिरइ नहिँ फेरा॥

दोहा।

रंग नाथ हउँ जा कर हाथ ओही के नाथ।
गहे नाथ सो खाँचई फेरत फिरइ न माथ॥१४४॥

मन-सकती = मनः-शक्ति = मन की शक्ति, अर्थात् जीव। सीउ = शिक्षा = सीख। पइ = अपि, यहाँ परन्तु। पेम = प्रेम। जीऊ = जीव। सिर = शिर। देइ = दत्त्वा = दे कर। पगु = प्रग = पग = पैर। धरई = (धरति) धरता है। मूए = मरे ऊए = म्टतक। मीचु = म्टत्यु। करई = (करोति) = करता है। सँकलपि = संकल्प्य = संकल्प कर = दे कर। दुख = दुःख। साँबरि = संबल = राह-खर्च। तउ = तदा = तब। पयान = प्रयाण = गमन = याचा। जान = जानइ = (जानाति)। कवँल = कमल। पिरीती = प्रीति = स्नेह। बिथा = व्यथा = पीडा। बीती = बीतइ (व्यत्येति) का भूत-काल में स्त्रीलिङ्ग का एक-वचन। समुद = समुद्र। बूँद = बिन्दु। परि-लेखा = परि-लिखइ (परि-लिखति) का भूत-काल। सात = सप्त। सत = सत् = सत्य-प्रेम। सँभारू = सम्भार = भार = बोझा। धरती = धरित्री = पृथ्वी। गरुअ = गुरु = गढू = भारी। पहारू = प्रहार वा प्रस्तार = पहाड। बाँधा = बाँधइ (बध्नाति) का भूत-काल। बेरा = बेडा = नाव। बरु = वर = बल्कि = चाहे। फिरइ = (स्फुरति) फिरता है = लौटता है। फेरा = फेरने से = लौटाने से॥ रंग = प्रेम-रङ्ग। नाथ = नाथा ऊआ (नाथृ बन्धने)। हउँ = अस्मि = हूँ। हाथ = हस्त। नाथ = बन्धन = नकेल। गहे = गृह्णन् = पकडे ऊए। खाँचई = (कर्षति) खीँचइ = खीँचता है। फेरत = फेरने से। माथ = मस्तक, यहाँ शिर॥

(राजा रत्न-सेन ने कहा, कि) गज-पति, यह (आप की) शिक्षा मन की शक्ति (जीव) से है, अर्थात् यदि जीव ठेकाने रहे, तो मन इस शिक्षा को मान सकता है॥ परन्तु जिस के (हृदय में) प्रेम ऊआ, अर्थात् प्रेम ने प्रवेश किया, तिस को कहाँ जीव, (क्योँकि एक म्यान में दो तलवार नहीँ रह सकती, एक वन में दो सिंह नहीँ रह सकते, एक नगर में दो राजाओँ का अधिकार नहीँ हो सकता, सो जीव से बडा प्रतापी जो प्रेम, सो मेरे हृदय में अधिकार कर लिया, अब जीव का कहाँ ठेकाना)॥ जो पहले-ही शिर दे कर, पैर धरता है, (१२५ वेँ दोहे में शुक के उपदेश से राजा ने संकल्प कर लिया था, कि पद्मावती के प्रेम-मार्ग में शिर काट कर दे दूँगा, और उस मार्ग में चलूँगा; इस पर राजा कहता है, कि मैं पहले-ही शिर दे कर तब इस प्रेम-मार्ग में चलने को तयार ऊआ। सो जो पहले-ही से शिर दे कर मार्ग में पैर को धरता है, वह तो मरा-ही है, और मरने पर तब मार्ग में चल रहा है, इस लिये मार्ग में परम क्लेश की मर्यादा है म्टत्यु सो) मरे ऊए को म्टत्यु क्या करती है, अर्थात् कुछ नहीँ कर सकती, मरे को क्या मारेगी॥ (मैं) सुख को

संकल्प कर (इस राह की) खर्ची दुःख-ही को लिया, अर्थात् पहले-ही से समझ लिया, कि इस प्रेम-मार्ग में दुःख-ही खाने पीने को मिलेगा; (ऐसा मन में दृढ कर) तब सिंहल की याचा किया॥ (हे गज-पति, मेरी इस बात को सुन कर, संभव है, कि आप मुझे मन में पागल समझते हों,) परन्तु (निश्चय समझिये, कि) निश्चय से भ्रमर-ही कमल की प्रीति जानता है; जिस में प्रेम की व्यथा बीती है, अर्थात् कमल-विरह से जो असह्य पीडा होती है, उसे भ्रमर भोग चुका है, तब कमल-प्रीति के सुख को जानता है, जिस से लुब्ध हो रात में कमल के संपुटित होने पर कैदी-सा पडा रहता है, परन्तु वहाँ से टरता नहीं। सो आप के ऊपर प्रेम-व्यथा नहीं बीती है, आप इस को नहीं जान सकते; कहावत है, कि 'न हि वन्ध्या विजानाति सूतिका-परिवेदनाम्' 'बाझ न जान प्रसव की पीरा'। 'जा के पैर न फटी बेवाई। वह का जानइ पीर पराई'॥ और जिस ने प्रेम का समुद्र देख लिया, तिस ने इस समुद्र (चार, चीर, इत्यादि) को बूँद लिखा है, अर्थात् तिस के मत से ये समुद्र, जिन का भयङ्कर वृत्तान्त आप ने सुनाया है, एक जल-विन्दु के समान हैं॥ सत्, अर्थात् मेरा सत्य-प्रेम सातो समुद्रोँ का सँभार किया है, अर्थात् सातो समुद्रोँ का जो दुःख-भार है, उसे मेरा सत्य-प्रेम सँभालेगा, (क्योंकि) यदि पृथ्वी है, (तो उस के आगे) पहाड की गुरुता (भार) क्या है, अर्थात् कुछ भी नहीं है। पृथ्वी सब पहाडोँ की गुरुता सँभाले-ही है; इसी प्रकार धरित्री-सदृश मेरा सत् (सत्य-प्रेम) पहाड-सदृश सातो समुद्रोँ के दुःख-भार को अवश्य सँभालेगा॥ जिन्होँ ने निश्चय से, जीव से सत-रूपी नाव को बाँधा है, अर्थात् जीव को पक्का कर सत-रूपी नाव को जो तयार कर लिया है; वे लोग (उस नाव पर चढ कर) चाहे जीव (चला) जाय (परन्तु) फिर फेरने से नहीं फिरते॥

(सो हे गज-पति) रंग, अर्थात् प्रेम-रङ्ग, (जिस का वर्णन १४१ वेँ दोहे में 'जेहि के हिअइ पेम-रँग जामा। का तेहि भूख नीँद बिसरामा॥' यह कर आये हैं) जिस का मैं नाथा हूँ, उसी के हाथ में नाथ है, अर्थात् नकेल है। (वही प्रेम-रङ्ग) नकेल को पकडे खीँच रहा है, (मेरा) शिर (माथ) फेरने से नहीं फिरता, अर्थात् आप की शिक्षा मन में आती है परन्तु क्या करूँ, लाचार हूँ, पद्मावती का प्रेम-रङ्ग मुझे नाथ कर अपने प्रबल कर से पद्मावती-ही की ओर खीँच रहा है, किसी प्रकार से मेरा शिर फेरने से नहीं फिरता है॥ १४४॥

चउपाई ।

पेम-समुदर अइस अउगाहा । जहाँ न वार न पार न थाहा ॥
जउ वह समुद गाह एहि परे । जउ अउगाह हंस हिअ तरे ॥
हउँ पदुमावति कर भिख-मंगा । दिसिटि न आउ समुद अउ गंगा ॥
जेहि कारन गिउ काँथरि-कंथा । जहाँ सो मिलइ जाउँ तेहि पंथा ॥
अब एहि समुद परेउँ होइ मरा । पेम मोर पानी कइ करा ॥
मर होइ बहा कतहुँ लेइ जाऊ । ओहि के पंथ कोउ धरि खाऊ ॥
अस मन जानि समुद मँह परऊँ । जउ कोइ खाइ बेगि निसतरऊँ ॥

दोहा ।

सरग सीस धर धरती हिआ सो पेम-समुंद ।
नयन कउडिआ होइ रहे लेइ लेइ उठहिँ सो बुंद ॥ १४५ ॥

पेम-समुदर = प्रेम-समुद्र = प्रेम का समुद्र । अइस = एतादृश = ऐसा । अउगाहा = अवगाढ = कठिन । वार = जिधर खडे हो उधर का तट । पार = दूसरी ओर का तट । थाहा = तल = थाह । जउ = यदि । समुद = समुद्र । गाह = गाध = थाह = जो अथाह न हो = जिसे थहा सकते हैं । अउगाह = अगाध = अतल-स्पर्श = जिस के तल का पता न लगे = जिस की गहराई का पता न लगे । हंस = एक पक्षि-विशेष, यहाँ प्राण । हिअ = हृदय । तरे = तरइ (तरति) का भूत-काल में बहु-वचन । पदुमावति = पद्मावती । भिख-मंगा = भिक्षुक = भिखारी = भीख माँगने-वाला । दिसिटि = दृष्टि = नेत्र = आँख । गंगा = गङ्गा, प्रसिद्ध पवित्र नदी । कारन = कारण = सबब = हेतु । गिउ = ग्रीवा = गला । काँथरि = कथरी = गुदरी । कंथा = कन्था = गुदरी का चोलना । मिलइ = मिले = मिलइ (मिलति) का लिङ् लकार में प्रथम-पुरुष का एक-वचन । मरा = मर = मृतक = मुर्दा । पेम = प्रेम । पानी = पानीय = जल । करा = कला = अंश = भाग । बहा = बहइ (वहति) का भूत-काल । कतहुँ = कुत्र हि = कुत्रापि = कहीं । धरि = धृत्वा = धर कर = पकड कर । खाऊ = खाउ = खावे = खाइ (खादति) का लिङ् का प्रथम-पुरुष में एक-वचन । जानि = ज्ञात्वा = जान कर । परऊँ = परइ (पतति) का लोट् में उत्तम-पुरुष का एक-वचन, यहाँ परऊँ = परउँ = पडता हूँ ।

खाइ = खावे = खाय = खाद (खादति) का लिङ् में प्रथम-पुरुष का एक-वचन। बेगि = वेग = शीघ्र। निसतरऊँ = निसतरइ (निस्तरति) का लोट् में उत्तम-पुरुष का एक-वचन॥ सरग = स्वर्ग = आकाश। सीस = शीर्ष = शिर। धर = धरा = धड = शिर के नीचे का शरीर-भाग। धरती = धरित्री = पृथ्वी। पेम-समुंद = प्रेम-समुद्र। कउडिआ = कपर्दिका = कौडी। उठहिँ = उठइ (उत्तिष्ठते) का बहु-वचन। बुंद = विन्दु॥

(राजा रत्न-सेन गज-पति से कहता है, कि) प्रेम का समुद्र ऐसा कठिन है, जहाँ न वार, न पार, न थाह है, अर्थात् उस के सीमा का पता-ही नहीँ है, कि कहाँ तक है, और न उस की गम्भीरता-ही किसी के मन में आती॥ (सो) यदि इस (एहि) (आप के कहे समुद्र) में पडने से (परे) वह (प्रेम-समुद्र) गाध हो यदि (वा) अगाध हो (परन्तु) हृदय के हंस, अर्थात् प्राण, (उस प्रेम-समुद्र को अवश्य) तरे हैँ, अर्थात् अवश्य तरैंगे, यह निश्चय है। हंस उडने में कभी थकते नहीँ, चाहें तो दिन रात उडा करें; इसी तात्पर्य से रत्न-सेन ने अपने प्राणों को हंस बनाया, कि ये चलने में थकने-वाले नहीँ; इस लिये अवश्य-ही प्रेम-समुद्र को तरैंगे। भारत में कथा है, कि एक वेर सब पक्षियों ने मिल कर हंस को अपना राजा बनाया; इस पर वैश्य-पुत्रों के बहकाने से काक ने कहा, कि हंस में कौन गुण है, राजा होने के योग्य मैं हूँ। इस विवाद पर काक और प्रधान हंस दोनों समुद्र के इस पार से उस पार और विना विश्राम लिये उस पार से इस पार आने के लिये उडे। काक इधर से जाते-ही थक कर, समुद्र में गिर पडा, और हंस, विना विश्राम के इस पार से उस पार चला गया, और उधर से इस पार चला आया; राह में मृत-प्राय जल में पडे काक को भी पीठ पर लादे हुये चला आया। इस से पक्षियों को निश्चय हो गया, कि हंस के उडने का वेग अमोघ है (भारत-कर्ण-पर्व, अध्याय ४१)॥ (रत्न-सेन कहता है, कि मैं) पद्मावती का भिखमंगा हूँ, अर्थात् मुझे जिस भिक्षा की इच्छा है, वह भिक्षा पद्मावती-ही के पास है, इस लिये मैं दूसरे के द्वार पर भिक्षुक बन कर, उस भिक्षा को नहीँ पा सकता; केवल पद्मावती-ही के द्वार का भिक्षुक हूँ, (इस लिये संसार के सुख-साधन-सामग्रियों के लिये प्रधान जो रत्न, उन से भरा) समुद्र, और (परलोक-सुख की दात्री) गङ्गा, (दोनों) (मेरी) दृष्टि में नहीँ आते, (क्योंकि जिस रत्न का मैं भिक्षुक हूँ, वह इन दोनों के पास नहीँ है)॥ (सो) जिस (पद्मावती-रत्न) के कारण गले में

कथरी का कन्था (पडा) है; वह (सो) जहाँ मिले उसी राह में मैं जाऊं, अर्थात् जाऊँगा ॥ (सो) अब (तो) इस (प्रेम-समुद्र) में मुर्दा हो कर, पडा हूं; जिस मैं, अर्थात् जिस समुद्र में मेरा प्रेम पानी का भाग है, अर्थात् जैसे दूध, दही, सुरा के समुद्रों मैं क्रम से जल के स्थान मैं दूध, दही, और सुरा हैं; उसी प्रकार इस प्रेम के समुद्र मैं जल के स्थान मैं मेरा प्रेम है ॥ (सो अब तो) मुर्दा हो कर (प्रेम-समुद्र मैं) बहा हूँ, (चाहे वह समुद्र) कहीं ले जाय; (चाहे) उस (पद्मावती) की राह मैं कोई पकड कर (धरि) खावे (मुझे इस की कुछ भी परवाह नहीं)॥ ऐसा मन मैं जान कर, (इस) समुद्र मैं पडता हूँ। यदि कोई (मुझे) खावे तो (भला है, क्योंकि इस अपार विरह-सागर से) शीघ्र निस्तरों, अर्थात् शीघ्र निस्तार पाऊं ॥

(मेरा) शिर तो स्वर्ग पर (टँगा) है, और धड धरती पर (पडी) है, अर्थात् शिर में जो मस्तिस्क (मगज़) है, वह नष्ट हो गया है, केवल धड बे-काम हो कर, धरती पर पडी है, (और) हृदय मैं वह (सो) प्रेम-समुद्र है, अर्थात् हृदय में वह प्रेम-समुद्र, तरल तरङ्ग मार रहा है। दोनों नयन (उस समुद्र के) कौडी हो रहे हैं; बूँदों को ले ले कर उठते हैं, अर्थात् पद्मावती के ध्यान से जब तक नयन बंद रहते हैं, तब तक जानों नयन-रूपी कौडी उस प्रेम-समुद्र मैं डूबी रहती हैं, और जब विरह-व्यथा से व्याकुल होने से उन नयनों मैं जल-विन्दु भर जाते हैं, तब जो नयन खुल जाते हैं, उन की छवि ऐसी है, जानों उस प्रेम-समुद्र की कौडियाँ प्रेम-विन्दु को ले ले कर ऊपर उठ आई हैं। कौडी, घोंघे के सदृश एक समुद्र का जल-जन्तु है, जो प्रायः सर्वत्र प्रसिद्ध है। भाषा मैं नयन शब्द पुलिङ्ग है, इस लिये K 3 पुस्तक के पाठ 'होइ रहे' को उत्तम समझ, मूल मैं निवेशन किया है। बहुत रोते रोते आँखों की काली पुतली मैं सफेदी आ जाती हैं, इस लिये आँखों मैं विशेष सफेदी आ जाने से कौडी की उपमा देना बहुत-ही योग्य है ॥ १४५ ॥

चउपाई ।

कठिन बिओग जोग दुख-दाहू। जरत मरत होइ ओर निबाहू ॥
डर लज्जा तहँ दुअ-उ गवाँनी। देखइ किछू न आगि न पानी ॥
आगि देखि ओहि आगइ धावा। पानि देखि तेहि सउँह धसावा ॥

जस बाउर न बुझाए बूझा। जउनहि भाँति जाइ का सूझा॥
मगर मच्छ डर हिअइ न लेखा। आपुहि चहइ पारभा देखा॥
अउ न खाहिँ ओहि सिंघ सँदूरा। काठ-हु चाहि अधिक सो झूरा॥
काया माया संग न आथी। जेहि जिउ सउँपा सोई साथी॥

दोहा।

जो किछु दरब अहा सँग दान दीन्ह संसार।
का जानी केहि सत सती दइउ उतारइ पार॥ १४६॥

बिओग = वियोग = विरह = जुदाई। जोग = योग। दुख = दुःख। दाह्र = दाह = ताप = जलन। जरम = जनम = जन्म। जरत = जरता है = जरइ = ज्वलति। ओर = अन्त = अ-लव। निबाह्र = निर्वाह। डर = भय। लज्जा = लाज = शर्म। दुअ-उ = द्वावपि = दोनों। गवाँनी = गमन कर जाती हैं = चली जाती हैं = खो जाती हैं। किछू = किञ्चित् = किछु = कुछ। आगि = अग्नि = आग। पानी = पानीय। आगइ = अग्रे = आगे। धावा = धाव = धावइ (धावति)। सउँह = सन्मुख = सामने। धसावा = धसा-आवा = धसा आता है, धसा = धसइ (ध्वंसते) का भूत-काल। आवा = आव = आवइ (आयाति) = आता है। बाउर = वातुल = बौरहा। बुझाए = बुझाने से = समझाने से। बूझा = बूझइ = (बुद्ध्यते)। जउनहि = य एव नु हि = जौन। भाँति = भङ्गी = रीति, जिस से संशय भग्न हो। सूझा = सूह्म = सुन्दर रूहा, यहाँ सूझा = देखा = सूझइ (शुध्यति) का भूत-काल। मगर = मकर = एक भयङ्कर जल-जन्तु। मच्छ = मत्स्य, रोह्र, पढ़िना इत्यादि। हिअइ = हृदये = हृदय में। लेखा = लेख = लिखइ (लिखति) = लिखता है = अर्थात् ख्याल करता है। पारभा = प्रभा = अपने प्यारे की कान्ति, जिस का कि प्रेम उत्पन्न हुआ है। खाहिँ = खाइ (खादति) का बहु-वचन। सिंघ = सिंह = प्रसिद्ध गज-वैरी जन्तु। सँदूरा = शार्दूल = एक प्रकार का व्याघ्र (शार्दूलद्वीपिनौ व्याघ्रौ, अमरकोश)। काठ-हु = काष्ठतोऽपि = काठ से भी। चाहि = च हि = निश्चय से। झूरा = झीर्ण = सूखा। काया = काय = शरीर। माया = पुत्र दारादि का स्नेह। आथी = अस्ति = सार वस्तु। जिउ = जीव। सउँपा = समर्पण किया। सोई = स एव = वही। साथी = सार्थी = सङ्गी॥ दरब = द्रव्य = धन। अहा = आसीत् = था। सँग = सङ्ग। सत = सत् = सत्पुरुष = सज्जन। सती = पतिव्रता = सुशीला

= साध्वी स्त्री । दइउ = देव = भगवान् = ईश्वर । उतारइ = उतारे = उतारइ (उत्तारयति) का लिङ् लकार में प्रथम-पुरुष का एक-वचन ॥

(कवि कहता है, कि) वियोग के योग से, अर्थात् विरहाग्नि के संयोग से कठिन दुख-दाह है, अर्थात् कठिन दुःख देने-वाला दाह (ताप) उत्पन्न होता है, (जिस से विरही) जन्म (भर) जरा करता है, अन्त में निर्वाह होता है, अर्थात् अन्त में प्राण देने-ही से छुटकारा पाता है, और कोई उपाय-ही नहीं, जिस से वह ताप शान्त हो। कवि का अभिप्राय है, कि योग साधते साधते मर कर, दूसरी काया पाने से, और सिद्ध हो जाने से, जिस का विरह हुआ है, उस के मिलने-ही से वह दाह शान्त होता है॥ तहाँ, अर्थात् विरहाग्नि-दाहावस्था में डर और लज्जा दोनों निकल जाती हैं, अर्थात् जैसे साधारण आग में सुवर्ण को तपाने से सुवर्ण-मिलित मालिन्य भस्म हो जाते हैं; उसी प्रकार विरहाग्नि के बीच में पड़ने से शरीरस्थ लोकापवाद-जन्य लज्जा, और प्राण जाने का भय, ये दोनों भस्म हो जाते हैं, (इस लिये वह विरही प्राणी) न आग, न पानी, कुछ भी नहीं देखता है (क्योंकि देखे तो तब जब प्राण का भय हो)॥ (वह विरही) आग देख कर, उस के आगे-ही दौडता है। पानी देख कर, उस के सामने धसा आता है॥ जैसे बौरहा समझाने से नहीं समझता, (चाहे) जौन भाँति से (कहो) क्या सूझा जाता है? अर्थात् क्या उस को कुछ सूझ पडता है? अर्थात् नहीं सूझ पडता, (उसी प्रकार से विरही को भी कुछ नहीं सूझ पडता)॥ (वह विरही) हृदय में मगर मच्छ के डर का लेखा नहीं करता, अर्थात् समुद्र में जाने से मगर मच्छ खा जायँगे; इस का उस को कुछ परवाह-ही नहीं; (वह) आप-ही प्रभा को देखा चाहता है, अर्थात् जिस के विरह-दाह से मर रहा है, उस के कान्ति-दर्शन-ही को वह सब से प्रधान समझता है॥ और उसे सिंह व्याघ्र भी नहीं खाते हैं (खाने के लिये जहाँ उस के निकट आये तहाँ विरहाग्नि-ज्वाल से उन के मुह जरने लगते हैं, इस लिये सिंह व्याघ्र भी विरही को नहीं खाते, यह कवि का तात्पर्य है)। विरहिणी के वर्णन में खानखाना ने भी यह बरवा लिखा है —

'बिरहिनि ढूँढन बन गइ बाघ भेंटान। बघवा सूँघि न खाएस बिरहिनि जान ॥'।

(और विरह-ज्वाल के ताप से) वह (विरही) काठ से भी अधिक निश्चयेन झूर, अर्थात् शुष्क रहता है॥ उस के संग में न (उस की) शरीर, न (घर की) माया,

न अस्ति (कुछ खाने पीने की चीज) कुछ भी नहीँ रहती, जिस को (उस ने अपना) जीव सौँप दिया है, वही (केवल उस का) साथी है, अर्थात् जिस के लिये घर बार छोड, प्राण देने को तयार है, वही उपास्य-देवता-सदृश उस का साथी है॥

(सो) जो कुछ द्रव्य संग में थी, सब को संसार में दे दिया, अर्थात् राजा रत्न-सेन ने, इस बुद्धि से, उस स्थान में जितने गज-पति के राज्य में सत्पात्र लोग थे सब में अपने साथ का धन दान दे कर, लुटा दिया, कि क्या जानें किस सत् (पुरुष) और सती (स्त्री) (के आशीर्वाद) से भगवान (समुद्र के) पार उतारे, क्योँकि शास्त्र में लिखा है, कि दान पुण्य से क्या नहीँ होता। कहावत है, कि एक वार अकबर ने बीरबर से पूँछा, कि संसार में सब से बढ कर कौन कर्म है, जो मृत्यु को भी कुछ काल के लिये हटा दे; इस पर बीरबर ने कहा, कि पृथ्वीनाथ, यह सामर्थ्य दान-ही में है जो कि मृत्यु को भी कुछ काल के लिये हटा देता है। इस पर बादशाह चुप हो रहे। कुछ दिन बीते बादशाह बीरबर को संग लिये वाटिका-विहार करते थे। अकस्मात् हाथ के ऊपर एक काक ने बीट कर दी, उस के धोने के समय अँगूठी में पानी न लगे इस बुद्धि से बादशाह ने अपने मोहर की अँगूठी को निकाल, बीरबर के हाथ में दिया और कहा, कि खबर्दार इसे खो मत देना, खो देने से जान से हाथ धो बैठोगे। निदान लौटने पर, स्मरण न रहने से बीरबर, अँगूठी अपने जेब में रक्खे, अपने घर आये, और बादशाह अपनी महल में पधारे। वहाँ बादशाह को स्मरण ऊआ, कि बीरबर के छकाने के लिये यह अवसर अच्छा उपस्थित ऊआ है; सो यह सोच किसी चतुर चार के द्वारा बीरबर के जेब में से उस मुदरी को चुरवा मँगाया, और जिस में किसी प्रकार से मुद्रिका न पाई जाय, यह विचार, उसे अपने हाथ से यमुना में फेंक दिया, और प्रातःकाल होते-ही मुद्रिका के लिये बीरबर के घर सिपाही को भेजा। बीरबर अपने जेब में मुद्रिका को न पा कर, बऊत घबराये, और सिपाही से कहा, कि बादशाह से प्रार्थना करो, कि सन्ध्या के समय दर्बार में मैं मुद्रिका के साथ स्वयमुपस्थित ऊँगा। सिपाही के चले जाने पर, सब घर बाहर ढूँढा, मुद्रिका कहीँ न मिली, तब बादशाह की आज्ञा स्मरण कर, बीरबर अपने जीने की आशा दूर कर, और यह विचार कर, कि अब मरण समय में दान पुण्य करना चाहिये, दीनोँ को दान देने लगे। दान-दुन्दुभि सुन कर, नाना प्रकार के लोग बीरबर के घर दौडे। एक मल्लाह भी एक विशाल मत्स्य को, जिसे तुरन्त-ही यमुना में फँसाया था,

ले कर, वहाँ पङँचा, और बीरबर को वह मत्स्य भेंट में दिया, जिस के बदले बीरवर से बङत कुछ पाया। बीरवर ने आज्ञा दिया, कि इस मत्स्य को पकावो, और जो गरीब, खाने लायक हेां, उन्हेँ और व्यञ्जनोँ के साथ इसे भी खिलावो। पकाने के लिये लोगोँ ने मत्स्य को फाडा तो उस के पेट में से वही बादशाही मोहर-वाली मुद्रिका निकली, जिसे ले कर, बडे आनन्द से बीरबर सन्ध्या को दर्बार में पङँचे, और बादशाह के हाथ में उस मुदरी को दी। बादशाह ने मुद्रिका को देख कर, बडे आश्चर्य में हो, बीरबर से कहा, कि इसे तो मैं ने स्वयं यमुना में फेंक दिया था तुम्हेँ कैसे मिली?। बीरबर ने कहा, कि पृथ्वी-नाथ, दान के प्रभाव से यह मुझे मत्स्य के पेट में से मिली; इस पर बादशाह को विश्वास ङआ, कि सत्य है, बडी बडी विपत्ति दान से हट जाती हैं॥ इसी बुद्धि से राजा रत्न-सेन ने भी सर्वस्व-दान दिया। आगे की चौपाई में कवि भी दान-महिमा-वर्णन के लिये उद्यत ङआ॥ १४६॥

चउपाई।

धनि जीअन अउ ता कर हीआ। ऊँच जगत महँ जा कर दीआ॥
दिआ सो सब जप तप उपराहीँ। दिआ बराबर जग किछु नाहीँ॥
एक दिआ तइँ दस-गुन लाहा। दिआ देखि सब जग मुख चाहा॥
दिआ करइ आगइ उँजिआरा। जहाँ न दिआ तहाँ अँधिआरा॥
दिआ मँदिर निसि करइ अँजोरा। दिआ नाहिँ घर मूसहिँ चोरा॥
हातिम करन दिआ जो सीखा। दिआ रहा धरमिन्ह महँ लीखा॥
दिआ सो काज दुहूँ जग आवा। इहाँ जो दिआ ओही जग पावा॥

दोहा।

निरमर पंथ कीन्ह तिन्ह जिन्ह रे दिआ किछु हाथ।
किछु न कोइ लेइ जाइहि दिआ जाइ पइ साथ॥१४७॥

धनि = धन्य। जीअन = जीवन। हीआ = हृदय। ऊँच = उच्च = ऊँचा। जगत = जगत् = संसार। दीआ = दान = दत्त, वा दीआ = दीपक = दीप = दीया = चिराग। उपराहीँ = उपरि हि = ऊपर। जग = जगत् = संसार। किछु = किञ्चित् = कुछ। तइँ = तें = से। दस = दश। गुन = गुण। दस-गुन = दश-गुण = दस-गुना। लाहा = लाभ =

फायदा। उँजिआरा = उज्ज्वलकार = उज्ज्वल। अँधिआरा = अन्धकार। मँदिर = मन्दिर = घर। निसि = निशि = रात्रौ = रात में। अँजोरा = उज्ज्वल = उजेला = प्रकाश। सूसहिँ = मूसइ (मुष्णाति) का बहु-वचन। चोरा = चोर। हातिम = मुसल्मानोँ मेँ एक प्रसिद्ध दानी। करन = कर्ण = भारत का प्रसिद्ध धीर, वीर, और दानी। सीखा = शिक्षा पाया, वा सीखा = शिखा = चोटी। धरमिन्ह = धर्मिणः = धर्मि-जन। लीखा = लेखा = गणना। काज = कार्य = काम। दुहूँ = दो हि = दोनोँ। आवा = आव = आवइ (आयाति)। इहाँ = इह = यहाँ॥ निरमर = निर्मल = उज्ज्वल = स्वच्छ = साफ। पंथ = पन्थाः = मार्ग = राह। जाइहि = जायगा = जाइ (याति) का भविष्यत्-काल मेँ एक-वचन। पइ = अपि = निश्चय से = अवश्य, वा पइ = पर। साथ = सार्थ = सङ्ग॥

(मलिक महम्मद कहते हैँ, कि) तिस (पुरुष) का धन्य जीवन और हृदय है, जिस का, कि दान, वा दीया (प्रताप) जगत् मेँ सब से ऊँचा, अर्थात् बढ कर है॥ वह (सो) दिया अर्थात् दान, वा दीया (प्रताप), सब जप (और) तप के ऊपर है। दान (दिया) वा दीया (प्रताप) के बराबर जगत् मेँ कुछ नहीँ है, अर्थात् संसार मेँ ऐसी कोई वस्तु नहीँ जो दान वा प्रताप की बराबरी करे। भारत, शान्तिपर्व, सर्ग २९ की कथा मेँ व्यास लोग ऊपरी कथा कहते हैँ, कि राजा रन्तिदेव कई दिन उपवास करने पर, खेत मेँ झडे हुए जवोँ को चुन लाये और उन से जो सत्तू तयार हुआ, उस का ब्राह्मण, अपने, पत्नी, पुत्र, और पुत्र की पत्नी के हेतु पाँच विभाग कर, पत्तलोँ मेँ परोस, ब्राह्मण का भाग अलग निकाल, जैसे-ही जेँवने के लिये बैठे, तैसे-ही राजा के धर्म को ध्वंस करने के लिये विश्वामित्र पहुँचे, और कहा, कि 'राजन् बुभुक्षितोऽस्मि' इस पर राजा ने ब्राह्मण का अलग रक्खा हुआ भाग उन के आगे बडे आदर से रख दिया। उस के खा जाने पर मुनि ने कहा, कि 'राजन् नैतावता भोजनेन तृप्तिर्जाता'। तब राजा ने क्रम क्रम से अपना, अपनी पत्नी का, तथा पुत्र का और पुत्र-बधू का, सब भाग विश्वामित्र को खिला कर, उन्हेँ आदर-पूर्वक विदा किया। और इधर क्षुधा-वेदना से चारो के प्राण स्वर्ग-प्रयाण के लिये उठ खडे हुए। इस कठिन दान को देख कर, देवोँ ने धन्य धन्य कह, दुन्दुभी बजाई, और चारो को विमान मेँ बैठा, मङ्गल-स्तुति करते स्वर्ग को ले गये। यहाँ विश्वामित्र के पत्तल पर जो उच्छिष्ट सत्तू पडा था, उस के खाने के लिये एक नेउरा आया। पत्तल चाटने के समय उस के नाभी से ऊपर शरीरार्द्ध-भाग मेँ जो उच्छिष्ट लगे, उस के कारण उस की आधी देह

सोने की हो गई। जब युधिष्ठिर ने राजसूय किया, और बहुत ब्राह्मणों को भोजन कराया, उस समय उस नेउरे ने यह सोच, कि उस यज्ञ में ब्राह्मणों की जूठी पत्तलों पर लोटने से मेरी बाकी आधी देह अवश्य सोने की हो जायगी, वहाँ आ कर, घूर पर पडी जूठी पत्तलों के ऊपर लोटना आरम्भ किया। युधिष्ठिर के साथ कोठे पर बैठे कृष्ण उस नेउरे के, वार वार लोट कर, शरीर के निरेखने पर खिल खिला कर हँस उठे। युधिष्ठिर कुछ आमर्ष से हँसी का कारण पूँछने लगे। युधिष्ठिर के हठ पकडने पर कृष्ण ने उस नेउरे को देखाया और कहा, कि देखो राजा रन्तिदेव के ब्राह्मण-भोजन के उच्छिष्ट में लोटने से इस की आधी देह सोने की हो गई है, अवशिष्ट देह को भी सोना बनाने के लिये तुमारे यज्ञ के ब्राह्मण-भोजन के उच्छिष्ट में लोट रहा है, और वार वार अपनी देह को निरख रहा है, कि सोने की हुई, कि नहीँ, परन्तु वह देह ज्योँ की त्योँ बनी है, सोने की नहीँ होती है। इस पर युधिष्ठिर ने लज्जित हो कर, कृष्ण से पूँछा, कि क्या मेरी यज्ञ निर्विघ्न पूरी नहीँ हुई। कृष्ण ने कहा, कि युधिष्ठिर, तुमारी यज्ञ अवश्य निर्विघ्न पूरी हुई, परन्तु राजा रन्तिदेव के यज्ञ की बराबरी नहीँ कर सकती। राजा रन्तिदेव ने अपना पेट काट कर, ब्राह्मण के मुख में हुत किया, सो उन की यज्ञ सर्वोत्तमोत्तम हुई। सच है दान के बराबर जगत् में कुछ नहीँ है, तहाँ भी ऐसा दान, जिस से कि प्राण पर आ बने॥ एक देने से दस-गुना लाभ होता है, अर्थात् जगत् में सब प्राणियोँ की यही इच्छा रहती है, कि कुछ नुक्सान हो जाय, परन्तु प्रतिष्ठा लाभ हो, सो आदर-पूर्वक एक से प्रतिष्ठा पाने के लिये तो उस को दान दिया, और उस ने दस जगह दानी की प्रशंसा किया, जिस से उस दानी की दश-गुणित प्रतिष्ठा हो गई। जैसे एक दीये से दस-गुना लाभ होता है, अर्थात् दसो दिशा की वस्तु प्रकाश से मिल जाती है। दिया (दान) को देख कर, (दानी के औदार्य पर) सब जगत् (उस दानी के) मुख को चाहता है, अर्थात् सब कोई चाहता है, कि ऐसे पुण्यात्मा के मुख का दर्शन हो। जैसे दीये को देख कर जग में सब कोई उस दीये के मुख को चाहता है, अर्थात् दीप-शिखा को लक्ष्मी-रूप समझ, सब कोई प्रणाम करने के लिये उस दीये के मुख का दर्शन चाहता है॥ दिया (दान) आगे उँजेला करता है, अर्थात् परलोक-मार्ग को देखाता है, जैसे दीया आगे (राह में) उँजेला करता है। जहाँ दिया (दान) नहीँ है, तहाँ अन्धकार है,

अर्थात् उस के लिये परलोक-मार्ग अन्धकार-मय है, जैसे जहाँ दिया (दीप) नहीं है तहाँ अन्धकार रहता है॥ दिया (दान) रात को घर में उँजेला करता है, अर्थात् रात को घर में दानी के सो जाने पर भी दान-प्रताप ऐसा प्रकाशित रहता है, कि उस के आतङ्क से चोर, चाईं, कोई भी, उस के पास नहीं पहुँच सकता; वह दान-प्रताप सदा उँजेला रखता है, जैसे दीया (दीप) रात को घर में उँजेला करता है। (जहाँ) दिया (दान) नहीं है (उस) घर को चोर मूसते हैं, अर्थात् न देने से कृपण के सञ्चित धन का यही परिणाम है, कि उसे दूसरा ले लेता है। भर्त्तृहरि ने भी लिखा है, कि—

'दानं भोगो नाशस्तिस्रो गतयो भवन्ति वित्तस्य।
यो न ददाति न भुङ्क्ते तस्य तृतीया गतिर्भवति॥' (भर्त्तृहरि-नीतिशतक)।

(भोग भी एक प्रकार का दान-ही है, किन्तु कुपात्र में देने से इस दान से कोई फल नहीं) जैसे दीया न रहने से घर को चोर मूस लेते हैं॥ हातिम और कर्ण ने जो दिया (दान) को सीखा, अर्थात् दान देने का जो अभ्यास किया; (इसी लिये आज तक उन दोनों का) दिये (दान)-ही से धर्मियों में गणना रही है, अर्थात् दान-कीर्त्ति-ही से आज तक उन के नाम धर्मि-गणना में वर्त्तमान हैं, वा, हातिम और कर्ण के, दिया (दीप, प्रताप) की जो शिखा (प्रज्वलित हुई है, उसी कारण वह) दिया (प्रताप) धर्मियों के बीच लिखा रहा है, अर्थात् उन के प्रताप का विशेष वर्णन धर्मियों के बीच आज तक इतिहासों में लिखा हुआ है॥ दिया (दान) जो है सो दोनों जगत्, अर्थात् इस लोक और परलोक दोनों, में काम आता है, जैसे जग में दिया (दीप=दीया) जो है सो दोनों, अर्थात् घर के भीतर बाहर दोनों, काम में आता है। यहाँ, अर्थात् इस लोक में, जो कुछ दिया हुआ है (वही) दूसरे जगत् में, अर्थात् पर-लोक में, पाया जाता है, अर्थात् अन्त समय कुछ भी नहीं काम आता और न कोई संग चले, एक दान-पुण्य-रूप धर्म-ही साथ देता है, और वही साथी हो कर, ईश्वर के यहाँ सहायक होता है। शास्त्र में भी लिखा है, कि 'धर्म एकः सहायः' जैसे यहाँ जिस का दिया (धर्म-दीप-प्रकाश) है वही परलोक में भी (प्रकाश के लिये उस धर्मी को) मिलता है॥

(कवि कहता है, कि) रे (मन, वा मित्र) जिस ने (अपने) हाथ से कुछ दिया, अर्थात् दान-पुण्य किया, (निश्चय समझो, कि) तिस ने (पर-लोक यात्रा में अपने लिये) निर्मल राह किया है, अर्थात् वही दान-दीप की उज्ज्वल-शिखा उस के अन्त

समय स्वर्ग जाने में निर्मल राह देखाती है। कोई कुछ भी नहीं ले जायगा, (पर) निश्चय से दिया (दान) अवश्य साथ जाता है, अर्थात् अन्त में सब कोई साथ छोड देता है परन्तु दान-धर्म-ही सदा साथ दिये रहता है ॥

हातिम मुसल्मानों में एक बडा प्रसिद्ध वीर, धीर, और दानी हो गया है। जैसे विक्रम की प्रशंसा में सिंहासन बत्तीसी, बैताल-पचीसी बनी हुई हैं; उसी प्रकार इस की प्रशंसा में पारसी में 'हातिम ताई' बनी है। इस के पिता का कुल तै वंश में था। इस लिये इसे लोग हातिम ताई कहते हैं, अर्थात् हातिम तै वंश का। एक सौदागर की कन्या हुस्नबानू से विवाह करने के लिये एक राज-पुत्र, मुनीरशामी, आतुर हुआ। परन्तु हुस्नबानू की प्रतिज्ञा थी, कि जो कोई मेरे स्थिर किये हुए सातो प्रश्नों का उत्तर करेगा उसी से मैं विवाह करूँगी। मुनीरशामी को, उत्तर न होने पर, हुस्नबानू ने वर्ष दिन की अवधि दी थी। यह रोता हुआ वन में गया, वहाँ हातिम से भेंट हुई। हातिम ने प्रतिज्ञा की, कि मैं तेरे बदले सातो प्रश्नों का उत्तर करूँगा। प्रतिज्ञानुसार बडे बडे दुःखों को भोग कर, हातिम ने उन उत्तरों को दिया और मुनीरशामी से हुस्नबानू का विवाह कराया। यह हातिम यमन नगर का राजा था। एक वार एक भेडिये ने एक प्रसूता हरिणी को, भक्षण करने के लिये, पकड लिया। अनाथ उस मृगी का बच्चा कैसे जीयेगा; इस विचार से भेडिये को दधीचि के ऐसा अपने चूतरों की मांस दे कर, हरिणी को छोडाया। यह ऐसा दानी, मानी और सत्यभाषी था, कि पशुओं में भी इस का यश फैल रहा था। जैसे ऋक्ष-पति जाम्बुवान् नें कृष्ण से अपनी कन्या जाम्बुवती का विवाह किया; उसी प्रकार जब हुस्नबानू के पहले प्रश्न (एक वेर देखा है, दूसरी वार देखने की अभिलाषा है) के उत्तर की खोज में इस ने वन-यात्रा किया है; उस समय इस का यश और नाम सुन, उस समय का ऋक्ष-पति नें इस के साथ अपनी कन्या का विवाह करना निश्चित किया। परन्तु हातिम ने अस्वीकार किया। इस पर ऋक्ष-पति ने हातिम को कैद किया। अन्त में एक दिव्य-पुरुष के कहने से हातिम ने उस ऋक्ष-पति की पुत्री से विवाह किया और उसी के प्रसाद से पहले प्रश्न के उत्तर को भी पाया। यह सब मनोहर कथा 'हातिम ताई' में हैं। मुन्शी नवलकिशोर ने इस का हिन्दी-अनुवाद भी छपवा दिया है जो 'आरायश-महफिल' (ارایش محفل) इस नाम से प्रसिद्ध है।

कुन्ती, विवाह होने के पहले एक दिन यमुना नहाने गई थी। उस की शोभा को देख, सूर्य उस पर आसक्त ऊए। उसी सूर्य के शुक्र से कर्ण की उत्पत्ति ऊई। सूर्य के प्रसाद से कुन्ती का कुमारी-धर्म नहीं नष्ट ऊआ। पीछे से यह पण्डु से व्याही गई। कुन्ती ने कर्ण को जन्मते-ही लोकापवाद-भय से यमुना में बहा दिया। यह बहते बहते प्रयाग में गङ्गा जी में आया। वहाँ से बहते बहते विहार में पऊँचा। वहाँ एक रथ-कार (लोहार वा बढई) की स्त्री राधा ने इसे पकडा और वंश में कोई पुत्र न रहने के कारण, अपना पुत्र मान लिया। राधा का पति इन्द्र-प्रस्थ में पण्डु के यहाँ रथ बनाने पर नोकर था। नोकरी पक्की हो जाने पर पीछे से राधा भी अपने पुत्र कर्ण को लिये, अपने पति के साथ इन्द्र-प्रस्थ में रहने लगी। दुर्योधन की मित्रता से कर्ण शस्त्र-निपुण और वडा प्रख्यात ऊआ। यह वडा-ही वीर, धीर, और दानी था। जिस घडी यह पूजा कर के उठता था, उस समय जो कोई सत्पात्र जो कुछ माँगता था, नाहीं नहीं करता था। इस का जन्म शरीरस्थ कवच और कुण्डल के साथ ऊआ था। एक वेर पूजा के समय इन्द्र ने आ कर, कवच और कुण्डल को माँगा। इस ने तुरन्त अपनी शरीर में से नोच कर, इन्द्र को कवच और कुण्डल दे दिया (भारत आदिपर्व, अध्या० ६७, श्लो० १४१-४३) इस स्थान पर व्यास लोग कर्ण के औदार्य पर अनेक कहानी सुनाते हैं।

युधिष्ठिर ने एक वेर कृष्ण से पूँछा, कि हमारे लोगों में कौन दानी है, कृष्ण ने कहा, कि कर्ण; इस पर युधिष्ठिर उदास ऊए। कुछ दिन बीते वर्षा-ऋतु में एक ब्राह्मण आ कर, कृष्ण के साथ कोठे पर बैठे युधिष्ठिर से विनय किया, कि महाराज, ब्राह्मणी को लडका ऊआ है, सो शीत-निवारणार्थ कुछ इन्धन चाहिए। युधिष्ठिर ने भण्डारी को आज्ञा दिया, कि ब्राह्मण को इन्धन दो। भण्डारी ने ब्राह्मण से कहा, कि इस समय भण्डारे में इन्धन नहीं है; मनुष्य वन में भेजा गया है; आप एक पहर के वाद आइये, यथेच्छ इन्धन मिलेगा। इस पर युधिष्ठिर ने भी ब्राह्मण से यही कहा, कि पहर भर के बाद आ कर, भण्डारी से यथेच्छ इन्धन ले जाइयेगा। वह ब्राह्मण वहाँ से फिर कर, कर्ण के घर पर आया जो युधिष्ठिर के घर के सामने-ही था। और उन से भी इन्धन के लिये प्रार्थना की। कर्ण ने भी इन्धन के लिये भण्डारी को आज्ञा दिया। दैवात् उन के यहाँ भी भण्डारे में इन्धन न रहा। इस लिये भण्डारी ने ब्राह्मण से विनय किया, कि देवता, पहर भर के वाद

इन्धन मिलेगा। इस पर कर्ण ने क्रुद्ध हो कर, भण्डारी को डाँटा, कि मूर्ख, पहर भर में तो संभव है, कि ब्राह्मणी शीत के कारण व्याकुल हो, सो मेरी चारपाइयों को चीर कर, आज के लिये ब्राह्मण को यथेच्छ इन्धन दे। इस पर भण्डारी ने कर्ण के कई चारपाइयों के पाटी गोडे चिरवा कर, ब्राह्मण को इन्धन दिया। इस पर कृष्ण ने युधिष्ठिर को देखा कर कहा, कि क्या आप के पास चारपाइयाँ न थीं, जिन से ब्राह्मण को आप इन्धन दे सकते? सो देखो कर्ण की उदारता। इसी लिये मैं ने तुमारे लोगों में सब से अधिक उदार कर्ण को कहा है। इस बात को सुन, युधिष्ठिर ने लज्जित हो, नीचे शिर कर लिया।

व्यासों की दूसरी कहानी ऐसी है—। बडे भोर कर्ण की सत्यता और दान-शीलता देखने के लिये एक वेर योगी बन कर, महादेव जी आये। जैसे-ही योगी द्वार पर पहुँचा, तैसे-ही अन्तःपुर से बाहर कर्ण उठा हुआ चला आता था। योगी से चार आँख होते-ही, प्रणाम करने के अनन्तर, बडे भोर योगी के आने का कारण पूँछा। योगी ने कहा, कि आप से कुछ माँगने आया हूँ, यदि आप तीन वेर वचन दें तो मै माँगूँ। कर्ण ने कहा, कि योगि-राज, आप माँगिये मैं निःसंशय दूँगा, दूँगा, दूँगा। इस प्रकार तीन वेर वाचा बँधा कर योगी ने कहा, कि तुमारे पुत्र विकर्ण को मांस खाने चाहता हूँ। उस में नियम यह, कि आप अपनी पत्नी के सामने उस का शिर काटिये, और आप की पत्नी उस कटे शरीर की बोटी बोटी चीर कर, पानी से अच्छी तरह धो कर, बटलो-ही में धर कर, पकावे। पकने पर वही थारी में परोसे, और आप मुझे जेवाँवें, और आप की वही पत्नी, जब तक मैं भोजन न कर लूँ, बैठी बेनिया डोलावे। परन्तु इतना ध्यान रक्खो, कि इस कृत्य के आदि से अन्त तक तुमारे और तुमारी पत्नी के आँखों से आँसू के एक बूँद न निकले। यदि किसी के आँख से एक बूँद भी टपकेगा तो मैं भोजन न करूँगा और शाप से तुमारी सब श्री भस्म कर डालूँगा। इस पर धैर्य धर, कर्ण घर के भीतर पत्नी के पास गया; और कदाचित् पुत्र के शिर काटने में यह विघ्न करे, और यथोचित योगी के नियम का न पालन करे, इस भय से, अनेक मनोहर मधुर वचनों से पत्नी की सेवा में लग गया। पति-व्रता पत्नी भी बडे आदर से पति के पैरों पर गिर कर, विनय करने लगी, कि नाथ, ऐसा कौन सा कार्य-भार आ पडा, जिस के लिये इस दासी की इतनी सेवा में आप के सब अङ्ग नाना प्रकार की भङ्गी में लगे

ऊए हैं। कर्ण ने कहा, कि यदि तुम राजी हो कर देने को कहो और कार्य में भाँजी न पडो, तो मैं करूँ। पत्नी ने कहा, कि प्राण-नाथ, मेरे लिये संसार में ऐसी सार वस्तु-ही नहीं जो आप की आज्ञा से बाहर हो; तन, मन, धन, परिवार-जन, सब आप का है; निःसंशय आज्ञा हो दासी सर्व प्रकार से आज्ञा पालन करेगी। पत्नी के इस वचन पर कर्ण ने योगी के वृत्तान्त को सुना कर, कहा, कि मैं यह सब करने का वचन उसे दे आया हूँ, अब, प्राण-प्रिये, तुमारी-ही देरी है; इस पर पति-आज्ञा को—

'गुरुरग्निर्द्विजातीनां वर्णानां ब्राह्मणो गुरुः।
पतिरेको गुरुः स्त्रीणां सर्वत्राभ्यागतो गुरुः॥'

इस मनु-वाक्य से सब से भारी समझ, वह भी पति के साथ सब काम करने को तयार ऊई। निदान योगी के नियमानुसार दोनों ने वैसा-ही कर देखाया। जब पुत्र-मांस परोस कर कर्ण योगी को जेवाँने लगा, और उस की पत्नी बेनियाँ डोलाने लगी, तब अत्यन्त प्रसन्न हो कर, धन्य धन्य कहते, महादेव जी प्रगट हो कर, उस के पुत्र विकर्ण को जिला दिया, और बऊत कुछ वर-प्रदान देते दम्पतियों की सत्यता को सराहते अपनी कैलासपुरी को पधारे। जैसे श्रवण, गोपीचन्द, भर्तृहरि के चरित्रों को लोग गाया करते हैं; तिसी प्रकार बऊत से लोग इस कर्ण-कहानी को भी अनेक मनोहर गीतों में गाया करते हैं॥ १४७॥

चउपाई।

सत न डोल देखा गज-पती। राजा दत्त सत्त दुहुँ सती॥
आपुन नाहिँ कया पइ कंथा। जीउ दीन्ह अगुमन तेहि पंथा॥
निहचइ चला भरम डर खोई। साहस जहाँ सिद्ध तहँ होई॥
निहचइ चला छाडि कइ राजू। बोहित दीन्ह दीन्ह सब साजू॥
चढा बेगि अउ बोहित पेले। धनि वेइ पुरुख पेम-पँथ खेले॥
पेम-पंथ जउ पहुँचइ पारा। बहुरि न आइ मिलइ तेहि छारा॥
तिन्ह पावा ऊतिम कबिलासू। जहाँ न मीचु सदा सुख बासू॥

दोहा ।

एहि जीअन कइ आस का जस सपना तिल आधु ।
मुहमद जिअत-हि जे मुए तिन्ह पुरुखन्ह कहँ साधु ॥ १४८ ॥

इति राजा-गजपति-संबाद-खंड ॥ १३ ॥

सत = सत्य = सत्य-प्रतिज्ञा = सत्य-सङ्कल्प । डोल = डोला = दोलित हुआ = डगा = डोलइ (दोलति) का भूत-काल । दत्त = दान । सत्त = सत्य = सत्य-व्रत । सती = समीचीन = सच्ची । कया = काय = शरीर । पइ = अपि = निश्चय । अगुमन = आगमने = आगमन-ही में = प्रारम्भ-ही में = आगे-ही । निहचइ = निश्चय = निःसंशय । चला = चलइ (चलति) का भूत-काल । भरम = भ्रम = संशय । डर = भय । खोई = खो कर = नष्ट कर । साहस = विना समझे बूझे कर बैठना = हिम्मत से विना विचारे काम करना । सिद्ध = सिद्धि = मनोरथ का पूरा होना । छाडि = छोड कर (सञ्छुद्य) । राजू = राज्य । बोहित = वोहित = जहाज = बडी नाव । दीन्ह = देइ (दत्ते) का भूत-काल । सब = सर्व । साजू = साज = सामग्री । चढा = चढइ (चरति) का भूत-काल । बेगि = वेगेन = शीघ्र । पेले = पेले गये = चलाये गये = पेलइ (पेलति) से कर्म में प्रत्यय है । धनि = धन्य । पुरुख = पुरुष = मनुष्य । पेम-पँथ = प्रेम-पथ = प्रेम का मार्ग । खेले = खेलहिँ = खेलइ = (खेलति) का बहु-वचन । जउ = यदि । पहुँचइ = पहुँचे । पारा = पार । बहुरि = भूयः = फिर । आइ = आगत्य = आ कर । मिलइ = मिलति । छारा = छार = भस्म = राख । ऊतिम = उत्तम । कबिलासू = कैलास, वा कबिलासू = क-विलास = ब्रह्मा का विलास, अर्थात् ब्रह्म-सुख । मीचु = मृत्यु । बासू = वास = स्थान ॥ जीअन = जीवन । आस = आशा = उम्मेद । जस = यथा = जैसे । सपना = स्वप्न । तिल = तिलान्न । आधु = अर्ध = आधा । साधु = समीचीन ॥

(वार वार समझाने पर भी) गज-पति ने देखा, (कि राजा का) सत्य-व्रत, अर्थात् सिंहल जाने का सत्य-सङ्कल्प न डगा । (और मन में निश्चय किया, कि) राजा का दत्त, अर्थात् दान (जो अभी निर्विघ्न समुद्र-पार होने के लिये किया है) और सत्य-सङ्कल्प दोनों सच्चे हैं, अर्थात् राजा के जी से लग गई है, कि मैं सिंहल को जाऊँ ॥ (कवि कहता है, कि सच है, जिस ने) आगे-ही से उस राह में (जाने के लिये अपना) जीव दे दिया है; उस की अपनी-ही शरीर नहीं है, (किन्तु) निश्चय से कन्या है, अर्थात् जीव दे देने पर शरीर कहाँ । जो शरीर देख पडती है, उसे शरीर

न समझो किन्तु कन्था समझो, जो कि निर्जीव और बे-काम है॥ (गज-पति मन में कहता है, कि राजा रत्न-सेन) संशय और डर को खो कर, अर्थात् भुला कर, निश्चय से, अर्थात् दृढता से, (सिंहल को) चला है, सो, जहाँ (ऐसा) साहस है तहाँ (अवश्य-ही) सिद्धि (मनोरथ-सिद्धि) होती है॥ सो राजा निश्चय से राज्य को छोड कर, (सिंहल को) चला है, (यह गज-पति ने अपने मन में निश्चय कर, रत्न-सेन को) जहाज दिया (और जहाज-उपयोगि) साज (सामग्री) को भी दिया॥ (राजा) शीघ्र (जहाज पर) चढा और जहाज चलाये गये। (कवि कहता है, कि) धन्य वे पुरुष हैं, जो कि प्रेम-मार्ग में खेलते हैं, अर्थात् जो कि सब से उत्तम मन-बहलाव प्रेम-मार्ग-ही को जानते हैं॥ यदि (कोई) प्रेम-मार्ग के पार पहुँचे, (तो वह) फिर (इस संसार में) आ कर, तिस (संसार के) भस्म में नहीं मिलता है, अर्थात् वह जन्म मरण से मुक्त हो प्रेम-मय पर-ब्रह्म में लीन हो जाता है॥ वे लोग (तिन्ह) उत्तम कैलास वा ब्रह्म-विलास को पाते हैं, जहाँ मृत्यु नहीं है (और) सदा सुख से स्थान है, अर्थात् जहाँ मृत्यु-भय से मुक्त हो, प्राणी सुख से अचल स्थान में विराजता है॥

(मुहम्मद कहते हैं कि) इस जीवन की क्या आशा, जैसे स्वप्न और तिल का आधा, अर्थात् जैसे स्वप्न की स्थिति बहुत थोडे काल तक रहती है, और एक तिल-ही छोटे परिमाण के कारण बहुत अल्प काल तक एक स्थान में रहता है, तहाँ तिल के आधे की स्थिति तो और भी बहुत अल्प है; एक चण में दृष्टि-गोचर हुआ, दूसरे चण में वायु-वेग से अन्यत्र चले जाने से अगोचर हो गया। इसी प्रकार मनुष्य का जीवन है। इस चण में वर्त्तमान है, दूसरे चण में नहीं जानते, कि इस की स्थिति कहाँ होगी। (इस लिये जब यह जीव चण-भङ्गुर है तब इस के ठहराने का यत्न सब निष्फल है, सो) जो लोग जीते-ही मर गये हैं, अर्थात् जो प्रेम-पथ में चले हैं, (क्योंकि प्रेम-पथ-ही में पहले शिर दे कर, तब मनुष्य चलता है; इस लिये जानों जीता-हो मरे के समान है) तिन्ही पुरुषों को (मैं) साधु, अर्थात् समीचीन, कहता हूँ। कवि का तात्पर्य है, कि जब निश्चय है, कि शरीर चण-भङ्गुर है तब यह प्रेम-पथ में यदि खोई जाय तो अत्युत्तम; इस लिये जो प्रेम-पथ में शरीर खोवे उसी को मैं सच्चा साधु महात्मा समझता हूँ॥ १४८॥

इति राज-गजपति-संवाद-खण्ड-नाम त्रयोदश-खण्डं समाप्तम्॥ १३॥

अथ बोहित-खंड ॥ १४ ॥

चउपाई ।

जस रथ रेँगि चलइ गज ठाटी । बोहित चले समुद गे पाटी ॥
धावहिँ बोहित मन उपराहीँ । सहस कोस एक पल मँह जाहीँ ॥
समुद अपार सरग जनु लागा । सरग न घालि गनइ बइरागा ॥
ततखन चाल्ह एक देखरावा । जनु धवला-गिरि परबत आवा ॥
उठी हिलोर जो चाल्ह नराजी । लहरि अकास लागि भुइँ बाजी ॥
राजा सँति कुअँर सब कहहीँ । अस अस मच्छ समुद मँह अहहीँ ॥
तेहि रे पंथ हम चाहहिँ गवँना । होहु सँजूत बहुरि नहिँ अवना ॥

दोहा ।

गुरु हमार तुम्ह राजा हम चेला तुम्ह नाथ ।
जहाँ पाउँ गुरु राखइ चेला राखइ माँथ ॥ १४९ ॥

जस = यथा = जैसे । रेँगि = (रिगि गतौ) रिङ्गण कर = रेँग कर । गज = हाथी । ठाटी = ठठम् = ठट = यूथ । गे = गये । पाटी = पाटनम् = पट । धावहिँ = धावइ (धावति) का बहु-वचन । उपराहीँ = उपरि-हि = ऊपर । सहस = सहस्र = हजार । कोस = क्रोश । पल = घटी का साठवाँ भाग । अढाई पल का एक मिनट होता है ।

जाहीँ = जाहिँ = जाइ (याति) का बहु-वचन। सरग = स्वर्ग। लागा = लग्न हुआ है = लगा है। घालि = गलि = गल कर = चीण हो कर, वा घालि = डाल कर। गनइ = (गणयति) = गिनता है। बइरागा = वैराग्येण = वैराग से। ततखन = तत्क्षणे = तिसी क्षण में। चाल्ह = चाल: = चेल्हवा = एक प्रकार का सफेद मत्स्य। देखरावा = देखने में आया। धवलागिरि = धवल-गिरि = धवलाचल = सफेद पहाड। परबत = पर्वत। उठी = उठइ (उत्तिष्ठते) का स्त्री-लिङ्ग में भूत-काल का एक-वचन। हिलोर = हिल्ल-लोल = हिलने से चञ्चल। नराजी = नाराज हुई = चिढी = चिढ गई। लहरि = लहरी = तरङ्ग। अकास = आकाश। लागि = लग कर = लग्न हो कर। भुइँ = भूमि। बाजी = बजइ (वजति = व्रजति) का स्त्री-लिङ्ग में भूत-काल का एक-वचन। सँति = सँती = से। कुअँर = कुमार = राज-कुमार। अस = एतादृश = ऐसे। मच्छ = मत्स्य। अहहीँ = अहहिँ = अहइ (अस्ति) का बहु-वचन। चाहहिँ = चाहइ (चहति, चदति। वा इच्छति) का बहु-वचन। गवँना = गमनम् = जाना। सँजूत = संयुत = सावधान। बहुरि = भूय: = पुन: = फिर। अवना = आगमनम् = आवना = आना॥ पाउँ = पाद = पैर। राखइ = राखे = (रचेत्) = रक्खे॥

जैसे रथ में गज का ठट्ट रँग कर चलता है, (उसी प्रकार सब) जहाज चले, (जिन से) समुद्र पट गये, अर्थात् समुद्र में जहाँ देखो तहाँ जहाज-ही जहाज देख पडते हैं, समुद्र का जल देख-ही नहीँ पडता॥ जहाज मन से भी ऊपर दौडते हैं, अर्थात् जहाजों की गति मनो-गति से भी अधिक है। एक पल में हजार कोस जाते हैं॥ समुद्र (ऐसा) अपार है, अर्थात् ऐसा अपार जल-राशि है, जानोँ आकाश (स्वर्ग) में लगा है, अर्थात् भूमि से आकाश तक जल-ही जल देख पडता है। (ऐसे भयङ्कर स्थान में राजा) गल कर (घालि), अर्थात् पद्मावती के विरह में चीण हो कर, वा अपने को डाल कर, वैराग्य से स्वर्ग को नहीँ गिनता है, अर्थात् पद्मावती-विरह-जन्य-वैराग्य के कारण मृत्यु (सरग = स्वर्ग) को नहीँ गिनता है॥ तिसी क्षण में एक चाल्ह देखने में आया। (उस की शरीर ऐसी देख पडी) जानोँ (चाल्ह नहीँ किन्तु) धवलाचल पर्वत आ गया हो॥ (जहाजों के देखने से) जो चाल्ह चिढ गया (तो पुच्छ और पक्ष के हिलाने से समुद्र में बडी) हिलोर उठी, (जिस के कारण) लहर आकाश में लग कर भूमि में आने लगी॥ (इस भयङ्कर-लीला को देख कर) सब राज-कुअँर राजा से कहते हैं, (कि अहो महाराज,) ऐसे ऐसे

(पर्वताकार) मत्स्य समुद्र मेँ हैँ ॥ (सो) अरे (भाई) तिसी राह मेँ (जिस मेँ ऐसे ऐसे भयङ्कर मत्स्य हैँ) हम लोग चलना (गमनम् = गवँना) चाहते हैँ, (सो सब कोई) सावधान हो (और निश्चय रक्खो, कि अब) लौट कर नहीँ आना होगा, अर्थात् सब कोई इसी राह मेँ गल पच जायँगे, लौट कर घर पहुँचने की कोई आशा नहीँ ॥

(कुअँर लोग कहते हैँ, कि) राजा, आप हमारे लोगोँ के गुरु हैँ, (इस लिये) आप स्वामी (नाथ) हैँ, (और) हम लोग चेला हैँ, (सो हम लोग इस भयङ्कर मार्ग से नहीँ डरते, अर्थात् हमारे लोगोँ का यह साश्चर्य-वचन सुन, आप यह मन मेँ न समझेँ, कि ये लोग आगे चलने से हिचकते हैँ। क्योँकि शास्त्र की मर्यादा है, कि) जहाँ गुरु पैर रक्खे, वहाँ चेला माथ रक्खे, अर्थात् जहाँ गुरु पैर से चलने की इच्छा करे, वहाँ चेले को शिर के बल चलना चाहिए। इन सब बातोँ से कुअँरोँ ने राजा से यह सङ्केत किया, कि आप स्वयं विचार कर लेँ, कि ऐसे भयङ्कर मार्ग मेँ चलना चाहिए, कि नहीँ, और हम लोग तो आप के अनुगामी होने को मनसा वचसा कर्मणा तयार हैँ ॥ १४९ ॥

चउपाई ।

केवट हँसे सो सुनत गवेँजा । समुद न जानु कुआँ कर मेँजा ॥
यह तउ चाल्ह न लागइ कोह्न । का कहिहहु जब देखिहहु रोह्न ॥
अब-हीँ तइँ तुम्ह देखे नाहीँ । जेहि मुख अइसे सहस समाहीँ ॥
राज-पंखि तेहि पर मेँडराहीँ । सहस कोस जेहि कइ परिछाहीँ ॥
जेइ वेइ मच्छ ठोर गहि लेहीँ । सावक-मुख चारा लेइ देहीँ ॥
गरजइ गगन पंखि जउ बोलहिँ । डोलहिँ समुद डयन जउ डोलहिँ ॥
तहाँ न चाँद न सुरुज असूझा । चढइ सो जो अस अगुमन बूझा ॥

दोहा ।

दस मँह एक जाइ कोइ करम धरम सत नेम ।
बोहित पार होइहि जउ तउ कूसल अउ खेम ॥ १५० ॥

केवट = कैवर्त्त = मलाह । हँसे = हँसइ (हसति) का भूत-काल मेँ बहु-वचन । सुनत = सुनते = शृण्वन्तः । गवेँजा = गोजन् = गौंगा = बतकही । न = नु = वितर्क ।

जानु = जानइ = (जानाति), वा जानु = जानुँ = जानेाँ । कुआँ = कूप = कूआँ । मँजा = मज्जा = अपवित्र जल, मज्जा के सदृश । तउ = तो । चाल्ह = चालः = चेल्हवा । लागइ = (लगति) लगता है । कोइ = क ह = कुछ भी । कहिहऊ = कहोगे = कहइ (कथयति) का भविष्य-काल में बड़-वचन । देखिहऊ = देखोगे = देखइ (दृश्यते) का भविष्य-काल में बहु-वचन । रोह = रोहितः = एक प्रकार का मत्स्य । तइँ = तक । अइसे = एतादृश = ऐसे । सहस = सहस्रोँ = हजारेाँ । समाहीँ = समाहिँ = समाइ (समाप्यते) का बहु-वचन । राज-पंखि = राज-पक्षी = बडे बडे पक्षी । पर = उपरि = ऊपर । मेँडराहीँ = मेँडराहिँ = मेँडराइ (मण्डलयति) का बहु-वचन । कोस = क्रोश । परिछाहीँ = परिच्छाया = परछाहीँ । जेइ = ये = जो लोग । तेइ = तान् = उन । मच्छ = मत्स्य । ठोर = क्षौरम् = चोँच । गहि = संगृह्य = गृहीत्वा = गह कर = पकड कर । सावक-मुख = बच्चे के मुह में । चारा = चार = भक्षण । गरजइ = (गर्जति) गर्जता है । पंखि = पक्षी । जउ = यदा = जब । बोलहिँ = बोलइ (वल्गति वा वदति) का बहु-वचन । डोलहिँ = डोलइ (दोलति) का बहु-वचन । डयन = डयनम् = डैना । चाँद = चन्द्र । सुरुज = सूर्य । असूझा = असूह्य = असूझ = न देखने योग्य, वा अशुद्ध । चढइ = (चलति) चढता है । अस = एतादृश = ऐसा । अगुमन = आगमने = आगे-ही = पहले-ही । बूझ = बूझइ (= बुध्यते) का भूत-काल में एक-वचन ॥ दस = दश । जाइ = (याति) जाता है । कोइ = कोऽपि = कोई । करम = कर्म । धरम = धर्म । सत = सत्य । नेम = नियम । होइहि = होगा । तउ = तब = तदा । कूसल = कुशल । खेम = क्षेम = कल्याण ॥

(चाल्ह को देख कर जो राज-कुअरोँ ने बतकही की) उस (सो) बतकही को सुनते-ही केवट हँसे, (और कहने लगे, कि आप लोग) समुद्र को कुआँ का मज्जा जानते हैँ न, अर्थात् जैसे कूएँ के थोडे घेरे में थोडा सा मैला पानी छोटे छोटे जल-जन्तुओं से संयुत रहता है; उसी प्रकार आप लोगोँ ने समुद्र को समझ लिया क्या?॥ (सो) यह चाल्ह तो कुछ भी नहीँ (दृष्टि में) लगता है, अर्थात् यह तो समुद्र के मत्स्योँ में कुछ भी भारी नहीँ है। (आप लोग जो इसी को बड़त भारी मान लिया, तो) जब (समुद्र का) रोह देखोगे तब क्या कहोगे, अर्थात् चाल्ह-दर्शन-ही में जब बुद्धि चकरा गयी, तब नहीँ कह सकते, कि रोह के देखने पर क्या गति होगी ॥ अभीँ तक आप लोगोँ ने (रोह को) नहीँ देखा, जिस के (रोह के) मुख में ऐसे (चाल्ह) हजारोँ समा जाते हैं, अर्थात् 'तिमिंगिल-गिलोऽप्यस्ति

तद्गिलोऽप्यस्ति राघवः’ (समुद्र में मछलियों के निगलने-वाला मत्स्य है, उस को भी निगलने-वाला दूसरा मत्स्य है और उस को भी निगलने-वाला राघव है)। (कहावत है, कि समुद्र में राघव और यादव नाम के दो परस्पर प्रतिस्पर्धी महापर्वताकार मत्स्य हैं, जो परस्पर एक एक को लडने के लिये ढूँढते फिरते हैं। जिस दिन दोनों से भेंट होगी और वे दोनों लडने लगेंगे, उसी दिन उन के प्रबल-वेग से समुद्र तरङ्गित हो कर, पृथ्वी के चारो ओर फैल जायगा, जिस से संसार में प्रलय हो जायगा)॥ तिस (रोहु) के ऊपर राज-पक्षी मँडराते हैं, जिन की परिछाहीं हजारों कोस तक की होती है॥ (और) जो, (कि) उस मत्स्य (रोहु) को ठोर से पकड लेते हैं, (और उसे) ले कर (अपने) बच्चे के मुह में चारा देते हैं॥ जब वे पक्षी (राज-पक्षी) बोलते हैं (तब प्रति-ध्वनि से) आकाश गर्जता है, अर्थात् आकाश गर्जने लगता है। (और) जब (उन के) डैने डोलते हैं, (तब) समुद्र डोलते हैं, अर्थात् समुद्र डोलने लगते हैं॥ (मल्लाह कहते हैं, कि आगे बडे बडे भयङ्कर समुद्र हैं) तहाँ न चन्द्र, (और) न सूर्य है, (सब) अन्धुझ हैं, अर्थात् तहाँ चाँद, सूर्य तारा-गण कुछ भी नहीं देख पडते। ऐसे (कठिन समुद्र) को जो पहले-ही समझ बूझ लेता है, अर्थात् पहले-ही से समुद्र की इस स्थिति को समझ बूझ कर, जो धैर्य धरता है, सो (पार होने के लिये जहाज पर) चढता है॥

(अपने) सत्य कर्म, सत्य धर्म, (और) सत्य नियम से, दस में कोई एक (समुद्र-पार) जाता है, (सो) जब (समुद्र-) पार जहाज हो जायगा, तब कुशल और क्षेम (समझना चाहिए)॥ १५०॥

चउपाई।

राजइ कहा कीन्ह सो पेमा। जेहि रे कहाँ कर कूसल खेमा॥
तुम्ह खेवहु जउ खेवइ पारहु। जइसइ आपु तरहु मोहिँ तारहु॥
मोँहि कूसल कर सोच न ओता। कुसल होत जउ जनम न होता॥
धरती सरग जाँत पर दोऊ। जो तेहि बिच जिउ बाँच न कोऊ॥
हउँ अब कुसल एक पइ माँगउँ। पेम-पंथ सत बाँधि न खाँगउँ॥
जउ सत हिअ तउ नयनहिँ दीआ। समुद न डरइ पइठि मरजीआ॥
तहँ लगि हेरउँ समुद ढिढोरी। जहँ लगि रतन पदारथ जोरी॥

दोहा।

सपत पतार खोजि जस काढेउ बेद गरंथ।
सात सरग चढि धावउँ पदुमावति जेहि पंथ॥१५१॥

इति बोहित-खंड॥१४॥

राजइ = राजा ने। कह = कहइ (कथयति) का भूत-काल में एक-वचन। कीन्ह = करइ (करोति) का भूत-काल। सो = स एव = वह। पेमा = प्रेम। कुसल = कुशल। खेमा = क्षेम। खेवऊ = खेवइ (खेवते) का लोट् में मध्यम-पुरुष का बहु-वचन। जउ = यदि। खेवइ = खेने में। पारऊ = पारइ (पारयति) का लोट् में मध्यम-पुरुष का बहु-वचन। जइसइ = जैसे-ही = यथैव। आपु = आप = आत्मा। तरऊ = तरइ (तरति) का लोट् में मध्यम-पुरुष का बहु-वचन। तारऊ = तरइ का लोट् में णिजन्त का रूप। सोच = शोच = अफसोस। ओता = तावान् = उतना। जनम = जन्म। धरती = धरित्री = पृथ्वी। सरग = स्वर्ग। जाँत = यन्त्र = जाँता = पीसने की चक्की। पट = पट्ट = पट = नीचे ऊपर की चक्की। बाँच = बँचइ = (वञ्चति) (वञ्चु गतौ)। कोऊ = क्वापि = कथमपि। कुसल = कुशल। माँगउँ = माँगइ (मङ्गते) का लट् में उत्तम-पुरुष का एक-वचन। पेम-पंथ = प्रेम-पथ = प्रेम की राह। सत = सत्य। बाँधि = बन्धयित्वा = बाँध कर। खाँगउँ = खाँगइ (खञ्जति) का लोट् में उत्तम-पुरुष का एक-वचन। हित्र = हृदय। तउ = तदा = तहिँ। दीआ = दीप = दीया। डरइ = (दरति) डरता है। पइठि = प्रविश्य = पैठ कर। मरजीआ = मर कर जीने-वाला = समुद्र में गोता लगाने-वाला = गोता-खोर। हेरउँ = हेरइ (हेडते) का लोट् में उत्तम-पुरुष का एक-वचन। ढिढोरी = ढक्का-ढोल कर के = ढिढोरा फेर कर = डौंडी फिरा कर। रतन = रत्न। पदारथ = पदार्थ = वस्तु। जोरी = जोडी = युग्म॥ सपत = सप्त = सात। पतार = पाताल। खोजि = सङ्खुज्य (खुज चौर्ये) वा संचुद्य = खोज कर = खोजइ (खोजति) से बना है। काढेउ = काढइ (कर्षति) का लोट् में प्रथम-पुरुष का एक-वचन। बेद = बेद, ऋग्, यजुर्वेद, साम, अथर्वण। गरंथ = ग्रन्थ। सात = सप्त। चढि = चढ कर। धावउँ = धावइ (धावति) का लोट् में उत्तम-पुरुष का एक-वचन॥

राजा (रत्न-सेन) ने (केवटौँ से) कहा, कि रे (केवट) जिस ने उस (सो) प्रेम को किया, अर्थात् जिस ने प्रेम-पथ मेँ पैर डाला (उस को) कहाँ का कुशल (और) क्षेम, अर्थात् उस को इस की चिन्ता नहीँ, कि कुशल और क्षेम हो ॥ (सो) तुम लोग यदि (जहाज को) खे सकते हो (तो) खेवो। जैसे आप तरो, (तैसे) मुझे (भी) तारो, अर्थात् जैसे तुम लोग आप पार उतरोगे, तैसे-ही मुझे-भी उतारो ॥ (जितना तुम लोगोँ को कुशल का सोच है) उतना मुझे कुशल का सोच नहीँ। यदि जन्म न होता तो कुशल होता, अर्थात् जब जन्म ले कर प्राणी संसार में आया तब कहाँ कुशल; कहावत प्रसिद्ध है, कि 'कुशल होत जउ जनम न होत।' इस लिये मुझे कुशल की कुछ-भी चिन्ता नहीँ ॥ (क्योँकि) धरती और स्वर्ग (ये) दोनोँ जाँत के पल्ले हैँ। जो (जीव) तिन (पल्लोँ) के बीच मेँ आया (फिर) (वह) जीव कथमपि नहीँ बचता है, अर्थात् विना मरे नहीँ रहता। कबीर-दास ने भी कहा है, कि;—

'दो चक्की के बीच मेँ साबित गया न कोय।
यही तमासा देखि के कबिरा दीन्हा रोय ॥'

मैँ (हउँ=हौँ=अहम्) अब निश्चय कर (पइ) एक कुशल माँगता हूँ, (कि) प्रेम-पथ मेँ सत्य बाँध कर खञ्ज न होऊँ, अर्थात् प्रेम-मार्ग मेँ चलने का जो सत्य-सङ्कल्प किया है, वह न टूटे ॥ (तुम लोगोँ ने जो वर्णन किया है, कि आगे बडा भयङ्कर समुद्र है, 'तहाँ न चाँद न सुरुज असूझा' सो इस की परवाह मुझे नहीँ है, क्योँकि) यदि हृदय मेँ सत्य है, तो (वही सत्य) नयनोँ मेँ दीप है, अर्थात् सत्य अन्धकार मेँ भी नयनोँ की ज्योति को अविहत रखता है। (सत्य-सङ्कल्प-ही से मोती निकालने के लिये) गोता-खोर समुद्र मेँ पैठ कर (भी) नहीँ डरता है, अर्थात् मोती पाने के सत्य-सङ्कल्प से, गोता-खोर समुद्र के भीतर भी आँखोँ की अविहत-ज्योति से मोती को निकाल लेता है ॥ (सो गोताखोर के ऐसा मैँ भी) ढिढोरा दे कर, तहाँ तक समुद्र को हेरूँ, अर्थात् ढूढूँगा, जहाँ तक, कि रत्न पदार्थ की जोडी है, अर्थात् जहाँ तक कि मेरी जोडी पद्मावती है, तहाँ तक डंका पीट कर समुद्र को ढूढूँगा। जिस का जी चाहे सो आ कर विघ्न करे और मुझे रोके; मैँ किसी से हारने-वाला और रुकने-वाला नहीँ ॥

जैसे (वेद व्यास ने) सातो पातालोँ को खोज कर, वेद-ग्रन्थोँ को काढा; तिसी प्रकार जिस राह मेँ पद्मावती है (वह राह यदि सातो स्वर्गोँ के ऊपर भी हो तो)

सातो स्वर्गों के ऊपर चढ कर (उस राह में) धाऊँ, अर्थात् दौडूँगा (तुमारे लोगों के डेरवावने से नहीं डरूँगा)। (सात पाताल और सात स्वर्ग के लिये १ दोहे की टीका देखो)॥ पुराणों में कथा है, कि नास्तिकों के कारण जब वेद जहाँ तहाँ छिन्न भिन्न हो गया, तब व्यास जी ने बडे परिश्रम से सर्वत्र से खोज खोज कर यावच्छक्य सब वेदों को फिर एकट्टा किया। इसी लिये आदर के लिये लोग व्यास को वेद-व्यास कहते हैं और भगवान् के चौबीस अवतारों में १७ वाँ अवतार मानते हैं। कवि ने प्रसिद्ध होने के कारण काढेउ क्रिया के कर्त्ता वेद-व्यास को दोहे में समावेश न होने से छोड दिया है। क्योंकि उस का अध्याहार करना कुछ कठिन नहीं। वेद-व्यास के लिये श्रीमद्भागवत, प्रथम-स्कन्ध, अध्याय ३, श्लोक २१।

'ततः सप्तदशे जातः सत्यवत्यां पराशरात्।
चक्रे वेदतरोः शाखा दृष्ट्वा पुंसोऽल्पमेधसः॥' ऐसा लिखा है॥ १५१॥

इति बोहित-खण्ड-नाम चतुर्दश-खण्डं समाप्तम्॥ १४॥

सत्य-ही सर्वत्र, आगे पीछे जहाँ जहाँ मगर, मच्छ, और कछुए रहते हैं, (रक्षा के लिये) ताका करता है, अर्थात् प्राणी का सत्य-ही सब हिंसक जन्तु से बचाने के लिये उस का पहरा दिया करता है॥ (जिस समय जहाज वेग से चले उस समय समुद्र में ऐसी) लहर उठने लगी जानों (लहर नहीं) पहाड खडे हैं। लहर स्वर्ग तक चढ कर, अर्थात् आकाश में बहुत ऊंचे तक जा कर, फिर (ऐसे झोंक से नीचे की ओर आती है, कि) पाताल में पडती है, अर्थात् पाताल के नीचे तक चली जाती है॥ (उस समय) जहाज (इधर उधर) डोलने लगते हैं (और) लहरें खाने लगते हैं, अर्थात् लहरों के सङ्ग जहाज भी नीचे ऊंचे आया जाया करते हैं, चण में नीचे और चण में ऊपर होते हैं, वा (लहरों के आघात से) चण में तडकते हैं, अर्थात् तड तड शब्द करते हैं, और फिर ऊपर की ओर तड तडा कर आते हैं॥ (कवि कहता है, कि) वह (सो) राजा (रत्न-सेन) सत्य को हृदय में बाँधा है, अर्थात् हृदय में दृढ सत्य-सङ्कल्प किया है, कि अवश्य-ही सिंहल को जाऊँगा। (सो) जिस को सत्य है (उस को वही सत्य) टेक कर, अर्थात् सँभार कर (उस के) कंधे पर पहाड को करता है, अर्थात् उस के कंधे पर पहाड धर देता है, और वह सत्य के आधार से उस पहाड (प्रेम-पहाड) को सुखेन उठा लेता है॥

सो राजा (अपने सत्य-सङ्कल्प से) खार समुद्र को लाँघ गया, अर्थात् खार समुद्र के पार हो गया, (और) चीर-समुद्र जहाँ है तहाँ (लोग) आये। (कवि कहता है, कि देखने में) वे सातो समुद्र मिले हैं (किन्तु उन के) जल भिन्न भिन्न हैं, अर्थात् जल के भिन्न भिन्न आकार और भिन्न भिन्न स्वादु से वे सातो भिन्न भिन्न नाम से पुकारे जाते हैं; नहीं तो वस्तुतः वे सातो मिले हुए हैं। सातो के मिलाने से कवि ने यह देखलाया, कि उन्ही जहाजों पर विना उतरे लोग चले जाते हैं। परन्तु पुराणों में दो दो समुद्रों के बीच बीच में एक एक द्वीप लिखा है, इस लिये मलिक महम्मद की यह कल्पना भारतवर्षीय विद्वानों के मत से विरुद्ध है। कदाचित् किसी मुसल्मानी ग्रन्थ में यह कल्पना हो तो आश्चर्य नहीं॥ १५२॥

चउपाई।

खीर-समुद का बरनउँ नीरू। सेत सरूप पिअत जस खीरू।
उलथहिँ मानिक मोती हीरा। दरब देखि मन होइ न थीरा।

मनुआ चाह दरब अउ भोगू। पंथ भुलाइ बिनासइ जोगू॥
जोगी मनहिँ उह-इ रिस मारइ। दरब हाथ कइ समुद पबारइ॥
दरब लेइ सो असथिर राजा। जो जोगी तेहि के केहि काजा॥
पंथिहि पंथ दरब रिपु होई। ठग बटपार चोर सँग सोई॥
पंथी सो जो दरब सउँ रूसे। दरब समेटि बहुत अस मूसे॥

दोहा।

खीर-समुद सब नाँघा आए समुद दधि माँह।
जो हहिँ नेह क बाउर ना तेहि धूप न छाँह॥ १५३॥

खीर-समुद = चीर-समुद्र = दूध का समुद्र। बरनउँ = वरनइ (वर्णयति) का लोट् में उत्तम-पुरुष का एक-वचन। नीरू = नीर = जल। सेत = श्वेत = सफेद। सरूप = स्वरूप = रूप = सूरत। पीअत = पिबन् सन् = पीने में। जस = यथा = जैसे। खीरू = खीर = चीर = दूध। उलथहिँ = उलथइ (उलुथ्यति) का बहु-वचन। मानिक = माणिक्य = लाल रत्न। मोती = मुक्ता = मौक्तिक। हीरा = हीर = हीरक। दरब = द्रव्य = धन। देखि = देख कर = देखइ (दृश्यते) से ल्यप्। थीर = स्थिर = अचल। मनुआ = मानव = मनुष्य, वा मनुआ = मनवा = मन। चाह = चाहइ (चहति)। भोगू = भोग। पंथ = पन्थाः = राह। भुलाइ = विलोप्य = भुलवा कर। बिनासइ = (विनाशयति) विनाश करता है, वा करती है। जोगू = योग = फकीरी। जोगी = योगी। उह-इ = वही। रिस = रिष्ट = अरिष्ट = अनिष्ट। मारइ = (मारयति) मारता है। पबारइ = (प्रवारयति) पबारता है = फेँकता है। असथिर = अस्थिर = चञ्चल। काजा = कार्य = काम। पंथिहि = पथिक को। पंथ = पथ में = राह में। रिपु = शत्रु = दुश्मन। ठग = स्थगः = छल से चोराने-वाला। बटपार = वाट-पाल = राह-रक्षा करने-वाले कोल भिल्ल। सँग = संग = सङ्ग = साथ। पथी = पान्थ = पथिक। सउँ = सोँ = से। रूसे = रूसइ (रुष्यति) का भूत-काल में बहु-वचन। समेटि = समेत्य = एकट्ठा कर के = बटोर कर। मूसे = मूसे गये = ठगे गये = मुष्ट हुए॥ नाँघा = नाँघइ (लङ्घते) का भूत-काल में एक-वचन। हहिँ = हइ (अस्ति) का बहु-वचन। नेह = स्नेह = प्रेम = प्रीति। क = का, वा, के। बाउर = वातुल = बौरहे। ना = न, वा ना = नर। धूप = तेज = घाम। छाँह = छाया॥

(कवि कहता है, कि) क्षीर-समुद्र का क्या वर्णन करूँ, अर्थात् उस की शोभा वर्णन से बाहर है। श्वेत (तो उस का) रूप है, (और जल का) पीने में (ऐसा स्वादु जान पडता है) जैसे दूध का॥

पुराणों के मत से इसी क्षीर-सागर में भगवान् विष्णु लक्ष्मी के साथ शेष-नाग के ऊपर सोते हैं, और इसी समुद्र में से चौदहो रत्न मथन करने पर निकले हैं, जिन के ये नाम हैं, कल्पद्रुम=कल्पवृक्ष १। वारुणी=मदिरा २। वारण=ऐरावत हस्ती ३। धेनु=काम-धेनु=गाय ४। धन्वन्तरि=वैद्य ५। धनु=शार्ङ्गधनु ६। शङ्ख=पाञ्चजन्य शङ्ख ७। चन्द्रमा ८। कमला (लक्ष्मी) ९। मणि=कौस्तुभ मणि १०। रम्भा=अप्सरा ११। अमृत १२। विष १३। वाजी=(उच्चैःश्रवा घोडा) १४। इस को रामसहाय कवि ने रत्नाकर नाम की सवैया छन्द में लिखा है—

'कलपद्रुम बारुनि बारन धेनु धनन्तरि औ धनु संख निसाकर।
कमला मनि रंभ सुधा बिष बाजि सबै प्रगटे प्रक एक गुनाकर॥
इन चौदह को सुख मानि लिये हरि संभु सुरासुर इंद्र दिवाकर।
हित ये न सहाय भये तब-हीँ जब-हीँ घट-जोनि पिये रतनाकर॥'

इसी पर कवि कहता है, कि इस समुद्र में लहर के उठने पर—

माणिक्य, मोती हीरा (इत्यादि रत्न) उलटते हैं, अर्थात् इधर से उधर उलटते पुलटते हैं, (जिन) द्रव्यों को देख कर (लोभ से) मन स्थिर नहीँ होता है, अर्थात् उन के लेने के लिये मन चञ्चल हो जाता है॥ (कवि कहता है, कि यह) मनुष्य वा मन द्रव्य और भोग को चाहता है; (जो द्रव्य, कि) राह (योग की राह) को भुलवा कर, योग का विनाश कर देता है, अर्थात् यह मन जहाँ द्रव्य और भोग-विलास में फँसा, तहाँ योग की राह भूली और योग नष्ट हुआ॥ (इस लिये) योगी मन से उसी रिष्ट को, अर्थात् उसी अनिष्ट-कारक द्रव्य को, मारता है, अर्थात् मन से उस की वासना हटा देता है। द्रव्य हाथ में कर के, अर्थात् अनायास हाथ में द्रव्य आ जाने पर भी, (उस द्रव्य को) समुद्र में फेँक देता है॥ द्रव्य को जो लेता है, वह (सो) राजा चञ्चल है, अर्थात् द्रव्य को लेने से राजा भी लोभी कहलाता है। (और) जो योगी है, तिस के लिये (द्रव्य) किस काम का, अर्थात् योगी के लिये द्रव्य किसी काम का नहीँ॥ पथ में पथिक के लिये द्रव्य शत्रु है। इसी (सोई) के कारण संग में ठग, बटपार और चोर लगते हैं॥ वे-ही (सो) पथिक (सच्चे हैं)

जो द्रव्य से रूस गये हैं, अर्थात् द्रव्य से मन को हटाये ज्ञए हैं, (क्योंकि) द्रव्य के समेटने से, अर्थात् द्रव्य को एकट्ठा करने से, बज्जत ऐसे (देखे गये हैं जो, कि) मूस गये, अर्थात् लुट गये॥

सब (कोई) चीर-समुद्र को लाँघे (और) दधि के समुद्र में आये। (लोग विश्राम क्यों नहीं लेते हैं; लगातार क्यों चले जाते हैं; इस पर कवि कहता है, कि) जो स्नेह के बौरहे हैं, अर्थात् प्रेम-रस के नशे से जो पागल हो गये हैं; तिन्हें न धूप न छाया, वा तिन मनुष्यों को न धूप न छाया कुछ भी नहीं समझ पडती, अर्थात् उन्हें दुःख और सुख दोनों का ज्ञान नहीं रहता, प्रेम-रस के नशे में मत्त रहते हैं; जिस पर प्रेम है, उसी के मिलने का दिन रात ध्यान लगा रहता है॥ १५३॥

चउपाई।

दधि समुदर देखत तस डहा। पेम क लुबुध दगध इमि सहा॥
पेम जो डाढा धनि वह जीऊ। दधि जमाइ मँथि काढइ घीऊ॥
दधि एक बूँद जाम सब खीरू। काँजी बूँद बिनासइ नीरू॥
साँस डीढ मन-मँथनी गाढी। हिअइ चोट बिनु फूट न साढी॥
जेहि जिउ पेम चँदन तेहि आगी। पेम बिहून फिरइ डरि भागी॥
पेम क आगि जरइ जउ कोई। ता कर दुख न अँबिरथा होई॥
जो जानइ सत आपुहि जारा। निसत हिअइ सत करइ न पारा॥

दोहा।

दधि समुंद पुनि पार भे पेमहि कहाँ सँभार।
भावइ पानी सिर परइ भावइ परहि अँगार॥ १५४॥

समुदर = समुद्र। तस = तथा = तैसा। डहा = दहा = डहइ, वा दहइ (दहति) का भूत-काल में एक-वचन। पेम = प्रेम। लुबुध = लुब्ध = लोभी। दगध = दग्ध = दाह। इमि = इदम् = इस। सहा = सहइ (सहते) का भूत-काल में एक-वचन। डाढा = डाहा = डाहइ (दाहयति) का भूत-काल में एक-वचन। धनि = धन्य। जीऊ = जीव।

जमाइ = जमाय कर, जन्मा कर। मँथि = मन्थयित्वा = मथ कर। काढइ = (कर्षति) काढता है। घीउ = घृत = घी। बूँद = बिन्दु। जाम = जमइ (जायते)। खीरु = क्षीर = दूध। काँजी = काञ्जी = मठा = मंठा। बिनासइ = (विनाशयति) विनाश करता है। नीरु = नीर = जल। साँस = श्वास। डीठ = दृढ = मजबूत। मन-मँथनी = मनो-मन्थिनी = मन-ही जो मथानी। मथानी = महने की लकडी = छोरी। गाढी = कठिन। हिअइ = हृदय। चोट = घाव = आघात। बिनु = विना। फूट = फुटइ (स्फुटति) फूटती है। साढी = सार = बालाई। चँदन = चन्दन। आगी = अग्नि = आग। बिहून = विहीन = विना। फिरइ = (स्फुरति) फिरता है। डरि = डरइ (दरति) से ल्यप् = डर कर। भागी = भागइ (भाजयति) से ल्यप् = भाग कर। जरइ = (ज्वलेत्) = जरे। दुख = दुःख। अँबिरथा = आवृथा = आव्यर्थ = बे-फायदा = बे-मतलब। जानइ = (जानाति) जानता है। जारा = जारइ। निसत = निःसत्य। सत = सत्, वा सत = शत = सौ। करइ = (करोति) करता है॥ समुंद = समुद्र। भे = भये। कहाँ = कथम्। सँभार = सम्भार। भावइ = भावेन = चाहे। परइ = (पतेत्) परे = पडे। अँगार = अङ्गार = अँगारा॥

(राजा जैसे-ही) दधि के समुद्र को (देखा) तैसे-ही देखते डह गया, अर्थात् उस की ज्वाला से भस्म हो गया, (परन्तु) प्रेम का लोभी इस दग्ध (होने के दुःख) को सहा, अर्थात् प्रेम की चाह से इस दुःख को कुछ न समझा, सह लिया॥ (कवि कहता है, कि) प्रेम ने जिस (जीव) को दग्ध कर दिया है; वह जीव धन्य है। (वही जीव इस प्रेम-रस की) दही जमा कर, (उसे) मथ कर, घी (प्रेम-तत्त्व-रूप अपने प्रियतम) को निकालता है॥ (यह न समझो, कि अपार प्रेम-रस का सागर कैसे दही-सदृश जमेगा) दही के एक बूँद से सब दूध जम जाता है, (अर्थात् जैसे दही के एक बूँद से सब दूध जम जाता है; उसी प्रकार यदि प्रेम-रस का एक बूँद भी गाढा हो कर, अपने प्रियतम के रूप-सौंख्य की संयोग-वासना से जम कर, दही हो जाय, तो वही दधि-विन्दु सारे प्रेम-रस सागर को भी जमा देगा)। (और) काँजी का एक विन्दु (दूध को कौन कहे) जल को भी नाश कर देता है, अर्थात् मठे के एक विन्दु से दूध तो फट कर बिगड-ही जाता है, किन्तु जल जो है वह भी उस के संयोग से अपेय हो जाता है। इसी प्रकार मठा के ऐसा एक प्रेम-रस-विन्दु, जो प्राणी के हाथ दैव-योग से लग गया है, पतला पड जाने से प्रेम-रस-सागर को

तो फाड कर बिगाडता-ही है किन्तु प्राणी के जीवन (नीर) को भी खाद-रहित कर देता है, जिस की ओर एक पखेरू भी भूल कर, एक नयन-कोर से भी नहीँ निरेखता। (प्रेम-सर दैव-वश जम कर, यदि दधि-स्वरूप हो भी गया, तो भी उस में से अपने प्रियतम-रूप, पुनीत, नवनीत का निकालना सहज नहीँ है)। साँस-(रूपी) दृढ (रज्जु) (और) गाढी मन-(रूप) मथानी रहने पर भी, अर्थात् प्राणायाम के बल से श्वास को दृढ और मन को अचलस्तम्भ के सदृश कडा कर लेने पर भी, विना हृदय के चोट से, अर्थात् दधि के मध्य में विना उस मथानी के आघात से, साढी नहीँ फूटती (जिस से कि नवनीत मिले)। कवि का तात्पर्य है, कि योग-विद्या से श्वास दृढ और मन अचल कर लेने से भी जब तक समाधि लगा कर, हृदय के मध्य, श्वास-रज्जु से फिरा फिरा कर मन-मथनी से आघात न करोगे, तब तक हृदय-दधि के अन्तर्गत परब्रह्म-रूप प्रियतम नवनीत का मिलना दुर्घट है॥ (दधि-समुद्र के दाह को राजा ने कैसे सह लिया। इस पर कवि की उक्ति है, कि) जिस के जी में प्रेम है, तिसे आग चन्दन है, अर्थात् प्रेम की आग में सब से बढ कर ज्वाला है। सो जिस का जीव उस ज्वाला से तप्त है, उस को और आग की ज्वाला शीतल लगती है। गर्मी स्वभावतः सर्वत्र सम-भाव से रहती है, इस लिये अधिक-तप्त पदार्थ, अल्प-तप्त पदार्थ से जब संयोग करेगा तो सम-भाव होने के लिये अधिक-तप्त पदार्थ अपनी गर्मी में से कुछ अंश न्यून-तप्त पदार्थ की गर्मी में मिला देगा। इस लिये अधिक-तप्त पदार्थ से न्यून-तप्त पदार्थ-ही और अधिक गर्म हो जायगा, और अधिक-तप्त पदार्थ, कुछ गर्मी का भाग निकल जाने से, अपने को कुछ शीतल समझेगा। इस लिये महा-प्रेमानल से झुलसा हुआ प्राणी को इतर अल्पानल-ज्वाल शीतल लगता है; यह कवि का कथन शास्त्र-संमत है। (जो) विना प्रेम का है, अर्थात् जिसे प्रेमानल का दाह नहीँ व्याप्त है, (वह अवश्य इतर अग्नि से) डर कर, (और) भाग कर, फिरता है, अर्थात् उस आग के आगे से लौट जाता है॥ (कवि कहता है, कि) यदि कोई प्रेम की आग से जरे, अर्थात् जर जाय, (तो) तिस का (यह भस्म-रूप) दुःख वृथा नहीँ होता है, अर्थात् जैसे सुवर्ण आग में डहने से, मल भस्म हो जाने से, और उत्तम कान्तिमान् हो जाता है, उसी प्रकार प्रेमाग्नि से सकल उपाधि के भस्म हो जाने पर पर-ब्रह्म रूप हो, प्राणी दिव्य-स्वरूप हो जाता है। इस लिये भस्म हो जाने का दुःख व्यर्थ नहीँ होता। उस के बदले वह

आकाश जरते हैं ॥ उसी समुद्र में जो आग उत्पन्न ऊई है, अर्थात् जो बडवानल है, उसी के एक विन्दु से, अर्थात् उसी अग्नि के एक कण से (हनुमान् जी द्वारा) लङ्का भस्म हो गई है ॥ (सो संसार में) जो विरह-(अनल) उत्पन्न ऊआ है। उसी से (बडवानल) काढा है, अर्थात् ब्रह्मा ने बडवानल को विरह के एक कणिका को निकाल कर, उसी से बनाया है। यह कवि की अतिशयोक्ति है। (सो वह विरह) जगत् में तैसा बढा ऊआ है, अर्थात् तैसा सर्वत्र व्याप्त है, कि (एक) चण (भी) नहीं बुझता है ॥

रात दिन विरही के हृदय में पैठ, सब अङ्ग को दहन किया करता है। श्री-हर्ष ने भी इस विरहानल की महिमा में लिखा है, कि सती विरहानल को बुझाने-ही के लिये हिमालय के घर जन्म लिया और महादेव के ललाट में जो संसार-दाहक ज्वाला-मय तीसरा नयन है, वह वस्तुतः सती-विरहानल है। और यह विरहानल साधारण अग्नि से बढ कर है; तब तो नारी-जन पति-विरहानल के दुःख से छुट-कारा पाने के लिये चितानल में मृत-पति के संग भस्म हो जाती हैं,

जनुरधत्त सती स्मरतापिता हिमवतो न तु तन्महिमादृता।
ज्वलति भालतले लिखितः सती-विरह एव हरस्य न लोचनम् ॥
दहनजा न पृथुर्दवथुव्यथा विरहजैव पृथुर्यदि नेदृशम्।
दहनमाशु विशन्ति कथं स्त्रियः प्रियमपासुमुपासितुमुद्धुराः ॥
(नैष० स० ४। श्लो० ४५-४६)।

सो जिन्ह को विरह (-अनल) है, अर्थात् जिन्हों ने विरहानल को सह लिया है, उस को साथ साथ लिये चलते फिरते हैं। तिन्हें (यह समुद्र की) आग नहीं देख पडती, अर्थात् वे लोग इस आग को कुछ नहीं समझते। (जो विरहानल को सह लिया है, वह इस आग के) सामने जरता है, और फिर कर पीठ नहीं देता है, अर्थात् इस को तुच्छ समझ कर, इस के भीतर बराबर चला जाता है ॥ संसार में (यह प्रसिद्ध है, कि) तरवार की धार कठिन है, (परन्तु) विरह की दमक (झारा) तलवार (की चमक) से (भी) अधिक है ॥

(कवि कहता है, कि जिस के विरह से यह अग्नि उत्पन्न होती है वह प्रेम-मय प्रियतम) यदि ऐसे अगम्य राह में न होता, (तो) श्रद्धा करने से सब कोई (उस प्रियतम को) पाता, अर्थात् तब तो सर्व साधारण को सुलभ हो जाने से इस

प्रेम-मय प्रियतम (वा पर-ब्रह्म) का माहात्म्य-ही न होता ॥ (सो) अरे (भाई) तिसी समुद्र में (जहाँ धरती सरग जरइ तेहि झारा), (उस विरहानल के बल से) राजा (निःसंशय पार जाने के लिये) पडा, (और) उस में जरा चाहता है, परन्तु (उस विरहानल के प्रभाव से राजा का) रोम भी न जरा ॥

जैसे कराहे में तेल खौलता है (तलफइ), तैसे-ही (इस समुद्र का) जल खौलता है। (परन्तु राजा), जो प्रेम का मलयाचल है, (तिस के) समीर (हवा) से समुद्र बिध गया, अर्थात् मलय-स्वरूप राजा के अङ्ग से मिल कर जो हवा समुद्र में लगी उस के कारण समुद्र भी सुगन्धित और शीतल हो गया। मलयाचल का धर्म है, कि अपने भीतर तो गन्धक इत्यादि द्रव्य और विष-धर सर्पादिकों के कारण जला करता है, और बाहर ऐसा सुगन्धित और शीतल रहता है, कि उस की हवा जिस को लगे वह सुगन्धित और शीतल हो जाय। इसी प्रकार, राजा विरहानल से तो भीतर दग्ध हो रहा है, परन्तु ऊपर योगियों के सदृश, ऐसी शान्त, सुगन्धित और शीतल काया को बनाये है, कि उस की हवा समुद्र में लग जाने से, अग्नि-मय समुद्र भी सुगन्धित और शीतल हो गया। यह कवि का गम्भीराशय है, और इस से राजा में विरहानल-दग्धत्व और मलयाचल-शीतलत्व ये दोनों धर्म आ जाने से पूर्णोपमा ऊई। (इस प्रकार समुद्र के ठंढे हो जाने से लोग सहज में इस समुद्र को भी पार कर गये; यह अध्याहार है)॥॥ १५५ ॥

चउपाई।

सुरा समुद मँह राजा आवा। महुआ मद-छाता देखरावा॥
जो तेहि पिअइ सो भावँरि लेई। सीस फिरइ पँथ पइगु न देई॥
पेम-सुरा जेहि के जिअ माँहा। कित बइठइ महुआ की छाँहा॥
गुरु के पास दाख रस रसा। बइरी बबुर मारि मन कसा॥
बिरहइ दगधि कीन्ह तन भाठी। हाड जराइ दीन्ह जस काठी॥
नयन नीर सउँ पोती किआ। तस मद चुआ बरा जउँ दिआ॥
बिरह सुरागनि भूँजइ माँसू। गिरि गिरि परहिँ रकत कइ आँसू॥

दोहा ।

मुहमद मद जो परेम का गए दीप तहँ राखि ।
सीस न देइ पतंग होइ तउ लहि जाइ न चाखि ॥ १५६ ॥

सुरा = मदिरा = मद्य । आवा = आवइ (आयाति) का भूत-काल में एक-वचन । मऊआ = मधूक = मऊए का फल, जिस से इस प्रान्त में शराब बनती है। मद-छाता = मद-छत्र = मद का छाता = मादक (नशैली) वस्तु का छाता। जैसे सिंघाडे का छाता पानी में फैला रहता है तिसी प्रकार इस जल-मऊए का मद से भरा छाता, अर्थात् पत्र । देखरावा = देखलाया । पिअइ = (पिबति) पीता है । भावँरी = भ्रामरी = घुमरी । शीस = शीर्ष = शिर । फिरइ = (स्फुरति) = फिरता है = घूमता है। पँथ = पथ में = राह में। पइगु = पग = प्रग = पैर। पेम-सुरा = प्रेम-सुरा = प्रेम का मद्य। पास = पार्श्व = निकट । दाख = द्राक्षा = अंगूर । रसा = लसा = लसइ (लसति) का भूत-काल। बइरी = वैरी = शत्रु। वा, बइरी = वदरी = वदरी = वैर वृक्ष। बबुर = बर्व्वर = एक कँटीला वृक्ष जो इस प्रान्त में बऊत प्रसिद्ध है। मारि = मारयित्वा = मार कर। कसा = कसइ (कर्षति) का भूत-काल में एक-वचन। बिरहइ = बिरह ने। दगधि = दग्ध्वा = दग्ध कर = दहका कर। तन = तनु = शरीर। भाठी = भट्टी = भस्त्रा। हाड = हड्डी = अस्थि। जराइ दीन्ह = जरा दिया। जस = जैसे = यथा। काठी = काष्ठ = लकडी। सउँ = सेाँ = से । पोती = पूत = पवित्र = आग से दहक कर डेगचे में मऊआ-गुड वाष्प हो कर जिस नली द्वारा चूते हैं, उस नली के चारो ओर पोचारे के लिये जल रहता है, जिस से मद्य का वाष्प ठंढा हो कर, जल-रूप में हो कर, नली के मुख से दूसरे पात्र में चूआ करता है। इस जल को पोचारे, वा पोतारे, वा पोती का जल कहते हैं। मद = मद्य = मदिरा। चुआ = चुअइ = (च्यवते) चूता है। बरा = बरइ (वर्त्तयति) का भूत-काल में एक-वचन। दिआ = दीप = दीया। सुरागनि = सुराग्नि = सुरा की अग्नि से। भूँजइ = (भज्जति, भ्रस्ज धातु से) भूँजता है। माँसू = मांस। गिरि गिरि = गिर गिर कर = गल गल कर। परहिँ = परइ (पतति) का बऊ-वचन। रकत = रक्त = लोहू। आँसू = अश्रु = आँस ॥ परेम = प्रेम। दीप = दीपक = दीया। राखि = रचयित्वा = रख कर। पतंग = कीट = फतंगा। तउ लहि = तब तक। जाइ (याति) जाता है। चाखि = चख (चषति) से बना = चाखा ॥

राजा सुरा (मदिरा) के समुद्र में आया। मऊआ मद के छाते को देखलाया, अर्थात् उस समुद्र में जहाँ देखो तहाँ मऊआ के छाते (पच) मद से भरे देख पडते हैं, जिन के मिलने से समुद्र का जल मदिरा हो गया है॥ (इस लिये) जो तिस (जल) को पीता है वह (सो) (नशे से) भावँरी लेने लगता है, अर्थात् घुमरी खाने लगता है। शिर फिरता है, अर्थात् शिर में चक्कर आने लगता है, (और वह पुरुष) राह में पैर नहीं देता है, अर्थात् उस पुरुष का राह में सीधा पैर नहीं पडता है॥ राजा उन मऊओं की छाया में बैठ कर विश्राम क्यों नहीं लेता है। इस पर कवि कहता है, कि जिस के हृदय में प्रेम-सुरा है, अर्थात् जो प्रेम-सुरा से छक गया है, वह मऊए की छाया में क्यों (कित = कुतः) बैठे (बइठइ = बैठे = उपविष्टो भवेत् = विशेत्)॥ (राजा इस समुद्र-सुरा को क्यों नहीं पीता है; इस पर कवि कहता है, कि) गुरु (शुक वा गोरखनाथ जिस को स्मरण कर चला है) के पास (राजा) अंगूर रस से रस गया है; अर्थात् गुरु की कृपा से द्राक्षा-रूप जो प्रेम उस से राजा की शरीर भर गई है, (और राजा ने) वैरी बबुर को मार कर, अर्थात् शरीरान्तर्गत मोह, लोभ, क्रोध इत्यादि जो वैरी, कण्टक-स्वरूप बबुर के सदृश उन्हें हटा कर, वा मोहादि जो बैर बबुर सदृश उन्हें हटा कर, (उस प्रेम-द्राक्षा को अच्छी तरह) मन में कस लिया, अर्थात् मन के भीतर भर लिया॥ विरह (अग्नि) को दगधा कर तनु (शरीर) को भट्ठी किया, (और) हड्डियों को ऐसा जराया जैसे कि काठ। (अपने) नयन जलों से पोचारा किया, अर्थात् उस भट्ठी में से वह प्रेम-द्राक्षा का रस वाष्प हो कर, जब गले की पिछली नस-नली से चला, तब उस को ठंढा करने और जल-रूप करने के लिये नयनाश्रुओं से पोचारा किया। (इस प्रकार से नयनों के द्वारा) तैसा मद (मदिरा = सुरा) चुआ जैसे दीप बरा हो, अर्थात् उस चूते सुरा का ऐसा उज्ज्वल तेजो-मय रूप है जैसे दीप की संचलित शिखा हो (इस लिये जिस के पास अंगूरी शराब है, वह मैली मऊए की बदबूदार शराब क्यों पीवे)॥ (यद्यपि राजा के हृदय में ऐसी अंगूरी शराब भरी है, तथापि मुख-द्वारा हृदय में न भरने से, राजा इस के स्वादु से वञ्चित है, क्योंकि यह तो गुरूपदेश से कान की राह से राजा के हृदय में भर गई है। इस लिये दूसरी राह से पेट में जाने से सुख के बदले राजा को दुःख-दायिनी हो गई है)। विरह (इस) सुराग्नि से, अर्थात् घी के स्थान में इसी सुरा को तपा अग्नि-मय कर, उस में (राजा के) मांस को भूँज

रहा है, (जिस के कारण राजा के नयनों से) रक्त की आँस गिर गिर पडती हैं (ऐसी व्याकुल-अवस्था में राजा की दशा अत्यन्त शोचनीय हो गई है) ॥

(मुहम्मद कवि कहते हैं, कि यद्यपि राजा के हृदय में प्रेम-सुरा भरी है, तथापि कर्णद्वारा उदर में जाने से यह अजीर्ण हो कर राजा को आकुल किये है। इस लिये 'विषस्य विषमौषधम्' इस सिद्धान्त से यदि और कहीं कुछ प्रेम-सुरा मिले, जिसे मुख-द्वारा राजा पीवे, तो प्रेम-सुरा का स्वादु पावे और अजीर्ण भी नसावे। परन्तु) प्रेम का मद (सुरा) जो है, सो (तो) तहाँ (पद्मावती वा पर-ब्रह्म) दीप (सिंहल-दीप, वा परब्रह्म-स्थान) में रख गया है, अर्थात् पद्मावती के दीप में वह स्नेह (प्रेम) स्नेह (तैल) के सदृश बरता ऊआ रक्खा है। (सो जब तक उस दीप में) पतंग हो कर गिर न दे, तब तक वह (स्नेह = प्रेम) चक्खा न जाय, अर्थात् जैसे दीप की शिखा में फतंगा जल जाता है। उसी तरह उस पद्मावती के दीप में जब तक जल न जाय, तब तक उस प्रेम-सुरा के स्वादु को नहीं पा सकता ॥ १५६ ॥

चउपाई।

पुनि किलकिला समुद मँह आए। गा धीरज देखत डरु खाए ॥
भा किलकिल अस उठइ हलोरा। जनु अकास टूटइ चहुँ ओरा ॥
उठइ लहरि परबत कइ नाईं। होइ फिरइ जोजन लख ताईं ॥
धरती लेत सरग लहि बाढा। सकल समुद जानउँ भा ठाढा ॥
नीर होइ तर ऊपर सोई। महा-अरंभ समुद जस होई ॥
फिरत समुद जोजन लख ताका। जइसइ फिरइ कोम्हार क चाका ॥
भा परलउ निअराना जउ-हीँ। मरइ सो ता कहँ परलउ तउ-हीँ ॥

दोहा।

गइ अउसान सबहिँ कइ देखि समुद कइ बाढि।
निअर होत जनु लीलइ रहा नयन अस काढि ॥ १५७ ॥

किलकिला = किल किल ऐसा जिस के शब्द में अनुकरण हो। गा = अगात् = गया। धीरज = धैर्य। डरु = डर = दर = भय। खाए = खाद (खादति) का भूत-काल में बज-वचन। भा = अभूत् = भया = ऊआ। उठइ = (उत्तिष्ठते) उठता है। हलोर =

हिल-लोल = इधर से उधर पानियोँ का चञ्चल होना। अकास = आकाश = आसमान। टूटइ = (त्रुय्यति) टूटता है। चऊँ = चारो। ओर = अपर-प्रान्त = किनारा। उडइ = (उड्डीयते) उडता है, उडती है। लहरि = लहरी, वा लहर = तरङ्ग। परबत = पर्वत = पहाड। नाईँ = निभ = सदृश। फिरइ = (स्फरति) फिरता है। जोजन = योजन, (चार क्रोश का एक योजन होता है)। लख = लक्ष = लाख। ताईँ = तक = तदन्त। धरती = धरित्री = पृथ्वी। लेत = लेता ऊआ। सरग = स्वर्ग = आकाश। लहि = लाभ कर, वा लहि = लगि = लग कर = तक। बाढा = बढइ (वर्द्धते)। ठाढ = ठढा = खडा = उत्थित। नीर = जल। तर = तल = नीचे। ऊपर = उपरि। महा-अरंभ = महारम्भ = महावेग = महात्वरा (आरम्भः सम्भ्रमस्त्वरा, अमरकोश, ३ काण्ड, सङ्कीर्ण-वर्ग)। जस = यथा = जैसे, वा जस = यश = यशो-गान। ताका = ताकने से = देखने से = तर्कतः = तर्क से। जइसइ = जैसे = यथा। कोम्हार = कुम्हार, वा कोहार = कुलाल। क = का। चाका = चक्र = चाक। परलउ = प्रलय = परलय। निअराना = निकट ऊआ = निकट आया = नगिचाना। (जैसे भूख से भुखाना, लालच से ललचाना, घाबड से घबडाना इत्यादि)। जउ-हीँ = ज्योँ-ही = जैसे-ही। मरइ = (मरति) मरता है। तउ-हीँ = त्योँ-ही = तैसे-ही॥ गइ = गई = स्त्री-लिङ्ग में भूत-काल का एक-वचन, इसी का पुं-लिङ्ग में रूप 'गा' होता है। अउसान = अवशान्ति = स्थिरता। बाढि = बाढ = वर्धनम्। निअर = निकट। होत = होते। लीलइ (निगिलति) = लीलता है = निगलता है। काढि = काढ कर = निकाल कर = निःकाश्य।

(लोग) फिर किलकिला समुद्र में आए, (समुद्र को) देखते-ही (लोगोँ का) धीरज (चला) गया, (और) डर खाए, अर्थात् डर गये॥ (उस समुद्र में) किलकिल ऐसा (शब्द) ऊआ, अर्थात् होता है, (और) हलोर उठता है। (उस हलोर में अररर ऐसा शब्द होता है)। जानोँ चारो ओर से आकाश टूट रहा है॥ लहर पर्वत के ऐसी उडती है, अर्थात् लहर में समुद्र से अलग पहाड के ऐसा बडे ऊँचे तक जल-पुञ्ज उड जाता है। (और वह लहर) लाख योजन तक हो कर फिरती है, अर्थात् लाख लाख योजन तक लहर में पानी उठ जाता है तब वहाँ से फिरता है॥ (जिस घडी पानी ऊपर को उठता है उस बेरा समुद्र) धरती लेते स्वर्ग तक बढ जाता है। (उस समय जान पडता है, कि) सर्वत्र (सकल-स्थान) जानोँ समुद्र (ही) खडा ऊआ है, अर्थात् भूमि से आकाश तक समुद्र-ही समुद्र देख पडता है॥ वही

(सोई) नीर, अर्थात् वही लहर का पानीय-पुञ्ज (आवर्त्त के वेग से) नीचे ऊपर होता है। (उस के कारण जान पडता है) जैसे समुद्र में महा-वेग होता हो, अथवा महा-वेग से समुद्र का यश होता हो, अर्थात् चारो ओर से यशो-गान की घोर-ध्वनि होती हो॥ देखने से, वा तर्क करने से, (जान पडता है, कि) लाख (लख) योजन तक (आवर्त्त से) पानी घूमता है, जैसे (कि) कोहार का चाक फिरता है॥ (ऐसा समुद्र) जैसे-ही नियराना (तैसे-ही) प्रलय हो गया, अर्थात् लोगोँ ने यही समझा, कि अब प्रलय आ गया, इस में कोई न बचेगा। (प्रलय में तो सब का नाश हो जाता है) इस में यदि मरँगे भी तो राजा और राज-कुअँर-ही मरँगे। फिर इस का नाम कवि ने प्रलय कैसे कहा। इस आशङ्का पर कवि कहता है, कि) (जो) मरता है तिस के लिये त्योहीँ, अर्थात् मरण-क्षण-ही में वह (सो) प्रलय है, अर्थात् जिस दिन जो मर जाता है, उस के लिये जानोँ प्रलय हो गया। कहावत है, कि 'आप डूबा जग डूबा'। प्रलय पुराणोँ में चार प्रकार का है, दैनं-दिन प्रलय१, जो कि प्राणियोँ के मरने से प्रतिदिन हुआ करता है। ब्राह्म-लय २, ब्रह्मा की रात्रि आ जाने से; इस प्रलय में सब जीवोँ को अपने उदर में ले कर, ब्रह्मा सो जाता है। प्राकृतिक प्रलय३, इस में ब्रह्मा इत्यादि सब का नाश हो जाता है; सब प्रकृति के अन्तर्गत हो जाते हैं। आत्यन्तिक प्रलय४, उस योगी का होता है, जो समाधि लगा कर, पाप-पुण्य को ज्ञानाग्नि से भस्म कर, पर-ब्रह्म में लीन हो जाता है। भास्कराचार्य ने अपने गोलाध्याय के भुवन-कोश में लिखा है, कि--

दिने दिने यन्म्रियते हि भूतैर्दैनंदिनं तं प्रलयं वदन्ति।
ब्राह्मं लयं ब्रह्म-दिनान्तकाले भूतानि यद्ब्रह्मतनुं विशन्ति॥
ब्रह्मात्यये यत् प्रकृतिं प्रयान्ति भूतान्यतः प्राकृतिकं कृतीन्द्राः।
लीनान्यतः कर्मपुटान्तरत्वात् पृथक् क्रियन्ते प्रकृतेर्विकारैः॥
ज्ञानाग्निदग्धाखिलपुण्यपापा मनः समाधाय हरौ परेशे।
यद्योगिनो यान्त्यनिवृत्तिमस्मादात्यन्तिकं चेति लयश्चतुर्धा॥

(भास्कर के लिये गणकतरङ्गिणी देखो)

इस तरह प्रलयोँ में चार भेद होने से स्पष्ट होता है, कि कवि ने 'मरइ सो ता कहँ परलउ तउ-हीँ'। इस से दैनंदिन प्रलय को लिया है॥

('सकल समुद जानउँ भा ठाढा' ऐसी) समुद्र की बाढ देख कर सब का धैर्य गया,

अर्थात् सब कोई धीरज छोड कर घबडा गये। (तरङ्ग-रूप) नयनोँ को ऐसा काढ रहा है, अर्थात् वार वार तरङ्ग-नयनोँ से ऐसा गुरेर रहा है; जानोँ नगीच होते-ही लील-ता है, अर्थात् अपने लहरोँ की ऐसी भयङ्कर लीला को देखला रहा है, जिस से यही जान पडता है, कि इस के नगीच हुए, कि निगला ॥१५७॥

चउपाई।

हीरा-मनि राजा सउँ बोला। इह-ई समुद आहि सत-डोला ॥
सिंघल-दीप जो नाहिँ निबाहू। इह-इ ठावँ साँकर सब काहू ॥
इह-इ किलकिला समुद गँभीरू। जेहि गुन होइ सो पावइ तीरू ॥
इह-इ समुदर-पंथ मँझ-धारा। खाँडइ कइ असि धार निरारा ॥
तीस सहसर कोस कइ पाटा। तस साँकर चलि सकइ न चाँटा ॥
खाँडइ चाहि पइनि पइनाई। बार चाहि पातरि पतराई ॥
इह-इ ठावँ कहँ गुरु सँग लीजिअ। गुरु सँग होइ पार तउ कीजिअ ॥

दोहा।

मरन जिअन एही पँथ एही आस निरास।
परा सो गएउ पतारहि तरा सो गा कबिलास ॥ १५८ ॥

हीरा-मनि = हीरा-मणि। सउँ = सोँ = से। बोला = बोलइ (बल्गति वा वदति) का भूत-काल में एक-वचन। इह-ई = यही = अयं हि। आहि = है (अस्ति)। सत-डोला = सत्य-दोलक = सत्य को डोलाने-वाला = सत्य को डगाने-वाला = सत्य को हिलाने-वाला = सत्य छोडाने-वाला। सिंघल-दीप = सिंहल-द्वीप। निबाहू = निर्वाह। ठावँ = स्थान। साँकर = सङ्कटम् = सङ्कट = कठिन = दुःखद। गँभीरू = गम्भीर = गहरा। गुन = गुण = विद्या = हुनर। वा गुण = डोर, जहाज की। पावइ = (प्राप्नोति) पाता है। तीरू = तीर = तट = किनारा, उस पार का। समुदर = समुद्र। समुदर-पंथ = समुद्र-पथ = समुद्र की राह। मँझ-धारा = मध्य-धारा = बीच की धारा। खाँडइ = खण्ड = तलवार = खड्ग। असि = एतादृशी = ऐसी। धार = धारा। निरारा = निरालय = बाहर = निकली = निनार = निराल = खास = अलग। तीस = त्रिंशत्। सहसर = सहस्र = हजार। कोस = क्रोश। पाटा = पाट = पाच। सकइ =

(शक्नोति) सकता है। चाँटा = चाट = चीँटा। चाहि = च हि = से भी। पदनि = पानी = पान जिस मेँ हो (अनेक वस्तुओँ को पानी मेँ मिला कर, उस मिश्रित पानी में पक्का करने के लिये शस्त्र को बुझाते हैँ। इस मिश्रित पानी को संहिता-कारोँ ने 'पान' के नाम से लिखा है। पान जिस मेँ हो सो पानी, जैसे दण्ड से दण्डी, दान से दानी, मान से मानी इत्यादि) अर्थात् चोखाई, वा तेजाई अथवा तीक्ष्णता। पदनाई = पदनि से धर्मबोधक शब्द बनाने के लिये तद्धित से 'आई' प्रत्यय लगा है, जैसे पाऊन से पऊनाई, मीत से मिताई, खट्टा से खटाई इत्यादि। बार = वाल = केश (चिकुरः कुन्तलो वालः कचः केशः शिरोरुहः, अमरकोश, काण्ड२, मनुष्य-वर्ग। श्लो. ६५९)। पातरि = पतला = पत्र के ऐसा = सूक्ष्म। पतराई = पतलापन (धर्मवाचक में पतरे से 'आई' प्रत्यय)। लीजिअ = लीजिये। तउ = तर्हि = तो। कीजिअ = कीजिये ॥ मरन = मरणम् = मरना। जिअन = जीवनम् = जीना। एही = यही। आस = आशा = उम्मेद। निरास = नैराश्य = ना उम्मेदी। परा = परइ (पतति) का भूत-काल मेँ एक-वचन। पतारहि = पाताल को। तरा = (तरति) तरइ का भूत-काल मेँ एक-वचन। कबिलास = कैलास = शिव-लोक ॥

हीरा-मणि (शुक) राजा (रत्न-सेन) से बोला, (कि) सत्य को डोलाने-वाला यही समुद्र है ॥ सिंहल-दीप मेँ जो निर्वाह नहीँ होता, अर्थात् जा नहीँ सकते, (उस का कारण यही है, कि) यही स्थान (किलकिला समुद्र) सब किसी को कठिन है, अर्थात् यात्रियोँ को यही रोक रखता है; इसी को देख कर लोग प्राण-भय से फिर जाते हैँ ॥ यही (बडा) गम्भीर किलकिला समुद्र है। जिस को (कोई अपूर्व) विद्या वा गोन (जहाज खीँचने की डोर) हो सो (इस के उस) तीर को पाता है ॥ यही समुद्र-पथ मेँ मध्य-धारा है, अर्थात् यही समुद्रोँ का मध्य-धारा-रूप समुद्र है, इसी मेँ सब से अधिक लहर और भयङ्कर धारा का वेग है। (इस की) खास तलवार के धार ऐसी धारा है, अर्थात् जैसे खड्ग की धारा के सम्मुख जाने से प्राणी टूक टूक हो जाता है; इसी प्रकार इस की धारा के सम्मुख पड जाने से, जीव, जन्तु, जहाज इत्यादि के टुकडे टुकडे हो जाते हैँ; वे टुकडे पाताल मेँ पऊँच जाते हैँ, क्योँकि पता नहीँ लगता, कि कहाँ चले गये ॥ तीस हजार क्रोश का (तो इस का) पाट है। (और यह) तैसा कठिन है, कि चीँटा भी (इस मेँ) नहीँ चल सकता। यहाँ चीँटा से चीँटा के ऐसा लघु पुरुष समझो, जो कि अपनी लघुता से पानी के नीचे नहीँ जाता, किन्तु पानी के ऊपर-ही तैरा

करता है, तिस के लिये भी इस समुद्र का पार होना कठिन है। अन्यथा चींटा एक साधारण जल भरे गडहे के पार नहीँ हो सकता, उस को समुद्र-तरण में असमर्थ होने से समुद्र की क्या विशेष महिमा ऊई॥ (इस समुद्र की धारा में) खड्ग की तीक्ष्णता से भी बढ कर तीक्ष्णता है। बार की पतराई से भी बढ कर पतला-पन है, अर्थात् इस की धारा में ऐसी तेजी और पतला-पन है, कि छोटा से छोटा और पतला से पतला भी जन्तु इस के सामने पडे, तो भी टूक टूक ऊए विना न बचे॥ इसी ध्यान के लिये गुरु को संग लीजिये, अर्थात् गुरु को संग लेना चाहिए, अर्थात् ध्यान से गुरु का स्मरण कर, गुरु को अपने हृदय में धर लेना चाहिए। (जब) गुरु संग में हो तब (इस को) पार कीजिये, अर्थात् ध्यान से गुरु को अपने हृदय मेँ धर कर, उसे संगी बना कर, तब इस को पार करना चाहिए॥

इस (समुद्र की) राह में मरना जीना (दोनो) है। इस (राह) में आशा, निराशा (दोनो) है, (क्योँ कि) (जो इस की धारा मेँ) पडा वह (सो) (तो) पाताल को चला गया (इस से मरना और निराशा दोनो ऊए), (और जो) तर गया, अर्थात् निर्विघ्न पार हो गया, सो कैलास में गया, अर्थात् आशा पूर्ण ऊई, और सदा के लिये जीना (अमरत्व) हो गया। वह प्राणी जीवन्मुक्त हो पर-ब्रह्म-स्वरूप हो गया॥ १५८॥

चउपाई।

राजइ दीन्ह कटक कहँ बीरा। सु-पुरुख होहु करहु मन धीरा॥
ठाकुर जेहि क सूर भा कोई। कटक सूर पुनि आपु-हि होई॥
जउ लहि सती न जिउ सत बाँधा। तउ लहि देइ कहार न काँधा॥
पेम-समुद मँह बाँधा बेरा। एइ सब समुद बूँद जेहि केरा॥
ना हउँ सरग क चाहउँ राजू। ना मोहिँ नरक सितँ किछु काजू॥
चाहउँ ओहि कर दरसन पावा। जेइ मोहिँ आनि पेम-पँथ लावा॥
काठहि काह गाढ का ढीला। बूड न समुद मगर नहिँ लीला॥

दोहा।

गहि समुदर धसि लीन्हेसि भा पाछइ सब कोइ।
कोइ काहु न सँभारई आपुनि आपुनि होइ॥ १५९॥

ऐसी शोभा है, जानों दन्त नहीं हैं, भौंरे दाँतों का रूप धारण कर विकशित मुख-कमल का रस लेते हैं। जब मुख-कमल बंद हो जाता है तब जानों वे दन्त-रूप भौंरे संपुटित हो जाते हैं, और हँसने पर मुख-कमल के प्रफुल्लित होने से देख पड़ने लगते हैं। मुख-कमल के पुराने अन्तरङ्ग मित्र दाँत हैं। अपरिचित को देख कर, यह मुख-कमल सङ्कोच से कदाचित् अपना शुद्ध-रस न पीने दे। इस लिये भौंरे, कपट से दाँतों का रूप धारण कर, रस लेते हैं। यह कवि की अतिशयोक्ति है॥ (उस मानसर में) हंस हँसते हैं, अर्थात् प्रसन्न वदन हैं, और (आपस में) क्रीड़ा करते हैं। मोती, हीरा (इत्यादि) रत्न को चुनते हैं, अर्थात् चुँग रहे हैं॥ (कवि कहता है, कि) जो ऐसा तप (और) योग साध आवे, अर्थात् जैसा राजा ने कष्ट सह कर, तप और योग साधा; उसी प्रकार जो तप योग साधन करे, (तो उस की) आशा पूरी होती है, (और वह) इस भोग को मानता है, अर्थात् मन माना प्रेम-रस का भोग करता है॥

भ्रमर जो मन से मानसर (मानस वा, मान्य-सर=उत्तम-तड़ाग) को लिया, अर्थात् हृदय से सब वासना विसार कर, नाना प्रकार के क्लेशों को सह कर, जो उत्तम सर में पहुँचा, (तो उसी कष्ट के बदले) आ कर (अनुपम) कमल का रस लिया, ('लीन्ह' क्रिया का दोनो ओर अन्वय करना चाहिए)। (और) घुन जो साहस (हिम्राउ) न कर सका, तैसा सूखा काठ खाता है, अर्थात् आलस्य से, हिम्मत हार कर, बैठ रहा। तिसी के कारण उस को नीरस सूखा काठ खाना पड़ता है। कबीरदास ने भी कहा है, कि

'जो ढूँढा तिन पाइयाँ गहिरे पानी पैठि।
वे बपुरी क्या पाइयाँ रहीं किनारे बैठि॥'

हठ-योग के मत से गुद, लिङ्ग, नाभी, हृदय, कण्ठ, भ्रू-मध्य और ब्रह्माण्ड इन स्थानों में शरीरान्तर्गत कमल हैं (बहुतों के मत से हृदय और कण्ठ में अभेद होने से छ-ही कमल हैं), जिन में योगी को क्रम क्रम से प्राण चढ़ाने में क्लेश होता है। अर्थात् गुद पर चढ़ाने की अपेक्षा लिङ्ग-कमल पर चढ़ाना कठिन। लिङ्ग-कमल पर चढ़ाने की अपेक्षा नाभी-कमल पर चढ़ाना कठिन। यों एक से एक कठिन हैं। सब से कठिन नीचे गुद से चढ़ाते भ्रू-मध्य-कमल में ले जाना है। यदि इस कमल पर प्राण चढ़ गया तो ब्रह्माण्ड-कमल के मध्य जहाँ सच्चिदानन्द से

भरा अमृत-सुख धरा है, और 'सोऽहं सोऽहं' जिसे योगी कहते हैं उस हंस-स्वरूप पर-ब्रह्म का जहाँ अनाहत ध्वनि से पूरित नाना रत्नमय स्थान है, जाने में कुछ भी देरी नहीं लगती। यहाँ यदि इन कमलों के स्थान में क्रम से खार, चीर, दधि, जलधि, सुरा, किलकिला और मानसर को मान लो, तो राजा (रत्न-सेन) अब भ्रू-मध्य-कमल (किलकिला) के ऊपर अपने प्राणों को चढा लाया। इस लिये अब पद्मावती-रूप सच्चिदानन्द के परम-धाम ब्रह्माण्ड सिंहल में पहुँचना कुछ कठिन नहीं है। गुद से प्राण चढाने में स्थल-विशेषों में प्राण के आने से योगी इस काय-व्यूह में नाना प्रकार का चमत्कार देखता है, जहाँ नाना प्रकार की हजारों सिद्धि, कर जोरे योगी के सामने सेवा के लिये खडी रहती हैं। परन्तु यदि भ्रमर के सदृश, योगी उन की माया में फँस कर उन्हीं स्थानों में अपने प्राण को न अटकावे, और सिद्धियों की चटक मटक में न आवे, हिम्मत कर, मानसर (ब्रह्माण्ड = ब्रह्म-रन्ध्र) तक चला जावे, तो अवश्य इस साहस के बदले ब्रह्म-रन्ध्र-कमलान्तर्गत पर-ब्रह्म-पराग-रस को पावे, जिस से अजर अमर हो, जीवन्मुक्त कहलावे। अन्यथा घुन के ऐसा प्राण सूखी काय-काठी में पडा उसी काठी-ही को खाता, काठी के साथ-ही नष्ट हो जाता है। इस प्रकार के रूपक से समुद्र-यात्रा-वर्णन सब हठ-योग-पच्च में लग जाता है।

शरीरान्तर्गत चक्रों के विषय में अनेक मत हैं। देवी-भागवत, सप्तम-स्कन्ध, अध्याय ३५ में भी इन चक्रों का विशेष-रूप से वर्णन है। कोई ऐसा भी कहते हैं।

आधारे लिङ्गनाभौ प्रकटितहृदये तालुमूले ललाटे
द्वे पत्रे षोडशारे द्विदशदशदले द्वादशार्द्धे चतुष्के।
वासान्ते बालमध्ये डफ-कठ-सहिते कण्ठदेशे स्वराणां
हं चं तत्त्वार्थयुक्तं सकलदलगतं वर्णरूपं नमामि॥

आधार = गुद-कमल, ४ दल, व, श, ष, स वर्णात्मक १। लिङ्ग-कमल, ६ दल, ब, भ, म, य, र, ल वर्णात्मक २। नाभी-कमल, १० दल, ड, ढ, ण, त, थ, द, ध, न, प, फ वर्णात्मक ३। हृदय-कमल, १२ दल, क, ख, ग, घ, ङ, च, छ, ज, झ, ञ, ट, ठ वर्णात्मक ४। तालु-मूल = कण्ठ-कमल, १६ दल, अ, आ, इ, ई, उ, ऊ, ऋ, ॠ, ऌ, ॡ, ए, ऐ, ओ, औ, अं, अः वर्णात्मक ५। ललाट-कमल, २ दल, ह, च वर्णात्मक ६। इस के परे ब्रह्म-रन्ध्र-कमल, जिस में हजार दल हैं॥ १६१॥

इति सप्त-समुद्र-खण्ड-नाम पञ्चदश-खण्डं समाप्तम्॥ १५।

44

अथ सिंघल-दीप-भाउ-खंड ॥ १९ ॥

चउपाई ।

पूँछा राजइ कहु गुरु सुआ। न जनउँ आजु कहा दहु उआ ॥
पवन बास सीतल लेइ आवा। काया दहत चँदन जनु लावा ॥
कब-हुँ न अइस जुडान सरीरू। परा अगिनि मँह मलय-समीरू ॥
निकसत आउ किरिन रबि रेखा। तिमिर गए निरमर जग देखा ॥
उठइ मेघ अस जानउँ आगइ। चमकइ बीजु गगन पर लागइ ॥
तेहि ऊपर जनु ससि परगासा। अउ सो चाँद कचपची गरासा ॥
अउरु नखत चहुँ दिसि उँजिआरी। ठावँहिँ ठावँ दीप अस बारी ॥

दोहा ।

अउरु दखिन दिसि निअर-हि कंचन मेरु देखाउ ।
जनु बसंत रितु आवइ तस बसंत जग आउ ॥ १९२ ॥

पूँछा = पूँछइ (पृच्छति) का भूत-काल में एक-वचन । राजइ = राजा ने। कहु = कहइ (कथयति) का लोट् में मध्यम-पुरुष का एक-वचन। सुआ = शुक = सुग्गा। जनउँ = जानउँ = जानइ (जानाति) का उत्तम-पुरुष में एक-वचन। आजु = आज = अद्य। दहु = दह = दहा = दशा = भाग्य। उआ = उअइ (उदयति) का भूत-काल में एक-वचन। बास = वास = वासना = सुगन्ध। सीतल = शीतल = ठंढी, वा, ठंढा। काया = काय = शरीर। दहत = दहन् = दहती = भस्म होती। चँदन = चन्दन। लावा

लगाया = लगइ (लगति) का णिजन्त का भूत-काल में एक-वचन। कब-ऊँ = कदापि हि = कभी। अइस = एतादृश = ऐसी। जुडान = जुडाई = ठंढी ऊई = जडी-भूत ऊई। सरीरू = शरीर। परा = परइ (पतति) का भूत-काल में एक-वचन। अगिनि = अग्नि = आग। मलय-समीरू = मलय-समीर = मलय का वायु। निकसत = निःक्रमन् = निकलती। आउ = आवइ (आयाति)। किरिन = किरण। रबि = रवि = सूर्य। रेखा = लेखा = पङ्क्ति = पाँति। तिमिर = अन्धकार = अँधेरा। निरमर = निर्मल = स्वच्छ। जग = जगत् = संसार। देखा = देख पडता है। उठइ = (उत्तिष्ठते) उठता है। मेघ = बादल। अस = एतादृश = ऐसा। आगइ = अग्रे = आगे। चमकइ = (चम् करोति) चमकता है। बीजु = विद्युत् = बिजली। गगन = आकाश। पर = उपरि = ऊपर। लागइ = लगइ (लग्यते) लगती है। ससि = शशि = चन्द्रमा। परगासा = परगासइ = (प्रकाशते) का भूत-काल में एक-वचन। चाँद = चन्द्र = चन्द्रमा। कचपची = कृत्तिका नक्षत्र जिस में छ तारे रहते हैं = जिस के तारे कचपच करते रहते हैं। गरासा = गरासइ (ग्रसते) का भूत-काल में एक-वचन। अउरु = अपर = इतर। नखत = नक्षत्र। चऊँ = चारो। दिसि = दिशि = दिशाओं में। उँजिआरी = उज्ज्वलता = उँजेला। ठावँ = स्थान। दीप = दीया = चिराग। बारी = बारइ (वर्त्तयति) का भूत-काल में स्त्रीलिङ्ग का एक-वचन॥ दखिन = दक्षिण। निअर-हि = निकट-ही। कंचन = काञ्चन = सुवर्ण। मेरु = प्रसिद्ध उत्तर दिशा का पर्वत जहाँ देवता लोग रहते हैं। देखाउ = देखाता है = देख पडता है। बसंत = वसन्त = ऋतुओं का राजा। बसंत = बसता ऊआ = बसा ऊआ। जग = जगत् = संसार, यहाँ सब स्थान॥

राजा ने (शुक से पूँछा, कि) हे शुक गुरु, कहो (तो आज हम लोग कहाँ आये, क्योंकि) आज नहीं जानता, (कि) कैसी (कहा = कथम्) दशा (भाग्य) उदय ऊई॥ (आज) वायु शीतल सुगन्ध को ले आया है। (जो) शरीर भस्म होती थी (उस में) जानों चन्दन लगाया गया है॥ ऐसी कभी शरीर नहीं ठंढी ऊई थी। (जान पडता है, कि) आग में मलय-वायु पडा है, अर्थात् आज मलय-वायु से मेरे शरीर की तपन बुझ गई है॥ रवि के किरण की पङ्क्ति निकलती आती है, अर्थात् प्रातःकाल हो रहा है। अन्धकार (नष्ट हो) गये; जगत् निर्मल (साफ) देख पडता है॥ आगे ऐसा (जान पडता है) जानों बादल उठा है। बिजली चमकती है, (और) आकाश पर लगती है, अर्थात् बिजली चमक चमक कर आकाश के ऊपर जा कर

लगती है ॥ तिस (बिजली) के ऊपर जानेाँ चन्द्रमा प्रकाश किया है। और (जो) चन्द्रमा है सो कचपची को (जानेाँ) गरासता है, अर्थात् खाता है ॥ (कचपची के अतिरिक्त) और नचत्रोँ की (भी) चारो दिशाओँ मेँ उँजियाली है। (उन की ऐसी शोभा है, जानेाँ) जगह जगह मेँ दीप के ऐसे (कोई चमकदार पदार्थ) बारे गये हैँ ॥

और दक्षिण दिशा मेँ नगीच-ही सुवर्ण का मेरु (पर्वत) देख पडता है। जानेाँ वसन्त ऋतु आती है तैसा, जगत् बसता आता है, अर्थात् आगे सब स्थान ऐसे शोभित हैँ, जानेाँ उन स्थानेाँ मेँ वसन्त ऋतु आ कर डेरा लगाये है। यह सब पद्मावती-पच मेँ सिंहल की लीला और ब्रह्म-रन्ध्र मेँ ब्रह्म-रन्ध्रस्थ-कमल की लीला राजा वा योगि-राज को देख पडती है, जिस का यथावत् वर्णन अगली चौपाइयोँ से विदित होगा ॥ १६२ ॥

चउपाई ।

तूँ राजा जस बिकरम आदी। तूँ हरिचंद बइनु सत-बादी ॥
गोपिचंद तुइँ जीता जोगा। अउ भरथरी न पूज बिओगा ॥
गोरख सिद्धि दीन्ह तोहि हाथू। तारी गुरू मछंदर-नाथू ॥
जीता पेम तेँ पुहुमि अकासू। दिसिटि परा सिंघल कबिलासू ॥
बेद्द जो मेघ गढ लाग अकासा। बिजुरी कनइ कोट चहुँ पासा ॥
तेहि पर ससि जो कचपचि भरा। राज-मँदिर सोनइ नग जरा ॥
अउर-उ नखत कहेसि चहुँ पासा। सब रानिन्ह कइ आहि अबासा ॥

दोहा ।

गगन सरोबर ससि कवँल कुमुद तराईँ पास।
तूँ रबि ऊआ भवँर होइ पवन मिला लेइ बास ॥ १६३ ॥

तूँ = त्वम्। बिकरम = विक्रम, उज्जयिनी का राजा। आदी = आदि = प्रथम = पहला। हरिचंद = हरिश्चन्द्र = त्रिशङ्कु का पुत्र = अयोध्या का एक राजा। बइनु = वैन्य = वेन का पुत्र राजा पृथु, बर्हिष्मती नगरी का राजा। सत-बादी = सत्य-वादी = सत्य-कहने-वाला = सत्य-वक्ता। गोपिचंद = गोपीचन्द्र = बङ्गाले का एक राजा (१२२ वेँ दोहे की टीका देखो)। जीता = जीतइ (जयति) का भूत-काल मेँ एक-वचन।

जोगा = योग। भरथरी = भर्तृहरि = राजा विक्रम का छोटा भाई (१३४ वेँ दोहे की टीका देखो)। पूज = पूजा = पूजइ (पूर्यते) का भूत-काल मेँ एक-वचन। बिओगा = वियोग = विरक्तता। गोरख = गोरक्ष-नाथ अवधूत जो मछंदर के प्रधान शिष्य थे (१२८ वेँ दोहे की टीका देखो)। हाथू = हाथ = हस्त। तारी = तारइ (तारयति) का स्त्री-लिङ्ग मेँ भूत-काल का एक-वचन। वा, तारी = ताली = कुञ्जी = चाभी। गुरू = गुरु = आचार्य। मछंदर-नाथू = मछंदर-नाथ = मत्स्येन्द्र-नाथ = गोरख के गुरु। पेम = प्रेम। पुहुमि = पृथिवी = भूमि। अकासू = आकाश = आसमान। दिसिटि = दृष्टि। परा = परइ (पतति) का भूत-काल मेँ एक-वचन। सिंघल = सिंहल-द्वीप। कबिलासू = कैलास = महादेव के रहने का स्थान = शिव-लोक। गढ = गाढ = दुर्ग = किला। लाग = लगइ (लगति) का भूत-काल मेँ एक-वचन। अकासा = आकाश। बिजुरी = विद्युत् = बिजली। कनइ = कणी = कणिका = कनी वज्र की। कोट = गढ। चहुँ = चारो। पासा = पार्श्व। ससि = शशि = चन्द्र। कचपचि = कचपची = कृत्तिका नक्षत्र। भरा = भरइ (भरति) का भूत-काल मेँ एक-वचन। राज-मँदिर = राज-मन्दिर = राजा का घर। सोनइ = स्वर्ण = सुवर्ण = सोना। नग = अमूल्य रत्नोँ के टुकडे। जरा = जडा = जटित। नखत = नक्षत्र। कहेसि = कहा = कहइ (कथयति) का भूत-काल मेँ एक-वचन। रानिन्ह = रानी का बहु-वचन, (रानी = राज्ञी = राज-महिषी)। आछि = अस्ति = है। अबासा = आवास = निवास-स्थान = रहने की जगह॥ गगन = आकाश। सरोबर = सरोवर = अच्छा तडाग = पोखरा। कवँल = कमल। कुमुद = कोईँ। तराईँ = तारायेँ = तारा-गण। ऊआ = उअइ (उदयति) का भूत-काल मेँ एक-वचन। भवँर = भ्रमर = भौँरा। पवन = वायु। मिला = मिलइ (मिलति) का भूत-काल मेँ एक-वचन। लेइ = ले कर। बास = वास = सुगन्ध॥

(शुक ने कहा, कि) राजा, तूँ जैसा आदि विक्रम, अर्थात् विक्रमादित्य था, तैसा-ही है। भारत-वर्ष मेँ प्राचीन परम्परा से बडी बडी राज-धानियोँ मेँ यह रीति आज तक चली आती है, कि दो चार पीढी के बाद फिर फिर राजाओँ के वे-ही नाम रक्खे जाते हैँ, जैसे जय-पुर मेँ राम-सिंह, माधव-सिंह, जय-सिंह, मान-सिंह ये-ही चार नाम राजाओँ के फिर फिर होते हैँ। कवि ने सब से पहला अतिशय प्रतापी विक्रम के बोध होने के लिये 'आदि' शब्द का उपादान किया है। तूँ सत्य-भाषी हरिश्चन्द्र (और) राजा पृथु (वैन्य) है, अर्थात् उन्होँ के ऐसा सत्य-भाषी

और यशस्वी है ॥ तैं ने योग में (राजा) गोपीचंद को जीता, अर्थात् जीत लिया। (क्योंकि उस ने माता की आज्ञा से लाचार हो कर योग लिया और तैं ने स्वतः अपनी इच्छा से योग लिया इस लिये तूँ बढ कर है)। और विरक्तता में, अर्थात् वैराग्य में, भर्तृहरि भी तेरी बराबरी में नहीं पूरे ऊए, अर्थात् तैं ने वैराग्य में राजा भर्तृहरि को भी जीत लिया (क्योंकि उन्हों ने अपनी पत्नी के दुराचार पर ग्लानि कर, वैराग्य धारण किया, और तूँ ने अपनी इच्छा से वैराग्य को लिया) ॥ तेरे हाथ में गोरख-नाथ ने सिद्धि (अष्ट-सिद्धि, अष्ट-सिद्धि के लिये २० वें दोहे की टीका में ४६ वाँ पृष्ठ देखो) को दिया, अर्थात् घर से चलती बेला जो तैं ने 'सिद्ध होइ कहँ गोरख कहा' (१२८ वाँ दोहा) इस से गोरख को गुरु मान उन का स्मरण किया, सो गुरु ने तेरी तपस्या से प्रसन्न हो तुझे सिद्धि दे कर सिद्ध बनाया। (और गुरु के नाते से तेरे दादा) गुरु (महानुभाव) मछंदर-नाथ ने (भी अपना पौच समझ तेरी शरीर को) तार दिया, अर्थात् इन महासागरों से पार कर दिया। वा (तुझे अपना पौच समझ उन सिद्धियों को) तारी (तुझे) दिया। इस अर्थ में पहले चरण में जो 'दीन्ह' क्रिया पद है उस का सिद्धि, और तारी, दोनों कर्म समझो ॥ तैं ने प्रेम से पृथ्वी (और) आकाश (दोनों) को जीत लिया, अर्थात् सिद्ध हो जाने से तेरे लिये यह लोक और पर-लोक दोनों सुलभ हो गये। कैलास (सदृश) सिंहल तेरी दृष्टि के सामने पडा, अर्थात् नजर आया, वा कैलास (शिव-लोक, यहाँ सच्चिदानन्द पर-ब्रह्म का स्थान) (और) सिंहल दोनों तेरी दृष्टि में आये, अर्थात् षट्-चक्राकार सागरों के पार हो जाने से और गोरख से सिद्धि मिलने से, इस लोक का स्वर्ग-स्थान सिंहल और पर-लोक का उत्तम-स्वर्ग कैलास दोनों देख पडे ॥ जो मेघ है, अर्थात् जिसे तुम मेघ समझते हो, वह (वेंद) (सिंहल में राजा गन्धर्व-सेन का) गढ है, जो कि आकाश में लगा है, अर्थात् अत्यन्त ऊँचा है। (और) कोट (गढ) के चारो ओर (चऊँ पासा) जो कनी हैं, अर्थात् शोभा के लिये उचित उचित स्थानों में जो वज्र की कणी लगाई गई हैं (वे-ही सब) बिजली हैं, अर्थात् वे-ही बिजली-सी चमकती हैं ॥ (और) तिस के ऊपर (जिसे तुम) कचपची से भरा (मुँह) चन्द्र (कहते हो) सो नगों से जडा सोने का राज-मन्दिर है, अर्थात् वही राजा गन्धर्व-सेन का मुख्य रहने का स्थान है, जिस में सुवर्ण-मण्डल चन्द्र और उस में जडे नग कचपची से जान पडते हैं ॥ और उस के चारो ओर (जिसे तुम) और नखत्र कहते हो, (वह) सब

रानियों का (अलग अलग) निवास-स्थान है, अर्थात् वह रनिवास है, जिस में अनेक नग-जटित मन्दिर इतर तारागण के ऐसे चमकते हैं॥

(शुक कहता है, कि राजा निश्चय समझो, कि) आकाश सरोवर में चन्द्र-कमल, (उस चन्द्र-कमल के पास) तारा-गण कुमुद हैं, और (आज) तूं (उस गगन सरोवर में) रवि उदय हुआ है। (सो आज जो तेरे अङ्ग में शीतल सुगन्ध वायु लग रहा है, उसे वायु न समझो, किन्तु तुमारे रवि-रूप के उदय से जो शशि-कमल खिल गया है, इस की प्रसन्नता में) भ्रमर पवन का रूप धर वास (सुगन्ध) को ले कर (आप से) मिला है। क्योंकि रवि-ही के कारण कमल के खिलने पर भ्रमर के सुगन्ध-वास-ग्रहण मनोरथ की सिद्धि होती है। इस लिये जिस के अनुग्रह से मनोरथ-सिद्धि हुई उस को भेंट देना उचित है। यह समझ भ्रमर पवन के कपट-वेष से उस वास को आप (रवि) के यहाँ भेंट लाया है। यह कवि का आन्तरिक अभिप्राय है। पद्मावती-पक्ष में, गगन से गन्धर्व-सेन का गढ-सरोवर, उस में शशि पद्मावती कमल, उस के पास की सखियाँ तारा-गण, कुमुद ('तुम्ह ससि होऊ तरायन साखी' दोहा ६४, पृष्ठ १०१) लेना चाहिये। और राजा रत्न-सेन ऐसा अपूर्व रवि वहाँ उदय हुआ, कि जिस के कारण उस शशि-(पद्मावती) कमल के साथ कुमुद भी (सखियाँ तारागण) जो रवि-दर्शन से सङ्कुचित हो जाते हैं, प्रफुल्लित हो गये॥ सच्चिदानन्द पर-ब्रह्म-पक्ष में गगन-ही सरोवर, और शशि-ही, कमल, और उस शशि के पास के तारा-गण कुमुद हैं। राजा सिद्ध होने से पूरा योगी हुआ। पुराणों में कथा है, कि योगी सिद्ध होने पर रवि-मण्डल को बेध कर ब्रह्म में लीन हो जाता है। इस लिये योगी में रवि से भी अधिक सामर्थ्य होने से राजा रत्न-सेन अपूर्व रवि हुआ, जिस से शशि और तारागण भी दीप्तिमान् हो कर खिल उठे। भारतवर्षीय ज्योतिषियों के मत से शशि और तारागणों में रवि-ही के तेज से तेज है। कमलाकर ने लिखा है, कि—

तेजसां गोलकः सूर्यो ग्रहर्क्षाण्यम्बुगोलकाः।
प्रभावन्तो हि दृश्यन्ते सूर्यरश्मिप्रदीपिताः॥
(सिद्धान्ततत्त्वविवेक बिम्बाधिकार, श्लो० २।)

योगी षट्-चक्र को बेध कर जब प्राण को सप्तम-चक्र ब्रह्माण्ड में चढाने लगता है, तब ब्रह्माण्ड, आकाश, और शशि, वाम-स्वर जो नासिका के बायें पूरे से निकलता है

जिसे योगी ईडा नाडी कहते हैं, उस के पास पास मस्तिष्क से मिले छोटे छोटे नस-तन्तु, तारा-गण और कुमुद। दक्षिण-स्वर, जो नासिका के दहने पूरे से निकलता है, जिसे योगी पिङ्गला नाडी कहते हैं, वह रवि। और उस के पास पास के मस्तिष्क से मिले छोटे छोटे नस-तन्तु विद्युत् सदृश उसे देखाई पडते हैं। फिर योगी यदि इन के दर्शन से घबडा न जावे; गुरूपदेश से आगे प्राण को चढाता जावे, तो आगे सुषुम्ना नाडी में प्राण जायगा। फिर वहाँ से उसे सुन्दर सुखद राज-मार्ग मिलता है, जो कि पर-ब्रह्म-स्थान तक प्राण को पहुँचा कर, पर-ब्रह्म में मिला देता है, और फिर विष्णु-ग्रन्थि, रुद्र-ग्रन्थि, और ब्रह्म-ग्रन्थि भी खुल जाती हैं॥

सुप्ता गुरुप्रसादेन यदा जागर्त्ति कुण्डली।
तदा सर्वाणि पद्मानि भिद्यन्ते ग्रन्थयोऽपि च॥
प्राणस्य शून्यपदवी तदा राजपथायते।
तदा चित्तं निरालम्बं तदा कालस्य वञ्चनम्॥
सुषुम्ना शून्यपदवी ब्रह्मरन्ध्रं महापथः।
श्मशानं शाम्भवी मध्यमार्गश्चेत्येकवाचकाः॥
तस्मात् सर्वप्रयत्नेन प्रबोधयितुमीश्वरीम्।
ब्रह्मद्वारमुखे सुप्तां मुद्राभ्यासं समाचरेत्॥
महामुद्रा महाबन्धो महावेधश्च खेचरी।
उड्डानं मूलबन्धश्च बन्धो जालन्धराभिधः॥
करणी विपरीताख्या वज्रोली शक्तिचालनम्।
इदं हि मुद्रादशकं जरामरणनाशनम्॥

(हठयोगप्रदीपिका, तृतीयोपदेश, श्लो० २-७)।

इस प्रकार पर-ब्रह्म-पक्ष, और पद्मावती-पक्ष, दोनों में सब कवि का कहा ठीक लग जाता है। और जो पिछले दोहे में कहा कि, उस स्थान में जानों वसन्त ऋतु आई है, उस की लीला भी इस दोहे में यथावत् वर्णित हो गई। जब पर-ब्रह्म वा पद्मावती की प्राप्ति हो गई, तब वहाँ जरा-मरण की निवृत्ति हो जाने से सदा एक आनन्द-रस रहने से सर्वदा वसन्त-ऋतु का रहना समुचित है॥

विक्रमादित्य, जिस का संवत् आज तक भारतवर्ष में प्रचलित है, उज्जयिनी वा धारा का राजा था, जिस के दान, पराक्रम, बुद्धि इत्यादि की महिमा सिंहासन-बत्तीसी

और बैताल-पचीसी में विशेष रूप से वर्णित है। ज्यौतिष-ज्योतिर्विदाभरण के अन्तिम लेख से यह सिद्ध होता है, कि इन के दरबार में

धन्वन्तरि-क्षपणका-ऽमरसिंह-शङ्कु-वेतालभट्ट-घटखर्पर-कालिदासाः।
ख्यातो वराहमिहिरो नृपतेः सभायां रत्नानि वै वररुचिर्नव विक्रमस्य ॥'

ये नवरत्न थे। परन्तु वराहमिहिर का समय ४२७ शाका है। इस लिये इस श्लोक के सत्य होने में महान् संशय है। ज्योतिर्विदाभरण का कर्त्ता कालिदास भी जान पडता है, कि रघुवंशादि-कर्त्ता कालिदास से भिन्न है। (गणक-तरङ्गिणी देखो)। निदान विक्रम के विषय में विशेष लिखना व्यर्थ है। कुछ इन के विषय में १३४ व दोहे की टीका में भी लिख आये हैं।

हरिश्चन्द्र राजा त्रिशङ्कु के पुत्त्र और अयोध्या के राजा थे। इन की सत्यता और उदारता जगत्प्रसिद्ध है। स्वप्न में भी यदि किसी को कुछ देना स्वीकार कर लेते थे तो प्रातःकाल उस को विना दिये नहीं रहते थे। इन की सत्यता को भङ्ग करने के लिये एक बेर विश्वामित्र ने अपनी सिद्धि के प्रभाव से इन्हे स्वप्न दिखलाया, कि एक बूढे ब्राह्मण को राजा ने अपना सब राज्य सङ्कल्प कर दिया। प्रातःकाल होने पर राजा घर से बाहर निकल उस ब्राह्मण की प्रतीक्षा में राज-कार्य छोड कर बैठे। उन की पत्नी शैव्या मध्याह्न समय जान स्वयं सुजान पति के स्थान में आई। कहने लगी; कि नाथ उच्छिष्ट प्रसाद के लिये यह दासी प्रार्थना करती है। राजा ने कहा, कि प्रिये स्वप्न में इस राज्य को एक ब्राह्मण के नाम से दान दे चुका हूँ, सो जब वह ब्राह्मण आवे, और उसे इस राज्य को सौंप कर, त्रिलोक से न्यारी काशी-पुरी में चलूँ, तब भोजन करूँ। राज-पाट, घर बाहर, धन धान्य, सब ब्राह्मण का हो चुका है, उस के धान्य को कैसे भोजन करूँ। पति के साथ पति-व्रता शैव्या भी सेवा करती बैठ गई। इतने-ही में विश्वामित्र पहुँचे और कहा, कि आप ने स्वप्न में मुझे सब राज्य दे दिया है, सो सत्य-पालन कीजिये। राजा ने कहा, कि इसी लिये मैं आप की प्रतीक्षा-ही में बैठा हूँ। राजा ने झारी से जल डाल कर, झट राज्य को सङ्कल्प कर दिया। और दान-साङ्गता सिद्धार्थ मन्त्री से कहा, कि ब्राह्मण को हजार अशर्फी खजाने से ला कर दो। इस पर विश्वामित्र ने कहा, कि अब तेरा कैसा खजाना; खजाने से तुझ से क्या संबन्ध। सो तूँ यदि अपने को सत्य-सन्ध समझता है तो अपने राज्य के बाहर से हजार अशर्फी ला कर मुझे दे, नहीं तो मैं शाप दूँगा,

तेरी पूर्व पुण्य सब नष्ट हो जायगी। इस पर राजा ब्राह्मण को बडे विनय के साथ काशी में ले आया और दासी-कर्म पर अपनी पत्नी को बेंच ५००) अशर्फी, और अपने को काशी जी में केदारघाट* श्मशान के अधिकारी डोमडे के हाथ दास-कर्म पर बेंच ५०० अशर्फी, यों हजार अशर्फी ले ब्राह्मण को सम्मान पुरःसर दे कर, विदा किया। राजा उस डोमडे के श्मशान पर मुर्दों के कर को उगाहता था। यही उस की नोकरी थी। अपनी नोकरी में भी राजा सत्य से ऐसा बँधा था, कि राजा का एकमात्र पुत्त्र रोहितास, जो कि बालवयः-कारण से माता-ही के साथ रहता था, सर्प के काटने से मर गया और शैव्या अपनी आधी धोती का कफन कर, उस को श्मशान में ले आई, तो राजा ने विना कर लिये फूँकने न दिया। शैव्या ने, यह विचार कर, कि चिर काल से अलग रहने के कारण और रूपान्तर हो जाने से कदाचित् ये मुझे पहचानते न हों, कहा, कि 'प्राण-नाथ मैं वही आप की आज्ञानु-वर्त्तिनी अभागिनी शैव्या हूँ, और यह मृतक आप का वही प्राणाधार एकलौता पुत्त्र रोहितास है, जिस के लिये रोज रोज खोज खोज कर नये चाँदी सोने के खिलोने लियें जाते थे। आप गोद में लिये मारे मोद के अङ्ग न समाते थे।' इस पर राजा ने यही कहा, कि 'प्रिये मैं किसी को भूला नहीं हूँ। सब को पहचानता हूँ। परन्तु मेरी नजर से सब से ऊपर सत्य-ही नजर पडता है। स्वामी से वचन दे चुका हूँ, कि आप की आज्ञा से विना कर लिये आग न दूँगा, और न मुर्दे को जलाने दूँगा।' इस पर अन्त में लाचार हो कर शैव्या ने नङ्गी हो कर, अपनी बची आधी धोती को उतार कर, कर देने के लिये कर फैलाने की मन में इच्छा की। दम्पतियों का ऐसा अचल सत्य-व्यवहार देख देवों ने पुष्प की वृष्टि की, और विमान को ले आये, उस पर दम्पतियों को स्वर्ग ले चलने के लिये बैठाना चाहा। राजा ने कहा, कि जितने दिनों के लिये मैं नोकरी स्वीकार कर चुका हूँ, उन में अभीं कुछ दिन बाकी हैं। सो सत्य-भङ्ग कर, मैं स्वर्ग को नहीं जाया चाहता। इस बात पर देव लोग उस डोम को भी विमान पर बैठा लिये, और कहने लगे, कि वहीं स्वर्ग में बाकी दिनों को इस डोम की नोकरी में पूरा करियेगा। इस राजा की कुछ कथा महाभारत, २ सभा पर्व, १२ अध्याय में ऐसी है। इन की उदारता पर ब्राह्मण का रूप धर विष्णु स्वयं परीचार्थ आये हैं। और हरिश्चन्द्र से कहा, कि 'मैं आप से कुछ माँगा

* बहुतों के मत से यह स्थान काशी में मचक्ना चडहा है जहाँ अब तक हरिश्चन्द्रेश्वर महादेव हैं।

चाहता हूँ'। राजा ने कहा 'निःसंशय कहिए'। विष्णु-ब्राह्मण ने कहा, कि 'आप का आधा दक्षिणाङ्ग शिर से पैर तक चाहता हूँ'। राजा ने आरे से आधी देह को देने के लिये चिरवाने लगा। आरा शिर को चीरते चीरते जब मस्तक के पास पहुँचा तब राजा की दहनी आँख से आँस का एक बूँद टपक पडा, इस पर ब्राह्मण ने कहा, कि 'आप दान के समय दुःखित हो गये सो अब मैं इस कलुषित दान को न लूँगा'। इस पर राजा ने कहा, कि 'महाराज मै दुःखित इस चिन्ता से हुआ हूँ, कि आधी देह तो आप के काम आई पर मेरी बची आधी देह व्यर्थ न जाय यह भी किसी के काम मैं आ जाय'। इस बात पर भगवान् राजा से बहुत प्रसन्न हुए और अभय प्रदान कर, विष्णुलोक को चले गये। विष्णुपुराण ४ अंश०। अध्या० ३। श्लो० १५ मैं भी इस राजा का नाम आया है। इसी को ले कर, और देवी भागवत, स्कन्ध ७, अध्या० १२-२७ की कथा को मिला कर कवि लोगों ने अपनी कल्पना के साथ, अनेक मनोरञ्जन कथा बनाई है। मेरे मित्र भारतेन्दु बाबू हरिश्चन्द्र जी ने भी हिन्दी मैं इस विषय का 'सत्य-हरिश्चन्द्र' नाटक ऐसा करुणा-रस पूरित बनाया है, कि पढने मैं पद पद पर, उन की विपद से रुलाई आती है। भागवत के ९ स्कन्ध, अध्याय ७ वें मैं भी संक्षेप से कुछ राजा हरिश्चन्द्र की कथा है। ये त्रेतायुग मैं सूर्यवंश मैं २८ वाँ राजा हुए हैं।

वेनु, यह परम्परा से भ्रष्ट पाठ है, क्योंकि वेनु अर्थात् वेन यह तो भारतवर्ष मैं महा अधम राजा हुआ है। इस के राज्य में धर्माधर्म का कुछ भी विचार नहीं था; लोग पशुवत् वृत्ति उठा ली थी। इसी पर मनु-स्मृति में लिखा है, कि

नोद्वाहिकेषु मन्त्रेषु नियोगः कीर्त्यते क्वचित्।
न विवाहविधावुक्तं विधवावेदनं पुनः॥
अयं द्विजैर्हि विद्वद्भिः पशुधर्मो विगर्हितः।
मनुष्याणामपि प्रोक्तो वेने राज्यं प्रशासति॥
स महीमखिलां भुञ्जन् राजर्षिप्रवरः पुरा।
वर्णानां सङ्करं चक्रे कामोपहतचेतनः॥
ततः प्रभृति यो मोहात् प्रमीतपतिकां स्त्रियम्।
नियोजयत्यपत्यार्थं तं विगर्हन्ति साधवः॥

(अध्याय ९, श्लो० ६५-६८)

इस लिये हम ने 'बदन' वैन्य का अपभ्रंश, पाठ रक्खा है।

वैन्य, वेन का पुत्र, राजा पृथु। वेन जब अपने राज्य में बहुत अत्याचार करने लगा, तब मुनि और देवता लोगों ने मिल कर उसे मार डाला। उस को सन्तान न था, इस लिये राजा होने के लिये उस से सन्तान पैदा करने के लिये सब प्रजा देव, मुनि लोग उस की मरी शरीर को मथने लगे। मथते मथते पहले उस की शरीर से महापाप-रूप काला निषाद उत्पन्न हुआ। फिर दूसरी वार मथन करने से महा-प्रतापी, यशस्वी, दानी, दयालु, सत्य-वादी राजा पृथु हुआ, जिसे वेन की शरीर से उत्पन्न होने के कारण लोग वैन्य कहते हैं। इस की कीर्त्ति-महिमा चतुर्थ-स्कन्ध भागवत के १५-२३ अध्याय तक वर्णित है। इसी ने पृथ्वी को दुह कर, इस से अनेक धान्य प्रजाओं के सुख के लिये उत्पन्न किया। पृथ्वी इस की भार्या थी। यद्यपि आज तक अनेक राजा हो गये, जो पृथ्वी को भोगते आये, तथापि पृथ्वी आज तक पृथु-ही की भार्या कहाती है। ऐसा मनु ने मनु-स्मृति में कहा है,

पृथोरपीमां पृथिवीं भार्यां पूर्वविदो विदुः।
स्थाणुच्छेदस्य केदारमाहुः शल्यवतो मृगम् ॥
(अध्याय ९, श्लो० ४४)

इस पृथु (वैन्य) की प्रशंसा में व्यास ने ४ स्कन्ध भागवत के २३ वें अध्याय के अन्त में लिखा है, कि

वैन्यस्य चरितं पुण्यं शृणुयात् श्रावयेत् पठेत्।
वैचित्रवीर्याभिहितं महन्माहात्म्यसूचितम् ॥
अस्मिन् कृतमतिर्मर्त्त्यः पार्थवीं गतिमाप्नुयात्।
अनुदिनमिदमादरेण शृण्वन् पृथुचरितं प्रथयन् विमुक्तसङ्गः।
भगवति भवसिन्धुपोतपादे स च निपुणां लभते रतिं मनुष्यः ॥

मछंदर-नाथ वही हैं, जो नेपाल में हुए हैं और संस्कृत में जिन्हें मत्स्येन्द्र-नाथ कहते हैं। इन्हीं के शिष्य गोरख-नाथ थे। नाथ-पंथियों में यह इतिहास है, कि शिव (महादेव) जी, जिन्हें नाथ-पंथी (गोरख-पंथी) आदि-नाथ कहते हैं, किसी समय किसी दीप में एक पुष्कर के तट पर सुखद एकान्त स्थान को देख कर, पार्वती को हठ योग का उपदेश देते थे। तट पर एक मत्स्य भी बैठा उन उपदेशों को निश्चल मन से सुनता था। अन्त में महादेव जी ने उसे भी सत्पात्र समझ, जल के सिञ्चन से सिद्ध-पुरुष बना दिया। प्रधान सिद्धों में आदि-नाथ

(महादेव) के बाद दूसरी गणना इन्हीँ की है। हठ-योग-प्रदीपिका मेँ प्रधान सिद्धोँ के ये नाम लिखे हैँ,

श्री-आदिनाथ-मत्स्येन्द्र-शाबरा-ऽऽनन्दभैरवाः ।
चौरङ्गी-मीन-गोरक्ष-विरूपाक्ष-बिलेशयाः ॥
मन्थानो भैरवो योगी सिद्धिर्बुद्धश्च कन्थडिः ।
कोरण्टकः सुरानन्दः सिद्धपादश्च चर्पटिः ॥
कानेरी पूज्यपादश्च नित्यनाथो निरञ्जनः ।
कपाली बिन्दुनाथश्च काकचण्डीश्वराह्वयः ॥
अल्लामः प्रभुदेवश्च घोडा चोली च टिण्टिणिः ।
भानुकी नरदेवश्च खण्डः कापालिकस्तथा ॥
इत्यादयो महासिद्धा हठयोगप्रभावतः ।
खण्डयित्वा कालदण्डं ब्रह्माण्डे विचरन्ति ते ॥
(उपदेश १। श्लो० ५-९)

मत्स्येन्द्र-नाथ की नव नाथोँ मेँ भी गणना है। नव नाथोँ के लिये १२८ वेँ दोहे की टीका देखो॥ १६३॥

चउपाई।

सो गढ देखु गगन तइँ ऊँचा। नयन देखि कर नाहिँ पहूँचा॥
बिजुरी चकर फिरहिँ चहुँ फेरे। अउ जमकात फिरहिँ जम केरे॥
धाइ जो बाजा कइ मन साधा। मारा चकर भएउ दुइ आधा॥
चाँद सुरुज अउ नखत तराई। तेहि डर अँतरिख फिरहिँ सबाई॥
पवन जाइ तहँ पहुँचा चहा। मारा तइस टूटि भुइँ बहा॥
अगिनि उठी जरि बुझी निआना। धुआँ उठा उठि बीच बिलाना॥
पानि उठा तहँ जाइ न छूआ। बहुरा रोइ आइ भुइँ चूआ॥

दोहा।

रावन चहा सउँह कइ (हेरा) उतरि गए दस माथ।
संकर धरा ललाट भुइँ अउरु को जोगी-नाथ॥ १६४॥

गढ = गाढ = दुर्ग = किला। देखु = देखइ (दृश्यते) का लोट् में मध्यम-पुरुष का एक-वचन। गगन = आकाश। तइँ = तैं = से। ऊँचा = उच्च। नयन = आँख। देखि = दृष्ट्वा = देख कर। कर = हाथ। नाहिँ = न हि = नहीं। पहुँचा = पहुँचा = पहुँचइ (प्रभुत्वति, प्राकृत पहुच्चइ) = पहुँचता है। बिजुरी = विद्युत् = बिजुली। चकर = चक्र। फिरहिँ = फिरइ (स्फुरति) का बहु-वचन। चहुँ = चारो। फेरे = ओर = प्रान्त। जमकात = यमकास्त्र = जोडे (दोहरे) अस्त्र। वा, जमकात = यमकर्त्तरी = यम की कैंची। जम = यम = प्राण लेने-वाले यमराज। धाइ = धाय कर = दौड कर (धावति से ल्यप्)। बाजा = बाजइ (व्रजति = वजति) का भूत-काल में एक-वचन। साधा = श्रद्धा = साध = इच्छा। आधा = अर्ध = खण्ड = टुकडा। चाँद = चन्द्र। सुरुज = सूर्य। नखत = नक्षत्र। तराई = तारा = तरई। डर = दर = भय। अँतरिख = अन्तरिक्ष = आकाश और भूमि के बीच में। सबाई = सब = सभी। पवन = वायु = हवा। पहुँचा = पहुँचना। चहा = चाहा = इच्छा किया = चहइ (चदति वा इच्छति) का भूत-काल में एक-वचन। मारा = मारइ (मारयति) का भूत-काल में एक-वचन। तइस = तथा = तैसा। टूटि = त्रुटित्वा = टूट कर। भुइँ = भुवि = पृथ्वी में। बहा = बहइ (वहति) का भूत-काल में एक-वचन। अगिनि = अग्नि = आग। उठी = उठइ (उत्तिष्ठते) का स्त्री-लिङ्ग में भूत-काल का एक-वचन। जरि = ज्वलित्वा = जर कर = बर कर। बुझी = बुझइ (बुतति) का स्त्री-लिङ्ग में भूत-काल का एक-वचन। निश्राना = निदान, निश्राना = निरन्य = विना अन्य = विना सहायक। धुआँ = धूम = धूआँ। उठि = उत्थाय = उठ कर। बिलाना = विलीन हो गया = लय हो गया = लोप हो गया। पानि = पानीय = पानी। छूआ = छुआ = छुअइ (स्पृश्यते) का भूत-काल में एक-वचन। बहुरा = बहुरइ (अवरोहति) का भूत-काल में एक-वचन। रोइ = रुदित्वा = रो कर। आइ = आगत्य = आ कर। चूआ = चुआ = चुअइ (च्यवते) का भूत-काल में एक-वचन॥ रावन = रावण। सउँह = शपथ = सौंह = कसम = प्रतिज्ञा। उतरि = उतर (उत्तरण) = कट। दस = दश। माथ = मस्तक = शिर। संकर = शङ्कर = महादेव। धरा = धरइ (धरति) का भूत-काल में एक-वचन। ललाट = भाल = मस्तक = माथा। जोगी-नाथ = योगि-नाथ = योगियों का राजा॥

(शुक कहता है, कि राजा) देख वह (सो) गढ आकाश से (भी) ऊँचा है। आँख से देख कर (भी वहाँ) हाथ नहीं पहुँचता है, वा आँख देख कर (भी)

नहीँ पङ्कँचती है, अर्थात् यह विवेक नहीँ कर सकती, कि कितना ऊँचा है॥ (उस गढ) के चारो ओर बिजुली के चक्र (रचा के लिये) फिरा करते हैँ। और यम-राज के दोहरे अस्त्र फिरा करते हैँ, वा (रचा के लिये) यम-कर्त्तरी फिरी करती है॥ जो (मनुष्य) मन में श्रद्धा कर, दौड कर, (वहाँ) गया; (जाते-ही उसे) चक्र (बिजुरी-चक्र) ने ऐसा मारा कि दो टुकडा ङ्कश्रा, अर्थात् चक्र ऐसा उसे मार देता है, कि (वह) दो टुकडा हो जाता है॥ चन्द्र, सूर्य, और नचत्र, तारा, सब तिसी (गढ के रचकोँ के) डर से (रात दिन) अन्तरिच में फिरा करते हैँ, अर्थात् घूमा करते हैँ॥ तहाँ (गढ तक) वायु जा कर, (गढ-पति के पास) पङ्कँचना चाहा, (परन्तु जाते-ही बिजुरी-चक्र-यमकास्त्रोँ ने) तैसा मारा, कि टूट (टूट) कर, अर्थात् छिन्न भिन्न हो कर, पृथ्वी में बहने लगा, अर्थात् अङ्ग-भङ्ग हो जाने से असमर्थ हो कर, पृथ्वी में इधर उधर डोलने लगा॥ (उस स्थान में पङ्कँचने के लिये प्रज्वलित और उच्च शिखा से) आग उठी, (परन्तु) निदान (अन्त) में, वा विना (गुरु) सहायक के जर कर, बुझ गई (वहाँ तक न पङ्कँच सकी)। (इस पर बाप की कसर निकालने के लिये उस अग्नि का पुत्र) धूआँ (पङ्कँचने के लिये) उठा। (परन्तु वह भी) उठ कर बीच-ही में बिलाय गया (पता भी न लगा, कि क्या हो गया)॥ तहाँ (जाने के लिये मेघ-व्याज से) पानी उठा, (और) जा कर (भी उस गढ-पति को) न छूआ, अर्थात् न छू सका। (इस लिये वहाँ से) रो कर फिरा, (और) भूमि में चू पडा, (बौरहा हो, नारी नारी में घूमने लगा; उच्च स्थान की लालसा मन से बिसार नीच-स्थान-ही में फिरने लगा)। यह सब कवि की उत्प्रेचा है॥

रावण शपथ कर (उस पद्मावती-प्रकृति-रूपा सीता के गढ, अर्थात् देह को) चाहा, (कि उस के साथ सुख विलास करूँ। सो इस इच्छापराध-ही के कारण उस के) दशो माथ उतर गये, अर्थात् उस के दशो शिर काटे गये। महादेव जी [जब राम और लच्मण वन में सीता को ढूँढते थे तब उस पद्मावती-प्रकृति-रूप, चिच्छक्ति विशिष्ट सीता के गढ (देह) को स्मरण कर] पृथ्वी में (अपने) ललाट को धर दिया, अर्थात् उस को सब से परे आद्या शक्ति का गढ समझ कर, दूर-ही से दण्डवत किया। रामायण में प्रसिद्ध कथा है, कि जब जानकी-हरण के अनन्तर वन में जानकी को ढूँढते राम जी चले हैँ, तहाँ मार्ग में सती-सहित महादेव से भेँट ङ्कई है। महादेव जी ने राम जी को बडा समझ, प्रणाम किया; इस पर कवि की उत्प्रेचा है, कि

महादेव ने राम को प्रणाम नहीँ किया, किन्तु, जिस आद्या शक्ति सीता की गढ (देह) ढूँढने मेँ राम व्याकुल थे उस को सब से परे जान, उसी को ध्यान कर, प्रणाम किया। सो जिस गढ के आगे महादेव ने, (जो नाथ-संप्रदाय-वालोँ मेँ प्रधान हैँ, और आदि-नाथ कहलाते हैँ) अपने माथ को धर दिया, (उस के पास पहुँचने मेँ), और कौन योगि-नाथ है? अर्थात् और कोई नहीँ है (महादेव के आदि-नाथ होने के विषय मेँ पिछले दोहे की टीका मेँ मत्स्येन्द्र-नाथ की कथा देखो)। कवि ने इन वर्णनोँ से देखलाया, कि जिस गढ (सिंहल वा ब्रह्माण्ड) के पास, पवन, अग्नि, वायु, पञ्चतत्त्व-मय प्राणियोँ मेँ सब से प्रतापी रावण, जिस ने वेदोँ के ऊपर व्याख्यान किया, और महादेव, जो योगि-राज हैँ, नहीँ पहुँच सकते, वह गढ अत्यन्त दुर्घट है, उस के पास पहुँचने की कोई नियत राह नहीँ। यदि गढ-पति (पद्मावती वा प्रकृति-रूपा चिच्छक्ति) प्रसन्न हो, तो चाहे जिस राह से, विना किसी के सलाह से, अपने पास बडे सुपास से बुला कर सुख से वास दे सकता है। अन्यथा कोई उपाय नहीँ, कि प्राणी उस अनगढ गढ के पास जाय। सातवाँ कमल-चक्र जो ब्रह्माण्ड है, उसे गढ मानने से, और पिछले दोहे की टीका मेँ ईडा, पिङ्गला आदि जो शशि, तारा-गण, रवि, विद्युत् इत्यादि मान आये हैँ, वैसे-ही यहाँ भी मान लेने से, और गढ-पति को प्रकृति अव्यक्त ब्रह्म समझ लेने से, सब वर्णन योग-पक्ष मेँ लग जाता है। इसी लिये प्रत्येक चौपाइयोँ की टीका मेँ उचित स्थान पर कोष्ठकान्तः पद्मावती और प्रकृति इत्यादि संनिवेश कर दिया है, जिस मेँ सहज मेँ दोनोँ पक्षोँ के अर्थ समझे जायँ ॥ १६४ ॥

चउपाई ।

तहाँ देखु पदुमावति रामा। भवँर न जाइ न पंखी नामा॥
अब सिधि एक देउँ तोहि जोगू। पहिलइ दरस होइ तउ भोगू॥
कंचन मेरु देखावसि जहाँ। महादेव कर मंडप तहाँ॥
ओहि क खंड जस परबत मेरू। मेरु-हि लागि होइ अति फेरू॥
माघ मास पाछिल पख लागे। सिरी-पंचमी होइहि आगे॥
उघरिहि महादेव कर बारू। पूजइ जाइ सकल संसारू॥
पदुमावति पुनि पूजइ आवा। होइहि ओहि मिसु दिसिटि मेरावा॥

दोहा ।

तुम्ह गवँनहु ओहि मंडप हउँ पदुमावति पास ।
पूजइ आइ बसंत जउ तउ पूजिहि मन आस ॥ १६५ ॥

तहाँ = तत्र । देखु = देखइ (दृश्यते) का लोट् में मध्यम-पुरुष का एक-वचन । पदुमावति = पद्मावती । रामा = सुन्दर रमणयोग्य युवती । वा, रामा = रमा = लक्ष्मी । भवँर = भ्रमर = भौँरा । पंखी = पक्षी । नामा = नाम । अब = अधुना = इदानीम् । सिधि = सिद्धि = उपाय । देउँ = देइ = (दत्ते) का उत्तम-पुरुष में एक-वचन । जोगू = योग्य = लायक । पहिलइ = प्रथम हि = पहले । दरस = दर्शन = देखा देखी । होइ = होवे = होय = होइ (भवति) का विध्यर्थ में एक-वचन । तउ = तदा = तब । भोगू = भोग = समागम-सुख । कंचन = काञ्चन = सुवर्ण = सोना । मेरु = उत्तर ध्रुव के नीचे का पर्वत जहाँ देवता लोग बसते हैं । देखावसि = देखावइ (दर्शयति) का मध्यम-पुरुष में एक-वचन । जहाँ = यत्र । मंडप = मण्डप = मन्दिर के बाहर का भाग जो कि छाया-दार रहता है । क = का । खंड = खण्ड = छोटे छोटे भाग = खंभे = आधार । जस = यथा = जैसे । परबँत = पर्वत । मेरू = मेरु । लागि = लगिला = लग कर । अति = अत्यन्त = बडा । फेरू = फेर = घेरा = प्रदक्षिणा-परिधि । माघ = दसवाँ चान्द्र-मास । मास = महीना । पाछिल = पिछला = पश्चिम = पश्चात् । पख = पक्ष । लागे = लगने में = लग्ने । सिरी = श्री । सिरी-पंचमी = श्री-पञ्चमी = वसन्त-पञ्चमी, भारतवर्ष में इसी दिन से वसन्तोत्सव आरम्भ होता है । होइहि = होइ (भवति = अस्ति) का भविष्यत्-काल में एक-वचन । आगे = अग्रे । उघरिहि = उघरइ (उद्घटति) का भविष्यत्-काल में एक-वचन । बारू = बार = द्वार = दरवाजा । पूजइ = पूजने । जाइ = (याति) जाता है । सकल = सब । संसारू = संसार = संसार में बसने-वाले जन । पुनि = पुनः । पूजइ = पूजने । आवा = आवइ = आयाति । मिसु = मिष = व्याज = बहाना । दिसिटि = दृष्टि = आँख = नजर । मेरावा = मिलाप = समागम ॥ गवँनहु = गमन करो = जाव । हउँ = अहम् = हौँ = मैं । पास = पार्श्व = निकट । पूजइ = पूजे = पूजइ (पूर्यते) का संभावना में एक-वचन । बसंत = वसन्त-पञ्चमी । जउ = यदि । पूजिहि = पूजइ (पूर्यते) का भविष्यत् में एक-वचन । आस = आशा = इच्छा = उम्मेद ॥

(हीरा-मणि शुक कहता है, कि) तहाँ, अर्थात् जिस गढ की प्रशंसा पीछे कर आये हैँ तहाँ, पद्मावती रमणी (वा पद्मावती प्रकृति-रूपा रमा चिच्छक्ति) है। (जिस रमणी के यहाँ) भ्रमर नहीँ जाता है, (और उस के यहाँ) पक्षी का नाम नहीँ है, अर्थात् वहाँ भ्रमर की गति नहीँ है; और उस के यहाँ उस के पिता गन्धर्व-सेन की आज्ञा से कोई पक्षी भी नहीँ रहने पाता। मैँ केवल था सो आप-ही के पास चला आया। (५७ वाँ दोहा, ८९ पृ० देखो)॥ (सो) तेरे योग्य मैँ अब एक सिद्धि देता हूँ, अर्थात् एक उपाय बताता हूँ, (जिस से) पहले (पद्मावती का) दर्शन हो। तब (पीछे उस के समागम का सुख) भोग (मिले)॥ (अब शुक उपाय बताता है) जहाँ तुम सोने का मेरु देखलाते हो ('अउरु दखिन दिसि नित्रर-हि कंचन मेरु देखाउ' १६२ वाँ दोहा) तिसी स्थान में महादेव का मण्डप है॥ उसी के खण्ड (छोटे छोटे भाग चारो ओर ऐसे हैँ) जैसे मेरु के पर्वत, अर्थात् मेरु के आधार-पर्वत हैँ। पुराणों में लिखा है, कि सुमेरु छत के ऐसा है, उस के चारो ओर पूर्वादि दिशा के क्रम से मन्दर, सुगन्ध, विपुल, और सुपार्श्व खंभे के ऐसे आधार पर्वत हैँ। भास्कराचार्य ने भी गोलाध्याय के भुवनकोश में पुराणानुसार लिखा है, कि 'विष्कम्भशैलाः खलु मन्दरोऽस्य सुगन्धशैलो विपुलः सुपार्श्वः' (भास्कर के लिये गणक-तरङ्गिणी देखो)। (और आधार-पर्वत) मेरु में, अर्थात् ऊपर की छत में, लग कर अत्यन्त घेरा हुआ है, अर्थात् आधार-खंभोँ को लगा कर मण्डप की गोलाई बहुत भारी बनाई गई है॥ माघ महीने में पिछला पक्ष लगने पर, अर्थात् शुक्ल-पक्ष लगने पर, आगे वसन्त-पञ्चमी होगी॥ (उसी दिन) महादेव (के मन्दिर) का दरवाजा खुलेगा। (उस दिन महादेव को) पूजने को सब संसार, अर्थात् सब लोग जाते हैँ॥ (उसी दिन) फिर पद्मावती (भी) पूजने को (वहाँ) आवेगी। उसी व्याज से (वहाँ-ही) दृष्टि-समागम होगा, अर्थात् उस दिन वहाँ तुम से और पद्मावती से आपस में देखा देखी होगी॥

(सो) तुम उसी (महादेव के) मण्डप में चलो (और) मैं पद्मावती के पास (जाता हूँ)। यदि (ईश्वरेच्छा से) वसन्त-पञ्चमी आ कर पूजे, अर्थात् निर्विघ्न पञ्चमी आ कर पूरी पड जाय; तब तक किसी के यहाँ यह भेद न खुले, तो (तुमारे) मन की आशा पूरी होगी॥ हठ-योग के साधने-वाले प्रायः वसन्त-पञ्चमी-ही से योग-क्रिया आरम्भ करते हैँ। इस लिये यहाँ मेरु से ब्रह्म-रन्ध्र और उस स्थान में स्थित शाम्भवी शक्ति को महादेव मानने से सब योग-पक्ष में लग जाता है (१६३ दोहे की टीका देखो)॥ १६५॥

चउपाई ।

राजइ कहा दरस जउ पावउँ । परबत काह गगन कहँ धावउँ ॥
जेहि परबत पर दरसन लहना । सिर सउँ चढउँ पाउँ का कहना ॥
मो-हूँ भाउ ऊँच सउँ ठाऊँ । ऊँचइ लेउँ पिरीतम नाऊँ ॥
पुरुखहि चाहिअ ऊँच हिआऊ । दिन दिन ऊँचइ राखइ पाऊ ॥
सदा ऊँच पइ सेइअ बारू । ऊँचइ सउँ कीजिअ बेवहारू ॥
ऊँचइ चढइ ऊँच खँड सूझा । ऊँचइ पास ऊँच मति बूझा ॥
ऊँचइ संग सँगति निति कीजिअ । ऊँचइ लाइ जीउ पुनि दीजिअ ॥

दोहा ।

दिन दिन ऊँच होइ सो जेहि ऊँचइ पर चाउ ।
ऊँच चढत जउ खसि परइ ऊँच न छाँडिअ काउ ॥ १९९ ॥

कहा = कहइ (कथयति) का भूत-काल मेँ एक-वचन । दरस = दर्शन । जउ = यदि = जौँ । पावउँ = पावइ (प्राप्नोति) का संभावना मेँ उत्तम-पुरुष का एक-वचन = पाऊँ । परबत = पर्वत । काह = क हि = क्या । गगन = आकाश । कहँ = को = ऊपर । धावउँ = धावइ (धावति) का संभावना मेँ उत्तम-पुरुष का एक-वचन = धाऊँ = दौडूँ । पर = उपरि । दरसन = दर्शन । लहना = लभन = लाभ = प्राप्ति । सिर = शिर । सउँ = सोँ = से । चढउँ = चढइ (उच्छर्दति, प्राकृत चड्डइ) का संभावना मेँ उत्तम-पुरुष का एक-वचन = चढूँ । पाउँ = पाद = पैर । का = किम् = क्या । कहना = कथनम् । मो-हूँ = मुझे भी । भाउ = भाइ (भाति) भाता है = सोहता है = अच्छा लगता है । ऊँच = उच्च = ऊँचा । ठाऊँ = स्थान । ऊँचइ = उच्चैः = बडे स्वर से = बडे जोर से । लेउँ = लेइ (लाति) का उत्तम-पुरुष मेँ एक-वचन । पिरीतम = प्रियतम = सब से प्रिय (प्यारा) । नाऊँ = नाम । पुरुखहि = पुरुष को । चाहिअ = चाहिए । ऊँच = ऊँचा = पक्का = दृढ = बडा । हिआऊ = हियाव = हृदयम्, प्राकृत हिअउं = साहस = हिम्मत । ऊँचइ = ऊँचे पर = उच्च पदवी पर । राखइ = रक्खे = रखइ (रचति) का विध्यर्थ मेँ प्रथम-पुरुष का एक-वचन । पाऊ = पाउ = पाव = पाद = पैर । सदा = सर्वदा = हमेशा = सब दिन । ऊँच = उच्च (पुरुष) = बडा आदमी । पइ = अपि = निश्चय कर । सेइअ = सेइये = सेवइ (सेवते) का

विधि मैँ मध्यम-पुरुष का बहु-वचन। बारू = बार = द्वार = डेवढी। ऊँचइ = उच्च (महा-धनी) = महाजन। कीजिअ = कीजिये = करिये = करइ (करोति) का विधि मैँ मध्यम-पुरुष का बहु-वचन। बेवहारू = व्यवहार = लेन देन। ऊँचइ = उच्च स्थान = कोठा, अटारी, वा धरहरा। चढइ = चढे = चढइ (उच्छर्दति) का संभावना मैँ प्रथम-पुरुष का एक-वचन। ऊँच = ऊँचा = दूर। खँड = खण्ड = भाग। सूझा = सूझइ (शुद्ध्यते) = सूझता है। ऊँचइ = ऊँचा (बुद्धि मैँ) = पण्डित = बहु-श्रुत। पास = पार्श्व = निकट। ऊँच = ऊँची = सब से बढ कर। मति = बुद्धि = अकिल। बूझा = बुझइ (बुध्यते) = बूझता है = जानता है। ऊँचइ = बडे (राजा, बाबू, सिद्ध, महन्त इत्यादि)। संग = सङ्ग = साथ। सँगति = सङ्गति = सङ्गमन = चलना। निति = नित्य = नित। ऊँचइ लाइ = ऊँचे को लगा कर = ऊँचे के लिये = बडे लोग के लिये। दीजिअ = दीजिये = देइ (दत्ते) का विधि मैँ मध्यम-पुरुष का बहु-वचन॥ ऊँच = बडा = प्रतिष्ठित। होइ = होता है। चाउ = चाह = इच्छा। चढत = चढने मैँ। खसि (खचति, प्राकृत खसइ से बना) = खसना = पतन = गिर। परइ = परे = पडे = परइ (पतति) का संभावना मैँ प्रथम-पुरुष का एक-वचन। छाँडिअ = छाडिये = छोडिये (छुडति) का विधि मैँ मध्यम-पुरुष का बहु-वचन। काउ = क्वापि = कभी॥

राजा ने (शुक से) कहा, कि यदि (पद्मावती का) दर्शन पाऊँ, (तो) पर्वत क्या आकाश को दौडूँ, अर्थात् तैँ ने जो महादेव के मण्डप-पर्वत पर जाने को कहा, वह तो अत्यन्त सुगम है। मैँ पद्मावती के लिये आकाश के ऊपर दौड सकता हूँ॥ (सो हे शुक,) जिस पर्वत पर (पद्मावती के) दर्शन की प्राप्ति है; (उस अनुपम पर्वत पर) मैँ शिर से चढूँ, पैर का क्या कहना, अर्थात् पैर की क्या बात; मैँ उस पर्वत पर शिर के बल चढ सकता हूँ॥ (क्योँकि उच्च वंश मैँ जन्म लेने से) मुझे भी ऊँचा स्थान अच्छा लगता है। (ऊँच सउँ ठाऊँ = उच्च से जो स्थान हो, अर्थात् प्रतिष्ठित लोग से जो स्थान भूषित हो)। (मैँ सच्चा प्रेमी हूँ; छिप लुक कर नहीँ, किन्तु) उच्च-स्वर से (अपने) प्रियतम का नाम लेता हूँ (सो ऊँचे-ही पर से प्रियतम का नाम पुकारना उत्तम है)॥ पुरुष को चाहिए, कि बडा साहस रक्खे, (जैसे रावण ने साहस किया, कि शिर तक काट कर हवन कर दिया, तब लङ्का का राजा हुआ)। (और) दिन दिन उच्च पदवी पर पैर रखता जाय (राखइ का दोनोँ कर्मोँ मैँ संबन्ध है), (जैसे विश्वामित्र, चत्रिय, ऋषि, राजर्षि होते होते ब्रह्मर्षि हो गये।

वाल्मीकि रामा० बा० का०। स० ५१-६५)॥ सर्वदा निश्चय कर के बडे के द्वार की सेवा करनी चाहिए (नीति में भी लिखा है, कि

'सेवितव्यो महान् वृक्षः फलच्छायासमन्वितः।
यदि दैवात् फलं नास्ति छाया केन निवार्यते'॥)

(जैसे जय और विजय सदा विष्णु के द्वार-पाल हैं)। ऊँचे से सर्वदा व्यवहार करना चाहिए (जिस में दशा हीन होने पर भी महाजन और महाधनी के कारण, वह अपने लेन देन का तगादा असभ्य व्यवहार से न करे, जिस के कारण तुम्हें क्लेश न हो)। यदि व्यवहार से संबन्ध लो, तो 'ऊँचे से संबन्ध करना चाहिए' यह अर्थ करना चाहिए, [जैसे हिमालय ने कन्या-दान दे कर, महादेव (अत्युच्च) से संबन्ध किया]॥ ऊँचे पर चढने से दूर (ऊँचे) तक के खंड, अर्थात् भूमि-खण्ड सूझ पडते हैं। ऊँचे (बुद्धि-वाले ज्ञानी और पण्डित) के पास रहने से ऊँची बुद्धि बूझ पडती है (जैसे उद्धव, हनुमान्, इत्यादि, भगवान् कृष्ण और राघवेन्द्र राम के पास रहने से उत्तम बुद्धि को पाये। व्यास लोगों की कहानी है, कि एक व्यक्ति आवँ की पीडा से आकुल हो पुरीषोत्सर्ग-ही की वेला में हा राम, हा राम, कह कह, कहँरता था। उसी समय उसी राह से दिव्य रूप के वेष से कहीं हनुमान् जी जाते थे सो ऐसे मल-मय स्थल में उस को विमल राम-नामोच्चारण करते देख, अनुचित समझ, क्रोधावेश से बडे बल से उसे पादतल से मार, आगे चले गये। रात्रि में जब राम के शरीर की सेवा में तत्पर हुए, तब राम की पीठ में बडे भारी गडहे को देख कर, हाथ जोड, बडे विनय से हनुमान् ने राम जी से गडहे पडने का कारण पूँछा। राम जी ने हँस कर कहा, कि यह गडहा तुमारे-ही कारण से पड गया है। आवँ की पीडा से जब वह आकुल हो, मुझे पुकार रहा था, तब तुम ने कैसे बल से उस गरीब पर लात चलाई थी। यदि वह चोट उस पर बैठती, तो वह रसातल को चला जाता; सो मैं ने उस को अपनी पीठ की ओट से बचा कर, तुमारी चोट को पीठ पर ली। उसी के कारण यह बडा गडहा है। सो हनुमान् तुम्हें आज से ध्यान देना चाहिए, कि मेरे लिये क्या विमल, क्या मल। जब प्राणी शुद्धान्तःकरण से मुझे स्मरण करे, मैं उसी क्षण में उस का अवलम्बन होता हूँ, यही मेरा विलक्षण पण है। इस पर हनुमान् जी को चेत हुआ, और आगे सावधान होने के लिये अपना कान उमेठा)॥ ऊँच-ही के संग में नित्य संगमन करिये, अर्थात् बडे बडे महानुभावों-ही के

संग मैँ सदा रहना चाहिए (क्योँकि उन के संग के प्रभाव से और उच्छिष्टादि प्रसाद से अधम भी उत्तम हो जाता है। नारद दासी-पुत्त थे। इन की माता साधुओँ का चौका वर्त्तन करती थी, और साधुओँ के उच्छिष्ट से अपना और नारद का पालन करती थी। साधुओँ के जूठे अन्न के भक्षण के प्रभाव से नारद महानुभाव हो गये। इन की महानुभावता को देख कर, इन्हेँ ब्रह्मा ने अपना पुत्त बनाया। वैरागियोँ मेँ प्रसिद्ध कहानी है, कि नाभा, जिस ने भक्त-माल बनाई है, एक ढरकारिन का लडका था, जो अयोध्या मेँ एक महानुभाव महन्त के मन्दिर के द्वार पर पडी रहती थी। जो कुछ साधुओँ के घूर पर पडे उच्छिष्ट पत्तलोँ पर पडा पावे, उसी से अपना और नाभा का पालन करे। उसी उच्छिष्ट के भक्षण के प्रभाव से नाभा महानुभाव हो गया। एक दिन महन्त जी स्नान कर भजन भाव करते थे। उसी समय एक उन के भक्त शिष्य की चावल से भरी नाव डूब रही थी, और उस भक्त ने अपने गुरु महन्त जी का स्मरण कर, कह रहा था, कि यदि आप की अनुकम्पा से नाव बच जाय, तो आधे चावलोँ को आप के चरणोँ मेँ साधु-सेवा के लिये अर्पण करूँगा। चिकालदर्शी महन्त जी, इस बात पर ईश्वर का ध्यान करने लगे, कि 'हे भगवन् उस का बेडा पार लगा दे'। इतने-ही मेँ नाभा, जो वहाँ खडा था, बोल उठा, कि 'महाराज आप की प्रार्थना को भगवान ने सुन कर, उस का बेडा पार लगा दिया'। इस पर महन्त ने विस्मित हो कर, कहा, कि 'अरे नाभा, तूँ वहाँ तक पहुँच गया'। नाभा ने हाथ जोड कर, कहा, कि 'आत्मनाथ आप के उच्छिष्ट के प्रसाद से अवश्य मैँ पहुँच गया'। फिर महन्त प्रसन्न हो कर, कहा, कि 'अब तूँ सिद्ध हो गया, भगवद्भक्तोँ के चरित्रोँ का वर्णन कर'। इसी आज्ञा से नाभा ने भक्त-माल बनाई। सच है बडोँ की, अर्थात् अच्छे महानुभावोँ की सङ्गति से क्या क्या नहीँ होता॥ इसी पर भर्त्तृ-हरि ने कहा है, कि

'जाड्यं धियो हरति सिञ्चति वाचि सत्यं
मानोन्नतिं दिशति पापमपाकरोति।
चेतः प्रसादयति दिक्षु तनोति कीर्तिं
सत्सङ्गतिः कथय किं न करोति पुंसाम्॥'

(नीतिशतक, श्लो० २२)।

ऊंचे को लगा कर, अर्थात् बडे लोगोँ के लिये, फिर जीव (तक) दे देना चाहिए

(जैसे इन्द्र के लिये दधीचि ने अपनी हड्डी दे कर, अपना प्राण गवाँया, जिस से आज तक सर्वत्र उस का यश छाया है, और इन्द्र भी उस का वज्र, असाधारण समझ, बडे आदर से आज तक धारण किये हैं)॥

जिस को उच्च पर चाह रहती है, अर्थात् जिस को यह इच्छा रहती है, कि मेरी प्रतिष्ठा और यश हो, वह दिन दिन ऊँचा, अर्थात् बढता (प्रतिष्ठा पाता) जाता है। ऊंचे चढने में, अर्थात् प्रतिष्ठा पाने के यत्न में, वा हाथी घोडे के चढने में, यदि (दैवात्) गिर पडे, (तो भी) कभी उच्च (प्रतिष्ठा-यत्न वा हाथी, घोडा, इत्यादि उच्च यान) को न छोडना चाहिए। क्योँकि जो घोडे पर चढता है, वही गिरता है, परन्तु गिर कर भी वह चढना नहीँ छोडता, क्योँकि घोडे चढने से कितनी मान मर्यादा है, यह उसे अच्छी तरह मालूम है, इस लिये घोडे से गिर कर, मर जाना अच्छा, पर घोडे का न चढना नहीँ अच्छा॥ १६६॥

चउपाई।

हीरा-मनि देइ बचा कहानी। चलेउ जहाँ पदुमावति रानी॥
राजा चलेउ सवँरि सो लता। परबत कहँ जो चलेउ परबता॥
का परबत चढि देखइ राजा। ऊँच मँडप सोनइ सब साजा॥
अंब्रित फल सब लागु अपूरी। अउ तहँ लागु सजीअनि मूरी॥
चउ-मुख मंडप चहूँ केवारा। बइठे देवता चहूँ दुआरा॥
भीतर मँडप चारि खँभ लागे। जिन्ह वेइ छुअइ पाप तिन्ह भागे॥
संख घंट घन बाजहिँ सोई। अउ बहु होम जाप तहँ होई॥

दोहा।

महादेव कर मंडप जगत जातरा आउ।
जस हीँछा मन जेहि कइ सो तइसइ फल पाउ॥ १६७॥

इति सिंघल-दीप-भाउ-खंड॥ १६॥

हीरा-मनि = हीरा-मणि, शुक। देइ = दत्त्वा = दे कर। बचा = वचन। कहानी = कथनम् = वृत्तान्त। चलेउ = चलइ (चलति) का भूत-काल में एक-वचन। पदुमावति =

पद्मावती । रानी = राज्ञी । सवँरि = संस्मृत्य = स्मरण कर = सुमिर कर । लता = वल्ली = प्राण-लता = प्राण की वल्ली । परबत = पर्वत । कहँ = को । जेा = जो = जैसे-ही । परवता = पार्वतीय = हीरा-मणि शुक । चढि = चलित्वा = चढ कर । देखइ (दृश्यते) = देखता है । मँडप = मण्डप । सोनइ = स्वर्ण का = सोने का । साजा = साजइ (सज्जयति) का भूत-काल में एक-वचन । अंब्रित = अमृत । फर = फल । लागु = लाग = लगइ (लगति) का भूत-काल में बहु-वचन = लगे हैं । अपूरी = आपूर्य = भर कर = भर पूर । सजीअनि = सञ्जीविनी = जिलाने-वाली । मूरी = मूली = मूलिका । चउ-मुख = चतुर्मुख = चार मुख का । चहुँ = चारो । केवारा = कपाट = केवाडा = दरवाजा । बइठे (उपविष्टाः) = बैठे हैं । दुआरा = द्वार = दरवाजा । भीतर = अभ्यन्तर । चौरि = चार । खंभ = स्तम्भ = खंभा । लागे = लगे = लगइ (लगति) का भूत-काल में बहु-वचन = लगे हैं । कुअइ (कुपति) = कूता है । पाप = दुष्कर्म से अनिष्ट । भागे = भगइ (वजति = व्रजति) का बहु-वचन = भागहिँ = भागते हैं । संख = शङ्ख = एक जलजन्तु की मृत अस्थि-मय देह, जिसे पूजा के समय लोग बजाते हैं । घंट = घण्ट पीतल का, जो देवता के मन्दिर में बजाया जाता है = घण्टा । घन = कांस्य (काँसे) के और बाजे (ततं वीणादिकं वाद्यमानद्धं मुरजादिकम् ॥ वंशादिकं तु सुषिरं कांस्यताला-दिकं घनम् । चतुर्विधमिदं वाद्यं वादित्रातोद्यनामकम् ॥ अम० को० । प्र० का० । नाट्यवर्ग । श्लो० २०३-२०४) = झाँझ, मँजीरा, विजय-घण्ट इत्यादि । बाजहिँ = बाजइ (वाद्यते) का बहु-वचन । बहु = बहुत । होम = हवन = आग में मन्त्रों को पढ पढ कर, घृत इत्यादि की आहुति डालना । जाप = जप मन्त्रों की अभीष्ट-सिद्धि के लिये । जगत = जगत् के लोग । जातरा = यात्रा = तीर्थ-यात्रा । आउ = आवइ (आयाति) = आता है । हौँछा = हि-इच्छा = निश्चय से इच्छा । तइसइ = तथा हि = तैसा-ही । पाउ = पावइ (प्राप्नोति) = पाता है ॥

हीरा-मणि (इस प्रकार से) वचन कहानी दे कर, अर्थात् वचन से उपाय बता कर, जहाँ पद्मावती रानी (रहती थी तहाँ) चला ॥ जैसे-ही पर्वत का रहने-वाला (शुक) चला, (तैसे-ही) राजा (भी) उस (सो) लता (पद्मावती) को स्मरण कर, पर्वत को चला, अर्थात् सिंहल-स्थ देव-मण्डप के यहाँ जाने के लिये पर्वत पर चढा ॥ राजा पर्वत पर चढ कर, क्या देखता है, (कि) ऊँचा मण्डप सब सोने से साजा हुआ है, अर्थात् उस महादेव के मन्दिर का मण्डप स्वर्ण-मय है ॥ (और उस के चारो ओर जो बाटिका है,

जिस का वर्णन २८ वें दोहे में कर आये हैं, कि 'गुआ सुपारी जाइफर सब फर फरे अपूरि' उस में) भर पूर सब अमृत फल लगे हैं। और तहाँ सञ्जीवनी मूरि (भी) लगी है (जिस से लक्ष्मण की शक्ति-जनित मूर्छा निवृत्त हो गई थी)॥ मण्डप चार मुख का है, अर्थात् मण्डप की चारो दिशा में एक एक द्वार है, (और) चारो (द्वारों में) केवाड़े (लगे) हैं। चारो दरवाजे पर देवता बैठे हैं, अर्थात् चारो दरवाजों पर अनेक देवमूर्त्ति बनी ऊई हैं। मण्डप के भीतर (छोटा सा और मण्डप है, जिस में) चार खंभे लगे हैं। (उसी में मुख्य महादेव जी हैं), जो लोग उन (खंभों) को छूते हैं, अर्थात् श्रद्धा से स्पर्श करते हैं, तिन के पाप भाग जाते हैं॥ वहाँ (सोई) पर, शङ्ख, घण्ट, घन (झाँझ, मँजीरा इत्यादि) बजा करते हैं। और तहाँ बड़, अर्थात् नाना प्रकार के, होम जाप होते हैं, अर्थात् मनोरथ पूरा होने से जिस जिस प्रकार की मनौती लोग किये रहते हैं, तिस तिस प्रकार के होम और जप हो रहे हैं॥

(उस) महादेव के मण्डप में जगत् के लोग याचा (तीर्थ-याचा) के लिये जाते हैं। जिस के मन में जैसी इच्छा रहती है, वह (सो) तैसा-ही फल पाता है, अर्थात् कोढी काया, बाँझ वंश, और दरिद्री धन इत्यादि पाते हैं॥ १६७॥

इति सिंहल-द्वीप-भाव-खण्ड-नाम षोडश-खण्डं समाप्तम्॥ १६॥

अथ मंडप-गवँन-खंड ॥ १७ ॥

चउपाई ।

राजा बाउर बिरह बिओगी। चेला सहस तीस सँग जोगी ॥
पदुमावति के दरसन आसा। दँडवत कीन्ह मँडप चहुँ पासा ॥
पुरुब बार होइ कइ सिर नावा। नावत सीस देव पहँ आवा ॥
नमो नमो नारायन देवा। का मोहिँ जोग सकउँ कइ सेवा ॥
तुइँ दयाल सब के उपराहीँ। सेवा केरि आस तोहि नाहीँ ॥
ना मोहिँ गुन न जीभ रस-बाता। तुइँ दयाल गुन निरगुन दाता ॥
पुरवहु मोरि दरस कइ आसा। हउँ मारग जोअउँ हरि साँसा ॥

दोहा।

तेहि बिधि बिनय न जानउँ जेहि बिधि अस्तुति तोरि।
करु सु-दिसिटि अउ किरिपा हीँछा पूजइ मोरि ॥ १६८ ॥

बाउर = वातुल = बौरहा। बिरह = विरह = वियोग। बिओगी = वियोगी, जिसे वियोग हो = वैरागी। चेला = शिष्य। सहस = सहस्र = हजार। तीस = त्रिंशत्। सँग = सङ्ग = साथ। जोगी = योगी। दरसन = दर्शन = देखना। आसा = आशा = इच्छा = उम्मेद। दँडवत = दण्डवत् = दण्ड के ऐसा भूमि में गिर कर प्रणाम। मँडप = मण्डप। चहुँ = चारो। पास = पार्श्व = ओर। पुरुब = पूर्व दिशा। बार = द्वार = दरवाजा।

सिर = शिर। नावा = नावइ (नमयति) का भूत-काल में एक-वचन। नावत = नावते = झुंकाते। सीस = शीर्ष = शिर। देव = देवता = महादेव। पहँ = पार्श्व = निकट। आवा = आवइ (आयाति) का पुंलिङ्ग में भूत-काल का एक-वचन। नारायन = नारायण = नारायणाय। देवा = देव = हे देव। वा, देवा = देवाय = महादेवाय = महादेव के लिये। जोग = योग = योग-क्रिया। सकउँ = सकइ (शक्नोति) का उत्तम-पुरुष में एक-वचन। सेवा = टहल = खिदमत। तुइँ = त्वम् = तुम। दयाल = दयालु = दया के घर। उपराहीँ = उपरि हि = ऊपर। गुन = गुण। जीभ = जिह्वा। रस-बाता = रस-वार्त्ता = रस की बात। निरगुन = निर्गुण = गुण-रहित। दाता = देने-वाले। पुरवज्ञ = पुरवइ (पूरयति) का लोट् लकार में मध्यम-पुरुष का बज्ञ-वचन। दरस = दर्शन। आसा = आस = आशा। हउँ = अहम् = मैं। मारग = मार्ग। जोअउँ = जोअइ (जोहइ = जुहोति) का उत्तम-पुरुष में एक-वचन। हरि = हर = प्रत्येक। साँसा = साँस = श्वास॥ बिधि = विधि = विधान = प्रकार। बिनय = विनय = प्रार्थना = स्तुति। जानउँ = जानइ (जानाति) का उत्तम-पुरुष में एक-वचन। असतुति = स्तुति। करु = करइ (करोति) का लोट् में मध्यम-पुरुष का एक-वचन। सु-दिसिटि = सु-दृष्टि = सुन्दर दृष्टि। किरिपा = कृपा = मेहर्बानी। हीँछा = हि-इच्छा = निश्चय से मनोरथ। पूजइ = पूजे (पूर्यते) = पूजइ का विध्यर्थ में प्रथम-पुरुष का एक-वचन॥

राजा ने विरह से बौरहा (और) विरक्त (वियोगी) हो, तीस सहस्र योगियोँ को सङ्ग में चेला बनाये [पहले कह आये हैं, कि सोरह सहस्र राज-कुमार योगी ज़ए, (१२६ वाँ दोहा देखो) और यहाँ तीस हजार कहते हैं। इस विरोध को मिटाने के लिये सोरह हजार राज-कुमार और चौदह हजार इतर साधारण लोगोँ की संख्या लेनी चाहिए इसी लिये १२६ वेँ दोहे मेँ 'राइ रंक सब भए बिओगी। सोरह सहस कुअँर भए जोगी॥' इस मेँ साधारण लोगोँ के ग्रहणार्थ राइ, रंक का उपादान है]॥ पद्मावती के दर्शन की आशा से, मण्डप के चारो ओर (आ कर) दण्डवत् किया॥ (मण्डप के) पूर्व-द्वार हो कर शिर को झुंकाया, और शिर को झुंकाते ही, अर्थात् शिर को झुंकाये-ही महादेव (देव) के पास आया॥ (आ कर बाहर से कहने लगा, कि) देवाय नारायणाय नमो नमः, अर्थात् नारायण-स्वरूप देव के लिये मेरी वार वार नमस्कार (योगी लोग सब देवताओं को नारायण-रूप समझ, आज तक 'नारायणाय नमो नमः' ऐसा ही प्रणाम करते हैं)। मेरे में क्या योग है? मैं क्या (आप की)

सेवा कर सकता हूँ, अर्थात् मेरे मैं न योग-बल है न सेवा-बल है जिन से मैं आप को प्रसन्न कर सकूँ ॥ (सो) आप सब के ऊपर दयाल हो, अर्थात् सब के ऊपर दया करने-वाले हो। तुम्हें सेवा की आशा नहीं, अर्थात् आप को सेवा की इच्छा नहीं, कि जब कोई मेरी सेवा करे तो मैं फल देऊँ, इस की आप को परवाह नहीं ॥ मेरे भी गुण नहीं और न जिह्वा मैं रस की बात है, अर्थात् न मेरे मैं ऐसा गुण न मनो-हर वाणी, जिस से यह भरोसा हो, कि मैं अवश्य ही अपने गुण और मनो-हर वाणी से आप को रिझा लूँगा। आप दयालु हो, निर्गुणों को गुण देने-वाले हो (हम ने यहाँ आदरार्थ सर्वत्र बहु-वचन का प्रयोग किया है, कवि ने देव को अद्वितीय समझ सर्वत्र 'तुइ' एक-वचन का प्रयोग किया है) ॥ (सो हे महादेव,) मेरी जो (पद्मावती के) दर्शन की इच्छा है, (उसे) पूरी कीजिये। मैं हर श्वास मैं, अर्थात् प्रति श्वासोच्छासान्तर्वर्त्ती काल मैं (पद्मावती के) मार्ग को जोहता हूँ। प्रतिक्षण मैं यही प्रतीक्षा कर रहा हूँ, कि कब पद्मावती आवे और दर्शन हो ॥

जैसे विधि की आप की स्तुति है, अर्थात् आप जिस प्रकार की स्तुति के योग्य हैं, तिस प्रकार से विनय करना मैं नहीं जानता। (सो मेरे ऊपर) सु-दृष्टि और कृपा करो (जिस मैं) मेरी निश्चय से इच्छा पूरी हो ॥ १६८ ॥

चउपाई।

कइ असतुति जउ बहुत मनावा। सबद अकूत मँडप महँ आवा ॥
मानुस पेम भएउ बइकुंठी। नाहिँ त काह छार एक मुंठी ॥
पेमहि माँह बिरह अउ रसा। मयन के घर मधु अंब्रित बसा ॥
निसत धाइ जउ मरइ तो काहा। सत जउ करइ बइठि होइ लाहा ॥
एक बार जउ मन देइ सेवा। सेवहि फल परसन होइ देवा ॥
सुनि कइ सबद मँडप झनकारा। बइठहु आइ पुरुब के बारा ॥
पिंडु चढाइ छार जेत आँटी। माटी होहु अंत जो माटी ॥

दोहा।

माटी मोल न किछु लहइ अउ माटी सब मोल।
दिसिटि जो माटी सउँ करइ माटी होइ अमोल ॥ १६९ ॥

असतुति = स्तुति । जउ = यदा = जब । बहुत = बहुतर । मनावा = मनावइ (मानयति) का पुंलिङ्ग में भूत-काल का एक-वचन । सबद = शब्द = आवाज । अकूत = आकूतम् = इच्छा-सूचक = अकस्माद् वाणी । मँडप = मण्डप । आवा = आवइ (आयाति) का पुंलिङ्ग में भूत-काल का एक-वचन । मानुस = मानुष = मनुष्य । पेम = प्रेम । बइकुंठी = वैकुण्ठी = वैकुण्ठ जिस को हो, अर्थात् देवता । त = तो । काह = का हि = क्या । छार = चार = राख = राखी । एक = एक । मुंठी = मुष्टि = मुट्ठी । बिरह = विरह = वियोगाग्नि । रसा = रस = अमृत-रस । मयन = मदन = काम-देव । वा, मधु-मक्खियों का मोम । मधु-अंब्रित = मध्वमृत = शहद जो अमृत । बसा = बसइ (वसति) का पुंलिङ्ग में भूत-काल का एक-वचन । वा, बसा = वसा = बर्रै । निसत = निःसत्, वा निःसत्य = जिस में सत् वा सत्य न हो । धाइ = धाय कर = दौड़ कर । जउ = यदि । मरइ = मरे = मरइ (मरति) का सम्भावना में प्रथम-पुरुष का एक-वचन । तो = तर्हि = तदा । काहा = काह = क्या । सत = सत् = सच्चा । बइठि = उपविश्य = बैठ कर । लाहा = लाभा = लाभ = प्राप्ति । बार = वार = सर्त्तव = दफे । सेवा = सेवइ (सेवते) का पुंलिङ्ग में भूत-काल का एक-वचन । परसन = प्रसन्न = खुश । देवा = देव = देवता । सुनि कइ = सुन कर । झनकारा = झणत्-कार = झन झन । बइठऊ = बइठइ (उपविशति) का आज्ञा में मध्यम-पुरुष का बहु-वचन । आइ = आगत्य = आ कर । पुरुब = पूर्व दिशा । बारा = वार = द्वार । पिंडु = पिण्ड = शरीर = देह । चढाइ = चढा कर । जेत = यतमा = जितना । आँटी = अँटे = आप्त हो = पर्याप्त हो । माटी = मट्टी = मृत् = मृत्तिका । अंत = अन्त में ॥ मोल = मूल्य = कीमत । किछु = किञ्चित् = कुछ । लहइ = (लभते) लाभ होता है = प्राप्त होता है । दिसिटि = दृष्टि ॥

(राजा) स्तुति कर जब (महादेव को) बहुत मनाया (मनावा), (तब) मण्डप में से अकस्मात् शब्द आया, अर्थात् राजा के लिये आकाश-वाणी हुई ॥ (कि) मनुष्य प्रेम(-ही) से देवता हुआ है, अर्थात् देवता हो जाता है, नहीं तो (मनुष्य) क्या है?, अर्थात् कुछ नहीं है; (केवल) एक मुट्ठी राख है ॥ प्रेम-ही के बीच विरह और रस (दोनों भरे) हैं । (जैसे) मदन के घर (मदन-मन्दिर = योनि) मधु (मदिरा) और अमृत (दोनों) बसते हैं, अर्थात् अनुचित रीति से उस घर में व्यवहार करने से मनुष्य को मधु (मदिरा) सदृश, बुद्धि और शरीर के नाश करने-वाले उपदंशादि अनेक रोग हो जाते हैं, और उचित रीति से व्यवहार करने में अमृत-रस-सदृश

भोर = भोरु = प्रातःकाल। साँझ = सन्ध्या । सिंगी = शृङ्गी = हरिण के सीँग का बाजा। निति = नित्य = नित। पूरी = पूरइ (पूरयति) का स्त्री-लिङ्ग में भूत-काल का एक-वचन। कंथा = कन्था = गुदडी । जरइ = (ज्वलति) जरती है। आगि = अग्नि। जनु = यथा = जैसे = यथा नु। लाई = लगाई = लगइ (लगति) का णिजन्त में रूप। बिरह = विरह = वियोग = जुदाई। धंधोर = धन-धुरा = धन शब्द का धुरा, अर्थात् लवर के साथ बहुत काष्ठ का जलना = होलिका = होली। जरत = जरता हुआ = बरता हुआ। बुझाई = बुझइ = बुतइ (बुदति) = बुझता है। रात = रक्त = लाल। निसि = निशि = रात्रि। मारग = मार्ग = राह। जागे = जागइ (जागर्त्ति) का पुंलिङ्ग में भूत-काल का बहु-वचन। चक्रित = चकित। वा चक्रित = चक्रीतः = कुलाल से प्राप्त, अर्थात् खेलौने का। चकोर = एक पक्षिविशेष, जो अग्नि का अँगारा खाता है, और रात को चन्द्र-ही की ओर दृष्टि किये रहता है, इस प्रान्त में सर्वत्र प्रसिद्ध है। कुंडल = कुण्डल = कर्ण-मुद्रा, जो कान में योगी लोग पहरे रहते हैं (१२८ वें दोहे की छठवीं चौपाई देखो)। सीस = शीर्ष = शिर। भुइँ = भूमि। लावा = लगाया = लगावइ (लगयति) का पुंलिङ्ग में भूत-काल का एक-वचन। पावँरि = पामरी = पादुका = पनही। पावा = पावँ = पाद = पैर। जटा = केशों के लटों का समूह। छोरि = सञ्छुद्य = छोर कर। बार = बाल = केश। बोहारउँ = बोहारूँ = बोहारइ (अवहरति) का सम्भावना में उत्तम-पुरुष का एक-वचन। पँथ = पन्थाः = राह। आउ = आवे = आवइ (आयाति) का सम्भावना में प्रथम-पुरुष का एक-वचन। बारउँ = बारूँ = बारइ (वारयति) का लोट् में उत्तम-पुरुष का एक-वचन॥ चारि-हु = चारो। चकर = चक्र = मण्डल = फिरइ (स्फुरति) = फिरता है = घूमता है। डँड = दण्ड = घटी। रहइ (रहति) = रहता है। थिर = स्थिर। मार = मार कर। भसम = भस्म = राख। पवन = वायु। सँग = सङ्ग = साथ। परान = प्राण। अधार = आधार = जिस के आसरे ठहरना हो॥

(आकाश-वाणी होने पर मण्डप के पूर्व-द्वार पर राजा) व्याघ्र-चर्म पर बैठ कर, और तपस्वी हो कर, अर्थात् शरीर के ऊपर भस्म को रमाय कर, (आसन मार) पद्मावती, पद्मावती जपने लगा॥ जिस (पद्मावती) के दर्शन के लिये (राजा) बैरागी हो गया है, उसी से दृष्टि और समाधि लग गई, अर्थात् पद्मावती-ही की ओर ज्ञान-दृष्टि कर, राजा ने समाधि को लगाया। किँगरी को लिये (राजा) व्यर्थ बजाया करता है (और) साँझ सबेरे नित्य सिंगी को भी पूरा किया, अर्थात् बजाया किया।

BIBLIOTHECA INDICA:

A

COLLECTION OF ORIENTAL WORKS

PUBLISHED BY THE

ASIATIC SOCIETY OF BENGAL.

NEW SERIES NO. 1172.

THE PADUMĀWATI

OF

MALIK MUHAMMAD JAISI,

EDITED, WITH A COMMENTARY, TRANSLATION, AND CRITICAL NOTES.

BY

G. A. GRIERSON, C.I.E., PH.D., I.C.S.,

AND

MAHAMAHOPADHYAYA SUDHAKARA DVIVEDI, F.A.U.

FASCICULUS V.

CALCUTTA:

PRINTED AT THE BAPTIST MISSION PRESS,

AND PUBLISHED BY THE

ASIATIC SOCIETY, 57, PARK STREET.

1907.

(व्यर्थ कहने का यह भाव है, कि ध्यान तो सर्वात्मना पद्मावती-ही की ओर है, परन्तु मेरा यह भेद लोगों पर न खुले, इस लिये जाहिरा साँझ सबेरे किंगरी, और सिंगी को बजाया करता है)॥ (पद्मावती के विरहानल से ऐसी राजा की शरीर तप्त हो गई है, कि उस तपन से (ऐसी) गुदरी जरती है, जानों (उस गुदरी में) आग लगाई गई हो। (कवि कहता है, कि सच है) बरता विरह(-अनल) का धँधोर नहीं बुझता॥ रात में (पद्मावती के) मार्ग में, अर्थात् ध्यान में जागने से नयन लाल (लाल) हो गए हैं, (उन की ऐसी शोभा है) जानों चकोर चकित हो कर, चन्द्रमा में लगा है (जिस के कारण नयन लाल हो गए हैं। राजा को चकित चकोर, और पद्मावती को शशि समझो) वा, जानों खेलौने का चकोर चन्द्रमा में लगा हो (जिस से पलक नहीं भजती, टकटकी लग गई है)॥ (राजा ने) कुण्डल को पकडे शिर को भूमि में लगाया, अर्थात् कानों की मुद्रा को हाथों से पकडे शिर को जमीन में रगडता है, (अपराध-क्षमा कराने के लिये कानों की मुद्रा को, अर्थात् कानों को हाथों से पकडे, शिर रगडता है), (और मन में यही कहता है, कि) जहाँ उस (पद्मावती) का पैर हो, (वहाँ उन पैरों की मैं) पनही होऊँ॥ जिस पथ से (पद्मावती) आवे (उस पथ को) जटा छोर कर (अपने) केशों से बोहारूँ, अर्थात् झारूँ, और तहाँ, अर्थात् तिस मार्ग में (पद्मावती के निमित्त अपने) शिर को वारूँ, अर्थात् काट कर बलि दूँ॥

(राजा का) मन चारो ओर (पद्मावती के लिये) चक्कर के ऐसा घूमता है, एक दण्ड (भी) मार कर, अर्थात् पद्मावती के ध्यान को बिसार कर, स्थिर नहीं रहता। (राजा यही चाहता है, कि) जहाँ प्राण का आधार (पद्मावती) है, (तहाँ) भस्म हो कर, अर्थात् शरीर को राख कर, पवन के संग पहुँचूँ, वा धाऊँ, यह अध्याहृत है॥ १७०॥

इति मण्डप-गमन-खण्ड-नाम सप्तदश-खण्डं समाप्तम्॥ १७॥

अथ पदुमावति-बिओग-खंड ॥ १८ ॥

चउपाई ।

पदुमावति तेहि जोग सँजोगा । परी पेम बस गहे बिओगा ॥
नौंद न परइ रइनि जो आवा । सेज केवाँछ जानु कोउ लावा ॥
डहइ चाँद अउ चंदन चीरू । दगध करइ तन बिरह गँभीरू ॥
कलप-समान रइनि तेहि बाढी । तिल तिल जो जुग जुग पर-गाढी ॥
गहे बीन मकु रइनि बिहाई । ससि-बाहन तब रहइ ओनाई ॥
पुनि धनि सिंघ उरेहइ लागइ । अइसी बिथा रइनि सब जागइ ॥
कहाँ हो भवँर कवँल-रस लेवा । आइ परहु होइ घिरिनि परेवा ॥

दोहा ।

सो धनि बिरह पतँग भइ जरा चहइ तेहि दीप ।
कंत न आउ भिरिँग होइ को चंदन तन लीप ॥ १७१ ॥

जोग = योग । सँजोग = संयोग । पेम = प्रेम । बस = वश । गहे = ग्रहण किया = पकड लिया (ग्रह उपादाने) । बिओग = वियोग = जुदाई । नौंद = निद्रा । परइ = पतति । रइनि = रजनी = रात्रि । सेज = शय्या । कवाँछ = कपि-कच्छु = केवाँच = एक लता-फल, जिस के छू जाने से देह में खजुली पैदा हो जाती है । जानु = जाने वा यथा ।

कोउ = कोऽपि = कोई। लावा = लगाया (लग संलग्ने का भूत काल)। डहइ = दहइ (दहति) = जलाता है। चाँद = चन्द्र। चीरू = चीर = कपडा। दगध = दग्ध = भस्म। करइ = करोति = करता है। तन = तनु = शरीर = देह। गँभीरू = गम्भीर = गहिरा। कलप = कल्प = चारो युग का एक हजार बार बीत जाना। बाढी = बढइ (वर्धते) का भूत-काल। जुग = युग = महा-युग = चारो युग का योग। पर-गाढी = प्र-गाढ = बहुत कठिन। बीन = वीणा = एक बाजा। मकु = मैं-ने कहा, यहाँ कदाचित् जिस में। बिहाई = बीते। ससि-बाहन = शशि-वाहन = चन्द्र की सवारी हरिण। तब = तदा। रहइ = रहता है (रह त्यागे का वर्त्तमान-काल) ओनाई = अवनम्य = उनय कर = झुक कर। पुनि = पुनः = फिर। धनि = धन्या (पद्मावती)। सिंघ = सिंह। उरेहइ = उल्लेखन = लिखने। लागइ = लगति = लगती है। असी = एतादृशी = ऐसी। बिथा = व्यथा = पीडा = तकलीफ। जागइ = जागती है (जागर्त्ति)। कहाँ = क ह = कुत्र। भवँर = भ्रमर। कवँल-रस = कमल-रस = कमल का रस। लेवा = लेनेवाला (लाति से बना हुआ)। आइ = एत्य = आ कर। परऊ = पडो (पततु)। होइ = भूत्वा = हो कर। घिरिनि = घिन्नी = चक्र। परेवा = पारावत = कबूतर॥

पतँग = पतङ्ग = कीट = कीडा। भइ = भई (बभूव)। जरा = जलना = ज्वलनम्। चहइ =(चहते वा इच्छति) चाहती है। दीप = दीया = चिराग। कंत = कान्त = पति। आउ = आयाति = आता है। भिरिंग = भृङ्ग = कीट विशेष जो और कीडों को भी अपने ही ऐसा बना लेता है। लीप = लीपे (लिपि धातु का लिङ् लकार का रूप)॥

तिस राजा रत्नसेन के योग (लेने) से पद्मावती को संयोग हुआ, अर्थात् राजा के योग-प्रभाव से पद्मावती को स्वप्न में राजा से भेंट हो गई, पद्मावती (जागने पर) प्रेम के वश हो गई, राजा की जुदाई ने पद्मावती को पकड लिया॥ रात को जो रत्नसेन आया उस से नींद नहीं पडती (इधर उधर तडपा करती है) जानों किसी ने पलँग में केवाँच लगा दिया हो॥ चन्द्रमा और चन्दन से बासे कपडे भी पद्मावती को जलाते हैं और पति का गहिरा विरह (जुदाइ) शरीर को भस्म करता है॥ तिस पद्मावती के लिये रात कल्प के बराबर बढ गई, तिल, तिल जो रात सो युग युग के ऐसी बहुत ही कठिन हो गई॥ (विचार कर, कि) कदाचित् रात कट जाय (इस लिये पद्मावती ने) बीन को (बजाने के लिये) लिया, (उस की आवाज सुन कर) चन्द्र-वाहन हरिण झुंक कर, रह गया अर्थात् वीणा के सुर से मोहित हो झुंक कर ठहर

गया इस लिये चाँद के ठहर जाने से रात और बढी ॥ (यह कठिनता देख) फिर धन्या पद्मावती सिंह की मूर्त्ति लिखने लगी, (कि इसे देख कर चन्द्र-वाहन हरिण चन्द्र को ले कर भागे जिस में तुरन्त रात बीते), पद्मावती इस प्रकार की पीडा से सब रात जागी ॥ (और मन में विलाप किया करती, कि) हे कमल-रस के लेनेवाले भ्रमर (कान्त) कहाँ हो, (क्यों नहीं) चक्र या कबूतर हो कर, आ कर (इस सेज पर) पडते हो ॥

वह धन्या पद्मावती विरह-आग की फतिंगा हो गई, तिस विरह के दीप (दीये) में जला चाहती है। भृङ्ग रूप हो कर कान्त नहीं आता है (जो कि अपने ही ऐसा कर अपने साथ में ले)। (फिर) कौन देह में चन्दन पोते (जिस से देह ठंढी हो जाय) ॥ १७१ ॥

चउपाई ।

परी बिरह-बन जानहुँ घेरी। अगम असूझ जहाँ लगि हेरी ॥
चतुर दिसा चितवइ जनु भूली। सो बन कवन जो मालति फूली ॥
कवँल भवँर उहइ बन पावइ। को मिलाइ तन-तपनि बुझावइ ॥
अंग अनल अस कवँल सरीरा। हिअ भा पिअर पेम कइ पीरा ॥
चहइ दरस रबि कीन्ह बिगासू। भवँर दिसिटि मँह कवँल अकासू ॥
पूँछइ धाइ बारि कहु बाता। तुइँ जस कवँल-कली रँग राता ॥
केसर बरन हिआ भा तोरा। मानहुँ मनहिँ भएउ किछु भोरा ॥

दोहा ।

पवन न पावइ संचरइ भवँर न तहाँ बईठ ।
भूलि कुरंगिनि कस भएउ मनहुँ सिंघ तुइँ डीठ ॥ १७२ ॥

बिरह = विरह = जुदाई । बन = वन = जङ्गल । जानऊँ = जाने = जानों = यथा । घेरी = घिरी = घिर गई = गृहीत ऊई । अगम = अगम्य = जाने लायक नहीं । असूझ = सूझने लायक नहीं । जहाँ = यावत् = यत्र । लगि = लगिला = लग कर । हेरी = आहरण किया = ढूँढा, वा देखा (हेड़ गतौ से यहाँ गति = प्राप्त)। चतुर = चत्वारि = चारो । दिसा = दिशा । चितवइ = चेतयति = देखती है । जनु = जानऊँ = जानों । भूली = भूल गई = भ्रम में पड गई । कवन = क नु = कौन । मालति = मालती = एक फूल ।

फूली = (फुल्ल विकसने से फुल्लति का भूत-काल)। कवँल = कमल। भवँर = भ्रमर। उह-ई = वही = स एव। पावइ = पावे (प्र उपसर्ग, आप्लृ व्याप्तौ से बना)। मिलाइ = मेलयित्वा = मिला कर। तन = तनु = देह। तपनि = तापन = ताप = जलन। बुझावइ = (बुन्ध-निशामने बुन्ध्यते से)। अनल = आग। अस = एतादृश = ऐसा। सरीरा = शरीर। हिअ = हृदय। पिअर = पीत = पीला। पेम = प्रेम। पीरा = पीडा। चहइ = चाहता है (चहते वा इच्छति से)। दरस = दर्शन। रवि = सूर्य। कीन्ह = किया (डुकृञ् करणे)। बिगासू = विकाश = प्रकाश। अकासू = आकाश = आसमान। पूँछइ = पूछती है (पृच्छति)। धाइ = धात्री = धाई = दाई। बारि = बाले = हे बेटी। कऊ = कथय = कह। बाता = वार्त्ता = बात। तुइँ = त्वम् = तूँ। जस = यादृक् = यथा = जैसे। कवँल-कली = कमल-कली। रँग = रङ्ग। राता = रक्त = लाल। केसर = केशर = एक सुगन्ध-पुष्प। बरन = वर्ण। हिआ = हृदय। भा = हुआ (बभूव)। तोरा = तेरा (तव)। मानहुँ = मन्ये = मानोँ। मनहिँ = मन मेँ। भएउ = भया (बभूव)। किछु = किञ्चित्। भोरा = भ्रम = संशय = शक॥

पवन = वायु = हवा। पावइ = पाता है (प्राप्नोति)। संचरइ = सञ्चलनम् = भीतर धसना। बईठ = = बैठता है (उपविशति)। कुरंगिनि = कुरङ्गी = हरिणी। कस = कैसा = कथम्। सिंघ = सिंह। डीठ = दृष्टवान् = देखा॥

पद्मावती विरह-वन मेँ पड गई, (उस मेँ से निकल नहीँ सकती) जानोँ (किसी से) घिर गई हो, जहाँ तक (आँख उठा कर, उस ने) देखा (तहाँ तक) अगम और असूझ ही जान पडा॥ चारो दिशा की ओर (इस प्रकार से) ताक रही है जानोँ (राह) भूल गई हो, जहाँ पर मालती (पति की शोभा) फूली है वह कौन वन है (इस का पता नहीँ मिलता)॥ जिस वन मेँ कमल है उस वन को तो भ्रमर पा जाता है (पर इस के पति को) कौन मिला कर इस के देह की जलन को बुझावे॥ कमल-शरीर मेँ अङ्ग अङ्ग आग ऐसी लग गई है, पति के प्रेम की पीडा से हृदय पीला हो गया॥ रवि (पति) ने प्रकाश किया (इस लिये पद्मावती) चाहती है, कि (उस रवि अर्थात् पति का) दर्शन हो; भ्रमर की दृष्टि मेँ कमल आकाश मेँ है अर्थात् पद्मावती-भ्रमर ने देखा कि पति-कमल आकाश मेँ छिपा हुआ है॥ (सबेरा होने पर) धाई ने पूछा, कि बेटी इस बात को तो कहो, कि क्या है क्योँकि तूँ ऐसी लाल रंग की थी जैसी कमल की कली॥ सो (आज) तेरा हृदय केशर के रंग (ऐसा पीला हो गया) है, मानोँ तेरे मन मेँ कुछ भ्रम हो गया हो॥

जहाँ हवा भीतर नहीं धसने पाता तहाँ भ्रमर (भी) नहीं बैठता अर्थात् तहाँ भ्रमर भी नहीं बैठ सकता। सो तूं भूली हरिनी के ऐसी क्यों हो गई, मानों सिंह ने तुझे देखा हो (जिस के डर से पीली हो गई) ॥ १७२ ॥

चउपाई।

धाइ सिंघ बरु खातेउ मारी। कइ तसि रहति अहि जस बारी ॥
जोबन सुनेउँ कि नवल बसंतू। तेहि बन परेउ हसति मइमंतू ॥
अब जोबन बारी को राखा। कुंजल बिरह बिधाँसइ साखा ॥
मइँ जानेउँ जोबन रस-भोगू। जोबन कठिन सँताप बिओगू ॥
जोबन गरुअ अपेल पहारू। सहि न जाइ जोबन कर भारू ॥
जोबन अस मइमंत न कोई। नवँइ हसति जउ आँकुस होई ॥
जोबन भर भादउ जस गंगा। लहरइ देइ समाइ न अंगा ॥

दोप।

परिउँ अथाह धाइ हउँ जोबन उदधि गँभीर।
तेहि चितवउँ चारि-हु दिसि को गहि लावइ तीर ॥ १७३ ॥

धाइ = धावौ = धाई। सिंघ = सिंह। बरु = वरम् = अच्छा। खातेउ = खाता (खादृ भक्षणे से बना है)। मारी = मार कर = मारयित्वा। कइ = कि = वा = अथवा। तसि = तथा = तैसी। रहति = रहती (रह त्यागे से बना है)। अहि = आसीत् = थी। जस = यथा = जैसी। बारी = बालिका = लडकी = थोडे उमर की। जोबन = यौवन = जवानी। सुनेउँ = सुना (श्रु श्रवणे से बना है)। नवल = नया। बसंतू = वसन्त ऋतु, यहाँ वसन्त-ऋतु का वन। बन = वन। परेउ = पडा (प्र-उपसर्ग पूर्वक पत् पतने से बना है)। हसति = हस्ती = हाथी। मइमंतू = मदमत्त = मद से मस्त। अब = अधुना = इदानीम्। बारी = बालिका = बाल, वा वाटिका। को = कः = कौन। राखा = रक्खे = रक्षेत्। कुंजल = कुञ्जर = हस्ती = हाथी। बिरह = विरह = पति की जुदाई। बिधाँसइ = विध्वंसयति = विध्वंस करता है = नाश करता है। साखा = शाखा = डार। मइँ = मैं ने। जानेउँ = जाना (ज्ञा अवबोधने से बना है)। भोगू = भोग। सँताप = सन्ताप = ताप।

बिश्रोगू = वियोग = जुदाई। गरुश्र = गुरु = भारी। श्रपेल = हठाने योग्य नहीं। पहारू = पहाड = प्रहार। सहि = सहन = बर्दाश्त। जाइ = जायते = जाता है। भारू = भार = बोझा। श्रस = ऐसा = एतादृश। कोई = कोऽपि। नवँइ = नमति = झुँकता है। जउ = यदि = जौं। श्राँकुस = श्रङ्कुश। होई = हो (भवेत्)। भर = भरी = पूरी। भादव = भादव = भाद्रपद, बरसात का महीना। गंगा = गङ्गा नदी। लहरइ = लहर = तरङ्ग। देइ = देता है = दत्ते। समाइ = समाता है = संमाति। श्रंगा = श्रङ्ग॥

परिउँ = पड गई। श्रथाह = श्रस्थल = श्रतल = श्रगाध। हउँ = श्रहम् = मैं। उदधि = समुद्र। गँभीर = गम्भीर = गहरा। तेहि = तिस से = तिस कारण से। चितवउँ = चेतयामि = देखती हूँ। चारि-ऊ = चारो। दिसि = दिशा। को = कः = कौन। गहि = गहीला = पकड कर। लावइ = लावे = ले श्रावे। तीर = तट = किनारा॥

(पद्मावती कहती है, कि) हे धाई सिंह मार कर, खा जाता तो श्रच्छा होता, श्रथवा जैसी लडकपन-में थी वैसी ही (श्रब भी) रहती तौ भी श्रच्छा॥ सुना था, कि जवानी नया वसन्त-ऋतु का वन है, सो उस वन में मद से मस्त (विरह-रूपी) हाथी (श्रा कर) पड गया श्रर्थात् डेरा ले लिया॥ सो श्रब (इस) जवानी-वाटिका को कौन रख सकता है, (क्योंकि) विरह-हाथी (हर एक) (श्रङ्ग-रूपी) शाखाश्रों को नाश कर रहा है॥ मैं जानती थी, कि जवानी (श्रच्छे) रस-भोग (का समय) है, (पर श्रब समझी, कि पति के) वियोग से जवानी कठिन सन्ताप है॥ जवानी भारी श्रटल पहाड है, जवानी का भार नहीं सहा जाता॥ जवानी के ऐसा कोई मद-मत्त नहीं है, यह (जवानी) हाथी (तभी) (नीचे की श्रोर) झुँकता है यदि श्रङ्कुश हो। जवानी भादव की भरी जैसी गङ्गा लहर मारती है, तैसी (इस देह में लहर मार रही है), श्रङ्ग में समाती नहीं (बाहर उमगी चाहती है)॥

हे धाई मैं गहरे जवानी-समुद्र के श्रथाह (जल) में पड गई हूँ तिसी कारण चारो दिशा देख रही हूँ, कि कौन पकड कर, मुझे किनारे ले श्रावे॥ १७३॥

चउपाई।

पदुमावति तूँ समुद सयानी। तोहि सरि समुद न पूजइ रानी॥
नदी समाहिँ समुद मँह श्राई। समुद डोलि कहु कहाँ समाई॥
श्रब-हीं कवँल-करी हिश्र तोरा। श्रइहइ भवँर जो तो कहँ जोरा॥

जोबन-तुरी हाथ गहि लीजिअ। जहाँ जाइ तहँ जान न दीजिअ॥
जोबन जोर मात गज अहई। गहहु ग्यान आँकुस जिमि रहई॥
अबहिँ बारि तुइँ पेम न खेला। का जानसि कस होइ दुहेला॥
गगन दिसिटि करु नाइ तराहीँ। सुरुज देखु कर आवइ नाहीँ॥

दोहा।

जब लगि पीउ मिलइ तोही साधु पेम कइ पीर।
जइस सीप सेवाती कहँ तपइ समुद मँझ नीर॥ १७४॥

पदुमावति = पद्मावती। तूँ = त्वम्। समुद = समुद्र। सयानी = सयान का स्त्रीलिङ्ग, सयान = सज्ञान = ज्ञान से भरा। सरि = सदृश = बराबरी। पूजइ = पूर्यते = पूरा पडता। रानी = राज्ञी। समाहिँ = समाइ का बहु-वचन, समाइ = संमाति = धसता है वा धसती है। मँह = मध्ये = बीच। आई = एत्य = आ कर। डोलि = आदोल्य = डोल कर = इधर उधर चल कर। कहु = कथय = कहो। कहाँ = क ह = कुच। अब-हीँ = अधुना = अभीँ। कवँल-करी = कमल-कली। हिअ = हृदय। अइहइ = आयास्यति = आवेगा। भवँर = भ्रमर। जो = जो = यः। तो = तव। कहँ = को। जोरा = जोडा = योग्य। तुरी = त्वरी = घोडा। हाथ = हस्त। गहि = ग्रहणम्। लीजिअ = लीजिए (ला उपादाने से बना है)। जहाँ = यत्र। जाइ = जावे (या प्रापणे का लिङ् का एक-वचन)। तहँ = तत्र। जान = जाने = यानम्। दीजिअ = दीजिए (दा दाने से बना है)। जोर = बली। मात = मत्त = मस्त। गज = हाथी। अहई = अस्ति = है। गहहु = गृहाण = पकडो। ग्यान = ज्ञान। आँकुस = अङ्कुश। जिमि = यथा = जैसे = जिस में। रहई = रहे (रह त्यागे का लिङ् के प्रथम पुरुष के एक वचन का रूप)। बारि = वाले = हे बेटी। तुइँ = त्वम् = तूँ। पेम = प्रेम। खेला = खेलइ का भूत, मध्यम-पुरुष का एक-वचन। जानसि = जानासि = जानती है। कस = कथम् = कैसा। होइ = होवे (भवेत्)। दुहेला = दुर्हेला = बुरी खेल = दुःख। गगन = आकाश = आसमान। दिसिटि = दृष्टि। करु = कुरु = करो। नाइ = अवनमय्य = झुँका कर = नवा कर। तराहीँ = तल = नीचे। सुरुज = सूर्य। देखु = देख = पश्य (दृशिर् प्रेक्षणे से बना है)। कर = हाथ। आवइ = आयाति = आता है।

जब = यावत्। लगि = लग्न। जब लगि = जब तक। पीउ = प्रिय = पति। मिलइ = मिले (मिल धञ्जमे से)। साधु = साधय। पीर = पीडा। जइस = जैसे = यथा। सीप = सीपी = शुक्ति। सवाती = खाती। तपइ = तपति = तपती है। मँझ = मध्य। नीर = पानी॥

(धाई कहती है, कि) हे पद्मावती तूँ समुद्र है और समझदार है, हे रानी तेरी बराबरी में समुद्र भी नहीँ पूरा पडता॥ नदी तो आ कर, समुद्र में समा जाती है, (पर) कहो तो समुद्र इधर उधर चल कर कहाँ समाय॥ अभीँ तेरा हृदय कमल की कली है, (खिलने पर) जो तेरे लिये (विधना ने) जोडा लिखा है वह (पति-रूपी) भ्रमर आवेगा॥ (अभीँ) जवानी-घोडे को हाथ से पकड लीजिए जहाँ जाना चाहे वहाँ मत जाने दीजिए। जवानी बली मस्त हाथी है, (उस के लिये) ज्ञान-अङ्कुश को पकडो जिस में (वह हाथी) रहे, इधर उधर न जाय॥ हे बेटी अभीँ तूँ ने प्रेम-खेल को नहीँ खेली है (इस लिये तूँ) क्या जाने, कि (प्रेम-खेल में) कैसा दुःख होता है॥ आकाश की ओर जो दृष्टि है उसे झुंका कर, नीचे की ओर कर। देख, सूर्य हाथ में नहीँ आता, अर्थात् नहीँ पकडा जाता॥

जब तक तुझे (सपने में) पति मिलता है तब तक प्रेम की पीडा को साध, अर्थात् सह। जैसे कि सीपी समुद्र के पानी के बीच (पडी) खाती के लिये तप करती है॥ (सीपी खाती के लिये १४१ वें दोहे की टीका देखो, इस ग्रन्थ का पृ० २८३-२८६)॥ १७४॥

चउपाई।

दहइ धाइ जोबन अउ जीऊ। होई परइ अगिनि मँह घीऊ॥
करवत सहउँ होत दुइ आधा। सहि न जाइ जोबन कइ दाधा॥
बिरहा सुभर समुद असँभारा। भवँर मेलि जिउ लहरहिँ मारा॥
बिरह नाग होइ सिर चढि डसा। अउ होइ अगिनि चाँद मँह बसा॥
जोबन पंखी बिरह बिआधू। केहर भएउ कुरंगिनि खाधू॥
कनक-पानि कत जोबन कीन्हा। अउटन कठिन बिरह ओहि दीन्हा॥
जोबन जलहि बिरह मसि छूआ। फूलहिँ भवँर फरहिँ भा सूआ॥

दोहा ।

जोबन चाँद उआ जस बिरह भएउ सँग राहु ।
घटतहि घटत छीन भइ कहे न पारउँ काहु ॥ १७५ ॥

दहइ = दहति = जलाता है । धाइ = धात्री = धाई । जोबन = यौवन = जवानी । अउ = अपि च = और । जीउ = जीव । होई = हो । परइ = पडा । अगिनि = अग्नि । मँह = मध्य । घीउ = घृत । करवत = करपत्र = आरा । सहउँ = सहे = सहती हूँ । होत = होती है (भवति) । दुइ = द्वौ = दो । आधा = अर्ध = खण्ड = टुकडा । दाधा = दाह । बिरहा = विरह = जुदाई । सुभर = शुभ्र = अच्छा = साफ = भारी । असँभारा = सँभारने लायक नहीं = सँभार = सम्भार । भवँर = भ्रमर = आवर्त्त = भौँर । मेलि = मेलयित्वा = मेल कर = डाल कर । जिउ = जीव । लहरहिँ = लहरोँ से = तरङ्गोँ से । मारा = मारयति = मारता है । नाग = सर्प = साँप । होइ = होइ = भूला = हो कर । सिर = शिरः । चढि = चढ कर = उच्चैराह्य । डसा = दशति = डसता है = काटता है । चाँद = चन्द्र । बसा = वसति = वास किया है । पंखी = पक्षी । बिआधू = व्याध = बहेलिया । केहर = केशरी = सिंह । कुरंगिनि = कुरङ्गी = हरिणी । खाधू = खाद्य = भक्षण = खाने की वस्तु । कनक = सुवर्ण = सोना । पानि = पानीय = पानी । कत = कुतः = कस्मात् = काहे को । अउटन = आवर्त्तन = औटना । जलहि = जल को = पानी को । मसि = मषी = स्याही । कूआ = कूअइ का प्रथम पुरुष में भूत-काल का एक-वचन । फूलहिँ = फूलइ का बहु-वचन (फुल्ल विकशने से बना है) । भवँर = भ्रमर । फरहिँ = फरइ का बहु-वचन (फलति से बना) । भा = बभूव = भया = हुआ, यहाँ हो कर । सूआ = शुक = सुग्गा ।

उगा = उद्गत हुआ = ऊगा । जस = यथा = जैसे । सँग = सङ्ग = साथ । राहु = एक दैत्य जो चन्द्र को निगल जाता है । घटतहि घटत = घटते घटते = कम होते होते (घट चेष्टायां घट्यते से) । छीन = क्षीण = दुर्बल । कहे = कहने से = कथनेन । पारउँ = पार हो सकती हूँ । काहु = कापि वा किसी से ॥

(पद्मावती कहती है, कि) हे धाई, (विरह) जवानी और जीव (दोनोँ) को जला रहा है (जानोँ) आग में घी पडा हो ॥ (देह जानोँ) आरे से दो टुकडे हुई जाती है (इस दुःख को भी) सहती हूँ; जवानी की जलन नहीं सही जाती ॥ पति की जुदाई भारी अपार समुद्र है वह जीव को भौँर में डाल कर लहरोँ से मार रहा है ॥

विरह साँप हो कर, शिर पर चढ, काट रहा है; और आग हो कर, चन्द्रमा में जा कर वास किया है (इस से चन्द्र-किरण मेरे ऊपर आग बरसाती हैं)॥ विरहिणी को चन्द्र-किरण आग ऐसी जान पडती है यह बात संस्कृत काव्यों में बहुत प्रसिद्ध है। श्रीहर्ष ने भी नैषध में लिखा है। जब चन्द्र-ताप से दमयन्ती व्याकुल हुई है तब सखी से कहती है, कि—

कुरु करे गुरुमेकमयोघनं बहिरितो मुकुरं च कुरुष्व मे।

विशति तत्र यदैव विधुस्तदा सखि सुखादहितं जहि तं द्रुतम्॥ (स०४ श्लो०५७)

जवानी पक्षी है उस के लिये विरह व्याधा है; विरह-रूपी सिंह का जवानी-हरिणी भक्षण है॥ (विधना ने) क्यों जवानी को सोने का पानी बनाया, जिस को कि विरह कठिन (कडी आँच में) औटन देता है, अर्थात् औटता है। जवानी-रूपी पानी को विरह-स्याही ने छू दिया (जिस से वह पानी मैला हो गया); (जवानी में) भ्रमर फूलते हैं और सूगे हो कर फलते हैं (जवानी के आरम्भ में स्तनाग्र पहले कुछ काले रहते हैं, वे ही जानों भ्रमर के ऐसे काले फूल हैं; फिर स्तन बढने पर शुक के ऐसे पीले हो जाते हैं, वे ही सुग्गे के ऐसे फल हैं॥)

जैसे ही जवानी-चन्द्र उदय हुआ तैसे ही संग में विरह-राहु लग गया; (इस कारण हे धाई) घटते घटते मैं क्षीण (दुर्बल) हो गई किसी से कह कर (अपनी दशा के) पार नहीं हो सकती॥ १७५॥

चउपाई।

नयन जो चाक फिरहिँ चहुँ ओरा। चरचइ धाइ समाइ न कोरा॥
कहेसि पेम जउ उपना बारी। बाँधहु सत मन डोल न भारी॥
जेहि जिउ मँह सत होइ पहारू। परइ पहार न बाँकइ बारू॥
सती जो जरइ पेम पिअ लागी। जउ सत हिअ तउ सीतल आगी॥
जोबन चाँद जो चउदस-करा। बिरह क चिनगि चाँद पुनि जरा॥
पवन-बंध सो जोगी जती। काम-बंध सो कामिनि सती॥
आउ बसंत फूल फुलवारी। देओ-बार सब जइहहिँ बारी॥

दोहा ।

तुम्ह पुनि जाहु बसंत लेइ पूजि मनावहु देउ ।
जीउ पाइ जग जनम कइ पीउ पाइ कइ सेउ ॥ १७६ ॥

नयन = आँख। चाक = चक्र = कोहार का चाक। चहुँ = चारो = चत्वारि। ओर = अपर, वा अवार = तरफ। चरचइ = चर्चयति = उपाय करती है = दुलारती है। समाइ = समाती है = संमाति। कोरा = क्रोड। कहेसि = कहा (कथ व्यक्तायां वाचि से बना है)। पेम = प्रेम। जउ = यदि = जौं। उपना = उत्पन्न हुआ। बारी = बालिका = बाला = बेटी। बाँधहु = बाँधइ का मध्यम-पुरुष में लोट् लकार का एक-वचन। सत = सत् = सत्य-धर्म। डोल = डोले = चले (दोल्ल सञ्चलने से)। भारी = भार जिस में हो। जिउ = जीव। मँह = मध्य। पहारू = प्रहार = पहाड। परइ = पडे (प्र उपसर्ग-पूर्वक पत्लृपतने से)। बाँकइ = बाँके = वक्र हो = टेढा हो। बारू = बाल। सती = पतिव्रता स्त्री = समीचीना। जरइ = जलती है (ज्वलति)। पिअ = प्रिय = पति। लागी = लग्न हो कर = लिये। हिअ = हृदय। तउ = तर्हि = तदा = तो। सीतल = शीतल = ठंढी। आगी = अग्नि = आग। जोबन = यौवन = जवानी। चाँद = चन्द्र। चउदस-करा = चतुर्दश-कला। बिरह = विरह = वियोग = जुदाई। चिनगि = चिल्कण = स्फुलिङ्ग = चिनगी। जरा = जलता है (ज्वल दीप्तौ से बना)। पवन-बंध = पवन बाँधनेवाला = हवा रोकनेवाला। जोगी = योगी। जती = यति। काम-बंध = काम रोकनेवाला। कामिनि = कामिनी = काम की इच्छा करनेवाली स्त्री। आउ = आयाति = आता है। बसंत = वसन्त-ऋतु। फूल = फूलती है (फुल्लति)। फुलवारी = पुष्प-वाटिका। देओ-बार = देव-द्वार। सब = सर्व। जइहहिँ = जइहइ (यास्यति) का बहु-वचन। बारी = बालिका = लडकियाँ।

तुम्ह = तुम = त्वम्। पुनि = पुनः = फिर। जाहु = जाओ (याहि)। लेइ = लेकर (णी प्रापणे से नीला)। पूजि = आपूज्य = पूज कर। मनावहु = मनाओ (मानयतु) का बहु-वचन। देउ = देव = देवता। जीउ = जीव। पाइ = प्राप्य = पा कर। जग = जगत् = संसार। जनम = जन्म। पीउ = प्रिय = पति। सेउ = सेवा।

(पद्मावती की) जो आँखेँ हैँ (सो) चारो ओर फिरने लगीँ; धाई उपाय करती है (बहुत दुलारती और धीरज देती है और गोद में लेती है पर पद्मावती) गोद में समाती नहीँ (गिरी पडती है)॥ धाई ने कहा, कि बेटी यदि (पति का) प्रेम

(हृदय में) उत्पन्न हुआ, (तो अभी) भारी सत से मन को बाँध रक्खो (जिस में इधर उधर) न चले॥ जिस के जो में सत्-पहाड होता है, (उस के ऊपर) पहाड (भी गिर) पडे (तो भी उस का) बाल नहीं बाँकता (टेढा होता)॥ सती जो प्रेम से पति के लिये जलती है, (उस के) हृदय में यदि सत्-धर्म है तो (उस को) आग ठंढी (जान पडती है)॥ जो जवानी चतुर्दश-कला अर्थात् चतुर्दशी का चन्द्र है, उस में विरहाग्नि की चिनगी पड जाने से फिर वह चन्द्र जला करता है। (चतुर्दशी के चन्द्र के लिये १६ दोहे की टीका देखो पृ० २२)। इस जलन से घबडाना न चाहिए)॥ जो हवा को रोक रखता है वही योगी, यती, कहाता है; और जो काम को रोक रक्खे वही स्त्री सती (कहाती) है॥ (योग-क्रिया करनेवाले को योगी कहते हैं; यति के लिये १० दोहे की चौपाइयों की टीका देखो पृ० ४६) वसन्त-ऋतु आता है (जब) फुलवारी फूल उठती हैं। (उस समय तब) सब लडकियाँ (दर्शन के लिये) देव-द्वार में जायँगी॥

फिर तुम (भी) वसन्त ले कर (वसन्त के फूलों के ऐसी सखियों को ले कर) जाओ और देवता को पूज कर मनाओ, (कि हे देव) संसार में जन्म कर जीव तो पाया (अब) पति पा कर (उस की) सेवा (करूँ ऐसा वर दान देओ)॥ १७६॥

चउपाई।

जब लगि अवधि चाह सो आई। दिन जुग बर बिरहिनि कहँ जाई॥
नींद भूख अह-निसि गइ दोऊ। हिअइँ मारि जस कलपइ कोऊ॥
रोअँ रोअँ जनु लागहिँ चाँटे। सूत सूत बेधहिँ जनु काँटे॥
दगधि कराह जरइ जस घीऊ। बेगि न आउ मलइ-गिरि पीऊ॥
कवन देओ कहँ जाइ परासउँ। जेहि सुमेरु हिअ लाइ गरासउँ॥
गुपुत जो फल साँसहिँ परगटे। अब होइ सुभर चहहिँ पुनि घटे॥
भए सँजोग जो रे अस मरना। भोगी गए भोग का करना॥

दोहा।

जोबन चंचल ढीठ हइ करइ निकाजइ काज।
धनि कुलवंति जो कुल धरइ कइ जोबन मन लाज॥ १७७॥

इति पद्मावति-बिओग-खंड॥ १८॥

जब लगि = यावत् = जब तक । अवधि = मिती = वसन्त-ऋतु का समय । सो = सः = वह । आई = आवे = (आ-उपसर्ग पूर्वक या प्रापणे से बना)। जुग = युग । बर = वर = बडा । बिरहिनि = विरहिणी । कहँ = को । जाई = जाता है = जायते । नींद = निद्रा । भूख = बुभुक्षा = खाने की इच्छा । अह-निसि = अहर्निश = दिन रात । गइ = गई = अगात् । दोऊ = दोनोँ = द्वावपि । हिअइँ = हृदये = हृदय मेँ । मारि = मारयित्वा = मार कर । जस = यथा = जैसे । कलपइ = कल्पति = काटता है (कृपु छेदने)। कोई = कोऽपि । रोअँ = लोम = रोआँ । जनु = जाने = जानेाँ । लागहिँ = लगइ (लगति) का बहु-वचन, लगते हैँ । चाँटे = चीँटे = चाटुक । सूत = सूत्र = एक परिमाण (दो सूत का एक पैन और चार पैन का एक इंच)। बेधहिँ = बेधइ (विध्यते) का बहु-वचन । काँटे = कण्टक । दगधि = दग्ध्वा = दग्ध हो कर = भस्म हो कर । कराह = कटाह = कराहा । घीऊ = घृत = घी । बेगि = वेगेन = जल्दी । आउ = आता है (आयाति)। मलइ-गिरि = मलय-गिरि = मलयाचल । पीऊ = प्रिय = पति । कवन = को नु = कौन । देओ = देव = देवता । जाइ = जा कर (या प्रापणे से बना है)। परासउँ = परसउँ (स्पृशानि) = छूऊँ । लाइ = लगा कर । गरासउँ = ग्रसउँ (ग्रसानि) = ग्रसूँ = निगल जायँ । गुपुत = गुप्त = छिपा । साँसहिँ = श्वासे = साँस मेँ । परगटे = प्रकट हुए = परगटइ (प्रकटयति) का प्रथम-पुरुष मेँ लिट् का एक-वचन । सुभर = शुभ्र = अच्छा । चहहिँ = चहइ (चदते वा इच्छति) का बहु-वचन। पुनि = पुनः = फिर । घटे = घटना = घटनम् (घट चेष्टायां से बना)। भए = भए । सँजोग = संयोग । अस = एतादृश = ऐसा । मरना = मरण । भोगी = भोग करने-वाला । गए = जाने पर । भोग = सुख-विलास । करना = करण ॥

जोबन = जवानी = यौवन । चंचल = चञ्चल । ढीठ = धृष्ट = ढीठा । हइ = अस्ति = है । करइ = करता है (करोति)। निकाजइ = निः कार्य का = बेकाम का । काज = कार्य । धनि = धन्य । कुलवंति = कुलवती = कुल-वधू । धरइ = धरती है (धरति)। कइ = कृत्वा = कर । लाज = लज्जा ।

जब तक वह (मन-)चाही मिती (वसन्त-ऋतु) आवे, (तब तक) विरहिणी (पद्मावती) को दिन बडे युग के ऐसा जाता है (बीतता है)॥ दिन रात नींद और भूख दोनोँ (चली) गई। (ऐसा जान पडता है, कि) कोई हृदय मेँ मार कर काट रहा हो ॥ जानोँ रोएँ रोएँ मेँ चीँटे लगे हैँ, और सूत सूत पर काँटे चुभते होँ ॥

जैसे कराह में भस्म हो कर, घी जलता हो (तैसे ही पद्मावती का जी जल रहा है) मलयाचल-रूप पति जल्दी से नहीं आता है (जिस से जी की जलन बुझे)॥ (पद्मावती कहती है, कि) किस देवता को जा कर, कूऊँ जिस से सुमेरु (सुमेरु ऐसा पति) को हृदय में लगा कर (इस जलन को) निगल जाऊँ अर्थात् बुझाऊँ। छिपे ऊए फल (जलन-रूप फल हा!) अब साँस की राह से प्रगट ऊए, अर्थात् गर्म साँस चलने लगी; सो अब (मैं) अच्छी (कान्ति की) हो कर, फिर घटना (मलिन ऊआ) चाहती हूँ॥ अरे यह जो संयोग सो ऐसा (आ गया जिस से अब) मरना होगा; सुख-विलास (का समय) बीत जाने पर भोग करनेवाले को (ले कर) क्या करना होगा॥

(कवि कहता है, कि) जवानी चञ्चल और ढीठी है; बेकाम ही का काम करती है। धन्य कुल-वधू है (कि इस) जवानी में मन में लज्जा कर (अपने) कुल को धरती है, अर्थात् नहीं छोडती॥ १७७॥

इति पद्मावती-वियोग-खण्डं नामाष्टादश खण्डं समाप्तम्॥ १८॥

अथ पदुमावति-सुत्रा-भेँट-खंड ॥ १९ ॥

चउपाई ।

तेहि बित्रोग हीरा-मनि आवा । पदुमावति जानहुँ जिउ पावा ॥
कंठ लाइ सूत्रा सो रोई । अधिक मोह जउ मिलइ बिछोई ॥
बुझा उठा दुख हिअइँ गँभीरू । नयनहिँ आइ चुआ होइ नीरू ॥
रही रोइ जउँ पदुमिनि रानी । हँसि पूछहिँ सब सखी सयानी ॥
मिले रहस चाहिअ भा दूना । कित रोइअ जउ मिला बिछूना ॥
तेहि क उतर पदुमावति कहा । बिछुरन दुख जो हिअइँ भरि रहा ॥
मिलत हिअइँ आएउ सुख भरा । वह दुख नयन नीर होइ ढरा ॥

दोहा ।

बिछुरंता जब भेँटइ सो जानइ जेहि नेह ।
सुक्ख सुहेला उग्गवइ दुक्ख झरइ जिमि मेह ॥ १७८ ॥

बिओग = वियोग । हीरा-मनि = हीरा-मणि शुक । आवा = आया = आयात् । जानहुँ = जाने = जानों । जिउ = जीव । पावा = पाया = प्राप्नोत् । कंठ = कण्ठ = गला । लाइ = लगा कर । सूआ = शुक = सूगा = सुग्गा । सो = सा = वह । रोई = रोअइ (रोदिति) का प्रथम-पुरुष में लिट् का एक-वचन । अधिक = बहुत । जउ = यदि = जौं । मिलइ = मिलता है (मिलति) । बिछोई = बिछोही = विच्छुरित = बिछुडा हुआ । बुझा = बुझइ (बुन्ध निशामने बुन्ध्यते से) का प्रथम-पुरुष में लिट् का एक-वचन । उठा = उदतिष्ठत् ।

दुख = दुःख। हिअइँ = हृदये = हृदय में। गँभीरू = गम्भीर = गहिरा। नयनहिँ = आँखों में। आइ = एत्य = आ कर। चुआ = चुअइ (च्यवते) का प्रथम-पुरुष में लिट् का एक-वचन। होइ = भूत्वा = हो कर। नीरू = नीर = पानी। रही = रहइ (रहते) का प्रथम-पुरुष में लिट् का एक-वचन। रोइ = रुदित्वा = रो कर। जउँ = ज्यौँ = जैसे-ही। पदुमिनि = पद्मिनी। हँसि = हसित्वा = हँस कर। पूछहिँ = पूछइ (पृच्छति) का प्रथम-पुरुष में लट् का बहु-वचन। सयानी = सयान (सज्ञान) का स्त्री-लिङ्ग। मिले = मिलने में (मिल सङ्गमे से)। रहस = क्रीडा = सुख। चाहिअ = चाहिए (चाहइ = इच्छति से बना)। भा = भया, यहाँ होना। दूना = द्विगुण। कित = किमुत = क्यौँ। रोइअ = रोइए (रोअइ = रोदिति से बना)। बिछूना = विच्छुरित = बिछुडा। क = का। उतर = उत्तर। कहा = कहइ (कथयति) का प्रथम-पुरुष में लिट् का एक-वचन। बिछुरन = विच्छुरण। भरि = भर कर। ढरा = ढरइ (अवधरति) का प्रथम-पुरुष में लिट् का एक-वचन॥

बिछुरंता = विच्छुरित = बिछुडा हुआ। जब = यदा। भैँटइ (मिलति वा अभ्यटति) = भैँटता है। जानइ = (जानाति) जानता है। नेह = स्नेह। सुक्ख = सुख। सुहेला = शोभित = सोहावना। उग्गवइ = उद्गच्छति = उदय होता है। दुक्ख = दुःख। झरइ = झरता है (झरति)। जिमि = यथा = जैसे। मेह = मेघ = बादल॥

तिसी (पति-)वियोग (की पीडा के समय में) हीरा-मणि शुक आ गया, (उस के देखने से) जानोँ पद्मावती जीव को पा गई। वह (पद्मावती) सुग्गे को गले में लगा कर रोई, (सच है) यदि बिछुडा मिले तो बहुत मोह होता है। (सुग्गे के बिछुडने का) दुःख बुझ गया और गहिरे हृदय से उठा; आँखों में आ कर पानी हो कर चू पडा। जैसे-ही पद्मिनी (पद्मावती) रानी रो कर (चुप हो) रही; (तैसे-ही) सब सयानी सखियाँ हँस कर पूछने लगीँ। (कि बिछुडे के) मिलने मेँ चाहिए कि दूना सुख हो; जब बिछुडा मिल गया (तब) क्यौँ रोना चाहिए। तिस के उत्तर में पद्मावती ने कहा कि बिछुडने का जो दुःख हृदय में भरा था (उस के स्थान मेँ बिछुडे के) मिलते-ही सुख आ गया और हृदय मेँ भर गया (सो वह दुःख हलका हो कर) आँखों से पानी हो कर गिर पडा॥

(कवि कहता है कि) जब बिछुडा हुआ (आ कर) भैँटने लगता है (उस समय की दशा) वही जानता है जिसे कि नेह है; (उस समय) सोहावना सुख उदय होने लगता है और दुःख झरने लगता है जैसे कि मेघ॥ १७८॥

चउपाई ।

पुनि रानी हँसि कूसर पूछा । कित गवँनेहु पौँजर कइ छूँछा ॥
रानी तुम्ह जुग जुग सुख पाटू । छाज न पंखिहि पौँजर ठाटू ॥
जउँ भा पंख कहाँ थिरु रहना । चाहइ उड़ा पाँख जउँ डहना ॥
पौँजर मँह जो परेवा घेरा । आइ मँजारि कीन्ह तहँ फेरा ॥
दिवस-क आइ हाथ पइ मेला । तेहि डर बनोबास कहँ खेला ॥
तहाँ बिआध आइ नर साधा । छूट न पाउ मीचु कर बाँधा ॥
वेइ धरि बेँचा बाम्हन हाथा । जंबू-दीप गएउँ तेहि साथा ॥

दोहा ।

तहाँ चितर चितउर-गढ चितर-सेन कर राज ।
टीका दीन्ह पुतर कहँ आपु लीन्ह सिउ-साज ॥ १७९ ॥

पुनि = पुनः = फिर । रानी = राज्ञी । हँसि = हसित्वा = हँस कर । कूसर = कुशल । पूछा = पूछइ (पृच्छति) का प्रथम-पुरुष मेँ लिट् का एक-वचन । कित = किमुत = क्योँ गवँनेऊ = गए (गमन से बना) । पौँजर = पञ्जर = पिँजडा । कइ = कृत्वा = कर । छूँछा = खाली (छो छेदने से) । जुग = युग = एक काल-परिमाण । पाटू = पट्ट = सिंहासन । छाज = सोहता है (सज्जते) । पंखिहि = पक्षी को । ठाट = स्थिति । जउँ = ज्योँ = जैसे-ही । भा = बभूव = हुआ । पंख = पक्ष = पंर । कहाँ = कुतः = काहे को । थिरु = स्थिर । रहना = रहणीयं (रहइ से बना है) । चाहइ = चाहता है (चदते या इच्छति) । उडा = [उडइ (उड्डीयते) से बना है] उडना । पाँख = पक्ष = पर । डहना = डयन = डैना । मँह = मध्य । परेवा = पारावत, यहाँ पक्षी । घेरा = गृहीत । आइ = एत्य = आ कर । मँजारि = मार्जारी = बिलैया । तहाँ = तत्र । फेरा = स्फुरण = फेरी । दिवस क = दिवस एक = एक दिन । हाथ = हस्त । पइ = अपि = निश्चय । मेला = मेले (मेलयेत्) = डाले । डर = दर = भय । बनोबास = वनवास । खेला = खेलइ (खेलति) का उत्तम-पुरुष मेँ लिट् का एक-वचन । बिआध = व्याध = बहेलिया । आइ = एत्य = आ कर । नर = नल = नरकट की नली = लग्गी जिस से बहेलिया खोँचा मारते हैँ । साधा = साधइ (साधयति) का प्रथम-पुरुष मेँ लिट् का एक वचन । छूट = छुटइ (छुट छेदने) ।

पाउ = पाता है (प्राप्यते)। मीचु = मृत्यु = मौत। बाँधा = बँधा = बद्ध। बेह = वह। धरि = धृत्वा = धर कर = पकड कर। बँचा = बँचइ (विक्रीणीते) का प्रथम-पुरुष में लिट् का एक-वचन। बाम्हन = ब्राह्मण। जंबू-दीप = जम्बू-द्वीप। गएउँ = गया (गाङ् गतौ से बना है)। साथा = सार्थ = सङ्ग॥

चितर = चित्र = विचित्र। चितउर-गढ = चित्तौर-गढ। चितउर = चित्रवर वा चित्रपुर। गढ = गाढ = दुर्ग = किला। चितर-सेन = चित्रसेन। कर = का। राज = राज्य। टीका = तिलक। पुतर = पुत्र = बेटा। आपु = आत्मा = स्वयम्। लीन्ह = लिया = लेइ (लाति) का प्रथम-पुरुष में लिट् का एक-वचन। सिउ = शिव = महादेव। साज = सज्जित वस्तु॥

फिर रानी ने हँस कर कुशल पूछा (और कहा कि) पिँजडे को खाली कर क्यों चले गए। (शुक ने कहा कि) हे रानी तुम युग युग सुख से सिंहासन (पर बैठो); पक्षी को पिँजडे की स्थिति नहीँ सोहती। जहाँ (जैसे-ही) पर हुआ (फिर) कहाँ ठहर कर रहना; जैसे-ही डैने में पर हुए (तैसे-ही पक्षी) उडना चाहता है। (मैँ) पक्षी जो पिँजडे में घिरा था, तहाँ बिलैया आ कर फेरी करने लगी। (मैँ ने सोचा कि) एक दिन आ कर निश्चय हाथ डालेगी; तिसी डर से वन-वास के लिये खेल किया अर्थात् चल दिया। तहाँ आ कर बहेलिये ने लग्गी को साधा; मौत का बँधा छूटने नहीँ पाता। (मैँ फँस गया) उस ने पकड कर एक ब्राह्मण के हाथ बँच दिया, उस (ब्राह्मण) के साथ साथ जम्बू-द्वीप में गया॥

तहाँ विचित्र चित्तौर-गढ में राजा चित्र-सेन की राज है, (उस ने) बेटे को तिलक (राज-गद्दी) दे कर आप स्वयं महादेव के साज को लिया, अर्थात् मर कर शिव-लोक को गया॥ १७९॥

चउपाई।

बइठ जो राज पिता के ठाऊँ। राजा रतन-सेन ओहि नाऊँ॥
का बरनउँ धनि देस दिआरा। जहँ अस नग उपना उँजिआरा॥
धनि माता अउ पिता बखाना। जेहि के बंस अंस अस आना॥
लखन बतीस-उ कुल निरमरा। बरनि न जाइ रूप अउ करा॥
बेइ हउँ लीन्ह अहा अस भागू। चाहइ सोनइ मिला सोहागू॥

सो नग देखि हीँछा भइ मोरी। हइ यह रतन पदारथ जोरी ॥
हइ ससि जोग इहइ पइ भानू। तहँ तोहार मइँ कीन्ह बखानू ॥

दोहा ।

कहाँ रतन रतना-गिरी कंचन कहाँ सुमेरु ।
दइउ जो जोरी दुहुँ लिखी मिली सो कउन-हुँ फेरु ॥ १८० ॥

बइठ = बैठा = बैठइ (विशति) का प्रथम-पुरुष में लिट् का एक-वचन । राज = राजा वा राज्य । पिता = बाप । ठाऊँ = स्थान । रतन-सेन = रत्न-सेन । नाऊँ = नाम । का = क्या = कथम् । वरनउँ = वर्णये = वर्णन करूँ । धनि = धन्य । देस = देश । दिश्रारा = दीपाकार = दीए के ऐसा उज्ज्वल । जहँ = जहाँ = यत्र । अस = एतादृश = ऐसा । नग = पत्थल, यहाँ रत्न । उपना = उत्पन्न हुआ (उत्पद्यते से लिट् का प्रथम-पुरुष में एक-वचन) । उँजिश्रारा = उज्ज्वल । बखाना = वर्णन-योग्य । बंस = वंश । अंस = अंश = अवतार । आना = आनइ (आनयति) का प्रथम-पुरुष में लिट् का एक-वचन । लखन = लक्षण । बतीस-उ = द्वात्रिंशदेव = बत्तीसो । (इस ग्रन्थ का ७६-७७ पृ० देखो) । निरमरा = निर्मल = साफ । जाइ = जाता है (याति) । करा = कला = तेज = कान्ति । हउँ = हौँ = मैं, यहाँ मुझे । अहा = आसीत् = थी ।, भागू = भाग्य । चाहइ = चहइ (चहते या इच्छति) = चाहता है । सोनइ = स्वर्ण = सोने में । मिला = मिलना = मेलनम् । सोहागू = सोहागा । देखि = देख कर (दृष्ट्वा) । हीँछा = हि-इच्छा = निश्चय, इच्छा । भइ = भई = हुई (बभूव) । मोरी = मेरी = मम । हइ = है (अस्ति) । यह = अयम् । रतन = रत्न । पदारथ = पदार्थ = वस्तु । जोरी = जोडी = योज्य । ससि = शशि = चन्द्र । जोग = योग्य । इहइ = यही = अयमेव । पइ = अपि = निश्चय । भानू = भानु = सूर्य । तोहार = तुम्हारा । मइँ = मैँ । बखानू = वर्णन ॥

रतना-गिरि = रत्न-गिरि = रत्न का पहाड । कंचन = काञ्चन = सुवर्ण = सोना । सुमेरु = सोने का पहाड । दइउ = देव वा दैव (भाग्य) = ब्रह्मा = विधि । दुहूँ = दोनोँ को = द्वयोरपि । लिखी = लिखइ (लिखति) का प्रथम-पुरुष में लिट् का एक-वचन । कउन-हूँ = किसी = केनापि । फेरु = फेर = स्फुरण = चाल ॥

पिता के स्थान पर जो राजा बैठा, उस राजा का रत्न-सेन नाम है । क्या वर्णन करूँ । दीपक के ऐसा (वह) देश धन्य है । जहाँ कि ऐसा उजला नग (रत्न-सेन) उत्पन्न हुआ ।

वर्णन के योग्य माता और पिता धन्य हैं। जिन के वंश में (ब्रह्मा ने) ऐसे अंश को ले आया अर्थात् ऐसे पुरुष को उत्पन्न किया। (रत्न-सेन में) बत्तीसो लक्षण हैं (इस ग्रन्थ का ७६-७७ पृ॰ देखो)। (रत्न-सेन का) निर्मल कुल, रूप और तेज बखाना नहीं जाता। (मेरी) ऐसी भाग्य थी कि उन्हों ने मुझे लिया (खरीदा), (क्योंकि) सोने में सोहागा (रत्न-सेन में पद्मावती) मिलने चाहता है। उस नग (रत्न-सेन) को देख कर, निश्चय कर मेरी इच्छा ऊई कि, यही रत्न पदार्थ (पद्मावती) की जोडी है। यही सूर्य निश्चय कर चन्द्र (पद्मावती) के योग्य है; (इस लिये) तहाँ पर मैं ने तुम्हारा वर्णन किया॥

(देखो) कहाँ रत्नाचल में रत्न और कहाँ सुमेरु में सोना। (पर) देव ने जो दोनों की जोडी लिखी थी (इस लिये) किसी न किसी चाल से दोनों की जोडी मिल गई। (सोने की अँगूठी में रत्न ही जडा जाता है, दोनों के मिलने-ही से शोभा बढती है। दक्षिण ध्रुव के पास रत्नाचल में रत्न होता है और उत्तर ध्रुव के पास सुमेरु में सोना। पर दोनों की जोडी लिखी थी। इस लिये अँगूठी में दोनों एकट्ठें हो जाते हैं। इसी प्रकार तुम दक्षिण दिशा सिंहल में और राजा रत्न-सेन उत्तर दिशा चित्तौर में। परन्तु यदि जोडी लिखी है तो अवश्य मिलना होगा)॥ १८०॥

चउपाई।

सुनि कइ बिरह-चिनगि ओहि परी। रतन पाउ जउ कंचन-करी॥
कठिन पेम बिरहा दुख भारी। राज छाडि भा जोगि भिखारी॥
मालति लागि भवँर जस होई। होइ बाउर निसरा बुधि खोई॥
कहेसि पतंग होइ धनि लेऊँ। सिंघल-दीप जाइ जिउ देऊँ॥
पुनि ओहि कोउ न छाडि अकेला। सोरह सहस कुअँर भए चेला॥
अउरु गनइ को संग सहाई। महादेओ-मढ मेला जाई॥
सूरुज पुरुस दरस कइ ताईं। चितवइ चाँद चकोर कि नाईं॥

दोहा।

तुम्ह बारी रस जोग जेहि कवँलहि जस अरघानि।
तस सूरुज परगास कइ भवँर मिलाएउँ आनि॥ १८१॥

सुनि कइ = श्रुत्वा = सुन कर। बिरह = विरह = वियोग = जुदाई। चिनगि = चित्-कण = आग की कनी = स्फुलिङ्ग। परी = परइ (पतति) का प्रथम-पुरुष में लिट् का एक-वचन। रतन = रत्न। पाउ = पाता है (प्राप्यते)। जउ = यदि। कंचन = कञ्चन = सोना। करी = कली = कलिका। कठिन = कडा। पेम = प्रेम। दुख = दुःख। भारी = जिस में भार (बोझा) हो। राज = राज्य। छाडि = छोड कर (आछोड्य)। भा = हुआ (बभूव)। जोगि = योगी। भिखारी = भिक्षुक (भिक्षालु)। मालति = मालती = एक बरसात का लता-पुष्प। लागि = लग कर (लगिला) = लिये। भवँर = भ्रमर। जस = यथा = जैसा। होई = होता है (भवति)। होइ = होइ = हो कर (भूत्वा)। बाउर = वातुल = बौरहा। निसरा = निःससार = निकला। बुधि = बुद्धि। खोई = खो कर = गवाँ कर। कहेसि = कहा (कथ व्यक्तायां वाचि से बना)। पतंग = पतङ्ग = फतिंगा। धनि = धन्या = पद्मावती। लेऊँ = लेवँ = लेइ (लाति) का सम्भावना में उत्तम-पुरुष का एक-वचन। सिंघल-दीप = सिंहल-द्वीप। जाइ = जा कर (याला)। जीउ = जीव। देऊँ = देवँ = देइ (दत्ते) का सम्भावना में उत्तम-पुरुष का एक-वचन। अकेला = एकलः = एकाकी। सोरह = षोडश। सहस = सहस्र। कुअँर = कुमार = राज-कुमार। भए = भए = हुए (बभूवुः)। चेला = शिष्य। गनइ = गने = गणयेत्। सहाई = सहाय = सहायक। महादेओ = महादेव। मढ = मठ = मन्दिर। मेला = मिले = डेरा किए (मिल सङ्गमे से)। जाई = जाइ = जा कर। सूरुज = सूर्य। पुरुस = पुरुष। दरस = दर्शन। कइ ताईं = के लिये। चितवइ = (चेतयति वा चिन्तयति) = देख रहा है। चाँद = चन्द्र। चकोर = एक पक्षी। नाईं = निभ = सदृश = बराबर ॥

बारी = बालिका थोडी अवस्था की या वाटिका। जोग = योग्य। कवँलहि = कमल में। अरघानि = आघ्राण = सुगन्ध। परगास = प्रकाश। मिलाएऊँ = मिलाया (मेलयेयम्)। आनि = आनीय = ले आ कर ॥

(इस बात को) सुन कर उस के (हृदय में) विरहाग्नि की कनी पड गई, (सच है) यदि कञ्चन की कली हो (तभी) रत्न को पाता है। प्रेम (होने) से विरह का दुःख कठिन और भारी होता है; (वह) राज्य छोड कर भिखारी हो गया। मालती के लिये भ्रमर की जैसी (दशा) होती है; (तैसे-ही) बुद्धि खो कर, पागल हो कर (घर से बाहर) निकला। कहा कि फतिंगा हो कर (उस) धन्या (पद्मावती) को लेऊँ और (उस के लिये) सिंहल-द्वीप में जा कर जी को देऊँ। फिर उसे कोई

अकेला न छोडे (इस लिये) सोरह हजार राज-कुमार चेला ऊए (और संग मेँ चले)। और संग मेँ जो सहायक (चले उन को) कौन गिने; (इस प्रकार वह) जा कर महादेव के मठ मेँ मिला है अर्थात् उतरा है। (वह) सूर्य-पुरुष (तुम्हारे) दर्शन के लिये (चारो ओर) देख रहा है, जैसे चकोर चन्द्र के लिये चारो ओर देखे॥

तुम थोडी अवस्था की जिस रस के योग्य हो जैसे कि कमल मेँ सुगन्ध-रस, तैसा-ही सूर्य को प्रकाश कर, अर्थात् तुम्हारी प्रशंसा से उस के हृदय मेँ विरह-रूपी सूर्य का प्रकाश कर (उस) भ्रमर (रत्न-सेन) को ले आ कर, मिलाया है॥ १८१॥

चउपाई।

हीरा-मनि जो कही यह बाता। सुनि कइ रतन पदारथ राता॥
जस सूरुज देखइ होइ ओपा। तस भा बिरह काम-दल कोपा॥
पइ सुनि जोगी केर बखानू। पदुमावति मन भा अभिमानू॥
कंचन जउ कसिअइ कइ ताता। तब जानहु दहुँ पीत कि राता॥
कंचन-करी न काँचुहिँ लोभा। जउ नग होइ पावइ तब सोभा॥
नग कर मरम सो जरिआ जाना। जुरइ जो अस नग हीर बखाना॥
को अस हाथ सिंघ-मुख घालइ। को यह बात पिता सउँ चालइ॥

दोहा।

सरग इँदर डरि काँपइ बासुकि डरइ पतार।
कहँ अस बर पिरिथुमीँ मोहिँ जोग संसार॥ १८२॥

हीरा-मनि = हीरा-मणि, शुक। कही = कहा का स्त्रीलिङ्ग (कहा, कथ व्यक्तायां वाचि से ऊआ)। बाता = वार्त्ता = बात। सुनि कइ = सुन कर = सुला। रतन = रत्न। पदारथ = पदार्थ = वस्तु (पद्मावती)। राता = रक्त = लाल। सूरुज = सूर्य। देखइ = देखता है (दृश्यते)। होइ = हो कर (भूला)। ओपा = आउप = आतप। तस = तथा = तैसेई। भा = ऊआ = बभूव। बिरह = विरह = वियोग। काम-दल = काम की सेना।

कोपा = कोपइ (कुप्यते) का प्रथम-पुरुष मेँ लिट् का एक-वचन। पइ = पर = परन्तु। जोगी = योगी। केर = का। बखानू = वर्णन। अभिमानू = अभिमान। कंचन = कञ्चन = सोना। जउ = यदि। कसिअइ = कसिए = कसइ (कषति से बना है) कइ = कर = कला। ताता = तप्त = गर्म। जानङ = जानिए (ज्ञायते)। दऊँ = दोनोँ मेँ = कि = अथवा। पीत = पीला। कंचन-करी = कञ्चन-कली। काँचुहिँ = काचे = काच मेँ। लोभा = लोभाता (लुभ धातु से)। नग = नगीना = रत्न। होत्र = होवे (भवेत्)। पावइ = पाता है (प्राप्यते)। सोभा = शोभा। मरम = मर्म = भेद। जरित्रा = जडिया = जडने-वाला = जोटक। जुरइ = जुटता है (जुट बन्धने)। हीर = हीरा। अस = ऐसा = एतादृश। हाथ = हस्त। सिंघ = सिंह। मुख = मुह। घालइ = घाले = डाले (घ-प्रस्रवणे) प्रा. घल्लइ। सउँ = से। चालइ = चलावे (चालयेत्)॥

सरग = स्वर्ग। इँदर = इन्द्र। डरि = डर कर = दरिला। काँपइ = काँपता है (कम्पते)। बासुकि = वासुकि = नाग (इस ग्रन्थ का १६५ पृ० देखो)। डरइ = डरता है (दरति)। पतार = पाताल (२ पृ० देखो)। अस = ऐसा = एतादृश। बर = वर = श्रेष्ठ = विवाहयोग्य। पिरिथुमीँ = पृथिव्याम् = पृथिवी मेँ। जोग = योग्य। संसार = जगत्॥

हीरा-मणि शुक ने जो यह बात कही, (उसे) सुन कर रत्न का पदार्थ (रत्न-सेन के योग्य पद्मावती) (तप कर) लाल हो गया। जैसे सूर्य के देखने से ओप (तप) चढ जाता है; तैसे-ही विरह (और भी तप्त) हो गया और काम की सेना (और भी) कोपित हुई। पर योगी का वर्णन सुन कर पद्मावती के हृदय मेँ अभिमान हुआ। कि यदि कञ्चन की कली को तपा कर कसिए तब जान पडता है कि पीला है कि लाल। कञ्चन की कली काँच मेँ नहीँ लोभाती; यदि (सच्चा) नगीना हो तभी शोभा को पाती है। जो जडनेवाला होता है वही (सो) नग का भेद जानता है; जो वर्णन के योग्य नगीना हीरा हो तो जुटे, अर्थात् यदि रत्न-सेन सच्चा पुरुष-रत्न हो तो उस का और मेरा साथ हो सकता है। (परन्तु) ऐसा कौन है जो सिंह के मुह मेँ हाथ डाले; कौन इस बात को पिता से चलावे अर्थात् कौन ऐसा निडर है जो मेरे पिता के कान मेँ इस बात को डाले॥

(जिस के) डर से इन्द्र स्वर्ग मेँ और वासुकि पाताल मेँ काँपता है (उस के सामने कौन इस बात को चला सकता है)। इस संसार और पृथिवी मेँ कहाँ ऐसा वर है जो मेरे योग्य हो॥ १८२॥

चउपाई ।

तूँ रानी ससि कंचन-करा। वह नग रतन सूर निरमरा ॥
बिरह बजागि बीच का कोई। आगि जो छुअइ जाइ जरि सोई ॥
आगि बुझाइ धोइ जल काढइ। वह न बुझाइ आगि अति बाढइ ॥
बिरह कि आगि सूर नहिँ टीका। रातिहिँ दिवस फिरइ अउ धीका ॥
खनहिँ सरग खन जाइ पतारा। थिर न रहइ तेहि आगि अपारा ॥
धनि सो जीउ दगध इमि सहा। अकसर जरइ न दोसर कहा ॥
सुलगि सुलगि भीतर होइ सावाँ। परगट होइ न कहा दुख नावाँ ॥

दोहा ।

कहा कहउ हउँ ओहि सउँ जेहि दुख कीन्ह न मेट।
तेहि दिन आगि करउँ एहि (बाहर) होए जेहि दिन सो भेँट ॥ १८३ ॥

तूँ = त्वम्। ससि = शशि = चन्द्रमा। कंचन-करा = कञ्चन-कला = सोने की कला। रतन = रत्न-सेन। सूर = सूर्य। निरमरा = निर्मल = साफ। बजागि = वज्राग्नि = बिजुरी की आग। बीच = मध्य। का = किमु = क्या। छुअइ = छूता है (स्पृशति)। जाइ = जाता है (याति)। जरि = जर = ज्वलित। सोई = स एव = वही। बुझाइ = बुझा कर (अपबुध्यते से)। धोइ = धो कर = आधूय। जल = पानी। काढइ = काढता है = निकालता है = निःकाशयति। अति = बहुत। बाढइ = बढती है (वर्धते)। टीका = टिकइ (टीकते, टीकृ गत्यर्थे) = टिकता है = ठहरता है। रातिहिँ = रात्रि = रात। दिवस = दिन। फिरइ = फिरता है (स्फुरति)। धीका = दहकइ (दह्यते) = दहका करता है। खनहिँ = क्षण में। सरग = स्वर्ग। पतारा = पाताल। थिर = स्थिर। रहइ = रहता है (रहति)। अपारा = अपार = जिस का पार न हो। धनि = धन्य। जीउ = जीव। दगध = दग्ध = दाह। इमि = एवम् = ऐसा। सहा = सहइ (सहते)। अकसर = एकसर = अकेला। जरइ = जलता है (ज्वलति)। दोसर = दूसरा = द्विः-सर। कहा = कहइ (कथयति) = कहता है। सुलगि = सुलग कर = सु-लग्य। भीतर = अभ्यन्तर। होइ = होइ = होता है (भवति)। सावाँ = श्याम = काला। परगट = प्रकट। होइ = होइ = हो कर (भूत्वा)। दुख = दुःख। नावाँ = नाम ॥

कहा = किमु हा = क्या। कहउँ = कहूँ (कथये)। हउँ = हैाँ = अहम् = मैँ। ओहि सउँ = उस से। मेट = मेटइ = मिटाता है (मठि शोके, मण्ठते)। करउँ = करूँ (करवाणि)। बाहर = बहिः। भेँट (भट भृतौ वा, अभ्यटति से) = मुलाकात ॥

(हीरा-मणि ने कहा कि) हे रानी (पद्मावती) तूँ चन्द्रमा और सोने की कला है और वह (रत्न-सेन) निर्मल सूर्य और नगीना है। (जो तुम कहती हो कि कौन बीच मेँ पडे और इस बात को पिता से कहे सो) बिरह-बिजुरी की आग के बीच क्या कोई पडे; (पडना दूर रहा) जो कोई (उस) आग को छूवे वही जल जाय। (साधारण) आग को पानी से बुझा कर (उस मेँ पडे सोने को) धो कर (आदमी) निकाल लेता है, (पर) वह (बिजुरी की) आग (पानी से) नहीँ बुझती (किन्तु) और अधिक बढती है। बिरह की आग से सूर्य नहीँ ठहरता है; रात दिन घूमा करता है और (जलन से) दहका करता है। (कवि की उत्प्रेक्षा है कि भगवान् की आँख से जिस दिन सूर्य बिछुडा, उसी दिन से जुदाई की आग से व्याकुल हो दिन रात तपा हुआ घूमा करता है, ठहरता नहीँ। पुराणोँ मेँ कथा है, कि सूर्य की उत्पत्ति भगवान् की आँख से है। तुलसी-दास ने भी विनय-पत्रिका मेँ लिखा है कि 'बिछुरे ससि रबि मन नयनन्ह तेँ', ८८ वाँ पद देखो)। क्षण मेँ स्वर्ग और क्षण मेँ पाताल जाता है; तिसी अपार (बिरह की) आग से स्थिर नहीँ रहता। धन्य वह जीव (रत्न-सेन) है जो ऐसे (आग की) दाह को सहता है; अकेला जला करता है (पर) दूसरे से नहीँ कहता। सुलग सुलग कर भीतर काला हो जाता है (पर) प्रगट हो कर दुःख का नाम (तक) नहीँ कहता है ॥

मैँ उस से (ब्रह्मा से) क्या कहूँ जिस ने दुःख को तो किया अर्थात् दिया (पर उस को) मिटाता नहीँ; (सो हे पद्मावति) जिस दिन वह (रत्न-सेन) भेँट करेगा उसी (तिसी) दिन इस आग को बाहर करूँ अर्थात् करूँगा (घबडाओ न अभीँ जहाँ तक बने इस आग को दबा कर हृदय मेँ रक्खो, भभकने न पावे) ॥ १८३ ॥

चउपाई।

सुनि कइ धनि जारी अस काया। तन भउ साँच हिअइँ भउ माया ॥
देखउँ जाइ जरइ जस भानू। कंचन जरइ अधिक होइ बानू ॥
अब जउ मरइ सो पेम बिओगी। हतिआ मोहिँ जेहि कारन जोगी ॥

हीरा-मनि जो कही तुम्ह बाता। रहिहउँ रतन-पदारथ राता॥
जउ वह जोग सँभारइ छाला। देइहउँ भुगुति देहउँ जय-माला॥
आउ बसंत कुसल सउँ पावउँ। पूजा मिस मंडप कहँ आवउँ॥
गुरु के बइन फूल मइँ गाँथे। देखउँ नयन चढावउँ माँथे॥

दोहा।

कवँल-भवँर तुम्ह बरना मइँ पुनि माना सोइ।
चाँद सूर कहँ चाहिअ जउ रे सूर वह होइ॥ १८४॥

सुनि कइ = सुन कर = श्रुत्वा। धनि = धन्या (पद्मावती)। जारी = जारइ (ज्वालयति) का प्रथम-पुरुष में लिट् का एक-वचन। अस = ऐसा = एतादृश। काया = काय = शरीर = देह।। तन = तनु = शरीर। भउ = भई (बभूव) = हुई। साँच = सच = सत्य। हिअइँ = हृदये = हृदय में। माया = मोह। देखउँ = देखें (पश्येयम्)। जाइ = जा कर = यात्वा। जस = यथा = जैसे। भानू = भानु = सूर्य। अधिक = बहुत। होइ = होइ = होता है (भवति)। बानू = वर्ण = रंग = रंगत। जउ = यदि। मरइ = मरे (मरेत्)। पेम = प्रेम। बिओगी = वियोगी = विरही। हतिआ = हत्या। कारन = कारण। जोगी = योगी। हीरा-मनि = हीरा-मणि। कही = कहा का स्त्री-लिङ्ग (कहा, कथ व्यक्तायां वाचि से)। बाता = वार्त्ता = बात। रहिहउँ = रहूँगी। रतन = रत्न। पदारथ = पदार्थ। राता = रक्त = लगी। जोग = योग। सँभारइ = सम्भरेत् = सँभाले। छाला = चैल = मृग-छाला = मृग-चर्म। देइहउँ = दूँगी = देऊँगी (दास्ये)। भुगुति = भुक्ति = भोग-विलास। देहउँ = देऊँगी। जय-माला = जय-माल = विजय की माला (स्वयंवर में स्त्री जिसे पसंद करती है उस के गले में जो माला पहना देती है, उसे जय-माला कहते हैं। यह प्रायः महुए के फूल की होती है, काव्यों में 'मधूक-माला' मिलता है)। आउ = आता है (आयाति)। बसंत = वसन्त-ऋतु। कुसल = कुशल। पावउँ = पावँ (प्राप्नुयाम्)। मिस = मिष = व्याज = बहाना। मंडप = मण्डप = देव-मन्दिर। आवउँ = आऊँगी (आयास्यामि)। गुरु = हीरा-मणि = शुक। बइन = वचन = बात। फूल = फुल्ल = पुष्प। मइँ = मैं। गाँथे = गाँथा = गाँथइ (ग्रथ्नाति) का उत्तम-पुरुष में लिट् का एक-वचन। नयन = आँख। चढावउँ = चढाऊँ (उच्चालयेयम्)। माँथे = मस्तक॥

बसइ = बसता है (वसति)। मीन = मछली। जल = पानी। धरती = धरित्री = भूमि। अंबा = आम्र = आम। अकास = आकाश। पिरीति = प्रीति। पइ = अपि = पर = परन्तु। दोउ = दोनोँ = द्वयोः। मँह = मध्य = मेँ। अंत = अन्त। होहिँ = होते हैँ (भवन्ति)। एक = एक। पास = पार्श्व = निकट॥

हीरा-मणि ने जो यह बात कही (कि तेरे योग्य पुरुष-रत्न ले आया हूँ, इस से पद्मावती के हाथ से हीरा-मणि ने) पान (बीडा) पाया, (जिस से उस का) मुह लाल हो गया। (वहाँ से बिदा हो कर) शुक (हीरा-मणि) चला; तब रानी (पद्मावती) ने कहा कि जो दूसरे का ज्ञआ वह (सो) कैसे रहे। जो नित्य चलने के लिये परोँ को सँवारा करता है, वह आज जो रहे (तो फिर) कल (उसे) कौन रक्खे, अर्थात् कोई नहीँ रख सकता। हे शुक, नहीँ जानती कि आज कहाँ से (आ कर मेरी) दशा उदय ज्ञई, (कि तुम) मिलने आए (और अब) मिल कर चले। मिल कर बिछुडना, मरने को ले आना है, अर्थात् मरण के समान है; यदि अन्त मेँ (तुम्हेँ) चलना ही था तो क्योँ आए। (शुक ने कहा कि, रानी (तुम्हारी) शपथ, या रानी (मैँ सच) कहता हूँ कि, भगवान का स्मरण करता मैँ (यहाँ) रह जाता; (पर) वचन से बँध कर (मैँ पद्मावती से समाचार कह अभीँ आता हूँ, ऐसी प्रतिज्ञा रत्न-सेन से कर) (यहाँ) कैसे रहूँ। (इस मेँ संशय नहीँ कि) तुम ने तिस की (भगवान की) दृष्टि (कृपा) से (मेरी) ऐसी सेवा की; जैसे कि स्वभाव ही से पक्षियोँ का मन वन की झाडियोँ को सेवता है; अर्थात् जैसे पक्षियोँ का मन वन की झाडियोँ मेँ लगा रहता है, उसी प्रकार तुम्हारा मन मेरे मेँ लगा रहता है॥

(सो रानी घबडाओ मत, देखो,) मछली भूमि मेँ जल मेँ बसती है और आम (ऊपर) आकाश मेँ बसता है, अर्थात् रहता है; पर दोनोँ मेँ जो प्रीति है (इस से) अन्त मेँ (दोनोँ) एक संग हो जाते हैँ। [मछली की मांस मेँ खटाई (नीबू या आम की फाँकी) मिलने से बज्ञत ही स्वादु होता है। इस पर किसी मैथिल-कवि ने कविता की है कि—

केचिद्वदन्त्यमृतमस्ति सुरालयेषु केचिद्वदन्ति वनिताधरपल्लवेषु।
ब्रूमो वयं सकलशास्त्रविचारदक्षा जम्बीर-नीर-परिपूरित-मत्स्य-खण्डे]

सो भगवान की दया होगी तो हम लोग फिर एकट्ठाँ हो जायँगे। यदि जीते जी न मिलेँगे तो मरने पर मछली और आम के ऐसा साथ होगा॥ १८५॥

चउपाई।

आवा सुआ बइठ जहँ जोगी। मारग नयन बिओग बिओगी॥
आइ परेवइँ कहा सँदेसू। गोरख मिला मिला उपदेसू॥
तुम्ह कहँ गुरू मया बहु कीन्हा। कीन्ह अदेस आदि कहँ दीन्हा॥
सबद एक होइ कहा अकेला। गुरु जस भिंग पनिग जस चेला॥
भिंगी ओहि पंखी पइ लेई। एकहि बार गहइ जिउ देई॥
ता कहँ गुरू करइ असि माया। नउ अउतार देइ नइ काया॥
होइ अमर अस मर कइ जीआ। भवँर कवँल मिलि कइ मधु पीआ॥

दोहा।

आवइ रितू बसंत जब तब मधुकर तब बासु।
जोगी जोग जो इमि करइ सिद्धि समापत तासु॥ १८६॥

इति पदुमावति-सुआ-भेँट-खंड॥ १९॥

आवा = आया = (आययौ)। सुआ = शुक = सुगा। बइठ = बैठा था = उपविष्ट। जहाँ = यत्र। जोगी = योगी। मारग = मार्ग = राह। नयन = आँख। बिओग = वियोग = विरह। बिओगी = वियोगी = विरही। आइ = एत्य = आ कर। परेवइँ = परेवा ने = पारावत ने, यहाँ पक्षी ने। कहा = कहइ (कथयति) का प्रथम-पुरुष में भूत-काल का एक-वचन। सँदेसू = सन्देश = सँदेसा। गोरख = गोरख-नाथ = गोरक्ष-नाथ। मिला = मिलइ (मिलति) का प्रथम-पुरुष में भूत-काल का एक-वचन। उपदेसू = उपदेश = शिक्षा। गुरू = गुरु। मया = माया = मोह = प्यार = कृपा। बहु = बहुत। अदेस = आदेश = आज्ञा। आदि = मुख्य = असल = पहली। सबद = शब्द = बात। होइ = होइ = हो कर (भूला)। अकेला = एकलः = एकाकी। भिंग = भृङ्ग = एक कीट। पनिग = पतङ्ग = फनगा = फतिंगा। चेला = शिष्य। भिंगी = भृङ्ग। पंखी = पक्ष जिस में हो = फतिंगे। पइ = अपि = निश्चय कर। लेई = लेइ = लेता है (लाति)। बार = वार। गहइ = गहता है (गृह्णाति) = पकडता है। जीउ = जीव। देई = देइ (ददाति वा दत्ते) = देता है। ता कहँ = तिस को। करइ = (करोति) करता है। असि = ऐसी = एतादृशी।

नउ = नव = नया । अउतार = अवतार = जन्म । नइ = नई = नवा । काया = काय = शरीर । होइ = (भवेत्) होवे । अमर = जो न मरे = मृत्यु-रहित । मर कइ = मर कर (मृत्वा) । जीआ = जीवेत् = जीवे । भवँर = भ्रमर । कवँल = कमल । मिलि कइ = मिल कर (मिलित्वा) । मधु = शहद । पीआ = पीवे (पिबेत्) ॥

आवइ = आता है (आयाति) । रितु = ऋतु । बसंत = वसन्त । मधुकर = भ्रमर । बासु = वास = सुगन्ध । जोग = योग । इमि = एवं = इस प्रकार । सिद्धि = मनोरथ-सिद्धि । समापत = समाप्त = पूर्ण = पूरी । तासु = तस्य = तिस का ॥

जहाँ योगी (रत्न-सेन) (शुक की) राह की ओर आँख लगाए और विरह से विरही हो कर बैठा था, (वहाँ पर) शुक (हीरा-मणि) आया । पक्षी (शुक) ने आ कर सँदेसे को कहा, कि गोरख मिला और (उस गोरख से) उपदेश भी मिला । (गोरख से यहाँ पद्मावती है । गोरख के लिये २४० पृ० देखो ।) तुम्हारे ऊपर गुरु (पद्मावती, गोरख-रूप) ने बहुत कृपा की; आज्ञा की (कि रत्न-सेन को चेला करूँगा) और पहली बात को भी दे दिया अर्थात् बता दिया । (पद्मावती ने) अकेले में हो कर एक बात कही; कि गुरु जैसा भृङ्ग और चेला जैसा फतिंगा है (भृङ्ग के लिये १५७ पृ० देखो) । भृङ्ग उस फतिंगे को निश्चय से लेता है, और एक ही वार पकडता है और (उस में अपना) जीव (डाल) देता है । तिस (फतिंगे) के ऊपर गुरु (भृङ्ग) ऐसी कृपा करता है, कि नया जन्म और नई शरीर दे देता है, अर्थात् अपनी जाति का बना देता है । इस प्रकार (फतिंगे के ऐसा) मर कर जीवे तो अमर होवे, और (तब) भ्रमर के ऐसा कमल में मिल कर मधु, अर्थात् कमल-रस, को पीवे ॥

जब वसन्त-ऋतु आती है तभी भ्रमर (देख पडते हैं), और तभी (फूलोँ में) सुगन्ध भी होती है; जो योगी इस प्रकार से (फतिंगे के ऐसा) योग को करता है, तिस की मनोरथ-सिद्धि पूरी हो जाती है ॥ १८६ ॥

इति पद्मावती-शुक-संमिलन-नामैकोनविंशति-खण्डं समाप्तम् ॥ १९ ॥

अथ बसंत-खंड ॥ २० ॥

चउपाई ।

दइअ दइअ कइ सो रितु गवाँई । सिरी-पंचमी पूजी आई ॥
भएउ हुलास नउल रितु माँहा । खन न सोहाइ धूप अउ छाँहा ॥
पदुमावति सब सखी हँकारी । जावँत सिँघल-दीप कइ बारी ॥
आजु बसंत नउल रितु-राजा । पंचमि होइ जगत सब साजा ॥
नउल सिँगार बनाफर कीन्हा । सीस परासहि सेँदुर दीन्हा ॥
बिगसि फूल फूले बहु बासा । भवँर आइ लुबुधे चहुँ पासा ॥
पिअर पात दुख झरे निपाते । सुख पल्लउ उपने होइ राते ॥

दोहा ।

अवधि आइ सो पूजी जो इच्छा मन कीन्ह ।
चलहु देउ-मढ गोहने चहउँ सो पूजा दीन्ह ॥ १८७ ॥

दइअ = देव । कइ = कर = कला ! रितु = ऋतु । (संस्कृत मेँ ऋतु पुंलिङ्ग है परन्तु हिन्दी मेँ पुंलिङ्ग और स्त्री लिङ्ग दोनो है, कवि लोग दोनोँ का प्रयोग करते हैँ)। गवाँई = बिताई (गम्लृ गतौ से)। सिरी = श्रीः । पंचमी = पञ्चमी । श्री-पञ्चमी = वसन्त-पञ्चमी = माघशुक्ला पञ्चमी = जिस दिन से वसन्तोत्सव आरम्भ होता है। पूजी = पूजइ (पूर्यते) से प्रथम-पुरुष मेँ भूत-काल का एक-वचन। आई = आइ = एत्य = आ कर। भएउ = भया (बभूव) = हुआ । हुलास = उल्लास = आह्लाद । नउल = नवल = नए ।

खन = चण। सोहाइ = सोहाद् (शोभते) = सोहता है। धूप = घाम = धाम = रविकिरण। छाँहा = छाहँ = छाया। हँकारी = हँकारइ (हं कारयति वा हक्कारयति) का भूत-काल = पुकरवाई = बोलाई। जावँत = यावन्तः = जितनी। सिंघल-दीप = सिंहल-द्वीप। कइ = को। बारी = बालिका = लडकियाँ। आजु = अद्य = आज। बसंत = वसन्त। रितु राजा = ऋतु-राज = ऋतुओँ का राजा। होइ = होता है (भवति)। जगत = जगत् = संसार। सब = सर्व। साजा = साज = सज्जित = तयारी। सिँगार = शृङ्गार। बनाफर = वनस्पति, प्राकृत में वनप्फडिआ। सीस = शीर्ष = शिर। परासहि = पलास के। सेँदुर = सिन्दूर = सेँधूर। बिगसि = विकाश्य = विकशित हो कर = खिल कर। फूल = फुल्ल = पुष्प। फूले = फूले हैँ (फुल्लन्ति)। बहु = बहुत। बासा = वास = सुगन्ध। भवँर = भ्रमर। लुबुधे = लोभे हैँ (लोभन्ते)। चहुँ = चारो = चत्वारि। पासा = पास = पार्श्व = ओर। पिअर = पीत = पीला। पात = पत्त्र = पत्ते। दुख = दुःख। झरे = झड पडे = गिर गए = झरइ (झरति) के प्रथम-पुरुष में भूत-काल का बहु-वचन। निपाते = निःपत्त्र = बेपत्ते के। पल्लउ = पल्लव = नए पत्ते। उपने = उत्पन्न हुए = उपनइ (उत्पद्यते) के प्रथम-पुरुष में भूत-काल का बहु-वचन। होइ = होइ = हो कर। राते = रक्त = लाल॥

अवधि = मिति = मिती। चलहु = चलो = चलइ (चलति) का आज्ञा में मध्यम-पुरुष का बहु-वचन। देउ-मढ = देव-मठ = देव-मन्दिर। गोहने = गोपन के लिये = रक्षा के लिये = साथ। चहउँ = चाहती हूँ (इच्छामि)॥

(पद्मावती ने) हे देव, हे देव, (इस शिशिर ऋतु को शीघ्र बिताओ, ऐसा कह कह कर) उस (सो) ऋतु (शिशिर) को बिताई; श्री-पञ्चमी आ कर पूरी हुई, अर्थात् पहुँची। नए (वसन्त) ऋतु में (बडा) आह्लाद हुआ; क्षण क्षण पर न घाम और न छाया सोहती है, अर्थात् घाम में जाओ तो घाम कडा मालूम होता है और छाया में आओ तो ठंढक लगती है (वसन्त का यही धर्म है)। पद्मावती ने सखिओं को और सिंहल-दीप में जितनी लडकियाँ थीं सब को बोलवाया। (और कहा कि) आज नए ऋतु-राज वसन्त की पञ्चमी है संसार में सब (उत्सव की) तयारी हो रही है। (वसन्त सब ऋतुओं का राजा है इसी लिये भगवान कृष्ण ने भगवद्गीता में कहा है कि 'ऋतूनां कुसुमाकरः')। वनस्पतियों ने भी नए शृङ्गार को किया है; (देखो) पलास के शिर में सेँदुर को दिया है। (वसन्त में पलास की डालियों में लाल लाल फूल उत्पन्न होते हैँ जिन्हें लोग टेँसू का फूल भी कहते हैँ। उन की ऐसी

शोभा है जानों वनस्पति ने पलास के शिर में सेंदुर दे कर शृङ्गार किया हो)। बहुत फूल सुगन्ध से भरे खिल कर फूले हैं; (उन के) चारो ओर भ्रमर आ कर सोभे हैं। दुःख-रूप पीले पत्ते झड पडे हैं (वृक्ष सब) बे-पत्ते के हो गए हैं; और सुख-रूप पल्लव लाल लाल हो कर उत्पन्न हो रहे हैं ॥

सो जो मैं ने मन में इच्छा की थी उस की मिती आ कर पूरी हुई, अर्थात् पहुँची; (सब कोई) साथ साथ देव-मठ में चलो; (इच्छा पूरी होने से देवता को, मानी हुई) सो (उस) पूजा को, दिया चाहती हूँ ॥ १८७ ॥

चउपाई।

फिरी आन रितु-बाजन बाजे। अउ सिँगार बारिन्ह सब साजे ॥
कवँल-करी पदुमावति रानी। होइ मालति जानहुँ बिगसानी ॥
तारा-मँडर पहिरि भल चोला। अउ पहिरइ ससि नखत अमोला ॥
सखी कुमोद सहस दस संगा। सबइ सुगंध चढाए अंगा ॥
सब राजा रायन्ह कइ बारी। बरन बरन पहिरहिँ सब सारी ॥
सबइ सरूप पदुमिनी जाती। पान फूल सेँदुर सब राती ॥
करहिँ कुरेल सुरंग रँगीली। अउ चोआ चंदन सब गीली ॥

दोहा।

चहुँ दिसि रही सु-बासना फुलवारी अस फूल।
वेइ बसंत सउँ भूलीँ गा बसंत ओहिँ भूल ॥ १८८ ॥

फिरी = फिरइ (स्फुरति) का प्रथम-पुरुष में भूत-काल का एक-वचन। आन = आज्ञा। रितु-बाजन = ऋतु के बाजे जो वसन्त-ऋतु में बजाए जाते हैं, ढोल, डफ इत्यादि। बाजन = वादन = वाद्य। बाजे = बजइ (वाद्यते) का प्रथम-पुरुष में भूत-काल का बहु-वचन। सिँगार = शृङ्गार। बारिन्ह = बारी (बालिका) का बहु-वचन। साजे = सजइ (सज्जते) का प्रथम-पुरुष में भूत-काल का बहु वचन। कवँल-करी = कमल-कली। मालति = मालती = एक लता-पुष्प जो बरसात में फूलती है। जानहुँ = जाने = जानों। बिगसानी = विकसित हुई = प्रसन्न हो कर खिल उठी = हँस दिया। तारा-मँडर =

तारा-मण्डल = तारा-गण = ताराओं का झुंड । पहिरि = परिधाय = पहर कर = पहन कर । भल = अच्छा = वर । चोला = चोलना = निचोल = चोली । पहिरइ = पहरती है (परिधत्ते) । ससि = शशि = चन्द्र । नखत = नक्षत्र । अमोला = अमूल्य । कुमोद = कुमुदिनी = कोईं । सहस = सहस्र । दस = दश । संगा = सङ्ग = साथ । सबइ = सभी । सुगंध = सुगन्ध । चढाए = चढाइ (उच्चालयति) का प्रथम-पुरुष में भूत-काल का बहु-वचन । अंगा = अङ्ग । रायन्ह = राय का बहु-वचन (राय राजा ही से बना है परन्तु अब राय को राजा से छोटा समझते हैं) । बरन = वर्ण = भाँति = तरह । पहिरहिँ = पहिरइ का बहु-वचन । सारी = साडी । सरूप = स्वरूप । पदुमिनी = पद्मिनी । जाती = जाति । पान = पर्ण । फूल = फुल्ल = पुष्प । सेंदुर = सिन्दूर । राती = रक्त = लाल । करहिँ = करइ (करोति) का बहु-वचन । कुरेल = कुलेल = खेल = क्रीडा । सु-रंग = सुरङ्ग = अच्छे रङ्ग से । रँगीली = रँगी हुई । चोआ = च्युत = चुआने से जो सुगन्ध-द्रव्य हो । चंदन = चन्दन । गीली = आर्द्र = भीँजी = गलित ॥

चहुँ = चारो = चत्वारि । दिसि = दिशि । रही = रहइ (रहते) का प्रथम-पुरुष में भूत-काल का एक-वचन । सु-बासना = सुगन्ध । फुलवारी = पुष्पवाटिका । भूलीँ = भूल गईं = [भुलइ (भल परिभाषणे भलते) से] । गा = गया = अगात् ॥

(चारो ओर) आज्ञा फिर गई, वसन्त-ऋतु के बाजे बजने लगे और सब लडकियाँ शृङ्गार को सजने लगीं । कमल-कली सी पद्मावती रानी जानों मालती हो कर विकशित हुई (कमल-कली लाल होती है, हँसने की उपमा श्वेत से दी जाती है । प्रसन्नता से कमल-कली सी पद्मावती हँस देने से श्वेत हो गई, सो जानों मालती हो गई । मालती का फूल श्वेत होता है) । पद्मावती ताराओं के ऐसी अच्छी चोली पहन कर, (चोली के कपडे में चारो ओर तारे के ऐसे बूटे निकाले हुए हैं जिन की शोभा ऐसी है जानों पद्मावती तारा-गणों ही को पहने हुई है), और अमूल्य (गहनों को) पहनती है, जैसे चन्द्र नक्षत्रों को पहने । (चन्द्र पद्मावती और नक्षत्र आभूषण हैं) कोईं (ऐसी) दश हजार सखी संग में हैं जो सब कि अङ्गों में सुगन्ध चढाए (लगाए) हुई हैं । सब राजा और रायों की लडकियाँ हैं; सब भाँति भाँति की साडियाँ पहने हुई हैं । सब सुन्दर हैं और जाति में पद्मिनी हैं; पान, फूल और सेंदुर से सब लाल (हो रही) हैं । (पद्मिनी के लिये पृ० ४७ देखो) (सब) अच्छे रंग से रँगी हुई कुलेल करती हैं और चोआ चन्दन से सब भीँजी हुई हैं ॥

चारो दिशा में सु-गन्ध छा रही है; ऐसा (जान पडता है कि) फुलवारी के (सब) फूल हैं। वे सखी सहेलियाँ वसन्त-ऋतु से भूली ऊई हैं और वसन्त-ऋतु उन में भूला ऊआ है, अर्थात् वसन्त की शोभा में सब सखियाँ मोहित हैं और सखियों की शोभा देख वसन्त भी मोहित हो गया है; वसन्त की शोभा और सखियों की शोभा एक एक से बढ कर हैं ॥ १८८ ॥

चउपाई।

भंइ आहाँ पदुमावति चली। छत्तिस कुरि भइँ गोहन भली ॥
भइ गउरी सँग पहिरि पटोरा। बाँभनि ठाउँ सहस अँग मोरा ॥
अगरवारि गज-गवँन करेई। बइसिनि पाँउ हंस-गति देई ॥
चंदेलिनि ठमकहिँ पगु ढारा। चलिँ चउहानि होइ झनकारा ॥
चलीँ सोनारि सोहाग सोहाती। अउ कलवारि पेम-मधु माती ॥
बानिनि देइ सेँदुर भल माँगा। कइथिनि चलीँ समाहिँ न आँगा ॥
पटइनि पहिरि सुरँग तन चोला। अउ बरइनि मुख खात तमोला ॥

दोहा।

चलीँ पउन सब गोहने फूल डार लेइ हाथ।
बीसुनाथ कइ पूजा पदुमावति के साथ ॥ १८९ ॥

भइ = भई (बभूव)। आहाँ = आह्वान = पुकारने की बोली। पदुमावति = पद्मावती। चली = चलइ (चलति) का प्रथम-पुरुष में भूत-काल का एक-वचन। छत्तिस = छत्तीस = षट्त्रिंशत्। कुरि = कुली = कुल की = जाति की। गोहन = गोपन = रचा = साथ। भली = अच्छी = वरा। गउरी = गौरी = पार्वती। सँग = सङ्ग = साथ। पहिरि = पहन कर (परिधाय)। पटोरा = पट्टोर्ण = पट्ट और ऊर्ण के वस्त्र = रेशमी और ऊनी कपडे। बाँभनि = ब्राह्मणी। ठाउँ = स्थान। सहस = सहस्र। अँग = अङ्ग। मोरा = मोरती है = ऐंठती है = मोडती है = मोरइ = मोडइ (मुड मर्दने से)। अगरवारि = अगरवालिन = अगरवाले की स्त्री। गज-गवँन = गज-गमन = हाथी की चाल। करेई = करइ (करोति) = करती है। बइसिनि = बैसिनि = वैश्या वा बैस ठाकुर की स्त्री।

पाँउ = पैर = प्रग = पाद । हंस-गति = हंस के ऐसी चाल । (हंस एक श्वेत जल-पक्षी है जो दूध-पानी को अलग अलग कर देता है)। देई = देइ (ददाति) = देती है। चंदेलिनि = चँदेले की स्त्री, (चँदेली में जो क्षत्रिय बस गए उन्हें चँदेला कहते हैं, चँदेली के लिये पृ० २७० देखो)। ठमकहिँ = ठमकइ (स्तम्भयति) का बहु-वचन, रुक रुक के चलती हैं। पगु = प्रग = पैर। ढारा = धारा = धरती हैं = रखती हैं (धृ धारणे से)। चलिँ = चलीँ = चलइ (चलति) का प्रथम-पुरुष में भूतकाल बहु-वचन। चउहानि = चौहान की स्त्री (चौहान एक प्रकार के क्षत्रिय हैं। दिल्ली का अन्तिम राजा पृथ्वीराज चौहान ही था)। होइ = होता है (भवति)। झनकार = झणत्कार = गहनों का झन झन शब्द। सोनारि = सोनारिन = सोनार की स्त्री। सोनार = सुवर्ण-कार। सोहाग = सौभाग्य। सोहाती = सोहती = शोभित। कलवारि = कलवारिन = कलवार की स्त्री, कलवार = शराब बनाने और बेंचनेवाले। पेम = प्रेम। मधु = मदिरा = शराब। माती = मत्त = मस्त। बानिनि = बनिआइन = बनिये की स्त्री, बनिया = वणिक्। सेंदुर = सिन्दूर। माँगा = माँग (माँग के लिये पृ० १६६ देखो)। कइथिनि = कायस्थ की स्त्री = ललाइन। समाहिँ = समाती नहीँ हैँ (संमाति) = समाइ का बहु-वचन। आँगा = अङ्ग। पटइनि = पटवे की स्त्री, पटवा = गहना गुहने-वाला = पट्टवाहक = रेशम रखने-वाला। सुरँग = सुरङ्ग = अच्छे रङ्ग का। तन = तनु = शरीर। चोला = चोल = निचोल = चोली वा चोलिया। बरइनि = बरई की स्त्री, बरई = पर्णी = पान-रखनेवाला एक प्रकार का तमोली। खात = खाती (खादृ भक्षणे से)। तमोला = ताम्बूल = पान ॥

पउन = पवन = हवा, वा पउन = पावन = पवित्र। फूल = फुल्ल = पुष्प। डार = डार = डाला = डलिया = डाली। लेइ = लेइ = ले कर (नीत्वा, वा ला धातु से ल्वा)। हाथ = हस्त। बीसुनाथ = विश्वनाथ = महादेव। साथ = सार्थ = सङ्ग ॥

'पद्मावती (महादेव पूजने) चली' (ऐसी) पुकार की बोली हुई; छत्तीसो कुल की अच्छी अच्छी सखियाँ साथ हुईं। रेशमी और ऊनी कपडे पहन कर पार्वती के ऐसी ब्राह्मणी (पुरोहितानी) संग हुई, (जो कि नेग लेने के लिये) हजारोँ स्थान पर, अर्थात् स्थान स्थान पर, (अपने) अङ्ग को मोडती है, अर्थात् नाक भौं सिकोडती है कि विना नेग लिये आगे न बढने दूंगी। अगरवालिन हाथी के ऐसा गमन करती है, अर्थात् बहुत धीरे धीरे चलती है; वैश्या वा बैसठकुराइन, हंस की गति ऐसी (भूमि में)

पैर को देती है अर्थात् रखती है। चंदेलिन (राह में) ठमक जाती हैं इधर उधर नखरा तिल्ला कर, पैर के गहनों को सँभार तब फिर) पैर को रखती हैं। चौहानिन (जब) चलती हैं (तब गहनों का अच्छा) झन झन शब्द होता है, अर्थात् चौहानिन गहनों से लदी हैं। सौभाग्य से सोहती सोनारिन और प्रेम-मदिरा से माती कलवारिन चलीं। बनिआइन और कैथिनि माँग में अच्छी तरह से सेंदुर दे कर चलीं (खुशी से) अङ्ग में नहीं समाती हैं। पटइनि देह में अच्छे रंग की चोलिया पहन कर और बरइनि मुह में पान खाते चलीं॥

सब हवा ऐसी वा पवित्र हाथ में फूलों की डलिया ले ले कर साथ साथ महादेव की पूजा (करने को) पद्मावती के साथ चलीं॥ १८९॥

चउपाई।

ठठेरिनि चलिँ बहु ठाठर कीन्हे। चलीँ अहीरिनि काजर दीन्हे॥
गूजरि चलिँ गोरस कइ माती। तंबोलिनि चलिँ रँग बहु राती॥
चलीँ लोहारिनि पइनइँ नयना। भाँटिनि चलीँ मधुर मुख बयना॥
गंधिनि चलीँ सुगंध लगाए। छीपिनि छीपइँ चीर रँगाए॥
रँगरेजिनि तन रातो सारी। चलीँ चोख सउँ नाउनि बारी॥
मालिनि चलीँ फूल लेइ गाँथे। तेलिनि चलीँ फुलाएल माँथे॥
कइ सिँगार बहु बेसवा चलीँ। जहँ लगि मूँदी बिकसीँ कलीँ॥

दोहा।

नटिनि डोमिनि ढोलिनी सहनाइनि भेरिकारि।
निरतत तंत बिनोद सउँ बिहँसत खेलत नारि॥ १९०॥

ठठेरिनि = ठठेर की स्त्री, ठठेर = वर्त्तन बनाने और बेंचने-वाले। ठाठर = ठाट = तयारी। अहीरिनि = अहीर की स्त्री, अहीर = आभीर = गाय पालने-वाले, इन्हें ग्वाल (गोपाल) भी कहते हैं। काजर = कज्जल। गूजरि = गुर्जरी = गूजर की स्त्री, गूजर = गुर्जर = एक प्रकार के अहीर। गोरस = गोदुग्ध = दूध। माती = मत्त = मस्त। तंबोलिनि = तमोलिन = तमोलिनि = तमोली की स्त्री, तमोली = ताम्बूली = ताम्बूल (पान) बेंचने-वाले। रँग = रङ्ग। राती = रक्त = अनुरक्त = रँगी हुई। लोहारिनि =

लोहादन = लोहार की स्त्री, लोहार = लोहकार = लोहे का काम करने-वाला। पइनइँ = पैनी (पेणृ गति-प्रेरण-श्लेषणेषु, भ्वादि, से बना) = तीक्ष्ण = तीखी। भाँटिनि = भाट की स्त्री, भाट = जो कि लोगोँ का गुण गाया करते हैँ (भटति वदति गुण-मिति भाटः)। मधुर = मीठी। बयना = वचन। गंधिनि = गंधी की स्त्री, गन्धी, जो गन्ध (सुगन्ध द्रव्य) बेँचे। लगाए = लगाए हुए (लग धातु से)। छीपिनि = छीपी की स्त्री, छीपी = छापा छापने-वाला = छीँट बनाने-वाला = चेपी = कुछ और वस्त्र मेँ मिला देने-वाला। छीपइँ = छीपी से। चीर = वस्त्र = कपडा। रँगाए = रँगाए हुए (रञ्ज रागे से)। रँगरेजिनि = रँगरेज की स्त्री, रँगरेज = कपडा रँगने-वाला। तन = तनु = शरीर = देह। राती = रक्त = लाल। सारी = साडी। चोख = तीखी = तीक्ष्ण। नाउनि = नाऊ (नाई) की स्त्री, नाऊ = नापित = बाल बनाने-वाला। बारी = बारिनि = बारी की स्त्री, बारी = पर्णी = पत्तल बनाने-वाला। मालिनि = माली की स्त्री, माली, फूलोँ की माला बनाने-वाला। गाँथे = ग्रन्थि मेँ = गठरी मेँ। तेलिनि = तेली की स्त्री, तेली = तेल बनाने और बेँचने-वाला। फुलायल = पुष्पतैल = फुलेल। माँथे = मस्तक पर = शिर पर। सिँगार = शृङ्गार। बेसवा = वेश्या = नगरनारी = वाराङ्गना = कसबी = रंडी। जहँ लगि = जहाँ तक। मूँदी = मुद्रित = बंद। बिकसीँ = विकशित हुईँ = खिलीँ = खिल उठीँ। कलीँ = कली का बहु-वचन ॥

नटिनि = नट की स्त्री, नट = तमाशा देखाने-वाले। डोमिनि = डोम की स्त्री, डोम = मुर्दे घोडे को ले जाने-वाले और खाने-वाले। ढोलिनी = ढोल की स्त्री, ढोल = ढोल बजाने-वाले = डफाली। सहनाइनि = सहनाई बजाने-वाले की स्त्री, सहनाई बजाने-वाला = हेला = मेहतर। भेरिकारि = भेरी (नगाडा) बजाने-वाले की स्त्री, भेरी बजाने-वाला = चमार = चर्मकार। निरतत = नृत्यन् = नाचते। तंत = तन्त्र = बाजा। बिनोद = विनोद = आनन्द = खुशी। बिहँसत = विहसन् = बिहँसती। खेलत = खेलन् = खेलती। नारि = नारी = स्त्री ॥

बहुत तयारी किए ठठेरिन चलीँ; (आँखोँ मेँ) काजर दिए अहीरिन चलीँ। दूध से मस्त गूजरी चलीँ; बहुत रंग से रँगी तमोलिन चलीँ। तीखी आँख-वालीँ लोहारिन चलीँ; मुख मेँ मीठी बात भरे भाँटिन चलीँ। सुगन्ध को लगाए गंधिन चलीँ; छीपी से कपडे को रँगाए छीपिन चलीँ; देह मेँ लाल साडी (पहन कर) रँगरेजिन चलीँ; नाउन और बारिन (बडी) चोखाई से चलीँ, अर्थात् बडी तीखी

चाल से चलीं (भीतर बाहर सदा काम करते ढीठी हो गई हैं इस लिये बडी तेजी से चलती हैं ; मर्दों का कान काटती हैं)। गठरिश्रों में फूल ले कर मालिन चलीं ; श्रोर शिर पर फुलेलों को ले कर तेलिन चलीं । शृङ्गार किए बहुत वेश्या चलीं ; जहाँ तक मूँदी कलिया थीं सब खिल गईं, अर्थात् जो जो लडकियाँ घर में सदा बंद रहा करती थीं सब बाहर निकल पडीं ॥

नटिन, डोमिन, ढोलिन, सहनाई श्रोर भेरी बजाने-वालीं (सब) स्त्रियाँ बाजे के श्रानन्द से नाचती, विहँसती, श्रोर खेलती (चलीं) ॥

कवि ने दोनों दोहाश्रों की चौपाइश्रों में ब्राह्मणी १। श्रगरवालिन २। बैसिन ३। चंदेलिन ४। चौहाइन ५। सोनारिन ६। कलवारिन ७। बनिश्राइन ८। कैथिन ९। पटइन १०। बरइन ११। ठठेरिन १२। श्रहीरिन १३। गुजरी १४। तँबोलिन १५। लोहारिन १६। भाँटिन १७। गंधिन १८। छीपिन १९। रँगरेजिन २०। नाउन २१। बारिन २२। मालिन २३। तेलिन २४। वेश्या २५। नटिन २६। डोमिन २७। ढोलिन २८। सहनाइन २९। भेरिकारिन (चमाइन) ३०। यह तीस जात की स्त्रियों को कहा। इन में वेश्या की कोई जाति न होने से २९ ही जाति हुई शेष ७ जाति 'जहँ लगि मूँदी बिकसीं कलीं' इस से समझ लेना चाहिए। श्राज कल प्रचलित ३६ जाति के लिये पृ० १५५ देखो ॥ १९० ॥

चउपाई ।

कवँल सहाय चलीं फुलवारी। फर फूलन्ह कइ इच्छा-बारी ॥
आपु आपु मँह करहिँ जोहारू। यह बसंत सब कहँ तेवहारू ॥
चहइ मनोरा झूमक होई। फर अउ फूल लिश्रउ सब कोई ॥
फागु खेलि पुनि दाहब होरी। सेँतब खेह उडाउब झोरी ॥
आजु साजि पुनि दिवस न दूजा। खेल बसंत लेहु कइ पूजा ॥
भा आयसु पदुमावति केरा। बहुरि न आइ करब हम फेरा ॥
तस हम कहँ होइहि रखवारी। पुनि हम कहाँ कहाँ यह बारी ॥

दोहा ।

पुनि रे चलब घर आपुन पूजि बिसेसर देउ ।
जेहि का होइइ खेलना आजु खेल हँसि लेउ ॥ १९१ ॥

कवँल = कमल । सहाय = सहायक । चलौं = चलइ (चलति) का प्रथम-पुरुष में भूत-काल का बहु-वचन । फुलवारी = फुल्लवाटिका = पुष्पवाटिका । फर = फल । फूलन्ह = फूल (फुल्ल) का बहु-वचन । कइ = की । बारी = वाटिका = बगीचा । आपु = आप (आत्मा) = अपने । करहिँ = करइ (करोति) का बहु-वचन । जोहारू = हे जीव-हार = प्रणाम । तेवहारू = तिहवार = पर्व । चहइ = चाह से = खुशी से । मनोरा = मनोहर = मनोहरा । झूमक = स्त्रियाँ साथ हो कर झूम झूम कर जो गाती हैं उस गान को झूमक कहते हैं । होई = होइ (भवति) = होता है । लिश्रउ = लिए । फागु = फाल्गुन का उत्सव । खेलि = खेल कर (खेलित्वा) । दाहब = जलावँगी = (दाहयिष्यामः) । होरी = होली = होलिका (फाल्गुन की पूर्णिमा को रात्रि में प्रत्येक ग्राम की सीमा में काठ सरपत का टाल लगाया जाता है; उसे होली या होलिका कहते हैं; गावँ के लोग एकट्ठाँ हो कर मन्त्र पढ कर उस में आग लगाते हैं, उस की प्रदक्षिणा करते हैं, और आपस में एक दूसरे को गाली देते हैं; होलिका-माहात्म्य में लिखा है कि उस दिन ग्राम में ढुण्ढि राक्षसी आती है और लडकों को दुःख देती है, इस लिये सीमा पर आग बारना और ललकार ललकार गाली देना जिस में वह डर से ग्राम में न आने पावे (भगलिङ्गाङ्कितैः शब्दैस्त्रासयेत् ढुण्ढिराक्षसीम्); यह रीति बढते बढते ऐसी बढ गई कि अब लोग आपस ही में गाली बकते हैं । पुराणों में यह भी कथा है कि हिरण्याक्ष दानव की बहिन होली थी; वह जब स्नान करने लगे तो उस के अञ्चल से आग निकले । हिरण्याक्ष ने अपने पुत्र प्रह्लाद को, जो कि पिता के मत से विरुद्ध वैष्णव हो गया था, जलाने के लिये स्नान के समय अपनी बहिन के गोद में डाल दिया; दैव-संयोग से उस दिन होली ही जल गई प्रह्लाद बच गया; प्रह्लाद के संगी लडके ताली पीट पीट कर खुशी से होली को गाली देने लगे । उसी दिन से प्रतिवर्ष लोग उस की नकल करने लगे । प्राचीन समय में यह रीति थी कि होली की जली हुई भस्म को एकट्ठाँ कर झोरियों में रख आपस में एक दूसरे के देह में पोतते थे और खुशी से गाली बकते थे, पर अब भस्म की जगह अबीर लगाते हैं । होलिका-माहात्म्य में लिखा है कि होली को जला कर उस दिन डोम को छूना चाहिए । सँतब = सैंतँगी = एकट्ठाँ करँगी (समेष्यति) ।

खेह = धूलि = धूर (खे आकाशे ईहा इच्छा यस्य) । उडाउब = उडावँगी = उडावइ का उत्तम-पुरुष में भविष्यत् काल में बहु-वचन । झोरी = थैली, वा झोल = जलने के समय

जो जलते ऊए टण पत्ते ऊपर उड कर फिर बुझ कर नीचे गिरते हैं। आजु = अद्य = आज। साजि = सजा कर = सज्जयित्वा। दूजा = द्वितीय = दूसरा। खेल = खेला = क्रीडा। भा = भया (ऊआ)। आयसु = आयस = आज्ञा। बऊरि = भूयः = फिर = बऊल। करब = करँगी (कर्त्तव्यम्)। फेरा = स्फुरण = भ्रमण। तस = तथा = तैसी। होइहि = होगी (भविष्यति)। रखवारी = रचा = रचण = रखवाली। बारी = वाटिका॥

रे = अरे। चलब = चलँगी (चलितव्यम्)। घर = गृह। आपुन = अपने। पूजि = पूजा कर (पूजयित्वा)। बिसेसर = विश्वेश्वर। देउ = देव = महादेव। होहइ = होवे (भवेत्)। खेल = खेलन। हँसि = हँस कर (हसित्वा)। लेउ = लेओ॥

कमल (पद्मावती) के सहाय के लिये फुलवारियाँ (सब सखी सहेलियाँ) चलीं; (ये सखी सहेलियाँ) फल फूलों की इच्छा-वारी हैं, अर्थात् ये ऐसी बाटिका हैं कि जो फल फूल की इच्छा हो सब देने-वाली हैं। अपने अपने में प्रणाम करती हैं (और कहती हैं कि) यह वसन्त सब का तिहवार है। चाह से मनोहर झूमक होता है या चाह से मनोहरा और झूमक होता है [किसी विशेष मङ्गल में सब से पहले जो गीत गा कर देव-पूजन करते हैं उस गीत को स्त्रियाँ मनोरा (मनोहरा) कहती हैं, और उस पूजन को मनोरा-पूजा कहती हैं (कहती हैं कि मनोरा पूजा जाता है)]। फाग खेल कर फिर होली जलाऊँगी; राख को समेट कर झोरी उडाऊँगी, अर्थात् झोरी की झोरी राख उडाऊँगी। आज के ऐसा दूसरा दिन नहीं है, आज तयारी कर, (और महादेव की) पूजा कर, वसन्त (वसन्तोत्सव) में खेल लेओ। पद्मावती की आज्ञा ऊई कि फिर हम लोग आ कर (यहाँ) न घूमँगी॥

हम लोगों की तैसी रख-वाली होगी कि फिर कहाँ हम लोग और कहाँ यह वाटिका होगी। अरे (सखिओ) (हम लोग) विश्वेश्वर महादेव की पूजा कर फिर अपने अपने घर चलँगी, सो जिस को खेलना हो आज हँसी खुशी से खेल लेओ॥ १९१॥

चउपाई।

काह्न गही आँब कइ डारा। काह्न बिरह चाँप अति झारा॥
कोइ नारँग कोइ झार चिरउँजी। कोइ कटहरि बडहर कोइ नउँजी॥
कोइ दारिउँ कोइ दाख सो खीरी। कोइ सदाफर तुरुँज जँभीरी॥
कोइ जइफर कोइ लउँग सुपारी। कोइ कमरख कोइ गुआ छोहारी॥

कोइ बिजउर कोइ नरिअर जूरी । कोइ इविँली कोइ महुअ खजूरी ॥
कोई हरिफा-रेउरि कसउँदा । कोइ अउँरा कोइ राइ-करउँदा ॥
काहु गही केरा कइ घउरी । काह्न हाथ परी निँउ-कउरी ॥

दोहा ।

काह्न पाई निअरइँ काह्न कहँ गइ दूर ।
काह्न खेल भएउ बिख काह्न अंब्रित-मूर ॥ १९२ ॥

काह्न = किसी ने । गही = गहा (जग्राह) का स्त्री-लिङ्ग । आँब = आम = आम्र । डारा = डार = डाल = दाल (जिस में दल अर्थात् पत्ते रहते हैं) = शाखा = दारु । बिरह = वियोग । चाँप = चम्पक (चम्पको हेमपुष्पकः, अमरकोशे वनौषधिवर्गे, श्लो० ४११) । अति = बहुत । झारा = झर = कडुआ । नारँग = नारङ्गी । झार = झाडी । चिरउँजी = चिरौंजी । कटहरि = कटहर = कण्टकिफल । बडहर = एक प्रसिद्ध फल (वृद्ध फल) । नउँजी = लौंजी लोची वा लकुट (लकुच) । दारिउँ = दाडिम = अनार । दाख = द्राक्षा = अङ्गूर । खीरी = खीरिनी = क्षीरिणी (जिस के फल में दूध हो) = एक बहुत प्रसिद्ध फल । सदाफर = सदाफल = सदाफलने-वाले । तुरुँज = तुरञ्ज = एक प्रकार का निम्बू । जँभीरी = जम्बीर निम्बू । जाइफर = जायफल = जातीफल । लउँग = लवङ्ग । सुपारी = सूपारिः = सुफली = सोपारी = पूगीफल । कमरख = एक प्रसिद्ध फल । गुआ = बङ्गाले की सोपारी = गुवाकः । छोहारी = छोहारा = चौहहर = एक प्रकार का खजूर । बिजउर = बीजालय = बिजौडिया निम्बू । नरिअर = नारिकेर । जूरी = जूरिका = अङ्कुर । इविँली = अम्लिका = चिञ्चा । महुअ = मधूक = महुआ । खजूरी = खर्जूरी = खजूर । हरिफा-रेउरि = हालफा-रेवडी = लवली । कसउँदा = कषायद = कसैला । अउँरा = अमलक = औंरा । राइ-करउँदा = राय-करौंदा = राज-कुरुविन्द । केरा = कदली = केला । घउरी = घौर = घवर = घन फल । निउँ-कउरी = निम-कौडी = निम्ब-कपर्दी = नीम का फल ॥

पाई = पावइ (प्राप्यते) का प्रथम-पुरुष में भूत-काल का एक-वचन । निअरइँ = निकटे = नगीच । गइ = गई = गया (अगात्) का स्त्री-लिङ्ग । बिख = विष = जहर । अंब्रित-मूर = अमृत-मूल = अमृत की जड ॥

किसी ने आम की डार को पकड लिया; किसी ने विरह के ऐसे बऊत कडुए चंपे (की डार को) पकडा [चंपे के वृक्ष के फूल का गंध बऊत कडुआ होता है, इसी लिये भ्रमर भी इस फूल का बास नहीं लेता इसी पर कवि की उत्प्रेक्षा है कि जैसा विरह (वियोग) कडुआ है उसी प्रकार चंपा भी बऊत कडुआ है] किसी ने नारङ्गी और किसी ने चिरौंजी की झाडी को पकडा; किसी ने कटहर, किसी ने बडहर और किसी ने लौंजी लीची की डार को पकडा। किसी ने अनार, किसी ने अङ्गूर और किसी ने खीरिनी की डार को पकडा; किसी ने सदाफल, किसी ने तुरुंज और किसी ने जम्बीर की डार को पकडा। किसी ने जायफल, किसी ने लौंग, किसी ने सोपारी, किसी ने कमरख, किसी ने गुआ और किसी ने छोहारे की डार को पकडा। किसी ने बिजौड, किसी ने नारिकेर की डार को और किसी ने जूरी को पकड लिया। किसी ने अमिली, किसी ने मऊआ और किसी ने खजूर की डार को पकडा। किसी ने हालफा-रेवडी, किसी ने कसैले औंरे और किसी ने रायकरौंदे की डार को पकडा। किसी ने केले के घौर को पकड लिया, और किसी के हाथ में निम-कौडी ही पडी ॥

किसी ने नगीच ही (अपनी इच्छी को) पाया और किसी के लिये वह इच्छा दूर (निकल) गई। किसी का खेल जहर हो गया और किसी के लिये (वही खेल) अमृत की जड हो गया; अर्थात् खेल में चोट लग जाने से बऊत सखियाँ गिर पडीं, उन के लिये खेल जहर हो गया; और बऊत सी सखियाँ बाजी जीत गईं, अमृत-फलों को भी पा गईं; इस लिये उन के लिये वही खेल अमृत हो गया। (२८ और ३४ दोहे की चौपाइओं को भी देखो) ॥ १९२ ॥

चउपाई।

पुनि बीनहिँ सब फूल सहेली। जो जेहि आस पास सब बेली ॥
कोइ केवरा कोइ चाँप नेवारी। कोइ केतकि मालति फुलवारी ॥
कोइ सतिबरग कूँद अउ करना। कोइ चवेँइलि नगेसरि बरना ॥
कोइ सो गुलाल सुदरसन कूजा। कोई सोनिजरद भल पूजा ॥
कोइ सो मउलसिरि पुहुप बकउरी। कोइ रूप-माँजरि अउ गउरी ॥

कोइ सिंगार-हार तेहि पाँहा। कोइ सेवती कदम कि छाँहा॥
कोइ चंदन फूलहिँ जनु फूली। कोइ अजान बीरउ तर भूली॥

दोहा।

(कोइ) फूल पाउ कोइ पाती जेहि क हाथ जो आँट।
(कोइ सो) हार चीर उरझाना जहाँ छुअइ तहँ काँट॥ १९३॥

बीनहिँ = बीनइ [वेणृ (वेनृ) गतिज्ञानचिन्तानिशामनवादित्रग्रहणेषु, वेणते, वेणति, वा वेनते, वेनति] का बहु-वचन। सहेली = सहचरी = सखी। आस = आशा = दिशा पास = पार्श्व = निकट = नगीच। बेली = वल्ली = लता। केवरा = केवडा = कैरव = एक प्रकार का कुमुद। चाँप = चाम्पेय = केसर (चाम्पेयः केसरो नाग केसरः काञ्चनाह्वयः, अमरकोशे वनौषधिवर्गे श्लो० ४१२)। नेवारी = नवमालिका = वसन्त का एक श्वेत-पुष्प (सप्तला नवमालिका, अमरकोशे वनौषधिवर्गे श्लो० ४२०)। केतकि = केतकी = प्रसिद्ध पुष्प। मालति = मालती = प्रसिद्ध पुष्प (सुमना मालती जातिः अमरकोशे वनौषधिवर्गे श्लो० ४२०)। फुलवारी = फुलवाटिका। सतिवर्ग = जिस में सैकडों पत्तियाँ हों = हजारा गेंदा (६० वाँ दोहा देखो)। कूँद = कुन्द (मुकुन्दः कुन्दकुन्दुरू, अमरकोशे वनौषधिवर्गे श्लो० ४६७) = एक प्रसिद्ध पुष्प। करना = एक प्रकार का निम्बू जिस का फूल सुगन्धित होता है। (३५ वाँ और ६० वाँ दोहा देखो)। चवँदलि = चमेली = एक प्रसिद्ध पुष्प। नगेसरि = नागकेसर (नागकेसरः काञ्चनाह्वयः अमरकोशे वनौषधिवर्गे श्लो० ४२०)। बरना = पुष्प-विशेष = वरणः (वरुणो वरणः सेतुस्तिक्तशाकः कुमारकः, अमरकोशे वनौषधिवर्गे श्लो० ३७३)। गुलाल = गुलाली-रंग का गुलाब (६० वाँ दोहा देखो)। सुदरसन = सुदर्शन = एक लता जिस के पत्ते चौडे होते हैं। कूजा = एक प्रकार का गुलाब। सोनिजरद = सोनजर्द, जिस का सोने-सा पीला फूल होता है (६० वाँ दोहा देखो)। पूजा = पूज्य = पूजा के योग्य। मउलसिरि = मौलसरी = मौसिरी = मुक्ताकेसर = वकुल। पुहुप = पुष्प = फूल। बकउरी = बकावली = गुल बकावली। रूपमाँजरि = रूपमञ्जरी = एक प्रसिद्ध पुष्प। गउरी = गौरी = श्वेतमल्लिका। सिंगार-हार = हर-शृङ्गार = पारिजात। पाँहा = पार्श्व = पास। सेवती = एक प्रसिद्ध पुष्प। कदम = कदम्ब। चंदन = चन्दन। फूलहिँ = फूलोँ से। अजान = अज्ञान = अज्ञात। बीरउ = वीरुध = विरवा = वृक्ष। तर = तल = नीचे॥

पाउ = प्राप्यते = पाता वा पाती है। क = के। हाथ = हस्त। जो = यः। अँाट = अँटता है = आस्तीयते। हार = मुक्ता-हार = मोती की माला। चीर = वस्त्र = कपडा। उरझाना = अरुझा = अरुझइ (आरुध्यते) का भूत-काल में एक-वचन। जहाँ = यत्र। छुअइ = छूती है (स्पृशति)। तहाँ = तत्र। काँट = काँटा = कण्टक॥

फिर सब सहेलियाँ, जिन की जिस दिशा में जो लतायें पास (पास) में थीं उन के फूलों को चुनने लगीं। किसी ने केवडे को, किसी ने केसर और नेवारी को, किसी ने फुलवारी के बीच केतकी और मालती को चुना। किसी ने हजारे (गेंदे), कुन्द और करने को, किसी ने चमेली, नागेश्वर और वरण को चुना। किसी ने गुलाब, सुदर्शन और कूजे फूल को, किसी ने रूप-मञ्जरी और गौरी को चुना। किसी ने अपने पास के पारिजात को, किसी ने कदम्ब की छाया में (लगी हुई) सेवती के फूल को चुना। कोई (सुगन्ध-द्रव्यों से ऐसी गमक रही हैं) जानों चन्दन के फूलों से फूली हुई हैं; कोई अजान वृक्ष के नीचे (उस की शोभा से) भूली हुई है, अर्थात् जिस का नाम नहीं जानती उस को पहचानने की इच्छा से उस के नीचे उस की शोभा में भूली हुई है॥

जिस के हाथ में जो आया (उसी को पाया इस लिये) किसी ने फूल को पाया और किसी ने पत्ती को। किसी का हार और (किसी का) कपडा (कँटीले वृक्ष में) उरझ गया। (इस लिये वह) जहाँ छूती है तहाँ काँटा ही काँटा जान पडता है॥१९३॥

चउपाई।

फर फूलन्ह सब डार ओढाईं। झुंड बाँधि कइ पंचम गाईं॥
बाजहिँ ढोल दुंदु अउ भेरी। माँदर तूर झाँझ चहुँ फेरी॥
सिंग संख डफ बाजन बाजे। बंसकार महुअरि सुर साजे॥
अउरु कहिअ जित बाजन भले। भाँति भाँति सब बाजत चले॥
रथहिँ चढीं सब रूप सोहाईं। लेइ बसंत मढ-मँडफ सिधाईं॥
नउल बसंत नउल वेइ बारी। सेंदुर बूका होइ धमारी॥
खनहिँ चलहिँ खन चाँचर होई। नाँच कोड भूला सब कोई॥

दोहा ।

सेँदुर-खेह उठा तस गगन भएउ सब राति ।
राति सकल महि धरती राति बिरिख बन पाति ॥ १९४ ॥

फर = फल । फूलन्ह = फूल (फुल्ल = पुष्प) का बज्ज-वचन । सब = सर्व । डार = डाल = डलरा = फल-फूल रखने का पात्र । श्रोढाईं = श्रोढाई का बज्ज-वचन; श्रोढाई = श्रोढइ (उपवेष्टते) का भूत-काल का एक-वचन । झूँड = झुंड = यूथ । बाँधि कइ = बाँध कर (बद्धा) । पंचम = पञ्चम-खर । गाईं = गाई का बज्ज-वचन, गाई = गावइ (गायति) का भूत-काल में एक-वचन । बाजहिं = बाजइ (वाद्यते) का बज्ज-वचन । ढोल = एक मुसल्मानी बाजा । दुंदु = दुन्दुभि । श्रउ = श्रपर = श्रार । भेरी = दुन्दुभी का एक भेद = नगारा । माँदर = मर्दल = मृदङ्ग का एक भेद । तूर = तूर्य = तुरही । झाँझ = झञ्झा । चज्जँ फेरी = चारो श्रोर । सिंग = शृङ्गी = सींग के बाजे । संख = शङ्ख = जन्तु विशेष के हड्डी का बाजा । डफ = डफला = एक मुसल्मानी प्रसिद्ध बाजा । बाजन = वाद्य = बाजा । बाजे = बजइ (वाद्यते) का भूत-काल में बज्ज-वचन । बंस-कार = वंशाकार = वंशी । मज्जश्ररि = मधुकरी = एक तुम्बी का प्रसिद्ध बाजा, जिस के खर से साँप मोहित हो जाता है । सुर = खर । साजे = सज्जित किए = तयार किए = साजइ (सज्जते) का भूत-काल में बज्ज-वचन । श्रउरु = श्रपर । कहिश्र = कहे जाते हैं (कथ्यन्ते) । जित = जितने (यावन्तः) । भले = वर (श्रेष्ठ) का बज्ज-वचन । भाँति = भङ्गी = रचना विशेष; भाँति भाँति = तरह तरह के । बाजत = बजते ज्जए (वदन्तः) । चले = चलइ (चलति) का भूत-काल में बज्ज-वचन । रथहिं = रथों पर । चढीं = (उच्चलन्त्यः वा उच्चर्दन्त्यः) चढी ज्जईं । रूप = सूरत । सोहाईं = शोभित ज्जईं । लेइ = ले कर (नीला वा ला धातु से ल्का) । बसंत = वसन्त-ऋतु । मठ = मठ । मंडफ = मण्डप । मठ-मंडफ = मठं (मन्दिर) का मण्डप; मण्डप = मन्दिर के द्वार के सामने छाया ज्जश्रा स्थान । सिधाईं = सिधावइ (सिधु गत्याम्, भ्वादि, सेधति) का स्त्री-लिङ्ग में भूत-काल का बज्ज-वचन । नउल = नवल = नया । वेइ = वे । बारी = वालिका = बाली । सेँदुर = सिन्दूर । बूका = बूका ज्जश्रा = चूर किया ज्जश्रा । होइ = होता है वा होती है (भवति) । धमारी = धमार = धर-मार, होली के दिनों में श्रपने मित्रों को पकड कर, उन के श्रङ्गों में श्रबीर को लगाने, उन से हँसी ठट्ठा करने श्रार गाली की गीत गाने को धमार कहते हैं ।

खनहिँ = क्षण में । चलहिँ = चलइ (चलति) का बहु-वचन । खन = क्षण । चाँचर = चर्चरी, होली में जगह जगह पर ठहर ठहर कर, दो गोल बाँध कर, डफ पर जो गाते हैं, उसे चाँचर कहते हैं । नाँच = नृत्य । कोड = कूद = कूर्दन = कूदना । भूला = भूल गए = भूलइ (भ्रमति, प्रा० भुल्लइ) का भूत-काल ॥

खेह (खे आकाशे ईहा चेष्टा यस्याः सा खेहा) = खेहा = धूर । उठा = उठइ (उत्तिष्ठते) का भूत-काल । तस = तथा = तैसा । गगन = आकाश । भएउ = भया (बभूव) । राति = रक्त = लाल । सकल = सब । महि = मही = भूमि । धरती = धरित्री = जमीन । बिरिख = वृक्ष । बन = वन । पाति = पत्री = पत्ती ॥

सब (सखियों) ने डलरे को फल फूल से ओढा दिया, अर्थात् फल फूलों से डालियों को भर लिया और गोल (झुंड) बाँध कर पञ्चम-स्वर से गाने लगीं । (जितने ऊँचे स्वर से कोयल बोलती है उस स्वर को पञ्चम कहते हैं)॥ चारो ओर ढोल, दुन्दुभी, भेरी, मृदङ्ग, तुरही और झाँझ बज रहे हैं । सींग के बाजे, शङ्ख, डफ, वंशी, और महुअर भी स्वर से भरे (सजे) बजने लगे ॥ और तरह तरह के जितने अच्छे बाजे कहे जाते हैं, सब बजते चले ॥ सब (सखियाँ) रथ पर चढीं, रूप से शोभित वसन्त को लिए, अर्थात् अपने रूप और आभूषण से जानों वसन्त-ऋतु की शोभा साथ में लिए, मठ-मण्डप की ओर चलीं ॥ (आज) वसन्त-ऋतु नूतन है और वे बालिका (सब सखियाँ) भी नूतन हैं, (इस लिये उत्साह से भरीं सब सखियाँ होली खेल रही हैं, जिस से) बूके हुए सेंदुर (अबीर) से धमार हो रहा है॥ क्षण में (सब सखियाँ आगे) चलती हैं, क्षण में (गोल बाँध कर गाने से) चाँचर होने लगता है, (इस प्रकार) सब कोई नाँच कूद में भूल गए ॥

सेंदुर की ऐसी (तस) धूर उठी कि सब आकाश लाल हो गया । पृथ्वी में सब धरती लाल हो गई और वन में वृक्षों की पत्तियाँ भी लाल हो गईं ॥ १९४ ॥

चउपाई ।

एहि बिधि खेलत सिंघल-रानी । महादेओ मढ जाइ तुलानी ॥
सकल देओता देखइ लागे । दिसिटि पाप सब तिन्ह के भागे ॥
एहि कबिलास सुनी अपछरी । कहाँ तइँ आईँ परमेसरी ॥
कोई कहइ पदुमिनी आईँ । कोइ कहइ ससि नखत तराईँ ॥

कोइ कह फूल कोई फुलवारी। भूले सबइ देखि सब बारी ॥
एक सरूप अउ सेँदुर सारी। जानहुँ दिश्रा सकल महि बारी ॥
मुरुछि परइ जावँत जे जोहइ। जानहुँ मिरिग दिश्रारहिँ मोहइ ॥

दोहा।

कोई परा भवँर होइ बास लीन्ह जनु चाँद।
कोइ पतँग भा दीपक होइ अध-जर तन काँप ॥ १९५ ॥

एहि = यहि = अनेन = इस। बिधि = विधि = प्रकार = तरह। खेलत = खेलन् = खेलते। सिंघल = सिंहल। रानी = राज्ञी। महादेश्रो = महादेव। मढ = मठ = मन्दिर। जाइ = जा कर (यात्वा)। तुलानी = तुलित हुई = पहुँची। सकल = सब। देश्रोता = देवता। देखइ = देखने (दृशि प्रेक्षणे से)। लागे = लगे (लग संलग्ने से)। दिसिटि = दृष्टि। पाप = दोष। भागे = भग गए = नष्ट हो गए। कबिलास = कैलास, यहाँ इन्द्र-लोक। सुनी = सुनइ (शृणोति) का भूत-काल में एक-वचन। अपछरी = अप्सरा। कहँ तइँ = कस्मात् = कहाँ तेँ। आईं = आवइ (आयाति) का भूत-काल में बहु-वचन। परमेसरी = परमेश्वरी। कोई = कोऽपि। कहइ = कथयति = कहता है। ससि = शशि = चन्द्र। नखत = नक्षत्र। तराईं = तारा-गण। भूले = भूल गए (भ्रम-सञ्चलने से)। सबइ = सर्वे = सभी। देखि = दृष्ट्वा = देख कर। बारी = बालिका = थोडी उमर की। सरूप = सुरूप = सुन्दर-रूप। सेँदुर = सिन्दूर = प्रसिद्ध अङ्गराग। सारी = सँवारी हैँ (वृ-वरणे से)। जानहुँ = जाने = जानोँ। दिश्रा = दीया = दीप। महि = मही = पृथ्वी। बारी = बारइ (ज्वलति) का भूत-काल। मुरुछि = मूर्छित्वा = मूर्छा खा कर = घुमर कर। परइ = पतति = पडता है। जावँत = यावन्तः = जितने। जे = ये = जो। जोहइ = जोहता है (जेह-यत्ने से)। मिरिग = मृग = हरिण। दिश्रार = दिवाकर = सूर्य, दिश्रारहिँ = दिवाकर से, सूर्य की चमक से = मृगतृष्णा से। मोहइ = मुह्यति = मोहता है ॥

परा = परइ (पतति) का भूत-काल में एक-वचन। भवँर = भ्रमर = भौँरा। बास = वास = सुगन्ध। लीन्ह = लेइ (लाति) का भूत-काल में एक-वचन। जनु = जाने = जानोँ। चाँप = दाब (चप धातु से)। पतँग = पतङ्ग = कीट। भा = हुआ (बभूव)। दीपक = दीया। अध-जर = आधा जरा = अर्ध-ज्वलित। तन = तनु = देह। काँप = काँपती है (कम्पते) ॥

इस प्रकार सिंहल की रानी पद्मावती, खेलती महादेव के मन्दिर के पास जा पऊँची॥ सब देवता (पद्मावती और सहेलिओं को) देखने लगे, (देखते ही पद्मावती और सहेलिओं के अङ्ग मेँ दृष्टि-किरण के लगते-ही) तिन्ह देवताओं के सब दृष्टि-दोष भाग गए, अर्थात् देवताओं की दिव्य-दृष्टि हो गई। (मन मेँ कहने लगे कि) यह सुना था कि इन्द्र-लोक मेँ अप्सरा रहती हैँ, (सो ये सब) परमेश्वरी रूप कहाँ से आ गईं॥ कोई कहता है कि पद्मिनी आई हैँ; कोई कहता है कि (साचात्) चन्द्र, नचत्र, और तारा-गण हैँ॥ कोई कहता है कि फूल हैँ, कोई कहता है कि पुष्प-वाटिका है; (इस प्रकार) बालिकाओं को देख कर सब (देवता) भूल गए॥ (उन्ह सबोँ के) एक तो सुन्दर रूप, दूसरे सेँदुर की बनावट से, जान पडता है कि सब पृथ्वी मेँ दीपक बारे ऊए हैँ॥ जितने देवता हैँ उन मेँ जो जो (बालिकाओं) को देखते हैँ सब घूमरी खा कर गिर पडते हैँ, जानोँ मृग-तृष्णा से हरिण मोह गए होँ॥

कोई भ्रमर हो कर गिर पडा जानोँ (सहेलियोँ के) सुगन्ध ने (उस को) दबा दिया। कोई दीये का फतिंगा हो गया, अर्थात् जैसे दीये की ज्योति मेँ पड कर फतिंगा तडपता है तैसे तडपने लगा; देह अध-जरी हो कर काँपने लगी॥ १९५॥

चउपाई।

पदुमावति गइ देओ-दुआरू। भीतर मँडफ कीन्ह पइसारू॥
देओहि साँसउ भा जिउ केरा। भागउँ केहि दिसि मंडफ घेरा॥
एक जोहार कीन्ह अउ दूजा। तिसरइ आइ चढाई पूजा॥
फर फूलन्ह सब मँडफ भरावा। चंदन अगर देओ अन्हवावा॥
भरि सेँदुर आगइ भइ खरी। परसि देओ पुनि पाएन्ह परी॥
अउरु सहेली सबइ बिआहीँ। मो कहँ देओ कतहुँ बर नाहीँ॥
हउँ निरगुन जेइ कीन्ह न सेवा। गुन निरगुन दाता तुम्ह देवा॥

दोहा।

बर सँजोग मोहिँ मिरवहु कलस जात हउँ मानि।
जेहि दिन हीछा पूजइ बेगि चढावउँ आनि॥ १९६॥

(प्रवारयति) का भूत-काल में एक-वचन। जइस = जैसे = यथा। परेवा = पारावत; यहाँ साधारण पक्षी। मरि भा = मर गया = मुर्दा हुआ। ईस = ईश = महादेव। अउरु = अपर = और। देवा = देव। बिनु = विना। जिउ = जीव। नाउत = नापित = नाऊ = नाई। ओझा = उपाध्याय = पुजारी। पूरि = पूरी = पूरिता। काल = मारनेहारा। भा = भया (बभूव)। गोझा = गुह्यक = एक प्रकार का पक्वान्न, जिस के भीतर मेवे इत्यादि भरे रहते हैं। जो = यः। देखइ = देखता है (दृशि प्रेक्षणे से)। जनु = जानों = जाने। बिसहर = विषधर = सर्प। डँसा = डसइ (दंशति) का भूत-काल में एक-वचन। देखि = दृष्ट्वा = देख कर। चरित = चरित्र = तमाशा। हँसा = हँसइ (हसति) का भूत-काल में एक-वचन। भल = वर = अच्छा। हम = अहम्। आइ = एत्य = आ कर। मनावा = मनावइ (मानयति) का भूत-काल में एक-वचन। गा = गया (अगात्)। सोइ = सो = स्वपित। मानइ = माने (मन्येत)। सेवा = टहल = खिदमत। पुरवइ = पुरवे = पूरा करे (पूरयेत्)। दुख = दुःख = तकलीफ। धोआ = धोवे = धो डाले [धावु-(गतिशुद्ध्योः) से]। मनि = मानि = मान कर = संमान्य। आए = आए (इण् गतौ से)। सोई = स एव = वही। तन = तनु = देह। सोआ = सोअइ (शेते) का भूत-काल में एक-वचन॥

जेहि = यस्य = जिसे। धरि = धृत्वा = धर कर = पकड कर। उठावहिँ = उठावइ (उत्थापयति) का बहु-वचन। सीस = शीर्ष = शिर। बिकल = विकल = बेचैन। डोल = डोलइ (दोलते) = डोलता है = हिलता है। धर = अधर-भाग = गले के विना देह-भाग। कोइ = कोई = कोऽपि। जानइ (जानाति) = जानता है। मुख = मुह। बकत = बकता है (वक्ति)। कु-बोल = कुत्सित-वाणी = अंड बंड बोली॥

रानी (पद्मावती) ने जैसा (विनय करना) जानती थी (वैसी) इच्छा कर कर विनय किया और फिर हाथ जोड कर (सामने) खडी हुई॥ (बहुत देरी पर) मण्डप में से अकस्मात् शब्द हुआ कि (अरे पद्मावती तेरी विनय-स्तुति) का उत्तर कौन देवे; देव तो (तेरे रूप-तेज से) मर गया॥ जैसे (कोई) पक्षी को काट कर (दो टुकडे कर) फेंक देवे, (उसी प्रकार दो टुकडे हो कर जब) ईश (महादेव) ही मर गया तो और देव कौन है (जो जीता हो)॥ (मन्दिर के) सब नाई ओझा (पद्मावती के दर्शन से) विना जीव के हो गए; (प्रसाद की) पूरिआँ जहर हो गईं और गोझे काल हो गए॥ जोई (पद्मावती को) देखता है (उस की ऐसी दशा हो जाती है) जानों साँप ने

डस लिया हो; यह तमाशा देख कर पद्मावती ने हँस दिया॥ (और कहने लगी कि) हम ने आ कर अच्छे देवता को मनाया (जो बोलता ही नहीँ), जान पडता है कि सो गया है (फिर) कौन मेरी सेवा को माने, अर्थात् जड क्या समझे कि मैँ ने कैसी उस की सेवा की॥ जिस को (बहुत ही बडा) मान कर आए, वही जब अपनी देह मैँ सो गया, तो (दूसरा) कौन इच्छा को पूरा करे और दुःख को धोवे॥

जिसी (नाज़ और ओझे) के शिर को पकड कर सखियाँ उठाती हैँ, वही विकल हो कर कुछ हिलता ही नहीँ (जानोँ काठ की मूर्त्ति हो गया है)। कोई जानता ही नहीँ है कि कहाँ धड है और कहाँ जीव; (कवि कहता है कि, अरे भाई, सब बौरहे हो कर) मुख से अंड बंड बोली बकते हैँ॥ १९७॥

चउपाई।

ततखन एक सखी बिहँसानी। कउतुक एक न देखहु रानी॥
पुरुब दार मढ जोगी छाए। न जनउँ कउन देस तइँ आए॥
जनु उन्ह जोग तंत अब खेला। सिद्ध होइ निसरे सब चेला॥
उन्ह मँह एक गुरू जो कहावा। जनु गुड देइ काहु बउरावा॥
कुअँर बतीस-उ लखन सो राता। दसएँ लखन कहइ एक बाता॥
जानहुँ आहि गोपिचँद जोगी। कइ सो आहि भरथरी बिओगी॥
वह जो पिँगला कजरी-आरन। यह सो सिँघला दहुँ केहि कारन॥

दोहा।

यह मूरति यह मुदरा　हम न देख अउधूत।
जानहुँ होहिँ न जोगी　कोइ राजा कर पूत॥ १९८॥

ततखन = तत्क्षणे = तिसी क्षण मेँ = उसी क्षण मेँ। बिहँसानी = बिहँसइ (विहसति) का भूत-काल मेँ एक-वचन, इस का दूसरा रूप 'बिहँसी' भी होता है। कउतुक = कौतुक = लीला = तमाशा = चमत्कार। न = नु = निश्चय कर = अवश्य। देखहु = देखो = देखइ (दृशि प्रेक्षणे से) का लोट् लकार मेँ मध्यम-पुरुष का एक-वचन। पुरुब = पूर्व।

भइ = भई (बभूव)। दिसिटि = दृष्टि। सउँ = सेाँ = से। ढरे = ढरइ (अवधरति) का भूत-काल में बहु-वचन। लीन्हा = लेइ (लाति) का भूत-काल में एक-वचन। जिउ = जीव। दीन्हा = देइ (दत्ते) का भूत-काल में एक-वचन। चहत = चाहता था। परा = पडा = परइ (पतति) का भूत-काल में एक-वचन। पालइँ = पाले = पालि: (पालि: स्त्र्यश्र्यङ्कपङ्क्तिषु, अमरकोषे नानार्थव० श्लो० १४०६)। सुधि = शोध = खबर। पिआलइँ = प्याले में। प्याला = मद्यपीने का पात्र = चषक। माँति = मत्त हो कर = मस्त हो कर। गोरख = गोरखनाथ, प्रसिद्ध अवधूत। चेला = शिष्य। तन = तनु = शरीर। छाडि = छाड कर = छोड कर (छुर छेदने से)। सरग = स्वर्ग। खेला = खेलति = (खेलइ) का भूत-काल में एक-वचन। किँगरी = किं-करी = सारंगी से छोटा चिकारे के ऐसा एक बाजा; आज कल पौरिए रखते हैँ; प्रथम बालक उत्पन्न होने पर लोगोँ के घर जा कर इसी किँगरी को बजाते हैँ। गहे = गहइ (गृह्णाति) से। हुत = था = आसीत्। बइरागी = वैरागी = जिस को विराग हो। मरतिहिँ = मरने की। बार = वार = वेला = समय। उहइ = वही = स एव। धुनि = ध्वनि = शब्द। लागी = लग गई = लगइ (लगति) का भूत-काल में एक-वचन॥

धंध = धन्धन = काम। लागइ = लगइ (लगति)। सपनेहुँ = स्वप्ने हि = सपने में भी। सूझ = सूझइ = सूझता है (शुध्यते)। तपसी = तपस्वी। साधहिँ = साधइ (साधयति) का बहु-वचन। करहिँ = करइ (करति) का बहु-वचन। बंध = बन्धन॥

(सखी की) उस बात को सुन कर (पद्मावती) रानी रथ पर चढी; (और कहने लगी कि) मढी में कहाँ ऐसा योगी है जिसे (चल कर) मैँ देखूँ॥ सखिओँ को संग ले कर तहाँ फेरा किया अर्थात् तहाँ पर गई, (उस समय ऐसी शोभा हुई जानों) अप्सराओँ ने योगिओँ को घेर लिया हो॥ (पद्मावती के) कपूर से नेत्र प्रेम-मद से भर गए; वैसी ही मद भरी दृष्टि भी हो गई, जिस की धारा (एक बार ही) योगी (रत्न-सेन) पर ढरक पडीँ॥ (पद्मावती ने अपनी) दृष्टि से योगी (रत्न-सेन) की दृष्टि को लिया, अर्थात् पद्मावती और योगी की चार आँखेँ हो गईँ; नजर से नजर मिल गई; (योगी ने पद्मावती के) आँख ही के रूप से अर्थात् आँख के रूपदर्शन ही से (अपनी) आँखो ही से अपने जी को दे दिया; अर्थात् नेत्र को देखते ही अपने नेत्र-द्वारा ही अपने जीव को निकाल कर पद्मावती को सङ्कल्प कर दिया॥ (राजा रत्न-सेन) जिस नशे को चाहता था उसी के पाले पड गया; एक ही प्याले में

अर्थात् एक ही वार के दर्शन में (बेहोश हो गया कुछ भी) खबर न रही॥ वह गोरख-नाथ का चेला मस्त हो कर गिर पडा; (गोरख-नाथ के लिये १२८ दोहे की टीका देखो) जीव देह त्याग कर स्वर्ग में खेलने लगा, अर्थात् स्वर्ग को चला गया॥ वह वैरागी (रत्न-सेन) जो किँगरी लिए था (उस में से) मरती-वेला वही (पद्मावती पद्मावती) धुनि होने लगी (मरती वेला पद्मावती का ध्यान आ जाने से मुख और किँगरी से पद्मावती पद्मावती ध्वनि निकलने लगी)॥

जिस का मन जिस काम में लग जाता है, (उस को) वही काम सपने में भी सूझता है; इसी लिये तपस्वी तप साधा करते हैं, और (ईश्वर के) प्रेम ही को मन का बन्धन करते हैं, जिस में मन उसी में बँधा रहे मरने के समय भी दूसरी ओर न जाय। मरने के समय मन जिस वस्तु का ध्यान करता है; दूसरे जन्म में उसी योनि में जाता है। इसी लिये महानुभाव योगी लोग सदा अपने मन को परमेश्वर में लगाए रहते हैं, जिस में मरती वेला भी उसी में लगा रहे जिस से ईश्वर-स्वरूप हो जाय (इस ग्रन्थ का २३१ पृ० देखो)। इस दोहे के १, ३ चरणों में सोरह सोरह मात्रा हैं इस लिये छन्दःशास्त्र में इस दोहे का नाम हरिपद है। बहुतों का मत है कि इसे दोहा न कहना चाहिए किन्तु यह स्वतन्त्र हरिपद नाम का छन्द ही है॥ १९९॥

चउपाई।

पदुमावति जस सुना बखानू। सहसहुँ करा देखेसि तस भानू॥
मेलेसि चंदन मकु खन जागा। अधिकउ सीत सीर तन लागा॥
तब चंदन आखर हिअ लिखे। भीख लेइ तुइँ जोग न सिखे॥
बार आइ तब गा तूँ सोई। कइसइ भुगुति परापति होई॥
अब जउँ सूर अहउ ससि राता। आएहु चढि सो गगन पुनि साता॥
लिखि कइ बात सखिन्ह सउँ कही। इहइ ठाउँ हउँ बारति अही॥
परगट होउँ तउ होइ अस भंगू। जगत दिआ कर होइ पतंगू॥

दोहा।

जा सउँ हउँ चखु हेरउँ सोई ठाउँ जिउ देइ।
एहि दुख कतहुँ न निसरउँ को हतिआ असि लेइ॥ २००॥

जस = जैसा = यादृश = यथा । सुना = सुनइ (शृणोति) का भूत-काल मैं एक-वचन । बखानू = बखान = वर्णन । सहसऊँ = सहस्र = हजारों । करा = कला = किरण । देखेंसि = देखा = देखइ का भूत-काल मैं प्रथम-पुरुष का एक-वचन । तस = तैसा = तादृश = तथा । भानू = भानु = सूर्य । मेलेसि = मेला = मेलइ (मेलयति) का भूत-काल मैं प्रथम-पुरुष का एक-वचन । मकु = मैं कहा = क्या जानैं । खन = क्षण । जागा = जागे = जागइ (जागर्त्ति) का विध्यर्थ मैं प्रथम-पुरुष का एक-वचन । अधिकउ = और = अधिक = अधिकतर । सोत = स्रोतस् = धारा । सीर = फार = हलाग्र । तन = तनु = देह । लागा = लगा = लगइ (लगति) का भूत-काल मैं प्रथम-पुरुष का एक-वचन । तब = तदानीम् = तदा । आखर = अक्षर । हिअ = हृदय । लिखे = लिखा = लिखइ (लिखति) का भूत-काल । भीख = भिक्षा । लेइ = लेना । तुइँ = त्वम् । सिखे = सिखा = सिखइ (शिक्ष्यते) का भूत-काल मैं उत्तम-पुरुष का एक-वचन । बार = द्वार = दरवाजा । आइँ = आईं = आवइ (आयाति) का भूत-काल मैं उत्तम-पुरुष का स्त्रीलिङ्ग मैं एक-वचन । गा = गया (अगात्) । तूँ = त्वम् । सोई = सो = स्वपित । कइसइ = कैसे = कथम् । भुगुति = भुक्ति = भोग । परापति = प्राप्ति = पराप्ति । होई = होवे (भवेत्) । अब = अधुना । जउँ = जौं = यदि । सूर = हे सूर्य । अहउ = हो । ससि = शशि । राता = रक्त = आरक्त = आशक्त । आएउ = आना (आ उपसर्ग पूर्वक या प्रापणे से) । चढि = चढ कर (उच्चाह्य) । गगन = आकाश । पुनि = पुनः = फिर । साता = सात = सप्त । लिखि कइ = लिख कर = आलिख्य । बात = वार्त्ता । सउँ = सेाँ = से । कही = कहइ (कथयति) का भूत-काल मैं स्त्रीलिङ्ग का एक-वचन । इहइ = यही = इसी । ठाउँ = ठावँ = स्थान । हउँ = अहम् = मैं । बारति = व्रत । अही = थी । परगट = प्रगट = प्रकट = जाहिर । होउँ = होऊँ (भवेयम्) । तउ = तदा = तर्हि = तो । अस = ऐसा = एतादृश । भंगू = भङ्ग = नाश । जगत = जगत् = संसार । दिआ = दीप । कर = का । पतंगू = पतङ्ग = फतिंगा ॥

जा = यस्य = जिस । हउँ = अहम् = मैं । चखु = चक्षुः = आँख । हेरउँ = हेरती हूँ (हेडामि) = हेरइ (हेडति) का उत्तम-पुरुष मैं एक-वचन । सोई = वही = स एव । देइ = देता है (दत्ते) । एहि = इसी । दुख = दुःख । कतऊँ = कुत्र हि = कहीं । निसरउँ = निसरइ (निःसरति) का उत्तम-पुरुष मैं एक-वचन । को = कौन । हतिआ = हत्या । असि = ऐसी = एतादृशी । लेइ = लेवे ॥

पद्मावती ने जैसा (उस योगी का) वर्णन सुना था तैसा ही सहस्र-किरण सूर्य के

ऐसा (उसे) देखा ॥ (उस के अङ्ग पर) चन्दन लगाया, कि क्या जानँ चण भर के लिये जाग उठे; (परन्तु सो बात न ऊई, चन्दन लगाने से) और भी अधिक (दृष्टि-किरण-रूप) फार के धार देह मेँ लगने लगे ॥ तब (पद्मावती ने उस के) हृदय मेँ चन्दन से अचरोँ को लिखा, कि तैँ ने भिचा के योग्य योग को नहीँ सीखा ॥ जब मैँ तेरे द्वार पर आई तब ढूँ सो गया तो तुझे कैसे भुक्ति (भोग-भिचा) की प्राप्ति हो ॥ अब तो हे सूर्य यदि तुम चन्द्र (मेरे) मेँ आसक्त हो तो फिर सात आकाश चढ कर आना ॥ (पद्मावती) इस बात को लिख कर सखियोँ से कहने लगी, कि इसी स्थान के लिये मैँ व्रत कर रही थी ॥ सो यदि (इस अवसर मेँ मैँ) प्रगट होती हूँ तो मेरा वैसा ही विनाश हो जायगा, अर्थात् वैसी ही दशा हो जायगी जैसी कि संसार मेँ दीप के फतंगे की होती है (कि भस्म हो कर प्राण दे देता है परन्तु दीप-शिखा से भेँट नहीँ होती) ॥ भूः, भुवः, स्वः, महः, जन, तप, और सत्य ए सात ऊपर के लोक सप्त आकाश कहे जाते हैँ । किसी कार्य-सिद्धि के लिये जो नियम किया जाता है कि जब तक कार्य-सिद्धि न हो तब तक मैँ जल ही पीकर रहूँगा वा निर्जल उपवास करूँगा इत्यादि, ऐसे नियम को व्रत कहते हैँ ।

(हे सखिओ) मैँ जिसी की ओर आँख उठा कर देखती हूँ, वही उसी स्थान मेँ जीव दे देता है; इसी दुःख से मैँ कहीँ (बाहर) नहीँ निकलती, कि कौन ऐसी हत्या को लेवे । हत्या एक महापाप है जो किसी के मारने से मनुष्य को लगता है, जैसे ब्राह्मण को मारने से ब्रह्महत्या, गौ को मारने से गोहत्या इत्यादि ॥ २०० ॥

चउपाई ।

कीन्ह पयान सबन्ह रथ हाँका । परबत छाडि सिँघल-गढ ताका ॥
भए बलि सबइ देओता बली । हतिआरिन हतिआ लेइ चली ॥
को अस हितू मुए गह बाहीँ । जउँ पइ जिउ आपुन तन नाहीँ ॥
जउ लहि जिउ आपुन सब कोई । बिनु जिएँ सबइ निरापुन होई ॥
भाइ बंधु अउ मीत पिआरा । बिनु जिएँ घडी न राखइ पारा ॥
बिनु जिएँ पीँड छार करि कूरा । छार मिलावइ सो हित पूरा ॥
तेहि जिएँ बिनु अब मर भा राजा । को उठि बइठि गरब सउँ गाजा ॥

दोहा ।

परी कया भुइँ रोअई कहाँ रे जिउ बलि भीउ ।
को उठाइ बइसारई बाजु पिरीतम जीउ ॥ २०१ ॥

कीन्ह = करइ (करोति) का भूत-काल। पयान = प्रयाण = यात्रा। सबन्ह = सब (सर्व) का बहु-वचन। हाँका = हाँकइ (अकयति, अक कुटिलायां गतौ से णिच्) का भूत-काल। परबत = पर्वत = पहाड। छाडि = छोड कर (सन्त्यज्य)। सिँघल = सिंहल। गढ = गाढ = दुर्ग = किला। ताका = ताकइ (तर्कयति) का भूत-काल। सबइ = सभी। देओता = देवता। बली = प्रबल। हतिआरिन = हत्या-कारिणी = हत्या करनेहारी। हतिआ = हत्या = पाप। लेइ = ले कर (ला धातु से)। चली = चलइ (चलति) का भूत-काल में स्त्रीलिङ्ग का एक-वचन। को = कौन = कः। अस = ऐसा = एतादृश। हित्र = हित = हितैषी। मुए = मरे का। गह = गहे (गृह्णीयात्) = पकडे। बाहीँ = बाहु = बाँह। जउँ = यदि = जौं। पइ = अपि = निश्चय। जिउ = जीव। आपुन = अपना। तन = तनु = देह। जउ लहि = जब लग = जब तक। बिनु = विना। जिअ = जीव। निरापन = जो अपना नहीँ = बेगाना = पराया। होई = होता है (भवति)। भाइ = भाई = भ्राता। बंधु = बन्धु। अउ = अपि च = और। मीत = मित्र। पिआरा = प्यारा। घडी = एक घडी = एक घटी। राखइ = रखने को। पारा = पार = समर्थ = शक्य। पौँड = पिण्ड = देह। छार = क्षार = भस्म। करि = कृत्वा = कर के। कूरा = कूट = ढेर। मिलावइ = मिलाता है (मेलयति)। पूरा = पूर्ण = पक्का। अब = इदानीम् = अधुना। मर = मुर्दा = मृतक। भा = भया = हुआ (बभूव)। उठि = उठ कर (उत्थाय)। बइठि = बैठ कर (उपविश्य)। गरब = गर्व = अभिमान। सउँ = सेाँ = से। गाजा = गाजे = गरजे = गाजइ (गर्जति) से ॥

परी = परइ (पतति) का भूत-काल में स्त्रीलिङ्ग का एक-वचन। कया = काय = देह। भुइँ = भूमि में। रोअइ = रोती है (रोदिति)। बलि = बलि राजा, जिस के छलने के लिये भगवान् विष्णु का वामनावतार हुआ है; पुराणोँ में प्रसिद्ध कथा है। भीउ = भीम = युधिष्ठिर के दूसरे भाई जो कि महाबली थे। उठाइ = उठा कर। बइसारइ = बैठावे (उपवेशयेत्)। बाजु = बरजे = रोके (वर्जयेत्)। पिरीतम = प्रियतम = सब से प्यारा ॥

सब किसी ने याचा की, रथ को हाँका; और पर्वत (देव मन्दिर का पर्वत) को छोड कर, सिंहल-गढ की ओर दृष्टि की ॥ सब बली देवता बलि हो गए अर्थात् पद्मावती के रूप से मोहित हो मृतक से हो गए; (इस प्रकार) हत्यारिन (पद्मावती) (सब की) हत्या को ले कर चली ॥ (कवि कहता है कि) कौन ऐसा हितैषी है जो मरे की बाँह पकडे; यदि जीव अपनी देह में नहीं है (तो कोई साथ देने-वाला नहीं) ॥ जब तक जीव है तभी तक सब कोई अपना है; जीव के विना सभी पराए हो जाते हैं ॥ भाई, बन्धु, और प्यारा मित्र, (सब) जीव के विना एक घडी भी नहीं रख सकते ॥ जो विना जीव की देह को (भस्म कर) राख की ढेरी कर राख में मिला देवे वही पूरा हितू है ॥ (जिस जीव ही से संसार में सब नाता है) उसी जीव के विना अब राजा मुर्दा हो गया; कौन उठ कर बैठे और गर्व से गरजे ॥

भूमि में पडी देह रो रही है (रो रो कर पुकारती है कि) अरे जीव, अरे राजा बलि और भीम, कहाँ हो (आ कर शरीर के सहायक हो); अरे (इस कु-अवसर में) कौन उठा कर (मुझे) बैठावे और कौन प्रियतम जीव को रोके (और डाँटे कि इस की देह को न छोड इसी में रह) ॥ २०१ ॥

चउपाई।

पदुमावति सो मँदिर पईठी। हँसत सिँघासन जाइ बईठी ॥
निसि सूती सुनि कथा बिहारी। भा बिहान अउ सखी हँकारी ॥
देओ पूजि जस आएउँ काली। सपन एक निसि देखेउँ आली ॥
जनु ससि उदउ पुरुब दिसि लीन्हा। अउ रबि उदउ पछिउँ दिसि कीन्हा ॥
पुनि चलि सूर चाँद पहिँ आवा। चाँद सुरुज दुहुँ भएउ मेरावा ॥
दिन अउ राति जानु भए एका। राम आइ राओन-गढ छेँका ॥
तस किछु कहा न जाए निखेधा। अरजुन-बान राहु गा बेधा ॥

दोहा।

जनहुँ लंक सब लूसी हनू बिधाँसी बारि।
जागि उठेउँ अस देखत सखि कहु सपन बिचारि ॥ २०२ ॥

सो = वह। मँदिर = मन्दिर = घर। पईठी = पैठी = पइठइ (प्रविशति) का भूत-काल में स्त्रीलिङ्ग का एक-वचन। हँसत = हँसती हुई = हसन्ती। सिंघासन = सिंहासन। जाइ = जा कर = संयाय। बईठी = बैठी = बइठइ (उपविशति) का भूत-काल में स्त्रीलिङ्ग का एक-वचन। निसि = निशि = रात्रि में। सूती = सूतइ (शेते) का भूत-काल में स्त्रीलिङ्ग का एक-वचन। सुनि = सुन कर (श्रुत्वा)। कथा = कहानी। बिहारी = विहारी = विहार की = सैर की। भा = भया = हुआ = (बभूव)। बिहान = सबेरा = व्युष = भोर। सखी = प्रिय-सखी, जिस से भली बुरी बात कहने में सङ्कोच न हो। हँकारी = हँकारइ (हुँ-कारयति) का भूत-काल में स्त्रीलिङ्ग का एक-वचन। देश्रो = देव। पूजि = पूज कर (पूजयित्वा)। जस = जैसेही = यथा। श्राएउँ = श्राई = श्रावइ (श्रायाति) का भूत-काल में स्त्रीलिङ्ग का एक-वचन। काली = कल = कल्यम्। सपन = स्वप्न = सपना। देखेउँ = देखा = देखइ का भूत-काल। श्राली = सखी। जनु = जानों = जाने। ससि = शशि = चन्द्र। उदउ = उदय। पुरुब = पूर्व। दिसि = दिशा। लीन्हा = लेइ (लाति) का भूत-काल। रबि = रवि = सूर्य। पछिउँ = पश्चिम। कीन्हा = करइ (करोति) का भूत-काल। पुनि = पुनः = फिर। चलि = चल कर = (चलित्वा)। सूर = सूर्य। चाँद = चन्द्र। श्रावा = श्रावइ (श्रायाति) का भूत-काल में एक-वचन। सुरुज = सूर्य। दुहुँ = दोनों में = द्वयोर्हि। भएउ = भया = हुआ (बभूव)। मेरावा = मिलाप = मेलाप = भेंट। राति = रात्रि। एका = एक। राम = अयोध्या के प्रसिद्ध राजा, दशरथ के पुत्र। राश्रोन = रावण। गढ = गाढ = दुर्ग = किला। राश्रोन-गढ = रावण का गढ = लङ्का। छँका = छँकइ (शकि शङ्कायाम् से णिजन्त, शङ्कयति) का भूत-काल। तस = तथा = तैसा। किछु = किञ्चत् = कुछ। कहा न जाए = कहा नहीं जाता। निखेधा = निखेधइ (निषेधयति) का भूत-काल। अरजुन = अर्जुन = युधिष्ठिर का तीसरा भाई, इन्द्र का अंश। बान = वाण। राहु = राहु के (सर्प के) श्राकार का एक लक्ष्य (निशाना)। गा = गया (अगात्)। बेधा = विद्ध = विध॥

जनउँ = जानों = जाने। लंक = लङ्का। लूसी = लुट गई (लूष हिंसायाम्, चुरादि)। हनू = हनूमान्। बिधाँसी = विधंसी = विधंसइ (विध्वंसयति) का भूत-काल। बारि = वाटिका। वा बारि = बार कर जला कर। जागि = जाग कर = जाग्रित हो कर। उठेउँ = उठी = उठइ (उत्तिष्ठते) का भूत-काल में स्त्रीलिङ्ग का उत्तम-पुरुष में एक-वचन। सखि = हे सखि। कहु = कहु (कथय)। बिचारि = विचार कर (विचार्य)॥

(देव-मन्दिर से आ कर) वह पद्मावती अपने मन्दिर में पैठी, अर्थात् प्रवेश की, और हँसती ऊई, जा कर सिंहासन पर बैठ गई। विहार (सैर) की कथा (सखिओं से) सुन कर रात को सूती; भोर होते-ही प्रिय-सखी को बुलाई। (और कहने लगी, कि) हे सखि कल देवता को पूज कर जैसे आई (उन सब बातों को तो तुम जानती ही हो; नई बात यह है कि आज) रात्रि में एक सपना देखी हूँ कि। जानों पूर्व दिशा से चन्द्रमा उदय को लिया है, अर्थात् उदय ऊआ है, और पश्चिम दिशा में सूर्य उदय किया है। फिर सूर्य चल कर चन्द्र के पास आया है; चन्द्र और सूर्य दोनों में मिलाप ऊआ है। जानों दिन और रात दोनों एक में मिल गए और राम ने आ कर लङ्का को घेर लिया है। (इस के अनन्तर) जैसा कुछ ऊआ जो कहा नहीं जाता, (उस बात के कहने का शास्त्रों में) निषेध है; (यही समझ लो) कि अर्जुन के बाण से राऊ (निशाना) बिध गया (द्रौपदी-रूपा जो मैं चन्द्र, तिस का उस सूर्य से विवाह हो गया)। द्रुपद ने द्रौपदी के विवाह के लिये स्वयंवर रचा था। उस में एक धनु और पाँच बाण रख दिए थे और एक यन्त्र के ऊपर आकाश में एक निशाना, जो कि बऊतों के मत से सर्पाकार वा मत्स्याकार था, लटका दिया गया था; यन्त्र में एक छेद कर दिया था। प्रतिज्ञा थी कि जो इस धनु को चढा कर, इन्हीं पाँच बाणों से निशाने को इस प्रकार से बेध दे, कि बाण यन्त्र के छेद में से होते ऊए निशाने को बेधे तो उसी के साथ द्रौपदी का विवाह हो, अर्थात् द्रौपदी उसी पुरुष की भार्या होगी। रङ्गशाला में द्रौपदी का भाई धृष्टद्युम्न ने ललकार कर कहा है कि—

इदं धनुर्लक्ष्यमिमे च बाणाः शृण्वन्तु मे भूपतयः समेताः ।
छिद्रेण यन्त्रस्य समर्पयध्वं शरैः शितैर्व्योमचरैर्दशार्धैः ॥
एतन्महत्कर्म करोति यो वै कुलेन रूपेण बलेन युक्तः ।
तस्याद्य भार्या भगिनी ममेयं कृष्णा भवित्री न मृषा ब्रवीमि ॥
(भारत, आदि पर्व, १८७ अध्या० श्लो० ३५-३६)।

जानों हनूमान ने वाटिका को (पद्मावती के भूषणों को) विध्वंस कर दिया है और लङ्का [पद्मावती की लङ्क=(कटि)] को नष्ट भ्रष्ट कर दिया है; ऐसा (स्वप्न) देखते-ही मैं जाग उठी। (सो) हे सखि, विचार कर (इस) सपने को कह, अर्थात् इस सपने का फल विचार कर, कह ॥ २०२ ॥

चित्रलेखा रात को द्वारिका मेँ जा कर सोते ऊए अनिरुद्ध को उठा लाई और ऊषा से मिला दी। इस पर द्वारिका मेँ अनिरुद्ध को न देख कर बऊत घबडाहट मची और इधर पुत्री के साथ अनुचित व्यवहार करने से बाणासुर ने अनिरुद्ध को कैद कर लिया। बऊत दिनोँ के बाद नारद से खबर पा कर, कृष्ण शोणितपुर गए और बाणासुर को पराजय कर, ऊषा के साथ अनिरुद्ध को द्वारिका मेँ ले आए। श्रीमद्भागवत के दशमस्कन्ध ६२-६३ अध्याय मेँ इस की सविस्तर कथा लिखी है॥

(सो रानी तुम घबडाओ मत) तुम को (सदा) सुख, सौभाग्य है और पान फूल के रस का भोग है; ऐसा सपने का संयोग, आज कल मेँ (सच) ऊआ चाहता है॥ २०३॥

इति वसन्त-खण्डं नाम विंश-खण्डं समाप्तम्॥ २०॥

अथ राजा-रतनसेन-सती-खंड ॥ २१ ॥

चउपाई।

कइ बसंत पदुमावति गई। राजहि तब बसंत सुधि भई ॥
जो जागा न बसंत न बारी। नहिँ सो खेल न खेलन-हारी ॥
ना उन्ह कइ वह रूप सोहाई। गइ हेराइ पुनि दिसिटि न आई ॥
फूल झरे सूखी फुलवारी। दिसिटि परी उकठी सब झारी ॥
केइँ यह बसत बसंत उजारा। गा सो चाँद अथवा लेइ तारा ॥
अब तेहि बिनु जग भा अँध-कूपा। वह सुख छाँह जरउँ हउँ धूपा ॥
बिरह दवाँ को जरत सिरावा। को पीतम सउँ करइ मेरावा ॥

दोहा।

हिअइ देख जो चंदन खेवरा मिलि कइ लिखा बिछोउ।
हाथ मीँजि सिर धुनि सो रोअइ जो निचिंत अस सोउ ॥ २०४ ॥

कइ = कर = कृत्वा। बसंत = वसन्त-ऋतु। गई = गया (अगात्) का स्त्रीलिङ्ग। तब = तदानीम्। सुधि = शोध = खबर। भई = भया का स्त्रीलिङ्ग (बभूव) = हुई। जागा = जागइ (जागर्त्ति) का भूत-काल। बारी = वाटिका, वा वालिका। खेल = खेला = क्रीडा। कइ = की। सोहाई = सोहइ (शोभते) का भूत-काल। गइ हेराइ = हेराय गई = हत हो गई = लोप हो गई। पुनि = पुनः = फिर। दिसिटि = दृष्टि। आई = आवइ (आयाति) का भूत-काल में स्त्रीलिङ्ग का एक-वचन। फूल = फुल्ल = पुष्प।

झरे = झरइ (झरति) का भूत-काल में प्रथम-पुरुष का बहु-वचन। सूखी = सूखइ (शुष्यति) का भूत-काल में स्त्रीलिङ्ग का प्रथम-पुरुष में एक-वचन। फुलवारी = पुष्पवाटिका। परी = परइ (पतति) का स्त्रीलिङ्ग में भूत-काल का एक-वचन। उकठी = उकठ गई = सूख गई। छारी = भस्म हो गई = चार हो गई = राख हो गई। केइँ = किस ने। बसत = बसते। उजारा = उजारइ (उज्जारयति) का भूत-काल में एक-वचन। गा = गया (अगात्)। चाँद = चन्द्र। अथवा = अस्त हो गया (अस्तमितः)। लेइ = ले कर (आलाय)। तारा = तारा-गण। अब = इदानीम्। बिनु = विना। जग = जगत् = संसार। भा = भया (बभूव)। अँध-कूपा = अन्ध-कूप। छाँह = छाया। जरउँ = जरइ (ज्वलति) का उत्तम-पुरुष में एक-वचन। हउँ = अहम् = मैं। धूप = घाम। बिरह = विरह = वियोग। दवाँ = दवानल = दवाग्नि। जरत = जरते (ज्वलन्)। सिरावा = सिरावे = सिरावइ (शीतयति) का सम्भावना में प्रथम-पुरुष का एक-वचन। पीतम = प्रियतम। सउँ = सेाँ = से। करइ = करे (कुर्यात्)। मेरावा = मिलाप = मेलापक॥

हिअइ = हृदये = हृदय में। देख = देखा = देखइ का भूत-काल में प्रथम-पुरुष का एक-वचन। खँवरा = खौरा हुआ = लगाया हुआ (खेट्ट सेवने से)। मिलि कइ = मिल कर। लिखा = लिखा हुआ। बिछोउ = बिछोह = विशोक = विशेष शोक, वा वियोग। हाथ = हस्त। मीजि = मीँज कर (आमर्द्य)। सिर = शिर। धुनि = धुन कर = कँपा कर (धुञ् कम्पने से)। रोअइ = रोता है (रोदिति)। निचिंत = निश्चिन्त = विना चिन्ता के। अस = ऐसा = एतादृश। सोउ = सोता है (शेते)॥

जब पद्मावती वसन्त कर, अर्थात् वसन्त ऋतु की शोभा फैला कर, चली गई; तब राजा (रत्न-सेन) को वसन्त-ऋतु की याद हुई, अर्थात् वसन्त-ऋतु की शोभा देखते-ही बेहोश हो गया था; होश होते-ही उस वसन्त की सुधि हुई। जो जागा (तो देखता है कि) न वसन्त है न वाटिका है वा न वे बालिकाएँ हैं; न वह खेल है, न वे खेलन-हारी (नवयौवना युवती) ही हैं। और न उन के शोभित रूप ही हैं; (वह पद्मावती) लोप हो गई, फिर दृष्टि में न आई। फूल झड पडे, फुलवारी सूख गई; (राजा की) दृष्टि सब भस्म हो कर राख हुई, और उकठी फुलवारी पर पडी। (रोने लगा कि हाय) किस ने इस बसते वसन्त को उजाड दिया; (हा वह) चन्द्र (पद्मावती का रूप) चला गया; (सब) ताराओं (सखिओं) को ले कर अस्त हो गया। अब उस के विना संसार अन्ध-कूप हो गया; (हा) वह (पद्मावती-रूप चन्द्र)

सुख से छाया में (जा कर बैठा) है, और मैं धूप में जलता हूँ। (हा इस) जरती हुई विरहाग्नि को कौन ठंढी करे, और कौन प्रियतम (पद्मावती) से भेंट करावे।

देखा कि हृदय में जो चन्दन घेवरा है उस में लिखा है कि मिल कर वियोग हुआ है, अर्थात् मैं तुम से मिलो पर तुमारे सो जाने से मिलना न मिलना बराबर हो गया; (इस लेख के पढते-ही) वह (रत्न-सेन) हाथ मल मल कर और शिर को पीट पीट कर रोने लगा, कि (हाय मैं ऐसा क्यों सो गया) ऐसा (वही) सोता है जो कि निचिंत (बेफिक्र) हो॥ २०४॥

चउपाई।

जस बिछोउ जल मीन दुहेला। जल हुति काढि अगिनि मँह मेला॥
चंदन आँक दाग होइ परे। बुझहिँ न ते आखर परजरे॥
जनु सर आगि होइ होइ लागे। सब बन दागि सिंघ बन दागे॥
जरहिँ मिरिग बन-खँड तेहि ज्वाला। अउ ते जरहिँ बइठ तेहि छाला॥
कित ते आँक लिखे जिन्ह सोआ। मकु आँकन्ह तेहि करत बिछोआ॥
जइस दुखँत कहँ साकूँतला। माधउनलहि कामकंदला॥
भएउ अंग नल जइस दमावति। नयनाँ मूँदि छपी पदुमावति॥

दोहा।

आइ बसता छपि रहा होइ फूलन्ह के भेस।
केहि बिधि पावउँ भवँर होइ कउनु सो गुरु उपदेस॥ २०५॥

जस = जैसे = यथा। बिछोउ = विच्छुरड = बिछुडना = वियोग। जल = पानी। मीन = मछली। दुहेला = दुःखी = दुखिया। हुति = से। काढि = काढ कर (आकृष्य) = खींच कर। अगिनि = अग्नि = आग। मेला = मेलइ (मेलयति) का भूत-काल में प्रथम-पुरुष का एक-वचन। आँक = अङ्क = चिह्न = अक्षर। दाग = निशान = दग्ध स्थान। होइ = हो कर (भूला)। परे = परइ (पतति) का भूत-काल में प्रथम-पुरुष का बहु-वचन। बुझहिँ = बुझइ (व्यवचायति = प्राकृत वोज्झेइ) का बहु-वचन। आखर = अक्षर। परजरे = परजरइ (प्रज्वलति) का भूत-काल में प्रथम-पुरुष का बहु-वचन। सर = शर = वाण। आगि =

अग्नि। लागे = लगइ, वा लागइ (लगति) का भूत-काल में प्रथम-पुरुष का बहु-वचन। बन = वन = जङ्गल। दागि = दग्ध्वा = जला कर। सिंघ = सिंह। दागे = दगधइ (दहति) का भूत-काल में प्रथम-पुरुष का बहु-वचन। जरहिँ = जरइ (ज्वलति) का बहु-वचन। मिरिग = मृग = हरिण। बन-खँड = वन-खण्ड = वनविभाग। ज्वाला = ज्वलन = तेज वा अग्नि। बइठ = बैठते हैँ (उपविशन्ति)। छाला = छाल = चैल = मृगचैल। कित = कुतः = क्योँ। लिखे = लिखे गए। सोग्रा = स्वपित = सोआ है। मकु = मैँ कहा = क्या जानैँ। आँकन्ह = आँक का बहु-वचन। करत = करते हैँ (कुर्वन्ति)। बिछोआ = विच्छुरित = वियोगी। जइस = जैसे = यथा। दुखँत = दुष्यन्त, एक प्रसिद्ध राजा। सकुँतला = शकुन्तला = मेनका की पुत्री, कण्व से जो पाली गई। माधउनलहि = माधवानल को; माधवानल एक प्रसिद्ध गुणी, जो सङ्गीतशास्त्र मैँ बहुत निपुण था। कामकंदला = एक वेश्या। नल = एक प्रसिद्ध राजा। दमावति = दमयन्ती = विदर्भदेश के राजा भीमसेन की पुत्री। नयनाँ = नयन का बहु-वचन = आँखैँ। मूँदि = मूँद कर (आमुद्य) = बंद कर। छपी = छपइ (औत्क्षिपत् प्रक्षेपणे से छिपते) का भूत-काल मैँ स्त्रीलिङ्ग का एक-वचन। पदुमावति = पद्मावती ॥

आइ = आ कर = एत्य। वसंता = वसन्त-ऋतु। छपि रहा = छिप रहा। फूलन्ह = फूल का बहु-वचन। भेस = वेष = सूरत। पावउँ = पावइ (प्राप्नोति) का सम्भावना मैँ उत्तम-पुरुष का एक-वचन। भवँर = भ्रमर = भौँरा। कउनु = को नु = कौन। उपदेस = उपदेश = शिक्षा ॥

जैसे जल के वियोग से मछली दुखिया हो और उसे पानी से निकाल कर आग मैँ डालैँ (उसी प्रकार राजा रत्नसेन की दशा हुई); (हृदय मैँ) चन्दन के (लिखे हुए) अक्षर के दाग पड गए वे अक्षर बुझते नहीँ प्रज्वलित हो गए। जानौँ (वे अक्षर) दाग के बाण हो हो कर (रत्न-सेन के हृदय मैँ) लगे हैँ; (वे अक्षर) सब वन को दाग कर वन मैँ सिंह को दागे हैँ (कवि की उत्प्रेक्षा है कि वन के वृक्षोँ मैँ स्थान स्थान पर जो चिन्ह हैँ उन्हेँ चिह्न न समझो, किन्तु वे उन्हीँ अक्षरोँ के दागे हुए चिन्ह हैँ और सिंह के अङ्ग मैँ जो स्थान स्थान पर काले चिन्ह हैँ वे भी उन्हीँ अक्षरोँ के दाग हैँ)। उन्हीँ (अक्षरोँ) की ज्वाला से वनविभाग मैँ (कभीँ कभीँ) हरिण जल जाते हैँ, अर्थात् उन्हीँ अक्षरोँ से दावाग्नि उत्पन्न होती है; और जो तिस (राजा के आसन) मृग-छाला पर बैठ जाते हैँ वे भी जरने लगते हैँ।

जो (पुरुष स्वस्थ हो कर) सोया था (उस के हृदय में) क्योँ वे अचर लिखे गए; क्या जानँ वे अचर ही विरह (दुःख) को करते हैँ, अर्थात् यदि अचर न लिखे होते तो राजा को विरह-दुःख न होता; अचरोँ ही के कारण राजा को ज्ञान ऊत्रा, कि पद्मावती आ कर चली गई, इस लिये विरह-दुःख का कारण अचर ही हैँ। जैसे दुष्यन्त को शकुन्तला ने, माधवानल को काम-कन्दला ने विरह-दुःख दिया। और जैसे दमयन्ती के वियोग से नल के अङ्ग की दशा ऊई (वैसी ही राजा रत्न-सेन की दशा ऊई); (राजा रत्न-सेन की) आँखोँ को बंद कर पद्मावती लोप हो गई॥

दुष्यन्त पुरुवंशियोँ मेँ प्रधान पुरुष थे; इन से विश्वामित्र के वीर्य से मेनका अप्सरा से उत्पन्न शकुन्तला का विवाह ऊत्रा था। प्रत्यच विवाह होने के पूर्व वन मेँ कण्व के आश्रम में दुष्यन्त और शकुन्तला से प्रथम भेँट ऊई थी और परस्पर वचनप्रमाण से एक प्रकार का विवाह हो गया था; पीछे से गर्भवती शकुन्तला जब राजा के पास गई तब राजा को शकुन्तला के साथ वन मेँ विवाह करना भूल गया इस लिये उस को भार्या न बनाया; इस से वह बऊत व्याकुल ऊई। पुत्री की ऐसी दशा देख मेनका उठा ले गई। फिर विवाह का होना स्मरण कर दुष्यन्त शकुन्तला के विरह से बऊत ही व्याकुल ऊत्रा था; भारत आदिपर्व, अध्याय ६८-७४ मेँ इस की सविस्तर कथा लिखी ऊई है; पद्मपुराण मेँ भी कुछ भिन्न प्रकार से इस की कथा है। कालिदास ने जो शाकुन्तल नाटक को बनाया है उस मेँ प्रायः पद्मपुराण ही की बऊत कथा है।

माधवानल एक ब्राह्मण था। कामकन्दला पर आसक्त हो गया था। उस के विरह से व्याकुल हो कर हा कामकन्दला, हा कामकन्दला, कहता इधर उधर बौरहा सा फिरा करता था। इस की सविस्तर कथा सिंहासन-बतीसी की २१ वीँ कहानी मेँ है। राजा नल वीर-सेन के पुत्र थे; और दमयन्ती विदर्भ-राज भीम-सेन की पुत्री थी; नल ने हंस से दमयन्ती की प्रशंसा सुन उस के विरह से बऊत ही व्याकुल ऊत्रा था। इस की कथा भारत वनपर्व ५२-८९ अध्यायोँ मेँ विस्तरपूर्वक है। इसी की छाया से श्रीहर्ष ने नैषध काव्य लिखा है॥

(राजा रत्न-सेन विलप रहा है कि) वसन्त (पद्मावती) आ कर फूलोँ के वेष मेँ हो कर छिप रहा, अर्थात् वसन्त-रूप पद्मावती फूल हो कर राज-मन्दिर मेँ चली गई; सो भ्रमर हो कर (उसे) किस प्रकार से पाऊँ; कौन ऐसा वह गुरु है जो (इस विषय मेँ) उपदेशे, अर्थात् शिचा दे॥ २०५॥

चउपाई ।

रोअइ रतन माल जनु चूरा । जहँ होइ ठाढ होइ तहँ कूरा ॥
कहाँ बसंत सो कोकिल बइना । कहाँ कुसुम अलि बेधी नइना ॥
कहाँ सो मूरति परी जो डीठी । काढि लीन्ह जिउ हिअइ पईठी ॥
कहाँ सो दरस परस जेहि लाहा । जउँ सो बसंत करीलहि काहा ॥
पात बिछोउ रूख जो फूला । सो महुआ रोअइ अस भूला ॥
टपकहिँ महुअ आँसु तस परही । होइ महुआ बसंत जउँ झरही ॥
मोर बसंत सो पदुमिनि बारी । जेहि बिनु भएउ बसंत उजारी ॥

दोहा ।

पावा नउल बसंत पुनि बहु आरति बहु चोपु ।
अइस न जाना अंत होइ पात झरहिँ होइ कोपु ॥ २०६ ॥

रोअइ = रोता है (रोदिति)। रतन = रत्न-सेन । माल = माला = मुक्ता-माला । चूरा = चूर्ण । ठाढ = खडा = स्थित । कूरा = कूट = ढेरी । बसंत = वसन्त । कोकिल = एक प्रसिद्ध काले वर्ण का पची जो वसन्त-ऋतु मेँ बोलता है; इसे पिक भी कहते हैँ; भाषा मेँ कोयल नाम से प्रसिद्ध है। बइना = बैन = वचन । कुसुम = पुष्प । अलि = भ्रमर । बेधी = बेधइ = (विध्यति) का भूत-काल मेँ स्त्रीलिङ्ग का एक-वचन । नइना = नयन = आँख । मूरति = मूर्त्ति । परी = परइ (पतति) का भूत-काल मेँ स्त्रीलिङ्ग का एक-वचन । डीठी = दृष्टि। काढि = काढ = कर्षण। लीन्ह = लेइ (लाति) का भूत-काल। जिउ = जीव । हिअइ = हृदय मेँ। पईठी = पैठि = पैठ कर (प्रविश्य)। दरस = दर्शन । परस = स्पर्श । जेहि = जिस का । लाहा = लाभ । जउँ = यदि = जौं । करीलहि = करील को, करील एक प्रकार का वृच है जो कि वृन्दावन मेँ बहुत प्रसिद्ध है, वसन्त मेँ सब वृचोँ मेँ नए पत्ते उत्पन्न होते हैँ परन्तु करील मेँ नए पत्ते नहीँ होते, यह वृच प्रायः बेपत्ते का होता है। पात = पत्ता = पत्र । बिछोउ = विच्छुरण = वियोग । रूख = वृच । फूला = फूलइ (फुल्लति) का भूत-काल मेँ पुंलिङ्ग का एक-वचन । महुआ = मधूक = एक प्रसिद्ध वृच । अस = ऐसा = एतादृश । भूला = भूला हुआ ।

टपकहिँ = टपकइ (प्रपतति) का बक्र-वचन । आँसु = अश्रु = आँस । तस = तैसा = तथा । परहीँ = परइ (पतति) का बक्र-वचन । जउँ = ज्योँ = यथा । झरहीँ = झरइ (झरति) का बक्र-वचन । बारी = वाटिका । उजारी = उजार = उज्जरण ॥

पावा = पावइ (प्राप्नोति) का भूत-काल । आरति = आर्त्त = दुःख = आतुरी । चोपु = चोप = वेग = इच्छा । अइस = ऐसा । जाना = जानइ (जानाति) का भूत-काल । अंत = अन्त मेँ = आखिर मेँ । कोपु = कोप = पल्लव ॥

रतन (राजा रत्न-सेन) रोने लगा (आँसुओँ की पङ्क्ति जान पडती है कि) जानोँ चूर हो कर, अर्थात् टूट कर मुक्ता-माला गिरती हो; जहाँ खडा होता है तहाँ ही मोतिओँ की ढेर हो जाती है। (विलपने लगा, कि हाय) वह वसन्त, वह कोकिल सा वचन, कहाँ है और जिस फूल ने नयन-भ्रमर को बेध दिया वह फूल कहाँ है। जिस मूर्त्ति पर दृष्टि पडी थी वह कहाँ है; (उस) मूर्त्ति ने हृदय मेँ पैठ कर जी को निकाल लिया। (मेरी ऐसी भाग्य) कहाँ जिस से (पद्मावती के) दर्शन और स्पर्श का लाभ हो; यदि वह वसन्त-ऋतु हो भी तो करील को क्या (भर्तृहरि ने भी नीति-शतक मेँ लिखा है कि 'पत्त्रं नैव यदा करील-विटपे दोषो वसन्तस्य किम्')। पत्तोँ के बिछुडने पर (और) जो वृक्ष हैँ वे फूलते हैँ (परन्तु) वह मऊआ ही है जो (पत्तोँ के बिछुडने पर मेरे) ऐसा भूला ऊआ रोता है (आँसुओँ के बूँद सा, बक्रत दिनोँ तक टपटप फूलोँ को टपकाया करता है)। मऊआ उसी प्रकार टपकते हैँ जैसे कि (मेरी) आँस; वसन्त-ऋतु मेँ जैसे मऊआ झरते हैँ (उसी प्रकार) मऊआ हो कर (मेरी आँस) झरती हैँ। मेरा वसन्त पद्मावती वाला है; जिस के विना (मेरे लिये) वसन्त उजाड हो गया॥

फिर बक्रत आर्त्त (नाद) और आतुरी से नूतन वसन्त को पाया; ऐसा नहीँ जाना, कि पल्लव हो कर, अन्त मेँ (सब) पत्ते झड जाते हैँ, अर्थात् यह न समझा था कि वसन्तागम मेँ पल्लव होते ही पत्ते झड जायँगे (पद्मावती आते ही फिर लौट जायगी)॥ २०६ ॥

चउपाई ।

अरे मलेछ बिसुआसी देवा। कित मइँ आइ कीन्ह तोरि सेवा ॥
आपुनि नाउ चढइ जो देई। सो तउ पार उतारइ खेई ॥

सुफल लागि पगु टेकेउँ तोरा। सुआ क सेवँरि तूँ भा मोरा॥
पाहन चढि जो चहइ भा पारा। सो अइसइ बूडइ मँझ धारा॥
पाहन सेवा कहा पसीजा। जरम न पलुहइ जउँ निति भीँजा॥
बाउर सोइ जो पाहन पूजा। सकति क भार लेइ सिर दूजा॥
काहे न पूजिअ सोइ निरासा। मुए जिअत मन जा करि आसा॥

दोहा।

सिंघ तरँदा जेइँ गहा पार भए तेहि साथ।
ते पइ बूडे बारि ही भेंड पूँछि जिन्ह हाथ॥ २०७॥

अरे = अरे = नीच सम्बोधन। मलेछ = म्लेच्छ। बिसुआसी = विश्वाशी = विश्व (संसार) को खाने-वाला। कित = कुतः = क्योँ। मइँ = मैँ। आइ = आ कर = एत्य। कीन्ह = करइ (करोति) का भूत-काल। तोरि = तोरी = तेरी। सेवा = टहल। आपुनि = अपनी। नाउ = नाव = नौका। चढइ = चढने। जो = यः। देई = देइ (दत्ते) = देता है। सो = सः = वह। तउ = तो = तर्हि। उतारइ = उतारता है (उत्तारयति)। खेई = खे कर (खेट्ट खेदायाम्)। सु-फल = सुन्दर फल के लिये। लागि = लग कर = लिये। पगु = प्रग = पैर। टेकेउँ = टेकइ (टङ्कति) का सम्भावना मेँ उत्तम-पुरुष का एक-वचन। सुआ = शुक। क = का। सेवँरि = शाल्मलि = सेमर; जिस के फल मेँ रस नहीँ रहता केवल रूई भरी रहती है। तूँ = त्वम्। भा = भया (बभूव)। पाहन = पाषाण = पत्थल। चढि = चढ कर। चहइ = चाहता है (इच्छति)। अइसइ = ऐसे ही = एतादृशो हि। बूडइ = बूडता है = डूबता है (ब्रुड मज्जने, ब्रुडति)। मँझ = मध्य। कहा = कथम् = कैसे। पसीजा = पसीजइ = पसीजे = प्रस्वेदित हो। जरम = जन्म। पलुहइ = पनपता है (पल्लवयति)। जउँ = जौँ = यदि। निति = नित्य। भीँजा = अभ्यञ्जित। बाउर = वातुल = बौरहा। सोइ = स एव = वही। पूजा = पूज = पूजइ (पूजयति)। सकति = शक्यते। क = क्व = कहाँ। भार = बोझा। लेइ = लेवे। सिर = शिर। दूजा = दूसरा = द्वितीय। काहे न = किमु न = क्योँ नहीँ। पूजिअ = पूजिए (पूजयेः) = पूजो। निरासा = निराशः = आशा से रहित = परमेश्वर। मुए = मरने पर। जिअत = जीते = जीवन्। जा करि = जिस की। आसा = आशा॥

सिंघ = सिंह। तरँदा = तैरिंद = तैरने-वाला जन्तु। जेइँ = जिन्हों ने। गहा = पकडा = गहद्द (गृह्णाति) का भूत-काल। भए = ऊए (= बभूवुः)। तेहि = तिसी के = उसी के। साथ = सार्थ = संग। पइ = अपि = निश्चय। बूडे = बूडइ का भूत-काल में प्रथम-पुरुष का बऊ-वचन। बारि ही = पानी में। भेंड = भेंडा = मेड = मेष। पूँछि = पुच्छ = पोंछ। जिन्ह = जिन्ह के। हाथ = हस्त॥

(राजा रत्न-सेन विलप कर कहने लगा, कि) अरे विश्व को (ठग ठग कर) खाने वाला म्लेच्छ देव; मैं ने क्यों आ कर तेरी सेवा की। जो अपनी नाव पर चढने देता है; वह तो खे कर पार उतार देता है (तैं ने क्यों मुझे डुबा दिया)। सुन्दर फल के लिये तेरे पैर को टेका (पकडा); (सो) तूं मेरे लिये शुक का सेमर ऊआ (शुक सेमर के फल को सरस जान उस में चोंच लगाता है परन्तु चोंच में नीरस रूई लपट जाने से रस के बदले दुःख ही पाता है)। (सच है) जो पत्थल (की नाव) पर चढ कर पार ऊआ चाहता है; वह ऐसे ही (मेरे ऐसे) बीच धारा में डूबता है। पत्थल सेवा से कैसे पसीजे। यदि नित्य (पानी से) भींगा रहे तौ भी जन्म भर में (वह) नहीं पनफता है, अर्थात् रत्ती भर भी नहीं बढता है। जो पत्थल पूजता है वही (सच्चा) पागल है; (परमेश्वर को छोड) दूसरा कहाँ (किसी का) भार ले सकता है। (इस लिये) उसी निराश्र परमेश्वर को क्यों न पूजिए; जिस की आशा मरने और जीने दोनों में लगी रहती है॥

जिन्हों ने तैरने-वाले जानवरों में जो सिंह अर्थात् श्रेष्ठ है उस को पकडा वे उस के साथ ही साथ पार हो गए; पर जिन के हाथ में भेंड की पुच्छ है, अर्थात् जो भेंड की पुच्छ पकड कर पार ऊआ चाहे, वे अवश्य पानी में डूब गए। (सो भेंड की पुच्छ-सदृश इस देवता के पैर को मैं ने व्यर्थ ही पकडा)॥ २०७॥

चउपाई।

देओ कहा सुनु बउरे राजा। देओहि अगुमन मारा गाजा॥
जो पहिलइँ अपुनइ सिर परई। सो का काहु क धरहरि करई॥
पदुमावति राजा कइ बारी। आइ सखिन्ह सउँ मँडफ उघारी॥
जइसइ चाँद गोहन सब तारा। परउँ भुलाइ देखि उँजिआरा॥
चमकइ दसन बीजु कइ नाईँ। नयन-चकर जमकात भवाँईँ॥

हउँ तेहि दीप पतँग होइ परा । जिउ जम काढि सरग लेइ धरा ॥
बहुरि न जानउँ दहुँ का भई । दहुँ कबिलास कि कहँ अपसई ॥

दोहा ।

अब हउँ मरउँ निसासी हिअइ न आवइ साँस ।
रोगिआ की को चालइ बइदहि जहाँ उपास ॥ २०८ ॥

देश्रो = देव । कहा = कहइ (कथयति) का भूत-काल में प्रथम-पुरुष का एक-वचन । बउरे = वातुल = बौरहे । देश्रोहि = देव को । अगुमन = आगमन = आगे ही = पहले । मारा = मारइ (मारयति) का भूत-काल का एक-वचन । गाजा = गर्जन = विद्युत् । पहिलइँ = पहले ही = प्रथम एव । सिर = शिर । परई = परइ (पतति) । का = क्या = किम् । काहू क = किसी का । धरहरि = धरहरिया = धर-धर = पकड कर रचा करना । करई = करे (कुर्यात्) । कइ = की । बारी = वालिका = वाला = कन्या । आइ = आ कर (एत्य) । सखिन्ह = सखी का बहु-वचन । सउँ = सेाँ = से । मँडफ = मण्डप । उघारी = उघारइ (उद्घाटयति) का भूत-काल, स्त्रीलिङ्ग, एक-वचन । जइसइ = जैसे = यथा । चाँद = चन्द्र । गोहन = गोपन = संग । परेउँ = परइ (पतति) सम्भावना में, उत्तम-पुरुष, एक-वचन । भुलाइ = भूल कर (भ्रान्त्वा) । देखि = देख कर = दृष्ट्वा । उँजिआरा = उज्ज्वलता = उँजेला । चमकइ = चमकता है (संस्कृत में लिट् के प्रथम-पुरुष का एक-वचन चकासे) । दसन = दशन = दाँत । बीजु = विद्युत् = बिजुरी । कइ = की । नाईं = निभ = सदृश । नयन = नेत्र । चकर = चक्र = चक्कर । जमकात = यम-कर्त्तरी = एक प्रकार की प्राण लेने-वाली कैंची । भवाँईं = भवाँवइ (भ्रामयति) का भूत-काल, स्त्रीलिङ्ग, प्रथम-पुरुष का बहु-वचन । हउँ = हौं = मैं । दीप = दीया = दीपक = चिराग । पतँग = पतङ्ग = फतिंगा = कीट । होइ = हो कर (भूत्वा) । परा = परइ (पतति) का भूत-काल, पुंलिङ्ग, उत्तम-पुरुष का एक-वचन । जिउ = जीव । जम = यम = यम-राज । काढि (आकृष्य) = खींच कर = निकाल कर । सरग = स्वर्ग । लेइ = ले कर = आलाय । धरा = धरइ (धरति) का भूत-काल, प्रथम-पुरुष, एक-वचन । बहुरि = भूयः = पुनः = फिर । जानउँ = जानइ (जानाति) का उत्तम-पुरुष, एक-वचन = जानता हूँ । दहुँ = दुहुँ = दोनों में से = किं वा । कबिलास = कैलास । कि = अथवा = किं वा । कहँ = कहाँ = कुत्र । अपसई = अपसरइ (अपसरति) का भूत-काल, स्त्रीलिङ्ग, एक-वचन ॥

अब = अधुना = इदानीम्। मरउँ = मरइ (मरति) का उत्तम-पुरुष में एक-वचन। निसासी = निःश्वासी = बेदम का। हिअइ = हृदय में। आवइ = आयाति = आती है। साँस = श्वास। रोगिआ = रोगी। चालइ = चलावे (चालयेत्)। बइदहि = वैद्य को। जहाँ = यत्र। उपास = उपवास = फाँका ॥

(रत्न-सेन के कटु-वचन कहने पर) देव ने कहा कि अरे पगला राजा सुन; देव को तो पहले ही बिजुरी ने मार दिया। जो पहले ही अपने शिर के बल गिर पडता है वह क्या किसी की धरहरिया करे। (सुन) राजा (गन्धर्व-सेन) की कन्या पद्मावती ने सखिओं के साथ मण्डप में आ कर, (अपने मुह को) खोला। (उस बेला में सखिओं के मुख के संग उस के मुख की ऐसी शोभा हुई) जैसे चाँद के साथ सब तारा हों; (सो उस) उँजेले को देख कर मैं भ्रम में पड गया। विद्युत् की नाईं (उस के) दाँत चमकते हैं, अर्थात् चमकते थे; आँखों के चक्र (जानों) यम-कर्त्तरी को फेरते थे। मैं उसी नयनचक्र-रूपी दीप में फतिंगा हो कर गिर पडा; यमराज ने (मेरे) जीव को निकाल कर, स्वर्ग में रख दिया। (मैं बेहोश हो गया) फिर नहीं जानता कि (वह पद्मावती) क्या हो गई; कैलास में चली गई कि कहाँ सरक गई (सो मैं नहीं कह सकता) ॥

अब मैं (स्वयं उस के लिये) बेदम का हो कर मर रहा हूँ; हृदय में साँस नहीं आती है; (सो हे राजा) जहाँ वैद्य ही उपवास कर रहा है वहाँ रोगी की कौन (बात) चलावे, अर्थात् मैं देवता हो कर जब मर रहा हूँ तब तुम्हारी सहायता क्या करूँ ॥ २०८ ॥

चउपाई।

अनु हउँ दोस देउँ का काहू। संगी कया मया नहिँ ताहू ॥
हतेउ पिआरा मीत बिछोई। साथ न लागि आपु गा सोई ॥
का मइँ कीन्ह जो काया पोखी। दूखन मोहिँ आपु निरदोखी ॥
फागु बसंत खेलि गइ गोरी। मो तनु लाइ आगि देइ होरी ॥
अब अस काहि छार सिर मेलउँ। छारइ होउँ फागु तस खेलउँ ॥
कित तप कीन्ह छाडि कइ राजू। आहर गएउ न भा सिध काजू ॥
पाएउँ नहिँ होइ जोगी जती। अब सर चढउँ जरउँ जस सती ॥

दोहा ।

आइ पिरीतम फिरि गया मिला न आइ बसंत ।
अब तन होरी घालि कइ जारि करउँ भसमंत ॥ २०९ ॥

अनु = पश्चात् = पीछे । हउँ = हौं = मैं । दोस = दोष । देउँ = देऊँ = देइ (दत्ते) का सम्भावना, उत्तम-पुरुष का एक-वचन । का = क्या = किमु । काह्न = किसी को । संगी = सङ्गी = साथी । कया = काय = शरीर = देह । मया = माया = मोह । ताह्न = तिस को भी । हतेउ = हतइ (हन्ति) का भूत-काल, पुंलिङ्ग, प्रथम-पुरुष का एक-वचन । पिआरा = प्यारा । मीत = मित्र । बिछोई = बिछुडा हुआ । साथ = सार्थ = सङ्ग । लागि = लग कर = लगिला । आपु = आप = स्वयम् = आत्मा । गा = गया (अगात्) । सोई = वह । मइँ = मैं । कीन्ह = करइ (करोति) का भूत-काल । काया = काय = शरीर । पोखी = पोखइ (पोषयति) का भूत-काल, स्त्रीलिङ्ग, प्रथम-पुरुष का एक-वचन । दूखन = दूषण = दोष । निरदोखी = निर्दोषी = दोष-रहित । फागु = फाल्गुनोत्सव = फगुआ । बसंत = वसन्त-ऋतु । खेलि = खेल कर = (खेलिला) । गइ = गई (अगात्) । गोरी = गौरी = सुन्दर युवती । मो = मेरी । तनु = शरीर = देह । लाइ = लाई = लगाई । आगि = अग्नि । देइ = दे कर = दत्त्वा । होरी = होलिका = होली । अब = अधुना = इदानीम् । अस = ऐसा = एतादृश । काहि = किस के । छार = चार = रचा = राखी = भस्म । सिर = शिर । मेलउँ = मेलइ (मेलयति) का सम्भावना में, पुंलिङ्ग, उत्तम-पुरुष का एक-वचन । छारइ = छार ही = भस्म ही । होउँ = होइ (भवति) का सम्भावना में पुंलिङ्ग, उत्तम-पुरुष का एक-वचन । तस = तैसा = तथा । खेलउँ = खेलइ (खेलति) का सम्भावना में पुंलिङ्ग, उत्तम-पुरुष का एक-वचन । कित = कुतः = क्यों । तप = तपः = तपस्या । छाडि कइ = छोड कर । राजू = राज्य । आहर = आहार = खाना पीना । गएउ = गया (अगात्) । भा = भया = हुआ (बभूव) । सिध = सिद्ध = पूरा । काजू = काय = काम । पाएउँ = पावइ (प्राप्नोति) का भूत-काल, पुंलिङ्ग, उत्तम-पुरुष का एक-वचन । होइ = हो कर (भूत्वा) । जोगी = योगी । जती = यति । सर = शर = शर-चिता । चढउँ = चढइ (उच्चलति) का पुंलिङ्ग, उत्तम-पुरुष का एक-वचन । जरउँ = जरइ (ज्वलति) का पुंलिङ्ग, उत्तम-पुरुष का एक-वचन । जस = जैसे = यथा । सती = साध्वी स्त्री = पतिव्रता ॥

आइ = आ कर (एत्य)। पिरीतम = प्रियतम = सब से प्यारा। फिरि = लौट। गया = अगात्। मिला = मिलइ (मिलति) का भूत-काल। तन = तनु = देह। घालि कइ = घाल कर = नाश कर = गला कर। जारि = जला कर (प्रज्वाल्य)। करउँ = करइ (करोति) का पुंलिङ्ग उत्तम-पुरुष का एक-वचन। भसमंत = भस्म = राख।

(देव-वचन सुन कर राजा कहने लगा कि जब बात बिगड गई तो) पीछे से मैँ क्या किसी को दोष देऊँ; जो शरीर की संगी (पद्मावती) है उस को भी तो मोह नहीँ है (मोह होता तो क्योँ मुझे छोड कर चली जाती)। (सो) प्यारा वियोगी मित्र (पद्मावती) ने (मुझे) मार डाला; साथ न लगा कर, अर्थात् साथ मेँ न हो कर, वह आप (मेरे पास से) चला गया। मैँ ने क्या किया जो देह को पोसा; (सब) दोष मेरे ही मेँ हैँ आप (वह पद्मावती) निर्दोष है। (वह) गौरी-रूपा (पद्मावती) वसन्त मेँ फाग खेल कर चली गई; आग दे कर मेरी शरीर होरी को लगा दिया, अर्थात् फूँक दिया। अब ऐसी (होली की) राख को किस के शिर मेँ लगाऊँ? (कोई हितू संसार मेँ नहीँ देख पडता सो अब) तैसा फाग खेलता हूँ कि (स्वयं मैँ) राख हो जाऊँ। मैँ ने राज्य छोड कर क्योँ (निराहार) तप को किया; (जिस से) आहार गया, अर्थात् भोजन विना मर गया और काम भी पूरा न हुआ। योगी, यती, हो कर भी (पद्मावती को) न पाया तो अब चिता पर चढता हूँ और जैसे पति-व्रता सती स्त्री (पति-वियोग से) जरती है; उसी प्रकार मैँ प्रिया-वियोग से जरता हूँ। (योगी, यति के लिये ३० वेँ दोहे की टीका देखो)।

प्रियतम (पद्मावती) आ कर लौट गया; वसन्त मेँ भी आ कर न मिला। (इस लिये) अब देह को गला कर, और होरी के ऐसा जला कर, भस्म कर देता हूँ॥ २०९॥

चउपाई।

ककनू पंखि जइस सर साजा। तस सर साजि जरइ चह राजा॥
सकल देओता आइ तुलाने। दहुँ कस होइ देओ-असथाने॥
बिरह अगिनि बजरागि असूझा। जरइ सूर न बुझाए बूझा॥
तेहि के जरत जो उठइ बजागी। तीनउँ लोक जरहिँ तेहि लागी॥

अब-हि कि घडी चिनगि पइ छूटिहि । जरिहि पहाड पहन सब फूटिहि ॥
देओता सबइ भसम होइ जाहीँ । छार समेटइ पाउब नाहीँ ॥
धरती सरग होइ सब ताता । हइ होई एहि राख बिधाता ॥

दोहा ।

मुहमद चिनगि परेम कइ सुनि महि गगन डेराइ ।
धनि बिरहिन अउ धनि हिआ जहँ अस अगिनि समाइ ॥ २१० ॥

ककनू = ककनुस (ققنوس یا ققنس)। यह अरबी या यूनानी शब्द है; एक पक्षी का नाम है; इसे फारसी में आतशजन (آتش زن) भी कहते हैँ । पंखि = पक्षी । जइस = जैसे = यथा । सर = शर = सरपत = शर की चिता । साजा = साज = साजइ (सज्जते) । तस = तैसे = तथा । साजि = सज्ज कर = तयार कर । जरइ = जरना । चह = चाहा = चहइ (इच्छति) का भूत-काल, पुंलिङ्ग प्रथम-पुरुष का एक-वचन । सकल = सब । देओता = देवता । आइ = आ कर (एत्य) । तुलाने = पहुँचे । दहुँ = देखैं । कस = कैसा = कथम् । होए = होइ = होता है (भवति) । देओ = देव । असथाने = स्थान मेँ । बिरह = विरह = वियोग । अगिनि = अग्नि = आग । बजरागि = वज्राग्नि । असूझा = देखने योग्य नहीँ = तीव्र । जरइ = (ज्वलति) जरता है । सूर = शूर = बहादुर (रत्न-सेन) । बुझाए = बुझाने से । बूझा = बूझ = बुझइ = बुझती है । जरत = जरते । उठइ = उठे (उत्तिष्ठेत्) । बजागी = वज्राग्नि । जरिहँ = जरँगे = जरइ (ज्वलति) का भविष्यकाल, प्रथम-पुरुष का बहु-वचन । लागी = लगने से । अब-हि = अभी । घडी = घटी = दण्ड = यहाँ समय । चिनगि = चिल्कण = स्फुलिङ्ग = आग की कनी । पइ = अवश्य = अपि । छूटिहि = छूटइ (क्षुद्यते) का भविष्य काल = छूटेगी । जरिहि = जरेगा । पहाड = प्रहार = पर्वत । पहन = पाहन = पाषाण = पत्थल । फूटिहि = फुटइ (स्फुटति) का भविष्यकाल = फूटेगा । सबइ = सभी । भसम = भस्म । जाहीँ = जायँगे । छार = क्षार = राख । समेटइ = समेटने से (संवर्त्तयति से)। पाउब = पावइ (प्राप्नोति) का भविष्यकाल = पावँगे । धरती = धरित्री = जमीन । सरग = स्वर्ग । होइ = होँगे । ताता = तप्त = गर्म । राख = रक्खे = रक्षेत् । बिधाता = विधाता = ब्रह्मा ॥

परेम=प्रेम। कइ=की। सुनि=सुन कर (श्रुत्वा)। महि=मही=पृथिवी। गगन=आकाश। डेराइ=(दरति)=डरता है। धनि=धन्य वा धन्या। बिरहिन=विरहिणी। हिआ=हृदय। जहँ=जहाँ=यत्र। अस=ऐसी=एतादृश। अगिनि=अग्नि। समाइ=समाती है (समेति)॥

ककनू पक्षी जैसे (लकड़िओँ का) चिता बनाता है; वैसे ही चिता बना कर राजा जरना चाहा॥ [यूनान में कहावत है कि ककनुस, फुट पैदा होता है; नर ही होता है इस की मदिया नहीँ होती। यह सङ्गीत-शास्त्र में बड़ा निपुण होता है; सब रागोँ को ठीक ठीक गाता है। जब यह पूरा हजार वर्ष का होता है तब लकड़िओँ का जालीदार खोता बना कर उस के भीतर बैठ जाता है और रागोँ को गाने लगता है; जब दीपक राग गाने लगता है तब खोते में आग भभक उठती है और यह ककनुस जल कर भस्म हो जाता है, फिर इस की राख पर बरसात का पानी पड़ने से एक अंडा पैदा होता है जिस में से फिर एक ककनुस उत्पन्न होता है। इसे वहाँ के लोग आतशजन (آتش زن) भी कहते हैँ; इस लिये संस्कृत में इसे अग्निजन्य कहते हैँ।] (राजा को जलते देख) सब देवता आ कर पहुँचे (और आपस में कहने लगे कि) आश्चर्य है, देव-स्थान में यह कैसी बात होती है। विरहाग्नि वज्राग्नि के ऐसी असूझ है, अर्थात् उस का तेज देखा नहीँ जाता; (उसी में) शूर (रत्न-सेन वीरपुङ्गव) जरता है, जो कि बुझाने से भी नहीँ बुझती। इस के जरते जो वज्राग्नि उठेगी उस के लगने से तीनोँ लोक (आकाश, पाताल, भूलोक) जल जायँगे। अभी इसी समय अवश्य चिनगिआँ छटकँगी (जिन से) पहाड़ जल जायगा और सब पत्थल फूट जायँगे (फूट फूट कर टुकड़े टुकड़े हो जायँगे)। सब देवता भस्म हो जायँगे। हम लोग उन की राख समेटने से भी नहीँ पावँगे। पृथ्वी और स्वर्ग सब तप जायँगे; (सो) हे विधाता (इस समय ऐसा) कोई है जो इस (राजा) को (जलने से) बचावे॥

महम्मद कवि कहते हैँ प्रेम(-अग्नि) की (ऐसी) चिनगी है (जिस का नाम ही) सुन कर, पृथ्वी और आकाश डर जाते हैँ। धन्य विरहिणी और धन्य (उस का) हृदय है जहाँ कि ऐसी अग्नि समा जाती है, अर्थात् प्रेमाग्नि से राजा तो जलने लगा, पर धन्य विरहिणी पद्मावती है जिस ने इस आग को समेट कर अपने हृदय में रख लिया; गुरुजनोँ में प्रकाश होने न दिया॥ २१०॥

चउपाई ।

हनुवँत बीर लंक जेइँ जारी। परबत उहइ अहा रखवारी॥
बइठ तहाँ होइ लंका ताका। छठएँ मास देइ उठि हाँका॥
तेहि कइ आगि उहउ पुनि जरा। लंका छाडि पलंका परा॥
जाइ तहाँ वेइँ कहा सँदेसू। पारबती अउ जहाँ महेसू॥
जोगी आहि बिओगी कोई। तुम्हरेइ मँडफ आगि तेइ बोई॥
जरे लँगूर सु-राते ऊहाँ। निकसि जो भाग भएउँ कर-मूहाँ॥
तेहि बजरागि जरइ हउँ लागा। बजर-अंग जरतहि उठि भागा॥

दोहा ।

राओन-लंका हउँ डही वेइँ मोहिँ डाढन आइ।
घनइ पहार होत हइ रावट को राखइ गहि पाइ॥ २११॥

इति राजा-रतन-सेन-सती-खंड॥ २१॥

हनुवँत = हनुमान् = हनुमंत। बीर = वीर = बहादुर। लंक = लङ्का = रावण-राजधानी। जेइँ = येन = जिस ने। जारी = जारइ (ज्वालयति) का भूत-काल, स्त्रीलिङ्ग प्रथम-पुरुष का एक-वचन। परबत = पर्वत = पहाड। उहइ = वही = उसी। अहा = था = आसीत्। रखवारी = रखवाली = रक्षापाल = रक्षा के लिये नियुक्त। बइठ = बैठा = बैठा हुआ = (उपविष्ट)। होइ = हो कर (भूला)। ताका = ताक = ताकइ (तर्कयति) = देखा करता है। छठएँ = षष्ठे = छठवेँ। मास = महीना। देइ = (दत्ते) देता है। उठि = उठ कर (उत्थाय)। हाँका = हाँक = हुङ्कार। कइ = की। आगि = अग्नि। उहउ = वह-भी। पुनि = पुनः = फिर। जरा = जलने लगा। छाडि = छोड कर (छुर वा छुट छेदने से)। पलंका = पर्यङ्क = पलँग = शय्या। परा = परइ (पतति) का भूत-काल, पुंलिङ्ग प्रथम-पुरुष का एक-वचन। जाइ = जा कर (आयाय)। वेइँ = उन्हों ने। कहा = कहइ (कथयति) का भूत-काल, पुंलिङ्ग प्रथम-पुरुष का एक-वचन। सँदेसू = सन्देश = सँदेसा। पारबती = पार्वती = पर्वत हिमालय की लडकी। जहाँ = यत्र। महेसू = महेश = महादेव। जोगी = योगी। आहि = है (अस्ति)। बिओगी = वियोगी = विरही।

कोई = कोऽपि। तुम्हारे-इ = तुम्हारे-ही। मँडफ = मण्डप। बोई = बोअइ (वपति) का भूत-काल, स्त्रीलिङ्ग प्रथम-पुरुष का एक-वचन। लँगूर = लाङ्गूल = पोंछ। सु-राते = सु-रक्त = सुन्दर ललित। जहाँ = वहाँ। निकसि = निकल कर (निःकाश्य)। भाग = भागा। कर-मूहाँ = कर-मुहाँ = काला मुख। बजरागि = वज्राग्नि। जरइ = जलने। हउँ = मैं। लागा = लगा। बजर-अंग = वज्राङ्ग = वज्र-देह ॥

राओन-लंका = रावण-लङ्का। डही = डहइ = दहइ (दहति) का भूत-काल, स्त्रीलिङ्ग प्रथम-पुरुष का एक-वचन। डाढन = डाढने = दाहने = जलाने। आइ = आई = आवइ (आयाति) का भूतकाल, स्त्रीलिङ्ग प्रथम-पुरुष का एक-वचन। घन इ = घन-ही = कठिन-ही। पहार = पहाड = प्रहार = पर्वत। रावट = आवर्त्तन = पिघल कर एक हो जाना = गल कर एक हो जाना = राख हो जाना। राखइ = रक्खे (रचेत्)। गहि = गह कर (गृहीत्वा) = पकड कर। पाइ = पाद = पावँ = पैर ॥

वीर हनूमान् जिन्हों ने लङ्का जारा था, उस पर्वत पर रखवाली के लिये रहा करते थे। (वह) वहीँ बैठे हुए वहीँ से लङ्का को देखा करते हैँ और छठएँ छठएँ मास मेँ उठ कर हाँक दिया करते हैँ (जिस मेँ लङ्का के राचस डरते रहेँ; उत्तर की ओर आ कर भारत के लोगोँ को दुःख न देँ)। तिसी की (रत्न-सेन के चिता की) आग से फिर वे भी जलने लगे; लङ्का को छोड (कैलास मेँ भगे और वहाँ जा कर जलन की वेदना से) पलँग के ऊपर जा कर पड गए। उन्होँ ने वहाँ जा कर जहाँ पार्वती और महादेव थे तहाँ इस सन्देश को कहा। कि कोई विरही योगी है उस ने (हे महादेव जी) तुम्हारे मण्डप मेँ आग को दी है। वहाँ पर मेरा सुन्दर ललित लाङ्गूल जल गया; निकल कर जो भागा तो आग की लवर लग जाने से कर-मुहाँ हो गया। उसी वज्राग्नि से मैँ जलने लगा; वज्राङ्ग (वज्र के ऐसा अङ्ग) जरते-ही मैँ (वहाँ से) उठ कर भागा ॥

रावण की लङ्का को तो मैँ ने जलाया और वह (आग) मुझे जलाने के लिये आई। (सो) कठोर पहाड पिघल कर राख होता है; कौन (रत्न-सेन के) पैर को पकड कर, (प्रार्थना कर, इस समय उस आग से सब के प्राणोँ को) बचावे ॥ २११ ॥

इति राजा-रत्न-सेन-सतखण्डं नामैकविंश-खण्डं समाप्तम् ॥ २१ ॥

अथ पारबती-महेस-खंड ॥ २२ ॥

चउपाई ।

ततखन पहुँचे आइ महेसू । बाहन बइल कुसटि करि भेसू ॥
काँथरि कया हडावरि बाँधे । मूँड माल अउ हतिआ काँधे ॥
सेस-नाग जो कंठइ माला । तनु बिभूति हसती कर छाला ॥
पहुँची रुदर-कवँल कइ गटा । ससि माँथइ अउ सुरसरि जटा ॥
चवँर घंट अउ डवँरू हाथा । गउरी पारबती धनि साथा ॥
अउ हनुवंत बीर सँग आवा । धरे भेस जनु बंदर-छावा ॥
अउतहि कहेन्हि न लावहु आगी । ता करि सपत जरहु जेहि लागी ॥

दोहा ।

कइ तप करइ न पारहु कइ रे नसाएहु जोगु ।
जिअत जीउ कस काढहु कहहु सो मोहिँ बिओगु ॥ २१२ ॥

ततखन = तत्क्षणे = तिसी क्षण में । पहुँचे = पहुँचइ (प्रभुत्यति से, प्रा० पहुच्चइ) का भूत-काल, आदरार्थ पुंलिङ्ग प्रथम-पुरुष का बहु-वचन । आइ = आ कर = एत्य । महेसू = महेश = महादेव । बाहन = वाहन = सवारी । बइल = बैल = बलीवर्द । कुसटि = कुष्ठी = कोढी । करि = कर के = कृत्वा । भेसू = वेष = सूरत । काँथरि = कन्था = गुदरी ।

कथा = काथ = शरीर । हडावरि = अस्थ्यवली = हड्डियों की लडी । बाँधे = बाँधइ (बध्नाति) का भूत-काल, पुंलिङ्ग प्रथम-पुरुष का बहु-वचन । मूँड = मुण्ड । माल = माला । हतिआ = हत्या = हत्या की मूर्त्ति । काँधे = स्कन्धे = कंधा = कंधे पर । सेस-नाग = शेष-नाग = प्रसिद्ध सहस्र शीर्ष का सर्प, जिस पर चीर सागर में लक्ष्मीसहित विष्णु सोते हैं । कंठइ = कण्ठे = कण्ठ में = गले में । तनु = शरीर = देह । बिभूति = विभूति = भस्म । हसती = हस्ती = हाथी । कर = का । छाला = चैल = चर्म । पहुँची = एक आभूषण जो गट्टे (कलाई) में पहनी जाती है; जोधन के दाने ऐसे दो तीन सोने के दाने, पाट में गुहा कर, कलाई में पहनते हैं; उसी को पहुँची कहते हैं; इस प्रान्त में सर्वत्र प्रसिद्ध है । रुदर = रुद्र । कवँल = कमल । रुदर-कवँल = रुद्राक्ष । गटा = गट्टा = कलाई । ससि = शशि = चन्द्र । माँथइ = मस्तक में । सुरसरि = सुर-सरित् = गङ्गा । जटा = केशों की लट । चवँर = चामर । घंट = घण्टा । डवँरू = डमरू = ढक्का । हाथा = हाथ = हस्त । गउरी = गौरी = गौर वर्ण की । पारबती = पार्वती । धनि = धन्या । साथा = साथ = संग । हनुवंत = हनुमान् = हनुमंत । बीर = वीर = शूर । सँग = साथ = संग । आवा = आवइ (आयाति) का भूत-काल, पुंलिङ्ग प्रथम-पुरुष का एक-वचन । धरे = धरइ (धरति) से = धरे हैं । बंदर = वानर । छावा = शाव = बच्चा । अउतहि = आते ही । कहेन्हि = कहे = कहइ (कथयति) का भूत-काल, पुंलिङ्ग प्रथम-पुरुष का बहु-वचन । लावहु = लगावो । आगी = आग = अग्नि । ता करि = तिस की । सपत = शपथ = कसम । जरहु = जरते हो । जेहि लागी = जिस के लिये ॥

कइ = कि । तप = तपः = तपस्या । करइ = करने में । पारहु = पार होते हो = पूरा कर सकते हो । नसाएहु = नाश किया = नसावइ (नाशयति) का भूत-काल, पुंलिङ्ग मध्यम-पुरुष का बहु-वचन । जोगु = योग । जिअत = जीते-ही । जीउ = जीव । कस = कथम् = किमर्थ = क्यों । काढहु = निकालते हो = काढइ (कर्षति) = का सम्भावना में पुंलिङ्ग मध्यम-पुरुष का बहु-वचन । कहहु = कहो = कहइ (कथयति) का विध्यर्थ में पुंलिङ्ग मध्यम-पुरुष का बहु-वचन । बिओगु = वियोग = दुःख ॥

महादेव, बैल के वाहन पर कोढी का वेष कर उसी चण (रत्न-सेन के पास) पहुँचे । शरीर की गुदडी में हड्डिओं की लडी बाँधे हैं; (मरे आदमिओं के) मूँड की माला (पहने हैं) और हत्या की मूर्त्ति कन्धे पर लिए हैं । शेष-नाग जो है उस की माला कण्ठ में है; शरीर में भस्म और हाथी का चर्म है । महिषासुर का पुत्त्र गजासुर

जब देवताओँ को बज़त दुःख देने लगा। तब देवोँ की प्रार्थना से महादेव ने उस को मारने के लिये त्रिशूल उठाया; और त्रिशूल गोद कर उस की शरीर को छत्र के ऐसा अपने शिर के ऊपर उठा लिया; इस पर उस ने कहा कि मैँ तुम्हारे ऊपर हो गया इस लिये मैँ जीता आप हार गए। इस वचन-चातुरी से महादेव ने प्रसन्न हो कर कहा कि वर माँग; गजासुर ने कहा कि भगवन् यदि प्रसन्न हो तो मुझे मार कर सु-गति दीजिए और मेरे चर्म को अपना वस्त्र बनाइए और आज से आप का एक नाम कृत्ति-वासाः (हाथी का चर्म, जिस का वस्त्र हो) हो। तब से महादेव गज का वस्त्र धारण करते हैँ; काशीखण्ड के ६४वेँ अध्याय मेँ इस की सविस्तर कथा लिखी ज़ई है। गट्टे मेँ रुद्राक्ष की पऊँची है; माथे पर चन्द्रमा और जटा मेँ गङ्गा है। हाथोँ मेँ चामर, घण्ट, और डमरू हैँ; गौरवर्ण की धन्या पार्वती साथ मेँ है। और संग मेँ हनुमान् वीर भी आए; वे ऐसी सूरत बनाए हैँ जानोँ वन्दर का बच्चा हो। (महादेव ने) आते-ही कहा कि आग न लगाओ; तुम्हेँ उसी की कसम है जिस के लिये कि जल रहे हो (थोडा ठहर जाओ बताओ तो)॥

कि तप करने मेँ पूरे नहीँ ज़ए कि (किसी कारण से) योग को नष्ट कर दिया; जीते ही क्योँ जी निकालते हो; उस वियोग-दुःख को मुझ से कहो ॥ २१२ ॥

चउपाई ।

कहेसि को मोहिँ बातहिँ बिरमावा। हतिआ केरि न डर तोहि आवा॥
जरइ देहु दुख जरउँ अपारा। निसितर परउँ जाइ एक बारा॥
जइस भरथरी लाग पिंगला। मो कहँ पदुमावती सिंघला॥
मइँ पुनि तजा राज अउ भोगू। सुनि सो नाउँ लीन्ह तप जोगू॥
एहि मढ सेएउँ आइ निरासा। गइ सो पूजि मन पूजि न आसा॥
तेइँ यह जिउ डाढे पर दाधा। आधा निकसि रहा घट आधा॥
जो अध-जर सो बिलंब न लावा। करत बिलंब बहुत दुख पावा॥

दोहा ।

एतना बोलि कहत मुख उठी बिरह कइ आगि।
जउँ महेस न बुझावत सकल जगत हुत लागि॥ २१३॥

कहेसि = कहा = कहइ (कथयति) का भूत-काल। बातन्हि = बातों में = वार्त्तासु। बिरमावा = बेलम्हाया = विलम्बित किया = भुलवाया। हतिआ = हत्या। डर = भय (दर)। आवा = आवइ (आयाति) का भूत-काल। जरइ = जलने। देहु = देओ। दुख = दुःख। जरउँ = जलता हूं (ज्वलामि)। अपारा = अपार = बेहद। निसितर = निस्तार = निस्तरण। परउँ = परइ (पतति) का उत्तम-पुरुष का एक-वचन। बारा = वार। जइस = जैसे = यथा। भरथरी = भर्त्तृहरि। लाग = लिये। पिङ्गला = दक्षिण-स्वर-नाडी, वा पिङ्गला = एक रानी। सिंघला = सिंहल। मइँ = मैं। पुनि = पुनः = फिर। तजा = तजइ (त्यजति) का भूत-काल, पुंलिङ्ग-उत्तम-पुरुष का एक-वचन। राज = राज्य। भोगू = भोग = विलास। सुनि = सुन कर (श्रुत्वा)। नाउँ = नाम = नावँ। लीन्ह = लेइ (लाति) का भूत-काल, पुंलिङ्ग-उत्तम-पुरुष का एक-वचन। तप = तपः = तपस्या। जोगू = योग। मढ = मठ = मन्दिर। सेएउँ = सेया = सेवइ (सेवते) का भूत-काल, पुंलिङ्ग-उत्तम-पुरुष का एक-वचन। आइ = आ कर = एत्य। निरासा = निराश = ना उम्मेद। गइ = गई (अगात्)। पूजि = पूज कर (सम्पूज्य)। पूजि = पूजी = पूरी हुई = पूजइ (पूर्यते) का भूत-काल, स्त्रीलिङ्ग-प्रथम-पुरुष का एक-वचन। डाढे = जलाने। दाधा = दग्ध किया = दाहइ (दाहयति) का भूत-काल। आधा = अर्ध। निकसि = निकल कर (निःकाश्य)। रहा = रहइ (रहति) का भूत-काल। अध-जर = अध-जरा = आधा जला = अर्धज्वलित। बिलंब = विलम्ब = देरी। लावा = लाव = लावइ = लगाता है। पावा = पाव = पावइ = पाता है॥

एतना = इतना = एतावती। बोलि = बोली = वाक्य। उठी = उठइ (उत्तिष्ठते) का भूत-काल, स्त्रीलिङ्ग प्रथम-पुरुष का एक-वचन। बिरह = विरह = वियोग-दुःख। कइ = की। आगि = अग्नि = आग। जउँ = जौं = यदि। महेस = महेश = महादेव। बुझावत = बुझाते। सकल = सब। जगत = जगत् = संसार। हत = हतती = मार डालती (हन् हिंसायाम् से)। लागि = लग कर (लगित्वा)॥

(महादेव की बात सुन कर राजा ने) कहा कि कौन (तुम) मुझे बातों में अटकाते हो। तुझे हत्या की डर नहीं होती, मैं अपार दुःख से जल रहा हूं (सो मुझे अब शीघ्र) जलने दो; (जिस में जल कर) एक बार ही निस्तार (स्थान) में पडूं, अर्थात् जल कर शीघ्र इस बखेडे से अलग हो जाऊं। (अच्छा मेरी कहानी सुनो) जैसे भर्त्तृहरि को पिङ्गला दक्षिणनाडी वा पिङ्गला रानी लग गई (उसी प्रकार)

सिंहल में मुझे पद्मावती लग गई । उस का नाम सुन कर मैं ने राज्य और भोग-विलास को छोड दिया ; तप और योग को लिया, अर्थात् उस के लिये तपस्या और योगाभ्यास करने लगा । निराश, अर्थात् सब आशा छोड कर (उसी के लिये) इस मठ में (महादेव को) सेया ; सो वह आ कर महादेव को पूज कर चली गई पर मेरे मन की आशा न पूरी हुई, अर्थात् समागमाभिलाष मन ही में रह गया । उसी ने इस जीव को जलाने पर जलाया है ; (अब यह जीव) आधा निकल कर आधा घट (शरीर) में रह गया है । (इस लिये) जो अध-जरा है वह विलम्ब नहीं लगाता ; विलम्ब करने से बहुत दुःख पाता है ॥

इतनी बोली कहते ही (राजा के) मुख से विरह की आग (भभक) उठी । यदि महादेव (दौड कर उस आग को) न बुझाते तो वह (चारो ओर) लग कर सब संसार को मार डालती ॥ २१३ ॥ (भर्तृहरि के लिये १२४ वें दोहे की टीका देखो)

चउपाई ।

पारबती मन उपना चाऊ । देखउँ कुअँर केर सत-भाऊ ॥
दहुँ यह बीच कि पेमहि पूजा । तन मन एक कि मारग दूजा ॥
भइ सु-रूप जानहुँ अपछरा । बिहँसि कुअँर कर आँचर धरा ॥
सुनहु कुअँर मो सउँ एक बाता । जस रँग मोहिँ न अउरहिँ राता ॥
अउ बिधि रूप दीन्ह हइ तो का । उठा सो सबद जाइ सिउ-लोका ॥
तब हउँ तो कहँ इँदर पठाई । गइ पदुमिनि तुइँ आछरि पाई ॥
अब तजु जरन मरन तप जोगू । मो सउँ मानु जरम भरि भोगू ॥

दोहा ।

हउँ आछरि कबिलास कइ जेहि सरि पूज न कोइ ।
मोहिँ तजि सवँरि जो ओहि मरसि कउनु लाभ तोहि होइ ॥ २१४ ॥

पारबती = पार्वती । उपना = उत्पन्न हुआ = उपनइ = उपजइ (उत्पद्यते) का भूतकाल, पुंलिङ्ग-प्रथम-पुरुष का एक-वचन । चाऊ = चाह = इच्छा । देखउँ = देखूँ = देखइ (दृश्यते) का सम्भावना में उत्तम-पुरुष का एक-वचन । सत-भाऊ = सत्य-भाव ।

दऊँ = देखें = क्या जानें। बीच = अन्तर। पेमहि = प्रेम को। पूजा = पूजइ (पूजयति) का पुंलिङ्ग-प्रथम-पुरुष का एक-वचन। तन = तनु = शरीर। मारग = मार्ग = राह। दूजा = दूसरा = द्वितीय। भइ = भई (बभूव)। सु-रूप = सुन्दर रूप = रूपवती। जानऊँ = जानें = जाने। अपछरा = अप्सरा। बिहँसि = विहँस कर (विहस्य)। कुअँर = कुमार = राज-कुमार। आँचर = अञ्चल = वस्त्र का किनारा = वस्त्र का टाँका। धरा = धरइ (धरति) का भूत-काल। सुनऊ = सुनइ (शृणोति) का विध्यर्थ में पुंलिङ्ग-मध्यम-पुरुष का बहु-वचन। मो सउँ = मुझ से। बाता = बात = वार्त्ता। जस = जैसा = यथा। रँग = रङ्ग = वर्ण। अउरहिँ = औरों में = अपरासु। राता = रक्त = ललित = अनुरक्त। बिधि = विधि = ब्रह्मा। रूप = सुन्दरता = खूबसूरती = आकृति। दीन्ह हइ = दिया है। तो का = तुम को। उठा = उठइ (उत्तिष्ठते) का भूत-काल, पुंलिङ्ग-प्रथम-पुरुष का एक-वचन। सबद = शब्द = वाणी। जाइ = जा कर = (प्रयाय)। सिउ-लोका = शिव-लोक = कैलास, यहाँ इन्द्र-लोक। तब = तदा। हउँ = अहम् = हौं = मैं, यहाँ मुझे। तो कहँ = तुझ को = तेरे लिये। इँदर = इन्द्र = देवताओं का राजा। पठाई = पठवइ (प्रेषयति) का भूत-काल। गइ = गई (अगात्)। पदुमिनि = पद्मिनी = पद्मावती। तुइँ = त्वं = तैं ने। आछरि = अप्सरा। पाई = पावइ (प्राप्नोति) का भूत-काल, स्त्रीलिङ्ग-प्रथम-पुरुष का एक-वचन। अब = इदानीम् = अधुना। तजु = त्यज = छोड। जरन = जलना = जरण। मरन = मरण = मरना। तप = तपः = तपस्या। जोगू = योग। मो सउँ = मुझ से। मानु = मानो = मानइ (मन्यते) का विध्यर्थ में पुंलिङ्ग-मध्यम-पुरुष का एक-वचन। जरम = जन्म। जरम भरि = जन्म भर। भोगू = भोग = विलास॥

हउँ = हौं = मैं। कबिलास = कैलास। कइ = की। सरि = सदृश = बराबरी। पूज = पूजइ (पूर्यते) = पूरा होता। तजि = तज कर (सन्त्यज्य) = छोड कर। सवँरि = सुमिर कर (संस्मृत्य) = खयाल कर। मरसि = तूँ मरता है। कउनु = को नु = कौन। लाभ = लब्धि = फायदा। होइ = हइ = है (अस्ति)॥

पार्वती के मन में इच्छा उत्पन्न हुई कि राज-कुमार (रत्न-सेन) का सत्य-भाव तो देखूँ। देखें कि इस (सत्य-भाव) में अन्तर है या (निरन्तर हो कर) प्रेम को पूज लिया है, वा प्रेम से भर गया है, अर्थात् वस्तुतः इस का मन पद्मावती के प्रेम में मग्न हो गया है अथवा झूठा ऊपर का आडम्बर मात्र है। तन मन एक हो गए हैं अथवा तनु का दूसरा मार्ग और मन का दूसरा मार्ग है, अर्थात् भीतर बाहर एक-ही

बात है या भीतर और और बाहर कुछ और ही है। (यह विचार कर पार्वती) ऐसी सुन्दरी ऊई जानों अप्सरा हो गई और हँस कर राज-कुमार के अँचरे को पकड लिया। (कहने लगी कि) कुअँर मुझ से एक बात सुनो; मेरी जैसी रंगत है ऐसी रंगत और किसी में नहीं है। और ब्रह्मा ने तुझे भी सुन्दर रूप दिया है; (सो तुमारी सुन्दरता की) बात शिव लोक में जा कर उठी। तब इन्द्र ने (तेरे लिये) मुझे भेजा; (सो) पद्मावती गई (तो कुछ चिन्ता नहीं उस के बदले) तैं ने अप्सरा पाई। अब जलना, मरना, तप और योग को छोड; मुझ से जन्म भर भोग विलास को मान, अर्थात् अब जन्म भर मुझ से भोग-विलास कर ॥

मैं वह कैलास की अप्सरा हूँ, जिस की बराबरी में कोई भी पूरा नहीं होता, अर्थात् मैं अनुपम सुन्दर अप्सरा हूँ। मुझे छोड कर, जो तूँ उस (पद्मावती) को स्मरण कर मर रहा है (इस में तुझे) कौन लाभ होता है? ॥ २१४ ॥

चउपाई।

भलेहि रंग आछरि तोहि राता। मोहिँ दोसरइ सउँ भाओ न बाता ॥
मोहिँ ओहि सवँरि मुअइ अस लाहा। नइन जो देखसि पूछसि काहा ॥
अबहिँ ताहि जिउ देइ न पावा। तोहि असि आछरि ठाढि मनावा ॥
जउँ जिउ दइहउँ ओहि कइ आसा। न जनउँ काह होइहि कबिलासा ॥
हउँ कबिलास काह लेइ करउँ। सो कबिलास लागि जेहि मरउँ ॥
ओहि के बार जीउ नहिँ बारउँ। सिर उतारि नेओछाओरि डारउँ ॥
ता कर चाह कहइ जो आई। दुअउ जगत तेहि देउँ बडाई ॥

दोहा।

ओहि न मोरि किछु आसा हउँ ओहि आस करेउँ।
तेहि निरास पीतम कहँ जिउ न देउँ का देउँ ॥ २१५ ॥

भलेहि = वरं हि = भद्रं हि = अच्छा। रंग = रङ्ग = वर्ण। आछरि = अप्सरा। तोहि = तेरा वा तेरे में। राता = रक्त = ललित। मोहिँ = मुझे = मम। दोसरइ = दूसरा = द्वितीय। भाओ = भाति = अच्छा लगता। बाता = वार्त्ता = बात। ओहि = उसे = तस्याः। सवँरि =

संस्मृत्य = स्मरण कर। सुअद् = मरने पर। अस = एतादृश = ऐसा। लाहा = लाभ = प्राप्ति। नइन = नयन = आँख। जो = यत् = जो। देखसि = पश्यसि = देखते हो। पूछसि = पृच्छसि = पूछते हो। काहा = कथम् = किम् = क्या। अबहिँ = इदानीं हि = अभी। ताहि = तस्याः = तिसे। जिउ = जीव। देइ = देने = दातुम्। पावा = प्राप्नोत् = पाया। तोहि = तेरे। असि = सदृश = तुल्य। ठाढि = स्थिता = खडी हो कर। मनावा = सममानयत् = मनाती है। जउँ = यदि = जो। दइहउँ = दास्यामि = दूँगा। कइ = की। आसा = आशा = उम्मेद। जनउँ = जानउँ = जाने = जानता हूँ। काह = किम् = क्या। होइहि = होइहि = होगा। कबिलास = कैलास, यहाँ स्वर्ग। हउँ = अहम् = मैं। लेइ = ले कर = आलाय। करउँ = करवाणि = करूँ। लागि जेहि = जिस के लिये = यदर्थ। मरउँ = मरता हूँ = मरामि। बार = द्वार। बारउँ = वलि दूँ। सिर = शिरः। उतारि = अवतार्य = उतार कर। नेओछाओरि = नेवछावर कर = न्यवच्छाद्य। डारउँ = डारूँ (दारये)। चाह = इच्छा। कहइ = कथयेत् = कहे। आई = आयाय = आ कर। दुअउ = दयोर्हि = दोनों में। जगत = जगत् = संसार। देउँ = दद्याम् = देऊँ। बडाई = वरल = वरता = श्रेष्ठता = वृद्धत्व॥

किछु = किञ्चित् = कुछ। आस = आशा। करेउँ = करोमि = करता हूँ। निरास = नैराश्य = निराशा। पीतम = प्रियतमा = सब से प्यारी। कहँ = को॥

(रत्नसेन ने उस अप्सरा से कहा कि) अप्सरा तेरा ललित वर्ण अच्छा हो (तो क्या), मुझे दूसरे से बात करना नहीँ भाता। मुझे उस के स्मरण करते (और उस के लिये) मरने पर (तयार) होते-ही ऐसा लाभ हुआ (जो कि तेरा दर्शन हुआ), (सो तूँ) जिसे आँख से देखती है उसे क्योँ पूछती है। अभीँ उस के लिये जीव देने नहीँ पाया। (इतने-ही में) तेरे ऐसी अप्सरा खडी हो कर मनाने लगी। यदि उस की आशा से जीव देऊँगा तो नहीँ जानता कि स्वर्ग में क्या होगा। मैं स्वर्ग ले कर क्या करूँ, जिस के लिये मैं मर रहा हूँ मेरे लिये वही स्वर्ग है। (जब वह ऐसी अनुपमा है तब) उस के द्वार क्या जीव को वलिदान न करूँ और शिर उतार (काट) कर उस पर नेवछावर कर न (भूमि पर) डारूँ। जो आ कर मुझ से उस की इच्छा को कहे अर्थात् वह क्या मुझ से चाहती है इस बात को मुझ से कहे, उस को दोनों इस लोक और परलोक में मैं बडाई दूँ।

उसे मेरी कुछ आशा नहीँ (किन्तु) मैं उस की आशा करता हूँ। उस के नैराश्य

से उस प्रियतमा (पद्मावती को) जीव न देऊँ तो क्या देऊँ, अर्थात् उस के लिये जीव ही का देना मैं उत्तम समझता हूँ ॥ २१५ ॥

चउपाई ।

गउरइ हँसि महेस सउँ कहा । निहचइ एहु बिरहानल दहा ॥
निहचइ यह ओहि कारन तपा । परिमल पेम न आछइ छपा ॥
निहचइ पेम पीर एहु जागा । कसइँ कसउटी कंचन लागा ॥
बदन पिअर जल डभकहिँ नइना । परगट दुअउ पेम के बइना ॥
यह एहि जरम लागि ओहि सीझा । चहइ न अउरहि उहई रीझा ॥
महादेओ देओन्ह के पिता । तुम्हरे सरन राम रन जिता ॥
एहु कहँ तस मया करेहू । पुरवहु आस कि हतिआ लेहू ॥

दोहा ।

हतिआ दुइ जो चढाएहु काँधइ अजहुँ न गइ अपराधु ।
तेसरि एहु लेहु माथइँ जउँ रे लेइ कइ लाधु ॥ २१६ ॥

गउरइ = गौरी ने = पार्वती ने । हँसि = विहस्य = हँस कर । महेस = महेश = महादेव । सउँ = से । कहा = कहइ (कथयति) का पुंलिङ्ग, प्रथम-पुरुष, भूत-काल का एक-वचन । निहचइ = निश्चयेन = निश्चय से । एहु = अस्य = इसे । बिरहानल = विरहानल = वियोगाग्नि = विरह की आग । दहा = दहइ (दहति) का पुंलिङ्ग, प्रथम-पुरुष, भूत-काल का एक-वचन । ओहि = तस्याः = उस के । कारन = कारण । तपा = तप किया (अतपत्) । परिमल = पुष्प-पराग = सुगन्ध द्रव्य । पेम = प्रेम । आछइ = अच्छेन = स्वच्छतया = अच्छी तरह से । छपा = छपइ (क्षिपति) का पुंलिङ्ग, प्रथम-पुरुष, भूत-काल का एक-वचन । पीर = पीडा = व्यथा = दर्द । जागा = जागइ (जागर्त्ति) का पुंलिङ्ग, प्रथम-पुरुष, भूत-काल का एक-वचन । कसइँ = कषन् = कसने से । कसउटी = कषवर्ती = कसौटी = सोना कसने का पत्थल । कंचन = काञ्चन = सोना । लागा = लगा (अलगत्) । बदन = वदन = मुख । पिअर = पीत = पीला । जल = पानी । डभकहिँ = डुबहिँ = बुडहिँ = बुडइ (ब्रुडति) का बहु-वचन । नइना = नयन = आँख । परगट = प्रकट = जाहिर । दुअउ = द्वे हि = द्वे अपि = दोनोँ । बइना = वचन = बैन । जरम = जन्म ।

सीझा = सीझइ (सिध्यति) का प्रथम-पुरुष, पुंलिङ्ग, भूत-काल का एक-वचन। चहइ = इच्छति = चाहता है। अउरहि = अपरं हि = और को। उहई = तस्या अपि = तस्य एव = उसी पर। रीझा = रीझइ (रध हिंसासंराद्धोः, रध्यति) का प्रथम-पुरुष, पुंलिङ्ग, भूत-काल का एक वचन। महादेओ = महादेव, सम्बोधन। देओन्ह = देवन्ह = देव का बहु-वचन। पिता = बाप। सरन = शरण। राम = दशरथ राजा के पुत्र, रावणहर्त्ता। रन = रण = सङ्ग्राम। जिता = जीता = जितइ (जयति) का प्रथम-पुरुष, पुंलिङ्ग, भूत-काल का एक-वचन। एहु कहँ = अस्यापि = इस पर भी। मया = माया = करुणा = कृपा। तस = तथा = तैसी। करेहु = करहु = करिए (कुरुत)। पुरवँहु = पूरयत = पूरा करिए। आस = आशा। हतिआ = हत्या = पाप। लेहु = लात = लीजिए॥

चढाएहु = चढाए (उच्चलति से)। काँधइ = स्कन्धे = कंधे पर। अजहुँ = अद्यापि = आज तक। गईँ = (अगाताम्) गईँ। अपराधु = अपराध = दोष। तेसरि = तीसरी = तृतीया। एहु = एहु = अस्या अपि = इसे भी। लेहु = लेहु = लीजिए। माथइँ = मस्तके = माथे पर। जउँ = यदि = जो। लेइ कर = लेने की। साधु = साध = श्रद्धा॥

पार्वती ने हँस कर महादेव से कहा, कि निश्चय इसे विरहाग्नि ने भस्म कर दिया है। निश्चय यह उस के लिये तप किया है, (क्योंकि) प्रेम (पुष्प) का परिमल अच्छी तरह से, अर्थात् किसी तरह से, नहीँ छिपता। निश्चय इसे प्रेम की व्यथा लगी है, (क्योंकि) कसने से कसौटी पर सोने का (वर्ण) लगता है (सो मैं अपराधरूप कसौटी पर रत्न-सेन सोने को कस कर परख लिया)। (इस का) मुख पीला हो गया है, आँखें जल में डूब रही हैं, अर्थात् आँखों में पानी भर गया है, दोनों से प्रेम के वचन प्रगट हो रहे हैं, अर्थात् प्रेम भरी बातों ही के कारण नेत्रों में जल भर गए हैं। यह इस जन्म में उसी (पद्मावती) के लिये सीझा है। दूसरे को नहीँ चाहता (यह) उसी पर रीझा है। हे महादेव, सब देवताओं के पिता, तुम्हारे शरण से राम ने सङ्ग्राम में (रावण को) जीता है। कहावत है कि राम ने महादेव के शरण में हो उन की विधिपूर्वक पूजा कर समुद्र के इसी पार उन की स्थापना की, इस पर महादेव जी राम पर प्रसन्न हो कर अपने भक्त रावण की सहायता के लिये उस पार लङ्का में नहीँ गए। वैसी-ही इस पर भी कृपा कीजिए, इस की आशा पूरी कीजिए नहीँ तो (इस के मर जाने की) हत्या लीजिए॥

जो दो हत्या (दोनों) काँधे पर चढाए हो वे दोष के कारण आज तक न गईं।

of lotuses (*padma*) (was exhaled from the new-born child, and) pervaded the earth, and bees and butterflies came round her on every side.

Such beauty had the maiden, that no other could be compared with her. Happy is the land where so fair a form is born.

52. The sixth[1] night came with its happy sixth night service, and with joy and dancing did it pass. When dawn appeared, came the paṇḍits, who drew out their holy books[2] and interpreted her birth. 'At the most propitious hour hath she been born. A moon hath risen which hath illumined the whole sky. The moon (in the sky) hath risen upon the world in the sign of the Virgin, and hence her name must be called Padmāvatī.[3] The sun[4] hath, as it were, met the philosopher's stone, and from its rays hath been born a diamond more glorious than they, and worthy of the diamond hath been born a still more perfect spotless jewel (*ratna*).[5] She hath been born in Siṁhala-dvīpa, and will go to death's abode from Jambū-dvīpa.'[6]

'E'en as when Rāma was born in Ayōdhyā, with the thirty-two[7] lucky marks; as Rāvaṇa was fascinated when he saw Rāma; so all when they see her will be fascinated, as the moth is by a candle.'

53. The astrologer had written the proper horoscope, and having blessed her returned home; and when the damsel was five[8] years old, they taught her to sit, as a pupil, and to read the *purāṇas*. Thus Padmāvatī became wise and learned, and the kings of all the world[9] heard of it. 'A girl is in the king's house at Siṁhala, very beautiful hath God made her incarnate. In the first place is she a Padminī, and, in the second, a Paṇḍit. We wonder

moon on Mahādēva's head is always represented as two days old. The full moon, on the contrary, is covered with marks, and is not so much worshipped as being impure. Compare note 9 on next page. Note that the poet treats the word *sasi*, moon, as feminine, contrary to Hindū custom.

[1] See *Bihār Peasant Life.* § 1406. It is believed that, on the sixth night after birth, Brahmā writes on the child's forehead its future fate. Hence, on this night, astrologers are called to prepare the infant's horoscope. The occasion is one of much rejoicing, and the greatest care is taken that no demon or ghost should approach the mother or child, and that nothing unlucky should happen. It is said that on the sixth night Yaçōdā held Kṛṣṇa crookedly to her breast, and that, in consequence, Kṛṣṇa squinted all his life.

[2] A Sanskrit MS. is usually kept wrapped up in a cloth. Hence the expression 'drew out.'

[3] According to Hindū astrologers each *nakṣatra*, or lunar asterism, has certain syllables allotted to it. The sign of the Virgin includes a portion of the asterism of *Uttara-phālgunī*, the whole of the asterism *Hast*, and half of the asterism *Citrā*, of which the syllables, in order are *ṭo, pa, pī, pū, ṣa, ṇa, ṭa, pē, pō.* Padmāvatī must have been born in the third *caraṇa* of *Uttara-phālgunī*, i.e., when 3 *aṁças*, 20 *kalās* of the sign of the Virgin had been passed by the moon, and hence her name had to commence with *Pa*.

[4] The sun is Gandharva-Sēna, her father; the philosopher's stone, Campāvatī, her mother; and the diamond, Padmāvatī, herself.

[5] The 'Jewel' (*ratna*) is, of course, Ratna-sēna, who was to woo and win Padmāvatī.

[6] Jambū-dvīpa here means India.

[7] Regarding the thirty-two marks, see p. 24, note 6.

[8] According to the *Jyautiṣa-phalita*, a child should commence the alphabet at the commencement of its fifth year.

[9] Literally 'of the four quarters.'

meet for what mate hath God created her thus. He in whose house fate hath written that Lakshmi [1] will be there, will get this learned fair one.' So suitors came from the seven continents, and bent before (the king), but they obtained no favourable answer, and went home one by one.

The King saith in his pride, 'I am Indra and my kingdom is Çiva's [2] heaven. Who is my equal ?[3] With whom shall I discuss marriage relations ?'

54. The Princess became twelve years of age, and when the King heard that she was full grown and fitted for a mate, he gave her for a dwelling his seven-storied palace,[4] and for her fellows did he give her maidens with whom she might sport in her happiness. All of them were young virgins, nor had any e'er lain with a man. They were like waterlilies blooming by the lotus.

Padmāvatī also had a parrot, a great Paṇḍit,[5] Hīrā-maṇi by name. God had given the bird such glory, that his eyes were like precious stones, and his face as it were rubies and pearls. Golden was the colour of this beauteous parrot. Yea, he was, as it were, gold that had been melted with borax.[6]

Together ever remained they. Together read they the holy books and the Vēdas. When Brahmā heard their reading so did it pierce his heart, that he himself nodded approval.

55. The child Padmāvatī was now of full age, and (God) had made her young limbs (straight as) glistening standards.[7] The scented odour of her limbs pervaded the universe, and the greedy bees came round her on all sides. The sandal breeze of Malaya invaded her dark serpentine locks,[8] and on her forehead sat the new-moon [9] two days old. Her brows were bows from which she aimed the arrows (of her coquettish glances) ; her eyes were like those of the large-eyed antelope, lost, and gazing (for its mates). Her nose was like unto a parrot's, and her face bloomed like the lotus ; the whole universe was charmed as it gazed upon her form. Her lips were rubies, her teeth were

1 Lakṣmī is, of course, the goddess of Good Fortune.

2 Again the confusion between Indra and Çiva.

3 According to the proverb '*bibāh, bair, aur prīti, samān mẽ sōh'tā hai,*' marriage, enmity, and love, are only proper with an equal. *Barōka* is for *barēkhī*, the *vara-parīkṣā*, or testing of the bridegroom. When a marriage is arranged, a sum of money is given to the bridegroom, and then he is bound to carry out the agreement. This ceremony has various names, such as *barēkhī*, *baracchā*, *sagāī*, or *chẽkā*, and is equivalent to a betrothal.

4 *i.e.*, a safe place, fit for a *zanānā*, to which men could not approach. This is important in the later portion of the story, when she is wooed by Ratna-sēna.

5 The expression *Paṇḍit* should be noted. The parrot, we shall see subsequently, was a Brāhmaṇa.

6 Borax is the usual flux for gold, and its use is said to improve the colour of the metal.

7 Here there are puns. The word *bārī* means either a young girl, or a garden. *Karī* means properly a young shoot, and can be metaphorically applied to mean limbs. The verse may, hence, be also translated, 'Padmāvatī, like a garden, was now full grown, and God had made its young shoots straight, &c.' In the next verses the metaphor is carried on. The garden is supplied with bees (lovers), and snakes (her raven tresses), and so on.

8 Mount Malaya is celebrated for two things, its sandal trees, and its snakes.

9 An emblem of purity. See note 5 on page 25.

diamonds, and her heart rejoiced 'neath her golden breast-oranges. Her waist surpassed the lion's and her gait that of the elephant; gods and men alike laid their heads in the dust when they saw her.[1]

No such was e'er seen upon the earth. The Apsarases (first learned to) gaze with unwinking eyes (through gazing at her).[2] For her did Yōgins Yatins, and Sannyāsins undergo austerities.[3]

56. [One day the princess Padmāvatī said to Hīrāmaṇi the parrot; 'Hear, O Hīrāmaṇi, and give unto me advice. Day by day cometh the God of Love and tortureth me. My father doth not push on the matter (of my marriage), and out of fear my mother cannot address him on the subject. From every land come suitors, but on none will my father cast his eye.[4] My youth hath become (irresistible) as the Ganges, and in every limb doth the bodiless[5] Cupid wound me.' Then replied Hīrāmaṇi,—'What is written by fate cannot be wiped out. Give me the order, and I will go forth and wander over all lands, and seek for a king worthy to be thy spouse.

'Until I return to thee, keep in restraint thy heart and thy thoughts.' There was there some wicked man, who heard the parrot, and, who after consideration, went and told the king].[6]

57. The king heard that (Padmāvatī's) countenance had become changed, because that the cunning parrot had given her knowledge (of good and evil). He gave his royal command to kill the bird, 'for he is talking of the sun (*i e.*, a husband) where the moon (Padmāvatī) has risen.' The parrot's enemies were the barber and the torch-bearer,[7] and when they heard the order, they ran upon him as if they were a cat; but the princess hid him so that the cat could not find him. 'My father's command,' she cried, 'is upon my head (and binding), but go ye and tell him my supplication with folded hands. No bird is a reasoning creature. He knoweth but how to eat

1 They recognized her as an incarnate deity. In the esoteric meaning of the poem she is Wisdom.

2 The Apsarases are the nymphs of Indra's heaven. According to tradition they are unable to close their eyes. This is the way they grow. The poet puts forward the conceit, that they acquired this habit from staring at Padmāvatī. The passage, literally translated, is 'The Apsarases kept their eyes in the ether (*akāça*)'. *I.e.*, they kept staring down from heaven, through the ether intervening, to see Padmāvatī.

3 Similarly, it is the poet's conceit that the holy men mentioned really performed all their austerities, not to obtain salvation but, to obtain a view of Padmāvatī's countenance. Regarding Yōgins, Yatins, and Sannyāsins, see note, on p. 17.

4 *i. e.*, approve of: *ākhi lagānā*, to fall in love with, is a common idiom.

5 *Kandarpa*, the Indian Cupid, was destroyed by Çiva, for endeavouring to excite his passion. Çiva turned his terrible third eye upon him, and burnt him to ashes. Ever since Cupid has had no bodily form.

6 This set of verses is almost certainly an interpolation, and has been added to explain what follows. Some sort of explanation is necessary, but the interpolation is clumsy enough. The language is not Malik Muhammad's, and the presence of the wicked male in the *zanānā* portion of the palace, is not explained.

7 The traditional enemies of every Brāhmaṇa; as he does not require their services as match-makers before his marriage. *Nāū bārī* might possibly be translated 'a damsel of the barber caste.'

and how to fly. That which a parrot reciteth is but what he hath been taught. How much sense hath a creature whose soul hath no eyes?

'If he see rubies and pearls, his soul knoweth them not. He fancieth that they are but pomegranates and grapes, and so doth he fill his beak with them.'

58. So they returned to the king with this reply, and the parrot did humbly address Padmāvatī, eating fear within his heart. 'Princess, mayst thou live happily for ages, but give unto me leave to betake myself to a forest home. When once the beauty of a pearl hath been fouled, how can its water e'er again be pure?[1] No safety is there for that servant, whom his master in his heart[2] is determined to kill. How can even the name of birds exist in the house where the death-cat danceth? In thy rule have I seen great happiness, so much that it could not be written if I were asked to recount it. Whate'er my heart desired, I ate, and I depart lamenting that I have not served thee (more).

'He killeth luckless ones, who feareth not his own faults. What sport can the plantain have, that dwelleth near the (thorny) jujube'?[3]

59. The princess then said in sorrow, 'If my life go, how can my body survive? Hīrāmaṇi, thou art the dove of my life, nor have I ever found thee wanting in thy service. I fain would not sift parting into thy service;[4] may I ever keep thee in the cage of my heart. I am human, and thou art my darling bird. Our love for each other is a pure one, and who then, can dare kill thee? What (a mean) love is that which fadeth in the body![5] That alone is love which departeth with one's life. Take thou the burden of my love and there will be no sorrow in thy heart, whether on the path of (that) love there be good or there be evil? How can that mountain-load of love upon thy shoulder be destroyed, for it is bound unto my life?'

The parrot would not stay, for it still feared in its soul that soon that death would come; 'for,' thought he, 'if a man's steersman be his enemy, he will some time sink the ship.'

1 *Pāni* = *āb*, the 'water' of a jewel.

2 *Anta* = *antaḥkaraṇa*.

3 If the plantain sportively flung its leaves about, they would be torn by the jujube's thorns.

4 A difficult sentence. If not corrupt, to be translated as above. An *ākhā* is a sieve, hence *ākhnā* means to sift. Padmāvatī means that she wishes to avoid sifting the bad flour of separation into, and mingling it with the good flour of long and faithful service. *Ākhnā*, may be derived from *ākhyān*, and may mean 'to speak.' The line would then mean 'if thou desirest to abandon thy service, I say thee nay.'

5 *i. e.*, while the body yet lives.

CANTO IV.

THE MĀNASARŌDAKA LAKE.

60. ONE day, on the full moon festival, Padmāvatī went to bathe in the Mānasarōdaka lake.[1] She called all her fellows, and, like a garden went they all.[2] Some were campakas,[3] and some companions were Indian jasmines,[4] others sweet fragrant screw-pines,[5] or citrons,[6] or honey-plants.[7] Some were sweet basils,[8] or red rose-apples,[9] and others posies[10] of smiling abelias.[11] Some were sweet maulasirīs,[12] glorious with blossom. Others were the Spanish[13] or the Indian jasmines[14] or dog-roses.[15] Some were oleasters,[16] and some were safflowers.[17] Others were weeping-nyctanthes[18] flowers, and others rose-chesnuts.[19] Some were kūjā-roses,[20] marigolds[21] and the Arabian jasmine.[22] Others were kadambas,[23] and sweet honey-plants.[24]

They all went along with the Aganosma,[25] and the lotuses and the water-lilies[26] bloomed. And the fragrance of their joy-(giving) nectar[27] penetrated the hearts of Gandharva-sēna's servants (who guarded them).

1 See xxxi, 1.

2 Compare the list of flowers in xxxv.

3 *Michelia champaca*, Linn.

4 *Jasminum pubescens*, Wild.

5 *Kētakī* or *Keōrā* = *Pandanus odoratissimus*.

6 *Citrus medica*, Linn.

7 *Hoya lanceolata*, Wall.

8 *Ocimum basilicum* L.

9 *Eugenia jambos*, Linn.

10 *Bakucana* is obl. plur. of *bakucā*, a bundle; cf. xxxv, 6.

11 *Abelia triflora*, Br.

12 *Mimusops elengi*, Linn.

13 *Jasminum grandiflorum*, L.

14 *Jasminum auriculatum*, Vahl.

15 *Rosa glandulifera*, Roxb.

16 *Elæagnas conferta*, Roxb.

17 *Crocus sativus*, Linn.

18 *Nyctanthes arbor tristis*, Linn.

19 *Mesua ferrea*, L.

20 *Rosa brunoniana*, Lindl.

21 *Calendula officinalis*, L.

22 *Jasminum sambac*, Ait.

23 *Anthocephalus cadamba*, Miq.

24 *Hoya lanceolata*, Wall.

25 *Aganosma caryophyllata*, Don. The clove-scented aganosma or *Mālatī*, which here represents Padmāvatī.

26 *i.e.*, the Companions.

27 Or ointments.

61. Sporting went they forth to the Mānasarōdaka lake, and stood upon its bank. As they looked at it frolicked they, and cried to Padmāvatī, 'My Princess, consider in thine heart, but a few days more have we to wait in our fathers' homes. If thou must sport, sport thou to-day, for thou can'st but sport while thou art a maiden in thy father's kingdom. On the morrow must we all depart to our husbands' dwellings,—then where will we be, and where the bank of this fair lake? Where will be our liberty of going and coming at our own sweet will, and where shall we meet together and sport? The husband's mother and sister will kill us with their (jealous) speeches, and his stern father will not let us slip out of doors.

'I know that my Love will be beloved and over all, but what can he do against them? Keep he us in bliss or in sorrow, still we must live with him.'

62. Frolicking do they meet, and mount the swing, and happily do the artless damsels rock themselves therein. 'Swing away while thou art in thy parent's house; for, once married, our Lords will no longer let us swing. He will (jealously) guard us in our father-in-law's house, (and put us) where we shall not e'en be able to wish for our parents' homes. Where will then be this sunshine, and where this shade? We shall ever remain indoors, and without our young friends. Some day he will consider and ask questions (of us) and blame us (for to-day's sport): what answer, what release, shall we obtain? How often will our mothers-in-law and our sisters-in-law contract their brows, and we shall remain shrivelled up, with both hands humbly joined? Where again shall we come to frolic thus? In our husbands' houses shall we have sorrow to bear till our deaths.

'How seldom shall we return to our parents' homes. How seldom will there be this sport in our husbands' houses. Each of us will be herself to herself, as a bird fallen into a fowler's basket.'

63. To the shore of the lake came the Padminī; and she untied her head-knot, and let her hair fall o'er her face.[1] 'Twas as though black serpents concealed and inhaled her moonface and the Princess's sandal-fragrant limbs. 'Twas as it were a black cloud which descended and o'ershadowed the world, or like the demon of eclipse coming to the moon for refuge. It was as though the sun were obscured by day, and the moon had taken the stars and appeared by night.[2] The very partridge[3] turned his eyes upon her face in error, for he thought that it was the moon shining through a fleece of clouds. Her teeth were the summer lightning, and her voice the cuckoo, her brows were the rainbow shining in the sky. Her eyes, two khañjan[4] birds, sported in the air, and bees imbibed the nectar of her orange-breasts.

The lake was troubled at her beauty, and his heart surged up (crying), 'May I but attain to touch her feet;' and with this pretext he advanced (upon the shore) his waves.

1 When a woman bathes, she undoes her hair and lets it fall over her face, as she cleans it (her hair).

2 The night is her black hair; the moon her face; and the stars her companions.

3 Fabled to be enamoured of the moon and always gazing at it.

4 Motacilla alba, a kind of wagtail, whose quick motion is often compared to the glances of a damsel's eye.

64. The damsels laid their bodices and veils upon the bank, and entered into the lake. Like jasmines, they reached the water, sporting and playing the play of love.[1] Their black[2] hair floated on the water like poisonous snakes, which bore lotuses in their mouths, and met the waves.[3] Up rose they like tender shoots on pomegranates or vines.[4] Yea, it was as if the very branches of love uplifted themselves. They were, as it were, tendrils prepared by the new spring, and become manifest, full of nectar. The lake could not contain the whole universe, for the moon had entered it with all the stars to bathe. Blessed was the lake in which Luna and the stars had risen; now, who will look at mere lotuses and lilies?

The very Ruddy goose[5] in solitude crieth out, 'Where can I find my love? By night there is a moon in the sky, and, by day, another in the water.'

65. They began to sport in the flood; the very swans in shame sat vanquished in grace upon the banks. Then, for their game, set they Padmāvatī to one side, and cried, 'Be thou, O moon, the umpire between the stars.'[6] They agreed upon a bet, and commenced their sport. Whoever lost should give her necklace as the stake.[7] Dark with dark, and fair with fair, each of the maidens took her fellow. 'Understand ye the game and play together, that thy necklace may not go into another's hand. When shall we play to-day's sport again? When the sport is over, where will any of us sport?' 'Happy' (saith Muḥammad) is that game which is played with love. (As the proverb saith) "Mastery and happiness (are rare companions)."'[8]

Muḥammad saith, 'If the ocean of love please thee, sport thou in it, (but so sport thou that), even as when flowers and oil are mixed, there may become a scented unguent.'

66. One of the damsels knew not the game[9] and became distraught because her jewelled necklace[10] was lost. She helplessly grasped a lotus stalk crying, 'To whom shall I lament my condition? Why I came here with

[1] *i.e.*, the sportive actions by which Love conquers the world.

[2] *Karila* may mean either black, or may be equivalent to *karilā*, the shoot of a bamboo. Either meaning will suit. The snakes are poisonous, because they carry death to the heart of man, not by biting, but by their mere look.

[3] The lotus are, of course, the maidens' faces.

[4] The Pomegranates and Vines are the maidens, the Shoots are their ornaments.

[5] Which is separated from its mate at night. See note 8, p. 18.

[6] *Tarāyana*, here, is a pun. It means both 'stars,' and 'divers.'

[7] The game they played is still common. Two women agree to play it, and one throws some small object into the water. They then both dive for it. If the original owner gets it, the match is a drawn one; if the other gets it, she keeps it. Then the other throws, and so on. Sometimes a third person throws an article into the water, and two dive for it. If neither gets it, the article is of course lost.

[8] *I.e.*, in playing a game, unless love is an ingredient, the winner alone is happy and the loser is unhappy.

[9] She forgot to warn her partner that she was about to throw the necklace, so the latter could not find it.

[10] The stanza is full of puns on the double meaning of *hāra*, a necklace, and *hāra* = *ḥāl*, condition.

169. 2. Ia U *chāra bhara muṇṭhī*. 3. K *maina ke ghaṭa bidhi ambrita*. 4. Ia U *sata saũ rahai baiṭhi*. 6. Ib has second half *pūrana hōihi jōga tumhārā*. U has *siŋgha-sabada maṇḍapha jhanakārā | puruba bāra hwai āsana mārā*. K has the second half like U. 7. Ia UK *bahuta kai ā̃ṭī*. 8. Is K *saba bōla*. Ia *bahu mōla*. 9. K *sisiṭi* (*çriṣṭi*).

170. 1. Ia *caḍhi tápā*. U *pai tápā*. 5. *cakrita*, so all MSS. exc. Ia which has *cakita*. 8. The following are the readings—

Iac *cāri-hi cakara phirata mana* · *ḍaṇḍa na rahi thira māra* |

Ibd *cāri-hu* „ „ „ *khōjata* *ḍā̃ḍa na rahai* „ „ |

Is „ *jū̃ga* „ „ „ „ „ „ „ „ |

U „ *cakara phirai mana* *thira* „ „ *ḍā̃ḍawāra* |

K *cārī cakara phirai mana* „ „ „ *ḍaḍamāna* |

K[2] *cārihu cakra phirai manu* *ḍā̃ḍa na rahai thira māri* |

K[3] *cāriu cirta phirai mana khōjata* „ „ „ „ |

9. Ia *hōũ bhasama pawana hoi jahā̃*. UK om. *hoi kai*.

Is inserts the following after 170—

Cau.|| *jaba janamī padumāwati rānī* | *tā dina ganaka kahā mana jānī* ||

jambū-dīpa dēsa eka áhā | *padumāwati kara tohā̃ besāha* ||

eka dina dhāī bāta calāwā | *larikāī jiu goha bari áwā* ||

jaba rati pati jō gāta samānā | *simbhu na simbhu dui uṭhē amāna* ||

sawā̃rata sō nisi bāsara jāī | *bhawana chayā sō kichu na sohāī* ||

biraha-bithā ati byākuli bārī | *hari hita lēpana bhāu na sarī* ||

jala suta sītala dēha cadhāī | *adhīka biraha tana lāga dohāi* ||

Dō.|| *banitā baiṭhi jo sumirai* *hari bhā̃ḍāra kara dēi* |

suruja cā̃da sakhi kaba milai *jō rati pati karēi* || 171*a* ||

171. 1. Ia *jehi joga*. K *pīrama pēma*. 3. Is *ḍahai aŋga*, K *tana barai gā̃bhīrū*.

4. The following are the readings—

Ia *kāla samāna raini haṭhi bāḍhī* | *tila tila kh t juga juga bora māḍhī* ||

Ib *kalapa* „ „ *tehi* „ | „ „ *jō* „ „ *para gāḍhī* ||

Ic „ „ „ *huta* „ | „ „ *mara* „ „ „ „ ||

Id „ „ „ *jahā̃* „ | „ „ *bhara* „ „ „ „ ||

Is „ „ „ *haṭhi* „ | „ „ *mara* „ „ *bara* „ ||

U *kāla* „ „ *ati* „ | „ „ *ēka bhayeu juga bāḍhī* ||

K „ „ „ *ohi* „ | „ „ *bhari juga kē sama kāḍhī* ||

5. Ia *raini sirāī*. Ib *bāhana rabi*. K *raini gawā̃i* | *sasi-bāhana tan raha arasāī* ||

6. The following are the readings—

Iacs UK *puni dhuni siŋgha urēhai lāgai* | *aisi bithā raini saba jāgai* ||

Ib „ „ „ *upahai* „ | „ *bhā̃ti* „ „ „ ||

Id „ *janu* „ *urēhai* „ | „ *bithā* „ „ „ ||

In all P we may read *saŋkha* instead of *siŋgha*, but N have all *siŋgha*. 7. Is and K[2] *kahā̃ so*.

172. 1. U *jarai biraha*. 2. Ic UK *mana bhūlī*. 3. UK *tapati*. 4. Ia *aŋga agini asa karai*. U *mukha bhā*. 5. Iads *mā̃hu kai so*. Ic *mā̃ha kinha tewāsā*. U *disiṭi soi rahai akāsā*. K *bhawā̃ra disiṭi kai āu akāsā*. 6. K *mana rātā*. 7. Ia *kachu jōrā*. Ib *phórā*. Icds U *bhōrā*. K *thōrā*.

173. Ia *kai tasi hatī*. U *kai tē rahati rahī ja°*. K *kasa na muī hōtiū jaba bārī* 2. Ia UK *biraha hasati*. 3. Is *jōbana parai*. U *kuñjara*.

174. 1. Iacd UK *tuī samuda*. Ib *subudhī*. Is *sumati*. 2. Ia *ḍōli kahū kā pahā jāī*. U *nadi sabai mila samūda mahā āī*. K[2] *nadi samāti samuda mahā āī*. 3. U *milahi bhawā̃ra* 4. U *bāga gahi*. 5. K[2] *gahu giāna*. Iads UK *hātha dekha kījia*. Iacs K *jāe na dījia*. K[2] and K[3] *jāi na dījai*. 7. *Nāi*, so all except Ia which has *nāwa*. Printed editions have *pāi*. Ia *sūra* and *āwata*. 8. Ia *jaba lagi to kahā̃ piu milai*.

BIBLIOTHECA INDICA:

A

COLLECTION OF ORIENTAL WORKS

PUBLISHED BY THE

ASIATIC SOCIETY OF BENGAL.

NEW SERIES, NOS. 877, 920, 951, 1024, 1172, & 1273.

THE PADUMAWATI

OF

MALIK MUḤAMMAD JAISI

EDITED, WITH A COMMENTARY, TRANSLATION, AND CRITICAL NOTES

BY

G. A. GRIERSON, C.I.E., PH.D., D.LITT., I.C.S. (*Retd.*).

AND

MAHĀMAHOPĀDHYĀYA SUDHĀKARA DVIVEDI, F.A.U.,

First Professor, Government Sanskrit College, Benares.

VOL. I.

TEXT, COMMENTARY, AND CRITICAL NOTES.

CANTOS I—XXV (VV. 1—286).

CALCUTTA:

PRINTED AT THE BAPTIST MISSION PRESS,

AND PUBLISHED BY THE

ASIATIC SOCIETY, 1, PARK STREET.

1911.

हैँ । ये धारा नगरी के राजा थे । भोजप्रबन्ध मेँ इनकी विस्तृत कथा लिखी है । गोरखनाथ के लिये १२८ वेँ दोहे की टीका देखो ॥ २१७ ॥

चउपाई ।

ततखन रतनसेन गहबरा । छाँडि डफार· पाउँ लेइ परा ॥
मातइ पितइ जरम कित पाला । जउँ अस फाँद पेम गिअ घाला ॥
धरती सरग मिले हुत दोऊ । कित निनार कइ दीन्ह बिछोऊ ॥
पदिक पदारथ कर हुत खोआ । टूटहिँ रतन रतन तस रोआ ॥
गगन मेघ जस बरसहिँ भली । पुहुमी पूरि सलिल होइ चली ॥
साएर उपटि सिखर गे पाटी । जरइ पानि पाहन हिअ फाटी ॥
पउन पानि होइ होइ सब गरहीँ । पेम फाँद केहु जनि परहीँ ॥

दोहा ।

तस रोअइ जो जरइ जिउ गरइ रकत अउ माँसु ।
रोअँ रोअँ सब रोअहिँ सोत सोत भरि आँसु ॥ २१८ ॥

ततखन = तत्क्षणे = तिसी समय = उसी समय । रतन-सेन = रत्न-सेन (राजा) । गहबरा = गह्वर हो गया = गहन हो गया, अर्थात् व्याकुल हो गया । छाँडि = छोड कर (संछुद्य) । डफार = पुक्का फार रोदन = गाल फार रोदन । पाउँ = पाद = पैर । लेइ = ले कर = पकड कर (आलाय) । परा = परइ (पतति) का प्रथम-पुरुष, पुंलिङ्ग, भूत-काल का एक-वचन । मातइ = माता ने । पितइ = पिता ने । जरम = जन्म दे कर । कित = कुतः = क्योँ । पाला = पालइ (पालति) का प्रथम-पुरुष भूत-काल, पुंलिङ्ग का एक वचन । जउँ = यदि = जो । अस = एतादृश = ऐसा । फाँद = फंदा = पाश = फसरी । पेम = प्रेम । गिअ = ग्रीवा = गला । घाला = घालइ (गेरइ = गारयति) का प्रथम-पुरुष, पुंलिङ्ग, भूत-काल का एक-वचन । धरती = धरित्री = पृथिवी । सरग = स्वर्ग । मिले = मिले ऊए (मिल सङ्गमे से) । ऊत = थे । दोऊ = द्वावपि = दोनो । निनार = निनय = निलय = भिन्न भिन्न । दीन्ह = दिया (अदात्) का बऊ-वचन । बिछोऊ = बिच्छुडन = वियोग । पदिक = रत्न-भूषण । पदारथ = पदार्थ । कर = हाथ । खोआ =

खोअद (खति) का उत्तम-पुरुष, भूत-काल, पुंलिङ्ग का एक-वचन। टूटहिँ = त्रुत्यन्ति = टूटते हैँ। रतन = रत्न = जवाहिर। रतन = रत्न-सेन (राजा)। तस = तथा = तैसे। रोआ = रोअद (रोदिति) का प्रथम-पुरुष, भूत-काल, पुंलिङ्ग का एक-वचन। गगन = आकाश। मेघ = बादल = मेह। जस = जैसे = यथा। बरसहिँ = वर्षन्ति = बरसते हैँ। भली = वरम् = भद्रम् = अच्छी तरह से। पुहुमी = पृथिवी। पूरि = पूर हो कर = आपूर्य। सलिल = जल = पानी। होद = भूत्वा = हो कर। चली = चलद (चलति) का प्रथम-पुरुष, स्त्रीलिङ्ग, भूत-काल का एक-वचन। साअर = सागर = जलस्थान। उपटि = उत्पत्य = भर कर। सिखर = शिखर = चोटी। गे = गए। पाटी = पट = भर। जरद = ज्वलति = जरता है। पानि = पानीय = पानी। पाहन = पाषाण = पत्थल। हिय = हृदय। फाटी = फटद (स्फुटति) का भूत-काल, फाटा पुंलिङ्ग के स्थान मेँ फाटी। पउन = पवन = वायु = हवा। सब = सर्व। गरहीँ = गरहिँ = गरद (गरति) का बहु-बचन = गलते हैँ। केह = केऽपि = कोई। जनि = मत। परहीँ = परद (पतति) का बहु-वचन, यहाँ परहिँ = पडँ॥

जिउ = जीव। गरद = गरति = गलता है। रकत = रक्त = लोह। माँसु = माँस = मांस। रोअँ = रोम = रोआँ। रोअहिँ = रुदन्ति = रोते हैँ। सोत सोत = सूत सूत। भरि = भृत्वा = भर कर। आँसु = अश्रु = आँस॥

उस क्षण रत्नसेन व्याकुल हो गया, पुक्का फार, उच्च स्वर निकाल निकाल कर, (महादेव का) पैर पकड कर, (गिर) पडा। (रो कर कहने लगा कि) यदि ऐसा ही गले मेँ प्रेम का फन्दा पडना (डालना) था तो माता-पिता ने पैदा (जनमा) कर क्योँ पाला। पृथ्वी और स्वर्ग दोनोँ मिले हुए थे, क्योँ (ईश्वर ने) अलग कर वियोग कर दिया। (हाय) जो रत्नाभरणरूप पदार्थ हाथ मेँ था (उसे) मैँ ने खो दिया अर्थात् आई हुई पद्मावती हाथ से निकल गई। (इस प्रकार से) रत्नसेन ने रोया, (आँसू के जल टपकते हैँ जैसे) रत्न (मोती) टूट टूट कर गिरते होँ। (वा) आकाश से जैसे मेघ बरसते हैँ (जिस से) अच्छी तरह पृथ्वी भर गई (पीछे भरने के बाद जानोँ वही पृथ्वी) पानी हो कर बह चली। (सब) स्थल भर कर (पहाडोँ) की चोटिआँ डूब गईँ; (रत्नसेन के आसूँ के) पानी जरते हैँ, जिन के लगने से पत्थल के कलेजे (हृदय) फट गए। हवा पानी हो हो कर गलते हैँ, (भगवान् करे कि) प्रेम-फन्द मेँ कोई न पडे॥

जिस का जीव (विरहाग्नि से) जलता है वह उसी तरह से रोता है, (और) उस के रक्त और मांस गलते हैं, अर्थात् गल गल कर गिरते हैं, सूत सूत (अङ्ग के अवयव) आँसू से भर (उस के) रोएँ रोएँ सब रोते हैं ॥ २१८ ॥

चउपाई ।

रोअत बूडि उठा संसारू । महादेओ तब भएउ मयारू ॥
कहेसि न रोउ बहुत तइँ रोआ । अब ईसुर भा दारिद-खोआ ॥
जो दुख सहइ होइ सुख ओ का । दुख बिनु सुख न जाइ सिउ-लोका ॥
अब तूँ सिद्ध भया सुधि पाई । दरपन कया छूटि गइ काई ॥
कहउँ बात अब हो उपदेसी । लागि पंथ भूले परदेसी ॥
जउँ लहि चोर सेँधि नहिँ देई । राजा केर न मूसइ पेई ॥
चढइ त जाइ बार वह खूँदी । परइ त सेँधि सीस सउँ मूँदी ॥

दोहा ।

कहउँ सो तोहि सिंघल गढ हइ खँड सात चढाउ ।
फिरइ न कोई जिअत जिउ सरग पंथ देइ पाउ ॥ २१९ ॥

रोअत = रुदन् = रोते । बूडि = बूड = डूब (ब्रुड संवरणे से) । उठा = उठइ (उत्तिष्ठते) का पुंलिङ्ग, प्रथम-पुरुष, भूत-काल का एक-वचन । संसारू = संसार = जगत् । महादेओ = महादेव । तब = तदा । भएउ = बभूव = भया = हुआ । मयारू = मायालय = दयालु । कहेसि = कहा (अकथयत्) । रोउ = रोओ (रोदीः) । बहुत = बहुतर = अधिक । तइँ = तैँ । रोआ = रोइअ (रोदिति) का प्रथम-पुरुष, भूत-काल का एक-वचन । अब = इदानीम् । ईसुर = ईश्वर । भा = बभूव = हुआ । दारिद = दरिद्र । खोआ = खोने-वाला । जो = यः । दुख = दुःख । सहइ = सहते = सहता है । होइ = (भवति) होता है । ओ का = उस को । जाइ = जाता है (याति) । सिउ-लोका = शिव-लोक = कैलास । तूँ = त्वम् । भया = (बभूव) हुआ । सुधि = शुद्धि = पवित्रता । पाई = पावइ (प्राप्नोति) का प्रथम-पुरुष, भूत-काल, स्त्रीलिङ्ग का एक-वचन । दरपन = दर्पण = आरसी = ऐना । कया = काय = शरीर । गइ = गई (अगात्) । काई = कायी = मैला । कहउँ = कहता हूँ (कथयामि) । बात = वार्त्ता । हो = हे = अहो ।

CONTENTS.

With much sorrow I here record the lamented death of my old friend and colleague Mahāmahōpādhyāya Paṇḍit Sudhākara Dvivēdī, the joint editor of this poem.

It was his custom, in the midst of other multifarious occupations, to write the admirable commentary as it was required by the printer, and the present fasciculus, the last few sheets of which have not had the benefit of his revision, contain the final instalment of his work.

Until arrangements can be made by the Asiatic Society of Bengal for another scholar to carry on his task, the publication of this edition of the Padumāwati is necessarily suspended.

As it stands, this first volume fulfils one of the objects with which the edition was undertaken. It gives a very complete example of the old Awadhī dialect spoken in the 16th century A.D. For those who wish to study the poem for its contents, there are published in India numerous uncritical editions of the text, which will meet their requirements.

GEORGE A. GRIERSON.

उपदेसी = उपदेशी = उपदेश-योग्य। लागि = लग कर (लगिला)। पंथ = पन्थाः = राह। भूले = भूलइ (भ्रमति) का प्रथम-पुरुष, भूत-काल, पुंलिङ्ग का बहु-वचन। परदेसी = परदेशी = परदेश के लोग। जउँ = यदि। लहि = लगि = तक = अवधि। चोर = चौर। सँधि = सन्धि। देई = देइ (दत्ते) = देता है। केर = का। मूसइ = मूसने (मुष धातु से)। पेई = पाई = पाता है (प्राप्नोति)। चढइ = चढे (उच्चलेत्)। त = तदा = तहिं = तो। बार = वार = द्वार। खूँदी = खुन्दन। परइ = पतेत् = पडे। सीस = शीर्ष = शिर। सउँ = से = तें। मूँदी = मुद्रित ॥

सो = सो = वह, यहाँ उस। तोहि = तुझ से। सिंघलगढ = सिंहल-गाढ = सिंहल का किला। हइ = है (अस्ति)। खँड = खण्ड = महल। सात = सप्त। चढाउ = (उच्चलन) = चढाव। फिरइ = लौटता है (परावर्त्तते, निवर्त्तते)। कोई = कोऽपि। जिअत = जीवन् = जीता। जिउ = जीव। सरग = स्वर्ग। दइ = दत्त्वा = दे कर। पाउ = पाद = पैर ॥

(रत्न-सेन के) रोते (आँसू से) संसार बूड उठा, तब महादेव दयालु हुए। (और) बोले कि बहुत रो चुका अब तूँ न रो, अब ईश्वर (तेरे) दरिद्र के खोने पर हुआ। जो दुःख सहता है उसे (पीछे से) सुख होता है, दुःख किए विना (कोई) सुख से शिवलोक में नहीं जाता। अब तूँ सिद्ध हो गया, तैं ने पवित्रता को पाया, शरीर-दर्पण की काई छूट गई। हे (रत्न-सेन) अब (एक) उपदेश-योग्य बात कहता हूँ, (जिस के) लिये परदेशी (लोग) राह में भटके हैं। जब तक चोर सँध नहीं देता तब तक राजा को नहीं मूसने पाता। यदि (वह चोर) चढे तो दरवाजे-ही पर खूँदा जाय; और (गिर) पडे तो सँध-ही में शिर गाडा (मूँदा) जाय ॥

तुझ से कहता हूँ, उस सिंहलगढ में सात महल की चढाई है, सो स्वर्ग की राह में पावँ दे कर, कोई जीता जीव नहीं लौटता है ॥ २१९ ॥

चउपाई।

गढ तस बाँक जइस तोरि काया। परखि देखु यह ओहि कइ छाया ॥
पाइअ नाहिँ जूझि हठ कीन्हे। जेइँ पावा तेइँ आपुहिँ चीन्हे ॥
नउ पउरी तेहि गढ मँझिआरा। अउ तहँ फिरहिँ पाँच कोटवारा ॥
दसउँ दुआर गुपुत एक नाँकी। अगम चढाउ बाट सुठि बाँकी ॥

दोहा ।

आपुहि मीचु जिअन पुनि आपुहि तन मन सोइ ।
आपुहि आपु करइ जो चाहइ कहाँ क दोसर कोइ ॥ २२१ ॥

इति पारबती-महेस-खंड ॥ २२ ॥

दसउँ = दशम = दसवाँ । दुआर = द्वार = दरवाजा । तारु = तार (ताल वृच) वा तालू । लेखा = हिसाब । उलटि = विपर्यय = उलट कर । दिसिटि = दृष्टि । जो = यः । लाउ = लाता है = लगाता है (लाति) । सो = सो = वह । देखा = देख = देखता है (पश्यति) । जाइ = जाय । साँस = श्वास । मन = मनः । बंदी = बन्धी = बन्धन में बँध जाना । जस = यथा = जैसे । धँसि = धँस कर । लीन्ह = लिया (ला देने से) । कान्ह = कृष्ण । कालंदी = कालिन्दी = यमुना । ठूँ = लम् । नाथ = नाथो (नाथ् बन्धने से) । माह = मारो । साँसा = श्वास । जउँ = यदि = जो । पइ = अपि = निश्चय । मरऊ = मरो (मरत) । आपु = आप = स्वयम् (आत्मा) । करु = कुरु = करो । नासा = नाश । परगट = प्रकट = प्रगट । लोकचार = लोकाचार = लोक का आचार । कऊ = कथय = कहो । बाता = वार्त्ता = बात । गुपुत = गुप्त । जा सउँ = जिस से । राता = रक्त = लगा । हउँ = अहम् = मैं । कहत = कथयन् = कहते । मेँटि = मिटा कर = भ्रष्ट कर । सब = सर्व । खोई = खो दिया । आहि = अस्ति = है । सोई = स एव = वही । जिअतहिँ = जीवन्नेव = जीते ही । मरइ = मरे = मरेत् । एक = एक । बारा = वार । पुनि = पुनः = फिर । को = कः = कौन वा किम् । को = कः । मारइ = मारने । पारा = पार = समर्थ । आपुहि = स्वयम् । चेला = शिष्य । अकेला = एकलः = एकाकी ॥

जिअन = जीवन । तन = तनु = शरीर । सोइ = स एव । करइ = करे (कुर्यात्) । चाहइ = चाहे (इच्छेत्) । कहाँ क = कहाँ का = कस्य कः । दोसर = द्वितीय = दूसरा । कोइ = कोऽपि = कोई ॥

तार वा तालू के लेखा सा दसवाँ द्वार है, अर्थात् जैसे तालवृच, अथवा शरीर में तालु-स्थान, ऊँचा है उसी तरह का दसवाँ दरवाजा है; जो उलट कर उस पर दृष्टि लगावे वह (उसे) देखता है। साँस से मन को बाँध कर जो जाय वह (वहाँ पर) जा सकता है, जैसे कि कृष्ण ने यमुना में धँस कर (कालिय नाग को) लिया (पकड़ा)।

तूँ साँस को मार और (उसी साँस से) मन को नाथ, यदि निश्चय मरा चाहता है तो अपने को नाश कर। प्रगट (तो) लोकव्यवहार की बात कह, और गुप्त जिस से मन लगा है उसी में मन लगाओ। (तैँ ने) मैँ मैँ कहता सब को मिटा कर खो दिया, (सो अब) यदि तूँ नहीँ हो अर्थात् अपने को मिटा दे तो तूँ सब वही है, अर्थात् सर्वाङ्गरूप से फिर तूँ पद्मावती ही हो जाय। अरे (रत्न-सेन) जो जीते ही एक वार मर जाय, फिर (उस के लिये) मौत क्या है और (उसे) कौन मार सकता है। वह आप ही गुरु और आप ही चेला है, वह (यद्यपि) आप अकेला है (तथापि वह) आप ही सब है॥

(वह) आप ही मृत्यु और आप ही जीवन है, वह आप ही शरीर और मन है। (वह) जो चाहे सो आप अपने को करे, (फिर) कहाँ का कौन (उस के) सामने दूसरा है, अर्थात् फिर वह अद्वितीय, घट घट व्यापक परब्रह्म-रूप ही है॥ २११॥

इति पार्वती-महेशखण्डं नाम द्वाविंशति-खण्डं समाप्तम्॥ २२॥

अथ राजा-गढ-छेँका-खंड ॥ २३ ॥

चउपाई ।

सिद्धि-गोटिका राजइ पावा । अउ भइ सिद्धि गनेस मनावा ॥
जब संकर सिधि दीन्ह को टेका । परी हूल जोगिन्ह गढ छेँका ॥
सबइ पदुमिनी देखहिँ चढी । सिंघल घेरि कीन्ह उठि मढी ॥
जस खर-फरा चोर मति कीन्ही । तेँहि बिधि सेँधि चाह गढ दीन्ही ॥
गुपुत जो चोर रहइ सो साँचा । परगट होइ जीउ नहिँ बाँचा ॥
पउरि पउरि गढ लाग केवारा । अउ राजा सउँ भई पुकारा ॥
जोगी आइ छेँकि गढ मेले । न जनउँ कउनु देस कहँ खेले ॥

दोहा ।

भएउ रजाएसु देखहु को अस भिखारी ढीठ ।
जाइ बरजि तिन्ह आवहु जन दुइ जाहिँ बसीठ ॥ २२२ ॥

सिद्धि = अष्टसिद्धि । गोटिका = गुटिका = गोली । राजइ = राजा ने = राज्ञा । पावा = पाया (प्राप्नोत्) । अउ = अपि च = और । भइ = (भवति) होई = होता है वा प्रथम-पुरुष, स्त्रीलिङ्ग, भूत-काल का एक-वचन । गनेस = गणेश । मनावा = (मानयति)

मनावद का प्रथम-पुरुष, पुंलिङ्ग, भूत-काल, एक-वचन। जब = यदा। संकर = शङ्कर = महादेव। सिधि = सिद्धि। दीन्ह = दिया का बहु-वचन। को = कौन। टेका = टेके = रोके (रोधयेत्)। परी = परइ (पतति) का प्रथम-पुरुष, स्त्रीलिङ्ग, भूत-काल का एक-वचन। हूल = हुङ्कार = हौरा = कोलाहल। जोगिन्ह = जोगी (योगी) का बहु-वचन। गढ = गाढ = दुर्ग = किला। छेंका = रोका = शङ्कित किया = छेंकइ (शङ्कते) का प्रथम-पुरुष, पुंलिङ्ग, भूत-काल का एक-वचन। सबइ = सर्वा हि = सभी। पदुमिनी = पद्मिनी। देखहिँ = देखइ (पश्यति) का बहु वचन। चढी = चढी हुई (उच्चलन्ती)। सिंघल = सिंहल। घेरि = घेरा (अग्रहीत्)। कीन्ह = किया का बहु-वचन। उठि = उत्थाय = उठ कर। मढी = मठ = मठी = देव-मन्दिर। जस = यथा = जैसे। खर-फरा = चर-फरा = आतुर = जल्दबाज। तेंहि बिधि = तिसी तरह = उसी तरह। सँधि = सन्धि। चाह = इच्छा। दीन्ही = देइ (दत्ते) का प्रथम-पुरुष, स्त्रीलिङ्ग, भूत-काल, बहु-वचन। गुपुत = गुप्त। जो = जो = यः। रहइ = रहे (तिष्ठेत्)। सो = सः = वह। साँचा = सत्य = सच। परगट = प्रगट = प्रकट। होइ = होय (भवेत्)। जीउ = जीव। बाँचा = बचे = उर्वर्यात् = अवशिष्येत। पउरि = पुरद्वारी = पौरी = प्रतोली। लाग = लगा = लग्न हुआ। केवारा = केवारा = कपाट। राजा सउँ = राजा से। भई = (भवति) होइ का प्रथम-पुरुष, स्त्रीलिङ्ग, भूत-काल का एक-वचन। पुकारा = पुकार = पुत्कार। जोगी = योगी। आइ = एत्य = आ कर। छेंकि = छेंक कर (आशङ्क्य) = शङ्कित कर = रोक कर। मेले = मिले हुए हैं (मिल सङ्गमे से) = एकट्ठाँ हो कर। जनउँ = जानउँ = जाने। कउनु = कौन = क नु। देस = देश। कहँ = को। खेले = खेले हैं = खेलयन्ति वा खेलन्ति ॥

भएउ = भया (बभूव)। रजाएसु = राजाज्ञा = राजादेश। देखहु = देखो (दृशि प्रेक्षणे से)। को = कः = कौन। अस = एतादृश = ऐसा। भिखारी = भिक्षुक। ढीठ = धृष्ट = ढीठा। जाइ = जा कर (यात्वा)। बरजि = वर्जन। तिन्ह = तिन्हैं। आवहु = आओ (आयाहि)। जन = आदमी। दुइ = दो (द्वौ)। जाहिँ = जायँ (याताम्)। बसीठ = दूत ॥

राजा ने (महादेव से) सिद्धि-गुटिका को पाया, गणेश को मनाया और सिद्धि (प्राप्त) हुई। जब महादेव ने सिद्धि दी (तो उस को) कौन रोके, योगिओं ने गढ को छेंक लिया यह कोलाहल हुआ। सब पद्मिनी (अटारिओं पर) चढी देख रही हैं, (योगिओं ने) देवमन्दिर से उठ कर सिंहल (गढ) को घेर लिया। जिस तरह जल्द-बाज चोर मति करता है अर्थात् आतुर चोर की जैसी बुद्धि होती है उसी

तरह योगी लोग (शीघ्र) गढ में सँध दिया चाहते हैं। वही सच्चा चोर है जो कि छिपा रहता है, (यदि चोर) प्रगट हो जाय तो जीव न बचे। गढ की हर एक पौरी पर दरवाजे बंद हो गए, और राजा से पुकार की गई। (कि) योगी गढ छेंक कर एकट्ठे ऊए हैं, नहीं जानते कि किस देश में खेला चाहते हैं ॥

राजा की आज्ञा ऊई कि देखो कौन ऐसे ढीठे भिखारी हैं, दो आदमी दूत ऐसे जायँ और उन्हें बरज आवें ॥ २२२ ॥

चउपाई ।

उतरि बसिठ दुइ आइ जोहारे । कइ तुम्ह जोगी कइ बनिजारे ॥
भण्उ रजाण्सु आगइ खेलहु । गढ तर छाँडि अनत होइ मेलहु ॥
अस लागेहु केहि के सिखि दीन्हे । आण्हु मरइ हाथ जिउ लीन्हे ॥
इहाँ इँदर अस राजा तपा । जउँ-हि रिसाइ सूर डरि छपा ॥
हहु बनिजार तो बनिज बेसाहहु । भरि बइपार लेहु जो चाहहु ॥
जोगी हहु तो जुगुति सउँ माँगहु । भुगुति लेहु लेइ मारग लागहु ॥
इहाँ देओता अस गण हारी । तुम्ह पतंग को आहि भिखारी ॥

दोहा ।

तुम्ह जोगी बइरागी कहत न मानहु कोहु ।
लेहु माँगि किछु भिच्छा खेलि अनत कहँ होहु ॥ २२३ ॥

उतरि = उत्तीर्य = उतर कर । बसिठ = बसीठ = वसिष्ठ, के ऐसा दूत । दुइ = दौ = दो । आइ = एत्य = आ कर । जोहारे = जोहार किए = प्रणाम किए (हे जीव-हार ऐसा कह कर प्रणाम किए)। कइ = कि। जोगी = योगी। कइ = कि = वा। बनिजारे = वणिज = बनिए। भण्उ = बभूव = ऊआ। रजाण्सु = राजादेश = राजाज्ञा। आगइ = आगे = अग्रे। खेलऊ = खेलो = खेलइ (खेलति) का, मध्यम-पुरुष, लोट लकार, बऊ-वचन। गढ = गाढ = दुर्ग = किला। तर = तल। छाँडि = (सञ्छुद्य) छोड कर। अनत = अन्यत्र। होइ = हो कर (भूत्वा)। मेलऊ = मिलो = एकट्ठा हो (मिल सङ्गमे से)। अस = एतादृश = ऐसा। लागेऊ = लगे = लग्न ऊए। केहि के = किस के। सिख = शिक्षा। दीन्हे = देने से (दा दाने से)। आण्ऊ = आए। मरइ = मरने के लिये = मरणाय। हाथ = हस्त।

जिउ = जीव = प्राण। लीन्हे = लिए ऊए (ला दाने से)। इहाँ = अत्र = यहाँ। इंदर = इन्द्र = देवताओं का राजा। तपा = तप = तपइ (तपति) = तपता है। जउँ = यदि। हि = निश्चयेन। रिसाइ = रिस करे = क्रुद्ध हो (रुष्येत्)। सूर = सूर्य। डरि = डर कर (आदर्य)। छपा = छप = छपे = छिपे (चिप प्रेरणे से)। हऊ = हो (भवथ)। तो = तो = तर्हि। बनिज = वाणिज्य। बेसाहऊ = बेसाहइ (क्रीणीते) का लोट लकार, मध्यम-पुरुष, बऊ-वचन। भरि = भर कर (भृत्वा)। बइपार = व्यापार। लेऊ = लेइ (लाति) का लोट लकार, मध्यम-पुरुष, बऊ-वचन। लेऊ = लेओ (ला दाने से)। चाहहु = चाहो (इच्छथ)। जुगुति = युक्ति = उपाय। सउँ = से। माँगऊ = माँगो। भुगुति = भुक्ति = भोजन। लेइ = ले कर (आलाय)। मारग = मार्ग = राह। लागऊ = लगिए = लगइ (लगति) का लोट लकार, मध्यम-पुरुष, बऊ-वचन। देओता = देवता। हारी = हार गए (हृ हरणे से)। पतंग = पतङ्ग = फतिंगे। को = क = कौन। आहि = हो। भिखारी = भिक्षुक = भिखमंगा॥

बइरागी = वैरागी। कहत = कहते (कथयन्)। मानऊ = मानिए = मानइ (मन्यते) का लोट लकार, मध्यम-पुरुष, बऊ-वचन। कोहु = क्रोध। माँगि = माँगना = याचना। किछु = कुछ = किञ्चित्। भिच्छा = भिक्षा = भीख। खेलि = (खेलित्वा) खेल कर। होऊ = होओ (भवत)॥

दो दूतों ने (गढ से) उतर कर, (योगिओं के पास) आ कर, (उन को) प्रणाम किए (और पूछे) कि तुम लोग योगी हो वा बनिजारे। राजा की आज्ञा ऊई है कि आगे जा कर खेलो, गढ के तल को छोड कर अन्यत्र जा कर एकट्ठाँ होओ। किस के सिखाने से इस तरह (गढ के नीचे) लगे हो, (क्या) जीव को हाथ में ले कर मरने आए हो। यहाँ इन्द्र के ऐसा राजा (गन्धर्व-सेन) तपता है, यदि सचमुच क्रोध करे तो सूर्य डर कर छिप जाय। (यदि) बनिए हो तो बनिज को खरीदो, (और अपने) व्यापार भर जो चाहो सो लेओ। यदि योगी हो तो युक्ति (कायदे वा रीति) से माँगो, भोजन लो और (भोजन) ले कर रास्ता पकडो। देवता ऐसे (लोग) तो यहाँ हार ही गए, तुम्ह लोग फतिंगे ऐसे भिखारी क्या हो, अर्थात् फतिंगे ऐस तुम फकीरों की क्या गिनती॥

तुम लोग योगी वैरागी हो, (मेरे) कहने पर क्रुद्ध न हो, कुछ भीख माँग लो (फिर) खेल कूद कर अन्यत्र कहीं चले जाओ॥ २२३॥

दोहा ।

वह रानी जेहि जोग हइ तेही राज अरु पाट ।
सुंदरि जाइ राज-घर जोगिहि बाँदर काट ॥ २२५ ॥

सुनि = श्रुत्वा = सुन कर । बसीठ = वसिष्ठ = दूत । उपनी = उत्पन्न ऊई । रीसा = रिस = रोष = क्रोध । जउ = जव = यव, एक प्रसिद्ध अन्न । पीसत = पीसते (पिष् संचूर्णने से) । घुन = घुण = काठ वा अन्न खानेवाला एक प्रसिद्ध कीडा । जाइहि = जायगा (यास्यति) । पीसा = पीस । जोगी = योगी । असि = एतादृश = ऐसा । कहइ = (कथयति) कहता है । कोई = कोऽपि । सो = सः = वह । कहु = कह (कथय) । बात = वार्त्ता । जोग = योग्य । तोहि = तुझे । होई = होय (भवेत्) । बड = बडा (वर) । राज = राजा । इँदर = इन्द्र । पाटा = पट्टा = सिंहासन । धरती = धरित्री = भूमि । परइँ = पडे (पतन्) । सरग = स्वर्ग । को = कः = कौन । चाटा = चाट = चाटता है (चट भेदने से, चटयति) । जउँ = यदि = जो । होइ = होवे (भवेत्) । तहँ = तत्र = तहाँ । चली = चलाई (प्रचार) । कूटिहिँ = कूटेंगे (कुटिष्यन्ति, कुट छेदने, तुदादि) । अबहिँ = इदानीं हि = अभीं । हसति = हस्ती = हाथी । सिंघली = सिंहली = सिंहल के । तहँ = तत्र = तहाँ । बजर = वज्र । गोटा = गोट = गोला । बिसरइ = बिसरे = भूल जाय (विस्मर्येत) । भुगुति = भुक्ति = भोजन । होउ = हो (भवतु) । रोटा = रोडा = लोष्ट = ढेला । जहँ लगि = जहाँ तक = यावत् । दिस्टि = दृष्टि । जाइ = जाय (यायात्) । पसारी = प्रसार = फैलाय । पसारसि = फैलाता है (प्रसारयसि) । हाथ = हस्त । भिखारी = भिक्षुक । आगू = आगे = अग्रे । देखि = देख कर (दृष्ट्वा) । पाउँ = पाद = पैर । धरु = धर (धर) । नाथा = नाथ = हे गोरखनाथी योगी । हेरु = हेर (हेड्रि अन्वेषणे से) । टूट = टूटे (त्रुट्येत) । जहँ = जहाँ = यत्र । माथा = मस्तक ॥

रानी = राज्ञी = राजा की पत्नी, यहाँ गन्धर्वसेन की कन्या । हइ = है (अस्ति) । पाट = पट्ट = सिंहासन । सुंदरि = सुन्दरी (पद्मावती) । जाइ = जायगी (यास्यति) । राज-घर = राज-गृह । जोगिहि = योगी को । बाँदर = बंदर (वानर) । काट = काटे (कर्त्तयेत्) ॥

(रत्न-सेन की बात) सुन कर दूत के मन में रोष उत्पन्न ऊआ, (कहने लगा कि खबर्दार ऐसा न कह, नहीं तो) जौ के पीसते घुन भी पीसा जायगा, अर्थात् तेरे संग

मैं भी मारा जाऊँगा। कोई योगी ऐसा नहीं कहता, जो तेरे योग्य बात हो उसे कह। वह (गन्धर्व-सेन) बडा राजा है (उस का) इन्द्र के ऐसा सिंहासन है, कौन ऐसा है जो जमीन पर पडा स्वर्ग को चाटना चाहे। यदि यह बात वहाँ (गन्धर्व-सेन के यहाँ) चलाई जाय (तो) अभीँ सिंहल के हाथी कूटँगे। और वज्र के गोले कूटँगे, (जिस से यह) भुक्ति-वासना भूल जायगी, तुम (मर कर) ढेले हो जाओगे। जहाँ फैलाने से नजर भी नहीँ पहुँचती तहाँ अरे भिखारी तूँ हाथ फैलाता है। अरे गोरख-नाथ के चेले, आगे देख कर पावँ रख, उस जगह न ढूँढ जहाँ कि माथ टूट जाय ॥

वह (पद्मावती) रानी जिस के योग्य है उसी को (यहाँ के) राज्य और सिंहासन हैं, (वह) सुन्दरी राजा के घर जायगी; योगी को बंदर काट खायगा ॥

एक माकन्दिका पुरी मेँ मौनी योगी भिक्षा माँगा करता था। दैवात् एक दिन एक बनिए के घर भिक्षा माँगने गया। उस की सुन्दरी कन्या को देख मोहित हो मौनव्रत को त्याग उस के विरह से व्याकुल हो गया। योगी की यह दशा देख वह बनिया योगी के पीछे पीछे दौडा। और ज्योँ ही वह अपनी मठ के पास पहुँचा त्योँ ही वह योगी के पास पहुँच कर प्रार्थना की किं महाराज मेरी कन्या को देख कर आप दुःखी क्योँ हुए। योगी ने कन्या को लेने के लिये उस से धूर्त्तता से कहा कि यह कन्या बडी अभागी है। विवाह होते ही तुमारा सर्वनाश करेगी। सो यदि अपना भला चाहो तो इसे रात को संदूक मेँ बंद कर गङ्गा जी मेँ बहा दो। बहाते समय संदूक के ऊपर एक बरता हुआ दीप रख देना। योगी के कहने से बनिए ने वैसा ही किया। इधर योगी ने अपने चेलोँ से कहा कि जाओ गङ्गा जी मेँ एक संदूक जिस के ऊपर चिराग जल रहा है बह रही है उसे ज्योँ की त्योँ उठा लाओ। इस बीच मेँ एक राजकुमार शिकार खेलते खेलते गङ्गा के किनारे पहुँचा और संदूक को बहते देख अपने नौकरोँ से पकडवा मँगाया। खोलने पर उस मेँ अति सुन्दरी स्त्री को देख, मोहित हो उसे अपनी रानी बनाया और उस संदूक मेँ एक बनैले भयङ्कर बंदर को जिसे कि बन से फँसा लाया था बंद कर गङ्गा जी मेँ बहा दिया। योगी के चेलोँ ने उस संदूक को पकड कर योगी के पास लाए। योगी संदूक देख कर बहुत खुश हुआ और कोठरी के भीतर ले जा कर चेलोँ से कहा कि बाहर से कोठरी बंद कर दो, मैं योग सिद्ध करूँगा, तुम लोग चुप चाप नीचे जा कर सोओ। निदान संदूक खोलने पर बंदर ने योगी को काट खाया। योगी कोठरी खोलने के

लिये बहुत चिल्लाया पर योगी की पूर्वाज्ञा से चेले चुप चाप नीचे सोए रह गए। इस प्रकार वह सुन्दरी राजा के घर गई और योगी के नाक कान को बंदर ने काट खाया। यह कथा, कथासरित्सागर के तृतीय लम्बक के प्रथम तरङ्ग के ३०-५३ श्लोकों में लिखी है ॥ २२५ ॥

चउपाई ।

जउँ जोगिहि सुठि बाँदर काटा। एकइ जोग न दोसरि बाटा ॥
अउरु साधना आवइ साधे। जोग-साधना आपुहि दाधे ॥
सिर पहुँचाउ जोग करि साथू। दिसिटि चाहि हो अगुमन हाथू ॥
तुम्हरइ जउँ रे सिंघली हाथी। मोरइ गुरू हसति होइ साथी ॥
हसति नसत जेहि करत न बारा। परबत करइ पाउँ कइ छारा ॥
गढ कइ गरब खेह मिलि गए। मंदिर उठइ ढहइ भए नए ॥
अंत जो चलना कोउ न चीन्हा। जो आवइ आपुन चह कीन्हा ॥

दोहा ।

जोगिहि कोहु न चाहिअ तब न मोहिँ रिस लागि ।
पेम-पंथ जेहि पानि हइ कहा करइ तेहि आगि ॥ २२६ ॥

जउँ = यदि। जोगिहि = योगी को। सुठि = सुष्ठु = अच्छी तरह। बाँदर = बंदर (वानर)। काटा = काटे (कर्त्तयेत्)। एकइ = एक एव = एक ही। जोग = योग। दोसरि = दूसरी (द्वितीय)। बाटा = वाट = पथ = राह। अउरु = अपर = दूसरी। साधना = साधन-वस्तु। आवइ = (आयाति) आती है। साधे = साधने से = साधन करने से (साधनेन)। जोग-साधना = योग-साधना। आपुहि = अपने को (आत्मनः)। दाधे = दग्ध करने से। सिर = शिरः = शिर। साथू = साथ (सार्थ)। दिसिटि = दृष्टि। चाहि = बढ कर। हो = अहो (संबोधनसूचक शब्द)। अगुमन = अग्रगमन = आगे। हाथू = हाथ = हस्त। तुम्हरइ = तुम्हारे। सिंघली = सिंहली = सिंहल के। हाथी = हस्ती। मोरइ = मोरं = मुझे। गुरू = गुरु, गोरख-नाथ। हसति = हस्तीं = हाथी। साथी = संगी (सार्थी)। नसत = नष्ट। जेहि = जिसे। करत = करते (कुर्वत्)। बारा = वार = विलम्ब। परबत = पर्वत = पहाड। करइ = (करोति) करता है। पाउँ = पावँ = पैर। कइ = की। छारा = चार = राख = भस्म। गढ = गाढ = दुर्ग = किला। गरब = गर्व = अभिमान। खेह = धूर।

मंदिर = मन्दिर = गृह। उठइ = (उत्तिष्ठते) उठता है। ढहइ = (ध्वंसते) ढहता है = गिर पडता है। भए = भए ऊए। नए = नव। अंत = अन्त मेँ। चलना = चलन = जाना। कोउ = कोऽपि = कोई। चीन्हा = चीन्हइ (चिन्हयति, चिन्हं लक्ष्म च लक्षणम्—अमरकोश) का प्रथम-पुरुष, भूत-काल, पुंलिङ्ग का एक-वचन। आपुन = अपना। चह = चहइ = (इच्छति) चाहता है। कीन्हा = करना॥

कोऊ = कोह = क्रोध। चाहिअ = चाहिए। मोहिँ = मुझे। रिस = रोष = क्रोध। लागि = लगी = लगइ (लगति) का प्रथम-पुरुष, भूत-काल, स्त्रीलिङ्ग का एक-वचन। पेम = प्रेम। पंथ = पन्थाः = राह। पानि = पानीय = पानी। हइ = है (अस्ति)। कहा = किमु = क्या। करइ = करे (कुर्यात्)। आगि = अग्नि = आग॥

(राजा रत्नसेन ने कहा कि) यदि योगी को अच्छी तरह से बंदर काटे, तो भी (योगी के) योग की एक ही राह है दूसरी नहीँ। और साधना साधने से आ जाती है, पर योग-साधना अपने को जला देने ही से आती है। योग को साथ मेँ कर, शिर को पहुँचाओ, और हे (वसीठ) दृष्टि से बढ कर, आगे हाथ हो (तब योग-सिद्धि हो)। यदि तुम्हारे (साथ) सिंहली हाथी हैँ, (तो) मेरे साथ भी गुरु (गोरख-नाथ) हाथी हैँ। जिस को (तुम्हारे) हाथिओँ को नाश करते देर नहीँ, और जो कि पर्वत को भी पावँ की धूर कर देता है। (गुरु के आगे) गढ के अभिमान खेह मेँ मिल गए हैँ, मन्दिर उठता है, ढह जाता है (और फिर ढह कर) नए हो जाते हैँ। अन्त मेँ जो (संसार से उठ) चलना है उस चलने को कोई नहीँ जानता, जो (यहाँ) आता है वह अपने ही ऐसा किया चाहता है॥

(हे दूत तुम ने जो कहा कि) योगी को क्रोध न चाहिए (सो ठीक है), तभी तो मुझे रिस नहीँ लगी। जिस की राह मेँ प्रेम-रूप पानी है, उस को आग क्या कर सकती है॥ २२६॥

चउपाई।

बसिठहि जाइ कही असि बाता। राजा सुनत कोहु भा राता॥
ठाउँहिँ ठाउँ कुअँर सब माखे। केइँ अब लगि जोगी जिउ राखे॥
अब-हूँ बेगि करहु संजोऊ। तस मारहु हतिआ किन होऊ॥
मँतिरिन्ह कहा रहहु मन बूझे। पति न होइ जोगिहिँ सउँ जूझे॥

बेइ मारहिँ तो काह भिखारी। लाज होइ जउँ मानिअ हारी॥
ना भल मुअइ न मारइ मोखू। दुहूँ बात तुम्ह लागिहि दोखू॥
रहइ देहु जउँ गढ तर मेली। जोगी कित आछहिँ बिनु खेली॥

दोहा।

रहइ देहु जो गढ तर जनि चालहु यह बात।
तिन्हहिँ जो पाहन भख करहिँ अस केहि के मुख दाँत॥ २२७॥

बसिठहि = बसीठ ने = दूत ने। जाइ = (संयाय) = जा कर। कही = कहइ (कथयति) का प्रथम-पुरुष, भूत-काल, स्त्रीलिङ्ग का एक-वचन। असि = एतादृशी = ऐसी। बाता = वार्त्ता = बात। सुनत = सुनते (शृण्वन्)। कोह = क्रोध। भा = हुआ (बभूव)। राता = रक्त = लाल। ठाउँहिँ ठाउँ = स्थान स्थान में। कुअँर = (राज) कुमार। माखे = आमर्ष में हो गए। केइ = किन लोगों ने। अब लगि = अब तक। जोगी = योगी। जिउ = जीव। राखे = रक्खे (रचित किए)। अब-हूँ = इदानीं हि = अब भी। बेगि = वेगेन = शीघ्र। करहु = करो (कुरुथ)। संजोउ = संयोग = युक्ति। तस = तथा = तैसा। मारहु = मारो (मारयथ)। हतिआ = हत्या = पाप। किन = किं न = क्यों न। होउ = होवे (भवेत्)। मँतिरिन्ह = मन्त्री का बहु-वचन। कहा = (अकथयत्)। रहहु = रहो (तिष्ठथ)। बूझे = बूझने पर = बोध होने पर। पति = पत्ति = लज्जा = मर्यादा। होइ = होती है (भवति)। जोगिहिँ सउँ = योगिओं से। जूझे = युद्ध करने से (युद्धेन)। बेइ = उन्हें। मारहिँ = मारें (मारयेम)। तो = तर्हि। काह = किम् = क्या। भिखारी = भिक्षुक। लाज = लज्जा। होइ = होय (भवेत्)। जउँ = यदि। मानिअ = मन्येत = मानिए। हारी = हार। ना = नहीं। भल = वर। मुअइ = मरने (मरणे)। मारइ = मारने में (मारणे)। मोखू = मोक्ष। दुहूँ = दोनों में (द्वयोर्हि)। बात = वार्त्ता। लागिहि = लगेगा (लगिष्यति)। दोखू = दोष। रहइ = रहने। देहु = दो। गढ = गाढ = दुर्ग = किला। तर = तल = नीचे। मेली = मिले = एकट्ठे हुए। कित = किम् = क्या। आछहिँ = अच्छे हैं। बिनु = विना। खेली = खेल॥

जनि = मत। चालहु = चलाओ (चालयथ)। पाहन = पाषाण = पत्थर। भख = भक्षण। करहिँ = करते हैं (कुर्वन्ति)। अस = एतादृश = ऐसा। केहि = किस। मुख = मुँह। दाँत = दन्त॥

दूत जा कर (रत्न-सेन की कही) ऐसी बात (गन्धर्व-सेन से) कही, राजा (गन्धर्व-सेन) सुनते ही क्रोध से लाल हो गया। जगह जगह पर सब राज-कुमार माख गए, (कहने लगे कि) किन लोगोँ ने अभी ँ तक योगी के जीव को रख छोडा है। अब भी जल्द उपाय करो, ऐसा मारो (कि सब मर जायँ) पाप क्योँ न हो। मन्त्रिओँ ने कहा कि ठहरो मन मेँ समझने दो, योगिओँ से लडने मेँ इज्जत नहीँ रहती। उन भिखारिओँ को मारिए तो क्या (फल), (और लड कर) हार मानिए तो (बडी) लज्जा हो। मरने मेँ भी भला नहीँ और मारने मेँ भी मोच नहीँ, दोनोँ बातोँ मेँ तुम लोगोँ को दोष लगेगा। यदि गढ के नीचे एकट्ठे ऊए हैँ तो रहने दो, खेल छोड और क्या योगी अच्छे हैँ, अर्थात् योगी लोग सेवाय खेल कूद के और क्या कर सकते हैँ॥

यदि गढ के नीचे हैँ तो रहने दो, इस (उठा देने की) बात को न चलाओ, जो (योगी लोग) पत्थर को खाते हैं, उन लोगोँ के ऐसे किस के मुँह मेँ दाँत हैँ॥ २२७॥

चउपाई।

गए जो बसिठ पुनि बहुरि न आए। राजइ कहा बहुत दिन लाए॥
न जनउँ सरग बात दहुँ काहा। काहु न आइ कही फिरि चाहा॥
पाँख न कया पउन नहिँ पाया। केहि बिधि मिलउँ होउँ केहि छाया॥
सवँरि रकत नइनहिँ भरि चूआ। रोइ हँकारेसि माँझी सूआ॥
परहिँ जो आँसु रकत कइ टूटी। अबहुँ सो राती बीर-बहूटी॥
उहइ रकत लिखि दीन्ही पाती। सुअइ जो लीन्ह चोँच भइ राती॥
बाँधा कंठ पडा जरि काँठा। बिरह क जरा जाइ कहँ नाठा॥

दोहा।

मसि नइना लिखनी बरुनि रोइ रोइ लिखा अकत्थ।
आखर दहहिँ न कोइ गहइ (सो) दीन्ह परेवा हत्थ॥ २२८॥

गए = गए। बसिठ = बसीठ = वसिष्ठ = दूत। पुनि = पुनः। बहुरि = भूयः = लौट कर। आए = (आययुः)। राजइ = राजा ने। कहा = अकथयत्। बहुत = बहुतर =

अधिक। लाए = लगाए। जनउँ = जानउँ = जाने = जानता हूँ। सरग = स्वर्ग। बात = वार्त्ता। दऊँ = क्या जानेँ। काहा = किम् = क्या। काऊ = किसी ने। आइ = आ कर (एत्य)। कही = कहइ (कथयति) का भूत-काल, प्रथम-पुरुष, स्त्रीलिङ्ग का एक-वचन। फिरि = फिर कर = लौट कर। चाहा = चाह = इच्छा। पाँख = पच = पर। काया = काय = शरीर। पउन = पवन = हवा। पाया = पाद = पैर। 'केहि = किस। बिधि = प्रकार = उपाय। मिलउँ = मिलूँ (मिलेयम्)। होउँ = होयँ (भवेयम्)। छाया = आश्रित। सवँरि = संस्मृत्य = स्मरण कर। रकत = रक्त। नइनहिँ = नयनोँ मेँ। भरि = भर कर (भृत्वा)। चूआ = चुअइ (च्यवति) का प्रथम-पुरुष, भूत-काल, पुंलिङ्ग का एक-वचन। रोइ = रो कर (रुदित्वा)। हँकारेसि = पुकारा (हमकारयत्)। माँझी = मध्यी = मध्यस्थ। सूआ = शुक = सुग्गा। परहिँ = पडती हैँ (पतन्ति)। आँसु = अश्रु = आँस। कइ = की। टूटी = टूट कर (त्रुटित्वा)। अबहूँ = अब भी (इदानीँ हि)। राती = ललित = लाल। बीर-बहूटी = वीर-वधू = इन्द्र-वधू। उहइ = वही = स एव। लिखि = लिख कर (लिखित्वा)। दीन्ही = देइ (दत्ते) का भूत-काल, प्रथम-पुरुष, स्त्रीलिङ्ग का एक-वचन। पाती = पत्री = चीठी। सुअइ = (शुकेन) = सुग्गेने। लीन्ह = लिया (ला दाने से)। चोँच = चञ्चु। भइ = भई (बभूव)। बाँधा = बाँधइ (बध्नाति) का प्रथम-पुरुष, भूत-काल, पुंलिङ्ग का एक-वचन। कंठ = कण्ठ = गला। पडा = पडइ (पतति) का प्रथम-पुरुष, भूत-काल, पुंलिङ्ग का एक-वचन। जरि = जर कर (ज्वलित्वा)। काँठा = कंठा = शुक के गले की धारी। बिरह = विरह = वियोग। क = का। जरा = जरा हुआ = जला हुआ। जाइ = जाय (यात्)। कहँ = कुत्र = कहाँ। नाठा = नष्ट॥

मसि = मषी = स्याही। नइना = नयन। लिखनी = लेखनी = कलम। बरुनि = बरोनी = वारणी (१०६ दोहे की टीका देखो)। रोइ रोइ = रो रो कर। लिखा = लिखइ (लिखति) का प्रथम-पुरुष, भूत-काल, पुंलिङ्ग का एक-वचन। अकत्थ = अकथ्य = कहने के न योग्य। आखर = अक्षर। दहहिँ = दहइ (दहति) का बहु-वचन। गहइ = (गृह्णाति) पकडता है। दीन्ह = दिया (अदात्)। परेवा = पारावत = यहाँ पक्षी शुक। हत्थ = हाथ = हस्त॥

राजा (रत्न-सेन) ने कहा कि, दूत बहुत दिन लगाए, जो गए सो फिर लौट कर न आए। नहीँ जानता कि (क्या हुआ), क्या जानेँ स्वर्ग मेँ बात है क्या, (क्योँकि) किसी ने आ कर फिर (अपनी) इच्छा न कही। (मेरी) शरीर मेँ न पर, न प्राण

(पवन) और न पैर है, किस तरह से मिलूँ, किस के शरण मैं जाऊँ। (पद्मावती के) स्मरण करते ही आँखों में रक्त भर कर चूने लगे, रो कर (रत्न-सेन ने) मध्यस्थ हीरामणि शुक को पुकारा। रक्त की आँस टूट टूट कर जो पडी हैं, उन्हीं से अब तक बीर-बहुटी लाल हैं। उसी अश्रु रक्त से लिख कर चिट्ठी को दिया, सुग्गे ने जो (उस रक्ताचर की चीठी) ली उसी से उस की चोंच लाल हो गई। (रत्न-सेन ने उस चीठी को शुक के) गले में बाँध दिया, (बाँधने से) गला जल गया (इसी से) कण्ठ में लाल धारी का कंठा पड गया। (चीठी में यही लिखा था कि,) विरह का जला हुआ नष्ट हो कर कहाँ जाय ॥

आँख की (आँस की) स्याही, और बरौनी की कलम से, (और भी बहुत विरह की बातें जो) कहने योग्य नहीं (सब) रो रो कर लिखा। अचर जलते हैं, कोई (जल जाने के डर से जिस पची को) पकडता नहीं, (उस को) सुग्गे के हाथ में दिया ॥ २२८ ॥

चउपाई ।

अउ मुख सउँ बच कहेसु परेवा । पहिलइ मोरि बहुत कइ सेवा ॥
पुनि सवँराइ कहेसु अस दूजे । जो बलि दीन्ह देओतन्ह पूजे ॥
सो अबहूँ तइसइ बलि लागा । कब लगि कया छून मढ जागा ॥
भलेहि ईस तुम्ह-हूँ बलि दीन्हा । जहँ तुम्ह भाउ तहाँ बलि कीन्हा ॥
जउँ तुम्ह मया कीन्ह पगु ढारा । दिसिटि देखाइ बान-बिख मारा ॥
जो अस जा कर आसा-मुखी । दुख मँह अइस न मारइ दुखी ॥
नइन भिखारि न मानहिँ सीखा । अगुमन दउरि लीन्ह पइ भीखा ॥

दोहा ।

नइनहिँ नइन जो बेधि गइ　नहिँ निकसहिँ वेइ बान ।
हिअइ जो आखर तुम्ह लिखे　ते सुठि घटहिँ परान ॥ २२९ ॥

अउ = अपि च = और। मुख सउँ = मुख से = मुँह से। बच = वचः = वचन। कहेसु = कहना (कथनीयम्)। परेवा = पारावत = पची। पहिलइ = प्रथम = पहले ही। मोरि = मेरी। बहुत = बहुतर = अतिशय। कइ = कर। सेवा = खुशामद = विनति = विनय।

पुनि = पुनः = फिर । सवँराइ = स्मरण करा कर (संस्मार्य) । अस = एतादृश = ऐसा । दूजे = दूसरी = द्वितीय । बलि = बलिदान । दीन्ह = दिया (अदात्) । देओतन्ह = देवता का बहु-वचन । पूजे = पूजइ (पूजयति) का प्रथम-पुरुष, भूत-काल, पुंलिङ्ग का बहु-वचन । अब-हुँ = इदानीं हि = अब भी । तइसइ = तथैव = तैसा ही । लागा = लगा है (लग्नः) । कब लगि = कब तक = कियत् कालम् । कया = काय = देह । सून = शून्य = खाली । मठ = मठ = देव-मन्दिर । जागा = जागे = जागइ (जागर्ति) का सम्भावना में, प्रथम-पुरुष, पुंलिङ्ग का एक-वचन । भलेहि = भले ही = अच्छी तरह से = वरम् । ईस = ईश = महादेव । तुम्ह-हूँ = तुम्ह भी = त्वमपि । दीन्हा = दीन्ह । जहँ = यत्र = जहाँ । तुम्ह = तुम्हें । भाउ = भाया = अच्छा मालूम हुआ (भा दीप्तौ से) । तहाँ = तत्र । कीन्हा = कीन्ह = किया (अकरोत्) । जउँ = यदि = जो । मया = माया = मोह = कृपा । पगु = प्रग = पैर । ढारा = धारा = धारण किया । दिसिटि = दृष्टि । देखाइ = देखा कर (प्रदर्श्य) । बान-बिष = विषवाण = विष से बुझाया हुआ वाण । मारा = मारइ (मारयति) का प्रथम-पुरुष भूत-काल, पुंलिङ्ग, एक-वचन । जा कर = जिस का । आसा = आशा = दिशा, वा उम्मीद । आसा-मुखी = दिशा वा उम्मेद की तरफ मुँह रखने-वाला । दुख = दुःख । मँह = मध्ये = में । अइस = एतादृश = ऐसा । मारइ = मारता है (मारयति) । दुखी = दुःखी = दुखिआ । नइन = नयन = आँख । भिखारि = भिखारी = भिक्षुक । मानहिँ = मानइ (मन्यते) का बहु-वचन । सीखा = शिक्षा = उपदेश । अगुमन = अग्रगमन = आगे । दउरि = दौड कर (संद्रुत्य वा द्रुत्वा) । लीन्ह = लिया (ला दाने से) । पइ = अपि = निश्चय । भीखा = भिक्षा = भीख ॥

बेधि गइ = बिध गई = विद्ध हो गई । निकसहिँ = (निष्क्रशति) निकसइ का बहु-वचन । वेइ = वे । बान = वाण । हिअइ = हृदय में (हृदये) । लिखे = (लिखति) लिखइ का मध्यम पुरुष, पुंलिङ्ग, भूत-काल का बहु-वचन । ते = वे । सुठि = सुष्ठु = अच्छी तरह से । घटहिँ = घटाते हैं । परान = प्राण ॥

(रत्न-सेन ने कहा कि) और पहले हमारी ओर से बहुत खुशामद कर, हे पारावत (शुक पक्षी) मुख से (चौठी की) बात कहना । फिर सुधि दिला कर ऐसा कहना कि, जिस ने देवताओं को पूजा और बलि को दिया, वह अब तक (अपने को) बलि देने के लिये उसी तरह से लगा हुआ है, अर्थात् तैयार है, (सो) शून्य (प्राण के बिना) देह कब तक मठ में जागती रहे (अन्त में सो गई) । तुम ने भी

अच्छी तरह से महादेव को बलि दी, जहाँ तुम्हें भाया तहाँ तुम ने बलि की, अर्थात् बलिदान दिया। यद्यपि तुम ने अनुग्रह कर (मेरे यहाँ) पैर को धारण किया, अर्थात् आप आईं, (तथापि) दृष्टि को देखा कर विष-वाण मार दिया। सो जो जिस का ऐसा आशामुखी हो, उस दुखिआ को वह ऐसे दुःख में नहीं मारता। (क्या किया जाय) भिख-मंगी आँखें भीख नहीं मानतीं, आगे-ही से दौड कर भीख को ले लिया॥

आखों से आँखें बिध गईं, वे (तुम्हारे विष-)वाण नहीं निकसते, हृदय में जो तुम ने अक्षर लिखे वे अच्छी तरह से प्राण को कम कर रहे हैं। (हृदय के अक्षर के लिये २०० दोहे को देखो)॥ २२९॥

चउपाई।

तेइ बिख-बान लिखउँ कहँ ताईं। रकत जो चुआ भीँज दुनिआई॥
जानु सो गारइ रकत पसेऊ। सुखी न जान दुखी कर भेऊ॥
जेहि न पीर तेहि का करि चीता। प्रीतम निठुर होइ अस नीता॥
का सउँ कहउँ बिरह कइ भाखा। जा सउँ कहउँ होइ जरि राखा॥
बिरह आगि तन जर बर जरई। नइन नीर सायर सब भरई॥
पाती लिखी सवँरि तुम्ह नावाँ। रकत लिखे आखर भए स्यावाँ॥
आखर जरहिँ न कोई छूआ। तब दुख देखि चला लेइ सूआ॥

दोहा।

अब सुठि मरउँ छूँछि गइ पाती पेम पिआरे हाथ।
भेँटि होति दुख रोइ सुनावत जीउ जात जउँ साथ॥ २३०॥

तेइ = तिस। बिख-बान = विष-वाण = विष के वाण। लिखउँ = लिखूँ (लिखानि)। कहँ ताईं = कहँ ताईं = कहाँ तक। रकत = रक्त = खून। जो = यत् = जो। चुआ = चुअइ (च्यवति) का प्रथम-पुरुष, पुंलिङ्ग, भूत-काल का एक-वचन। भीँज = भीँगा = अभिषिक्त हुआ। दुनिआई = दुनिआ। जानु = जाने = जानें। सो = वह = सः। गारइ = (गारयति) गारता है। पसेऊ = प्रस्वेद = पसीना। सुखी = सुखिआ। जान = जानइ (जानाति) = जानता है। दुखी = दुःखी = दुखिआ। कर = का। भेऊ = भेद।

पीर = पीडा = व्यथा। का करि = किस की। चीता = चिन्ता = फिक्र। प्रीतम = प्रियतम। निठुर = निष्टुर = कठोर। होद = (भवति) होता है। अस = एतादृश = ऐसा। नीता = नीत। कहउँ = कहूँ (कथयानि)। बिरह = विरह = वियोग। भाखा = भाषा = वाणी। जरि = जल कर (प्रज्वल्य)। राखा = राख = रचा = भस्म। आगि = अग्नि। तन = तनु = शरीर। जर = जड। बर = वट = बर का पेंड। जरद = (ज्वलति) जलता है। नदन = नयन = आँख। नीर = पानी। सायर = सागर = जलस्थान। सब = सर्व। भरद = (भरति) भरता है। पाती = पत्री = चिट्ठी। लिखी = लिखद (लिखति) का प्रथम-पुरुष, भूत-काल, स्त्रीलिङ्ग का एक-वचन। सवँरि = (संस्मृत्य) स्मरण कर। नावँ = नावँ = नाम। आखर = अक्षर। भए = भए (बभूवुः)। स्यावँ = श्याम = काले। जरहिँ = जरद का बहु-वचन। छूआ = छुअद (स्पृशति) का प्रथम-पुरुष, भूत-काल, पुंलिङ्ग का एक-वचन। तब = तदा। दुख = दुःख। देखि = (दृष्ट्वा) देख कर। चला = चलद (चलति) का प्रथम-पुरुष, पुंलिङ्ग भूत-काल का एक-वचन। लेद = ले कर (आदाय)। सूआ = शुक = सुग्गा ॥

अब = इदानीम् = अधुना। सुठि = सुष्टु = अच्छी तरह से। मरउँ = मरता हूँ (मरामि)। छूँछि = छूँछी = खाली (रिक्त)। गइ = गई (अगात्)। पेम = प्रेम। पिआरे = प्रिय। हाथ = हस्त। भेँटि = भेँट = समागम। होति = होती (भवेत्)। रोद = रो कर (रुदित्वा)। सुनावत = सुनावता (श्रावयेत्)। जीउ = जीव। जात = जाता (यात्)। जउँ = यदि। साथ = सार्धं ॥

उस विष-बाण (की कथा) कहाँ तक लिखूँ, (उस से विद्ध होने से आँखोँ से) जो रक्त चुआ, उस से दुनिआ भीँग गई। कवि कहता है कि जान पडता है कि वह (रत्न-सेन) खून का पसीना गार रहा है, (सच है) सुखी दुःख का भेद नहीँ जानता। जिसे पीडा नहीँ उसे किस की चिन्ता, प्रियतम निष्टुर होता है, ऐसी नीति है। मैँ (अपनी) विरह की वाणी किस से कहूँ, जिस से कहता हूँ वही जल कर राख हो जाता है। विरहाग्नि से बर के जड ऐसी देह जलती है, आँखोँ के पानी से सब जलस्थल भर रहे हैँ। (हे पद्मावती) तेरे नाम को स्मरण कर (मैँ ने इस) पत्री को लिखी है, रक्त के लिखे अक्षर (विरहाग्नि से) काले हो गए। कवि कहता है कि अक्षर जल रहे हैँ (उन्हेँ जल जाने के डर से) कोई छूता नहीँ है, तब (अन्त मेँ रत्न-सेन का) दुःख देख कर शुक (हीरामणि) (उस पत्री को) ले कर चला ॥

(रत्न-सेन कहता है कि हाय) मेरी प्रेम-पत्री प्यारे (पद्मावती) के हाथ में खाली गई, अर्थात् पत्री के साथ मेरा जीव नहीं गया, (इसी पछतावे से) अब अच्छी तरह से मरता हूँ, यदि पत्री के साथ जीव जाता तो भेंट होती और (रो) रो कर मेरे दुःख को सुनाता ॥ २३० ॥

चउपाई।

कंचन तार बाँधि गिअँ पाती। लेइ गा सुआ जहाँ धनि राती ॥
जइसइ कवँल सुरुज कइ आसा। नीर कंठ लहि मरइ पिआसा ॥
बिसरा भोगु सेज सुख बासू। जहाँ भवँर सब तहाँ हुलासू ॥
तब लगि धीर सुना नहिँ पीऊ। सुनतहि घरी रहइ नहिँ जीऊ ॥
तब लगि सुख हिअ पेम न जामा। जहाँ पेम गा सुख बिसरामा ॥
अगर चँदन सुठि दहइ सरीरू। अउ भा अगिनि कया कर चीरू ॥
कथा कहानी सुनि सुठि जरा। जानहुँ घिउ बइसंदर परा ॥

दोहा।

बिरह न आपु सँभारइ मइल चीर सिर रूख।
पिउ पिउ करत रात दिन पपिहा भइ मुख सूख ॥ २३१ ॥

कंचन = काञ्चन = सुवर्ण। तार = तागा = सूत्र। बाँधि = बाँध कर (बन्धयित्वा)। गिअँ = ग्रीवा = गला। पाती = पत्री। लेइ = ले कर (आलाय)। गा = गया (अगात्)। सुआ = शुक = सुग्गा। जहाँ = यत्र। धनि = धन्या, पद्मावती। राती = रक्ता = रत्न-सेन के ध्यान में मग्ना। जइसइ = यथा = जैसे। कवँल = कमल। सुरुज = सूर्य। कइ = की। आसा = आशा = उम्मीद। नीर = जल। कंठ = कण्ठ। लहि = लब्ध्वा = पा कर। मरइ = मरता है (मरति)। पिआसा = पिपासा = प्यास। बिसरा = बिसरइ (विस्मरति) का प्रथम-पुरुष, भूत-काल, पुंलिङ्ग का एक-वचन। भोगु = भोग = सुखविलास। सेज = शय्या = पलँग। बासू = वास। भवँर = भ्रमर = भौँरा। सब = सर्व। तहाँ = तत्र। हुलासू = उल्लास। तब लगि = तब तक। धीर = धैर्य = ढाढस। सुना = सुनइ (शृणोति) का प्रथम-पुरुष, भूत-काल, पुंलिङ्ग का एक-वचन। पीऊ = प्रिय। सुनतहि = सुनते-ही (शृण्वन् हि)। रहइ = रहता है (तिष्ठति)। जीऊ = जीव। हिअ = हृदय में। पेम =

प्रेम । जामा = जमइ (जायते) का प्रथम-पुरुष, भूत-काल, पुंलिङ्ग का एक-वचन। बिसरामा = विश्राम । अगर = अगुरु = एक सुगन्ध काष्ठ । चँदन = चन्दन = एक प्रसिद्ध सुगन्ध काष्ठ । सुठि = सुष्ठु = अच्छी तरह = अत्यन्त । दहइ = दहता है (दहति) = भस्म करता है । सरीरू = शरीर = देह । भा = भया = हुआ (बभूव) । अगिनि = अग्नि = आग । कया = काय = शरीर । कर = का । चीरू = चीर = वस्त्र । कहानी = कथानीक । सुनि = सुन कर (श्रुत्वा) । जरा = जरइ (ज्वलति) का प्रथम-पुरुष, भूत-काल, पुंलिङ्ग का एक-वचन । जानङँ = जाने = जानों । घिउ = घृत = घी । बइसंदर = वासंदर = वैश्वानर = आग । परा = परइ (पतति) का प्रथम-पुरुष, भूत-काल, पुंलिङ्ग का एक-वचन ॥

बिरह = विरह = वियोग = जुदाई । आपु = आप = स्वयम् । सँभारइ = सँभारता है (सम्भारयति) । मइल = मैला = मलिन = मलयुक्त । चीर = वस्त्र । सिर = शिर । रूख = रूक्ष = रूखा । पिउ = प्रिय । करत = करते (कुर्वत्) । रात = रात्रि । पपिहा = पपीहा = चातक = एक प्रसिद्ध पक्षी जो स्वाती ही का जल पीता है । भइ = भई (बभूव) । मुख = मुँह । सूख = शुष्क हुआ = सूख गया = सुखइ का भूत-काल ॥

(अपने) गले में सोने के तार से पक्षी को बाँध कर, जहाँ रत्न-सेन के ध्यान में लगी पद्मावती थी (वहाँ पर हीरा-मणि) शुक (पक्षी को) ले गया। जैसे सूर्य की आशा से कमल, कण्ठ तक पानी पा कर भी (रवि-किरणरूप जल के) प्यास से मरता रहता है, (उसी तरह रत्न-सेन के विना पद्मावती मरती थी)। (पद्मावती को) भोग, सय्या, सुख का वासस्थान, (सब) भूल गया, जहाँ भ्रमर (रत्न-सेन) था, वहाँ ही पर सब भोग-विलास चला गया। जब तक प्रिय (के आगमन) को नहीं सुना था, तब तक धैर्य था, (आगमन) सुनते-ही (अब) घडी (घरी = घटी) भर भी जीव (स्थिर) नहीं रहता है। जब तक हृदय में प्रेम नहीं जमा था तभी तक सुख था, जहाँ प्रेम जमा कि सुख के साथ विश्राम गया। अगर और चन्दन शरीर को भस्म करते हैं, और देह पर का वस्त्र आग हो गया है। (रत्न-सेन की) कथा कहानी सुन (सुन) कर और भी जीव जल रहा है, जानों आग में घी पडा हो ॥

बिरह से (पद्मावती) अपने को नहीं सँभारती है, कपडा मैला हो गया है, शिर (के बाल) रूखे हो गए हैं; रात दिन पी, पी (प्रिय, प्रिय) करती पपीहा हो गई है, (और) मुँह सूख गया है ॥ २३१ ॥

चउपाइ।

ततखन हीरामनि गा आई। मरत पिआस छाँह जनु पाई॥
भल तुम्ह सुआ कीन्ह हइ फेरा। गाढ न जानेउँ प्रीतम केरा॥
बाटहि जानहुँ बिखम पहारा। हिरदइ मिला न होइ निनारा॥
मरम पानि कर जान पिआसा। जो जल मँह ता कहँ का आसा॥
का रानी यह पूँछहु बाता। जनि कोइ होइ पेम कर राता॥
तुम्हरे दरसन लागि बिओगी। अहा सो महादेओ मढ जोगी॥
तुम्ह बसंत लेइ तहाँ सिधाई। देओ पूजि पुनि ओ पहँ आई॥

दोहा।

दिसिटि बान तस मारेहु घाइ रहा तेहि ठाउँ।
दोसरि बार न बोला लेइ पदुमावति नाउँ॥ २३२॥

ततखन = तत्क्षणे = उसी समय। हीरामनि = हीरामणि (शुक)। गा = गया (अगात्)। आई = आ कर (एत्य)। मरत = मरता (मरन्)। पिआस = पिपासा = प्यास। छाँह = छाया। जनु = जाने = जानों। पाई = पावइ (प्राप्नोति) का प्रथम-पुरुष, भूत-काल, स्त्रीलिङ्ग का एक-वचन। भल = वर = भला। सुआ = शुक = सुग्गा। कीन्ह = किया (अकरोत्)। हइ = है (अस्ति)। फेरा = स्फुरण = पुनरागमन। गाढ = कठिन = कष्ट। जानेउँ = जानी (अजानम्)। प्रीतम = प्रियतम। केरा = का। बाटहि = बाट मेँ = राह मेँ। जानहुँ = जाने = जानों। बिखम = विषम = नीचा ऊँचा। पहारा = पहाड = प्रहार = पर्वत। हिरदइ = हृदये = हृदय मेँ। मिला = मिला हुआ = मिलित। होइ = होता है (भवति)। निनारा = निरालय = अलग = निर्गत। मरम = मर्म = भेद। पानि = पानीय = पानी। जान = जानइ (जानाति) जानता है। पिआसा = प्यासा हुआ = पिपासु। जो = यः। जल = पानी। मँह = मध्ये = मेँ। ता कहँ = तिस को। का = किम् = क्या। आसा = आशा = उम्मीद। रानी = राज्ञी = पद्मावती। यह = इदम्। पूँछहु = पूछती हो (पृच्छथ)। बाता = वार्त्ता = बात। जनि = मत = न। कोइ = कोऽपि = कोई। होइ = होय = होवे (भवेत्)। पेम = प्रेम। कर = का। राता = रक्त =

सक । दरसन = दर्शन । लागि = लिये = वास्ते = लग्न । बिओगी = वियोगी = विरही । अहा = था = आसीत् । सो = वह = सो । महादेओ = महादेव । मढ = मठ = मन्दिर । जोगी = योगी । बसंत = वसन्त ऋतु । लेइ = ले कर (आलाय) । तहाँ = तत्र । सिधाई = सिधावइ (सेधति) का प्रथम-पुरुष, भूत-काल, स्त्रीलिङ्ग का एक-वचन । देओ = देव = देवता । पूजि = पूज कर (आपूज्य) । पुनि = पुनः = फिर । ओ पहँ = उस के यहाँ । आई = आवइ (आयाति) का प्रथम-पुरुष, भूत-काल, स्त्रीलिङ्ग का एक-वचन ॥

दिसिटि = दृष्टि । बान = वाण । तस = तथा = तैसा । मारेहु = मारा = मारइ (मारयति) का मध्यम-पुरुष, भूत-काल, स्त्रीलिङ्ग का एक-वचन । घाइ = घाव = घात । रहा = था = आसीत् । तेहि = तिसी = उसी । ठाउँ = स्थान = ठावँ । दोसरि = दूसरी = द्वितीया । बार = वार = मर्तब । बोला = बोलइ (वदति) का प्रथम-पुरुष, भूत-काल, पुंलिङ्ग का एक-वचन । पदुमावति = पद्मावती । नाउँ = नाम = नावँ ॥

उसी समय हीरामणि (शुक) आ गया, जानों प्यास से मरता छाँह पा जाय (ऐसी दशा पद्मावती की हुई) । (कहने लगी कि) हे शुक अच्छा किया जो तुम्ह ने फेरा की, मैं (अपने) प्रियतम के कष्ट को नहीं जानी (कि क्या उस पर बीत रही है) । (मेरे लिये उस के मिलने को) राह में जानों विषम पहाड पडा हुआ है, (तो भी) हृदय में मिला (वह किसी तरह से) अलग नहीं होता । प्यासा पानी का मर्म जानता है, जो पानी में है उस के लिये क्या (पानी की) आशा । (शुक ने उत्तर दिया कि) रानी इस बात को क्या पूछती हो; (भगवान करे कि) प्रेम का अनुरागी कोई न हो । वह (रत्न-सेन) विरही योगी तुम्हारे दर्शन के लिये महादेव के मन्दिर में (ठहरा) था । तुम वसन्त ऋतु (सखिओं) को ले कर वहाँ पधारी और देवता पूज कर फिर उस के पास आई ॥

तुम ने ऐसा दृष्टि-वाण मारा कि (उस) घात से (वह बेचारा) उसी जगह रह गया, (एक वार) पद्मावती (ऐसा तुमारा) नाम ले कर (मूर्छित हो गया फिर) दूसरी वार न बोला ॥ २३२ ॥

चउपाई ।

रोअँहिँ रोअँ बान वेइ फूटे । सोतहिँ सोत रुहिर मुख छूटे ॥
नइनन्ह चली रकत कइ धारा । कंथा भीँजि भएउ रतनारा ॥

सूरुज बूडि उठा परभाता। अउ मँजीठ टेँसू बन राता ॥
भएउ बसंत रात बनफती। अउ राते सब जोगी जती ॥
पुहुमि जो भीँज भई सब गेरू। अउ तहँ अहा सो रात पखेरू ॥
राती सती अगिनि सब काया। गगन मेघ राते तेहि छाया ॥
ईँगुर भा पहार तस भीँजा। पइ तुम्हार नहिँ रोअँ पसीजा ॥

दोहा।

तहाँ चकोर कोकिला तिन्ह हिअ मया पईठि।
नइन रकत भरि आए तुम्ह फिरि कीन्ह न दीठि ॥ २३३ ॥

रोअँहिँ रोअँ = रोम रोम। बान = वाण। वेइ = वे। फूटे = फूटइ (स्फुटति) का प्रथम-पुरुष, भूत-काल, पुंलिङ्ग का बहु-वचन। सोतहिँ सोत = सोते सोते = स्रोत स्रोत। रुहिर = रुधिर। मुख = मुँह। छूटे = छूटइ (छुटति) का प्रथम-पुरुष, भूत-काल, पुंलिङ्ग का बहु-वचन। नइनन्ह = नयनन्ह = आँखोँ से। चली = चलइ (चलति) का प्रथम-पुरुष, भूत-काल, स्त्रीलिङ्ग का एक-वचन। रकत = रक्त = रुधिर = खून = लोहू। कइ = की। धारा = प्रवाह। कंथा = कन्था = गुदरी। भीँजि = भीँग कर (अभ्यज्यते)। भएउ = हुआ (बभूव)। रतनारा = रक्तवर्ण = लाल। सूरुज = सूर्य। बूडि = बूड कर = डूब कर (संब्रुड्य)। उठा = उठइ (उत्तिष्ठते) का प्रथम-पुरुष, भूत-काल, पुंलिङ्ग का एक-वचन। परभाता = प्रभात = प्रातःकाल। मँजीठ = मञ्जिष्ठा। टेँसू = किंशुक = पलास। बन = वन। राता = रक्त। बसंत = वसन्त ऋतु। रात = रक्त। बनफती = वनस्पति। राते = रक्त हो गए। सब = सर्व। जोगी = योगी। जती = यतिः। पुहुमि = पृथ्वी = भूमि। भीँज = भीँजी = भीँगी। भई = हुई (बभूव)। गेरू = गैरिक। तहँ = तत्र = तहाँ। अहा = था = आसीत्। सो = सः = वह। पखेरु = पक्षी। राती = रक्तवर्ण की। सती = साध्वी स्त्री = पतिव्रता, जो मृतपति के साथ चिता पर भस्म हो जाती है। अगिनि = अग्नि = आग। काया = काय = देह। गगन = आकाश। मेघ = बादल। ईँगुर = हिङ्गुल। भा = भया = हुआ (बभूव)। पहार = प्रहार = पहाड = पर्वत। तस = तथा = तैसा। पइ = अपि = पर। पसीजा = पसीजइ (प्रस्विद्यति) का प्रथम-पुरुष, भूत-काल पुंलिङ्ग का एक-वचन ॥

तहाँ = तच । चकोर = एक प्रसिद्ध पची, जो अङ्गार खाता है। कोकिला = एक प्रसिद्ध पची । तिन्ह = तिन्ह के = उन के । हिय = हृदय । मया = माया = दया । पईठि = पैठी = प्रविष्ट ऊई । नइन = नयन । भरि = भर = पूर्ण । आए = आवइ (आयाति) का प्रथम-पुरुष, भूत-काल, पुंलिङ्ग का बज्ज-वचन । फिरि = फिर कर । कीन्ह = किया (अकरोत्) । दीठि = दृष्टि = नजर ॥

उन वाणों से रोएँ रोएँ फूट गए, (उन के) मुखों से रुधिर के सोते के सोते छूटे। आँखों से रक्त की धारा (बह) चली, कन्था भीँग कर लाल हो गया। प्रातःकाल का सूर्य (उसी रक्त-धारा से) बूड उठा और वन के मँजीठ और टेंसू लाल हो गए। (उसी रक्त-धारा से) वसन्त ऋतु मेँ वनस्पतिआँ लाल हो गईं, और योगी यती सब लाल हो गए, अर्थात् उन के गेरुआ वस्त्र उसी रक्तधारा से लाल हो गए हैं। (उस धारा से) पृथ्वी जो भीँगी उसी से भूमि मेँ गेरू ऊए (कवि के मत से गेरू स्त्रीलिङ्ग है इसी से भइ का प्रयोग किया है) और उस जगह जितने पची थे सब लाल हो गए। (उसी रक्त-धारा से) अग्नि मेँ सती की सब शरीर लाल हो गई, (उसी धारा की) छाया पडने से आकाश मेँ मेघ लाल रङ्ग के ऊए। (उसी रक्त-धारा से) पहाड ऐसा भीँग गया कि उस मेँ ईंगुर (की खानि) हो गई, (यह सब कवि की उत्प्रेचा है), ये सब तो ऊए पर तुम्हारा एक रोआँ भी न पसीजा ॥

उस स्थान मेँ चकोर और कोकिला जो थे उन के हृदय मेँ दया आई, (दया से) उन की आँखों मेँ रुधिर भर आए पर तुम फिर कर (उस की ओर) दृष्टि न की। चकोर और कोकिला की आँखेँ लाल लाल होती हैँ वहाँ कवि की उत्प्रेचा है कि दया-ही के कारण रक्ताश्रु भर जाने से उन की आँखेँ लाल हो गई हैँ ॥ २३३ ॥

चउपाई ।

अइस बसंत तुम्हइँ पइ खेलहु । रकत पराए सेँदुर मेलहु ॥
तुम्ह तउ खेलि मँदिर कहँ आईँ । ओहि क मरम पइ जानु गोसाईँ ॥
कहेसि मरइ को बारहिँ बारा । एकहि बार होउँ जरि छारा ॥
सर रचि चहा आगि जो लाई । महादेओ गउरइ सुधि पाई ॥
आइ बुझाइ दीन्ह पँथ तहवाँ । मरन खेल कर आगम जहवाँ ॥

उलटा पंथ पेम कइ बारा। चढइ सरग सो परइ पतारा ॥
अब धँसि लीन्ह चहइ तेहि आसा। पावइ आस कि मरइ निरासा ॥

दोहा ।

पाती लिखि जो पठाई लिखा सबइ दुख रोइ ।
दहुँ जिउ रहइ कि निसरइ काह रजाप्रसु होइ ॥ २३४ ॥

अइस = एतादृश = ऐसा। बसंत = वसन्त-ऋतु। तुम्हइँ = तुम्हीँ। पइ = अपि। खेलहु = खेलती हो (खेलथ)। रकत = रक्त = रुधिर। पराए = परस्य = दूसरे के। सेँदुर = सिन्दूर = सेँधुर। मेलहु = मेलती हो = लगाती हो (मेलयथ)। तउ = तो। खेलि = खेल कर (खेलिला)। मँदिर = मन्दिर = गृह। कहँ = को। आईँ = आवइ (आयाति) का मध्यम-पुरुष, भूत-काल, स्त्रीलिङ्ग का बहु-वचन। ओहि क = उस का, मरम = मर्म = भेद। जानु = जान = जानता है (जानाति)। गोसाईँ = गोस्वामी = भगवान्। कहेसि = कहा (अकथयत्)। मरइ = मरे (मरेत्)। को = कः = कौन। बारहिँ बारा = वरम्बार। होउँ = होऊँ (भवानि)। जरि = जल कर (प्रज्वल्य)। छारा = छार = भस्म = राख। सर = शर = शरशय्या = चिता। रचि = रच कर (आ-रचय्य)। चहा = चाहा = चाहइ (इच्छति) का प्रथम-पुरुष, भूत-काल, पुंलिङ्ग का एक-वचन। आगि = अग्नि = आग। लाई = लगावेँ (लगयेः)। महादेओ = महादेव। गउरइ = गौरी ने। सुधि = शोध = खबर। पाई = पावइ (प्राप्नोति) का प्रथम-पुरुष, भूत-काल, स्त्रीलिङ्ग का एक-वचन। आइ = आ कर (एत्य)। बुझाइ = बुझा कर (निर्वाप्य)। दीन्ह = दिया (अदात्)। पँथ = पथ = पन्थाः = राह। तहवाँ = तहाँ = तत्र। मरन = मरणार्थ। खेल = लीला। आगम = आगमन। जहवाँ = जहाँ = यत्र। उलटा = उद्वर्त्तन = विपरीत। पेम = प्रेम। कइ = के। बारा = द्वार। चढइ = चढे (उच्चलेत् वा आरोहेत्)। सरग = स्वर्ग। सो = सः = वह। परइ = पडे (पतेत्)। पतारा = पाताल। अब = इदानीम् = अधुना। धँसि = धँस कर (आध्वंस्य)। लीन्ह = लेना। चहइ = चाहता है (इच्छति)। आसा = आशा = उम्मीद। पावइ = पावे (प्राप्नुयात्)। कि = वा = अथवा। मरइ = मरे (मरेत्)। निरासा = निराश = नैराश्य = नाउम्मीद ॥

पाती = पत्री। लिखि = लिख कर (लिखिला)। पठाई = पठवइ (प्रेषयति वा प्रस्थापयति) का प्रथम-पुरुष, भूत-काल, स्त्रीलिङ्ग का एक-वचन। लिखा = लिखइ

(लिखति) का प्रथम-पुरुष, भूत-काल, पुंलिङ्ग का एक-वचन । सबइ = सभी । दुख = दुःख । रोइ = रो कर (रुदित्वा)। दऊँ = देखेँ = क्या जानेँ। जिउ = जीव। रहइ = रहता है (तिष्ठति) । निसरइ = निकलता है (निःसरति) । काह = किम् = क्या । रजाएसु = राजाज्ञा । होइ = होती है (भवति) ॥

(शुक पद्मावती से कह रहा है कि) ऐसा वसन्त निश्चय है कि तुम्ही खेलती हो, दूसरे के रुधिर का सेँदुर लगाती हो। तुम तो खेल कर घर चली गई पर उस (रत्न-सेन) का हाल भगवान-ही जानता है। (उस रत्न-सेन ने) कहा कि वारंवार (पद्मावती के ध्यान से) कौन मरता रहे, एक-ही वार जल कर राख हो जाऊँ (तो अच्छा)। (ऐसा विचार कर) चिता रच कर, ज्योँ-ही आग लगा कर जलना चाहा, त्योँ ही महादेव और पार्वती (गौरी) ने खबर पाई (कि रत्न-सेन जल रहा है)। आ कर, आग को बुझा कर, उस पथ को दिया, अर्थात् बताया, जिस मेँ कि मरने के खेल का आगम है। (कवि कहता है कि) प्रेम-दार की राह उलटी है, स्वर्ग को चढे तो पाताल मेँ गिरे। (राजा रत्न-सेन) अब उस (पद्मावती) की आशा से, (गढ मेँ) धँस कर। (उस राह को) लेना चाहता है ; (उस राह मेँ) आशा को पावे या नैराश्य हो कर मरे ॥

(रत्न-सेन ने) जो पत्री भेजी थी (उस मेँ) सभी दुःख रो रो कर लिखा था, (उस मेँ यह भी लिखा था कि) देखेँ जीव रहता है कि जाता है (देखेँ) राजा (गन्धर्व-सेन) की क्या आज्ञा होती है ॥ २ ३ ४ ॥

चउपाई ।

कहि कइ सुअइ छोडि दइ पाती । जानहुँ दीप छुअत तस ताती ॥
गिअहिँ जो बाँधे कंचन तागे । राते स्यावँ कंठ जरि लागे ॥
अगिनि साँस सँग निसरी ताती । तरुअर जरहिँ तहाँ को पाती ॥
रोइ रोइ सुअइ कही सब बाता । रकत क आँसुहिँ भा मुख राता ॥
देखु कंठ जरि लागु सो गेरा । सो कस जरइ बिरह अस घेरा ॥
जरि जरि हाड भए सब चूना । तहाँ माँस को रकत बिहूना ॥
वेइ तोहि लागि कया असि जारी । तपत मीन जल रहइ न पारी ॥

दोहा।

तेहि कारन वह जोगी भसम कीन्ह तन दाहि।
तूँ अस निठुर निछोही बात न पूँछी ताहि ॥ २३५ ॥

कहि कइ = कह कर (कथयित्वा)। सुश्रद् = शुक ने। छोडि दइ = छोड दी। दइ = दी = दई (अदात्)। जानऊँ = जाने = जानें। दीप = दीपक = दीया = चिराग। छुश्रत = छूते (स्पृशन्)। तस = तथा = तैसी। ताती = तप्त = गर्म। गिअहिँ = ग्रीवा में = ग्रीवायाम्। बाँधे = बँधे थे = बद्ध थे। कंचन = काञ्चन = सुवर्ण। तागे = सूत। राते = रक्त = लाल। स्यावँ = श्याम = काला। जरि = जल कर (प्रज्वल्य)। लागे = लगे = लग्न हो गए। अगिनि = अग्नि = आग। साँस = श्वास। सँग = संग = साथ। निसरी = निसरइ (निःसरति) का प्रथम-पुरुष, भूत-काल, स्त्रीलिङ्ग का एक-वचन। तरुअर = तरुवर = बडे वृक्ष। जरहिँ = जरइ (ज्वलति) का बहु-वचन = जलते हैँ। तहाँ = तत्र। को = क्या = किम्। रोइ = रो कर (रुदित्वा)। कही = कहइ (कथयति) का प्रथम-पुरुष, भूत-काल, स्त्रीलिङ्ग का एक-वचन। वाता = वार्त्ता = बात। रकत = रक्त = रुधिर। क = की। आँसुहिँ = आँसुओं से = अश्रुभिः। भा = भया (बभूव) = हुआ। मुख = मुँह। राता = रक्त = लाल। देखु = देख (पश्य)। कंठ = कण्ठ = गला। लागु = लगा = लग्न हुआ। सो = वह। गेरा = गिरा दिया। कस = कथम् = कैसा। जरइ = जलता है (ज्वलति)। बिरह = विरह = वियोग। अस = एतादृश = ऐसा। घेरा = घेर लिया। हाड = अस्थि = हड्डिआँ। भए = हुए (बभूवुः)। चूना = चूर्ण। तहाँ = तत्र। माँस = मांस। को = किम् = क्या। बिहूना = विहीन। वेइ = उन्हों ने। तोहि लागि = तेरे लिये। कया = काय = शरीर = देह। असि = एतादृशी = ऐसी। जारी = जारइ (ज्वालयति) का प्रथम-पुरुष, भूत-काल, स्त्रीलिङ्ग का एक-वचन। तपत = तप्त। मीन = मछली। जल = पानी। रहइ = रहने को। पारी = पारइ (पारयति) का प्रथम-पुरुष, भूत-काल, स्त्रीलिङ्ग का एक-वचन ॥

कारन = कारण। जोगी = योगी। भसम = भस्म = राख। कीन्ह = किया (अकरोत्)। तन = तनु = देह। दाहि = दाह कर (दग्ध्वा)। तूँ = त्वम्। निठुर = निष्ठुर = क्रूर। निछोही = निःचोभी = निर्लोही। बात = वार्त्ता। पूँछी = पूँछइ (पृच्छति) का प्रथम-पुरुष, भूत-काल, स्त्रीलिङ्ग का एक-वचन ॥

शुक ने (इतनी बात) कह कर (पद्मावती के आगे, गले से) खोल कर पत्री को रख दी, (पत्री) छूने से ऐसी तप्त जान पड़ती है जैसे कि दीप। (दो फेरे) सोने के ताग जो गले में बाँधे गए थे (वे पत्री की आग से) जल कर कण्ठ में लाल काले (कण्ठे) हो गए, कवि की उत्प्रेक्षा है कि शुक के गले में लाल काले जो कण्ठे हैं वे पत्री की आग से ताग के जल जाने से हैं। (शुक की) गर्म श्वास के साथ आग भभक उठी जिस से बड़े बड़े वृक्ष जलने लगे, तहाँ (वृक्ष की) पत्तिओं की क्या गिनती है। शुक (हीरा-मणि) ने रो रो कर सब बात कही, रक्त की आँसुओं से मुख लाल हो गया। (शुक कहता है कि, पद्मावती) देख, कण्ठ जलने लगा तब (इस पत्री को) गिरा दिया, सो (जिस के हाथ की पत्री है वह) ऐसी विरहाग्नि के घेरे से कैसा जरता है (यह तूँ ही समझ)। (उस रत्न-सेन के) सब हाड जल जल कर चूने हो गए, वहाँ रक्त के विना मांस की क्या बात है। उन्हों ने तेरे लिये इस तरह से देह को भस्म कर दिया; (सो तूँ ही कह कि) जलती मछली पानी में रह सकती है?॥

तेरे लिये उस योगी ने देह को जला कर, राख कर दी, (पर) तूँ ऐसी निर्मोही है कि उस से बात तक न पूछी ॥ २३५ ॥

चउपाई।

कहेसि सुआ मो सउँ सुनु बाता। चहउँ तो आजु मिलउँ जस राता॥
पइ सो मरमु न जानइ भोरा। जानइ प्रीति जो मरि कइ जोरा॥
हउँ जानति हउँ अब-हूँ काँचा। ना जेहि प्रीति रंग थिरु राँचा॥
ना जेहि होइ भवँर कर रंगू। ना जेहि दीपक होइ पतंगू॥
ना जेहि करा भिंगि कइ होई। ना जेहि अबहि जिअइ मरि सोई॥
ना जेहि पेम अउटि एक भएउ। ना जेहि हिअइ माँह डर गएउ॥
ना जेहि भएउ मलइ गिरि बासा। ना जेहि रबि होइ चढेउ अकासा॥

दोहा।

तेहि का कहिअ रहन खन जो हइ पीतम लागि।
जहाँ सुनइ तहँ लेइ धँसि कहा पानि का आगि॥ २३६॥

कहेसि = कहा (अकथयत्)। सुआ = शुक। मो सउँ = मुझ से। सुनु = सुन (शृणु)। बाता = वार्त्ता = बात। चहउँ = चाहूँ (इच्छामि)। तो = तर्हि। आजु = आज = अद्य। मिलउँ = मिलूँ (मिलामि)। जस = यथा = जैसे। राता = रक्त = अनुरक्त। पइ = अपि = पर। सो = सः = वह। मरसु = मरम = मर्म = भेद। जानइ = जानता है (जानाति)। भोरा = भुलना = बौरहा = गवाँर = वातुल। प्रीति = प्रेम। जो = यः = जो। मरि कइ = मर कर (मृत्वा)। जोरा = जोरइ (जोटयति) का प्रथम-पुरुष, भूत-काल, स्त्रीलिङ्ग का एक-वचन। हउँ = अहम् = मैं। जानति = जानती (ज्ञाता)। हउँ = हूँ (अस्मि)। अब-हूँ = इदानीमपि = अधुनापि = अब भी। काँचा = कच्चा (कच्यः कच बन्धने से)। ना = न = नहीं। रंग = रङ्ग = वर्ण। थिर = स्थिर = ठहराऊ। राँचा = रचा गया, वा रचा = रचइ (रचयति) का प्रथम-पुरुष, भूत-काल, पुंलिङ्ग का एक-वचन। होइ = होता है (भवति) भवँर = भ्रमर = भौंरा। रंगू = रङ्ग = वर्ण। दीपक = दीप = दीया। पतंगू = पतङ्ग = फतिंगा। करा = कला। भिंगि = भृङ्गी = बिलनी = एक कीट विशेष। होई = होइ (भवति)। अबहि = अभीँ। जिअइ = जीवता है (जीवति)। मरि = मर कर (मृत्वा)। सोई = स एव = वही। पेम = प्रेम। अउटि = आवर्त्त्य = औट कर। एक = एक। भएऊ = भया (बभूव) = हुआ। हिअइ = हृदय। माँह = मध्ये = मेँ। डर = दर = भय। गएऊ = गया (अगात्)। मलइ = मलय। गिरि = पर्वत। बासा = वास। रबि = रवि = सूर्य। होइ = हो कर (भूत्वा)। चढेउ = चढा (उच्चलित हुआ)। अकासा = आकाश = स्वर्ग ॥

का = किम् = क्या। कहिअ = कहिए (कथ्यते)। रहन = रहना। खन = क्षण। हइ = है (अस्ति)। पीतम = प्रियतम। लागि = लिये। जहाँ = यत्र। सुनइ = सुने (शृणुयात्)। तहँ = तहाँ। लेइ = लेता है (लाति)। धँसि = धँस कर (प्रध्वंस्य)। कहा = किम् = क्या। पानि = पानीय = पानी। का = किम् = क्या। आगि = अग्नि = आग ॥

(पद्मावती ने) कहा कि, हे शुक मुझ से बात सुन, जैसा (वह मेरे में) अनुरक्त है (इस बात के सुनने से) चाहूँ तो आज ही मिलूँ। पर वह गवाँर (प्रीति का) मर्म नहीं जानता, जो मर कर प्रीति को जोडता है वही (प्रीति को) जानता है। मैं जानती हूँ, अभीं वह कच्चा है, जिस में स्थिर प्रीति-वर्ण नहीं रचा गया। जिस में (अभीं) भौंर का रङ्ग नहीं आया, जो कि (अभीं) दीए का फतिंगा न हुआ। जिस में अभीं भृङ्गी की कला न हुई, जो कि वह अभीं मर कर नहीं जीआ है।

(भङ्गी के लिये ७८ वें दोहे की टीका देखो)। जिस की (देह में) चोट कर प्रेम एक नहीं हुआ है, अर्थात् मिल नहीं गया है, जिस के हृदय में से डर नहीं गया है। जिस को मलयाचल का वास नहीं हुआ, अर्थात् मलय-चन्दन की प्राप्ति नहीं हुई, जो सूर्य हो कर, आकाश पर नहीं चढा॥

जो प्रियतम के लिये (उपस्थित) है, उस को क्या रहने का क्षण कहा जाता है, अर्थात् वह क्या एक क्षण भी ठहरता है; उस को क्या पानी क्या आग, जहाँ (प्रियतम का नाम) सुने वहीँ धँस कर (प्रियतम-प्राप्ति का सुख) ले॥ २३६॥

चउपाई।

पुनि धनि कनक पानि मसि माँगी। उतर लिखत भीँजी तनु आँगी॥
तेहि कंचन कहँ चहिअ सोहागा। जउँ निरमल नग होइ सो लागा॥
हउँ जो गइउँ मढ मंडप भोरी। तहवाँ तुइँ न गाँठि गहि जोरी॥
गा बिसँभारि देखि कइ नइना। सखिन्ह लाज का बोलउँ बइना॥
खेलहि मिसु मइँ चंदन घाला। मकु जागसि तो देउँ जइ-माला॥
तबहुँ न जागा गा तूँ सोई। जागइँ भेँटि न सोअइँ होई॥
अब तउ ससि होइ चढेउँ अकासा। जो जिउ देइ सो आवइ पासा॥

दोहा।

तब लगि भुगुति न लेइ सका रावन सिअ एक साथ।
कउन भरोसइँ अब कहउँ जीउ पराए हाथ॥ २३७॥

पुनि = पुनः = फिर। धनि = धन्या (पद्मावती)। कनक = सुवर्ण। पानि = पानी = पानीय। मसि = मषी = स्याही। माँगी = माँगइ (याचते) का प्रथम-पुरुष, भूत-काल, स्त्रीलिङ्ग का एक-वचन। उतर = उत्तर = जवाब। लिखत = लिखते (लिखन्)। भीँजी = भीँजइ (अभ्यञ्जते) का प्रथम-पुरुष, भूत-काल, स्त्रीलिङ्ग का एक-वचन। तनु = शरीर = देह। आँगी = अँगिआ (अङ्गिनी) = चोलिआ = चोली। तेहि = तिस। कंचन = काञ्चन = सुवर्ण। कहँ = को। चहिअ = चाहिए। सोहागा = सोहागा = (शुभाङ्ग)। जउँ = यदि = जो। निरमल = निर्मल = स्वच्छ = साफ। नग = रत्न का खण्ड, जो अँगूठी इत्यादि में

जड़ा जाता है। होइ = होय = होवे (भवेत्)। सो = वह = सः। लागा = लाग = लगता है (लगति)। हउँ = अहम् = मैं। गइउँ = गई (अगाम्)। मढ = मठ = देव-मन्दिर। मंडप = मण्डप = मन्दिरद्वार के बाहर की शाला। भोरी = बौरही। तहवाँ = तहाँ = तत्र। तुइँ = त्वम् = तूँ। गाँठि = ग्रन्थि = गाँठ। गहि = गृहीत्वा = गह कर = पकड़ कर। जोरी = जोरइ (जोटयति) का, प्रथम-पुरुष, भूत-काल, स्त्रीलिङ्ग का एक-वचन। गा = गया (अगात्)। बिसँभारि = बेसँभार (विसम्भार)। देखि कइ = देख कर (दृष्ट्वा)। नइना = नयन = आँख। सखिन्ह = सखी का बहु-वचन। लाज = लज्जा। का = किम् = क्या। बोलउँ = बोलूँ (वदानि)। बइना = वचन। खेलहि = खेल के = खेलायाः। मिसु = मिष = व्याज = बहाना। मइँ = मैं। चंदन = चन्दन = सुगन्ध द्रव्य। घाला = घालइ (गारयति) का प्रथम-पुरुष, भूत-काल, पुंलिङ्ग का एक-वचन। मकु = मैं ने कहा = कि। जागसि = जागे = जागइ (जागर्त्ति) का मध्यम-पुरुष, सम्भावना में पुंलिङ्ग का एक-वचन। तो = तर्हि। देउँ = देऊँ (ददानि)। जइ-माला = जय-माला। तबहूँ = तदापि = तौ भी। जागा = जागइ (जागर्त्ति) का प्रथम-पुरुष, भूत-काल, पुंलिङ्ग का एक-वचन। गा = गया (अगात्)। तूँ = त्वम्। सोई = सोय = शयित = शयन। जागइँ = जागने से (जागरणेन)। भेँटि = भेँट = सम्भवेत = समागम। सोअइँ = सोने से (शयनेन)। होई = होइ = होता वा होती है (भवति)। अब तउ = अब तो = इदानीं तु। ससि = शशी = चन्द्र। होइ = हो कर (भूत्वा)। चढउँ = चढी (उच्चलितास्मि)। अकास = आकाश। जो = यः। जिउ = जीव। देइ = दे = देवे (दद्यात्)। सो = सः = वह। आवइ = आवे (आयात्)। पास = पार्श्व = पास॥

तब लगि = तब तक। भुगुति = भुक्ति = भोजन। सका = सकइ (शक्नोति) का प्रथम-पुरुष, भूत-काल, पुंलिङ्ग का एक-वचन। राओन = रावण = प्रसिद्ध लङ्का का राजा। सिअ = सीता = प्रसिद्ध पतिव्रता, राम-पत्नी, जनक की कन्या। एक = एक। साथ = सार्थ। कउन = क्व नु = किस। भरोसइँ = भरोसे से (भराशया)। कहउँ = कहूँ (कथयेयम्)। जीउ = जीव। पराए = परस्य = दूसरे के। हाथ = हस्त॥

फिर धन्या (पद्मावती) ने सोने की पानी की स्याही, अर्थात् सोने की स्याही माँगी, उत्तर लिखती बेरा (प्रियतम के अनुराग से, रोमाञ्च और पसीना आ जाने से) देह की चोलिआ भीँग गई। (लिखने लगी कि) उस सोने में सोहागा मिलना चाहिए यदि (वह सोना चाहे कि मैं) निर्मल होऊँ (तव) उस में नग लगा हो,

अर्थात् तब उस मैं नग लगाया जाता है। मैं बौरही जब मठ-मण्डप मैं गई, उसी जगह तैँ ने क्यों न (मुझ से) गाँठ जोडी। (मेरी) आँखों को देख कर तूँ बेसँभार, अर्थात् बेहोश, हो गया, (मैं उस समय) सखिओं की लाज से क्या बात बोलूँ। मैं ने खेल के बहाने से (तेरे ऊपर) चन्दन को डाल दिया, कि तूँ जागे तो मैं जय-माला (तुझे) देऊँ। तब भी तूँ न जागा, सो गया, (सो) जागने से भेंट होती है सोने से नहीं। अब तो मैं चन्द्र हो कर आकाश (धरहरे) पर चढी हूँ; जो जीव दे, अर्थात् मर कर स्वर्ग पर चढे, वह मेरे पास आवे, (जीव रहते स्वर्ग पर आना असम्भव है)॥

सीता के एक साथ मैं (रह कर भी) तब तक रावण ने भुक्ति (स्वर्ग-सुख) को न ले सका (जब तक कि जीव को न दिया)। सो अब किस भरोसे से कहूँ (कि मैं कैसे मिलूँगी), जीव तो दूसरे के, अर्थात् पिता के हाथ मैं है॥ २३७॥

चउपाई ।

अब जउँ सूर गगन चढि आवइ। राहु होइ तउ ससि कहँ पावइ॥
बहुतइँ अइस जीउ पर खेला। तूँ जोगी केहि माँह अकेला॥
बिकरम धँसा पेम कइ बारा। चंपावति कहँ गएउ पतारा॥
सुदइ बच्छ मगधावति लागी। कँकन पूरि होइ गा बइरागी॥
राज कुअँर कंचन-पुर गएऊ। मिरगावति कहँ जोगी भएऊ॥
साध कुअँर गंधावति जोगू। मधु मालति कहँ कीन्ह बिओगू॥
पेमावति कहँ सर सुर साधा। उखा लागि अनिरुध बर बाँधा॥

दोहा।

हउँ रानी पदुमावती सात सरग पर बास।
हाथ चढउँ हउँ ताहि के प्रथम करइ अपुनास॥ २३८॥

अब = इदानीम्। जउँ = यदि = जो। सूर = सूर्य, वा शूर = बहादुर रत्न-सेन। गगन = आकाश। चढि = चढ कर = आरुह्य = प्रचाल्य। आवइ = आवे (आयात्)। राहु = प्रसिद्ध दैत्य। होइ = होवे = भवेत् = हो। तउ = तर्हि = तो। ससि = शशि = चन्द्र। कहँ = को। पावइ = पावे = प्राप्नुयात्। बहुतइँ = बहुत लोग = बहवो हि। अइस = ऐसे = एतादृश। जीउ = जीव। पर = उपरि। खेला = अखेलत्। तूँ = त्वम्।

जोगी = योगी। केहि = कस्य = किस। माँह = मध्ये = मैं। अकेला = एकलः = एकाकी। बिकरम = विक्रम = उज्जयिनी का प्रसिद्ध राजा। धँसा = पैठा [ध्वंसु अवस्रंसने (भ्वादि) से]। पेम = प्रेम। कइ = के। बारा = बार = द्वार। चंपावति = चम्पावती = एक पाताल की राज-कन्या। कहँ = के। गप्रउ = गया (अगात्)। पतारा = पाताल। सुदइ बच्छ = सुदेव वत्स = वत्सदेव। मंगधावति = मगधावती = मागधी = मगधराज की कन्या। लागी = लिये। कँकन = कङ्कण = कडा। पूरि = आपूर्य = पहन कर। होइगा = हो गया। बइरागी = वैरागी = विरागी। राज-कुअँर = राज-कुमार = राज-पुत्र। कंचन-पुर = कञ्चन-पुर। मिरगावति = मृगावती = एक राज-कन्या। भप्रज = भया (बभूव)। साध = साधा (असाधयत्)। कुअँर = कुमार = राज-पुत्र। गंधावति = गन्धावती = एक राज-कन्या। जोगू = योग। मधु = मधुकर = एक राजा। मालति = मालती = एक राज-कन्या। कीन्ह = किया (अकरोत्)। बिओगू = वियोग। पेमावति = प्रेमावती = मोहनी। सर = शर = फूस की चिता। सुर = देव = महादेव। साधा = असाधयत्। उखा = ऊषा = वाणासुर की कन्या। अनिरुध = अनिरुद्ध = कृष्ण का पौत्र = प्रद्युम्न का पुत्र। बर = वर = विवाहयोग्य पुरुष। बाँधा = बाँधा गया॥

हउँ = मैं। पदुमावती = पद्मावती। सात = सप्त। सरग = स्वर्ग। पर = उपरि। बास = वास = रहने का स्थान। हाथ = हस्त। चढउँ = चढती हूँ। ताहि के = तिस के। प्रथम = पहले। अपुनास = अपना नाश॥

अब तो सूर्य (रत्न-सेन) यदि आकाश पर चढ कर आवे और राहु होवे तो शशि (पद्मावती) को पावे अर्थात् शशि के साथ का सुखानुभव करे। (मेरे लिये) ऐसे-ही बहुत से लोग जीव पर खेल गए, अर्थात् उद्योग कर मर गए, हूँ अकेला योगी किस गिनती में है। प्रेम के द्वार में विक्रम धँसा, (और) चम्पावती के लिये पाताल में चला गया। वत्सदेव मगधावती के लिये (हाथों में) कङ्कण पहन कर वैरागी हो गया। राज-कुअँर मृगावती के लिये कञ्चन-पुर गया और योगी हो गया। कुअँर ने गन्धावती के लिये योग साधा। मधुकर ने मालती को वियोग, अर्थात् व्याकुल, किया, अर्थात् विरहिणी किया। सुर ने प्रेमावती के लिये चिता लगाई, अनिरुद्ध ऊषा के लिये बाँधा गया॥

मैं पद्मावती रानी हूँ सात स्वर्ग (धरहरे) के ऊपर मेरा वास है, जो पहले अपने को खोवे (नाश करे) उस के हाथ मैं आती हूँ (चढती हूँ)॥

तुम्हारी मनकामना पूरी करेगा। कुअँर उस के पास जा कर उस की सेवा में लगा। बज्जत दिनों पर वह प्रसन्न हो कर कहा कि क्या चाहते हो। कुअँर ने कहा कि योगि-राज गन्धावती को चाहता हूँ। इस पर उस ने कहा कि यह मेरी सामर्थ्य से बाहर है तुम मेरे गुरु के पास जाओ। कुअँर उस के गुरु के पास जा कर उस की सेवा करने लगा और उस के प्रसाद से शुक हो कर गन्धावती से मिला। गन्धावती तौल में एक फूल से बढ गई इस पर उस के पिता को उस पर पर-पुरुष संयोग का संशय ज्ञआ। बज्जत खोज करने पर उस ने चाहा कि सुग्गे को मार डालें पर गन्धावती ने उसे उडा दिया। वह कुअँर मनुष्य वेष से वहीँ रहने लगा अन्त में स्वयंवर के समय गन्धावती ने उसी के गले जय-माल डाल कर उसी से विवाह किया। संभव है कि इसी कहानी को बढा कर किसी ने गन्धावती नाम की कोई पुस्तक लिखी हो॥

मधु-मालती—मोहनपुर में मधुकर नाम का राजा रहता था। एक दिन राजा अहेर करने गया वहाँ एक हरिण के पीछे दौडा। बज्जत दूर जाने पर हरिण लोप हो गया। राजा एक वृक्ष की घनी छाँह के नीचे कपडे को बिछा कर आराम करने लगा। बज्जत दिनों के बिछुडे दो सुग्गे दैवात् उस वृक्ष पर आए। दोनों से भेंट होने पर दोनों प्रसन्न हो कर आपस में बात चीत करने लगे। एक ने कहा कि मित्र तुम से बिछुड कर एक वृक्ष पर बैठा था तहाँ अचानक एक व्याधे ने मुझे फँसा लिया। उस ने प्रेम-नगर की हाट में रूप-राजा के यहाँ मुझे बेंच दिया। राजा ने अपनी कन्या मालती से कहा कि इस सुग्गे को पालो। उस ने मुझे बडे प्यार से पाला। वह ऐसी सुन्दरी है कि मैं वर्णन नहीं कर सकता। एक दिन वह सरोवर में स्नान करने गई। घर को सूना पा कर मेरे पिँजरे पर बिलैया झपटी। भाग्य-वश पिँजरे से भाग कर उड आया। मधुकर मालती का नाम सुन प्रेम से विकल हो गया। मधुकर ने उस सुग्गे से कहा कि नीचे उतर कर मेरे पास आओ और मालती कैसे मिलेगी इस का उपाय बताओ। राजा के बज्जत कहने पर सुग्गे ने मालती के पास जा कर राजा का सँदेसा सुनाया। मधुकर का नाम सुन कर मालती भी उस के मिलने की चाह से बज्जत व्याकुल ज्जई। मालती की दशा पर सुग्गा फिर लौटा और मालती की फुलवारी में रहने लगा। धाई ने मालती की दशा देख कर सब वृत्तान्त पूछी। मालती ने धाई के कहने से प्रेम बनिजारे के साथ सुग्गे को भेज कर मधुकर को बुला कर उस के साथ विवाह किया। इस की सविस्तर कथा इन्द्रावती के मधुकरखण्ड में नूर महम्मद ने लिखी है। नागरी प्रचारिणी ग्रन्थमाला में इन्द्रावती छापी गई है॥

सुर-प्रेमावती—इस नाम से मुझे यह कथा नहीँ मिली है। बहुत लोग कहते हैँ कि प्रेमावती मोहनी का नामान्तर है। समुद्र मथने के समय जब अमृत निकला है तब उस के लिये देवता और राचस लडने लगे। इस पर भगवान् मोहनी स्त्री का रूप बन कर आए। सब लोग उस पर मोहित हो गए, अमृत का घट उसी को दे दिया। मोहनी ने छल से सुरा राचसेाँ मेँ और अमृत देवताओँ मेँ बाँट दिया। एक दिन महादेव ने भगवान् से कहा कि मैँ आप का मोहनी रूप देखा चाहता हूँ। बहुत कहने पर भगवान् विष्णु ने मोहनी रूप देखाया। महादेव मोहित हो उस के पीछे पीछे दौडने लगे। अन्त मेँ मोहनी अन्तर्धान हो गई। इस पर व्याकुल हो उस के लिये महादेव जी मरने के लिये तयार हुए। पुराणोँ मेँ यह कथा मिलती है। मैँ नहीँ कह सकता कि प्रेमावती से मोहनी-ही है वा दूसरी। संभव है कि प्रेमावती कोई राज-कन्या हो और सुर देवता रूप कोई राजा रहा हो ॥

अनिरुद्ध—ऊषा। शोणित-पुर के राजा बाणासुर की कन्या ऊषा थी। एक दिन इस ने स्वप्न मेँ अनिरुद्ध को देखा। उस के व्याकुल होने पर उस की सखी चित्र-लेखा ने सब के चित्र खीँच खीँच कर उसे देखाया। अन्त मेँ अनिरुद्ध के चित्र को उस ने पहचाना और कहा कि यही चित-चोर रात को स्वप्न मेँ मेरे पास आया था। चित्र-लेखा द्वारिका से सोते हुए अनिरुद्ध को उठा लाई और ऊषा से मिलाई। खबर लगने पर बाणासुर ने अनिरुद्ध को कैद किया। फिर पीछे कृष्ण ने यदुवंशियोँ के साथ आ कर, बाणासुर से लड कर, अनिरुद्ध को छुडाया। यह कथा श्रीमद्भागवत के दशमस्कन्ध मेँ विस्तार के साथ लिखी है ॥ २३८ ॥

चउपाई ।

हउँ पुनि अहउँ अइसि तोहि राती। आधी भेँटि पिरीतम पाती ॥
तोहि जउँ प्रीति निबाहइ आँटा। भवँर न देखु केत मँह काँटा ॥
होहु पतंग अधर गहि दीआ। लेहु समुँद धँसि होइ मरजीआ ॥
राति रंग जिमि दीपक बाती। नइन लाउ होइ सीप सेवाती ॥
चातक होइ पुकारु पिआसा। पीउ न पानि सेवाति क आसा ॥
सारस होहु बिछुरि जस जोरी। रइनि होहु जस चकइ चकोरी ॥
होहु चकोर दिसिटि ससि पाँहा। अउ रबि होहु कवँल ओहि माँहा ॥

दोहा ।

हम-हुँ अदसि हउँ तो सउँ सकसि त प्रीति निबाहु ।
राहु बेधि अरजुन होइ जिति दुरपदी बिआहु ॥ २३९ ॥

हउँ = अहम् = मैं । पुनि = पुनः = फिर । अहउँ = हूं (अस्मि) । अदसि = एतादृशी = ऐसी । तोहि = तेरे में । राती = रक्त = अनुरक्त । आधी = अर्ध । भेंटि = भेंट = समवेत = मुलाकात । पिरीतम = प्रियतम । पाती = पत्री = चिट्ठी । तोहि = तुझे । जउँ = यदि = जो । प्रीति = प्रेम । निबाहइ = निर्वाह करना = निबाहना । आँटा = आँट = अँटइ (समेति) । भवँर = भ्रमर = भौंरा । देखु = देख = देखता है (पश्यति) । केत = केतक = केतकी = एक प्रसिद्ध पुष्प । मँह = मध्ये = में । काँटा = कण्टक । होऊ = होओ (भवथ) । पतंग = पतङ्ग = फतिंगा । अधर = ओठ । गहि = गह कर (गहीला) = पकड कर । दीआ = दीप = चिराग । लेऊ = लेओ (लाथ) । समुँद = समुद्र । धँसि = धँस कर (आध्वंस्य) । होइ = हो कर (भूत्वा) । मरजीआ = मर कर जीने-वाला = गोताखोर = समुद्र में गोता लगाने-वाला । राति = रक्त = लाल । रंग = रङ्ग = वर्ण । जिमि = यथा = जैसे । दीपक = दीप = दीआ । बाती = वर्त्ती = बत्ती । नइन = नयन = आँख । लाउ = लगावो (लगय) । होइ = हो कर (भूत्वा) । सीप = शुक्ति । सेवाती = स्वाती = वर्षा की एक नक्षत्र । चातक = पपीहा = एक प्रसिद्ध पक्षी । पुकारु = पुकार (फुत्कारय) । पिआसा = पिपासित = प्यासा । पीउ = पी (पिब) । पानि = पानी (पानीय) । क = की । आसा = आशा = उम्मीद । सारस = एक प्रसिद्ध जल-पक्षी । बिछुरि = बिछुड कर = विच्छुरित हो कर । जस = यथा = जैसे । जोरी = जोडी = युगल । रइनि = रजनी = रात्रि । जल = पानी । चकइ = चकई = चक्रवाकी = चकवा (चक्रवाक) की स्त्री । चकोरी = चकोर पक्षी की स्त्री । दिसिटि = दृष्टि । ससि = शशी = चन्द्र । पाँहा = पार्श्व = निकट । रबि = रवि = सूर्य । कवँल = कमल । ओहि माँहा = उस में ॥

हम-ऊँ = अहमपि = हम भी । अदसि = एतादृशी = ऐसी । हउँ = हूं (अस्मि) । तो सउँ = तुझ से । सकसि = सकते हो (शक्नोसि) । त = तर्हि = तो । प्रीति = प्रेम । निवाऊ = निबाह (निर्वाहय) । राऊ = राऊ (सर्प वा मत्स्य) के आकार का लक्ष्य (निशाना) । बेधि = बेध कर (विद्ध्वा) । अरजुन = अर्जुन = युधिष्ठिर के भाई, भारत के प्रसिद्ध योद्धा । जिति = जीत कर (जित्वा) । दुरपदी = द्रौपदी = युधिष्ठिरादि पाँचो पाण्डवों की स्त्री । बिआऊ = व्याह (विवाहय) ॥

फिर मैं भी तुझ में ऐसी-ही अनुरक्त हूँ, (अनुरक्त होने-ही से आधी भेंट के लिये तेरे पास चिट्ठी भेजी है क्योंकि कहावत है कि) पत्री प्रियतम की आधी मुलाकात है। यदि तूँ प्रीति-निर्वाह कर सकता है तो भ्रमर यह नहीँ देखता कि, केतकी में (कितने) काँटे हैँ। ओठों से दीप (ज्योति) को पकड कर, फतिंगा हो जाओ, अर्थात् दीप-ज्योति-सम मैं जो हूँ उस के लिये फतिंगा हो जाओ, गोताखोर हो कर समुद्र में धँस कर (मोती-रूप मुझे) लेओ। जैसे दीए की बत्ती लाल रंग की होती है, वैसे-ही खाती के लिये सीप हो कर (मेरे में) आँखों को लगाओ। कहावत है कि यद्यपि सीप समुद्र में रहती है तथापि खाती-ही का पानी पीती है, उसी पानी के पीने से उस में मुक्ता पैदा होती है। चातक हो कर प्यास के दुःख से खाती के पानी की आशा से "पीव, पीव" पुकार, अर्थात् मेरे लिये प्यासा हो कर दिन रात मेरे नाम को पुकारा कर। कहावत है कि चातक खाती-ही का पानी पीता है, इस के ऊपर तुलसी-सतसई में अनेक दोहे लिखे हैँ। (१४१ वँ दोहे की टीका देखो)। जोडी बिछुडने पर जैसी सारस की दशा होती है वैसा-ही मेरे लिये तुम सारस हो। सारस के जोडे में बङत-ही प्रीति होती है, एक के वियोग से दूसरा प्राण दे देता है, इसी पर वाल्मीकि-रामायण का पहला स्लोक बनाया गया है। रात्रि में (पति-वियोग के कारण) पानी में चकई और चकोरी की जो दशा होती है वैसा-ही तुम भी हो। कहावत है कि चकवे और चकोर के जोडे में रात्रिसमय वियोग हो जाता है। चकोर हो कर चन्द्र पर दृष्टि लगाओ; (कहावत है कि रात को चकोर चन्द्र-ही को देखा करता है) अर्थात् मुझे चन्द्र समझ कर तुम चकोर हो जाओ; और रवि जो है उस में कमल हो जाओ, अर्थात् मुझे रवि ज्ञान कर उस के लिये तुम कमल हो जाओ॥

हम भी तुम से ऐसी-ही (प्रीति लगाई ऊई) हैँ, (सो) तूँ भी, यदि कर सकता है, तो प्रीति को निबाह। अर्जुन हो कर राऊ (मत्स्याकार लक्ष्य) को वेध कर, (और सब को) जीत कर, द्रौपदी से विवाह कर, अर्थात् मुझ से विवाह कर। राऊ के लिये १०४ दोहे की टीका देखो॥ २३९॥

चउपाई।

राजा इहाँ तइस तप झूरा। भा जरि बिरह छार कर कूरा॥
मउन लगाए गण्उ बिमोही। भा बिनु जिउ जिउ दीन्हेसि ओही॥

गहि पिंगला सुखुमना नारी । सुन्न समाधि लागि गइ तारी ॥
बूँद-हि समुँद होइ जस मेरा । गा हेराइ तस मिलइ न हेरा ॥
रंग-हि पानि मिला जस होई । आपुहि खोइ रहा होइ सोई ॥
सुश्रइ आइ देखा भा नासू । नइन रकत भरि आएउ आँसू ॥
सदा पिरीतम गाढ करेई । वह न भूल भूँला जिउ देई ॥

दोहा ।

मूरि सजीओनि आनि कइ अउ मुख मेला नीर ।
गरुर पाँख जस झारइ अँबिरित बरसा कीर ॥ २४० ॥

इहाँ = यहाँ = अत्र । तइस = तैसा = तथा । तप = तपः = तपस्या । झूरा = झूर हो गया = शुष्क हो गया । भा = भया (बभूव) = हुआ । जरि = जल कर (प्राज्वल्य)। बिरह = विरह = वियोग । छार = चार = राख । कूरा = कूट = ढेर । मउन = मौन = चुप । गएउ = गया = (अगात्) । बिमोही = विमोह = मूर्छित । बिनु = विना । जिउ = जीव । दीन्हेसि = दिया (अदात्)। ओही = उसे । गहि = गह कर (गृहीला) = पकड कर । पिंगला = पिङ्गला = नासिका का दहिना स्वर । सुखुमना = सुषुम्णा = नासिका के दोनों स्वर । नारी = नाडी । सुन्न = शून्य = ब्रह्माण्ड । समाधि = ध्यान में मग्न हो जाना, संसार से चित्तवृत्ति को हटा लेना (चित्तवृत्तिनिरोधः समाधिः, ऐसा योगशास्त्र में लिखा है)। लागि गइ = लग गई । तारी = ताली = तालिका = कुञ्जी । बूँद-हि = बूँद से (बिन्दुतः)। समुँद = समुद्र। होइ = होता है (भवति)। जस = यथा = जैसे । मेरा = मेल = संग । गा = गया (अगात्)। हेराइ = लोप (हेडृ अन्वेषणे से)। तस = तथा = तैसे । मिलइ = मिलता है (मिलति)। हेरा = हेरने से = ढूँढने से (हेडृ अन्वेषणे से)। रंग-हि = रङ्ग में । पानि = पानी (पानीय)। मिला = मिलित । होई = होइ = होता है (भवति)। आपु-हि = अपने को (आत्मनः)। खोइ = खो = नाश । रहा = रहइ (तिष्ठति) का प्रथम-पुरुष, भूत-काल, पुंलिङ्ग का एक-वचन । होइ = हो कर (भूला)। सोई = सा एव = वही । सुश्रइ = शुक ने । आई = आ कर (एत्य)। देखा = देखइ (पश्यति) का प्रथम-पुरुष, भूत-काल, पुंलिङ्ग का एक-वचन । भा = भया (बभूव) = हुआ । नासू = नाश । नइन = नयन = आँख । रकत = रक्त = खून = रुधिर । भरि = भर = पूर्ण । आएउ = आया (आयात्)। आँसू = आँस (अश्रु)।

सदा = हमेशा। पिरीतम = प्रियतम = प्यारा। गाढ = कठिन = कष्ट। करेई = करइ (करोति) = करता है। भूल = भूलइ (भ्रमति) = भूलता है। भूला = भूला हुआ = भ्रान्त। जिउ = जीव। देई = देइ = देता है (दत्ते)॥

मूरि = मूली = मूलिका। सजीओनि = सञ्जीवनी = जिलानेवाली। आनि कइ = आन कर (आनीय)। मेला = मेलइ (मेलयति) का प्रथम-पुरुष, भूत-काल, पुंलिङ्ग का एक-वचन। नीर = पानी। गरुर = गरुड = प्रसिद्ध पक्षी, विष्णु का वाहन। पाँख = पक्ष = पर। जस = यथा = जैसे। झारइ = झारता है (झारयति)। अँबिरित = अमृत। बरसा = बरसइ (वर्षति) का प्रथम-पुरुष, भूत-काल, पुंलिङ्ग का एक-वचन। कीर = शुक॥

यहाँ राजा तप से ऐसा सूख गया कि, विरहाग्नि से जल कर राख का ढेर हो गया। चुप साधे मूर्छित हो गया, जीव उस (पद्मावती) को दे दिया, (आप) विना जीव का हो गया। पिङ्गला और सुखम्णा नाडी को पकड कर (ऊपर खींच लिया इसी से) शून्य (ब्रह्माण्ड) में, अर्थात् ब्रह्मरन्ध्रस्थान में समाधि लग गई (और ब्रह्म-कपाट में) ताली लग गई, अर्थात् जिस ब्रह्मछिद्र से प्राण ऊपर चढ गया वह छिद्र बंद हो गया। योगी लोग इसी तरह से ब्रह्माण्ड पर प्राण चढाते हैं। (इस ग्रन्थ का २५१–२५२ पृष्ठ देखो।) जैसे समुद्र में एक जल-विन्दु का मेल हो जाय (तो फिर उस का पता नहीं लगता, उसी तरह (राजा रत्न-सेन पद्मावती के ध्यान में) लोप हो गया, ढूँढने से भी नहीं मिलता। जैसे (किसी) रंग में पानी मिला होता है (पर पानी की सूरत नहीं देख पडती) उसी तरह (राजा रत्न-सेन) अपने को खो कर, वही (पद्मावती) हो कर रह गया है। शुक (हीरा-मणि) ने आ कर देखा कि, (राजा का तो) नाश हो गया, (देख कर) आँखों में रक्ताश्रु भर गई। (मन में कहने लगा कि हाय विरही) सदा (अपने) प्रियतम के लिये कष्ट करता है, वह प्रियतम नहीं भूलता पर आप भूला हुआ (उस के लिये) जीव देता है॥

सञ्जीवनी मूली ला कर और (उस के रस के साथ राजा के) मुख में पानी डाला, जैसे गरुड अपने पंख को झारता है उसी तरह सुग्गे ने (राजा के मुख के ऊपर) अमृत की दृष्टि की॥ २४०॥

चउपाई।

सुआ अहा जेहि आस सो पावा। बहुरी साँस पेट जिउ आवा॥
देखेसि जागि सुअइ सिर नावा। पाति दीन्ह मुख बचन सुनावा॥

गुरू सबद दुइ सरवन मेला। गुरू बोलाउ बेगि चलु चेला॥
तोहि अलि कीन्ह आपु भा केवा। हउँ पठवा कइ बीच परेवा॥
पउन साँस तो सउँ मन लाई। जोवइ मारग दिसिटि बिछाई॥
जस तुम्ह कया कीन्ह अगि-डाहू। सो सब गुरु कहँ भएउ अगाहू॥
तब उडंत-छाला लिखि दीन्हा। बेगि आउ चाहउँ सिधि कीन्हा॥

दोहा।

आवहु स्यावँ सुलक्खनँ जीउ बसइ तुम्ह नाउँ।
नइनहिँ भीतर पंथ हइ हिरदहि भीतर ठाउँ॥ २४१॥

सुआ = शुक = सुग्गा। अहा = था (आसीत्)। जेहि = जिस। आस = आशा। सो = सो = वह = सः। पावा = पावइ (प्राप्नोति) का प्रथम-पुरुष, भूत-काल, पुंलिङ्ग का एक-वचन। बहुरी = फिरी = लौटी (न्यवर्त्ति = व्यवर्त्ति)। साँस = श्वास। पेट = पेटिका। जिउ = जीव। आवा = आवइ (आयाति) का प्रथम-पुरुष, भूत-काल, पुंलिङ्ग का एक-वचन। देखेसि = देखा (अपश्यत्)। जागि = जाग कर (जागृत्वा)। सुअइ = शुक ने। सिर = शिर। नावा = नावइ (नामयति) का प्रथम-पुरुष, भूत-काल, पुंलिङ्ग का एक-वचन। पाति = पाती = पत्री = चिट्ठी। दीन्ह = दिया (अदात्)। मुह = मुँह = मुख। बचन = वचन = बात। सुनावा = सुनावइ (श्रावयति) का प्रथम-पुरुष, भूत काल, पुंलिङ्ग का एक-वचन। गुरू = गुरु। सबद = शब्द। दुइ = दो = द्वयम्। सरवन = श्रवण = कान। मेला = मेलइ (मेलयति) का प्रथम-पुरुष, भूत-काल, पुंलिङ्ग का एक-वचन। बोलाउ = बुलाता है (ह्वलयति)। बेगि = वेग = शीघ्र। चलु = चल (चल)। चेला = शिष्य। तोहिँ = तुझे। अलि = भ्रमर = भौँरा। कीन्ह = किया (अकरोत्)। आपु = आप = स्वयम्। भा = भया (बभूव) = हुआ। केवा = कमल वा केवडा। हउँ = अहम्, यहाँ मुझे। पठवा = पठवइ (प्रेषयति) का प्रथम-पुरुष, भूत-काल, पुंलिङ्ग का एक-वचन। कइ = कर। बीच = मध्य। परेवा = पारावत = पक्षी। पउन = पवन = वायु। साँस = श्वास। तो सउँ = तुझ से। लाई = लगाई = लगावइ (लगयति) का प्रथम-पुरुष, भूत-काल, स्त्रीलिङ्ग का एक-वचन। जोवइ = जोहता है (जेहति) प्रा० जोएदि। मारग = मार्ग। दिसिटि = दृष्टि। बिछाई = बिछा कर (विस्तीर्य)। जस = यथा = जैसे।

कया = काय = शरीर। कीन्ह = किया (अकरोत्)। अगि-डाह = अग्नि-दाह = अग्नि से दाह। सो = सः = वह। सब = सर्व। गुरु कहँ = गुरु को। भण्उ = भया (बभूव) = ऊआ। अगाह = आगाह = विदित। तब = तदा। उडंत-छाला = उड्डयन-चैल = उडने-वाली छाल = जिसे शरीर में रखने से मनुष्य को उडने की शक्ति होती है। लिखि = लिख कर (लिखिला)। दीन्हा = दिया (अदात्)। आउ = आव (आयाहि)। चाहउँ = चाहता हूँ (इच्छामि)। सिधि = सिद्ध। कीन्हा = करना (करणम्)।

आवह = आइए = (आयाय)। स्यावँ = श्याम। सुलक्खनँ = सुलक्षण = जिस में सुन्दर लक्षण हों। जीउ = जीव। बसद् = बसता है (वसति)। नाउँ = नाम = नावँ। नइनहिं = नयनों के = आँखों के। भीतर = अभ्यन्तर। पंथ = पन्थाः = राह। हद् = है (अस्ति)। हिरदहि = हृदय के। ठाउँ = ठावँ = स्थान ॥

जिस आशा में (कि राजा जी जाय) शुक था, उस आशा को पाया, अर्थात् रत्न-सेन जी उठा, पेट में साँस फिर आई और जीव (प्राण) भी लौट आया। (राजा रत्न-सेन ने) जाग कर (सुग्गे को) देखा, सुग्गे ने भी (राजा के सामने) शिर झुँकाया, (पद्मावती की) चिट्ठी दी, और मुँह से (पद्मावती का) सँदेसा सुनाया। (कहा कि) गुरु (पद्मावती) ने (तुम्हारे) कान में दो शब्द डाला है, (एक शब्द तो यह है कि) गुरु (तुझे) बोलाता है, (और दूसरा शब्द यह कि कहो) चेला जल्द आवे। (गुरु ने) तुझे भ्रमर बनाया है और आप कमल ऊआ है, और मुझ पक्षी को मध्यस्थ कर (तेरे पास) भेजा है। (गुरु ने) तुझ से, श्वास-वायु के द्वार से, मन को लगाया है, दृष्टि को फैला कर (बिछाई) तेरी राह जोह रहा है। जिस तरह तुम्ह ने अपनी देह को आग में भस्म कर दिया, वह सब गुरु को मालूम ऊआ है। तब (इस पक्षी को) उडंत-छाला (के ऐसा) लिख दिया है, (और कहा है कि) जल्द आव, मैं (तुझे) सिद्ध किया चाहता हूँ ॥

(और भी कहा है कि) हे सुलक्षण श्याम (कृष्ण-स्वरूप) (शीघ्र) आओ, (मेरा) जीव तुम्हारे नाम में बस गया है; (तुम्हारे लिये) आँखों के भीतर राह और हृदय के भीतर स्थान है ॥ २४१ ॥

चउपाई।

सुनि कइ असि पदुमावति मया। भा बसंत उपनी नइ कया ॥
सुआ क बोलि पउन होइ लागा। उठा सोइ हनुवँत होइ जागा ॥

चाँद मिलन कइ दीन्हेसि आसा । सहसहु करा सूर परगासा ॥
पतरि लीन्ह लेइ सीस चढावा । दिसिटि चकोर चाँद जनु पावा ॥
आस पिआसा जो जेहि केरा । जउँ झिझिकार ओही सो हेरा ॥
अब यह कउन पानि मइँ पीआ । भा तन पाँख पनग मरि जीआ ॥
उठा फूलि हिरदइ न समाना । कंथा टूक टूक बिहराना ॥

दोहा ।

जहाँ पिरीतम वेइ बसहिँ यह जिउ बलि तेहि बाट ।
जउँ सो बोलावइ पाउँ सउँ हउँ तहँ चलउँ ललाट ॥ २४२ ॥

सुनि कइ = सुन कर (श्रुत्वा)। असि = ऐसी = एतादृशी । पदुमावति = पद्मावती । मया = माया = दया = कृपा । भा = भया (बभूव) = हुआ । बसंत = वसन्त-ऋतु । उपनी = उत्पन्न हुई (उत्पन्ना)। नइ = नई (नव)। कया = काय = शरीर = देह । सुआ = शुक = सुग्गा । क = की । बोलि = बोली = वाणी । पउन = पवन = वायु । होइ = हो कर (भूत्वा)। लागा = लगा = लगइ (लगति) का प्रथम-पुरुष, भूत-काल, पुंलिङ्ग का एक-वचन । उठा = उठइ (उत्तिष्ठते) का प्रथम-पुरुष, भूत-काल, पुंलिङ्ग का एक-वचन। सोइ = सो कर (आशीय)। हनुवंत = हनुमान् । जागा = जागइ (जागर्त्ति) का प्रथम-पुरुष, भूत-काल, पुंलिङ्ग का एक-वचन । चाँद = चन्द्र । मिलन कइ = मिलने की = मेलनस्य । दीन्हेसि = दिया (अदात्)। आसा = आशा = उम्मीद । सहसहु = सहस्रैः = हजारोँ । करा = कला वा किरण । सूर = सूर्य । परगासा = प्रकाश किया (प्राकाशयत्)। पतरि = पत्री = चिट्ठी । लीन्ह = लिया [अलात्)। लेइ = ले कर (आलाय)। सीस = शीर्ष = शिर । चढावा = चढावइ (उच्चालयति) का प्रथम-पुरुष, भूत-काल, पुंलिङ्ग का एक-वचन । दिसिटि = दृष्टि । चकोर = एक प्रसिद्ध पक्षी, जो चन्द्र से अत्यन्त प्रेम रखता है । जनु = जाने = जानोँ । पावा = पावइ (प्राप्नोति) का प्रथम-पुरुष, भूत-काल, पुंलिङ्ग का एक-वचन । आस = आशा । पिआसा = पिपासित = प्यासा । जो = यः । जेहि केरा = जिस का वा जिस के । जउँ = यदि । झिझिकार = झझकारे = झट-कारे (झट् कारयेत्)। ओही = उसी को । सो = सः = वह । हेरा = हेरइ (हेडते) का प्रथम-पुरुष, भूत-काल, पुंलिङ्ग का एक-वचन । अब = अधुना = इदानीम् । यह = अयम् वा इदम् ।

कउन = क नु = कौन। पानि = पानी (पानीय)। मइँ = मैं। पीआ = पीअइ (पिबति) का उत्तम-पुरुष, भूत-काल, पुंलिङ्ग का एक-वचन। भा = (बभूव) = भया = ऊआ। तन = तनु = देह। पाँख = पक्ष = पर। पनग = पन्नग = साँप। मरि = मर कर (मृत्वा)। जीआ = जीअइ (जीवति) का प्रथम-पुरुष, भूत-काल, पुंलिङ्ग का एक-वचन। फूलि = फूल कर (सम्फुल्ल्य)। हिरदइ = हृदय। समाना = समाइ (संमाति) का प्रथम-पुरुष, भूत-काल, पुंलिङ्ग का एक-वचन। कंथा = कन्था = गुदरी। टूक टूक = खण्ड खण्ड = टुकडे टुकडे। बिहराना = बिहरइ (विहरति) का प्रथम-पुरुष, भूत-काल, पुंलिङ्ग का एक-वचन॥

जहाँ = यत्र। पिरीतम = प्रियतम। वेइ = वे = ते। बसहिँ = बसइ (वसति) का बऊ-वचन। जिउ = जीव। बलि = बलिदान। तेहि = तिस। बाट = वाट = मार्ग = राह। बोलावइ = बोलावे (आह्वयेत्)। पाउँ सउँ = पायँ से। हउँ = अहम् = मैं। तहँ = तहाँ = तत्र। चलउँ = चलूँ (चलानि) = जाऊँ। ललाट = मस्तक = माथा॥

ऐसी पद्मावती की करुणा भरी वाणी को सुन कर, (राजा रत्न-सेन के लिये) वसन्त (का समय) हो गया, नई शरीर उत्पन्न हो गई। शुक की वाणी (देह में ठंढी) हवा सी लगी, सोता ऊआ, हनुमान के ऐसा उठा और जाग गया। चन्द्र (पद्मावती) ने मिलने की आशा दी (इस लिये) सूर्य (रत्न-सेन) हजारों कला वा किरणों से प्रकाशित ऊआ। चिट्ठी को लिया, ले कर शिर पर चढाया, (ऐसा प्रसन्न ऊआ) जानों चकोर की दृष्टि ने चन्द्र को प्राप्त कर लिआ हो। (कवि कहता है कि, सच है) जो जिस की आशा का प्यासा है, वह, यदि झिझिकारा भी जाय, तो भी उसी को ढूँढा करता है। (राजा कहता है कि) अब मैं यह कौन पानी को पी लिया, (जिस से) शरीर में पर जम गए (जिस से उडने की शक्ति हो गई), और मरा ऊआ (मैं) साँप जो उठा। हृदय फूल उठा (देह में) नहीं समाता, और कंथा टुकडे टुकडे हो कर फट गया॥

(रत्न सेन कहने लगा कि) जहाँ वह प्रियतम (पद्मावती) बसता है, उस राह में यह जीव बलि है; यदि वह (पद्मावती) पैर से बोलावे वहाँ मैं शिर से चलूँ॥ २४२॥

चउपाई।

जो पँथ मिला महेसइ सेई। गएउ सो मुंद उहइ धँसि लेई॥
जहँ वह कुंड बिखम अउगाहा। जाइ परा जहँ पाओ न थाहा॥

बाउर अंध पेम कर लागू। सउँह धँसइ किछु सूझ न आगू॥
लीन्हेसि धँसि सुआँस मन मारा। गुरू मछंदर-नाथ सँभारा॥
चेला परइ न छाँडइ पाछू। चेला मच्छ गुरू जस काछू॥
जनु धँसि लीन्ह समुँद मरजीआ। उघरइ नइन बरइ जनु दीआ॥
खोजि लीन्ह सो सरग दुआरा। बजर जो मूँदे जाए उघारा॥

दोहा।

बाँक चढाउ सरग गढ चढत गएउ होइ भोर।
भइ पुकार गढ ऊपर चढे सेँधि देइ चोर॥ २४३॥

जो = यः। पँथ = पंथ = पन्थाः = राह। मिला = मिलइ (मिलति) का प्रथम-पुरुष, भूत-काल, पुंलिङ्ग का एक-वचन। महेसइ = महेश (महादेव) को। सेई = सेवा कर (संसेव्य)। गएउ = गया (अगात्)। सो = वह। मुंद = मुद्रित = बंद। उहइ = उसी को। धँसि = धँस कर (आध्वंस्य)। लेई = लेने के लिये। जहँ = जहाँ = यत्र। कुंड = कुण्ड। बिखम = विषम = कठिन = नीँचा ऊँचा। अउगाहा = अगाध = अथाह। जाइ = जा कर (संयाय)। परा = परइ (पतति) का प्रथम-पुरुष, भूत-काल, पुंलिङ्ग का एक-वचन। पाओ = पावइ (प्राप्नोति) = पाता है। थाहा = थाह = स्थल = तल। बाउर = वातुल = बौरहा। अंध = अन्ध = अंधा। पेम = प्रेम। लागू = लगा = लग्न ऊआ। सउँह = सौंह = संमुख। धँसइ = धँसता है (ध्वंस्यते)। किछु = कुछ = किञ्चित्। सूझ = सूझइ (शुध्यति) = सूझता है। आगू = आगे = अग्रे। लीन्हेसि = लिया (अलात्)। सुआँस = श्वास = साँस। मारा = मारइ (मारयति) का प्रथम-पुरुष, भूत-काल, पुंलिङ्ग का एक-वचन। गुरू = गुरु। मछंदर-नाथ = मत्स्येन्द्र-नाथ। सँभारा = सँभारइ (सम्भारयति) का प्रथम-पुरुष, भूत-काल, पुंलिङ्ग का एक-वचन। चेला = शिष्य। परइ = पडता है (पतति)। छाँडइ = छोडता है (छोडयति)। पाछू = पीछा = पृष्ठे। मच्छ = मत्स्य। जस = जैसा = यथा। काछू = कछुआ (कच्छप)। जनु = जाने = जानौँ। लीन्ह = लिया (अलात्)। समुँद = समुद्र। मरजीआ = मर कर जीने-वाला = गोता खोर = गोता लगाने-वाला। उघरइ = उघरे = उघरइ (उद्घटते) का प्रथम-पुरुष, भूत-काल, पुंलिङ्ग का बज्ज-वचन। नइन = नयन = आँख। बरइ = बरे = बरइ (ज्वलति) का प्रथम-पुरुष, भूत-काल, पुंलिङ्ग का बज्ज-वचन।

जनु = जाने = जानोँ। दीश्रा = दीप = चिराग। खोजि लीन्ह = खोज लिया = ढूँढ लिया। सो = वह। सरग = स्वर्ग। दुश्रारा = द्वार = दरवाजा। बजर = वज्र। मूँदे = मुद्रित थे = बंद थे। जाए = जाइ (याति) यहाँ जाए = गए। उघारा = उद्घटित = खुला॥

बाँक = वक्र = टेढा। चढाउ = चढाव (उच्चलन)। गढ = गाढ = किला = दुर्ग। चढत = चढते (उच्चलन्); गएउ होइ = हो गया। भोर = व्यह = सबेरा। भइ = भई (बभूव) = ऊई। पुकार = हँकार (पुं-वा ऊं-कार)। ऊपर = उपरि। चढे = चढइ (उच्चलति, आरोहति) का प्रथम पुरुष, भूत-काल, पुंलिङ्ग का बक्र वचन। सँधि = सन्धि। देइ = दे कर (दत्वा)। चोर = चौर॥

महादेव की सेवा करने से जो (रत्न सेन को) पथ (राह) मिला था (२१९— २२० दोहे को देखो) वह मुद्रित, अर्थात् बंद था, उसी को (रत्न-सेन) धँस कर लेता है, अर्थात् लेना चाहता है। जहाँ पर वह विषम और अगाध कुण्ड था, वहाँ पर जा कर पडा, जहाँ कि थाह नहीँ पाता है। (कवि कहता है कि,) प्रेम के लाग, अर्थात् प्रेम के लगने से (मनुष्य) पागल और अंधा हो जाता है, सामने-ही धँसता है, आगे, अर्थात् सामने, कुछ भी नहीँ सूझता है कि, (आग है कि पानी)। (रत्न-सेन ने) धँस कर (राह को) लिया, अर्थात् राह को पा गया, मन में श्वास को मार लिया, अर्थात् हृदय के भीतर श्वास को रोक लिया, (और) गुरु मोछंदर-नाथ को सँभारा, अर्थात् स्मरण किया (मोछंदर-नाथ के लिये १६२ दोहे की टीका देखो)। (कवि कहता है कि) चेला गिर पडे (तो भी गुरु का) पीछा नहीँ छोडता, गुरु कच्छप ऐसा (अचल) होता है और चेला मछली के ऐसा (चञ्चल)। जैसे गोताखोर समुद्र में धँस कर (तीव्र दृष्टि से देख कर मोती को) लिया, अर्थात् निकाल लेता है (उसी तरह रत्न-सेन के) नयन खुल गए जानों दीप बरे (ऐसे तीव्र हो गए)। सो (रत्न-सेन ने) स्वर्ग, अर्थात् ऊपर चढने का दरवाजा खोज लिया, जो दरवाजे वज्र (कपाट) से बंद थे खुल गए॥

गढ के स्वर्ग, अर्थात् ऊपर जाने के लिये (बऊत) टेढा (कठिन) चढाव था, चढते चढते भोर हो गया, (चौकीदारों की) पुकार ऊई कि, चोर सेँध दे कर ऊपर चढे हैँ॥ २४३॥

चउपाइ।

राजइ सुना जोगि गढ चढे। पूँछी पास पँडित जो पढे॥
जोगी गढ जो सेँधि देइ आवहिँ। कहहु सो सबद सिद्धि जिन्ह पावहिँ॥

अथ मंची-खंड ॥ २४ ॥

चउपाई ।

राँधि जो मंची बोलइ सोई। अइस जो चोर सिद्ध पइ कोई ॥
सिद्ध निसंक रइनि पइ भवँहीँ। ताकहँ जहाँ तहाँ उपसवहीँ ॥
सिद्ध निडर पइ अइसइ जीआ। खरग देखि कइ नावँहिँ गीआ ॥
सिद्ध जाहिँ पइ जिउ बधि जहाँ। अउरहि मरन पंख अस कहाँ ॥
चढहिँ जो कोपि गगन उपराहीँ। थोरइ साज मरहिँ सो॰ नाहीँ ॥
जंबुक कहँ जउँ चढिअहि राजा। सिंघ साजि कइ चढिअ त छाजा ॥
सिद्ध अमर काया जस पारा। छरहिँ मरहिँ पइ जाहिँ न मारा ॥

दोहा ।

छरहिँ काज किरिसुन कर साजा राजा धरहिँ रिसाइ ।
सिद्ध गिद्ध जेहिँ दिसिटि गगन पर बिनु छर किछु न बसाइ ॥ २४५ ॥

राँधि = आराध्य = आराधना कर = पूज कर = प्रणाम कर । जो = जो = यः । मंची = मन्त्री । बोलइ = वदति = बोलता है। सोई = स एव = वही। अइस = एतादृश = ऐसा । चोर = चौर । पइ = अपि = निश्चय से । कोई = कोऽपि । निसंक = निःशङ्क = बेडर । रइनि = रजनी = रात । भवँहीँ = भ्रमन्ति = भ्रमण करते हैँ । ताकहिँ =

तर्कयन्ति = ताकते हैं = देखते हैं। जहाँ = यत्र। तहाँ = तत्र। उपसवहीं = उपसर्पन्ति = चले जाते हैं। निडर = निर्दर = निर्भय। अइसइ = एतादृशो हि = ऐसे ही। जीआ = जीव = प्राणी। खरग = खड्ग = तलवार। देखि कइ = दृष्ट्वा = देख कर। नावँहिँ = नमयन्ति = झुकाते हैं। गीआ = ग्रीवा = गला। जाहिँ = यान्ति = जाते हैं। जिउ = जीव = प्राण। बधि = हत्वा = बध कर। अउरहि = अपरस्य = दूसरे को। मरन = मरण = मृत्यु। पंख = पक्ष = पर। अस = एतादृश = ऐसा। कहाँ = क हि। चढहिँ = उच्चलन्ति = चढते हैं। कोपि = सङ्कुप्य = कोप कर = क्रोध कर। गगन = आकाश। उपराहीं = उपरि हि = ऊपर। थोरइ = स्तोकेन = थोडे। साज = सज्जन = तयारी। मरहिँ = मरन्ति = मरते हैं। सो = सः, यहाँ = वे। नाहीं = नहि। जंबुक = जम्बुक = सियार। कहँ = को। जउँ = यदि = जो। चढिअहि = चढिए = उच्चलेत्। सिंघ = सिंह। साजि कइ = सज कर = तयारी कर। चढिअ = चढिए = उच्चलेत्। त = तर्हि = तो। छाजा = शोभित हो। काया = काय = शरीर। जस = यथा = जैसे। पारा = पारद। छरहिँ = चरन्ति = छरते हैं। मारा = मारे ॥

काज = कार्य = काम। क्रिरिसुन = कृष्ण = कृष्ण-चन्द्र। कर = का। साजा = सज्जित। धरहिँ = धरन्ति = धरते हैं। रिसाइ = रिस कर = रोष कर। गिद्ध = गृध्र = मांस खाने-वाला प्रसिद्ध पक्षी। जेहिँ = येषाम् = जिन की। दिसिटि = दृष्टि = नजर। पर = उपरि। बिनु = विना। छर = चर = नाश। किछु = किञ्चित् = कुछ। बसाइ = वशमेति = बसाता है = चलता है ॥

(गन्धर्व-सेन को) प्रणाम कर जो मन्त्री था वह बोलता है कि, ऐसा जो चोर वह निश्चय कर कोई सिद्ध है। सिद्ध बेडर रात में घूमा करते हैं, जहाँ देखते हैं, अर्थात् इच्छा करते हैं, वहीं चले जाते हैं। सिद्ध निडर होते हैं और ऐसे जीव हैं कि खड्ग देख कर (उस के सामने अपना) गला झुँका देते हैं। निश्चय कर सिद्ध जहाँ चाहते हैं वहाँ जीव का नाश कर चले जाते हैं, दूसरे को कहाँ ऐसा मरना और पक्ष है (जो आकाश पर जाय)। जो सिद्ध क्रोध कर आकाश पर चढते हैं, वे थोडी (सेना की) तयारी से नहीं मरते। हे राजा यदि स्यार पर चढाई करना हो तो सिंह (के मारने) की तयारी कर चढिए तो उचित हो। सिद्ध की शरीर अमर है जैसे कि पारा, (ए दोनों) छर जाते हैं, अर्थात् टुकडे टुकडे हो जाते हैं, पर (किसी के) मारे नहीं मरते ॥

सिद्ध कृष्ण भगवान का भी सजा सजाया काम बिगाड देते हैँ। क्रोध कर राजा लोगोँ को भी पकड लेते हैँ। सिद्धरूप गिद्ध जिन की दृष्टि आकाश के ऊपर रहती है उन से (अपने) नाश के सेवाय कुछ नहीँ बसाती अर्थात् कुछ नहीँ चलती॥

दशमस्कन्ध श्रीमद्भागवत के ५७ अध्याय मैँ कथा है कि उदास हो कर द्वारिका से महात्मा अक्रूर के चले जाने पर कृष्ण से कुछ भी न हो सका। द्वारिका के लोग आधि व्याधि और अवर्षण से बहुत ही पीडित हो गए। अन्त मैँ कृष्ण के उपदेश से जब लोग प्रार्थना कर अक्रूर को द्वारिका मैँ ले आए तब सब रोग नष्ट हुए और वृष्टि भी हुई॥

सिद्ध गोरख-नाथ जब कामाचा मैँ गए तो वहाँ एक दुष्टा स्त्री ने व्यभिचार की इच्छा से भिचा माँगते हुए गोरख के एक गरीब चेले को पकड रक्खा। गोरख ने क्रोध से उस राज्य के सब लोगोँ को पत्थर कर दिया। अन्त मैँ जब वहाँ का राजा गिडगिडा कर गोरख के पैरोँ पर पडा तब गोरख ने कृपा कर सब का उद्धार किया। इस प्रकार भारतवर्ष मैँ सिद्धोँ की सैकडोँ कहानिआँ प्रसिद्ध हैँ ॥ २४५ ॥

चउपाई।

आवहु करी गुदर मिस साजू। चढहु बजाइ जहाँ लगि राजू॥
होहु सँजोइल कुअँर जो भोगी। सब दर छेँकि धरहु अब जोगी॥
चउबिस लाख छतर-पति साजे। छपन कोटि दर बाजन बाजे॥
बाइस सहस सिंघली चाले। गिरिह पहार पुहुमि सब हाले॥
जगत बराबर देइ सब चाँपा। डरा इँदर बासुकि हिअ काँपा॥
पदुम कोटि रथ साजे आवहिँ। गिरि होइ खेह गगन कहँ धावहिँ॥
जनु भुइँ-चाल चलत तहँ परा। कुरमहि पीठि टूटि हिअ डरा॥

दोहा।

छतरहिँ सरग छाइ गा सूरज गएउ अलोपि।
दिनहिँ राति असि देखी चढा इँदर होइ कोपि॥ २४६॥

आवहु = आयात = आओ। करी = करिए। गुदर = गुदरी = कन्था। मिस = मिष = बहाना। साजू = साज = तयारी। चढहु = उच्चलत = चढो। बजाइ = संवाद्य =

बजा कर। जहाँ लगि = जहाँ तक। राजू = राज्य। होऊ = भवत = हो। सँजोइल = संसज्जित = तयार। कुअँर = कुमार = राज-कुमार। जो = जो = ये। भोगी = भोग करने-वाले = जागीर पाने-वाले। सब = सर्व। दर = दरी = घाँटी। छेंकि = छेकयित्वा = छेंक कर = रोक कर। धरऊ = धरत = धरो। अब = अधुना = इदानीम्। जोगी = योगी। चउबिस = चतुर्विंशति = चौबीस। लाख = लच। छतर-पति = छत्रपति। साजे = सज्जित किए गए। छपन = षट्पञ्चाशत् = छप्पन। दर = दल = सेना। बाजन = वाद्य। बाजे = बजे = बजाए गए। बाइस = द्वाविंशति। सहस = सहस्र = हजार। सिंघली = सिंहली = सिंहल के हाथी। चाले = चलाए गए। गिरिह = ग्टह = घर। पहार = प्रहार = पहाड। पुहुमि = पृथ्वी = भूमि। हाले = हिले = हिलने लगे। जगत = जगत् = संसार। बराबर = एकतार = लगातार। देंइ = देइ = दत्वा = दे कर। चाँपा = चाँपइ (चापयति) का भूत-काल, पुंलिङ्ग, एक-वचन। डरा = डरइ (दरति) का भूत-काल, पुंलिङ्ग, एक-वचन। इंदर = इन्द्र = देवराज। बासुकि = वासुकि = एक प्रकार का सर्प। हिअ = हृदय। काँपा = चकम्पे = काँप उठा। पदुम = पद्म = सौ करोड। कोटि = करोड। साजे = सज्जित किए। आवहिँ = आयान्ति = आते हैँ। गिरि = पर्वत। होइ = भूत्वा = हो कर। खेह = धूलि = धूर। गगन = आकाश। कहँ = को। धावहिँ = धावन्ति = दौडते हैँ। जनु = जानौँ। भुइँ-चाल = भूमिचाल = भूकम्प = भूडोल। चलत = चलते। तहँ = तहाँ = तच। परा = परइ (पतति) का भूत-काल, पुंलिङ्ग का एक-वचन। कुरमहि = कूर्म की = कछुए की। पीठि = पृष्ठ = पीठ। टूटि = टूटी = टूटइ (त्रुटयति) का भूत-काल, स्त्रीलिङ्ग, एक-वचन ॥

छतरहिँ = छत्रौँ से = छाताओँ से। सरग = स्वर्ग। छाइ गा = छा गया = छादित हो गया। सूरुज = सूर्य। गएउ = अगात् = गया। अलोपि = अलोप = अदृश्य। दिनहिँ = दिन मैँ। राति = रात्रि = रात। अस = एतादृशी = ऐसी। देखी = देखइ (दृश्यते) का भूत-काल, स्त्रीलिङ्ग, एक-वचन। चढा = चढइ (उच्चलति) का भूत-काल, पुंलिङ्ग, एक-वचन। कोपि = सङ्कुप्य = कोप कर = क्रोध कर ॥

(मन्त्री ने कहा कि) आइए गुदर अर्थात् गुदरी वाले योगिओँ के बहाने तयारी करिए, जहाँ तक राज्य है (सब कोई) बाजा बजा कर, अर्थात् डंका दे कर, चढिए। जो जागीरदार कुअँर हैँ सब तयार होँ और सब घाटिओँ को रोक कर योगी को पकडेँ। चौबीस लाख छत्रपति तयार हुए, सेना मैँ छप्पन करोड बाजे बजने लगे।

बादस हजार सिंहली हाथी चलाए गए (जिस से) पृथ्वी पर के सब घर और पहाड हिल उठे। सब (हाथी, घोडे, पैदल) बराबर (पैर) दे कर जगत् (भूमि) को चाँपा (जिस से) इन्द्र डर गया, वासुकि नाग का हृदय काँपने लगा। सजे ऊए करोड पद्म रथ आए, (जिन से) पहाड धूर हो कर आकाश में उडने लगे। (सेना के) चलते जानों वहाँ पर भूडोल आ गया, कछुए की पीठ टूट गई और उस का हृदय डर गया। पुराणों में कथा है कि भगवान कच्छप का अवतार ले कर पृथ्वी को अपनी पीठ पर रक्खे ऊए हैं जिस से वह नीचे नहीं जाती। सेना से कच्छप की पीठ का टूटना यह अतिशयोक्ति है जैसा विहारी ने सतसई में लिखा है कि—

"अहो पथिक कहियो तुरत गिरिधारी सों टेरि।
दृग झरि लाई राधिका बच्यो चहै ब्रज फेरि॥"

तोष कवि ने भी कहा है,—

गोपिन के अँसुआन के नीर पनारे भए बहि के भए नारे।
नारे भए सो भईं नदिआँ नदिआँ नद ह्वै गए काटि करारे॥
बेगि चलो जू चलो ब्रज को कवि तोष सुनो ब्रज-राज दुलारे।
वे नद चाहत सिंधु भए अब सिंधु तें ह्वैहैं जलाहल सारे॥

(छत्रपतिओं के) छाते से स्वर्ग छा गया सूर्य अलोप गया, दिन में रात ऐसी देख पडने लगी। (जान पडा कि) इन्द्र देवराज क्रोध कर (जगत् को विध्वंस करने के लिये) चढा है॥ २४६॥

चउपाई।

देखि कटक अउ मइमत हाथी। बोले रतन-सेन के साथी॥
होत आउ दर बहुत असूझा। अस जानत हहिँ होइहइ जूझा॥
राजा तूँ जोगी होइ खेला। इहइ दिवस कहँ हम भए चेला॥
जहाँ गाढ ठाकुर कहँ होई। संग न छाडइ सेवक सोई॥
जो हम मरन दिवस मन ताका। आज आइ सो पूजी साका॥
बरु जिउ जाउ जाए जनि बोला। राजा सत्त सुमेरु न डोला॥
गुरू केर जउँ आएसु पावहिँ। सउँह होइ हम चकर चलावहिँ॥

दोहा ।

आजु करहिँ रन भारथ　सत्त बचा दइ राखि ।
सत्त करइ सब कउतुक　सत्त भरइ पुनि साखि ॥ २४७ ॥

देखि = दृष्ट्वा = देख कर । कटक = सेना । अउ = अपि । मदमत = मदमत्त = मद से मस्त । हाथी = हस्ती । बोले = बोलइ (वदति) का भूत-काल, पुंलिङ्ग, बहु-वचन । रतन-सेन = रत्न-सेन । साथी = सार्थ = संगी । होत = होता = भवन् । आउ = आयाति = आता है । दर = दरी = घाँटी । बहुत = बहुच, वा बहुतर । असूझा = अदृश्य = अँधेरा = असुद्ध । अस = ऐसा = एतादृश । जानत = जानते । हहिँ = स्मः = हैं । होइहइ = भविष्यति = होगा । जूझा = युद्ध । ठँ = लम् । जोगी = योगी । होइ = भूला = हो कर । खेला = खेलइ (खेलइ) का भूत-काल, पुंलिङ्ग, एक-वचन । इहइ = इह हि = इसी । दिवस = दिन । कहँ = को । हम = अहम्, यहाँ वयम् । भए = हुए = बभूविम । चेला = शिष्य । जहाँ = यत्र । गाढ = कठिन । ठाकुर = ठक्कुर = मालिक । होई = होवे = भवेत् । संग = सङ्ग = साथ । छाडइ = छोटयति = छोडता है । सेवक = दास । सोई = स एव = वही । जो = यः । मरन = मरण । मन = मनसि = मन में । ताका = ताकइ (तर्कयति) का भूत-काल, पुंलिङ्ग, एक-वचन । आज = अद्य । आइ = एत्य = आ कर । सो = सः = वह । पूजी = पूरी हुई । साका = शक = वर्ष । बरु = वरम् = बल्कि । जिउ = जीव = प्राण । जाउ = यातु = जाय । जाग्र = जाय । जनि = यो न = जिन = मत । बोला = बोली = वचन । सत्त = सत्ता = सत्य । सुमेरु = सोने का पहाड जो उत्तर ध्रुव के नीचे है । डोला = डोल = डोलइ (दोलति) । गुरु = गुरु । केर = का । जउँ = यदि = जो । पावहिँ = पावँ = प्राप्नुयाम् । सउँह = सम्मुख = सामने । चकर = चक्र । चलावहिँ = चलावँ = चालयेयम् ॥

आजु = आज = अद्य । करहिँ = करँ = कुर्याम् । रन = रण = संग्राम । भारथ = भारत । बचा = वचन । दइ = देव = भगवान । राखि = राख = रखता है (रचति) । कउतुक = कौतुक = क्रीडा । भरइ = भरति = भरता है । पुनि = पुनः = फिर । साखि = साची = गवाह ॥

सेना और मदमत्त हाथियों को देख कर राजा रत्न-सेन के साथी (कुअँर लोग) बोले, कि घाटियों में बहुत अँधेरा होता आता है, ऐसा जान पडता है कि युद्ध

होगा । हे राजा तूँ (तै ने) योगी हो कर खेल किया, हम लोग इसी दिन के लिये चेले ऊए हैँ । जहाँ मालिक के ऊपर कष्ट पडे वहाँ पर जो संग न छोडे वही (सच्चा) सेवक है । हम लोग जिस मरणदिन को मन में अनुमान किया था, आज वह साका (वर्ष) पूरी ऊई । (ईश्वर से प्रार्थना है कि) जीव जाना अच्छा पर वचन (बात) न जाय, हे राजा सत्य (वचन) और सुमेरु नहीँ हिलता, अर्थात् नहीँ डगमगाता । यदि गुरु की आज्ञा पावैँ तो हम लोग सामने हो कर चक्र चलावैँ ॥

(हम लोग) आज भारत के ऐसा सङ्ग्राम करैँ । भगवान् सत्य वचन को रखता है । सत्य ही सब कौतुक करता है और सत्य ही साखी भरता है, अर्थात् मनुष्य का सच्चा गवाह सत्य ही है; शास्त्र में भी लिखा है कि सत्ये सर्वं प्रतिष्ठितम् । जल, वायु, पृथ्वी, अग्नि, और सूर्यादि ग्रह सब सत्य ही से अपने अपने कामोँ में लगे हैँ । कहावत है कि साँच को आँच क्या, अर्थात् सच्चे को आग की आँच क्या है ॥

गोरखनाथी और नान्हकशाही साधु लोग अपने शिर की पगडी में एक लोहे का वृत्ताकार हथिआर रखते हैँ । उसी को चक्र कहते हैँ । इसे हाथ की अँगुली से घुमा कर शत्रु के गले पर फेँकते हैँ । वह गला काटता ऊआ आगे निकल जाता है । सुनते हैँ कि पहले यह इस चाल से फेँका जाता था जिस से यह शत्रु का गला काटता और चक्कर लगाता ऊआ घूम कर फिर अपने मालिक के पास लौट आता था । भगवान कृष्ण का सुदर्शन चक्र सर्वत्र प्रसिद्ध है ॥

कौरव पाण्डवोँ का भारत सङ्ग्राम व्यासकृत महाभारत में प्रसिद्ध है जहाँ सत्य-धुरन्धर, धर्मराजावतार, युधिष्ठिर ने भी कृष्ण के कहने से द्रोणाचार्य के मारने के लिये 'अश्वत्थामा हतो नरो वा कुञ्जरः' यह झूठी बात कह कर अपने को कलङ्कित किया ॥ २४७ ॥

चउपाई ।

गुरू कहा चेला सिध होह्न । पेम बार होइ करी न कोह्न ॥
जा कहँ सीस नाइ कइ दीजिअ । रंग न होय ऊभ जउँ कीजिअ ॥
जेहि जिउ पेम पानि भा सोई । जेहि रँग मिलइ तेही रँग होई ॥
जउँ पइ जाइ पेम सउँ जूझा । कित तपि मरहिँ सिद्ध जेइँ बूझा ॥
यह सत बहुत जो जूझि न करिअइ । खरग देखि पानी होइ ढरिअइ ॥

पानिहि काह खरग कइ धारा। लउटि पानि सोई जो मारा ॥
पानी सँति आगि का करई। जाइ बुझाइ पानि जउँ परई ॥

दोहा ।

सीस दीन्ह मइँ अगुमन पेम पाअ सिर मेलि ।
अब सो पिरीति निबाहउँ चलउँ सिद्ध होइ खेलि ॥ २४८ ॥

गुरू = गुरु । कहा = कहइ (कथयति) का भूत-काल, पुंलिङ्ग, एक-वचन । चेला = शिष्य । सिध = सिद्ध । होउ = होऊ = भवत = हो । पेम = प्रेम । बार = वार = द्वार । होइ = भूत्वा = हो कर । करी = करिए = कुर्यासम् । कोह = कोह = क्रोध । जा कहँ = यस्य = जिस को । सीस = शीर्ष = शिर । नाइकइ = आनमय्य = झुका कर । दीजिअ = दीजिए = दीयेत । रंग = रङ्ग = वर्ण । होय = हो = भवेत् । ऊभ = उद्वेग = घबडाहट = भय । जउँ = यदि । कीजिअ = कीजिए = क्रियेत । जेहि = यस्य = जिस । जिअ = जीव । पानि = पानीय = पानी । भा = अभूत् = हुआ । रँग = रंग । मिलइ = मिले = मिलेत् । तेही = तिसी । होई = होवे = भवेत् । पइ = अपि = निश्चय कर । जाइ = जाय = यात् । सउँ = सें = से । जूझा = युद्ध । कित = कुतः = कस्मात् = क्यों । तपि = प्रतप्य = तप कर । मरहिँ = मरें = मरेयुः । जेइँ = जिन्हों ने । बूझा = बूझइ (बुध्यति) का भूत-काल, पुंलिङ्ग, एक-वचन । यह = अयम्, वा इदम् । सत = सत्य । जूझि = युद्ध । करिअइ = कीजिए = कुर्यासम् । खरग = खड्ग । देखि = दृष्ट्वा = देख कर । ढरिअइ = ढरिए = धारा के ऐसा होइए । (धृङ् अवस्थाने से अङ् प्रत्यय कर फिर टाप् करने से धारा बनता है उसी से, ढरइ (धरति) होता है ।) पानिहि = पानी को । काह = क्या = किम् । कइ = की । धारा = धार । लउटि = उलट कर = अवलुप्य । पानि = पानी । सोई = वही । मारा = मारइ (मारयति) का भूत-काल, पुंलिङ्ग, एक-वचन । सँति = सँती = से । आगि = अग्नि । का = किम् । करई = करइ (करोति) । जाइ = याति = जाती है । बुझाइ = बुझ । परई = पतेत् = पडे ॥

दीन्ह = अदाम् = दिया । अगुमन = अग्रतः । पाअ = पाद = पैर । सिर = शिर । मेलि = मेलयित्वा = डाल कर । पिरीति = प्रीति । निबाहउँ = निर्वाहयामि = निबाहता हूँ । चलउँ = चलामि = चलता हूँ । खेलि = खेलयित्वा = खेल कर ॥

गुरु (रत्न-सेन) ने कहा कि चेले लोग सिद्ध हो जाओ, प्रेम-द्वार में हो कर अर्थात् पैठ कर, क्रोध न करना चाहिए। जिस के लिये झुका कर शिर दीजिए, (वहाँ) यदि भय कीजिए तो (फिर) रंग नहीं होता, अर्थात् भय करने से मनुष्य बदरंग हो कर फीका पड जाता है। जिस के हृदय में वह (सच्चा) प्रेम का पानी (उत्पन्न) हुआ, उस (पानी) में जो रंग मिले वह वही (प्रेम-)रंग हो जाय, अर्थात् प्रेम-रस में किसी रंग के पडने से उस में विकार नहीं होता वह ज्यों का त्यों बना रहता है। यदि प्रेम से युद्ध होता हो तो सिद्ध लोग, जिन्हों ने (प्रेम को) बूझ लिया है, क्यों तपस्या कर के मरते। यही बहुत सत्यता है जो युद्ध न कीजिए, अर्थात् इस अवसर पर युद्ध न करना यही सब से बढ कर सच्ची बहादुरी है, (इस अवसर पर) खड्ग को देख कर पानी हो कर ढरक जाना चाहिए। पानी के लिये खड्ग की धारा क्या है, अर्थात् कुछ नहीं है, (पानी को) जो मारता है वही उलट कर पानी हो जाता है, अर्थात् पानी को मारने के लिये जो पानी में पैठता है वह पानी के भीतर ही गल कर पानी हो जाता है। पानी से आग क्या कर सकती है, अर्थात् क्रोधाग्नि शान्त-रूप पानी के पडते ही बुझ कर ठंढी हो जाती है, जहाँ पानी पडा कि (वह) बुझ जाती है ॥

प्रेम के पैर में शिर डाल कर मैं ने पहले ही से (अपने) शिर को दे दिया है, अब तो मैं उस प्रीति को निबाहता हूँ, और सिद्ध हो कर खेल कर (उस प्रेम-द्वार में) चलता हूँ ॥ २४८ ॥

चउपाई ।

राजहि छेंकि धरे सब जोगी । दुख ऊपर दुख सहइ बिओगी ॥
ना जिउ धडक धरत हइ कोई । न जनउँ मरन जिअन कस होई ॥
नाग-फाँस उन्ह मेली गीआ । हरख न बिसमउ एकउ जीआ ॥
जेइँ जिउ दीन्ह सो लेउ निरासा । बिसरइ नहिँ जउँ लहि तन साँसा ॥
कर किंगरी तेइ तंत बजावा । नेह गीत बैरागी गावा ॥
भलेहिँ आनि गिअ मेली फाँसी । हिअइँ न सोच रोस रिस नासी ॥
मइँ गिअ-फाँद ओही दिन मेला । जेहि दिन पेम-पंथ होइ खेला ॥

दोहा।

परगट गुपुत सकल महि पूरि रहा सब ठाउँ।
जहँ देखउँ ओहि देखउँ दोसर नहिँ कहँ जाउँ॥ २४९॥

राजहि = राजा को। छेँकि = छेकयित्वा = छेँक कर = रोक कर। धरे = धरइ (धरति) का भूत-काल, पुंलिङ्ग, बहु-वचन। सब = सर्व। जोगी = योगी। दुख = दुःख। ऊपर = उपरि। सहइ = सहते = सहता है। बिओगी = वियोगी = विरही। ना = न। जिउ = जीव। धडक = धडका = धडधडाहट। धरत हइ = धरइ (धरति) धरता है। कोई = कोऽपि। जनउँ = जाने = जानता हूँ। मरन = मरण। जिअन = जीवम। कस = कथम् = कैसा। होई = भवति होता है। नाग-फाँस = नाग-पाश = सर्पाकार फंदा। उन्ह = उन्हों ने। मेली = मेलइ (मेलयति) का भूत-काल, स्त्रीलिङ्ग, एक-वचन। गीआ = ग्रीवा = गला। हरख = हर्ष = खुशी। बिसमउ = विस्मय = चिन्ता। एकउ = एकोऽपि = एक भी। जीआ = जीव। जेइँ = यैः = जिन्हों ने। दीन्ह = अदात् = दिया। सो = सः = वह। लेउ = लातु = लेवे। निरासा = नैराश्येन = निराश से। बिसरइ = बिसरे (विस्मर्यते) = भूल्दे। जउँ लहि = जब तक। तन = तनु = शरीर। साँसा = श्वास। कर = हाथ। किँगरी = किन्नरी = एक तरह की चिकारी जिसे पौरिया वा योगी हाथ में लिए बजाया करते हैं। तेइ = तिस ने। तंत = तन्तु = तार। बजावा = बजावइ (वादयति) का भूत-काल, पुंलिङ्ग, एक-वचन। नेह = स्नेह = प्रीति। गीत = गान। बैरागी = विरागी = योगी। गावा = गावइ (गायति) का भूत-काल, पुंलिङ्ग, एक-वचन। भलेहिँ = वरम् = अच्छा। आनि = आनीय = आन कर। गिअ = ग्रीवा = गला। मेली = मेलइ (मेलयति) का भूत-काल, स्त्रीलिङ्ग, एक-वचन। फाँसी = पाशी = फाँसी लगाने की रस्सी। हिअइँ = हृदय में। सोच = शोच = चिन्ता। रोस = रोष = क्रोध। रिस = रिष्ट = शुभ। नासी = नसइ (नश्यति) का भूत-काल, स्त्रीलिङ्ग, एक-वचन। मइँ = मैं = अहम्। फाँद = पाश = फंदा। ओही = उसी। मेला = मेलइ (मेलयति) का भूत-काल, पुंलिङ्ग, एक-वचन। जेहि = जिस। पेम = प्रेम। पंथ = पन्थाः = राह। होइ = भूत्वा = हो कर। खेला = खेलइ (खेलति) का भूतकाल, स्त्रीलिङ्ग, एक-वचन॥

परगट = प्रकट = जाहिर। गुपुत = गुप्त = छिपा। सकल = सब = समग्र। महि = पृथ्वी = भूमि। पूरि = पूर = पूर्ण। रहा = रहइ (रहति) का भूत-काल, पुंलिङ्ग,

एक-वचन । सब = सर्व । ठाउँ = ठावँ = स्थान । जहँ = जहाँ = यत्र । देखउँ = पश्यामि = देखता हूँ । ओहि = उसी को । दोसर = दूसरा = द्वितीय । कहँ = कहाँ = कुत्र । जाउँ = यानि = जाऊँ ॥

सब (कुअँर) योगिओं ने राजा (रत्न-सेन) को पकड रक्खा, (बेचारा) वियोगी (रत्न-सेन) दुःख के ऊपर दुःख सह रहा है। (मुझे) कोई पकड रहा है इस बात का खटका (राजा के) जीव में नहीं है, (राजा कहने लगा कि) मैं नहीं जानता कि मरना और जीना कैसा होता है। उस (पद्मावती) ने गले में नाग-पाश डाल दिया है, (अब) हर्ष और विस्मय एक भी जी में नहीं है। जिस ने जी दिया है, वही नैराश्य कर (जी को) ले ले, (मुझे कुछ परवाह नहीं) जब तक शरीर में श्वास है तब तक (वह) न भूले (यही मेरी प्रतिज्ञा है)। (ऐसा कह) उस वैरागी (रत्न-सेन) ने हाथ से किँगरी के तारों को बजाने और स्नेह गीत को गाने लगा। (गीत का अर्थ यही था कि) उस (पद्मावती) ने अच्छा किया जो ला कर मेरे गले में फाँसी डाली, (अब) मेरे दिल में शोच नहीं क्रोध और शुभेच्छा भी नष्ट हो गई। मैं तो उसी दिन अपने गले में फंदे को डाल दिया जिस दिन प्रेम-राह में पड कर खेलने को चला, अर्थात् योगी का सवाँग बनाया ॥

(मेरी समझ में तो वह प्राणप्रिया पद्मावती) समग्र पृथ्वी में क्या प्रगट क्या छिपे सब स्थानों में पूर्ण (विराजमान) हो रही है, जहाँ देखता हूँ तहाँ उसी को देखता हूँ (मेरे लिये) दूसरा (हई) नहीं है, (इस लिये) कहाँ जाऊँ ॥ २४९ ॥

चउपाई ।

जब लगि गुरु मइँ अहा न चीन्हा । कोटि अँतर पट हुत बिच दीन्हा ॥
जउँ चीन्हा तउ अउरु न कोई । तन मन जिउ जोबन सब सोई ॥
हउँ हउँ कहत धोख अँतराहीँ । जो भा सिद्ध कहाँ परछाहीँ ॥
मारइ गुरू कि गुरू जिआवा । अउरु को मार मरइ सब आवा ॥
सूरी मेलि हसति गुरु पूरू । हउँ नहिँ जानउँ जानइ गूरू ॥
गुरू हसति पर चढा सो पेखा । जगत जो नास्ति नास्ति सब देखा ॥
अंध मीन जस जल मँह धावा । जल जीअन पुनि दिसिटि न आवा ॥

दोहा ।

गुरू मोर मोरइ सिर देइ तुरंगहि ठाठ ।
भीतर करहि डोलावई बाहर नाँचइ काठ ॥ २५० ॥

जब लगि = जब तक = यावत् । मइँ = मैं । अहा = था, अहइ (अस्ति) का भूत-काल, पुंलिङ्ग, एक-वचन । चीन्हा = चीन्हइ (चिह्नयति) से संज्ञा बनाई गई है । कोटि = करोड । अँतर = अन्तर । पट = वस्त्र वा पट्ट = केवाडा = पर्दा । हुत = था । बिच = बीच = मध्य । दीन्हा = दिया हुआ । जउँ = यदि वा जब । तउ = तदा = तब । अउरु = अपर । कोई = कोऽपि । तन = तनु = शरीर । मन = मनः = मानस । जिउ = जीव । जोबन = यौवन = जवानी । सोई = वही = स एव । हउँ = अहम् = मैं । कहत = कथयन् = कहते । धोख = धोखा = भ्रम । अँतराहीँ = अन्तरे हि = भीतर में । जो = जब, वा यदि । भा = बभूव = हुआ । कहाँ = कुत्र । परछाहीँ = परिच्छाया । मारइ = मारे = मारयेत् । गुरू = गुरु । जिआवा = जीवयेत् = जिलावे । को = को = कः = कौन । मार = मारने । मरइ = मरने । आवा = आवइ (आयाति) का भूत-काल, पुंलिङ्ग, एक-वचन । सूरी = शूली = फाँसी । मेलि = मेलयित्वा = मेल कर = डाल कर । हसति = हस्ती = हाथी । पूरू = पूर = पूरइ = पूरयति = पूरा करता है । हउँ = मैं = अहम् । जानउँ = जानामि = जानता हूँ । जानइ = जानाति = जानता है । गूरू = गुरु । चढा = उच्चलन् = चढा हुआ । सो = सः = वह । पेखा = पेख = प्रेक्षति = पेखता है, देखता है वा परीक्षा करता है । जगत = जगत् = संसार । जो = जो = यत् । नास्ति = नहीं है = नष्ट है । देखा = देख = देखइ (पश्यति) = देखता है । अंध = अन्ध = अंधा । मीन = मछली । जस = यथा = जैसे । जल = पानी । मँह = मध्ये = में । धावा = धाव = धावइ (धावति) = दौडता है । जल = जड = मूर्ख । जीअन = जीवन = पानी = जल । पुनि = पुनः = फिर । दिस्टि = दृष्टि = नजर । आवा = आव = आवइ (आयाति) = आता है ॥

मोर = मेरा = मम । मोरइ = मोरे = मेरे = मम । सिर = शिरः । देइ = दत्त्वा = दे कर । तुरंगहि = तुरङ्गस्य = घोडे को । ठाठ = ठाट = संस्थान = साज । भीतर = अभ्यन्तर । करहि = कला को (कलायाः) = कल को । डोलावई = डोलावइ (दोलयति) = डोलाता है = घुमाता है । बाहर = बाह्य । नाँचइ = नृत्यति = नाँचता है । काठ = काष्ठ = लकडी, यहाँ काठ सी शरीर ॥

फनगा = पाँखी । करवत = करपच = आरा । सिर = शिरः । सारद = सारे = रचे = सारयेत् । मरत = मरते । मोरउँ = मोरूँ = फेरूँ = मूर्द्धानि । अंग = अङ्ग = देह ॥

(रत्न-सेन कहता है कि) वह पद्मावती गुरु है और मैं (उस का) चेला हूँ, जिस (गुरु) के कारण मैं ने योग-शास्त्र को खेला अर्थात् सीखा। उस के द्वार को छोड कर दूसरा (द्वार) नहीँ जानता, जिस दिन मिले उसी दिन (मेरी) याचा पूरी होगी। (यदि वह मिले तो) प्राण को निकाल कर मस्तक को जमीन पर रक्खूँ, उस के लिये हृदय में आसन देऊँ। कौन ऐसा है जो मुझे ले कर उस के पैर को कुआवे, और नया जन्म दे कर नई शरीर करे। वह प्राण से भी अधिक प्यारी है, (यदि) माँगे (तो) प्राण दे कर बलिदान करूँ। यदि शिर माँगे तो गले के साथ शिर को देऊँ, यदि जी मारे तो और भी अधिक झुँक जाऊँ। मुझे अपने प्राण का लोभ नहीँ है, प्रेम-द्वार में हो कर, अर्थात् पैठ कर, (केवल) उसी को, अर्थात् उसी के, दर्शन को माँगता हूँ, अर्थात् यही चाहता हूँ कि कोई उपकारी उस का दर्शन करा दे ॥

(मेरे लिये) उस का दर्शन दीए के ऐसा है और अरे (कुअँर लोग) मैं भिखारी (उस दीए में जलने-वाला) फतिंगा हूँ। यदि वह मेरे शिर पर आरा रक्खे, अर्थात् चलावे, तो मरते मरते अंग न मोरूँ, अर्थात् प्राण निकलते निकलते भी आरे के सामने से न हटूँ ॥ २५१ ॥

चउपाई ।

पदुमावति कवँला ससि जोती। हँसइ फूल रोअइ तब मोती ॥
बरजा पितइ हँसी अरु रोजू। लाए दूत होइ निति खोजू ॥
जउ हिँ सुरुज कहँ लागेउ राहू। तउ हिँ कवँल मन भएउ अगाहू ॥
बिरह अगस्ती बिसमउ भएऊ। सरवर हरख सूखि सब गएऊ ॥
परगट ढारि सकइ नहिँ आँसू। घटि घटि माँसु गुपुत होइ नासू ॥
जस दिन माँझ रइनि होइ आई। बिगसत कवँल गएउ कुम्हिलाई ॥
राता बदन गएउ होइ सेता। भवँर भवँति रहि गई अचेता ॥

दोहा ।

चितहिँ जो चितर कीन्ह धनि रोअँ रोअँ अंग समेटि ।
सहस साल दुख आहि भरि मुरुछि परी गइ मेटि ॥ २५२ ॥

पदुमावति = पद्मावती। कवँला = कमल (ससि = शशि = चन्द्र। जोती = ज्योतिः = प्रकाश। हँसइ = हसति = हँसती है। फूल = फुल्ल। रोअइ = रोदिति = रोती है। तब = तदा। मोती = मुक्ता = मौक्तिक। बरजा = बरजइ (वर्जयति) का भूत-काल, पुंलिङ्ग एक-वचन। पितइ = पित्रा = पिता ने। हँसी = हास्य। अरु = अपि च = और। रोजू = रुज = रोग वा रोज। लाए = लगाए। दूत = भेदी। होइ = होता है। निति = नित्य = रोज। खोजू = खोज = शोध। जउहिँ = जबहि = यदा हि। सुरुज = सूर्य। कहँ = को। लागेउ = लगा = लगइ (लगति) का भूत-काल, पुंलिङ्ग, एक-वचन। राहु = राहु। तउहिँ = तबहि = तदा हि = तभी से। कवँल = कमल। भएउ = भया = बभूव = हुआ। अगाहु = आगाह = खबर। बिरह = विरह = वियोग। अगस्ती = अगस्त्य ऋषि। बिसमउ = बेसमय = विना समय। भएऊ = भएउ = हुआ। सरवर = सरोवर = तडाग। हरख = हर्ष। सूखि = शुष्क = सूख। सब = सर्व। गएऊ = गया (अगात्)। परगट = प्रगट = प्रकट। ढारि = धारायित = धारा के ऐसा (धातु विसरणे से)। सकइ = शक्नोति = सकती है। आँसू = अश्रु = आँस। घटि घटि = घट घट कर = कम हो हो कर। माँसु = मांस = माँस। गुपुत = गुप्त = लोप। होइ = भवति = होती है। नासू = नाश। जस = यथा = जैसे। माँझ = मध्ये = में। रइनि = रजनी = रात। आई = आवइ (आयाति) का भूत-काल, स्त्रीलिङ्ग, एक-वचन। बिगसत = विकाश होते। कुम्हिलाइ = कुमलिन = कुम्लान। राता = रक्त = लाल। बदन = वदन = मुख। सेता = श्वेत = सफेद। भवँर = भ्रमर = आवर्त्त। भवँति = भ्रमन्ति = घूमती। रहि गई = हो गई। अचेता = अचेतन = बेहोश॥

चितहिँ = चित्त में। चितर = चित्र = तसबीर। कीन्ह = किया (अकृत)। धनि = धन्या (पद्मावती)। रोअँ रोअँ = रोअँ रोअँ = रोम रोम = रोआँ रोआँ। अँग = देह के अवयव। समेटि = समेत्य = समेट कर = सङ्कुचित कर। सहस = सहस्र = हजार। साल = सालइ (शल्यति) का भूत-काल पुंलिङ्ग, एक-वचन। दुख = दुःख। आहि = आह। भरि = भृत्वा = भर कर। मुरुछि = मूर्छा खा कर = संमूर्च्छ्य = मूर्छित हो कर। परी = परइ (पतति) का भूत-काल, स्त्रीलिङ्ग, एक-वचन। गइ = गई = अगात्। मेटि = मिट = मट्टी = मृत्तिका॥

पद्मावती कमल और चन्द्र-ज्योति है, हँसती है तो फूल चूता है और रोती है तब (आँसुओं से) मोती टपकती है। पिता ने हँसी और (विरह) रोग को रोक दिया, अर्थात् पिता का हुक्म हुआ कि यह हँसी ठट्ठा न करने पावे और अकेली

बैठ कर रोवे भी न, (पिता ने) भेदिओं को लगा दिया, रोज खोज होने लगी। जैसे ही सूर्य को राहु लगा, अर्थात् सूर्य-स्वरूप रत्न-सेन को राहु-रूप गन्धर्वसेन के सेना के लोग पकड़ने की इच्छा की उसी समय कमल (पद्मावती) के मन में यह खबर पहुँच गई। विरह अगस्त्य बेसमय (उदित) हुआ, सब हर्ष-रूप तडाग सूख गया। (पिता के भय से) जाहिरा में आँसू को नहीं गिरा सकती, (पर) मांस कम होते होते लोप हो कर नष्ट हो गई, अर्थात् दुबली हो गई, मांस गल गई, खाली हड्डी भर रह गई। जैसे दिन में रात हो आई (इस लिये) प्रफुल्लित कमल (पद्मावती) कुम्हिला गया। ललित मुँह सफेद हो गया, (जल के) भवँर ऐसी घूमती घूमती अचेत हो गई॥

अंग के रोएँ रोएँ को समेट कर जो धन्या पद्मावती ने (अपने) चित्त के भीतर (रत्न-सेन की) तसबीर की, अर्थात् बनाई (इस से) हजारों बाणों के सालने के ऐसा दुःख हुआ; आह भर के मूर्छा खा कर गिर पडी और मिट गई॥

देवा-सुर-सङ्ग्राम में जब भगवान् मोहिनी-रूप धारण कर देवताओं में अमृत परोसने लगे तब सूर्य और चन्द्र के बीच में राहु दैत्य छिप कर बैठ गया था, अमृत पान करते ही सूर्य चन्द्र के बताने से भगवान ने सुदर्शन चक्र से उस का शिर काट डाला परन्तु अमृत के प्रभाव से दोनों टुकडे अमर हो कर आकाश में चलने लगे। धड को राहु और शिर को केतु कहते हैं। सूर्य और चन्द्र के कारण से राहु का शिर काटा गया इसी लिये वह बदला लेने के लिये अवसर पा कर सूर्य और चन्द्रमा को गरासता है। यह पुराणों में प्रसिद्ध कथा है॥

वर्षा-ऋतु के अन्त में अगस्त्य तारा, जिसे अंगरेजी में Canopus कहते हैं, उदय होता है। इस के उदय होते ही वर्षा की समाप्ति होती है और पोखरी, पोखरे, सूखने लगते हैं; तुलसी-दास ने भी अपने रामायण के किष्किन्धाकाण्ड में लिखा है कि—

उदित अगस्त पंथ-जल सोखा। जिमि लोभहि सोखइ संतोखा॥

प्रसिद्ध है कि रात को खिले हुए कमल कुम्हिला जाते हैं, कमल के फूल का मुँह बंद हो जाता है॥ २५२॥

चउपाई।

पदुमावति सँग सखी सयानी। गनि कइ नखत पीर ससि जानी॥
जानहिँ मरम कवँल कर कोई। देखि बिथा बिरहिनि कइ रोई॥

बिरहा कठिन काल कइ कला। बिरह न सहइ काल पर भला ॥
काल काढि जिउ लेइ सिधारा। बिरह काल मारे पर मारा ॥
बिरह आगि पर मेलइ आगी। बिरह घाउ पर घाउ बजागी ॥
बिरह बान पर बान बिसारा। बिरह रोग पर रोग सँचारा ॥
बिरह साल पर साल नवेला। बिरह काल पर काल दुहेला ॥

दोहा।

तन राओन होइ गढ चढा बिरह भएउ हनुवंत।
जारे ऊपर जारई तजइ न कइ भसमंत ॥ २५३ ॥

पदुमावति = पद्मावती। सँग = संग। सखी = सहेली। सयानी = सज्ञाना = चतुर। गनि-कइ = गणयित्वा = गन कर। नखत = नक्षत्र। पीर = पीडा। ससि = शशि = चन्द्र। जानी = जानइ (जानाति) का भूत काल, स्त्रीलिङ्ग, एक-वचन। जानहिँ = जानन्ति = जानती हैँ। मरम = मर्म = भेद। कवँल = कमल। कर = का। कोईँ = कुमुदिनी। देखि = दृष्ट्वा = देख कर। बिथा = व्यथा = पीडा। बिरहिनि = विरहिणी। कइ = की। रोईँ = रोअइ (रोदिति) का भूत-काल, स्त्रीलिङ्ग, बहु-वचन। बिरहा = विरह = वियोग। कठिन = कठोर। काल = प्राण लेने-वाला = यम-दूत। कला = अंश = अवतार। सहइ = सहते = सहना है। पर = परन्तु। भला = वर = अच्छा। काढि = कर्षयित्वा = खीँच कर। जिउ = जीव। लेइ = ले कर (आलाय)। सिधारा = सिधार = सिधारइ (सेधति) = सिधारता है = चला जाता है। मारे = मारने। पर = उपरि = ऊपर। मारा = मार = मारइ (मारयति) = मारता है। आगि = आग = अग्नि। मेलइ = मेलयति = मेलता है = डालता है। आगी = आग। घाउ = घात = क्षत = घाव। बजागी = वज्राग्नि = बिजली की आग। बान = वाण। बिसारा = बिसार = बिसारइ (विसारयति) = विशेष कर सारता है = विशेष कर फेँकता है। सँचारा = सँचार = सँचारइ (सञ्चालयति) = सँचारता है = फैलाता है। साल = शाल = शल्य = दुःख। नवेला = नवल = नया। दुहेला = दुर्हेल = भयङ्कर = कठिन ॥

तन = तनु = शरीर। राओन = रावण। होइ = होइ = भवति = है। गढ = गाढ = दुर्ग = किला। चढा = चढइ (उच्चलति) का भूत-काल, पुंलिङ्ग, एक-वचन। भएउ =

बभूव = भया = ऊत्र्या । हनुवंत = हनुमंत = हनुमान्, प्रसिद्ध रामायण के महावीर और राम के सेवक। जारे = जारने। ऊपर = उपरि (ज्वलनोपरि)। जारई = जारद (ज्वलयति) = जारता है। तजइ = त्यजति = तजता है = छोडता है। कइ = छला = कर। भसमंत = भस्म = राख ॥

पद्मावती के साथ की नक्षत्र-रूप चतुरी सखी गन कर, अर्थात् रुख देख कर शशि (पद्मावती) की पीडा को जान गई। कमल (पद्मावती) का भेद कोई (सखिआँ) ही जानती हैं, विरहिणी (पद्मावती) की पीडा देख कर (सब सखिआँ) रोने लगीं। (आपस में कहने लगीं कि) विरह (पति-वियोग) कठिन काल का अवतार है, विरह नहीं सहा जाता (इस लिये उस से) बल्कि काल भला है। काल (तो) प्राण खींच कर, और ले कर चला जाता है, अर्थात् जीव केवल ले कर मरी शरीर को छोड देता है। पर विरह-काल (तो) मारने पर मारता है। विरह आग पर आग डालता है, वज्राग्नि विरह घाव पर घाव करता है। विरह बाण के ऊपर बाण फेंकता है, विरह रोग पर रोग फैलाता है। विरह साल पर नया साल है, विरह काल पर भयङ्कर काल है ॥

शरीर रावण का गढ (लङ्का) ऊई है, विरह हनुमान् ऊत्र्या है और (उस गढ पर) चढा है,। जारने के ऊपर जार रहा है (शरीर को) भस्म कर के (भी) नहीं छोडता है ॥

सहवासी विजानीयात् चरित्रं सहवासिनाम्, इस नियम से साथ कीं रहने-वालीं कोईंरूप सखिआँ ही कमल (पद्मावती) का भेद जानती हैं ॥ यह कवि का लिखना बऊत उचित है ॥

रामायण-सुन्दर-काण्ड में हनुमान् का लङ्का जारना प्रसिद्ध है, तुलसी-दास ने भी लिखा है कि 'उलटि पलटि लंका कपि जारा। कूदि परा पुनि सिंधु मँझारा' ॥ इस लिये मलिक महम्मद का तनु लंका, विरह हनुमान् और जारे ऊपर जारई यह कहना बऊत ही रोचक है ॥ २५३ ॥

चउपाई।

कोइ कुमोद कर परसहिँ पाया। कोइ मलयागिरि छिडकहिँ काया ॥
कोइ मुख सीतल नीर चुआवहिँ। कोइ अंचल सउँ पउन डोलावहिँ ॥

कोइ मुख अबिँरित आनि निचोआ। जनु बिख दीन्ह अधिक धनि सोआ॥
जोवहिँ साँस खनहिँ खन सखी। कब जिउ फिरइ पउन अउ पँखी॥
बिरह काल होइ हिअइँ पईठा। जीउ काढि लेइ हाथ बईठा॥
खन एक मूँठि बाँध खन खोला। खनहिँ जीभ मुख जाइ न बोला॥
खनहिँ बजर कै बानन्ह मारा। कँपि कँपि नारि मरइ बिकरारा॥

दोहा।

कइसेहु बिरह न छाडइ भा ससि गहन गिरास।
नखत चहूँ दिसि रोअहिँ अँधिअर धरति अकास॥ २५४॥

कोइ = कोई = कापि। कुमोद = कुमुदिनी = कोईँ। कर = हाथ। परसहिँ = स्पृशन्ति = परसती हैँ = छूती हैँ। पाया = पाद = पैर। मलयागिरि = मलयगिरि का चन्दन। छिडकहिँ = शेकन्ते = छिडकती हैँ। मुख = मुँह। सीतल = शीतल = ठंढा। नीर = जल = पानी। चुआवहिँ = च्योतयन्ति = चुआती हैँ। अंचल = अञ्चल = आँचर। सउँ = सेँ = से। पउन = पवन = हवा। डोलावहिँ = दोलयन्ति = चलाती हैँ। अबिँरित = अमृत। आनि = आनीय = आन कर। निचोआ = निचोअ = निचोती हैँ = निच्योतयन्ति = गारती हैँ। जनु = जाने = जान पडता है। बिख = विष = जहर। दीन्ह = दिया = अदात्। अधिक = ज्यादा = और भी। धनि = धन्या (पद्मावती)। सोआ = सोअइ (स्वपिति) का भूत-काल, स्त्रीलिङ्ग, एक-वचन, सोई के स्थान मेँ अनुप्रास मिलाने के लिये सोआ किया गया। जोवहिँ = जोवइ (जोहते) का बहु-वचन, जोहती हैँ = देखती हैँ वा द्युत दीप्तौ से संद्योतयति का बहु-वचन। साँस = श्वास। खनहिँ खन = क्षणे क्षणे = क्षण क्षण पर। सखी = सहेली। कब = कदा। जिउ = जीव = प्राण। फिरइ = परिवर्त्तयति = फिरता है। अउ = अपि च। पँखी = पक्षी। बिरह = विरह = प्रियवियोग। काल = मारने-वाला = यम-दूत। होइ = होइ = भूला = हो कर। हिअइँ = हृदय मेँ। पईठा = पइठा = पैठा = पइठइ (प्रविशति) का भूत-काल, पुंलिङ्ग, एक-वचन। काढि = कर्षयित्वा = खीँच कर = निकाल कर। लेइ = लेइ = आलाय = ले कर। हाथ = हस्त। बईठा = बइठा = बैठा = बइठइ (विशति) का भूत-काल, पुंलिङ्ग, एक-वचन। खन = क्षण। एक = एक। मूँठि = मुट्ठी = मुष्टि। बाँध = बाँधइ (बध्नाति) = बाँधता है।

खोला = खोल = खोलइ (खोलति) = खोलता है। खनहिँ = चण में। जीभ = जिह्वा। मुख = मुँह। जाइ = याति = जाती है = निकलती है। बोला = बोल = बोली = बात। बजर = वज्र। बानन्ह = बान (वाण) का बहु-वचन। मारा = मार = मारइ (मारयति) = मारता है। काँपि काँपि = कम्पयित्वा कम्पयित्वा = काँप काँप कर। नारि = नारी (पद्मावती)। मरइ = मरति = मरती है। बिकरारा = विकराल = भयङ्कर ॥

कइसेहु = कथमपि = कैसेहु = किसी तरह से। छाडइ = छोडता है = छन्दति। भा = भया = बभूव = हुआ। ससि = शशि = चन्द्र। गहन = ग्रहण। गिरास = ग्रास। नखत = नचत्र। चहुँ दिसि = चतुर्दिशु = चारो दिशा। रोअहिँ = रोदन्ति = रोती हैं। अँधिअर = अँधिआर = अन्धकार = अँधेरा। धरति = धरती = धरित्री। अकास = आकाश = आस्मान ॥

कोई कुमुदिनी (सखिआँ) हाथ से (पद्मावती के) पैर को छू रही हैं (कि ठंढा तो नहीं हो गया), कोई शरीर पर मलय-चन्दन को छिडक रही हैं। कोई मुँह में ठंढा पानी चुआ रही हैं, कोई (अपने) आँचर से हवा कर रही हैं। कोई मुँह में अमृत, अर्थात् संजीवनी जडी को निचोड रही हैं, (वह औषधि ऐसी हो गई) जानों विष दिया गया, वह धन्या (पद्मावती) और भी सो गई, अर्थात् बेहोश हो गई। सखिआँ चण चण पर साँस देखती हैं, कि कब जी आता है और पवन पची (का संयोग होता) है, अर्थात् देखें कब शरीर में प्राण फिर कर आता है। (पद्मावती के) हृदय में विरह काल हो कर पैठ गया है, जी को निकाल कर, हाथ में ले कर बैठा हुआ है। एक चण में मुट्ठी को बाँध लेता है (तब पद्मावती बेजीव की हो जाती है), एक चण में (मुट्ठी को) खोल देता है (तब पद्मावती की साँस कुछ चलने लगती है), एक चण में मुख की जीभ से कुछ बोली नहीं बोली जाती, अर्थात् एक चण में जीभ ऐंठ जाती है, मुँह से बोली नहीं निकलती। एक चण में (वह विरह-काल) वज्र के वाणों से (पद्मावती को) मारता है, (जिस से) वह नारी (पद्मावती) काँप काँप कर बेकरार (विकराल) हो जाती है ॥

विरह किसी तरह से (पद्मावती को) नहीं छोडता है (जानों) ग्रहण में चन्द्र का ग्रास हो गया, अर्थात् चन्द्र-रूपा पद्मावती कान्तिहीन हो गई। चारो ओर से नचत्र-रूप (सखिआँ) रो रही हैं, धरती और आकाश में अँधेरा छा गया ॥ २५४ ॥

चउपाई।

घरी चारि इमि गहन गिरासी। पुनि बिधि जोति हिअइँ परगासी॥
निसँसि ऊभि भरि लीन्हेसि साँसा। भइ अधार जीअन कइ आसा॥
बिनवँहिँ सखी छूटि ससि राहू। तुम्हरी जोति जोति सब काहू॥
तूँ ससि-बदन जगत उँजिआरी। केइ हरि लीन्ह कीन्ह अँधिआरी॥
तूँ गजगाविँनि गरब गहीली। अब कस अस छाडइ सत ढीली॥
तइँ हरि लंक हराई केहरि। अब कस हारि करसि हइ हे हरि॥
तूँ कोकिल-बइनी जग मोहा। को ब्याधा होइ गहइ बिछोहा॥

दोहा।

कवँल करी तूँ पदुमिनि गइ निसि भएउ बिहान।
अबहुँ न संपुट खोलेसि जो रे उठा जग भान॥ २५५॥

घरी = घटी = २४ मिनट। चारि = चार = चत्वारि। इमि = एवम् = इस तरह से। गहन = ग्रहण। गिरासी = ग्रस्त हुई। पुनि = पुनः = फिर। बिधि = विधि = ब्रह्मा। जोति = ज्योतिः = प्रकाश। हिअइँ = हृदय में। परगासी = परगासइ (प्रकाशयति) का भूत-काल, स्त्रीलिङ्ग, एक-वचन। निसँसि = निश्वस्य = उसास ले कर = उच्छ्वास ले कर। ऊभि = ऊब कर = घबडा कर = उद्विज्य। भरि = भर कर = भृत्वा। लीन्हेसि = लिया = अलात्। साँसा = श्वास। भइ = भई = होइ (भवति) का भूत-काल, स्त्रीलिङ्ग, एक-वचन। अधार = आधार। जीअन = जीवन। कइ = की। आसा = आशा = उम्मीद। बिनवँहिँ = विनमन्ति = विनय करती हैं। सखी = सहेली। छूटि = छूटा। ससि = शशि = चन्द्र। राहू = राहु। तुम्हरी = तुम्हारी = आप की। काहू = को। तूँ = त्वम् = तुम। ससि-बदन = शशि-वदना = चन्द्र-मुखी। जगत = जगत् = संसार। उँजिआरी = उज्ज्वलता। केइ = केइ = केन = किस ने। हरि = हर = चुरा। लीन्ह = लिया = अलात्। कीन्ह = किया = अकृत। अँधिआरी = अन्धकार = अँधेरा। गजगाविँनि = गजगामिनी = हाथी के चाल ऐसी चलने-वाली। गरब = गर्व = अभिमान। गहीली = ग्रहिला = आग्रह करने-वाली। अब = अधुना = इदानीम्। कस = कथम् = क्यों। अस = एतादृश = ऐसा। छाडइ = छोडती है (छन्दति)। सत = सत्ता वा सत्य। ढीली = अधीर्य = ढीली हो कर।

तइँ = त्वम् = तैँ । हरि = हृत्वा = हरण कर । लंक = लङ्क = कटि = कमर । हराई = हरावइ (हारयति) का भूत-काल, स्त्रीलिङ्ग, एक-वचन । केहरि = केशरी = सिंह । हारि = हार कर = आहार्य । करसि हइ = करती है (करोषि) । हे हरि = हे हरे । कोकिल-बइनी = कोकिल-वचनी = कोकिला-सी बोलने-वाली । जग = जगत् = संसार । मोहा = मोही = मोहइ (मोहयति) का भूत-काल, मध्यम-पुरुष, स्त्रीलिङ्ग, एक-वचन । को = कौन = कः । ब्याधा = व्याध । होइ = होइ = हो कर = भूत्वा । गहइ = ग्रसति = ग्रसता है । बिछोहा = विक्षुब्धा = वियोगिनी = विरहिणी ॥

कवँल = कमल । करी = कली = कलिका । पदुमिनि = हे पद्मिनि । गइ = गई = अगात् । निसि = निशा = रात । भएउ = भया = बभूव = हुआ । बिहान = व्युह = सबेरा । अबहूँ = अब भी = इदानीमपि । सम्पुट = बंद मुख । खोलेसि = खोली = खोलइ (खोलति) का भूत-काल, मध्यम-पुरुष, स्त्रीलिङ्ग, एक-वचन । उठा = उठइ (उत्तिष्ठते) का भूत-काल, पुंलिङ्ग, एक-वचन । जग = जगत् वा जग = जगि = जागला = जाग कर । भान = भानु = सूर्य ॥

इस तरह से (पद्मावती) चार घडी तक ग्रहण में ग्रस्त थी, फिर ब्रह्मा ने हृदय में ज्योति की प्रकाश की, अर्थात् फिर हृदय में प्राण आया । उच्छ्वास ले कर, ऊब कर, और (हृदय में) भर कर (ठंढी) साँस ली, (सब सखिओं का) आधार हुई और जीने की आशा हुई । सब सखिआँ विनय करने लगीँ कि 'राहु से चन्द्रमा छूट गया, (हे रानी) तेरी ही ज्योति से सब किसी को ज्योति है । तूँ चन्द्रमुखी संसार की उँजिआरी है, (नहीँ जानतीँ कि) किस ने (उस उँजिआरी को) हर लिया था और अँधेरा कर दिया था । तूँ गज-गामिनि, गर्वीली और हठीली है, अब क्योँ इस तरह से ढीली हो कर (अपने) सत को छोडती है । तैँ ने कमर को चुरा कर सिंह को हरा दिया, अर्थात् सिंह की कमर से भी तेरी कमर पतली है, अब क्योँ हार कर हे हरि, हे हरि करती है, अर्थात् अब क्योँ जी में हार कर हे हरि, हे भगवान्, हाय भगवान् कह कह कर कराहती है । तूँ जग के मोहने-वाली कोकिल-वचनी है, कौन व्याध हो कर (तुझ) विरहिणी को पकडता है ॥

हे पद्मिनि तूँ कमल-कली है सो रात बीत गई, सबेरा हुआ अब तक भी सम्पुट को नहीँ खोली, अर्थात् अब तक तेरी मुख-कमल-कली नहीँ खुली (विकसित हुई), क्योँकि रे (पद्मावति देख) जगत् में सूर्य उठ आया, वा सूर्य जग कर उदय हुआ ॥ २५५ ॥

चउपाई।

भान नाउँ सुनि कवँल बिगासा। फिरि कइ भवँर लीन्ह मधु बासा॥
सरद चाँद मुख जीभ उघेली। खंजन नइन उठे कइ केली॥
बिरह न बोल आउ मुख ताई। मरि मरि बोलि जीउ बरिआई॥
दवइ बिरह दारुन हिअ काँपा। खोलि न जाइ बिरह दुख झाँपा॥
उदधि समुँद जस तरँग देखावा। चखु घूमहिँ मुख बात न आवा॥
यह सुठि लहरि लहरि पर धावा। भवँर परा जिउ थाह न पावा॥
सखी आनि बिख देहु त मरऊँ। जिउ नहिँ पेट ताहि डर डरऊँ॥

दोहा।

खनहिँ उठइ खन बूडइ अस हिअ कवँल सँकेत।
हीरामनिहि बोलावहु सखी गहन जिउ लेत॥ २५६॥

भान = भानु = सूर्य। नाउँ = नाम। सुनि = श्रुत्वा = सुन कर। कवँल = कमल। बिगासा = बिगसा = बिगसइ = बिकसइ (विकाशते) का भूत-काल, पुंलिङ्ग, एक-वचन। फिरि कइ = फिर कर = लौट कर। भवँर = भ्रमर = भौंरा। लीन्ह = लिया = अलात्। मधु = पुष्परस = मकरन्द। बासा = वास = सुगन्ध। सरद = शरत् = शरत् ऋतु। चाँद = चन्द्र = चंद। मुख = मुँह। जीभ = जिह्वा। उघेली = उघारी = उघेरइ वा उघारइ (उद्घाटयति) का भूत-काल, स्त्रीलिङ्ग, एक-वचन। खंजन = खञ्जन = खञ्जरीट = एक प्रसिद्ध पंछी जो शरत् ऋतु में देख पडता है। नइन = नयन = आँख। उठे = उठइ (उत्तिष्ठते) का भूत-काल, पुंलिङ्ग, द्वि-वचन। कइ = कर। केली = केलि = क्रीडा। बिरह = विरह = प्रियवियोग। बोल = बोली = बात। आउ = आवइ (आयाति) = आती है। ताई = तावइ (त्रायते) का भूत-काल, स्त्रीलिङ्ग, एक-वचन = ताय गई = मूँद गई = बंद हो गई। मरि मरि = मर मर कर = मारं मारम्। बोलि = बोली = बात। जीउ = जीव = प्राण। बरिआई = वरबलेन = प्राबल्येन = हठ से = जबर्दस्ती से। दवइ = दव = दवाग्नि = वन की आग। दारुन = दारुण = कठिन। हिअ = हृदय = दिल। काँपा = काँपइ (कम्पते) का भूत-काल, पुंलिङ्ग, एक-वचन। खोलि = खोला। जाइ = याति = जाता है। दुख = दुःख। झाँपा = झाँपइ (झम्पति) का भूत-काल, पुंलिङ्ग एक-वचन।

उदधि = उदक (जल) जिस में रहे। समुँद = समुद्र। जस = जैसे = यथा। तरँग = तरङ्ग = लहर। देखावा = देखावइ (दर्शयति) का भूत-काल, पुंलिङ्ग, एक-वचन। चखु = चक्षुः = आँख। घूमहिँ = घूर्मयन्ति = घूमती हैं। बात = वार्त्ता = बोली। आवा = आवइ (आयाति) = आती है। यह = अयम्, वा इदम्। सुठि = सुष्ठु = अच्छा। लहरि = लहर = लहरी = तरङ्ग। धावा = धाव = धावइ (धावति) = धावती है = दौडती है। भवँर = भ्रमर = भौंर। परा = पडा हुआ = पतित। जिउ = जीव = प्राण। थाह = स्थल = जमीन। पावा = पाव = पावइ (प्राप्नोति) = पाता है। सखी = हे आली। आनि = आनीय = आन कर = ला कर। देऊ = देओ = दद्याः। त = तर्हि = तो। मरऊँ = मरूँ = मराणि। पेट = पिटक = उदर। ताहि = तिस के। डर = दर = भय। डरऊँ = डरती हूँ (दरामि = विभेमि)॥

खनहिँ = चण में। उठइ = उत्तिष्ठते = उठता है = ऊपर आता है। खन = चण में। बूडइ = ब्रुडते = बूडता है = डूब जाता है। अस = ऐसा = एतादृश। हिअ = हृदय। सँकेत = संकेत = संकष्ट = महादुःख। हीरामनिहि = हीरामणेः = हीरामणि (शुक) को। बोलावहु = बोलावइ (वादयति) का विध्यर्थ में मध्यम-पुरुष का बहु-वचन। सखी = हे आली। गहन = ग्रहण। लेत = लेइ (लाति) = लेता है॥

सूर्य का नाम सुन कर (पद्मावती) कमल खिल उठा, भ्रमर लौट कर (उस के) रस का बास लेने लगा, अर्थात् शरीर में प्राण आ जाने से शरीर की सुगन्ध चारो ओर फैल गई जिस से फिर भ्रमर लौट कर बास लेने लगे। शरद काल के चन्द्र ऐसे मुख ने जीभ खोली, खञ्जन नयन, अर्थात् खञ्जन से नयन क्रीडा कर उठे, अर्थात् खुले। खञ्जन, और मछली की चञ्चलता ले कर कवि लोग आँख की उपमा खञ्जन और मछली से देते हैं। गिरिधरदास ने भी लिखा है कि 'सफरी से चल नैन'। विरह से मुख बंद हो गया, बोल नहीं आती है, प्राण मर मर कर जबर्दस्ती से बोली (कुछ) बात कहता है। कठिन विरहाग्नि से हृदय काँपने लगा, विरहदुःख ने (फिर मुख को) बंद कर दिया, (मुँह) खोला नहीं जाता। सुखादु पानी के समुद्र ऐसा (विरह ने) तरंग को देखाने लगा, आँख घूमने लगी, मुँह से बात नहीं आती। पुराणों में कथा है कि जिस समुद्र का सुखाद पानी है उसी में वडवानल है जिस कारण से उस समुद्र में बडे बड तरँग उठते हैं। भास्कराचार्य ने भी अपनी सिद्धान्त-शिरोमणि के गोलाध्याय में लिखा है कि "स्वादुदकान्तर्वडवानलोऽसौ"। बडे तरंग ही के

कारण कवि ने 'उदधि समुँद' का प्रयोग किया है। यहाँ उदधि से समुद्र ग्रहण करने से पुनरुक्ति दोष होता है इस लिये उदधि से 'सुन्दरपानी-वाला' यही अर्थ करना चाहिए। इस अच्छे (समुद्र) में लहर पर लहर दौडती है, अर्थात् उठती है, और में पडा जी थाह नहीं पाता है। (पद्मावती कहती है, कि) हे सखि विष ला कर दे दे तो मर जाऊँ (जिस से) पेट में जी न रहे, (क्योंकि उसी जी के रहने के) डर से डरती हूँ, अर्थात् जब तक पेट में जी है तब तक यह डरा करता है और उसी के डर से मैं भी डरती हूँ॥

एक क्षण में जी उठता है, अर्थात् होश में आ जाता है दूसरे क्षण में (विरह सागर में) डूब जाता है, अर्थात् बेहोश हो जाता है। इस तरह से (हे सखि) हृदय-कमल में बहुत-ही कष्ट है। (हे सखि) (विरह) ग्रहण जी लेता है। (शीघ्र) हीरामणि (शुक) को बुलाओ॥ २५६॥

चउपाई।

पुरइनि धाइ सुनत खन धाईं। हीरामनिहि बेगि लेइ आईं॥
जनहुँ बइद ओखद लेइ आवा। रोगिआ रोग मरत जिउ पावा॥
सुनत असीस नइन धनि खोली। बिरह बइन कोइल जिमि बोली॥
कवँलहि बिरह बिथा जसि बाढी। केसरि बरन पिअरि हिअ गाढी॥
कित कवँलहि भा पेम अँकूरू। जउँ पइ गहन लीन्ह दिन सूरू॥
पुरइनि छाँह कवँल कइ करी। सकल बिभास आस तुम्ह हरी॥
पुरुख गँभीर न बोलहिँ काहू। जउँ बोलहिँ तउ अउरु निबाहू॥

दोहा।

एतना बोल कहत मुख पुनि होइ गई अचेत।
पुनि कइ चेत सँभारी उहइ बकत मुख लेत॥ २५७॥

पुरइनि = पर्णिनी = जल का पुष्प विशेष जिस के पत्र चारो ओर से जल को छिपाए रहते हैं। धाइ = धाई = धात्री = बचपन में दूध पिलाने-वाली। सुनत = सुनते-ही। खन = क्षण। धाईं = धावइ (धावति) का भूत-काल, स्त्रीलिङ्ग, बहु-वचन।

हीरामनिहि = हीरामणि को । बेगि = बेगेन = शीघ्र । लेइ = ले कर = आलाय । आईँ = आवइ (आयाति) का भूत-काल, स्त्रीलिङ्ग का बक्र-वचन । जनङ्क = जानोँ = जाने = जान पडता है । बइद = वैद्य = बैद । ओखद = औषध = दवा । आवा = आवइ (आयाति) का भूत-काल, पुंलिङ्ग, एक-वचन । रोगिआ = रोगी । रोग = बीमारी । मरत = मरन् = मरते । जिउ = जीव = प्राण । पावा = पावइ (प्राप्नोति) का भूत-काल, पुंलिङ्ग, एक-वचन । असीस = आशीस = आशीर्वाद । नइन = नयन = आँख । धनि = धन्या (पद्मावती) । खोली = खोलइ (खोलति) का भूत-काल, स्त्रीलिङ्ग, एक-वचन । बिरह = विरह = प्रियवियोग । बइन = वचन = बैन । कोइल = कोकिला = कोयल = पिक । जिमि = यथा = जैसे । बोली = बोलइ (वदति) का भूत-काल, स्त्रीलिङ्ग, एक-वचन । कवँलहि = कमल मेँ (पद्मावती को) । बिथा = व्यथा = पीडा । जसि = जैसी = यथा । बाढी = बाढइ (वर्धते) का भूत-काल, स्त्रीलिङ्ग, एक-वचन । केसरि = केशर = एक प्रसिद्ध पुष्प की पखडी । बरन = वर्ण = रङ्ग । पिअरि = पीली = पीत । हिअ = हृदय । गाढी = गाढ का स्त्रीलिङ्ग = गहिरी । कित = कुतः = क्योँ । भा = बभूव = भया = ङआ । पेम = प्रेम । अँकूरू = अङ्कुर = अँखुआ । जउँ = यदि = जो । पइ = अपि = निश्चय । गहन = ग्रहण । लीन्ह = लिया = अलात् । सूरू = सूर्य । छाँह = छाया । कइ = की । करी = कली । सकल = सब । बिभास = विभास = प्रकाश = तेज = कान्ति । आस = आशा = उम्मीद । तुम्ह = तुम ने । हरी = हरइ (हरति) का भूत-काल, स्त्रीलिङ्ग, एक-वचन । पुरुख = पुरुष = मनुष्य । गँभीर = गभीर = गम्भीर । बोलहिँ = वदन्ति = बोलते हैँ । काह्न = कस्यापि = किसी को वा क्वापि = कभीँ । तउ = तर्हि = तो । अउरु = अपि च = और । निबाहि = निबाह = निबाहहिँ (निर्वाहयन्ति) = निवाहते हैँ ॥

एतना = एतावती = इतनी । बोल = बोली = बात । कहत = कथयन्ती = कहते । मुख = मुँह । होइ गई = हो गई । अचेत = अचेतन = बेहोश । पुनि = पुनः = फिर । कइ = कर = से । चेत = चेतन = होश । सँभारी = सँभारइ (सम्भारयति) का भूत-काल, स्त्रीलिङ्ग का एक-वचन । उहइ = वही । बकत = बकते = कहते । लेत = लेते ॥

(हीरामणि को ले आओ इस बात के) सुनने-ही के क्षण मेँ पुरइनि (ऐसी) धाई दौडीँ और झट हीरामणि को ले आईँ । (हीरामणि का उस समय मेँ ले आना ऐसा ङआ) जानोँ वैद्य ने औषध को ले आया और जानोँ रोग से मरते मरते रोगी ने प्राण पाया । (हीरामणि ने आते-ही आशीस दी) धन्या (पद्मावती) ने आशीस सुनते-ही

आँख खोली और कोयल ऐसी विरह वचन बोली। कमल में अर्थात् मेरे में जैसी जैसी विरह व्यथा बढने लगी (वैसा वैसा मेरी देह का) रंग केशर सा होता गया, (अब) हृदय में गाढी पिअराई (छा गई) है। यदि दिन ही में निश्चय कर ग्रहण ने सूर्य को ले लिया, अर्थात् यदि दिन में सूर्य को ग्रहण से अदृश्य होना था, तो क्यों कमल (मेरे) में प्रेम का अङ्कुर उत्पन्न हुआ। पुरइनि (धाइओं) की छाया में (सुख से) कमल-कली (मैं) थी, (उस की) तुम ने सब आशा और कान्ति को हर लिया, अर्थात् तुम ने उस सूर्य रत्न-सेन का नाम सुना कर, मेरे में प्रेमाङ्कुर पैदा किया फिर उस सूर्य रत्न-सेन को अदृश्य कर अब मेरी सब आशा और कान्ति नष्ट कर डाली। गम्भीर पुरुष (कभी) किसी से नहीं बोलते अर्थात् किसी को वचन नहीं देते, और यदि देते हैं, तो निर्वाह करते हैं अर्थात् वचन दे कर उस का पालन करते हैं, तुम ने वचन दिया है मुझ को उस सूर्य रत्न-सेन का दर्शन कराओ॥

इतनी बात मुख से कहते कहते (पद्मावती) फिर बेहोश हो गई, (कुछ देर में) उसी (बात) को बकते और उसी (रत्न-सेन के नाम) को मुख से लेते फिर अपने होश को सँभाली, अर्थात् फिर होश में आई॥ २५७॥

चउपाई।

अउरु दगध का कहउँ अपारा। सुनइ सो जरइ कठिन असि झारा॥
होइ हनिवंत बइठ हइ कोई। लंका डाहि लागु तनु सोई॥
लंका बुझी आगि जउँ लागी। यह न बुझइ तस उपज बजागी॥
जनहुँ अगिनि के उठहिँ पहारा। वेइ सब लागहिँ अंग अँगारा॥
कँपि कँपि माँसु सुराग पुरोआ। रकत कि आँसु माँसु सब रोआ॥
खन एक मारि माँसु अस भूँजा। खनहिँ जिआइ सिंघ अस गूँजा॥
यह रे दगध हुति उतिम मरीजिअ। दगध न सहिअ जीउ बरु दीजिअ॥

दोहा।

जहँ लगि चंदन मलइ-गिरि अउ साएर सब नीर।
सब मिलि आइ बुझावहिँ बुझइ न आगि सरीर॥ २५८॥

अउरु = अपर = और। दगध = दग्ध = दाह = जलन। का = किम् = क्या। कहउँ = कहूँ (कथयानि)। अपारा = अपार = बेहद्द। सुनइ = शृणोति = सुनता है। सो = सो = सः = वह। जरइ = ज्वलति = जलता है। कठिन = कठोर। असि = ऐसी = एतादृशी। झारा = झार = तेजी = तीव्रता = तिखाई = तीक्ष्णता। होइ = हो कर (भूत्वा)। हनिवंत = हनुमान्। बइठ = बैठा = उपविष्ट। हइ = है (अस्ति)। कोई = कोऽपि। लंका = लङ्का = रावण की राजधानी। डाहि = दग्ध्वा = दाह कर = जला कर। लागु = लाग = लगा है (लगति)। तनु = शरीर = देह। सोई = स एव = वही। बुझी = बुझइ (बुतते) का भूत-काल, स्त्रीलिङ्ग, एक-वचन। आगि = अग्नि। जउँ = यदि। लागी = लगइ (लगति) का भूत-काल, स्त्रीलिङ्ग, एक-वचन। बुझइ = (बुतते) = बुझती है। तस = तथा = तैसी। उपज = उपजी = उत्पन्न ऊई। बजागी = वज्राग्नि। जनऊँ = जाने = जानों = जान पडता है। अगिनि = अग्नि = आग। उठहिँ = उत्तिष्ठन्ते = उठते हैँ। पहारा = पहाड = प्रहार। वेइ = वे। लागहिँ = लगन्ति = लगते हैँ। अंग = अङ्ग = देह। अँगारा = अङ्गार। कँपि = कम्पयित्वा = कँप कर। माँसु = मांस = माँस। सुराग = सुरुङ्गा = सुरङ्ग। पुरोआ = पुरोअइ (प्रवयति) का भूत-काल, पुंलिङ्ग, एक-वचन। रकत = रक्त = लोहू। कि = की। आँसु = अश्रु = आँस। रोआ = रोअ = रोअहिँ = रुदन्ति = रोती हैँ। खन = क्षण। एक = एक। मारि = मारयित्वा = मार कर। अस = ऐसा = एतादृश। भूँजा = भूँजइ (भ्रज्जति) का भूत-काल, पुंलिङ्ग, एक-वचन। खनहिँ = क्षण मेँ। जिआइ = आजीव्य = जिला कर। सिंघ = सिंह, प्रसिद्ध जन्तु। गूँजा = गूँजइ (गर्जति) का भूत-काल, पुंलिङ्ग, एक-वचन। ऊति = से। उतिम = ऊतिम = उत्तम। मरीजिअ = मरजाना। सहिअ = सहना चाहिए (सह्येत)। जीउ = जीव = प्राण। बरु = वरम् = श्रेष्ठ = भला। दीजिअ = दीजिए (दीयेत)॥

जहँ लगि = जहाँ तक। चंदन = चन्दन। मलइ-गिरि = मलय-गिरि = मलयाचल। अउ = और = अपि च। साएर = सागर = जलस्थान। नीर = जल = पानी। मिलि = मिलित्वा = मिल कर। आइ = एत्य = आ कर। बुझावहिँ = बुझावेँ। बुझइ = बुझती है। सरीर = शरीर = देह॥

(पद्मावती फिर कहने लगी कि) और अपार दाह को क्या कहूँ (इस की) ऐसी कठिन तेजी है कि (इस के नाम को) जो सुनता है वही जलने लगता है। (जान पडता है कि) कोई हनुमान हो कर, (शरीर मेँ) बैठा है और वह हनुमान लङ्का को जला कर

(अब मेरी) शरीर में लगा है, अर्थात् शरीर जलाने के लिये शरीर में पैठा है। यदि लङ्का में आग लगी तो (कुछ काल में) बुझ गई, (परन्तु) यह ऐसी वज्राग्नि उत्पन्न हुई है कि बुझती ही नहीं। जान पडता है कि (शरीर के भीतर से) आग के पहाड उठते हैं और वे सब अङ्गों में अङ्गार से लगते हैं। (जान पडता है कि) काँप काँप कर, अर्थात् गल गल कर, माँस सुरङ्ग में चली जाती हैं, (उस दुःख से) सब माँस रक्ताश्रु के बहाने रो रही हैं। ऐसा (जान पडता है कि कोई) एक क्षण में मार कर माँस को भूँजता है, फिर दूसरे क्षण में जिला कर (भय दिखाने के लिये) सिंह के ऐसा गर्जता है। अरे (हीरामणि) इस दाह से अच्छा तो मर जाना है, जीव दे देना अच्छा पर इस दाह का सहना नहीं अच्छा ॥

(संसार में) जहाँ तक मलयाचल चन्दन हैं और सब जलस्थल में जितने पानी हैं, सब एकट्ठाँ हो (मेरे पास आ कर यदि बुझावैं तौ भी शरीर की आग नहीं बुझती) ऐसा मुझे जान पडता है। यहाँ पर यह कवि की अतिशयोक्ति है ॥ २५८ ॥

चउपाई।

हीरामनि जो देखी नारी। प्रीति बेलि उपनी हिअ बारी ॥
कहेसि कस न तुम्ह होहु दुहेली। अरुझी पेम प्रीति कइ बेली ॥
प्रीति-बेलि जनि अरुझइ कोई। अरुझा मुअइ न छूटइ सोई ॥
प्रीति-बेलि अइसइ तनु डाढा। पलुहत सुख बाढत दुख बाढा ॥
प्रीति-बेलि कइ अमर सो बोई। दिन दिन बढइ खीन नहिँ होई ॥
प्रीति-बेलि सँग बिरह अपारा। सरग पतार जरइ तेहि झारा ॥
प्रीति अकेलि बेलि चढि छावा। दोसर बेलि न सरिवरि पावा ॥

दोहा।

प्रीति-बेलि उरझाइ जब　तब सो छाँह सुख साख।
मिलइ पिरीतम आइ कइ　दाख बेलि रस चाख ॥ २५९ ॥

हीरामनि = हीरामणि (शुक)। देखी = देखइ (पश्यति) का भूत-काल, स्त्रीलिङ्ग, एक-वचन। नारी = स्त्री, वा नाडी हाथ की। प्रीति = स्नेह। बेलि = वल्ली = लता।

उपनी = उपनइ (उत्पद्यते) का भूत-काल, स्त्रीलिङ्ग, एक-वचन। हिग्र = हृदय। बारी = बालिका (पद्मावती) वा वाटिका = बाग। कहेसि = कहा = अकथयत्। कस = कथम् = क्यों। होऊ = हो (भवत)। दुहेली = दुर्हेली = दुःखिता। अरुझी = अरुझइ (अवरुध्यते) का भूत-काल, स्त्रीलिङ्ग, एक-वचन। पेम = प्रेम। कइ = की। बेली = वल्ली। जनि = न = मत। अरुझइ = अरुझे (अवरुध्येत)। कोई = कोऽपि। अरुझा = अरुझा हुआ = अवरुद्ध। मुअइ = मरता है = मरति। छूटइ = छूटता है (छुट्यते)। सोई = स हि = वह। अइसइ = ऐसे ही = एतादृश। तनु = शरीर। डाढा = डाढ = दाहइ (दहति) = जलाती है। पलुहत = पल्लवित = लगने में। बाढत = बढते = वर्धयन्। दुख = दुःख। बाढा = बाढइ (वर्धते) का भूत-काल, पुंलिङ्ग का एक-वचन। कइ = के यहाँ को। अमर = जो मरे नहीं। सो = सो = वह (परमात्मा, भगवान्)। बोई = बोअइ (वपति) का भूत-काल. स्त्रीलिङ्ग, एक-वचन। बढइ = वर्धते = बढती है। खीन = क्षीण = नाश। होई = भवति = होती है। संग = सङ्ग = साथ। बिरह = विरह = प्रियवियोग। अपारा = अपार = बेहद्द। सरग = स्वर्ग। पतार = पाताल। जरइ = ज्वलति = जलता है। तेहि = तिस के = उस के। झारा = झार = तेजी = तीव्रप्रभाव। अकेलि = अकेली = एकला। चढि = चढ कर (उच्चल्य)। छावा = छाव = छावइ (छादयति) = छावती है। दोसर = दूसरी = द्वितीया। सरिवरि = बराबरी = सादृश्य = साम्य। पावा = पाव = पावइ (प्राप्नोति) = पाती है॥

उरझार = उरझइ (अवरुध्यते) = अरुझती है। जब = यदा तब = तदा। छाँह = छाया। साख = शाखा। मिलइ = मिले (मिलेत्)। पिरीतम = प्रियतम = सब से प्यारा। आइ कइ = एत्य = आ कर। दाख = द्राक्षा = अङ्गूर। चाख = चखे (चषेत्) = चक्खे॥

हीरामणि ने जो नाडी वा नारी (पद्मावती) देखी तो (समझ लिया कि इस के) हृदय-वाटिका में प्रीति की बेलि उत्पन्न हुई, वा इस बालिका के हृदय में प्रीति-बेलि उत्पन्न हुई। (देख कर शुक ने) कहा कि (तुमारे हृदय में) प्रीति-बेलि अरुझ गई फिर तुम क्यों न दुखिआ हो। (ईश्वर करे) कोई प्रीति-बेलि में न अरुझे, (क्योंकि) अरुझने-वाले के मरने पर भी वह प्रीति-बेलि नहीं छूटती, अर्थात् मरने पर भी प्रीति-बेलि से छुटकारा नहीं होता। (जैसी तुमारी शरीर जल रही है) उसी तरह प्रीति-बेलि शरीर को जलाती है, प्रीति-बेलि के उत्पन्न होने में तो सुख जान पडता है (परन्तु यह ज्यों ज्यों) बढती जाती है (त्यों त्यों) उसी के साथ दुःख बढता जाता है।

परमात्मा ने प्रीति-बेलि को अमर कर के बोया है। यदि बोई के स्थान में पोई पाठ हो तो पोई=पोअइ (पचति) का भूत-काल, स्त्रीलिङ्ग का एक-वचन समझना और तब 'प्रीति-बेलि को अमर कर के पोया है अर्थात् बनाया है' ऐसा अर्थ करना। (यह) दिन दिन बढती है चीण नहीँ होती। प्रीति-बेलि के साथ साथ अपार विरह भी रहता है जिस के झार (कटुता) से स्वर्ग और पाताल (दोनोँ) जलते हैँ। प्रीति-बेलि अकेली चढ कर (स्वर्ग और पाताल को) छा लेती है, दूसरी बेलि इस की समता को नहीँ पाती है॥

जब प्रीति-बेलि (हृदय मेँ) अरुझ जाती है, तब सुख-रूप शाखा उस की छाया मेँ पड जाती है, अर्थात् प्रीति-बेलि के छा लेने से सुख-शाखा उस की छाया मेँ पड कर दब जाती है, (जब) प्रियतम आ कर मिले (तब) द्राचा-बेलि के रस को चक्खे, अर्थात् द्राचा-रस सदृश प्रियतम मिले तब प्रीति-बेलि-रस से दुःखित प्राणी सुख पावे नहीँ तो जन्म भर प्रीति-बेलि मेँ अरुझा तडप तडप कर कराहता रहे॥ २५९॥

चउपाई।

पदुमावति उठि टेकइ पाया। तुम्ह हुति हो प्रीतम कइ छाया॥
कहत लाज अउ रहइ न जीऊ। एक दिसि आगि दोसरि दिसि सीऊ॥
तुम्ह सो मोर खेवक गुरु देऊ। उतरउँ पार तेही बिधि खेऊ॥
सूर उदइ-गिरि चढत भुलाना। गहने गहा कवँल कुम्हिलाना॥
ओहट होइ मरउँ तेहि झूरी। यह सुठि मरन जो निअरहि दूरी॥
घट मँह निकट बिकट भा मेरू। मिलेहु न मिलइ परा तस फेरू॥
दामवती नल हंस मिलावा। तब हीरामनि नाउँ कहावा॥

दोहा।

मूरि सजीवनि दूरि इमि साली सकती बानु।
प्रान मुकुत अब होत हइ बेगि देखावहु आनु॥ २६०॥

पदुमावति=पद्मावती। उठि=उत्थाय=उठ कर। टेकइ=टेकती है (टीकयति)। पाया=पाय=पैर=पाद। तुम्ह हुति=तुम से। हो=अहो। प्रीतम=प्रियतम।

कइ = की । छाया = छाहँ । कहत = कहते (कथयन्) । लाज = लज्जा । अउ = अपि = और । रहइ = रहति = रहता है । एक = एक । दिसि = दिशि = दिशा में । आगि = अग्नि । दोसरि = दूसरी = द्वितीया । सीऊ = सीत = शीत = पानी । सो = सो = सः = वह । मोर = मेरा = मम । खेवक = खेवने-वाले । गुरुदेऊ = गुरुदेव । उंतरउँ = उत्तरामि = उतरूँ । तेही = तेही = तिस । बिधि = विधि = प्रकार । खेऊ = खेवइ (खेवते) का विध्यर्थ में मध्यम-पुरुष, पुंलिङ्ग का एक-वचन । सूर = सूर्य । उदइ-गिरि = उदय-गिरि = उदयाचल । चढत = चढते = उच्चलन् । भुलाना = भुलइ (भ्रमति) का भूत-काल, एक-वचन । गहने = ग्रहणे = ग्रहण में । गहा = ग्रस्त हुआ (जगहे) । कवँल = कमल । कुम्हिलाना = कुम्हिलाइ का भूत-काल, पुंलिङ्ग का एक-वचन = कुम्लान हुआ = बुरी तरह से मलिन हुआ । ओहट = अरहट्ट = रहँट = पुरवट । होइ = हो कर = भला । मरउँ = मरती हूँ (मरामि) । झूरी = झूर हो कर = सूख कर = झरिला = झर कर । सुठि = सुष्ठु = अच्छा । मरन = मरण = मरना । निअरहि = निकटे हि = निकट में । दूरी = दूर । घट = शरीर । मँह = मध्ये = में । निकट = नगीच । बिकट = विकट = कठिन । भा = भया = बभूव = हुआ । मेरू = मेरु = मेरुदण्ड । मिलेऊ = मिलने पर । मिलइ = मिलति = मिलता है । परा = पडा = परइ (पतति) का भूत-काल, पुंलिङ्ग, एक-वचन । तस = तथा = तैसा । फेरू = फेर = फेरा । दामवती = दमयन्ती । नल = राजा नल । हंस = प्रसिद्ध मानस सर का पची । मिलावा = मिलावइ (मेलयति) का भूत-काल, पुंलिङ्ग, एक-वचन । तब = तदा = तो । हीरामनि = हीरामणि (शुक) । नाउँ = नाम । कहावा = कहावइ (कथ्यते) का भूत-काल, पुंलिङ्ग, एक-वचन ॥

मूरि = मूली । सजीवनि = सञ्जीवनी = जिलाने-वाली । दूरि = दूर । इमि = इस तरह से = इस प्रकार से । साली = सालइ (शल्यति) का भूत-काल, स्त्रीलिङ्ग, एक-वचन । सकती = शक्ति । बानु = बान = बाण । प्रान = प्राण = जीव । मुकुत = मुक्त = छूटता । अब = इदानीम् = अधुना । होत हइ = होता है । बेगि = वेगेन = शीघ्र । देखावहु = देखाओ (दर्शयत) । आनु = आनय = आनो = ले आओ ॥

पद्मावती उठ कर (हीरामणि के) पैर को टेकने लगी, अर्थात् उस के पैर पर अपना शिर रख दिया (और कहने लगी कि) अहो (शुक) तुम्हीं से प्रियतम की छाया है, अर्थात् तुम्हारे ही उद्योग से अपने प्रियतम की परछाहीं देख सकती हूँ । कहने में लज्जा आती है और (कहे विना) जी रहता नहीं, एक तरफ आग और

दूसरी तरफ पानी है (क्या करूँ किधर जाऊँ)। तुम मेरे गुरुदेव खेवक हो, इस रीति से खेओ जिस में (इस विरहसागर के) पार उतर जाऊँ। (तुम ने सुना होगा कि) सूर्य (रत्न-सेन) उदयाचल (गढ) पर चढते भूल गया, (अब) ग्रहण में पकड गया (इसी से) कमल (मैं) कुम्हिला गया, इसी कारण मैं रहँट हो कर भी सूख कर मर रही हूँ, अर्थात् दिन रात आँसू के जल से नहा रही हूँ तौ भी सूख कर मरती हूँ, जैसे जल के भीतर रह कर भी सूर्य के विना कमल मुरझा जाता है। यह अच्छा मरना है (जो प्रियतम के) नगीच में रह कर भी दूर पर हूँ, अर्थात् अलग हूँ। घट (शरीर) में नगीच ही मेरुदण्ड रहने पर भी (उस का मिलना) कठिन हो गया। (गुद-मूल से शिर तक शरीर में पीठ की ओर जो एक हड्डी चली गई है उसी में लगा हुआ भीतरी ओर मेरुदण्ड है इसी में छ कमल हैं। यदि योगाभ्यास से मेरुदण्ड को ठीक ठीक पहचान कर प्राण उन कमलों में चढ जाय तो फिर सिद्ध हो कर अमर हो जाना सहज है।) ऐसा फेर पड गया है कि मिलने पर भी (वह मेरुदण्ड, अर्थात् रत्न-सेन) नहीं मिलता है।) जैसे हंस ने दमयन्ती और नल को मिला दिया (ऐसे ही तुम मुझे राजा रत्न-सेन से मिला दो) तब तो हीरामणि तुमारा नाम कहने योग्य (नहीं तो काच से भी अधम तुमारा नाम समझूँगी)। विदर्भ देश के राजा भीम-सेन की कन्या दमयन्ती थी और निषध देश का राजा नल था। नल ने अपने बाग के तडाग में एक विचित्र हंस को देख कर पकड लिया। उस के रोने पर करुणा में आ कर छोड दिया। छुटने पर हंस ने प्रसन्न हो कर कहा कि राजा आप ने दया कर जो मुझे छोड दिया इस के प्रत्युपकार में मैं जगत्-सुन्दरी दमयन्ती से आप का विवाह करा दूँगा। फिर हंस ने दमयन्ती के यहाँ जा कर नल की प्रशंसा कर बडे उद्योग से दोनों को मिलाया। इस की कथा भारत और श्रीहर्षरचित नैषध काव्य में विस्तार से लिखी है। जिस समय नल से बिदा हो कर हंस दमयन्ती के यहाँ चलने लगा है, उस समय नल के आशीर्वाद की कविता श्रीहर्ष ने नैषध में ऐसी की है—

तव वर्त्मनि वर्त्ततां शिवं पुनरस्तु त्वरितं समागमः।
अयि साधय साधयेप्सितं स्मरणीयाः समये वयं वयः॥

(पद्मावती बिलपती है कि) सञ्जीवनी मूली (राजा रत्न-सेन) दूर है (और यहाँ पर मुझे) इस तरह से शक्ति-बाण, अर्थात् शक्ति-साल रही है, (अरे हीरामणि)

अब प्राण छूटने चाहता है, शीघ्र (रत्न-सेन को) देखाओ (शीघ्र उसे) ले आओ। रावण के बेटे मेघनाद की ब्रह्म-दत्त शक्ति (साँगी) प्रसिद्ध है जिस के आघात से लक्ष्मण अचेत हो गए थे। उन के जिलाने के लिये हनुमान द्रोणाचल को उठा लाए थे जिस पर कि सञ्जीविनी जडी थी। रामायण में यह कथा प्रसिद्ध है ॥ २६० ॥

चउपाई।

हीरामनि भुइँ धरा लिलाटू। तुम्ह रानी जुग जुग सुख पाटू ॥
जेहि के हाथ जरी अउ मूरी। सो जोगी नाहीँ अब दूरी ॥
पिता तुम्हार राज कर भोगी। पूजइ बिपर मरावइ जोगी ॥
पवँरि पंथ कोतवार बईठा। पेम क लुबुध सुरंग पईठा ॥
चढत रइनि गढ होइ गा भोरू। आवत बार धरा कइ चोरू ॥
अब लेइ देन गए ओहि सूरी। तेहि सौँ अगाह बिथा तुम्ह पूरी ॥
अब तुम्ह जीउ कया वह जोगी। कया क रोग जान पइ रोगी ॥

दोहा।

रूप तुम्हार जीउ लेइ आपन पिंड कमावा फेरि।
आपु हेराइ रहा तेहि खंडहि काल न पावइ हेरि ॥ २६१ ॥

हीरामनि = हीरामणि (शुक)। भुइँ = भुवि = पृथ्वी में = जमीन में। धरा = धरइ (धरति) का भूत-काल, पुंलिङ्ग का एक-वचन। लिलाटू = ललाट = मस्तक। तुम्ह = आप = आत्मा। रानी = राज्ञी। जुग = युग। पाटू = पाट = पट्ट = सिंहासन। जेहि = जिस। हाथ = हस्त। जरी = जडी। अउ = और। मूरी = मूली। सो = सः = वह। जोगी = योगी। नाहीँ = नहीँ = न हि। अब = अधुना = इदानीम्। दूरी = दूर। पिता = बाप। तुम्हार = तुम्हारा = आप का। राज = राज्य। कर = का। भोगी = भोग करने-वाला। पूजइ = पूजयति = पूजता है। बिपर = विप्र = ब्राह्मण। मरावइ = मारयति = मरवाता है। पवँरि = पवँरी = पौरी = पुरद्वार। पंथ = पन्थाः = राह। कोतवार = कोतवाल = कोटपाल। बईठा = बइठा = बैठा = बइठइ वा बैठइ (विशति) का भूत-काल, पुंलिङ्ग, एक-वचन। पेम = प्रेम। क = का। लुबुध = लुब्ध = लोभी। सुरंग = सुरङ्गा। पईठा = पइठा = पैठा = पइठइ वा पैठइ (प्रविशति) का भूत-काल, पुंलिङ्ग, एक-वचन।

चढत = चढते (उच्चलन्) । रइनि = रजनी = रात । गढ = गाढ = दुर्ग = किला । होइ गा = हो गया । भोरू = भोर = सबेरा । आवत = आते = आयन् । बार = द्वार = दरवाजा । धरा = धरइ (धरति) का भूत-काल, पुंलिङ्ग, एक-वचन । कइ = कर = कृत्वा । चोरू = चोर । अब = इदानीम् = अधुना । लेइ = ले कर = आलाय । देन = देने । गए = जाइ (याति) का भूत-काल, पुंलिङ्ग, बहु-वचन । ओहि = उसे । सूरी = शूली = फाँसी । तेहि सौं = तिसी से = उसी से । अगाह = अगाध = बेहद्द । बिथा = व्यथा = पीडा । तुम्ह = तुम्हें । पूरी = पूरइ (पूर्यते) का भूत-काल, स्त्रीलिङ्ग, एक-वचन । जीउ = जीव = प्राण । कया = काय = शरीर । रोग = मर्ज । जान = जानइ (जानाति) = जानता है । पइ = अपि = निश्चयेन । रोगी = रोगिआ = जिसे रोग हुआ हो ॥

रूप = सूरत । आपन = अपना वा अपनी । पिंड = पिण्ड = देह । कमावा = कमाया = कमाइ का भूत-काल, पुंलिङ्ग, एक-वचन । फेरि = फिर = पुनः । आपु = आप = स्वयम् । हेराइ = हेराद = हरित । रहा = रहइ (रहति) का भूत-काल, पुंलिङ्ग, एक-वचन । खंडहि = खण्ड में । काल = प्राण लेने-वाला यमदूत । पावइ = प्राप्नोति = पाता है । हेरि = हिण्डित्वा = हेर कर = ढूँढ कर ॥

हीरामणि ने जमीन पर (अपने) मस्तक को रक्खा (और आशीर्वाद दिया कि) हे रानी तुम्हें युग युग सुख और सिंहासन है । जिस के हाथ में (जिलाने-वाली) जडी और मूली है, वह (राजा रत्न-सेन) योगी अब दूर नहीं है । तुम्हारा पिता (केवल) राज्य का भोगी है, ब्राह्मण को तो पूजता है (पर) योगी को मरवाता है । पुरद्वार की राह पर कोतवाल बैठा था, (वहाँ) प्रेम का लोभी (रत्न-सेन योगी) सुरंग लगा कर पैठा । रात में गढ पर चढते चढते भोर हो गया, (ऊपर) दरवाजे पर आते आते (कोतवाल के सिपाहिओं ने) चोर समझ कर पकड लिया । अब (लोग) उसे (रत्न-सेन को) पकड कर फाँसी देने गए हैं, इसी से तुम्ह भी अगाध पीडा से भर गई । अब तुम्ह जीव और वह योगी शरीर है, अर्थात् योगी का प्राण तुम हो और उस की खाली बेप्राण की शरीर वहाँ पर पडी है, निश्चय समझो कि रोगिआ ही शरीर के रोग को जानता है, अर्थात् तुम्ह दुखिआ हो तुम्ही समझती हो कि उस बेचारे दुखिआ पर क्या बीतता होगा ॥

तुम्हारा रूप और अपना प्राण ले कर (रत्न-सेन ने) फिर से (योगाभ्यास के बल से) अपनी शरीर को बनाया है, अर्थात् अपनी देह को नई कर डाला है

जिसे कि योगी लोग काय-कल्प कहते हैं। (इसी से) उस खण्ड में, अर्थात् नए देह के अवयव में आप हेराय गया है (दूसरी देह हो जाने से) ढूँढने से भी (उसे) काल नहीं पाता है (इसी लिये अभीं तक जीता है)॥ २६१॥

चउपाई।

हीरामनि जो बात यह कही। सुरुज के गहन चाँद पुनि गही॥
सुरुज के दुख जो ससि भइ दुखी। सो कित दुख मानइ करमुखी॥
अब जउँ जोगि मरइ मोहिँ नेहा। मोहिँ ओहि साथ धरति गगनेहा॥
रहइ तो करउँ जरम भरि सेवा। चलइ तो यह जिउ साथ परेवा॥
कउनु सो करनी कहु गुरु सोई। पर-काया परबेस जो होई॥
पलटि सो पंथ कउनु बिधि खेला। चेला गुरू गुरू होइ चेला॥
कउनु खंड अस रहा लुकाई। आवइ काल हेरि फिरि जाई॥

दोहा

चेला सिद्धि सो पावई गुरु सउँ करइ उछेद।
गुरू करइ जउँ किरिया कहइ सो चेलहि भेद॥ २६२॥

हीरामनि = हीरामणि (शुक)। जो = जो। बात = वार्त्ता। यह = अयम्, वा इयम्, वा इदम्। कह = कहइ (कथयति) का भूत-काल, स्त्रीलिङ्ग, एक-वचन। सुरुज = सूर्य। के = के। गहन = ग्रहण। चाँद = चन्द्र। पुनि = पुनः = फिर। गही = गहइ (गृह्यते) का भूत-काल, स्त्रीलिङ्ग, एक-वचन। दुख = दुःख। ससि = शशि = चन्द्र। दुखी = दुःखित। सो = सा = वह। कित = कुतः = कस्मात् = क्यों। मानइ = मन्येत = माने। करमुखी = कृष्णमुखी = जिस का काला मुँह हो। अब = इदानीम् = अधुना। जउँ = यदि = जो। जोगि = जोगी = योगी। मरइ = मरेत् = मरे। मोहिँ = मोहिँ = मेरे। नेहा = नेह = स्नेह। ओहि = ओहि = उस का। साथ = सार्थ = संग। धरति = धरती = धरित्री = पृथ्वी। गगनेहा = गगन में = आकाश में। रहइ = रहे (रहेत्)। तो = तो = तर्हि। करउँ = कुर्याम् = करूँ। जरम = जन्म। भरि = भर = पूरा। सेवा = खिदमत = टहल। चलइ = चले (चलेत्)। जिउ = जीव = प्राण। परेवा = पारावत = पक्षी। कउनु = कौन = को नु। करनी = करणी = कर्त्तव्यता।

कहु = कह = कथय। सोई = सोऽपि = वह, यहाँ उसे। पर-काया = परकाय = दूसरे की शरीर। परबेस = प्रवेश = जाना। होई = होय (भवेत्)। पलटि = परिवर्त्य = उलट कर। पंथ = पन्थाः = राह। बिधि = विधि = रीति = प्रकार। खेला = खेल = क्रीडा। चेला = शिष्य। गुरू = गुरु। होइ = होइ = हो = भवेत्। खंड = खण्ड = भूमि-खण्ड। अस = ऐसा = एतादृश। रहा = रहइ (रहति वा तिष्ठति) का भूत काल, पुंलिङ्ग, एक वचन। लुकाई = लुका कर = लुक्कायित हो कर = छिप कर। आवइ = आयाति = आता है। काल्ह = प्राण लेने-वाला यम-दूत। हेरि = हिण्डित्वा = हेर कर = ढूँढ कर। फिरि जाई = फिर जाता है = प्रयाति = लौट जाता है ॥

सिद्धि = अणिमादि अष्ट सिद्धि, जिन से जो चाहे सो कर ले। पावई = पावइ = प्राप्नोति = पाता है। सउँ = सेाँ = से। करइ = करे = कुर्यात्। उछेद = उच्छेद = नाश = सर्वनाश। जउँ = यदि = जो। किरिपा = कृपा = दया। कहइ = कथयति = कहता है। चेलहि = चेला को। भेद = मर्म बात = हाल ॥

हीरामणि ने जो यह पिछले दोहे में बात कही (कि सूर्य का ग्रहण हो गया, अर्थात् रत्न-सेन पकड गया, तो) सूर्य के ग्रहण होने से, अर्थात् रत्न-सेन के पकड जाने का वृत्तान्त सुनने से, फिर चन्द्र (पद्मावती) भी ग्रस्त हो गई। सूर्य के दुःख से चन्द्रमा में जो दुःख हुआ, उस दुःख को कर-सुखी (सूर्य) क्यों माने, अर्थात् ग्रस्त सूर्य (रत्न-सेन) को क्या मालूम कि मेरे दुःख से चाँद (पद्मावती) के ऊपर कैसा वज्रपात के ऐसा दुःख पडा है। (पद्मावती कहने लगी, कि) यदि मेरे स्नेह से योगी (रत्न-सेन) मर जाय तो मेरा और उस का साथ यहाँ पृथ्वी और आकाश दोनों स्थानों में रहेगा। यदि पृथ्वी पर वह योगी (रत्न-सेन) रहे तो जन्म भर (उस की) सेवा करूँ (यदि परलोक में) चले तो यह मेरा प्राण पखेरू भी (उस के) साथ चलेगा। वह कौन सी क्रिया है जिस से परकाय में (प्राण का) प्रवेश हो, उस क्रिया को हे गुरु (शुक) कह, अर्थात् बताव। किस तरह से खेल अर्थात् काम किया जाय और वह कौन पथ है जिस से पलट कर चेला गुरु और गुरु चेला हो जाय। ऐसे कौन भूमि-खण्ड में (वह रत्न-सेन) लुका रहा है, जहाँ कि काल आता है और ढूँढ कर (लाचार हो कर न पाने से) लौट जाता है ॥

वही चेला सिद्धि को पाता है जो कि गुरु से सर्वनाश करता है अर्थात् गुरु के उपदेश से सब विघ्नों का नाश करता है। गुरु यदि कृपा करे तो चेला से सब-

भेद कह दे। अर्थात् चेला उस सिद्धि को तभी पा सकता है जब निष्कपट हो सर्वनाश कर गुरु की शरण में आवे और गुरु उसे शुद्ध समझ कर कृपा कर उस सिद्धि मिलने के उपाय को ठीक ठीक बता दे ॥ २६२ ॥

चउपाई ।

अनु रानी तुम्ह गुरु वह चेला। मोहिँ पूँछेहु कइ सिद्ध नवेला ॥
तुम्ह चेला कहँ परसन भईँ। दरसन देइ मँडफ चलि गईँ ॥
रूप तुम्हार सो चेलइ डीठा। चित समाइ होइ चितर पईठा ॥
जीउ काढि तुम्ह लेइ उपसई। वह भा कया जीउ तुम्ह भई ॥
कया जो लागु धूप अउ सीऊ। कया न जानु जानु पइ जीऊ ॥
भोग तुम्हार मिला वह जाई। ओहि कइ बिथा सो तुम्ह कहँ आई ॥
तुम्ह ओहि घट वह तुम्ह घट माँहा। काल कहाँ पावइ ओहि छाँहा ॥

दोहा ।

अस वह जोगि अमर भा पर-काया परवेसु ।
आवइ काल तुम्हहिँ तिन्ह (देखे) फिरि कइ करइ अदेसु ॥ २६३ ॥

अनु = आन = शपथ = कसम = अणक । रानी = राज्ञी । तुम्ह = आप । गुरु = उस्ताद । वह = सः । चेला = शिष्य । मोहिँ = मुझ से । पूँछेऊ = पूँछइ (पृच्छति) का भूत-काल, स्त्रीलिङ्ग, बहु-वचन । कइ = कर = कला । सिद्ध = सिद्ध पुरुष, जो चाहे सो कर डाले । नवेला = नवल = नया । कहँ = को, यहाँ से । परसन = प्रसन्न = खुश । भईँ = हुईँ (बभूविथ)। दरसन = दर्शन । देइ = दत्वा = दे कर । मँडफ = मण्डप । चलि गईँ = चली गईँ । रूप = सूरत । तुम्हार = आप का । सो = वह = सः । चेलइ = चेला ने । डीठा = देखा = दृष्टिगोचर किया = ददृशे । चित = चित्त । समाइ = समेत्य = समाय कर । होइ = हो कर = भूत्वा । चितर = चित्र = तसवीर । पईठा = पइठा = पैठा = पइठइ (प्रविशति) का भूत-काल, पुंलिङ्ग, एक-वचन । जीउ = जीव = प्राण । काढि = कर्षयित्वा = खींच कर । लेइ = ले कर (आलाय)। उपसई = उपससर्प = उपससार = चली गईं = हट गईँ । भा = बभूव = हुआ । कया = काय = शरीर । भई = होइ (भवति) का भूत-काल, स्त्रीलिङ्ग, एक-वचन । लागु = लाग = लागइ (लगति) = लगता है ।

धूप = घाम। अउ = अपि च = और। सीऊ = शीत = ठंढक। जानु = जान = जानइ (जानाति) जानता है। पइ = अपि = निश्चय। भोग = सुखसामग्री। मिला = मिलइ (मिलति) का भूत-काल, पुंलिङ्ग का एक-वचन। वह = उस में। जाई = जा कर (यात्वा)। ओहि कइ = उस की। बिथा = व्यथा = पीडा। तुम्ह कहँ = तुम को। आई = आवइ (आयाति) का भूत-काल, स्त्रीलिङ्ग, एक-वचन। ओहि = उस के। घट = शरीर। माँहा = माँह = मध्य = में। काल = प्राण निकालने-वाला यम-दूत। कहाँ = कुत्र। पावइ = पावे (प्राप्नुयात्)। छाँहा = छाँह = छाया = परछाहीँ॥

अस = ऐसा = एतादृश। जोगि = योगी = जोगी। अमर = जो मरे न। परकाया = परकाय = दूसरे की शरीर। परबेसु = प्रवेश। आवइ = आयाति = आता है। तुम्हहिँ = तुम्हेँ। तिन्ह = तिन्हेँ। फिरि कइ = फिर कर = लौट कर। करइ = करोति = करता है। अँदेसु = अंदेश = अँदेसा = चिन्ता॥

(हीरामणि ने कहा कि) रानी तुम्हारा शपथ है, तुम्ह गुरु और वह (रत्न-सेन) तुम्हारा चेला है। आन शपथ के अर्थ में तुलसी-दास ने भी अयोध्याकाण्ड में लिखा है— 'सपथ तुम्हार भरत कइ आना। हेतु न दूसर मैं कछु जाना'। (उसे) नया सिद्ध कर (अब) मुझ से पूछी हो। आप (उस) चेले के ऊपर प्रसन्न हुईं, (महादेव के) मण्डप में (उसे) दर्शन दे कर चली गईं। उस चेले (रत्न-सेन) ने तुम्हारे रूप को देखा, (देखते ही वह रूप) चित्त में समाय कर तसबीर हो कर (भीतर) पैठ गया। आप (उस का) जीव निकाल कर (उस मण्डप से) हट गईं, (अब) वह (रत्न-सेन) तो शरीर हुआ और आप (उस शरीर का जीव) हुईं। शरीर में जो धूप और शीत लगते हैं उन्हें शरीर नहीं जानती निश्चय कर जीव जानता है, अर्थात् प्राण ही धूप और शीत का अनुभव करता है जड शरीर को धूप-शीत का कुछ भी ज्ञान नहीं। तुम्हारा भोग-विलास जा कर उसे मिला और उस की वह पीडा तुम्हारे यहाँ चली आई। तुम्ह उस की शरीर में और वह तुम्हारी शरीर में है, अर्थात् परकायप्रवेशविद्या से तुम्ह उस की देह में और वह तुम्हारी देह में प्रवेश कर गया है, (इस लिये) काल उस की परछाहीँ भी कहाँ पावे, अर्थात् वह रत्न-सेन योगी परकायप्रवेशविद्या से तुम्हारे (परब्रह्म-स्वरूप रूप) में लीन हो गया, इस लिये अब काल उस के प्रतिबिम्ब को भी नहीं पा सकता। वह अजर अमर ब्रह्मगुफा में पैठ कर ब्रह्म-रूप हो गया, वहाँ पर काल की गति ही नहीं फिर वह बेचारा कैसे उस की छाया को पा सकता है॥

इस तरह से वह योगी परकायप्रवेशविद्या से अमर हो गया। काल (प्राण लेने के लिये) तुम्हारे और उन के (रत्न-सेन के) पास आता है (पर आप लोगों का यथार्थ रूप न पा कर) लौट कर चिन्ता करता है, अर्थात् झंखता है कि यम-राज की आज्ञा से प्राण लेने के लिये आया पर यहाँ रूप मिलता ही नहीं, अब क्या करूँ, और कहाँ ढूँढूँ ॥ २६३ ॥

चउपाई ।

सुनि जोगी कइ अम्मर करनी। नेउरी बिरह-बिथा कइ मरनी ॥
कवँल-करी होइ बिगसा जीऊ। जनु रबि देखि छूटि गा सीऊ ॥
जो अस सिद्ध को मारइ पारा। नीँऊ रस तइँ जो होय छारा ॥
कहउ जाइ अब मोर सँदेसू। तजहु जोग अब होहु नरेसू ॥
जनि जानहु हउँ तुम्ह सउँ दूरी। नइनहिँ माँझ गडी वह सूरी ॥
तुम्ह परसेत घटइ घट केरा। मोहिँ जिउ घटत न लागइ बेरा ॥
तुम्ह कहँ राज-पाट मइँ साजा। अब तुम्ह मोर दुअउ जग राजा ॥

दोहा ।

जउँ रे जिअहिँ मिलि केलि करहिँ मरहिँ तो एकइ दोउ ।
तुम्ह पिअ जिउ जनि होउ किछु मोहिँ जिउ होउ सो होउ ॥ २६४ ॥

इति मंचौ-खंड ॥ २४ ॥

सुनि = श्रुत्वा = सुन कर। जोगी = योगी। कइ = की। अम्मर = अमर। करनी = करणी = कर्म। नेउरी = नेउरइ (निवरति) का भूत-काल, स्त्रीलिङ्ग, एक-वचन। बिरह-बिथा = विरह-व्यथा = विरह की पीडा। मरनी = मरण = मृत्यु। कवँल-करी = कमल-कली = कमल की कली। होइ = हो कर = भूत्वा। बिगसा = बिगसइ (विकाशते) का भूत-काल, पुंलिङ्ग, एक-वचन। जीऊ = जीव = प्राण। जनु = जाने = जानता हूं = जानोँ। रबि = रवि = सूर्य। देखि = दृष्ट्वा = देख कर। छूटि गा = छूट गया। सीऊ = शीत = ठंढक। अस = ऐसा = एतादृश। सिद्ध = सिद्ध-पुरुष, जो चाहे सो कर डाले। को = को = कौन। मारइ = मारे (मारयेत्)। पारा = पारद = तुङ्गबीज।

नीँऊ = निंबू = निबुआ। तइँ = तैँ = से। होय = होय = होता है (भवति)। छारा = छार = खार = राख = भस्म। कहउ = कहो (कथयत)। जाइ = गत्वा = यात्वा = जा कर। अब = इदानीम् = अधुना। मोर = मेरा = मम। सँदेसू = सन्देश = सँदेसा। तजऊ = तज देओ = छोड देओ (त्यजथ)। जोग = योग। होऊ = होओ (भवथ)। नरेसू = नरेश = राजा। जनि = न = मत। जानऊ = जानइ (जानाति) का विध्यर्थ में मध्यम-पुरुष, बऊ-वचन। हउँ = अहम् = मैँ। सउँ = से = तैँ। दूरी = दूर। नइनहिँ = नयनोँ = नयनयोः = आखोँ। माँझ = मध्य = मेँ। गडी = गडइ (गडति) का भूत-काल, स्त्रीलिङ्ग, एक-वचन। वह = सा। सूरी = शूली = फाँसी। तुम्ह = तुम्हारा = आप का। परसेत = प्रस्वेद = पसीना। घटइ = घटे = कम हो। घट = शरीर। केरा = का। मोहिँ = मेरे = मम। जिउ = जीव = प्राण। घटत = घटते = कम होते = निकलते। लागइ = लगता है (लगति), यहाँ लगेगा। बेरा = वेला = समय = काल। कहँ = को। राज-पाट = राज-पट्ट = राज-सिंहासन। मइँ = मैँ। साजा = साजइ (सज्जयते) का भूत-काल, पुंलिङ्ग का एक-वचन। दुअउ = दोनोँ = द्वयोः। जग = जगत् = लोक। राजा = पति॥

जउँ = यदि = जो। जिअहिँ = जीएँ (जीवेयम्)। मिलि = मिल कर = मिलित्वा। केलि = केलि = क्रीडा = भोग-विलास। करहिँ = करेँ (कुर्याम्)। तो = तो = तर्हि। एकइ = एक ही। दोउ = दोनोँ = द्वावपि। पिअ = प्रिय = पति। होउ = होवे = भवेत्। किछु = कुछ = किञ्चित्॥

(हीरा-मणि से) योगी (रत्न-सेन) की अमर-करणी सुन कर, (पद्मावती की) विरह-व्यथा की मृत्यु हट गई। प्राण कमल-कली हो कर (फिर) विकशित ऊआ, जानोँ सूर्य देख कर शीत छूट गया। (पद्मावती कहने लगी कि) यदि ऐसा सिद्ध हो गया, तो (अब) पारे को कौन मारे, जो कि नीबू के रस से भस्म हो जाता है, अर्थात् जब सिद्ध हो गया, तो उसी के मिलने से सब मनोरथ सिद्ध हो जायगा, पारे के मारने से क्या प्रयोजन, क्योँकि मारा ऊआ पारा तो नीबू के रस से भस्म, अर्थात् राख हो जाता है; फिर उस मेँ कुछ शक्ति ही नहीँ रहती। वैद्यशास्त्र मेँ पारा मारने की विधि लिखी ऊई है, उस विधि से बडे प्रयास से पारा मारा जाता है। मरे ऊए पारे के सेवन से अनेक रोग दूर हो जाते हैँ। मरे ऊए पारे को बडे यत्न से रखना पडता है। यदि उस मेँ नीबू का रस पड जाय, तो वह राख हो जाता है;

उस की सब शक्ति नष्ट हो जाती है। इस पर पद्मावती कहती है कि ऐसा जो रत्न-सेन सिद्ध हो गया तो उसी का सेवन करूँगी, उसी से सब रोग दूर करूँगी; जो पारा (क्षुद्र मनुष्य) नीबू के रस से (क्षुद्र मनुष्य के भोग-विलास से) राख हो जाता है अब उसे कौन मारे। (हे हीरा-मणि) अब जा कर तुम मेरे सँदेसे को कहो कि (पद्मावती ने कहा है कि) अब योग का त्याग करो (तपस्या पूरी हो गई) और अब राजा हो। यह न जानो कि मैं तुम से दूर हूँ, वह (तुम्हारी) शूली मेरी आँखों में गडी ऊई है। तुम्हारी शरीर के पसीने के घटने में (चाहे देर हो तो हो, पर) मेरे प्राण के घटने में, अर्थात् निकलने में, देर न लगेगी। आप के लिये मैं राज-सिंहासन सज चुकी, अब आप यह लोक पर-लोक दोनों में मेरे राजा अर्थात् स्वामी हैं॥

(अरे हीरा-मणि जा कर बेखटके कह दे कि) जब तक जीएँ मिल कर भोग-विलास करें, और मरें तो एक ही साथ रहें। हे (प्राण) प्रिय, आप के जीव को कुछ न हो, जो हो सो मेरे जीव को हो॥ २६४॥

इति मन्त्रि-खण्ड-नाम चतुर्विंश-खण्डं समाप्तम्॥ २४॥

अथ सूरी-खंड ॥ २५ ॥

चउपाई।

बाँधि तपा आनेउ जहँ सूरी। जुरी आइ सब सिंघल पूरी ॥
पहिलइँ गुरू देइ कहँ आना। देखि रूप सब कोउ पछिताना ॥
लोग कहहिँ यह होअइ न जोगी। राजकुअँर कोउ अहइ बिओगी ॥
काहु लागि भएउ हइ तपा। हिअइँ सो माल करइ मुख जपा ॥
जस मारइ कहँ बाजा तूरू। सूरी देखि हँसा मन सूरू ॥
चमके दसन भएउ उँजिआरा। जो जहँ तहाँ बीजु अस मारा ॥
जोगी केर करहु पइ खोजू। मकु न होअइ यह राजा भोजू ॥

दोहा।

सब पूँछहिँ कहु जोगी जाति जरम अउ नाओँ।
जहाँ ठाओँ रोअइ कर हँसा सो कहु केहि भाओ ॥ २६५ ॥

बाँधि = बद्धा = बाँध कर। तपा = तपस्वी = तपसी। आनेउ = आनयत् = ले आए। जहँ = यत्र = जहाँ। सूरी = शूली = फाँसी। जुरी = युक्ताऽभूत् = एकट्ठी हुई। आइ = एत्य = आ कर। सब = सर्व। सिंघल = सिंहल। पूरी = पुरी = पुर के रहने-वाले। पहिलइँ = प्रथमे = पहले। गुरू = गुरु = रत्न-सेन। देइ कहँ = देने के लिये = शूली देने के लिये। आना = आनयत् = ले आए। देखि = दृष्ट्वा = देख कर। रूप = सूरत। कोउ = कोऽपि = कोई। पछिताना = पश्चात्ताप = पछताने लगे (यहाँ पर बहु-वचन

समझना) । लोग = लोकाः । कहहिँ = कथयन्ति = कहते हैँ । यह = अयम् । होश्रइ = होवे = भवेत् । जोगी = योगी । राज-कुअँर = राज-कुमार = राज-पुत्त्र । अहइ = अस्ति = है । बिओगी = वियोगी = विरही । काह्न लागि = कस्या अर्थम् = किसी के लिये । भण्उ = भया = अभूत् । हइ = अस्ति = है । हिअइँ = हृदयं = हृदय में । सो = सो = वह । माल = माला । करइ = करोति = करता है । मुख = मुँह । जपा = जप । जस = जैसे ही = यदैव । मारइ कहँ = मारने के लिये । बाजा = बजा = अवादीत् । तूरू = तूर्य = तुरही । हँसा = अहसत् = हँस दिया । मन = मनसः = मन से । सूरू = सूर्य = रत्न-सेन, वा सूरू = शूर = बहादुर रत्न-सेन । चमके = चमक उठे = चकमे । दसन = दशन = दाँत । उँजिआरा = उज्ज्वलन = उँजेरा = प्रकाश । जो = यः । तहाँ = तत्र । बीजु = विद्युत् = बिजुरी । अस = एतादृश = ऐसा । मारा = ममार = मार दिया । केर = का । करऊ = कुरुत = करिए । पइ = अपि = निश्चय । खोजू = खोज = अन्वेषण । मकु = मैं ने कहा = क्या जानें । भोजू = भोज = धारा नगरी का प्रसिद्ध संस्कृतानुरागी राजा ॥

सब = सर्वे । पूँछहिँ = पृच्छन्ति = पूछते हैँ । कहु = कथय = कह । जाति = ज्ञाति । जरम = जन्म । अउ = अपि च = और । नाओँ = नावँ = नाम । ठाओँ = ठावँ = स्थान । रोअइ कर = रोने का । केहि भाओँ = किस भाव से = किस अभिप्राय से = केन भावेन ॥

तपस्विओँ को (लोग) बाँध कर जहाँ शूली खडी की गई थी (वहाँ) ले आए। (उस के देखने के लिये) सब सिंहल पुरी एकट्ठी हुई, अर्थात् सिंहल के सब लोग एकट्ठे हुए। (सब से) पहले गुरु (रत्न-सेन को शूली) देने के लिये (लोग) ले आए, सब लोग उस के रूप को देख कर पछताने लगे। लोग कहते हैँ कि यह योगी नहीँ है कोई विरही राज-कुमार है। किसी के लिये तपस्वी हो गया है, हृदय में वह माला (ऐसी) है, (उसी के नाम का) जप मुख से करता है। जैसे ही मारने के लिये अर्थात् शूली देने के लिये तुरही बजी, (और शूली देखाई गई उसी चण) शूली को देख कर मन से, अर्थात् (लोगोँ को देखाने के लिये बाहर और बात और मन में और बात नहीँ किन्तु सच्चे) हृदय से हँसने लगा। (हँसने से) दाँत चमक उठे। (सब जगह) उँजेला हो गया, जो जहाँ खडे थे सब (जानोँ) बिजली के मारे हुए हैँ। (सब आपस में चौंक कर कहने लगे कि) योगी का खोज करो, क्या जानें यह राजा भोज न हो ॥

विक्रम के बाद उज्जयिनी में राजा भोज हुआ है इस ने धारा नगरी बसाई है और यह बडा ही संस्कृतानुरागी था। भोज-प्रबन्ध में इस की बडी बडी कथा लिखी हुई है॥

सब पूछने लगे कि योगी, अपनी जाति, जन्म-स्थान और नाम को कह (बताओ) (क्योंकि हम लोगों को बडा अचरज है) जहाँ रोने का स्थान है वहाँ कह किस अभिप्राय से हँसा॥ २६५॥

चउपाई।

का पूँछहु अब जाति हमारी। हम जोगी अउ तपा भिखारी॥
जोगिहि कवन जाति हो राजा। गारिहि कोह न मारहि लाजा॥
निलज भिखारि लाज जिन्ह खोई। तिन्ह के खोज परउ जनि कोई॥
जा कर जीउ मरइ पर बसा। सूरी देखि सो कस नहिँ हँसा॥
आजु नेह सउँ होइ निबेरा। आजु पुहुमि तजि गगन बसेरा॥
आजु कया-पिंजर बँध टूटा। आजु परान-परेवा छूटा॥
आजु नेह सउँ होइ निरारा। आजु पेम सँग चला पिआरा॥

दोहा।

आजु अवधि सरि पूजी कइ जो चलउँ मुख रात।
बेगि होहु मोहिँ मारहु का चालहु बहु बात॥ २६६॥

का = क्यों = किमर्थम्। पूँछहु = पूँछते हो = (पृच्छन्ति) पूछइ का विध्यर्थ में मध्यम-पुरुष का बहु-वचन। अब = इदानीम् = अधुना। जाति = ज्ञाति। हमारी = मेरी का बहु-वचन। हम = हौं (अहम्) का बहु-वचन। जोगी = योगी। अउ = अपर = और। तपा = तपस्वी = तपसी। भिखारी = भिक्षुक। जोगिहि = योगिन: = योगी को। कवन = क्व नु = कौन। हो = अहो सम्बोधन। गारिहि = गाले: = गाली से। कोह = क्रोध। मारहि = मारणेन = मारने से। लाजा = लज्जा। निलज = निर्लज्ज। जिन्ह = जिन्हों ने। खोई = खोअइ (क्षयति) का भूत-काल, स्त्री-लिङ्ग, एक-वचन, प्रथम-पुरुष। तिन्ह के = तेषाम्। खोज = अन्वेषणे = ढूँढने में। परउ = पतेत् = पडे। जनि = जातु न = कदाचित् न = मत। कोई = कोऽपि। जा कर = यस्य = जिस का।

जीउ = जीव। मरइ पर = मरने पर। बसा = बसइ (वसति) = बसता है। सूरी = शूली। देखि = दृष्ट्वा = देख कर। सो = सो = वह। कस = कथम्। हँसा = हँसे = हसेत्। आजु = अद्य = आज। नेह = स्नेह। सउँ = से। होइ = भवति = होता है। निबेरा = निवृत्ति। पुहुमि = पृथ्वी = भूमि। तजि = त्यक्त्वा = तज कर = छोड कर। गगन = आकाश। बसेरा = वास। कया-पिंजर = काय-पिञ्जर = शरीर-पिंजडा। बंध = बन्धन। टूटा = टूट = टूटइ = त्रुट्यति = टूटता है। परान-परेवा = प्राण-पारावत = प्राण-पत्ती। छूटा = छूटइ = छूट (छोटति) = छूटता है। निरारा = निरालय = अलग। पेम = प्रेम। सँग = सङ्ग = साथ। चला = चल = चलइ (चलति) चलता है। पिआरा = प्यारा = प्रिय ॥

अवधि = सीमा = हद्द। सरि = सरित् = नदी। पूजी = पूजइ (पूर्यते) का भूत-काल, प्रथम-पुरुष, स्त्री लिङ्ग, एक-वचन। कइ = कृत्वा = कर के। चलउँ = चलामि = चलता हूँ। मुख = मुँह। रात = रक्त = लाल। बेगि = वेग = शीघ्र। होऊ = भवथ = हो। मोहिँ = मोहिँ = मुझे। मारऊ = मारयथ = मारिए। चालऊ = चालयथ = चलाते हो। बात = वार्त्ता ॥

(राजा रत्न-सेन ने कहा कि) अब हमारी जाति क्या पूछते हो, हम योगी और तपस्वी भिखारी हैँ। हे राजा, योगी की कौन जात (जिसे) मारने से न क्रोध और गाली से न लज्जा। भिखारी, जिन्होँ ने लाज खो दिया है, निर्लज्ज होते हैँ, उन्ह के खोज मेँ कोई मत पडो। जिस का जीव मरने पर बस गया वह शूली देख कर क्योँ न हँसे। आज स्नेह से निबटेरा (निवृत्ति) होता है, आज भूमि छोड कर आकाश मेँ वास होता है। आज शरीर-पिँजडे का बन्धन टूटता है (इस लिये) आज प्राण-पत्ती छूटता है। आज स्नेह से अलग होना होता है, आज प्यारा (प्राण) प्रेम के साथ चलता है ॥

आज (प्रेम-)अवधि-रूप नदी भर गई (इस लिये अपना) मुँह लाल कर चलता हूँ, अर्थात् प्रेम-नदी-धारा मेँ पड कर मुँह नहीँ मोडा उस के भर जाने से मरता हूँ। लोग यह तो कहेँगे कि जिस राह मेँ रत्न-सेन पडा उस मेँ प्राण तक दे दिया पर मुँह नहीँ मोडा। इस लिये मैँ अपना मुँह लाल कर के चलता हूँ। जौँ मुँह मोडता तो अवश्य काला मुँह कर के जाता। (रत्न-सेन कहता है कि) बेगि होऊ अर्थात् जल्दी करो, (अभी) मुझे मारो; क्योँ बहुत बात चलाते हो ॥

योगी लोग परब्रह्म के प्रेम में डूब कर नीचे से षट् चक्र और अष्ट कमलों में क्रम क्रम से प्राण चढाते जब ब्रह्मगुफा के पास ब्रह्माण्ड में प्राण को ले जाते हैं तब अप्सरा-उर्वशी और काम की तरह तरह की मन हरने-वाली लीला सब उस योगी के प्राण को ऊपर न चढने के लिये विघ्न करते हैं। उस घडी जो योगी न घबडाय और उस लीला में फँस कर अपने को फाँसी पर न चढावे तो ब्रह्म-रन्ध्र में अपने प्राण को घुसा कर, उस परब्रह्म के दर्शन को पा कर, आप सच्चिदानन्द हो जाय और प्रकृति-रूप पद्मावती से भेंट कर सायुज्य मुक्ति को पावे। इस लिये मलिक महम्मद ने यहाँ रूपकालङ्कार किया है कि योगी रत्न-सेन ब्रह्मगुफा के दरवाजे पर आ चुका है, राजा गन्धर्व-सेन की फाँसी-लीला अप्सरा-उर्वशी इत्यादि लीला के समान हैं जिन्हें देख कर कुछ भी नहीं डरता। जिस प्रकृति-परब्रह्म-रूप पद्मावती के ध्यान में मग्न है उस के बल से उन लोगों की शूली-रचना से कुछ भी नहीं डरता है, बल्कि इस तुच्छ शूली को देख कर हँसता है कि मैं तो आप मरने पर अर्थात् इस मलिन काया के छोडने पर तयार हूँ, शूली की मुझे क्या डर है ॥ २६६ ॥

चउपाई।

कहहिँ सवँरु जेहि चाहसि सवँरा। हम तोहि करहिँ केति कर भवँरा ॥
कहेसि ओही सवँरउँ हरि फेरा। मुअइँ जिअत आहइँ जेहि केरा ॥
जहाँ सुनउँ पदुमावति रामा। यह जिउ नेवछावरि तेहि नामा ॥
रकत क बूँद कया जत अहहीँ। पदुमावति पदुमावति कहहीँ ॥
रहहिँ त बूँद बूँद महँ ठाऊँ। परहिँ त सोई लेइ लेइ नाऊँ ॥
रोअँ रोअँ तनु ता सउँ ओधा। सूतहि सूत बेधि जिउ सोधा ॥
हाडहि हाड सबद सो होई। नस नस माँह उठइ धुनि सोई ॥

दोहा।

खाइ बिरह गा ता कर गूद माँसु कइ खान।
हउँ होइ साँच रहा अब वह होइ रूप समान ॥ २६७ ॥

कर = का । आसन = बैठने की स्थिति । टरा = टरइ (चलति) का भूत-काल, प्रथम-पुरुष, एक-वचन । अउ = अपि = और । हँसि = हसित्वा = हँस कर । पारबती = पार्वती = महादेव की स्त्री । सउँ = से । कहा = कहइ (कथयति) का भूत-काल, प्रथम-पुरुष, एक-वचन । जानऊँ = जाने = जान पडता है । सूर = सूर्य वा शूर = बहादुर । गहन = ग्रहण । गहा = जाटहे = गहा गया = पकड गया । आजु = अद्य = आज । चढइ = उछलने = चढने में । गढ = गाढ = दुर्ग = किला । ऊपर = उपरि । तपा = तपस्वी = योगी । राजइँ = राज्ञा = राजा ने । तब = तदा । छपा = छपइ (चपति) का भूत-काल, प्रथम-पुरुष, एक-वचन । जग = जगत् = संसार । देखइ = दर्शनार्थ = देखने । कउतुक = कौतुक = लीला = खेल । कइ = के । आजू = आज = आजु । कीन्ह = अकृत = किया । मारइ कहँ = मारने के लिये । साजू = सज्जन = तयारी । सुनि = श्रुत्वा = सुन कर । पाँय्‌न = पायँ का बहु वचन, पायँ = पाद = पैर । परी = परइ (पतति) का भूत-काल, स्त्रीलिङ्ग, एक-वचन । चलऊ = चलथ = चलिए । महेस = महेश = महादेव । देखाहँ = देखेँ = पश्येव । एक = एक । घरी = घटी = चौबिस मिनिट, यहाँ एकचण = चणभर । भेस = वेष = रूप । भाट = भट = कवित्त में यश पढने-वाला । भाटिन = भाट की स्त्री । कर = का । कीन्हा = कीन्ह = अकृत = किया । हनुवंत = हनुमान् = राम का प्रसिद्ध भक्त, लङ्का जलाने-वाला । बीर = वीर = योद्धा = बली । सँग = संग = सङ्ग = साथ । लीन्हा = अलात् = लिया = लीन्ह । आइ = एत्य = आ कर । गुपुत = गुप्त, गुपुत होइ = गुप्त हो कर = छिप कर । देखन = देखने में । लागे = लग्न ऊए = लग गए । दऊँ = देखें । मूरति = मूर्त्ति । कस = कथम् = कैसी । सती = सच्ची । सभागे = भाग्यवान = भाग्य के सहित ॥

कटक = सेना = फौज । असूझ = जो समझ न पडे कि कितनी है = अपार = अगोध । देखि कइ = दृष्ट्वा = देख कर । (आपनि) = आत्मनः = अपनी । राजा = गन्धर्व-सेन । गरब = गर्व = गह्वर = अभिमान । करेइ = करइ (करोति) = करता है । दइउ = देव = भगवान् । क = की । दसा = दशा = हाल = गति = लीला । देखिअइ = देखी जाती है । दऊँ = न जानें = दो में से एक । का कहँ = कस्य = किस को । जइ = जय = विजय = जीत । देइ = दद्यात् = दे ॥

जैसे ही योगिओं पर ऐसा दुःख पडा (उसी चण) महादेव का आसन टल गया, (पार्वती की ओर मुँह को फेर लिया) । और हँस कर पार्वती से कहा कि जान पडता है

सूर रत्न-सेन (सूर्य) ग्रहण के ऐसा पकड गया, अर्थात् जैसे ग्रहण में राहु से सूर्य पकडा जाता है उसी तरह यह रत्न-सेन भी राजा गन्धर्व-सेन के सिपाहिओं से पकड गया। आज तपस्वी (रत्न-सेन) को गढ के ऊपर चढने में राजा गन्धर्व-सेन ने पकड लिया, तब (वह) सूर (रत्न-सेन वा सूर्य) छिप गया। आज जगत (सिंहल-वासिओं) ने तमाशा देखने के लिये तपस्वी (रत्न-सेन) को मारने के लिये तयारी की है। (यह) सुन कर पार्वती (महादेव के) पैरों पर पडी (और कहने लगी कि) हे महादेव जी चलिए एक घडी (इस तमाशे को) देखें। (आपस में सलाह कर) महादेव ने भाट का और पार्वती ने भाटिन का रूप बनाया और हनुमान् वीर को संग में ले लिया। आ कर, छिप कर देखने लगे कि देखें (उस) भाग्यवान् (रत्न-सेन की) कैसी सच्ची मूर्त्ति है॥

राजा गन्धर्व-सेन अपनी असूझ सेना को देख कर (अपने मन में) गर्व करता है (कि मेरे बराबर बली संसार में दूसरा कौन है, पर) देव की गति नहीं देखी जाती, न जानें वह किस को जय दे॥ २६८॥

चउपाई।

अस बोलईं रहा होइ तपा। पदुमावति पदुमावति जपा॥
मन समाधि अस ता सउँ लागी। जेहि दरसन कारन बइरागी॥
रहा समाइ रूप ओहि नाऊँ। अउरु न सूझ बार जहँ जाऊँ॥
अउ महेस कहँ करउँ अदेसू। जेहि एहि पंथ दीन्ह उपदेसू॥
पारबती सुनि सत्त सराहा। अउ फिरि मुख महेस कर चाहा॥
हइँ महेस पइ भई महेसी। कित सिर नावँहिँ यह परदेसी॥
मरतेहुँ लीन्ह तुम्हारइ नाऊँ। तुम्ह चुप कीन्ह सुनहु एहि ठाऊँ॥

दोहा।

मारत हइँ परदेसी राखि लेहु एहि बेरि।
कोइ काहु कर नाहीं जो होइ जाइ निबेरि॥ २६९॥

अस = एतादृश = ऐसा। बोलईं = बोल। रहा = तस्थौ। होइ = होइ = भूत्वा = हो कर। तपा = तपस्वी। पदुमावति = पद्मावती। जपा = जजाप = जपने लगा। मन =

मनः। समाधि = चित्तवृत्तिनिरोध = सब तरफ से चित्त को हटा लेना। ता सउँ = तिस से। लागी = लगइ (लगति) का भूत-काल, स्त्रीलिङ्ग, एक-वचन। जेहि = जेहि = यस्याः = जिस के। दरसन = दर्शन। कारन = कारण। बइरागी = बैरागी = विरागी। समाइ = समापित = समाय। रूप = सूरत। ओहि = ओहि = उस के = तस्याः। नाऊँ = नावँ = नाम। अउरु = अपर = और। सूझ = शुध्यति = सूझता है। बार = द्वार = दरवाजा। जहँ = यत्र = जहाँ। जाऊँ = यानि। अउ = और = अपि। महेस = महेश = महादेव। कहँ = का। करउँ = करोमि = करता हूँ। अदेसू = आदेश = आज्ञा। एहि = अस्मिन् = इस। पंथ = पन्थाः = राह। उपदेसू = उपदेश = शिक्षा। पारबती = पार्वती = महादेव की स्त्री। सुनि = श्रुत्वा = सुन कर। सत्त = सत्यता = सत्ता। सराहा = सराहइ (श्लाघते) का भूत-काल, पुंलिङ्ग, एक-वचन। फिरि = घूम कर। मुख = मुँह। कर = का। चाहा = चाहइ (इच्छति) का भूत-काल पुंलिङ्ग, एक-वचन। हइँ = हहिँ = सन्ति = हैँ। पइ = अपि = निश्चय से। भई = होइ (भवति) का भूत-काल, स्त्रीलिङ्ग, एक-वचन। महेसी = महेशी = पार्वती। कित = कुतः = कस्मात् = क्योँ। सिर = शिर। नावँहि = नामयेयुः = नवावैँ। यह = एते = ये। परदेसी = परदेशी = दूसरे देश के रहने-वाले। मरतेऊँ = मरते समय भी = मरती बेरा भी। लीन्ह = अलात् = लिया। तुम्हारइ = तुम्हारा ही = भवतां हि। तुम्ह = आप। चुप = मौन। कीन्ह = अकृत = किया। सुनकु = शृणुथ = सुनिए। ठाऊँ = स्थान = ठावँ॥

मारत हइँ = मारयन्ति = मारते हैँ। राखि लेकु = रक्षथ = रख लेओ = बचा लेओ। बेरि = बेरा = अवसर। कोइ = कोऽपि = कोई। काकु कर = किसी का = कस्यापि। जो = यः। होइ जाइ = हो जाय। निबेरि = निपटाने-वाला = निवारण करने-वाला॥

ऐसी बोली पर तपस्वी (रत्न-सेन) ठहर गया और पद्मावती पद्मावती जपने लगा। (कहने लगा कि) मन मेँ पद्मावती से समाधि ऐसी लग गई, जिस के लिये कि बैरागी हुआ हूँ। उसी (पद्मावती) के नाम में (मेरा) रूप समा गया है, और दूसरा द्वार नहीँ सूझ पडता जहाँ जाऊँ। और महादेव का कहा करता हूँ जिन्होँ ने इस राह मेँ (जाने के लिये) उपदेश दिया। (इस बात को) सुन कर पार्वती ने (राजा रत्न-सेन के) सत्य को सराहा, अर्थात् राजा रत्न-सेन की पद्मावती मेँ सच्ची प्रीति है, इस बात की प्रशंसा की और फिर कर महादेव जी के मुँह को देखने लगी (कि इन के मन मेँ क्या है)। (कवि कहता है कि एक तो) महादेव ही

(राजा रत्न-सेन के पक्ष पर) हैँ (और अब) निश्चय से पार्वती भी (राजा के पक्ष पर) ऊई (तो फिर) ये परदेशी (योगी लोग) क्योँ (हार मान कर राजा गन्धर्व-सेन के सामने) शिर झुकावैँ। (पार्वती बडे आग्रह से कहने लगी कि हे नाथ) सुनो मरने समय भी तुम्हारा ही नाम ले रहा है, सो आप चुप अर्थात् मौन व्रत धारण किए हो (ऐसी बेरा में आप को यह उचित नहीँ कि मौन-व्रत धारण करैँ ॥)

(ये गन्धर्व-सेन के सिपाही) परदेशी (योगिओँ) को मारते हैँ, इस बेरा (इन योगिओँ को) रख लेओ अर्थात् बचा लेओ, (इस अवसर में) कोई किसी (योगी) का नहीँ है जो कि निवारण करने-वाला हो, अर्थात् ऐसा कोई आप के सेवाय दूसरा नहीँ देख पडता जो कि इस अवसर में इन योगिओँ का प्राण बचावे ॥ २६९ ॥

चउपाई ।

लेइ सँदेस सुअटा गा तहाँ। सूरी देन गए लेइ जहाँ॥
देखि रतन हीरामनि रोआ। रतन ग्यान ठगि लोगन्ह खोआ॥
देखि रोदन हीरामनि केरा। रोअहिँ सब राजा मुख हेरा॥
माँगहिँ सब बिधिना पहुँ रोई। करु उपकार छोडावइ कोई॥
कहि सँदेस सब बिनति सुनाई। बिकल बहुत किछु कहा न जाई॥
काढि परान बइसि लेइ हाथा। मरइ तो मरउँ जिअउँ तेहि साथा॥
सुनि सँदेस राजा तब हँसा। प्रान प्रान घट घट मँह बसा॥

दोहा ।

हीरामनि अउ भाट दसउँधी भए जिउ पर एक ठाउँ।
चलहु जाइ कह बतकही जहाँ बइठु हहिँ राउ॥ २७० ॥

लेइ = लेइ = आलाय = ले कर। सँदेस = सन्देश = सँदेसा = खबर। सुअटा = शुक = सुग्गा। गा = अगात् = गया। तहाँ = तत्र। सूरी = शूली। देन = देने। गए = जग्मुः। जहाँ = यत्र। देखि = देख कर = दृष्ट्वा। रतन = रत्न = रत्न-सेन। हीरामनि = हीरामणि शुक। रोआ = रुरोद = रोया। ग्यान = ज्ञान। ठगि = स्थगिता = ठग कर। लोगन्ह = लोग (लोक) का बऊ-वचन। खोआ = खोअइ का भूत-काल, पुंलिङ्ग, एक-वचन। रोदन = रोदन = रोना। केरा = का। रोअहिँ = रुदन्ति = रोते हैँ।

सब = सर्व । मुख = मुँह । हेरा = हेरद (हेडूते) का भूत-काल, पुंलिङ्ग, एक-वचन । माँगहिं = याचन्ते = माँगते हैं । बिधिना = विधि = ब्रह्मा । पहँ = पहँ = से । रोई = रुदिला = रो कर । कह = कुरु = कर । छोडावद = छोडावे (छोटयेत्) । कोई = कोऽपि । कहि = कथयिला = कह कर । बिनति = विनति = विनय । सुनाई = सुनावद (श्राव-यति) का भूत-काल, स्त्रीलिङ्ग, प्रथम-पुरुष, एक-वचन । बिकल = विकल = दुःखित । बज्जत = बज्जतर । किछु = कुछ = किञ्चित् । कहा = कथन । जाई = जायते । काढि = कर्षयित्वा = खींच कर = निकाल कर । परान = प्राण । बदसि = बैठी = उपविष्टा । लेद = ले कर = श्रालाय । हाथा = हाथ = हस्त । मरद = मरे = म्रियेत । तो = तर्हि = तो । मरउँ = मरूँ = मराणि । जिअउँ = जीवेयम् = जीवैं । तेहि = तस्याः = तिस के । साथा = साथ = सार्थ = सङ्ग । सुनि = श्रुत्वा = सुन कर । तब = तदा । हँसा = हँसद (हसति) का भूत-काल, पुंलिङ्ग, प्रथम-पुरुष, एक-वचन । प्रान = प्राण । घट = शरीर । मँह = मध्ये = में । बसा = बस = वसति = बसता है ॥

अउ = अपि = और । भाट = स्तुति करने-वाला (महादेव) दसउँधी = दशधी = साधारण मनुष्य से जिस की दश गुनी बुद्धि हो । आज कल भाटों में एक जाति राय और दूसरी दसौंधी कहाती है । भए = भए = बभूवतुः = ज्जए । जिउ = जीव । पर = उपरि । एक = एक । ठाउँ = ठावँ = स्थान । चलज्ञ = चलेँ । जाद = आयाय = आ कर । कह = कहँ । बतकही = वार्त्ताकथनम् = बातचीत । बदठु हहिँ = बैठे हैं = उपविशन्ति = तिष्ठन्ति । राउ = राजा ॥

(इसी बीच में) हीरामणि शुक (पद्मावती का) सँदेसा ले कर गया जहाँ कि (लोग) (राजा रत्न-सेन को) शूली (फाँसी) देने ले गए थे । हीरामणि रत्न-सेन को (ऐसी दुर्दशा में) देख कर रोने लगा कि (हाय) लोगों ने रत्न-सेन को ठग कर (इस के) ज्ञान को खो दिया । हीरामणि का रोना देख कर सब रोने लगे और राजा रत्न सेन का मुँह देखने लगे । सब (लोग) रो कर ब्रह्मा से (हाथ जोड जोड कर) माँगते हैं कि (हे विधि, इस समय) उपकार कर (और ऐसी प्रेरणा कर कि) कोई (आ कर राजा रत्न-सेन को शूली से) छोडावे । (शुक ने पद्मावती का सब सँदेसा) कह कर (उस की) विपत्ति सुनाई कि (पद्मावती) बज्जत विकल है, कुछ कहा नहीं जाता । (घट के भीतर से) प्राण को निकाल कर हाथ में ले कर बैठी है, (और कहती है कि राजा रत्न-सेन) मरे तो मैं भी मरूँ (और जीवे तो)

उसी के साथ मैं भी जीऊँ। तब (पद्मावती के इस) संदेस को सुन कर राजा रत्न-सेन ने हँस दिया (और कहने लगा कि मेरा) प्राण (उस के) प्राण में और (मेरी) शरीर (उस की) शरीर में बस गई है। (इतना कह कर राजा रत्न-सेन चुप हो गया, आँख बंद कर पद्मावती का ध्यान कर समाधि में हो गया)॥

(यह राजा की दशा देख कर) हीरामणि शुक और दसौंधी भाट (महादेव जी) (दोनों) एक स्थान पर (एकट्ठे हो, सलाह कर) जीव (देने) पर (तयार हुए। कहने लगे कि) चलो जहाँ राजा गन्धर्व-सेन बैठे हैं वहाँ जा कर (कुछ) बात (तो) कहैं ॥ २७० ॥

चउपाई ।

राजा रहा दीठि कइ अउँधी । रहि न सका तब भाट दसउँधी ॥
कहेसि मेलि कइ हाथ कटारी । पुरुस न आछहिँ बइठि पिटारी ॥
कान्ह कोपि कइ मारा कंसू । गूँग कि फूँक न बाजइ बंसू ॥
गँधरब-सेन जहाँ रिस बाढा । जाइ भाट आगइँ भा ठाढा ॥
ठाढ देखि सब राजा राऊ । बाएँ हाथ दीन्ह बर-भाऊ ॥
गँधरब-सेन तुँ राजा महा । हउँ महेस मूरति- अस कहा ॥
जोगी पानि आगि तूँ राजा । आगिहि पानि जूझ नहिँ छाजा ॥

दोहा ।

आगि बुझाई पानि सउँ तूँ राजा मन बूझ ।
तोरइ बार खपर हइ (लीन्हे) भिखिआ देहि न जूझ ॥ २७१ ॥

रहा = रहइ (तिष्ठति) का भूत-काल, पुंलिङ्ग, प्रथम-पुरुष, एक-वचन। दीठि = दृष्टि = आँख। कइ = कर = करला। अउँधी = औंधी = अधः = नीचे। रहि = रह = ठहर = स्थिर। सका = सकइ (शक्नोति) का भूत-काल, पुंलिङ्ग, प्रथम-पुरुष, एक-वचन। तब = तदा। भाट = स्तुति करने-वाला। दसउँधी = दशधी = भाटों की एक जाति। कहेसि = अकथयत् = कहा। मेलि = मेलयिला = मेल कर = ले कर। हाथ = हस्त। कटारी = कटार = कर्त्तरी। पुरुस = पुरुष = मर्द। आछहिँ = शोभन्ते = सोहते हैं।

कालि = कालिय नाग जिस की कथा श्रीमद्भागवत दशमस्कन्ध में प्रसिद्ध है। जेइँ = येन = जिस ने। नाथा = नाथइ (नाथते) का भूत-काल, पुंलिङ्ग, प्रथम-पुरुष, एक-वचन। बरँभा = बरह्मा = ब्रह्मा = सृष्टि के रचने-वाले त्रिदेव में एक देव। चतुर-मुख = चतुर्मुख = जिसे चार मुँह हो। जासू = यस्य = जिस को। अउ = अपि = और। पातार = पाताल। बलि = राजा बलि। बासू = वासुकि-नाग = आठ नागों में एक प्रसिद्ध नाग। मेघ = पानी बरसाने-वाले बादल। डरहिँ = डरइ (दरति) का बहु-वचन = डरते हैं। बिजुरी = विद्युत् = बिजली। जिन्ह = येषाम् = जिन को। डीठी = दृष्टि = आँख = नेत्र। कुरुम = कूर्म = कच्छप = पृथ्वी का आधार = भगवान का एक अवतार। धरती = धरित्री = भूमि। जेहि = यस्य = जिस की। पीठी = पृष्ठ = पीठ। मंदर = मन्दर = एक पहाड जिस से समुद्र मथा गया है। मेरू = मेरु = सोने का प्रसिद्ध पर्वत जिस पर देवता वास करते हैँ। चंद = चन्द्र = चाँद। सुरुज = सूर्य। गगन = आकाश। कुबेरू = कुबेर = रावण का बडा भाई, धन का देवता। चहउँ = इच्छेयम् = चाहँ। तो = तहिँ = तो। भंजउँ = भञ्जेयम् = नाश करूँ = तोड डालूँ। गहि = गृहीला = ग्रहण कर = पकड कर। केसा = केश = बाल। कीट = कीडे, रँगने-वाले। पतंग = कीडे, उडने-वाले। नरेसा = नरेश = राजा लोग॥

बोला = बोलइ (वदति) का भूत-काल, पुंलिङ्ग, प्रथम-पुरुष, एक-वचन। नरेस = नरेश = राजा। सुनु = शृणु = सुन। गरब = गर्व = अभिमान। छाजा = छाज = छाजइ (सज्जते वा शोभते) सोहता है = छाजता है। जीउँ = जीवे = जीव में। कुंभकरन = कुम्भकर्ण = रावण का भाई। कइ = की। खोपडी = करोटी = मस्तक के ऊपर का हिस्सा। बूडत = बूडने से = (ब्रुड धातु से) डूबने से। बाँचा = बच गया। भीउँ = भीम = युधिष्ठिर से छोटा और अर्जुन से बडा पाँचो पाण्डवों में एक प्रसिद्ध कुन्ती का पुत्र॥

(राजा गन्धर्व-सेन की) आज्ञा हुई कि (यह) कौन अभागा भाट है जिस ने बाएँ हाथ से (मुझे) आशीर्वाद दिया है। (और) मेरे शहर में ऐसा कौन योगी है जो कि सँध दे कर चोरी करने के लिये गढ पर चढता है। (मुझ से) इन्द्र डरता है, नित (मेरे सामने) माथ झुँकाता है। जिस कृष्ण ने कालिय नाग को नाथा है वह (मुझ से) डरता है। जिस ब्रह्मा को चार मुँह है वह (मुझ से) डरता है, और पाताल में बलि और वासुकि नाग (मुझ से) डरते हैँ। जिन की आखोँ में बिजली बसती है वे मेघ (भी मुझ से) डरते हैँ। जिस को पीठ पर धरती है

वह कच्छप (भी मुझ से) डरता है। मुझ से धरती, मन्दर और मेरु डरते हैं, आकाश में चन्द्र, सूर्य और कुवेर डरते हैं। चाहूँ तो (शिर के) बाल पकड कर सब को (पटक कर) तोड डालूँ (मार डालूँ)। (जब मैं इन लोगों को कुछ नहीं समझता, तो) और (मेरे सामने) कीडे, फतंगे ऐसे राजा लोग कौन हैं॥

(राजा गन्धर्व-सेन की अभिमान भरी बात को सुन कर) भाट बोला कि राजा गन्धर्व-सेन, सुन, जी में गर्व नहीं सोहता। भीम (जिसे अपने बल का बहुत ही अभिमान था) कुम्भकर्ण की खोपडी में डूबते डूबते बच गया॥

कश्यप को अदिति स्त्री से जो पुत्र हुए वे देवता कहाते हैं। उन में सब से जेठा इन्द्र, देवताओं का राजा, अमरावती नगरी में रहता है। पुराणों में प्रसिद्ध कथा है कि जो पृथ्वी का राजा सौ अश्वमेध करे वह इन्द्र हो जाय। इसी लिये जब किसी राजा को ९९ अश्वमेध यज्ञ पूरी हो जाती है, तब इन्द्र डर कर सौवें अश्वमेध में विघ्न करता है जिस में वह पूरी न हो।

कृष्ण की कथा श्रीमद्भागवत में प्रसिद्ध है। इन के पिता वसु-देव और माता कंस की बहिन देवकी हैं॥

ब्रह्मा क्षीरशायी भगवान के नाभिकमल से उत्पन्न हुआ है। पुराणों में कथा है कि प्रलय काल में भगवान क्षीर-सागर में शेष के ऊपर सो जाते हैं। फिर जब उन की इच्छा सृष्टि करने की होती है, तब उन की नाभी से एक कमल का वृक्ष उत्पन्न होता है। उस का नाल जब जल के ऊपर आता है तब उस में पुष्प उत्पन्न होता है। उसी कमल के फूल में सृष्टि करने के लिये ब्रह्मा उत्पन्न होता है।

बलि प्रह्लाद का पुत्र है। ऐसा दानी राजा कोई नहीं हुआ। अपने दान और यज्ञ के प्रभाव से इस ने इन्द्र की पदवी को ले लिया। इन्द्र बहुत दुःखी हुआ। इस पर अदिति के गर्भ से भगवान ने वामन-रूप उत्पन्न हो कर बलि को छल कर, इन्द्र को फिर स्वर्ग का राजा और बलि को पाताल का राजा बनाया। पुराणों में प्रसिद्ध कथा है।

वासुकि के लिये इस ग्रन्थ का १६५ पृष्ठ देखो।

मेघ पानी बरसाने-वाले इन्द्र के अनुचर हैं।

ज्यौतिषी लोग अपने पञ्चाङ्ग में नव मेघ लिखते हैं, जिन के नाम— आवर्त्त १। संवर्त्त २। पुष्कर ३। द्रोण ४। काल ५। नीलक ६। वरुण ७। वायु ८। तम ९। ये हैं।

मकरन्द-कल्पलता में लिखा है—

शाके ऽष्टगुणिते नन्दैर्भाजिते शेषतो घनः । आवर्त्त एकशेषे स्यात् संवर्त्ताख्यो द्विशेषके ॥ त्रिशेषे पुष्करो द्रोणश्चतुःशेषे प्रकीर्त्तितः । कालनामा पञ्चशेषे षट्शेषे नीलकः स्मृतः ॥ वरुणः सप्तशेषे स्याद्वायुरष्टावशेषके । नवशेषे तमो नामा क्रमान्मेघा नव स्मृताः ॥

कच्छप एक भगवान का अवतार है। पुराणों में कथा है कि जब चीर-सागर मथने जाने लगा उस समय मन्दर मथानी के ठहरने के लिये भगवान ने कच्छप का रूप धारण किया। फिर कच्छप और वराह (शूकरावतार) ये दोनों पृथ्वी को नीचे गिरने से रोके हुए हैं। शेष भी अपने हजार फनों से पृथ्वी को रोके हुए है जिस में पृथ्वी नीचे न चली जाय ॥

कथा है कि एक वार युधिष्ठिर के छोटे भाई भीमसेन अभिमान से अपने साथिओं से कहते बरसात में कहीं चले जाते थे कि कुम्भकर्ण में कुछ भी बल न था। जौं आज वह होता तो मैं एक हाथ से उसे उठा कर समुद्र पार फेंक देता। इस बतकही में ऊपर आँख किए अभिमान से भरे बडे उमंग से आगे आगे चले जाते थे। नीचे की ओर नजर न रहने से अकस्मात् एक पानी भरे बडे ताल में गिर कर डूबने लगे। साथिओं के बडे जतन से मरते मरते निकले। फिर पीछे से पता लगाने पर जान पडा कि कुम्भकर्ण की खोपडी पानी से भरी हुई बडे ताल ऐसी हो गई है। तुलसी-दास के रामायण में भी किसी ने चेपक में लिखा है कि 'जोजन तीन सीस की फेरी' अर्थात् कुम्भकर्ण के शिर की फेरी (खोपडी) तीन योजन याने बारह कोस की थी। भारतवर्ष में भीमसेन के अभिमान-भंग की यह कथा घर घर प्रसिद्ध है पर मुझे अभी तक इस का पता न लगा कि यह कथा किस पुराण की है ॥ २७२ ॥

चउपाई।

राओन गरब बिरोधा रामू। उहई गरब भएउ सँगरामू ॥
तेहि राओन अस को बरिवंडा। जेहि दस सीस बीस बहु-दंडा ॥
सूरज जेहि कइ तपइ रसोई। बइसंदर निति धोती धोई ॥
सूक सउँटिआ ससि मसिआरा। पउनु करइ निति बार बोहारा ॥
मीचु लाइ कइ पाटी बाँधी। रहा न ओ सउँ दोसरि काँधी ॥

जो अस बजर टरइ नहिँ टारा ।　सोउ मुआ दुइ तपसिन्ह मारा ॥
नाती पूत कोटि दस अहा ।　रोअनिहार न एकउ रहा ॥

दोहा ।

ओछ जानि कइ काहुही　जनि कोइ गरब करेइ ।
ओछे पारइँ दइउ हइ　जीत-पतर जो देइ ॥ २७३ ॥

राअोन = रावण = प्रसिद्ध लङ्का का राजा । गरब = गर्वेण = गर्व से अभिमान से । बिरोधा = बिरोधइ (विरोधयति) का भूत-काल, पुंलिङ्ग, प्रथम-पुरुष, एक-वचन । रामू = राम = भगवान का प्रसिद्ध एक अवतार = दशरथ का पुत्र । उहई = वही = तेनैव । भएउ = बभूव = हुआ । सँगरामू = सङ्ग्राम = युद्ध । तेहि = तस्य = तिस । अस = ऐसा = एतादृश । को = कः = कौन । बरिवंडा = बलवन्त = बलवान् । जेहि = यस्य = जिसे । दस = दश । सीस = शीर्ष = शिर । बीस = विंशति । बाहु-दंडा = बाहु-दण्ड = भुज-दण्ड । सूरज = सूर्य । कइ = की । तपइ = तपति = तपता है । रसोई = रसवती । बइसंदर = बैश्वानर = आग । निति = नित्य । धोती = धौत वस्त्र । धोई (धावयति) = धोअइ = का भूत-काल, स्त्रीलिङ्ग, प्रथम-पुरुष, एक-वचन । सूक = शुक्र तारा । सउँटिआ = सोंटिआ = सोंटाबर्दार = द्वारपाल । ससि = शशि = चन्द्रमा । मसिआरा = मशालची = मशाल देखाने-वाला । पउनु = पवन = हवा = वायु । करइ = करोति = करता है, यहाँ करता था । बार = द्वार = दरवाजा । बोहारा = बोहारइ (व्याहारयति) = बोहार । मीँचु = मृत्यु = मौत । लाइ करि = आलाय = ले कर = पकड कर । पाटी = पट्टिका = पट्टी । बाँधी = बाँधइ (बध्नाति) का भूत-काल, स्त्रीलिङ्ग, प्रथम-पुरुष, एक-वचन । रहा = आसीत् । ओ सउँ = तत्सदृश = उस के ऐसा । दोसरि = द्वितीय = दूसरा । काँधी = कन्धादेने-वाला = बराबरी करने-वाला । जो = यः । बजर = वज्र । टरइ = टरता = चलता । टारा = टालने से = चलाने से । सोउ = सोऽपि = वह भी । मुआ = ममार = मर गया । दुइ = द्वौ = दो । तपसिन्ह = तपसी (तपस्वी) का बहु-वचन । मारा = मारइ (मारयति) का भूत-काल, पुंलिङ्ग, प्रथम-पुरुष, बहु-वचन । नाती = नप्ता = कन्या का पुत्त्र, या पौत्र, पुत्र का लडका । पूत = पुत्त्र = बेटा । कोटि = करोड । दस = दश । अहा = आसीत्, यहाँ आसन् = थे । रोअनिहार = रोनेवाला । एकउ = एकोऽपि = एक भी । रहा = ठहरा = तस्थौ ॥

ओक = तुच्छ = छोटा । जानि कइ = ज्ञात्वा = जान कर । काऊही = कस्यापि = किसी को । जनि = न = नहीँ । कोइ = कोऽपि = कोई । करेइ = कुर्यात् = करे । पारइँ = पच्चे = पच में । दइउ = देव = भगवान । हइ = है = अस्ति । जीत-पतर = जयपत्र = विजय का परवाना । देइ = दत्ते = देता है ॥

रावण ने गर्व कर राम से विरोध किया, उसी गर्व के कारण (राम-रावण से) सङ्ग्राम हुआ। उस रावण के ऐसा कौन बलवान था जिसे कि दश शिर और बीस भुज-दण्ड थे। जिस की रसोईँ में सूर्य तपता था, अर्थात् आग का काम सूर्य से लिया जाता था, आग धोती धोती थी। (सप्तशती दुर्गास्तोत्र के ४ अध्याय के ५२ श्लोक में शुंभ-निशुंभ की प्रशंसा में लिखा है कि 'वह्निरपि ददौ तुभ्यमग्निशौचे च वाससी'।) शुक्र सोँटेदार, चन्द्रमा मशालची, और वायु दरवाजे पर झाड़ू देता था। (जिस रावण ने) मौत को पकड कर (चारपाई की) पाटी में बाँध रक्खा था, उस रावण का बराबरी करने-वाला दूसरा कोई भी नहीँ था। जो (रावण) वज्र के ऐसा था, किसी के टालने से नहीँ टलता था, वह भी (गर्व ही के करने से) मरा, दो तपसिओँ (राम-लक्ष्मण) ने (उसे) मार डाला। (जिस रावण को) दश करोड नाती और बेटे थे (उस की दुर्गति ऐसी हुई कि मरने पर उस के नाम पर) एक भी रोने-वाला न ठहरा अर्थात् नाती बेटे में कोई भी न रहा जो उस के नाम पर दो चार बूँद आँसू टपकाता ॥

(भाट कहता है कि हे राजा गन्धर्व-सेन, ऐसा जान कर) किसी को छोटा समझ कर (उचित है कि) कोई अभिमान न करे। भगवान छोटे का पच्छ करता है, जो कि विजय-पत्र देता है, अर्थात् विजय-पत्र देने-वाला है ॥ २७३ ॥

चउपाई ।

अउरु जो भाट उहाँ हुत आगे । बिनइ उठा राजा रिस लागे ॥
भाट आहि ईसुर कइ कला । राजा सब राखहिँ अरगला ॥
भाट मौँचु जो आपनि दीसा । ता सउँ कउनु करइ रिस रीसा ॥
भएउ रजाएसु गँधरब-सेनी । काह मौँचु कइ चढा निसेनी ॥
काहे अनबानी अस धरई । करइ बिटंड भटंत न करई ॥

जाति करा कित अउगुन लावसि। बाएँ हाथ राज बरभावसि॥
भाट नाउँ का मारउँ जीवा। अबहूँ बोल नाइ कइ गीवा॥

दोहा।

तूँ रे भाट यह जोगी तोहि एहि कहाँ क संग।
कहाँ छरइ अस पावा कहा भएउ चित भंग॥ २७४॥

अउरु = अपर = और। जो = जो = यः। भाट = भट = स्तुति करने-वाला। उहाँ = तत्र = वहाँ। हुत = आसीत् = था। आगे = अग्रे = सामने। बिनइ = विनीय = विनय कर। उठा = उत्तस्थौ। रिस = रोष = क्रोध। लागे = लग्ने = लगने पर। आहि = अस्ति = है। ईसुर = ईश्वर = भगवान या महादेव। कइ = की। कला = अंश = अवतार। सब = सर्व। राखहिँ = राखइ (रक्षति) का बहु-वचन = रखते हैँ। अरगला = अर्गला = अगडी = अवरोधक = बन्धन। मीँचु = मृत्यु = मौत। आपनि = अपनी = आत्मनः। दीसा = दीस = देखइ (पश्यति) = देखता है। ता सउँ = तिस से = उस से। कउनु = को नु = कौन! करइ = कुर्यात् = करे। रिस = रोषेण। रीसा = रोष = क्रोध। भएउ = बभूव = हुई। रजाएसु = राजाज्ञा = हुक्म। गँधरब-सेनी = गन्धर्व-सेनी = गन्धर्व-सेन की। काह = किम् = क्या। चढा = चढइ (उच्चलति) का भूत-काल, प्रथम-पुरुष, एक-वचन। निसेनी = निश्रेणी = सीढी। काहे = कथं वा किमर्थम्। अनबानी = अनुचितवाणी = कुवाणी, वा अणुवाणी = छोटी बोली। अस = एतादृश = ऐसी। धरई = धरति = धरता है। बिटंड = वितण्डावाद = बखेडा। भटंत = भटता = भाट का काम। करई = करइ = करता है = करोति। जाति = ज्ञाति = जात। करा = कला। कित = कुतः = क्योँ। अउगुन = अवगुण = दोष। लावसि = लागयसि = लगाता है। बाएँ = वाम। हाथ = हस्त। राज = राज्ञः = राजा को। बरभावसि = वरं भावयसि = आशीर्वदसि = आशीर्वाद देता है। नाउँ = नावँ = नाम। का = किम् = क्या। मारउँ = मारूँ = मारयेयम्। जीवा = जीव = प्राण। अबहूँ = अद्यापि = इदानीमपि = अब भी। बोल = वद। नाइ कइ = विनमय्य = झुँका कर = नवा कर। गीवा = ग्रीवा = गला॥

तूँ = त्वम् = तैँ। रे = अरे = नीच सम्बोधन। जोगी = योगी। तोहि = त्वत्तः = तुझ से। एहि = अस्मात् = इस से। कहाँ = कस्य। क = का। संग = सङ्ग = साथ।

कहाँ = कुच । छरद = छरने के लिये = नाश करने के लिये = चरणार्थ । पावा = पावइ (प्राप्नोति) का भूत-काल, प्रथम-पुरुष, एक-वचन । कहा = कथम् = क्यौं । चित = चित्त = मन । भंग = भङ्ग = विकार ॥

और (फिर) जो वहाँ भाट आगे (खडा) था (वह) राजा गन्धर्व-सेन के क्रोध होने पर विनय कर के खडा हो गया । (और फिर क्रोध में आ कर कहने लगा कि) भाट ईश्वर की कला है, सब राजा लोग (भाट को) अर्गला के लिये (अनुचित कार्य के रोकने के लिये) रखते हैं । जो भाट (सदा) अपनी मौत देखा करता है, उस से कौन क्रोधी क्रोध कर सकता है, अर्थात् जो मौत को नहीं डरता उस पर कोई क्या क्रोध करे । (भाट की ऐसी खरी बात सुन कर) गन्धर्व-सेन की आज्ञा हुई कि (अरे भाट) क्या मौत की सीढी पर चढा है । क्यौं ऐसी अनुचित वाणी (मन में) रखता है, क्यौं बखेडा करता है, क्यौं नहीं भाट के ऐसी बात करता । (तेरी) जात (ईश्वर की) कला है (उस में) क्यौं दोष लगाता है, क्यौं राजा को बाएँ हाथ से आशीर्वाद देता है । तेरा नाम भाट है, (इस लिये) क्या तेरे जीव को मारँ, (सावधान हो जा) अब भी गर्दन को झुका कर (उचित बात को) बोल ॥

अरे तूँ तो भाट और यह योगी, तुझ से और इस (योगी) से कहाँ का सङ्ग । (अपने को) नाश करने के लिये कहाँ ऐसा (योगी का) भङ्ग पाया. क्यौं (तेरा) चित्त भङ्ग हो गया ॥ २७४ ॥

चउपाई ।

जो सत पूँछसि गँधरब-राजा । सत पइ कहउँ परइ किन गाजा ॥
भाटहि कहा मौँचु सन डरना । हाथ कटार पेट हनि मरना ॥
जंबुदीप जो चितउर देसू । चितर-सेन बड तहाँ नरेसू ॥
रतन-सेन यह ता कर बेटा । कुल चहुआन जाइ नहिँ मेटा ॥
खाँडे अचल सुमेरु पहारू । टरइ न जउँ लागइ संसारू ॥
दान सुमेरु देत नहिँ खाँगा । जो ओहि माँग न अउरहि माँगा ॥
दाहिन हाथ उठाएउँ ताही । अउरु को अस बरभावउँ जाही ॥

दोहा ।

नाउँ महापातर मोहिँ　　तेहि क भिखारी ढीठ ।
जउँ खरि बात कहत रिस (लागइ)　खरिअइ कहहिँ बसीठ ॥ २७५ ॥

जो = जौँ = यदि । सत = सत्य = सच । पूँछसि = पृच्छसि = पूछता है । गँधरब-राजा = गन्धर्व-राज = गन्धर्व-सेन राजा । पइ = अपि = निश्चय कर । कहउँ = कथयामि = कहता हूँ । परइ = पतेत् = पडे । किन = किमु न = क्योँ न । गाजा = गर्ज्या = गरजने-वाली = बिजली । भाटहि = भटस्य = भाट को । कहा = किम् = क्या । मीँचु = मृत्यु = मौत । सन = से । डरना = दरण = भय करना । हाथ = हस्त । कटार = कर्त्तक = काटने-वाला । पेट = पिटक = उदर । हनि = हत्वा = हन कर = मार कर । मरना = मरण । जंबुदीप = जम्बूदीप । जो = यः । चितउर = चित्रवर, वा = चित्रपुर = चितौर गढ । देसू = देश । चितर-सेन = चित्र-सेन । बड = बर = बडा । तहाँ = तत्र । नरेसू = नरेश = राजा । रतन-सेन = रत्न-सेन । यह = अयम् । ता कर = तस्य = तिस का = उस का । बेटा = वत्स = वेत्र = आधार = पुत्र । कुल = वंश । चहुआन = चतुःस्थान = चौहान । जाइ = जायते । मेटा = मार्ष्टि स्म = मिटाया । खाँडे = खण्डक = काटने-वाला या खाँडा = खड्ग = तलवार । अचल = अटल । सुमेरु = सोने का सब से श्रेष्ठ पर्वत । पहारू = प्रहार = पहाड । टरइ = चलति = टरता है । जउँ = यदि = जौँ । लागइ = लगेत् = लगे । संसारू = संसार । देत = देने में । खाँगा = कम = शुष्क = खुक्ख = खाली खङ्ग (खजि गतिवैकल्ये) । ओहि = तस्मात् = उस से । माँग = माँगइ (याचते) । अउरहि = अपरस्मात् = और से = दूसरे से । माँगा = माँगता = जाँचता । दाहिन = दक्षिण = दहिना । उठाएउँ = उत्थापयामास = उठाया । ताही = तिसे = उसे । को = कः = कौन । अस = एतादृश = ऐसा । बरभावउँ = वरं भावयेयम् = आशीर्वाद देऊँ ॥

नाउँ = नाम = नावँ । महापातर = महापात्र । मोहिँ = मम = मेरा । क = का । भिखारी = भिक्षुक । ढीठ = धृष्ट = ढीठा । खरि = खरी = सच्ची = खर । बात = वार्त्ता । कहत = कथयतः = कहने से । रिस = रोष = क्रोध । (लागइ) = लगति = लगती है । खरिअइ = खरी-ही = सच्ची-ही । कहहिँ = कथयन्ति = कहते हैँ । बसीठ = दूत = वशिष्ठ ॥

(भाट बोला कि) जौँ राजा गन्धर्व-सेन तूँ सच पूछता है (तो मैं) निश्चय कर सच कहता हूँ, (उस सच के कहने से मेरे ऊपर) बिजली क्योँ न पडे (पर मैं सच

कहना नहीँ छोडूँगा)। भाट को क्या मौत से डरना, (भाट के) हाथ में कटार है (सच कहने पर जौं आप को बुरा लगे तो आप क्या मुझे मारेंगे मुझे तो) पेट में कटार मार कर (आप) मरना है। (अब मैं सच बात कहता हूँ, सुन,) जम्बूदीप में जो चितौर देश है, वहाँ का (सब से) बडा राजा चित्र-सेन था। यह रत्न-सेन उस का बेटा है, (यह) चौहान वंश का है (जो कर्म में लिखा रहता है वह) मिटाया नहीं जाता। तलवार चलाने में सुमेरु पहाड ऐसा अचल है, जौं सारा संसार लगे तौ भी टरने-वाला नहीं। दान देने में सुमेरु के ऐसा है (कभी ऐसा नहीँ कि धन) घटे; जो कोई उस से माँगता है वह दूसरे से नहीं माँगता, अर्थात् राजा रत्न-सेन के दान से वह सन्तुष्ट हो जाता है, फिर उस को दूसरे से माँगने की जरूरत नहीं पडती। (हे राजा गन्धर्ब-सेन, सुन, मैं आशीर्वाद देने के लिये अपना) दहिना हाथ उस के (आगे) उठा चुका हूँ, (अब) दूसरा ऐसा कौन है जिसे (दहिने हाथ से) आशीर्वाद दूँ ॥

मेरा नाम महापात्र है मैं उसी (रत्न-सेन) का ढीठा भिखारी हूँ (उसी के आगे दहिना हाथ उठाने-वाला हूँ)। यद्यपि खरी बात कहने से (सुनने-वाले को) क्रोध हो जाता है, पर दूत (बुरा लगे तो लगे) सच्ची ही बात कहते हैं ॥

विश्वनाथ महापात्र ने काव्यप्रकाश बनाया है। ये बडे कवि थे इसी लिये ग्रन्थकार ने आदर के लिये केवल पदवी मात्र से भाट का नाम महापात्र रक्खा हो तो आश्चर्य नहीं ॥ २७५ ॥

चउपाई ।

ततखन सुनि महेस मन लाजा । भाट कला होइ बिनवा राजा ॥
गँधरब-सेन तुँ राजा महा । हउँ महेस मूरति सुनु कहा ॥
पइ जो बात होइ भलि आगइँ । कहा चाहि का भा रिस लागइँ ॥
राज-कुअँर यह होइ न जोगी । सुनि पदुमावति भएउ बिओगी ॥
जंबूदीप राज-घर बेटा । जो हइ लिखा सो जाए न मेटा ॥
तोरइ सुअइँ जाइ एहि आना । अउ जा कर बरोक तुइँ माना ॥
पुनि यह बात सुनी सिउ लोका । करहु बिआह धरस बड तो का ॥

दोहा।

खपर लिए उहई पइ माँगइ   मुएहु न छाडइ बारु।
बूझि देखु जो कनक कचउरी   देहु भीख नहिँ मारु॥ २७६॥

ततखन = तत्क्षणे = उस क्षण में। सुनि = श्रुत्वा = सुन कर। महेस = महेश = महादेव। लाजा = लज्जित हुआ। भाट = भट = स्तुति करने-वाला। कला = अंश = रूप। होइ = भूत्वा = हो कर। बिनवा = बिनवइ (विनमति) का भूत-काल, प्रथम-पुरुष, एक-वचन। गँधरब-सेन = गन्धर्ब-सेन। तुँ = त्वं = त्वम्। महा = महान् = बड़ा। हउँ = हौं = अहम् = मैं। मूरति = मूर्त्ति। सुनु = शृणु = सुन। कहा = कहते हैं = कहा गया है = कथ्यते। पइ = अपि = निश्चय कर। जो = यः, यहाँ या। बात = वार्त्ता। होइ = भवति = होती है। भलि = भली = वर = अच्छी। आगइँ = अग्रे = आगे। कहा चाहि = कहना चाहिए। का = क्या = किम्। भा = बभूव = भया = हुआ। रिस = रोष = क्रोध। लागइँ = लगने से = लग्नतः। राज-कुअँर = राज-कुमार। यह = अयम्। होइ = अस्ति = है। जोगी = योगी। पदुमावति = पद्मावती। भएउ = बभूव = भया = हुआ। बिओगी = वियोगी = विरही। जंबूदीप = जम्बूदीप। राज-घर = राज-गृह = राज-घराना। बेटा = वत्स वा वेच। लिखा = लेख। सो = सः = वह। जाए = जाय = जायते। मेटा = मिटाया = मार्ष्टि स्म (मृजू शुद्धौ से)। तोरइ = तवैव = तेरा ही। सुअइँ = शुकेन = सुग्गे ने। जाइ = आयाय = जा कर। एहि = अमुम् = इसे। आना = आनयत् = ले आया। अउ = अपि = और। जा कर = यस्य = जिस का। बरोक = वरेचण = बरच्छा = बरेखी। तुइँ = त्वया = तैँ ने। माना = मानइ (मन्यते) का भूत-काल, प्रथम-पुरुष, पुंलिङ्ग, एक-वचन। पुनि = पुनः = फिर। सुनी = सुनइ (शृणोति) का भूत-काल, प्रथम-पुरुष, स्त्रीलिङ्ग, एक-वचन। सिउ = शिव = महादेव। लोका = लोक। करऊ = कुरुथ = करिए। बिआह = विवाह = व्याह। धरम = धर्म। बड = बडा = बृहत्। तो का = तव = तुझे॥

खपर = खर्पर = खप्पड। लिए = लिए हुए। उहई = वही = तामेव। माँगइ = याचते = माँगता है। मुएहु = मृतेऽपि = मरने पर भी। छाडइ = छोडे (छोटयेत्) यहाँ छोडेगा। बारु = द्वार = वार। बूझि = सम्बुध्य = समझ कर = बूझ कर। देखु = पश्य = देख। कनक = सोना। कचउरी = कचौरी = तामा सोने का मेल। देऊ = दद्य = देओ। भीख = भिक्षा। मारु = मारय = मारो॥

उसी समय (राजा गन्धर्व-सेन के यहाँ बडे बडे लोग जो बैठे थे सभी ने भाट की बात की निन्दा करने लगे। उस निन्दा को) सुन कर महादेव (भाट) का मन लज्जित हो गया, (और) भाट की कला अर्थात् चाल ऐसे हो कर राजा गन्धर्व से विनय करने लगे, अर्थात् भाट के ऐसा दहिने हाथ से गन्धर्व-सेन, को आशीर्वाद दे कर भाट विनय करने लगा। राजा गन्धर्व-सेन, सुन, तूँ बडा राजा है (और लोग) मुझे (भाट को) महेश की मूर्त्ति कहते हैं। पर (ऐसी चाल है कि) जो बात आगे के लिये भली हो, उस को कहना चाहिए, क्रोध लगने से क्या ऊआ, अर्थात् सुनने-वाले को क्रोध लगे तो लगे, पर भली बात को जरूर कहना चाहिए। भारवी ने माघकाव्य में सच लिखा है कि 'हितं मनोहारि च दुर्लभं वचः'। हित की बात मनोहर भी हो यह दुर्लभ है। यह राज-कुमार है योगी नहीं, पद्मावती (की सुन्दरता) सुन कर विरही हो गया है। जम्बूद्वीप के राज-घराने का बेटा है, जो (कर्म में) लिखा है वह मिटाया नहीं जाता। तेरेई सुग्गा (हीरामणि) (जम्बू-द्वीप में) जा कर इस को ले आया है, और (यह वही राज-कुमार है) जिस का तैं (पद्मावती के साथ ब्याह करने के लिये) बरच्छा माना है अर्थात् बरच्छा किया चाहता है। फिर यह बात शिव-लोक में (भी) सुनी गई है (वहाँ भी इस के साथ पद्मावती का व्याह योग्य समझा गया है। सो आप इस के साथ पद्मावती का) व्याह कीजिए। (ऐसा करने से) आप को बडा धर्म होगा॥

(यह) खप्पर लिए उसी (पद्मावती) को माँगता है, मरने पर भी (तुम्हारा) दरवाजा न छोडेगा। राजा तूँ बूझ कर देख जो यह (सच्चा) सोना है (या) कचौडी है। (मेरा कहना मान इसे) भीख देओ, मारो मत, अर्थात् पद्मावती के साथ इस का व्याह कर दो, मारो मत। यही पद्मावती के योग्य वर है॥ २७६॥

चउपाई।

भाट भेस ईसुर जस भाखा। हनुवँत बीर रहइ नहिँ राखा॥
लीन्ह चूरि ततखन वइ सूरी। धरि मुख मेलेसि जानहुँ मूरी॥
महादेओ रन घंट बजावा। सुनि कइ सबद बरम्ह चलि आवा॥
चढे अतर लेइ बिसुन मुरारी। इँदर-लोक सब लाग गोहारी॥
फन-पति फन पतार सउँ काढा। असटउ कुली नाग भा ठाढा॥

तेइँतिस कोटि देश्रोता साजा। अउ छाँनबइ मेघु-दल गाजा॥
छपन कोटि बइसुंदर बरा। सवा लाख परबत फरहरा॥

दोहा।

नवइ नाथ चलि आवहीँ अउ चउरासी सिद्ध।
अहुटि बजर जर धरती गगन गरुर अउ गिद्ध॥ २७७॥

भाट = भट = स्तुति करने-वाला। भेस = वेष = रूप। ईसुर = ईश्वर = महादेव। जस = यथा = जैसे। भाखा = भाखइ = (भाषते) का भूत-काल, पुंलिङ्ग, प्रथम-पुरुष, एक-वचन। हनुवँत = हनुमान्। बीर = वीर = योद्धा। रहइ = तिष्ठति = रहता है। राखा = रखने से = रक्षणतः। लीन्ह = अलात् = लिया। चूरि = चूर्ण = चूर। ततखन = तत्क्षणे = तिस क्षण में = उस क्षण में। वइ = वह वा उस। सूरी = शूली। धरि = धृत्वा = धर कर = पकड कर। मुख = मुँह। मेलेसि = अमेलयत् = मेल दिया = डाल दिया। जानउँ = जाने = जानौँ। मूरी = मूली = मूलिका = मुरई = एक खाने का कन्द। महादेश्रो = महादेव। रन = रण = सङ्ग्राम। घंट = घण्टा। बजावा = बजावइ (वादयति) का भूत-काल, पुंलिङ्ग, प्रथम-पुरुष, एक-वचन। सुनि कइ = श्रुत्वा = सुन कर। सबद = शब्द = आवाज। बरम्ह = ब्रह्मा। चलि आवा = आयात् = चला आया। चढे = चढइ (उच्चलति) का भूत-काल, पुंलिङ्ग, प्रथम-पुरुष, बहु-वचन। अतर = अस्त्र = जो कि मन्त्र से चलाया जाय। लेइ = आलाय = ले कर। बिसुन = विष्णु। मुरारी = मुरारि = मुर के शत्रु। इंदर-लोक = इन्द्र-लोक। सब = सर्व। लाग = लगइ (लगति) का भूत-काल, पुंलिङ्ग, प्रथम-पुरुष, एक-वचन। गोहारी = गोहार = गोपन = रक्षण = रक्षा करना। फनपति = फणिपति = साँपोँ का राजा = शेष नाग। फन = फणा सउँ = से। काढा = काढइ (कर्षति) का भूत-काल, पुंलिङ्ग, प्रथम-पुरुष, एक-वचन असटउ = अष्टौ = आठो। कुली = कुल के। नाग = साँप = सर्प। भा = बभूव = भया = ऊआ, यहाँ ऊए। ठाढा = खडा = उत्थान। तइँतिस = तैंतीस = त्रयस्त्रिंशत्। कोटि = करोड। देश्रोता = देवता। साजा = साजइ (सज्जते) का भूत-काल, पुंलिङ्ग, प्रथम-पुरुष, एक-वचन। अउ = अपि = और। छाँनबइ = षण्णवति = छानबे। मेघु-दल = मेघ-दल = मेघोँ की सेना = बादलोँ के झुंड। गाजा = गाजइ (गर्जति = गरजइ) का भूत-काल, पुंलिङ्ग, प्रथम-पुरुष, एक-वचन। छपन = षट्पञ्चाशत् = छप्पन। बइसुंदर =

बैश्वानर = आग। बरा = बरइ (वरति) का भूत-काल, पुंलिङ्ग, प्रथम-पुरुष, का एक-वचन। सवा लाख = सपादलक्ष। परबत = पर्वत। फरहरा = फरहरइ (स्फुरति) का भूत-काल, पुंलिङ्ग, प्रथम-पुरुष, एक-वचन॥

नवइ = नवापि = नवो। नाथ = नाथान्त सिद्ध-पुरुष, गोरख-नाथादि। चलि = चल कर = चलिला। आवहीँ = आयान्ति = आते हैं। चउरासी = चतुरशीति = चौरासी। सिद्ध = सिद्ध-पुरुष। अऊटि = औटन = आवर्त्तन। बजर = वज्र = बिजली। जर = जरइ (ज्वलति) = जरता है वा जरती है। धरती = धरित्री = भूमि। गगन = आकाश = आसमान। गरुर = गरुड = मांसखाने-वाला प्रसिद्ध पक्षी, जिसे इस प्रान्त में ढकपखेर कहते हैं। गिद्ध = गृध्र = मांसखाने-वाला प्रसिद्ध पक्षी॥

जैसे-ही भाट के वेष में महादेव ने (पिछले दोहे की बात) कही, (वैसे-ही) वीर हनुमान रखने से अर्थात् रोकने पर भी नहीं रहे (झट उठ खडे हुए)। उसी क्षण में उस शूली को चूर कर डाला, (और) पकड कर मुँह में डाल लिया जानों (कोई) मूली मुँह में डाल कर खाता हो। महादेव ने रण का घंटा बजाया, जिस का शब्द सुन कर (ब्रह्म-लोक से दौडे) ब्रह्मा चले आए। मुरारि विष्णु अस्त्र ले कर (लडने के लिये) चढाई किए; इन्द्र-लोक के सब लोग (रत्न-सेन की) रक्षा करने लगे। पाताल से शेष नाग ने अपने फन को निकाला, आठो कुल के नाग (आ कर) खडे हुए। तैंतिस करोड देवता (लडने की) तयारी करने लगे और छानबे बादलों के झुंड गरजने लगे। छप्पन करोड आग बरने लगी, सवा लाख पर्वत फरकने लगे॥

नवो-नाथ और चौरासी सिद्ध भी (वहाँ) चले आए। बिजली के औटने से भूमि जलने लगी। गरुड और गिद्ध (नर-मांस खाने के लिये) आकाश में मँडराने लगे॥

हनुमान = केशरी के वीर्य से अञ्जना के गर्भ से उत्पन्न हुए हैं, रामायण में इन की कथा प्रसिद्ध है॥

महादेव, ब्रह्मा और विष्णु ये पुराणों में प्रसिद्ध तीन देवता हैं॥

इन्द्र-लोक में इन्द्र रहता है। वह देवताओं का राजा है, इस के लोक को स्वर्ग लोक कहते हैं। इस की राजधानी अमरावतीपुरी और सभा सुधर्मा है। इस ने गौतम की स्त्री अहल्या का सत बिगाडा था। इस लिये गोतम के शाप से इस की देह में हजार योनि हो गई थी। पीछे लङ्का विजय करने पर राम के वर से

वे सहस्र योनि सहस्र आँख हो गईं। इसी से इस का नाम सहस्राक्ष हुआ। रामायण में इसकी सविस्तर कथा लिखी हुई है ॥

फणिपति शेषनाग के ऊपर प्रलयकाल में भगवान विष्णु लक्ष्मी के साथ सोते हैं। शेष ही ने पतञ्जलि हो कर अष्टाध्यायी का भाष्य और कपिल हो कर योगशास्त्र को बनाया है ॥

अष्टकुली नाग के लिये इस ग्रन्थ का १६५ पृ० देखो ॥

ऋग्वेद में ग्यारह भूमि के, ग्यारह पाताल के और ग्यारह स्वर्ग के सब तैंतीस देवता लिखे हैं। पर पुराणों में एक एक के करोड करोड सन्तान मान कर तैंतीस करोड देवता लिखे हैं ॥

ज्यौतिष के मेघमाला नाम ग्रन्थ में मन्दर के उत्तर १२ मेघ, बारह महीने के १२ मेघ, कैलास, विकट, जठर, मेरु, शृङ्ग, पारिजात, हिमवान्, और गन्धमादन पर्वत पर के दश दश मेघ सब ८४ लिखे हैं। ग्रन्थकार ने एक प्रलय काल का सांवर्त्तक और दूसरा मेघदूत का पुष्पकावर्त्त ले कर ८६ लिखा है, ऐसा जान पडता हैं। श्रीमद्भागवत दशमस्कन्ध के २५ अध्याय में लिखा है कि इन्द्र ने प्रलय करने-वाले सांवर्त्तादिक मेघों को ले कर व्रज पर चढाई किया था ॥

अग्नि— श्रीमद्भागवत षष्ठस्कन्ध—१८ अध्याय के ३ श्लोक की टीका में 'पञ्च वा एते ऽग्नयो यच्चितय इति' यह श्रीधर लिखते हैं। इस से पाँच आग, और चतुर्थ-स्कन्ध के १ अध्याय के ५९—६० श्लोक—

स्वाहाभिमानिनश्चाग्नेरात्मजांस्त्रीनजीजनत् ।
पावकं पवमानं च शुचिं च हुतभोजनम् ॥
तेभ्यो ऽग्नयः समभवंश्चत्वारिंशच्च पञ्च च ।
त एवैकोनपञ्चाशत् साकं पितृपितामहैः ॥

इन से ४९ अग्नि हैं। दोनों के जोडने से ५४ अग्नि और स्मार्त्ताग्नि, श्रौताग्नि दो और अधिक करने से ५६ अग्नि होते हैं। इन के, तैंतिस देवताओं के सन्तान ऐसा, कोटि कोटि सन्तान मान कर ग्रन्थकार ने ५६ करोड अग्नि को लिखा है। वेदों में और कर्मकाण्डग्रन्थों में अनेक अग्नि के भेद लिखे हैं ॥

पर्वत— पद्म-पुराण के उत्तर-खण्ड के दूसरे अध्याय में लिखा है कि सवा लाख पर्वतों के बीच में वदरिकाश्रम स्थित है। वहाँ नर और नारायण जी रहते हैं।

महेश उवाच ।

एकलक्षं पञ्चविंशत्सहस्राः पर्वतास्तथा ।
तेषां मध्ये महत्पुण्यं बद्रिकाश्रममुत्तमम् ॥ १ ॥
नरो नारायणो देवो यत्र तिष्ठति नारद ।
तस्य स्वरूपं तेजश्च वक्ष्यामीह च सांप्रतम् ॥ २ ॥

(वेङ्कटेश्वर छापेखाने की छपी पुस्तक, खेतवाडी-मुंबई)।

नवोनाथों के लिये इस ग्रन्थ का २४१ पृ० देखो।

गोरख-नाथिओं में चौरासी सिद्ध हैं जिन के नाम नीचे लिखे हुए हैं।

सिद्ध-नाथ १। बद्धपद्म-नाथ २। दृढ-नाथ ३। वीर-नाथ ४। पवनमुक्त नाथ ५। धीर-नाथ ६। श्वास-नाथ ७। पश्चिमतान-नाथ ८। वातायन-नाथ ९। मयूर नाथ १०। मत्स्येन्द्र-नाथ ११। कुक्कुट-नाथ १२। भद्र-नाथ १३। अर्धपाद-नाथ १४। पूर्णपाद-नाथ १५। दक्षिण-नाथ १६। शव-नाथ १७। अश्व-नाथ १८। धनुष-नाथ १९। पादशिरा-नाथ २०। द्विपादशिरा-नाथ २१। स्थिर-नाथ २२। वृक्ष-नाथ २३। अर्धवृक्ष-नाथ २४। चक्र-नाथ २५। ताल-नाथ २६। ऊर्ध्वधनुष-नाथ २७। वामसिद्ध-नाथ २८। स्वस्तिक-नाथ २९। स्थितविवेक-नाथ ३०। उत्थितविवेक-नाथ ३१। दक्षिणतर्क-नाथ ३२। पूर्वतर्क-नाथ ३३। निःश्वास-नाथ ३४। अर्धकूर्म-नाथ ३५। गरुड-नाथ ३६। व्याघ्र-नाथ ३७। वामत्रिकोण-नाथ ३८। प्रार्थना-नाथ ३९। दक्षिणसिद्ध-नाथ ४०। पूर्णत्रिकोण-नाथ ४१। वामभुज-नाथ ४२। भयङ्कर-नाथ ४३। अङ्गुष्ठ-नाथ ४४। उत्कट-नाथ ४५। वामाङ्गुष्ठ नाथ ४६। ज्येष्ठिका-नाथ ४७। वामार्धपाद-नाथ ४८। वामभुजपाद-नाथ ४९। भुजपाद-नाथ ५०। वामवक्र-नाथ ५१। वामजानु-नाथ ५२। वामशाख-नाथ ५३। त्रिस्तम्भ-नाथ ५४। वामपादापान-नाथ ५५। वामहस्तचतुष्कोण-नाथ ५६। गोमुख-नाथ ५७। गर्भ-नाथ ५८। एकपादवृक्ष-नाथ ५९। मुक्तहस्तवृक्ष-नाथ ६०। हस्तवृक्ष-नाथ ६१। द्विपादपार्श्व-नाथ ६२। कन्दपीडन-नाथ ६३। प्रौढ-नाथ ६४। उपधान-नाथ ६५। ऊर्ध्वसंयुक्तपाद-नाथ ६६। अर्धशव-नाथ ६७। उत्तानकूर्म-नाथ ६८। सर्वाङ्ग-नाथ ६९। अपान-नाथ ७०। योनि-नाथ ७१। मण्डूक-नाथ ७२। पर्वत-नाथ ७३। शलभ-नाथ ७४। कोकिल-नाथ ७५। लोल-नाथ ७६। उष्ट्र-नाथ ७७। हंस-नाथ ७८। प्राण-नाथ ७९। कार्मुक-नाथ ८०। आनन्दमन्दिर-नाथ ८१। खञ्जन-नाथ ८२। ग्रन्थिभेदन-नाथ ८३। भुजङ्ग-नाथ ८४। इन लोगों ने, जिस जिस आसन से हठ-योग सिद्ध किए हैं, उन्हीं

आसन-संबन्धी नाम हैँ। जैसे जिस ने सिद्धासन से हठ-योग सिद्ध किया उस का नाम सिद्ध-नाथ पडा। कहीँ कहीँ इन के दूसरे नाम भी मिलते हैँ। काशी के श्रीरामशास्त्री-भारद्वाज के शिष्य ब्रह्मचारी नृसिंहशर्मा ने मुंबई "कर्नाटक" मुद्रालय में सन् १८९८ ई० में एक "चौरासी-आसन" नाम की पुस्तक छपवाई है। उस में चौरासी आसनोँ के अवान्तर भेद से ९७ आसन चित्र के साथ दिखलाए हैँ। परन्तु ज्यौतिषशास्त्र में सिद्ध शब्द से आज कल २४ संख्या लेते हैँ। जैनिओँ में चौबीस जिन देव सिद्ध हुए हैँ इस लिये जान पडता है कि आज कल प्रचलित ज्यौतिष-ग्रन्थोँ में 'जिन' या 'सिद्ध' वा 'अर्हत्' से चौबीस का ग्रहण करते हैँ॥

गोरक्ष-पद्धति में भी चौरासी लाख आसनोँ में से ८४ ही को मुख्य माना है।

चतुराशीतिलक्षाणामेकैकं समुदाहृतम्।

ततः शिवेन पीठानां षोडशोनं शतं (८४) कृतम्।

बहुत लोग दोहे के 'चउरासी सिद्ध' से चौरासी आसनोँ के द्वार से जो सिद्ध हैँ, उन्हेँ लेते हैँ॥ २७७॥

चउपाई।

जोगी धरि मेले सब पाछइँ। अउरु माल आए रन काछइँ॥
मंत्रिन्ह कहा सुनहु हो राजा। देखहु अब जोगिन्ह के काजा॥
हम जो कहा बड ता कर जूझू। होत आउ दर बहुत असूझू॥
खन एक मँह छरहट होइ बीता। दर मँह छरहिँ रहइ सो जीता॥
कइ धीरज राजा तब कोपा। अंगद आइ पाँओ रन रोपा॥
हसति पाँच जो अगुमन धाए। ते अंगद धरि सूँड फिराए॥
दीन्ह अडारि सरग कहँ गए। लउटि न बहुरे तहँ के भए॥

दोहा।

देखत रहे अचंभउ जोगी हसति बहुरि नहिँ आए।
जोगिन्ह कर अस जूझब पुहुमि न लागहिँ पाए॥ २७८॥

जोगी = योगी। धरि = धृत्वा = धर कर = पकड कर। मेले = मेलइ (मेलयति) का भूत-काल, पुंलिङ्ग, प्रथम-पुरुष, बहु-वचन। सब = सर्व। पाछइँ = पृष्ठे = पीछे। अउरु = और = अपर। माल = मल्ल = कुश्ती लडने-वाले। आए = उपेयुः। रन =

रण = सङ्ग्राम । काछहँ = कच्छित = कछ कसे = लँगोटा कसे । मंचिन्ह = मन्त्रिभिः = मन्त्रिओं ने । कहा = अकथयत् । सुनज = शृणुथ = सुनिए । हो = अहो = हे = उच्च सम्बोधन । देखज = पश्यथ = देखिए । अब = इदानीम् = अधुना । जोगिन्ह = जोगी का बज-वचन । के = का का बज-वचन । काजा = कार्य = काम । हम = हौं वा मैं का बज-वचन । जो = यः = जो । बड = बृहत् = बडा । ता कर = तस्य = तिस का = उस का । जूझू = युद्ध । होत = होता = भवन् । आउ = आयाति = आता है । दर = दल = सेना । बजत = बजतर = अधिक । असूझू = असूझ = अगाध = जिस की गणना न हो । खन = चण । एक = एक । मँह = मध्ये = में । छरहट = चरहट्टा = मरने की बाजार । होइ = भूला = हो कर । बीता = बीत = बीतता है = व्येति । छरहिँ = चरन्ति = मरते हैं । रहइ = तिष्ठति = रहता है । सो = सः = वह । जीता = जीत = जयति = जीतता है । कइ = कृत्वा = कर के । धीरज = धैर्य । तब = तदा । कोपा = चुकोप = कोप किया = क्रोध किया । अंगद = अङ्गद = बालि का पुत्र, सुग्रीव का भतीजा । आइ = एत्य = आ कर । पाँओ = पाद = पैर । रोपा = रोपइ (रोपयति रुह, बीजजन्मनि प्रादुर्भावे से) का भूत-काल, पुंलिङ्ग, प्रथम-पुरुष, एक-वचन । हसति = हस्ती = हाथी । पाँच = पृच्छ । अगुमन = अग्रगमन = पहले । धाए = धावइ (धावति) का भूत-काल, पुंलिङ्ग, प्रथम-पुरुष, बज-वचन । ते = वे । सूँड = शुण्ड = हाथी का हाथ । फिराए = फिरावइ (भ्रमयति) का भूत-काल, पुंलिङ्ग, प्रथम-पुरुष, बज-वचन । दीन्ह = अदात् = दिया । अडारि = अधारण = प्रक्षेपण = फेंक । सरग = स्वर्ग । कहँ = को । गए = जाइ (याति) का भूत-काल, पुंलिङ्ग, बज-वचन । लउटि = परावर्त्य = लौट कर । बजरे = फिरइ (परिवर्त्तयति) का भूत-काल, पुंलिङ्ग, प्रथम-पुरुष, बज-वचन । तहँ = तत्र । भए = बभूवुः = ज़ए ॥

देखत = पश्यन् = देखते । रहे = तस्थुः = थे । अचंभउ = अचंभा = आश्चर्य । बजरि = फिर = भूयः । आए = आए । कर = का । अस = एतादृश = ऐसा । जूझब = योद्धव्य = जूझना = लडना । पुज़मि = भूमि = पृथ्वी । लागहिँ = लगन्ति = लगते हैं । पाँए = पाँय = पैर = पाद ॥

(पहले कहे ज़ए ब्रह्मादिक ने) योगिओं को पकड कर पीछे कर दिए, और रण में लँगोटा कस कस सब (ब्रह्मादि) माल उतर पडे । (गन्धर्व-सेन के) मन्त्रिओं ने कहा कि हे राजा, (मेरी बात) सुनिए, अब योगिओं के काम को देखिए । हम ने जो

(पहले-ही आप से) कहा कि योगियों का संग्राम बड़ा (भयङ्कर) होता है, (सो देखिए) असूझ बहुत दल होता आता है, अर्थात् असंख्य सेना चली आती है। एक क्षण में मुर्दों की बाजार लगी चाहती है, दल में (लोग) मरा चाहते हैं, सो जो जीतेगा वही (दल में) रहेगा। (मन्त्रियों की इतनी बात सुन कर) राजा (गन्धर्व-सेन) ने तब क्रोध किया, (इतने-ही में) रण में आ कर अङ्गद ने (लड़ने के लिये) पैर को जमाया। पहले जो (राजा गन्धर्व-सेन के) पाँच हाथी (अङ्गद की ओर पकड़ने को) दौड़े, अङ्गद ने उन्हें सूँड पकड़ कर फिराया (और फिरा कर आकाश में फेंक दिया। वे (उड़ कर) स्वर्ग को चले गए, फिर न लौटे, वहीं के हो गए॥

योगी लोग इस आश्चर्य को देखते रह गए कि वे हाथी फिर नहीं (जमीन पर) आए। (कवि कहता है कि) योगियों का ऐसा लड़ना होता है कि जमीन पर पैर नहीं लगता, अर्थात् योगी लोग आसमान-ही से लड़ते हैं, जमीन पर नहीं उतरते॥

अङ्गद की कथा रामायण में प्रसिद्ध है। ये राम का दूत बन कर रावण की सभा में गए थे, और प्रतिज्ञा की थी कि रावण, मेरे टेके हुए पैर को जौं घसका दो, तो मैं सीता को हार जाता हूँ, राम जी विना लड़े लौट जायँगे॥ २७८॥

चउपाई।

कहहिँ बात जोगिहिँ हम पाई। खन एक मँह चाहत हहिँ धाई॥
जउँ लहि धावहिँ अस का खेलहु। हसतिन्हँ केर जूह सब पेलहु॥
जस गज पेलि होइ रन आगइँ। तस बगमेल करहु सँग लागइँ॥
हसति कि जूह जउहिँ अगुसारी। हनुवँत तउहिँ लँगूर पसारी॥
जउहिँ सो सइन जीति रन आई। सबहि लपेटि लँगूर चलाई॥
बहुतक टूटि भए नउ खंडा। बहुतक जाइ परे ब्रहमंडा॥
बहुतक फिरा करहिँ अँतरीखा। अहे जो लाख भए ते लीखा॥

दोहा।

बहुतक परे समुँद मँह परत न पावा खोज।
जहाँ गरब तहँ बेरा जहाँ हँसी तहँ रोज॥ २७९॥

कहहिँ = कथयन्ति = कहते हैँ । बात = वार्त्ता । जोगिहिँ = योगिनाम् = योगिश्रों का । हम = हौँ (मैँ) का बक्ठ-वचन । पाई = पावइ (प्राप्नोति) का भूत-काल, स्त्रीलिङ्ग, प्रथम-पुरुष, बक्ठ-वचन । खन = चण । एक = एक । मँह = मध्ये = में । चाहत हहिँ = इच्छन्ति = चाहते हैँ । धाई = धावनम् = धावा मारना । जउँ लहि = जब तक = यावद्धि । धावहिँ = धावन्ति = दौडते हैँ = धावा मारते हैँ । अस = एतादृश । का = कि । खेलक्ठ = खेलन्तु = खेलो । हसतिन्ह केर = हस्तिनाम् = हाथिश्रों का । जूह = यूथ = झुंड । सब = सर्वे । पेलक्ठ = पीलयन्तु = पेलो = ऊलाश्रो । जस = यथा = जैसे । गज = हस्ती = हाथी । पेलि = पीलयित्वा = पेल कर = ऊला कर । होइ = भवेत् = हो । रन = रण = सङ्ग्राम । आगइँ = अग्रे = आगे । तस = तथा = तैसे । बगमेल = वागमेल = वाग से वाग को मिलाना = मुठ भेर = डट जाना = ऊपर पक्ठँच जाना । करक्ठ = कुर्वन्तु = करो । सँग = संग = साथ । लागइँ = लगे ऊए = लगन्तः । हसति = हस्ती = हाथौ । कि = की । जउहिँ = यदा हि = जैसे-ही । अगुसारी = अग्रसरण = आगे गमन । हनुवँत = हनुमान् = हनुमंत । तउहिँ = तदा हि = तैसे-ही । लँगूर = लाङ्गूल = पोंक = पुच्छ । पसारी = पसारइ (प्रसारयति) का भूत-काल, स्त्रीलिङ्ग, प्रथम-पुरुष, एक-वचन । सो = सः = वह । सइन = सेनायाम् = सेना में । जीति = जीतने के लिये = जयार्थ । आई = आवइ (आयाति) का भूत-काल, स्त्रीलिङ्ग, प्रथम-पुरुष, एक-वचन । सबहि = सर्वेषाम् = सब को । लपेटि = प्रपुष्य = लपेट कर । चलाइ = चलावइ (चालयति) का भूत-काल, स्त्रीलिङ्ग, प्रथम-पुरुष, एक-वचन । बक्ठतक = बक्ठतरकः = वक्ठत एक = बक्ठत तो । टूटि = त्रुटित्वा = टूट कर । भए = बभूवुः = ऊए = हो गए । नउ-खंडा = नव-खण्ड = नव टुकडे । जाइ = यात्वा = जा कर । परे = परइ (परति) का भूत-काल, पुंलिङ्ग, प्रथम-पुरुष, बक्ठ-वचन । ब्रहमंडा = ब्रह्माण्ड = आकाश । फिरा करहिँ = भ्रमन्तः सन्ति = फिरा करते हैँ = घूमा करते हैँ । अँतरीखा = अन्तरिच । अहे = आसन् = थे = रहे । जो = यः = जो । लाख = लच । ते = वे । लीखा = लीचा = लीख ॥

समुँद = समुद्र । परत = पडत-ही = पतन्त एव । पावा = पावइ (प्राप्नोति) का भूत-काल, पुंलिङ्ग, प्रथम-पुरुष, एक-वचन । खोज = चिह्न = निशान = पता । जहाँ = यत्र । गरब = गर्व = अभिमान । तहँ = तत्र । बेरा = बैंडा = वक्र = कठिनता । हँसी = हास्य = ठट्ठा । रोज = रुज = रोग ॥

(राजा गन्धर्व-सेन के पच-वाले) कहने लगे कि हम लोग जोगिश्रों के (मतलब को) पा गए, अर्थात् समझ गए, (ये लोग) एक चण में (हमारी सेना के ऊपर) धावा मारा चाहते हैं। जब तक (ये लोग) धावा मारें (तब तक) ऐसा खेलो कि (धावा न करने पावें, इसी बीच में इन की सेना में) हाथिश्रों का झुंड पिला दो। जैसे हाथी पिल कर रण के आगे हों, वैसे-ही सब लोग साथ में लगे ऊए मुठ भेर करो, अर्थात् शत्रुश्रों से भिड जाओ। जैसे-ही हाथिश्रों का झुंड (रत्न-सेन की सेना के) आगे आया, वैसे-ही हनुमान ने अपने लंगूर को फैलाया। जैसे-ही वह झुंड (रत्न-सेन की) सेना में जीतने के लिये रण-चेत्र में आया, (वैसे-ही) हनुमान ने सब को लंगूर में लपेट कर (ऊपर की ओर) चलाया। बऊत टूट कर नव टुकडे हो गए, बऊत जा कर ब्रह्माण्ड में पडे। बऊत अन्तरिच में घूमने लगे, जो लाख थे वे लीख हो गए, अर्थात् लाखों हाथी लीख के ऐसे छितिर बितिर हो गए ॥

बऊत समुद्र में जा कर पडे, पडते-ही उन का पता न लगा (कि क्या हो गए)। (कवि कहता है कि) जहाँ अभिमान है वहीं कठिनता पडती है, अर्थात् घमंडी-ही के ऊपर विपत्ति पडती है, (और) जहाँ हँसी होती है वहीं (लडाई का) रोग होता है। कहावत है कि 'रोग की जड खाँसी और झगडे की जड हाँसी'। कवि का अभिप्राय है कि भाट और मन्त्रिश्रों के समझाने पर भी राजा गन्धर्व-सेन ने न माना, घमंड से भरा लडने-ही लगा, जिस का फल यह ऊआ कि जिन हाथिश्रों का बडा घमंड था वे हनुमान के फैंकने से लीख के ऐसे टुकडे टुकडे हो कर छितिर-बितिर हो गए ॥ २७९ ॥

चउपाई।

फिरि आगइँ का देखइ राजा। ईसुर केर घंट रन बाजा ॥
सुना संख सो बिसुन जउँ पूरा। आगइँ हनुवँत केर लँगूरा ॥
लीन्हइँ फिरहिँ सरग ब्रह्मंडा। सरग पतार लोक म्रितमंडा ॥
बलि बासुकि अउ इँदर नरंदू। गरह नखत सूरज अउ चंदू ॥
जावँत दानउ राकस पुरी। अहुठउ बजर आइ रन जुरी ॥
जिन्ह कर गरब करत हुत राजा। सो सब फिरि बइरी होइ साजा ॥
जहवाँ महादेओ रन खरा। नारी घालि आइ पाँ परा ॥

दोहा ।

केहि कारन रिस कीजिअ हउँ सेवक अउ चेर ।
जेहि चाहिअ तेहि दीजिअ बारि गोसाईँ केर ॥ २८० ॥

फिरि = पुनः = भूयः । आगइँ = अग्रे = आगे । का = किम् = क्या । देखइ = पश्यति = देखता है । ईसुर = ईश्वर = महादेव । केर = का । घंट = घण्टा । रन = रण = सङ्ग्राम । बाजा = बाजइ (वाद्यते) का भूत-काल, पुंलिङ्ग, प्रथम-पुरुष, एक-वचन । सुना = सुनइ (शृणोति) का भूत-काल, पुंलिङ्ग, प्रथम-पुरुष, एक-वचन । संख = शङ्ख । सो = सो = सः = वह । बिसुन = विष्णु = भगवान । जउँ = यथा = जैसे-ही । पूरा = पूरइ (पूर्यते) का भूत-काल, पुंलिङ्ग, प्रथम-पुरुष, एक-वचन । हनुवँत = हनुमान = हनुमन्त । लँगूरा = लाङ्गूल = पूछ = पुच्छ । लीन्हइँ = लीन्हे = लिए । फिरहिँ = भ्रमन्ति = फिरते हैँ । सरग = स्वर्ग । ब्रहमंडा = ब्रह्माण्ड । पतार = पाताल । म्रितमंडा = मृत्युमण्डित = मर्त्यलोक । बलि = पाताल का प्रसिद्ध राजा । बासुकि = नाग की एक जाति । अउ = अपि = और । इँदर = इन्द्र । नरंदू = नरेन्द्र = राजा । गरह = ग्रह । नखत = नक्षत्र । सूरज = सूर्य । चंदू = चन्द्र । जावँत = यावन्तः = जितने । दानउ = दानव = दनु के सन्तान । राकस = राक्षस, जो मनुष्य को खाते हैँ । पुरी = नगरी । अऊठउ = आवर्त्त्य = ऊटने-वाला । बजर = वज्र = बिजली । आइ = एत्य = आ कर । जुरी = जुरइ = (युज्यते) का भूत-काल, स्त्रीलिङ्ग, प्रथम-पुरुष, एक-वचन । जिन्हकर = येषाम् = जिनका । गरब = गर्व = घमंड = अभिमान । करत ऊत = करता था । सब = सर्व । बदरी = वैरी = शत्रु । होइ = भूला = हो कर । साजा = साजइ (सज्जते) का भूत-काल, पुंलिङ्ग, प्रथम-पुरुष, एक-वचन । जहवाँ = जहाँ = यत्र । महादेओ = महादेव । खरा = खडा = उत्थित । नारी = स्त्री । घालि = गिरा कर = अवधार्य (धृ चरणदीप्त्योः से) । पाँ = पाद = पैर । परा = परइ (पतति) का भूत-काल, पुंलिङ्ग, प्रथम-पुरुष, एक-वचन ॥

केहि = कस्य = केन = किस ? कारन = कारण । रिस = रोष = क्रोध । कीजिअ = क्रियन्ते = करते हैँ । हउँ = अहम् = मैँ । सेवक = दास । चेर = चेटः = चेटक = टहलुआ । जेहि = यस्य = जिसे । चाहिअ = चाहिए = इच्छ्यते । तेहि = तस्य = तिसे = उसे । दीजिअ = दीयताम् = दीजिए । बारि = बाला = बालिका = कन्या = लडकी । गोसाईँ = गोस्वामी = मालिक । केर = की ॥

फिर (इस के) आगे राजा क्या देखता है कि रण में महादेव का घंटा बजा। (उस घंटे की आवाज ज्यों ही सुनी गई (त्यों ही) विष्णु ने (अपनी) उस (पाञ्च-जन्य) शंख को (स्वर से) पूरा, अर्थात् मुँह में लगा कर फूँक को भरा (जिस से बहुत भारी शब्द हुआ। (फिर इस के) आगे हनुमान के लंगूर में शत्रु की सेना के सब हाथी घोडे योद्धा लिपटे हुए (उसी लंगूर में) पडे स्वर्ग से ब्रह्माण्ड में, स्वर्ग से पाताल में और (पाताल से) मर्त्य लोक में घूमा फिरते हैं। बलि, वासुकि, और (देवताओं का राजा) इन्द्र, मनुष्यों के राजा, (भौमादि) ग्रह, नक्षत्र, सूर्य और चन्द्र, (सब) पुरियों के जितने दानव और राक्षस, (सब को) औटने-वाला वज्र, ये सब (महादेव के घंटा के बजते ही) आ कर रण में जुट गए। राजा गन्धर्व-सेन जिन लोगों का गर्व करता था वे सब उलट कर (राजा गन्धर्ब-सेन के) शत्रु हो कर (उन्ही के ऊपर लडने के लिये) तयारी करने लगे। (इस आश्चर्य को देख कर राजा गन्धर्व-सेन घबडा गया) जहाँ रण में महादेव खडे थे (वहाँ महादेव जी के पैर पर अपनी) स्त्री (चम्पावती) को गिरा कर (आप भी वहाँ पर) आ कर (महादेव जी के) पैर पर गिर पडा॥

(और गिडगिडाने लगा कि आप) किस कारण से क्रोध करते हैं। मैं तो (आप का) दास और टहलुआ हूँ। (आप) गोसाईं की (वह पद्मावती) बेटी है, जिसे चाहिए उसे दीजिए। मैं जो आप की इच्छा में कुछ बाधा करूँ तो अवश्य मेरे ऊपर क्रोध कीजिए॥

महादेव प्रसिद्ध तीन देवताओं में एक देवता हैं जो सृष्टि का नाश करते हैं।

विष्णु भी प्रसिद्ध तीन देवताओं में एक देवता हैं जो सृष्टि का पालन करते हैं।

हनुमान की कथा रामायण में प्रसिद्ध है।

स्वर्ग के लिये इस ग्रन्थ का ३ पृ० देखो।

पाताल के लिये इस ग्रन्थ का ३ पृ० देखो।

बलि के लिये इस ग्रन्थ का ४३८ पृ० और २०२ दोहे की टीका देखो।

वासुकि के लिये इस ग्रन्थ का १६५ पृ० देखो।

इन्द्र देवताओं का राजा, अदिति का ज्येष्ठ पुत्र, पुराणों में स्वर्ग का राजा कहा जाता है।

ग्रह से यहाँ पर भौम, बुध, बृहस्पति, शुक्र और शनैश्चर हैं।

नक्षत्र प्रसिद्ध ज्योतिषशास्त्र में सत्ताइस हैं, परं यहाँ पर कवि ने नक्षत्र से सब ताराओं को लिया है ।

दानव और राक्षस में भेद है इसी लिये मनुस्मृति के १ अध्याय ३७ वेँ श्लोक में लिखा है कि

यक्षरक्षःपिशाचांश्च गन्धर्वाप्सरसोऽसुरान् ।
नागान् सर्पान् सुपर्णांश्च पितॄणां च पृथग् गणान् ॥ २८० ॥

चउपाई ।

तउ महेस उठि कीन्ह बसीठी । पहिलइँ कडुइ अंत होइ मीठी ॥
तूँ गँधरब राजा जग पूजा । गुन चउदह सिख देइ को दूजा ॥
हीरामनि जो तुम्हार परेवा । गा चितउर गढ कीन्हेसि सेवा ॥
तेहि बोलाइ पूछहु ओहि देसू । अउ पूछहु जोगिन्ह कर भेसू ॥
हमरे कहत रहइ नहिँ मानू । वह बोलइ सोई परवाँनू ॥
जहाँ बारि तहँ आउ बरोका । करहु बिआह धरम बड तो का ॥
जो पहिले मन मान न काँधी । परखि रतन गाँठी तब बाँधी ॥

दोहा ।

रतन छपाए ना छपइ पारख होइ सो परीख ।
घालि कसउटी दीजिअइ कनक कचउरी भीख ॥ २८१ ॥

तउ = तदा = तर्हि । महेस = महेश = महादेव । उठि = उत्थाय = उठ कर । कीन्ह = अकृत = किया । बसीठी = विशिष्टत्व = दूतत्व = दूत का काम । पहिलइँ = पहले = प्रथमे । कडुइ = कटु = कडुई । अंत = अन्त्य = आखिर । होइ = भवति = होती है । मीठी = मिष्ट । तूँ = त्वम् = तैँ । गँधरब = गन्धर्व = गन्धर्व-सेन । जग = जगत् = संसार । पूजा = पूज्य । गुन = गुण । चउदह = चतुर्दश = चौदह । सिख = शिक्षा । देइ = दद्यात् = देवे । को = कः = कौन । दूजा = द्वितीय = दूसरा । हीरामनि = हीरामणि शुक । जो = जो = यः । तुम्हार = तुम्हारा = तव । परेवा = पारावत = पक्षी । गा = अगात् = गया । चितउर = चित्र-वर वा चित्र-पुर । गढ = गाढ = दुर्ग = किला । कीन्हेसि = अकृत =

किया। सेवा = टहल = खिदमत। तेहि = तम् = तिसे = उसे। बोलाद = आहूय = आवाद्य = बुला कर। पूछहु = पृच्छथ = पूछिए। ओहि = तस्य = उस का। देसू = देश। अउ = अपि = और। जोगिन्ह कर = योगिनाम् = योगिओं का। भेसू = वेष। हमरे = अस्माकम् = हमारे। कहत = कथने = कहने में। रहइ = रहता है (तिष्ठति)। मानू = मान = आदर। वह = सः। बोलइ = वदेत् = बोले। सोई = स एव = वही। परवाँनू = प्रमाण। जहाँ = यत्र। बारि = बालिका = बाला = कन्या। तहँ = तत्र = तहाँ। आउ = आयात् = आया। बरोका = बर ओका = उस का वर। करहु = कुरुथ = कीजिए। बिआह = विवाह = ब्याह। धरम = धर्म = पुण्य। तो का = तवक = तुझे = तुझ को। मन = मनसि। मान = मानइ = मन्यते। काँधी = स्कन्धी = कन्धा देनेवाला = आधार देने-वाला। परखि = परीक्ष्य = परीक्षा कर = परख कर। रतन = रत्न। गाँठी = ग्रन्थि = गाँठ। तब = तदा। बाँधी = बाँधइ (बध्नाति) का भूत-काल, स्त्रीलिङ्ग, प्रथम-पुरुष, एक-वचन॥

छपाए = छिपाने से = क्षपयन्। ना = न = नहीं। छपइ = क्षपति = छिपता है। पारख = पारखी = परीक्षक। होइ = भवेत् = स्यात् = हो। सो = सो = वह। परीख = परीक्षेत = परखे। घालि = घाल कर = कर्षयित्वा = कस कर। कसउटी = कषवटी = कसौटी। दीजिअइ = दीयेत = दीजिए। कनक = सुवर्ण = सोना। कचउरी = कचौरी = सोने ताँबे का मेल। भीख = भिक्षा॥

(जब राजा गन्धर्व-सेन अपनी रानी के समेत महादेव के पैरों पर पड अपना अपराध क्षमा कराया) तब महादेव जी उठ कर दूतत्व करने लगे (और कहने लगे कि जो बात) पहले कडुई लगती है वह अन्त में मीठी होती है। हे गन्धर्व-सेन राजा, तूँ जग में पूजनीय है, चौदहो (विद्या के) गुण (तेरे में) हैं, दूसरा कौन है जो तुझे सिखावें। जो तेरा हीरामणि पक्षी है वह चितौर गढ गया था (और उसी ने यह तेरी) सेवा की है, अर्थात् उसी ने तेरी कन्या के योग्य इसे लाया है। उस (शुक) को बुला कर उस (रत्न-सेन) के देश को पूछो, और योगिओ के वेष को (भी) पूछो. अर्थात् उस से पूछो कि ये सब योगिओं के वेष बनाए कौन हैं। मेरे कहने से मान न रहे, अर्थात् मेरे कहने का प्रमाण तूँ न माने, तो (जो) वह कहे उसी का प्रमाण करो। जहाँ (तेरी) कन्या है वहाँ ही उस का वर आ गया, (अब इस के साथ) ब्याह कर दो (ऐसा करने से) तुम्हें बडा धर्म होगा। जो आधार

कि उस हीरामणि को बुलाओ, (क्योंकि हीरामणि पण्डित है) पण्डित से बुराई नहीं होती। (बुलाने के लिये) आज्ञा हुई, (आज्ञा होते ही) हजारों नोकर (बुलाने के लिये) दौडे (और) शीघ्र हीरामणि को ले आए। (नोकरों ने राजा के) आगे ला कर पिंजडे को खोला, बहुत दिनों का रूसा हुआ (हीरामणि पिंजडे से) निकल कर (राजा से) मिला। बहुत प्रकार की स्तुति करते हुए (वह) मिला, (उन स्तुतिओं को सुन कर) राजा के हृदय में शान्ति हुई (क्रोध ठंढा हो गया)। जानों आग से जरते हुए के ऊपर पानी पड गया, (राजा का) हृदय फुलवारी हो कर आनन्द से भर गया। (हीरामणि से) मिल कर राजा ने हँस कर बात पूछी कि क्यों (तेरी) शरीर पीली हुई और मुँह लाल ॥

तुम चारो वेदों के पण्डित हो, शास्त्र और वेद को पढे हो। (कहो तो सही, ये) जोगी कहाँ चढे हैं, क्यों (इन सब को यहाँ) ला कर गढ को (छिन्न) भिन्न किया, अर्थात् क्यों गढ में सँध दिलाया ॥

ऋक्, साम, यजुः, और अथर्व ये चार वेद प्रसिद्ध हैं।

न्याय, वैशेषिक, पूर्वमीमांसा, उत्तर मीमांसा (वेदान्त), सांख्य, और योग ये षट् शास्त्र, और व्याकरण, ज्यौतिष, निरुक्त, कल्प, शिक्षा और छन्द ये षडङ्ग भी कभीँ कभीँ शास्त्र कहे जाते हैं ॥ २८२ ॥

चउपाई।

हीरामनि रसना रस खोला। देइ असीस अउ असतुति बोला ॥
इँदर राज-राजेसुर महा। सउँहीं रिस किछु जाइ न कहा ॥
पइ जेहि बात होइ भलि आगइँ। सेवक निडर कहइ रिस लागइँ ॥
सुआ सुफल अबिँरित पइ खोजा। होइ न बिकरम राजा भोजा ॥
हउँ सेवक तुम्ह आदि गोसाईँ। सेवा करउँ जिअउँ जब ताईँ ॥
जेइँ जिउ दीन्ह देखावा देसू। सो पइ जिअ महँ बसइ नरेसू ॥
जो मन सवँरइ एकइ तूँही। सोई पंखि जगत रत-मूही ॥

दोहा।

नइन बइन सरवन बुधी सबइ तोर परसाद।
सेवा मोर इहइ निति बोलउँ आसिरबाद ॥ २८३ ॥

हीरामनि = हीरामणि । रसना = जिह्वा = जीभ । रस = रस भरी बात । खोला = खोलइ (खलयति = उद्घाटयति) का भूत-काल, पुंलिङ्ग, प्रथम-पुरुष, एक-वचन । देइ = दत्त्वा = दे कर । असीस = आशीर्वाद । अउ = अपि = और । असतुति = स्तुति । बोला = बोलइ (वदति) का भूत-काल, पुंलिङ्ग, प्रथम-पुरुष, एक-वचन । इंदर = इन्द्र । राज-राजेसुर = राजराजेश्वर = राजाओं के राजाओं का ईश्वर । महा = महान् = बडा । सउँहीं = सम्मुखे हि = सामने । रिस = रोष = क्रोध । किछु = किञ्चित् = कुछ । जाइ = जाता । कहा = कथनम् । पइ = अपि = निश्चयेन । जेहि = यस्य = जिस । बात = वार्त्ता । होइ = भवति = होता है । भलि = भला = अच्छा = वर । आगइँ = अग्रे = आगे । सेवक = दास । निडर = निर्दर = निर्भय । कहइ = कथयति = कहता है । लागइँ = लगे = लग्ने । सुआ = शुक = सुग्गा । सुफल = अच्छा फल । अबिँरित = अमृत । खोजा = खोजइ (अन्वेषति) का भूत-काल, पुंलिङ्ग, प्रथम-पुरुष, एक-वचन । होइ = अस्ति = है । बिकरम = विक्रम = विक्रमादित्य = उज्जयिनी का प्रसिद्ध एक राजा । भोजा = भोज = धारानगरी का प्रसिद्ध एक राजा । हउँ = हौं = अहम् = मैं । तुम्ह = आप । आदि = प्रथम = प्रधान । गोसाईं = गोस्वामी = मालिक = प्रभु । सेवा = टहल = खिदमत । करउँ = करवाणि = करूँ । जिअउँ = जीवानि = जीऊँ । जब ताईं = यावत् = जब तक । जेइँ = यैः = जिन्हों ने । जिउ = जीव । दीन्ह = अदात् = दिया । देखावा = देखावइ (दर्शयति) का भूत-काल, पुंलिङ्ग, प्रथम-पुरुष, एक-वचन । देसू = देश । सो = सः = वह । जिअ = जीव । मँह = मध्ये = में । बसइ = वसति = बसता है । नरेसू = नरेश = राजा । जो = यः । मन = मनसि = मन में । एकइ = एकः = एक । तूँही = त्वं हि । सोई = स एव = वही । पंखि = पक्षी = पंखी = पंछी = चिडिया । जगत = जगत् = संसार । रत-मूँही = रक्त-मुखी = लाल मुँह की ॥

नइन = नयन = आँख । बइन = वचन । सरवन = श्रवण = कान । बुधी = बुद्धि । सबइ = सर्व हि = सभी । तोर = तव = तेरा । परसाद = प्रसाद । मोर = मम = मेरी । इहइ = इयमेव = यही । निति = नित्य = रोज । बोलउँ = बदामि = बोलता हूँ । आसिरबाद = आशीर्वाद = शुभवचन ॥

हीरामणि ने जीभ से रस को खोला, अर्थात् अमृत-वाणी बोलना आरम्भ किया, (राजा गन्धर्व-सेन को) आशीर्वाद दे कर और स्तुति कर बोलने लगा। (कि) हे इन्द्र, हे बडे राज-राजेश्वर, (प्रभु को) सामने क्रोध से (भरा देख) कुछ कहा नहीं जाता,

अर्थात् आप के क्रोध से डरता हूँ इस से मुँह से बोल नहीँ निकलती। पर जो बात आगे भली हो (उसे) बेधडक हो कर सेवक को कहना चाहिए, (मालिक को) रिस लगे तो लगे। सुग्गा निश्चय कर सुन्दर अमृत फल ही का खोजने-वाला है, (यह) न विक्रम है न राजा भोज है। मैँ तो आप प्रथम स्वामी का दास हूँ, जब तक जीऊँ (तब तक आप की) सेवा करूँ (यही मेरा सङ्कल्प है)। पर जिस ने जीव दिया, अर्थात् मेरा प्राण बचाया, और (मेरे इस) देश को देखाया, वह राजा निश्चय कर जीव मेँ बसता है। जो पची 'एक तूँ ही' है 'एक तूँ ही' है वही मन से सुमिरा करता है, वही पची संसार मेँ लालमुँही है। अर्थात् जो एक को प्रभु मान कर मनसा, वाचा, और कर्मणा, से उसी की सेवा मेँ रहता है, उसी के मुँह की लाली सदा बनी रहती है॥

आँख, वचन, कान और बुद्धि सब तेरे प्रसाद से (मेरे मेँ) हैँ, मेरी यही सेवा है कि नित्य (आप के लिये) शुभवचन बोला करूँ॥

राजा विक्रम के लिये इस ग्रन्थ का ३५२-३५३ पृ० देखो॥

राजा भोज प्रसिद्ध संस्कृतानुरागी विक्रम के बाद धारानगरी का राजा हुआ था। एक एक श्लोक पर लाख लाख रुपए दिए हैँ। इस की विस्तार से कथा भोजप्रबन्ध मेँ लिखी है॥

अवध और राजपुताने मेँ एक प्रसिद्ध पची है, जिस की बोली मेँ 'एकइ तूँ ही' 'एकइ तूँ ही' ऐसी धुनि जान पडती है। इसी लिये उस पची का नाम ही 'एकइ तूँ ही' पड गया है। कहावत है कि वह पची भगवान की स्तुति किया करता है, कि हे भगवान इस संसार मेँ (सच्चा अविनाशी) एक तूँ ही है॥ २८३॥

चउपाई।

जउ पंखी रसना रस रसा। तेहि क जीभ अबिँरित पइ बसा॥
तेहि सेवक के करमहिँ दोसू। सेवा करत करइ पति रोसू॥
अउ जेहि दोस न दोसहि लागा। सो डरि तहाँ जीउ लेइ भागा॥
जउँ पंखी कहवाँ थिर रहना। ताकइ जहाँ जाइ जो डहना॥
सपत दीप फिरि देखेउँ राजा। जंबू-दीप जाइ पुनि बाजा॥
तहँ चितउर गढ देखेउँ ऊँचा। ऊँच राज सरि तोहि पहूँचा॥
रतन-सेन यहु तहाँ नरेसू। आएउँ लेइ जोगी कर भेसू॥

दोहा।

सुआ सुफल पइ आना　हइ ता तेँ मुख रात।
कया पीत सो तेहि डर　सवँरउँ बिकरम बात ॥ २८४ ॥

जउ = यदि = जौं। पंखी = पक्षी = पंछी = चिडिया। रसना = जिह्वा = जीभ। रस = स्वादु की वस्तु। रसा = रसइ (रस्यति) का भूत-काल, पुंलिङ्ग, प्रथम-पुरुष, एक-वचन। तेहि = तस्य = तिस। क = की। जीभ = जिह्वा। अविँरित = अमृत। पइ = अपि = निश्चयेन। बसा = बसइ (वसति) का भूत-काल, पुंलिङ्ग, प्रथम-पुरुष, एक-वचन। सेवक = दास = टहलुआ। करमहिँ = कर्मणाम् = कर्मों का। दोसू = दोष। सेवा = टहल = खिदमत। करत = कुर्वन् = करते। पति = प्रभु = मालिक। रोसू = रोष = क्रोध। अउ = अपि = और। जेहि = यस्य = जिस के। दोस = दोष। दोसहि = दोष को। लागा = लगा = लगइ (लगति) का भूत-काल, पुंलिङ्ग, प्रथम-पुरुष, एक-वचन। सो = वह = सः। डरि = आदर्य = डर कर। तहाँ = तत्र = वहाँ। जीउ = जीव = प्राण। लेइ = आलाय = ले कर। भाग = भागइ (अभ्यगच्छति) का भूत-काल, पुंलिङ्ग, प्रथम-पुरुष, एक-वचन। जउँ = यदि = जौं। कहवाँ = कहाँ = कुत्र। थिर = स्थिर। रहना = अर्हणा = योग्यता। ताकइ = तर्क्यते = ताकता है = देखता है। जहाँ = यत्र। जाए = जाइ = याति। जाता है। जो = यत्। उडना = उड्डयन = डैना। सपत = सप्त = सात। दीप = द्वीप। फिरि = भ्रमिला = घूम कर। देखेउँ = अपश्यम् = देखा। राजा = राजन् = हे राजा। जंबूदीप = जम्बूदीप। जाइ = याला = जा कर। पुनि = पुनः = फिर। बाजा = बजइ (वाद्यते) का भूत-काल, पुंलिङ्ग, प्रथम-पुरुष, एक-वचन। तहँ = तहाँ = तत्र। चितउर = चित्रवर या चित्रपुर = चित्तौर। गढ = गाढ = दुर्ग = किला। ऊँचा = उच्च। ऊँच = ऊँचा = उच्च। राज = राज्य। सरि = सादृश्य = बराबरी। तोहि = तव = तुम्हारी। पहुँचा = पहुँचइ (प्राप्नोति) का भूत-काल, पुंलिङ्ग, प्रथम-पुरुष, एक-वचन। रतन-सेन = रत्न-सेन। यह = यह = अयम्। नरेसू = नरेश = राजा। आएउँ = अगच्छम् = आया। लेइ = आलाय = ले कर। जोगी = योगी। कर = का। भेसू = वेष ॥

सुआ = शुक = सुग्गा। सुफल = अच्छा फल। पइ = अपि = निश्चय कर। आना = आनइ (आनयति) का भूत-काल, पुंलिङ्ग, प्रथम-पुरुष, एक-वचन। हइ = अस्ति = है।

ता तँ = तस्मात् = उस से । मुख = मुँह । रात = रक्त = लाल । कया = काय = शरीर । पीत = पीली । सो = सः = वह । तेहि = तस्य = तिस । डर = दर = भय । सवँरउँ = स्मरामि = याद करता हूँ । बिकरम = विक्रम = उज्जयिनी का प्रसिद्ध राजा । बात = वार्त्ता ॥

जब पची की जीभ में रस रस गया (तब) उस की जीभ में निश्चय कर अमृत बस गया । सेवा करते जौँ मालिक क्रोध करे तो उस सेवक के कर्माँ का दोष समझना चाहिए । और जिस दोष के न (होने पर भी वह) दोष (सेवक के ऊपर) लगाया गया, इस लिये (यह सेवक) डर कर (अपना) प्राण ले कर भागा । (अर्थात् मैं सदा पद्मावती को सुन्दर उपदेश ही देता था । उस पर भी मेरे ऊपर यह दोष लगाया गया कि यह पद्मावती को बुरी राह दिखला रहा है । इस डर से मैं अपना जीव ले कर आप के यहाँ से भागा ।) जब पची ऊआ तब उस को कहाँ स्थिर रहना, जब डैना है तब जहाँ देखे वहाँ ही पऊँच जाता है । (हे राजा गन्धर्व-सेन मैं आप के यहाँ से भाग कर) सातो दीपोँ को घूम घूम कर देखा, फिर जम्बूद्वीप में जा कर पऊँचा । वहाँ (सब से) बडा चित्तौर गढ देखा, (वह) बडा राज्य आप की बराबरी में पऊँचा है । वहाँ का यह रत्न-सेन राजा है, (उसी को) योगी के वेष में ले कर आया हूँ ॥

(मैं) शुक निश्चय कर अच्छे फल को लाया हूँ, इसी से (मेरा) मुँह लाल है । (और) राजा विक्रम की बात याद कर उसी डर से (मेरी) देह पीली हो गई है ॥

सातो द्वीप के लिये इस ग्रन्थ का ३ पृ० देखो । कथा है कि राजा विक्रम के यहाँ एक शुक था । उस ने एक दिन राजा से कहा कि जौँ आप कुट्टी देते तो अपने जन्मस्थान को देख आता और आप के लिये एक अमृत-फल भी लेता आता । राजा ने इस बात को सुन सुग्गे को छोड दिया । वह बऊत दिनोँ तक वन की सैर कर राजा के पास अमृत-फल लिये लौटा । राजा ने विचारा कि इस की बीज से पेँड पैदा करेँ जिस से अनेक फल पैदा किए जायँ । माली को पेँड तयार करने के लिये उस फल को दिया । माली ने दो चार वर्ष में पेँड तयार किया । समय पर उस में फल आए । राजा ने कहा कि पकने पर मेरे पास लाना । दैव-संयोग से रात को वह फल चू कर जमीन पर आया । उसे एक साँप ने अपनी जीभोँ से अच्छी तरह से चाटा, जिस से वह विष से भर गया । सबेरे

माली उस फल को पानी से धो कर डाली में ले गया। राजा ने अपने लोगों के विचार से उस अजान फल के एक टुकडे को कुत्ते को खिलाया। वह खाते ही मर गया। इस पर राजा ने क्रोध कर कि यह दुष्ट सुग्गे ने मुझे मारने के लिये विष-फल लाया था, उस सुग्गे को मरवा डाला। फिर पीछे से बहुत दिनों तक वह पेंड विष-वृक्ष नाम से प्रसिद्ध हुआ। एक दिन बुढिया मालिन ने अपने पति से रूठ कर मरने की इच्छा से उस विष-फल को खा लिया। खाते ही सोरह वर्ष की जवान हो गई। इस लीले को देख कर उस का पति माली ने भी खाया। वह भी खाते ही बीस वर्ष का जवान हो गया। राजा को जब ये सब बातें मालूम हुईं तब हाथ मल मल कर पछताने लगा कि हाय मैं विना जाने नाहक अपराध के विना ही अपने सुग्गे को मरवा डाला ॥ २८४ ॥

चउपाई।

पहिलइँ भएउ भाट सत-भाखी। पुनि बोला हीरामनि साखी ॥
राजहि भा निसचइ मन माना। बाँधा रतन छोरि कइ आना ॥
कुल पूछा चउहान कुलीना। रतन न बाँधइँ होइ मलीना ॥
हीरा दसन पान रँग पाके। विहँसत सबहिँ बीजु बर ताके ॥
मुँदरा स्रवन मइन सउँ चाँपे। राज-बइन उघरे सब झाँपे ॥
आना काटर एक तुखारू। कहा सो फेरइ भा असवारू ॥
फेरा तुरइ छतीसउ खूरी। सबहिँ सराहा सिंघल-पूरी ॥

दोहा।

कुअँर बतीसउ लक्खना सहस करा जस भानु।
कहा कसउटी कसिअइ कंचन बारह बानु ॥ २८५ ॥

पहिलइँ = पहले = प्रथमे। भएउ = बभूव = भया = हुआ। भाट = भट = ख्याति करने-वाला। सत-भाखी = सत्य-भाषी = सच बोलने-वाला। पुनि = पुनः = फिर। बोला = बोलइ (वदति) का भूत-काल, पुंलिङ्ग, प्रथम-पुरुष, एक-वचन। हीरामनि = हीरामणि (शुक)। साखी = साक्षी = गवाह। राजहि = राज्ञः = राजा को। भा = बभूव = भया = हुआ। निसचइ = निश्चय = विश्वास। माना = मानइ (मन्यते) का

भूत-काल, पुंलिङ्ग, प्रथम-पुरुष, एक-वचन । बाँधा = बाँधा हुआ = बद्ध । रतन = रत्न = रत्न-सेन । छोरि कइ = छोडयित्वा = छोड कर । आना = आनइ (आनयति) का भूत-काल, पुंलिङ्ग, प्रथम-पुरुष, एक-वचन । कुल = वंश । पूछा = पूछइ (पृच्छति) का भूत-काल, पुंलिङ्ग, प्रथम-पुरुष, एक-वचन । चउहान = चहुआन = चतुःस्थान् = अग्नि से पैदा हुए चार चत्रिय वंशों में से एक प्रसिद्ध चत्रिय वंश । कुलीना = कुलीन = प्रतिष्ठित । बाँधइँ = बाँधने से = बन्धनेन । होइ = भवति = होता है । मलीना = मलिन = मैला । हीरा = हीर = हीरक (रत्न) । दसन = दशन = दाँत । पान = पर्ण । रँग = रङ्ग = रंग । पाके = पक्व = पके । बिहँसत = विहसन् = बिहँसते । सबहिँ = सर्वै = सबों ने । बीजु = विद्युत् = बिजली । बर = वर = श्रेष्ठ । ताके = तर्क्य = जान पडे = अनुमान किए गए । मुँदरा = मुद्रा = गोरख-नाथी-पंथिओं का एक कान में पहरने का पदार्थ । स्रवन = श्रवण = कान । मदन = मदन = मोम । सउँ = से । चाँपे = चापित = दबाए हुए । राज-बइन = राज-वचन = राजा की बोल । उघरे = उद्घटित = खुले । सब = सर्व । झाँपे = झम्पित = ढँपे हुए = बंद किए हुए = छिपाए हुए । आना = आनइ (आनयति) का भूत-काल, पुंलिङ्ग, प्रथम-पुरुष, एक-वचन । काटर = कर्त्तक = कट्टर = काटने-वाला । तुखारू = तीव्र तुरङ्ग = तीखा घोडा । कहा = अकथयत् । सो = सः = वह । फेरइ = फेरे = भ्रामयेत् । असवारू = अश्ववार = सवार । फेरा = फेरइ (भ्रामयति) का भूत-काल, पुंलिङ्ग, प्रथम-पुरुष, एक-वचन । तुरइ = तुरग = घोडा । छतीसउ = षट्‌त्रिंशदपि = छत्तीसो । खूरी = खुरविन्यास = पैरों की चाल । सराहा = सराहइ (श्लाघते) का भूत-काल, पुंलिङ्ग, प्रथम-पुरुष, एक-वचन । सिंघल-पूरी = सिंहल-पुरी = सिंहल-पुर के रहने-वाले ॥

कुअँर = कुमार = राज-कुमार । बतीसउ = बत्तीसो = द्वात्रिंशदपि । लक्खना = लक्षण । सहस = सहस्र = हजार । करा = कला = किरण = कर । जस = यथा = जैसे । भानु = सूर्य । कहा = किमु = क्या । कसउटी = कषवटी = कसौटी = सोना परीक्षा करने का एक विशेष पत्थर का टुकडा । कसिअइ = कसिए = कष्येत । कंचन = काञ्चन = सुवर्ण = सोना । बारह = द्वादश । बानु = वर्ण ॥

पहले भाट सच बोलने-वाला हुआ फिर हीरामणि ने (भी) गवाही में (वही बात) कही । (भाट और सुग्गे की एक ही बात होने से) राजा (गन्धर्व-सेन) को निश्चय हो गया (और यह राजा अच्छे वंश का है यह बात) मन ने मान ली ।

बाँधे हुए रत्न-सेन को छोड कर (लोग राजा गन्धर्व-सेन के पास) ले आए। (राजा गन्धर्व-सेन ने) कुल पूछा (और पूछने पर मालूम हुआ कि) प्रतिष्ठित चौहान है, (कवि कहता है कि) रत्न बाँधने से मैला नहीँ होता, अर्थात् रत्न जब तक बाँधा रहेगा तब तक छिपा रहेगा खुलने पर उस की कान्ति से झट लोग समझ लेंगे कि यह बढिआँ जवाहिर है। हीरा ऐसे दाँत पान के रँग से पके हुए हैँ, अर्थात् पान के रंग से सुशोभित हैँ, विहँसने पर सभी ने देखा कि (जानाँ) बिजली से भी बढ कर हैँ। कानाँ मेँ मोम से मुद्रा चपकाए हुए हैँ, अर्थात् कान फाड के मुद्रा नहीँ पहनाई हुई है किन्तु मोम से नकली मुद्रा चिपकाई हुई है, राजा की जितनी बातेँ ढँपी हुई थीँ सब खुल गईँ। (राजा गन्धर्व-सेन की आज्ञा से लोग) एक कट्टर (और बडे) तेज घोडे को ले आए। (राजा गन्धर्व-सेन ने अपने प्रधान से कहा कि कहो) यह (योगी) घोडे को फेरे। (इस बात के सुनते ही राजा रत्न सेन उस घोडे पर) सवार हुआ। (राजा रत्न-सेन ने) उस घोडे को छत्तीसो चाल से फेरा, (उस फेरने को देख कर) सब सिंहलपुर के रहने-वाले वाह वाह करने लगे॥

(ध्यान कर देखने से प्रसिद्ध हो गया कि) यह बत्तीसो लक्षणाँ से युत राज-कुमार है, जैसे हजार किरण-वाला सूर्य। (लोग कहने लगे कि) बारह वर्ण-वाले सोने को क्या कसौटी पर कसना (वह तो आप चमका करता है)॥

कथा है कि वसिष्ठ ऋषि के यज्ञ से पृथ्वी की रक्षा के लिये यज्ञ की अग्नि में से चार प्रकार के क्षत्रिय उत्पन्न हुए।

चौहान १। प्रमार २। चालुक्य ३। परिहार ४। (नागरी-प्रचारिणी सभा सीरिज़ नं० ४—८ के रासोसार का ६—८ पृ० देखो)।

घोडे को बारह समय पर निपुण सवार कोडे से एक वार धीरे, दो वार कुछ जोर और तीन वार बडे जोर से बारह स्थानाँ मेँ मारते हैँ। इस तरह से घोडे के फेरने मेँ छत्तिस भेद होते हैँ इन के जाननेवाला चतुर सवार कहाता है।

शिशुपालवध महाकाव्य—पंचमसर्ग के दशवेँ श्लोक की टीका मेँ मल्लिनाथ ने लिखा है कि—

"अत्र कशाः कशाघातास्तासां त्रयमुत्तममध्यमाधमेषु यथा संख्यंमृदुसमनिष्ठुर सकृद्द्विचिकरणरूपं त्रितयं तस्य विचारः। एतेषु निमित्तेष्वश्वैर्वं ताड्य इति विमर्षः तद्वता तज्ज्ञेन।

यथाह भोजः ।

मृदुनैकेन घातेन दण्डकालेषु ताडयेत् ।
तीक्ष्णं मध्यं पुनर्द्वाभ्यां जघन्यं निष्ठुरैस्त्रिभिः ॥
उपवेशेऽथ निद्रायां स्खलिते दुष्टचेष्टिते ।
बडवालोकनौत्सुक्ये बहुगर्वितह्रेषिते ॥
सन्त्रासे च दुरुत्थाने विमार्गगमने भये ।
शिक्षात्यागस्य समये सञ्जाते चित्तविभ्रमे ॥
दण्डः प्रयोज्यो वाहानां कालेषु द्वादशस्वपि ।
ग्रीवायां भीतमाहन्यात् त्रस्तं चैव च वाजिनम् ॥
विभ्रान्तचित्तमधरे त्यक्तशिक्षं च ताडयेत् ।
प्रह्रेषितं स्कन्धबाह्वोर्वडवालोकिनं तथा ॥
उपवेशे च निद्रायां कटिदेशे च ताडयेत् ।
दुश्चेष्टितं मुखे हन्यादुन्मार्गप्रस्थितं तथा ॥
जघने स्खलितं हन्यान्नेत्रमार्गे दुरुत्थितम् ।
यः कुष्ठप्रकृतिर्वाजी तं सर्वत्रैव ताडयेत् ॥"

उसी जगह "पुला नाम प्लुताद्यनेकापरनामा हयानां गतिविशेषः । तदुक्तं हयलीलावत्याम् ।

प्लुतां प्लवङ्गतिमाहुर्याधारा पुलनाभिधा ।
पुनरेनां रखोपान्तां पुलामित्याह देशिकः ॥" यह भी लिखा है ।

जयादित्य के अश्ववैद्य की टीका में शुक का वचन है—

गतयः षड्विधा धाराः स्कन्दितं रेचितं प्लुतम् ।
धौरीतकं वल्गितं च तासां लक्ष्म पृथक् पृथक् ॥

इन छओं गतिओं में अल्प, मध्य, और अधिक वेग करने से अठारह भेद होते हैं । फिर अठारह में सुख से पैर रखता है या दुःख से ये दो दो भेद से सब गति छत्तीस तरह की हो जाती हैं । जयादित्य का टीकासहित अश्ववैद्य बंगाल की एशिआटिक सोसाइटी में छपा है ॥

मनुष्य के बत्तीसो लक्षणों के लिये इस ग्रन्थ का ७६–७७ पृ० देखो ।

बारह वर्ण-वाले सोने के लिये इस ग्रन्थ का १५१ पृ० देखो ॥ २८५ ॥

चउपाई ।

देखि सुरुज बर कवँल सँजोगू। असतु असतु बोला सब लोगू ॥
मिला सो बंस अंस उँजिआरा। भा बरोक अउ तिलक सँवारा ॥
अनिरुध कहँ जो लिखी जइमारा। को मेटइ बानासुर हारा ॥
आजु बरी अनिरुध कहँ ऊखा। देओ अनंद दइति सिर दूखा ॥
सरग सूर भुइँ सरवर केवा। बन-खँड भवँर भएउ रसलेवा ॥
पछिउँ क बार पुरुब कइ बारी। लिखी जो जोरी होइ न निनारी ॥
मानुस साज लाख पइ साजा। साजा बिधि सोई पइ बाजा ॥

दोहा ।

गए जो बाजन बाजत जेहि मारन रन माँह ।
फिरि बाजे ते बाजे मंगलचार उनाँह ॥ २८६ ॥

इति सूरी-खंड ॥ २५ ॥

देखि = दृष्ट्वा = देख कर । सुरुज = सूर्य । बर = वर = श्रेष्ठ = विवाह योग्य पुरुष। कवँल = कमल । सँजोगू = संयोग्य = लायक । असतु = अस्तु । बोला = बोलइ (वदति) का भूत-काल, पुंलिङ्ग, प्रथम-पुरुष, एक-वचन । सब = सर्व । लोगू = लोग = लोक = प्राणी । मिला = मिलइ (मिलति) का भूत-काल, पुंलिङ्ग, प्रथम-पुरुष, एक-वचन । सो = वह = सः । बंस = वंश । अंस = अंश = अवतार । उँजिआरा = उज्ज्वल । भा = बभूव = भया = हुआ । बरोक = वर परीक्षा = बरेखी । अउ = अपि = और । तिलक = टीका । सँवारा = सँवारइ (संमार्जयति) का भूत-काल, पुंलिङ्ग, प्रथम-पुरुष, एक-वचन । अनिरुध = अनिरुद्ध = कृष्ण का पोता प्रद्युम्न का बेटा । कहँ = को । जो = यत् । लिखी = लिखई (लिखति) का भूत-काल, स्त्रीलिङ्ग, प्रथम-पुरुष, एक-वचन । जइमारा = जयमाला = विजय-माला । को = कः = कौन । मेटइ = मेटे = मृदमेतु । बानासुर = बाणासुर = बलि का बेटा । हारा = हारइ (हारयति) का भूत-काल, पुंलिङ्ग, प्रथम-पुरुष, एक-वचन । आजु = आज = अद्य । बरी = बरइ (वृणोति) का भूत-काल, स्त्रीलिङ्ग, प्रथम-पुरुष, एक-वचन । ऊखा = ऊषा = बाणासुर की बेटी ।

दश्रो = देव = देवता । अनंद = आनन्द = खुशी । दइति = दैत्य = दिति से उत्पन्न । सिर = शिर । दूखा = दूखइ (दुष्यति) का भूत-काल, पुंलिङ्ग, प्रथम पुरुष, एक-वचन। सरग = स्वर्ग = आकाश । सूर = सूर्य । भुइँ = भूमि = पृथ्वी । सरवर = सरोवर = उत्तम तडाग = अच्छा पोखरा = अच्छा तालाव । केवा = कमल । बन-खँड = वन-खण्ड = वन-भाग । भवँर = भ्रमर = भौँरा । भण्उ = बभूव = हुआ = भया । रस-लेवा = रस लेने-वाला = रसग्राहक = रसलः । पछिउँ = पश्चिम = पच्छिम । क = का । बार = बाल = बालक = वर । पुरुब = पूर्व = पूरब । कइ = की । बारी = बालिका = लडकी । जोरी = जोडी = युग = युग्म । होइ = भवति = होती है । निनारी = अलग-निर्नला । मानुस = मानुष = मनुष्य । साज = सज्जन = तयारी । लाख = लच । पइ = अपि = निश्चय कर । साजा = साजइ (सज्जते) का भूत-काल, पुंलिङ्ग, प्रथम-पुरुष, एक-वचन । बिधि = विधि = ब्रह्मा । सोई = स एव = वही । बाजा = बाजइ (वाद्यते) का भूत-काल, पुंलिङ्ग, प्रथम-पुरुष, एक-वचन ॥

गए = अगुः । बाजन = वादन = बाजा । बाजत = बजते = वदन् । जेँहि = यस्य = जिसे मारन = मारणार्थ = मारने के लिये । रन = रण = सङ्ग्राम । माँह = मँह = मध्ये = मेँ । फिरि = फिर कर = भ्रमित्वा = घूम कर । बाजे = बाजइ (वाद्यते) का भूत-काल, पुंलिङ्ग, प्रथम-पुरुष, बहु-वचन । ते = वे । बाजे = बाजन = वादन । मंगलचार = मङ्गलाचार = मङ्गल की रीति । उनाँह = उनद्ध = संनद्ध = संबन्ध ॥

कमल (पद्मावती) के लायक (रत्न-सेन) सूर्य वर को देख कर सब लोग 'एवमस्तु' 'एवमस्तु' अर्थात् 'यह योग्य वर है' 'यह योग्य वर है' ऐसा बोलने लगे । (कवि कहता है कि इस प्रकार से) वह उज्ज्वल वंश का अंश मिला, (फिर) बरच्छा हुआ और (विवाह के लिये) तिलक रचा गया । अनिरुद्ध को जो (ब्रह्मा ने ऊषा की) जय-माला लिखी थी उस को कौन मिटावे, (अन्त में) वाणासुर हार ही गया । आज ऊषा ने अनिरुद्ध को वरा, देवताओँ मेँ आनन्द हुआ, दैत्योँ का शिर दुखने लगा, अर्थात् आज पद्मावती ने रत्न-सेन को वरा, पद्मावती के पच के लोग आनन्दित हुए और विरोधिओँ का शिर दुखने लगा । (कवि कहता है कि देखो) स्वर्ग मेँ सूर्य रहता है, पृथ्वी पर सरोवर मेँ कमल रहता है (जिस से कमल खिल उठता है), और वनविभाग से भौँरा आ कर (उस कमल का) रस लेने वाला हुआ, अर्थात् सिंहल की रहने-वाली पद्मावती हीरामणि शुक सूर्य से खिल उठी और समुद्र पार

चित्तौरगढ-रूप दुर्गम वन से रत्न-सेन भौंरा आ कर उस का रस लेने-वाला ऊआ। पश्चिम का वर और पूर्व की कन्या (इन दोनों की) जोडी जो (ब्रह्मा ने) लिखी वह अलग नहीँ हो सकती है। मनुष्य निश्चय कर लाखों तयारी करता है, पर ब्रह्मा ने जो रची है वह (बात) होती है ॥

जो बजते ऊए बाजे रण में जिस के मारने के लिये गए थे वे ही फिर (उसी के) विवाह-संबन्ध के मङ्गलचार में बजने लगे, अर्थात् दैवी गति जानी नहीँ जाती कि क्या होगी। किसी कवि ने सच लिखा है कि—

गिरौ कलापी गगने पयोदा लचान्तरेऽर्कस्य जलेषु पद्माः।
इन्दुर्दिवस्थे कुमुदस्य बन्धुर्यो यस्य मित्रं न हि तस्य दूरे ॥

बरोक के लिये इस ग्रन्थ का ८३ पृ० देखो।

अनिरुद्ध, ऊषा और बाणासुर के लिये इस ग्रन्थ का ४४३-४४४ पृ० देखो।

वामनपुराण के ९२ अध्याय में लिखा है कि राजा बलि के रसातल जाने पर उस का पुत्र बाणासुर पृथ्वी में शोणितपुर बनवा कर राज करने लगा ॥ २८६ ॥

इति स्हरी-खण्डं नाम पञ्चविंश-खण्डं समाप्तम् ॥ २५ ॥

208. 1. Ia *māreu*, U *marā na gājā*. 2. K *jabahi agani apunai sira*. Ia U *aurah kahā* (U *kā*) *bujhāwai jarai* (U *jarā* with *parā* in the preceding half verse). 4. Ia K *sãga* for *saba*. 6. U *phaniga* for *patãga*. Is *jama gahā*, U *jama līnha*. 8. Ia *ajahū̃*, Ic *abahū̃* U *ajahū̃ kãpinī mō hiai*, K *abahū̃ marau̇ na cēta tanu*. Is *na pāwaū̃ sā̃sa*.

209. 2. Ib *hitū* for *hateu*. K *hōta*. 4. Iac *mohi tanu āgi lāi kai hōrī*. Is *mohi jia*. 5. Ia *asa jāni*. 6. Is *līnha āhara*, so all except Ib (*ōhara*), and K *kehi gati bhau*. 7. Ic *sara sāji*. U *caḍhi aba citai jaraū̃ jyõ sātī*. 9. Ia U *aba yaha hōri ghāli tanu*.

210. 1. Is *gagana* for *kakanū* (ققنوس). Is U *sara baiṭhi*, Id *sara caḍhi baiṭhi jarai*. 4. Id *tehi kē āgi*. 5. Is *abahū̃......tē*. U *aba dēkhahu tasa cinagi chūṭai*. 7. U *hai kōū jō rākhi*. K *hai kōi unha rākhi*. 9. Ics U *birahī*.

211. 1. Ics U *rahā rakhawārī*. 2. Icds *tahā̃ bhā*. Ib *eka hā̃kā*, U *soi hā̃kā*. 4. *jāi kahā tinha tahā̃ sā̃dēsū*. 5. Icd *jōgī ēka*. 6. Iad *jo rātē*, U *so lāgeu ūhā̃*. Ic *nisari* for *nikasi*. 7. Ia *jari uṭhatahi*. Ib *bajara āgi tehi jarai na bhāgā*. Ic *jari uṭhā to bhāga*. 9. Ia *kanaka pahāra jarā rāwata*, Ib *bhaē* (or *ghanē*) *pahāra jarā rāwaṭa*. Is *kanai pahāra jarata hai*. U *kanaka pahāra jarata hai*. K *kanaka pahāra hōta hai rāwaṭa*. K² *tīnau lōka jarata hai*, K³ *ga pahāraē saba hōta hai*. Others as in text.

212. 2. Iacds K *ruṇḍa*. The *muṇḍa* of Ib and U makes the best sense. 6. Ia *kapi kai rūpa so adhika sohāwā*.

213. 2. Ic K *paraū̃ maraū̃*, Is *paraū̃ jaraū̃*, U *paraū̃ ēkahi bārā*. Ic *nisari parāna jāi*. 9. Ia *jaū̃ mahēsa nahi āwata*, Is *jaū̃ mahēsa nahi amia bujhāwata*. K *jau mahēsa nahi āi bujhāwata*, K² *jau na mahēsa bujhāwata*, K³ *jau na mahēsa nahī amia bujhāwata sakala jagata hoi lāgi*.

214. 1. Is K *upajā*. 4. Ia UK *sata bā̃ta*. 5. Ia *sunī so cā̃da jāi siu lōkā*. Ic *sunā so sabada*. 9. UK *mohi taji ohi jaū̃ sawā̃rahu*.

215. U *bhalehi rūpa*. Is *āchari tātā*. 6. Ia *jiu bali dīnhā*, । *sira utāri neochāori kīnhā*; U *jiu maĩ wāraū̃*. Ib *sīsa utāri nichā?*, U *sīsa kāṭi neochāori sāraū̃*. K² K³ *sira utāri nevachāori sāraū̃*. 7. Ias *dēū̃ baḍhāī*.

216. 2. All N give *parimala*. Ia has *prēmala prēma rahai tehi chapā*. Other P. are doubtful. They may be read as *parabala*. 3. Is *kasata*. 4. *ḍabhakahī*, so Ias U. Ib *ṭapakahī*, Ic *dēkhahī*, Id *baha-kai*, K *ḍahaḍaha*. 5. Ia *yaha ohi lāgi janama kai sījhā*. Ids U *ohi lāgi janama puni* (Is *tō*, U *taĩ*) *sījhā*. K *ohi lāgi tribēnī sījhā*. 7. Ib has *ehu* for *ēhū̃*, and inserts *tumha* after *tasa*. Ia U *siu* for *tasa*. Id *aba ēhū kahā̃ mayā*. 8 Ib has *hatiā du eka caḍhāehu māthaĩ, mahā dukha aparādhu*. Ids *abahū̃* for *ajahū̃*. Ic transfers *kā̃dhaĩ* to second half line and has *kā̃dhaĩ tohi aparādhu*. 9. The first half runs as follows in the varions copies :—

Ia	*tīsari ēhū lēhu tumha*.
Ibd	*tīsara ēhu laihu kai māthaĩ*.
Ic	*tīsara bhūlahu aba* (sic).
Is	*tīsari lēhu ēhu kai kā̃dhaĩ*.
U	*tīsara yahau lēhu sira*.
K	*tīsara hoi lei aba*.
K²	*tisarī ihau lēhu māthē*.
K³	*tisarī ihau lēhu kī māthē*. We have followed Ibd.

For secod half, Ia has *jau lāwai kai*, Ib *kai purawahu ehi sādhu*, U *jaure lewai kai sādhu*.

217. 1. Ib *lēkhā*, Is U *rākhā*, for *lākhā*. 5. Ia *basaha* for *baila*. Ib *kaha rājai sata*. Ias *girijā-pati sō āhi*. Ic *girijā-suta tapa āhi*, U *yaha* for *sata*. K *kākara suta pati āha mahēsū*. 6. Ia U *jō jiu cāha rahai soi nārī*, । *taji mahēsa kita hōta bhakhārī*. ॥ 7. Ia substitutes 6 for this, thus,—*cinhai sō jo karai asa khōjā* । *para kāyā para dēsa sājōgā* ॥ Ids U *jabahī bhā*. U *phērā* for *mērā*. 9. Is *cēlā siddha*. Ia transposes this dōhā with No. 218.

218. 2. Ias *jaũ pai asa phā̃da pēma kē ghālā,* U *jinha asa khēla prēma kai ghālā.* 4. Ia second half *dhara nahī̃ mū̃ta ratana tasa rōā.* 6. Ia *Jarai pahāra nīra taī̃ ā̃ṭī.* 7. Ia *jarai nīra tasa marai bihūnā* । *parabata jarai hōi jasa cūnū.* ॥ 8 Ia *jō jō sunai so rōai dhara nahi rakata kai ā̃su* । U *tasa rōai jasa mēgha ghana,* K[2] *tasa rōai jō jārai jiu* । *garai rakata au mā̃su.* K[3] *tasa roai au khōai* ...

219. Ib *tū̃ rōā.* K *bhā parasana dukha dārua.* 4. Ic *taī̃.* 5. Iac *bāta sunahu upadēsī.* K[2] *kahaū̃ hāta aha haũ upadēsī.* K[3] *kahaũ hāta suna hō upadēsī.*

220. 1. Iak *dēkhu dahū̃ kā kara chāya.* U *nirakhi.* 3. Ia *nau paurī kahā̃ lāgu kewārā* K *ḍiṭhiārā* Id *diwasahi phirahī̃.* Is U *pai tahā̃ phirahī̃.* 5. Ia *jasa kari bhēda caḍhai hai cā̃ṭi.* UK *caḍhai gura cā̃ṭī.* 6. Iak *gaḍha tara surā̃ga kuṇḍa tehi mā̃hā̃.* So Is U but *kuṇḍa augāhā.* Ia K *tahawā̃ pantha agama augāhā* U *jahā̃ na wāra pāra nahi thāhā.* 8. Ids have *dhasi marai* for *dhasai.* Ia *jasa marajiā samūda māha ḍhū̃ḍhi uṭhai lei sīpu.* 9. Ia *khōji lēhu caḍhi saraga saũ tū caḍhu, &c.* K[2] *ḍhū̃ḍhi lēi sō saraga dvārī tau caḍhasī* ... K[3] *ḍhū̃ḍhi lēi jō saraga dvāri au caḍhai....*

221. 2. Ia *jāe so tahā̃ sā̃sa mana sā̃dhē* । ...... *kānha mana, bā̃dhē.* Ib *tahā̃ so jāe.* Ic *jāe sōijō asa mana.* Ia K insert after No. 2 the following:

gau patāra kūlī puni nāthā । *apuruba kawāla āu taba hā̃tha* ॥

3. Is *tū̃ paru nātha.* Ia *jaũ pai karasi āpu kahā̃ nāsā* ॥ Is *marahu āhi.* U *karahu* for *marahu.* 4 Ia *karu bātā.* 5. Ias *kahaba* for *kahata.* Is *au tū̃ āhi nāhī̃ saba.* U *āpu hai sōī* 6. Is U *muai* for *marai.* Ia *puni kahā̃.* Is U *puni kata mīcu marai kō mārā.* 7. Ia K om. this line, see above. U *āpuhi gurū suā yaha cēlā.* 9 Ia *āpuhi āpu jo karasi taī̃.* K[2] *āpuhi āpu karai jo au dūsara na kōi.* K[3] *āpuhi āpu karai yaha kahā̃ sō dūsaru kōi.*

222. 2. K *chā̃ḍi manṭra.. jōginha.* 3. Ia K *saba gaḍha chē̃ka gaī taji mā̃ḍhī.* Is *gaī or kīnha.* 4. Ia *khara-bharā* for *khara-pharā.* 6. Ib *rājā saũ bhai jāe pukārā.* 7. Icd *kaunu kahā̃ kahā̃.* 8. Ia K *asa ko,* Ib *kō so.* Ic U *ko bhikhārī asa.* 9. Ic *bēgi* for *jāi.* Ia *paṭhahu basīṭha,* K[2] *dai jāhu basīṭha,* K[3] *dai bhē̃ji basīṭha.*

223. 1. U *basīṭha so āi.* 2. Ic *dūra hoi mēlahu.* Is *yaha gaḍha chā̃ḍi.* 5. Ia *lēhu jita cāhahu.* K *phirahu besāhi lēi jo cāhahu.* 6. U *bhuguti dēhī̃.* 7. Ia *ihā̃ dēo asa gaē johārī* । *tumha jōgī kehi mānahu bhikhārī* (sic). K[2] *ihā̃ deotā asa gaē johārī* । *tumha patagga kō ahahu bhikhārī.* K[3] *ihā̃ deotā asa gaē johārī* । *tumha patagga kā ahahu bhikhārī.*

224. 1. Is U *anu haũ bhikhi jo.* 2. Ib *ghara bārī.* 4. Is UK *asa āhi na dūjā.* 7. U *yaha prīti nihōrā.* 8. U *bāra āwahī̃ jehi, etc.* 9. Ic *āsa nahī̃.* U *āsana gahē̃.* K has an altogether different and very corrupt dōhā. K[2] and K[3] *ḍiḍha ātana*

225. 1. K. *jau sā̃ga pīsā.* 2. U *jōga jehi hōī.* 5. Ia *saba bajara,* Id *puni oajara.* 8. Ib *jōgata kī,* UK *jōgati.* 9. Ia *sundara bara nahi rāja.* Ib *sundari cāhi.* K[2] *sundari parī,* K[3] *sundari jāi.*

226. 2. U *prēma sādhi nā kōū sādhai.* 4. Ic *hasati baḍa sāthī.* Id *hamaraī sata gurū hai sāthī.* 6. The MS. are as follows :—

Ia *kurakuṭi hai jō pāihi bārū* । *tehi uṭhāi kai karai pahārū* ॥
UK *kurakuṭi rahai jo pāū tarērī* । *parai* (K *uṭai*) *naina uṭhi sakai na hērī* ॥
Ib *jō gaḍha garaba karahī tē kīē* । *mandira uṭhai ḍahai bhai nāyē* ॥
Icd *gaḍha kai garaba khē̃ha mili kīē* । *mandira uṭhai ḍahai bhai nayē* ॥
Is *jo guru ē gaḍha jāwā̃ta bhaē* । *jo gaḍha garaba karahi tē gaē* ॥
K[2] *jau re garuē gaḍha jawatu bhaē* । *jau gaḍha garaba karahī tau gaē* ॥
K[3] *mandila ḍhāhi uṭhāwai naē* । *gaḍha kara garaba kheha mili gaē* ॥

We have followed Icd. 7. UK *jā kē gaḍai na nisarai sōī* । *hā̃sai jo garaba marai sō rōī* ॥

227. 2. *jōgihi kahā̃ rākhē.* 3. Ic *kita hōū.* 4. *pati,* so Iad UK. Ib *bata,* Ic ? *tapa,* Is *mati.* 7. Ia *jō jōgī āē sō khēlē.* Ic *jōgī āē so asahī khēlē.* K *jōgī hōihi jāihi khēlē.*

228. 3. Ib UK insert before 3 *paṅkha na mō kahā̃ dīnha gosāī̃* । *paṅkha hōta tau jātiũ ḍāī* ॥ UK also omit 7, but Ib has it. 4. Ib *pā̃chaī sūā.* 9. Ia *na chua sakai sō,* Ib *na*

kōi chuai sō. Is *na kēhu gahai sō*. U *na jāi gahi*. K² *ākhara likhē pēma kē*. K³ *hātha achara nahi chui sakē*.

229. 1 Ia *kahehu*, Ic *kahau*. 2. Ia *kahehu*. Ic *kahau*. Is has *bali* throughout, so UK, P give no indication. 4 Ia *īsa tumha-hī*, Ib *īsa-hū̃ tumha*. Ib *īsa tumha mohi*. Is *aisa haũ tumha*. U *pahilaī-hī kōhū̃ bala dīnhā*. K *sō aba-hī tapasī bala*. K² *bhalehi aisa bala tumha kahā̃ dīnhā*. K³ *bhalehu tumhahu aisa bali dīnhā*.

230. 1. K *sō dukha-bāta likhaũ*. 2 Ia, *tana jō kara saba rakata*. 3 Some copies make this line the 5th. U *biraha bijāra jarai bana*. Is *tana jarata na jarai*. Ia substitutes *wā-saũ kahaũ dūkha kau nāmā̃* | *jā-saũ hōe duhū̃ juga kāmā̃*, and makes the line No. 5. 4. Ia *citā...hōi anacitā*. Ic *cintā......nintā*, V. *nitā ...mitā*. 5. Ia *kai bātā... hōi dukha tātā*. 6. K *tua* for *tumha*. Ia *rakata ke anka likhē bhai syāmā̃*. 7. Is *kāhū* for *kōī*. Ia *ata dukha*. 8. Is *aba tau maraũ*. 9 Ia *tehi sātha*.

231. 2. Ia *sūra* for *suruja*. 3. Ia *sā̃ga tahā̃*, Is *bhaũra tahā̃ basai hulāsū*. 5. Is *kā sukha bisarāmā*. 9. Ic *bhau*, Id *jyō̃* for *bhai*.

232. 1. Ia *āsa jala pāī*. 2. Id *na jāē*. Is *na jānahū*, U *kaṭhina jīu sō prītama kērā*. 3. U *bīcahī jānahu*, Iac *agama* for *bikhama*, Ia U *milana*. 4. Is *kā trāsā*. 5. Ia *tumha pū̃°*. Ic *jiu pū̃°*. U *pēma mada mātā*. 8. Is *bāna sara mārehu*. 9. Ia *dōsari bōli*, Ib *bāra jo bōlā*, Ic *dūjī bāra jō māra*. U *ēka bāra phiri bōlisa*.

For the whole of this set K has:—

Hīrāmani āwā tehi māhā | *jānahu pyāsē sītala chāhā* ||
Bhala tuha suā kīnha hai phērā | *kahā rajāesu prītama kērā* ||
Bāta o haṭa bica gagana pahārā | *hirdaā milā no hōi ninārā* ||
Aisa na tuha cita lāu bidēsī | *kahasi na tehi ka sā̃ dēsa sā̃dēsī* ||
Kā rānī pūchahu ohi bātā | *jani kai hōi viraha kai mātā* ||
Toharē darasana lāgi biyōgī | *ahai so mahādēo maṭha jōgī* ||
Tu basanta kai ihā̃ sidhāī | *ohi kā marama to jānu gosāī* ||
Dōsari bōla na bōlai lihai padumāwati nāu ||
Disiṭi bānā asa mārehu ghāela bhā tehi ṭhāo ||
So K² and K³ ||

233. 1. Is *bāna jana phū°* Ia *rudhira*, U, *jasa chūṭī*. 2. Is *nainahu*. 3. K. *sūruja udaī*. 4 Iac K, *banaspatī*. U *banipatī*. 5. Is *puhumī pūji bhaī*, U *bhūmi*. The second half varies. The reading given is that of Ib.

Ia *au saba tahā̃ jo rāta pakhērū* ||
Icd *autahī bana saba rāta pakhērū* ||
Is *au tahā̃ sō rāta pakhērū* (sic) ||
U *au rātē tahā̃ bahuta pakhērū* ||
K *rātē nirakhata sabai pakhērū* ||
K² *jahā̃ rā̃ga rāta bhae tahā̃ pakhērū* ||
K³ *au tahā̃ rahē so rāta pakhērū* ||

6. Ia, *jala kāyā*, Ic. *tehi kāyā*, Is. U. *sahi kāyā*. Is *mēgha rātau*. 7. Ia UK *saba bhījā*. Is *jahā̃ bhījā*. 8. Id *jahā̃ cakōra*, UK *cakōra au kōkilā*. 9. Ic *bhari rōai*.

234. 1. Ic. *sīsa parāō̃*. 2. Ia *tau jānu*, Icd *jasa jānu*. K has second half *dēo pūji puni ō rahā̃ āī*. 3. K *ēkahi bāra hōū nistārā*. 4. Ia *cāha ēka jo lāī*. 5. Is *gaḍha āgama*. U *gama āgama*, K *tahā̃* | *mana kara khēla agama kara jāhā̃*. 6. UK *kara bārā*. Iac K *au parai*. Id *jō parai*. 7 Ia *cāha*, Is *caḍhai*, for *cahai*. Ic *pāwai sā̃sa ki marai nisāsā*. 9. Ia U *nikasai*, K *nikarai*. Ia UK *kahā* for *kāha*.

235. 1. Ia *kai sandēsu chōḍi dahi pātī*; *dipa*, all P have دبّ, which Ib vocalises, *dibba*, Is has *dīvya*, UK have *dipa*. All printed editions translate *dibba* by *nihāī* or 'anvil.' Ia *jasa tātī*. 2 Icd *bandhē*, K *kanṭha jana lā°*. 3. Is *tasa nisarai pātī......kā wātī*, U *tasa nikasai tātī ...aura kō pātī*, K *sā̃ga nikasai pātī......kē wātī*. 4. Ia *yaha bātā*, Ids *mukha*.

bātā. Ic *āsu bhaeu*, Id *āsū bhā*. 5. *gērā*, so Is. All P may be either *gērā* or *kērā*, U has *mērē* K *kērā*. Ic *dēkhi jo kanṭha lāgi jari gērā* (or *kērā*). U *dēkhahu kanṭha lāgi kai mērē* K *dēkhā kanṭha jasa lāgu su kera*. In second half, Is *kā ghēra*, U *kē*, K *kai*. 6. Iac *jari jari biraha hāḍa bhai cūnā*. Is *mānusa kā rakata*, Ia UK *māsa kā rakata*. 7. Id *tarapata* for *tapata*, Ids U *dēi na pārī*. 8. UK *tohi kārana jōgī bhā*, Ia *kīnha āga dāhi*. 9. Ic *tumha*, Id *taī*. UK *bhuguti dēsi na tāhi*. K² *bāta na puchē tāhi* K³ *bāta na pūchasi tāhi*.

236. 1. Ia *kahau*, K *kahau suā tō sō nija bātā*, Ia *so āju...hoi rātā*, so U *hoi ratā*. Id *cāhaū āju*. K *wahi rāta*. 2. Ia *jānai sōi*, U *jānai marama*. 3. Iacd *ajahū*. Is K *nā jahu*, and so throughout the following lines, U *ajahū na* (*prīti*), and so throughout the following lines. 5. Ia *ajahū jiai*. 6. Is *hia mahā kai ḍara*. 8. Ia *rahaba*. K *tehi kā kahi thira rahanā*. Id *jō hia*, U *jō jehi*. 9. Ias *jahā wahā sunahī lēhi*, Ic *jahawā sunai*. Id *jhūṭhi sunahi*. K *jahā nāū sunai*. We have adopted the text of Ib U.

237. 2. Ia *lāgu sohāgā*. Iab *hōi to lāgā*, Is *hoi sālāgā*. 3. Ia *siu manḍapa*. Ic *manḍapa tōrī*, U *jōri gaiū maḍha manḍapa hōrī*, K *gai jōgī maḍha manḍapa hōrī*. *Tahawāi* &c., so Ibds. Ia *tahāwahā khana gāṭhī taī jōrī*. Ic *tahawā kasa na gāṭhi*, U *tahā taī naina gāṭhi nahi jōrī*, K *tahawā naina gāṭhi tuha jōrī*. 4. Ic *tu bisābhāri so dēkhata nainā*. Ia *mukha āu na bainā* 5. Ia *maku khana jāgu dēū*. 6. Ib U have for second half line *kaisai bhuguti parāpati hōī*. 7. Ia *rabi hoi caḍhai*, K *sasi mai caḍheū*. U *āwahu pāsā*. 8. Iab *taba tū*. Ics *rāma sīa*. 9. Ia *kachu kahaū*, Ia K *aba milaū*, U *aba milai*.

238. 1. Ic U *jō hō sūra*, Ias UK *caḍhi dhāvahu...hōhu.. pāwahu*. 2. Ia *tū bhikhāri*. Ib *tū rē jōga kō āha akēla*. K *tū jōgī kā āha*. 3. *campāwati*, so Ib U Ias K *sapanāwat*, Icd *sampāwati*. 4. *sudai baccha*, so I as U Ibd سدی بچهه Ic, سدابچهه (without any points, K *rudumacha* (sic). Id *kanakapūra*, Is *kaṅkanapura*, UK *gagana upari*. 6. *gandhāwati*, so Ib. Ia, *kumudāwati*, Icd K, *manōhara*, Is *kaḍāwati*, U *kundāwati*. 7. *sara sura*, so all except Is *śrīdhara*, U *sīdhara*, K *siradhara*. Icd *ga bādhā*. 9. Iad *jiu nāsa*, UK *karai jo āpuhi nāsa*. K² and K³ *prathama karai apanāsa*.

239. 1. Ia *haū puni aisī tō saū rāti*. Cf below, V. 8. 2. Ia *nibāhasi*, Ic *yaha jaū prīti......kētakī kāṭā*. 5. Id *pīwi na pāni*. Is U *piai, na pāni*, R *piahi*. 6. Is *jimi jōrī*. 7. Ia UK *dala māhā*, Is *jala māhā*. 8. The readings vary as follows :—

Ia *hamahū ahaū asi tō saū*	*sakasi to ōra nibāhu* ।
Ib *hamahū aisi haū tō saū*	*utara likhā jasa āhu* ।
Ic *hamahū aisi haū tō saū*	*sakasi to ōra nibāhu* ।
Id *hamahū aisi tohi rātī*	*sakasi to prīti nibāhu* ।
Is *ahaū aisē jaū rātē*	*sakasi to prīti nibāhu* ।
U *jasa haū sası tō saū kahaū*	*sakahu to prīti nibāhu* ।
K *hau asi dēkhahu tau sō* (sic)	*sakahu to ōra nibāhu*
K² *haū aisī tohi rātī*	*ūtara likhā nibāhu*.
K³ *haū aisī haū tōhi kō*	*sakahu to prīti nibāhu*.

We have followed the majority.

9. U *rāhu bēdhi jaū pārathē*.

240. 1. Ia *aisa tapa*, U *baiṭhi tapa*. Ic *haū asa maī gayā bimōhī* (sic). Id U *mauna gāwāē*. Is *jauna lawāē*, Ias U *nirajīu jīu dayo* (Ias *disa*) *ōhī*. 3. Ia *sukhana*, Is *sukhanā*, Icd *sukhamā*. 4. Iab *gāherāi puni*. 9. Iab *jhāri kai*.

241. 1. There are wide discrepancies in the first half of this verse as follows :—

Ia *murchita āsa pāsa jo pāwā* ।
Ibc *mua jehi āsa pāsa so pāwā* ।
Id *mari jahā āsa pāsa so pāwā* ।
Is *suā ahā jehi āsa so pāwā* । (the reading adopted).
U *suā ju āi hātha tani lāwā* ।
K *suā jo āi hātha tana lāwā* ।

For *bahurī*, Ic *līnhesi*, Is *phiri kai*, K *palaṭā sā̃sa āsa jiu āwā*. K² *phirī suāsa pē̃ṭa jiu āwā*. K³ *bahura suāsa pē̃ṭa jiu lāwā*.

2. Ibs *dēkhesi jāgi suā hai ṭhāḍhā* । *gurū ka bacana dēkhu* (Is *sunē̃*) *mukha kāḍhā* ।

3. Here again there are wide discrepancies. Ib gives two alternative readings (Ib 1 and Ib 2) for this and the next line.

Ia *guru kara bacana sarō̃ dui mēlā* ।
Ib K¹ *gurū sabada dui sarawana mēlā* ।
Ibs K² *sabada bōli kai sarō̃* (Is *sravana*) *ughēlā* ।
Ic *guru kā sabada sarō̃ dui mēlā* ।
Id *sabada ēka jo sunahi akēlā* ।
U *guru kā bacana srawana lae mēlā* ।

For the second half, Ibl and U have *kīnhi so disiṭi bēgi calu cēlā* ॥

4. Ia *bhai kēwā*. Ibl *hai bīca*. Ib2 Is and K² omit this verse, and substitute the following, which is also given as an alternative reading by Icd. All these (except Ic) agree in placing this substituted verse at the end of the set of seven *caupāīs*.

Ib2 अउ दरसन कहँ नइन पसारी । दरसन चाहउँ रूप तुम्हारी ॥

IcsK² अउ अस कह हउँ नइन पसारी । &c.

Id अउ अस कहँ मइँ नइन पसारी । &c.

5. K *pauna sātha tō kahā̃ sā̃ga lāē*. Ic *disiṭī chipāī*, Is *bujhāī*.

7. The first two words are in all N. तबउडंत P all differ. They have

Ia تبارۆنت
Ib آد انت
Ic تب اونت

Id تب آونت. In all these و may also be read as ڈ. For the second half Ic UK have *pala mohā̃ āu*, Ia *bēgi calāu cahaũ*, Id *bēgi jo āu*, Is *pagu cali āu*.

8. Ia *sulacchanē̃*.

242. 1. Iac UK *suni padumāwati kai asi mayā* (Ia K *māyā*), Ia *nau kāyā*, K *nai kāyā* UK *paluhī̃* for *upanī*. 2. Ia *sōi saṅkhahi*, Icd. *asa jāgā*. 3. Iac *milai kahā̃*, Id *cā̃da kalaṅkahi dīnhī āsā*. Icd *sahasa kalā sūruja*. 4. Ia *pātī līnhi ūsa lai lāwā*, Ic *pātī lai kai*, Id *pātī lai lai*. Ic *jimi pāwā*. 5. Ib *aisa piāsā*, U *āsa nirāsā kou kehū kēra*, Ib *jō jehi gāra*, IdK *jō jhīkāra*, U *ujiyara sōi jāhi saũ hērā*, Ia *ohī disa hērā*. 6 Ia *sunatahī̃ kauna pauna sikha kīā*, Ids *pauna*, U *gauna pauna*, K *aba tō tahā̃ gauna bhai dīā*. 8. Id *hahī̃ basai*. 9. Ia *maĩ sō calaũ*, Ib *haũ tahā̃ dharaũ*, Is *hama tahā̃ calahī̃*. K² *haũ tahũ caḍhaũ lilāṭa*. K³ *hama cali āu lilāṭa*.

243. 2. Ia *tahā̃ pāyasa thāhā*, Ic *parā tahā̃*, Id *parā janu*, Is *pāī thāhā*, U *janu pāwai na thāhā*, K *jahā̃ pāi athāhā*. 3. Ib *prīti kō lāgū*, Icd U *prīti kara*, Ic *saũha dhasā na sūjē āgū*. 4. U *dhā̃si jasi sā̃sa na mārā*, K *līnha sā̃sa jasa sīdhanha mārā*. 5. Ic *tarai*. Ia *mā̃cha*, Ib *cēlā pā̃chhi gurū*, Is U *gurū bhā kā̃chū*. 6. Ic *jimi dhā̃si*, U *jasa dhā̃si*. Ic *jimi dīā*. 7. Is *ḍhū̃ḍi līnha*, U *khōli līnha*. Ia *bajara kewāra so jāe*. Id U *bajara mū̃da sō gā ūghārā*. 8. Ia UK *saraga kara*, Ib *saraga asa*, Is *surā̃ga gaḍha*, Ia *caḍhata raini bhā bhōra*, Is U *caḍhata hōi gā bhōra*. K² *caḍhata gaeu hoi bhōra*. K³ *caḍhatai bhai ga bhōra*.
9. Ids *pukāra rājā saũ*.

244. 1. Ib *pū̃chī bāta*, Is *pū̃chī pāsa patrī jō*, UK *pū̃chā rāja-pā̃ḍita au* (K *jala*) *paḍhē* 2. Ia *karanī kauna siddhi*, Id *kahahu jo*, Is *jehi pāwahī*, UK *kahahu sajāi kauna sō* (K *wai pā°*. 4. Ia *sīsa para*. 5. Ia *saraga jāi sūrī para sikhē*, Icd *caḍhē saraga sūrī*. 6. Ia *pai* for *para*, Ias UK *tāhi na dōkhū*. 7. Ia *cōra pakari bēdhati*, U *cōra parāwa*, K *cōra pagāra*. 8. Ic *jasa ehi rāja mā̃dira kahā̃ dīnha raini hoi sē̃dhi*, UK *jasa rē rāja* (K *oi cōra*) *bhā̃ḍāra kahā̃*. 9. Ia *tasa inha mōkha hoi taba*, Ic *tasa tinha tapa mōkha hai*, Id *taisa caḍhē puni*.

U *taba tinha mōkhu hōi jaũ*, K *tasa unha mōkha hōiai*, Ia *jaba sūrī saũ bēdhi*, K *jaba mara sūrī bēdhi*. K[2] *māria sūrī bēdhi*. K[3] *mārahu sūrī bēdhi*

245. 1. Ia *aisā cōra*. 2. Ia *nisaṅka aisā jo bhā°*. K *tākahī jahā̃ tahā̃ uḍi jāwahī*, with *bhāwahī* in the preceding half line. 3. Icd *siddha ḍarai nahi*. 4. Ia *jāi tā kī* (sic) *mana jahā̃*. Ib *hia* for *pai*, K *jia mahā̃ jahā̃*. 5. Ias *caḍhā*. Ib *pai nāhī*, Is *tē nāhī*, U *dharai wai nāhī*. 6. There are great variations.

Ia *mānata gida dharai tō rājā* ı *siddha dharai to kaccī kājā* ıı
Ib *jambū kahana calai jō rājā* ı etc. as in text
(or) *chambaka kahā̃ jō cāhai rājā* ı
(both readings given)
Ic *campaka para jaũ caḍhiau rājā* ı *siṅgha sāji kai caḍhia sājā* ıı
Id *campaka jo dharai hoihō rājā* ı *sīgha kai sāji charai tehi rājā* ıı
Is as in text.
U as in text, except *dharihō* for *caḍhiau* ı *siṅgha samāja caḍhai tau chājā* ıı
K as in text except *dharai koi rājā* ı As in text, except *caḍhai* for *caḍhia* ıı
K[2] *jambuka kahai so caḍhē rājā*.

7. Ia *chalahī marai bali jāi na mārā*. Ib *jarai na jārai marai na mārā*.
8, 9. Ia *chalahi chalā bali bāwana* *mēlā bādhi taṅgara* ı
chalahi chalā laṅkēsara *chanata nalā kai bāra* ıı

The latter half of the second line is very doubtful. No vowels are marked.

8. Id *rājā caḍahi*, Is has for second half *charahadanasāi*, from which some syllables are missing. U for second half *chārau̇ milai sukhāi*, K. *rājā chārā sōī*.

9 Ib *siddha karahī jehī disiṭi*. Id U *binu chara māri na jāi*. K *binu chara māri na hōī*.

246. Ia آوُه کرنه کودر مس ساجا
Ib آوهو کروی گدّر مس ساجو
Ic آوه کوی کدر مس ساجو
Id آوه کوي کیدر منس ساجو
Is आवऊ करी गुदर मिस साजू ।
U आवऊ करइँ गुदर मिस आजू ।
K आवऊ करी गुदार मिसु आजू ।
K[2] आवऊ करिए गुदर मिसि साजू ।
K[3] आवऊ करी गुदर मिसु साजू ।

Iacd do not distinguish between گر and کر

Ibcd *caḍhī*. 2. Ibc *hōhī*, Ia K *sā̃jōwa*. Is *sabhōgī*, Ibc *dharahī*. 3. Ia *kōṭi kaṭaka dala bājē*. 4. Ia *sakala pahāra sahata mahi hālē*. Ibc *pahāra parbata*. A printed commentary says that *puai* = *pahāra* = *giri*. 6. Ia *hā̃kē āwahī*.

247. 2. Ib *jānata hoihai puni jū°*, Id *asa jānata kichu*. 5. Ia *niti tākā*, Ic *jia tākā*, U *hia tākā*. 6. Iab *para* for *baru*. Ia *jāu jāu*, Ic UK *jāe jāe*. 7. Ib *cakara phirāwahī*. 8. Ia UK *satta bica*. Ibd *jia rākhi*.

248. 1 Ia *caḍhi karī na*, Ib *hoi jūjhi na*, with v. l. *karī* for *jūjhi*, UK *karia na*. 2 K. *dijai*. Ia *raṅga na rahai*. Ib *jūjhi* for *ūbha*. U *hoe ūbhai*, K *raṅgā na rahai jo ūca karījai*. 4. U *jaũ pai nāi*. Is *pēma pā̃tha sūjhā* Iac U *karahī* for *marahī*, which Id also gives as a v. l. Is *pēma jei būjhā* 5. U *jūjhi nikariai*. 6. Id *sōī puni*, U *pāni taisaī jani mārā*, K *pāni nahī hōe niārā*. 8. Ia *pēma pāni*, Ic *pēma pantha*.

249. 2. Ia *nā ḍara jiu dharata*, U *ḍaraki*, K *ḍarai*. Ib *janai*, Ia *nāhī̃ marana*. 3. Ic *phā̃sa dhari mēlī*. Ia *bisamai*. 4. Ib *dēu*, *lēhu*. Ia *jaba lagi tana*, Ic *jo āhi tana*. 5. Is *kī̃garī taba tēi bajāwā*, U *nēhu bajāwā*. K. *nēhu guputa*. Ibs *bairāginha*. 6. Ics *pahilahī̃*. 8. Iacd *rahā sō nāū̃*. 9. Ia *jahā̃ jāū̃ ohi*, Is *jahā̃ tākaū̃*, U *jahā̃ tahā̃*.

250. 1. Ia *jau lahi gurū ahā nahī̃ cīnhā*. Ia انتریت ناسون کیدھا. Ib *taba lagi kōṭi ā̃tarapaṭa dīnhā*, Is *ā̃tarapaṭa bica hata*, U *bica bica*, K *bica taba dīnhā*. 2. Ia *tana mana jībana jōbana sōī*, Ic *puni sōī*, U *tanu manu dhanu jiu jōbana sōī*. 3. Is *haū̃ tō*, Ic *maī̃ maī̃*. K *uparāhī̃*. 5. Is U *kara pūrū*, all P vocalized plainly *guru*. Ia has *sāī̃ mōra asti guru pūrū*, Id *sūri dīnha masta guru*, K *guru mēlī hastī kahā̃ pūrū*. 6. Ia *guru asti*, Ib *caḍhā bisēkhā*, Ib *nāsti kai dēkhā*, U *nāsti asti*, K *asti nāsti*. 7. Iac U *jala* for *puni*. Verse 8 is as follows :—

Ia کرو مور موری هئین * دئین ترنک—م دهاتھ

Ib گُرو مور مورین سو * دینهین جس ترنکھ دهاتھ

Ic کُرو مور مورین هت * دینهین ترنکھ دهاتھ

Id کرو مور مورین هین دینھ ترنکھ دهاتھ

Is गुरू मोर मोरे छिन दिहे तुरंगहि ढाठ।

U गुरू मार मोरें सिरहिँ। दिए कुंरंगहिँ ढठि।

K गुरुमोरमोरसिर देइ तुरंगहि ढाठ ।

K[2] गुरू मोर मोरे सिर दीन्ह तुरंगम ढाटि ।

K[3] गुरू मोर हिरदै बसे गहे तुरंगहि ढाट ।

Iacd do not distinguish between کر and گر.

251. 1. Is K *padumāwati kara cēlā*. 2. Ibds *ohi nāū̃ na jānaū̃*. 3. Is *baiṭhaka* dēū- 4. Instead of *lai so*, U has *āni* and K *lēi*. Iabc *nau autāra*. 6. Is U *sai* for *saī̃*, Ic K *sō*. 7. Ia *bāra caḍhi*, Id *bāra bhai*. 8. UK *darasa dikhāwahu* (K *diyāwahu*) *tāhi kara*. Is *haū̃ so bhikhāri*, K *haū̃ jōgī jaisē pataṅga* (sic). 9. K *sira dei mohī*.

252. 2 Ia *nahī̃ rōjū*. 3. Iad U *jabahī̃ . . . tabahī̃*, Ia UK *kawāla kahā̃*. 4. Ias UK *bisamai*. Iad UK *hie gaeū̃*. 5. Ib *gaṭa gaṭa mā̃su*, K *rakata* for *guputa*, Ia *kara nāsū*, U *bhā nāsū*. 6. Ia *lāgu kumhilāī*, Ib *lāgu sukhāī*, Ic *gaeu murujhāī*. 7. Ias U *bhawā̃ti bhawā̃ti*, Iac *hoi gai*. 8 Ia *citara jo kīnha bicitara dhani rōma rōma gā bhē̃ṭi*, Ib *cita kīnha dhani*, Ic *cētahi jo*, Is *citahī to citara kīnha dhani rōwā̃ rōwā̃ rā̃ga bhē̃ṭi*. U *rōma rōma ā̃ga nitta*. 9. Ia *sīsa sāla*, Is *sahasa sahasa dukha hia bhari*, Ic *dukha ubharī*, U *dukha āhi kai muruchi parī gā mitta*.

253. 1. Id *gaṅgana nakhata* (so also a v. l. in Ib). 3. Ib U *kāma kai kalā*. Ias *baru bhalā*. 5. Ia *mēlata*. 6. Ibc *bāna pasārā*. 7. Ib K *kāla para kāla*. 9 Is *jārē para jārai sō*. U *jārai para taba jārai*. Ia *kara na sakai bhasamanta*.

254. 1. Ia *kumōda lai*, Ic *kumōda koi*, Id *kumōḍa parasahī̃ mukha pāyā*, Is *ku° parasahī gai pāyā*, U *kōi kumōdina parasai*, K *kumōda dai*. 3. Ia *koi awīrita dhari nīra nicōā*, . . . *adhika baru*. 6. Ic *khina eka dasana bā̃dha*. Is *gahē jībha*, K *gahesi jībha*. 7. For *bajara*, Ic has بیلد, Ic بیجھ Id بیجھ, Is बैभा. U *jānahu biraha bāna saū̃ mārā*, K *jānahu bīj(u) bāna saha mārā*. 9. *ā̃dhēra*, so Ib. Ia *andhā*, Ic *andhara*, U *adhara*, Is *rōahī̃*. Id *bhā ā̃dhiāra akāsa*, K *ā̃dhiārā dharati akāsa*. K[2] *adhiara dharati akāsa*. K[3] *ā̃tarikha dharati akāsa*.

255. 1. Ia K *jō gahana*. K *puni budhi cēti hiaī̃*. 2. Id *gahesi suāsā*. K *ūbhi līnh dhani sāsā*. Ia U *bhā adhāra kuchhu jiuna ka āsā*, Icd *adhāra kucchu ji kara āsā*. 4. Ia *kaī̃ hari līnha jo kīnha ā̃dhārā*. 5. Iac *karati gahēlā* (Ic *gahīlā*). Ia *aba kata sata chā̃ra hoi duhēlā*, Ib *aba kaisaī̃*. Ic *saba ḍhīlī*, Is *tasa ḍhīlī*, U *aba kasa āsa chā̃ḍi sati ḍhīlī*, K *aba*

kasa sata chāḍī tana ḍhīlī. 6. Ia *tumharī laŋka harī kā kēhara*, Ib *laŋka harī kēhārī . . . karesi hēhārī.* Icd *tū̃ hari laŋka harī aba kēharī*, Is *tumharī laŋka.* Ia *aba kata hāri karesi kā hēhara*, Ic *hāri parī jī hēhari*, Is *aba kyaĩ hari kahau sasi hēhari*, U *aba tū̃ hahā karesi kasa hēhara*, K *aba kata tua saka rahī jō hēhari.* 7. Is has *nichōhā* for *bichōhā*, Ic is doubtful, all others clearly *bichōhā*, Ia *kaĩ byādhā hoi gahana*, Ib *hoi gaeu*, Icd *hoi kīnha*.

K केइ नौनार कै दीन्ह बिछोहा ।

K² कै ब्याधी गहनी नौछोही ।

K³ केइ ब्याधा छोइ गहा बिछोहा ।

8. K *rāti bitā bhā bihāna* (*sic*). 9. Ias U *khōlahu.* Ia *jaū̃ re uā jaga*, Ic *ueu jaga*, U *jōreu wā jaga*, K *bēgi uthā jaba bhāna.*

256. 1. Ic *bahu bāsā*, U *rasa bāsā.* 2. Id *mukha-canda ughēlī*, Is U *mukha jānu ughēlī.* 3. K *mukha tāhī.* Ib *piu gai bōli*, Id *mari mari nāri*, Is *mari mari jiai bōla bariāī*, U *mari mari bōli jiaī*, K *mari mari wō jīwana bara nāhī.* 4. U *dūni biraha*, K *dahai biraha.* Is *bōli na jāe.* 5. K *biraha samū̃da.* The second half reads as follows in the various MSS.

Ia چکھہ کھوتھنہ (? گھوتھنہ) مکھہ بچن نہ آوا

Ib ھیین کوٹ مکھہ ایک ناوا

Ic چکھہ کہومنھہ مکہہ بکت نہ آوا

Id چکھہ کھونڈہہ مکہہ ایک نہ آوا

Is चखु छूटहिँ मुख एक न आवा ॥

U चखु कोटि निमिख एक न आवा ॥

K चखु कोटिन्ह मुख एक न आवा ॥

K² चाख छुमत मुख बोलि न आवा ॥

K³ चख छूटइ मुख बात न आवा ॥

6. Ias *jiu hātha parāwā*, U *jiu hātha na āwā.* 7. Ic *bikha dēhu to khāū̃.* Ia *pēṭa hiaĩ ḍara*, Ic *pēṭa jo marata sakāū̃*, Is *pēṭa tabahi ḍara*, UK *pēṭa marana kā ḍaraū̃.* 8. Ib *asa bhai kawā̃la.* 9. U. *bēgi gahana*, K *sakhī biraha jiu lēta.*

257. 1. IaK *puraini sakhī*, Ic *cērī dhāī*, Ia U *uṭhi dhāī*, Id *sakhī sabahi jo uṭhi kai dhāī.* Ia UK *hīrāmani lai āi bolāī.* 2. Ia *rogiaī*, Ic *rōga so marata jiāwā.* 4. K *jiu bāḍhī . . . . hia kāḍhi.* 5. Ia *lēta dina*, Id *līnha dhani.* 6 Ib gives *piāsa* as v. l. for *bibhāsa*; Ic has *vithā* for *bibhāsa.* In all MSS. except Ic *bibhāsa* is quite clear. K *āsa tua bhari*, Ic *sakala bithā birahini kē lēhī.* 7. K *janama nibāhū̃.* 8. Ib *hoi gai nāri acēta.* 9. Ia K *cēta sā̃bhāri jaū̃ uṭhī bakatā wai mukha lēta.* Is *puni jaū̃ cēta sā̃bhāri cita bakatā*, &c. as Ia K. U *birahini cēta sā̃bhārī uhai guputa mukha lēta.*

258. 2. Ia *baiṭha tana khōī*, Ibc *ḍāhi karai tana sōī*, Is *ḍāhi lāi tana khōī.* 3. Ia *yaha na bujhai āgi tasa jāgi*, Ic *ā̃ca bajāgī*, Id *ū̃ca bajāgī*, Is *yaha na bujhāi upanī bajāgī*, U *bujhāi upajī bajarāgī.* 4. K has second half *dahai dēha saba lāgu apārā.* 5. Ibs *kaṭi kaṭi mā̃su*. Ias U *saba dhōā*, K *rakata ke ā̃sunha tē̃ mukha dhōā.* 7. Ia *dagadha tē̃ utima maranā̃ | dagadha ke sahahī jīu kā karanā̃.* Is *dagadha baru*, U *dagadha tē̃ utima*, K *dagadha saū̃.* U *jiu pai dījia.*

259. 1. Iad *upajī*, UK *jia bhārī.* 2. Ia *arujhī pēma pirītama bēlī*, K *kāma prīti.* 5. Iabcs omit *so*, thus spoiling the metre. Id *amara jo.* Iads, *bōī* for *pōī.* 8. Is *taba pāwai sukha*, U *sōi chāha.* 9. Is U *milai jaū̃ prītama.*

260. I. Is *tumha tē hō.* U *tumha tō hahu pri°.* 2. Icd *dosari disi pīū̃*, which Ib also notes as a v. l. 3. Ib notes this verse as extra, and adds an eighth *caupāī* lower.

down. Iad UK omit this verse and substitute one lower down, see below. 4. Iacd *gahanē līnha.* Ics *cā̃da kū̃bhilānā.* 5. Ia *ō huti bhai maraū̃ tasa jhūrī.* Is *nahī̃ jhūrī.* Ibs *maaū̃* for *marana.* 6. Ia *milā na jāe parā.* After this line Iabd UK insert the following:—

दसईं (Ia UK दसउँ) अवस्था अब (Iad अस, K सब) मोहि भारी ।

दसईं लखन होउ (K कोइ) उपकारी ॥

7. Icd *dāmani nalahi jo* (Id *jasa*) *hamsa,* Is *dāmahi nala jō hamsa.* In K[2] it is 4th line, and runs as follows:—

दमही नल जस हंस मिलावा K[3] दमावती नल हंस मेरावा

8. Ia *mūri sajīwana āni kai.* UK *dūri ati.* Ias K *sāli sakati hia* (K *jasa*) *bāna.* 9. Ia *prāna rahahī̃ ghaṭa jātu aba . . . . bhānu.* Ic *bēgi milāwahu,* Is *dekhāwahu bhānu,* U *milāwahu bhānu.*

261. 3. Id *rāja ghara.* Ia U *pūjai bipara so mārai jōgī,* Id *pūjai āsa,* Is *pūjai bēda.* 4. Iad *pawā̃ri pawā̃ri kotawāra.* Ib *kotawāra jo baiṭhā . . . . surā̃ga dai paiṭhā.* 5. UK *ānā bā̃dhi dharā.* 6. Ia *aba ohi dēi gaē lai sūrī । ohi kai bithā sōga tumha pūrī ॥* 7. Ic *tuma sō jiu kāyā waha jōgī.* Ia K *rōga jīu bhā rōgī,* Ic *jīu lai,* Id U *jīu pai.* 9. Ia *āpu lukāi.*

262. 1. Ia *saba bāta jaū̃ kahī.* For (Ib) *puni,* Iac *kē,* Id *kahā̃,* Is *gai,* K *mō.* U *suruja gahana canda gahagahī.* 2. Ia *suruja ke dukha tarunī bhai dukhī.* U *suruja ki dukha saū̃,* Ics *hō dukhī,* K *suruja ke gahana.* 3. Ia *dharana gā̃ganēhā.* Id *sātha jo dharata sinēhā.* Is *gananēhā.* 4. Ias UK *janama* for *jarama.* 5. Ia *karanī kahahu kaunu kina sōī.* Id *sō karani kara kahu guru sōī.* U *kaunu so karanī jō guru hōī.* K *guna sōī.* U *paravēsa hai sōī.* 6. Ia U *guru bhā cēlā,* Id *guru waha cēlā.* 7. Ia *rahai lukāī,* Id *kahahu khanḍa,* K *chapāī* for *lukāī,* Ic U *kāla ḍhū̃ḍhi phiri.* 9. Ia *guru karai jaū̃ māyā.* UK *kiripā mayā guru karai.* Ibc *cēlā bhēda.* Is *kahai to.*

263. This set of chaupāīs and on to No. 266 are not in Is, the pages being missing. 1. Ib *āna rānī,* K *sunu rānī tumha guru maī̃ cēlā.* This second half commences as follows in the various MSS. Ia *pūjehu* (?) *minatahi* (منتهه) *siddha,* Ibd as printed. Ic *mayā mōha kē siddha,* U *būjhi mohi kai,* K *bujhu mayā karu.* 2. Iac *tumha jō* (Ic *sō*) *cēlahi parasana.* Ia U *darasana dēna.* 3. Ia *jo* for *so,* Ib *rūpa gurū sō,* Icd *tumhāra tahā̃ waī ḍīṭhā,* UK *tumhāra jabahi waha ḍī°.* Iac U *baīṭhā* for *paīṭhā.* 4. Ia *ohi kai kayā.* 6. Ia *bithā sōga tumha āī.* 7. Ia *tumha ohi kai ghaṭa waha tumha māhā̃,* K *waha tū̃ tū̃ waha aba ghaṭa. mahā̃.* Ia *kāla na jānai āchai kāhā̃.* Ic *kāla na jānai pāwai chāhā̃.* 9. The following are the various readings:—

Ia	*āwai*	*kāla*	*gurū*	*tinha*	*dēkhē.*
Ib	„	„	*tumahī* „		„
Ic	„	„	*tahā̃ tumha*		„
Id	„	„	*tumha nahi*		„
U	*āi*	*kāla*	*tumha*	*hēri*	*kai.*
K	*āwā*	*kāla*	*tuha*	*dēkhai.*	
K[2]	*āwai*	*kāla*	*tumhahī tahā̃ dēkhai.*		
K[3]	„	„	*guru tahā̃ dē bahurai kayā adēsa.*		

U *bahurā kai ādēsa* K *bahurā karī adēsa.*

264. Not in Is. See No. 263. 1. Ia *bithā kai baranī,* K *bithā dukha haranī.* 3. U *jō bhā siddha,* K *tehi ehi bidhi kō.* The second half is as follows:—

Ia جگين سدهه دنيهه سوئي رکهوارا

Ib نيو رسي جيءُ هوى چهارا

Ic نيورس نهه جي هوے حهارا

Id نيئو رس تهه جئي هوي چهارا

U नवौओरसौ होइ तिँहिँ भारा ॥

K नवो रसौ जनि होइ विकारा ॥

K2 निह रस तजिए ओही छारा ॥

K3 नीऊ रसहुति जरइ होइ छारा ॥

4. Icd K *bhaehu narēsū.* 5. Iac *tumha mō saũ*, Id *mō saũ tumha.* 6. Ia *tumha paragaṭa*, Ib *para siddha*, Ic *parahasta*, Id *parasasta*, U *parasvēta*, K *parasāda*. All printed editions have *parasēta* with glosses stating that the word means '*pasīnā*.' We have followed this, on the authority of U. Ia *mohi jiu ghaṭata ghaṭata*, Ib *mohi guputa jiu ghaṭa bahu bērā*. Ic *mohi ghaṭa jīu ghaṭata nahī̃ bērā.* Id *jō ghaṭa jīu ghaṭata yaha bērā*, U *mohi jiu ghaṭata na lāgē bērā*, K *mō jiu ghaṭana na lāgai bērā.* 8. Ia *mili sukha.* Ibd *mili kala rahahī̃.* U *jō rē jiyahu mila kēla kara.* Id *marahī̃ ēka sāga dōu.* K *marahī̃ to saṅgahi dōa.*

9. Ia تمهه جلي جان کچهو هوي

Ib تمهه پي جين جن هؤو کچهو

Ic تمهه لي جيهه صن هوى کچهه

Id تمهه جيو سيو (?) نهوي کچهه

U तुम पिय जिय जनु होऊ कछु ।

K तुह जिउ जनि कछु होउ बिधि ।

K2 तुम्ह पै जीउ न होइ कुछु मोहि जिउ होइ सो होउ ॥

K3 तुम्ह जीअ पेम हौँ जाना हम जिअ होइ सो होउ ॥

Iad *hōi* for *hōu* both times.

265. Not in Is. See No. 263. 1. Iab *ānī jahā̃.* U *jurī tahā̃.* 3. K *ahai biōgī.* Others *bhōgī.* 4. Ia *hiaī̃ japa-māla.* Ic. *hiaī̃ jō māla.* Ib *garai makha japā.* K has for the second half *parimala prēma rahai nahī̃ chapā.* 7. Ib *lēhu pai khōjū.* 8. Ic *rē jōgī* Ibcd *jarama*, others (IaK) *janama.* 9. K *roibē kara.* U *hā̃sā sō kawanē bhāū.*

266. Not in Is. See No. 263. 3. Iac *parai.* IaUK *mati kōī*, Ic *kā kōī.* 5. Ic *āju pēma.* Ia *karaũ nibērā.* 7. Ib *āju pēma*, K *āju nēma.* Iac *hōū ninārā.* U has for the first half *ājuhi jagata hōi ādhiārā.* U *calai piārā.* 8. IaU *awadhi pahũcāī sira, kaī so calā* (Ia *calaū*). Id *gaē jāū mukha.* K *calaũ mukha kai rāta.* 9. Ia *kā pū̃chata hahu jāti.* Ic *kā pū̃chahu aba bāta.* U *kā pū̃chahu yaha bāta.* K *kā pū̃chahu kusalāta.*

267. Is has the first three lines, and then goes on with the last six lines of 269. Id puts No. 268 before this. 1. Is *kahesi.* For *karahī̃*, Ia *karaba*, Is *kārana.* For *kēti kara*, Is *kētuki*, U *kētu kara.* 2. IaU *sawā̃raũ sōi nāū hari phērā.* 3. Icd *au suwā̃raū Padumāwati.* 4. Id *jaba* for *jata.* 5. The second half runs as follows in the different MSS.

IaUK *parahī̃ uṭhahī̃ sōī lai nāū̃.*
Ibd *parahī̃ to sōī lai lai nāū̃*
Ic *parahī̃ to sōi lēta waha nāū̃.*

We have followed Ibd. 6. Ia *tā saũ sīdhā* । *sūta sūta saba ō saũ bīdhā* ॥ Ic *sūta sūta tanu tā saũ ōdhā* । *kahata kahata rō rō wai sōdhā* ॥ K has *jasa bōdhā* for *jiu sōdhā.* 8. K *biraha gāta kahā̃.* IcdU *kī hāni*, with *samāni* in the rhyme. K *kī ghrāni*, with similar rhyme. 9. Id *sā̃ca dhara rahā.* IaK *haū̃ aba rahā sā̃ca hoi,* U *hō aba rahā sā̃ci hōai.* IbK *ohi kē rūpa.*

268. From here to No. 277 the various MSS. differ widely in the arrangement of the sets of *caupāīs* and *dōhās.* We have mainly followed the arrangement of Ib. The present set is not in U. 1. Iad *jabahī̃* for *jauhī̃.* Is *māra* for *gāḍha.* 2. Ib *suruja* for *sūra.* IasK *gagā̃na kasa áhā̃,* Ib has *gā̃gana,* corrected on the margin to *gahana,* Id *gā̃gana risa gahā.* 3. Ia *gahana* for *gahā.* Ia *puni chapā,* Is *ḍara chapā.* 4. Ia *kā kautuka ājū,* Ic *calu dēkhai eka kautuka tahā̃* । *dharatī tapā mārai kahā̃ jahā̃* ॥ Id *hai ājū* K *gai ājū.* Ia *jahā̃ tapā.* 5. Ic *calu kusā maī̃ dē.°* IsK *dēkhia.* 7. Ia *dēkhana.* Ia *dhani mūrati kasa sūrati bhāgē.* Icd *dahū̃ sumirata kasa satī sohāgē* (Id *sabhāgē*). Is *sunē sabhāgē.* K *dahu sumirata kai satī sabhāgē.* 8. Ia om. *āpani.* 9. Ic *jiu dēi.*

269. This is complete only in Ib and Ic. The latter misplaces it. Is gives all but the first three lines (see No. 267). Id in place of this set repeats the *caupāīs* of 268, but gives the right *dōhā,* 2. Ic *samādhi ṭā saū̃ dhuni lāgī.* Ib *pāsa jahā̃ jāū̃.* 4. Ib *jehi mahā̃ pantha.* 5. Is *au bhari.* 6. Is *hia mahēsa waha bhaē mahēsī, kata.* Is *tē̃ paradēsī,* Ic *tē pa°.* 7. Ic *mana mahā̃ līnha.* Is *sunata ehi.* Ic has second half *tumha kasa mushṭa dharī tehi ṭhāū̃.* 8. Is *mārita.* Is *ehi bāru.* 9. Is *kōnu kāhū̃,* Is *jaū̃ hoi jāi nināru.*

270. This occurs only in Ib U and K. 1. Ib *lai so sādēsa sua gaeu táhā̃.* K *gau táhā̃.* U *sūrī dēi.* K *surī dēna lē āē jahā̃.* 2. K *lōganha jōā.* 3. K *muha hērā.* 4. K *bara bidhinā sō rōī.* U *bidhinā̃ pai rōī.* K *kari upakāra.* 5. K *bipati sunāī.* 6. UK *baiṭhi.* UK *jiaī̃ to jiaū̃ marai tau* (K *maraū̃ eka*) *sāthā.* 8. U *bhaē̃ dōu eka ṭhāū̃.* 9. Ib *calahu jāi tehī̃ kahahī̃.* K *jahā̃ baiṭhā hahī̃ rāū̃.*

271. This occurs in all MSS. except Is, but with widely differing readings. UK omit the third line, and substitute another between the sixth and seventh. Ib transposes the second and fourth lines. 1. Ic *kahi kai rahā,* Id U *suni kai rahā.* Ia K *ratana sēna kara bhāṭa dasaū̃dhī* । *bhāṭahī̃ kahā rahai risa aū̃dhī* ॥ Ib *sahi na sakā.* 2. Ic *kahā mēli kari.* U *ghālesi hātha kaṭārā mū̃ṭhī* । *uṭhā so kōpi sūra asa ūṭhī* ॥ K *ghālē hātha kaṭāra so mūṭhī* । *uṭhā kōpi jaba sūrī ūṭhī* ॥ 3. Ib *kōpi mārā puni kansū.* Ia *aba jānā eha purukha ka ansū.* Ibd have :—

Ib گونگ کہ پہونک بنا جي بنْسوُ

Id گونک کي بہونک بنا جي بنسو

Id does not distinguish between ک and گ. Ib is quite clear. This line is not in UK. K² K³ गुंगे कि फूँक न बाजइ बंसु 4. Iabo *gā̃dharapa.* Ia *tahā̃ risa.* UK *risa bharā.* For the second half UK have *gahai kaṭāra jāi* (K *āi*) *bhā kharā.* 5. For first half UK have *cahai kīnha tahā̃ āpuhi ghāū̃.* 6. UK *bānā birada bōla asa kahā* । *gandhrapa sēna tū̃ rājā mahā* । Ia has second half *sōhai risa kachu jāi na kahā.* Ibcd as in text. Between this and the next line UK insert *haū̃ mūrati mahēsa kai kalā* । *rājā saba rākhai aragalā* ॥ 7. UK *siddha pāni tū̃ āgi* (K *agni*) *asūjhā* । *agina* (K *agni*) *kōha pānī saū̃ būjhā* ॥ 8. After *pāni saū̃* Ic adds *jūjha na,* and K *jūjhai.* The readings of the last line are as follows :—

Ia *jōgī bāra khapara lai māni kai*	*bhīkha dēhi mana jūjha.*
Ib *tōraī bāra khapara hai līnhē*	*bhikhiā dēhi na jūjha.*
Icd ,, ,, ,, *lai māni kai*	,, ,, ,,
U *jōgī bāra jo āwā*	*bhīkha dēi mati jūjha.*
K ,, ,, *khapara līnha hai*	*bhicchā dēhi na jūjha.*

We have followed Ib.

To sum up the above. U and K differ so widely from the other MSS. that we here give the text of U. That of K closely agrees as indicated above.

चउपाई ।

सुनि कै रहा दीठि कइ अउँधी । रहि न सका तब भाट दसउँधी ॥
घालेसि हाथ कटारा मूँठी । उठा सो कोपि सूर अस ऊठी ॥
गंध्रप सेन जहाँ रिस भरा । गहइ कटार जाइ भा खरा ॥
चहइ कीन्ह तहँ आपुहि घाऊ । बाएँ हाथ दीन्ह बर भाऊ ॥
बाना बिरद बोल अस कहा । गंध्रप सेन तुँ राजा महा ॥
हउँ सूरति महेस कइ कला । राजा सब राखइ अरगला ॥
सिद्ध पानि तूँ आगि असूझा । अगिन कोह पानी सउँ जूझा ॥

दोहा ।

आगि बुझाइ पानि सउँ तूँ राजा मन बूझि ।
जोगी बार जो आवा भीख देइ मति जूझि ॥

272. Is has only *caupāīs* 3 to 6. The remaining *caupāīs* and the *dōhā* in Is are taken from an imperfect and incorrect set of six *caupāīs* and a *dōhā* in Ib. 1. Ib *ubhāū*. Ia *hātha rāu bara*. U *dēi bara*. K *rājahi bara*. Ic substitutes for the entire line *bōlā gandhrapa sēna risāī। kaisaī jōga ko bhāṭa abhāī॥* 2. Ib *āwai gaḍha*. U *jō gaḍhi caḍhai sẽdhi dai cōrī*. 3. Is *ḍarai mohi nā°*, IcK *ḍarai nāwāĩ mohi māthā*. U *kānha ḍarai*. Icds *sēsa* for *kāli*. 4. Ia *caturbhuja*. IaK *pātāla ḍarai kabilāsū*. 5. Ia *kumbha* for *kuruma*. 6. Ic *ḍarai au mandila*, U *ḍarai mandira sumērū*. Ib *gagana sumērū*. Id *gagana gãbhīrū*. K *cãda surja au ḍarai kubērū*. 7. The following are the various readings :—

Ia *cāhau tō mãgaũ dhai kēsā।* *auru ko kīṭa patayga narēsā॥*
Ib *sabaĩ deotā karai adēsū।* *auru ganai kō patãga narēsū॥*
Ic *cahaũ ta saba gahi mãgaũ kēsā।* *aurū kīṭa patayga narēsā॥*
IdK ,, ,, ,, ,, ,, ,, । *au kō* ,, ,, ,, ॥
U *cāhaũ tō mãgaũ dhai kēsā।* *auru kōṭi patayga narēsā॥*
K[2] *cāhaũ haũ bhanjaũ gahi kēsā।* *auru ko guputa patayga narēsā॥*

8. UK *bōlā bhāṭa kahaũ sata* (K *tasa*) *rōsa na lāgē jīũ*. Is *na kījai jīũ*. 9. K *tajā garaba bala bhīũ*. Ic has an altogether different *dōhā*, viz :—

sura nara rikhi guni gãdharapa *asura sūra jita dēu।*
paragaṭa guputa sirisiṭī *karahĩ sabai mili sēu॥*

This is made up of portions of an imperfect set of *caupāīs* in Ib.

273. 1. Ic has duplicate first lines. It first has a line the same as Is, and then a line the same as the text. Is substitutes *bōlai bhāṭa phūra hama jhūṭhē। jaũ yaha garaba dēu tohi rūṭhē॥* For the second half IaUK *garabahi bharā kīnha* (K *kiā*) *sãgarāmū*. Ic *uhai bhaeu* 2. UK *rāwana asa jaga kō*. Id *rāona saũ*. Is *bhua daṇḍā*. UK *bhuja daṇḍā*. *jehi sūruja tapa karai rasōī*. Icd *suruja jai niti tapai*. K *jā ke suruja tapa karai rasōī*. K *baisudarā jehi dhōbī hōī*. 5. UK *bãdhā*. Id *rahā na dōsara ō saũ kãdhī*. U *rahā na jaga mahā̃ dōsara kãdhā*. K *tahā na dōsara ohi sama kãdhā*. 6. Id *risa* for *asa*. Ia *muā so dui tapasinha kara mārā*. U *muā sōu tapasī kara mārā*. K *sōu muā tapasī kā mārā*. 7. K *dui ahā*. IaU *na kōū ráhā*. IcK *na kōī ráhā*. 9. Ib *ōchē sāta*. Id *ōchē bāra*. K *ōchē kē disa daiu*. U *jayati patra tehi dēi*. Ib *jai dēi*. Ic *tehi dēi*. Ia substitutes for the last *dōhā*—

dai kai disa nahi dēkhai dahũ kā kahā̃ jai dēi.

274. Not in Is. K here gives three sets of *caupāīs* and *dōhās* all to the same effect, but in slightly different versions, with the lines in the present set scattered through them. 1. IaU *suni kai bhāṭa bhāṭa jaba* (U *kai*) *jātī*. Ib *ahahi jo*. K *ṭhāra huta*. IaU *rājā kahā̃ uṭhi* (U *racchā kai kai*) *kīnha bināи*. Ic *puni ūṭhā*, Id *bir uṭhā*, K *binai uṭhā*. Ib *rājahi*. 2. IaU omit this line, and substitute another before line 7. Ic *bhāṭa ahai*. K *bhāṭa jāti*. 3. Icd *mīcu āpana pai dīsā*. K *mīcu apanē mana dīsā*. Ia *tā saũ kā kījai rīsā*. Ib *tā kahā̃*. U *tā saũ aba kā kījai rīsā*. K *tuha sō kaunu karai dai rīsā*. 4. IaU have second half *kahā̃ caḍhā asa* (U *yaha*) *mīcu nasēnī*. K *kā tohi jīu mīcu mana ṭhēnī*. 5. This is as follows in the different MSS. :—

Ia کهـان آی بـانی اس کـرئی * کـرون بتند بهات اس مرئی

Ib کاه اتی بـانی جس مـــرءی * کرءی بتّهانک بهتّنت نه کـرءی

Ic کاه اونی بـالی اس مـــرسے * کرس بتّیند بهوم نهه کـــرسے

Id کاه اونی بائین اس مـــریے * کرس بتند بهوم تهه کـــریے

U कहा आगि पानी सउँ करई। करइ बिडम्भ भाट नहिँ मरई॥

K काहे अनबानी अस धरई। करइ बिटंड भटंत न करई॥

K[2] कहइ न प्रानि पिअसि कह मरई। करइ बिटंड भाट तन अहई॥

K[3] एन्ह सउँ रीस न करिए राजा। करहिँ बिटंड बात के काजा॥

6. Ia *jāti ko rāu auguna lāwai*, Ib *jāti kaunu kita*, Ic *jāti karā̃*, U *jāti karā kunu au°*, K *jāti ka bhāṭ au au°*. Here IaU insert *satta* (U *satya*) *na kahai* (U *kahō*) *kaṭāwō̃ mātha* (U *hāthā*) *kahā̃ parā* (U *parē*) *jōgina kē sāthā*. 7. IaUK *bhāṭahi kā aba* (K *kata*) *mārau̐ jīwā* । *pūchahu kahai* (K *bōlu*) *nāi kai gīwā* ॥ Ic has *bhāṭa ṭhāṭa mukha ambirita mānī* । *kīṭa kapaṭa risa kathā kahānī* ॥ 8. Id *kahā̃ kara saŋga*. 9. K[2] K[3] *charai*. U *mati bhaŋga*.

275. Not in Is. Ic has a different set here, with the same purport, but worded differently. 1. IaUK have a different first line, as follows :—

jaũ rājā sata (Ia *tumha*) *pūchahu antū* । *satta kahaũ jōginha* (Ia *jō hai*) *biritantū* ॥

2. IaU *bhāṭa kahā maranē-saũ ḍarai*, K *bhāṭa kahā maranahi jiu ḍarau̐*, with, for the second half, IaUK *mīcu nāũ suni agumana* (K *aga tehi*) *marai*. 3. For *jō*, Ia *sō*, Id *ō*, U *hai*. K. *jambu-dīpa citaura gaḍha dēsū*. 4. U omits this line and substitutes the verse noted lower down. 5. IaK omit this line, and substitute the same line noted lower down. 6. Ib *samũda sumēru na kāhū khā̃gā*, Id *dāna samunda dēta*, UK *dāna sumēru samunda na khā̃gā*. For second half K *tehi ka bhāṭa haũ ōhī mā̃gā*. After this IaU insert the following, which K also has, but after the next line :—

tehi ka bhāṭa haũ bōlō bānā । *nāũ mahāpātara au rānā* (K *nāũ mahāpratāpa pradhāna*) ॥

7. IaU *dahinai hātha wahī baribhāũ*, K *dahina hātha ō kahā̃ baramhāō*, with for second half IaUK *dosarai kahā̃ nahi janama uṭhāũ* (K *uṭhāō*). Ib *auru ko aisa uṭhāwaũ jāhī*. 8. IaK *ohi chuṭi auru na mā̃gaũ jehi ka bhikhārī ḍhīṭha*. U *waha taji* etc. as IaK. 9. Ib *jaũ kahi bāta*, U *bāta kahai risa lāgai*. For second half K *khari puni kahai basīṭha*.

276. Not in IaUK. 1. Ic *tatakhana sunā mahā mana*. Ids *bhāṭa karā*. Id *binawai*. 2. Ib *asa kahā̃*. 3. Id omits this verse, see below. Ib *pīchahi bhāṭa hōi bhala-āgaī*. Ics *kahā cahai*. 4. Ic *suni padumini kahā̃*. 5. Ic *jō hui likhā*. Id *jāe nahī* is *so kōi na*. 6. Id *waha jā kara*. Ibs *barōka*, Ic *biōga tuī*, Id *biōga tasa*. *karu so biāha*. Ib *dharama aba tō kā̃*. After this Id repeats *caupāī* 275, 2, to make up for the missing third *caupāī* above. 8. Ic *khapara liē sō mā̃gai*. 9. Instead of *jō*, Id *jāi*, Is *dahū̃*.

277. Ic omits the first two lines, and adds two others after the seventh *caupāī*. IaK. substitute the following for the first two lines :—

Ia *jōgi na hōi so āhi narēsū* । *au parasana tehi siddha mahēsū* ॥
bhāratha hōi jūjha jaũ ōdhā । *āhi sahāi hōhī saba jōdhā* ॥

K *jōgi na āhi so ahai narēsū* । *au parasana tehi siddha mahēsū* ॥
bhāratha hōi jūjhi jaba kōdhā । *hoi sahāe āe saba jōdhā* ॥

1. Ib *īsura asa*, Is *īsura jō*. IcsU *hanuwā̃ta bīra rahai na*. 3. Is *mahādēo taba*, UK *mahādēo asa*. *suni sō*, IdUK *siŋgi sabada baramhā*. 4. For *caḍhē*, Is *calā*. For *atara*, ic *cakara*, Id Ib *dēo-lōka*. 5. Ibs *bāsuki phana patāra*. 6. IaK *chānawai kōṭi mēghu dala*, Ib *chānawai mēghu āwa dala gājā*, Ic *chappana kōṭi mēghu*. Isd U *mēghu suni gā°*. 7. For *bárā*, IdU *párā*, Is *wārā* (sic), K *járā*. For *pharahárā*, Is *bhirihárā*, U *kharabhárā*, K *bharahárā*. Here, as above explained, Ic adds two lines which are palpably made up to fill the lacuna. As they are far from legible, it is not worthwhile attempting to reproduce them here. 8. U *nawā nātha jōgī calā*. 9. The commencement differs in the various copies. Thus :—

Ia K[3] *āju mahā rana bhāratha*
Ibd *ahuṭi bajara jara dharatī*
Ics *āju mahābhāratha rana*
U *ahuṭhi bajra bhai dharatī*
K *ahuṭha hātha dhara dharatī*
K[2] *ahuṭha bujaru dharuti jurē*

We have followed Ibd. Iacs *calā* for *gāgana*.

278. Ic has the lines of this verse in different order. 1. This is 6 in Ic, which has *mahādēo lai jōgī pāchai* । *uṛa-kai māla āi rana kāchai* ॥ 2. This is 1 in Ic. Icd *kahā chatarapati rājā*. IasUK *sājā for kājā*, IaUK *kara* for *kē*. 3. This is 2 in Ic. Ib *bidyā-kara jūjhū*, IdU *bidā-kara*, Is *bighna-kara*. Is *hota āwata hai jagata asūjhū*, K *hōta asūjha so jagata*. 4. This is 7 in Ic, which also has *jhuramuṭa* for *charahaṭa*. For second half Ic *rana mā̃ha khēta rahai*, U *dara mañjhāra rahai sō jītā*, K *dila mā̃ha raini rahai* &c. 5. This is 3 in Ic. For second half, Ic *aŋgada sama sō pā̃ō rōpā*, K *rana gaḍha āi*. Ib *bhaō rōpā*, U *taba rōpā*. 6. This is Ic 4. 7. This is Ic 5. All N. have *aḍāri*, the P. readings are as follows :—Ia ادار Ib اورر or اودر Ic چلاى Id اودار 8. K *ajāna hau jōgī*. Id om. *jōgī*. 9. U *jōginha kara asa jūjhi lakhi kē ina ḍōla tehi ṭhā̃wa* with *ā̃wa* in the preceding rhyme. K *asa jō cahata padumini lāgai pā̃e*. Id *ā̃guwai pā̃e*.

279. 1. Is *jōgi*. U has a different line here, *viz.*, *khina eka tahā̃ bhaī sōkhaī* । *jayati patra jōgina kī bhaī* ॥ In second half, Icds *mā̃ha cahata*, K *kahi kai māha hēta hia dhāī*. Ib has for the last two words *tinha khāī*. 2. Iad *jōgī dhāwata asa*, U *jaba wai dhāwai taba asa khēlaū*, with *pēlaū* in the rhyme, K *jau dhāwahī aisa kai khēlahu*. Iab *kai*, Id *rana* for *kā*. 3. Icds *hasti* for *pēli*. U *jasa gaja mēla*. IsK *eka bagamēla*. Is *hōi*, U *karaī*, for *karahu*. 4. Ia *mati kai hasti sunḍa agusārī*. Ic *jauhi samūha hasti agu°*, Id *tata khina jō ḍarai agu°*, Is *mati kai jabahī saina agu°*, U *mati kai jabahī anī agu°* K *hasti kera jūha raini agu°*. U *dīnha* for *tauhī*. 5. Ia *jūjhi karai jita rana mā̃ha āi*, Ic *aura jaisai sanamukha hoi dhāī* । *hanūmanta laṅgūra calāī* ॥ Id *jahā̃ lahi saina*, Is *jabahi so*, U *sainā jō jītē rana āī*, K *jabā̃ siu sabhā jatana jana āī*. 6. U *katēka* for *bahutaka* here and elsewhere. 9. Ibs and (?) Iac *bērā*, Id *binati*, U *bairī*, K *bapurā*. Iac have بيرا, with no dots under the first letter. Ic may possibly be read *sērā*.

280. 1. Ia *puni* for *phiri*, Icd *āgai hoi kā*. 2. Ia *sunā jo saṅkha bisuna jaba pūrā*, Id *sēnā saṅkha jau bisuna pūrā*. Ic *dēkhai* for *āgaī*. 3. Ic *āi jurī jita sura barh°*. Isd *liaī ī* For *saraga*, Id *gagana*, Is *surāga*. 4. K om. this, and adds another line before 7. In second half, Ia *sēwā karahī nakhata au candū*, Is *gērahai* (sic) *nakhata*. 5. For *ahuṭhau*, Ib *ahuṭau*, Id *āṭhau*, U *ahukhē̃*. All others quite plainly *ahuṭhau*. 6. Ic *jā kara*. Is *hata rājā*, U *hō rājā*. Ic *tinha phiri sāja bīra karu sājā*, Id *tē saba*. K *sō saba lēi bīra hoi sājā*. For *sājā*, Ia *bājā*, Is *gajā*. After this line, K inserts *pārabatī mana cintā bhaeū* । *aba kasa karaū kauna bidhi laeū* ॥ 7. IcU *jahā̃ so* for *jahawā̃*, *huta* for *rana*.

Ia *nārī ghālī pāõ pārā*, Ic *kaī* (?) *paṭa ghāli rāu paga pārā*, Is *jāi* for *ai*, U *nāri samēta pāi lai pārā*, K *nāri ghāli jā pāend pārā*. 9. Id *bhāwai* for *cāhia*. Is *dījiu*, Is *bāra*.

281. 1. Ia *sunu binatī saũ karaũ basīṭhī*, U *au asi binatī kahaũ ba°*, K *tasa binatī maĩ karaũ basīṭhā*, with *mīṭhā* in the rhyme. For *hoe*, Ibc *hō*, Is *bhau*, U *sō*. For *jaga*, Ibs *saba*. 3. Ia *jō tumhara*, K *hīrāmani hai tehi ka pa°*. For second half, *kīnha jo phūṭa* (?) *karata tinha sēwā*, Ibs *gaeu tahā̃ au kī°*, U *sō bulāi kina pūchahu dēwā*, K *tinha hankāri pūchahu kina dēwā*, Icd as printed. 4. IaUK *waha jānata hai gā waha* (Ia *tā kara*) *dēsā* । *au ānesi jōginha kai bhēsā* ॥ Id has second half *ohi jōgī kai ṭhīka* (?) *narēsū*. Is *jasa bhēsū*. Lines 5, 6, 7 differ in nearly all the copies, as follows :—

Ia آنت جون له کهـــال کیُن کنتهـــا * راجـــا کـوئي نچهـــادت پنتّهـــا
راخ روب کـــل ســوــک کاتهـي * رتن دیکهـــه کو باندهـــه نـکانتهـي
جهـــان بـــار تنهـــه آو بـــروکا * کـــری بیـــاهـــه دهـــرم بد او کا

Ib هم ري کهت رهي نهه مانون * وه بـولي ســوءِي پــروانـــون
تـم بدّ راجـــا ادات گیـــانے * سمجهه ندیکهو من سوجـانے
هیـــرامن تس کری بکهـــانون * رتن سین راجا جس بهـــانون

Ic همـرین کهت رهي تیهه مـــانون * جو وه کهـــے سوي پر مـــانون
جنهـــه بـــاري تنهـــه او براوکان * کـــروُ بیاه دهـــرم بدّ توکان
جو تُمهـــار من مـــان نه کاندهُ * پرکهـــه رتن کانٹهے تب باندهُ

Id همـــوے کهت رهی نهه مانون * جـــو وه کهـــے ســوئي پروانون
جهـــان بار تنهـــه اوپر اوکان * کـــري بـیـــاه دهـــرم بدّ اوکان
جولهه مورا تپـــارین کاندهي * پرکهي رتن کانٹهه تب باندهي

Is हमरे कहत रहइ नहि मानू। वह बोलइ सोई परवानू॥
जहाँ बारि तहँ आउ बरोका। करु सो बिआह धरम बड तो का॥
जउँ पहिलेँ मन मान तउ काँधी। परिखी रतन गाँठि तब बांधी॥

U जोगि उघाल न आनत कंथा। राजा कोउ न छाँडत पंथा॥
जहाँ बारि तहँ आउ बरोका। करइ बिआह धरम बड ओ का॥
हमरे कहत रहइ नहिँ मानूँ। वह का बचन होइ परवाँनूँ॥

K आनत जौ न घालि सिर कंथा। राजा कोइ न छाडत पंथा॥
राजा रूप नग कुल सो काँठी। परिखि रतन अब बाधऊ गाँठी॥
जहाँ बारि तहँ आउ बरोका। करइ बियाह धरम बड ॥

K2 हमरे कहे न रहइ वह मानू। वह जो बोलहिँ सोइ परवानू॥
जहाँ बारि तहँ आउ बरोका। करिअ बिआह धरम बड ओका॥
जउ पहिले मन मान त काँधी। परखी रतन गाँठि तउ बाँधी॥

K[3] हमरे कहत रहइ नहिं माना । जो तुम्ह कहहु होइ परवाना ॥

जहाँ बारि तहँ नाउ बरोखा । करइ बिश्वाँहि धरम सत मोखा ॥

अउ हौ मानत धोखा । परखि रतन तब गाँठि बँधोखा ॥

It will be seen that Ia UK form one group, and the others another.

8. Ia *parakha hōe so*, U *parakha na hāra parīkha*. 9. Ia *bā̃dhi gā̃ṭhi sō dījiai*, U *bā̃dhi gā̃ṭhi pai dī°*, K *gā̃ṭhi bā̃dhi sō hī jiai*. UK *kanaka kaṭōrē*.

282. After 1, Ia UK insert the following verse, omitting verse 5. Id also has this verse, and also inserts verse 5 on the margin.

Ia *hīrāmani hai pā̃ḍita parēwa* । *kīnhesi Padumāwati kai sēwā* ॥
Id *hīrāmani huta* „ „ । *kiyau nāsa para saũ taji sēwā* ॥
UK *hīrāmani hai* „ „ । *au unha kīnha hamārī sēwā* ॥

After this Ia UK vary the order of the verses. 2. This is 4 in Ia UK, which have *nēgī* for *sōī*, and have for second half *ēka kahata dhāē dasa nēgī*. 3. The various readings are :—

Ibs *bhai agiā jana sahasaka dhāē* । *hīrāmanihī̃ bēgi lai āē* ॥
Id *ēka kahata sahasana dasa dhāē* । „ „ „ „ ॥
Ic *dhāwata ēka jāna sau dhāē* । „ „ „ „ ॥
Ia *hama sē rūṭhi gawā huta sōī* । *paṇḍita hutē dhōkha nahī̃ hōī* ॥
UK „ „ *rūsi gayā* „ „ । „ „ „ „ „ ॥

We have followed Ibs. 4. This is 5 in Ia UK. IaK *āni so* (K *āi jo*) *khōlā bēgi mā̃jūsā*. Ic *tehi* for *bahu*. 5. Ia UK omit this verse. Ids *tehi* for *bahu*. 7. IaK *kaṇṭha lāi pū̃chī*, Ic U *puni rājaī hā̃si pū̃chesi bātā*, Id *rājaī puni pū̃chī*, Is *mili rājaī pū̃chī ēka bātā*. Ia U *piara* for *pīta*. 8. U *tumha sayāna au paṇḍita*. IasK *paḍhē sāstra au bēda*. 9. Here again there are variations as follows :—

Ib *kahā̃ caḍhē jōginha kari*
Ic „ *charē* „ *gaḍha*
Id „ *caḍhē* „ *kahā̃*
Is „ *calē* „ *kara*
IaU „ *parē* „ *sā̃ga*
K „ „ „ *kara*.
K[2] „ *caḍhē* „ *kā*
K[3] „ *caḍhāē* „ *āni kīnha* Id *asa bhēda*.

283. 1. UK *hīrāmani kara-añjula kīnhā* । *bēda bhēda paḍhi āsisa dīnhā* ॥ 2. IaK *rājāesu* for *rājēsura*. K *saũha diṣṭi kachu*. 3. Is *kahai cahai kā bhā risa lāgaī*. IaK *hōhu na bikārama*, Ic *hai tumha hōhu bikarrama* (sic) *bhōjā*. 6. Ia makes this 5 and has for second half *tāhi jiu kahata basai narēsū* (sic). Ics *sōī jiu mahā̃ basai*. U *cita* for *jia*. 7. Ia K *tū̃ saba kachu au sabha para tū̃-hī* । *haũ kachu nāhi paŋkhi ratimūhī* ॥ 8. Iabd insert *au* before *sarawana*. Ib om. *budhī*. 9. has as follows :—

Ia UK *kahā̃ jībha asa pāwaũ*
Ib *mōra hai dina parata*
Ics *sēwā mōri ihai niti*
Id *kāhu jāni kai āpanā*

284. This set of *caupāīs* is wanting in U, and Ia K, have a similar but independent set. Ia is as follows :—

हउँ अस सेवक तुम्ह पति दसा। एक छाडि चित अउर न बसा॥
तेहि सेवक के करमहिँ दोसू। सेवा करत करइ पति रोसू॥
देखेउँ दोस जो दासहिँ लागा। तेहि डर निकसि जीउ ॥
पंखिहिँ का रहनाँ थिर काजू। सपत दीप फिरि देखेउ राजू॥
अब हउँ जंबू दीप पहुँचा। देखेउँ राज जगत पर ऊँचा॥
तहवा मइँ चितउर गढ देखा। महाराज नहिँ जाए बिसेखा॥
रतन सेन तहवाँ बड राजा। देखेउँ पुरुख राज पर छाजा॥

The variants of K are:—2. *dōsa jo sĕwaka karamaka dōsū*. 3. *dōsa na dā°. tehi ḍara banōbāsa kahā̃ bhāgā*. 4. *kā* comes between *thira* and *kājū*. Instead of *phiri*, *uḍi*. 6. *tahā̃ maĩ gaḍha citaura dēkhā* (sic). 7. *ratana sēna yaha baḍa tahā̃ rājā*.

As for the other MSS.—1. Id *jō asa sēwaka tumha pati dásā*। *tehi kē jiaĩ awīrita*. Ic *lai básā*. 2. Icd *sēwā karata ṭhākura hō rōsū*. Is *taba rōsū*. 3. Id *jehi pai dōsa*. Ic. *sēwaka ḍarahī̃ jīu*, Id *sēwaka ḍarai*, Is *tahā̃ so ḍarai jīu*. 4. Ics *jaũ bhā paṅkhi kahā̃ thira*. Id *haũ paṅkhī*. The second half is as follows:—

Ib *tākai uḍā pā̃kha jaũ dahanā*.
Ic ,, *jāe jahā̃ jō* ,,
Id *tākaũ jahā̃ jāũ* ,, ,,
Is *tākai* ,, *jāe jaũ* ,,

Ic *phiri* for *puni*. 6. Ic *sira tōki*. 7. Icd *baḍa* for *yahu*. 8. Ic *suphala lai khōjī*, K *pai khōjai*. Ics *hai tehi guna mukha*, K *tāhi bhaeu mukha*. 9. Ib *pīta asa tehi*. Ia *piara bhau tehi*, K *kayā̃ so pīta jo bikarama mana na bicārahu bāta*.

285. 2. Iacd *rājā*. UK *nihacai*. K *tahā̃ ānā*. 4. Ic *rasa pākē*. Ib *bihasata dasana*, U *bihasata badana*. U *asa tākē*. 5. K for *maina*, *nuina*. Ic *maina dai*. 6. *kāṭara*, so IbdsU, Ia *khatara jo*, Ic *khāṭara*, K *kaṭakara*. 7. K *phērā ṭurai unha dēkhā kharē*। *sakala sarāhahī̃ siṅghala karē*॥ Ib *sabahī̃ bakhānā*. 8. K *batīsa jo lacchanā*, Iac *lacchanā*. IaK *kalā*. 9. UK *jaisa kasauṭī para kasai adhika caḍhai tehi bānu*.

286. Before this Ibds K K3 insert a set of *caupāīs* and a *dōhā*. They differ widely amongst themselves, and the whole passage is very corrupt. We give below the readings of Is.

चउपाई।

बोल गोसाईँ कर मइ माना। एही जुगुति उतरु कइ आना॥
माना बोल हरख जिउ बाढा। अउ बरोक भा टीका काढा॥
टीका साथ कोटि नग पावा। बहुत पटंबर साथ चलावा॥
दूनउ मेरए मनावा भला। बिग्रह आपु आपु कहँ चला॥
लीन्ह उतारइ जो हत जोगू। जो तप करइ सो मानइ भोगू॥
जउँ कोइ अइस जीव पर छेवा। देओता आइ करहिँ तेहि सेवा॥
दिन दस (जो[1]) जोरे दुखं देखा। भा जुग जुग सुख तहाँ न

[1] Not in text, supplied from K, K3 has जिउ

दोहा।

रतन सेनि बर एउ कहँ पदुमावति क बिआऊ।
मंदिर बेगि अगुसारऊ मंदर तूर उछाऊ॥

Ib K K^3 nearly agree with the above, but hardly a single line of Id coincides. Ic omits 286, and inserts two sets of *caupāīs* and *dōhās* partly made up out of the above.

The following variations occur in 286. 3. Ia K *likhā*. After 3 U inserts *bōla gosāī* *tara mana* *pūjā jōga uā jaga bhānā* ॥ 4. U *anuruda kahai jo likhi huta ūkhā*. 5. U *bhā* for *bhāī*, *bana kara* for *banakhāḍa*. 6. Is *likhā jo daia na hōi ninārī*, U *likhā mēṭa kō karai ninārī*, K *bikhā* (sic) *milai kō karai ninārī*. 7. U om. this. Ia *kāju* for *sājā*. K *bhākhā* for *sājā*. For second half, Ia *sōi hōi jō bidhi uparājā*, K *hōi sōi jō bidhi likhi rākhā*. 8. K *mārana kō rana*. 9. Is U *cāra uchāhu*.